Fodor's 1993 Affordable Europe

D1413001

Portions of this book appear in *Fodor's Europe '93*.

Fodor's Travel Publications, Inc.
New York • Toronto • London • Sydney • Auckland

Fodor's Affordable Europe

Editor: Paula Rackow
Contributors: Katrine Osa Aaby, Robert Andrews, Barbara Angelillo, Nikola Antonov, Victor Aquilina, Ernest Beck, Christopher Billy, Robert Blake, Jules Brown, Linda Burnham, Andrew Collins, Nancy Coons, Karen Cure, Adrian Foreman, Clive Freeman, Caroline Haberfeld, George Hamilton, Emma Harris, Simon Hewitt, Alison Hoffman, Kerin Hope, Alannah Hopkin, Amanda Jacobs, Edie Jarolim, Elizabeth Konstantinova, Keneva Kunz, Graham Lees, Jillian Magalaner, Leo Mangasarian, Delia Meth-Cohn, Kristin Moehlmann, Richard Moore, Denise Nolty, Jeffrey Obser, Brian Owens, Alex Parsons, Ulla Plon, Karina Porcelli, Mark Potok, Marcy Pritchard, Elaine Robbins, Kate Sekules, Eric Sjogren, Susan Spencer, Samantha Stenzel, Aaron Sugarman, Enrique Tessieri, Robert Tilley, Julie Tomasz, Nancy van Itallie
Creative Director: Fabrizio La Rocca
Cartographer: David Lindroth
Cover Design: Tigist Getachew
Cover Photograph: Catherine Karnow/Woodfin Camp

Design: Vignelli Associates

Special Sales

Contents

Maps

Contents

Foreword

The Affordables are aimed at people like you and me—people with discriminating tastes and limited budgets.

This is a new series that combines essential budget travel information with all the great editorial features of a Fodor's gold guide: quality writing, authoritative hotel and restaurant reviews, detailed exploring tours, and wonderful maps.

The idea behind these guides is that you, the budget traveler, have the same curiosity, good taste, and high expectations as those who travel first class, and you need information with the same depth and detail as readers of Fodor's gold guides. But as a budget traveler you also need to know about low-cost activities, meals, and lodging, and especially how to get around by train or bus.

Some of you, of course, will spend a bit more on a hotel with full service and amenities but will eat simply; others will be willing to go the hostel route in order to splurge on meals; yet others will save by sticking to public transportation and picnic lunches in order to do some serious shopping. We've tried to include enough options so that each of you can spend your money in the way you most enjoy spending it.

The Affordables, therefore, tell you about activities you can enjoy for free—or close to it. They also place a special emphasis on bargain shopping—what to buy and where to find it.

These are not guides for the hotdog-on-the-run-it's-okay-to-sleep-on-a-park-bench crowd, but for those of you who insist on at least two good, healthy meals a day and a safe, comfortable place to put your head at night. The hotels we recommend offer good value, and there are no dives, thank you—only clean, friendly places with an acceptable level of comfort, convenience, and charm. There's also a wide range of inexpensive and moderately priced dining options, mostly small, family-run restaurants offering healthy, home-cooked, regional cuisine.

Equally important, the Affordables organize all travel according to convenient train and bus routes, and include point-to-point directions that get you to each town and attraction. No matter how you're traveling—by car, train, or bus—your Fodor's Affordable will tell you exactly how to get there. We even locate train routes on maps—a feature every cost-conscious traveler will appreciate, but which (if we may wave our own flag) you won't find in any other budget guide.

Fodor's has made every effort to provide you with accurate, up-to-date information, but time always brings change, and consequently the publisher cannot accept responsibility for errors that may occur. Hours and admission fees in particular may change, so, when it matters to you, we encourage you to call ahead.

We also encourage you to write and share your travel experiences with us—pleasant and unpleasant. When a hotel or restaurant fails to live up to its billing, please let us know, and we'll investigate the complaint and revise our entries when the facts warrant it. Send your letters to The Editor, Fodor's Affordables, 201 East 50th Street, New York, NY 10022.

Have a great trip!

Michael Spring
Editorial Director

Europe

Reykjavik
ICELAND

NORWAY
Bergen

SCOTLAND

NORTHERN
IRELAND

Edinburgh

North Sea

Skagerrat

Belfast

IRELAND

Irish Sea

GREAT BRITAIN

DENMARK

Dublin

WALES

ENGLAND

Hamburg

Cardiff

HOLLAND

Amsterdam

The Hague

Rotterdam

GERMA

London

English Channel

Brussels

Bonn

ATLANTIC OCEAN

BELGIUM

Frankfurt

Paris

LUXEMBOURG

FRANCE

Zürich

Munich

Bern

Salzburg

SWITZERLAND

Lyon

LIECHTENSTEIN

Milan

Lju

Venice

PORTUGAL

ANDORRA

Marseille

Nice

Monaco

Florence

Lisbon

Madrid

Barcelona

Corsica

SPAIN

Seville

Granada

Balearic Islands

Sardinia

Tyrrhenian S

Gibraltar

Mediterranean Sea

MOROCCO

ALGERIA

0   400 miles

0   600 km

TUNISIA

Money-Saving Tips

If you have discriminating tastes but a limited budget, this book is for you. One of Fodor's new Affordables, it combines essential budget travel information about low-cost meals, lodgings, and activities with the same editorial depth that the Fodor's gold guides lavishes on activities in all price categories: the knowledgeable writing, authoritative hotel and restaurant reviews, detailed exploring tours, and helpful maps.

This is not a book for someone intending to subsist on fast food and sleep on park benches, but for those who want at least a couple of good meals each day and a safe, comfortable place to spend the night. In *Affordable Europe 1993* you'll find no dives—only hotels that offer good value— clean, friendly places with an acceptable level of comfort, convenience, and even charm. There's also a wide range of inexpensive and moderately priced dining options, often small, family-run restaurants offering home-cooked, local cuisine. Want to do some shopping? We emphasize bargains and value—and tell you where to buy what you want, and can afford.

A few key strategies can dramatically cut the cost of your European vacation.

- In the planning stages, consult discount travel clubs and travel agencies and other organizations that specialize in discounted hotel and airfares. Some travel clubs are especially good at arranging cut-rate deals with suppliers. Others offer smaller discounts through partial rebates of commissions. Try **Discount Travel International** (114 Forrest Ave., Narberth, PA 19072, tel. 215/668–7184); **Moment's Notice** (425 Madison Ave., New York, NY 10017, tel. 212/486– 0503); **Travelers Advantage** (CUC Travel Service, 49 Music Square W, Nashville, TN 37204, tel. 800/548–1116); and **Worldwide Discount Travel Club** (1674 Meridian Ave., Miami Beach, FL 33139, tel. 305/534–2082). The *Half-Price Europe Book* ($42 plus postage and handling from Entertainment Publications, 2125 Butterfield Rd., Troy, MI 48084, tel. 800/477–3234) includes discount coupons for hotels, restaurants, rental cars, shops, tours, and special events. Since it's fairly expensive, some travel experts suggest you buy it only if you plan to use the hotel discounts, bearing in mind that many establishments offer only a limited number of rooms at discount prices, and for limited times of year.

- Make a budget, providing for accommodations, food, transportation, and cultural and recreational activities. Allow a certain amount of spending money each day, and on the road, try not to exceed that amount. There's no reason to set the same limit every day—you may want to live the Spartan life for a while, then indulge yourself later—say, eating sandwiches and staying at a youth hostel one day to save enough for a concert or a night at the theater the next.

- Remember that when you travel can make a tremendous difference in how much it will cost. European tourism peaks in summer, and prices are high then. If you can be flexible, travel during low season—between November and March, except in ski resort areas—or in the shoulder season—April, May, and mid-September through October. Airfares usually cost more on weekends, so fly midweek. Also, since hotels in big cities are often filled with business travelers during the week and charge their highest rates then, you may save money by visiting on weekends. You can also save by spending more time in regions that draw fewer tourists. This will mean less time in Paris, London, Rome, or at popular seaside resorts, but vacations in the countryside may prove even more rewarding.

- Consider all kinds of lodging options. Moderately priced hotels can be found through unexpected sources. For example, the prestigious **Steigenberger Reservation Service** (United States and Canada: tel. 800/223–5652; Great Britain: tel. 0800/28–93–92 and 071/486–5754), best known for booking luxury hotels worldwide, now represents three-star hotels with a touch of character—such as a 14th-century converted watermill in Berlin—in the medium-price range. Although Europe offers an abundance of inexpensive hotels, there are other possibilities, including hostels, pensions, university rooms, bed-and-breakfasts, and cottages or apartments that can be rented by the week or month. Hotel rooms with shower or bath cost more than rooms with neither. But opting to go without doesn't guarantee low prices: It may cost you $3–$6 to bathe or shower down the hall—so ask about charges in advance.

- If you're traveling alone on a group tour, avoid the single supplement fee. Solo travelers looking to reduce their expenses can contact one of several organizations that help to match up travel companions, including **Odyssey Network** (118 Cedar St., Wellesley, MA 02181, tel. 617/237–2400), and the large **Travel Companion Exchange** (Box 833, Amityville, NY 11701, tel. 516/454–0880). (Such single supplements are not an issue for independent travelers, since European lodgingplaces often have special lower-priced rooms designed for solo travelers, or accommodate singles in double rooms at as much as half the rate for two.)

- Consider camping out. If you enjoy the outdoors, you might plan on spending some or all of your nights at the affordable campsites located throughout Europe. Camping equipment is likely to be more expensive in Europe, so bring what you need from home.

- Don't make phone calls from your hotel. If you do, you'll pay a hefty surcharge. When calling home, prepare yourself with change or a phone card, then find a pay phone and dial direct. This may sound inconvenient, but it's a *lot* cheaper than an operator-assisted call.

- Spend your food dollars carefully. You can eat well but still save money on food at reasonably priced bistros and brasseries, as well as restaurants serving "foreign" cuisine. You're likely to find less expensive restaurants in the country-side, or on the outskirts of town. You can also buy your food at a store and have a picnic in a park or an early dinner in your room. In big cities especially, this is a good way to lower your dining expenses without resorting to fast food. The traditional "Continental breakfast" is pretty skimpy by American standards, and unless it is obligatory to eat where you've lodged, start the day with something from a local bakery, then order your coffee at the counter of the nearest bar. It's also generally cheaper to plan on lunch being your main meal for the day; at mid-day $10 can buy a three- or even four-course feast. In the evening, $6 a head will cover a light meal of bread, cheese, ham, fruit, and wine.

- Don't cash your traveler's checks at shops, hotels, or tourist attractions. Rates are usually better in banks.

- Shop wisely. Bargains can be found at small crafts and antiques shops, where owners are sometimes amenable to negotiating. Ask at your hotel or the tourist bureau about flea markets. Take advantage of the various countries' VAT refund schemes. At many stores, if you spend more than a specific amount on a given purchase, you can claim a refund—all you have to do is ask, though some stores—especially larger ones—offer this service only upon request.

- Consider a public transportation pass for getting around in major cities. In most European cities, you can buy passes for unlimited travel on municipal buses and trains, good for a certain number of days. There may also be discounts on tickets purchased in quantity. If you plan to rely at all on public transportation while in a given city, these passes will save you money.

- Be savvy about planning rail travel. Individual tickets aren't always more expensive than rail passes such as EurailPass or Eurail Flexipass. If you don't plan to cover a lot of ground, it can actually be cheaper to buy separate tickets for each leg of your trip. Traveling overnight by rail is a money saver since you can sleep on the train instead of in a hotel. But if you do spend the night on a train, take precautions against theft—sleep on top of your wallet or valuables, or take shifts with a companion.

- Compare rental companies if you plan on traveling by car. The multinational American companies don't always offer the best deals. You may do better with North American tour operators that arrange for cars from European rental companies such as Europe by Car, Foremost Euro-Car, and Kemwell. Weekly touring packages offer unlimited mileage and a much better rate than the day-to-day deals. To qualify for most of these touring rates, you need to keep the car for at least five days, so plan your itinerary accordingly.

- Plan less-expensive activities. Hiking and bicycling are often more rewarding than typical sightseeing, and cost less. And remember that while admission to castles, châteaus, and monuments averages $4–$5, you can visit the churches, cathedrals, and formal gardens you will find in most towns and cities at no charge. Museums may cost $1–$6 to enter, unless you go on discount days—but visiting art galleries is free. Avoid cabarets, nightclubs, and even relatively modest discos, which tend to be expensive.

- Before shelling out money on high-price theater and concert tickets, look into what's free. You may find performances in churches or *son-et-lumière* performances, sound-and-light extravaganzas staged outdoors in summer. Don't hesitate to ask about discounts—not all are advertised, so inquire before paying. Try for weekend rates, student and age-related price reductions, and promotional deals. Admission to movies in Paris, for instance, is reduced for Monday shows. Half-price theater tickets for same-day performances are fairly common in most European cities, and museum admission fees are often reduced on Sundays and occasionally Wednesdays.

Traveling on a budget doesn't necessarily mean limiting your entire trip to what you can do inexpensively. Some people will spend more on a full-service hotel with amenities and eat on the cheap; others will splurge on meals and stay in hostels; some will bankroll some serious shopping by sticking to public transportation and picnic lunches; still others will choose to scrimp wherever they can so as to afford a rental car. Your priorities are up to you; what we've done is include enough information about all the options so you can choose to spend your money in the way you most enjoy spending it. Yes, Europe '93 can be expensive. But after you've looked through the chapters that follow you may well be surprised just how affordable it can be.

1 Essential Information

Before You Go

Government Tourist Offices

Austria Austrian National Tourist Office. **In the United States:** 500 Fifth Ave., 20th Floor, New York, NY 10110, tel. 212/944–6880; 500 N. Michigan Ave., Suite 1950, Chicago, IL 60611, tel. 312/644–5556; 11601 Wilshire Blvd., Suite 2480, Los Angeles, CA 90025, tel. 213/477–3332; 1300 Post Oak Blvd., Suite 960, Houston, TX 77056, tel. 713/850–9999.
In Canada: 1010 Sherbrooke St. W, Suite 1410, Montreal, Quebec H3A 2R7, tel. 514/849–3709; 200 Granville St., Suite 1380, Vancouver, British Columbia V6C 1S4, tel. 604/683–5808; 2 Bloor St. E, Suite 3330, Toronto, Ontario M4W 1A8, tel. 416/967–3381.
In the United Kingdom: 30 St. George St., London W1R OAL, tel. 071/629–0461.

Belgium Belgian National Tourist Office. **In North America:** 745 Fifth Ave., Suite 714, New York, NY 10151, tel. 212/758–8130.
In The United Kingdom: Premier House, 2 Gayton Rd., Harrow, Middlesex HA1 2XU, tel. 081/861–3300.

Bulgaria Bulgarian National Tourist Office. **In North America:** Balkan Holidays (authorized agent), 161 E. 86th St., New York, NY 10028, tel. 212/573–5530.
In the United Kingdom: 18 Princes St., London W1R 7RE, tel. 071/499–6988.

Czechoslovakia Czechoslovak Travel Bureau and Tourist Office (Čedok). **In North America:** 10 E. 40th St., New York, NY 10016, tel. 212/689–9720.
In the United Kingdom: 17–18 Old Bond St., London W1X 4RB, tel. 071/629–6058.

Denmark Danish Tourist Board. **In the United States:** 655 Third Ave., New York, NY 10017, tel. 212/949–2333.
In Canada: Box 115, Station N, Toronto, Ontario M8V 3S4, tel. 416/823–9620.
In the United Kingdom: Sceptre House, 169–173 Regent St., London W1R 8PY, tel. 071/734–2637.

Finland Finnish Tourist Board. **In the United States:** 655 Third Ave., New York, NY 10017, tel. 212/949–2333.
In Canada: 1200 Bay St., Suite 604, Toronto, Ontario M5R 2A5, tel. 416/964–9159.
In the United Kingdom: 66–68 Haymarket, London, SW1Y 4RF, tel. 071/839–4048.

France French Government Tourist Office. **In the United States:** 610 Fifth Ave., New York, NY 10020, tel. 212/315–0888 or 212/757–1125; 645 N. Michigan Ave., Chicago, IL 60611, tel. 312/337–6301; 2305 Cedar Springs Rd., Dallas, TX 75201, tel. 214/720–4010; 9454 Wilshire Blvd., Beverly Hills, CA 90212, tel. 213/271–6665.
In Canada: 1981 McGill College Ave., Suite 490, Montreal, Quebec H3A 2W9, tel. 514/288–4264; 1 Dundas St. W, Suite 2405, Box 8, Toronto, Ontario M5G 1Z3, tel. 416/593–4717.
In the United Kingdom: 178 Piccadilly, London W1V OAL, tel. 071/629–1272.

Germany **German National Tourist Office. In the United States:** 122 E. 42nd St., New York, NY 10168, tel. 212/661–7200; 444 S. Flower St., Suite 2230, Los Angeles, CA 90071, tel. 213/688–7332. **In Canada:** 175 Bloor St. E, Suite 604, Toronto, Ontario M4W 3R8, tel. 416/968–1570. **In the United Kingdom:** Nightingale House, 65 Curzon St., London W1Y 7PE, tel. 071/495–3990.

Gibraltar **Gibraltar Government Tourist Office. In the United Kingdom:** Arundel Great Court, 179 The Strand, London WC2R 1EH, tel. 071/836–0777.

Great Britain **British Tourist Authority. In the United States:** 40 W. 57th St., New York, NY 10019, tel. 212/581–4700; 625 N. Michigan Ave., Suite 1510, Chicago, IL 60611, tel. 312/787–0490; World Trade Center, 350 S. Figueroa St., Suite 450, Los Angeles, CA 90071, tel. 213/628–3525; 2305 Cedar Springs Rd., Suite 210, Dallas, TX 75201, tel. 214/720–4040. **In Canada:** 94 Cumberland St., Suite 600, Toronto, Ontario M5R 3N3, tel. 416/925–6326. **In the United Kingdom:** Thames Tower, Black's Rd., Hammersmith, London W6 9EL, tel. 081/846–9000.

Greece **Greek National Tourist Organization: In the United States:** 645 Fifth Ave., New York, NY 10022, tel. 212/421–5777; 611 W. 6th St., Suite 2198, Los Angeles, CA 90017, tel. 213/626–6696; 168 N. Michigan Ave., Chicago, IL 60601, tel. 312/782–1084. **In Canada:** 1233 Rue de la Montagne, Montreal, Quebec H3G 1Z2, tel. 514/871–1535; 1300 Bay St., Toronto, Ontario M5R 3K8, tel. 416/968–2220. **In the United Kingdom:** 4 Conduit St., London W1R 0DJ, tel. 071/734–5997.

Hungary **Hungarian Travel Bureau (IBUSZ). In North America:** 1 Parker Plaza, Suite 1104, Fort Lee, NJ 07024, tel. 201/592–8585. **In the United Kingdom:** Danube Travel Ltd. (authorized agent), 6 Conduit St., London W1R 9TG, tel. 071/493–0263.

Ireland **Irish Tourist Board. In the United States:** 757 Third Ave., New York, NY 10017, tel. 212/418–0800 or 800/223–6470. **In Canada:** 160 Bloor St. E, Suite 934, Toronto, Ontario M4W 1B9, tel. 416/929–2777. **In the United Kingdom:** Ireland House, 150 New Bond St., London W1Y 0AQ, tel. 071/493–3201.

Italy **Italian Government Travel Office (ENIT). In the United States:** 630 Fifth Ave., Suite 1565, New York, NY 10111, tel. 212/245–4822; 500 N. Michigan Ave., Suite 1046, Chicago, IL 60611, tel. 312/644–0990; 360 Post St., Suite 801, San Francisco, CA 94108, tel. 415/392–6206. **In Canada:** 1 Place Ville Marie, Suite 1914, Montreal, Quebec H3B 3M9, tel. 514/866–7667. **In the United Kingdom:** 1 Princes St., London W1R 8AY, tel. 071/408–1254.

Luxembourg **Luxembourg Tourist Information Office. In North America:** 801 Second Ave., New York, NY 10017, tel. 212/370–9850. **In the United Kingdom:** 36–37 Piccadilly, London W1V 9PA, tel. 071/434–2800.

Malta **Malta National Tourist Office. In North America:** Maltese Consulate, 249 E. 35th St., New York, NY 10016, tel. 212/725–2345.

In the United Kingdom: Mappin House, Suite 300, 4 Winsley St., London W1N 7AR, tel. 071/323-0506.

Monaco **Monaco Government Tourist and Convention Bureau. In North America:** 845 Third Ave., New York, NY 10022, tel. 212/759-5227.
In the United Kingdom: 3/18 Chelsea Garden Market, Chelsea Harbour, London SW10 0XE, tel. 071/352-2103.

Netherlands **Netherlands Board of Tourism. In the United States:** 355 Lexington Ave., New York, NY 10017, tel. 212/370-7367; 225 N. Michigan Ave., Suite 326, Chicago, IL 60601, tel. 312/819-0300; 90 New Montgomery St., Suite 305, San Francisco, CA 94105, tel. 415/543-6772.
In Canada: 25 Adelaide St. E, Suite 710, Toronto, Ontario M5C 1Y2, tel. 416/363-1577.
In the United Kingdom: 25-28 Buckingham Gate, London SW1E 6LD, tel. 071/630-0451.

Norway **Norwegian Tourist Board. In North America:** 655 Third Ave., New York, NY 10017, tel. 212/949-2333.
In the United Kingdom: Charles House, 5/11 Lower Regent St., London SW1Y 4LR, tel. 071/839-6255.

Poland **Polish National Tourist Office (Orbis). In North America:** 500 Fifth Ave., New York, NY 10110, tel. 212/867-5011; 333 N. Michigan Ave., Chicago, IL 60601, tel. 312/236-9013.
In the United Kingdom: 82 Mortimer St., London W1N 7DE, tel. 071/580-8028.

Portugal **Portuguese National Tourist Office. In the United States:** 590 Fifth Ave., New York, NY 10036, tel. 212/354-4403.
In Canada: 2180 Yonge St., Toronto, Ontario M4S 2B9, tel. 416/250-7575.
In the United Kingdom: 22-25A Sackville St., London W1X 1DE, tel. 071/494-1441.

Romania **Romanian National Tourist Office. In North America:** 573 Third Ave., New York, NY 10016, tel. 212/697-6971.
In the United Kingdom: 17 Nottingham Pl., London W1M 3RD, tel. 071/224-3692.

Spain **Spanish National Tourist Office. In the United States:** 665 Fifth Ave., New York, NY 10022, tel. 212/759-8822; 845 N. Michigan Ave., Chicago, IL 60611, tel. 312/642-1992; San Vicente Plaza Bldg., 8383 Wilshire Blvd., Suite 960, Beverly Hills, CA 90211, tel. 213/658-7188.
In Canada: 102 Bloor St. W, Suite 1400, Toronto, Ontario M5S 1M8, tel. 416/961-3131.
In the United Kingdom: 57-58 St. James's St., London SW1A 1LD, tel. 071/499-0901.

Sweden **Swedish Tourist Board. In North America:** 655 Third Ave., New York, NY 10017, tel. 212/949-2333.
In the United Kingdom: 29-31 Oxford St., 5th floor, London W1R 1RE, tel. 071/437-5816.

Switzerland **Swiss National Tourist Office. In the United States:** 608 Fifth Ave., New York, NY 10020, tel. 212/757-5944; 260 Stockton St., San Francisco, CA 94108, tel. 415/362-2260.
In Canada: 154 University Ave., Suite 610, Toronto, Ontario M5H 3Y9, tel. 416/971-9734.
In the United Kingdom: Swiss Centre, 1 New Coventry St., London W1V 8EE, tel. 071/734-1921.

For each transaction there's a 2% fee (minimum $2, maximum $6). Call 800/227–4669 for information.

Cardholders can also cash personal or counter checks at any American Express office for up to $1,000, of which $500 may be claimed in cash and the balance in traveler's checks carrying a 1% commission.

Wiring Money To send or receive up to $10,000, you can use an **American Express MoneyGram,** and you don't have to have an American Express card. The sender goes to an American Express MoneyGram agent, specifies an amount, pays up to $1,000 with a credit card (anything over that in cash), and telephones the receiver with the reference number he is given. The receiver goes to the nearest MoneyGram agent, presents identification and the reference number, and picks up cash. Fees are 5% to 10%, depending on the amount and method of payment (AE, D, MC, V are accepted). For agent locations, call 800/543–4080.

You can also use **Western Union** (tel. 800/325–6000). A friend at home can bring either cash or a check to the nearest office or pay over the phone with a credit card. Delivery usually takes two business days, and fees are roughly 5% to 10%.

Passports and Visas

Americans All U.S. citizens need a current **passport** to enter the 25 countries covered in this guide. To obtain a new passport, apply in person; renewals can be obtained in person or by mail. First-time applicants should apply to one of the 13 U.S. Passport Agency offices at least five weeks in advance of their departure date. In addition, local county courthouses, many state and probate courts, and some post offices accept passport applications. Necessary documents include: (1) a completed passport application (Form DSP-11); (2) proof of citizenship (certified birth certificate issued by the Hall of Records of your state of birth or naturalization papers); (3) proof of identity (valid driver's license or state, military, or student ID card with your photograph and signature); (4) two recent, identical, 2-inch-square photographs (black-and-white or color head shot with a white or off-white background); and (5) a $65 application fee for a 10-year passport (those under 18 pay $40 for a 5-year passport). You may pay with a check, money order, or exact cash amount; no change is given. Passports are mailed to you in about 10–15 working days. To renew your passport by mail, you'll need to send a completed Form DSP-82, two recent, identical passport photographs, your current passport (if less than 12 years old and issued after your 16th birthday), and a check or money order for $55.

At press time, U.S. citizens need a **visa** to enter Romania. Many countries require a visa for stays longer than three months; apply at the country's embassy in Washington, DC. Since the United States does not have diplomatic relations with Albania, visa applications must go through the Albanian Mission in Paris or Rome. Only Americans of Albanian descent are allowed to enter the country and only on private visits to their relatives.

Canadians All Canadians need a **passport** to enter the 25 countries in this guide. Send the completed application (available at any post office or passport office) to the Bureau of Passports (Suite 215, West Tower, Guy Favreau Complex, 200 René Lévesque Blvd.

W, Montreal, Quebec H2Z 1X4). Include $25, two photographs, a guarantor, and proof of Canadian citizenship. Applications can be made in person at the regional passport offices in Edmonton, Halifax, Montreal, Toronto, Vancouver, or Winnipeg. Passports are valid for five years and are nonrenewable.

A **visa** is required by Canadian citizens traveling to Albania, Bulgaria, Czechoslovakia, Hungary, and Poland. A visa is required to enter Romania, but they can be purchased upon entering the country. Obtain it from the nearest embassy.

Britons All British citizens need a **passport;** applications are available from travel agencies or a main post office. Send the completed form to your nearest regional passport office or to the Passport Office, Clive House, 70–78 Petty France, London SW1H 9HD (tel. 071/279–3434). The application must be countersigned by your bank manager or by a solicitor, barrister, doctor, clergyman, or justice of the peace who knows you personally. In addition, you'll need two photographs and the £15 fee. The occasional tourist may opt for a British Visitor's Passport. It is valid for one year and allows entry into other European Community (EC) countries only. It costs £7.50 and is nonrenewable. You'll need two passport photographs and identification. Apply at your local post office.

A **visa** is required for British citizens entering Bulgaria, Poland, and Romania; the British Tourist Authority recommends calling the consulate of every country you visit to inquire about visas if you think one may be required. Apply at the nearest embassy or consulate.

Customs and Duties

On Arrival Arrival formalities vary from country to country and are detailed in each chapter. In addition to specific duty-free allowances, most countries allow travelers also to bring in cameras and a reasonable amount of film and electronic equipment; most do not allow fresh meats, plants, weapons, and narcotics.

On Departure If you are bringing any foreign-made equipment from home, such as a camera, it's wise to carry the original receipt with you or to register such equipment with U.S. Customs before you leave (Form 4457). Otherwise you may end up paying duty on your return.

U.S. residents may bring home duty-free up to $400 worth of foreign goods, as long as they have been out of the country for at least 48 hours and they haven't made an international trip in 30 days. Each member of the family is entitled to the same exemption, regardless of age, and exemptions may be pooled. For the next $1,000 worth of goods, a flat 10% rate is assessed; duties vary with the merchandise for anything over $1,400. Included for travelers 21 or older are 1 liter of alcohol, 100 cigars (non-Cuban), and 200 cigarettes. Only 1 bottle of perfume trademarked in the United States may be brought in. However, there is no duty on antiques or art over 100 years old. Anything exceeding these limits will be taxed at the port of entry and may be taxed additionally in the traveler's home state. Unlimited amounts of goods from designated "developing" or GSP countries also may be brought in duty-free; check with the U.S. Customs Service (Box 7407, Washington, DC 20044). Gifts valued at under $50 may be mailed to friends or relatives at home duty-free, but not more than one package per day to any one addressee and not including perfumes costing more than $5 or tobacco or liquor. Before your trip, be sure to obtain *Know Before You Go,* a free, invaluable customs brochure that outlines what returning residents may and may not bring back to this country, and at what cost. Contact U.S. Customs Service (1301 Constitution Ave., Washington, DC 20229).

Exemptions for returning **Canadians** range from $20 to $300, depending on the length of stay out of the country. For the $300 exemption, you must have been out of the country for one week. For any given year, you are allowed one $300 exemption. You may bring in duty-free up to 50 cigars, 200 cigarettes, 2.2 pounds of tobacco, and 40 ounces of liquor, provided these are declared in writing to customs on arrival and accompany the traveler in hand or checked-through baggage. Personal gifts should be mailed as "Unsolicited Gift—Value under $40." Request the Canadian Customs brochure "I Declare" for further details.

British residents, *see* Customs and Duties in Great Britain.

Staying Healthy

There are no serious health risks associated with travel in Europe. However, the Centers for Disease Control (CDC) in Atlanta cautions that most of southern Europe is in the "intermediate" range for risk of contracting traveler's diarrhea. Part of this may be due to an increased consumption of olive oil and wine, which can have a laxative effect on stomachs used to a different diet. The CDC also advises that international travelers swim only in chlorinated swimming pools if there is any question about contamination of local beaches and freshwater lakes.

If you have a health problem that might require purchasing prescription drugs while in Europe, ask your doctor to prescribe the drug by its generic name. Brand names vary widely from one country to another.

The International Association for Medical Assistance to Travelers (IAMAT) is a worldwide association offering a list of approved English-speaking doctors whose training meets British and American standards. Contact IAMAT for a list of European physicians and clinics that belong to this network. **In the United States:** 417 Center St., Lewiston, NY 14092, tel. 716/754–4883. **In Canada:** 40 Regal Rd., Guelph, Ontario, N1K 1B5. **In Europe:** 57 Voirets, 1212 Grand-Lancy, Geneva, Switzerland. Membership is free.

Shots and Medications Inoculations are not needed for Europe. The American Medical Association (AMA) recommends Pepto-Bismol for minor cases of traveler's diarrhea.

Insurance

Travelers may seek insurance coverage in four areas: health and accident, lost luggage, wrong flight, and trip cancellation. Your first step is to review your existing health and homeowner policies; some health insurance plans cover health expenses incurred while traveling, some major medical plans cover emergency transportation, and some home-owner policies cover the theft of luggage.

Health and Accident Several companies offer coverage designed to supplement existing health insurance for travelers:

Carefree Travel Insurance (Box 310, 120 Mineola Blvd., Mineola, NY 11501, tel. 516/294–0220 or 800/323–3149) provides coverage for emergency medical evacuation and accidental death and dismemberment. It also offers 24-hour medical phone advice.

International SOS Assistance (Box 11568, Philadelphia, PA 19116, tel. 215/244–1500 or 800/523–8930), a medical assistance company, provides emergency evacuation services, worldwide medical referrals, and optional medical insurance.

Travel Guard International, underwritten by Transamerica Occidental Life Companies (1145 Clark St., Stevens Point, WI 54481, tel. 715/345–0505 or 800/782–5151), offers reimbursement for medical expenses with no deductibles or daily limits, and emergency evacuation services.

Wallach and Company, Inc. (Box 480, Middleburg, VA 22117–0480, tel. 703/687–3166 or 800/237–6615) offers comprehensive medical coverage, including emergency evacuation services worldwide.

Lost Luggage and Trip Cancellation Airlines are responsible for lost or damaged property only up to $1,250 per passenger on domestic flights, and $9.07 per pound (or $20 per kilo) for checked baggage on international flights, and up to $400 per passenger for unchecked baggage on international flights. If you're carrying valuables, either take them with you on the airplane or purchase additional insurance for lost luggage. Some airlines will issue additional luggage insurance when you check in, but many do not. Insurance for lost, damaged, or stolen luggage is available through travel agents or directly through various insurance companies. Two that issue luggage insurance are **Tele-Trip** (Box 31685, 3201 Farnam St., Omaha, NE 68131–0618, tel. 800/228–9792), a subsidiary of Mutual of Omaha, and **The Traveler** (Ticket and Travel Dept., 1 Tower Sq., Hartford, CT 06183–5040, tel. 203/277–0111 or 800/243–3174). Tele-Trip operates sales booths at airports and issues insurance through travel agents. Tele-Trip will insure checked luggage for up to 180 days; rates vary according to the length of the trip. The Travelers Insurance will insure checked or hand luggage for $500 to $2,000 valuation per person, for a maximum of 180 days. Rates for 1–5 days for $500 valuation are $10; for 180 days, $85. Other companies with comprehensive policies include **Access America, Inc.,** a subsidiary of Blue Cross–Blue Shield (Box 11188, Richmond, VA 23230, tel. 800/334–7525 or 800/284–8300); and **Travel Guard International** (*see* Health and Accident Insurance, *above*).

In the United Kingdom, for free general advice on all aspects of holiday insurance, contact the **Association of British Insurers** (Aldermary House, 10–15 Queen St., London EC4N 1TT, tel. 071/248–4477). A provider of holiday insurance is **Europ Assistance** (252 High St., Croydon, Surrey CR0 1NF, tel. 081/680–1234).

Before you go, itemize the contents of each bag in case you need to file an insurance claim. Be certain to put your home or business address on each piece of luggage, including carry-on bags.

If your luggage is lost or stolen and later recovered, the airline will deliver the luggage to your home free of charge.

Trip Cancellation Consider purchasing trip-cancellation insurance if you are traveling on a promotional or discounted ticket that does not allow changes or cancellations. You are then covered if an emergency causes you to cancel or postpone your trip. Trip cancellation insurance is usually included in combination travel insurance packages available from most tour operators, travel agents, and insurance agents. Flight insurance, which covers passengers in the case of death or dismemberment, is often included in the price of a ticket when paid for with American Express, MasterCard, or other major credit cards.

Renting Cars

It's best to arrange a car rental before you leave. You won't save money by waiting until you arrive in Europe, and you may find that the type of car you want is not available at the last minute. If you're flying into a major city and planning to spend some time there before using your car, save money by arranging to pick it up on the day of your departure. If you're arriving and departing from different airports, look for a one-way car rental with no return fees. If you're traveling to more than one country, make sure your rental contract permits you to take the car across borders and that the insurance policy covers you in every country you visit. Be prepared to pay more for a car with an automatic transmission; because they are not as readily available as those with manual transmission, reserve in advance.

Budget rental companies serving Europe include **Europe by Car** (1 Rockefeller Plaza, New York, NY 10020, tel. 212/245–1713, 800/223–1516 or in CA 800/252–9401); **Foremost Euro-Car** (Suite 306, 5430 Van Nuys Blvd., Van Nuys, CA 91401, tel. 818/786–1960); and **Kemwel** (106 Calvert St., Harrison, NY 10528, tel. 800/678–0678). Other major firms with European rentals include **Avis** (tel. 800/331–1212); **Hertz** (tel. 800/654–3001); and **National** or **Europcar** (tel. 800/CAR-RENT).

Driver's licenses issued in the United States and Canada are valid in Europe. Non-EEC nationals must have Green Card insurance (*see* By Car in Getting Around Europe, *below*). You might also take out an International Driving Permit before you leave in order to smooth out difficulties if you have an accident or as an additional piece of identification. Permits are available for a small fee through local offices of the **American Automobile Association** (AAA) and the **Canadian Automobile Association** (CAA), or from their main offices (AAA, 1000 AAA Dr., Heathrow, FL 32746, tel. 800/336–4357; and CAA, 2 Carlton St., Toronto, Ontario M5B 1K4, tel. 416/964–3002).

Britons driving in Europe should have a valid driver's license. Green Card insurance is a wise buy, though not compulsory for EEC nationals. All drivers must carry their car registration documents and a red warning triangle.

Student and Youth Travel

The **International Student Identity Card** (ISIC) entitles students to youth rail passes, special fees on local transportation, student charter flights within Europe, and discounts at museums, theaters, sports events, and many other attractions. If purchased in the United States, the $14 card also entitles the holder to $3,000 in emergency medical insurance, plus $100 a day for up to 60 days of hospital coverage. Apply to the **Council on International Educational Exchange** (CIEE, 205 E. 42nd St., 16th floor, New York, NY 10017, tel. 212/661–1414). In Canada, the ISIC is available for CN$13 from **Travel Cuts** (187 College St., Toronto, Ontario M5T 1P7, tel. 416/979–2406).

The **Youth International Educational Exchange Card** (YIEE), issued by the **Federation of International Youth Travel Organizations** (FIYTO, 81 Islands Brugge, DK-2300 Copenhagen S, Denmark), provides similar services to nonstudents under 26 years of age. In the United States, the card is available from CIEE (*see above*). In Canada, the YIEE card is available from the **Canadian Hostelling Association** (CHA, 1600 James Naismith Dr., Suite 698, Gloucester, Ontario K1B 5N4, tel. 613/748–5638).

An **International Youth Hostel Federation** (IYHF) membership card is the key to inexpensive dormitory-style accommodations at thousands of youth hostels around the world. Hostels provide separate sleeping quarters and are situated in a variety of locations, including converted farmhouses, villas, restored castles, and specially constructed modern buildings. There are more than 5,000 hostel locations in 70 countries around the world. IYHF memberships, which are valid for 12 months from the time of purchase, are available in the United States through **American Youth Hostels** (AYH, Box 37613, Washington, DC 20013, tel. 202/783–6161). The cost for a first-year membership is $25 for adults 18 to 54. Renewal thereafter is $20. For youths (17 and under) the rate is $10, and for senior citizens (55 and older) the rate is $15. Family membership is available for $35. Every national hostel association offers special reductions for members visiting its country, such as discounted rail fare or free bus travel, so be sure to ask for an international concessions list when you buy your membership. IYHF also publishes an extensive directory of youth hostels around the world. Economical bicycle tours for small groups of adventurous, energetic students are another popular AYH student travel service. For information on these and other AYH services and publications, contact the AYH at the address above.

In the United Kingdom, contact the **Youth Hostel Association of England and Wales** (YHA, Trevelyan House, 8 St. Stephen's Hill, St. Albans, Herts AL1 2DY, tel. 0727/55215).

Council Travel, a CIEE subsidiary, is the foremost U.S. student travel agency and specializes in low-cost charters and serves as the exclusive U.S. agent for many student airfare bargains and student tours. The 72-page *Student Travel Catalog* and "Council Charter" brochure are available free from any Council Travel office in the United States (enclose $1 postage if ordering by mail). Contact CIEE headquarters at the address above, or Council Travel offices in Amherst, Austin, Berkeley, Boston, Cambridge, Chicago, Dallas, La Jolla, Long Beach, Los Angeles, New York, Portland, Providence, San Diego, San Francisco, and Seattle, to name a few.

Students who would like to work abroad should contact CIEE's **Work Abroad Department** at the address given above. The council arranges various types of paid and voluntary work experiences overseas for up to six months. CIEE also sponsors study programs in Europe, Latin America, and Asia, and publishes many books of interest to the student traveler, including *Work, Study, Travel Abroad: The Whole World Handbook* ($12.95 plus $1.50 book-rate postage or $3 first-class postage) and *Volunteer! The Comprehensive Guide to Voluntary Service in the U.S. and Abroad* ($8.95 plus $1.50 book-rate postage or $3 first-class postage).

The Information Center at the **Institute of International Education** (IIE, 809 UN Plaza, New York, NY 10017, tel. 212/883–8200) has reference books, foreign university catalogues, study-abroad brochures, and other materials that may be consulted by students and nonstudents alike, free of charge. The Information Center is open weekdays 10–4.

IIE administers a variety of grant and study programs offered by U.S. and foreign organizations, and publishes a well-known annual series of study-abroad guides, including *Academic Year Abroad, Vacation Study Abroad,* and *Study in the United Kingdom and Ireland.* The institute also publishes *Teaching Abroad,* a book of employment and study opportunities overseas for U.S. teachers. For a current list of IIE publications, along with prices and ordering information, write to the IIE Publications Service at the address given above. Books must be purchased by mail or in person; telephone orders are not accepted. General information on IIE programs and services is available from its regional offices in Atlanta, Chicago, Denver, Houston, San Francisco, and Washington, DC.

For information on the Eurail Youthpass, *see* Rail Passes in Getting Around Europe by Train, *below.*

Traveling with Children

Publications *A Capital Guide for Kids: A London Guide for Parents with Small Children* by Vanessa Miles (Allison & Busby, 6a Noel St., London W1V 3RB; £1.95). *Children's Guide to London* by Christopher Pick (Cadogan Books, 16 Lower Marsh, London SE1 7RJ; $8.50). *Family Travel Times* is an 8- to 12-page newsletter published 10 times a year by TWYCH (Travel with Your Children, 45 W. 18th St., 7th floor tower, New York, NY 10011, tel. 212/206–0688). Subscription includes access to back issues and twice-weekly opportunities to call in for specific advice. *Kids' London* by Elizabeth Holt and Molly Perham (St. Martin's Press, $5.95). "Young People's Guide to Munich" is a free pamphlet available from the German National Tourist Office (122 E. 42nd St., New York, NY 10168, tel. 212/661–7200). *Traveling With Children—And Enjoying It* (published by The Globe Pequot Press, Box 833, Old Saybrook, CT 06475, tel. 800/243–0495; $11.95 plus $2 shipping).

Family Travel **American Institute for Foreign Study** (AIFS, 102 Greenwich
Organizations Ave., Greenwich, CT 06830, tel. 203/869–9090) offers programs for college students and interested adults. For information on programs for high-school-aged students and their families, contact the **Educational Travel Division, American Council for International Studies** (19 Bay State Rd., Boston, MA 02215, tel. 617/236–2015 or 800/825–AIFS).

Families Welcome! (Box 16398, Chapel Hill, NC 27516, tel. 800/326–0724) is a travel agency that arranges England and France tours brimming with family-oriented choices and activities.

The French Experience (370 Lexington Ave., New York, NY 10017, tel. 212/986-3800) is an organization that understands family needs.

Grandtravel (600 Wisconsin Ave., Suite 706, Chevy Chase, MD 20815, tel. 301/986-0790 or 800/247-7651) offers dozens of international tours for grandparents and their children.

Getting There On international flights, children under two not occupying a seat pay 10% of adult fare. Various discounts apply to children two to 12 years of age. Regulations about infant travel on airplanes are in the process of changing. Until they do, however, if you want to be sure your infant is secure and traveling in his or her own safety seat, you must buy a separate ticket and bring your own infant car seat. (Check with the airline in advance; certain seats aren't allowed. Or write for the booklet "Child/Infant Safety Seats Acceptable for Use in Aircraft," from the Federal Aviation Administration, APA-200, 800 Independence Ave. SW, Washington, DC 20591, tel. 202/267-3479.) Some airlines allow babies to travel in their own car seats at no charge if there's a spare seat available; otherwise safety seats will be stored and the child will have to be held by a parent. (If you opt to hold your baby on your lap, do so with the infant outside the seatbelt so he or she won't be crushed in case of a sudden stop.)

Also inquire about special children's meals or snacks. *Family Travel Times* includes "TWYCH's Airline Guide," which contains a rundown of the children's services offered by 46 airlines.

Hotels **Novotel** hotels in Europe permit up to two children to stay free in their parents' room. Many Novotel properties have playgrounds. (International reservations, tel. 800/221-4542.)

Sofitel hotels in Europe offer a free second room for children during July and August and over the Christmas holiday, depending upon availability. (International reservations, tel. 800/221-4542.)

Happy Family Swiss Hotels are 22 properties in Switzerland that have joined together to welcome families, offering outstanding programs for children at reduced prices. A brochure on these hotels is available from the Swiss National Tourist Office (608 Fifth Ave., New York, NY 10019, tel. 212/757-5944).

Club Med (40 W. 57th St., New York, NY 10019, tel. 800/258-2633) has "Baby Clubs" (from age four months), "Mini Clubs" (for ages four to six or eight, depending on the resort), and "Kids Clubs" (for ages eight and up during school holidays) at many of its resort villages in France, Italy, Switzerland, and Spain.

Villa Rentals **At Home Abroad, Inc.** (405 E. 56th St., Suite 6H, New York, NY 10022, tel. 212/421-9165).
Villas International (605 Market St., Suite 510, San Francisco, CA 94105, tel. 415/281-0910).
Hideaways, Int'l (Box 1270, Littleton, MA 01460, tel. 508/486-8955).
B. & D. de Vogue (250 S. Beverly Dr., Suite 203, Beverly Hills, CA 90212, tel. 310/247-8612 or 800/727-4748).
Meeting Points (5515 S.E. Milwaukee Ave., Portland, OR 97207, tel. 503/233-1224).
Vacances en Campagne/Vacanze in Italia/Heritage of England (Box 297, Falls Village, CT 06031, tel. 203/824-5155 or 800/533-5405).

agrees to be a courier must accompany shipments between designated points. There are two sources of information on courier deals: (1) A telephone directory lists courier companies by the cities to which they fly. Send $5 and a self-addressed, stamped, business-size envelope to Pacific Data Sales Publishing, 2554 Lincoln Blvd., Suite 275-F, Marina Del Rey, CA 92091. (2) For a copy of a booklet called "A Simple Guide to Courier Travel," send $15.95 (includes postage and handling) to Box 2394, Lake Oswego, OR 97035. For more information, call 800/344–9375.

Charters Charter flights offer the lowest fares but often depart only on certain days, and seldom on time. Though you may be able to arrive at one city and return from another, you may lose all or most of your money if you cancel your trip. Don't sign up for a charter flight unless you've checked with a travel agency about the reputation of the packager. It's particularly important to know the packager's policy concerning refunds should a flight be canceled. One of the most popular charter operators to Europe is **Council Charter** (205 E. 42nd St., New York, NY 10017, tel. 212/661–0311 or 800/800–8222), a division of CIEE (Council on International Educational Exchange). Other companies advertise in Sunday travel sections of newspapers.

Consolidators Somewhat more expensive—but up to 50% below the cost of APEX fares—are tickets purchased through consolidators, companies that buy blocks of tickets on scheduled airlines and sell them at wholesale prices. Here again, you may lose all or most of your money if you change plans, but at least you will be on a regularly scheduled flight with less risk of cancellation than on a charter. Once you've made your reservation, call the airline to confirm it. Among the best-known consolidators are **UniTravel** (Box 12485, St. Louis, MO 63132, tel. 314/569–2501 or 800/325–2222) and **Access International** (101 W. 31st St., Suite 1104, New York, NY 10001, tel. 212/465–0707 or 800/825–3633). Others advertise in Sunday newspaper travel sections.

Travel Clubs Another option is to join a travel club that offers special discounts to its members. Three such organizations are **Moment's Notice** (425 Madison Ave., New York, NY 10017, tel. 212/486–0500), **Discount Travel International** (114 Forrest Ave., Narberth, PA 19072, tel. 215/668–7184 or 800/334–9294), and **Worldwide Discount Travel Club** (1674 Meridian Ave., Suite 300, Miami Beach, FL 33139, tel. 305/534–2082). These cut-rate tickets should be compared with APEX tickets on the major airlines.

Airlines The U.S. airlines that serve the major cities in Europe are **TWA** (tel. 800/892–4141); **United** (tel. 800/538–2929); **Continental** (tel. 800/231–0856); **American Airlines** (tel. 800/433–7300); **Northwest** (tel. 800/447–4747); and **Delta** (tel. 800/241–4141).

Many European national airlines fly directly from the United States to their home countries. The biggest advantage in arriving on a home airline is that the landing privileges are often better, as are the facilities provided at main airports. Here are the U.S. telephone numbers of those airlines that have representation in the United States; most of the numbers are toll-free.

Austria: Austrian Airlines (tel. 800/843–0002)
Belgium: Sabena Belgian World Airlines (tel. 800/950–1000)
Czechoslovakia: Czechoslovak Airlines (CSA, tel. 212/682–5833)

Denmark: Scandinavian Airlines (SAS, tel. 800/221–2350)
Finland: Finnair (tel. 800/950–5000)
France: Air France (tel. 800/237–2747)
Germany: Lufthansa (tel. 800/645–3880)
Great Britain: British Airways (tel. 800/247–9297); Virgin Atlantic (tel. 800/862–8621)
Greece: Olympic Airways (tel. 212/838–3600)
Holland: KLM Royal Dutch Airlines (tel. 800/777–5553)
Hungary: Malév Hungarian Airlines (tel. 212/757–6446)
Iceland: Icelandair (tel. 800/223–5500)
Ireland: Aer Lingus (800/223–6537)
Italy: Alitalia (tel. 800/223–5730)
Malta: Air Malta (tel. 415/362–2929)
Norway: Scandinavian Airlines (SAS, tel. 800/221–2350)
Poland: LOT Polish Airlines (tel. 212/869–1074)
Portugal: TAP Air Portugal (tel. 800/221–7370)
Romania: Tarom Romanian Airlines (tel. 212/687–6013)
Spain: Iberia Airlines (tel. 800/772–4642)
Sweden: Scandinavian Airlines (tel. 800/221–2350)
Switzerland: Swissair (tel. 800/221–4750)

Flying Time From New York: 6½ hours to London and 7–8 hours to Scandinavian capitals. From Chicago: 8½ hours to London, 10–11 hours to Scandinavian capitals. From Los Angeles: 10 hours to London, 12–13 hours to Scandinavian capitals.

Enjoying the Flight If you're lucky enough to be able to sleep on a plane, it makes sense to fly at night. Many experienced travelers, however, prefer to take a morning flight to Europe and arrive in the evening, just in time for a good night's sleep. Because the air on a plane is dry, it helps, while flying, to drink a lot of nonalcoholic beverages; drinking alcohol contributes to jet lag, as does eating heavy meals on board. Feet swell at high altitudes, so it's a good idea to remove your shoes at the beginning of your flight. Sleepers usually prefer window seats to curl up against; those who like to move about the cabin ask for aisle seats. Bulkhead seats (in the front row of each cabin) have more legroom, but seat trays are attached to the arms of your seat rather than to the back of the seat in front.

Smoking As of February 1990, smoking was banned on all scheduled routes within the 48 contiguous states, within the states of Hawaii and Alaska, to and from the U.S. Virgin Islands and Puerto Rico, and on flights of under six hours to and from Hawaii and Alaska. The rule applies to both domestic and foreign carriers.

On a flight where smoking is permitted, you can request a non-smoking seat during check-in or when you book your ticket. If the airline tells you on the day of the flight that there are no seats available in the nonsmoking section, insist on one: Department of Transportation regulations require U.S. carriers to find seats for all nonsmokers, provided they meet check-in time restrictions. These regulations apply to all international flights on domestic carriers; however, the Department of Transportation does not have jurisdiction over foreign carriers traveling out of, or into, the United States.

Luggage Regulations Airlines generally allow each passenger two pieces of check-in luggage and one carry-on piece on international flights from North America. Each piece of check-in luggage cannot exceed 62 inches (length + width + height) or weigh more than 70 pounds. The carry-on luggage cannot exceed 45 inches (length + width + height) and must fit under the seat or in the overhead luggage compartment.

For information on luggage insurance, *see* Insurance in Before You Go, *above.*

Labeling Luggage Put your home or business address on each piece of luggage, including hand baggage. If your lost luggage is recovered, the airline will deliver it to your home, at no charge to you.

From the United Kingdom by Plane

Air travel from Britain to continental Europe has undergone a quiet revolution during the past few years. Thanks in part to the ever-growing demand for inexpensive charter flights, in part to the British government's determination to break down the cozy system of intergovernmental fare setting, and above all to a stronger sense of a shared European identity, more and more Britons regard flying as an everyday means of transportation rather than as an occasional luxury. The result, as expected, is more flights, greater choice, and lower fares.

But it isn't all good news. For one thing, not all European governments share Britain's enthusiasm for more competitive fares. Of long-term concern is the evident inability of European air networks to cope with an explosion in passenger numbers. And, at least at peak periods, more people traveling means more congestion and more delays.

It's not just those in the cheaper seats who suffer, either. Scheduled flights are just as likely to be delayed as charter flights, though they are, it's true, mostly spared the major delays that can afflict the summertime charter flights. Nonetheless, Europe's more militant air-traffic controllers have never been slow to grasp that the most effective way to draw attention to increased work loads and, in many cases, antiquated air-traffic control systems is to go on strike when maximum disruption is guaranteed—in other words, at the busiest times. Shots of beleaguered tourists gamely bedding down for another night at the airport have become a commonplace on Britain's TV screens. France, Spain, and Greece currently head the list of countries with the most strike-happy air controllers.

None of which is intended to suggest that flying from Britain to the Continent is something that can be recommended only to those who don't mind not sleeping for three days. And not least, of course, because everyone agrees that Europe's prosperity depends more than ever on good communications, with air travel well up there in the forefront.

Though some would certainly argue that it's all long overdue, the past few years have seen a welcome and widespread recognition that vastly increased investment and a determination to rethink the answers are crucial if Europe is to have the air networks it deserves. A unified European air-traffic control system in place of the current nationally operated systems may still be only a gleam in the eye of Utopian-minded Europhiles, but a new generation of air-traffic control systems is, at last, being installed in many countries. Once in place, they should improve dramatically the capacity of today's overworked machines. Likewise, in the certain knowledge that routine delays will eventually kill the goose that lays the golden egg, airlines, tour operators, and charter companies have exerted increasing pressure on governments to ensure that strikes become the exception, not the rule.

Scheduled Airlines If flying from a convenient airport, avoiding night flights at awkward hours, and relative reliability are more important to you than just finding the cheapest flight, scheduled flights are a better option than charters. London, with its two main airports—Heathrow and Gatwick—and three subsidiary airports—Luton, Stanstead, and London City—is Europe's biggest air hub. Frequent scheduled services connect it with virtually every major European city and resort. British Airways (BA) is the largest single operator, but all other leading international European airlines have flights to and from their own countries. There is never less than one flight a day to all the European capitals; in most cases, many more.

Competition from up-and-coming airlines such as British Midland, determined to grab customers from BA, has increased the options available to travelers. These smaller airlines have pioneered routes to European capitals from regional British airports. Manchester, for instance, has become a busy northern hub for several carriers, with shuttle flights to London and several flights a day to Amsterdam and other European points. Other major European airlines also have flights from several regional British airports. Air France, for example, has daily flights from Edinburgh to Paris. Similarly, SAS has a daily flight from Edinburgh to Copenhagen. (Both Glasgow and Edinburgh are linked to London by frequent shuttle flights operated by BA, British Midland, and others.)

Most airlines' weekday schedules cater principally to business flyers, who want to fly at clearly defined peak times (generally weekdays, first thing in the morning and late afternoon/early evening). As a result, lower fares are available outside these peak times. Look for better fares on midday flights, and check into weekend fares. Some are less than half the regular economy fares, though note that nearly all require that you spend at least one Saturday night at your destination. As a basic rule of thumb, remember that the cheaper a fare is, the more likely it is to carry restrictions. Always make sure you find out what these are before you buy your ticket.

The busiest routes also tend to be the cheapest. There are evermore competitive fares on offer between London and Paris and London and Frankfurt. Likewise, fares between London and Brussels are also lower than the European average, mile for mile. Fares between London and Amsterdam can be a bargain, the cheapest in Europe. What's more, there are excellent onward connections from Amsterdam to other European cities.

Finally, remember, too, that few European flights are longer than four hours; the majority, in fact, rarely top two hours. Such short journeys make flying business-class or first-class, where it exists, an unnecessary luxury for most travelers. It's also worth bearing in mind that on most European airlines business class is open to anyone with a full-fare economy (coach class) ticket.

Charter Airlines Charter airlines offer much cheaper fares to Europe than do the scheduled carriers, but the rules that bind them are more restrictive. While the British government turns a blind eye to sales of seat-only charter tickets, some European governments still require proof that you have bought an inclusive package vacation rather than just a flight. Most of the seat-only agencies will therefore give you a voucher stating that you have accommodations at a certain hotel. This is to comply with the rules—it won't necessarily get you a bed, even if you can find the hotel in question!

Greece specifically has expressed its determination to stamp out seat-only traffic by threatening passengers using such tickets with fines or deportation under international rules on charter sales. Its implementation of this rule has, though, been patchy so far.

Charter flights are by far the cheapest form of air transportation to main vacation destinations—particularly in the Mediterranean—and some of the charter fares available to last-minute buyers compare favorably even with bus or rail fares. Moreover, to destinations such as Spain, Greece, and Italy, charter flights can give significant savings over scheduled fares. These are countries whose governments have vigorously resisted the introduction of cheaper scheduled fares and that remain zealously protective of their national airlines.

The main drawback of traveling by charter is rigid timetabling. Your return flight will be 7, 14, or 21 days from your departure date. The cheapest flights leave at inconvenient times—mainly in the early hours of the morning—and, in London, from airports a long way from the city center, such as Luton. The other major disadvantage is that charter flights are much more prone to delay than are scheduled flights. Delays of up to two days have been known, though these are admittedly exceptional. But on most flights it nonetheless makes sense to expect some delay, even if it's only an hour or so.

Arrival airports are often resorts rather than capital or major cities. In Spain, most charters fly to the Mediterranean coast rather than to Madrid or Seville; in Portugal, most flights arrive in the Algarve resort area rather than Lisbon. In Greece, this system can be an advantage rather than a drawback—most flights go to the islands rather than to Athens, so if your destination is, for example, Mykonos or Crete, you can fly there direct by charter without having to transfer to a domestic flight or ferry at Athens.

Charters bought at the last minute can be extremely cheap—check in travel agents' windows or in the classified sections of the London *Evening Standard* for cheap late-booking deals. Some of these may be so inexpensive that you may consider discarding the round-trip half of the ticket and traveling onward in Europe from your arrival point, rather than coming back to London.

From the United Kingdom by Car

Nearly all ferries from Britain to the Continent take cars. Which route you take, therefore, will be determined by a combination of your eventual destination and the amount of driving you want to do. The shortest routes are the fastest and the most popular: from Dover, Ramsgate, or Folkestone to Calais, Boulogne, and Ostend. These are the most convenient routes for much of France and Belgium, as well as central and southern Germany, Austria, Switzerland, Italy, and southeast Europe.

If you're heading to western France or to Spain and Portugal, then Dieppe, Le Havre, Caen, Cherbourg, and St. Malo are better routes. Similarly, though the cost is much higher (though equally, the driving is greatly reduced) you should consider putting your car on the train in France or taking the ferry to Santander in northern Spain. The best routes to Holland and north Germany are from Dover and Felixstowe to Zeebrugge; from Sheerness to Vlissingen; and from Harwich to the Hook of Holland and Hamburg. If you're heading for Scandinavia, there are sailings from Harwich and Newcastle to Esbjerg in Denmark, Gothenburg in Sweden, and Stavangar and Bergen in Norway. There are regular sailings to Dublin from Holyhead and to Rosslare from Fishguard and Pembroke in Wales.

Unless you're traveling in the dead of winter, and sometimes even then, it's essential to book well in advance (*see* By Ferry/ Ship, *below*, for addresses). Rates vary according to the length of your vehicle, the time of your crossing, and whether you plan to travel in peak, shoulder, or low season. Morning and evening crossings in the summer months are most expensive, and national holidays should be avoided where possible.

Both the **Automobile Association** (Fanum House, Basingstoke, Hants. RG21 2EA; tel. 0345/500600) and the **Royal Automobile Club** (RAC House, Box 100, South Croydon CR2 6XW, tel. 081/ 686–2525) operate on-the-spot breakdown and repair services across Europe. Replacement cars can be provided in case of accidents. Both companies will also transport cars and passengers back to Britain in case of serious breakdowns. The AA's 5-Star Cover costs £43 for up to 5 days, £60.50 for up to 12 days, and £85.50 for up to 31 days. Nonmembers are charged an extra £3; basic membership costs £45. The RAC's Euro-Cover costs £36 for up to 10 days and £46 for up to 31 days. Again, nonmembers are charged an extra £3; basic membership costs £31.

For advice on whether to bring your own car or to buy or rent one on your trip, *see* Renting, Leasing, and Purchasing Cars in Before You Go, *above*.

From the United Kingdom by Ferry/Ship

Ferry routes for passengers and vehicles link the North Sea, English Channel, and Irish Sea ports with almost all of Britain's maritime neighbors.

To France and Belgium By far the fastest and, for most visitors, the most convenient routes are those across the English Channel to France and Belgium. The principal routes are Dover–Calais (operated by **P&O European Ferries, Sealink,** and **Hoverspeed**); Dover–Boulogne (operated by P&O European Ferries and Hoverspeed); Dover–Zeebrugge (operated by P&O European Ferries); Dover–Ostend (operated by P&O European Ferries); Folkestone–Boulogne (operated by Sealink); and Ramsgate–Dunkirk (operated by **Sally Line**). Crossing times vary from 75 minutes for the Dover–Calais sailings to four hours for the Dover–Ostend sailings, depending on sea states. Make reservations well in advance for peak periods (Easter, July, and August).

The passengers-only Dover–Ostend Jetfoil (book through P&O European Ferries) is a good bet if you're traveling by train. It makes the crossing in only 100 minutes. But note that it is both more expensive than the regular ferries and much more liable to cancellation in bad weather.

There is a wide choice of other sailings to France: Newhaven–Dieppe (operated by Sealink); Portsmouth–Le Havre or Cherbourg (operated by P&O European Ferries); Southampton–Cherbourg (operated by Sealink); Portsmouth–Caen (operated by **Brittany Ferries**); Portsmouth–St. Malo (operated by Brittany Ferries); Poole–Cherbourg (operated by Brittany Ferries, summer only); and Plymouth–Roscoff (operated by Brittany Ferries). Journey times are longer (ranging from four hours for the Newhaven–Dieppe route to nine hours for the Portsmouth–St. Malo route) and fares higher, but you can avoid a great deal of unnecessary driving across northern France. Again, make reservations well in advance for peak periods.

To Spain and Portugal   Brittany Ferries, which runs the St. Malo service, also sails from Plymouth to Santander in northern Spain. The crossing takes 24 hours and the line's cruise ferries offer economy and luxury cabins, as well as entertainment facilities that include a cinema and restaurants. If you are traveling by car and plan to tour Spain, this route offers you the option of looping back through France and returning to Britain without retracing your tracks. Onward travel into Spain without a car, however, will be time-consuming and is really an option only for those with plenty of time to spare.

Holland, North Germany, and Scandinavia   There are excellent ferry routes linking British east coast ports with Europe's North Sea coast. Crossings are longer than English Channel routes, and most North Sea ferry lines have adopted the ferry-cruise concept, with cabins with various degrees of comfort and on-board facilities that can include duty-free shopping, bars, restaurants, discos, and casinos.

For Holland and north central Germany, the best routes are Sherness–Vlissingen (operated by **Olau Line**) and Harwich–Hook of Holland (operated by Sealink). If you're based farther north in England, the Hull–Rotterdam route (operated by **North Sea Ferries**) is also good. North Germany is best served by the Harwich–Hamburg route (operated by **Scandinavian Seaways**), the only direct ferry link with Germany. Services to Scandinavia include Harwich–Esbjerg, Denmark, and Newcastle–Esbjerg (both operated by Scandinavian Seaways); Harwich–Gothenburg, Sweden, and Newcastle–Gothenburg (both also operated by Scandinavian Seaways); Newcastle–Stavanger and Bergen, Norway (operated by **Color Line** and Scandinavian Seaways).

To Ireland   The principal ferry routes to Ireland are Holyhead–Dublin (operated by **B&I**); Holyhead–Dun Laoghaire (operated by Sealink); and Fishguard/Pembroke–Rosslare (operated by Sealink); and Pembroke–Rosslare (operated by B&I). There's a service between Swansea and Cork (operated by **Swansea Cork Ferries**) that runs from March through September. For Northern Ireland, take the Stranraer–Larne ferry (operated by P&O European Ferries and Sealink).

Useful Addresses   For information on the services mentioned above, contact:

B&I Line UK Ltd. (East Princes Dock, Liverpool L3 0AA, tel. 051/236–8325).

Brittany Ferries (Mill Bay Docks, Plymouth PL1 3EW, tel. 0752/221321).

Color Line (Tyne Commission Quay, North Shields NE29 6EA, tel. 091/296–1313).

Hoverspeed (Maybrook House, Queens Gardens, Dover, Kent CT17 9UQ, tel. 0304/240241).

North Sea Ferries (King George Dock, Hedon Rd., Hull HU9 5QA, tel. 0482/795141).

Olau Line (104 Anchor La., Sheerness Docks, Sheerness, Kent ME12 1SN, tel. 0795/666666).

P&O European Ferries (Channel View Rd., Dover, Kent CT17 9TJ, tel. 0303/223000).

Sally Line (Argyle Centre, York St., Ramsgate CT11 9PL, tel. 0843/595522).

Scandinavian Seaways (Scandinavia House, Parkeston Quay, Harwich, Essex CO12 4QG, tel. 0255/241234).

Sealink (Charter House, Park St., Ashford, Kent TN24 8EX, tel. 0223/646801).

Swansea Cork Ferries (Kings Dock, Swansea SA1 8RU, tel. 0792/456116).

From the United Kingdom by Train

Air travel may offer the fastest point-to-point service, car travel the greatest freedom, and bus transportation the lowest fares, but there is still an unparalleled air of romance about setting off for Europe by train from one of the historic London stations.

Boat trains timed to meet ferries at Channel ports leave London from Victoria, Waterloo, Paddington, and Charing Cross stations and connect with onward trains at the main French and Belgian ports. Calais and Boulogne have the best quick connections for Paris (total journey time about six to seven hours using the cross-Channel Hovercraft); the Dover–Ostend Jetfoil service is the fastest rail connection to Brussels (about 5½ hours, station to station), with good rail connections to Germany, northern France, and Poland.

Boat trains connecting with ferries from Harwich to the Dutch and Danish North Sea ports leave from London/Liverpool Street; there are good rail connections from the Dutch ports to Amsterdam and onward to Germany and Belgium and south to France.

For the Republic of Ireland, trains connecting with the ferry services across the Irish Sea leave from London/Paddington.

One-way and round-trip city-to-city tickets, including rail and ferry fares, can be booked in the United States through **BritRail,** either directly or through your travel agent. If you are traveling on one of the European rail passes bookable in the United States or in Britain, you may be entitled to free or discounted ferry crossings (*see* Getting Around Europe By Train, *below*).

Useful Addresses For European rail information, contact **InterCity Europe,** the international wing of **BritRail,** at London/Victoria station: information, tel. 071/834–2345; bookings can be made by phone using American Express, MasterCard, and Visa (tel. 071/828–0892).

From the United Kingdom by Bus

Freeways (motorways) in the United Kingdom link London with the English Channel ferry ports and make bus travel—connecting with fast ferry, Jetfoil, or Hovercraft crossings—only a little slower than rail travel on the shorter routes into Europe.

Bus travel to cities such as Paris, Brussels, Amsterdam, Rotterdam, and Bruges is by fast and comfortable modern buses with reclining seats, air-conditioning, video entertainment, and airplane-style refreshment carts. There are frequent departures from central London pickup points. Fares by bus are a good deal less than the equivalent rail fare.

Euroways/Eurolines—an international consortium of bus operators—offers a range of day and night services linking London with Amsterdam, Paris, Antwerp, Brussels, and other points en route. Night services to Paris take about 10¼ hours; overnight journey time to Amsterdam is a little more than 13 hours.

Faster **Citysprint** daytime crossings use the Dover–Ostend Jetfoil service en route to Amsterdam, reducing journey time to a little more than eight hours. The fast Hoverspeed crossing to France cuts the day trip time to Paris to just under seven hours. There are also one-day round-trips to Antwerp and Brussels and "Eurobreakaway" holiday packages with accommodations for two or three nights in Paris, Amsterdam, and Brussels.

National Express uses Sealink ferries to the Republic of Ireland. A connecting bus service in Ireland is operated by **Bus Eireann.** Sailings are from Fishguard to Rosslare—a 3½-hour crossing. The onward service goes via Waterford and Cork to Killarney and Tralee.

There are summer buses to the Spanish vacation resorts, aimed mainly at British families on a tight vacation budget. If you, too, are on a budget, these can be an inexpensive way of getting to Spain. The same is true for the winter coaches that run to Europe's less expensive ski destinations, notably Andorra and some Italian resorts.

The state of war in Yugoslavia at press time (summer 1992) means that the road route to Greece through that country is not an option.

Both Euroways/Eurolines and Hoverspeed City Sprint services are bookable in person at **National Express** offices at Victoria Coach Station (52 Grosvenor Gardens, London SW1W 0AU, opposite Victoria Rail Station) and at the **Coach Travel Centre** (13 Regent St., London SW1, for credit card reservations, tel. 071/730–3499; inquiries, tel. 071/730–0202). Or book at any National Express agent throughout Britain.

Getting Around Europe

By Train

European railway systems vary from the sublime to the ridiculous in terms of comfort and convenience. France, Germany, and the United Kingdom lead the field in developing high-speed trains, although the latter has fallen behind the other two. The **French National Railroads'** (SNCF's) Train à Grande Vitesse (TGV), for example, takes just 4½ hours to cover the 871 km (540 miles) from Paris to Marseille on the Mediterranean.

Rail Europe (Box 10383, Stamford, CT 06904) has a new catalogue that outlines trains, rental car, and hotel programs in 23 European countries. There are 17 plans listed for vacationers, and Rail Europe's Flexhotel program supplies hotel vouchers good for accommodations at 430 Best Western hotels. Also, Rail Europe has introduced a series of new "Rail–and–drive" programs that combine rail and rental car travel in 17 European countries.

BritRail operates high-speed InterCity trains—with a top speed of 202 kph (125 mph)—on its north-south routes between London and Scotland. Normal fares apply on the BritRail high-speed services, but there is a supplementary fare for travel on French TGV services.

The German rail system **Deutsche Bundesbahn** (DB, known in the United States as GermanRail) last year wrested the world rail speed record from the French, and its high-speed InterCity trains make rail travel the best public transportation option within Germany.

Swiss trains are not the fastest in Europe, but they are the most punctual and reliable, making onward travel connections remarkably stress-free.

International trains link most European capital cities, including those of Eastern Europe; service is offered several times daily. Generally, customs and immigration formalities are completed on the train by officials who board when it crosses the frontier.

Most European systems operate a two-tier, sometimes three-tier, class system, with first class substantially the most expensive. The only outstanding advantage of first class is that it is likely to be less crowded on busier routes. Train journeys in Europe tend to be shorter than in the United States—trains are much faster and distances much shorter—so first-class rail travel is usually a luxury rather than a necessity. Some of the poorer European countries retain a third class, but avoid it unless you are on a rock-bottom budget.

A number of European airlines and railways operate fast train connections to their hub airports, and these can sometimes be booked through the airline's computer reservation service. The *Lufthansa Express* connects Frankfurt and Köln/Bonn airports and is a splendid two-hour scenic journey along the Rhine valley.

Trains in Sweden and Norway offer supreme comfort, but greater distances and the more rugged terrain make for longer journey times; if you are on a tight schedule, you may prefer to take internal flights.

In Italy, there are some excellent rail services between major cities—but be sure that the train you book *is* a main intercity service, not one that stops at every minor station. Off the major lines, Italian rail services are slower and less frequent.

Trains are generally to be avoided in Spain and Portugal as point-to-point transportation—though there are some attractive scenic routes and special tourist trains. In Greece anyone but the most fanatical rail traveler will find the more frequent, modern, and comfortable buses preferable to the trains, which are slow, unreliable, crowded, and dirty.

Rail travel is vital to most Eastern European countries, and services within and between them are better and more comfortable than you might expect. Though usually much slower than the more modern Western European trains, service is frequent and reliable.

Scenic Routes While the high-speed expresses are an ideal and comfortable way of getting from one place to another, travelers who delight in train travel for its own sake will find plenty to please them in Europe's smaller rail lines.

In Norway and Sweden, almost any train journey offers a superb view of some of Europe's most grandiose scenery. The trains of Switzerland, Austria, and Czechoslovakia are also a comfortable way to view impressive mountain vistas.

In Switzerland, the *Glacier Express* running between the Alpine resorts of Zermatt, St. Moritz, and Davos is a regular train that has been taken over almost entirely by tourists attracted by the dramatic scenic route. It makes one round-trip a day in winter, and three in summer; reservations are essential.

In Portugal, rail travel is not ideal, but there are some charming journeys to be made on small local trains. For instance, the rail line north from Oporto to Viana do Castelo and the Spanish border passes through picturesque small towns and crosses over two remarkable river bridges built by Gustav Eiffel, designer of Paris's famed landmark. Branch lines from the same route run through some of Europe's prettiest and least-developed rural countryside.

Special tourist trains operate in many countries in Europe, a number of them using historic rolling stock or original steam engines. The *Venice Simplon-Orient Express* uses the original sleeping and dining cars and coaches of Europe's most romantic train. In Scotland, the *Royal Scot* travels the spectacular glens of the Highlands with antique cars from the heyday of rail travel.

In Spain, a tourist special runs in the summer months through the pretty north coast country of Cantabria and Asturias, leaving from Santander. From Seville, the luxurious *Andalus Express* uses four vintage cars built in the 1920s and operates five-day rail cruises via Cordoba and Granada to Málaga. The train features its own bar—open to 3 AM—with live music and dancing, restaurant cars, and a video and game room.

National tourist offices in the United States or London and national rail network offices are the best sources of information on these tourist specials.

Rail Passes Almost all European countries offer discount rail passes; details are given in the appropriate country chapter. Here is a listing of the rail passes available before you leave.

The **EurailPass,** valid for unlimited first-class train travel through 17 countries (Austria, Belgium, Denmark, Finland, France, Germany, Greece, Holland, Hungary, Ireland, Italy, Luxembourg, Norway, Portugal, Spain, Sweden, and Switzerland), is the best-value ticket for visitors from outside Europe.

den and Norway; **Stena Line,** which operates between Norway and Sweden (book through Sealink); and **TT-Line,** which operates between Sweden and Germany (book through Olau Lines).

Local ferries ply the Norwegian fjords and are an excellent way of seeing the country, whether you are traveling by car or on public transportation; a fjord trip in midsummer, the time of the Midnight Sun in northern Norway, should not be missed.

Main international Baltic ports are Copenhagen, Gothenburg, Malmö, Stockholm, Helsinki, Kristiansand, and Oslo—also Travemünde in Germany.

Useful Addresses **Viking Line** (Scantours, 8 Spring Gardens, Trafalgar Sq., London SW1A 2BG, tel. 071/930–9510).
For other Baltic ferry lines mentioned here, *see* From the United Kingdom by Ferry/Ship, *above.*

Scotland Ferry services are important, too, in the Scottish Western Isles, where the **Caledonian Macbrayne Ltd.** (Head Office, The Ferry Terminal, Gourock, Renfrewshire PA19 1QP, Scotland; tel. 0475/33755) has enjoyed a virtual monopoly for many years on its services linking the islands to the mainland port of Oban. The northern Scottish islands of the Orkney and Shetland groups are served by sea from Scrabster on the north coast of mainland Scotland—near John O'Groats.

Greece Interisland ferries play an important part in the Mediterranean, too, particularly among the Greek islands. Many island communities have formed cooperative companies to operate services linking their island with others and with Piraeus, the port of Athens. While all Baltic ferries offer high standards of comfort, even luxury—at commensurately high fares—Mediterranean ferry lines observe widely different standards. On Greek ships, for example, you can travel in a first- or second-class cabin or rough it in deck class for a much lower fare. The same is true for the international ferries plying between the Italian ports of Bari and Brindisi and the Greek ports of Corfu, Igoumenitsa, and Patras. The age of Greek ferry boats varies widely, too. Some are of pre–World War II vintage, while others—like the *Naxos,* which sails between Piraeus and Crete—are modern vessels. For Greek ferry information, contact the **Greek National Tourist Office** in New York or London (*see* Government Tourist Offices in Before You Go, *above*).

Flying Dolphin Lines operates fast hydrofoil service from Piraeus to points popular with Athenian vacationers, including the Saronic Gulf islands and resorts on the eastern Peloponnese.

River Travel Major river systems crisscross Europe. Among the many attractive river trips available are a number of luxury cruises on the Rhine and Danube rivers.

The Danube passes through European countries in Western and Eastern Europe, and international cruises are possible. Contact the **German National Tourist Office** for details. There is also an international hydrofoil service that operates several times a day on the Danube between Budapest in Hungary and Bratislava in Czechoslovakia. Information and booking are available through **Ibusz,** the Hungarian state travel agency, or **Čedok,** its Czech equivalent, in New York or London. For details of Rhine trips, contact **KD German Rhine Line** (170 Hamil-

ive scenic routes and special tourist trains. In Greece anyone but the most fanatical rail traveler will find the more frequent, modern, and comfortable buses preferable to the trains, which are slow, unreliable, crowded, and dirty.

Rail travel is vital to most Eastern European countries, and services within and between them are better and more comfortable than you might expect. Though usually much slower than the more modern Western European trains, service is frequent and reliable.

Scenic Routes While the high-speed expresses are an ideal and comfortable way of getting from one place to another, travelers who delight in train travel for its own sake will find plenty to please them in Europe's smaller rail lines.

In Norway and Sweden, almost any train journey offers a superb view of some of Europe's most grandiose scenery. The trains of Switzerland, Austria, and Czechoslovakia are also a comfortable way to view impressive mountain vistas.

In Switzerland, the *Glacier Express* running between the Alpine resorts of Zermatt, St. Moritz, and Davos is a regular train that has been taken over almost entirely by tourists attracted by the dramatic scenic route. It makes one round-trip a day in winter, and three in summer; reservations are essential.

In Portugal, rail travel is not ideal, but there are some charming journeys to be made on small local trains. For instance, the rail line north from Oporto to Viana do Castelo and the Spanish border passes through picturesque small towns and crosses over two remarkable river bridges built by Gustav Eiffel, designer of Paris's famed landmark. Branch lines from the same route run through some of Europe's prettiest and least-developed rural countryside.

Special tourist trains operate in many countries in Europe, a number of them using historic rolling stock or original steam engines. The *Venice Simplon-Orient Express* uses the original sleeping and dining cars and coaches of Europe's most romantic train. In Scotland, the *Royal Scot* travels the spectacular glens of the Highlands with antique cars from the heyday of rail travel.

In Spain, a tourist special runs in the summer months through the pretty north coast country of Cantabria and Asturias, leaving from Santander. From Seville, the luxurious *Andalus Express* uses four vintage cars built in the 1920s and operates five-day rail cruises via Cordoba and Granada to Málaga. The train features its own bar—open to 3 AM—with live music and dancing, restaurant cars, and a video and game room.

National tourist offices in the United States or London and national rail network offices are the best sources of information on these tourist specials.

Rail Passes Almost all European countries offer discount rail passes; details are given in the appropriate country chapter. Here is a listing of the rail passes available before you leave.

The **EurailPass,** valid for unlimited first-class train travel through 17 countries (Austria, Belgium, Denmark, Finland, France, Germany, Greece, Holland, Hungary, Ireland, Italy, Luxembourg, Norway, Portugal, Spain, Sweden, and Switzerland), is the best-value ticket for visitors from outside Europe.

The ticket is available for periods of 15 days ($430), 21 days ($550), one month ($680), two months ($920), and three months ($1,150). For two or more people traveling together, a 15-day rail pass costs $340. Between April 1 and September 30, you need a minimum of three in your group to get this discount. For those under 26, there is the **Eurail Youthpass,** for one or two months' unlimited second-class train travel at $470 and $640. The pass must be bought from an authorized agent before you leave home. Apply through your travel agent, through **Rail Europe** (226-230 Westchester Ave., White Plains, NY 10604, tel. 914/682–5172 or 800/345–1990), or one of the following: French National Railroads, GermanRail, or Italian State Railways (*see* Useful Addresses, *below*).

For travelers who like to spread out their train journeys, there is the **Eurail Flexipass.** With the 15-day pass ($280), travelers get five days of unlimited first-class train travel but they can spread that travel out over 21 days; a 21-day pass gives you 9 days of travel ($450), and a one-month pass gives you 14 days ($610).

For European travelers under 26, the **Inter Rail card** is an unbeatable value. It is available to people who have been resident in Europe for at least six months, and for one calendar month gives unlimited rail travel in 24 countries for £180. It also gives half-price travel within the United Kingdom and discounts of up to 50% on some ferry services to and from the United Kingdom. There are 15-day and one-month cards that allow for unlimited travel in 24 countries for £180, and £260, respectively. All cards are available from rail stations.

Useful Addresses Full information on rail services within the countries listed here is available from the addresses below. Otherwise, contact the national tourist office of the country concerned.

In the United States **Belgian National Railroads** (745 Fifth Ave., New York, NY
and Canada 10151, tel. 212/758–8130).
BritRail Travel International Inc. (630 Third Ave., New York, NY 10017, tel. 212/575–2667; 94 Cumberland St., Toronto, Ontario M5R 1A3; 409 Granville St., Vancouver, BC V6C 1T2).
French National Railroads (610 Fifth Ave., New York, NY 10020, tel. 212/582–2110; 9465 Wilshire Blvd., Beverly Hills, CA 90212; 11 E. Adams St., Chicago, IL 60603; 2121 Ponce de Leon Blvd., Coral Gables, FL 33114; 360 Post St., Union Sq., San Francisco, CA 94108; 1500 Stanley St., Montreal, Quebec H3A 1Re; 409 Granville St., Vancouver, BC V6C 1T2).
GermanRail (122 E. 42nd St., Suite 1904, New York, NY 10168–0072, tel. 212/922–1616; 625 Statler Office Bldg., Boston, MA 02116, 617/542–0577; 95–97 W. Higgins Rd., Suite 505, Rosemont, IL 60018; 112 S. Ervay St., Dallas, TX 75201; 11933 Wilshire Blvd., Los Angeles, CA 90025; 442 Post St., 6th floor, San Francisco, CA 94102; 8000 E. Girard Ave., Suite 518S, Denver, CO 80231; 2400 Peachtree Rd. NE, Lenox Towers, Suite 1299, Atlanta, GA 30326, tel. 404/266–9555; and Bay St., Toronto, Ontario M5R 2C3).
Italian State Railways (666 Fifth Ave., New York, NY 10103, tel. 212/397–2667).

In the United **Belgian National Railways** (Premier House, 10 Greycoat Pl.,
Kingdom London SW1P 1SB, tel. 071/233–0360).
French Railways (French Railways House, 179 Piccadilly, London, W1V OBA, tel. 071/491–9731).

German Federal Railways (10 Old Bond St., London W1X 4EN, tel. 071/499–0578).
Netherlands Railways (Egginton House, 25–28 Buckingham Gate, London SW1E 6LD, tel. 071/630–1735).
Norwegian State Railways Travel Bureau (21–24 Cockspur St., London SW1Y 5DA, tel. 071/930–6666).
Swiss Federal Railways (Swiss Centre, 1 New Coventry St., London W1V 8EE, tel. 071/734–1921).

For information about rail networks in other European countries, contact their tourist boards in London.

By Bus

If you have opted for land rather than air travel, the choice between rail and bus is a major decision. In countries such as Britain, France, Germany, and Holland, bus travel was, until recently, something of a poor man's option—slow, uncomfortable, and cheap. Today, though, fast modern buses travel on excellent highways and offer standards of service and comfort comparable to those on a train—but still at generally lower fares. Between major cities and over long distances, trains are still preferable and almost always faster, but buses will take you to places that trains often do not reach.

In several southern European countries—including Portugal, Greece, and much of Spain—the bus has supplanted the train as the main means of public transportation, and is often quicker, more frequent, and more comfortable than the antiquated rolling stock of the national rail system. Choose the bus over the rail in these countries unless there is a particular scenic rail route or a special tourist train you want to use. But be prepared to discover that the bus is now more expensive than the lowly railway. Competition among lines is keen, so compare services such as air-conditioning or reclining seats before you buy.

Information Information on bus transportation in most countries is available from national or regional tourist offices. For reservations on major bus lines, contact your travel agent at home. For smaller bus companies on regional routes, you may have to go to a local travel agency or to the bus line office.

Note that travel agencies may be affiliated with a certain line and won't always tell you about alternative services—you may have to do some legwork to be sure of getting the best service.

By Ferry/Ship

Bounded by the sea on three sides and crossed by a number of major rivers, Europe offers an abundance of choices for anyone who loves water travel.

The Baltic In the north, ferries ply daily between most of the major Baltic ports in Western Europe, as well as between Finnish ports and those of Russia. Baltic crossings are not for those in a hurry—several of them last overnight—and shipping lines operate luxury cruise-ferry vessels with all kinds of entertainment facilities and duty-free shopping.

Major lines include **Silja,** which operates between Finland and Sweden/Germany (book through Scandinavian Seaways); **Viking Line,** which operates between Finland and Sweden (book through Scantours); **Color Line,** which operates between Sweden and Norway; **Stena Line,** which operates between Norway and Sweden (book through Sealink); and **TT-Line,** which operates between Sweden and Germany (book through Olau Lines).

Local ferries ply the Norwegian fjords and are an excellent way of seeing the country, whether you are traveling by car or on public transportation; a fjord trip in midsummer, the time of the Midnight Sun in northern Norway, should not be missed.

Main international Baltic ports are Copenhagen, Gothenburg, Malmö, Stockholm, Helsinki, Kristiansand, and Oslo—also Travemünde in Germany.

Useful Addresses **Viking Line** (Scantours, 8 Spring Gardens, Trafalgar Sq., London SW1A 2BG, tel. 071/930–9510).
For other Baltic ferry lines mentioned here, *see* From the United Kingdom by Ferry/Ship, *above.*

Scotland Ferry services are important, too, in the Scottish Western Isles, where the **Caledonian Macbrayne Ltd.** (Head Office, The Ferry Terminal, Gourock, Renfrewshire PA19 1QP, Scotland; tel. 0475/33755) has enjoyed a virtual monopoly for many years on its services linking the islands to the mainland port of Oban. The northern Scottish islands of the Orkney and Shetland groups are served by sea from Scrabster on the north coast of mainland Scotland—near John O'Groats.

Greece Interisland ferries play an important part in the Mediterranean, too, particularly among the Greek islands. Many island communities have formed cooperative companies to operate services linking their island with others and with Piraeus, the port of Athens. While all Baltic ferries offer high standards of comfort, even luxury—at commensurately high fares—Mediterranean ferry lines observe widely different standards. On Greek ships, for example, you can travel in a first- or second-class cabin or rough it in deck class for a much lower fare. The same is true for the international ferries plying between the Italian ports of Bari and Brindisi and the Greek ports of Corfu, Igoumenitsa, and Patras. The age of Greek ferry boats varies widely, too. Some are of pre–World War II vintage, while others—like the *Naxos,* which sails between Piraeus and Crete—are modern vessels. For Greek ferry information, contact the **Greek National Tourist Office** in New York or London (*see* Government Tourist Offices in Before You Go, *above*).

Flying Dolphin Lines operates fast hydrofoil service from Piraeus to points popular with Athenian vacationers, including the Saronic Gulf islands and resorts on the eastern Peloponnese.

River Travel Major river systems crisscross Europe. Among the many attractive river trips available are a number of luxury cruises on the Rhine and Danube rivers.

The Danube passes through European countries in Western and Eastern Europe, and international cruises are possible. Contact the **German National Tourist Office** for details. There is also an international hydrofoil service that operates several times a day on the Danube between Budapest in Hungary and Bratislava in Czechoslovakia. Information and booking are available through **Ibusz,** the Hungarian state travel agency, or **Čedok,** its Czech equivalent, in New York or London. For details of Rhine trips, contact **KD German Rhine Line** (170 Hamilton Ave., White Plains, NY 10601) or in the United Kingdom (28 South St., Epsom, Surrey KT18 7PF, tel. 0372/742033).

Though a great deal less spectacular than either the Rhine or the Danube, the smaller rivers of Belgium, Holland, France, and other Western European countries can also provide a relaxed and fascinating vacation. **Floating Through Europe** (271 Madison Ave., New York, NY 10016, tel. 212/685–5600) specializes in these kinds of tours.

By Car

Touring Europe by car has tremendous advantages over other ways of seeing the Continent. You can go where you want, when you want, traveling at your own pace, free of the petty restrictions of timetables. But there are pitfalls, too. For the American driver, used to a uniform system of signs and traffic rules from coast to coast, and accustomed to being able to ask directions in English, Europe can be a bewildering experience. On the excellent freeways of northern and central Europe, it's possible to drive through three or four countries in less time than it would take to cross one of the larger of the U.S. states— which means that in one day you may have to cope with perhaps four different languages and four sets of traffic rules!

Frontiers You may be surprised at the relatively casual approach many European countries have toward border controls for drivers. At many frontiers, you may simply be waved through; it is quite possible, for example, to drive from Amsterdam to Germany, via Belgium and France, without once being stopped for customs or immigration formalities. There are, however, spot checks at all borders, and at some—particularly those checkpoints used by heavy commercial truck traffic—there can be long delays at peak times. Ask tourist offices or motoring associations for latest advice on ways to avoid these tie-ups. If you are driving a rented car, the rental company will have provided you with all the necessary papers; if the vehicle is your own, you will need proof of ownership, certificate of roadworthiness (known in the United Kingdom as a Ministry of Transport [MOT] road vehicle certificate), up-to-date vehicle tax, and a Green Card proof of insurance, available from your insurance company (fees vary depending on destination and length of stay).

Rules of the Road In the United Kingdom, the Republic of Ireland, and Gibraltar, cars drive on the left. In other European countries, traffic is on the right. Beware the transition when coming off ferries from Britain or Ireland to the Continent (and vice versa)!

By Plane

Licenses to operate on a given international or internal route are issued by governments, and international route licenses are in most cases still issued on the basis of bilateral agreements between the two countries in question. This means that bus stop–style services, like those so common in the United States, do not yet exist in Europe, though they may begin to appear in the near future. So-called fifth freedom licenses, which grant airlines the right to land and pick up passengers at intermediary points on a given route, are jealously guarded by governments and consequently are hard to come by. This makes touring Europe entirely by air a costly process, and the best bet, if you plan to visit a number of European countries, is to combine air travel with other transportation options.

Hub Airports As in the United States, airlines are developing hub and spoke-style services within Europe. The idea is that you take a trans-atlantic flight to an airline's hub, then continue on its intra-European services to other European cities. Thus, **SAS** is actively developing Copenhagen as a Scandinavian hub; the Dutch airline **KLM** is doing the same at Amsterdam's Schiphol; **British Airways** at London's Heathrow and Gatwick; and **Lufthansa** at Frankfurt. If you plan to fly to other European cities, one of these hubs is your obvious choice.

Domestic Services Most Western European countries have good internal services linking the capital city with major business and industrial centers and with more remote communities. In Germany, France, and Spain, regional flights tend to connect major business cities rather than areas of touristic interest—though in Spain there is a considerable overlap between the two.

In such countries as Sweden, Norway, Greece, and to some extent the United Kingdom, however, air services are a vital link between remote island and mountain communities and are often subsidized by the central government. In Greece, for example, you can fly very inexpensively between Athens and the islands—though not *between* islands.

Before booking an internal flight, consider the alternatives. Flights from London to Edinburgh take about one hour—airport to airport—while the competing BritRail InterCity train takes 4½ hours. But if you add in the hour needed to get from central London to the airport, the need to check in as much as one hour before departure, the inevitable flight delays, the time spent waiting for luggage on arrival, and the transfer time back into town from Edinburgh Airport—you'll find you may not have saved any more than an hour in travel time for a considerably higher fare. When looking into air travel as an option, remember that distances between European cities can be deceptively short to an eye accustomed to U.S. routings.

Formalities For scheduled flights, you will be asked to check in at least one hour before departure; for charter flights, generally two hours. These are guidelines; if you are traveling with just hand luggage, it is possible to check in as late as 30 minutes before take-off time. European luggage allowances are based on the total weight of your checked luggage, not, as in the United States, on the number of bags. The usual allowance is 44 pounds.

You may be pleasantly surprised by the Green Channel/Red Channel customs system in operation at most western European airports and at other international frontier posts. Basically, this is an honor system: If you have nothing to declare, you walk through the Green Channel without needing to open your bags for inspection. There are, however, random spot checks, and penalties for abusing the system can be severe. If in doubt, go through the Red Channel.

Eastern Europe Eastern European countries need hard Western currency so badly that they try not to set airfares at intolerably high levels. Most routes are operated in tandem with Western carriers, however, and anyone with an eye to comfort and safety will prefer the latter.

Useful Addresses Major national airlines for the following European countries can be contacted at their London addresses:

Aer Lingus (Ireland) (Aer Lingus House, 83 Staines Rd., Hounslow, Middlesex TW3 3JB, tel. 081/569–5555).

Air France (158 New Bond St., London W1Y 0AY, tel. 071/499–9511).

Alitalia (Italy) (205 Holland Park Ave., London W11 4XB, tel. 071/602–7111).

Austrian Airlines (50/51 Conduit St., London W1R 0NP, tel. 071/439–0741).

British Airways (Box 10, Heathrow Airport, Hounslow, Middlesex TW6 2JA, tel. 081/897–4000).

Czechoslovak Airlines (72 Margaret St., London W1N 7LF, tel. 071/255–1898).

Finnair (14 Clifford St., London W1X 1RD, tel. 071/408–1222).

Iberia (Spain) (130 Regent St., London W1R 5FE, tel. 071/437–5622).

KLM Royal Dutch Airlines (190 Great Southwest Rd., Feltham, Middlesex TW14 9RL, tel. 081/750–9000).

LOT Polish Airlines (313 Regent St., London W1R 7PE, tel. 071/580–5037).

Lufthansa (Germany) (23–26 Piccadilly, London W1V 0EJ, tel. 071/408–0442).

Olympic Airways (Greece) (Trafalgar House, Hammersmith International Centre, 2 Chalkhill Rd., London W6 8SB, tel. 081/846–9080).

SAS Scandinavian Airlines (52/53 Conduit St., London W1R 0AY, tel. 071/734–4020).

Swissair (Swiss Centre, 10 Wardour St., London W1V 4BJ, tel. 071/439–4144).

By Bicycle

Bicycling in Europe can be sheer pleasure or unadulterated torment—depending on when you go, where you go, and what you try to do.

If you're planning a European bike trip, you are probably experienced enough not to need advice on equipment and clothing. But it needs to be said that some European countries are far more user-friendly than others toward bicyclists. In countries like Holland, Denmark, Germany, and Belgium, bikes are very much part of the landscape—mainly because the landscape tends to be uniformly flat. City streets and many main roads in these countries have special bike lanes set aside, and car drivers are used to coping with large numbers of bicycle riders.

Cycling is a major sport in Italy, Spain, and Portugal, as well as in France, and there are regular "Tour" road races. Cyclists also get a good deal in the Eastern Bloc countries, where for economic reasons, the bicycle is still an everyday form of transportation.

Northern Scandinavia and Iceland, plus the Alpine countries Austria and Switzerland, with their steep terrain, are destinations only for the serious cyclist. The Scandinavian countries have plenty of excellent-value campsites. Ireland has emptier roads and a gentler landscape than Sweden or Norway and is a pleasant country to bicycle in, though the temptation to sample just one more Guinness at each wayside pub can be a hazard in itself.

Of the wealthier European countries, Britain has the most shameful record when it comes to providing facilities for bicyclists or considering their interests. Riding in London traffic is a stomach-churning experience requiring nerves of steel. Except in remoter areas—such as the north of Scotland—main roads are overcrowded and often dangerous to cyclists.

Bicycle Transport Transporting your bicycle from the United Kingdom to Europe holds no big problems—some ferry lines transport bicycles free, others charge a nominal fee. Shop around. Surprisingly, you can transport your bicycle by air as checked baggage—you won't have to pay extra so long as you are within the 44-pound total baggage allowance.

Most European rail lines will transport bicycles free of charge or for a nominal fee, though you may have to book ahead. Check with the main booking office. One of the joys of biking in Europe is being able to bike one way and return by train or to board a train with your bike when you need to cover long distances or simply when you need to take a rest. SNCF (French Railways) converted wagons on four of its Motorail services from Boulogne to carry bicycles for the first time in 1988. Transporting your bike by bus is also possible.

Renting Bicycles Bicycles can be rented by the day or week in most European capitals and are most readily available in cities like Amsterdam and Copenhagen, where cycling is part of the way of life. Local tourist boards are the best source of information on reliable rental agencies with safe bicycles to rent; remember to check on local traffic rules and make sure your insurance covers you in case of an accident. **GermanRail (DB)** rents bicycles at selected stations in summer—get further information from GermanRail or the German National Tourist Office in New York.

2 Austria

Though Austria has become considerably more expensive in recent years, there are still bargains to be found, and discovering them can be one of the diversions of a vacation in Austria. The country is highly accessible by public transport of one form or another. The rail network is well maintained, and trains are fast, comfortable, and punctual. Highways are superb and well marked. Public transportation in the cities, although not cheap, is safe, clean, and convenient. In short, the visitor to Austria spends more time having fun than coping with the logistics of getting from A to B.

What Austria lacks in size, it more than makes up for in diversity. Its Alps and mountain lakes in the central and southern provinces rival those of neighboring Switzerland; the vast Vienna Woods remind some of the Black Forest; the steppes of the province of Burgenland blend with those across the border in Hungary; and the vineyards along the Danube rival those of the Rhine and Mosel river valleys. In addition, nowhere else is there a Vienna or a Salzburg—or such pastry shops!

The Austrians are for the most part friendly and welcoming. They are an outdoor people, given to heading off to the ski slopes, the mountains, the lakes, and the woods at a moment's notice. At the same time, they can be as melancholy as some of the songs of their wine taverns would suggest. Communication is seldom a problem, since most Austrians speak another language besides their native German, usually English.

What you'll discover in conversation with Austrians is that they are more for evolution than revolution, so change is gradual, and old values tend to be maintained. Graceful dancers do execute the tricky "left waltz" on balmy summer evenings in Vien-

Austria

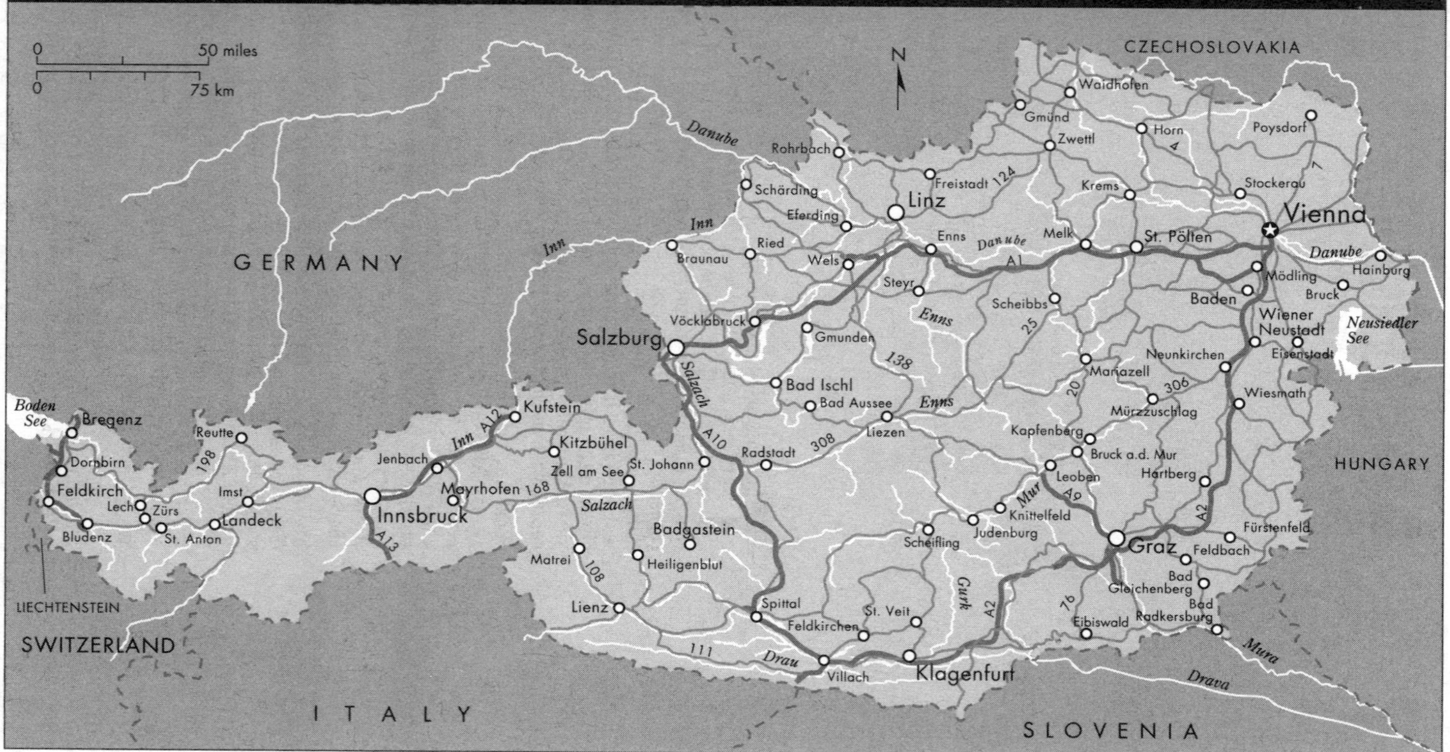
0
50 miles
0
75 km
N
CZECHOSLOVAKIA
GERMANY
HUNGARY
SLOVENIA
ITALY
SWITZERLAND
LIECHTENSTEIN
Boden See
Neusiedler See
Danube
Inn
Enns
Salzach
Mur
Gurk
Drau
Drava
Mura
Vienna
Linz
Salzburg
Innsbruck
Graz
Klagenfurt
Waidhofen
Gmünd
Zwettl
Horn
Poysdorf
Stockerau
Krems
Rohrbach
Freistadt
Schärding
Eferding
Ried
Braunau
Wels
Enns
Steyr
Melk
St. Pölten
Scheibbs
Mödling
Hainburg
Bruck
Baden
Wiener Neustadt
Eisenstadt
Neunkirchen
Mariazell
Mürzzuschlag
Wiesmath
Vöcklabruck
Gmunden
Bad Ischl
Bad Aussee
Liezen
Radstadt
Kapfenberg
Bruck a.d. Mur
Leoben
Knittelfeld
Judenburg
Scheifling
Hartberg
Fürstenfeld
Feldbach
Bad Gleichenberg
Bad Radkersburg
Eibiswald
St. Veit
Feldkirchen
Spittal
Villach
Lienz
Matrei
Heiligenblut
Badgastein
St. Johann
Zell am See
Kitzbühel
Kufstein
Jenbach
Mayrhofen
Reutte
Imst
Landeck
St. Anton
Zürs
Lech
Bregenz
Dornbirn
Feldkirch
Bludenz
A1
A2
A9
A10
A12
A13
4
7
20
25
76
108
111
124
138
168
198
306
308

na, and you may find an entire town celebrating some event, complete with brass band in lederhosen.

Essential Information

Before You Go

When to Go Austria has two main tourist seasons. The summer season starts at Easter and runs to about mid-October. The most pleasant months weather-wise are May, June, September, and October. June through August are the peak tourist months, and aside from a few overly humid days when you may wish for the wider use of air-conditioning, even Vienna is pleasant; the city literally moves outdoors in summer. The winter cultural season starts in October and runs into June; the winter sports season gets under way in December and lasts until the end of April, although you can ski in selected areas well into June and on some of the highest glaciers year-round. Some events—the Salzburg Festival is a prime example—make a substantial difference in hotel and other costs. Nevertheless, bargains are available in the (almost nonexistent) off-season.

Climate Summer can be warm; winter, bitterly cold. The southern region is usually several degrees warmer in summer, several degrees colder in winter. Winters north of the Alps can be overcast and dreary, whereas the south basks in winter sunshine.

The following are the average daily maximum and minimum temperatures for Vienna.

Jan.	34F	1C	**May**	67F	19C	**Sept.**	68F	20C
	25	−4		50	10		53	11
Feb.	38F	3C	**June**	73F	23C	**Oct.**	56F	14C
	28	−3		56	14		44	7
Mar.	47F	8C	**July**	76F	25C	**Nov.**	45F	7C
	30	−1		60	15		37	3
Apr.	58F	15C	**Aug.**	75F	24C	**Dec.**	37F	3C
	43	6		59	15		30	−1

Currency The unit of currency is the Austrian schilling (AS), divided into 100 groschen. There are AS 20, 50, 100, 500, 1,000, and 5,000 bills; AS 1, 5, 10, and 20 coins; and 1-, 2-, 10-, and 50- groschen coins. The 1- and 2-groschen coins are scarce, and the AS20 coins are unpopular—though useful for some cigarette machines. The 500- and 100-schilling notes look perilously similar; confusing the two can be an expensive mistake.

At press time (summer 1992), there were about AS9.4 to the dollar and about AS20 to the pound sterling.

Credit cards are widely used throughout Austria, although not all establishments take all cards. American Express has money machines in Vienna at Parkring 10 (actually in Liebenberggasse, off Parkring) and at the airport.

Cash traveler's checks at a bank, post office, or American Express office to get the best rate. All charge a small commission; some smaller banks or "change" offices may give a poorer rate *and* charge a higher fee. All change offices at airports and the main train stations in major cities cash traveler's checks. Bank-operated change offices in Vienna with extended hours are located on Stephansplatz and in the Opernpassage. The Bank Austria Zentralsparkasse machines on Stephansplatz and on Kärntnerstrasse 51 (to the right of the opera) and at the Raiffeisenbank on Kohlmarkt (at Michaelerplatz) change bills in other currencies into schillings, but rates are poor and a hefty commission is automatically deducted.

You may bring in any amount of foreign currency or schillings and take out any amount with you.

What It Will Cost   Austria is not inexpensive, but since inflation is negligible, costs remain fairly stable. Vienna and Salzburg are the most expensive cities, along with such fashionable resorts as Kitzbühel, Seefeld, Badgastein, Bad Hofgastein, Velden, Zell am See, and Pörtschach. Many smaller towns offer virtually identical facilities at half the price.

Drinks in bars and clubs are priced considerably higher than in cafés or restaurants. Austrian prices are inclusive; that is, service and tax are included.

Sample Prices   Cup of coffee, AS22; half-liter of draft beer, AS27–AS30; glass of wine, AS32; Coca-Cola, AS22; open sandwich, AS20; theater ticket, AS200; concert ticket, AS250; opera ticket, AS600; one-mile taxi ride, AS27.

Customs on Arrival   Austria's duty-free allowances are as follows: 200 cigarettes or 100 cigars or 250 grams of tobacco, 2 liters of wine and 1 liter of spirits, 1 bottle of toilet water (about 300-milliliter size), 50 milliliters of perfume for those aged 18 and over arriving from other European countries. Visitors arriving from the United States, Canada, or other non-European points may bring in twice the above amounts.

Language   German is the official national language. In larger cities and most resort areas, you will have no problem finding those who speak English; hotel and restaurant staff, in particular, speak English reasonably well. Most younger Austrians speak at least passable English, even if fluency is relatively rare.

Getting Around

By Train   Trains in Austria are fast and efficient, and most lines have now been electrified. Hourly express trains run on the key Vienna–Salzburg route. All principal trains have first- and second-class cars, as well as smoking and nonsmoking areas. Overnight trains have sleeping compartments, and most trains have dining cars. If you're traveling at peak times, a reserved seat—available for a small additional fee—is always a good idea.

Fares   If you're visiting other European countries, a **Eurail Pass** (*see* Getting Around Europe, in Chapter 1, for details), valid throughout most of Europe, is the best deal. Austria has only two discount tickets. A **Bundesnetzkarte** offers unlimited travel for a month and costs AS5,100 for first class and AS3,400 for second class. The alternative is a **Rabbit** card, which is good for unlimited travel on any four days within a 10-day period. The cost is AS1,600 for first class and AS1,070 for second class unless you're under 27, in which case it costs AS990 for first class, AS660 for second class. Check on rates, as these are subject to change. Full details are available from travel agents or from the Austrian National Tourist Office.

By Bus Service is available to virtually every community accessible by highway. Winter buses have ski racks. Vienna's central bus terminal (Wien-Mitte/Landstrasse Hauptstrasse, opposite the Hilton) is the arrival/departure point for international bus routes; in most other cities the bus station is adjacent to the train station.

By Boat Boats ply the Danube from Passau in Germany all the way to Vienna and from Vienna to Bratislava (Czechoslovakia), Budapest (Hungary), and the Black Sea. Only East European boats run beyond Budapest. Overnight boats have cabins; all have dining. The most scenic stretches in Austria are from Passau to Linz and through the Wachau Valley (Melk, Krems). From Vienna, there are day trips you can take upstream to the Wachau and downstream to Bratislava and Budapest. There are also special moonlight dancing and jazz excursions. Make reservations from **DDSG** (the Danube Steamship Company) in Vienna (tel. 0222/217100) or travel agents.

By Bicycle Bicycles can be rented at many train stations and returned to any of them. Most trains and some postal buses will take bikes as baggage. Bikes can be taken on the Vienna subway on weekends. Marked cycling routes parallel most of the Danube.

Staying in Austria

Telephones
Local Calls Pay telephones take AS 1, 5, 10, and 20 coins. A three-minute local call costs AS1. Emergency calls are free. Instructions are in English in most booths. Add AS1 when time is up to continue the connection. If you will be phoning frequently, get a phone "credit card" at a post office. This works in all *Wertkartentelefon* phones; the cost of the call will be deducted from the card automatically. Cards cost AS95 for AS100 worth of phoning, AS48 for calls totaling AS50.

Phone numbers throughout Austria are being changed. A sharp tone indicates no connection or that the number has been changed.

International Calls It costs more to telephone *from* Austria than it does to telephone *to* Austria. Calls from post offices are least expensive. Hotels time all calls and charge a "per unit" fee according to their own tariff, which can add AS100 or more to your bill. To avoid this charge, call overseas and ask to be called back. To make a collect call—you can't do this from pay phones—dial the operator and ask for an *R* (pronounced "err")-*Gespräch*.

International Information Dial 09. Most operators speak English; if yours doesn't, you'll be passed to one who does.

Mail
Postal Rates Airmail letters to the United States and Canada cost AS11.50 minimum; postcards cost AS8.50. Airmail letters to the United Kingdom cost AS7; postcards cost AS6. An aerogram costs AS12.

Receiving Mail American Express offices in Vienna, Linz, Salzburg, and Innsbruck will hold mail at no charge for those carrying an American Express credit card or American Express traveler's checks.

VAT Refunds Value-added tax (VAT) at 20% is charged on all sales and is automatically included in prices. If you purchase goods worth AS1,000 or more, you can claim the tax back as you leave or once you've reached home. Ask shops where you buy the goods to fill out and give you the necessary papers. Get them stamped at the airport or border by customs officials (who may ask to see the goods). You can get an immediate refund of the VAT at the airport or at main border points, less a service charge, or you can return the papers by mail to the shop(s), which will then deal with the details. The VAT refund can be credited to your credit-card account or paid by check.

Opening and Closing Times

Banks. Doors open weekdays 8–noon or 12:30 and 1:30–3 or 4. Hours vary from one city to another. Principal offices in cities stay open during lunch.

Museums. Opening days and times vary considerably from one city to another and depend on the season, the size of the museum, budgetary constraints, and assorted other factors. Your hotel or the local tourist office will have current details.

Shops. These open weekdays from 8 or 9 until 6 and Saturday until noon or 1 only, except the first Saturday of every month, when they stay open until 5. Some shops in larger cities are open on Thursday evenings until 8 PM. Many smaller shops close for one or two hours at midday.

National Holidays January 1; January 6 (Epiphany); April 11, 12 (Easter); May 1 (May Day); May 20 (Ascension); May 30, 31 (Pentecost); June 10 (Corpus Christi); August 15 (Assumption); October 26 (National Day); November 1 (All Saints' Day); December 8 (Immaculate Conception); December 25, 26.

Dining Take your choice of sidewalk *Wurstl* (frankfurter) stands, *Imbisstube* (quick-lunch stops), cafés, Heuriger wine restaurants, self-service restaurants, modest *Gasthäuser* neighborhood establishments with local specialties, and full-fledged restaurants in every price category. Most establishments post their menus outside. Shops that sell coffee beans (such as Eduscho) also offer coffee by the cup at prices that are considerably lower than those in a café. Many Anker bakery shops also offer tasty *Schmankerl* (snacks) and coffee, and often butcher shops sell a variety of cooked meats—a great basis for a picnic lunch.

Mealtimes Austrians often eat up to five meals a day: a very early Continental breakfast of rolls and coffee; a slightly more substantial breakfast *(Gabelfrühstück)* with eggs or cold meat, possibly even a small goulash, at mid-morning (understood to be 9, sharp); a main meal at noon; afternoon coffee *(Jause)* with cake at teatime; and, unless dining out, a light supper to end the day. Cafés offer breakfast; most restaurants open somewhat later. Lunches usually cost more in cafés than in restaurants. Use the humble Wiener Schnitzel to judge prices: if it's offered for less than A565, you've found yourself a budget eatery.

Dress A jacket and tie are generally advised for restaurants in the top price categories. Otherwise casual dress is acceptable, although in Vienna formal dress (jacket and tie) is preferred in some moderate restaurants at dinner. When in doubt, it's best to dress up.

Ratings Prices are per person and include soup and a main course, usually with salad, and a small beer or glass of wine. Prices also include taxes and service (you may wish to leave small change, in addition). Best bets are indicated by a star ★.

Category	Major City	Other Areas
Moderate	AS200–AS500	AS170–AS400
Inexpensive	AS150–AS200	AS130–AS170
Budget	under AS150	under AS120

Lodging Austrian hotels and pensions are officially classified using from one to five stars. These grades broadly coincide with our own four-way rating system. No matter what the category, standards for service and cleanliness are high. All hotels in the moderate category have either a bath or shower in the room; even the most inexpensive accommodations provide hot and cold water, with bath and toilets down the hall. Accommodations include conventional hotels, country inns *(Gasthof)*, motels (considerably less frequent), and the more modest pensions.

Ratings All prices quoted here are for two people in a double room. Though exact figures vary, a single room generally costs more than 50% of the price of a comparable double room. Breakfast—which can be anything from a simple roll and coffee to a full and sumptuous buffet—is usually included in the room rate. Best bets are indicated by a star ★.

Category	Major City	Other Areas
Moderate	AS850–AS1,250	AS700–AS1,000
Inexpensive	AS700–AS850	AS600–AS700
Budget	under AS700	under AS600

Tipping Railroad porters get AS10 per bag. Hotel porters or bellhops get AS5 per bag. Doormen get AS10 for hailing a cab and assisting. Room service gets AS10 for snacks and AS20 for full meals. Maids get no tip unless your stay is a week or more, or special service is rendered. In restaurants, 10% service is included. Add anything from AS5 to AS50, depending on the restaurant and the size of the bill.

Vienna

Arriving and Departing

By Plane All flights use Schwechat Airport, about 16 kilometers (10 miles) southwest of Vienna (tel. 0222/71110–2231).

Between the Airport and Downtown Buses leave from the airport for the city air terminal by the Hilton on Wien-Mitte-Landstrasse Hauptstrasse every half hour from 5 to 8:30 AM and every 20 minutes from 8:50 AM to 7:30 PM, then every half hour to 11:30 PM. Buses also run every hour from the airport to the Westbahnhof (west train station) and the Südbahnhof (south train station). Be sure you get on the right bus! The one-way fare for all buses is AS60.

By Train Vienna has four train stations. The principal station, Westbahnhof, is for trains to and from Linz, Salzburg, and Innsbruck. Trains from Germany and France arrive here, too. The Südbahnhof is for trains to and from Graz, Klagenfurt, Villach, and Italy. Franz-Josefs-Bahnhof is for trains to and from

Prague, Berlin, and Warsaw. Go to Wien-Mitte (Landstrasse) for local trains to and from the north of the city. Budapest trains use the Westbahnhof and Südbahnhof, and Bratislava trains use Wien-Mitte and Südbahnhof, so check.

By Bus If you arrive by bus, it will probably be at the central bus terminal, Wien-Mitte, opposite the city air terminal (and the Hilton).

By Boat All Danube riverboats dock at the DDSG terminal on Mexikoplatz. There's an awkward connection with the U-1 subway from here. Some boats also make a stop slightly upstream at Heiligenstadt, Nussdorf, from which there is an easier connection to the U-4 subway line.

Getting Around

Vienna is fairly easy to explore on foot; as a matter of fact, much of the heart of the city—the area within the Ring—is largely a pedestrian zone. The Ring itself was once the city ramparts, torn down just over a century ago to create today's broad, tree-lined boulevard. Public transportation is comfortable, convenient, and frequent, though not cheap.

Tickets for bus, subway, and streetcar are available in most stations. Tickets in multiples of five are sold at cigarette shops, known as Tabak-Trafik, or at the window marked "Vorverkauf" at central stations such as Karlsplatz or Stephansplatz. A block of five tickets costs AS75, a single ticket AS20. If you plan to use public transportation frequently, get a **24-hour ticket** (AS45), a **three-day tourist ticket** (AS115), or an **eight-day ticket** (AS235). Maps and information are available at Stephansplatz, Karlsplatz, and Praterstern U-Bahn stations.

By Bus or Inner-city buses are numbered 1A through 3A and operate
Streetcar weekdays to about 7:40 PM, Saturday until 2 PM. Reduced fares (buy a **Kurzstreckenkarte;** it gives four trips for AS30) are available for these routes as well as designated shorter stretches (roughly two to four stops) on all other bus or streetcar lines. Streetcars and buses are numbered according to route, and they run until about midnight. Night buses marked N follow special routes every hour on Saturdays and nights before holidays; the fare is AS25. The central terminal point is Schwedenplatz. The Nos. 1 and 2 streetcar lines run the circular route around the Ring, clockwise and counterclockwise, respectively.

By Subway Subway lines (U-Bahn; stations are marked with a huge blue "U") are designated U-1, U-2, U-3, U-4, and U-6 and are clearly marked and color-coded. Additional services are provided by a fast suburban train, the S-Bahn, indicated by a stylized blue "S" symbol. Both are tied into the general city fare system.

Important Addresses and Numbers

Tourist City Tourist Office (Kärntnerstr. 38, behind the opera, tel.
Information 0222/513–8892). Open daily 9–7.

Embassies U.S. (Gartenbaupromenade [Marriott Bldg.], tel. 0222/51451). **Canadian** (Dr. Karl Lueger-Ring, tel. 0222/533–3691). **U.K.** (Jauresg. 12, tel. 0222/713–1575).

Emergencies **Police** (tel. 133), **Ambulance** (tel. 144), **Doctor** (American Medical Society of Vienna, Lazaretteg. 13, tel. 0222/424568 or 408-3811).

Exploring Vienna

Vienna has been described as an "old dowager of a town," not a bad description for this onetime center of empire. It's not just the aristocratic and courtly atmosphere, with monumental doorways and stately facades of former palaces at every turn. Nor is it just that Vienna has a higher proportion of middle-aged and older citizens than any other city in Europe, with a concomitant sense of stability, quiet, and respectability. Rather, it's these factors, combined with a love of music; a discreet weakness for rich food (especially cakes); an adherence to old-fashioned and formal forms of address; a high, if unadventurous, regard for the arts; and a gentle mourning for lost glories, that produce a stiff but elegant, slightly other-worldly, sense of dignity.

The Heart of Vienna Most main sights are in the inner zone, the oldest part of the city, encircled by the **Ring**, once the city walls and today a broad boulevard. Before setting out, be sure to check opening times of museums carefully; they can change unpredictably. If you will be visiting a number of museums, you can save money by purchasing an AS150 Museum Pass, which will give you entries worth AS210 (get it at the first museum you visit). Carry a ready supply of AS10 coins, too; many places of interest have coin-operated tape machines that provide English commentaries. As you wander around, train yourself to look upward; some of the most memorable architectural treasures are on upper stories and roof lines.

Numbers in the margin correspond to points of interest on the Vienna map.

Vienna's role as imperial city is preserved in the complex of buildings that make up the former royal palace. Start your tour at Albertinaplatz, behind the opera house. Head down Augustinerstrasse. To the right is the "Memorial to Victims of Fascism," disputed in part because the sculptor was once an ❶ admitted Communist. On your left is the **Albertina,** home to the world's largest collection of drawings, sketches, engravings, and etchings. There are works here by Dürer—these are perhaps the highlight of the collection—Rembrandt, Michelangelo, Corregio, and many others. *Augustinerstr. 1, tel. 0222/534830. Admission: AS30. Open Mon., Tues., Thurs. 10–4; Wed. 10–6; Fri. 10–2; weekends 10–1; closed Sun. in July and Aug.*

Beethoven was a regular visitor at the Palais Lobkowitz across the street on Lobkowitzplatz. The renovated palace now ❷ houses the **Theater Museum.** Exhibits cover the history of theater in Vienna and the rest of Austria. A children's museum in the basement is reached by a slide! *Lobkowitzpl. 2, tel. 0222/512–3705. Admission: AS15. Open Tues.–Sun. 9–5.*

❸ Go back to Augustinerstrasse to the 14th-century **Augustinerkirche,** a favorite on Sundays, when the 11 AM mass is sung in Latin. The Habsburg rulers' hearts are preserved in a cham-
❹ ber here. Nearby is the **Nationalbibliothek** (the National Library), with its stunning Baroque great hall. Don't overlook

Albertina, **1**
Augustinerkirche, **3**
Donner Brunnen, **18**
Hofburg, **6**
Hofburgkapelle, **9**
Hoher Markt, **27**
Imperial
Apartments, **7**
Kapuzinerkirche, **17**
Karlskirche, **14**
Kirche am Hof, **24**
Kunsthistorisches
Museum, **12**
Maria am Gestade, **26**
Mozart
Erinnerungsräume, **22**
Nationalbibliothek, **4**
Naturhistorisches
Museum, **11**
Neue Hofburg
Museums, **10**
Pestsäule, **19**
Peterskirche, **20**
Ruprechtskirche, **28**
Sacher Hotel, **16**
Schatzkammer, **8**
Schloss Belvedere, **30**
Schönbrunn
Palace, **29**
Schottenkirche, **23**
Spanische
Reitschule, **5**
Staatsoper, **15**
Stephansdom, **21**
Tabak Museum, **13**
Theater Museum, **2**
20th Century
Museum, **31**
Uhrenmuseum, **25**

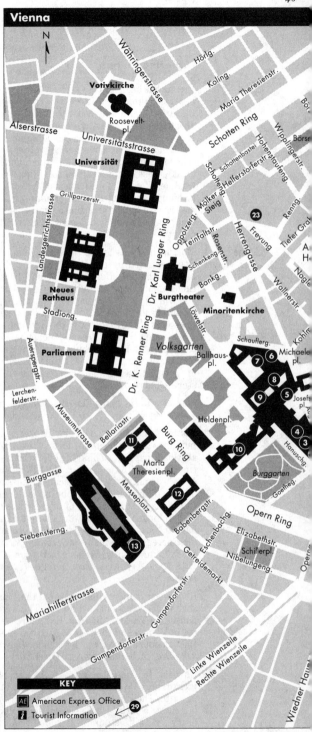

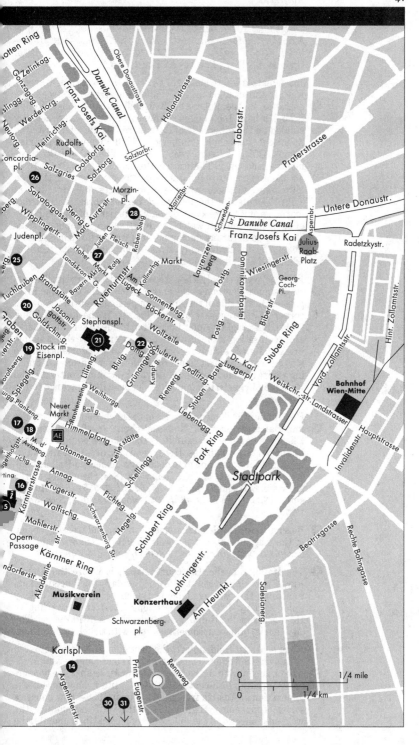

otten Ring
Gozelinkog.
Gonzaga.
sslingg.
Neuerg.
Werderforg.
Heinrichsg.
concordia-pl.
Salzgries
Rudolfs-pl.
Golsdorfg.
Salztorg.

26

berg.
Salvatorgasse
Wipplingertr.
Sterng.
Marc Aurel-str.
Morzin-pl.
Raben Steig

Judenpl.

28

Juden G. Fleisch
Hoher Markt Roig.
Bauern Mkt G.
Landskron
Fischhof

27

25

Tuchlauben Brandstätte
Jasomir-gottst.g.
Goldschm.g.
Rotenturmstr.
Am Elugeck Sonnenfelsg.
Bäckerstr.
Kollnerig.
Markt
Laurenzer-berg
Postg.

20

Graben
erstr.
berg
19 Stock im Eisenpl.
Stephanspl.

21

22

Blutg.
Domg.
Schulerstr.
Wollzeile
Grünangerg.
Kumpf g.
Riemerg.
Zedlitzg.
Bastei Luegerpl.
Dr. Karl

Dominikanerbastei
Biberstr.
Georg-Coch-Pl.

Stuben Ring

Weiskchr.-str.

Vord. Zollamtsstr.
Hint. Zollamtsstr.

Bahnhof Wien-Mitte

Radetzkystr.

Julius-Raab-Platz

Untere Donaustr.

Wiesingerstr.

Schweden-br.
Danube Canal
Franz Josefs Kai

Marienbr.

Obere Donaustrasse
Hollandstrasse
Taborstr.
Praterstrasse

Danube Canal
Franz Josefs Kai
Salztorbr.

morzahaeerg.
Spiegelg.
urgg.Plankeng.

17 **18**

M. d
Arvanag.
nghofgtr.
richg.

Neuer Markt
AE

Reauhensteig Weihburgg.
Ball g.
Himmelpfortg.
Johannesg.
Lilieng.
Stuben
Liebenbg.
Seilerstätte

Park Ring

tina-

16

5

Kärntnerstrasse
Krugerstr.
Walfischg.
Mahlerstr.
Annag.
Fichteg.
Schellingg.
Hegelg.
Schwarzenburg Str.

Schubert Ring

Stadtpark

Beatrixgasse
Rechte Bahngasse

Hauptstrasse
Invalidenstr.

Opern Passage
Kärntner Ring
Akademie-str.
ndorferstr.

Musikverein

Konzerthaus

Am Heumkt.

Schwarzenberg-pl.

Lothringerstr.

Salesianerg.

Karlspl.

14

Argentinierstr.

Rennweg
Prinz Eugenstr.

30 **31**

0   1/4 mile
0   1/4 km

the fascinating collection of globes on the third floor. *Josefsplatz 1, tel. 0222/534–10–397. Admission: AS15. Open May–Oct., Mon.–Sat. 10–4; Nov.–Apr., Mon.–Sat. 10:30– noon. Globe museum: tel. 534–10–297. Admission: AS10. Open Mon.–Wed., Fri. 11–12, Thurs. 2–3.*

Josefsplatz is where much of *The Third Man* was filmed, specifically in and around the Palais Pallavicini across the street. The entrance to the **Spanische Reitschule,** the Spanish Riding School, is here, too, though the famed white horses are actually stabled on the other side of the square. For tickets, write the Spanische Reitschule (Hofburg, A-1010 Vienna) or Austrian Tourist Office (Friedrichstr. 7, A-1010 Vienna) *at least* three months in advance. There are performances on Sunday at 10:45 AM from March through June, and from September through November, with some evening performances on Wednesdays at 7 PM. Tickets for the few short performances on Saturday mornings at 9 AM are available only from ticket offices and travel agencies. You can watch the 10 AM–noon training sessions Tuesday to Saturday during much of the performance season; tickets are available only at the door (Josefsplatz, Gate 2; adults AS60, children AS15).

From here you're only a few steps from Michaelerplatz, the circular square that marks the entrance to the **Hofburg,** the royal palace. On one side of the square, opposite the entrance, on the corner of Herrengasse and Kohlmarkt, is the **Loos building** (1911), designed by Adolf Loos. Step inside to see the remarkable restoration of the foyer. Outside, it's no more than a simple brick-and-glass structure, but architectural historians point to it as one of the earliest "modern" buildings in Europe—a building where function determines style. In striking contrast is the Baroque **Michaelertor,** opposite, the principal entrance to the Hofburg.

Head under the domed entrance of the Michaelertor to visit the **imperial apartments** of Emperor Franz Josef and Empress Elisabeth. Among the exhibits is the exercise equipment used by the beautiful empress. Here, too, is the dress she was wearing when she was stabbed to death by a demented Italian anarchist on the shores of Lake Geneva in 1898; the dagger marks are visible. *Michaelerplatz 1, tel. 0222/587–5554–515. Admission: AS25. Open Mon.–Sat. 8:30–noon, 12:30–4; Sun. 8:30– 12:30.*

Be sure to see the **Schatzkammer,** the imperial treasury, home of the magnificent crown jewels. *Hofburg, Schweizerhof, tel. 0222/533–7931. Admission: AS60. Open Wed.–Mon. 10–6.*

The **Hofburgkapelle,** the court chapel, is where the Vienna Boys Choir sings mass at 11 AM on Sunday. You'll need tickets to attend; they are available at the chapel from 5 PM Friday (queue up by 4:30 and expect long lines) or by writing to Hofmusikkapelle, Hofburg, Schweizerhof, A-1010 Vienna. The city tourist office can sometimes help with ticket applications.

Head south to Heldenplatz, the vast open square punctuated with oversized equestrian statues of Prince Eugene and Archduke Karl, in front of the **Neue Hofburg Museums.** The ponderously ornate 19th-century edifice—Hitler announced the annexation of Austria from the balcony in 1938—now houses a series of museums. Highlights are the Waffensammlung (the weapons collection), the collections of musical instruments, the ethnographic museum, and the exciting Ephesus museum, with finds from the excavations at that ancient site. The musical instruments collection has been undergoing refurbishing for years; check to see if it's finally open again. *Neue Hofburg, Heldenplatz 1, tel. 0222/521770. Admission: AS30; free first Sun. of each month. Open Wed.–Mon. 10–4.*

Walk west again under the unmonumental Hero's Monument and across the Ring, the broad boulevard encircling the inner
⑪ city, to the imperial museum complex. The **Naturhistorisches Museum** (Natural History Museum) is on your right, the
⑫ **Kunsthistorisches Museum** (Art History Museum) is on your left. The latter is one of the great art museums of the world; this is not a place to miss. The collections focus on old-master painting, notably Brueghel, Cranach, Titian, Canaletto, Rubens, and Velazquez. But there are important Egyptian, Greek, Etruscan, and Roman exhibits, too. *Burgring 5, tel. 0222/521770. Admission: AS45; free first Sun. of each month. Open Tues.–Sun. 10–6, alternate Tues. and Fri. 10–9.*

At the Mariahilferstrasse end of the Messepalast complex is
⑬ the small and fascinating **Tabak Museum,** the Tobacco Museum. *Mariahilferstr., tel. 0222/961716. Admission: AS20. Open Wed.–Fri. 10–3, Tues. 10–7, weekends 9–1.*

Head east down the Ring, with the Kunsthistorisches Museum on your right. Looming up to the right, over Karlsplatz, is the heroic facade and dome, flanked by vast twin columns, of the
⑭ **Karlskirche.** It was built around 1715 by Fischer von Erlach. The oval interior is surprisingly small, given the monumental facade: One expects something more on the scale of St. Peter's in Rome. The ceiling has airy frescoes, and stiff shafts of gilt radiate like sunbeams from the altar.

Take the pedestrian underpass back under the Ring to Opern-
⑮ platz. This is the site of the **Staatsoper,** one of the best opera houses in the world and a focus of Viennese social life. Tickets are expensive and rare, so you may have to settle for a backstage tour. The tour schedule for the day is usually posted outside the doors on the Operngasse side and will depend on the activities going on inside.

Head up Kärntnerstrasse, Vienna's main thoroughfare, now a busy pedestrian mall. On your left is the creamy facade of
⑯ the **Sacher Hotel.** Take a look inside at the plush red-and-gilt decor, a fin de siècle masterpiece. The hotel is also the home of the original Sachertorte—the ultimate chocolate cake. Back on Kärntnerstrasse, around the corner from the Sacher, is the city tourist office. Leading off Kärntnerstrasse, to the left, is the little street of Marco d'Aviano-Gasse. Follow it to
⑰ **Kapuzinerkirche,** in whose crypt, called the **Kaisergruft** or the imperial vault, the serried ranks of long-dead Habsburgs lie. The oldest tomb is that of Ferdinand II; it dates from 1633. The most recent tomb is that of Empress Zita, widow of Austria's last kaiser, dating from 1989.

⑱ In the center of the square is the ornate 18th-century **Donner Brunnen,** the Providence Fountain. The figures represent main rivers that flow into the Danube; Empress Maria Teresa thought the figures were obscene and wanted them removed or properly clothed. Turn north into Plankengasse, then, at the bright yellow Protestant churches, head east into the narrow Dorotheergasse.

⑲ Continue to reach pedestrians-only Graben. The **Pestsäule,** or Plague Column, shoots up from the middle of the street, looking like a geyser of whipped cream touched with gold. It commemorates the Black Death of 1697; look at the graphic depictions of those who fell victim to the ravages of the terrible disease. A small turning to the right, just past the column, **⑳** leads to the Baroque **Peterskirche.** The little church, the work of Johann Lukas von Hildebrandt, finished in about 1730, has what is probably the most theatrical interior in the city. The pulpit is especially fine, with a highly ornate canopy, but florid and swirling decoration is everywhere. Many of the decorative elements are based on a tent form, a motif suggested by the Turkish forces that camped outside the city walls during the great siege of Vienna at the end of the 17th century.

Walk down Goldschmiedgasse to Stephansplatz, site of the **㉑** **Stephansdom** (St. Stephen's Cathedral). Its towering Gothic spires and gaudy 19th-century tiled roof are still the dominant feature of the Vienna skyline. The oldest part of the building is the 13th-century entrance, the soaring **Riesentor,** or Giant Doorway. Inside, the church is mysteriously dark, filled with an array of monuments, tombs, sculptures, paintings, and pulpits. Despite extensive wartime damage—and numerous Baroque additions—the building radiates an authentically medieval atmosphere. Climb up the 345 steps of **Alte Steffl,** Old Steven, the south tower, for a stupendous view over the city. An elevator goes up the north tower to **Die Pummerin,** the Boomer, a 22-ton bell first cast in 1711 from cannons captured from the Turks. Take a 30-minute tour of the crypt to see the entrails of the Habsburgs, carefully preserved in copper jars.

㉒ On a narrow street east of the cathedral is the house where Mozart lived from 1784 to 1787. Today it's the **Mozart Erinnerungsräume,** the Mozart Museum. It was here that the composer wrote *The Marriage of Figaro*—thus the nickname Figaro House—and here, some say, that he spent the happiest years of his life. *Domgasse 5, tel. 0222/513–6294. Admission: AS15. Open Tues.–Sun. 9–12:15 and 1–4:30.*

Other Corners Walk back down the Graben and the narrow Naglergasse and **of Vienna** turn left into the Freyung. On your left is the **Palais Ferstl,** now a stylish shopping arcade. At the back is the skillfully restored **Café Central,** once headquarters for Vienna's leading literary **㉓** figures. Cross the Freyung to the dominant **Schottenkirche.** The monks who were brought to found it were actually Irish, not Scottish. They started a school as well, which shares the courtyard to the left with a pleasant garden restaurant in summer. Turn back through the Freyung to **Am Hof,** a remarkable square with the city's Baroque central fire station, possibly the **㉔** world's most ornate. Cross the square to the **Kirche am Hof.** The interior is curiously reminiscent of many Dutch churches.

Continue to Judenplatz and turn right into Parisergasse to the **㉕** **Uhrenmuseum** (Clock Museum), located in a lovely Renaissance house. *Schulhof 2, tel. 0222/533–2265. Admission: AS15. Open Tues.–Sun. 9–4:30.*

Turn down the Kurrentgasse and, via Fütterergasse, cross the Wipplingerstrasse into Stoss im Himmel (literally, a "thrust to **㉖** heaven"). To your left down Salvatorgasse is **Maria am Gestade,** originally a church for fishermen on the nearby canal. Note the ornate "folded hands" spire. Return along Wip-

㉗ plingerstrasse, across Marc Aurel-Strasse, to **Hoher Markt,** with a central monument celebrating the betrothal of Mary and Joseph. Roman ruins are displayed in the museum on the south side of the square. *Hoher Markt 3, tel. 0222/535–5606. Admission: AS15; free on Fri. morning. Open Tues.–Sun. 9–12:15 and 1–4:30.*

On the north side of Hoher Markt is the amusing **Anker-Uhr,** a clock that tells time by figures moving across a scale. The figures are identified on a plaque at the lower left of the clock; it's well worth passing by at noon to catch the show. Go through ㉘ Judengasse to the **Ruprechtskirche** (St. Rupert's). The oldest church in Vienna, dating from the 11th century, is small; damp; dark; and, unfortunately, usually closed, though you can peek through a window.

Vienna Environs It's a 15-minute ride from the city center on subway line U-4 ㉙ (stop either at Schönbrunn or Hietzing) to **Schönbrunn Palace,** the magnificent Baroque residence built between 1696 and 1713 for the Habsburgs. Here Kaiser Franz Josef I was born and died. His "office" (kept as he left it in 1916) is a touching reminder of his spartan life; other rooms, however, reflect the elegance of the monarchy. The ornate public rooms are still used for state receptions. A guided tour covers 45 of the palace's 1,441 rooms; among the curiosities are the Chinese room and the gym fitted out for Empress Elisabeth, where she exercised daily to keep her figure. *Schönbrunner Schlosstr., tel. 0222/81113–238. Admission: AS50. Guided tours only. Open Nov.–Mar., daily 9–4; Apr.–June, and Oct., daily 8:30–5, July–Sept., daily 8:30–5:30.*

Once on the grounds, don't overlook the **Tiergarten** (Zoo). It's Europe's oldest menagerie and, when established in 1752, was intended to amuse and educate the court. It contains an extensive assortment of animals, some of them in their original Baroque enclosures. *Tel. 0222/877–1236. Admission: AS30. Open Apr.–Sept., daily 9–6; Oct.–Mar., daily 9–4:30.*

Follow the pathways up to the **Gloriette,** that Baroque ornament on the rise behind Schönbrunn, and enjoy superb views of the city. Originally this was to have been the site of the palace, but projected construction costs were considered too high. *Admission: AS10. Open May–Oct., daily 8–6.*

The **Wagenburg** (Carriage Museum), near the entrance to the palace grounds, holds some splendid examples of early transportation, from children's sleighs to funeral carriages of the emperors. *Tel. 0222/823244. Admission: AS30. Open Oct.–Apr., Tues.–Sun. 10–4; May–Sept., Tues.–Sun. 10–6.*

㉚ Take the D streetcar toward the Südbahnhof to reach **Schloss Belvedere** (Belvedere Palace), a Baroque complex often compared to Versailles. It was commissioned by Prince Eugene of Savoy and built by Johann Lukas von Hildebrandt in 1721–22. The palace is made up of two separate buildings, one at the foot and the other at the top of a hill. The lower tract was first built as residential quarters; the upper buildings were reserved for entertaining. The gardens in between are among the best examples of natural Baroque ornamentation found anywhere. Both sections now house outstanding art museums: the gallery of 19th- and 20th-century art in the Upper Belvedere (Klimt, Kokoschka, Schiele, Waldmüller, Markart) and the Baroque museum (including medieval Austrian art) in the Lower Belvedere. *Prinz-Eugen-Str. 27, tel. 0222/784158. Admission: AS30. Open Tues.–Sun. 10–5.*

Continue across the Gürtel from the Upper Belvedere southward to the **20th Century Museum,** containing a small but extremely tasteful modern art collection. *Schweizer Garten, tel. 0222/782550. Admission: AS30. Open Thurs.–Tues. 10–6.*

You can reach a small corner of the **Vienna Woods** by streetcar and bus: Take a streetcar or the subway U-2 to Schottentor/ University and, from there, the No. 38 streetcar (Grinzing) to the end of the line. Grinzing itself is out of a picture book; alas, much of the wine offered in the taverns is less enchanting. (For better wine and ambience, try the village of Nussdorf, reached by streetcar D.) To get into the woods, change in Grinzing to the No. 38A bus. This will take you to Kahlenberg, which provides a superb view over the Danube and the city. You can take the bus or hike to Leopoldsberg, the promontory over the Danube from which Turkish invading forces were repulsed during the 16th and 17th centuries.

Off the Beaten Track

Vienna's **Bermuda Triangle** (around Judengasse/Seitenstettengasse) is jammed with everything from good bistros to jazz clubs. Also check the tourist office's museum list carefully: There's something for everyone, ranging from Sigmund Freud's apartment to the Funeral and Burial Museum. The **Hundertwasserhaus** (Kegelgasse/Löwengasse; streetcar N), an astonishing apartment complex designed by artist Friedenreich Hundertwasser, with turrets, towers, odd windows, and uneven floors, will be of interest to those who do not think that architectural form has to follow function.

Children will enjoy the charming **Doll and Toy Museum,** next door to the Clock Museum (*see* Exploring Vienna, *above*). It's filled with trains, dollhouses, and troops of teddy bears. *Schulhof 4, tel. 0222/535–6860. Admission: AS60 adults, AS30 children. Open Tues.–Sun. 10–6.*

Shopping

Shopping Districts Tourists gravitate to the **Kärntnerstrasse,** but the Viennese do most of their shopping on the **Mariahilferstrasse.**

Department Stores **Gerngross, Herzmansky,** and **Stafa** (all on Mariahilferstrasse) are the major outlets.

Food and Flea Markets The **Naschmarkt** (between Rechte and Linke Wienzeile; weekdays 6 AM–mid-afternoon, Sat. 6–1) is a sensational open-food market, offering specialties from around the world. The **Flohmarkt** (flea market) operates year-round beyond the Naschmarkt (subway U-4 to Kettenbrückengasse) and is equally fascinating (Sat. 8–4). Bargaining here goes on in any number of languages. An **Arts & Crafts Flea Market** with better offerings operates on Saturday (2–6 or 2–7) and Sunday (10–6) alongside the Danube Canal near the Salztorbrücke. One of the best seasonal local markets for handicrafts is on **Spittelberggasse,** particularly just before Christmas.

Dining

The simpler restaurants and **Gasthäuser** usually offer the best value. Look for blackboards outside listing daily specials, often a midday menu of soup and main course, possibly a dessert as well. Follow local habits—have your main meal at noon, a lighter meal in the evening—and you'll economize. Generally the farther you get from the first district, the more modest the restaurants. Restaurants around the university cater to student tastes and budgets.

Moderate   **Bastei-Beisl.** A comfortable, wood-paneled restaurant offering good traditional Viennese fare. Outdoor tables are particularly pleasant on summer evenings. *Stubenbastei 10, tel. 0222/512-4319. Reservations usually not necessary. AE, DC, MC. Closed Sun.*

Bei Max. The decor is somewhat bland, but the tasty Carinthian specialties—*Kasnudeln* and *Fleischnudeln* (a kind of cheese- and meat-filled ravioli) in particular—keep this friendly restaurant packed. *Landhausgasse 2/Herrengasse, tel. 0222/637359. Reservations advised. No credit cards. Closed Sat., Sun., Aug.*

★ **Gigerl.** It's hard to believe you're right in the middle of the city at this imaginative and charming wine restaurant that serves hot and cold buffets. The rooms are small and cozy but may get smoky and noisy when the place is full—which it usually is. The food is typical of wine gardens on the fringes of the city: roast meats, casserole dishes, cold cuts, salads. The wines are excellent. The surrounding narrow alleys and ancient buildings add to the charm of the outdoor tables in summer. *Rauhensteingasse 3, tel. 0222/513-4431. Reservations advised. AE, DC, MC, V.*

Melker Stiftskeller. This is one of the city's half-dozen genuine wine taverns, or kellers; the food selection is limited but good, featuring pig's knuckle. House wines from the Wachau are excellent. *Schottengasse 3, tel. 0222/533-5530. Reservations usually not necessary. MC. Evenings only; closed Sun.*

★ **Ofenloch.** This place is always packed, which speaks well not only of the excellent specialties from some Viennese grandmother's cookbook but also of the atmosphere. Waitresses are dressed in appropriate period costumes, and the furnishings add to the color. At times the rooms may be too smoky and noisy for some tastes. If you like garlic, try *Vanillerostbraten*, a rump steak with as much garlic as you request. *Kurrentgasse 8, tel. 0222/533-8844. Reservations required. AE, DC, MC, V.*

Stadtbeisl. Good standard Austrian fare is served at this popular eatery, which is comfortable without being pretentious. The service gets uneven as the place fills up, but if you are seated outside in summer, you probably won't mind. *Naglergasse 21, tel. 0222/533-3507. Reservations advised. No credit cards.*

Zu den drei Hacken. This is one of the few genuine Viennese *Gasthäuser* in the city center; like the place itself, the fare is solid if not elegant. Legend has it that Schubert dined here; the ambience probably hasn't changed much since then. There are tables outside in summer, although the extra seating capacity strains both the kitchen and the service. *Singerstr. 8, tel. 0222/5125895. No reservations. AE, V. Closed Sat. dinner and Sun.*

Zu ebener Erde und erster Stock. Ask for a table upstairs in this exquisite, tiny, utterly original Biedermeier house, which serves good, standard Austrian fare; the downstairs space is really more for snacks. *Burggasse 13, tel. 0222/936254. Reservations advised. AE. Closed Sun. and late July–late Aug.*

Inexpensive **Figlmüller.** Known for its schnitzel, Figlmüller is always
★ packed. Guests share the benches, the long tables, and the experience. Food choices are limited, but nobody seems to mind. Only wine is offered to drink, but it is good. The small "garden" is now enclosed and is just as popular as the tables inside. *Wollzeile 5 (passageway), tel. 0222/512–6177. No reservations. No credit cards. Closed Sat. dinner and Sun.*

Ilona-Stüberl. Head to Ilona-Stüberl for a cozy Hungarian atmosphere—without the gypsy music. Be prepared to douse the fire if you ask for a dish with hot peppers! The tables outside in summer are pleasant but somewhat public. *Bräunerstr. 2, tel. 0222/533–9029. Reservations advised. AE, DC, MC, V. Closed Sun.*

Budget **Einstein.** Diners are seated at one of a warren of semiprivate booths set off with dark wood dividers in the restaurant section, or at typical small tables in the café area. Fare is mainly Austrian, with occasional international touches. Try the excellent cream of garlic soup, or the *Suppentopf,* a thick stew that's a meal in itself, and have a genuine *Budweiser* beer on the side. *Rathausstr. 4, tel. 0222/422626. No reservations. No credit cards. Open weekdays 7 PM–2 AM, Sat. 10 PM–2 AM, Sun. 10 PM–midnight.*

Naschmarkt. These informal cafeteria-style restaurants, done in pseudo–Art Deco, are run (quite well) by the city and offer daily specials of prepared and grilled-to-order dishes plus regular features such as sandwich platters and a good salad bar. Soups are excellent, particularly the goulash in winter, gazpacho in summer. *Schwarzenbergplatz 16, tel. 0222/505–3839. No reservations. No credit cards. Open weekdays 6:30 AM–9 PM, weekends 9–9. Schottengasse 1, tel. 0222/533–5186. No reservations. No credit cards. Open weekdays 9–7:30, weekends 10:30–5.*

Rosenberger Marktrestaurant. Downstairs under a huge artificial tree a cluster of cafeteria-style food stations offers soups, excellent grilled specialties, salads, and desserts, all attractively presented and prepared to order. Look for seasonal specialties such as asparagus and fresh chilled melon. Stow your belongings in one of the free lockers, then find a seat in any of the side rooms, some decorated with musical instruments, some with antique kitchenware and dishes. *Maysedergasse 2/ Fürichgasse 3, tel. 0222/512–3458. No reservations. Open daily 11–11. Bistroette café open 8 AM–11 PM. No credit cards.*

Schnitzelwirt. Though inelegant and small, this neighborhood Gasthaus is known throughout the city for its immense schnitzels. Choose from other Austrian specialties, such as roast pork, as well. *Neubaugasse 52, tel. 0222/933771. Reservations advised. No credit cards. Open weekdays 10–10, Sat. 10–2:30, 5–10 PM. Closed Sun. and holidays.*

Lodging

Vienna's inner city is the best base for visitors because it's so close to most of the major sights, restaurants, and shops. This accessibility translates, of course, into higher prices, although there are still values to be found. Without wandering too far or sacrificing too much in the way of comfort, you can still find budget lodgings, and the efficient public transport can deliver you to still cheaper accommodations outside the center. For details and price-category definitions, *see* Lodging in Staying in Austria.

Moderate ★ **Austria.** This older hotel is on a quiet side street in a historic area. It is popular with tourists. *Wolfengasse 3/Fleischmarkt, tel. 0222/51523. 51 rooms, 40 with bath or shower. Facilities: bar. AE, DC, MC, V.*

★ **Kärntnerhof.** Though tucked away in a tiny, quiet side street, Kärntnerhof is nevertheless centrally located. It's known for its particularly friendly staff. The rooms are functionally decorated but clean and serviceable. *Grashofgasse 4, tel. 0222/512–1923. 45 rooms, 34 with bath or shower. AE, DC, MC, V.*

Pension Christine. This quiet pension, just steps from Schwedenplatz and the Danube Canal, offers mainly smallish modern rooms, warmly decorated with attractive dark-wood furniture set off against beige walls. Room 524 is particularly spacious and inviting. *Hafnersteig 7, tel. 0222/533–2961. 32 rooms with bath or shower. MC.*

★ **Pension Zipser.** This 1904 house, with an ornate facade and gilt-trimmed coat of arms, has become a favorite with regular visitors to Vienna. It is slightly less central than some others on our list, but very comfortable. *Langegasse 49, tel. 0222/420828. 46 rooms with bath or shower. Facilities: bar. AE, DC, MC, V.*

★ **Post.** Taking its name from the city's main post office, opposite, this is an older but updated hotel that offers a fine location, a friendly staff, and a good café. *Fleischmarkt 24, tel. 0222/515830. 107 rooms, 77 with bath or shower. AE, DC, MC, V.*

Schweizerhof. This is more of a pension than a hotel, but the location is excellent and the smallish rooms are certainly adequate. *Bauernmarkt 22, tel. 0222/533–1931. 55 rooms with bath or shower. AE, DC, MC, V.*

Wandl. The house is old and some of the rooms are small, but the Wandl's location and reasonable prices compensate for most of its deficiencies. *Petersplatz 9, tel. 0222/534550. 134 rooms with bath or shower. No credit cards.*

Budget **Felicitas.** You can look forward to a comfortable stay in this personable pension on a quiet street close to museums and transportation. The upstairs rooms are furnished in a variety of schemes, ranging from stark white modern decor with colorful accents to older pieces that will some day be called antiques. *Josefsgasse 7, tel. 0222/427212. 9 rooms, 1 with shower. No credit cards.*

Kirschbichler. Rooms in this simple, tidy family-run pension are freshly done with dark wood furniture against beige walls. You're one subway stop from the *Wien-Mitte* station here. Ask for one of the rooms on the courtyard side: they're quieter. There's no breakfast, but tea and coffee are provided. *Landstrasser Hauptstr. 33, tel. 0222/712–1068. 15 rooms with shower. No credit cards.*

★ **Kugel.** You're halfway between the West railroad station and the city center in this older but recently redecorated hotel. The breakfast/TV room is somewhat shabby, but guest rooms are furnished in modern, light wood pieces; those with the attractively tiled full baths will push the price up somewhat, those with only a shower remain comfortably within budget range. *Siebensterngasse 43, corner Neubaugasse 46, tel. 0222/933355 or 0222/931330. 38 rooms, most with shower or full bath. Facilities: bar, TV room. No credit cards.*

Stadtpark. You're within steps of the *Wien-Mitte* station (and the city air terminal) in this family-run pension, which was created in the 1920s by combining several adjoining apartments. Furnishings are eclectic; some rooms are spacious, others on the smaller side. Rooms with bath are slightly more expensive than those without. The breakfast buffet is a generous one. *Untere Viaduktgasse 59/Landstrasser Hauptstrasse 7, tel. 0222/713–3123. 20 rooms, 15 with bath. No credit cards.*

★ **Wild.** This friendly, family-run pension on several floors of an older apartment house offers the best value in town. Rooms are simple but modern, with furniture made from light-colored woods and pine-paneled ceilings. Each cluster of rooms has a kitchenette where you can prepare coffee and snacks. The breakfast room-TV lounge is bright and attractive, and the hotel is near the major museums. *Lange Gasse 1, tel. 0222/435174. 14 rooms, none with bath. Facilities: sauna, solarium, fitness room. AE, DC, MC, V.*

The Arts

Theater and Opera Check the monthly program published by the city; posters also show opera and theater schedules. Tickets for the Opera, Volksoper, and the Burg and Akademie theaters are available at the central ticket office to the left rear of the Opera (**Bundestheaterkassen,** Hanuschgasse 3, tel. 0222/514440; open weekdays 9–5, weekends 9–1). Tickets go on advance sale a week before performances. Unsold tickets can be obtained at the evening box office. Plan to be there at least one hour before the performance; students can buy remaining tickets at lower prices, so they are usually out in force. Tickets can be ordered six days in advance from anywhere in the world by phone (tel. 0222/513–1513; AE, DC, MC, V). Theater is offered in English at **Vienna English Theater** (Josefsgasse 12, tel. 0222/402–1260) and **International Theater** (Porzellangasse 8, tel. 0222/316272).

Music Most classical concerts are in either the **Konzerthaus** (Lothringerstr. 20, tel. 0222/712–1211) or **Musikverein** (Dumbastr. 3, tel. 0222/505–8190). Tickets can be bought at the box offices (AE, DC, MC, V). Pop concerts are scheduled from time to time at the **Austria Center** (Am Hubertusdamm 6, tel. 0222/236–9150; U-1 subway to Vienna International Center stop).

Film Films are shown in English at **Burg Kino** (Opernring 19, tel. 0222/587–8406), **de France** (Schottenring 5, tel. 0222/345236), **Top Kino** (Rahlgasse 1, tel. 0222/587–5557), and **Film Museum** (Augustinerstr. 1, tel. 0222/533–7054). To find English-language movies, look for "OF" (Originalfassung) or "OmU" (original with subtitles) in the newspaper listings.

Nightlife

Cabarets Most cabarets are expensive and unmemorable. Two of the best are **Casanova** (Dorotheergasse 6, tel. 0222/512–9845), which emphasizes striptease, and **Moulin Rouge** (Walfischgasse 11, tel. 0222/512–2130).

Discos **Atrium** (Schwarzenbergpl. 10, tel. 0222/505–3594) is open Thursday through Sunday and draws a lively younger crowd. **Queen Anne** (Johannesgasse 12, tel. 0222/512–0203) is central, popular, and always packed. The **P1** disco (Rotgasse 3, tel.

0222/535–9995) vies with the **U-4** (Schönbrunnerstr. 222, tel. 0222/858307) for top ranking among the young set.

Nightclubs A casual '50s atmosphere pervades the popular **Café Volksgarten** (Burgring 1, tel. 0222/630518), situated in the city park of the same name; tables are set outdoors in summer. The more formal **Eden Bar** (Liliengasse 2, tel. 0222/512–7450) is considered one of Vienna's classiest night spots; don't expect to be let in unless you're dressed to kill. Live bands, dancing, and snacks are offered at **Chattanooga** (Graben 29, tel. 0222/533–5000).

Wine Taverns For a traditional Viennese night out, head to one of the city's atmospheric wine taverns, which sometimes date as far back as the 12th century. You can often have full meals at these taverns, but the emphasis is mainly on drinking. **Melker Stiftskeller** (*see* Dining, *above*) is one of the friendliest and most typical of Vienna's wine taverns. Other well-known ones: **Antiquitäten-Keller** (Magdalenenstr. 32, tel. 0222/566–9533; closed Aug.), which has a backdrop of classical music; **Augustinerkeller** (Augustinerstr. 1, tel. 0222/533–1026), open at lunchtime as well as during the evenings, in the same building as the Albertina collection; **Esterhazykeller** (Haarhof 1, tel. 0222/533–3482), a particularly mazelike network of rooms; **Piaristenkeller** (Piaristengasse 45, tel. 0222/429152), somewhat touristy, with zither music; and **Zwölf-Apostelkeller** (Sonnenfelsgasse 3, tel. 0222/512–6777), near St. Stephen's Cathedral.

Salzburg

Arriving and Departing

By Plane For information, phone Salzburg airport, tel. 0662/852091.

Between the Airport and Downtown Buses leave for the Salzburg train station at Südtirolerplatz every 15 minutes during the day, every half hour at night. Journey time is 18 minutes.

By Train Salzburg's main train station is at Südtirolerplatz. Train information, tel. 0662/1717; telephone ticket orders and seat reservations, tel. 0662/1700.

By Bus The central bus terminal (information: tel. 0662/167) is in front of the train station.

Getting Around

By Bus and Trolleybus Service is frequent and reliable; route maps are available from the tourist office or your hotel. Save money by buying a Salzburg-1 (24-hour) or Salzburg-3 (72-hour) ticket that is good on all trolley and bus lines, on the funicular up to the fortress, on the Mönchsberg lift, and on the rail line north to Bergheim; half-price tickets for children 6–15. Local transportation information, tel. 0662/205–5131.

Tourist Information

Salzburg's official tourist office, **Stadtverkehrsbüro,** has an **information center** at Mozartplatz 5, tel. 0662/847568, and at the main train station, tel. 0662/871712. The main office is at Auerspergstrasse 7, tel. 0662/889870.

Exploring Salzburg

Numbers in the margin correspond to points of interest on the Salzburg map.

Salzburg is best known as the birthplace of Wolfgang Amadeus Mozart and receives its greatest number of visitors during the annual Music Festival in July and August. Dominated by a fortress on one side and a minimountain (Mönchsberg) on the other, this Baroque city is best explored on foot. Many areas are pedestrian precincts. Some of the most interesting boutiques and shops are found in the dozens of alleys and passageways that link streets and squares. And take an umbrella: Salzburg is noted for sudden, brief downpours that start as abruptly as they stop.

The Salzach River separates the old and new towns; for the best perspective on the old, climb the **Kapuziner** hill (pathways from the Linzerstrasse or Steingasse). Once back down at river level, walk up through Markartplatz to the **Landestheater,** where light opera and operettas are staged during the winter months; the larger houses used during the festival are closed most of the year. Wander through the Baroque **Mirabell** gardens in back of the theater and enjoy a dramatic view of the Old City, with the castle in the background. If you are pressed for time, you can pass up the **Baroque Museum.** *Admission: AS30. Open Tues.– Sat. 9–noon and 2–5, Sun. 9–noon.*

However, be sure to look inside **Schloss Mirabell.** It houses public offices, including that of the city's registrar; many couples come here for the experience of being married in such a sumptuous setting. The foyer and staircase, decorated with cherubs, are good examples of Baroque excess. Chamber music concerts are given in the Baroque hall upstairs in summer. *Mirabellplatz, tel. 0662/8072–2258. Open Mon.–Thurs. 8–4, Fri. 8–1.*

Head left down Schwarzstrasse, back toward the center of the city. On your left is the famed **Mozarteum,** a music academy (Schwarzstr. 26, tel. 0662/874492) whose courtyard encloses the summerhouse in which Mozart wrote his opera *The Magic Flute.* Cross over the Markartsteg footbridge to the Old City side of the Salzach river. Turn right and walk a short distance up the Kai to the **Carolino Augusteum Museum.** This is the city museum, whose collections include art, archaeology, and musical instruments. *Museumsplatz 1, tel. 0662/843145. Admission: AS30; combined ticket with toy museum in Bürgerspital (see below), cathedral excavations, and Folklore Museum: AS40. Open Tues. 9–8, Wed.–Sun. 9–5.*

Returning to city level, follow the Gstättengasse to the **Bürgerspital,** which houses a toy museum within its Renaissance arcades. *Bürgerspitalplatz 2, tel. 0662/847560. Admission: AS30; combined ticket with Carolino Augusteum. Open Tues.–Sun. 9–5.*

Ahead is Herbert-von-Karajan-Platz, whose central **Pferdeschwemme** (Horse Fountain) is its most notable feature. Built into the side of the mountain itself is the **Festspielhaus,** a huge complex where Salzburg's annual festival, the Festspiel, is held. *Hofstallgasse 1, tel. 0662/80450. Admission: AS30. Guided tours (not during rehearsals) weekdays at 2. No tours in July and Aug.*

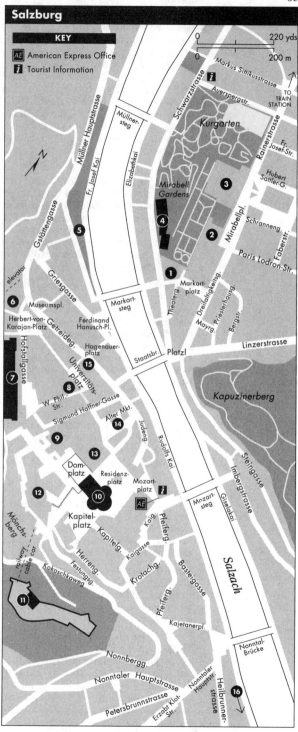

Salzburg

KEY

AE American Express Office

i Tourist Information

From the Festspielhaus, turn left into the Wiener-Philhar-
moniker-Strasse. The **Kollegienkirche** (Collegiate Church) on
the left is the work of Fischer von Erlach and is one of the best
examples of Baroque architecture anywhere; be sure to look inside. On weekday mornings the Universitätsplatz, in front of
the church, is crowded with market stands. Cut under the covered passageway and turn right into Sigmund Haffner-Gasse.

At the corner on the left stands the 13th-century **Franzis-
kanerkirche** (Franciscan Church), an eclectic mix of architectural styles, with Romanesque and Gothic accents. Nearby, at
Domplatz, is the Salzburg **Dom** (cathedral), a magnificently
proportioned building; note the great bronze doors as you
enter.

To reach the fortress on the hill above, walk under the arcade to
the right side of the church and up the narrow Festungsgasse at
the back end of Kapitalplatz. From here, you can either follow
the footpath up the hill or take a five-minute ride on the
Festungsbahn, the inclined railway cable car. On a sunny day, a
far more pleasurable—and strenuous!—route is to hike up the
Festungsgasse, turning frequently to enjoy the changing panorama of the city below.

Once you've reached the **Festung Hohensalzburg** itself, you can
wander around on your own (admission: AS20) or take a tour
(AS45). The views from the 12th-century fortress are magnificent in all directions. The main attraction is **St. George's Chapel,** built in 1501. A year later, in 1502, the Festung acquired the
200-pipe barrel organ, which plays daily in summer at 7 AM, 11
AM, and 6 PM. *Mönchsberg, tel. 0662/8042–2133. Open June–
Sept., daily 9:30–6:30; Oct.–May, daily 9:30–4:30. Guided
tour schedule varies.*

Back down in the city, follow the wall to **Stiftskirche St. Peter**
(St. Peter's Abbey). The cemetery lends an added air of mystery to the monk's caves cut into the cliff. The catacombs attached to the church can be visited by guided tour. *Just off
Kapitalplatz, tel. 0662/844–5780. Admission: AS10. Tours
May–Sept., daily 10–5, Oct.–Apr., daily 11–noon and 1:30–
3:30.*

Head around the cathedral to the spacious Residenzplatz, a
vast and elegant square. The **Residenz** itself includes prince-
archbishop's living quarters and representative rooms. *Residenzplatz 1, tel. 0662/8042–2690. Admission: AS40. Tours
Sept.–June, weekdays at 10–11, 2, and 3; July–Aug., daily every 20 mins. from 10 to 4:40.*

The **Residenzgalerie,** in the same building complex, has an outstanding collection of 16th- to 19th-century European art.
*Residenzplatz 1, tel. 0662/8042–2270. Admission: AS40. Com-
bined ticket with state rooms: AS60. Open daily 10–5. Closed
on Wed. Oct.–mid-Mar.*

From the lower end of Residenzplatz, cut across into the **Alter
Markt,** which still serves as an open market. Salzburg's nar-
rowest house is squeezed into the north side of the square. Turn
left into Griesgasse, a tiny street packed with boutiques and
fascinating shops. At the head of the tiny Rathausplatz is **Mozart's birthplace,** now a museum. *Getreidegasse 9, tel. 0662/
844313. Admission: AS50. Open daily 10–5; during festival,
daily 10–6.*

Wander along Getreidegasse, with its ornate wrought-iron shop signs and the Mönchsberg standing sentinel at the far end. Don't neglect the warren of interconnecting side alleys: These include a number of fine shops and often open onto impressive inner courtyards that, in summer, are guaranteed to be filled with flowers.

16 One popular excursion from Salzburg is to **Schloss Hellbrunn,** about 5 kilometers (3 miles) outside the city. Take bus line 55. The castle was built during the 17th century, and its rooms have some fine trompe l'oeil decorations. The castle's full name is Lustschloss Hellbrunn—Hellbrunn Pleasure Castle. It was designed for the relaxation of Salzburg's prince-bishops and includes the **Wasserspiele,** or fountains, conceived by someone with an impish sense of humor. Expect to get sprinkled as water shoots up from unlikely spots, such as the center of the table at which you're seated. The Baroque fountains are also fascinating. Both the castle and the fountain gardens can be included on a tour. *Tel. 0662/820372. Admission: AS48. Tours Apr. and Oct., daily 9–4:30; May–Sept., daily 9–5. Evening tours July–Aug. at 6, 7, 8, 9, and 10 PM.*

The Hellbrunn complex houses the **Tiergarten** (zoo), which is outstanding because of the way in which the animals have been housed in natural surroundings. *Tel. 0662/820176. Admission: AS40. Open Oct.–Mar., daily 9–4; Apr.–Sept., daily 8:30–6.* You can also visit the small **folklore museum.** *Admission: AS15. Open Easter–Oct., daily 9–5.*

Dining

Salzburg is a tourist town, meaning that prices are high, particularly in the city center, and the popular, low-price restaurants are always crowded. Try going a little ahead of or later than the noontime rush. Where noted, make reservations in advance, particularly during festival time.

Moderate **Alt Salzburg.** After an attempt to reach for the stars, this atmospheric restaurant has settled back to offer good local fare in its elegant red-and-white rooms. Try the traditional *Tafelspitz* (Austrian pot roast). *Bürgerspitalgasse 2, tel. 0662/841476. Reservations required. AE, DC, MC, V. Closed Sun.*

★ **Zum Mohren.** Arched ceilings in the lower rooms add atmosphere to this historic house. Duck and venison are specialties. *Judengasse 9, tel. 0662/842387. Reservations advised. No credit cards. Closed Sun. and holidays.*

Inexpensive **Mundenhamer.** Cream walls with dark wood accents and a tiled
★ floor create a fresh look in this popular eatery. The gulasch soup is just spicy enough, and the steak sandwiches and vegetarian specialties are highly recommended. Half-portions, available from 9:30 PM, are perfect late-night snacks. *Rainerstr. 2, tel. 0662/875693. Reservations useful. DC, MC, V. Closed Sun., holidays.*

★ **Wilder Mann.** The atmosphere may be too smoky for some (choose the outside courtyard in summer), but the beamed ceiling and antlers are genuine, as are the food and value. Try the *Tellerfleisch* (boiled beef) or game in season. *Getreidegasse 20/ Griesgasse 17 (passageway), tel. 0662/841787. Reservations advised. No credit cards. Closed Sun.*

Budget **Fasties.** There are two branches of this starkly modern, friend-
★ ly snack bar, where you'll find foods ranging from sandwiches
and salads to tasty hot noodle dishes. The high stools are not
the most comfortable, but that's the tradeoff for the quality of
food and the reasonable prices. *Lasserstr. 19, tel. 0662/873876.
Open weekdays 11–7:30. Pfeifergasse 3, tel. 0662/844774. Open
weekdays 8 AM–9 PM, Sat. 8–3; 8 AM–9 PM Mon.–Sat. mid-
June–mid-Oct. No credit cards.*

Sternbräu. During the summer, the spacious self-service garden is a favorite in this complex of restaurants, but there's
atmosphere to spare in the other rooms, such as the wood-
paneled *Bierstube.* Try any of the typical Austrian specialties
such as sausages or *Stelze* (knuckle of pork). *Griesgasse 23, tel.
0662/842140. No reservations. No credit cards. Open daily 8
AM–11 PM.*

Zum fidelen Affen. If you don't have a reservation, you'll have
to fight Salzburg's young businesspeople for a table in this popular but somewhat smoky beer bar/restaurant, decked out with
rough wooden floors and tables. Try the filling *schinken-
fleckerl* (a baked ham and pasta dish) or ask for the vegetarian
specialties, such as spinach strudel. *Preisterhausgasse 8, tel.
0662/877361. Reservations advisable. No credit cards. Open
Mon.–Sat. 5:30–11 PM.*

Lodging

Reservations are always advisable and are essential at festival
time (both Easter and summer), particularly for low-price accommodations. Be sure to get confirmation of reservations in
writing. For details and price-category definitions, *see* Lodging in Staying in Austria, *above.*

Moderate **Amadeus.** Rooms are done with tastefully simple natural wood
★ and rustic accessories in this family-run house dating from the
1500s. The central location is just minutes from the sites across
the river. *Linzer Gasse 43–46, tel. 0662/871401. 23 rooms with
bath or shower. AE, DC.*

Blaue Gans. Reasonable rates at a 500-year-old building in the
heart of the old city make this a popular choice. The enticing
prospects suggested by the baroque facade are not carried
throughout the place, unfortunately: Rooms are unimaginative, some even a little dingy, and the service is nothing special.
Being able to step out onto the Getreidegasse next door to the
famous Goldene Hirsch makes all the difference, however, so
book early. *Getreidegasse 43, tel. 0662/841317. 45 rooms, 29
with bath. Facilities: restaurant. AE, DC, MC, V.*

★ **Trumer Stube.** Guests repeatedly recommend this family-run
pension, mentioning the friendly atmosphere and helpful staff.
It's in a well-kept old building down a narrow, winding street
near Mirabellplatz. The breakfast room is bright and cheerful;
the simple but pleasant guest rooms are scrupulously clean and
are redecorated every four years. *Bergstr. 6, tel. 0662/874776.
22 rooms with shower. No credit cards.*

Wolf. The cozy rooms in this small family-run hotel just off
Mozartplatz are arranged on several upper floors, connected
by narrow, winding stairs, and decorated with a pleasing mix
of Oriental carpets and country furniture. The friendly, helpful
staff is only one reason that it's so difficult to book a room here.
*Kaigasse 7, tel. 0662/843453. 12 rooms with bath or shower.
AE.*

Inexpensive
★

Markus Sittikus. Rooms here are light and attractive, and many on the top floor get lovely morning sunlight. The train station is nearby, and the staff is friendly and helpful. This is a popular hotel, so book early. *Markus-Sittikus-Str. 20, tel. 0662/ 871121–0. 41 rooms with bath or shower. AE, DC, MC, V.*

Budget

Bergland. You're a bit farther from the city center in this simple pension, but still within walking distance of the main sights. If Bergland is full, you'll probably be referred to one of the other nearby, but slightly more expensive, pensions. *Rupertgasse 15, tel. 0662/872318. 18 rooms with shower. No credit cards. Closed Nov.–Dec. 20.*

Goldene Krone. Since rooms are plain and a bit worn, and breakfast is definitely on the spartan side, this hotel's only real draw is the central location. The least expensive rooms open onto ventilation shafts, others have views of a church, so you may want to check before signing in. *Linzer Gasse 48, tel. 0662/ 872300. 27 rooms, most with shower. No credit cards.*

Schwarzes Rössl. Once a favorite with regulars to Salzburg, this old *gasthof* is now student quarters for most of the year and rented to the public when unoccupied. Rooms are not elegant, but they are fresh and immaculate, and the location, close to nightime action, is excellent. *Priesterhausgasse 6, tel. 0662/ 874426. 51 rooms, all with bath. AE, DC, MC, V. Closed Oct.– June.*

The Arts

Festivals

Tickets for the festival performances are almost impossible to get once you are in Salzburg. Write ahead to **Salzburger Festspiele** (Postfach 140, A-5010 Salzburg).

Opera, Music, and Art

Theater and opera are presented in the **Festspielhaus** (*see* Exploring, *above*), opera and operetta at the **Landestheater** (Schwarzstr. 22, tel. 0662/871–5120), and concerts at the **Mozarteum** (Schwarzstr. 26, tel. 0662/873154). Chamber music—in costume—is performed in **Schloss Mirabell.** Special art exhibits in the **Carolino** (*see* Exploring, *above*) are often outstanding.

Innsbruck

Arriving and Departing

By Plane

The airport is 3 kilometers (2 miles) to the west of the city. For flight information, phone 0512/22220.

Between the Airport and Downtown

Buses (Line F) to the city center (Maria-Theresien-Str.) run every 20 minutes and take about 20 minutes. Get your ticket from the bus driver; it costs AS15.

By Train

All trains stop at the city's main station at Südtiroler-Platz. Train connections are available to Munich, Vienna, Rome, and Zurich. For train information, phone 0512/1717. Ticket reservations, tel. 0512/1700.

By Bus

The terminal is in front of the main train station.

Getting Around

By Bus and Most bus and streetcar routes begin or end at Südtiroler-Platz,
Streetcar site of the main train station. The bus is the most convenient
way to reach the five major ski areas outside the city. Many hotels offer free transportation with direct hotel pickup; for those
staying in the Old City, the buses leave from in front of the
Landestheater. Check with your hotel or the tourist offices for
schedules.

Tourist Information

The city's two main tourist offices are at Burggraben 3 (tel.
0512/5356—Innsbruck) and Wilhelm-Greil-Strasse 17 (tel.
0512/532–0170—Tirol).

Exploring Innsbruck

*Numbers in the margin correspond to points of interest on the
Innsbruck map.*

At the center of the province of Tirol lies the quaint and well-
preserved capital city of Innsbruck. Squeezed by the mountains and sharing the valley with the Inn River, Innsbruck is
compact and very easy to explore on foot. The ancient city—it
received its municipal charter in 1239—no doubt owes much of
its fame and charm to its unique situation. To the north, the
steep, sheer sides of the Alps rise like a shimmering blue-and-
white wall from the edge of the city, an awe-inspiring backdrop
to the mellowed green domes and red roofs of the picturesque
Baroque town.

Modern-day Innsbruck retains close associations with three
historical figures: Emperor Maximilian I and Empress Maria
Theresa, both of whom are responsible for much of the city's
architecture, and Andreas Hofer, a Tirolean patriot. You will
find repeated references to these personalities as you tour the
city. A good starting point is the **Goldenes Dachl** (the Golden
Roof), which made the ancient mansion whose balcony it covers
famous. (It's actually made of gilded copper tiles.) The building
now houses an **Olympic Museum,** which features videotapes of
the Innsbruck winter Olympics. *Herzog Friedrich-Str. 15, tel.
0512/536–0575. Admission: AS22. Open daily 10–5:30. Closed
on Mon. Nov.–Feb.*

A walk up the Hofgasse brings you to the **Hofburg,** the Rococo
imperial palace, with its ornate reception hall decorated with
portraits of Maria Theresa's ancestors. *Rennweg 1, tel. 0512/
587186. Admission: AS30. Open mid-May–mid-Oct., daily
9–4; mid-Oct.–mid-May, Mon.–Sat. 9–4.*

Close by is the **Hofkirche,** the Imperial Church, built as a
mausoleum for Maximilian. The emperor is surrounded by
24 marble reliefs portraying his accomplishments, as well
as 28 oversize statues of his ancestors, including the legendary
King Arthur. The above-mentioned Andreas Hofer is also
buried here. Don't miss the silver chapel with its ornate
altar. The **Tiroler Volkskunstmuseum** (Tirolean Folk Art Museum) is housed in the Hofkirche, too, and shows costumes,
rustic furniture, and farmhouse rooms decorated in styles
ranging from Gothic to Rococo. *Universitätsstr. 2, tel. 0512/
584302. Admission: AS20 (Hofkirche), AS40 (Volkskunst-*

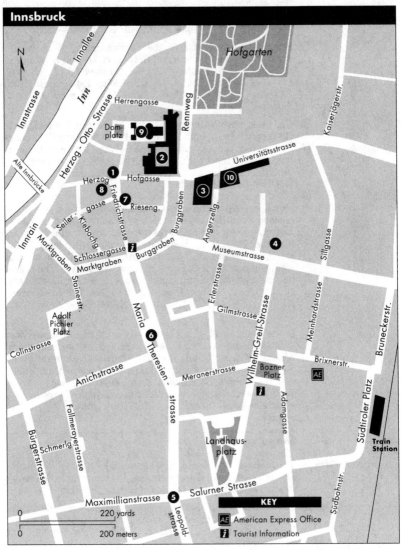

Innsbruck

Major Attractions
Annasäule, **6**
Ferdinandeum, **4**
Goldenes Dachl, **1**
Hofburg, **2**
Hofkirche, **3**
Triumphpforte, **5**

Other Attractions
Dom zu St. Jakob, **9**
Helblinghaus, **8**
Stadtturm, **7**
Tiroler Volkskunst-museum, **10**

KEY
AE American Express Office
i Tourist Information

museum); combined ticket: AS50. Hofkirche open daily 9–5; Volkskunstmuseum open Mon.–Sat. 9–5, Sun. 9–noon.

❹ Follow Museumstrasse to the **Ferdinandeum,** which houses Austria's largest collection of Gothic art, as well as paintings from the 19th and 20th centuries. *Museumstr. 15, tel. 0512/ 594–8971. Admission: AS50. Open May–Sept., daily 10–5; Thurs. eve. 7–9; Oct.–Apr., Tues.–Sat. 10–noon and 2–5, Sun. and holidays 10–1.*

❺ Cut back down Wilhelm Greil-Strasse to the **Triumphpforte** (Triumphal Arch), built in 1765, and walk up Maria Theresien-
❻ Strasse past the **Annasäule** (Anna Column) for a classic "post-card" view of Innsbruck with the Alps in the background.

Off the Beaten Track

Just 3 kilometers (2 miles) southeast of the city and easily reached by either bus or streetcar is **Schloss Ambras,** one of Austria's finest and best-preserved castles. Originally dating from the 11th century, it was later rebuilt as a residence for the archduke Ferdinand of Tirol (from 1564 to 1582), so most of what you now see is in German Renaissance style. The collection includes numerous pictures, weapons, armor, objets d'art, and furniture. *In the village of Ambras (streetcar line 3 or bus K), tel. 0512/48446. Admission: AS30. Open May–Sept., Wed.–Sun. 10–5.*

In the mountains high above the city is the unique **Alpine Zoo,** with alpine animals and birds in their native environment and even an aquarium. And, of course, there's a restaurant at the top. You can either hike up or take the Hungerberg funicular, then the cable car. A combination funicular-cable entry card is available at the Hungerberg ticket office. *Weiherburggasse 37, tel. 0512/892323. Admission: AS56. Open summer 9–6; winter 9–dusk.*

Shopping

Shopping Districts Many shops are found in the historic streets of Maria-Theresien-Strasse, Museumstrasse, Brixnerstrasse, Meraner-strasse, and among the arcades of Herzog Friedrich-Strasse.

Gift Ideas The best-known and best-loved local specialties include Tirole-an hats (those little pointed green felt ones, garnished with a feather), Loden cloth, lederhosen, dirndls, wood carvings, and mountain and skiing equipment.

Dining

For details and price-category definitions, *see* Dining in Staying in Austria.

Moderate **Goethestube.** The wine tavern of the city's oldest inn, the Goldener Adler, is one of Innsbruck's best. It was here that Goethe (who lent his name to the tavern) sipped quantities of red South Tirolean wine during his stays in 1786 and 1790. *Herzog Friedrich-Str. 6, tel. 0512/586334. Reservations not necessary. AE, DC, MC, V.*

★ **Hirschenstuben.** Old-fashioned hospitality and dark-wood trimmings are found in force at this charming local favorite.

Kiebachgasse 5, tel. 0512/582979. Reservations advised. AE, DC, MC, V. Closed Sun.

Ottoburg. A rabbit warren of rooms, in a 13th-century building, the Ottoburg is exactly right for an intimate, cozy lunch or dinner. It's packed with Austriana and is 100% genuine. Go for the trout if it's available. *Herzog Friedrich-Str. 1, tel. 0512/574652. Reservations advised. AE, DC, MC, V.*

Stieglbräu. Lovers of good beer will be delighted to find this popular rustic spot, which, in addition to its thirst-quenching ales, provides good, solid Austrian fare. Portions are huge, the garden exceptionally pleasant. *Wilhelm Greilstr. 25, 0512/584338. No credit cards.*

Inexpensive   **Weinhaus Happ.** Some of the smaller rooms upstairs in this historic house may be a bit smoky, and service falters if groups arrive, but local specialties such as game in season are excellent. *Herzog Friedrich-Str. 14, tel. 0512/582980. Reservations advised. AE, DC, MC, V. Closed Sun.*

Weisses Rossl. A friendly family atmosphere with a Tirolean accent marks this pleasant restaurant. The food is simple but excellent. *Kiebachgasse 8, tel. 0512/583057. No credit cards. Closed Sun.*

Budget   **Inn 95.** The diners in this casual spot, mainly from the adjacent hostel, are mostly young and not very critical, but you'll still find fair value in the daily noontime specials. The *knödel* (dumplings) are filling and good. *Innstr. 95, tel. 0512/86515. No credit cards. Closed Sun., holidays.*

Steden. The clientele and the smoky, wood-paneled rooms offer pure local atmosphere, although the quality of the food doesn't live up to the setting. Nevertheless, the daily specialties are a bargain, and the roast pork is particularly tasty. *Anichstr. 15, tel. 0512/580890. No credit cards. No dinner Sat. Closed Sun., holidays.*

Lodging

The best accommodation bargains during the winter are those included in ski package deals; during the summer, student dorms are transformed into modest hotels, though they are not necessarily the cheapest nor most central.

For details and price-category definitions, *see* Lodging in Staying in Austria.

Moderate   **Goldene Krone.** The Triumphal Arch is at the doorstep, and
★   stunning postcard views are to the left and right of this well-located older hotel. Rooms are modest, but spotless and comfortably furnished, and the buffet breakfast is adequate. You're a short walk (or one tram stop) from the rail station. *Maria-Theresien-Str. 46, tel. 0512/586160. 36 rooms with bath or shower. AE, DC, MC, V.*

Rössl in der Au. This student dorm offers convenient, reasonably priced quarters in summer, plus views across the river to the old city. Rooms are modern, if somewhat spartan. *Höttinger Au, tel. 0512/286846 or 0512/226460. 140 rooms with bath. Facilities: garage, parking. No credit cards.*

★   **Weisses Kreuz.** The comfortable rooms in this historic house in the arcaded old city are furnished with rag rugs and natural woods. The family management is friendly and helpful, and there's a convenient ground-floor ski storage room. *Herzog*

Friedrich-Str. 31, tel. 0512/594790. 39 rooms, 28 with bath or shower. Facilities: restaurant. AE, V.

Inexpensive **Binder.** A short bus trip from the center of town shouldn't be too high a price to pay for less costly comfort at this small, friendly hotel. *Dr.-Glatz-Str. 20, tel. 0521/42236 or 0521/59631. 32 rooms, some with bath or shower. Facilities: parking, garage. MC, V.*

Budget **Innbrücke.** The pink facade of this 550-year-old house on the river across from the old city conceals simple but attractive rooms furnished in light wood, with patterned wallpaper and carpeting; those in front, which have bay windows, are particularly appealing. *Innstr. 1, tel. 0512/281934. 20 rooms, some with bath. No credit cards.*

Schwarzer Bär. This comfortable, informal Gasthaus offers rooms with natural pine ceilings and the occasional Oriental carpet. The modernized old building is across the river from the old city. *Mariahilfstr. 16, tel. 0512/294900. 10 rooms, some with bath. No credit cards.*

★ **Weisses Lamm.** When booking, try for a room at the front and center of the hotel overlooking the river and the old city—and remember that there's no elevator to the upper floors. Rooms have dark furnishings and patterned wallpaper; baths are tiled in dark brown and white. The in-house restaurant, with its beamed ceiling and rustic decor, has a good reputation for local specialties. *Mariahilfstr. 12, tel. 0512/283156. 15 rooms with bath or shower. No credit cards.*

The Arts

Most hotels have a monthly calendar of events (in English). The **Central Ticket Office** is on Centralpassage (tel. 0512/536–0506). Tickets to most events are also available at the main tourist office, Burggraben 3 (tel. 0512/5356). Opera, operetta, musicals, and concerts take place at the **Tiroler Landestheater** (Rennweg 2, tel. 0512/520–7430) and **Kongresshaus.**

3 Belgium

Good things come in small packages. Belgium, which occupies the stretch of the land bordering the North Sea between France and Holland, measures just over 250 kilometers (150 miles) from Oostende in the west to the German border, less than 160 kilometers (100 miles) from Antwerp in the north to the French border. This is good news for the budget-conscious traveler, because it means that virtually all points of interest can be reached on one-day rail trips from the capital. With more than 10 million people, Belgium is the second most densely populated country in the world. Both Parisians and Amsterdammers tend to think of Belgium as a substandard version of "pure" French or Dutch culture. However, Belgium has a distinctive culture, or rather, two: Flemish and Walloon. The Flemish, who speak Dutch (Flemish), inhabit the northern half of the country and account for 56% of the population. The French-speaking Walloons live in the other half. The capital, Brussels, is officially designated a dual-language area.

Belgium is the world's most heavily industrialized country, with only 5% of the working population engaged in agriculture (though they still manage to produce 165 different cheeses and any number of fine sausages). Besides being natural entrepreneurs, the Belgians also work very hard—partly to make up for what has so long been denied them. In the course of history, the Belgians have been ruled by the Romans, French, Spanish, Austrians, Dutch, English, and Germans. Many of Europe's greatest battles have been fought on Belgian soil—from Waterloo and earlier to the long-slogging encounters of World War I. During World War II, this territory witnessed both the initial blitzkrieg of Nazi Panzer units and Hitler's final desperate counterattack against the advancing Allies in the Ardennes—

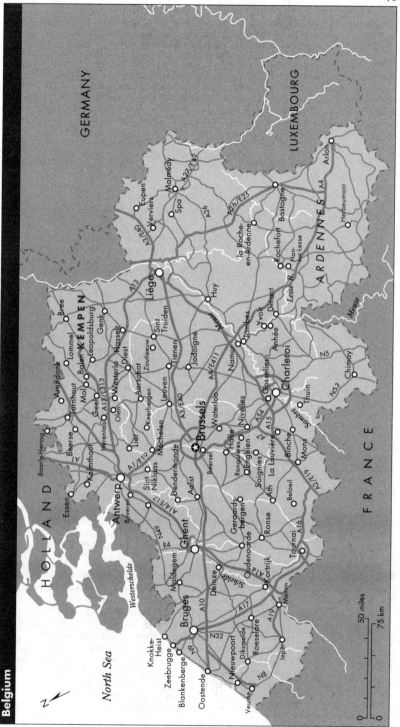

70

Belgium

an offensive that has gone down in history as the Battle of the Bulge.

The south of the country is a wild, wooded area, with mountains rising to more than 620 meters (2,000 feet). In the Dutch-speaking north, on the other hand, the land is flat and heavily cultivated, much as it is in neighboring Holland. Here stand the medieval Flemish cities of Ghent and Bruges, with their celebrated carillons and canals—not to mention the 68 kilometers (42 miles) of sandy beaches that make up the country's northern coastline. Due north of Brussels lies Antwerp, the country's dynamic seaport. This city, where the painter Rubens lived, is now the world's leading diamond-cutting center.

Brussels stands in the very center of the country. A booming, expanding, and often expensive city, it is now the capital of Europe. Here the European Community (EC) has its headquarters. Over the past few years a number of new hotels have been constructed in Brussels for budget travelers. Away from the capital hotel prices are at least 20% lower, with particularly advantageous prices at resort hotels on the coast and in the Ardennes.

As befits a bourgeois culture, the Belgians are great believers in the quality of life. In practice, this means that meals, parks, cars, and houses are large. Homes are highly individualistic and comfortable; trendy designer bars are cozy as well as chic.

But Belgians are not just creatures of the senses. A robust culture is celebrated in paintings by Bruegel and Rubens, Magritte, and Delvaux; by exciting Gothic, Renaissance, and Art Nouveau architecture; and by the best jazz in Europe. Belgium is no self-publicist, but quietly and confidently waits to be discovered.

Essential Information

Before You Go

When to Go The tourist season runs from early May to late September and peaks in July and August, when the weather is best. In recent years, however, off-season travel has become increasingly popular. In the coastal resorts, some hotels and restaurants remain open all year.

Climate Temperatures range from around 65 F in May to an average 73 F in July and August. In winter, temperatures drop to an average of about 40 to 45 F. Snow is unusual except in the mountains of the Ardennes, where cross-country skiing is a popular sport in February and March.

The following are the average daily maximum and minimum temperatures for Brussels.

Jan.	40F	4C	May	65F	18C	Sept.	69F	21C
	30	-1		46	8		51	11
Feb.	44F	7C	June	72F	22C	Oct.	60F	15C
	32	0		52	11		45	7
Mar.	51F	11C	July	73F	23C	Nov.	48F	9C
	36	2		54	12		38	3
Apr.	58F	14C	Aug.	72F	22C	Dec.	42F	6C
	41	5		54	12		32	0

Currency The unit of currency in Belgium is the franc. There are bills of 100, 500, 1,000, and 5,000 francs in addition to coins of 1, 5, 20, and 50 francs. Do not confuse the new 50-franc coin and the old 5-franc coin. At press time (spring 1992), the exchange rate was about BF33 to the dollar and BF60 to the pound sterling.

Traveler's checks and credit cards are the safest and simplest ways to carry money. American Express, Bank of America, Barclays, Eurocheques, and Thomas Cook traveler's checks are all honored in Belgium. All major credit cards are widely accepted, too. Avoid exchanging money on weekends or at hotels and restaurants unless you're prepared to pay a big premium.

What It Will Cost A recent study suggests that the cost for a prudent but not penny-pinching week in Brussels will come to about $600 per person. This includes two gourmet meals, five fixed-priced menus, seven light meals, and a shared double room in a moderately priced hotel. Major Brussels hotels also offer substantially reduced summer rates.

Sample Prices A cup of coffee in a café will cost BF45–BF60; a glass of beer, BF35–BF85; and a glass of wine, about BF100. Train travel averages BF6 per mile, the average bus/metro/tram ride costs BF40, theater tickets cost about BF500, and movie tickets about BF200.

Customs on Arrival Visitors from EC countries can bring in 300 cigarettes or 75 cigars or 400 grams of tobacco, 5 liters of still wine and 1½ liters of spirits or 3 liters of aperitif wine, and 75 grams of perfume. Other goods imported from the EC may not exceed BF17,000 in value. Visitors from non-EC countries can bring in 200 cigarettes or 50 cigars or 250 grams of tobacco, 2 liters of still wine and 1 liter of spirits or 2 liters of aperitif wine, and 50 grams of perfume. Other goods from non-EC countries may not exceed BF2,000 in value. There are no restrictions on the import or export of currency.

Language Language is a sensitive subject that has led to the collapse of at least two governments. There are three national languages in Belgium: French, spoken primarily in the south of the country (Wallonia); Dutch or Flemish, spoken in the north; and German, spoken in a small area in the east. Brussels is bilingual, with both French and Flemish officially recognized, though French predominates. Many people speak English in Brussels and in the north (Flanders). If your French is good but your Flemish nonexistent, it is politic to speak English to Flemings, especially in Antwerp or Flanders. In Wallonia you may have to muster whatever French you possess, but in tourist centers you will be able to find people with at least basic English.

Getting Around

By Train Fast and frequent trains connect all main towns and cities. If you intend to travel frequently, buy a **Tourrail Ticket,** which allows unlimited travel for any five days during a 17-day period. If you are over 26, the cost of the five-day pass is BF3,080 second-class. For those under 26, the pass costs BF1,990 second-class. The **Benelux Tourrail Ticket,** good throughout Belgium, Luxembourg, and the Netherlands, allows unlimited travel for five days in a 17-day period at a cost of BF1,800 second-class; for those under 26, BF1,350 second-class. Young people from 12 to 26 can purchase a **Go Pass** for BF990, valid for nine one-way trips in a six-month period on the Belgian rail network. All of the above are available at any Belgian train station.

Special weekend round-trip tickets are valid from Friday noon to Monday noon: A 40% reduction is available on the first traveler's ticket and a 60% reduction on companions' tickets. During the tourist season there are similar weekday fares to the seaside and the Ardennes.

By Bus There is a wide network of local and regional buses throughout Belgium. Details of services are available at train stations and tourist offices.

By Bicycle You can rent a bicycle from Belgian railways at 48 stations throughout the country; train travelers get reduced rates. A special brochure is available at most stations. Bicycling is especially popular in the flat northern and coastal areas. Bicycle lanes are provided in many Flemish cities, but bicycling in Brussels is madness.

Staying in Belgium

Telephones Pay phones work with 5- and 20-franc coins or with Telecards,
Local Calls available in a number of denominations starting from BF200. The Telecards can be purchased at any post office and at many newsstands. Most phone booths that accept Telecards have a list indicating where these cards are sold. An average local call costs BF10 or BF20.

International Calls The least expensive method is to buy a high-denomination Telecard and make a direct call from a phone booth. A five-minute phone call to the United States at a peak time will cost about BF750 by this method. International calls can also be made at most hotels, but nearly all have a service charge that may double the cost. It's always wise to ask what the service charge is before placing the call. Operator-assisted international calls can also be made at most post offices.

Operators The numbers for operator assistance and information vary from one city to another; it's best to ask at a hotel or post office or to consult a telephone directory.

Mail Airmail letters to the United States cost BF37 for the first 20
Postal Rates grams; postcards, BF28. Airmail letters to the United Kingdom are BF14 for the first 20 grams.

Receiving Mail You can have mail forwarded directly to your hotel. If you're uncertain where you'll be staying, have mail sent in care of **American Express** (1 pl. Louise, B-1000 Brussels). Cardholders are spared the $2-per-letter charge.

Shopping
Sales-Tax Refunds When you buy goods for export, you can ask most shops to fill out special forms covering VAT or sales tax. An itemized invoice showing the amount of VAT will also do. When you leave Belgium, you must declare the goods at customs and have the customs officers stamp the documents. Once you're back home, you simply send the stamped forms back to the shop and your sales tax will be refunded. This facility is available in most boutiques and large stores and covers most purchases of more than BF2,000.

Opening and Closing Times **Banks.** Banks are open weekdays from 9 to 4; some close for an hour at lunch. Exchange facilities are usually open on weekends, but you'll get a better rate during the week.

Museums. Most museums are open from 10 to 5 six days a week. Closing day is Monday in Brussels and Antwerp, Tuesday in Bruges. Check individual listings.

Shops. Stores are open weekdays and Saturdays from 10 to 6 and generally stay open later on Friday. Hours vary from store to store, so it's best to check in advance. Bakeries and some small food shops are open on Sunday.

National Holidays January 1; April 12 (Easter Monday); May 1 (May Day); May 20 (Ascension); May 31 (Pentecost Monday); July 21 (National Holiday); August 15 (Assumption); November 1 (All Saints' Day); November 11 (Armistice); December 25–26.

Dining Nearly all Belgians take eating seriously and are discerning about fresh produce and innovative recipes. Fixed-price menus are available in virtually all restaurants and often represent very considerable savings. Menus and prices are always posted outside. Belgian specialties include *lapin à la bière* (rabbit in beer), *faisan à la brabanconne* (pheasant with chicory), *waterzooi* (a rich chicken or fish hotpot), and *carbonnades* (chunky stews). A Belgian peculiarity is that dogs are allowed into most restaurants.

Local specialties include truly marvelous asparagus from Mechelen, at their best in May; *salade Liègoise,* a hot salad with beans and bacon (Liège); wild strawberries and freshwater fish from the Meuse River (Namur); different permutations of sprouts, chicory, and pheasant (Brussels); and shrimps, oysters, and mussels (Flanders).

Belgian snacks are equally appetizing. The waffle *(gaufre/ wafel)* has achieved world fame, but *couques* (sweet buns), *speculoos* (spicy gingerbread biscuits), and *pain d'amandes* (nutty after-dinner biscuits) are less well known. For lunch, cold cuts, rich pâtés, and *jambon d'Ardenne* (Ardenne ham) are popular, often accompanied by goat's cheese and rye or wholemeal bread.

Mealtimes Most hotels serve breakfast until 10. Belgians usually eat lunch between 1 and 3, some making it quite a long, lavish meal. However, the main meal of the day is dinner, which most Belgians eat between 7 and 10; peak dining time is about 8.

Dress Belgians tend to be fairly formal and dress conservatively when dining out in the evenings. Generally speaking, the more prestigious the restaurant, the more formal the dress. Younger Belgians favor stylish, casual dress in most restaurants.

Ratings Prices are per person and include a first course, main course, dessert, tip, and sales tax, but no wine. Best bets are indicated by a star ★.

Category	All Areas
Moderate	BF1,000–BF2,000
Inexpensive	BF500–BF1,000
Budget	under BF500

Lodging You can trust Belgian hotels, almost without exception, to be clean and of a high standard. The more modern hotels in city centers can be very expensive, but there are smaller, well-appointed hotels, offering lodging at excellent rates. The family-run establishments in out-of-the-way spots, such as the Ardennes, can be surprisingly inexpensive. Complete hotel lists, including pensions, are available at tourist offices.

Pensions Pensions offer a double room with bath or shower and full board from BF2,500 to BF3,500 in Brussels and from BF2,000 to BF3,000 elsewhere. These terms are often available for a minimum stay of three days.

Youth Hostels For information about youth hostels, contact **Fédération Belge des Auberges de la Jeunesse** (tel. 02/215–31–00). In the United States: **American Youth Hostels, Inc.,** Box 37613, Washington, DC 20013. In the United Kingdom: **Camping and Caravan Club Ltd.,** 11 Lower Grosvenor Pl., London SW1, or **Youth Hostels Association International Travel Bureau,** 14 Southampton St., London WC2.

Camping Belgium is well supplied with camping and caravan sites. For details, contact the **Royal Camping and Caravaning Club of Belgium** (rue Madeleine 31, B-1000 Brussels, tel. 02/513-12-87).

Ratings Hotel prices are inclusive and are usually listed in each room. All prices are for two people in a double room. Best bets are indicated by a star ★.

Category	All Areas
Moderate	BF3,500–BF5,500
Inexpensive	BF2,500–BF3,500
Budget	under BF2,500

Tipping Tipping has been losing its hold in Belgium over the past few years because a service charge is almost always figured into the bill. For example, a tip of 16% is included in all restaurant and café bills. The tip is also included in taxi fares. Porters in railway stations ask a fixed per-suitcase price, BF30 in the day and BF35 at night. For moderately priced hotels, BF50 should be an adequate tip for bellhops and doormen. At the movies, tip the usher BF20, whether or not he or she shows you to your seat. In restaurants, cafés, movie theaters, theaters, train stations, and other public places, you should tip the washroom attendant BF10.

Brussels

Arriving and Departing

By Plane All international flights arrive at Brussels's Zaventem Airport, about a 30-minute drive or a 16-minute train trip from the city center. **Sabena, American, Delta, TWA, United,** and **Tower Air** all fly into Brussels from the United States. **Sabena, British Airways,** and newcomer **British Midland,** often cheaper and just as good, dominate the short-haul London (Heathrow)–Brussels route. **Air UK** flies to Brussels from London (Stansted), and **Danair** from London (Gatwick). Several regional centers in the United Kingdom also have direct flights to Brussels.

0345 55 4 554
0345 666 777

Between the Airport and Downtown There is regular train service from the airport to the Gare du Nord (North Station) and the Gare Centrale (Central Station), which leaves every 20 minutes. The trip takes 16 minutes and costs BF140 (second-class round-trip); you can buy a ticket at a booth in the luggage area. The first train from the airport runs at 6 AM and the last one leaves at 11:46 PM. *10 minutes ferry kim*

By Train and Boat/Jetfoil From London, the train service connects with the Dover–Oostende ferry or jetfoil services. From Oostende, the train takes you to Brussels. The whole journey by jetfoil takes just under five hours, but is longer by boat. For reservations and times, contact **P & O Ferries** in London (tel. 081/575–8555). A one-way London–Brussels ticket costs £21, excluding the £6–£9 (depending on the season) jetfoil supplement.

There are three main stations in Brussels: the Gare du Nord, Gare Centrale, and Gare du Midi (South Station). There is also a Gare du Quartier Léopold on the east side of the city. The Gare Centrale is most convenient for the downtown area, but is served mostly by commuter trains. For train information, telephone 02/219–26–40 or inquire at any station.

By Bus and Hovercraft/Ferry From London, the Hoverspeed City Sprint bus connects with the Dover–Calais Hovercraft, and the bus then takes you on to Brussels. The journey takes 6½ hours; a one-way ticket costs £28. For reservations and times, contact **Hoverspeed** (tel. 081/554–7061). Overnight services by **National Express–Eurolines** (tel. 071/730–0202) take the ferry and also cost £28 one way.

0304 240
241

Getting Around

By Métro, Tram, and Bus The métro, trams (streetcars), and buses run as part of the same system. All three are clean and efficient, and a single ticket costs BF40. The best buy is a 10-trip ticket, which costs BF250, or a 24-hour card costing BF160. You need to stamp your ticket in the appropriate machine on the bus or tram; in the métro, your card is stamped as you pass through the automatic barrier. You can purchase these tickets in any métro station or at newsstands. Single tickets can be purchased on the bus. All services are few and far between after 10 PM.

Detailed maps of the Brussels public transportation network are available in most métro stations and at the Brussels tourist office in the Grand' Place (tel. 02/513–89–40).

Important Addresses and Numbers

Tourist Information The main tourist office for **Brussels** is in the Hôtel de Ville on the Grand' Place (tel. 02/513–89–40), open Monday–Saturday 9–6. The main tourist office for the rest of **Belgium** is near the Grand' Place (rue Marché-aux-Herbes 61, tel. 02/504–03–90) and has the same opening hours. There is a tourist office at **Waterloo** (chaussée de Bruxelles 149, tel. 02/354–99–10); it is open April–November 15, daily 9:30–6:30 and November 16– March, daily 10:30–5.

Embassies **U.S.** (blvd. du Régent 27, B–1000 Brussels, tel. 02/513–38–30). **Canadian** (av. de Tervuren 2, B–1000 Brussels, tel. 02/735–60– 40). **U.K.** (rue d'Arlon 85, B–1040 Brussels, tel. 02/287–62–11).

Emergencies **Police** (tel. 101); **Accident** (tel. 100); **Ambulance** (tel. 02/649– 11–22); **Doctor** (tel. 02/648–80–00 and 02/479–18–18); **Dentist** (tel. 02/426–10–26).

Exploring Brussels

Brussels is a city of individualists. Walk along almost any street, and you will be surprised at how different each house is from its neighbor, often embellished in *Art Nouveau* style, in contrast with impersonal office blocks. Stop in the Grand' Place during a *son-et-lumière* (sound-and-light) show and your mood softens, or watch from a cozy bar, its tables stacked high with pancakes or covered with bottles of Duvel beer. Brussels is an odd mixture of the provincial and the international. Underneath the bureaucratic surface, the city is a subtle meeting of the Walloon and Flemish cultures. As the heart of the ancient Duchy of Brabant, Brussels retains its old sense of identity and civic pride. A stone's throw from the steel-and-glass towers, there are cobbled streets, canals where old barges still discharge their freight, and forgotten spots where the city's eventful and romantic past is plainly visible through its 20th-century veneer.

Numbers in the margin correspond to points of interest on the Brussels map.

The Grand' Place Begin in the **Grand' Place,** one of the most ornate market
❶ squares in Europe. There is a daily flower market and a colorful Sunday-morning bird market. On summer nights, the entire square is flooded with music and colored light. The Grand' Place also comes alive during local pageants, such as the *Mayboom;* the *Ommegang*, a splendid historical pageant (early July); and the biennial *Tapis de Fleurs*, when the entire square is covered by a carpet of flowers (mid-August, next in 1994).

The bombardment of the city by Louis XIV's troops left only
❷ the **Hôtel de Ville** (town hall) intact. Civic-minded citizens started rebuilding the Grand' Place immediately, but the highlight of the square remains the Gothic town hall. The central tower, combining boldness and light, is topped by a statue of St-Michel, the patron saint of Brussels. Among the magnificent rooms are the Salle Gothique, with its beautiful paneling; the Salle Maximilienne, with its superb tapestries; and the Council Chamber, with a ceiling fresco of the *Assembly of the Gods* painted by Victor Janssens in the early 15th century. *Admission: BF75. Open Tues.–Fri. 9:30–12:15 and 1:45–5 (in winter until 4), Sun. 10–noon and 2–4.*

Brussels

N

Gare du Nord

Jardin Botanique

Gare Central

440 yds
400 m

Canal de Charleroi

79

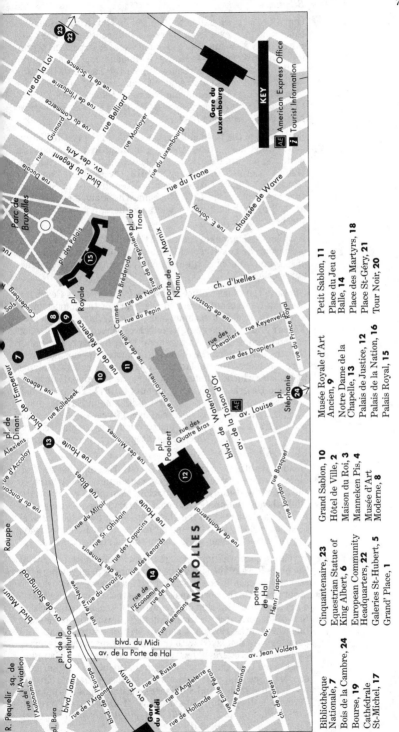

❸ Opposite the town hall is the **Maison du Roi** (King's House)—though no king ever lived there—a 16th-century palace housing the **City Museum.** The collection includes important ceramics and silverware—Brussels is famous for both—church sculpture, and statues removed from the facade of the town hall, as well as an extravagant collection of costumes for Manneken Pis (*see* Exploring Brussels, *below*). *Grand' Place, tel. 02/511–27–42. Admission: BF80. Open weekdays 10–12:30 and 1:30–5, weekends 10–1.*

❹ Southwest of the town hall, on the corner of the rue de l'Etuve and rue du Chêne, stands the famous **Manneken Pis,** a fountain with a small bronze statue of a chubby little boy urinating. Made by Jerome Duquesnoy in 1619, the statue is known as "Brussels's Oldest Citizen" and is often dressed in costumes that are kept in the City Museum. The Manneken was kidnapped by 18th-century invaders (soldiers, not tourists!) but was returned promptly.

Leaving the Manneken, cross the Grand' Place in the direction of the Marché-aux-Herbes. If you are planning to visit the rest of Belgium, stop in at the regional tourist office (rue Marché-aux-Herbes 61).

Opposite the tourist office, take the Petite rue des Bouchers, the main restaurant street in the heart of the tourist maelstrom. In Brussels fashion, each restaurant advertises its wares by means of large signs and carts packed with a selection of game and seafood. As a general rule, however, remember that the more lavish the display, the poorer the cuisine. From
❺ here, explore the network of galleries called **Galeries St-Hubert,** which includes the Galerie de la Reine, Galerie du Roi, and Galerie des Princes, all built in 1847. Their harmonious glass-top design was the first of its kind in Europe; moreover, the galleries were designed by a 17-year-old. Written on the central galleries is the motto "Omnibus Omnia" (Everything for Everyone), which is not altogether appropriate, given the designer prices.

❻ Head south along the rue Marché-aux-Herbes and the rue Madeleine until you come to the **equestrian statue of King Albert.** To the left of the statue is the Central Station and to the right, the
❼ **Bibliothèque Nationale** (National Library). Walk through the formal gardens next to the National Library and look back at the ornate clock, with moving figures, over the lower archway. Try to hear—and see—it at noon, when it strikes the hour.

Place Royale If you continue walking through the gardens, you will arrive at the **place Royale,** the site of the Coudenberg palace, where the sovereigns once lived. Here you have a superb view over the
❽ lower town. On the northwest corner of the square is the **Musée d'Art Moderne** (Museum of Modern Art), housed in an exciting feat of modern architecture. On entry, a vertiginous descent into the depths reveals a sudden well of natural light. The paintings are displayed with the light and space they deserve. Although there are a few paintings by Matisse, Gauguin, Degas, and Dali, the surprise lies in the quality of Belgian modern art. See Magritte's luminous fantasies, James Ensor's masks and still lifes, and Spilliaert's coastal scenes. Do not miss Permeke's deeply brooding *Fiancés* or Delvaux's Surrealist works. *Pl. Royale 1, tel. 02/513–96–30. Admission free. Open Tues.–Sun. 10–noon and 1–5.*

⑨ Next door is the **Musée Royale d'Art Ancien** (Royal Museum of Ancient Art). Here the collection is of Flemish and Dutch paintings, ranging from magnificent 15th- and 16th-century works—Cranach, Matsys, and Bruegel the Elder, among them—to Rubens (several fine canvases), Van Dyck, and David. Do not miss Bruegel's dramatic *La Chute d'Icare (The Fall of Icarus)* or Hieronymus Bosch's *Le Dernier Jugement (The Last Judgment)*, a malevolent portrait of humanity. *Rue de la Régence 10. Admission free. Open Tues.–Sun. 10–noon and 1–5.*

As you stand in the place Royale facing back the way you came, the rue de la Régence runs on your left up to the Palais de Jus-
⑩ tice. The Sablon lies along this street, on the right. The **Grand Sablon,** the city's most sophisticated square, is alive with cafés, restaurants, and antiques shops. Toward the end of the square is the **church of Notre Dame du Sablon,** built in flamboyant Gothic style. Although much of the original workmanship was lost in restoration, it remains one of the city's best-loved churches. At night, the brilliant church windows illuminate the Grand Sablon and the Petit Sablon behind.

⑪ A small garden square, the **Petit Sablon** is surrounded by 48 statues representing Brussels's medieval guilds. Each craftsman carries an object that reveals his trade: The furniture maker holds a chair, for instance; the wine merchant, a goblet.

On the Petit Sablon is the **Musée Instrumental** (Museum of Musical Instruments). A huge collection of over 1,000 musical instruments is on display. Half of them are unique, and a few go back to the Bronze Age. The guide can often be persuaded to play one of the pianos. *Petit Sablon 17, tel. 02/512–08–48. Admission free. Open Tues., Thurs., and Sat. 2:30–4:30, Wed. 4–6, Sun. 10:30–12:30.*

Immediately behind the Petit Sablon is the **Palais d'Egmont,** at different times the residence of Christina of Sweden, Louis XV, and Voltaire. It is now used by the Belgian Ministry of Foreign Affairs for official meetings. If security allows, you can enter the Jardin d'Egmont, another small park, on this side. Come out of the entrance on rue du Grand Cerf and turn left toward the boulevard de Waterloo, a wide street full of bars and designer shops.

Palais de Justice to the Black Tower At the end of the rue de la Régence is the **Palais de Justice.** Often described as the ugliest building in Europe, the palais is de-
⑫ signed to impress upon you the majesty of justice. It's located on the site of the former Gallows Hill. If you climb the more than 500 steps to the cupola, you will get an excellent view of the countryside around Brussels, weather permitting.

Down a rather steep hill from the Palais de Justice is the working-class **Marolles** district, where the artist Pieter Bruegel
⑬ died in 1569. His imposing marble tomb is in **Notre Dame de la Chapelle,** his local church on rue Haute. From place de la
⑭ Chapelle, take rue Blaes to the flea market in **place du Jeu de Balle.** On the way, you will pass a number of rough Belgian bars and North African food shops. Until this century, bourgeois Belgians considered this labyrinth of small alleys a haven for thieves and political refugees. Although the Marolles continues to welcome immigrants and outsiders, it has lost its danger but kept its slightly raffish character.

Return via the Sablon to the place Royale. Directly ahead of
⑮ you is the **Parc de Bruxelles** (Brussels Park) with the **Palais Royal** (Royal Palace) at the end closer to you. (The palace is usually open during August and a few days before and after. Dates
vary from year to year.) You can walk through the park to the
⑯ **Palais de la Nation** (Palace of the Nation) at the opposite end,
where the two houses of the Belgian Parliament meet. When
Parliament is not sitting, you can visit the building. *Guided
tours weekdays 10–noon and 2–5 (Sat. until 4).*

Surrounding the park are elegant turn-of-the-century houses.
The prime minister's office is next to the Parliament building.
A walk downhill (rue des Colonies) toward the downtown area
⑰ and a short right-hand detour bring you to the **Cathédrale St-
Michel.** The cathedral's chief treasure is the beautiful stained-
glass windows designed by Bernard van Orley, an early 16th-
century painter at the royal court. In summer the great west
window is floodlit from inside to reveal its glories. In the crypt,
you can see the remnants of the original 12th-century church.

Situated between the cathedral and the galleries is **La Mort
Subite** (Sudden Death) (rue Montagne-aux-Herbes-Potagères
7, tel. 02/513–13–18), the city's most genuine beer hall. Locals
sit on long benches and select drinks from the best beer list in
Brussels, including foamy *bière blanche* (white lager beer),
strong *trappiste* (brewed by monks), *framboise* (made with
raspberries), and heady *kriek* (a cherry beer).

⑱ Continue downhill to the **place des Martyrs,** a dignified square
over a mass grave for local patriots who died in the 1830 battle
to expel the Dutch. This dilapidated square, where renovation
is finally beginning, is at odds with the rue Neuve, the busy
shopping street that runs along one side. Cross the rue Neuve
and continue on to the boulevard Adolphe-Max. Turn left and
⑲ then right, in front of the imposing **Bourse** (stock exchange), to
place Ste-Catherine.

⑳ The 12th-century **Tour Noir** (Black Tower) here is part of the
city's first fortifications. Under the square runs the river
Senne, channeled underground in the last century when the
pollution of the canal basins and the stench from the open sew-
ers became too great. As a result of its watery past, place Ste-
Catherine and the old fish market (quai aux Briques) that
extends north from it still have the city's best seafood restaurants. If you have enough energy, take the rue de la Vierge
㉑ Noire to **place St-Géry,** the next square south. This whole area
is undergoing exciting renovation as Bruxellois gradually real-
ize the charms of the 17th-century buildings in this old port setting. Once an island, St-Géry has recently returned to its
watery roots: The river Senne has been uncovered and the
canalside houses, restored.

Parc du Another walk on the north side of the Parc de Bruxelles takes
Cinquantenaire you from the Palais de la Nation down the rue de la Loi toward
and Bois de la the Cinquantenaire (if the walk is too long for you, take the mé-
Cambre tro). On the way, you'll pass in front of the **European Communi-
㉒ ty Headquarters** at the Rond Point Schuman. The vast 13-story
cruciform building, now undergoing restoration to remove as-
bestos ceilings and partitions, houses the European Commission. The council offices are located nearby.

㉓ The **Cinquantenaire** is a huge, decorative archway, built in 1905
in a pleasant park. The buildings on either side of the archway

house the **Royal Museums of Art and History.** Displays include Greek, Roman, and Egyptian artifacts and toys. *Parc du Cinquantenaire 10, tel. 02/741–72–11. Admission free. Open weekdays 9:30–12:30 and 1:30–4:45, weekends 10–4:45.*

The new **Autoworld Museum,** also in the Cinquantenaire, has one of the world's most handsome collections of vintage cars. *Parc du Cinquantenaire 11, tel. 02/736–41–65. Admission: BF150. Open daily 10–6 (Nov.–Mar. until 5).*

㉔ South of the Palais de Justice is the **Bois de la Cambre,** a popular, rambling park on the edge of town. Take tram No. 94 from Sablon or place Stéphanie for a pleasant 10-minute ride along avenue Louise. Just before the bois is the former **Abbaye de la Cambre,** a 14th-century church with cloisters, an 18th-century courtyard, and a terraced park. The Bois de la Cambre is a good place for a family outing, with a lake, boat trips, pony rides, and an outdoor roller-skating rink.

Beyond the bois is the **Boitsfort racecourse,** and eastward lies the **Forêt de Soignes,** 27 square kilometers (17 square miles) of forest, mostly beech trees, with walking and riding paths.

Waterloo No history buff can visit Brussels without making the pilgrimage to the site of the **Battle of Waterloo,** where Napoleon was finally defeated on June 18, 1815. It is easily reached from the city and lies 19 kilometers (12 miles) to the south of the Forêt de Soignes; take a bus from place Rouppe or a train from Gare Centrale to Waterloo station. In July and August, a red tourist train (tel. 02/354–78–06) runs from Waterloo station to all the main sights (Visitors' Center, tel. 02/385–19–12; open Apr.–Oct. 9:30–6:30; Nov.–Mar. 10:30–4).

Wellington's headquarters, now a museum, presents the complex battle through illuminated 3-D maps, scale models, and military memorabilia, including the general's personal belongings. *Admission: BF60. Open Apr.–mid-Nov., Tues.–Sun. 9:30–6:30; mid-Nov.–Mar., Tues.–Sun. 10:30–5.*

The **Battle Panorama Museum,** beside the battlefield, is a rotunda displaying a huge, naturalistic painting of one stage of the battle. *Admission: BF70. Open daily 9:30–6.*

Beside it is the pyramid-shape **Lion Monument,** erected by the Dutch. After climbing 226 steps, you'll find one of the bleakest views in the country before you. With a little imagination, you can quickly conjure up the desolation of the battlefield scene.

Musée du Caillou (Napoleon's Headquarters) is worth visiting to understand the French perspective of the battle. Tours of the site are led by multilingual guides. *Admission: BF60. Open Wed.–Mon. 9–5.*

The Battle of Waterloo is reenacted every five years (next time in 1995) around June 15. A thousand local citizens dress as French, Prussian, and English soldiers and realistically shoot one another with old muskets. Unlike the real battle, which ended in over 40,000 deaths, this one ends in a large buffet, a son-et-lumière show, and a fireworks display. Check the dates with the Brussels or Waterloo tourist office.

Off the Beaten Track

The Maison d'Erasme is a beautifully restored 15th-century house where Erasmus, the great humanist, lived in 1521. Every detail of this atmospheric house is authentic, with period furniture and paintings by Holbein, Dürer, and Hieronymous Bosch. The custodian will convince you of the relevance of Erasmus's works to peace in our time. *Rue du Chapitre 31, tel. 02/521–13–83. Admission: BF20. Open Wed.–Thurs. and Sat.–Mon., 10–noon and 2–5.*

The new **Musée de la Bande Dessinée** celebrates the comic strip, emphasizing such famous Belgian graphic artists as Hergé, Tintin's creator. Hergé apparently invented the *ligne claire*, a simple, bold style of drawing. The display is housed in Victor Horta's splendid Art Nouveau building, once a department store. Horta's juggling of steel, glass, and light has created an exciting backdrop. *Les anciens magasins Waucquez, rue des Sables 20, tel. 02/219–19–80. Tram Nos. 92, 93, 101. Admission: BF120. Open Tues.–Sun. 10–6.*

The **Musée Horta** (Horta Museum) was once the home of the Belgian master of Art Nouveau, Victor Horta. From the attic to the cellar, every detail of the house displays the exuberant curves of Art Nouveau style. Horta, who designed the house for himself, wanted to put nature back into daily life. Here his floral motifs, organic style, and refined curves of iron and stone succeed magnificently. *Rue Américain 25, tel. 02/537–16–92. Admission: BF100. Open Tues.–Sun. 2–5:30. Tram No. 92 or bus No. 60.*

Shopping

Gift Ideas
Chocolates
For "everyday" chocolate, try the Côte d'Or variety, available in any chocolate shop or larger store. For the delicious pralines—rich chocolates filled with every fruit, liqueur, or nut imaginable—try the brands made by Godiva, Neuhaus, or Leonidas. Although Godiva is better known abroad, Leonidas offers a better value for your money and is rated more highly by the Belgians. Leonidas shops are scattered throughout the city. The most exclusive pralines are handmade at the shops named Mary, Wittamer, or Nihoul.

Lace
To avoid disappointment, ask the store assistant outright whether the lace is handmade Belgian or made in the Far East. As preparation, visit the **Lace Museum** (rue de la Violette 6, near the Grand' Place). **La Maison F. Rubbrecht,** on the Grand' Place, sells authentic, handmade Belgian lace. For a large choice of old and modern lace, try **Manufacture Belge de Dentelles** (Galerie de la Reine 6–8).

Shopping Districts
For boutiques and stores, the main districts are in the **ville basse** (low town), the **Galeries St-Hubert** (luxury goods or gift items), **rue Neuve** (inexpensive clothes), and **City 2** and the **Anspach Center** (large covered shopping complexes). In City 2, **FNAC** is a cherished French institution: As well as being an outlet for books, records, cameras, and stereo equipment at the best prices in town, it is also a trendy cultural and exhibition center.

You'll find designer names and department stores (such as **Sarmalux**) in the **ville haute** (high town). **Avenue Louise** is its center, complete with covered galleries; **Galerie Louise;** and **Galerie de la Toison d'Or,** the appropriately named street of the Golden Fleece!

Markets On Saturdays (9–5) and Sundays (9–1), the Sablon square is transformed into an **antiques market.** In early December it runs a traditional **European Christmas Market** with crafts from 12 countries. The **flower market** on the Grand' Place (Tues.–Sun. 8–4) is a colorful diversion. **Midi Market** is far more exotic (by Gare du Midi train station). On Sunday morning (5 AM–1 PM) the whole area becomes a colorful *souk* (bazaar) as the city's large North African community gathers to buy and sell exotic foods and household goods. The **Vieux Marché** (Old Market) in place du Jeu de Balle is a rough flea market worth visiting for the authentic atmosphere of the working-class Marolles district. The market is open daily 7–2. To make real finds, get there as early in the morning as you can.

Dining

Apart from hearty Belgian cuisine, Brussels is proud of its foreign restaurants: Chefs from at least 50 countries work in the city, and many Asian restaurants provide a tasty and inexpensive alternative to European fare. Servings are plentiful everywhere. Most places feature a *plat du jour* (daily special) at a reasonable price. If you are interested in local gourmet restaurants, ask the tourist office on the Grand' Place for its booklet "Gourmet Restaurants" (BF50), updated annually. It includes many affordable places.

For details and price-category definitions, *see* Dining in Staying in Belgium.

Moderate **Aux Armes de Bruxelles.** This restaurant is one of the few to escape the "tourist trap" label in this hectic little street. Inside, a lively atmosphere fills three rooms. Service is fast and friendly, and portions are large. Specialties include *waterzooi de volaille* (a rich chicken stew) and *moules au vin blanc* (mussels in white wine). *Rue des Bouchers 13, tel. 02/511–21–18. Reservations advised. AE, DC, MC, V. Closed Mon. and June.*

La Manufacture. Here's the latest trendy brasserie housed in a cleverly transformed workshop, with tables of polished stone, brick walls, and friendly servers dressed in long leather aprons. It features stylish fare, such as goat cheese salad or sautéed red mullet fillets, accompanied by great crusty bread. The two-course lunch menu is a bargain. *Rue Notre-Dame du Sommeil 12, tel. 02/502–25–25. Reservations advised. AE, DC, MC, V.*

La Quincaillerie. The name means "the hardware store"—and the character has been retained, with tables perched on the balcony and a zinc oyster bar downstairs. At BF875, the three-course *menu du patron* is a bargain. Excellent game dishes are nicely presented by a staff who, like the clientele, is young and pleasant. *Rue du Page 45, tel. 02/538–25–53. Reservations advised. AE, DC, MC, V.*

Inexpensive **Adrienne.** Just around the corner from Avenue de La Toison d'Or this buffet restaurant serves cold cuts, vegetables, salads, and a separate dessert buffet. On warm days you can sit on the terrace. *Rue Capitaine Crespel 1A, tel. 02/511–93–39. Reservations advised lunch. AE, DC, MC, V.*

Chez Leon. Opened in 1905, it has expanded into a row of eight old houses. Heaping plates of mussels and other Belgian specialties, like eels in a green sauce, are served nonstop from noon to midnight all year round. *Rue des Bouchers 18, tel. 02/ 511–14–15. No reservations. No credit cards.*

★ **Falstaff.** Some things never change, and Falstaff is one of them. This huge tavern, with an interior that is pure Art Nouveau, fills up for lunch and keeps going until 5 AM, with an ever-changing crowd from students to pensioners. Cheerful waitresses punch in your orders for onion soup, filet mignon, salads, and other straightforward dishes on electronic order pads. Falstaff II at No. 25 has the same food but not the ambience. *Rue Henri Maus 19, tel. 02/511–87–89. Reservations advised. AE, DC, MC, V.*

La Grande Porte. An old warren of interconnecting rooms provides a rustic setting for hearty and often rambunctious eating. Part of the appeal lies in the copious portions. The specialties include *carbonade à la flamande* (beef and onions stewed in beer); *ballekes à la marollienne* (spicy meatballs); steaks served with rice and/or french fries; and *salade folle* (mixed green salad with cold cuts), a meal in itself. *Rue Notre-Seigneur 9, tel. 02/539–21–32. Reservations advised. DC. Closed July.*

Budget **Boccaccio.** At this super-friendly hole-in-the-wall the Moroccan owner and his Spanish wife serve up generous portions of pasta and other Italian specialties. *Rue du Marché-aux-Fromages 14, tel. 02/512–29–29. AE, DC, MC, V.*

Le Faste Fou. On a side street near Place Louise, it has counter service downstairs and table service in the sparsely furnished upstairs dining room. Generous salads predominate, with hot meals a bit more expensive. *Rue du Grand-Cerf 21, tel. 02/511–38–32. AE, DC, MC, V.*

Le Pain Quotidien. This trendy bakery, newly installed in an old building, offers crusty, old-fashioned bread, as well as sandwiches, huge salads, and generous slices of pie, which you eat at a communal refectory table. *Rue Antoine Dansaert 16, tel. 02/502–23–61. No reservations. No credit cards.*

There are a large number of snack bars, some of them serving quite good food. One of the newest, already popular, is **The Front Page** (rue Duquesnoy 47, tel. 02/512–74–10). Virtually all cafés also serve simple fare, like spaghetti or omelets.

Lodging

The *Hotel Guide*, published every year by Tourist Information Brussels (TIB), provides the most reliable and up-to-date information on prices and services. In general, finding accommodations is not difficult. There has been a boom in hotel construction lately, adding several more hotels in all price categories. Avoid the cheap hotel districts near Gare du Midi and Gare du Nord train stations. Hotels can be booked at the tourist office on the Grand' Place (tel. 02/513–89–40), and a deposit is required (deductible from the final hotel bill).

For details and price-category definitions, *see* Lodging in Staying in Belgium.

Moderate **Arenberg.** Recently renovated, this hotel enjoys a central location near the central station. The noted restaurant offers lunch for only BF450 and can cater to special dietary requirements. Weekend rates are available. *Rue d'Assaut 15, tel. 02/511–07–*

70. *156 rooms with bath. Facilities: restaurant, coffee shop, bar, secretarial service, garden. AC, DC, MC, V.*

Cadettt. This 1991 addition to the Swiss Mövenpick chain does spell its name with three *t*'s. The large, bright rooms have blond wood furniture. The atrium bar and restaurant serves copious Swiss breakfasts and a limited selection of Mövenpick specialties. *Rue Paul Spaak 15, tel. 02/645-61-11. 128 rooms with bath. Facilities: restaurant, bars, sauna, fitness room, non-smoking rooms, parking. AE, DC, MC, V.*

Club House. Situated near the avenue Louise business and shopping district, this convenient hotel is tucked away down a quiet side street. The hotel is modern, the service is friendly, and the facilities are above average for a hotel in this price bracket. It is close to a number of good bars and restaurants. Weekend rates are available. *Rue Blanche 4, tel. 02/537-92-10. 83 rooms, most with kitchenette and bath. Facilities: parking, bar, conference facilities, garden. AE, DC, MC, V.*

Inexpensive   **Arlequin.** Owned and operated by a friendly young couple, this smallish hotel can be reached through an arcade that branches off the restaurant-packed Petite rue des Bouchers, a stone's throw from the Grand' Place. *Rue de la Fourche 17-19, tel. 02/514-16-15. 60 rooms with bath or shower. Facilities: breakfast room. AE, DC, MC, V.*

Gerfaut. In this 1991 hotel, the light beige rooms are of reasonable size, and three- and four-bedded rooms are available at modest supplements. A buffet breakfast is included in the price. Public transport is available. *Chaussée de Mons 115-117, tel. 02/522-19-22. 48 rooms with bath or shower. Facilities: bar, parking. AE, DC, MC, V.*

Orion. This residential hotel opened in 1990 in the old fish market, which has become a lively restaurant district. The reception area is always staffed, but you make your own bed. Linen is changed weekly. Rooms are decorated in a cheerful, crisp red-and-white modern scheme. There are fully equipped kitchenettes in the studio rooms and two-room apartments and a quiet interior courtyard. *Quai au Bois-à-Brûler 51, tel. 02/221-14-11. 169 rooms with bath. Facilities: parking. AE, DC, MC, V.*

Budget   **Sabina.** At this well-located hotel, where the wallpaper and carpets make a bit of a gusty impression, the rooms are small but cozy. *Rue du Nord 78, tel. 02/218-26-37. 24 rooms, 20 with bath or shower.*

Sun Hotel. Just off the Chaussee d'Ixelles, the Sun, renovated in 1987, makes a smart impression, but rooms are smallish and bathrooms cramped. *Rue du Berger 38, tel. 02/511-21-19. 22 rooms with shower or bath. Facilities: Breakfast room, snacks, parking. AE, DC, MC, V.*

Truite d'Argent. The smallest hotel in Brussels, in a quiet street off the fish market, has modern, well-equipped rooms and two restaurants: a small bistro, Les Caprices de Sophie, reserved for residents at dinner, and an expensive fish restaurant round the corner. *Rue du Peuplier 5, tel. 02/219-95-46. 6 rooms. Facilities: 2 restaurants, AE, DC, MC, V.*

Two modern youth hostels feature rooms for just two people. They are the **Auberge Bruegel** (rue St. Esprit 2, tel. 02/511-04-36) and the **Auberge Jacques Brel** (rue de la Sablonniere 30, tel. 02/218-01-87).

The Arts

The traditional performing arts—ballet, opera, theater—are well represented in Brussels. There is also a wide range of English-language entertainment, including movies and, on occasion, theater. The best way to find out what's going on is to buy a copy of the English-language weekly magazine *The Bulletin*. It's published every Thursday and sold at newsstands for BF75. For a fuller picture, see the Thursday *"Arts et Divertissements"* pull-out section in *Le Soir*, the French-language newspaper. It is often available from the Brussels tourist office.

Music Major classical music concerts are generally held at the **Palais des Beaux-Arts** (rue Ravenstein 23, tel. 02/507–82–00). Alternatively, there are many free Sunday morning concerts at various churches, including the Cathédrale St-Michel and the Petite Église des Minimes (rue des Minimes 62). Major rock and pop concerts are given at Forest National (av. du Globe 36, tel. 02/347–03–55).

Theater At Brussels's 30 theaters, actors perform in French, Flemish, and occasionally in English. Puppet theater is a Belgian experience not to be missed. In Brussels, visit the intimate **Théâtre Toone VII** (impasse Schuddeveld, Petite rue des Bouchers 21, tel. 02/511–71–37). In this atmospheric medieval house, satirical plays are performed in a Bruxellois dialect.

Film Movies are mainly shown in their original language, so many are in English. **The Acropole** (Galeries de la Toison d'Or, tel. 02/511–43–28) is a complex of several theaters and features comfortable armchairs and first-run movies. For unusual movies or screen classics, visit the **Musée du Cinéma** (Cinema Museum) (rue Baron Horta 9, tel. 02/513–41–55). Five movies are shown daily, at only BF50 each.

Nightlife

Disco The **Crocodile Club** (rue Duquesnoy 5, tel. 02/511–42–15) at the Royal Windsor Hotel appeals to young adults and business travelers. **Le Garage** (rue Duquesnoy 16, tel. 02/512–66–22) draws a younger crowd.

Bars The diversity is greater here than in many other European capitals. These are just a few of the best: **La Fleur en Papier Doré** (rue des Aléxiens 53, tel. 02/511–16–59) is a quiet bar that attracts an artistic audience to drink local beer and look at the ancient walls covered with surreal paintings and old etchings.

Cirio (rue de la Bourse 18, tel. 02/512–13–95) is a pleasantly quiet bar with nice decor.
Rick's Café (av. Louise 344, tel. 02/647–75–30) is as popular with homesick Americans as it is with the British expatriate community. It serves fairly expensive American and Tex/Mex food.

Jazz Brussels lays claim to being Europe's jazz capital. Buy the monthly *Jazz Streets* magazine to find out details. Among the best venues are **Travers** (rue Traversière 11, tel. 02/218–40–86), **Preservation Hall** (rue de Londres 3 bis, tel. 02/511–03–04), and the **Bierodrome** (pl. Fernand Cocq 21, tel. 02/512–04–56), a smoky rough-and-ready club in Ixelles, a lively part of the city. Entrance prices start at BF50.

Antwerp

Arriving and Departing

By Plane   Antwerp International Airport lies just 3 kilometers (2 miles) southeast of the city. For flight information, call 03/218-12-11.

Between the Airport and Downtown   Buses bound for Antwerp's central station leave about every 20 minutes; travel time is around 15 minutes. Taxis are readily available as well.

By Train   Express trains run between Antwerp and Brussels; the trip takes 35 minutes. Antwerp Central Station is at Koningin Astridplein 27 (tel. 03/233-39-15). Four trains leave every hour from Antwerp's central stations.

Getting Around

By Streetcar   In the downtown area, the streetcar (or tram) is the best, and most common, means of transportation. Some lines have been rebuilt underground (look for signs marked "M"); the most useful line runs between the central station (métro stop Diamant) and the Groenplaats (for the cathedral). For detailed maps of the transportation system, stop at the tourist office.

Tourist Information

The tourist office is near the cathedral (Grote Markt 15, tel. 03/232-01-03). It is open Monday–Saturday 9–6, Sunday 9–5.

A booklet on walks, including the famous "Rubens Walk," is available from the tourist office. Various other popular walks are signposted throughout the city.

Exploring Antwerp

Antwerp, lying on the Scheldt River 50 kilometers (31 miles) north of Brussels, is the world's fifth-largest port and the main city of Belgium's Flemish region. For 1993, it has been designated Europe's Capital of Culture by the EC. This has entailed the restoration of public buildings, the refurbishing of museums and theaters, and the organization of a large number of exibitions, dance and theatrical performances, and many other festivities. In addition to the year-long celebrations, Antwerp's year in the European limelight will give it the legacy of a greatly improved cultural infrastructure. This bustling sophisticated city has long been used to wealth. With its tradition of Jewish merchants and an ancient diamond-cutting trade, Antwerp has not looked back since the 1860s, when it freed the port from Dutch control.

Numbers in the margin correspond to points of interest on the Antwerp map.

① Antwerp's **central station** is a good place to start exploring the city. This elegant neoclassical building, restored to its former glory, is surrounded by cafés and cinemas. To the east of the **②** station is **Antwerp Zoo,** one of the world's most reputable, which celebrates its 150th anniversary this year. The huge, well-designed zoo complex also includes a winter garden, a planetarium, a good restaurant, and two natural-history muse-

Antwerp

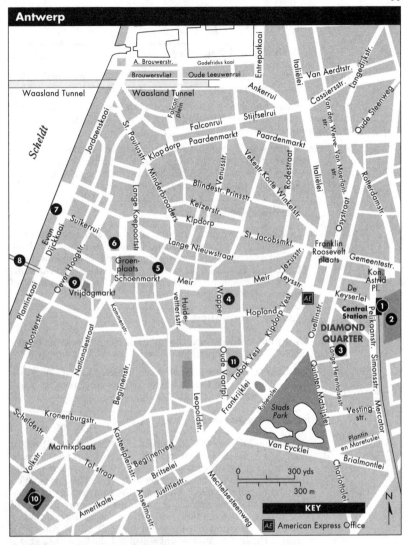

KEY

AE American Express Office

0 — 300 yds

0 — 300 m

N

Antwerp Zoo, **2**

Central Station, **1**

Diamond Museum, **3**

Koninklijk Museum voor Schone Kunsten, **10**

Nationaal Scheepvaart-museum, **7**

Onze-Lieve Vrouw, **6**

Plantin-Moretus Museum, **9**

Rubenshuis, **4**

St. Annatunnel, **8**

Torengebouw, **5**

Vogelmarkt, **11**

ums. *Koningin Astridplein 26, tel. 03/231–16–40. Admission: BF330 adults, BF205 children. Open July–Aug., daily 8:30– 6:30; Sept.–Feb., daily 9–5; Mar.–June, daily 8:30–6.*

Near the central station, along the Pelikaanstraat and the streets running off it, lies the **Diamond Quarter.** You can visit the diamond exhibition and see diamond cutters at work at the ❸ **Diamond Museum.** *Lange Herentalsestraat 31–33. Admission free. Open daily 10–5. Cutting and polishing demonstrations Sat. 2–5.*

The broad De Keyserlei leads west from the central station to the main shopping area, the **Meir.** South of the Meir, on ❹ Wapper, is **Rubenshuis** (Rubens House). The artist lived here from 1610 until his death in 1640. It's an atmospheric place, very much a patrician's home of the period, enriched with paintings by Rubens and his contemporaries. *Wapper 9. Admission: BF75. Open daily 10–5.*

❺ One of Europe's earliest skyscrapers, the 24-story **Toren-gebouw,** stands at the western end of the Meir. Pass to the left of this building, down the Schoenmarkt, and into the wide ❻ Groenplaats, with its statue of Rubens. The towering **Onze-LieveVrouw** (Cathedral of Our Lady), whose restoration has just been completed, stands at the opposite end of the square. Built in Gothic style, it has seven naves and 125 pillars and is the largest church in Belgium. It also has three masterpieces by Rubens. *Admission: BF40. Open weekdays 10–6, Sat. 10–3, Sun. 1–4.*

From the cathedral, walk the short distance north along the Suikerrui to the river. To your right is the fortresslike **Steen,** the oldest building in Antwerp. Dating from the 12th century, ❼ the Steen now houses the **Nationaal Scheepvaartmuseum** (Maritime Museum), which has many beautiful models of ships, especially of the East India clippers. *Steenplein 1, tel. 03/232–08– 50. Admission: BF75. Open daily 10–5.*

Walking along the river south of the Steen, you come to a foot ❽ tunnel, the **St. Annatunnel,** leading to the left bank of the river (the entrance is close to the Plantin-Moretus Museum, *see below*). From the riverside park, you get the best view of the city's great spires and wharves.

Return through the tunnel and walk east until you come to the ❾ **Plantin-Moretus Museum,** a famous printing works founded in the 16th century. The building is a fine example of Renaissance architecture and is magnificently furnished. Among its treasures are many first editions, engravings, and a copy of Gutenberg's Bible, the *Biblia Regia. Vrijdagmarkt 22. Admission: BF75. Open daily 10–5.*

From the Plantin, walk through the Vrijdagmarkt, where there is a **furniture and secondhand market** every Wednesday and Friday morning. Continue up the Oude Koornmarkt to the Groenplaats and catch a tram to the **Koninklijk Museum voor** ❿ **Schone Kunsten** (Royal Museum of Fine Arts). It lies in the southern part of the city and houses more than 1,500 paintings by old masters, including a magnificent array of works by Rubens, Van Dyck, Hals, and Bruegel. A major exhibition (Mar. 27–June 27, 1993) celebrates the 400th anniversary of the birth of Antwerp painter Jacob Jordaens. The second floor houses one of the best collections of the Flemish school anywhere in the world. The first floor is given over to more modern paintings. The neoclassical building also has an adequate snack bar. *Leopold de Waelplaats 1–9. Admission free. Open Tues.–Sun. 10–5.*

⑪ On Sunday morning you can see the famous **vogelmarkt**, or bird market, on the south side of the city on the Oude Vaartplaats. You'll find everything from birds and domestic pets to plants, clothes, and food.

Dining

Local specialties include herring and eel dishes and *witloof* (endives) cooked in a variety of ways. As for drink, there are 20 local beers; a city gin called *jenever;* and a strong liqueur, *Elixir d'Anvers.*

For details and price-category definitions, *see* Dining in Staying in Belgium.

Moderate **Rooden-Hoed.** Seafood is featured in this traditional cozy res-
★ taurant, reputed to be Antwerp's oldest. Specialties include eels and mussels, in season. Try the *paling in t'groen* (eel in green sauce). The restaurant recommends its dry, white wines from Alsace. *Oude Koornmarkt 25, tel. 03/233–28–44. Reservations advised. AE, MC. Closed Wed. and Thurs.*

Sawadee. Evoking a long-standing Far East connection, the menu here is well stocked with delicious Thai dishes. The restaurant operates on an upper floor of an old house, worth seeing in itself. *Britselei 16, tel. 03/233–08–59. Reservations advised. AE, DC, MC, V. Closed Tues.*

Inexpensive **In de Schaduw van de Kathedraal.** As the name states, this bud-
★ get restaurant, serving traditional food, lies "in the shadow of the cathedral." Try the seafood dishes, especially mussels in season. There is a terrace for outside dining. *Handschoenmarkt 17, tel. 03/232–40–14. Reservations accepted. AE, DC, MC, V. Closed Tues.*

Jan Zonder Vrees. Named for the legendary Jan Without Fear, this attractive restaurant is situated in a 14th-century house, formerly a brothel. Now it serves waterzooi, rabbit in beer, and other specialties. *Krabbenstraat 2, tel. 03/232–90–80. Reservations accepted. AE, V.*

Budget **City Garden.** Located in the attractive triangular Stadspark (City Park) near the Diamond Center, it's a modern tavern, where service is quick as befits a restaurant much used by tour groups. The cuisine runs to standard fare like steak, chicken, and brochette. *Rubenslei 37, tel. 03/226–08–36. AE, DC, MC, V. Closed dinner winter.*

De Molen. The name means "The Mill," which is what it once was. The restaurant is situated in a green area on the left bank of the river, near a camping site and the St. Anna beach, where Antwerpers go to sunbathe. Many of them like to repair to the rustic De Molen for a meal—mussels are a specialty—and the nice view of the city across the river. *Jachthavensweg 2, tel. 03/219–32–08. AE, DC, MC, V.*

Lodging

All hotels are modern, so expect comfort, rather than period charm. For details and price-category definitions, *see* Lodging in Staying in Belgium.

Moderate   **Alfa Theater.** This plush, centrally located hotel is part of the reliable Alfa chain. The restaurant offers an appealing blend of nouvelle-cuisine presentation and Belgian portions. Try the lobster mousse. *Arenbergstr. 30, tel. 03/232–39–70. 83 rooms with bath. Facilities: bar, restaurant, conference facilities. AE, DC, MC.*

Inexpensive   **Arcade.** This is a modern, impersonal hotel designed along the lines of a university campus. Its location, overlooking the week-end marketplace, makes it ideal for visiting the old district. *Meistr. 39 (Theaterplein), tel. 03/231–88–30. 150 rooms with shower. Facilities: bar, access for the disabled, conference facilities. MC, V.*

Waldorf. This pleasant, modern hotel is located near the diamond center. The smallish rooms are attractively decorated in gray and brown. *Belgielei 36, tel. 03/230–99–50. 100 rooms with bath. Facilities: restaurant, bar. AE, DC, MC, V.*

Budget   **Drugstore Inn.** This clean and decent hotel is on a noisy, busy square next to the Central Station. Though it was redecorated a couple of years ago, the rooms remain small. Ask for a room at the back. Women traveling alone should perhaps look elsewhere because of the raffish neighborhood. *Koningin Astridplein 43, tel. 03/231–21–21. 27 rooms with bath. AE, MC, V.*

Bruges

Arriving and Departing

Country codes

By Train   Trains run hourly at 28 and 59 minutes past the hour from Brussels (Gare du Midi) to Bruges. The London–Brussels service stops here as well. The train station is south of the canal 32 that surrounds the downtown area; for information, tel. 050/38–23–82. Travel time from Brussels is 53 minutes.

By Bus   National buses do not connect with Bruges, but individual bus tours from Brussels stop here on day excursions.

Getting Around

On Foot   By far the easiest way to explore the city is on foot because the downtown sights are fairly close together.

Guided Tours

Boat Trips   Boat trips along the city canals are run by several companies and depart from five separate landings. Boats ply the waters March–November, 10–6. There is no definite departure schedule; boats leave when enough people have gathered, but you'll never have to wait more than 15 minutes or so. The following are just two of the companies in operation: **P.C.B. Stael** (tel. 050/33–21–71) and **Coudenys** (tel. 050/33–51–03).

Orientation Tours Fifty-minute minibus trips of the city center leave every hour on the hour from the Market Square in front of the Belfry. Tours are given in seven languages (individual headphones). Cost: BF275 (children 180). For further information and a full list of companies, check with the tourist office.

Tourist Information

The **Bruges Tourist Office** (Burg 11, tel. 050/44–86–86).

Exploring Bruges

Bruges (or, more correctly, Brugge) is a perfectly preserved medieval museum, deservedly called "the Venice of the North." Bruges was ignored for centuries after the Zwin River silted up, and the port became a romantic Flemish backwater. This past misfortune is its present glory. Little has changed in this city of interlaced canals, overhung with humpbacked bridges and weeping willows. Bruges has a large student population, which is reflected in the lively bars and summer concerts in the historic squares. The **Burg**, an intimate medieval square, is the inspiring setting for summer classical concerts.

Numbers in the margin correspond to points of interest on the Bruges map.

1
2 The best place to start a walking tour is the **Markt** (Market Square). From the top of the **Belfort** (Belfry)—"Thrice destroyed and thrice rebuilt," as Longfellow tells us—there's a panoramic view of the town. The belfry has a carillon notable even in Belgium, where they are a matter of civic pride. On summer evenings, the Markt is brightly lit. *The Belfort. Admission: BF80. Open Apr.–Sept., daily 10–5:15; Oct.–Mar., daily 10–11:45 and 1:30–4:15. Carillon concerts Oct.–mid-June, Sun., Wed., and Sat. 2:15–3; mid-June–Sept., Mon., Wed., and Sat. 9–10 PM, Sun. 2:15–3.*

3 On the eastern side of the Markt stands the **Provinciaal Hof,** the neo-Gothic provincial government building. Walk east from the Markt along Breidelstraat, to the Burg, a square at the center
4 of ancient Bruges. On the left is the **Landshuis** (Provost's House), built in 1665. Across the square is a row of magnificent
5 buildings—the **Stadhuis** (town hall), dating from the 14th cen-
6 tury, its wonderfully ornate facade covered with statues; **Oude Griffie,** the former Recorder's House dating from the 1530s, and also ornamented with impressive windows; and the
7 **Heilig-Bloed Basiliek** (the Basilica of the Holy Blood), built to enshrine the vial containing Christ's blood, and a church so fascinating that it alone would warrant a visit to Bruges. Here, too, is a **Heilig-Bloed Museum** (Museum of the Holy Blood), with many treasures associated with the cult. *Stadhuis—Admission: BF40. Open daily 9:30–noon and 2–6. Heilig-Bloed Basiliek—Worship of the Blood, Fri. 8:30–11:45 and 3–4. Free guided visits daily 2–5. Museum—Admission: BF20. Open daily 9:30–noon and 2–6.*

8 Walk through a passage between the town hall and the Oude Griffie and you'll come to the **Dijver,** the city canal. Canal boat trips leave from here. *Boats leave on demand. Average trip 30 minutes. Cost: BF130.*

Bruges

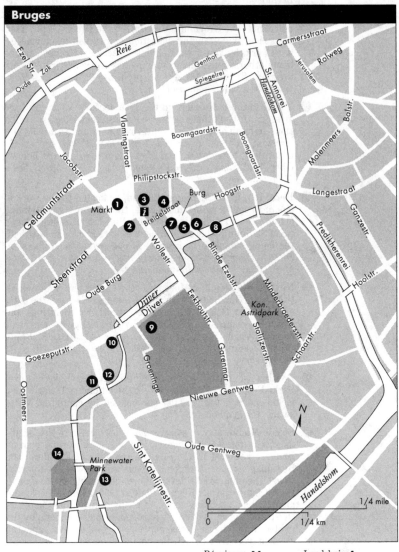

Béguinage, **14**

Belfort, **2**

Dijver, **8**

Groeninge
Museum, **9**

Gruuthuse
Museum, **10**

Heilig Bloed
Basiliek, **7**

Landshuis, **4**

Markt, **1**

Memling Museum, **11**

Minnewater, **13**

Onze-Lieve
Vrouwekerk, **12**

Oude Griffie, **6**

Provinciaal Hof, **3**

Stadhuis, **5**

❾ Walking south along the Dijver, you'll soon reach a group of museums. The **Groeninge Museum,** on the Dijver Canal, has a very rich, wide-ranging collection of Flemish masterpieces, with works by Van Eyck, Memling, Bosch, and Bruegel, among many others, plus some contemporary works. *Dijver 12. Admission: BF100. Open Apr.–Sept., daily 9:30–6; Oct.–Mar., Wed.–Mon. 9:30–noon and 2–5.*

❿ The **Gruuthuse Museum,** in the 15th century a palace of the aristocratic Gruuthuse family, contains archaeological exhibitions and a display of lace from all over Belgium. *Dijver 17. Admission: BF100; combined ticket for BF250 covers the Groeninge, Gruuthuse, and Memling museums (see below). Open Apr.–Sept., daily 9:30–noon and 2–6; Oct.–Mar., Wed.–Mon. 9:30–noon and 2–5.*

⓫ Here, too, is the **Memling Museum,** dedicated to the work of one of Bruges's most famous sons, the painter Hans Memling (1430–90), and housed in the former Sint Jans Hospital (Hospital of St. John), where the artist was nursed back to health after being wounded in France. *Mariastraat 38. Admission: BF100. Open Apr.–Sept., daily 9:30–noon and 2–6; Oct.–Mar., Thur.–Tues. 9:30–noon and 2–5.*

⓬ Next to the Memling Museum is the **Onze-Lieve Vrouwekerk** (Church of Our Lady), with, at 116 meters (375 feet), the highest tower in Belgium, a notable collection of paintings and carvings—especially a *Madonna* by Michelangelo—and some splendidly colorful tombs. *Mausoleums—Admission: BF30. Open weekdays 10–11:30 and 2:30–5, Sun. 2:30–5. No visits during services.*

⓭ Continue south to the enchanting **Minnewater** (Lake of Love) Park. From the Minnewater visit the adjoining 16th-century lockkeeper's house, usually surrounded by contented white swans, the symbol of the city.

⓮ Beside Minnewater, a picturesque bridge leads to the **Béguinage,** the former almshouses and the most serene spot in Bruges. Founded in 1245 by the countess of Flanders, the Béguinage was a home for religious women who took partial vows. The nuns lived a devout life while serving the community. Although the last Béguines left in 1930, a Benedictine community has replaced them. The Béguinage has kept its cloistered charm. Notice the harmonious pattern made by the gabled white houses, the expanse of green lawn, and the crooked trees that stretch diagonally across your view.

Dining

For details and price-category definitions, *see* Dining in Staying in Belgium.

Moderate **Oud Brugge.** Many of the city's restaurants are found in atmospheric ancient buildings, and this is one of them. Tasty local dishes are served under yet more vaulted ceilings. *Kuiperstraat 33, tel. 050/33–54–02. Reservations advised. No credit cards.*

Inexpensive **Gistelhof.** The Gistelhof serves hearty fish stews and other local dishes in historic Flemish surroundings. *West Gistelhof 23, tel. 050/33–62–90. Reservations accepted. AE, DC, MC, V.*
Straffe Hendrik. On an attractive square near the Beguinage,

this tap room is part of a family-run brewery. It serves a cold lunch buffet, Flemish beer soup, and other specialties. *Walplein, tel. 050/33-26-97. No credit cards.*

Budget **Taverne Curiosa.** A steep flight of stairs takes you down from one of the main shopping streets to this medieval cellar. A smoked seafood platter is always on the menu, and other specialties include inventive omelets. The ambience is pleasantly relaxed. *Vlamingstraat 22, tel. 050/34-23-34. V. Closed July.*

Zegeklokke. This is a modern restaurant in an old building, just around the corner from the Markt. The service is friendly, the meals light and inexpensive. *Hallestraat 4, tel. 050/33-94-46. AE, DC, MC, V.*

Lodging

In proportion to its size, Bruges has a large number of hotels; in fact, many more than Antwerp. For details and price-category definitions, *see* Lodging in Staying in Belgium.

Moderate **Duc de Bourgogne.** Set in a stunning location at the bend of a canal, the Duc has rooms that are all tastefully furnished in 17th-century style. There is also a fine restaurant—try the many fish dishes—with a remarkable view. *Huidenvetttersplein 12, tel. 050/33-20-38. 18 rooms with bath. Facilities: restaurant. AE, DC, MC, V.*

Inexpensive **Ter Brughe.** If it's atmosphere and period charm you want, you won't be disappointed by this delightful canalside hotel, a 15th-century survival, with friendly service and a cozy atmosphere. There's no restaurant. *Oost-Gisthelhof 2, tel. 050/34-03-24. 24 rooms with bath. DC, MC, V. Closed Jan.-Feb.*

Budget **De Pauw.** At this spotless, family-run hotel, the quaintly furnished rooms have names rather than numbers, and breakfast comes with six different kinds of bread. *St. Gilliskerkhof 8, tel. 050/33-71-18. 8 rooms, 6 with bath. AE, DC, MC, V.*

Jacobs. This hotel is on the same square as De Pauw, and shares many of its characteristics. It is larger, however, and the clientele a bit younger. The rooms have blond-wood furniture, and although not large are quite comfortable. *Baliestraat 1, tel. 050/33-98-31. 26 rooms, 24 with bath. Bar and breakfast room. AE, MC, V.*

4 Bulgaria

Bulgaria is a small, austere country that lies in the eastern half of the Balkan Peninsula. It is a land whose mountains, seascapes, and rustic beauty have attracted European travelers for centuries. From the end of World War II until recently, it was the closest ally of the former Soviet Union and presented a rather mysterious image to the Western world. This era ended in 1989 with the overthrow of Communist party head Todor Zhivkov. Since then, Bulgaria has gradually opened itself to the West as it struggles along the path toward democracy and a free-market economy.

Although stricken by shortages, with most of the shops still half empty, Bulgaria offers some of the lowest prices in Europe. Nearly everything costs 30%–60% less than in the other European countries. With its low standard of living and a very high free-market rate of convertible currency, Bulgaria offers much in the way of cheap dining, shopping, lodging, and public transportation. Only a few luxury hotels and hotel restaurants are priced at international levels.

Endowed with long Black Sea beaches, the rugged Balkan range in its interior, and fertile Danube plains, Bulgaria has much to offer the tourist year-round. Its tourist industry is quite well developed and is being restructured to shield visitors better from shortages of goods and services and the other legacies of rigid central planning.

The Black Sea coast along the country's eastern border is particularly attractive, with secluded coves and old fishing villages, as well as wide stretches of shallow beaches that have been developed into self-contained resorts. The interior landscape offers great scenic beauty, and the traveler who enters it will find a tranquil world of forested ridges, spectacular val-

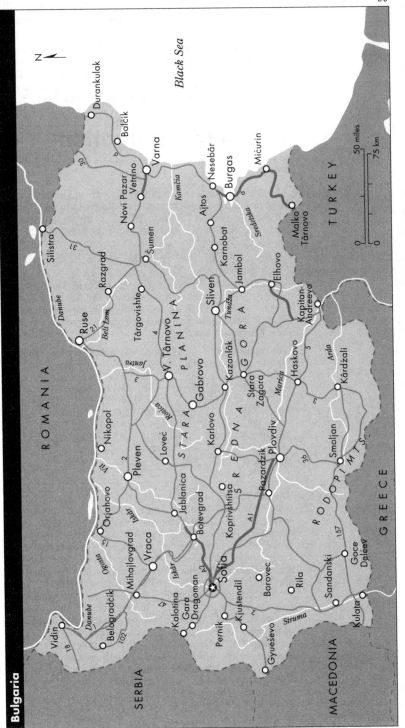

Bulgaria

leys, and rural communities where folklore is a colorful part of village life.

The capital, Sofia, is picturesquely situated in a valley near Mount Vitosha. There is much of cultural interest here, and the city has good hotels and restaurants serving international cuisine. The other major draw is Varna, the site of one of Europe's first cultural settlements and the most important port in Bulgaria.

Essential Information

Before You Go

When to Go The ski season lasts from mid-December through March, while the Black Sea coast season runs from May to October, reaching its crowded peak in July and August. Fruit trees blossom in April and May; in May and early June the blossoms are gathered in the Valley of Roses (you have to be up early to watch the harvest); the fruit is picked in September, and in October the fall colors are at their best.

Climate Summers are warm, winters are crisp and cold. The coastal areas enjoy considerable sunshine; March and April are the wettest months inland. Even when the temperature climbs, the Black Sea breezes and the cooler mountain air prevent the heat from being overpowering.

The following are the average daily maximum and minimum temperatures for Sofia.

Jan.	35F	2C	May	69F	21C	Sept.	70F	22C
	25	– 4		50	10		52	11
Feb.	39F	4C	June	76F	24C	Oct.	63F	17C
	27	– 3		56	14		46	8
Mar.	50F	10C	July	81F	27C	Nov.	48F	9C
	33	1		60	16		37	3
Apr.	60F	16C	Aug.	79F	26C	Dec.	38F	4C
	42	5		59	15		28	– 2

Currency The unit of currency in Bulgaria is the lev (plural leva), divided into 100 stotinki. There are bills of 1, 2, 5, 10, 20, 50, and 100 leva; coins of 1, 2, and 5 leva; and coins of 1, 2, 5, 10, 20, and 50 stotinki. At press time (spring 1992), as part of efforts at economic reform, hard-currency payments for goods and services are no longer permitted. The only legal tender for commercial transactions and tourist services in Bulgaria is the lev. These services include air, train, and long-distance bus travel; all accommodations, from camping to hotels; and car rentals and Balkantourist package tours. You may import any amount of foreign currency, including traveler's checks, and exchange it at branches of the Bulgarian State Bank, commercial banks, Balkantourist hotels, airports, border posts, and other exchange offices, which quote their daily selling and buying rates. The rate quoted by the Bulgarian State Bank at press time is 20 leva to the U.S. dollar, 37 leva to the pound sterling.

It is forbidden either to import or to export Bulgarian currency. Unspent leva must be exchanged at frontier posts on departure before you go through passport control. You will need to present your official exchange slips to prove that the currency was legally purchased.

The major international credit cards are accepted in the larger stores, hotels, and restaurants.

What It Will Cost   Prices in Bulgaria have been low for years, but this is changing as the government tries to revive the economy and open it up to the West. If you choose the more moderate hotels, accommodations won't be very expensive. It is possible to cut costs even more by staying in a private hotel or private room in a Bulgarian house or apartment—also arranged by Balkantourist or other tourism companies—or by camping. The favorable cash exchange rate, linked to foreign-currency fluctuations, makes such expenses as taxi and public transport fares, museum and theater admission, and meals in most restaurants seem comparatively low by international standards. A little hard currency, exchanged at this rate, goes a long way. Shopping for imported and domestic wares in the duty-free shops also helps to keep travel expenses down. The following price list, correct as of spring 1992, can therefore be used only as a rough guide.

Sample Prices   Trip on a tram, trolley, or bus, .70 lev–2 leva; theater ticket, 4 leva–15 leva; coffee in a moderate restaurant, 5 leva–8 leva; bottle of wine in a moderate restaurant, 18 leva–48 leva.

Museums   Museum admission is very inexpensive, ranging from 30 stotinki to 5 leva (less than 1¢ to 25¢).

Visas   All visitors need a valid passport. Those traveling in groups of six or more do not require visas, and many package tours are exempt from the visa requirement. Americans do not need visas when traveling as tourists. Other tourists, traveling independently, should inquire about visa requirements at a Bulgarian embassy or consulate before entering the country, since fees may be higher for visas obtained at the border.

Customs on Arrival   You may import duty-free into Bulgaria 250 grams of tobacco products, plus 1 liter of hard liquor and 2 liters of wine. Items intended for personal use during your stay are also duty-free. Travelers are advised to declare items of greater value—cameras, tape recorders, etc.—so there will be no problems with Bulgarian customs officials on departure.

Language   The official language, Bulgarian, is written in Cyrillic and is very close to Old Church Slavonic, the root of all Slavic languages. English is spoken in major hotels and restaurants, but is unlikely to be heard elsewhere. It is essential to remember that in Bulgaria, a nod of the head means "no" and a shake of the head means "yes."

Getting Around

By Train   Buy tickets in advance at a ticket office—there is one in each of the major centers—and avoid long lines at the station. Trains are very busy; seat reservations are obligatory on expresses. All medium- and long-distance trains have first- and second-class carriages and limited buffet services; overnight trains between Sofia and Black Sea resorts have first- and second-class sleeping cars and second-class couchettes. From Sofia there are six main routes—to Varna and to Burgas on the Black Sea coast, to Plovdiv and on to the Turkish border, to Dragoman and the Yugoslav border, to Kulata and the Greek border, and to Ruse on the Romanian border. The main line is powered by electricity. Plans to electrify the rest are under way.

By Plane **Balkanair** (Balkan Bulgarian Airlines) has regular services to Varna and Burgas; during the summer season it also serves Ruse on the Romanian border and Targovishte (near Veliko Târnovo in the Balkan Mountains). Book through Balkantourist offices, though this can take time, and overbooking is not unusual. Group travel and air-taxi services are available through the privately run Hemus Air, Air Via, and Jes Air. Business flights to other destinations in the country are also arranged by Hemus Air.

By Bus The routes of the crowded buses are mainly planned to link towns and districts not connected by rail. Within the cities a regular system of trams and trolley buses operates for a single fare of .70 lev–2 leva. Ticket booths, at most tram stops, sell single or season tickets; you can also pay the driver. The tourist information offices have full details of routes and times.

By Boat Modern luxury vessels cruise the Danube from Passau in Austria to Ruse. Hydrofoils link main communities along the Bulgarian stretches of the Danube and the Black Sea, and there are coastal excursions from some Black Sea resorts. A ferry from Vidin to Calafat links Bulgaria with Romania.

Staying in Bulgaria

Telephones Calls can be made from hotels or from public telephones in the post office in each major town or resort. Elsewhere, there is a new system of international telephones—modern, direct-dial phones with no coin slots—that operate only with special cards paid for in leva. Directions for buying the cards are given, often in English, on the phones.

Mail Letters and postcards to the United States cost 1 lev, 75 stotinki to the United Kingdom.

Opening and Closing Times **Banks.** The Foreign Trade Bank is open weekdays 8–3.

Museums. Museums are usually open 8–6:30 but are often closed on Monday or Tuesday.

Shops. Shops are open Monday–Saturday 9–1 and 3–7.

National Holidays January 1 (New Year's); March 3 (Independence Day); April 11 (Easter Sunday); May 1 (Labor Day); May 24 (Bulgarian Culture Day); December 24, 25, 26 (Christmas).

Dining There is a choice of hotel restaurants with their international menus, Balkantourist restaurants, or the inexpensive restaurants and cafeterias run privately and by cooperatives. The best bets are the small folk-style restaurants that serve national dishes and local specialties. The word *picnic* in a restaurant name means that the tables are outdoors. Standards have improved, but food is still rarely served piping hot, and visitors should be prepared for loud background music.

Specialties Balkan cooking revolves around lamb and pork, goat and sheep cheese, potatoes, peppers, eggplant, tomatoes, onions, carrots, and spices. Fresh fruit, vegetables, and salads are particularly good in season, and so are the soups. Bulgaria invented yogurt (*kiselo mleko*), with its promise of good health and longevity, and there are excellent cold yogurt soups during the summer. Rich cream cakes and syrupy *baklava* are served to round out a meal.

Bulgarian wines are good, usually full-bodied, dry, and inexpensive. The national drink is *rakia*—a plum or grape brandy called *slivova* or *grosdova*—but vodka is popular, too. Coffee is strong and is often drunk along with a cold beverage, such as cola or a lemon drink. Tea is taken with lemon instead of milk.

Dress In Sofia, formal dress (jacket and tie) is customary only at expensive restaurants. Casual dress is appropriate elsewhere.

Ratings Prices are per person and include a first course, main course, dessert, and tip, but no alcohol. Best bets are indicated by a star ★.

Category	All Areas
Moderate	30 leva–60 leva
Inexpensive	15 leva–30 leva
Budget	under 15 leva

Credit Cards Increasingly, even restaurants in the Moderate category are accepting credit cards, although the list of cards accepted may not always be correctly posted. Before you place an order, check to see whether you can pay with your card.

Lodging There is a wide choice of accommodations, ranging from hotels—most of them dating from the '60s and '70s—to apartment rentals, rooms in private homes, hostels, and campsites. Although hotels are improving, they still tend to suffer from temperamental wiring and erratic plumbing, and it is a good idea to pack a universal drain plug, as plugs are often missing in hotel bathrooms. In moderate and inexpensive hotels, bathrooms often look unusual. Don't be surprised if strangely placed plumbing turns the entire bathroom into a shower. Due to frequent power cuts, especially in the winter, flashlights and other battery-powered utilities are strongly recommended.

Hotels Until recently, most hotels used by Western visitors were owned by Balkantourist and Interhotels. At press time (summer 1992), many of the government-owned or -operated hotels listed below were on the verge of privatization. The conversion is expected to take up to five years. Hotels may be closed for renovation for extended periods or may be permanently shut down. Visitors are strongly urged to call hotels ahead to get the latest information. Some hotels were always privately run or run by municipal authorities or organizations catering to specific groups (Sipka for motorists, Orbita for young people, Pirin for hikers). Most have restaurants and bars; the large, modern ones have swimming pools, shops, and other facilities. Some coastal resorts have complexes where different categories of hotels are grouped, each with its own facilities.

Rented Accommodations Rented accommodations are a growth industry, with planned, modern complexes as well as picturesque cottages. Cooking facilities tend to be meager, and meal vouchers are included in the deal. An English-speaking manager is generally on hand.

Private Accommodations Staying in private homes, arranged by Balkantourist, is becoming a popular alternative as a means not only of cutting costs but of offering increased contact with Bulgarians. There are one-, two- and three-star private accommodations. Some offer a bed or bed and breakfast only; some provide full board. Three-star rooms are equipped with kitchenettes. Booking offices are located in most main tourist areas. In Sofia, contact Balkantourist at 27 Stambolijski Boulevard (tel. 2/88–52–56), or go to the private accommodations office at 37 Dondukov Boulevard.

Hostels   Hostels are basic, but clean and cheap. Contact **Orbita** (45a Stambolijski Boulevard, Sofia, tel. 2/87–95–52 or 2/80–15–03).

Campsites   There are more than 100 campsites, many near the Black Sea coast. They are graded one, two, or three stars, and the best of them offer hot and cold water, grocery stores, and restaurants. Balkantourist provides a location map.

Ratings   The following hotel categories are for two people in a double room with half-board (breakfast and a main meal). Best bets are indicated by a star ★. You must show your exchange slips to prove that your money was legally changed.

Category	Sofia	Other Areas
Moderate	1,000–2,000 leva	800–1,500 leva
Inexpensive	200–1,000 leva	200–800 leva
Budget	under 200 leva	under 200 leva

Tipping   To tip, round out your restaurant bill 5%–8%.

Sofia

Arriving and Departing

By Plane   All international flights arrive at Sofia airport. For information on international flights, tel. 2/79–80–35; domestic flights, tel. 2/72–24–14.

Between the Airport and Downtown   Bus No. 84 (nonstop) serves the airport. Fares for taxis taken from the airport taxi stand run about 40 leva–100 leva for the 10-kilometer (6-mile) ride into Sofia. Avoid the taxi touts; they tend to overcharge or to insist on payment in hard currency.

By Train   The central station is at the northern edge of the city. For information, tel. 2/3–11–11 or 2/59–71–87. The ticket offices in Sofia are in the underpass of the National Palace of Culture (1 Bulgaria Sq., tel. 2/59–71–87) or at the Rila International Travel Agency (5 Gurko St., tel. 2/87–07–77). There is a taxi stand at the station.

Getting Around

By Bus   Buses, trolleys, and trams run fairly often. Buy a ticket from the ticket stand near the streetcar stop and punch it into the machine as you board. (Watch how the person in front of you does it.) For information, tel. 2/3–12–41.

On Foot   The main sites are centrally located, so the best way to see the city is on foot.

Important Addresses and Numbers

Since late 1990, a national commission has been working to re-name cities, streets, and monuments throughout the country. Names given in the following sections were correct as of summer 1992 but are subject to change.

Tourist Information — Balkantourist Head Office (tel. 2/4–33–31) is at 1 Vitosha Boulevard; the tourist and accommodations office (tel. 2/88–44–30) is at 37 Dondukov Boulevard. It also has offices or desks in all the main hotels.

Embassies — U.S. (1 Stambolijski Blvd., tel. 2/88–48–01). U.K. (65 Levski Blvd., tel. 2/88–53–61).

Emergencies — Police: Sofia City Constabulary (tel. 166), ambulance (tel. 150), fire (tel. 160), doctor: Clinic for Foreign Citizens (Mladost 1, 1 Eugeni Pavlovski St., tel. 2/7–53–61), "Pirogov" Emergency Hospital (tel. 2/5–15–31).

Exploring Sofia

Sofia is set on the high Sofia Plain, ringed by mountain ranges: the Balkan range to the north; Lyulin Mountains to the west; part of the Sredna Gora Mountains to the southeast; and, to the southwest, Mount Vitosha, the city's playground, which rises to 2,325 meters (7,500 feet). The area has been inhabited for about 7,000 years, but the visitor's first impression is of a modern city with broad streets, light traffic, spacious parks, and open-air cafés. As recently as the 1870s it was part of the Ottoman Empire, and one mosque still remains. Most of the city, however, was planned after 1880. There are enough intriguing museums and high-quality musical performances to merit a lengthy stay, but if time is short, you need only two days to see the main sights and another day, at least, for Mount Vitosha.

Numbers in the margin correspond to points of interest on the Sofia map.

1 **Ploshtad Sveta Nedelya** (St. Nedelya Square) is a good starting point for an exploration of the main sights. The south side of the **2** square is dominated by the 19th-century **Tzarkva Sveta Nedelya** (St. Nedelya Church). Go behind it to find Vitosha Boulevard, a lively pedestrian street with plenty of stores, cafés, and dairy bars.

The first building along this boulevard, on the west side of the **3** street, is the former Courts of Justice, now the **Natzionalen Istoricheski Musei** (National History Museum). Its vast collections, vividly illustrating the arts history of Bulgaria, include priceless Thracian treasures, Roman mosaics, enameled jewelry from the First Bulgarian Kingdom, and glowing religious art that survived the years of Ottoman oppression. The courts are due to return to this location as soon as a new home is found for the National History Museum collection. *Vitosha Blvd., tel. 2/88–41–60. Open Tues.–Thurs. and weekends 10:30–6:30; Fri. 2–6:30.*

Return to the southeast side of St. Nedelya Square, and in the courtyard of the Sheraton Sofia Balkan Hotel you will see the **4** **Rotonda Sveti Georgi** (rotunda of St. George). Built in the 4th century as a Roman temple, it has served as a mosque and

Sofia

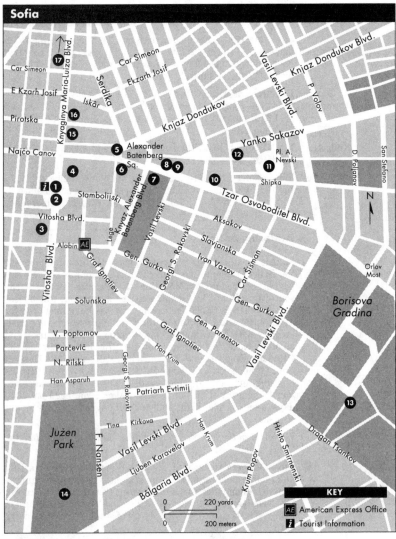

Banya Bashi
Djamiya, **16**

Borisova Gradina, **13**

Hram-pametnik
Alexander Nevski, **11**

Mavsolei Georgi
Dimitrov, **7**

Nacionalen Dvoretz na
Kulturata **14**

Natzionalen
Archeologicheski
Musei, **6**

Natzionalen
Etnografski Musei, **8**

Natzionalen
Istoricheski Musei, **3**

Natzionalna
Hudozhestvena
Galeria, **9**

Partiyniyat Dom, **5**

Ploshtad Sveta
Nedelya, **1**

Rotonda Sveti
Georgi, **4**

Tsentralen
Universalen
Magazin, **15**

Tsentralni Hali, **17**

Tzarkva Sveta
Nedelya, **2**

Tzarkva Sveta
Sofia, **12**

Tzarkva Sveti
Nikolai, **10**

church, and recent restoration has revealed medieval frescoes. It is not open to the public. Head east to the vast and traffic-free Alexander Batenberg Square, which is dominated by the ⑤ **Partiyniyat Dom** (the former headquarters of the Bulgarian Communist party).

Facing the square, but entered via Alexander Stambolijski Boulevard, is the former Great Mosque, which now houses the ⑥ **Natzionalen Archeologicheski Musei** (National Archaeological Museum). The 15th-century building itself is as fascinating as its contents, which illustrate the culture of the different peoples who inhabited Bulgaria up to the 19th century. *Tel. 2/88–24–05. Open Tues.–Sun. 10–noon and 2–6.*

⑦ On the next block to the east is the former **Mavsolei Georgi Dimitrov** (Georgi Dimitrov Mausoleum), which until 1990 contained the embalmed body of the first general secretary of the Bulgarian Communist party, who died in Moscow in 1949 and was known as the "Father of the Nation." His remains have been moved to the Central Cemetery, and there is talk of converting the mausoleum into a museum.

Across from the mausoleum is the former palace of the Bulgari-⑧ an Czar, which currently houses the **Natzionalen Etnografski Musei** (National Ethnographical Museum), with displays of costumes, handicrafts, and tools that illustrate the agricultural way of life of the country people until the 19th century. *Alexander Batenberg Sq., tel. 2/88–51–15. Open Wed.–Sun. 10–noon and 1:30–5:30.*

⑨ In the west wing of the same building is the **Natzionalna Hudozhestvena Galeria** (National Art Gallery). It houses a collection of the best works of Bulgarian artists, as well as a foreign art section that contains some graphics of famous artists. *6A Yanko Sakazov St., tel. 2/88–35–59. Open Wed.–Mon. 10:30–7.*

⑩ Nearby stands the ornate Russian **Tzarkva Sveti Nikolai** (Church of St. Nicholas), erected 1912–14.

From here you'll enter Tzar Osvoboditel Boulevard, with its monument to the Russians, topped by the equestrian statue of Russian Czar Alexander II. It stands in front of the National Assembly. Behind the National Assembly, just beyond Shipka Street, you'll be confronted by the neo-Byzantine structure with glittering onion domes whose image you may recognize from almost every piece of tourist literature and which really ⑪ does dominate the city. This is the **Hram-pametnik Alexander Nevski** (Alexander Nevski Memorial Church), built by the Bulgarian people at the beginning of this century as a mark of gratitude to their Russian liberators. Inside are alabaster and onyx, Italian marble and Venetian mosaics, magnificent frescoes, and space for a congregation of 5,000. Attend a service to hear the superb choir, and, above all, don't miss the fine collection of icons in the **Crypt Museum**. *Admission: 30 stotinki. Open Wed.–Mon. 10:30–6:30.*

Cross the square to the west to pay your respects to the much ⑫ older **Tzarkva Sveta Sofia** (Church of St. Sofia), which dates to the 6th century, though remains of even older churches have been found during excavations. Its age and simplicity are in stark contrast to its more glamorous neighbor.

Return to Tzar Osvoboditel Boulevard and continue east to the
⑬ **Borisova Gradina** (Boris's Garden), with its lake and fountains,
woods and lawns, huge sports stadium, and open-air theater.
From the park take Dragan Tsankov west (back toward St.
Nedelya Square) briefly, before going left on Patriarh Evtimij,
toward Južen Park. The formal gardens and extensive woodlands here are to be extended as far as Mount Vitosha.

At the entrance to the park stands a large modern building, the
⑭ **Natzionalen Dvoretz na Kulturata** (National Palace of Culture),
with its complex of halls for conventions and cultural activities.
Its underpass, on several levels, is equipped with a tourist information office, shops, restaurants, discos, and a bowling alley. *1 Bulgaria Sq., tel. 2/5-15-01. Admission: 30 stotinki.
Open 10:30-6:30. Closed Tues.*

Back at St. Nedelya Square, follow Knyaginya Maria-Luiza
Boulevard to the train station. The large building on the right
⑮ is the recently refurbished **Tsentralen Universalen Magazin**
(Central Department Store). *2 Knyaginya Maria-Luiza Blvd.
Open Mon.-Sat. 8-8.*

Just beyond is a distinctive building, a legacy of Turkish domi-
⑯ nation, the **Banya Bashi Djamiya** (Banja Basi Mosque); it is
closed to visitors. Nearby you will see the Public Mineral
⑰ Baths. Across the boulevard is the busy **Tsentralni Hali** (Central Market Hall), which is closed for renovations until the end
of 1992.

Off the Beaten Track

The little medieval church of **Boyana,** about 10 kilometers (6
miles) south of the city center, is well worth a visit. The church
itself is closed for restoration, but a replica, complete with copies of the exquisite 13th-century frescoes, is open to visitors.

The **Dragalevci Monastery** stands in beechwoods above the
nearby village of Dragalevci. The complex is currently a convent, but you can visit the 14th-century church with its outdoor
frescoes. Shepherds can often be seen tending their flocks in
the surrounding woods. From here take the chair lift to the delightful resort complex of **Aleko,** and another nearby chair lift
to the top of Malak Rezen. There are well-marked walking and
ski trails in the area. Both Boyana and Dragalevci can be
reached by taking the No. 64 bus.

Shopping

Gifts and Souvenirs There are good selections of arts and crafts at the shop of the
Union of Bulgarian Artists (6 Tzar Osvoboditel Blvd.) and at the
Bulgarian Folk Art Shop (14 Vitosha Blvd.). You will find a
range of souvenirs at **Sredec** (7 Lege St.), **Souvenir Store** (7
Stambolijski Blvd.), and **Prizma Store** (2 Tzar Osvoboditel
Blvd.). If you are interested in furs or leather, try **4 Slavjanska
St., 7 Car Kalojan St.,** or **2 Tzar Osvoboditel Blvd.** For recordings
of Bulgarian music, go to **Maestro Atanassov** (8 Tzar Osvobo-
ditel Blvd.).

Shopping Districts The latest shopping center is in the subway of the modern **National Palace of Culture,** where stores sell fashions, leather
goods, and all forms of handicrafts. The pedestrians-only area
along **Vitosha Boulevard** features many new, small shops.

Department Stores Sophia's biggest department store is the newly renovated **Central Department Store** at 2 Knyaginya Maria-Luiza Boulevard.

Dining

Eating in Sofia can be enjoyable and even entertaining if the restaurant has a nightclub or folklore program. Be prepared to be patient and make an evening of it, as service can be slow at times. Or try a *mehana*, or tavern, where the atmosphere is informal and service sometimes a bit quicker. For details and price-category definitions, *see* Dining in Staying in Bulgaria.

Moderate   **Boyansko Hanche.** Local and national specialties are the main features in this restaurant and folklore center, 10 kilometers (6 miles) from downtown (take bus No. 63). *Near Bojanske church, tel. 2/56–30–16. No credit cards.*

★ **Coop-35 Vitosha.** Continental cuisine is served in a friendly, homey atmosphere that makes it a good choice for both business dinners and more intimate dining. *Dragalevci District, 1 Narcis St., tel. 2/67–11–84. No credit cards.*

Corea. This place is known for its Far Eastern ambience and Korean specialties. *24 Assen Zlatarov St., tel. 2/44–34–36. No credit cards.*

Ropotamo. With its central location and reasonable prices, Ropotamo is a good bet for visitors on a budget. *63 Trakia Blvd., tel. 2/72–22–10. AE, DC, MC, V.*

Rozhen. Conveniently located near the National Palace of Culture, this cozy, two-tier restaurant features traditional Bulgarian cuisine. *74 Vitosha Blvd., tel. 2/52–11–31. AE, DC, MC, V.*

Rubin. This eating complex in the center of Sofia has a snack bar and an elegant restaurant that serves Bulgarian and international food. A full meal can sometimes push the cost into the Expensive bracket. *4 St. Nedelya Sq., tel. 2/87–20–86. No credit cards.*

Vodeničarski Mehani. The English translation is "Miller's Tavern," which is appropriate, since it's made up of three old mills linked together. It is at the foot of Mount Vitosha and features a folklore show and a menu of Bulgarian specialties. Nightclub open till 4 AM. *Dragalevci District (bus No. 64), tel. 2/67–10–21. No credit cards.*

Inexpensive   **Bulgarska Gostba.** The name means "Bulgarian meal." Home-
★ made traditional dishes are served in a rustic-looking interior. *34 Vitosha Blvd., tel. 2/87–91–62. No credit cards.*

Zherzavna. Candlelight, stone walls, and wood tables set the scene for Zherzavna's country cuisine. *26 Levski Blvd., tel. 2/87–91–62. No credit cards.*

Zlatnite Mostove. This restaurant on Mount Vitosha has live music in the evenings. *Vitosha District, 19 km (12 mi) from the city center, no phone. No credit cards.*

Budget   **Sofiisko Pivo.** This large restaurant 15 kilometers (10 miles)
★ from the center of town serves Bulgarian food and a wide selection of beer. *Vladaya District, tel. 2/57–82–18. No credit cards.*

Stadion. Known as a dissidents' hangout, frequented by the current president, Stadion has a central location and reasonable prices that make it a convenient place for a rest after a sight-seeing tour. *41 Graf Ignatiev St., tel. 2/87–77–94. No credit cards.*

Also recommended are the cheap and friendly club-restaurants, which since 1991 have been open to nonmembers: **Klub na Jurnalistite** (Club of the Journalists, 4 Graf Ignatiev St., tel. 2/87–30–83); **Klub na pisatelite** (Writers Club, 5 Angel Kanchev St., tel. 2/88–00–31); **Klub na Hudojnicite** (Artists Club, 6 Shipka St., tel. 2/43–431); **Klub na Filmovite Deici** (Filmmakers Club, 37 Exarkh Yosif St., tel. 2/80–22–25).

Lodging

The following hotels maintain a high standard of cleanliness and are open year-round unless otherwise stated. If you arrive in Sofia without reservations, go to Interhotels Central Office (4 Sveta Sofia St.), Balkantourist (37 Dondukov Blvd.), Bureau of Tourist Information and Reservations (35 Eksarh Josif St.), the National Palace of Culture (1 Bulgaria Sq.), or the central rail station. For details and price-category definitions, *see* Lodging in Staying in Bulgaria.

Moderate **Bulgaria.** Despite its central location, this small hotel is quiet and a bit old-fashioned. *4 Tzar Osvoboditel Blvd., tel. 2/87–19–77. 72 rooms, some with bath or shower. Facilities: restaurant, coffee shop, bar. AE, DC, MC, V.*

★ **Deva-Spartak.** This small new hotel is located behind the National Palace of Culture. It offers excellent sports facilities. *Vlado Georgiev St., tel. 2/66–12–61. Facilities: restaurant, indoor and outdoor swimming pools, Spartak sports complex, shop. AE, DC, MC, V.*

Evropa Palas Hotel. A convenient center-of-downtown location makes it a low-cost alternative to the Sheraton. *6 Kaloyan St., tel. 2/88–18–61. 86 rooms with shower. Facilities: restaurant, folk tavern, art gallery. AE, DC, MC, V.*

Hemus. This is a smaller place near the Vitosha Hotel. Guests can take advantage of the facilities of its larger neighbor while saving money for the casino or nightclub. *31 Cherni Vrah Blvd., tel. 2/6–39–51. 240 rooms, most with bath or shower. Facilities: restaurant, folk tavern, nightclub, shops. AE, DC, MC, V.*

Pliska-Cosmos. Part of the Balkan Airlines hotel chain, the Pliska-Cosmos, located at the entrance to Sofia, has been recently renovated. *87 Trakia Blvd., tel. 2/71–281. 200 rooms with shower. Facilities: restaurant, bar, shops. AE, DC, MC, V.*

Inexpensive **Serdika.** The centrally located Serdika has an old Berlin-style restaurant that serves German specialties. *2 Yanko Sakazov Blvd., tel. 2/44–34–11. 140 rooms, most with bath or shower. Facilities: restaurant. No credit cards.*

Budget **Prostor.** The airy winter-garden is a particularly pleasant pub-
★ lic room. Nestled high atop Mt. Vitosha, 20 kilometers (12 miles) from the city, Prostor provides excellent views of Sofia. Take bus no. 65 or 66 to the Dragalevci District. *Tel. 2/67–11–73. 107 rooms with bath. Facilities: restaurant, bar, nightclub, pool, fitness center, shop. AE, DC, MC, V.*

Sindbad. This centrally located hotel is well known for its good restaurants, which specialize in Bulgarian grilled meats and clay-pot cookery. *34 Totleben Blvd., tel. 2/54–29–95. 52 rooms with bath. Facilities: 2 restaurants, café, nightclub. No credit cards.*

Sredec. This hotel attached to a water-sports center is located

18 kilometers (11 miles) from the center of Sofia, at Pancherevo Lake. To get there, take bus no. 1, 2, or 3 to the Pancherevo district. *Samokovsko Chausse, tel. 98/2–34–23. 30 rooms with bath. Facilities: restaurant, coffee shop. No credit cards.*

The Arts

The standard of music in Bulgaria is high, whether it takes the form of opera, symphonic, or folk music, which has just broken into the international scene with its close harmonies and colorful stage displays. Contact Balkantourist or the **Concert Office** (2 Tzar Osvoboditel Blvd., tel. 2/87–15–88) for general information.

You don't need to understand Bulgarian to enjoy a performance at the **Central Puppet Theater** (14 Gourko St., tel. 2/88–54–16) or at the **National Folk Ensemble** (check with the tourist office for details).

There are a number of fine art galleries: The art gallery of the **Sts. Cyril and Methodius International Foundation** has a collection of Indian, African, Japanese, and Western European paintings and sculptures (Alexander Nevski Sq., tel. 2/88–21–81; open Wed.–Mon. 10:30–6). The art gallery of the **Union of Bulgarian Artists** has exhibitions of contemporary Bulgarian art (6 Shipka St., tel. 2/44–61–15; open daily 9–8).

The **Odeon, Serdika,** and **Vitosha cinemas** show recent foreign films in their original languages with Bulgarian subtitles.

Nightlife

Nightclubs The following hotel bars have floor shows and a lively atmosphere: **Bar Sofia** (Grand Hotel Sofia, 1 Narodno Sobranie Sq., tel. 2/87–88–21); **Bar Variety Ambassador** (Vitosha Hotel, 100 James Boucher Blvd., tel. 2/6–24–51); **Bar Variety** (Park Hotel Moskva, 25 Nezabravka St., tel. 2/7–12–61); **Bar Fantasy** (Sheraton Sofia Hotel Balkan, 1 St. Nedelya Sq., tel. 2/87–65–41).

Discos There is a disco, nightclub, and bowling alley at the **National Palace of Culture** (1 Bulgaria Sq.). Other choices are **Orbylux** (76 James Boucher Blvd., tel. 2/66–89–97), known as the classiest disco in town; **Angel** (centrally located at Narodno Sobranie Sq.); **Sky Club** (63 Hristo Botev Blvd., tel. 2/54–81–40), a big, two-tier disco; and **La Strada** (2-A Dimitar Polyanov St., tel. 2/46–75–70), which is most popular among teenagers .

Gamblers can try their luck at the casino in the **Vitosha Hotel** (100 James Boucher Blvd., tel. 2/62–41–51) or at the **Sheraton Sofia Hotel** (1 St. Nedelya Sq., tel. 2/82–65–43).

The Black Sea Golden Coast

Bulgaria's most popular resort area attracts visitors from all over Europe. Its sunny, sandy beaches are backed by the easternmost slopes of the Balkan range and by the Strandja Mountains. Although the tourist centers tend to be huge state-built complexes with a somewhat lean feel, they have modern amenities. Sunny Beach, the largest of the resorts, with more than 100 hotels, has plenty of children's amusements and play areas; baby-sitters are also available.

The historic port of Varna is a good center for exploration. It is a focal point of land and sea transportation and has museums, a variety of restaurants, and some nightlife. The fishing villages of Nesebâr and Sozopol are more attractive. Lodgings tend to be scarce in these villages, so private accommodations, arranged on the spot or by Balkantourist, are a good option. Whatever resort you choose, all offer facilities for water sports and some have instructors. Tennis and horseback riding are also available.

Getting Around

Buses make frequent runs up and down the coast and are inexpensive. Buy your ticket in advance from the kiosks near the bus stops. **Cars** and **bicycles** can be rented; bikes are particularly useful for getting around such spreading resorts as Sunny Beach. A **hydrofoil** service links Varna, Nesebâr, Burgas, and Sozopol. A regular **boat** service travels the Varna–Sveti Konstantin (St. Konstantin)–Golden Sands–Albena–Balčik route.

Tourist Information

There is a Balkantourist office in most towns and resorts.

Albena (tel. 57/21–52 or 57/23–12).
Burgas (1 Gani-Ganev St., tel. 56/4–29–32).
Nesebâr (18 Yana Luskova St., tel. 55/41–38–17).
Sunny Beach (tel. 55/41–23–46 or 554/23–12 or 23–15).
Sveti Konstantin and Golden Sands (tel. 52/6–56–27).
Varna (main office, 3 Moussala St., tel. 52/22–55–24; private accommodations office, 3 Kniaz Boris I Blvd.).

Exploring the Black Sea Golden Coast

Varna **Varna,** Bulgaria's third-largest city, is easily reached by rail (about 7½ hours by express) or road from Sofia. There is plenty to see in the port city of Varna. The ancient city, named Odessos by the Greeks, became a major Roman trading center and is now an important shipbuilding and industrial city. The main sights can be linked by a planned walk.

Begin with the **Museum of History and Art,** one of the great—if lesser known—museums of Europe. The splendid collection includes the world's oldest gold treasures from the Varna necropolis of the 4th millennium BC, as well as Thracian, Greek, and Roman treasures and richly painted icons. *41 Osmi Primorski Polk Blvd., tel. 52/23–70–57. Open Tues.–Sun. 10–5.*

Near the northeastern end of Osmi Primorski Polk Boulevard are numerous shops and cafés; the western end leads to Mitropolit Simeon Square and the monumental **Cathedral** (1880–86), whose lavish murals are worth a look. Running north from the cathedral is Vladislav Varnenchik Street, with shops, movie theaters, and eateries. Opposite the cathedral, in the City Gardens, is the **Old Clock Tower,** built in 1880 by the Varna Guild Association. On the south side of the City Gardens,

The Black Sea Golden Coast

N

Durankulak

Dobrich

Balčik

Shabla

Albena

Kavarna

Novi Pazar

Vetrino

A2

Zlatni Pjasâci
(Golden Sands)

Sveti Konstantin

Varna

Goljama

Staro Orjahovo

Kamčija

Bjala

Kamčija

Obzor

Black Sea

Orizare

Slânčev Brjag
(Sunny Beach)

Ajtos

Nesebâr

Pomorie

Burgas

Sozopol

Sredecka

Djuni

Primorsko

Mičurin

Ahtopol

TURKEY

0 — 40 miles
0 — 60 km

on Nezavisimost Square, stands the magnificent Baroque
Stoyan Bucharov National Theater.

Leave the square to the east and walk past the Moussala Hotel.
The tourist information office is at 3 Moussala Street (tel. 52/
22–55–24). Nearby, on the corner of Kniaz Boris I Boulevard
and Shipka Street, are the remains of the **Roman fortress wall**
of Odessos. Kniaz Boris I Boulevard is another of Varna's shopping streets. At No. 44 you can buy handcrafted souvenirs from
one of the outlets of the Union of Bulgarian Artists.

Walk south along Odessos Street to Han Krum Street. Here
you'll find the Holy Virgin Church of 1602 and the substantial
remains of the **Roman Thermae**—the public baths, dating from
the 2nd to the 3rd century AD. Buy the excellent English guidebook here to get the most out of your visit.

Not far from the baths, moving west, is old Drăzki Street, recently restored and comfortably lined with restaurants, taverns, and coffeehouses.

Head toward the sea and November 8 Street. The old prison
building at No. 5 houses the **Archaeological Museum** (open
Tues.–Sun. 10–5). Continue to Primorski Boulevard and follow
it, with the sea on your right, to No. 2 for the **Naval Museum**
(tel. 52/24–06; open daily 8–6:30), with its displays of the early
days of navigation on the Black Sea and the Danube. The museum is at the edge of the extensive and luxuriant **Marine Gardens,** which command a wide view over the bay. In the gardens
there are restaurants, an open-air theater, and the fascinating

Copernicus Astronomy Complex (tel. 2/82–94; open weekdays 8–noon and 2–5) near the main entrance.

Sveti Konstantin Eight kilometers (5 miles) north along the coast from Varna is **Sveti Konstantin,** Bulgaria's oldest Black Sea resort. Small and intimate, it spreads through a wooded park near a series of sandy coves. Today a luxury resort offers hydrotherapy on the spot where warm mineral springs were discovered in 1947.

In contrast to the sedate atmosphere of **Sveti Konstantin** is lively **Zlatni Pjasâci** (Golden Sands), a mere 8 kilometers (5 miles) to the north, with its extensive leisure amenities, mineral-spring medical centers, and sports and entertainment facilities. Just over 4 kilometers (2 miles) inland from Golden Sands is **Aladja Rock Monastery,** one of Bulgaria's oldest, cut out of the cliff face and made accessible to visitors by sturdy iron stairways.

From Sveti Konstantin, if time permits, take a trip 16 kilometers (10 miles) north to **Balčik.** Part of Romania until just before World War II, it is now a relaxed haven for Bulgaria's writers, artists, and scientists. On its white cliffs are crescent-shaped tiers populated with houses, and by the Balčik Palace, the beautiful **Botanical Gardens** are dotted with curious buildings, including a small Byzantine-style church.

Albena, the newest Black Sea resort, is located between Balčik and Golden Sands. It is well known for its long, wide beach and clean sea. The most luxurious among its 35 hotels is the **Dobrudja,** with extensive hydrotherapy facilities.

Slânčev Brjag Another popular resort, this time 36 kilometers (22 miles) south of Varna, is **Slânčev Brjag** (Sunny Beach). It is enormous and especially suited to families because of its safe beaches, gentle tides, and facilities for children. During the summer there are kindergartens for young vacationers, children's concerts, and even a children's discotheque. Sunny Beach has a variety of beachside restaurants, kiosks, and playgrounds.

Nesebâr is 5 kilometers (3 miles) south of Sunny Beach and accessible by regular excursion buses. It would be hard to find a town that exudes a greater sense of age than this ancient settlement, founded by the Greeks 25 centuries ago on a rocky peninsula reached by a narrow causeway. Among its vine-covered houses are richly decorated medieval churches. Don't miss the frescoes and the dozens of small, private, cozy pubs that opened recently all over Nesebâr.

Continue traveling south along the coast. The next town of any size is **Burgas,** Bulgaria's second main port on the Black Sea. Burgas is rather industrial, with several oil refineries, though it does have a pleasant **Maritime Park** with an extensive beach below.

For a more appealing stopover, continue for another 32 kilometers (20 miles) south to **Sozopol,** a fishing port with narrow cobbled streets leading down to the harbor. This was Apollonia, the oldest of the Greek colonies in Bulgaria. It is now a popular haunt for Bulgarian and, increasingly, foreign writers and artists who find private accommodations in the rustic Black Sea–style houses, so picturesque with their rough stone foundations and unpainted wood slats on the upper stories. It is also famous for the Apollonia Arts Festival, held each September.

Ten kilometers (6 miles) farther south is the vast, modern resort village of **Djuni,** where visitors can stay in up-to-date cottages, in the modern Monastery Compound, or in the Seaside Settlement. The wide range of amenities—cafés, folk restaurants, a sports center, shopping center, yacht club, and marina—make it another attractive vacation spot for families.

Dining and Lodging

For details and price-category definitions, *see* Dining and Lodging in Staying in Bulgaria. Gradually, even restaurants in the moderate category are beginning to accept credit cards. Check with a restaurant before ordering.

Albena
Dining

Bambuka (Bamboo Tree). This open-air restaurant serves international and Bulgarian cuisine and seafood. *Albena Resort, tel. 5772/24–04. No credit cards. Moderate.*

Gergana. This cozy beachside restaurant serves grilled seafood from the Black Sea and Bulgarian dishes such as white sheep's cheese cooked in a clay pot with eggs, vegetables, and spices. *Albena Resort, tel. 5772/29–10. No credit cards. Budget.*

★ **Orehite.** Enjoy Bulgarian specialties and seafood while you watch Orehite's famous fire-dancing show. *Albena Resort, tel. 5772/22–50. No credit cards. Budget.*

Lodging

Dobrudja Hotel. This is a big, comfortable hotel with a mineral-water health spa. *Albena Resort, tel. 5722/20–20. 272 rooms with bath. Facilities: restaurants, nightclub, coffee shops, bars, shops, indoor and outdoor swimming pools, fitness center, hydrotherapy. AE, DC, MC, V. Moderate.*

Kardam. This hotel near the center of the resort offers basic, no-frills accommodations. *Albena Resort, tel. 5772/29–27. 115 rooms with bath. Facilities: bar. AE, DC, MC, V. Budget.*

Mura. One of the largest hotels in Albena, Mura is an exceptional budget establishment in that it accepts credit cards. It is located in the center, near many sports facilities and discos. *Albena Resort, tel. 5772/22–36. 173 rooms with bath. Facilities: restaurant, bar, shop. AE, DC, MC, V. Budget.*

Burgas
Dining

Starata Gemia. The name of this restaurant translates as "old boat," appropriate for a beachfront restaurant featuring fish specialties. *39 Pârvi Maj St., tel. 56/4–57–08. No credit cards. Moderate.*

Lodging

Bulgaria. The Bulgaria is a high-rise Interhotel in the center of town. It features its own nightclub with floor show and a restaurant set in a winter garden. *21 Pârvi Maj St., tel. 56/4–28–20. 200 rooms, most with bath or shower. AE, DC, MC, V. Moderate.*

Slânčev Brjag
Dining

Hanska Šatra. Situated in the coastal hills behind the sea, this combination restaurant and nightclub has been built to resemble the tents of the Bulgarian khans of old. It has entertainment well into the night. *4.8 km (3 mi) west of Slânčev Brjag Resort, tel. 554/28–11. No credit cards. Moderate.*

Ribarska Hiza. This lively beachside restaurant specializes in fish and has music until 1 AM. *Northern end of Slânčev Brjag Resort, tel. 554/24–37. No credit cards. Inexpensive.*

Viatarna Melnica. National dishes such as *kavarma* (spicy minced pork or beef and vegetables in a sauce of fried onions, thyme, mint, and red pepper, all baked in a clay pot) are served at this restaurant 2 kilometers (1.3 miles) from the center of the resort. *Slânčev Brjag Resort, tel. 554/28–12. No credit cards. Budget.*

Yujni Noshti. Relax on the beach in wicker furniture at this restaurant whose name means "Southern Nights." International dishes and Bulgarian meals make up the bill of fare. *Slânčev Brjag Resort, tel. 554/28–51. No credit cards. Budget.*

Lodging **Burgas.** Large and comfortable, this hotel lies at the southern end of the resort. *Slânčev Brjag Resort, tel. 554/23–58. 250 rooms with bath or shower. Facilities: restaurant, 2 pools, sports hall, coffee shop, bar. AE, DC, MC, V. Moderate.*

★ **Globus.** Considered by many to be the best in the resort, this hotel combines a central location with modern facilities. *Slânčev Brjag Resort, tel. 554/22–45. 100 rooms with bath or shower. Facilities: indoor pool, restaurant, sports hall, coffee shop, bar. AE, DC, MC, V. Moderate.*

Kuban. Near the center of the resort, this large establishment is just a short stroll from the beach. *Slânčev Brjag Resort, tel. 554/23–09. 216 rooms, most with bath or shower. Facilities: restaurants, coffee shops. AE, DC, MC, V. Moderate.*

Čajka. This hotel offers the best location at a low cost. *Slânčev Brjag Resort, tel. 554/23–08. 36 rooms, some with bath or shower. No credit cards. Inexpensive.*

Shipka. A superb location in the heart of Slânčev Brjag makes this large high-rise hotel a standout. *Slânčev Brjag Resort, tel. 554/28–48. 143 room with bath. Facilities: bar, shop. AE, DC, MC, V. Budget.*

Trakia. A 20-minute walk from the beach, this somewhat characterless low-rise hotel outside the center can be reached by an electric train that stops nearby. The ride takes five minutes. *Slânčev Brjag Resort, tel. 554/27–47. 182 rooms with bath. Facilities: restaurant, bar, shop. AE, DC, MC, V. Budget.*

Sveti Konstantin **Bulgarska Svatba.** This folk-style restaurant with dancing is on
Dining the outskirts of the resort; charcoal-grilled meats are especial-
★ ly recommended. *Sveti Konstantin Resort, tel. 52/86–12–83. No credit cards. Moderate.*

Manastirska Izba. Centrally located, this eatery is a modest but pleasant restaurant with a sunny terrace. *Sveti Konstantin Resort, tel. 56/6–11–77. No credit cards. Moderate.*

Lodging **Čajka.** Čajka means "sea gull" in Bulgarian, and this hotel has a bird's-eye view of the entire resort from its perch above the northern end of the beach. *Sveti Konstantin Resort, tel. 52/86–13–32. 130 rooms, most with bath or shower. No restaurant. No credit cards. Moderate.*

Sandrovo. Once the residence of foreign guests of the government, this hotel in the 1960s-era Euxinograd Palace complex is sheathed in walnut paneling, decorated with wood reliefs, and furnished with traditional Bulgarian carved-wood furniture. *Sveti Konstantin Resort, tel. 52/86–12–41. 75 rooms, most with bath. Facilities: restaurant, café, bar. AE, DC, MC, V. Moderate.*

Narcis. Located in a park near the sea, this spa hotel offering balneotherapy is open year-round. Other treatments available include bioenergy therapy, phytotherapy, mineral-mud applications, and underwater massage. *Sveti Konstantin Resort, tel. 52/86–12–25. 60 rooms with bath. Facilities: indoor mineral-water pool, whirlpool, massage room. No credit cards. Budget.*

Varna
Dining

Morsko Kazino. This spacious restaurant offers Bulgarian and international cuisine, including seafood. *In Marine Garden, tel. 52/22–21–49. No credit cards. Moderate.*

Okean. Fish and seafood specialties are served in this restaurant in the center of the city. *4 San Stefano St., tel. 52/24–162. No credit cards. Moderate.*

Starata Kušta. This restaurant's name means "the old house." Part of a new catering complex, along with several bars and restaurants, it provides national specialties in a pseudo old-time atmosphere. *14 Drăzki St., tel. 52/23–90–65. No credit cards. Moderate.*

Lodging
★

Odessa. Expect just the basics at this four-story hotel next to the Marine Garden. *4 Primorski Blvd., tel. 52/22–83–81. 93 rooms with bath. Facilities: restaurant, bar, shops. AE, DC, MC, V. Inexpensive.*

5 Czechoslovakia

Czechoslovakia is a traveler's dream. It has layer upon layer of historical beauty, enlivened with cultural treasures and a rapidly changing social scene, all at prices that make the most budget-conscious tourist feel wealthy. Following the dramatic but peaceful revolution of November 1989, which overthrew the Communist regime that had been in power for 40 years, Czechoslovakia is once again taking up its historical place in the center of Europe. Being at the crossroads of East and West has never been particularly advantageous from a political point of view. The country has always been prey to invaders and occupiers—from the Tartars during the 13th century and the Habsburgs until 1918 to the Soviets since the end of World War II. This history has bred a parallel saga of heroic Czechs and Slovaks fighting for freedom—St. Vaclav; Jan Hus; Tomáš Masaryk; Alexander Dubček; and now, playwright-president Vaclav Havel.

In the throes of empire and international intrigue, culture has thrived in the Czechoslovak capital, Prague. The city developed its characteristic architectural magic in the flowering of Bohemian Gothic, during the era of Charles IV, king of Bohemia and Holy Roman Emperor, in the 14th century. Later, as the seat of the Habsburg emperor Rudolf II, Prague became famous as a haven for scientists, dominated by the genius of Johannes Kepler and Tycho Brahe.

Even in more recent times the relaxation from political pressures has led to a cultural flowering. The 1968 Prague Spring, when it seemed that the Communists were committed to a more humane socialism, led to a spate of experimental films (under such directors as Miloš Forman and Vera Chytilová) and innovative literature (Milan Kundera, Bohumil Hrabal, and others). Under Havel's presidency, Czechoslovak artists and writers

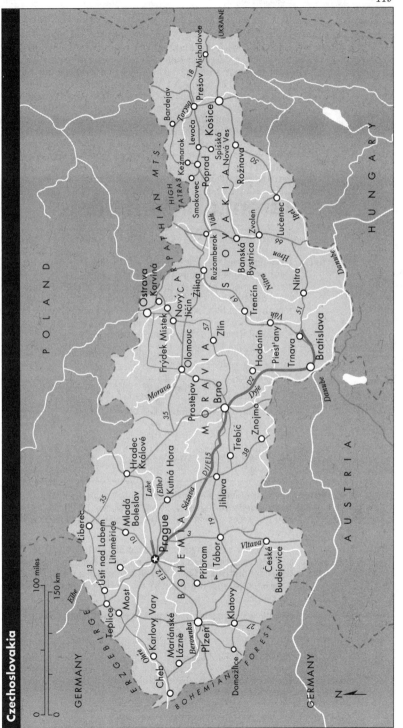

Czechoslovakia

have assumed a newly important role of cultural renewal in a land that had been decimated by despair.

Ironically, with no threatening foreign powers outside their borders, the Czechs and Slovaks were busy, at press time, dismantling their common state for lack of any compelling reason to keep the two peoples united politically. However, the changes are not expected to cause any special inconvenience to travlers. For the tourist, Czechoslovakia still bears the scars of 40 years of Communism—but, unlike much of the West, towns have remained much as they were, and streets are safe and have a refreshing lack of commercial hype. Tourist amenities certainly lack polish, and service can be frustratingly bad. The beauty of the cities and countryside and the heritage of history, art, and architecture compensate for these discomforts.

Essential Information

Before You Go

When to Go Organized sightseeing tours run from April or May through October. Some monuments, especially castles, either close entirely or open for shorter hours during the winter. Hotel rates drop during the off-season except during festivals. May, the month of fruit blossoms, is the time of the Prague Spring Music Festival. During the fall, when the forests are glorious, Bratislava and Brno hold their music festivals.

Climate The following are the average daily maximum and minimum temperatures for Prague.

Jan.	49F	10C	May	82F	28C	Sept.	84F	29C
	7	-13		36	2		38	4
Feb.	53F	11C	June	88F	31C	Oct.	71F	22C
	10	-12		44	7		29	-2
Mar.	64F	18C	July	91F	33C	Nov.	57F	14C
	18	-8		49	9		24	-5
Apr.	73F	23C	Aug.	89F	32C	Dec.	50F	10C
	29	-2		47	8		14	-10

Currency The unit of currency is the crown, or koruna, written as Kčs, and divided into 100 haléř. There are bills of 10, 20, 50, 100, 500, and 1,000 Kčs and coins of 5, 10, 20, and 50 haléř and 1, 2, and 5 Kčs.

The koruna was made convertible at the beginning of 1991, which means that a single unified rate of exchange was established for all transactions. At press time (spring 1992), the Koruna was trading at around 27 Kčs to the dollar and 52 Kčs to the pound.

Credit cards are widely accepted in establishments used by foreign tourists.

What It Will Cost Costs are highest in Prague and only slightly less in the High Tatra resorts and main spas, though even in these places you can now find very reasonable accommodations in private rooms. The least expensive areas are southern Bohemia and central and eastern Slovakia.

Sample Prices	Cup of coffee, 10 Kčs; beer (½ liter), 10½ Kčs–15 Kčs; Coca-Cola, 10 Kčs–15 Kčs; ham sandwich, 15 Kčs; 1-mile taxi ride, 100 Kčs.
Museums	Admission to museums, galleries, and castles ranges from 5 Kčs to 50 Kčs.
Visas	U.S. and British citizens do not need visas to enter Czechoslovakia. Visa requirements have been temporarily reintroduced for Canadian citizens; check whether this is still the case with the consulate. Apply to the Consulate of the Czech and Slovak Federal Republic, 50 Rideau Terrace, Ottowa, Ontario K1M 2A1, tel. 613/749–4442.
Customs on Arrival	Valuable items should be entered on your customs declaration. You can bring in 250 cigarettes (or their equivalent in tobacco), 2 liters of wine, 1 liter of spirits, ½ liter of eau de cologne, and gifts to the value of 1,000 Kčs.
On Departure	You can take out gifts and souvenirs to the value of 1,000 Kčs, as well as goods bought at Tuzex hard-currency shops (keep the receipts). Crystal and some other items not bought at hard-currency shops may be subject to a tax of 100% of their retail price. Only antiques bought at Tuzex or specially appointed shops may be exported.
Language	English is spoken fairly widely among both the young and those associated with the tourist industry. You will come across English speakers elsewhere, though not frequently. German is widely understood throughout the country.

Getting Around

By Train	There is an extensive rail network throughout the country. As elsewhere in Eastern Europe, fares are low and trains are always crowded. Also, you have to pay a supplement on all express trains (this does not apply if you bought your ticket outside Czechoslovakia). Most long-distance trains have dining cars; overnight trains between main centers have sleeping cars.
By Plane	Czechoslovakia has a remarkably good internal air service linking Prague with eight other towns, including Brno, Bratislava, Poprad (for the High Tatras), Karlovy Vary, and Piešťany. Prices are very low.
	Make reservations at Čedok offices or directly at **ČSA**, Czechoslovak Airlines (tel. 02/2146).
By Bus	A wide-ranging bus network provides quicker service than trains at somewhat higher prices (though they are still very low by Western standards). Buses are always full, and, on long-distance routes especially, reservations are advisable.

Staying in Czechoslovakia

Telephones *Local Calls*	These cost 1 Kčs from a pay phone. Lift the receiver, place the coin in the holder, dial, and insert the coin when your party picks up.
International Calls	You'll pay through the nose if you make calls from your hotel. There's automatic dialing to many countries, including North America and the United Kingdom. Special international pay booths in central Prague will take 5 Kčs coins and 100 Kčs telephone cards (available at newsstands), but your best bet is to go

to the main post office (Jindřišská 24, near Wenceslas Square). For international inquiries, dial 0132 for the United States, Canada, or the United Kingdom.

Mail
Postal Rates

Airmail letters to the United States cost 7 Kčs up to 10 grams, postcards 5 Kčs. Airmail letters to the United Kingdom cost 4 Kčs up to 20 grams, postcards 3 Kčs.

Receiving Mail

Mail can be sent to Poste Restante at the main post office in Prague (Jindřišská 24) or to any other main post office. There's no charge. The American Express office on Wenceslas Square in Prague will hold letters addressed to cardholders or holders of American Express traveler's checks for up to one month free of charge.

Opening and Closing Times

Banks and Museums. Banks are open weekdays 8–2. Museums are usually open Tues.–Sun. 10–5.

Shops. Shops are generally open weekdays 9–6 (9–8 on Thurs.); some close between noon and 2. Many are also open Sat. 9–noon (department stores, 9–4).

National Holidays

January 1; April 12 (Easter Monday); May 9 (Liberation Day); July 5; October 28 (Independence Day); December 25, 26.

Dining

If you prepay your hotel, try to avoid being stuck with Čedok meal vouchers. With few Čedok-run hotels left, these are only a frustration. For meals not limited by vouchers, you can choose among restaurants, wine cellars *(vinárna)*, the more down-to-earth beer taverns *(pivnice)*, cafeterias, and a growing number of coffee shops and snack bars. Eating out is popular, and in summer you should reserve in advance. Most restaurants are remarkably reasonable, but privatization is beginning to push up prices in a few places. Check on the menu outside to avoid being caught in a tourist trap.

Prague ham makes a favorite first course, as does soup, which is less expensive. The most typical main dish is roast pork (or duck or goose) with sauerkraut and dumplings. Dumplings in various forms, generally with a rich gravy, accompany many dishes. Fresh green vegetables are rare, but there are plenty of the pickled variety.

Mealtimes

Lunch is usually from 11:30 to 2 or 3; dinner from 6 to 9:30 or 10. Some places are open all day, and you might find it easier to find a table in off-hours.

Dress

In Prague, a jacket and tie are recommended for Very Expensive and Expensive restaurants, as well as for some of the stylish establishments in the Moderate category. Informal dress is appropriate elsewhere.

Ratings

Prices are reasonable by American standards, even in the more expensive restaurants. Czechs don't normally go in for three-course meals, and the following prices apply only if you're having a first course, main course, and dessert (excluding wine and tip). Best bets are indicated by a star ★.

Category	Prague	Other Areas
Moderate	200 Kčs–350 Kčs	100 Kčs–250 Kčs
Inexpensive	140 Kčs–200 Kčs	70 Kčs–100 Kčs
Budget	under 140 Kčs	under 70 Kčs

Lodging There's a choice of hotels, motels, private accommodations, and campsites. Many older properties are gradually being renovated, and the best have great character and style. There is still an acute shortage of hotel rooms during the peak season, so make reservations well in advance. Many private room agencies are now in operation, and as long as you arrive before 9 PM, you should be able to get a room. The standards of facilities and services hardly match those in the West, so don't be surprised by faulty plumbing or indifferent reception clerks.

Hotels These are officially graded with from one to five stars. Many hotels used by foreign visitors—Interhotels—belong to Čedok and are mainly in the three- to five-star categories. These will have all or some rooms with bath or shower. Čedok can also handle reservations for some non-Čedok hotels, such as those run by Balnea (the spa treatment organization); CKM (the Youth Travel Bureau); and municipal organizations, some of which are excellent.

Hotel bills can be paid in crowns, though some hotels still try to insist on hard currency.

Private Accommodations The best private accommodation service is AVE in the main train station. They keep a list of over 2,000 rooms; the average cost is $25–$40 for a double. The office is open daily from 6 AM to 10:30 PM. Čedok also offers private room services.

Camping Campsites are run by a number of organizations. A free map and list are available from Čedok.

Ratings Prices are for double rooms, generally not including breakfast. Prices at the lower end of the scale apply to low season. At certain periods, such as Easter or during festivals, there may be an increase of 15%–25%. Best bets are indicated by a star ★.

Category	Prague	Other Areas
Moderate	1500 Kčs–3000 Kčs	450 Kčs–1500 Kčs
Inexpensive	1000 Kčs–1500 Kčs	350 Kčs–450 Kčs
Budget	under 1000 Kčs	under 350 Kčs

Tipping Czechs and Slovaks are not usually blatant about the fact that tips are expected. Small sums of hard currency, though not officially encouraged, will certainly be most welcome. Otherwise, in Moderate or Inexpensive restaurants, add a few Kčs; in more expensive ones, add 10%. For taxis, add 10 Kčs. In the better hotels, doormen should get 5 Kčs for each bag they carry to the check-in desk; bellhops get up to 10 Kčs for taking them up to your rooms. In Moderate or Inexpensive hotels, you'll have to lug them yourself.

Prague

Arriving and Departing

By Plane All international flights arrive at Prague's Ruzyně Airport, about 20 kilometers (12 miles) from downtown. For arrival and departure times, tel. 02/367814 or 02/367760.

Between the
Airport and
Downtown
Czechoslovak Air Lines (ČSA) provides bus services linking the airport with Town Terminal Vltava (Revoluční 25) and major hotels. Buses depart every 20 minutes during the day, every half hour evenings and on weekends. The trip into Prague costs 6 Kčs and takes about 30 minutes. A special shuttle service serves main hotels and costs 50 Kčs; buy the ticket before boarding. The cheapest way to get into Prague is by regular bus No. 119; the cost is 4 Kčs, but you'll need to change to the subway at the Dejvická station for the last leg of the trip. By taxi, expect to pay 300 Kčs–400 Kčs.

By Train
The main station for international and domestic routes is Hlavni nádraží (tel. 02/229252), ul. Vítězného unora, not far from Wenceslas Square. Some international trains arrive at Holešovice, on the same metro line (C) as the main station.

By Bus
The main bus station is Florenc (at Na Florenci, tel. 02/221445), not far from the train station.

Getting Around

Public transportation is a bargain. Jizdenky (tickets) cost 4 Kčs and can be bought at hotels, newsstands, and from dispensing machines in the metro stations. For the metro, punch the ticket in the station before boarding; for buses and trams, punch the ticket inside the vehicle. You can also buy one-day passes allowing unlimited use of the system for 25 Kčs, two-day for 40 Kčs, three-day for 50 Kčs, and five-day for 70 Kčs. The passes can be purchased at the main metro stations and at newsstands.

By Subway
Prague's three modern subway lines are easy to use and spotlessly clean. They provide the simplest and fastest means of transportation, and most new maps of Prague mark the routes.

By Tram/Bus
You need to buy a new ticket every time you change vehicles. Express buses (marked with green badges) serve the suburbs and cost 4 Kčs.

Important Addresses and Numbers

Tourist
Information
The main Čedok office (Na přikopě 18, tel. 02/2127111) is close to Wenceslas Square. Next door is the **Prague Information Service** (Na příkopě 20, tel. 02/544444). One of the best sources of information is the **American Hospitality Center,** just off Old Town Square (Malé náměstí 14, tel. 02/2367486 or 02/267770).

Embassies
U.S. (Tržiště 15, Malá Strana, tel. 02/536641). **Canadian** (Mickiewiczova 6, Hradčany, tel. 02/3120251). **U.K.** (Thunovská 14, Malá Strana, tel. 02/533347).

Emergencies
Police (tel. 158 or 2121); **Ambulance** (tel. 155); **Doctor: Fakultní poliklinika** (Karlovo náměstí 32, tel. 02/299381) or **Diplomatic Health Center for Foreigners** (Na homolce 724, Prague 5, weekdays tel. 02/5292–2146, evenings and weekends tel. 02/5292–1111).

Exploring Prague

Prague is one of the most enchanting cities in Europe. Like Rome, far to the southwest, Prague is built on seven hills, sprawling within the confines of a broad loop of the Vltava River. The riverside location, enhanced by a series of graceful bridges, makes a great setting for two of the city's most notable features: its extravagant, fairy-tale architecture and its memorable music. Mozart claimed that no one understood him better than the citizens of Prague, and he was only one of several great masters who lived or lingered here.

It was under Charles IV (Karel IV) during the 14th century that Prague briefly became the seat of the Holy Roman Empire—virtually the capital of Western Europe—and acquired its distinctive Gothic imprint. At times you'll need to look quite hard for this medieval inheritance; it's still here, though, under the overlays of graceful Renaissance and exuberant Baroque.

Prague escaped serious wartime damage, but it didn't escape neglect. Because of the long-term restoration program now under way, some part of the city is always under scaffolding. But what's completed—which is nearly all that's described in the following itineraries—is hard to find fault with as an example of sensitive and painstaking restoration.

Numbers in the margin correspond to points of interest on the Prague map.

The Nové Město and Staré Město

① **②** **③** **Václavské náměstí** (Wenceslas Square) is the Times Square of Prague. Confusingly, it's not actually a square at all but a broad boulevard sloping down from the **Národní muzeum** (National Museum) and the equestrian **statue of St. Wenceslas.** The lower end is where all the action is. Na příkopě, once part of the moat surrounding the Old Town, is now an elegant pedestrian mall. Čedok's main office and Prague Information Service **④** are along here, on your way to the **Prašná brána** (Powder Tower), a 19th-century neo-Gothic replacement of the medieval original.

⑤ Turn into Celetná and you're on the old **Royal Route,** once followed by coronation processions past the foreboding Gothic **⑥** spires of the Týn Church through **Staroměstské náměstí** (Old **⑦** Town Square), down **Karlova,** across **Karlův most** (Charles Bridge), and up to the castle. Along this route, you can study every variety or combination of Romanesque, Gothic, Renaissance, and Baroque architecture. Two good examples are the town buildings at 12 Celetná and 8 Karlova. On Staroměstské náměstí, the crowds regularly gather below the famous **Clock Tower,** where, on the hour, the complex 16th-century mechanism activates a procession that includes the Twelve Apostles. Note the skeleton figure of Death that tolls the bell.

⑧ In the **Old Jewish Cemetery** in **Josefov** (Joseph's Town, the old Jewish quarter), ancient tombstones lean and jostle each other; below them, in a dozen layers, are 12,000 graves. As you stand by the tomb of the scholar Rabbi Low, who died in 1609, you may see, stuffed into the cracks, scraps of paper bearing prayers and requests. It's said that many Jews hid their valuables here before being transported to the concentration camps. Be sure to visit the tiny Gothic **Staronová synagóga** (Old-New Synagogue), which, along with the cemetery, forms part of the **⑨** **State Jewish Museum** (Státní Židovské muzeum). *Červená 101. Admission: 20 Kčs. Open Sun.–Fri. 9–4:30 (9–5 in summer); closed Sat. and religious holidays.*

When you stand on Charles Bridge, you'll see views of Prague that would still be familiar to the 14th-century architect Peter Parler and to the sculptors who added the 30 Baroque statues in the early 18th century (a few have been replaced). They're

Prague

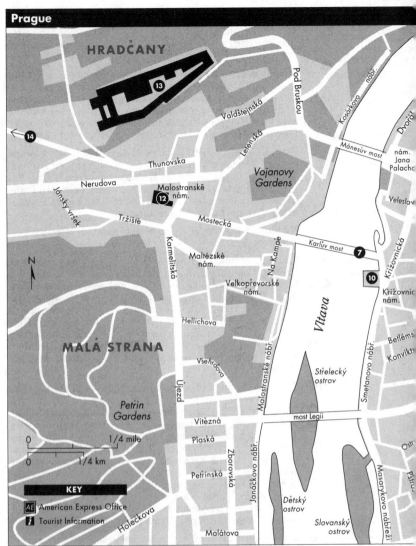

Betlémska kaple, **11**
Chram svatého
Mikuláše, **12**
Karlův most, **7**
Loreto, **14**
Národní muzeum, **2**
Old Jewish
Cemetery, **8**
Prague Castle, **13**
Prašná brána, **4**
Royal Route, **5**
Smetana Museum, **10**
Staroměstské
náměstí, **6**
State Jewish
Museum, **9**
Statue of
St.Wenceslas, **3**
Václavské náměstí, **1**

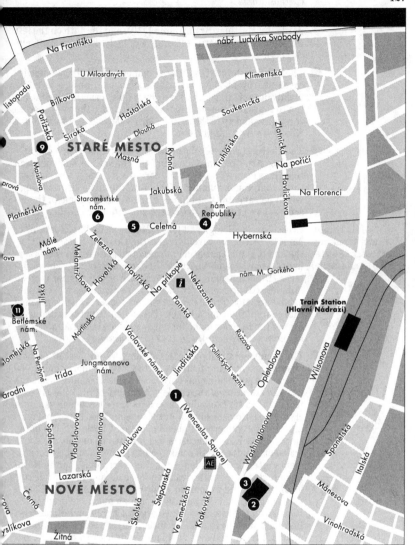

worth a closer look, especially the 12th on the left (St. Luitgarde, by Matthias Braun, circa 1710), and the 14th on the left (in which a Turk guards suffering saints, by F. M. Brokoff, circa 1714).

⑩ The **museum** devoted to Prague composer **Bedřich Smetana,** located nearby at Novotného lávka, is small, and its exhibits mainly documentary. But it's a lovely quiet oasis in which to listen to tapes of Smetana's music—and admire the views across the Vltava and up to the castle. *Novotného lávka. Admission: 7 Kčs. Open Wed.–Mon. 10–5.*

⑪ The **Betlémska kaple** (Bethlehem Chapel) has been completely reconstructed since Jan Hus thundered his humanitarian teachings from its pulpit in the early 15th century to congregations that could number 3,000. But the little door through which he came to the pulpit is original, as are some of the inscriptions on the wall. *Betlémské náměstí. Open daily 9–6.*

Malá Strana Cross Charles Bridge and follow Mostecká up to Malostranské
and Hradčany náměstí. After the turbulence of the Counter-Reformation at
(Lesser Quarter the end of the 16th century, Prague witnessed a great flower-
and Castle) ing of what became known as Bohemian Baroque. The archi-
⑫ tects (Dientzenhofer, father and son) of the **Chram svatého Mikuláše** (Church of St. Nicholas) were among its most skilled exponents. If you're in Prague when a concert is being given in this church, fight for a ticket. The lavish sculptures and frescoes of the interior make for a memorable setting. *Malostranské náměstí. Open daily 10–4 (9–6 in summer).*

⑬ The monumental complex of **Hradčany** (Prague Castle) has witnessed the changing fortunes of the city for more than 1,000 years. The scaffolding has only recently been removed from the latest restoration of the castle's **Cathedral of St. Vitus.** It took from 1344 to 1929 to build, so you can trace the whole gamut of styles from Romanesque to Art Nouveau. This is the final resting place for numerous Bohemian kings. Charles IV lies in the crypt. Good King Wenceslas has his own chapel in the south transept, studded with semiprecious stones. Knightly tournaments often accompanied coronation ceremonies in the **Royal Palace,** next to the cathedral, hence the broad Riders' Staircase leading up to the grandiose **Vladislav Hall** of the Third Courtyard. Oldest of all the buildings, though much restored, is the Romanesque complex of **St. George's Church and Monastery.** Behind a Baroque facade, it houses a superb collection of Bohemian art from medieval religious sculptures to decadent Baroque paintings. *Hradčanské náměstí. Admission to each museum building in the castle: 10 Kčs. All are open Tues.–Sun. 10–5.*

⑭ The Baroque church and shrine of **Loreto** is named for the Italian town to which the Virgin Mary's House in Nazareth was supposedly transported by angels to save it from the infidel. The crowning glory of its fabulous treasury is the glittering monstrance of the *Sun of Prague,* set with 6,222 diamonds. Arrive on the hour to hear the 27-bell carillon. *Loreta 12. Admission: 10 Kčs. Open Tues.–Sun. 9–noon and 1–4:30.*

Shopping

Tuzex Stores Ask Čedok for the latest list of these hard-currency-only outlets and their specialties. One of the main ones, at Železná 18, sells imported goods, glass, and porcelain. The branch at Štěpánská 23 specializes in fashion and leather goods.

Specialty Shops Look for the name **Dilo** for objets d'art and prints; **ULUV** or **UVA** for folk art. At Na příkopě 12 you'll find excellent costume jewelry. **Moser** (Na příkopě 12) is the most famous for glass and porcelain.

Shopping Districts Many of the main shops are in and around Wenceslas Square (Václavské náměstí) and Na příkopě, as well as along Celetná and Pařížská.

Department Stores Three central stores are **Bilá Labut'** (Na poříčí 23), **Družba** (Václavské nám. 21), and **Kotva** (nám. Republiky 8).

Dining

Eating out in Prague is a very popular pastime, so it's advisable to make reservations whenever possible, especially for dinner. For details and price-category definitions, *see* Dining in Staying in Czechoslovakia.

Moderate **Dům Slovenské Kultury.** You'll get good, hearty fare served in a relaxed, no-frills atmosphere at this "House of Slovak Culture," located behind Národní Třída in the New Town. The homemade sausage, accompanied by hearty Slovak wine, is excellent. The large *palačinky* (crêpes) for dessert are some of the best in Prague. *Purkyňova 4, tel. 02/298842. Reservations advised. AE.*

Myslivna. Don't be put off by the antlers on the wall or the fur-lined chairs; the food defies the clichés. Try leg of venison in wine sauce with walnuts or wild boar, all prepared to please the eye and palette. *Jagellonská 21, Vinohrady, tel. 02/276209. Reservations advised. AE, DC, MC, V.*

U Lorety. Sightseers will find this an agreeable spot—peaceful except for the welcoming carillon from neighboring Loreto Church. The service here is discreet but attentive, the tables are private, and the food is consistently excellent. Venison and steak are specialties. *Loretánské náměstí 8, near the Castle, tel. 02/536025. Reservations advised. AE, DC, MC, V. Closed Mon. (and Tues. in winter).*

U Sloupu. This popular neighborhood restaurant close to the Flora metro stop serves innovative versions of typical Czech dishes. *Lucemberska 11, tel. 02/271457. Reservations advised. AE, DC, MC, V.*

Vikárka. This was an eating house beside St. Vitus Cathedral as far back as the 16th century. It offers good-value local cooking in a historic setting. *Vikářská 6, in the Castle, tel. 02/535158. Reservations accepted. AE, DC, MC, V. Open only until 7:30. Closed Mon. in winter.*

Inexpensive **Que Huong.** This unassuming Vietnamese restaurant has a good selection of food and quick, friendly service. *Havelská 29, tel. 02/225584. Reservations advised 3 days in advance during summer. No credit cards.*

U Medvídků. Enjoy South Bohemian and old Czech specialties here in a noisy but jolly atmosphere. Try the goulash with sliced bread dumplings. *Na Perštýně 7, Staré Město, tel. 02/2358904. Reservations not necessary. No credit cards. Closed Sun.*

U Pinkasů. The two great attractions here are the draft beer and the goulash—you can also add your signature to the wall with the countless others before you. *Jungmannovo náměstí 15, Staré Město, tel. 02/265770. Reservations not necessary. No credit cards.*

★ **U Sv. Tomáše.** Although it's touristy, this restored ancient tavern overflows with atmosphere. Try the famous dark ale and such good, down-to-earth fare as roast pork with cabbage and dumplings. *Letenská 12, Malá Strana, tel. 02/530064. Reservations advised. No credit cards. Closed Sun.*

Budget **Deminka Restaurant and Cafe.** With its chandeliers and tall ceilings, this restaurant has a low-key elegance, and the standard Czech fare served here is of unusually high quality. There is seating outdoors in the summer, but only for beer. It's a short walk from Wenceslas Square, behind the National Museum. *Skretova 1, tel. 02/2362831. Reservations advised. Dress: casual. No credit cards.*

Kavarna Slavia. This large, upscale Art Deco café on the Vltava attracts theatergoers, business people, artsy types, and others from all parts of the world (some tourists). There's live music (elevator tunes) in the evening. You can try a variety of coffees, wines, and aperitifs in the sometimes smoky surroundings. The café also serves ice-cream sundaes and a cheese plate. Check out the frescoes on the ceiling above the bar. There is a restaurant attached. *Národní třída, opposite National Theater, tel. 02/261250. No reservations. No credit cards.*

Moravská Vináma. Not too touristy despite its central location, this vináma has a bar and a restaurant that serves large, tasty portions of Moravian specialties in average surroundings. The Victorian Mix is a delicious pork-and-vegetable dish. *Obecní dům, nám. Republiky 1090. No phone. Closed Sun. lunch.*

Restaurace U Buldoka. This classic, intimate Prague pub, hidden away west of the Vltava in the old district of Smichov, offers a variety of Czech specialties at rock-bottom prices. Take tram 4, 7, 14, or 16 to the first stop on the far side of the river (the ride affords sweeping views of Prague Castle and the city's bridges). *Preslova 1, tel. 02/544638. Reservations advised. Dress: casual. No credit cards.*

Restaurace U Supa. Good solid Czech food and beer attract Czechs and foreigners to this friendly and comfortable fast-service restaurant. The high vaulted ceiling in the front room gives an Old World air to the place, and in the back room a sad-faced musician plays your favorite synthesized polkas. *Celetná 28, off Staroměstská nám., tel. 02/223042. No credit cards.*

Sate Grill. Indonesian noodles, pork and chicken saté, and gyros go for $1–$2 each in this slick private eatery. Outdoor seating offers a sliver of a view down the Hradčany slope. Menus are available in English. *3 Pohořelec, above Loretánské nám. No phone. No credit cards.*

U Vejvodu. Hidden in the tiny streets of the Old Town, this pub serves excellent beer and the usual variations on pork, cabbage, and dumplings. The front room is reserved for nonsmokers. *Vejvoda 2, no phone. Reservations not necessary. No credit cards.*

Lodging

The cheaper hotels in Prague can be a little on the shabby side. Private accommodations are often a better option. The best service is offered by **AVE** (tel. 02/2362560, fax 02/2362956; open daily 7–10), in the main train station (Hlavní nádraží) near the arrivals area. Prices start at about $14 per person per night. Be sure to specify a room in central Prague, or you may spend much of your time commuting back and forth. The **City of Prague Accommodation Service** (tel. 02/2310202, fax 02/ 2314076; open daily until 8), on Hastelská náměsti in the Old Town, also provides this service. The **Čedok** branch at Panska 5 (tel. 02/225657) has arranged private accommodations for many years and also has a good selection of rooms. If all else fails, just take a walk through the Old Town. The number of organizations offering "Accommodation" (Unterkunft in German) is astounding.

Moderate **Ambassador.** This is another oldie from the turn of the century, renovated in 1983. It's right on Wenceslas Square. *Václavské náměstí 5, tel. 02/2143111. 170 rooms with bath. Facilities: disco. AE, DC, MC, V.*

International. Situated about 5 kilometers (3 miles) from the center, the International is known as the Russian Ritz for its 30-year-old architectural pretensions! High-season prices can edge this one up into the Expensive category. *Náměstí Družby 1, tel. 02/321051. 327 rooms with bath. Facilities: garden, miniature golf, nightclub. AE, DC, MC, V.*

Panorama. Out in the sticks in an ugly building, the Panorama has two saving graces: it is on a subway line and it has a top-floor swimming pool with a great view. *Milevská 7, tel. 02/ 416111. 432 rooms with bath. Facilities: saunas, pool, solarium, nightclub. AE, DC, MC, V.*

Inexpensive **Bohemia.** The location of this hotel, close to Staroměstské náměsti, makes up for its shabbiness. The rooms are clean, comfortable, and not too small. For a better breakfast than that served at the hotel, try the café at the Hotel Paříž, opposite. *Kralodvorska 4, tel. 02/2313920. 63 rooms, most without bath. Breakfast not included. Facilities: restaurant. No credit cards.*

Central. This family-run hotel was built in the 1920s and is popular with students, who appreciate the reasonable price and great location but don't mind the in-house disco (which keeps things hopping late into the night). The tiny rooms are functional and clean. *Rybna 8, tel. 02/2324351. 107 rooms, some with bath. Breakfast not included. Facilities: restaurant, wine bar. No credit cards.*

Meteor. The lobby and public areas have had a face-lift recently, and the marble and glass that greet you upon entering will raise your expectations—but the corridors and rooms won't live up to them. However, the location, a couple of blocks from the Powder Tower in the New Town, more than justified the reasonable price. *Hybernska 6, tel. 02/224202. 83 rooms without bath. Facilities: restaurant, bar. Breakfast not included. No credit cards.*

Budget **Hotel Axa.** Five minutes from the Florenc bus station, this hotel has a tram stop right outside its door with direct service to Václavské náměstí. The management is rather oblivious. Reserve one week ahead, earlier in summer. *Na poříčí 40, tel. 02/ 232–72–34. 133 rooms, many with bath. Facilities: restaurant, bar, nightclub. No credit cards.*

Hotel Hybemia. This hotel's shabby exterior is currently undergoing a face-lift, which no doubt will also raise the rates. Beware of the stern receptionist and the erratic prices. Add about $6.25 for a room with a bath. The train station is only five minutes away. *Hybernska 24, tel. 02/22–04–31. From Hlavní nádraží, walk down Opletalova and turn left on Hybernska. 70 rooms, few with bath. Facilities: restaurant, bar, lounge. No credit cards.*

Pensione. Catering mostly to German motorists, this newly renovated pension in outer Žižkov has small rooms with shared bathrooms clustered around the courtyard. You can cook your own meals in one of the kitchens. The management works hard to keep the place clean and efficient. Located 10 minutes by bus from the town center, it costs about $17 per person in a double room. *Hájkova 19, tel. 02/27–84–55. From Hlavní nádraží take bus No. 168 to Čemínova stop; walk 2 blocks, then left to Hájkova. No credit cards.*

Penzión Louda. The helpful proprietors at this hotel offer clean, comfortable rooms with something of a view from the hills north of the city center. Breakfast is included. It's about 15 minutes by tram from the center of town. *Kubišova 10, tel. 02/84–33–02 or 02/84–32–98. Metro Holešovice, then bus No. 102, 144, 157, 175, or 200 or tram No. 5, 12, 17, 24, 25, or 37 to Hercovka. 9 rooms. No credit cards. Reservations advised.*

The Arts

Prague's cultural life is one of its top attractions and its citizens like to dress up for it, but performances are usually booked far ahead. You can get a monthly program of events from the Prague Information Service, Čedok, or many hotels. The two English-language newspapers, *The Prague Post* (weekly) and *Prognosis* (bimonthly), carry detailed entertainment listings. The main ticket agencies are **Bohemia Ticket International** (Karlova 8 and Na příkopě 16, tel. 02/228738) and **Čedok** (Bílkova 6, tel. 02/2318255); for concerts, try **Sluna** (in Alfa passageway, Václavské náměstí). It's much cheaper, however, to buy tickets at the box office.

Concerts   Performances are held in the **National Gallery** in Prague Castle; the **National Museum;** the **Gardens** below the castle (where music comes with a view); the **churches of St. Nicholas** in both the Old Town Square and in Malá Strana; and **St. James's Church** on Malá Stupartská (Staré Město), where the organ plays amid a flourish of Baroque statuary.

Year-round concert halls include **Dvořák Hall** (the House of Artists, náměstí Jana Palacha), **Smetana Hall** (Obecní dum, Náměstí Republiky 5), and **Palác Kultury** (Kvetna 65).

Opera and Ballet   Opera is of an especially high standard in Czechoslovakia. The main venues in the grand style of the 19th century are the beautifully restored **National Theater** (Národní třida 2, tel. 02/205364) and **Smetana Theater** (Vitězného února 8, tel. 02/269746). The even older **Theater of Estates** (Ovocný trh 1, tel. 227281; formerly the Týl Theater) is occasionally used for opera performances.

Theater   You won't need to know the language at **Divadlo na Zábradlí** (Theater on the Balustrade, Anenské náměstí 5, tel. 02/2360449), home of the famous Black Theater mime group when it is (rather rarely) in Prague. **Laterna Magika** (Magic Lantern, Národní třída 40, tel. 02/260033) is a popular extravaganza combining live actors, mime, and sophisticated film techniques.

Puppet Shows These are brought to a high art form at the **Špejbl and Hurvínek Theater** (Římská 45).

Nightlife

Cabaret **The Alhambra** (Václavské náměstí 5, tel. 02/220467) has a three-part floor show. More moderately priced is **Variété Praha** (Vodičkova 30, tel. 02/23143). You'll find plenty of fellow foreigners at both.

Discos The best-known and most crowded is at the **Ambassador** hotel (*see* Lodging, *above*). There's one at each of the three hotels on the Vltava River: **Admirál** (Hořejši nábřeží), **Albatros** (nábřeží L. Svobody), and **Racek** (Dvorecká louka).

Bohemian Spas

The Bohemian countryside is a restful world of gentle hills and thick woods. It is especially beautiful during fall foliage or in May, when the fruit trees that line the roads are in blossom. In such settings lie the two most famous of Czechoslovakia's scores of spas: Karlovy Vary and Mariánské Lázně. During the 19th and early 20th centuries, the royalty and aristocrats of Europe who came to ease their overindulged bodies (or indulge them even more!) knew these spas as Karlsbad and Marienbad.

To the south, the higher wooded hills of Sumava, bordering Germany, have their own folklore and give rise to the headwaters of the Vltava. You'll follow its tortuous course as you enter South Bohemia, which has probably spawned more castles than any other region of comparable size. The medieval towns of South Bohemia are exquisite, though be prepared to find them in various stages of repair or decay. In such towns was the Hussite reformist movement born during the early 15th century, sparking off a series of religious conflicts that eventually embroiled all of Europe.

Getting Around

There are excellent and very cheap bus connections to Karlovy Vary and Mariánské Lázně from the Florenc bus station in Prague. Service between the two towns is also frequent. Train service to Karlovy Vary is slower (and only slightly cheaper); most trains to Germany pass through Mariánské Lázně. Trains leave Prague from the main station, Hlavní nádraží.

Exploring Bohemian Spas

Karlovy Vary, or Karlsbad, was named after Charles IV, who, while out hunting, was supposedly led to the main thermal spring of Vřídlo by a fleeing deer. In due course, the spa drew not only many of the crowned heads and much of the blue blood of Europe but also leading musicians and writers. The same parks, promenades, and colonnades still border the little river Teplá, beneath wooded hills. For all its later buildings and proletarian patients, Karlovy Vary still has a great deal of elegance. The waters from the spa's 12 springs are uniformly foultasting. The thing to do is sip them from traditionally shaped cups while nibbling rich Karlovy Vary wafers (*oplatky*), then resort to the "13th spring," Karlovy Vary's tangy herbal liqueur called *Becherovka*.

Karlovy Vary and **Mariánské Lázně** have Czechoslovakia's two best golf courses. As a spa, Mariánské Lázně is younger and smaller, yet its more open setting gives it an air of greater spaciousness. It was much favored by Britain's Edward VII, though from all accounts, he didn't waste too much time on strict diets and rigorous treatments.

Dining and Lodging

For details and price-category definitions, *see* Dining and Lodging in Staying in Czechoslovakia.

Karlovy Vary   **Adria.** Conveniently located by the bus station and small train station, this is a faded but adequate relic of the spa's glorious past. It's frequently full, due to its prime location. *Koněvova, tel. 017/237–65. 30 rooms, none with bath. No credit cards. Budget.*

Astoria. This older private spa is now trying to make it as a hotel and will probably succeed, given its excellent location near the "Sprudel" and main colonnade. In keeping with spa tradition, the rooms and public areas are comfortable but sterile. *Vridelni 23, tel. 017/282248. 80 rooms. No breakfast. No credit cards. Inexpensive.*

Atlantic. This hotel is right in the middle of town and is run by the nearby Hotel Central. The turn-of-the-century building was renovated recently, but it still bears its characteristic grotesque porcelain statues on the roof. *Divadelni náměstí, tel. 017/24715. 38 rooms, some with bath. AE, DC, MC, V. Moderate.*

Otova. You probably won't fall in love with the stern, modern architecture or the formal exterior. But for your money you get spotlessly clean and quiet rooms, and an excellent location right across from the colonnade. *Vridelni 4. Facilities: restaurant, wine bar. Breakfast included. No credit cards. Inexpensive.*

Mariánské Lázně   **Kavkaz.** You'll either love or hate the imposing 19th-century
★ "Empire" style of this former spa turned hotel just behind the main colonnade area. The rooms are airy and large, and the public areas are elegant. *Goethovo nám. 9, tel. 0165/31413. Facilities: restaurant. Breakfast not included. No credit cards. Inexpensive–Moderate.*

Europa. This former workers' spa-retreat is now a pleasant turn-of-the-century hotel conveniently located downtown. The hotel restaurant is very German, with game dishes such as wild boar and venison. *Trěbízského 101, near Čedok, tel. 0165/20–64. 30 rooms, some with bath. Facilities: restaurant. Reservations advised. No credit cards. Inexpensive.*

Kossuth. This is another complex of former union houses offering convenience and moderate prices. More modest than the Europa, this slightly worn-out hotel on a quiet street houses tourists mostly from within the country and the Eastern bloc. *Ruská 77, tel. 0165/28–61. 60 rooms, some with bath. No credit cards. Inexpensive.*

Bratislava

Getting Around

There are frequent buses and trains running between Prague and Bratislava; both options are cheap and take about five hours. There are also several trains and buses daily from Vienna, a little more than an hour away. In Bratislava there are buses and streetcars; ticket machines operate by most stops, and tickets cost 4 Kčs.

Tourist Information

Bratislava has its own tourist-information service, **Bratislava Information and Propagation Service** (BIPS, Laurinska 1, tel. 07/333715 or 07/334370; open weekdays 8–4, Sat. 8–1). **Čedok** (Sturova 13, tel. 07/52002; open weekdays 9–6. Sat. 9–noon) can provide help with accommodations and information on Bratislava and the surrounding area.

Exploring Bratislava

Many visitors are disappointed by Bratislava. Expecting a Slovak version of Prague, they discover a shabby, very East-bloc city with more than its share of high-rise housing projects. The winding streets of Bratislava's Old Town center and the handsome castle on the hill look decidedly secondary in their crumbling beauty. This is definitely a city that people live in, and not a museum. But if you're prepared to look beyond the urban ugliness, you'll find much of historical and aesthetic interest.

It may come as a surprise that for 300 years **Bratislava** was the capital of Hungary (after Buda and Pest fell to the Turks during the 15th century). The Hungarians knew it as Pozsony and the Habsburgs, who subsequently took it over, as Pressburg. It wasn't until 1918 that it regained its Slavic name.

During the 18th century, royal and noble families built patrician houses that still add much charm to the narrow streets of the old town, currently undergoing restoration below the **castle.** The castle has been virtually rebuilt since World War II and is a good point from which to get your bearings as you look down on the broad waters of the Danube, the Gothic spire of the **Cathedral of St. Martin**—where Hungarian kings and queens were crowned—and the huddled roofs of the old town.

Down in the old town there's architectural interest on almost every street, particularly on the square of Primaciálne námestie, with its Gothic-Renaissance **Old Town Hall** and its elegant **Primate's Palace.** The palace has some lovely 17th-century tapestries (made in the royal workshops at Mortlake near London), depicting the legend of Hero and Leander. *Primaciálne námestie. Open Tues.–Sun. 9–5.*

Follow busy Old World Michalská ulica up to the **Michalská brána** (Michael's Gate), the last remaining city gate of the original three. The bottom part of the tower is the original Gothic, built in the 14th century; the octagonal section was added in the early 16th century, and the flamboyant copper onion tower, topped with a statue of St. Michael, was an addition from the 18th century.

It's worth walking up to the **Hrad** (castle) to see the view over the Danube—if not for the endless apartment blocks on the Petrzalka side of the river, then to see over to Austria, to the right. The castle has been continually rebuilt since its establishment in the 9th century. Hungarian kings expanded it into a large royal residence and the Habsburgs turned it into a successful fortress against the Turks. Its current design, a square with four corner towers, dates from the 17th century, although it had to be rebuilt completely after a fire in 1811. Inside the castle is the **Slovenské narodné muzéum** (Slovak National Museum), displaying antique coins, glass, and weapons. *Hrad, Zámocká ul., tel. 07/311444. Admission: 50 Kčs adults, 25 Kčs children and students. Open Tues.–Sun. 10–5.*

Dining and Lodging

For details and price-category definitions, *see* Dining and Lodging in Staying in Czechoslovakia.

Dining **Kláštorna vináreň.** Old-town dining can be a delight in the vaulted cellars of this old monastery. The food is on the heavy side but goes down well with the excellent Slovak dry red wine. *Františkanská ul. 1, tel. 07/330430. Reservations advised. No credit cards. Closed Sun. Moderate.*

Rybársky cech. The name means "Fishermen's Guild," and this restaurant is in the guild's house on the river embankment below the castle. It has its own aquarium, and, as you'd expect, the emphasis is on fish specialties, prepared by two award-winning chefs. Try the carp. *Žižkova 1, tel. 07/313049. Reservations advised. No credit cards. Closed Sat. Moderate.*

★ **U Zlatého Kapra.** Situated in a beautiful Baroque house in the heart of the Old Town, this multilevel restaurant specializes in carp and other fish dishes. *Prepostská 6, tel. 07/331612. Reservations advised. No credit cards. Moderate.*

Veľkí Františkáni. Trendy and popular with foreigners, this large restaurant and wine cellar features local wine from barrels; you can also listen to music and enjoy your drink outdoors in summer. *Františkánske nám. 10, tel. 07/333–073. No reservations. No credit cards. Inexpensive.*

Amadeus. This unpretentious cafeteria-style restaurant serves food that's guaranteed meatless—a rarity in Czechoslovakia. Tucked in the whitewashed cellar of an old Baroque house, this restaurant boasts a visit from Mozart in its illustrious past. There is a new menu each day, plus salads and free tea. Although the prices are rock bottom, the place is clean and cheery. *Venturska ul. 10, tel. 07/331593. No credit cards. Closed Sat. Budget.*

Pizzeria Umbria. On one of the busier streets near downtown, this small place has given a curious twist to the art of pizza-making with its 15 varieties of pies, including one topped with pork cracklings and another with beans. It's really hot in this place in summer, but there is a no-smoking room (a rarity in this area), as well as a youthful clientele. *Špitálska 31, tel. 07/57–353. No reservations. No credit cards. Budget.*

Terno. On the fourth floor of Dom Odievania (House of Clothing) on the main square, this downtown restaurant offers some hidden surprises. Once you get past the sleazy lounge, the terrace café has a great rooftop view, and the chef offers some interesting variations on Slovak cuisine. Try the cholesterol-laden *šustrovo tajomstvo* (shoemaker's secret—pork chops in an omelet), followed by a round of *kominárske gule* (chimney sweep's balls—plum dumplings). Terno is rarely crowded, due to its inconspicuous location. *Nám. SNP 29, tel. 07/33–47–92. Closed Sat. dinner and Sun. No credit cards. Budget.*

TV Restaurant. Climb Kamzík hill north of the city and take the elevator (5 Kčs) up the TV tower to this revolving restaurant, which has the best view in town. As the conveyorbelt section of the floor slowly revolves, you will see the entire region from your table. Now privately owned, the restaurant does its best to accommodate foreign visitors, serving an elaborate array of meat dishes. Try the "turkey chest filled up with ham in wined sauce" accompanied by the "sterilized salad" and other wonders of translation. *Kamzík. Electric bus No. 213 to last stop then walk up road (or hike through forest) about 20 min. to TV tower. Budget.*

Lodging Bratislava's hotel situation is bad. The few hotels that exist are expensive and, in general, service is unfriendly. Čedok and BIPS can help you find private rooms, which will be far cheaper (about $15) and possibly more pleasant.

Carlton. This large, centrally located hotel still exudes old-fashioned graciousness, despite the obvious decline in decor and service standards. Rooms are large and comfortable, although rather dowdy. *Hviezdoslavovo nám. 2, 81609 Bratislava, tel. 07/335141, telex 09349. 215 rooms, ½ with bath. Facilities: restaurant, 2 cafés, 3 bars, nightclub. Breakfast included. AE, DC, MC, V. Moderate.*

Kjev. This 1970s high rise, located in a concrete jungle of a square close to the Old Town, embodies the communist aesthetic for luxury hotels. Despite its impersonal and at times tasteless decor the rooms are large, bright, and clean and the service reasonably polite. *Rajska 2, 81448, tel. 07/52041 or 07/57081, telex 07/092301. 199 rooms with bath. Facilities: restaurant, café, 3 bars, nightclub, sauna. Breakfast included. AE, DC, MC, V. Moderate.*

Flóra. One of the cheapest deals around is located on the outskirts near Zlaté Piesky (Golden Sands) lake and recreation area and is convenient for sports but for little else. Although it's small and a little run-down, the Flóra has friendly management who know some English and German. Doubles are cheap and fill up quickly during summer. Bring toilet paper—not all bathrooms have it. *Senecká cesta, tel. 07/21–41–54 or 07/21–41–22. From train station take tram No. 2 to last stop. 20 rooms with bath. Facilities: restaurant. No credit cards. Budget.*

6   Denmark

While it's true that Denmark is one of the world's most expensive countries, your visit needn't be. Seeing the country as the Danes themselves do, through the window of small cafés and from the seat of a bicycle, costs little more than a visit in other parts of Europe.

The Danes are friendly and helpful folk who have even coined a term—*hyggelig*—for the feeling of well-being that comes from their own brand of cozy hospitality. The stereotype of melancholic Scandinavia doesn't hold here: not in the café-studded streets of the larger cities, where musicians and peddlers hawk their wares to passersby; not in the tiny coastal towns, where the houses are the color of ice-cream flavors; not in the jam sessions that erupt in the Copenhagen jazz clubs, nor in the equally joyous "jam" sessions involved in the production of *smørrebrød* (the famous open-face Danish sandwich). Even the country's indoor/outdoor museums, where history is reconstructed through full-scale dwellings out in the open, indicate that Danes don't wish to keep life behind glass.

Denmark is the only Scandinavian country without wild tracts of forest and lake. This is a land of well-groomed agriculture, where every acre is rich in orchard and field. Nowhere are you far from water, as you drive on and off the ferries and bridges linking the three regions of Jutland, Funen, and Zealand.

It is the sea surrounding the land that has helped shape Denmark's history. The Vikings were magnificent seafarers and had seen much of the world by the 8th century. Today the Danes remain expert navigators, using the 4,480 kilometers (2,800 miles) of coastline for sport—there are regattas around Zealand and Funen—as well as for fishing and trading.

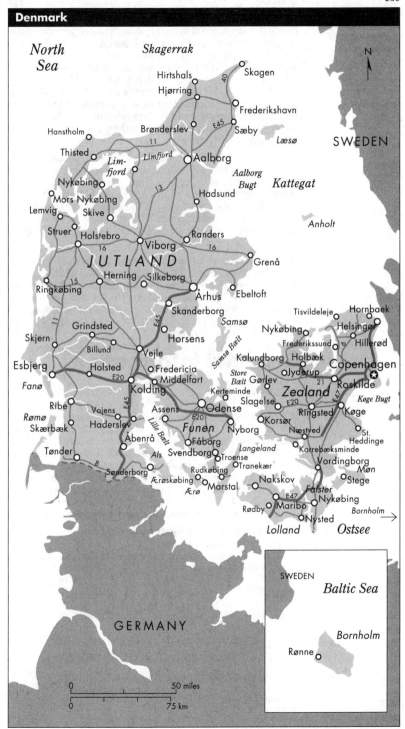

Denmark

North Sea

Skagerrak

N

Hirtshals
Hjørring
Skagen
Frederikshavn
Brønderslev
Sæby
Læsø
Hanstholm
Thisted
Lim-fjord
Limfjord
Aalborg
SWEDEN
Nykøbing
Mors Nykøbing
Skive
Hadsund
Aalborg Bugt
Kattegat
Lemvig
Struer
Holstebro
Viborg
Randers
Anholt
JUTLAND
Herning
Silkeborg
Grenå
Ringkøbing
Århus
Ebeltoft
Skanderborg
Samsø
Horsens
Tisvildeleje
Hornbaek
Nykøbing
Helsingør
Skjern
Grindsted
Frederikssund
Hillerød
Billund
Vejle
Samsø Bælt
Kalundborg
Holbæk
Esbjerg
Holsted
Fredericia
Middelfart
Gørlev
Jyderup
Copenhagen
Fanø
Kolding
Store Bælt
Roskilde
Ribe
Vojens
Kerteminde
Slagelse
Zealand
Køge Bugt
Rømø
Haderslev
Assens
Odense
Nyborg
Korsør
Ringsted
Køge
Skærbæk
Åbenrå
Funen
Næstved
St. Heddinge
Tønder
Als
Svendborg
Langeland
Karrebæksminde
Sønderborg
Troense
Tranekær
Vordingborg
Møn
Ærøskøbing
Rudkøbing
Stege
Ærø
Marstal
Nakskov
Falster
Rødby
Maribo
Nykøbing
Bornholm →
Nysted
Lolland
Ostsee

GERMANY

SWEDEN
Baltic Sea

Bornholm

Rønne

0   50 miles
0   75 km

Long one of the world's most liberal countries, Denmark has a highly developed social welfare system. The hefty taxes are the subject of grumbles and jokes, but Danes remain proud of their state-funded medical and educational systems, as well as their high standard of living. Evidence of the strong sense of community spirit is the uniquely Danish institution of the People's High School, or Folkehøjskole, where pupils live in and where the shared experience is deemed as important as the courses taken. In the summer, adults and even entire families attend these "schools for life," studying anything from weaving to the philosophy of Wittgenstein.

The country that gave the world Isak Dinesen, Hans Christian Andersen, and Søren Kierkegaard has a long-standing commitment to culture and the arts. In what other nation does the royal couple translate the writings of Simone de Beauvoir or the queen design postage stamps for Christmas? The Danish Ballet, founded in Copenhagen in 1722, is world-renowned, while the provinces boast numerous theater groups and opera houses.

Perhaps Denmark's greatest charm is its manageable size—about half that of Maine. This feature, combined with one of the world's largest concentrations of bicycles and an undeniably flat landscape, will lead the visitor to the same conclusion reached by Danes long ago: the best way to explore this country is atop a bike, spinning through colorful Copenhagen and the peaceful island of Funen.

Essential Information

Before You Go

When to Go Most travelers visit Denmark during the warmest months, July and August, but there are advantages to going in May, June, or September, when sights are less crowded and many establishments offer off-season discounts. However, few places in Denmark are ever unpleasantly crowded, and when the Danes make their annual exodus to the beaches, the cities have even more breathing space. Visitors may want to avoid the winter months, when the days are short and dark and when important attractions, Tivoli included, close for the season.

Climate The following are the average daily maximum and minimum temperatures for Copenhagen.

Jan.	36F	2C	May	61F	16C	Sept.	64F	18C
	28	- 2		46	8		51	11
Feb.	36F	2C	June	67F	19C	Oct.	54F	12C
	28	- 2		52	11		44	7
Mar.	41F	5C	July	71F	22C	Nov.	45F	7C
	31	- 1		57	14		38	3
Apr.	51F	11C	Aug.	70F	21C	Dec.	40F	4C
	38	3		56	14		34	1

Currency The monetary unit in Denmark is the krone (kr. or DKK), which is divided into 100 øre. At press time (summer 1992), the krone stood at 5.37 kr. to the dollar and 11.33 kr. to the pound sterling. Most well-known credit cards are accepted in Denmark, though the American Express card is accepted less frequently than others. Traveler's checks can be changed in banks and in many hotels, restaurants, and shops.

What It Will Cost Denmark's economy is stable, and inflation remains reasonably low, without wild fluctuations in exchange rates. While Denmark is slightly cheaper than Norway and Sweden, the standard and the cost of living are nonetheless high, especially for such luxuries as alcohol. Prices are highest in Copenhagen, while the least expensive areas are Funen and Jutland.

Sample Prices Cup of coffee, 14–20 kr.; bottle of beer, 15–25 kr.; soda, 10–15 kr.; ham sandwich, 24 kr.; 1-mile taxi ride, 20 kr.

Customs on Arrival If you purchase goods in a country that is a member of the European Community (EC) and pay that country's value-added tax (VAT) on those goods: You may import duty-free 1½ liters of liquor or 3 liters of strong wine (under 22%), plus 5 liters of other wine; 300 cigarettes or 150 cigarillos or 75 cigars or 400 grams of tobacco. Other articles may be brought in up to a maximum of 2,800 kr.; you are also allowed 75 grams of perfume.

If you are entering Denmark from a non-EC country or if you have purchased your goods in an airport, on a ferryboat, or in another airport not taxed in the EC, you must pay Danish taxes on any amount of alcoholic beverages greater than 1 liter of liquor or 2 liters of strong wine, plus 2 liters of other wine. For tobacco, the limit is 200 cigarettes or 100 cigarillos or 50 cigars or 250 grams of tobacco. Other articles (including beer) are allowed up to a maximum of 350 kr.; you are also allowed 75 grams of perfume.

Language A wit once said that Danish was not so much a language as "a disease of the throat." It is a difficult tongue for foreigners, except those from Norway and Sweden, to understand, let alone speak. Danes are good linguists, however, and almost everyone, except elderly people in rural areas, speaks English well.

Getting Around

By Train and Bus Traveling by train or bus is easy because Danish State Railways (DSB) and a few private companies cover the country with a dense network of train services, supplemented by buses in remote areas. Hourly intercity trains connect the main towns in Jutland and Funen with Copenhagen and Zealand, using high-speed diesels, called Lyntog (lightning trains), on the most important stretches. All these trains make the one-hour ferry crossing of the Great Belt (Store Bælt), the waterway separating Funen and Zealand. You can reserve seats on intercity trains and Lyntog, and you *must* have a reservation if you plan to cross the Great Belt. Buy tickets at stations for trains, buses, and connecting ferry crossings. You can usually buy tickets on the bus itself. For most cross-country trips, children between four and 11 travel free, though they must have a seat reservation (30 kr.). Ask about discounts for senior citizens and groups.

Fares The **Nordpass** (Nordic Tourist Ticket) is a good buy for 21 days of unlimited travel by rail and on some sea routes in Denmark, Norway, Sweden, and Finland. The price for an adult traveling second-class is 1,690 kr., 1,260 kr. for young adults (12–26), and 840 kr. for children (4–11).

By Boat Denmark has an excellent ferry service, with both domestic and international routes. There is frequent service to Germany, Poland, Sweden, Norway, and the Faroe Islands (in the Atlantic Ocean, north of Scotland), as well as to Britain. Domestic ferries provide services between the three areas of Jutland, Funen, and Zealand and to the smaller islands, 100 of which are inhabited. Danish State Railways and several private shipping companies publish timetables in English, and you should reserve on domestic as well as overseas routes. Ask about off-season discounts.

By Bicycle It is said that the Danes have the greatest number of bikes per capita in the world, and indeed, with its flat landscape and uncrowded roads, Denmark is a cycler's paradise. You can rent bikes at some train stations and many tourist offices, as well as from private firms. Additional information on cycling can be supplied by the **Danish Cyclists' Association** (Dansk Cyklist Forbund) (Rømersgade 7, DK 1363 Copenhagen, tel. 33/32–31–21). Danish tourist offices publish the pamphlet "Cycling Holiday in Denmark."

Staying in Denmark

Telephones Pay phones take 1-, 5-, and 10-kr. coins. Dial first, then insert
Local calls your coins when you make your connection. You must use the area codes even when dialing a local number.

International Calls Dial 009, then the country code, the area code, and the number. Hotels add a hefty service charge, so it's best to use a pay phone.

Operators and To speak to an operator, most of whom speak English, dial
Information 0033; for an international operator, dial 0039.

Mail Surface and airmail letters, as well as aerograms, to the United
Postal Rates States cost 4.75 kr. for 20 grams; postcards also cost 4.75 kr. Letters and postcards to the United Kingdom and other EC countries cost 3.50 kr. You can buy stamps at post offices or from shops that sell postcards.

Receiving Mail If you do not know where you will be staying, have mail sent to American Express or Poste Restante at any post office. American Express charges noncardholders 10 kr. for each letter. If no post office is specified, letters will be sent to the main post office in Copenhagen (Tietensgade 37).

Shopping Visitors from a non-EC country can save 20% by obtaining a
VAT Refunds refund of the value-added tax (VAT) at over 1,500 shops displaying a Tax Free sign on the window. If the shop sends your purchase directly to your home address, you pay only the sales price, exclusive of VAT, plus dispatch and insurance costs. If you want to take the goods home yourself, pay the full price in the shop and get a VAT refund at the Danish duty-free shopping center at the Copenhagen airport. You can obtain a copy of the *Tax-Free Shopping Guide* from the tourist office.

Opening and **Banks.** In Copenhagen, banks are open weekdays 9:30–3 and
Closing Times Thursdays until 6. Several *bureaux de change*, including the ones at Copenhagen's central station and airport, stay open until 10 PM. Outside Copenhagen, banking hours vary, so check locally.

Museums. As a rule, museums are open 10–3 or 11–4 and are closed on Mondays. In winter opening hours are shorter, and some museums close for the season. Check the local papers or ask at tourist offices for current times.

Shops. Shops are generally open weekdays 9–5:30; most stay open on Fridays until 7 or 8 and close on Saturdays at 1 or 2.

National Holidays January 1; April 9–11 (Easter); May 7 (Common Prayer); May 20 (Ascension); May 30 (Pentecost); June 5 (Constitution Day; shops close at noon); and December 24–26.

Dining Danes take their food seriously, and Danish food, however simple, is excellent, with an emphasis on fresh ingredients and careful presentation. Fish and meat are both of top quality in this farming and fishing country, and both are staple ingredients of the famous smørrebrød. Some smørrebrød are huge meals in themselves: Innocent snackers can find themselves faced with a dauntingly large (but nonetheless delicious) mound of fish or meat, slathered with pickle relish, all atop *rugbrød* (rye bread) and *franskbrød* (wheat bread). Another specialty is *wiener brød* (a Danish pastry), an original far superior to anything that dares call itself "Danish pastry" elsewhere.

All Scandinavian countries have versions of the cold table, but Danes claim that theirs, *det store kolde bord*, is the original and the best. It's a celebration meal; the setting of the long table is a work of art—often with paper sculpture and silver platters—and the food itself is a minor miracle of design and decoration.

In hotels and restaurants the cold table is served at lunch only, though you will find a more limited version at hotel breakfasts—a good bet for budget travelers because you can eat as much as you like.

Liquid refreshment is top-notch. Denmark boasts more than 50 varieties of beer made by as many breweries; the best-known come from Carlsberg and Tuborg. Those who like harder stuff should try *snaps*, the famous aquavit traditionally drunk with cold food. Do as the locals do, and knock it back after eating some herring. The Danes have a saying about the herring-snaps combo: "The fish should be swimming."

Mealtimes The Danes start work early, which means they generally eat lunch at noon. Evening meals are also eaten early, but visitors can be certain of being able to eat and drink until 10 or 11.

Dress The Danes are a fairly casual lot, and few restaurants require a jacket and tie. Even in the most chic establishments, the tone is elegantly casual.

Ratings Meal prices vary little between town and country. While approximate gradings are given below, remember that careful ordering can bring down the price of a meal at a more expensive restaurant. Prices are per person and include a first course, main course, and dessert, plus taxes and tip, but not wine. Best bets are indicated by a star ★.

Category	All Areas
Moderate	120–200 kr.
Inexpensive	80–120 kr.
Budget	under 80 kr.

Lodging Accommodations in Denmark range from the spare and comfortable to the resplendent. Even inexpensive hotels offer simple designs in good materials and good, firm beds. Many Danes prefer a shower to a bath, so if you particularly want a tub, ask for it, but be prepared to pay more. Farmhouse and *kro* (inn) accommodations offer a terrific alternative to more traditional hotels. Except in the case of rentals, breakfast and taxes are usually included in prices, but check when making a reservation.

Hotels While luxury hotels in the city or countryside offer rooms of a high standard, less expensive accommodations are uniformly clean and comfortable.

Inns A cheaper and charming alternative to hotels are the old stage-coach kro inns scattered throughout Denmark. You can save money by contacting **Kro Ferie** (Søndergade 31, 8700 Horsens, tel. 75/62–35–44) to invest in a book of Inn Checks, valid at 66 inns. Each check costs 325–425 kr. per person or 495 kr. per couple and includes one overnight stay in a double room with bath, breakfast included.

Farm Vacations These are perhaps the best way to see how the Danes live and work. You stay on a farm and share meals with the family; you can even get out and help with the chores. There's a minimum stay of three nights; bed-and-breakfast is 150–220 kr., while half board runs 242. (Full board can be arranged.) Contact the **Horsens Tourist Office** (Søndergade 26, DK 8700 Horsens, Jutland, tel. 75/62–38–22) for details.

Youth Hostels The 100 youth hostels in Denmark are excellent, and they're open to everyone regardless of age. If you have an International Youth Hostels Association card (obtainable before you leave home), the average rate is 60 kr. Without the card, there's a surcharge of 22 kr. For more information on youth hostels, contact **Danmarks Vandrehjem** (Søndergade 31, 8700 Horsens, tel. 32/52–29–08).

Rentals Many Danes rent out their summer homes, and a stay in one of these is another good way to see the countryside on your own terms. A simple house with room for four will cost from 1,000 kr. per week. Contact the Danish Tourist Board for details.

Camping Denmark has over 500 approved campsites, with a rating system of one, two, or three stars. You need an International Camping Carnet or Danish Camping Pass (available at any campsite and valid for one year). For more details on camping and discounts for groups and families, contact **Campingrådet** (Olof Palmes Gade 10, DK 2100 Copenhagen, tel. 31/42–32–22). Information is also available from **Dansk Vandrelang** (Kultorvet 7, DK 1175 Copenhagen, tel. 33/12–11–65).

Ratings Prices are for two people in a double room and include service and taxes and usually breakfast. Best bets are indicated by a star ★.

Category	Copenhagen	Other Areas
Moderate	670–800 kr.	500–600 kr.
Inexpensive	600–670 kr.	420–500 kr.
Budget	under 600 kr.	under 420 kr.

Tipping   The egalitarian Danes do not expect to be tipped. Service is included in bills for hotels, bars, and restaurants. The exception is hotel porters, who get around 5 kr. per bag; you should also leave 1 or 2 kr. for the use of a public toilet.

Copenhagen

Arriving and Departing

By Plane   The main airport for both international and domestic flights is Copenhagen Airport, 10 kilometers (6 miles) from the center of town.

Between the Airport and Downtown   There is frequent bus service to the city; the airport bus to the central station leaves every 15 minutes, and the trip takes about 25 minutes. You pay the 27-kr. fare on the bus. Public buses are half the price and run as often. Bus No. 32 or No. 32H takes you to Rådhus Pladsen, the city-hall square.

By Train   Copenhagen's central station is the hub of the train networks. Express trains leave every hour, on the hour, from 6 AM to 10 PM for principal towns in Funen and Jutland. Find out more from **DSB Information** at the central station (tel. 33/14–17–01). You can make reservations at the central station (tel. 33/14–88–00) and most other stations and through travel agents. In Copenhagen, for those with Inter-Rail cards there is an Inter-Rail Center (open July–mid-Sept., 7 AM–midnight) at the central station that offers rest and a bath.

Getting Around

By Bus and Suburban Train   The best bet for visitors is the **Copenhagen Card,** affording unlimited travel on buses and suburban trains (S-trains), admission to over 40 museums and sights around Zealand, and a reduction on the ferry crossing to Sweden. You can buy the card, which costs about 115 kr. (one day), 180 kr. (two days), or 225 kr. (three days), at tourist offices and hotels and from travel agents.

Buses and suburban trains operate on the same ticket system and divide Copenhagen and the surrounding areas into three zones. Tickets are validated on the time system: On the basic ticket, which costs 9 kr. for an hour, you can travel anywhere in the zone in which you started. You can obtain a discount by buying a packet of 10 basic tickets for 80 kr. Get zone information from the 24-hour information service: tel. 36/45–45–45 for buses, 33/14–17–01 for S-trains. Buses and S-trains run from 5 AM (6 AM on Sundays) to 12:30 AM.

By Bicycle   More than half the 5 million Danes are said to ride bikes, which are popular with visitors as well. Bike rental costs 30–50 kr. a day, with a deposit of 100–200 kr. Contact **Danwheel-Rent-a-Bike** (Colbjørnsensgade 3, tel. 31/21–22–27) or **Urania Cykler** (Gammel Kongevej 1, tel. 31/21–80–88).

Important Addresses and Numbers

Tourist Information The main tourist information office is **Danmarks Turistråd** (Danish Tourist Board) (H. C. Andersens Boulevard 22, DK 1553 Copenhagen, tel. 33/11–13–25). Located opposite city hall, it is open May–Sept., weekdays 9–6, Sat. 9–2, Sun. 9–1; Oct.–Apr., weekdays 9–5, Sat. 9–noon, closed Sun. In summer there are also offices at Elsinore, Hillerød, Køge, Roskilde, Gilleleje, Hundersted, and Tisvildeleje. Youth information in Copenhagen is available at **Huset** (Rådhusstraede 13, tel. 33/15–65–18).

Embassies U.S. (Dag Hammarskjöldsallé 24, tel. 31/42–31–44). **Canada** (Kristen Benikowsgade 1, tel. 33/12–22–99). **U.K.** (Kastelsvej 40, tel. 31/26–46–00).

Emergencies **Police, Fire, Ambulance** (tel. 000). **Doctor** (8 AM–4 PM, tel. 33/93–63–00; after hours, tel. 33/12–00–41. Fees payable in cash only; night fees around 250 kr.). **Dentist: Dental Emergency Service,** Tandlægevagten, 14, Oslo Plads, near Østerport station (no telephone; emergencies only; cash only).

Exploring Copenhagen

When Denmark ruled Norway and Sweden in the 15th century, Copenhagen was the capital of all three countries. Today it is still the liveliest Scandinavian capital, with about 1 million inhabitants. It's a city meant for walking, the first in Europe to recognize the value of pedestrian streets in fostering community spirit. As you stroll through the cobbled streets and squares, you'll find that Copenhagen combines the excitement and variety of big-city life with a small-town atmosphere. If there's such a thing as a cozy metropolis, you'll find it here.

Nor are you ever far from water, be it sea or canal. The city itself is built upon two main islands, Slotsholmen and Christianshavn, connected by drawbridges. Walk down Nyhavn Canal, an area formerly haunted by a fairly salty crew of sailors. Now it's gentrified, and the 18th-century houses lining it are filled with chic restaurants. You should linger, too, in the five main pedestrian streets collectively known as "Strøget," with shops, cellar galleries, and crafts workshops, and street musicians and vendors by the dozen. In summer Copenhagen moves outside, and the best views of city life are from the sidewalk cafés in the shady squares.

Rådhus Pladsen and Slotsholmen *Numbers in the margin correspond to points of interest on the Copenhagen map.*

The best place to start a stroll is the Rådhus Pladsen (City Hall Square), the hub of Copenhagen's commercial district. The ❶ mock-Renaissance building dominating it is the **Rådhus** (city hall), completed in 1905. A statue of Copenhagen's 12th-century founder, Bishop Absalon, sits atop the main entrance. Inside you can see the first World Clock, an astrological timepiece invented and built by Jens Olsen and put in motion in 1955. If you're feeling energetic, take a guided tour up the 350-foot tower for a panoramic view. *Rådhus Pladsen, tel. 33/66–25–82. Open weekdays 10–3. Tours in English: weekdays at 3, Sat. at 10. Tower tours: Mon.–Sat. at noon; additional tours June–Sept. at 10. Admission: tour 20 kr., tower 10 kr.*

2 On the right of Rådhus Pladsen is **Lur Blower's Column,** topped by two Vikings blowing an ancient trumpet called a *lur.* The artist took a good deal of artistic license—the lur dates from the Bronze Age, 1500 BC, while the Vikings lived a mere 1,000 years ago. The monument is a starting point for sightseeing tours of the city.

If you continue to the square's northeast corner and turn right, you will be in Frederiksberggade, the first of the five pedestri-
3 an streets that make up the **Strøget,** Copenhagen's shopping district. Walk past the cafés and trendy boutiques to the double square of **Gammel and Nytorv,** where, on April 16, golden apples (really gilded metal balls) dance on the water jets in the fountain to celebrate the queen's birthday.

Turn down Rådhusstræde toward Frederiksholms Kanal. Here
4 you'll find the entrance to the **National Museet** (National Museum), with extensive collections that chronicle Danish cultural history to modern times and display Egyptian, Greek, and Roman antiquities. Viking enthusiasts will want to see the Runic stones in the Danish cultural history section. *Frederiksholms Kanal 12, tel. 33/13–44–11. Admission: 20 kr. adults, 15 kr. students and senior citizens, free for children under 16. Open June 16–Sept. 15, Tues.–Sun. 10–4; Sept. 16–June 15, Tues.–Fri. 11–3, weekends noon–4.*

Cross Frederiksholms Kanal to Castle Island, dominated by
5 the massive gray **Christiansborg Slot** (Christiansborg Castle). The complex, which contains the Folketinget (Parliament House) and the Royal Reception Chambers, is situated on the site of the city's first fortress, built by Bishop Absalon in 1167. While the castle that stands was being built at the turn of the century, the National Museum excavated the ruins beneath the site. *Christiansborg ruins, tel. 33/92–64–92. Admission: 12 kr. adults, 5 kr. children. Open May–Oct., daily 9:30–3:30; closed Nov.–Apr., Mon. and Sat. Folketinget, tel. 33/37–55–00. Admission free. Tours every hour on Sun., 10–4. Reception Rooms. Admission: 25 kr. adults, 10 kr. children. Open May–Oct., Tues.–Sun., English tours at 11, 1, and 3; Oct.–May, Tues.–Thurs., and Sun., English tours at 11 and 1.*

6 Also on Castle Island, just north of the castle, is **Thorvaldsens Museum.** The 19th-century Danish sculptor Bertel Thorvaldsen, buried at the center of the museum, was greatly influenced by the statues and reliefs of classical antiquity. In addition to his own works, there is a collection of paintings and drawings by other artists illustrating the influence of Italy on Denmark's Golden Age artists. *Porthusgade 2, tel. 33/32–15–32. Admission free. Open Tues.–Sun. 10–5.*

7 Nearby, **Det Kongelige Bibliotek** (Royal Library) houses the country's largest collection of books, newspapers, and manuscripts. Look for early records of the Viking journeys to America and Greenland and the statue of the philosopher Søren Kierkegaard in the garden. *Christians Brygge 8. Admission free. Open weekdays 9–7, Sat. 10–7.*

8 Close to the library is the **Teaterhistorisk Museum** (Theater History Museum), in the Royal Court Theater of 1766. You can see extensive exhibits on theater and ballet history, then wander around the boxes, stage, and dressing rooms to see where it all happened. *Christianborg Ridebane 18, tel. 33/11–51–76.*

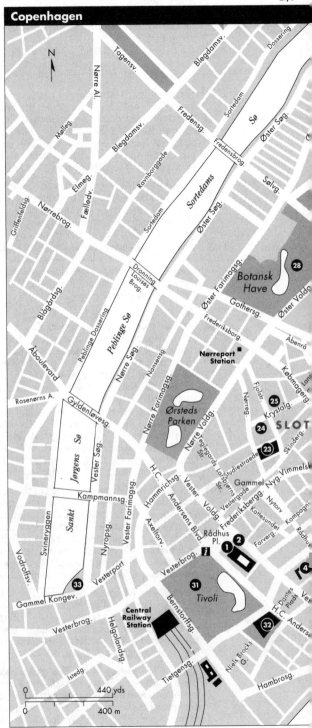

Copenhagen

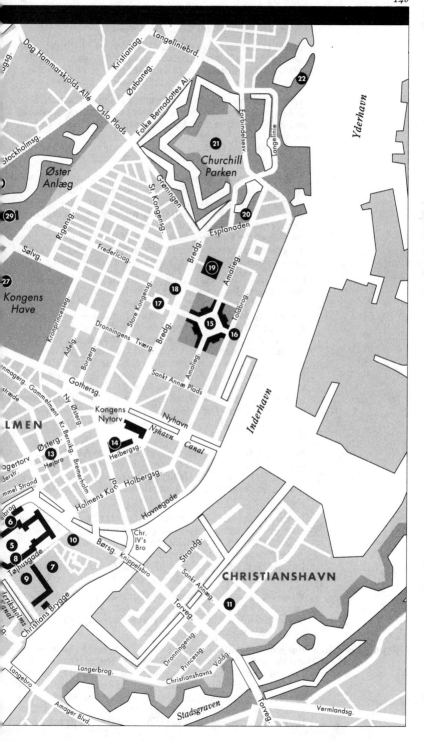

Dag Hammarskjölds Alle
Stockholmsg.
Kristianiag.
Langelieniebrd.
Øsibaneg.
Oslo Plads
Øster Anlæg
Folke Bernadottes Al.
Langelinie
Forbindelsesv.
Yderhavn

22

21
Churchill Parken

Grønningen
St. Kongensg.
Rigensg.
Fredericiag.

29

Sølvg.

27
Kongens Have

Bredg.
Amalieg.
Esplanaden

20

19

Kronprincesseg.
Store Kongensg.
18
17

Adelg.
Borgerg.
Dronningens Tværg.
Bredg.
15
16
Amalieg.
Toldbrog.

Gothersg.
Sankt Annæ Plads

nmager.
Gammelmønt
Ny Østerg.
Kr. Bernikg.
Bremerholm
straede
Gothersg.

LMEN
Kongens Nytorv
Nyhavn
Nyhavn
Canal

Østerg.
13
Højbro
14
Heibergsg.

agertorv
dersir.
Holmens Kan
Holbergsg.

mmel Strand
Havnegade

Inderhavn

lbrog.
6
5
8
Tøjhusgade
9
10
7
Børsg.
Chr. IV's Bro
Knippelsbro

Strandg.
Sankt Annæg.

CHRISTIANSHAVN

rtilleriholms
Christians Brygge
anal
g.

11

Langebro
Langerbrog.
Amager Blvd.

Dronningensg.
Princessg.
Christianshavns Voldg.

Torveg.

Stadsgraven

Torveg.
Vermlandsg.

Admission: 20 kr. adults, 10 kr. senior citizens and students, 5 kr. children. Open Wed. 2–4, Sun. noon–4.

Also at this address are the **Royal Stables**, which display vehicles used by the Danish monarchy from 1776 to the present. *Tel. 33/12–38–15. Admission: 10 kr. adults, 5 kr. children 6–15. Open Oct.–Apr., Sat.–Sun. 2–4; May–Sept., Fri.–Sun. 2–4.*

❾ Across the street that bears its name is **Tøjhuset Museum** (Royal Armory), with impressive displays of uniforms, weapons, and armor in an arched hall 200 yards long. *Tøjhusgade 3, tel. 33/11–60–37. Admission: 20 kr. adults, 5 kr. children 6–17. Open mid-Sept.–mid-June, Tues.–Fri. 1–3, weekends noon–4; mid-June–mid-Sept., Tues.–Sun. 10–4.*

❿ A few steps from Tøjhuset is the old stock exchange, **Børsen,** believed to be the oldest still in use—although it functions only on special occasions. It was built in the 16th-century monarch King Christian IV, a scholar and warrior, and architect of much of the city. The king is said to have had a hand at twisting the tails of the four dragons that form the structure's distinctive green copper spire. With its steep roofs, tiny windows, and gables, the building is one of Copenhagen's treasures.

From Børsen, look east across the drawbridge (Knippelsbro) that connects Slotsholmen with Christianshavn, one of the old-
⓫ est parts of Copenhagen, to the green-and-gold spire of **Vor Frelser's Kirke** (Our Savior's Church). The Gothic structure was built in 1696. Local legend has it that the staircase encircling it was built curling the wrong way around, and that when its architect reached the top and saw what he had done, he jumped. The less impulsive will enjoy the spectacular view from the top. *Skt. Annægade, tel. 31/57–27–98. Admission: 10 kr. adults, 4 kr. children. Open Mar. 15–May, Mon.–Sat. 9–4:30, Sun. noon–3:30; June–Aug., Mon.–Sat. 9–4:30, Sun. noon–4:30; Sept.–Oct., Mon.–Sat. 9–3:30, Sun. noon–3:30. Nov.–Mar. 14, Mon.–Sat. 10–1:30, Sun. noon–1:30. Tower closed Dec.–March 14.*

Head back to Strøget, turning left along the Amagertov section. Toward the end and to the right (5 Niels Hemmingsens
⓬ Gad) is the 18th-century **Helligånds Kirken** (Church of the Holy Ghost). The choir contains a marble font by the sculptor Thorvaldsen.

In Østergade, the easternmost of the streets that make up
⓭ Strøget, you cannot miss the green spire of **Nikolaj Kirke** (Nikolaj Church). The building that currently stands was built in the 20th century; the previous structure, which dated to the 13th century, was destroyed by fire in 1728. Today the church's role is secular—it's an art gallery and an exhibition center.

While Strøget is famous as a shopping area, and elegant stores abound, it's also where Copenhagen comes to stroll. Outside the posh displays of the fur and porcelain shops, the sidewalks have the festive aura of a street fair.

Royal Palace Area **Kongens Nytorv** (the King's New Market) is the square mark-
⓮ ing the end of Strøget. The **Kongelige Teater** (Danish Royal Theater), home of Danish opera and ballet as well as theater, sits on the south side. The Danish Royal Ballet remains one of the world's great companies, with a repertoire ranging from classical to modern. On the western side of the square you'll see the stately facade of the hotel D'Angleterre, the grande dame

of Copenhagen hotels. When former president Ronald Reagan visited Denmark, he couldn't stay there for security reasons but asked for a tour of the place just the same.

The street leading southeast from Kongens Nytorv is **Nyhavn.** The recently gentrified canal was a longtime haunt of sailors. Now restaurants and boutiques outnumber the tattoo shops, but on hot summer nights the area still gets rowdy, with Scandinavians reveling amid a fleet of old-time sailing ships and well-preserved 18th-century buildings. Hans Christian Andersen lived at both nos. 18 and 20.

Turn left at the end of Nyhavn to see the harbor front and then make an immediate left onto Sankt Annæ Plads. Take the third ⑮ right onto Amaliegade. Continue straight ahead for **Amalienborg Palace,** the principal royal residence since 1784. When the royal family is in residence during the fall and winter, the Royal Guard and band march through the city at noon to change the palace guard. The palace interior is closed to the public.

Rest a moment on the palace's harbor side, amid the trees and ⑯ fountains of **Amaliehavn Gardens.** Across the square, it's just a ⑰ step to Bredgade and the **Marmorikirken** (Marble Church), a 19th-century Baroque church with a dome that looks several sizes too large for the building beneath it.

⑱ Bredgade is also home to the exotic onion domes of the **Russiske Ortodoxe Kirke** (Russian Orthodox Church). Farther on is the ⑲ **Kundindustrimuseet** (Museum of Decorative Art), with a large selection of European and Oriental handicrafts, as well as ceramics, silver, and tapestries. *Bredgade 68, tel. 33/14–94–52. Admission: 30 kr. adults, 20 kr. students and senior citizens, children under 16 free, July, Aug., Sun., and holidays; otherwise free. Permanent exhibition open Tues.–Sun. 1–4; special exhibitions open Tues.–Sun. 10–4.*

A little farther, turn right onto Esplanaden and you'll come to ⑳ **Frihedsmuseet** (Liberty Museum), situated in Churchill Parken. It gives an evocative picture of the heroic Danish Resistance movement during World War II, which managed to save 7,000 Jews from the Nazis by hiding them in homes and hospitals, then smuggling them across to Sweden. *Esplanaden, tel. 33/13–77–14. Admission free. Open Sept. 16– April, Tues.–Sat. 11–3, Sun. 11–4; May–Sept. 15, Tues.–Sat. 10–4, Sun. 10–5.*

At the park's entrance stands the English church, St. Alban's, ㉑ and, in the center, the **Kastellet** (Citadel), with two rings of moats. This was the city's main fortress in the 18th century, but, in a grim reversal during World War II, the Germans used it as the headquarters of their occupation of Denmark. *Admission free. Open 6 AM–sunset.*

Continue on to the Langelinie, which on Sunday is thronged ㉒ with promenading Danes, and at last to **The Little Mermaid** (Den Lille Havrue), the 1913 statue commemorating Hans Christian Andersen's lovelorn creation, and the subject of hundreds of travel posters.

Around the Strøget From Langelinie, take the train or bus from Østerport station back to the center. Walk north from the Strøget on Nørregade ㉓ until you reach **Vor Frue Kirke** (The Church of Our Lady), Copenhagen's cathedral since 1924. The site itself has been a place of worship since the 13th century, when Bishop Absalon built a chapel here. The spare neoclassical facade is a 19th-century revamp that repaired the damage incurred during Nelson's famous bombing of the city in 1801. Inside you can see Thorvaldsen's marble sculptures of Christ and the Apostles, and Moses and David in bronze. *Nørregade, Frue Plads, tel. 33/15-10-78. Open Mon.-Sat. 9-5, Sun. noon-5. Closed during mass.*

㉔ Head north up Fjolstraede until you come to the main **university** building, built in the 19th century on the site of the medieval bishops' palace. Past the university, turn right onto
㉕ Krystalgade. On the left is the **synagogue,** designed by the famous contemporary architect Gustav Friedrich Hetsch. Hetsch drew on the Doric and Egyptian styles to create the arklike structure.

㉖ Just across Købmagergade is the **Runde Tårn,** a round tower built as an observatory in 1642 by Christian IV. It is said that Peter the Great of Russia drove a horse and carriage up the 600 feet of the inner staircase. You'll have to walk, but the view is worth it. *Købmagergade, tel. 33/93-66-60. Admission: 12 kr. adults, 5 kr. children. Open Dec.-May and Sept.-Oct., daily 10-5; June-Aug. 10-8.*

Turn right at Runde Tårn onto Landemærket, then left onto Åbenrå. If your appetite for museums is not yet sated, turn right out of Åbenrå until you reach Gothersgade, where anoth-
㉗ er right, onto Øster Voldgade, will bring you to **Rosenborg Slot.** This Renaissance castle—built by Renaissance man Christian IV—houses the Crown Jewels, as well as a collection of costumes and royal memorabilia. Don't miss Christian IV's pearl-studded saddle. *Øster Voldgade 4A, tel. 33/15-32-86. Admission: 30 kr. adults, 5 kr. children. Open Apr.-May, daily 11-3; June-Aug. daily 10-4; Sept.-Oct. daily 11-3; Nov.-Mar., Tues., Fri., and Sun. 11-3.*

The palace is surrounded by gardens, and just across Øster
㉘ Voldgade is **Botansk Have,** Copenhagen's 25 acres of botanical gardens, with a rather spectacular Palm House containing tropical and subtropical plants. There's also an observatory and a geological museum. *Admission free. Open May-Aug., daily 8:30-6; Sept.-Apr., daily 8:30-4. Palm House open daily 10-3.*

㉙ Leave the gardens through the north exit to get to the **Statens Museum for Kunst** (National Art Gallery), where the official doorman greets you wearing a uniform with buckled shoes and a cocked hat. The collection ranges from modern Danish art to works by Rubens, Dürer, and the Impressionists. Particularly fine are the museum's 20 Matisses. *Sølvgade 48-50, tel. 33/91-21-26. Admission: 20 kr. adults, children under 16 free. Open Tues.-Sun. 10-4:30.*

㉚ A nearby building houses the **Hirschprung Collection** of 19th-century Danish art. The cozy museum features works from the Golden Age, in particular those by a group of late-19th-century painters called the Skagen school. *Stockholmsgade 20, tel. 31/42-03-36. Admission: 20 kr. adults, 10 kr. students and senior citizens, children under 16 free. Open Wed.-Sat. 1-4, Sun. 11-4.*

From Stockholmsgade, turn right onto Sølvgade and then left onto Øster Søgade, just before the bridge. Continue along the canal (the street name will change from Øster Søgade to Nørre Søgade to Vester Søgade) until you reach the head of the harbor. Walk straight ahead and turn left onto Vesterbrogade.

31 On the right lies Copenhagen's best-known attraction, **Tivoli.** In the 1840s, the Danish architect Georg Carstensen persuaded King Christian VIII that an amusement park was the perfect opiate of the masses, preaching that "when people amuse themselves, they forget politics." In the comparatively short season, from May to September, about 4 million people come through the gates. Tivoli is more sophisticated than a mere funfair: It boasts a pantomime theater and open-air stage; elegant restaurants; and numerous classical, jazz, and rock concerts. On weekends there are elaborate fireworks displays and maneuvers by the Tivoli Guard, a youth version of the Queen's Royal Guard. Try to see Tivoli at least once by night, when the trees are illuminated along with the Chinese Pagoda and the main fountain. *Admission: 31 kr. adults, 20 kr. children. Open Apr. 24–Sept. 15, daily 10 AM–midnight.*

32 At the southern end of the gardens, on Hans Christian Andersens Boulevard, is the **Ny Carlsberg Glyptotek** (New Carlsberg Picture Hall). This elaborate neoclassical building houses a collection of works by Gauguin and Degas and other Impressionists, as well as Egyptian, Greek, Roman, and French sculpture. *Dantes Plads 7, tel. 33/91–10–65. Admission: 15 kr. adults, children free; adults free on Wed. and Sun. Open Sept.–Apr., Tues.–Sat. noon–3, Sun. 10–4; May–Aug., Tues.–Sun. 10–4.*

33 Tucked between St. Jorgens Lake and the main arteries of Vesterbrogade and Gammel Kongevej is the new **Tycho Brahe Planetarium.** The modern cylindrical building is filled with astronomy exhibitions and an Omnimax Theater, which takes visitors on a visual journey up through space and down under the seas. *Gammel Kongevej 10, tel. 33/12–12–24. Admission: 60 kr. for exhibition and theater, noon–5; 50 kr. for exhibition and theater, 6–10 PM; exhibition only, 10 kr. Reservations advised for theater. (According to planetarium officials, the movie is not suitable for children under 7.) Open daily 10:30–9.*

Excursions from Copenhagen

Helsingør– Kronborg Castle Shakespeare immortalized the town and castle when he chose **Kronborg Castle** as the setting for *Hamlet.* Dating from 1582, the gabled and turreted structure is about 600 years younger than the fortress we imagine from the setting of Shakespeare's tragedy. Well worth seeing is the 200-foot-long dining hall, the luxurious chapel, and the royal chambers. The ramparts and 12-foot walls are a reminder of the castle's role as coastal bulwark—Sweden is only a few miles away. The town of **Helsingør**—about 29 miles north of Copenhagen—has a number of picturesque streets with 16th-century houses. There is frequent train service to Helsingør station. *Helsingør, tel. 49/21–30–78. Admission: 16 kr. adults, 8 kr. children. Open May–Sept., daily 10:30–5; Oct. and Apr., Tues.–Sat. 11–4; Nov.–Mar., Tues.–Sun. 11–3.*

Louisiana A world-class modern art collection is housed in a spectacular building on the "Danish Riviera," the North Zealand coast. Even those who can't tell a Rauschenberg from a Rembrandt should make the 35-kilometer (22-mile) trip to see the setting:

It's an elegant, rambling structure set in a large park. In the permanent collection, Warhols vie for space with Giacomettis and Picassos. There are temporary exhibits, as well as concerts and films. In the summer, Danes bring their children and picnic in the sculpture garden. There's also a cafeteria, where you get a great view of the Calder mobile, the sound, and, on a clear day, Sweden.

Louisiana is well worth the half-hour train ride from Copenhagen to Humlebæk. The museum is a 10-minute walk from the station. *Gammel Strandvej 13, Humlebæk, tel. 42/19–07–19. Admission: 40 kr. adults, children free. Open Mon., Tues., and Thurs.–Sun. 10–5, Wed. 10–10.*

Roskilde History enthusiasts should take advantage of the frequent train service from Copenhagen to the bustling market town of **Roskilde,** 30 kilometers (19 miles) west of the city. A key administrative center during Viking times, it remained one of the largest towns in northern Europe through the Middle Ages. Its population has dwindled, but the legacy of its 1,000-year history lives on in the spectacular cathedral. Built on the site of Denmark's first church, the **Domkirke** (cathedral) has been the burial place of Danish royalty since the 15th century. Inside, four chapels house 38 kings and queens. Strewn with marble tombs, the interior has the feeling of a stately but surreal warehouse. The outside, which has received numerous additions over the centuries, provides a crash course in Danish architecture through the ages: The latest chapel dates from 1985. *Domkirkeplasden, Roskilde. Admission: 3 kr. adults, 1 kr. children. Open Apr.–Sept., weekdays 9–5:45, Sat. 11:30–5:45, Sun. 12:30–5:45; Oct.–Mar., weekdays 10–3:45, Sat. 11:30–3:45, Sun. 12:30–3:45.*

A 10-minute walk south and through the park takes you to the water and to the **Viking Ship Museum.** Inside are five Viking ships, discovered at the bottom of the Roskilde Fjord in 1962. Detailed placards in English chronicle Viking history. There are also English-language films on the excavation and reconstruction. *Strandengen, Roskilde, tel. 42/35–65–55. Admission: 20 kr. adults, 14 kr. children. Open Apr.–Oct., daily 9–5; Nov.–Mar., daily 10–4.*

Rungstedlund About halfway between Copenhagen and Helsingør is **Rungstedlund,** the former manor of Karen Blixen. The author of *Out of Africa* and several accounts of aristocratic Danish life, Blixen wrote under the pen name Isak Dinesen. The manor, where she lived as a child and to which she returned in 1931, recently opened as a museum, and includes manuscripts, as well as photographs and memorabilia documenting her years in Africa and Denmark. The estate is a half-hour train ride from Copenhagen, followed by a 10-minute walk from Rungsted station. *Rungsted Strandvej III, Rungsted Kyst, tel. 42/57–10–57. Admission: 30 kr. adults, children free. Open May–Sept., daily 10–5; Oct.–Apr., weekdays and Sun. 1–4.*

Shopping

Gift Ideas While Copenhagen is a mecca for shoppers in search of impeccable designs and top-notch quality, budget shoppers may find bargains elusive. Several ideas for inexpensive gifts include simple table decorations—a porcelain candle holder or ashtray or the long-lasting candles, often handmade, for which Scandinavia is famous. Denmark also produces tasteful reproductions of Viking ornaments and jewelry, in bronze as well as silver and gold.

Specialty Shops Synonymous with shopping are Strøget's pedestrian streets. For glass, try **Holmegaard** at Østergade. Just off the street is Pistolstræde, a typical old courtyard that's been lovingly restored and filled with intriguing boutiques. **PosterLand** is the home of one of the largest collections of art prints and posters in northern Europe. There are such specialists as **Royal Copenhagen Porcelain,** which has a small museum attached, as does **Georg Jensen,** one of Denmark's most famous silversmiths.

Off the eastern end of Strøget on Ny Østergade, the **Pewter Center** has a large pewterware collection, and on Gammel Strand there's another pewter designer, **Selangor Designer,** founded in 1885. Back along Strøget, **Birger Christensen** will offer you a glass of sherry while you look at the furs, unless you decide to take your patronage to their competition, **A. C. Bang.** **FONA** is the place to buy Bang and Olufsen stereo systems, so renowned that they are in the permanent design collection of New York's Museum of Modern Art.

Dining

Food remains one of the great pleasures of a stay in Copenhagen, a city with over 2,000 restaurants. Traditional Danish fare spans all the price categories: You can order a light lunch of the traditional *smørrebrød*, snack from a *store kolde bord* (cold buffet), or dine out on lobster and Limfjord oysters. Those who are strapped for cash can enjoy fast food Danish style, in the form of *pølser* (hot dogs) sold from trucks on the street. Team any of this with some pastry from a bakery (look for them under the sign of the upside-down gold pretzel), and you've got yourself a meal on the go.

For details and price-category definitions, *see* Dining in Staying in Denmark.

Moderate **Café Restaurant Philippe.** Brooding youths backed by corny
★ French music and love-struck couples pitching woo across checkered tablecloths supply this cozy restaurant with savoir faire. The Franco-Danish kitchen serves hearty salads, fresh fish, and meat dishes—among the choices are warm goat cheese salad, homemade pasta with mussel sauce, entrecôte Parisienne in mustard sauce, and duck stuffed with truffles in cognac sauce. *Gråbrødretory 2, tel. 33/32–92–92. Reservations advised. AE, DC, MC, V. Closed Sun. lunch, Dec. 23–Jan. 1.*
★ **Copenhagen Corner.** Diners get a great view of the Rådhus Pladsen here, and terrific smørrebrød besides. Plants hang from the ceiling; waiters hustle platters of herring, steak, and other Danish/French dishes; and businessmen clink glasses. In summer you can eat outside. *Rådhus Pladsen, tel. 33/91–45–45. Reservations advised. AE, DC, MC, V. Closed Dec. 24.*
Havfruen. A life-size wooden mermaid swings langorously from the ceiling in this snug fish restaurant in Nyhavn. Copenhagen natives love the maritime-bistro ambience and the French-inspired fish specialties. *Nyhavn 39, tel. 33/11–11–38. Reservations advised. DC, MC, V. Closed Sun.*
★ **Ida Davidsen.** A Copenhagen institution, this world-renowned lunch place has become synonymous with smørrebrød. A buffet displays heartbreakingly beautiful sandwiches, piled high

with caviar, salmon, smoked duck, and other elegant ingredients. *Skt. Kongensgade 70, tel. 33/91–36–55. Reservations advised. DC, MC, V. Lunch only. Closed weekends and July.*

Peder Oxe. Located in an 18th-century square in the old center of town, the Peder Oxe is classically elegant, with whitewashed walls, wooden floors, an open fireplace, and crisp damask tablecloths. It's usually crowded with diners from every walk of life. All main courses include a self-service salad bar. *Gråbrødertorv 11, tel. 33/11–00–77. Reservations accepted. DC, MC, V.*

Inexpensive **Café Asbæk.** Attached to a modern art gallery, this little establishment makes creative use of fresh ingredients. The menu changes every day, while the art on the walls changes with every new exhibition. Try the desserts, made on the premises. *Ny Adelgade 8, tel. 33/12–24–16. Reservations accepted. AE, DC, MC, V.*

Flyvefiske. Silvery stenciled fish swim along blue and yellow walls in this bright and airy vegetarian restaurant. More experimental than Green's (*see below*), the changing daily menu includes salads, nuts, legumes, and fish. Frequent specialties include an apple and beet salad with nuts, giant capers, and mustard dressing, and salmon with shiitake mushrooms, fresh herbs, and fish sauce. There's also a baked marzipan–apple cake served with fresh fruit. The downstairs café, which offers modified plates from the same menu, falls under the budget category. *Lars Bjørnstræde, tel. 33/14–95–15. Reservations not required. No credit cards. Closed Sat. dinner, Sun., and holidays.*

Four Seasons. The name is an unlikely one for the Mexican restaurant, but owner-waiter-host-clothing designer Suael Sundoo enjoys making opposites attract. In his tiny, basement restaurant, Mexican dishes like huevos rancheros and beef-stuffed tortillas are tempered for mild Danish tastes—but you can always ask for the hot sauce. *Valkendorfsgade 36, tel. 33/32–80–32. Reservations recommended on weekends. AE, DC, MC, V. Closed Sun., Dec. 24–Jan. 1.*

Green's. A vegetarian buffet by day and a restaurant by night, Green's serves healthy food with much emphasis on grains, natural sweeteners, and fresh fruit and vegetables. It's frequented by chic bohemians who welcome the classical music and friendly service of the youthful staff. *Grønnegade 12–14, tel. 33/15–16–90. Reservations accepted. MC, V. Closed Sun.*

Kasmir. This quiet, carpeted restaurant is a favorite with locals, who come for the unusual vegetarian and fish menu. Specialties include tandoori salmon, spicy red dahl, a hearty lentil soup, and basic side dishes like *bhajis* (fried vegetables in tomato sauce), *raita* (yogurt and cucumbers), and *nan* (thick flat rounds of bread). *Nørrebrogade 35, tel. 35/37–54–71. Reservations recommended on the weekends. AE, MC, V. Closed Dec. 24 and 25.*

Krasnapolsky. It's near the university, and there's a brooding youth at every table. The food is light and inventive—market-fresh produce is used religiously. Not as healthy as the quiches and sandwiches, but equally delicious, are the cakes and tarts, made in-house. *Vestergade 10, tel. 33/32–88–00. Reservations accepted. No credit cards.*

Budget **Cafe Smukke Marie.** This subterranean café beneath a movie theater has bright red and green frescoed walls decorated with stenciled curlicues. The funky atmosphere and generous por-

tions attract students and young couples, who drape themselves over marble tables to munch on hot pastrami and swiss
sandwiches, as well as hot meat-and-potato plates. *Knabro-
stræde 19, tel. 33/15-95-66. No reservations. No credit cards.*

Quatro Fontane. Chatty Italian waiters and a very affordable
menu make one of Copenhagen's best Italian restaurants a
boisterous affair, packed tight with locals and students. The
list of homemade pastas includes cheese or beef ravioli or
cannelloni, and linguine topped with a variety of sauces. The
pizza is excellent, the ice cream shameless—and both are also
available from the carryout in Frederiksberg. (Falkonér Allé,
tel. 38/39-49-82). *Guldbergsgade 3, tel. 31/39-39-31. Reservations recommended, especially on weekends. No credit cards.*

Riz Raz. Located on a corner off Strøget, this Middle Eastern
restaurant is a favorite with locals, who pack it to bursting on
weekends. The all-you-can-eat buffet is heaped with lentils, tomatoes, potatoes, olives, humus, warm pita bread, *kufte* (Middle Eastern meatballs), yogurt and cucumbers, pickled
vegetables, bean salads, and occasionally even pizza.
*Kompagnistræde 20, tel. 33/15-05-75. Reservations recom-
mended, essential on weekends. DC, MC, V. Closed Dec. 24-
25, Jan. 1.*

Lodging

Copenhagen is well served by a wide range of hotels, and you
can expect your accommodations to be clean, comfortable, and
well run. Most Danish hotels include a substantial breakfast in
the room rate, but this isn't always the case with foreign
chains: Inquire when making reservations. During summer
reservations are always recommended, but if you should arrive
without one, try the booking service at the *Vaerelseavivisning
kiosk* (Rooms Service booth) in the central station. This service
will also locate rooms in private homes, with rates starting at
about 140 kr. for a single. Young travelers should head for "Use
It" (Huset) at Rådhusstræde 13 (tel. 33/15-65-18); after hours,
they can check the bulletin board outside for suggestions for accommodations.

For details and price-category definitions, *see* Lodging in Staying in Denmark.

Moderate **Ascot.** A charming old building in the city's downtown area, the
Ascot features an elegant wrought-iron staircase and an excellent breakfast buffet. The rooms have colorful geometric-pat-
terned bedspreads and cozy bathrooms. Many have been
recently remodeled; a few have kitchenettes. *Studiestræde 57,
tel. 33/12-60-00. 105 rooms, 10 apartments, all with bath. Facilities: restaurant (breakfast only), bar. AE, DC, MC, V.*

Copenhagen Admiral. A converted 18th-century granary, the
Admiral has a massive and imposing exterior. Inside, sturdy
wooden beams harmonize with an ultramodern decor. A few
duplex suites are in the Expensive category. *Toldbrogade 24-
28, tel. 33/11-82-82. 366 rooms with bath. Facilities: restaurant, bar, café, shop, sauna. AE, MC, V.*

Excelsior. Housed in a circa-1890 building, this hotel was renovated in 1989. The bedrooms are done in bold blue and white,
with modern murals on the walls. The tranquil deck-garden in
the back is lovely. *Colbjørnsgade 4, tel. 31/24-50-85. 59 rooms,
42 with bath. Facilities: restaurant (breakfast only), bar. AE,
DC, MC, V. Closed two weeks at Christmas.*

Mayfair. Like its neighbors, the Webers and the Triton, this hotel is located near Copenhagen's half-hearted red-light district and busy, shop-lined Vesterbrogade. Guests are greeted by an austere, English-style lobby where they can sip complimentary coffee before heading to rooms decorated with dark wood furniture and gold-toned upholstery. *Helgolandsgade 3, 1653 KBH V, tel. 31/31–48–01. 102 rooms with bath, 4 suites. Facilities: bar, meeting room, breakfast. AE, DC, MC, V.*

Sophie Amalie Hotel. While the no-frills philosophy is the same, this is a less severe version of its sister hotel, the Copenhagen Admiral. The pretty, pink lobby has a fountain and bar, and the cozy, pastel-toned rooms overlook the harbor, Amalienborg Palace, or the modest town skyline. *Skt. Annæ Plads 21, 1250 KBH K, 33/13–34–00. 134 rooms with bath, 17 suites. Facilities: restaurant, bar, meeting rooms, parking, sauna, solarium, breakfast. AE, CB, MC, V.*

Triton. Streamlined and modern, the Triton has a cosmopolitan clientele and a central location. The large rooms, in blond wood and warm tones, are equipped with every modern convenience, and many of the bathrooms have been recently updated. The buffet breakfast is exceptionally generous. *Helgolandsgade 7–11, tel. 31/31–32–66. 123 rooms with bath. Facilities: restaurant (breakfast only), bar. AE, DC, MC, V.*

Webers Hotel. This recently renovated hotel offers downtown style and conveniences, like classical decor and a small gym, in the working-glass neighborhood of Vesterbro. Crystal chandeliers flash in the lobby, while guest rooms are bright and new, with zippy geometric upholstery and posters. *Vesterbrogade 11B, 1620 KBH V, tel. 31/31–14–32. 100 rooms with bath. Facilities: bar, meeting rooms, gym, sauna, solarium, patio with garden, breakfast. AE, DC, MC, V.*

Inexpensive **Missionhotellet Nebo.** This hotel is comfortable and even prim, despite the dubious location, between the main train station and Istedgade's seediest porn shops. Well-maintained by a friendly staff, the dormlike guest rooms are furnished with industrial carpeting, polished pine furniture, and striped gray duvet covers. Baths and toilets are in the hallway; downstairs there's a breakfast restaurant with a tiny courtyard. *Istedgade 6, 1653 KBH V, tel. 31/21–12–17. Facilities: breakfast.*

Skovshoved. A charming hotel about 8 kilometers (5 miles) from the center of town, the Skovshoved has as neighbors a few old fishing cottages beside the yacht harbor. Licensed since 1660, it has retained its Old World charm, though it is fully modernized. Individual rooms vary from spacious ones overlooking the sea to smaller rooms overlooking the courtyard. The restaurant provides gourmet dishes but ranks in the Expensive category. *Strandvejen 267, Charlottenlund, tel. 31/64–00–28. 20 rooms with bath. Facilities: conference room. AE, DC, MC, V.*

Verstersøhus. What this hotel lacks in charm, it makes up for in location: It's across the street from swan-filled lakes and just a 10-minute walk to Strøget. Rooms are simple, with '60s-style furniture, but they're also convenient, especially for budget-minded families who want an apartment with a kitchenette. *Vestersøgade 58, 1601 KBH V, tel. 31/11–38–70. 44 rooms, 35 with shower, 15 with kitchenette. Facilities: breakfast. AE, DC, MC, V. Closed Dec. 24–Jan. 2.*

Viking. A comfortable, century-old former mansion close to Amalienborg Castle, Nyhavn, and the Little Mermaid, the Viking is convenient to most sights and public transportation. The rooms are surprisingly spacious. *Bredgade 65, tel. 33/12–45–50. 90 rooms, 19 with bath. Facilities: restaurant (breakfast only). AE, DC, MC, V.*

Budget **Missionshotelet Ansgar.** The neighborhood, Copenhagen's red-light district, is nothing to write home about, but accommodations are clean, albeit worn in this hotel, which was under renovation at press time (summer 1992). The location may be, er, colorful, but it is convenient—around the corner from the main train station and a 10-minute walk to Tivoli. *Colbjørnsesgade 29, 1653 KBH V, tel. 31/21–21–96. 86 rooms, 68 with shower. Facilities: breakfast. AE, DC, MC, V. Closed Dec. 24–Jan. 2.*

The Arts

Copenhagen This Week has good information on musical and theatrical events, as well as on films and exhibitions. Concert and festival information is available from the **Dansk Musik Information Center (DMIC,** Vimmelskaftet 48, tel. 33/11–20–66). Copenhagen's main theater and concert season runs from September through May, and tickets can be obtained either directly from theaters and concert halls or from ticket agencies; ask your hotel concierge for advice.

Music **Tivoli Concert Hall** (Vesterbrogade 3, tel. 33/15–10–12), home of the Zealand Symphony Orchestra, offers more than 150 concerts (many free of charge) each summer, featuring a host of Danish and foreign soloists, conductors, and orchestras.

Theater, Opera, The **Royal Theater** (Kongens Nytorv, tel. 33/14–10–02) regu-
and Ballet larly holds performances alternating among theater, ballet, and opera. For English-language theater, attend a performance at the **Mermaid Theater** (27 Skt. Peder Stræde, tel. 33/11–43–03).

Film Copenhagen natives are avid movie buffs, and since the Danes rarely dub films or television imports, you can often see original American and British movies and TV shows.

Nightlife

Many of the city's restaurants, cafés, bars, and clubs stay open after midnight, some as late as 5 AM. Copenhagen is famous for jazz, but you'll find night spots catering to musical tastes ranging from bop to ballroom music. Younger tourists should make for the **Minefield,** the district around the Nikolaj Kirke, which has scores of trendy discos and dance spots, with admission only the price of a beer. **Privé** (Ny Østergade 14) and **U-Matic** (Vestergade 10) are particularly popular with the young set.

A few streets behind the railway station is Copenhagen's red-light district, where sex shops share space with Indian grocers. While the area is fairly well lighted and lively, women may feel uncomfortable going there alone at night.

Nightclubs Some of the most exclusive nightclubs are in the biggest hotels: **Fellini's** in the SAS Royal (Hammerichsgade 1, tel. 33/14–14–12), **After Eight** at SAS Scandinavia (Amager Blvd. 70, tel. 33/11–23–24), and the **Penthouse** at the Sheraton (Vester Søgade 6, tel. 33/14–35–35).

Jazz Copenhagen has a worldwide reputation for sophisticated jazz clubs. These are a few of the best: **De Tre Musketerer** (Nikolaj Plads 25); **Jazzhus Monmartre** (Nørregade 41), widely held to be one of the best on the Continent; **Jazzhus Slukefter** (Tivoli); **La Fontaine** (Kompagnistræde 11); and **Kridhuset** (Nørregade 1).

Odense

It was Hans Christian Andersen, the region's most famous native, who dubbed Funen "The Garden of Denmark." Part orchard, part farmland, Funen is sandwiched between Zealand and Jutland, and with its tidy, rolling landscape, seaside towns, manor houses, and castles, it is one of Denmark's loveliest islands.

Its capital is 1,003-year-old Odense in the north, one of Denmark's best-known cities and the birthplace of Hans Christian Andersen. It has two museums detailing his life and works.

Getting Around

Frequent trains run between Copenhagen and Odense; the trip takes between two and three hours. Once you arrive, you'll want to explore by foot. Most of the sights are in the old heart of town, within a mile radius. For those sights a bit out of the way, like the open-air Funen Village, there is local bus and, where appropriate, boat service.

Tourist Information

The tourist office at **Odense** (Rådhuset, tel. 66/12–75–20) can provide information about the **Odense Eventyr Pass** (Adventure Pass), which provides admission to most museums and sights, free bus transportation, and discounts for city tours and plays. The two-day pass costs 70 kr. for adults and 35 kr. for children under 14.

Exploring Odense

Plan on spending at least one night here in Denmark's third-largest city: in addition to its museums and pleasant pedestrian streets, Odense gives one a good feel for a provincial capital.

If you can't take quaintness, don't go to the **H. C. Andersens Hus** (Hans Christian Andersen Museum). The surrounding area has been carefully preserved, with cobbled pedestrian streets and low houses with lace curtains. Inside, the detailed exhibits use photos, diaries, drawings, and letters to convey a sense of the man and the time in which he lived. Among the most evocative rooms is one furnished exactly like his Copenhagen study; notice the immense size of his long, narrow boots, casually tossed into a corner. Attached to the museum is an extensive library with Andersen's works in more than 100 languages, where you can listen to fairy tales on tape. *Hans Jensenstræde 37–45, tel. 66/13–13–72. Admission: 20 kr. adults, 10 kr. children under 14. Open Apr., May, and Sept., daily 10–5; June–Aug., daily 9–6; Oct.–Mar., daily 10–3.*

Nearby is the **Carl Nielsen Museum**, a modern structure with multimedia exhibits on Denmark's most famous composer

(1865–1931) and his wife, the sculptress Anne Marie Carl-Nielsen. *Claus BergsGade 11, tel. 66/13–13–72, ext. 4670. Admission: 10 kr. adults, 2 kr. children. Open daily 10–4.*

Montegården, Odense's museum of cultural and urban history fills four houses built from the Renaissance to the 18th century, all grouped around a shady cobbled courtyard. The innovative exhibits inside feature dioramas, an extensive coin collection, clothed dummies, and tableaux. *Overgade 48–50. Admission: 5 kr. adults, 1 kr. children. Open daily 10–4.*

Brandt's Passage, off Vestergade, is a heavily boutiqued walking street. At the end of it, in what was once a textile factory, is a four-story art gallery, the Brandts Klædefabrik, incorporating the **Museum for Photographic Art,** the **Graphic Museum,** and other spaces, with temporary exhibits for video art. It's well worth the short walk to see Funen's version of a Soho loft. *37–43 Brandts Passage, tel. 66/13–78–97. Admission: 20 kr. to each museum; 30 kr. for entrance to both. Open Tues.–Sun. 10–5.*

Don't neglect **Den Fynske Landsby** (Funen Village), 3 kilometers (2 miles) south; an enjoyable way of getting there is to travel down the Odense River by boat. The open-air museum-village is made up of 20 farm buildings, including workshops, a vicarage, a water mill, and a windmill. There's a theater, too, which in summer stages adaptations of Andersen's tales. *Sejerskovvej 20, tel. 66/13–13–72. Admission: 10 kr. adults, 2 kr. children. Open Apr.–May and Sept.–Oct., daily 9–4; June–Aug., daily 9–6:30; Nov.–Mar., Sun. and holidays only, 10–4.*

Odense's newest attraction is **Hollufgård,** a multipurpose cultural center, originally built in the 16th century as a private manor. Today, it includes a Bronze- and Viking-Age village, nature trails, Denmark's only 27-hole golf course, and a sculpture workshop. To reach Hollufgård, take Bus 26 or 62 south from the town center. *Kulturcenter Hollufgård, Hestehaven 201, tel. 66/13–13–72, ext. 4638. Admission: 15 kr. adults, 5 kr. children. Green fees vary. Open May–mid-Oct., Tues.–Sun. 10–5; mid-Oct.–Apr., Sun. 11–4.*

Dining and Lodging

Odense boasts a wide range of hotels and inns, many of which offer off-season (October through May) rates, as well as special weekend deals. The city is also endowed with campsites and a youth hostel set in an old manor house. The Tourism Board has also designed a "Meet the Danes" program, where visitors stay overnight with a family that roughly corresponds in age and interests. For details and price-category definitions, *see* Dining and Lodging in Staying in Denmark.

Dining **Frank A.** Guarded by a meter-tall wooden bulldog named
★ Tobias, this merry meeting place is dominated by its display of high kitsch curios and paintings, and an unfathomable collection of bric-a-brac. Friendly waiters serve drinks and French-inspired Danish dishes like ham schnitzel with creamed potatoes and pepper steak flambé to a mostly local crowd. *Jernbanegade 4, tel. 66/12–27–57. Reservations accepted. DC, MC, V. Moderate.*

★ **Spisehuset.** Frescoed walls and French posters add polish to this country-style restaurant. The menu changes daily, and may include French-Danish offerings like warm salad with veal sweetbreads and medallions of beef with a port wine sauce. *Pogstræde 31, tel. 65/91-55-31. Reservations advised. AE, DC, MC, V. Moderate.*

Air Pub. This friendly, airplane-theme bar and restaurant is one of Odense's most popular meeting places. Because it's also located on one of the pedestrian streets, it's the perfect lunch spot for a quick sandwich and beer. *Kongensgade 41, tel. 66/14-66-08. No reservations. No credit cards. Inexpensive.*

Den Grimme Ælling. The name of this restaurant, translated as the Ugly Duckling, really isn't appropriate here. The family-style interiors are homey, with pine furnishings. Thanks to an all-you-can-eat buffet heaped with cold and warm dishes, it's very popular with locals and visitors. *Hans Jensens Stræde 1, tel. 65/91-70-30. Reservations recommended. DC, MC. Inexpensive.*

Målet. A spirited local clientele frequents this sports club and restaurant filled with soccer memorabilia. Schnitzels are the specialty, prepared with mushrooms, paprika, or even Italian and Madagascar style. *Jernbanegade 17, tel. 66/17-82-41. No reservations. No credit cards. Budget.*

Lodging **Missionshotellet Ansgar.** The rooms are a trifle boxlike but clean and comfortable nonetheless. This hotel offers solid lodgings (with satellite television) near the station. *Østre Stationsvej 32, tel. 66/11-96-93. 44 rooms with bath. MC, V. Moderate.*

Ydes Hotel. This no-frills hotel near the train station and pedestrian streets has white, unadorned rooms furnished with functional desks and brown–velour-topped twin beds. Downstairs, there's a small breakfast restaurant and bar. *Hans Tausensgade 11, 5000 Odense C, tel. 66/12-11-31. 28 rooms, 22 with shower. Facilities: breakfast. Inexpensive.*

Hotel Kahema. Buzzing with students, backpackers, and budget-minded travelers, this centrally located hotel trades charm for cheap simplicity. The rooms are ascetic dorms, with metal twin beds and hand-me-down spreads and furniture—but they are spotless. *Dronningsgade 5, 5000 Odense C, tel. 66/12-28-21. 14 rooms, none with shower. Facilities: communal kitchen for light cooking. Budget.*

7   Finland

Prices in Finland have dropped with respect to the other Nordic countries. A devaluation of the Finnmark in fall 1991 made the country more accessible to budget travelers. Even if Finland is the cheapest Nordic country, it is still expensive by Continental European standards. But don't let the high price levels get you down! If you look and search carefully, you can find good bargains in Finland.

If you like majestic open spaces, fine architecture, and civilized living, then Finland is for you. It is a land of lakes, 187,888 at the last count, and forests. It is a land where nature is so prized that even the design of city buildings reflects the soaring spaces of the countryside.

The music of Sibelius, Finland's most famous son, tells you what to expect from this Nordic landscape. Both can swing from the somber nocturne of midwinter darkness to the tremolo of sunlight slanting through pine and bone-white birch or from the crescendo of a sunset before it fades into the next day's dawn. Similarly, the Finnish people reflect the changing moods of their land and climate. They can get annoyed when described as "children of nature," but the description is apt. Their affinity with nature has produced some of the world's greatest designers and architects. Many American cities have buildings designed by Alvar Aalto and the Saarinens, Eliel and son Eero. In fact, Eliel and his family moved to the United States in 1923 and became American citizens—but it was to a lonely Finnish seashore that Saarinen had his ashes returned.

Until 1917, Finland (the Finns call it *Suomi)* was under the domination of its nearest neighbors, Sweden and Russia, who fought over it for centuries. After more than 600 years under Swedish rule and 100 under the czars, the country inevitably

Finland

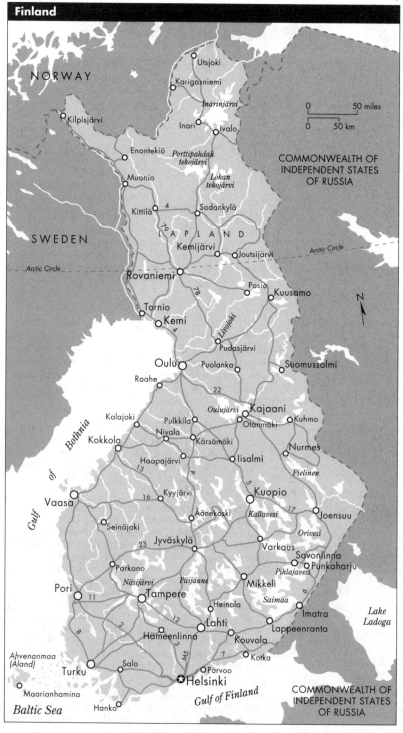

NORWAY

Utsjoki

Karigasniemi

Inarinjärvi

Kilpisjärvi

Inari
Ivalo

Enontekiö

Porttipahdan tekojärvi

Muonio

Lokan tekojärvi

Kittilä   4
Sodankylä

SWEDEN

L A P L A N D

7-9

Kemijärvi

Joutsijärvi

Arctic Circle

Rovaniemi

Arctic Circle

Posio

Kuusamo

Tornio

78

Kemi

N

Iijoki

Pudasjärvi

Oulu

Puolanka

Suomussalmi

Raahe

22

Kalajoki

Oulujärvi
Kajaani

Kokkola

Pulkkila

Otanmäki
Kuhmo

Nivala

Kärsämäki

Nurmes

Haapajärvi

Iisalmi

13

4

Pielinen

Kyyjärvi

5

Kuopio

16

Kallavesi

17

Vaasa

Äänekoski

Joensuu

Seinäjoki

Orivesi

23
Jyväskylä

Varkaus

Savonlinna

Bothnia

Parkano

Pihlajavesi
Punkaharju

Näsijärvi

Päijänne

Mikkeli

Pori

11

Tampere

Saimaa

of

8

Heinola

2

12

Imatra

Lahti

Gulf

Lappeenranta

Lake Ladoga

Hämeenlinna

3

Kouvola

Ahvenanmaa
(Åland)

Salo

M5

7

Kotka

Turku

Porvoo

Maarianhamina

★ Helsinki

Baltic Sea

Hanko

Gulf of Finland

COMMONWEALTH OF
INDEPENDENT STATES
OF RUSSIA

COMMONWEALTH OF
INDEPENDENT STATES
OF RUSSIA

0   50 miles
0   50 km

bears many traces of these two cultures, including a small (6%) but influential Swedish-speaking population and a scattering of Russian Orthodox churches.

But the Finns themselves are neither Scandinavian nor Slavic. All that is known of their origins—they speak a Finno-Ugric tongue, part Finnish, part Hungarian—is that they are descended from wandering groups of people who probably came from west of the Ural Mountains before the Christian era and settled on the swampy shores of the Gulf of Finland.

There is a tough, resilient quality in the Finns. No other people fought the Soviets to a standstill as the Finns did in the Winter War of 1939–40. This resilience, in part, stems from the turbulence of the country's past, but also comes from the people's strength and determination to work the land and survive the long winters. No wonder there is a poet-philosopher lurking in most Finns, one who sometimes drowns his melancholic, darker side in the bottle. For the Finn is in a state of constant confrontation—with the weather, the land, and most recently a huge eastern neighbor that is engulfed in political and economic turmoil. The Finn is stubborn, patriotic, and self-sufficient, yet he is not aggressively nationalistic. On the contrary, rather than being proud of past battles, the Finn is proud of finding ways to live in peace. His country's neutrality and his own personal freedom are what he tenaciously holds on to and will never easily relinquish.

The average Finn doesn't volunteer much information, but that's due to reserve, not indifference. Make the first approach and you may have a friend for life. Finns like their silent spaces, though, and won't appreciate back-slapping familiarity—least of all in the sauna, still regarded by many as a spiritual, as well as a cleansing, experience.

Essential Information

Before You Go

When to Go The tourist summer season runs from mid-June until mid-August, a magnificently sunny and generally dry time marked by unusually warm temperatures in recent years. This is when most Finns move to summer homes, called *kesämökki*, at the seaside or lakefront to enjoy the "white nights," the long nights of the midnight sun. Outside this period, many amenities and attractions either close or operate on much reduced schedules. But there are advantages to visiting Finland off-season, not the least being that you avoid the mosquitoes, which can be fearsome, especially in the north. Also, hotel rates, especially in vacation villages, may drop by 15% to 40%, and the fall colors (from early September in the far north, October in the south) are spectacular. January through March (through April in the north) is the main cross-country skiing season, and in the lengthening spring days you can get a great suntan. Spring is brief but magical, as the snows melt, the ice breaks up, and nature explodes into life almost overnight.

Climate Generally speaking, the spring and summer seasons begin a month earlier in the south of Finland than they do in the far north. You can expect warm (not hot) days in Helsinki from mid-May. The midnight sun can be seen from May to July, depending on the region. In midwinter there is a corresponding period when the sun does not rise at all, but it is possible to see magnificent displays of the Northern Lights. Even in Helsinki, summer nights are brief and never really dark, whereas in midwinter daylight lasts only a few hours.

The following are average daily maximum and minimum temperatures for Helsinki.

Jan.	26F	– 3C	May	56F	13C	Sept.	56F	13C
	17	– 8		44	6		46	8
Feb.	26F	– 3C	June	66F	19C	Oct.	49F	9C
	17	– 8		51	10		39	4
Mar.	34F	1C	July	73F	23C	Nov.	39F	4C
	23	– 5		57	14		30	– 1
Apr.	44F	6C	Aug.	66F	19C	Dec.	32F	0C
	32	0		55	13		21	– 6

Currency The unit of currency in Finland is the Finnmark (FIM), divided into 100 penniä. There are bills of FIM 10, 50, 100, 500, and 1,000. Coins are 10 and 50 penniä, and FIM 1 and FIM 5. At press time (summer 1992), the exchange rate was about FIM 3.87 to the dollar and FIM 7.73 to the pound sterling. Credit cards are widely accepted, even in many taxicabs. Traveler's checks can be changed only in banks.

What It Will Cost The cost of hotels and restaurants in Finland matches the standard of living: Both are high! Expect to pay considerably higher prices on lodging here than in southern Europe, and even more for meals. Prices are highest in Helsinki; otherwise they vary little throughout the country. Taxes are already included in hotel and restaurant charges, and there is no airport departure tax. However, the price of many goods includes an 18% sales tax, less on food (*see* Shopping in Staying in Finland, *below*).

Sample Prices Cup of coffee, FIM 5; glass of beer, FIM 10–FIM 20; Coca-Cola, FIM 7; ham sandwich, FIM 20–FIM 30; 1-mile taxi ride, FIM 30.

Customs on Arrival Europeans age 16 and over entering Finland may bring in 200 cigarettes or 250 grams of other tobacco; visitors from outside Europe may bring in twice as much. All visitors aged 20 or over may also bring in 2 liters of beer, 1 liter of alcohol under 22% volume, and 1 liter over 22% volume; or 2 liters of beer and 2 liters of alcohol under 22%. Visitors aged 18 or over may import 2 liters of beer and 2 liters of alcohol under 22% volume. Goods up to a value of FIM 1,500 may be imported, but be sure to check restrictions on the amount and type of foodstuffs allowed. Dogs and cats may be brought into Finland quarantine-free when they have a veterinarian's certificate stating that they have had an antirabies vaccine at least 30 days and not more than 12 months prior to importation. For those traveling on to Sweden and Norway, however, there is a four-month quarantine.

Language The official languages of Finland are Finnish and Swedish, though only a small minority (about 6%) speak Swedish. English is widely spoken among people in the travel industry and by many younger Finns, though they're often shy about using it. Nearly all tourist sites and attractions provide texts in English.

Getting Around

By Train Finland's extensive rail system reaches all main centers of the country and offers high standards of comfort and cleanliness.

Fares A special **Finnrail Pass** entitles you to unlimited travel for one, two, or three weeks; second-class prices are FIM 470 (one week), FIM 730 (two weeks), and FIM 920 (three weeks); first-class tickets are FIM 705 (one week), FIM 1,095 (two weeks), and FIM 1,380 (three weeks). Children pay half fare. These tickets can be purchased both inside and outside the country. In Finland, the Finnrail Pass is available from the Finnish State Railways (VR). In the United States, they can be purchased by calling 800/677-6454 or from **Holiday Tours of America** (tel. 212/832-8989); in the United Kingdom, from **Finlandia Travel** (tel. 071/409-7333). Other reductions apply to children, groups of three or more, and senior citizens. Reservations are essential on special fast trains.

By Plane **Finnair** (tel. 90/818800) operates an elaborate network of flights linking 21 towns in Finland. For $300, a **Holiday Ticket** guarantees you unlimited travel for 15 days; visitors aged 12–24 can get a **Youth Holiday Ticket** for $250. Other discounts apply to family groups, children, and senior citizens. These tickets are available in most countries, and in Finland they can be purchased at major travel agencies.

By Bus Bus travel plays a leading role in Finland, and the country's bus system provides the most extensive travel network of all; it can take you virtually anywhere. A **Coach Holiday Ticket,** available from bus stations and travel agencies, entitles you to 1,000 kilometers (625 miles) of bus travel for FIM 300 for two weeks. Additional discounts apply to children, family groups, and senior citizens.

By Boat Helsinki and Turku have regular sea links with the Åland Islands in the Baltic Sea. From mid-June to mid-August you can cruise the labyrinthine lakes of the Finnish interior. Try to include at least one of these trips in your itinerary. Complete timetables are available from the Finnish Tourist Board.

By Bicycle Planned bicycle routes are provided in many areas. The main advantages for the cyclist are the lack of steep hills and the absence of heavy traffic. Bikes can be rented in most tourist centers. The Finnish **Youth Hostel Association** (Yrjönkatu 38B, Helsinki, tel. 90/694-0377) offers accommodation packages of four, seven, or 14 days to tie in with visitors' cycling tours.

Staying in Finland

Telephones Hotels charge a substantial fee for all calls. You can avoid this
Local Calls fee by using the pay phones provided in most lobbies. Have some FIM 1 and FIM 5 coins ready. Note that the Finnish letters å, ä, and ö come at the end of the alphabet; this may be useful when looking up names in the telephone book.

International Calls An inexpensive way to make an international call is to go to a telegraph office; these are marked "Lennätin" or "Tele" and usually adjoin the post office. An operator will assign you a private booth and collect payment at the end of the call. Except in a few remote areas, there is direct dialing to Britain and the United States.

Operators and Information For information about telephone charges, dial 92023; for number inquiries in the Helsinki area, 012; for other areas, 020.

Mail
Postal Rates At press time (summer 1992), airmail rates to North America were FIM 3.40 for a letter of up to 10 grams and FIM 2.90 for postcards. Letters and postcards to the United Kingdom cost FIM 2.90.

Receiving Mail If you're uncertain about where you'll be staying, be sure that mail sent to you is marked "Poste Restante" and addressed to the Main Post Office, Mannerheimintie 11, 00100 Helsinki, or to major post offices in other towns. American Express (Travek Travel Bureau, Katajanokan Pohjoisranta 9, tel. 90/12511) offers a free clients' mail service and will hold mail for up to one month. The Finland Travel Bureau also provides a free mail service for foreigners: Mail should be addressed to its Mail Department, Box 319, 00101 Helsinki, and collected from the office at Kaivokatu 10A.

Shopping
Sales Tax Refunds If you purchase goods worth more than FIM 100 in any of the many shops marked "tax-free for tourists," you can get a 10%–16% refund when you leave Finland. Show your passport and the store will give you a check for the appropriate amount that you can cash at most departure points.

Opening and Closing Times **Banks.** Open weekdays 9:15–4:15.

Museums. Opening hours vary considerably, so check individual listings. Most close one day a week, usually Monday. Many museums in the countryside are open only during the summer months.

Shops. Most are open weekdays 9–6, Saturday 9–2. Department stores and supermarkets sometimes stay open until 8 from Monday through Friday.

Sightseeing. Schedules for most attractions vary widely outside the main tourist season. Check local tourist offices for opening days and hours.

National Holidays January 1; January 6 (Epiphany Day); April 9–12 (Easter); May 1 (May Day); May 20 (Ascension); May 29–31 (Pentecost); June 25–26 (Midsummer's Eve and Day); November 6 (All Saint's Day); December 6 (Independence Day); December 25–26.

Dining Even if dining in Helsinki is expensive by Continental European standards, there is hope for the tourist who is looking for a tasty meal in the Inexpensive and Budget price categories. In Helsinki, many people take advantage of the numerous and inexpensive ethnic restaurants and fast-food pizzerias. At lunchtime there are real bargains too. Restaurants offer special fixed-price menus (from around 11 AM to 2 or 3 PM), which can be 50% cheaper than what is normally found on the more expensive à la carte menu.

Check out the numerous small *baari* (cafés) or *grilli* (grills). You can find bargain meals here, but the quality of food varies considerably. Many large supermarkets have rotisseries and they sell chicken and pork spare ribs at cheap prices. Finland's high standards of hygiene make it possible for visitors to eat out at grill stands. At budget prices, these offer basic Finnish fast food at its best, including hamburgers and sausages.

As in other parts of Scandinavia, the *voileipäpöytä* (cold table) is often a work of art as well as a feast. It's usually available at lunchtime. Special Finnish dishes include *poronkäristys* (reindeer casserole); salmon, herring, and various freshwater fish; and *lihapullia* (meatballs) with a tasty sauce. Crayfish parties are popular between the end of July and early September. For a delicious dessert, try cloudberries (related to blackberries) and other forest fruits.

Mealtimes The Finns eat early; lunch runs from 11 or noon to 1 or 2, dinner from 4 to 7 (a bit later in Helsinki). Fixed-price menus, available at these times, are far more moderately priced than the à la carte choices served outside these hours.

Dress Casual attire is acceptable for restaurants in all price categories.

Ratings Prices are per person and include first course, main course, dessert, and service charge—but not wine. All restaurant checks include a service charge (*sisältää palvelupalkkion*). If you want to leave an additional tip—though it really isn't necessary—it's enough to round the figure off to the nearest FIM 5 or FIM 10. Best bets are indicated by a star ★ .

Category	Helsinki	Other Areas
Moderate	over FIM 75	over FIM 65
Inexpensive	FIM 34–FIM 75	FIM 30–FIM 65
Budget	under FIM 34	under FIM 30

If you select the fixed-price menu, which usually covers two courses and coffee and is served at certain hours in many establishments, the cost of the meal can be as little as half these prices.

Lodging The range of accommodations available in Finland includes hotels, motels, boarding houses, private homes, rented chalets and cottages, farmhouses, youth hostels, and campsites. There is no official system of classification, but standards are generally high. If you haven't reserved a room in advance, you can make reservations at the **Hotel Booking Center** at Helsinki's Railway Station (Asema aukio, tel. 90/171133) or through a travel agency; the booking fee is FIM 10. There are added reductions of up to 50% in Helsinki-area hotels from June 19 through August 16 when you buy a Helsinki Card. These cards are sold by the Hotel Booking Center and the Helsinki City Tourist Office (Pohjoisesplanadi 19, tel. 90/169–3757 or 90/174088). Don't forget that hotel rates are usually 30%–40% cheaper in the summer than in the winter months. There are also special weekend rates.

Hotels Nearly all hotels in Finland are modern or will have been recently renovated; a few occupy fine old manor houses. Most have rooms with bath or shower. Prices generally include breakfast and often a morning sauna and swim. The **Finncheque** voucher system, operating in many hotels from June through August, offers good discounts. Only the first night can be reserved, but subsequent reservations can be made free from any Finncheque hotel. For additional information, inquire at the Hotel Booking Center or local tourist board.

Several hotel groups, such as Cumulus, Sokos-Hotels, Rantasipi, and Arctia, offer special packages, and unless there's a festival going on, some hotels reduce their prices substantially in July.

Summer Hotels University students' accommodations are turned into "summer hotels" from June through August; they offer modern facilities at slightly lower-than-average prices.

Boarding Houses These provide the least expensive accommodations and are
and Private Homes found only outside Helsinki. Local tourist offices have lists.

Rentals The choice is huge, and the chalets and cottages are nearly always in delightful lakeside or seashore settings. For comfortable (not luxurious) accommodations, count on paying FIM 800–FIM 2,800 for a four-person weekly rental. A central reservations agency is **Lomarengas** (Malminkaari 23C, Helsinki, tel. 90/3516–1321, or Mikonkatu 25, Helsinki, tel. 90/170611).

Farmhouses These are located in attractive settings, usually near water. A central reservations agency is **Suomen 4H-liitto** (Abrahaminkatu 7, tel. 90/642233).

Youth Hostels These range from empty schools to small manor houses. There are no age restrictions, and prices range from FIM 34 to FIM 75 per bed. The Finnish Tourist Board can provide a list of hostels.

Camping There are about 350 Finnish campsites, all classified into one of three grades. All offer showers and cooking facilities, and many include cottages for rent. A list is available from the Finnish Tourist Board.

Ratings Prices are for two people in a double room and include breakfast and service charge. Best bets are indicated by a star ★.

Category	Helsinki	Other Areas
Moderate	over FIM 350	over FIM 270
Inexpensive	FIM 150–FIM 350	FIM 150–FIM 270
Budget	under FIM 150	under FIM 150

Tipping The Finns are less tip-conscious than other Europeans. (For restaurant tips, *see* Dining, *above*.) Train and airport porters have a fixed charge. The obligatory checkroom fee of FIM 3–FIM 4 is usually clearly indicated; if not, give FIM 3–FIM 10, depending on the number in your party. FIM 5 is a standard tip for all minor services.

Helsinki

Arriving and Departing

By Plane All international flights arrive at Helsinki's Vantaa Airport, 20 kilometers (12 miles) north of the city. For arrival and departure information, call 90/9700–8100.

Between the Finnair buses leave two to four times an hour for the city termi-
Airport and nals, located at the Inter-Continental hotel (Töölönkatu 21, tel.
Downtown 90/40551) and the Railway Station. The trip takes about 25 min-
utes and costs FIM 18. A local bus service (No. 615), which
takes about 40 minutes, goes to the Railway Station and costs
FIM 14.

By Train Helsinki's Railway Station is in the heart of the city. For train
information, phone 90/101–0115.

By Bus The terminal for many local buses is the Railway Station
square, Rautatientori. The main long-distance bus station is
located off Mannerheimintie between Salomonkatu and
Simonkatu. For information, phone 90/602122.

By Sea The Silja Line terminal for ships arriving from Stockholm is at
Olympialaituri, on the west side of the South Harbor. The
Finnjet-Silja Line and Viking Lines terminal for ships arriving
from Travemünde and Stockholm is at Katajanokka, on the east
side of the South Harbor.

Getting Around

The center of Helsinki is compact and best explored on foot.
However, the Helsinki City Tourist Office provides a free Helsinki route map that shows all public transportation. As far as
public transportation tickets go, your best buy is the **Helsinki
Card,** which gives unlimited travel on city public transportation as well as free entry to many museums, a free sightseeing
tour, and a variety of other discounts. It's available for one,
two, or three days (FIM 75, FIM 105, and FIM 125; about half-
price for children). You can buy it at most hotels and at the Helsinki City Tourist Office.

By Subway Helsinki's only subway line runs from the city center (Kamppi)
to Mellunmäki, in the eastern suburbs. It runs from around
5:45 AM to 11:20 PM, and each ride costs FIM 8; you can transfer
for free if you do so within an hour from the start of travel. Each
trip costs FIM 7 if you buy a 10-trip ticket. Tickets are available from some kiosks and vending machines.

By Streetcar These run from 6 AM to 1:30 AM, depending on the line. They can
be very handy, but be sure to get route advice because route
maps are practically nonexistent. The fare is the same as for the
subway. The 3T streetcar follows a figure-eight circuit around
the city center and, during summer, provides commentary on
an electric screenboard in several languages.

By Boat In summer there are regular boat services from the South Harbor market square to the islands of Suomenlinna and Kor-
keasaari.

Important Addresses and Numbers

Tourist The **Helsinki City Tourist Office** is near the South Harbor
Information (Pohjoisesplanadi 19, tel. 90/169–3757); open September 16–
May 15, Monday 8:30–4:30, Tuesday–Friday 8:30–4; May 16–
September 15, weekdays 8:30–6, Saturday 8:30–1. The **Finnish
Tourist Board's Tourist Information Office** (covering all Fin-
land) is nearby at Eteläesplanadi 4, tel. 90/403011; open May–
September, weekdays 9–5, Saturday 9–1; October–April,
weekdays 9–6.

Embassies U.S. (Itäinen Puistotie 14, tel. 90/171931). **Canadian** (Pohjois-esplanadi 25B, tel. 90/171141). **U.K.** (Itäinen Puistotie 17, tel. 90/661293).

Emergencies **General** (tel. 000); **Police** (tel. 000); **Ambulance** (tel. 000); **Doctor** (tel. 008); **Dentist** (tel. 90/736166).

Exploring Helsinki

Helsinki is a city of the sea. It was built on peninsulas that stab into the Baltic, and streets and avenues curve around bays, bridges arch over to nearby islands, and ferries reach out to islands farther offshore. Sweet-tasting salt air hovers over the city, and the sounds from the vessels steaming into port resonate off the city's buildings.

Like other European capitals, Helsinki has expanded its boundaries and now absorbs about one-sixth of the Finnish population, and the suburbs sprawl from one peninsula to another. Helsinki residents must know the peninsulas in order to know their city. However, most of the city's sights, hotels, and restaurants cluster on one peninsula, thus forming a compact hub that is of special interest to the traveler.

Unlike most other European capitals, Helsinki is "new." About 400 years ago, King Gustav Vasa of Sweden decided to woo trade from the Estonian city of Tallinn and thus challenge the monopoly of the Hanseatic League. To do this, he commanded the people of four Finnish towns to pack up their belongings and relocate at the rapids on the river Vantaa. This new town became Helsinki.

For three centuries, Helsinki had its ups and downs as a trading town. Turku, to the west of Helsinki, remained the capital and the center of the country's intellectual pursuits. Ironically, not until Finland was thrust under the dominance of Russia did Helsinki's fortunes improve. Czar Alexander I wanted Finland's political center closer to Russia and, in 1812, selected Helsinki as the new capital. Shortly after the capital was moved from Turku to Helsinki, Turku suffered a monstrous fire. So great was the inferno that the university was also moved to Helsinki. From then on Helsinki's future was secure.

Fire was indeed fortuitous for the future of Helsinki. Just before the czar's proclamation, a fire had swept through the town, permitting the construction of new buildings suitable for a nation's capital. The German-born architect Carl Ludvig Engel was commissioned to rebuild the city, and, as a result, Helsinki has some of the purest neoclassical architecture in the world. Add to this foundation the stunning outlines of the Jügend period (early 20th century) and the modern buildings designed by talented Finnish architects, and you have a European capital city that is as architecturally eye-catching as it is different from its Scandinavian neighbors or the rest of Europe.

Numbers in the margin correspond to points of interest on the Helsinki map.

Helsinki is an easy city to visit on foot. Not only are the key sights on one peninsula but most of them are also contained in the area between the Railway Station and the central Market Square (Kauppatori).

Across from the city tourist office and beside the South Harbor is the **Kauppatori.** Sometimes it seems that half the city is here seeking the best buys for the day or simply catching up on the gossip. All around are stalls selling everything from colorful, freshly cut flowers to ripe fruit, from vegetables trucked in from the hinterland to handicrafts made in small villages. Look at the fruit stalls—mountains of strawberries; raspberries; blueberries; and, if you're lucky, *suomuuraimet* (cloudberries), which grow largely above the Arctic Circle in the midnight sun. Closer to the dock are fresh fish, caught that morning in the Baltic Sea and still flopping. The market is a hive of activity and, in a sense, the heartbeat of everyday life in Helsinki. Stop at one of the food stalls and, as you sip your coffee, notice the **statue of Havis Amanda** standing in the square. This beautiful lady is loved by all Finns, and every May Day eve she is embraced by students who wade through the protective moat to crown her with their white caps.

The market ends at 2 PM, and, in the summer, the fruit and vegetable stalls are replaced with arts-and-crafts stalls. This happens at 3:30 PM and lasts until about 8 PM.

Another heartbeat of Helsinki is across the street, on the other side of Pohjoisesplanadi. The uniformed guards will prevent you from entering, but the building is the **Presidential Palace,** and next to it are the city hall and various administrative offices. Across from the palace is the waterfront, where ferries and sightseeing boats set out into the bay. On a summer's day it is a sailor's vision: sails hoisted and taut to the wind, yacht clubs beckoning, and island waters to explore. The redbrick edifice perched above the east side of the market is the Orthodox **Uspenski Cathedral.**

Just behind the cathedral is the district of **Katajanokka.** Here the 19th-century brick warehouses are slowly being renovated to form a complex of boutiques, arts-and-crafts studios, and restaurants. You'll find innovative designs at these shops, and the restaurants tend to offer lighter fare, which can make this a tempting area to stop for lunch. While in Katajanokka, you might enjoy a visit to **Wanha Satama,** a small complex of cafés and food stores attached to an art gallery.

A one-minute stroll north of city hall will take you into **Senaatintori** (Senate Square), the heart of neoclassical Helsinki and one of the most graceful squares in Europe, dominated by the domed **Lutheran Cathedral** (Tuomiokirkko). The square is the work of Ludvig Engel. The harmony created with the Tuomiokirkko, the university, and the state council building places you amid one of the purest styles of European architecture. Senaatintori has a dignified, stately air, enlivened in summer by sun worshipers who gather on the wide steps leading up to Tuomiokirkko and throughout the year by the bustle around the relatively new **Senaati Shopping Center** on the square's south side.

Most of the streets leading off Senaatintori contain government and administrative offices. Worth noting is **Snellmaninkatu,** a street named after J. V. Snellman. Known for awakening the Finnish national spirit, he was instrumental in persuading the Russian overlords to officially recognize the Finnish language and accept the idea of a separate Finnish cur-

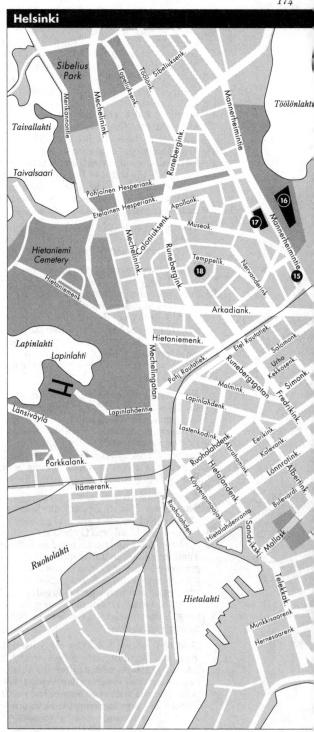

Helsinki

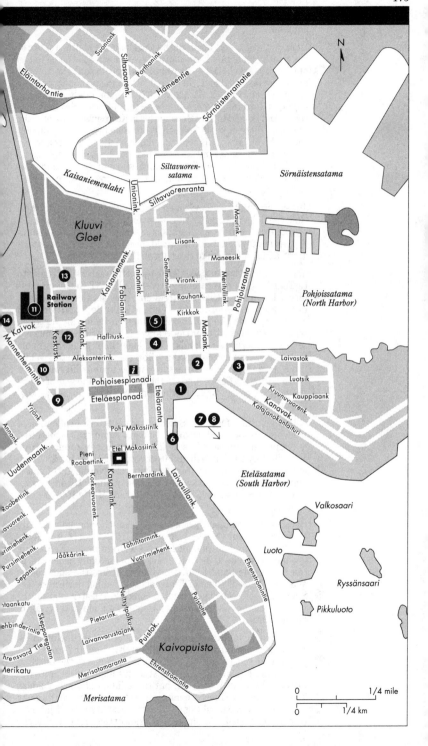

N

Eläintarhantie

Suonionk.

Siltasaarenk.

PorthaninK.

Hämeentie

Sörnäistenrantatie

Kaisaniemenlahti

Unionink.

Siltavuoren-
satama

Siltavuorenranta

Sörnäistensatama

Kluuvi
Gloet

Maurink.

Liisank.

Maneesik.

Snellmanink.

Vironk.

Rauhank.

Merituluink.

Kirkkok.

Pohjoisranta

Pohjoissatama
(North Harbor)

13

Railway
Station

11

14 Kaivok.

Mannerheimintie

Kaisaniemenk.

Unionink.

Fabianink.

Mikonk.

Keskusk.

12

Hallitusk.

Aleksanterink.

5

4

Mariank.

2

3

Laivastok.

Luotsik.

Kruunuvuorenk.

Kauppiaank.

Kanavak.

Katajanokanlaituri

10

9

Yrjonk.

Annank.

Pohjoisesplanadi

Eteläesplanadi

i

Eteläranta

1

Pohj Makasiinik.

Etel Makasiinik.

7 8

6

Uudenmaank.

Roobertink.

avuorenk.

rimiehenk.

Pursimiehenk.

Sepank.

Pieni
Roobertink.

Kasarmink.

Korkeavuorenk.

Bernhardink.

Laivasillank.

Eteläsatama
(South Harbor)

Valkosaari

Luoto

Ryssänsaari

taankatu

ehbinderintie

Skepparegatan

hrensvärd Tie

Merikatu

Jääkärink.

Tähtitornink.

Vuorimiehenk.

Neitsytpolku

Pietarink.

Laivanvarustajank.

Puistok.

Ehrenströmintie

Pikkuluoto

Puistotie

Kaivopuisto

Merisatamaranta

Ehrenströmintie

Merisatama

0   1/4 mile

0   1/4 km

rency. It is Snellman's statue that stands in front of the Bank of Finland.

Back on the market, head southward along the western shore of the South Harbor on Eteläranta Street. You'll soon come to the old brick **Market Hall**—it's worth taking a look at the voluminous displays of meat, fish, and other gastronomic goodies (open weekdays 8–5, Saturday 8–2). A little farther on is the **Olympia Terminal,** where the huge ferries from Sweden, Estonia, and Poland berth. Beyond this is **Kaivopuisto,** the elegant parkland district much favored by Russian high society during the 19th century. It is now popular as a strolling ground for Helsinki's citizens and as a residential area for diplomats. You'll find the U.S. and French embassies and British ambassador's residence clustered among the greenery, interspersed with statues.

Just around the headland you'll spot a peculiarly Finnish tradition: special platforms jutting out over the water (either the sea or a lake), on which people gather to scrub their carpets. Laundry, as in other parts of the world, becomes a lively, communal affair and an occasion to catch up on the latest gossip.

You can avoid the long walk back by cutting across Kaivopuisto to Tehtaankatu and catching streetcar No. 3T to the marketplace. From here, there's a frequent ferry service to **Suomenlinna.** *Suomenlinna* means "Finland's Castle," and for good reason. In 1748 the Finnish army helped build this fortress, which grew so much over the years that today Suomenlinna is a series of interlinked islands. For a long time the impregnable fortress was referred to as the "Gibraltar of the North." While it has never been taken by assault, its occupants did surrender twice without a fight—once to the Russians in the war of 1808–19 and then to the British, who bombarded the fortress, causing fires.

Although still a fortress, Suomenlinna is today a collection of museums, parks, and gardens. In early summer it is engulfed in mauve and purple mists of lilacs, the trees introduced from Versailles by the Finnish architect Augustin Ehrensvärd. One of the museums you may care to visit is the **Nordic Arts Center,** which exhibits and promotes Scandinavian art. *Admission free. Open Sept.–Apr., Tues.–Sun. 10–5; May–Aug., Tues.–Sun. 11–6.*

Back on the mainland, head west from the marketplace up **Pohjoisesplanadi** (North Esplanade). To your left, the leafy linden trees and statues of Finnish writers in the Esplanade gardens provide a peaceful backdrop for daily concerts at the Esplanade bandstand. On your right are the showrooms and boutiques of some of Finland's top fashion designers (*see* Shopping, *below*). The circular **Swedish Theater** marks the junction of the Esplanade and Helsinki's main artery, Mannerheimintie.

If you take a right up Keskuskatu, you'll come to **Stockmann's,** Helsinki's most famous store, well worth a shopping stop. Next you'll come to the **Railway Station** and its square, the bustling commuting hub of the city. The station's huge red-granite figures are by Emil Wikström, but the solid building they adorn was designed by Eliel Saarinen, one of the founders of the early 20th-century National Romantic style. The **Ateneum,** Finland's central art museum, is on the south side of the square facing the

⑬ National Theater. *Admission: FIM 10 adults, children free. Open year-round Tues. and Fri. 9–5, Wed. and Thurs. 9–9, weekends 11–5.*

⑭ In front of the main post office west of the station is the **statue of Marshal Mannerheim** gazing down Mannerheimintie, the major thoroughfare named in his honor. Perhaps no man in Finnish history is so revered as Marshal Baron Carl Gustaf Mannerheim, the military and political leader who guided Finland through much of the turbulent 20th century. When he died in Switzerland on January 28, 1951, his body was flown back to his native land to lie in state in the cathedral. For three days, young war widows, children, and soldiers filed past his bier by the thousands. Never in Finland's history has there been such an expression of national feeling.

⑮ ⑯ About half a mile along, past the colonnaded red-granite **Parliament House,** stands **Finlandia Hall,** one of the last creations of Alvar Aalto. If you can't make it to a concert there, take a guided tour. Finlandia Hall will be shut for interior renovations from 1994 to February 1995. Behind the hall lies the inland bay of Töölönlahti and, almost opposite, the **National** ⑰ **Museum,** another example of National Romantic exotica in which Eliel Saarinen played a part. *Admission: FIM 10 adults, FIM 5 children. Open May–Sept., daily 11–4; Oct.–Apr., Mon.–Sat. 11–3, Sun. 11–4; free admission on Tues. year-round 6–9 PM.*

⑱ Tucked away in a labyrinth of streets to the west is the strikingly modern **Temppeliaukio Church.** Carved out of solid rock and topped with a copper dome, this Helsinki landmark is a center for religious activities, church services, concerts, and lectures. From here it's only a short distance back to Mannerheimintie, where you can pick up any streetcar for the downtown area. *Lutherinkatu 3. Open June–Aug., weekdays 10–8, Sun. hours vary; Sept.–May, Mon. 10–8, Tues. 10–12:45 and 2:15–8, Wed.–Sat. 10–6.*

Shopping

Shopping Districts and Specialty Shops You should find everything you need on **Pohjoisesplanadi** (North Esplanade) and **Aleksanterinkatu,** in the **Forum Shopping Mall** at Mannerheimintie 20, or on the pedestrian mall **Iso Roobertinkatu.** You can make purchases until 10 PM, seven days a week, in the shops along the Tunneli underpass leading from the Railway Station.

Some of the shops in **Senaatti Center** and along Eteläesplanadi and Pohjoisesplanadi are open on Sundays from noon to 4 in summer. Along the latter you'll find some of Finland's top design houses: **Arabia-Nuutajärvi** ceramics and glass at No. 25; **Pentik** leather, **Aarikka** accessories, and wooden toys at No. 27 and Eteläesplanadi 8; I-Shop (Iittala) glass at No. 27A; **Marimekko** fashions at No. 31; and Artek furniture and ceramics at Eteläesplanadi 18. For more information, contact Design Forum Finland (Eteläesplanadi 8 or Fabianinkatu 10, Helsinki, tel. 90/629290).

Helsinki's three top jewelry boutiques are almost adjacent: **Galerie Björn Weckström,** Unioninkatu 30; **Kalevala Koru,** Unioninkatu 25; and **Kaunis Koru,** Senaatti Center.

Department Stores   **Stockmann's,** a huge store that fills an entire block between Aleksanterinkatu, Mannerheimintie, and Keskuskatu, is your best bet if you want to find everything under one roof.

Markets   The **Kauppatori market** beside the South Harbor (*see* Exploring Helsinki, *above*) is an absolute must. Also try to find time for the variety of goods at the **Hietalahti flea market,** located at the west end of Bulevardi on Hietalahti. (*Open Mon.–Sat. 7 AM–2 PM.*) The more basic **Hakaniemi Kauppahalli** market is just north of the center on Hakaniemi Tori (square) along Siltasaarenkatu.

Dining

For details and price-category definitions, *see* Dining in Staying in Finland.

Moderate   **Katariina.** Katariina is a popular Helsinki restaurant with a reputation for serving good Finnish and international fare. The cellar of the restaurant used to be a police detention center, where drunkards and criminal suspects were locked up. *Aleksanterinkatu 22–24, tel. 90/656722. Reservations advised. AE, DC, MC, V. Closed weekends during July.*

Kosmos. Located only a short walking distance from Stockmann's is Kosmos, which serves good food at reasonable prices for Helsinki. The restaurant is a favorite among artists, writers, and journalists during the evenings, and it's popular among business people during lunchtime. One of Kosmos's specialties is sweetbread. *Kalevankatu 3, tel. 90/607603. Reservations advised. AE, DC, MC, V. Closed weekends and national holidays.*

Omenapuu. This cozy family restaurant, set in the midst of a busy shopping district, features special dishes for weight watchers. *Keskuskatu 6, second floor, tel. 90/630205. Reservations advised for lunch. AE, DC, MC, V.*

Rivoli. Rivoli is divided into two restaurants that share the same menu. The seafood section is friendly and more low-key while the other section has a sophisticated atmosphere and is decorated in elegant white and black tones. Rivoli specializes in Finnish and international dishes. *Albertinkatu 38, tel. 90/643455. Reservations advised. AE, DC, MC, V. Closed Christmas, Easter, and June 25–26.*

Stockmann Terrace. Located on the top floor of Helsinki's biggest department store, the Stockmann Terrace specializes in meat, fish, vegetarian, and pasta dishes. A popular dish is pepper steak. *Pohjoisesplanadi 41, tel. 90/665566. No reservations required. AE, DC, MC, V. Closed Sun. and national holidays.*

Inexpensive   **Kynsilaukka (Garlic).** Garlic is the pungent theme of this restaurant, where the rustic decor suits the menu. *Fredrikinkatu 22, tel. 90/651939. Reservations advised. AE, DC, MC, V.*

Perho Mechelin. This is the restaurant connected with Helsinki's catering school. During summer the emphasis is on Finnish food, particularly salmon and reindeer. *Mechelininkatu 7, tel. 90/493481. Reservations advised. AE, DC, MC, V. Closed Christmas and June 25–26.*

Pizzeria Dennis. This restaurant is a small but attractive Italian establishment that serves some of the best pasta and pizza in town. *Fredrikinkatu 36, tel. 90/694–5271. No reservations. DC, MC, V. Closed Christmas and June 25–26.*

Sukothai. Sukothai is a small restaurant decorated in light colors that serves the best Thai food in Helsinki. Portions are not enormous but they are very tasty, and the service is friendly. *Runeberginkatu 32, tel. 90/446774. Reservations advised. MC, V. Closed Christmas and June 25–26.*

Wellamo. The decor at this restaurant draws upon changing exhibitions by new artists. Try the lamb steak in garlic butter. *Vyökatu 9, tel. 90/663139. Reservations advised. AE, MC, V. Closed Mon., Christmas, and June 25–26.*

Zinnkeller. The pleasant German decor and paraphernalia enhances the tasty, affordable, and generous portions of German and Hungarian dishes. Game weeks are organized once a year and are a specialty of the restaurant. *Meritullinkatu 25, tel. 90/135–4148. No reservations required. AE, DC, MC, V. Closed Christmas, Easter, June 25–26, and July.*

Budget **Helsinki University.** The university cafeterias offer the cheapest food in town at lunchtime (meals cost FIM 17–FIM 21) and are open to the general public. *Hallituskatu 11–13, second floor (Porthania building), tel. 191–2558 and Hietaniemenkatu 14 (Domus Academica building), tel. 90/1311–4313. No reservations. No credit cards. Porthania: closed Sun. Sept. 8–May 22; closed weekends May 24–Sept. 6; closed national holidays. Domus: closed weekends June 1–Aug. 16; closed national holidays.*

Snacky. Snacky is a drive-through fast-food stand that is popular among taxi drivers and young people cruising Helsinki at night. It's usually located at Shell service stations. *Shell Leppäsuo, Leppäsuontie, tel. 90/406942; Shell Herttoniemi, Hitsaajankatu 18, tel. 90/755–5347; Shell Itäkeskus, Visbynkatu 1, tel. 90/337515; also at Nauvontie 6, tel. 90/477–2535. No reservations. No credit cards.*

Lodging

Standards of service and amenities in nearly all Helsinki hotels are reliable. The main criteria for inclusion here are price and location. For details and price-category definitions, *see* Lodging in Staying in Finland.

Moderate **Anna.** The Anna, a 1925 town house, has light, cheerful rooms well insulated against traffic noise. It's within easy reach of the town center, but has no restaurant (café only). Nonsmokers will appreciate the designated nonsmoking floor and smoke-free public areas. *Annankatu 1, tel. 90/648011. 60 rooms with shower. Facilities: sauna. AE, MC, V. Closed Christmas and New Year's Day.*

Aurora. Located 1½ kilometers (1 mile) from the city center right across the Linnanmäki amusement park is Aurora. Reasonable prices, cozy rooms, and good facilities have made the hotel popular, especially with families. *Helsinginkatu 50, tel. 90/717400. 70 rooms with shower, 6 with bath. Facilities: restaurant, sauna, pool, squash courts, health spa, solarium. AE, DC, MC, V. Closed Dec. 23–Jan. 2.*

Hospiz. The Hospiz is located on a quiet, central street and is unpretentious but comfortable. *Vuorikatu 17B, tel. 90/173441. 160 rooms with bath or shower. Facilities: sauna, restaurant. AE, DC, MC, V.*

Marttahotelli. This hotel was fully renovated in 1990. The rooms are small but pleasantly decorated. It's only a 10-minute walk from the Railway Station. *Uudenmankatu 24, tel. 90/*

646211. 45 rooms with shower or bath. Facilities: sauna. AE, DC, MC, V. Closed Christmas and June 25–26.
Ursula. This unpretentious hotel is a 20-minute walk from the Railway Station near the Hakaniemi market square. Ursula was fully refurbished three years ago. *Paasivuorenkatu 1, tel. 90/750311. 32 rooms with shower. Facilities: nonsmoking rooms, breakfast room. AE, DC, MC, V. Closed Christmas.*

Inexpensive **Academica.** The Academica is a town house with simple but adequate rooms, a 10-minute walk from the town center. *Hietaniemenkatu 14, tel. 90/1311–4265 or 90/402–0206. 217 rooms, most with shower. Facilities: sauna, pool, indoor tennis, disco. AE, MC, V. Closed Sept.–May.*
Erottajanpuisto Matkailukoti. This hostel is centrally located and has clean, quiet rooms without toilet or shower. *Uudenmaankatu 9, tel. 90/642169. 15 rooms. No credit cards. Sometimes closed during Christmas.*
Omapohja. This hotel is located right next to the Railway Station. Rooms are simple but clean. *Itäinen Teatterikuja 3, tel. 90/666211. 15 rooms, 4 with shower. MC, V. Closed Christmas and June 25–26.*
Satakuntatalo. Satakuntatalo is only a five-minute walk from the Railway Station. Friendly service, clean rooms (without shower), and self-service laundry have made it popular among Americans. Some rooms can get traffic noise. Breakfast is included. *Lapinrinne 1A, tel. 90/695851. 67 rooms, 4 with shower. Facilities: restaurant, saunas. AE, MC, V. Open June 1–Aug. 31.*
Skatta. Located in the elegant neighborhood of Katajanokka Island, and 2 kilometers (1¼ miles) from the Railway Station, is modest Skatta. Each room has a kitchenette. *Linnankatu 3, tel. 90/659233 or 90/669984. 24 rooms with shower. Facilities: café, sauna, gym. DC, MC, V. Sometimes closed during Christmas.*

Budget **Stadionin Maja.** Located 3 kilometers (1.8 miles) from the Railway Station, this modest youth hostel is the cheapest place in town to sleep. There are good bus and streetcar connections. *Pohjois Stadiontie 3B, tel. 90/496071. 164 beds. Facilities: self-service kitchen, laundry, breakfast room. No credit cards. Closed Christmas.*
Vantaa Hostel. This hostel is conveniently located only 5 kilometers (3 miles) from the Helsinki-Vantaa Airport. A section of the hostel offers 24 rooms with private shower at higher rates. *Vantaa, Valkoisenlähteentie 52, tel. 90/8393310. 7 rooms. Facilities: breakfast room. No credit cards. Sometimes closed during Christmas.*

The Arts

For a list of events, pick up the free publications "Helsinki This Week" or "Helsinki Today," available in hotels and tourist offices. For recorded program information in English, dial 058. A central reservations office for all events is **Lippupalvelu,** Mannerheimintie 5, tel. 90/9700–4700 or 90/664466 when calling from abroad. Call **Tiketti,** Yrjönkatu 29C, tel. 90/693–2255, when making reservations for small concerts and restaurants.

Theater Although all performances are in Finnish or Swedish, summertime productions in such bucolic settings as **Suomenlinna Island, Kekuspuisto Park, Mustikkamaa Island,** the **Rowing**

Stadium (operettas), and the **Savoy Theater** (ballet and music performances) make enjoyable entertainment. The splendid new **Opera House** opens in 1993 in a waterside park by **Töölönlahti** just a few hundred feet from Finlandia Hall.

Concerts The two main locations for musical events are **Finlandia Hall** (tel. 90/40241) and **Temppeliaukio Church** (*see* Exploring, *above*). Free organ recitals are given on Sundays at 8 PM in the cathedral, and there's daily entertainment at the bandstand in the **Esplanade** gardens.

Festivals Finland holds many festivals throughout the country, especially during the summer months. The **Helsinki Festival** is said to be the biggest in Scandinavia. For more than two weeks during August to September, the city is turned over to the arts. Scores of musical happenings and art exhibitions are organized throughout Helsinki. Each Helsinki Festival has a theme (last year's focused on the three Baltic States). Contact Helsinki Festival, Unioninkatu 28, tel. 90/659688. For more information on festivals, call Finland Festivals, Mannerheimintie 40, B49, tel. 90/445763 or 90/445686.

Nightlife

The price of drinks at nightclubs and discos can be expensive when compared to Continental Europe. The high price of alcohol is attributable to the Finnish (and Nordic) alcohol policy, which is strictly controlled by the state. Those who do not want to spend a lot of money on alcohol when visiting one of these establishments should just order a bottle of beer.

Nightclubs The most popular nightclubs in town are **Helsinki Club** (Helsinki Hotel, Hallituskatu 12, tel. 90/131401) and **Hesperia Nightclub** (Hesperia, Kivelänkatu 2, tel. 90/43101). **Fizz** (Arctia Hotel Marski, Mannerheimintie 10, tel. 90/68061) and **Pressa** (Eteläinen Rautatiekatu 4, tel. 90/691–3161) are also popular. Pressa offers live shows and is located in the Ramada Presidentti Hotel.

Discos The liveliest and most popular are **Old Baker's** (Mannerheimintie 10, tel. 90/641579) and **Fanny & Alexander** (Pitkänsillanranta 3, tel. 90/701–4424). The most popular among young people is **KY Exit** (Pohjoinen Rautatiekatu 21, tel. 90/407238). If you are looking for tropical salsa music, try **La Havanna** (Erottajankatu 7, tel 90/680–2668).

The Lakelands

This is a region of lakes, forests, and islands in southeastern and central Finland. The light in these northern latitudes has a magical softness, and the vistas are constantly changing.

For centuries the lakeland region was a buffer between the warring empires of Sweden and Russia. After visiting the people of the lakelands, you should have a basic understanding of the Finnish word *sisu* (guts), a quality that has kept Finns independent, fiercely guarding their neutrality.

Getting Around

Savonlinna is the best-placed town in the Lakelands and can make a convenient base from which to begin exploring. You can fly to the Savonlinna area from Helsinki in 40 minutes; a connecting bus takes you the remaining 16 kilometers (10 miles) into town. By train, the journey takes 5½ hours; by bus, 6 hours.

Take advantage of the excellent network of air, rail, bus, and boat transportation. Take the boat from Savonlinna to Kuopio in 12 hours (**Roll Line**, tel. 971/262–6744). From Kuopio, take the 320-kilometer (200-mile) cross-country bus ride via Jyväskylä to Tampere. Continue by boat to Hämeenlinna in eight hours (**Finnish Silverline**, tel. 931/124803). The final leg by bus or train back to Helsinki takes about 1½ hours.

Tourist Information

Savonlinna (Puistokatu 1, tel. 957/13492). Open January–May, weekdays 9–4; June–late August, daily 8 AM–10 PM; late August–September, daily 8–6; October–December, weekdays 9–4.

Exploring the Lakelands

Savonlinna The center of **Savonlinna** is a series of islands linked by bridges. First, stop at the tourist office for information; then cross the bridge east to the **open-air market** that flourishes alongside the main passenger quay. It's from here that you can catch the boat to Kuopio. In days when waterborne traffic was the major form of transportation, Savonlinna was the central hub of the passenger fleet serving Saimaa, the largest lake system in Europe. Now the lake traffic is dominated by cruise and sightseeing boats, but the quayside still bustles with arrivals and departures every summer morning and evening.

A 10-minute stroll from the quay to the southeast brings you to Savonlinna's most famous sight, the castle of **Olavinlinna**. First built in 1475 to protect Finland's eastern border, the castle retains its medieval character and is one of Scandinavia's best-preserved historic monuments. Still surrounded by water that once formed part of its defensive strength, the fortress rises majestically out of the lake. The Savonlinna Opera Festival is held in the courtyard each July. The combination of music and setting is spellbinding. You will need to make reservations well in advance (tel. 957/514700 or 957/13492), both for tickets and for hotel rooms, since Savonlinna becomes a mecca for music lovers. And music is not the only activity; arts and crafts are also strongly featured in exhibits around town. *Castle admission: FIM 14 adults, FIM 7 children; includes a guided tour. Open June–Aug., daily 9–5; Sept.–May, daily 10–3.*

Close to the castle is the 19th-century steam schooner, *Salama,* which houses an excellent museum on the history of lake traffic, including the fascinating floating timber trains that are still a common sight on Saimaa today. *Admission: FIM 10 adults, FIM 6 children. Open mid-June–mid-Aug., daily 10–8; mid-Aug.–May, Tues.–Sun. 11–5.*

The most popular excursion from Savonlinna is to **Retretti**. You can take either a two-hour boat ride or a 30-minute, 29-kilometer (18-mile) bus trip. The journey by bus takes you along the 8-kilometer (5-mile) ridge of **Punkaharju**. This amazing ridge of pine-covered rocks, which rises out of the water and separates the lakes on either side, predates the Ice Age. At times it narrows to only 25 feet, yet it still manages to accommodate a road and train tracks. Retretti itself is a modern art complex of unique design, which includes a new cavern section built into Punkaharju ridge. It's also a magnificent setting for concerts in summer. *Admission: FIM 60 adults, FIM 55 senior citizens and students, FIM 25 children. Open July, daily 10–7; May 23–June and Aug., daily 10–6.*

Dining and Lodging

For details and price-category definitions, *see* Dining and Lodging in Staying in Finland.

Savonlinna
Dining

Majakka. Centrally located, Majakka goes in for home cooking and a family atmosphere. *Satamakatu 11, tel. 957/21456. Reservations required during festival season. AE, DC, MC, V. Moderate.*

Ravintola Hopeasalmi. Right next to the market square is a 100-year-old steamboat that has been converted into a restaurant. Ravintola Hopeasalmi is divided into three sections: a dining room, pizzeria (which is inexpensive), and a pub. The restaurant in the dining section specializes in such local fish dishes as the delicious *muikku*, a small, local freshwater fish. *Kauppatori, tel. 957/21701. Reservations advised during July. V. Open daily from May 1–mid-Sept.; closed the rest of the year. Moderate.*

Ravintola Retretti. Popular in summer when tourists visit the Retretti Art Center, the restaurant specializes in Finnish fare. Buffets are regularly offered June to August and during the Christmas season. *Punkaharju, tel. 957/311761. Reservations advised during the summer months. DC, MC, V. Closed Jan. Moderate.*

Bella-Ristorante. This restaurant specializes in Finnish and Italian home cooking, and has a friendly family atmosphere and good service. It's located 1½ kilometers (1 mile) west of the market square. *Tulliportinkatu 2, tel. 957/21286. No reservations necessary. AE, DC, MC, V. Closed Christmas. Inexpensive.*

Martina. Martina offers Finnish and Italian dishes. *Pilkkakoskenkatu 2, tel. 957/21222. No reservations necessary. V. Closed Christmas. Inexpensive.*

Paviljonki. Paviljonki is connected with the Savonlinna restaurant school. Located 1 kilometer (½ mile) west of the city center, the restaurant serves homemade Finnish dishes. *Rjalahdenkatu 4, tel. 957/520960. V. Inexpensive.*

Grilli Carlos. This restaurant specializes in Finnish home cooking. Portions are generous. *Olavinkatu 17, tel. 957/23357. No reservations. No credit cards. Closed Sun. and during national holidays. Budget.*

Pizzeria Capero. Pizzeria Capero is one of Savonlinna's two proper pizzerias. It seats about 50 people and is conveniently located in the heart of Savonlinna. *Olavinkatu 51, tel. 957/23955. No reservations. AE, DC, MC, V. Closed Sun. and Christmas. Budget.*

Uskudar Kebab. Savonlinna's only fast-food kebab restaurant. *Pilkkakoskenkatu 3, tel. 957/514206. No reservations. No credit cards. Closed Christmas and June 25–26. Budget.*

Lodging

Pietari Kylliäinen. Pietari Kylliäinen is centrally located in Savonlinna. The rooms are cozy and decorated in light tones, although some can get traffic noise. *Olavinkatu 15, tel. 957/ 575–0500. 48 rooms with shower. Facilities: restaurant, sauna, massage. AE, DC, MC, V. Closed for 2 weeks during Christmas. Moderate.*

Valtion Hoteli. A manor house with small rooms decorated in the old Finnish country style, the hotel is located in Punkaharju, a half-hour drive from Savonlinna. *Punkaharju, 957/ 311761. 30 rooms. Facilities: restaurant. DC, MC, V. Closed from the beginning of Sept. to mid-May. Moderate.*

Hospits. Located in the city center and on Lake Saimaa is Hospits, which is owned by the Savonlinna YMCA. It was fully renovated in 1992. *Linnankatu 20, 957/22443. 20 rooms, some with shower. Facilities: breakfast room, sauna. V. Inexpensive.*

Malakias. Around 1½ kilometers (1 mile) from the center of town is Malakias, a student dormitory that is converted into a hotel during the summer months (June 26–August 9). Rooms are large and unpretentious. *Pihlajanvedenkuja 6, tel. 957/ 23283. 220 rooms, with shower, toilet, and kitchenette for every 2 rooms. AE, DC, MC, V. Closed Aug. 10–June 25. Inexpensive.*

Vuorilinna Summer Hotel. Guests at this modern hotel use the facilities, including the restaurant, of the nearby Casino Spa Hotel. *Kasinonsaari, tel. 957/57500. 160 rooms, with shower for every 2 rooms. AE, DC, MC, V. Closed Sept.–May. Inexpensive (Moderate in July).*

Malakias Youth Hostel. Located in Malakias hotel, the hostel offers the same large rooms but without bed sheets or towels. Open from June 26–August 9. *Pihlajanvedenkuja 6, tel. 957/ 23283. 100 beds during June and Aug.; 50 beds in July. AE, DC, MC, V. Budget.*

Vuorilinna Youth Hostel. Every year part of the Vuorilinna Summer Hotel is converted into this youth hostel. The rooms are the same but without bed sheets or towels. The hostel is open only June 1–22 and August 8–30. *Kasinonsaari, tel. 957/ 57500. 100 beds with kitchenette, toilet, and shower for every 2 rooms. AE, DC, MC, V. Budget.*

8 France

Hotels and restaurants in France offer some of the best value in Western Europe—and the French economy has recently been in good shape, with inflation climbing just over 3% a year. Even in the heart of Paris it is possible to find a double room with shower for under $40 a night; good-value hotels abound in every country town. You can have a fine three-course meal in a restaurant for under $10. For $20 you can often have a virtual feast, usually with wine and as much bread as you wish thrown in at no extra cost.

France's rail system is another plus for the budget traveler. Not only is the network comprehensive; trains run on time and are comfortable, fast, and relatively cheap. Travel in France is geared to train lovers; drivers have to face highway tolls and exorbitant gas prices, and only the wealthy can afford to hire a car. Domestic air travel is also costly. Long-distance buses are almost nonexistent, and hitch hiking is difficult.

One thing the French do well—probably because it's instinctive and they don't need to think about it—is live. The essence of French *savoir-vivre* is simplicity. Everyday things count: eating, drinking, talking, dressing, shopping. Get in the mood: Daily rituals are meant to be enjoyed. Food is the best example. The French don't like rushing their meals. They plan them in advance, painstakingly prepare them, look forward to them over an *apéritif*, admire the loving presentation of each dish, savor each mouthful. The pace is unhurried and the wine flows steadily.

Make the most of the simple pleasure to be had from basking in the sunshine outside a café. Admire the casual elegance of the passersby or the old men in their time-honored berets. Even the most mundane things can become objects of beauty in

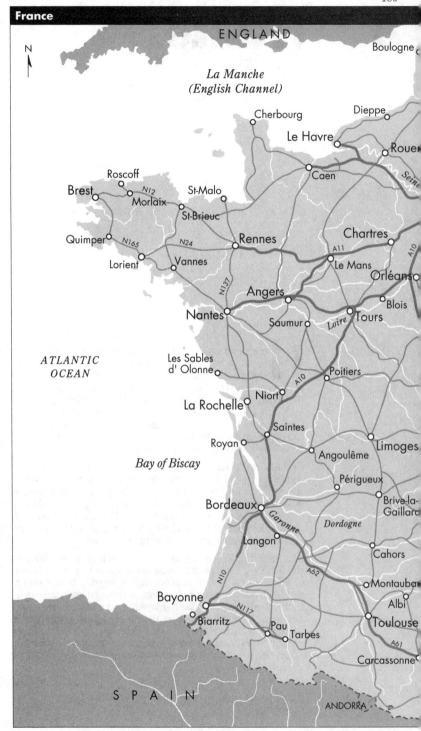

France

ENGLAND

Boulogne

La Manche
(English Channel)

N

Cherbourg

Dieppe

Le Havre

Rouen

Seine

Roscoff

Caen

Brest

Morlaix

St-Malo

N12

St-Brieuc

Chartres

Quimper

N165

N24

Rennes

A11

Le Mans

Orléans

A10

Lorient

Vannes

N137

Angers

Blois

Nantes

Saumur

Loire

Tours

ATLANTIC
OCEAN

Les Sables
d' Olonne

Poitiers

Niort

A10

La Rochelle

Saintes

Limoges

Royan

Angoulême

Bay of Biscay

Périgueux

Brive-la-
Gaillarde

Bordeaux

Garonne

Dordogne

Langon

Cahors

N10

A62

Montauban

Bayonne

Albi

Biarritz

N117

Toulouse

Pau

Tarbes

A61

Carcassonne

SPAIN

ANDORRA

BELGIUM

Corsica

Calvi
Bastia
Corte
Ajaccio
N198
Bonifacio

alais

A26 Lille

Arras
miens

Cambrai
St. Quentin

LUXEMBOURG

Beauvais

A1

Reims
A4

Metz

GERMANY

Paris

Châlons-sur-
Marne

Nancy

Strasbourg

Troyes

A31

Colmar

Sens

Auxerre

Mulhouse

Bourges

A6

Dijon

Belfort

Besançon

Nevers

Beaune

A71

SWITZERLAND

Montluçon

Mâcon

Bourg-en-
Bresse

Saône

Clermont-
Ferrand

Lyon

Rhône

rillac

Le Puy

A7

Chambéry

ITALY

Grenoble

A43

odez

Montélimar

Rhône

Millau

Avignon

Nîmes

Aix-en-Provence

Monte Carlo
Nice
Cannes

A9

Montpellier

Marseille

A8

Narbonne

Toulon

Perpignan

0   50 mi

Mediterranean Sea

Corsica

0   75 km

French eyes. The daily market is a festival of colors and textures, with fruit and vegetable stalls artistically and imaginatively composed. Shop windows are works of art.

Most French towns and villages are quietly attractive and historic. Chances are that the ornate *mairie* (town hall) has been there since the Revolution, and the church or cathedral since the Middle Ages. The main streets tend to be lined with sturdy trees planted before living memory. The 20th century is kept firmly at bay. Modern buildings—such as supermarkets—are banished to the outskirts or obliged to fit in with the architecture of the town center.

Whatever you may have been led to believe, France is a welcoming country. Don't be misled by the superficial coldness of the French: They are a formal people who don't go out of their way to speak to strangers (except in anger). Above all, don't suppose that all Frenchmen are like Parisians—it's not true. Most of the French are more approachable and friendly.

Still, deep down, most of the French are chauvinists who are proud of *La douce France*, worship Napoleon, and feel that the Liberty-Equality-Fraternity motto of the French Revolution confers moral superiority upon their country—as they showed during the patriotic celebrations in 1989 that marked the bicentennial of the Revolution.

Essential Information

Before You Go

When to Go On the whole, June and September are the best months to be in France. Both months are free of the mid-summer crowds. June offers the advantage of long daylight hours, while slightly cheaper prices and frequent Indian summers (often lasting well into October) make September an attractive proposition. Try to avoid the second half of July and all of August, or be prepared for inflated prices and huge crowds on the beaches. Don't travel on or around July 14 or August 1, 14, or 31. In addition, July and August heat can be stifling in southern France. Paris can be stuffy in August, too. But, on the other hand, it's pleasantly deserted (although many restaurants, theaters, and small shops are closed).

The skiing season in the Alps and Pyrenees lasts from Christmas through Easter—steer clear of February (school vacation time) if you can. Anytime between March and November will offer you a good chance to soak up the sun on the Riviera. If you're going to Paris or the Loire, remember that the weather is unappealing before Easter. If you're dreaming of Paris in the springtime, May (not April) is your best bet.

Climate Be prepared for changes in climate if you wish to visit different parts of France. North of the Loire (including Paris), France has a northern European climate—cold winters, pleasant if unpredictable summers, and frequent rain. Southern France has a Mediterranean climate: mild winters, long, hot summers, and sunshine throughout the year. The more continental climate of eastern and central France is a mixture of these two extremes: Winters can be very cold and summers very hot. France's Atlantic coast has a temperate climate even south of the Loire, with the exception of the much warmer Biarritz.

The following are the average daily maximum and minimum temperatures for Paris.

Jan.	43F	6C	May	68F	20C	Sept.	70F	21C
	34	1		49	10		53	12
Feb.	45F	7C	June	73F	23C	Oct.	60F	16C
	34	1		55	13		46	8
Mar.	54F	12C	July	76F	25C	Nov.	50F	10C
	39	4		58	14		40	5
Apr.	60F	16C	Aug.	75F	24C	Dec.	44F	7C
	43	6		58	14		36	2

The following are the average daily maximum and minimum temperatures for Marseille.

Jan.	50F	10C	May	71F	22C	Sept.	77F	25C
	35	2		52	11		58	15
Feb.	53F	12C	June	79F	26C	Oct.	68F	20C
	36	2		58	14		51	10
Mar.	59F	15C	July	84F	29C	Nov.	58F	14C
	41	5		63	17		43	6
Apr.	64F	18C	Aug.	83F	28C	Dec.	52F	11C
	46	8		63	17		37	3

Currency The unit of French currency is the franc, subdivided into 100 centimes. Bills are issued in denominations of 20, 50, 100, and 500 francs (frs); coins are 5, 10, 20, and 50 centimes and 1, 2, 5, and 10 francs. The small, copper-colored 5-, 10-, and 20-centime coins have considerable nuisance value, but can be used for tips in bars and cafés.

International credit cards and traveler's checks are widely accepted throughout France, except in rural areas. At press time (spring 1992), the dollar was worth 5.50 frs, the Canadian dollar was worth 4.70 frs, and the pound sterling was worth 9.80 frs.

What It Will Cost Gasoline prices are above the European average, and there are tolls on major highways. Train travel, though, is a good buy.

Hotel and restaurant prices compensate for travel expenses. Prices are highest in Paris, on the Riviera, and in the Alps during the ski season. But even in these areas, you can find pleasant accommodations and excellent food for surprisingly reasonable prices.

All taxes must be included in posted prices in France. The initials TTC *(toutes taxes comprises*—taxes included) are sometimes included on price lists but, strictly speaking, they are superfluous. Restaurant and hotel prices must *by law* include taxes and service charges: If they are tacked onto your bill as additional items, you should complain.

Sample Prices Cup of coffee, 4–7 frs; glass of beer, 7–10 frs; soft drink, 8–12 frs; ham sandwich, 12–15 frs; one-mile taxi ride, 20–25 frs.

Visas Citizens of the United States, Canada, and Britain do not require a visa to visit France.

Customs on Arrival Travelers from the United States and Canada may bring into France 400 cigarettes or 100 cigars or 100 grams of tobacco, 1 liter of liquor of 22% volume and 2 liters of wine, 0.50 liters of perfume and 0.25 liters of toilet water, and other goods to the value of 300 frs.

Adults traveling from the United Kingdom may bring into France 300 cigarettes or 150 cigarillos or 75 cigars or 400 grams of tobacco; 1.5 liters of liquor over 22% volume or 3 liters of liquor under 22% volume or 3 liters of fortified/sparkling wine, plus 4 liters of still wine; 0.9 liters of perfume and 0.375 liters of toilet water; plus other goods to the value of 2,400 frs.

Language The French study English for a minimum of four years at school, but few are fluent in their conversation. English is widely understood in major tourist areas, and in most tourist hotels there should be at least one person who can converse with you. Be courteous, patient, and speak slowly: France, after all, has visitors from many countries and is not heavily dependent for income on English-speaking visitors as, for example, is Spain.

Even if your own French is rusty, try to master a few words: The French are more cooperative when they think you are at least making an effort to speak their language.

Getting Around

By Train **SNCF,** the French national railroad company, is generally recognized as Europe's best national train service: fast, punctual, comfortable, and comprehensive. The high-speed TGVs, with a top speed of 190 mph, are the best domestic trains, heading south–east from Paris to Lyon, the Riviera, and Switzerland; west to Nantes; and south–west to Bordeaux. Most TGV trains require passengers to pay a supplement—usually 20–40 frs, but a bit more during peak periods. Also, you need a seat reservation—easily obtained at the ticket window or from an automatic machine. Seat reservations are reassuring but seldom necessary on other French trains, except at certain busy holiday times.

You need to punch your train ticket in one of the waist-high orange machines you'll encounter alongside platforms. Slide your ticket in faceup and wait for a "clink" sound. If nothing happens, try another machine. (The small yellow tickets and automatic ticket barriers used for most suburban Paris trains are similar to those in the métro/RER.)

It is not necessary to take an overnight train, even if you are traveling from one end of France to the other; but if you take one, you have a choice between *wagons-lits* (sleeping cars), which are expensive, and *couchettes* (bunks), which sleep six to a compartment (sheet and pillow provided) and are more affordable (around 80 frs). Ordinary compartment seats do not pull together (as in Germany) to enable you to lie down. There are special summer night trains from Paris to Spain and the Riviera geared for a younger market, with discos and bars to enable you to dance the night away.

Fares Various reduced-fare passes are available from major train stations in France and from travel agents acting as agents for SNCF. If you are planning a lot of train travel, we suggest that you buy a special **France Vacances** card (around 1,400 frs for nine days). Families and couples are also eligible for big discounts. So are senior citizens (over 60) and young people (under

26), who qualify for different discount schemes. Having paid for your pass, you can get 50% reductions during blue periods (most of the time) and 20% most of the rest of the time (white periods: noon Friday to noon Saturday; 3 PM Sunday to noon Monday). On major holidays (red periods) there are no reductions. A calendar showing the red, white, and blue periods is available at any station. The **Carte Kiwi** (395 frs) enables children and up to four accompanying adults to travel half-price. Note that there is no reduction for booking an *aller-retour* (round-trip) ticket rather than an *aller simple* (one-way).

By Plane   France's domestic airline service is called **Air Inter.** Most domestic flights from Paris leave from Orly. Contact your travel agent or Air Inter (tel. 45–39–25–25). Train service is always cheaper and may be faster, though, particularly when you consider the time it takes to travel between the airport and city center, so check train schedules before committing yourself to a flight.

By Bus   Because of excellent train service, long-distance buses are rare and found mainly where train service is inadequate. Bus tours are organized by the **SNCF** and other tourist organizations, such as **Horizons Européens:** Ask for their brochures at any major travel agent, or contact France-Tourisme at 3 rue d'Alger, 75001 Paris, tel. 42–61–85–50.

By Boat   France has Europe's busiest inland waterway system. Canal and river vacations are popular: Visitors can either take an organized cruise or rent a boat and plan their own leisurely route. Contact a travel agent for details or ask for a "Tourisme Fluvial" brochure in any French tourist office. Some of the most picturesque stretches are to be found in Brittany, Burgundy, and the Midi. The Canal du Midi between Toulouse and Sète, constructed in the 17th century, is a historic marvel. Additional information is available from French national tourist offices, **France-Anjou Navigation** (Quai National, 72300 Sablé-sur-Sarthe), or **Bourgogne Voies Navigables** (1 quai de la République, 89000 Auxerre).

By Bicycle   There is no shortage of wide empty roads and flat or rolling countryside in France suitable for bike riding. The French themselves are great cycling enthusiasts—witness the Tour de France. Bikes can be rented from a total of 260 train stations for around 40 frs a day; you need to show your passport and leave a deposit of about 500 frs (unless you have a Visa or MasterCard). You do not always need to return the bike to the same station. Bikes may be sent as accompanied luggage from any station in France; some trains in rural areas don't even charge to transport bikes. Tourist offices will supply details on the more than 200 local shops that have bikes for rent, or obtain the SNCF brochure "Guide du Train et du Vélo."

Staying in France

Telephones   The French telephone system is modern and efficient. Phone
Local Calls   booths are plentiful; they are nearly always available at post offices and cafés. A local call in France costs 73 centimes plus 12 centimes per minute; half-price rates apply between 9:30 PM and 8 AM and between 1:30 PM Saturday and 8 AM Monday.

Pay phones work with 1-, 2-, and 5-fr coins (1 fr minimum). Lift the receiver, place the coin(s) in the appropriate slot, and dial.

Unused coins are returned when you hang up. Many French pay phones are now operated by *télécartes* (phone cards), which you can buy from post offices and some shops (cost: 40 frs for 50 units; 96 frs for 120). These cards save money and time.

All French phone numbers have eight digits; a code is required only when calling the Paris region from the provinces (dial 16–1 and then the number) and for calling the provinces from Paris (dial 16, then the number). Note that the number system was changed in 1985 and that you may come across some seven-digit numbers in Paris and some six-digit ones elsewhere. Add 4 to the front of such Paris numbers and the former two-digit area code to provincial ones.

International Calls Dial 19 and wait for the tone, then dial the country code (1 for the United States and Canada, 44 for the United Kingdom), area code (minus any initial 0), and number. If you make phone calls from your hotel room, expect to be greatly overcharged.

Operators To find a number within France or to request other information, dial 12. For international information, dial 19–33 plus the country code.

Mail Airmail letters to the United States and Canada cost 4 frs for 20
Postal Rates grams. Letters to the United Kingdom cost 2.50 frs for up to 20 grams, as they do within France. Postcards cost 2.20 frs within France and if sent to EC countries (2.30 frs for surface or 3.70 frs for airmail to North America). Stamps can be bought in post offices and cafés sporting a red "Tabac" sign outside.

Receiving Mail If you're uncertain where you'll be staying, have mail sent to American Express, Thomas Cook, or Poste Restante at most French post offices. American Express has a $2 service charge per letter.

Shopping A number of shops, particularly large stores in cities and holi-
VAT Refunds day resorts, offer value-added tax (VAT) refunds to foreign shoppers. You are entitled to an export discount of 13% or 23%, depending on the item purchased, though this often applies only if your purchases in the same store reach a minimum 2,800 frs (for residents of EC countries) or 1,200 frs (all others, including Americans and Canadians).

Bargaining Shop prices are clearly marked and bargaining is not a way of life. Still, at outdoor markets, flea markets, and in antiques stores, you can try your luck. If you're thinking of buying several items in these places, you have nothing to lose in cheerfully suggesting to the proprietor, *"Vous me faites un prix?"* ("How about a discount?").

Opening and **Banks.** In general, banks are open weekdays 9:30–4:30, but
Closing Times times vary. Most close for an hour to an hour and a half for lunch.

Museums. Most museums are closed one day a week (usually Tuesday) and on national holidays. Usual times are from 9:30 to 5 or 6. Many museums close for lunch (noon–2); many are open afternoons only on Sunday.

Shops. Large shops in big towns are open from 9 or 9:30 to 6 or 7 without a lunch break. Smaller shops often open earlier (8 AM) and close later (8 PM), but take a lengthy lunch break (1–4). This siesta-type schedule is more typical in the south of France. Corner grocery stores, often run by immigrants, frequently stay open until around 10 PM.

National Holidays January 1; April 12 (Easter Monday); May 1 (Labor Day); May 8 (VE Day); May 20 (Ascension); May 31 (Pentecost); July 14 (Bastille Day); August 15 (Assumption); November 1 (All Saints Day); November 11 (Armistice); December 25.

Dining Eating in France is serious business, at least for two of the three meals each day. For a light meal, try a *brasserie* (steak and french fries remain the classic), a picnic (a *baguette* loaf with ham, cheese, or pâté makes a perfect combination), or one of the fast-food places that have sprung up in urban areas over recent years.

French breakfasts are relatively modest—strong coffee, fruit juice if you insist, and croissants. International chain hotels are likely to offer American or English breakfasts, but in cafés you will probably be out of luck if this is what you want.

Mealtimes Dinner is the main meal and usually begins at 8. Lunch begins at 12:30 or 1.

Dress Jacket and tie are recommended for Very Expensive and Expensive restaurants, and at some of the more stylish Moderate restaurants as well. When in doubt, it's best to dress up. Otherwise casual dress is appropriate.

Precautions Tap water is perfectly safe, though not always very appetizing (least of all in Paris). Mineral water is a palatable alternative; there is a vast choice of *eau plate* (plain) as well as *eau gazeuse* (fizzy).

Ratings Prices are per person and include a first course, main course, and dessert plus taxes and service (which are always included in displayed prices), but not wine. Best bets are indicated by a star ★.

Category	All Areas
Moderate	175–250 frs
Inexpensive	100–175 frs
Budget	under 100 frs

Lodging France has a wide range of accommodations, from rambling old village inns to stylishly converted châteaux. Prices must, by law, be posted at the hotel entrance and should include taxes and service. Prices are always by room, not per person. Ask for a *grand lit* if you want a double bed. Breakfast is not always included in this price, but you are usually expected to have it and often are charged for it whether you have it or not. In smaller rural hotels, you may be expected to have your evening meal at the hotel, too.

The quality of rooms, particularly in older properties, can be uneven; if you don't like the room you're given, ask to see another. If you want a private bathroom, state your preference for *douche* (shower) or *baignoire (bath)*—the latter always costing more. Tourist offices in major train stations can reserve hotels for you, and so can tourist offices in most towns.

Hotels Hotels are officially classified from one-star to four-star-deluxe. France has—but is not dominated by—big hotel chains: Examples in the upper price bracket include Frantel, Holiday Inn, Novotel, and Sofitel. The Ibis and Climat de France chains are more moderately priced. Chain hotels, as a rule, lack atmosphere, with the following exceptions:

Logis de France. This is a group of small, inexpensive hotels that can be relied on for comfort, character, and regional cuisine. Look for its distinctive yellow and green sign. The Logis de France paperback guide is widely available in bookshops (cost: around 65 frs) or from Logis de France (83 av. d'Italie, 75013 Paris).

France-Accueil is another chain of friendly low-cost hotels. You can get a free booklet from France-Accueil (85 rue Dessous-des-Berges, 75013 Paris).

Rentals   *Gîtes Ruraux* offers families or small groups the opportunity for an economical stay in a furnished cottage, chalet, or apartment. These can be rented by the week or month. Contact either the **Fédération Nationale des Gîtes de France,** 35 rue Godot-de-Mauroy, 75009 Paris, tel. 47–42–20–20 (indicate the region that interests you), or the French Government Tourist Office in New York or London (*see* Before You Go in Chapter 1, Essential Information).

Bed-and-Breakfasts   These are known in France as *chambres d'hôte* and are increasingly popular in rural areas. Check local tourist offices for details.

Youth Hostels   With inexpensive hotel accommodations in France so easy to find, you may want to think twice before staying in a youth hostel—especially as standards of French hostels don't quite approximate those in neighboring countries. Contact **Fédération Unie des Auberges de Jeunesse** (10 rue Notre-Dame-de-Lorette, 75009 Paris).

Villas   The French Government Tourist Offices in London and New York publish extensive lists of agencies specializing in villa rentals. You can also write to **Rent-a-Villa Ltd.** (3 W. 51st St., New York, NY 10019) or, in France, **Interhome** (15 av. Jean-Aicard, 75011 Paris).

Camping   French campsites have a good reputation for organization and amenities but tend to be crowded in July and August. More and more campsites now welcome advance reservations, and if you're traveling in summer, it makes sense to book in advance. A guide to France's campsites is published by the **Fédération Française de Camping et de Caravaning,** 78 rue de Rivoli, 75004 Paris.

Ratings   Prices are for double rooms and include all taxes. Best bets are indicated by a star ★.

Category	All Areas
Moderate	350–500 frs
Inexpensive	200–350 frs
Budget	under 200 frs

Tipping   The check in a bar or restaurant will include service, but it is customary to leave some small change unless you're dissatisfied. The amount varies, from 30 centimes for a beer to a few francs after a meal. Tip taxi drivers and hairdressers about 10%. Give ushers in theaters 1–2 frs. Cloakroom attendants will expect nothing if there is a sign saying *Pourboire in-*

terdit—no tip; otherwise give them 5 frs. Washroom attendants usually get 5 frs—a sum that is often posted.

Bellhops should get 10 frs per item.

If you stay in a moderately priced hotel for more than two or three days, it is customary to leave something for the chambermaid—perhaps 10 frs per day. Expect to pay 10 frs for room service—but nothing is expected if breakfast is routinely served in your room. If the chambermaid does some ironing or laundering for you, leave an additional 5 frs in the room.

Service station attendants get nothing for giving you gas or oil, and 5 or 10 frs for checking tires. Train and airport porters get a fixed sum (6–10 frs) per bag. Museum guides should get 5–10 frs after a guided tour. It is standard practice to tip guides (and bus drivers) after an excursion.

Paris

Arriving and Departing

By Plane International flights arrive at either Charles de Gaulle Airport (Roissy), 24 kilometers (15 miles) northeast of Paris, or at Orly Airport, 16 kilometers (10 miles) south of the city. For information on arrival and departure times, call individual airlines.

Between the Airport and Downtown **From Charles de Gaulle:** Buses leave every 15 minutes from 5:40 AM to 11 PM. The fare is 38 frs and the trip takes 40 minutes (up to 1½ hours during rush hour). You arrive at the Arc de Triomphe or Porte Maillot, on the Right Bank by the Hotel Concorde-Lafayette.

From Orly: Buses leave every 12 minutes from 6 AM to 11 PM and arrive at the Air France terminal near Les Invalides on the Left Bank. The fare is 31 frs, and the trip takes between 30 and 60 minutes, depending on traffic.

Both airports provide free bus shuttles to the nearest train stations, where you can take the RER service to Paris. The advantages of this are speed, price (31 frs to Paris from Charles de Gaulle in Roissy, 24 frs from Orly), and the fact that the RER trains link up directly with the métro system. The disadvantage is having to lug your bags around. Taxi fares from airports to Paris range from 150 to 200 frs.

By Train Paris has five international stations: Gare du Nord (for northern France, northern Europe, and England via Calais or Boulogne); Gare de l'Est (for Strasbourg, Luxembourg, Basle, and central Europe); Gare de Lyon (for Lyon, Marseille, the Riviera, Geneva, Italy); Gare d'Austerlitz (for the Loire Valley, southwest France, Spain); Gare St-Lazare (for Normandy, England via Dieppe). The Gare Montparnasse serves western France (mainly Nantes and Brittany) and is the terminus for the new TGV Atlantic service from Paris to Bordeaux. For train information, tel. 45–82–50–50. You can reserve tickets at any Paris station regardless of the destination. Go to the Grandes Lignes counter for travel within France or to the Billets Internationaux (international tickets) desk if you're heading out of France.

By Bus Long-distance bus journeys within France are uncommon, which may be why Paris has no central bus depot. The leading

Paris-based bus company is **Eurolines Nord** (3 av. de la Porte de la Villette, 19e, tel. 40–38–93–93).

Getting Around

Paris is relatively small as capital cities go, and most of its prize monuments and museums are within walking distance of one another. A river cruise is a pleasant way to get an introductory overview. The most convenient form of public transportation is the métro, with stops every few hundred yards; buses are a slower alternative, though they do allow you to see more of the city. Taxis are not expensive but not always easy to hail, either. Car travel within Paris is best avoided because parking is chronically difficult.

By Métro There are 13 métro lines crisscrossing Paris and the nearby suburbs, and you are seldom more than a five-minute walk from the nearest station. It is essential to know the name of the last station on the line you take, since this name appears on all signs within the system. A connection (you can make as many as you please on one ticket) is called a *correspondance*. At junction stations, illuminated orange signs, bearing the names of each line terminus, appear over the corridors leading to the various correspondances. Illuminated blue signs, marked *sortie*, indicate the station exit.

The métro service starts out from each terminus at 5:30 AM and continues until 1:15 AM—when the last métro on each line reaches its terminus. Some lines and stations in the seedier parts of Paris are a bit risky at night—in particular Line 2 (Porte-Dauphine–Nation) and the northern section of Line 13 from St-Lazare to St-Denis/Asnières. The long, bleak corridors at Jaurès and Stalingrad are a haven for pickpockets and purse snatchers. But the Paris métro is a relatively safe place, as long as you don't walk around with your wallet hanging out of your back pocket or travel alone (especially women) late at night.

The métro network connects at several points in Paris with RER trains that race across Paris from suburb to suburb: RER trains are a sort of supersonic métro and can be a great time-saver. All métro tickets and passes are valid for RER and bus travel within Paris. Métro tickets cost 5.50 frs each, though a *carnet* (10 tickets for 34.50 frs) is a far better value. Alternatively, you can buy a *coupon jaune* (weekly) or *carte orange* (monthly) ticket, sold according to zone. Zones 1 and 2 cover the entire métro network (cost: 54 frs per week or 190 frs per month). If you plan to take a suburban train to visit monuments in the Ile de France, you should consider a four-zone ticket (Versailles, St-Germain-en-Laye; 98 frs per week) or a six-zone ticket (Rambouillet, Fontainebleau; 123 frs per week). For these weekly or monthly tickets, you need to obtain a pass (available from train and major métro stations) and provide two passport-size photographs.

The *Formule 1* ticket is valid for one day's second-class travel (23–70 frs, depending on the number of zones), while the *Paris –Visite* card is valid for first-class travel over 3 days (80 frs Paris only, 150 frs with suburbs) or 5 days (130/185 frs).

Access to métro and RER platforms is through an automatic ticket barrier. Slide your ticket in flat and pick it up as it pops up farther along. Keep your ticket; you'll need it again to leave the RER system.

By Bus Most buses run from around 6 AM to 8:30 PM; some continue until midnight. Night buses operate from 1 AM to 6 AM between Châtelet and nearby suburbs. They can be stopped by hailing them at any point on their route. The buses and the métro use the same tickets, but they must be bought either from métro stations or tobacco shops. You need to show weekly/monthly/special tickets to the driver as you get on; if you have individual yellow tickets, you should state your destination and be prepared to punch one or more tickets in the red and gray machines on board the bus.

Important Addresses and Numbers

Tourist Information Paris Tourist Office (127 av. des Champs-Elysées, tel. 47–23–61–72). Open daily 9 AM–8 PM. (Closed Dec. 25, Jan 1.) Offices in major train stations are open daily 8–8.

Embassies U.S. (2 av. Gabriel, 75008 Paris, tel. 42–96–12–02). **Canada** (35 av. Montaigne, 75008 Paris, tel. 47–23–01–01). **U.K.** (35 rue du Faubourg St-Honoré, 75008 Paris, tel. 42–66–91–42).

Emergencies **Police:** dial 17 for emergencies. Automatic phone booths can be found at various main crossroads for use in police emergencies *(Police-Secours)* or medical help *(Services Medicaux)*; **Ambulance** (tel. 18 or 43–78–26–26); **Doctor** (tel. 47–07–77–77); **Hospitals: American Hospital** (63 blvd. Victor-Hugo, Neuilly, tel. 46–41–25–25); **British Hospital** (48 rue de Villiers, Levallois-Perret, tel. 47–58–13–12); **Dentist** (tel. 43–37–51–00; open 24 hours).

Exploring Paris

Paris is a compact city. With the possible exception of the Bois de Boulogne and Montmartre, you can easily walk from one sight to the next. Paris is divided in two by the River Seine, with two islands (Ile de la Cité and Ile St-Louis) in the middle. The south—or Left—Bank has a more intimate, bohemian flavor than the haughtier Right Bank. The east–west axis from Châtelet to the Arc de Triomphe, via the rue de Rivoli and the Champs-Elysées, is the principal thoroughfare for sightseeing and shopping on the Right Bank.

Monuments and museums are sometimes closed at lunchtime (usually noon–2) and one day a week (Monday or Tuesday): Check before you make the trip. A special **Carte Musées** pass, covering access to Paris museums and monuments, can be obtained from museums or métro stations (price: one-day pass, 50 frs; three days, 100 frs; five days, 150 frs). And remember that cafés stay open all day, making them the goal of foot-weary tourists in need of coffee, a beer, or a sandwich. Bakeries are another reliable source of sustenance.

Though attractions are grouped into four logical touring areas, there are several "musts" that most first-time visitors will not want to miss: the Eiffel Tower, the Champs-Elysées, the Louvre, and Notre-Dame. If time is a problem, you can explore Notre-Dame and the Latin Quarter; head to place de la Concorde and enjoy the vista from the Champs-Elysées to the Louvre; then take a boat trip along the Seine for a waterside rendezvous with the Eiffel Tower and a host of other monuments. You could finish off with dinner in Montmartre and consider it a day well spent.

Numbers in the margin correspond to points of interest on the Paris map.

Notre-Dame and the Left Bank

1 The most enduring symbol of Paris, and its historical and geographical heart, is **Notre-Dame Cathedral,** around the corner from Cité métro station. This is the logical place from which to start any tour of the city—especially as the tour starts on the Ile de la Cité, one of the two islands in the middle of the Seine, where Paris's first inhabitants settled around 250 BC. Notre-Dame has been a place of worship for more than 2,000 years; the present building is the fourth on this site. It was begun in 1163, making it one of the earliest Gothic cathedrals, although it was not finished until 1345. The facade seems perfectly proportioned until you notice that the north (left) tower is wider than the south. The interior is at its lightest and least cluttered in the early morning. Bay-by-bay cleaning is gradually revealing the original honey color of the stone. Window space is limited and filled with shimmering stained glass; the circular rose windows in the transept are particularly delicate. The 387-step climb up the towers is worth the effort for a perfect view of the famous gargoyles and the heart of Paris. *Admission: 30 frs adults, 16 frs children. Towers open daily 10–5. Treasury (religious and vestmental relics) open Mon.–Sat. 10–6, Sun. 2–6. Admission: 15 frs adults, 10 frs students, 5 frs children.*

The pretty garden to the right of the cathedral leads to a bridge that crosses to the city's second and smaller island, the **Ile St-Louis,** barely 600 meters (656 yards) long and an oasis of inner-city repose.

2 The rue des Deux Ponts bisects the island. Head left over the Pont de la Tournelle. To your left is the **Tour d'Argent,** one of the city's most famous restaurants.

3 Continue along quai de la Tournelle past Notre-Dame, then turn left at rue St-Jacques. A hundred yards ahead, on the right, is the back end of the **Eglise St-Séverin,** an elegant and unusually wide 16th-century church. Note the spiraling column among the forest of pillars behind the altar.

4 Turn left out of the church, cross the bustling boulevard St-Germain, and take rue de Cluny to the left. This leads to the **Hôtel de Cluny.** Don't be misled by the name. This is a museum devoted to the late Middle Ages and Renaissance. Look for the *Lady with the Unicorn* tapestries and the beautifully displayed medieval statues. *6 pl. Paul-Painlevé. Admission: 15 frs. Open Wed.–Mon. 9:45–12:30 and 2–5:15.*

5 Head up rue de la Sorbonne to the **Sorbonne,** Paris's ancient university. Students here used to listen to lectures in Latin, which explains why the surrounding area is known as the Quartier Latin (Latin Quarter). The Sorbonne is the oldest university in Paris—indeed, one of the oldest in Europe—and has for centuries been one of France's principal institutions of higher learning.

6 Walking up rue Victor-Cousin and turning left into rue Cujas, you come to the **Panthéon.** Its huge dome and elegant colonnade are reminiscent of St. Paul's in London but date from a century later (1758–89). The Panthéon was intended to be a church, but during the Revolution it was swiftly earmarked as a secular hall of fame. Its crypt contains the remains of such national heroes as Voltaire, Rousseau, and Zola. The interior is empty and austere, with principal interest centering on Puvis de Chavanne's late 19th-century frescoes, relating the life of Geneviève, patron saint of Paris. *Admission: 24 frs adults, 13 frs senior citizens, 5 frs children. Open daily 10–noon and 2–5.*

Behind the Panthéon is **St-Etienne du Mont,** a church with two claims to fame: its ornate facade and its curly Renaissance rood-screen (1521–35) separating nave and chancel—the only one of its kind in Paris. Don't forget to check out the fine 17th-century glass in the cloister at the back of the church.

Take the adjoining rue Clovis, turn right into rue Descartes, then left at the lively place de la Contrescarpe down rue Rollin.
7 Cross rue Monge to rue de Navarre. On the left is the **Arènes de Lutèce** (always open during daylight hours, admission free), a Gallo-Roman arena rediscovered only in 1869; it has since been landscaped and excavated to reveal parts of the original amphitheater, and counts as one of the least-known points of interest in Paris.

8 Rue de Navarre and rue Lacépède lead to the **Jardin des Plantes** (Botanical Gardens), which have been on this site since the 17th century. The gardens have what is reputedly the oldest tree in Paris, a robinia planted in 1636 (allée Becquerel), plus a zoo, alpine garden, hothouses, aquarium, and maze. Natural science enthusiasts will be in their element at the various museums, devoted to insects (Musée Entomologique), fossils and prehistoric animals (Musée Paléontologique), and minerals (Musée Minéralogique). *Admission: 12–25 frs. Museums open Wed.–Mon. 2–5.*

Head back up Rue Lacépède from the Jardin des Plantes. Turn left into rue Gracieuse, then right into rue Ortolan, which soon crosses the rue Mouffetard—site of a colorful market and many restaurants. Continue along rue du Pot-de-Fer and rue Rataud. At rue Claude-Bernard, turn right; then make your first left up rue St-Jacques.

9 Set slightly back from the street is the **Val de Grâce,** a domed church designed by the great architect Jules Hardouin-Mansart and erected in 1645–67 (after the Sorbonne church but before the Invalides). Its two-tiered facade, with capitals and triangular pedestals, is directly inspired by the Counter-Reformation Jesuit architectural style found more often in Rome than in Paris. The Baroque style of the interior is epitomized by the huge twisted columns of the baldachin (ornamental canopy) over the altar.

Continue to the **Closerie des Lilas** along nearby boulevard de Port-Royal. This celebrated brasserie retains more style than some of its cousins farther down the once bohemian, now unexciting, boulevard du Montparnasse, whose modern landmark, the 203-meter (656-foot) Tour Montparnasse, is visible in the distance.

From the crossroads by the Closerie des Lilas, there is an enticing view down the tree-lined avenue de l'Observatoire toward the **Palais du Luxembourg.** The palace was built by Queen
10 Maria de' Medici at the beginning of the 17th century in answer to Florence's Pitti Palace. It now houses the French Senate and

Paris

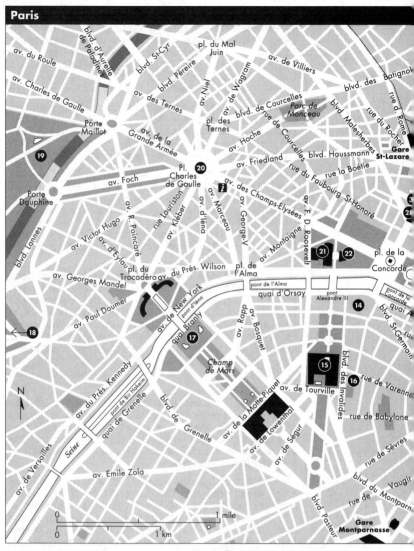

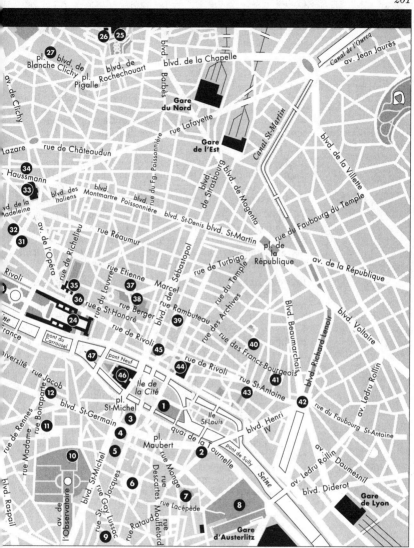

is not open to the public. In the surrounding gardens, mothers push their baby carriages along tree-lined paths among the majestic fountains and statues.

Head through the gardens to the left of the palace into rue de Vaugirard. Turn left, then right into rue Madame, which leads down to the enormous 17th-century church of **St-Sulpice.** Stand back and admire the impressive, though unfinished, 18th-century facade, with its unequal towers. The interior is overwhelmingly impersonal, but the wall paintings by Delacroix, in the first chapel on the right, are worth a visit.

Rue Bonaparte descends to boulevard St-Germain. You can hardly miss the sturdy pointed tower of **St-Germain-des-Prés,** the oldest church in Paris (begun around 1160, though the towers date to the 11th century). Note the colorful nave frescoes by the 19th-century artist Hippolyte Flandrin, a pupil of Ingres.

The spirit of writers Jean-Paul Sartre and Simone de Beauvoir still haunts the **Café de Flore** opposite the church, though this, and the neighboring **Aux Deux Magots,** have more tourists than literary luminaries these days. Still, you can linger over a drink while watching what seems to be all of Paris walking by.

Rue de l'Abbaye runs along behind St-Germain-des-Prés to place Fürstemberg, a charming little square where fiery Romantic artist Eugène Delacroix (1798–1863) had his studio. If you go there on a summer evening, you'll sometimes find young Frenchmen singing love songs to guitar accompaniment. Turn left into rue Jacob and continue along rue de l'Université. You are now in the heart of the Carré Rive Gauche, the Left Bank's district of art dealers and galleries.

About a quarter of a mile along rue de l'Université, turn down rue de Poitiers. Ahead is the sandstone bulk of the **Musée d'Orsay.** Follow it around to the left to reach the main entrance. The new Musée d'Orsay—opened in late 1986—is already one of Paris's star tourist attractions, thanks to its imaginatively housed collections of the arts (mainly French) spanning the period 1848–1914. Exhibits take up three floors, but the visitor's immediate impression is one of a single, vast hall. This is not surprising: The museum was originally built in 1900 as a train station. The combination of hall and glass roof with narrow, clanky passages and intimate lighting lends Orsay a human, pleasantly chaotic feel. You may get lost inside, but you won't mind too much.

The chief artistic attraction, of course, is the Impressionist collection, transferred from the inadequate Jeu de Paume museum across the river. Other highlights include Art Nouveau furniture, a faithfully restored Belle Epoque restaurant (formerly part of the station hotel), and a model of the Opéra quarter beneath a glass floor. *62 rue de Lille, tel. 40–49–48–14. Admission: 30 frs, 15 frs Sun. Open Tues., Wed., Fri., Sat. 10–5:30; Thurs. 10–9:15; Sun. 9–5:30.*

If the lines outside the Musée d'Orsay prove daunting, take a peek into the **Légion d'Honneur** museum across the way, a stylish mansion with a collection of French and foreign medals and decorations. *Admission: 10 frs. Open Tues.–Sun. 2–5.*

Farther along on rue de l'Université is the 18th-century **Palais Bourbon,** home of the French National Legislature (Assemblée Nationale). The colonnaded facade commissioned by Napoleon is a sparkling sight after a recent cleaning program (jeopardized at one stage by political squabbles as to whether cleaning should begin from the left or the right). There is a fine view from the steps across to place de la Concorde and the Madeleine.

Follow the Seine down to the exuberant **Pont Alexandre III.** The Grand and Petit Palais are to your right, across the river. To the left, the silhouette of **L'Hôtel des Invalides** soars above expansive if hardly manicured lawns. The Invalides was founded by Louis XIV in 1674 to house wounded (or "invalid") war veterans. Although only a few old soldiers live here today, the military link remains in the form of the **Musée de l'Armée**—a vast collection of arms, armor, uniforms, banners, and pictures. The **Musée des Plans-Reliefs** contains a fascinating collection of scale models of French towns made by the military architect Vauban in the 17th century.

The museums are far from being the only reason for visiting the Invalides. It is an outstanding Baroque ensemble, designed by Bruand and Mansart, and its church possesses the city's most elegant dome as well as the tomb of Napoleon, whose remains are housed in a series of no less than six coffins within a tomb of red porphyry. A *son-et-lumière* (sound and light) performance in English is held in the main courtyard on evenings throughout the summer (admission: 35 frs). *Admission to museums and church: 27 frs adults, 14 frs children. Open daily 10–6 (10–5 in winter).*

Alongside is the **Musée Rodin.** Together with the Picasso Museum in the Marais, this is the most charming of Paris's individual museums, consisting of an old house (built 1728) with a pretty garden, both filled with the vigorous sculptures of Auguste Rodin (1840–1917). The garden also has hundreds of rosebushes, with dozens of different varieties. *77 rue de Varenne. Admission: 20 frs, 10 frs Sun. Open Tues.–Sun. 10–5.*

Take avenue de Tourville to avenue de La Motte-Picquet. Turn left, and in a few minutes you will come face-to-face with the **Eiffel Tower.** It was built by Gustave Eiffel for the World Exhibition of 1889. Recent restorations haven't made the elevators any faster—long lines are inevitable—but decent shops and two good restaurants have been added. Consider coming in the evening, when every girder is lit in glorious detail. Such was Eiffel's engineering precision that even in the fiercest winds the tower never sways more than 11½ centimeters (4½ inches). Today, of course, it is the best-known Parisian landmark. Standing beneath it, you may have trouble believing that it nearly became 7,000 tons of scrap-iron when its concession expired in 1909. Only its potential use as a radio antenna saved the day; it now bristles with a forest of radio and television transmitters. If you're full of energy, you can stride up the stairs as far as the tower's third floor, but only the elevator will take you right to the top. The view from 1,000 feet up will enable you to appreciate the city's layout and proportions. *Admission: on foot, 8 frs; elevator, 17–49 frs, depending on the level. Open July–Aug., daily 10 AM–midnight; Sept.–June, Sun.–Thurs. 10 AM–11 PM, Fri., Sat. 10 AM–midnight.*

West Paris and the Louvre Our second itinerary starts at the **Musée Marmottan.** To get there, take the métro to La Muette, then head down chaussée de la Muette, through the small Ranelagh park to the corner of rue Boilly and avenue Raphaël. The museum is a sumptuous early 19th-century mansion, replete with many period furnishings, and probably is the most underestimated museum in Paris. It houses a magnificent collection of paintings by Claude Monet—including some of his huge, curving *Waterlily* canvasses—along with other Impressionist works and some delicately illustrated medieval manuscripts. *2 rue Louis-Boilly. Admission: 25 frs adults, 10 frs children and senior citizens. Open Tues.–Sun. 10–5:30.*

Continue along rue Boilly and turn left on boulevard Suchet. The next right takes you into the **Bois de Boulogne.** Class and style have been associated with "Le Bois" (The Woods) ever since it was landscaped into an upper-class playground by Haussmann in the 1850s. The attractions of this sprawling 891-hectare (2,200-acre) wood include cafés, restaurants, gardens, waterfalls, and lakes. You could happily spend a day or two exploring, but for the moment we suggest that you pass Auteuil racetrack on the left and then walk to the right of the two lakes. An inexpensive ferry crosses frequently to an idyllic island. Rowboats can be rented at the far end of the lake. Just past the boathouse, turn right on the route de Suresnes and follow it to Porte Dauphine, a large traffic circle.

Cross over to avenue Foch, with the unmistakable silhouette of the Arc de Triomphe in the distance. Keep an eye out for the original Art Nouveau iron-and-glass entrance to Porte Dauphine métro station, on the left. Then continue along avenue Foch, the widest and grandest boulevard in Paris, to the **Arc de Triomphe.** This 51-meter (164-foot) arch was planned by Napoleon to celebrate his military successes. Yet when Empress Marie-Louise entered Paris in 1810, it was barely off the ground and an arch of painted canvas had to be strung up to save appearances. Napoleon had been dead for more than 20 years when the Arc de Triomphe was finally finished in 1836. In 1988–89 it underwent a thorough face-lift to ward off signs of decay.

Place Charles de Gaulle, referred to by Parisians as **L'Etoile** (The Star), is one of Europe's most chaotic traffic circles. Short of a death-defying dash, your only way to get over to the Arc de Triomphe is to take the pedestrian underpass from either the Champs-Elysées (to your right as you arrive from avenue Foch) or avenue de la Grande Armée (to the left). France's Unknown Soldier is buried beneath the archway; the flame is rekindled every evening at 6:30.

From the top of the Arc you can see the "star" effect of Etoile's 12 radiating avenues and admire two special vistas: one, down the Champs-Elysées toward place de la Concorde and the Louvre, and the other, down avenue de la Grande Armée toward La Tête Défense, a severe modern arch surrounded by imposing glass and concrete towers. Halfway up the Arc there is a small museum devoted to its history. *Museum and platform. Admission: 30 frs adults, 16 frs senior citizens, 5 frs children. Open daily 10–5.*

The Champs-Elysées is the site of colorful national ceremonies on July 14 and November 11; its trees are often decked out with French tricolors and foreign flags to mark visits from heads of state. It is also where the cosmopolitan pulse of Paris beats strongest. The gracefully sloping 2-kilometer (1¼-mile) boulevard was originally laid out in the 1660s by André Le Nôtre as a garden sweeping away from the Tuileries. There is not much sign of that as you stroll past the cafés, restaurants, airline offices, car showrooms, movie theaters, and chic arcades that occupy its upper half. Farther down, on the right, is the **Grand Palais,** which plays host to Paris's major art exhibitions. Its glass roof makes its interior remarkably bright. *Admission varies. Usually open 10:30–6:30.*

The Grand Palais also houses the **Palais de la Découverte,** with scientific and mechanical exhibits and a planetarium. Entrance is in the avenue Franklin-Roosevelt. *Admission: 20 frs adults, 10 frs students; additional 13 frs (9 frs students) for planetarium. Open Tues.–Sun. 10–6.*

Directly opposite the main entrance to the Grand Palais is the **Petit Palais,** built at the same time (1900) and now home to an attractively presented collection of French paintings and furniture from the 18th and 19th centuries. *Admission: 12 frs adults, 6 frs students. Open Tues.–Sun. 10–5:40.*

The flowerbeds, chestnut trees, and sandy sidewalks of the lower section of the Champs-Elysées are reminders of its original leafy elegance. Continue down to place de la Concorde, built around 1775 and scene of more than a thousand deaths at the guillotine, including those of Louis XVI and Marie-Antoinette. The obelisk, a gift from the viceroy of Egypt, was erected in 1833.

To the east of the place de la Concorde is the **Jardin des Tuileries:** formal gardens with trees, ponds, and statues. Standing guard on either side are the **Jeu de Paume** and the **Orangerie,** identical buildings erected in the mid-19th century. The Jeu de Paume, home of an Impressionist collection before its move to the Musee d' Orsay, has been completely transformed. Its spacious, austere, white-walled rooms now house temporary exhibits of contemporary art, usually at its most brazen. The Orangerie contains fine early 20th-century French works by Monet, Renoir, Marie Laurencin, and others. *Admission to Jeu de Paume: 40 frs adults, 20 frs students. Open Wed.–Mon. 10–5. Admission to Orangerie: 25 frs, 13 frs Sun. Open Wed.–Mon. 9:45–5.*

Pass through the Tuileries to the Arc du Carrousel, a rather small triumphal arch erected more quickly (1806–08) than its big brother at the far end of the Champs-Elysées. Towering before you is the **Louvre,** with its glass pyramids. The Louvre, originally a royal palace, is today the world's largest and most famous museum. I. M. Pei's pyramids are the highlight of a major modernization program; in the course of their construction the medieval foundations of the palace were unearthed and are maintained and displayed as an integral part of the museum's collection. The pyramids stand as the easternmost landmark of a majestic vista stretching through the Arc du Carrousel, Tuileries, place de la Concorde, the Champs-Elysées, and the Arc de Triomphe all the way to the giant arch of La Défense, 4 kilometers (2½ miles) west of the capital.

The Louvre was begun as a fortress in 1200 (the earliest parts still standing date from the 1540s) and completed under Napoleon III in the 1860s. The Louvre used to be even larger; a wing facing the Tuileries Gardens was razed by rampaging revolutionaries during the bloody Paris Commune of 1871.

Whatever the aesthetic merits of Pei's new-look Louvre, the museum has emerged less cramped and more rationally organized. Yet its sheer variety can seem intimidating. The main tourist attraction is Leonardo da Vinci's *Mona Lisa* (known in French as *La Joconde)*, painted in 1503. The latest research, based on Leonardo's supposed homosexuality, would have us believe that the subject was actually a man! The *Mona Lisa* may disappoint you; it's smaller than most imagine, it's kept behind glass, and it's invariably encircled by a mob of tourists.

Turn your attention instead to some of the less-crowded rooms and galleries nearby, where Leonardo's fellow Italians are strongly represented: Fra Angelico, Giotto, Mantegna, Raphael, Titian, and Veronese. El Greco, Murillo, and Velázquez lead the Spanish; Van Eyck, Rembrandt, Frans Hals, Brueghel, Holbein, and Rubens underline the achievements of northern European art. English paintings are highlighted by works of Lawrence, Reynolds, Gainsborough, and Turner. Highlights of French painting include works by Poussin, Fragonard, Chardin, Boucher, and Watteau—together with David's *Coronation of Napoleon*, Géricault's *Raft of the Medusa*, and Delacroix's *Liberty Guiding the People.*

Famous statues include the soaring *Victory of Samothrace* (3rd century BC), the celebrated *Venus de Milo* (end of 2nd century BC), and the realistic Egyptian *Seated Scribe* (c. 2000 BC). Be sure to inspect the Gobelins tapestries, the Crown Jewels (including the 186-carat Regent diamond), and the 9th-century bronze statuette of Emperor Charlemagne. *Admission 30 frs adults, 15 frs students and Sun., children under 18 free. Open Wed.–Mon. 9–6 (9–9:45 PM Mon. and Wed.).*

Montmartre If you start at the Anvers métro station and head up rue de Steinkerque, with its budget clothing shops, you will be greeted by the most familiar and spectacular view of the Sacré

㉕ Coeur basilica atop the Butte Montmartre. The **Sacré-Coeur** was built in a bizarre, mock-Byzantine style between 1876 and 1910. It is no favorite with aesthetes, yet it has become a major Paris landmark. It was built as an act of national penitence after the disastrous Franco-Prussian War of 1870—a Catholic show of strength at a time when conflict between Church and State was at its most bitter.

The large, rather gloomy interior is short on stained glass but long on golden mosaics; *Christ in Glory*, above the altar, is the most impressive. The basilica's many cupolas are dominated by a dome and an 80-meter (260-foot) bell tower that contains the Savoyarde, one of the world's largest bells, cast in Annecy, Savoy, in 1895. The view from the dome is best on a clear day, when all the sights of Paris are spread out before you.

㉖ Around the corner is the **place du Tertre,** full of would-be painters and trendy, overpriced restaurants. The painters have been setting up their easels on the square for years; don't be talked into having your portrait done unless you really want to—in which case, check the price first.

Despite its eternal tourist appeal and ever-growing commercialization, Montmartre has not lost all its traditional bohemian color. Walk down rue Norvins and descend the bustling rue Lepic to place Blanche and one of the favorite haunts of Toulouse-Lautrec and other luminaries of the Belle Epoque—

㉗ the legendary **Moulin Rouge** cabaret.

Montmartre is some distance from the rest of the city's major attractions, so go left up boulevard de Clichy as far as **place Pigalle,** then take the métro to Madeleine.

Central Paris The **Eglise de la Madeleine,** with its array of uncompromising
28 columns, looks like a Greek temple. The only natural light inside comes from three shallow domes; the walls are richly but harmoniously decorated, with plenty of gold glinting through the dim interior. The church was designed in 1814 but not consecrated until 1842, after efforts to turn the site into a train station were defeated. The portico's majestic Corinthian colonnade supports a huge pediment with a sculptured frieze of the *Last Judgment.* From the top of the steps you can admire the vista down rue Royale across the Seine. Another vista leads up boulevard Malesherbes to the dome of **St-Augustin,** a mid-19th-century church notable for its innovative use of iron girders as structural support.

Place de la Madeleine is in the heart of Paris's prime shopping
29 30 district: Jewelers line rue Royale; **Fauchon's** and **Hédiard's,** behind the Madeleine, are high-class delicatessens.

Continue down boulevard de la Madeleine and turn right into rue des Capucines. This nondescript street leads to rue de la
31 Paix. Immediately to the right is **place Vendôme.** This is one of the world's most opulent squares, a rhythmically proportioned example of 17th-century urban architecture that shines in all its golden-stoned splendor since being sandblasted several years ago. Other things shine here, too, in the windows of jewelry shops that are even more upscale (and discreet) than those
32 in rue Royale—fitting neighbors for the top-ranking **Ritz** hotel. The square's central column, topped by a statue of Napoleon, is made from the melted bronze of 1,200 cannons captured at the Battle of Austerlitz in 1805.

Rue de la Paix leads to the place de l'Opéra. Dominating the
33 northern side of the square is the imposing **Opéra,** the first great work of the architect Charles Garnier, who in 1860 won the contract to build the opera house. He used elements of neoclassical architecture—bas reliefs on facades and columns—in an exaggerated combination that borders on parody. The lavishly upholstered auditorium, with its delightful ceiling painted by Marc Chagall in 1964, seems small—but this is because the stage is the largest in the world, accommodating up to 450 players. *Admission: 17 frs. Open daily 11–4:30.*

34 Behind the Opéra are **les grands magasins,** Paris's most venerable department stores. The nearer of the two, the **Galeries Lafayette,** is the more outstanding because of its elegant turn-of-the-century glass dome. But **Printemps,** farther along boulevard Haussmann to the left, is better organized and has an excellent view from its rooftop cafeteria.

Take the métro at Chaussée d'Antin, near the Galeries Lafayette, and travel three stops (direction Villejuif) as far as
35 **Palais-Royal.** This former royal palace, built in the 1630s, has a charming garden, bordered by arcades and boutiques, that many visitors overlook.

36 On the square in front of the Palais-Royal is the **Louvre des Antiquaires,** a chic shopping mall full of antiques dealers. It deserves a browse whether you intend to buy or not. Afterward, head east along rue St-Honoré and left into rue du Louvre.

Skirt the circular **Bourse du Commerce** (Commercial Ex-
❸❼ change) and head toward the imposing church of **St-Eustache,**
(1532–1637), an invaluable testimony to the stylistic transition
between Gothic and Classical architecture. It is also the "cathe-
❸❽ dral" of **Les Halles**—the site of the central market of Paris until
the much-loved glass-and-iron sheds were torn down in the late
'60s. The area has since been transformed into a trendy—and
already slightly seedy—shopping complex, Le Forum.

Head across the topiary garden and left down rue Berger. Pass
the square des Innocents, with its Renaissance fountain, to
boulevard de Sébastopol. Straight ahead lies the futuristic,
❸❾ funnel-topped **Centre Pompidou** (Pompidou Center)—a must
for lovers of modern art. The Pompidou Centre, also known as
the Beaubourg, was built in the mid-1970s and named in honor
of former French president Georges Pompidou (1911–74). This
"cultural Disneyland" is always crowded, housing a **Museum of
Modern Art,** a huge library, experimental music and industrial
design sections, a children's museum, and a variety of activities and exhibitions. Musicians, magicians, fire-eaters, and
other street performers fill the large forecourt near the entrance. *Admission: Museum of Modern Art, 27 frs, free Sun.;
50 frs for daily pass covering all sectors of the center. Open
Mon., Wed.–Fri. noon–10; weekends 10–10.*

Continue east to the **Marais,** one of the most historic quarters
of Paris. The spacious affluence of its 17th-century mansions,
many restored to former glory, contrasts with narrow winding
streets full of shops and restaurants. Rue de Rambuteau leads
from the Centre Pompidou into rue des Francs-Bourgeois.
Turn left on rue Elzivir to rue Thorigny, where you will find
❹⓿ the Hôtel Salé and its **Musée Picasso.** This is a convincing ex-
periment in modern museum layout, whether you like Picasso
or not. Few of his major works are here, but many fine, little-
known paintings, drawings, and engravings are on display. *5
rue Thorigny. Admission: 21 frs. Open Thurs–Mon. 9:15–
5:15; Wed. 9:15 AM–10 PM.*

Double back down rue Elzivir and turn left along rue des
❹❶ Francs-Bourgeois until you reach the **place des Vosges.** Built in
1605, this is the oldest square in Paris. The square's harmonious proportions, soft pink brick, and cloisterlike arcades give it
an aura of calm. In the far corner is the **Maison de Victor Hugo,**
containing souvenirs of the great poet's life and many of his surprisingly able paintings and ink drawings. *6 pl. des Vosges. Admission: 12 frs. Open Tues.–Sun. 10–5:40.*

Rue Birague leads from the middle of the place des Vosges
down to rue St-Antoine. About 250 yards along to the left is the
❹❷ **place de la Bastille.** Unfortunately, there are no historic vestiges here; not even the soaring column, topped by the figure of
Liberty, commemorates the famous storming of the Bastille in
1789 (the column stands in memory of Parisians killed in the up-
risings of 1830 and 1848). Only the new **Opéra de la Bastille,**
which opened in 1989, can be said to mark the bicentennial.

Retrace your steps down rue St-Antoine as far as the large
❹❸ Baroque church of **Saint-Paul-Saint-Louis** (1627–41). Then con-
❹❹ tinue down the rue de Rivoli to the **Hôtel de Ville.** This magnificent city hall was rebuilt in its original Renaissance style after
being burned down in 1871, during the violent days of the Paris

Commune. The vast square in front of its many-statued facade is laid out with fountains and bronze lamps.

Avenue de Victoria leads to place du Châtelet. On the right is

45 the **Tour St-Jacques.** This richly worked 52-meter (170-foot) stump is all that remains of a 16th-century church destroyed in 1802.

From Châtelet take the pont-au-Change over the Seine to the

46 Ile de la Cité and the **Palais de Justice** (law courts). Visit the turreted **Conciergerie,** a former prison with a superb vaulted 14th-century hall (Salles des Gens d'Armes) that often hosts temporary exhibitions. The **Tour de l'Horloge** (clock tower) near the entrance on the quai de l'Horloge has a clock that has been ticking off time since 1370. Around the corner in the boulevard du Palais, through the imposing law court gates, is the **Sainte-Chapelle,** built by St-Louis (Louis IX) in the 1240s to house the Crown of Thorns he had just bought from Emperor Baldwin of Constantinople. The building's lead-covered wood spire, rebuilt in 1854, rises 75 meters (246 feet). The somewhat garish lower chapel is less impressive than the upper one, whose walls consist of little else but dazzling 13th-century stained glass. *Conciergerie and Sainte-Chapelle. Admission: joint ticket 40 frs; single ticket 24 frs. Open daily 10–6; winter 10–5.*

From boulevard du Palais turn right on quai des Orfèvres. This

47 will take you past the quaint place Dauphine to the **square du Vert Galant** at the westernmost tip of the Ile de la Cité. Here, above a peaceful garden, you will find a statue of the Vert Galant: gallant adventurer Henry IV, king from 1589 to 1610.

Off the Beaten Track

Cemeteries aren't every tourist's idea of the ultimate attraction, but **Père Lachaise** is the largest, most interesting, and most prestigious in Paris. It forms a veritable necropolis with cobbled avenues and tombs competing in pomposity and originality. Steep slopes and lush vegetation contribute to a powerful atmosphere; some people even bring a picnic lunch. Leading incumbents include Chopin, Molière, Proust, Oscar Wilde, Sarah Bernhardt, Jim Morrison, Yves Montand, and Edith Piaf. Get a map at the entrance and track them down. *Av. du Père-Lachaise, 20e; métro Gambetta. Open daily 8–6, winter 8–5 .*

Shopping

Gift Ideas   Paris is the home of fashion and perfume. Old prints are sold in *bouquinistes* (stalls) along the Left Bank of the Seine. For state-of-the-art home decorations, the shop in the **Musée des Arts Décoratifs** in the Louvre (107 rue de Rivoli) is well worth visiting.

Boutiques   Only Milan can compete with Paris for the title of Capital of European Chic. The top shops are along both sides of the Champs-Elysées and along the avenue Montaigne and the rue du Faubourg St-Honoré. If you're on a tight budget, search for bargains along the shoddy streets around the foot of Montmartre (*see* Exploring, *above*), or near **Barbès-Rochechouart** métro station. The streets to the north of the Marais, close to **Arts-**

et-Métiers métro, are historically linked to the cloth trade, and many shops offer garments at wholesale prices.

Department Stores The most famous department stores in Paris are **Galeries Lafayette** and **Printemps,** on boulevard Haussmann. Others include **Au Bon Marché** near Sèvres-Babylone (métro on the Left Bank) and the **Samaritaine,** overlooking the Seine east of the Louvre (métro Pont-Neuf).

Food and Flea Markets The sprawling **Marché aux Puces de St-Ouen,** just north of Paris, is one of Europe's largest flea markets. Best bargains are to be had early in the morning (open Sat.–Mon.; métro Porte de Clignancourt). There are smaller flea markets at the Porte de Vanves and Porte de Montreuil (weekends only).

Dining

Eating out in Paris should be a pleasure, and there is no reason why choosing a less expensive restaurant should spoil the fun. After all, Parisians themselves eat out frequently and cannot afford five-star dining every night, either. For details and price-category definitions, *see* Dining in Staying in France.

Left Bank
Moderate **Vagenende.** Dark wood, gleaming mirrors, and obsequious waiters take the Vagenende dangerously close to turn-of-the-century pastiche. It claims to be a bustling brasserie, but don't believe it: Service is far too unhurried and the dining room far too cozy. You can be sure of having a copious and enjoyable meal (foie gras, oysters, and chocolate-based desserts are outstanding), with a stroll outside along the cheerful boulevard St-Germain to walk it off. *142 blvd. St-Germain, 6e, tel. 43–26–68–18. Reservations advised. AE, DC, MC, V. Closed Feb. 1–8.*

Inexpensive **Petit St-Benoît.** This is a wonderful place—small, amazingly inexpensive, always crowded, and with decor that's plain to the point of barely existing. The food is correspondingly basic, but quite good for the price. Expect to share a table. *4 rue St-Benoît, 6e. No reservations. Dress: informal. No credit cards. Closed weekends.*

Petit Zinc. This long-established haunt has recently moved to rue St-Benoît. Its imperturbable white-aproned waiters and unpretentious Belle Epoque decor lend it an authentically Parisian atmosphere, at the foot of the church of St-Germain-des-Prés. The seafood is good here; *pintade* (guinea fowl) is recommended, and game and poultry are served in robust sauces. It is open until 3 AM. *11 rue St-Benoît, 6e, tel. 46–33–51–66. Reservations advised. AE, DC, MC, V.*

Suffren. Next to the Ecole Militaire at the far end of the Champ de Mars, is this archetypal brasserie: lively, good value, with oysters, fish, and other seafood in abundance. Foreigners are treated with a welcome lack of condescension. *84 av. de Suffren, 15e, tel. 45–66–97–86. Reservations accepted. V. Closed Mon.*

Budget **Bistro de la Gare.** The 6th Arrondissement boasts two members of this popular chain. Of them, the one on boulevard Montparnasse is the better, not because the food is noticeably finer—it's much the same in all the restaurants—but because of the decor. It's crowded with Art-Nouveau trimmings, and the expansive glass window is classified as a historic monument. *59 blvd. du Montparnasse, 6e, tel. 45–48–38–01. Reservations not required. Dress: informal. MC, V.*

Thoumieux. This is a large, 1920s-style restaurant, not far from the Eiffel Tower, that has been in the same family for three generations. The cuisine comes exclusively from the southwest of France (meaning that rich duck dishes predominate). Try the fixed-price menu for maximum value. *79 rue St-Dominique, 7e, tel. 47-05-49-75. Reservations advised. Dress: informal. MC, V. Closed Mon.*

West Paris
Moderate

Le Boeuf Gros Sel. Salt beef is the undisputed champion of the menu here. The food, like the simple decor, is plain and ultra-traditional. Save room for the *tarte tatin*, the French version of apple pie. *299 rue Lecourbe, 15e, tel. 45-57-36-53. Reservations advised. Dress: informal. MC, V. Closed Sun., Mon. lunch, and Aug.*

Inexpensive

Bistrot d'André. This classic bistro, not far from Aquaboulevard, stands close to the former site of the Citroën automobile factory, and car mementos—mainly plaques and old photos—line the walls. The wooden chairs and maroon-velvet benches conjure up a mood of prewar Paris, and jovial Hubert Gloaguen, the moustached *patron*, hosts half the quartier most nights. Bistro cooking at its sturdiest and most reliable includes snails, andouillette, confit de canard, and chicken with tarragon. An aperitif (try the kir with red wine) and four courses plus coffee comes to under 150 francs, and a decent bottle of Burgundy won't push your check skyward either. *232 rue St-Charles, 15e, tel. 45-57-89-14. Reservations advised. Dress: casual. MC, V. Closed Sat. lunch and Sun. Inexpensive.*

Relais de la Sabretèche. It's worth traveling deep into the residential 16th arrondissement, near the Porte de St-Cloud, for a restaurant that offers both unbeatable value and appealing, country-house decor. Consider the four-course set menu (served lunchtime and at dinner until 9 PM) for about 100 frs. For a similar sum, you can wash the meal down with a St-Estèphe or Châteauneuf-du-Pape (ask for a bottle from the cellar or it will be too warm). The service is discreet to the point of forgetfulness. *183 blvd. Murat, 16e, tel. 46-47-91-39. Reservations advised. V. Closed Sun. dinner, Mon.*

Budget

Fontaine de Mars. The Fontaine de Mars is a simple little family-style restaurant located in the otherwise expensive area around the Eiffel Tower. The low-priced lunch menu is popular with the local residents—always a good sign. Alternatively, and more expensively, take your pick from a wide choice of traditional country-style dishes, like beef in sea salt or beef casserole. Eat outside by the little fountain in the summer. *129 rue St-Dominique, 7e, tel. 47-05-46-44. Reservations recommended. Dress: informal. MC, V. Closed Sat. evening, Sun., and Aug.*

Montmartre and
Central Paris
Moderate
★

Brasserie Flo. Flo is an authentic, bustling brasserie that effortlessly recaptures the spirit of 1900. Sausages and sauerkraut are served with large glasses of Alsatian beer. The atmosphere gets livelier (some would say noisier) throughout the evening. Closing time is 1:30 AM. *7 cour des Petites-Ecuries, 10e, tel. 47-70-13-59. Reservations advised. AE, DC, V. Closed Christmas.*

Clodenis. A small, elegant restaurant down the slope from the Sacré Coeur, Clodenis serves excellent fish dishes and has some fixed-price menus for less than 200 frs. The decor—soft lighting, small tables, and beige wallpaper—is easy on the eye. *57* *rue Caulaincourt, 18e, tel. 46–06–20–26. Reservations advised. AE, DC, MC, V. Closed Sun., Mon.*

Coconnas. The irresistible combination of summer dining beneath the 16th-century arcades of the place des Vosges and traditional, high-quality food based on duck, steak, and chicken have rapidly made the Coconnas a hit with tourists and Parisians alike. The inside dining room is tastefully decked out with old prints and sturdy wooden furniture. *2 bis pl. des Vosges, 4e, tel. 42–78–58–16. Reservations advised. MC, V. Closed mid-Dec.–mid-Jan.*

Inexpensive **Jo Goldenberg.** The doyen of Jewish eating places in Paris, Jo Goldenberg is in the heart of that most Jewish district, the Marais. Its two-level restaurant, with modern paintings, is always good-natured and crowded. The food is solid and cheap and heavily influenced by Central Europe (ground beef and salami). This makes it a great place to dine on a winter evening, but a bit heavy going in summer. The Israeli and Eastern European wines are rarely available elsewhere in France. *7 rue des Rosiers, 4e, tel. 48–87–20–16. Reservations advised. AE, DC, V.*

Budget **Chartier.** This is the down-to-earth Belle Epoque cousin of the Vagenende (*see* Left Bank). Again, there are mirrors and fancy lamps, but here you'll be rushed and crowded; the waiter's white apron will be stained; and your check will be written on the tablecloth. This is the gastronomic equivalent of roughing it, but as this is Paris, you can have steak, fries, and a glass of wine for almost the same price as the burger meal at the fast-food places nearby. The good food belies the price. *7 rue du Faubourg-Montmartre, 9e, tel. 47–70–86–29. No reservations. No credit cards. Closes 9:30 PM.*

Trumilou. Overlooking the Seine opposite the Ile St-Louis, this very French little bistro is a real find. Despite the harsh lighting, the mood is boisterous and welcoming, with many regulars among the diners. Bright and splashy paintings line the walls. The food is resolutely traditional, with time-honored favorites like *boeuf bourguignon* and sweetbreads. *84 quai de l'Hôtel de Ville, 4e, tel. 42–77–63–98. Reservations accepted. Dress: informal. MC, V. Closed Mon.*

Lodging

Paris is popular throughout the year, so make reservations early. The cost of renovating many hotels for the 1989 bicentennial celebrations has been passed on to the consumer, so be prepared for higher prices. For details and price-category definitions, *see* Lodging in Staying in France.

Left Bank and **Sorbonne.** This pretty, early 18th-century hotel, located right
Ile St-Louis by the Sorbonne, was transformed in 1988 when its handsome
Moderate stone facade was cleaned. As part of the cleanup, fresh flowers are now put in every room, augmenting their existing simple elegance. There's no restaurant or bar, but the receptionist is English, so you'll have no trouble making dining and entertainment plans. Try for a room overlooking the little garden. *6 rue Victor-Cousin, 5e, tel. 43–54–58–08. 10 rooms with bath, 27 with shower. MC, V.*

Inexpensive **Albe.** You won't have much room here, and the level of comfort
★ is basic. But the setting is ideal for exploring the Latin Quarter; the pedestrian rue de la Harpe is central, bustling, and full

of small restaurants (mainly Greek and North African). Try to insist on a (slightly) quieter room at the back of the hotel. *1 rue de la Harpe, 5e, tel. 46–34–09–70. 43 rooms, some with bath or shower. AE, MC, V.*

Esméralda. You'll find this delightful 17th-century inn just across the river Seine from Notre-Dame. The rooms are small but full of character: Don't be afraid to ask for one with a view of the cathedral. There are also three inexpensive singles in the eaves. *4 rue St-Julien-le-Pauvre, 5e, tel. 43–54–19–20. 19 rooms, with bath or shower. Facilities: sauna. No credit cards.*

Budget **Dhély's.** Who would have thought that you could find such a reasonably priced hotel so close to the lively, bohemian Place St-Michel? Tucked away behind a portico on the tiny rue de l'Hirondelle, the clean, white facade of this hotel is a pleasure to stumble upon. New showers were recently installed in small bathrooms. Be sure to reserve well in advance. *22 rue de l'Hirondelle, 6e, tel. 43–26–58–25. 14 rooms, some with shower. No credit cards.*

West Paris **Argenson.** This friendly, family-run hotel provides what may
Moderate well be the best value in the swanky 8th Arrondissement. Some of the city's greatest sights are just a 10-minute walk away. Old-time charm in the form of period furnishings, molded ceilings, and floral arrangements is not compromised by some modern touches, such as the new bathrooms that were installed in 1988. The best rooms are numbers 23, 33, 42, 43, and 53. *15 rue d'Argenson, 8e, tel. 42–65–16–87. 48 rooms with bath or shower. DC, MC, V.*

Mayflower. This small, cozy hotel is just behind the Champs-Elysées, near Etoile. The Laura Ashley wallpaper and bedspreads give the rooms (all renovated in 1988) a wholesome English look. On the first floor, you'll find a comfortable reading room where breakfast and drinks are served. *3 rue Chateaubriand, 8e, tel. 45–62–57–46. 24 rooms with bath. MC, V.*

Inexpensive **Ceramic.** These are the lowest rates you'll ever pay this close to the Arc de Triomphe and Champs-Elysées. The hotel sports an impressive 1904 tiled facade that embodies Belle-Epoque ambience, and the reception area, replete with crystal chandeliers and velvet armchairs, is glamorous. Those guest rooms that face the street, such as rooms 412, 42, and 442, have huge bay windows and intricate plaster moldings. Rooms facing the courtyard are quiet and rather average. *34 ave. de Wagram, 8e, tel. 42–27–20–30. 53 rooms with bath or shower. MC, V.*

Queen's Hotel. Queen's is one of only a handful of hotels located in the desirable residential district around rue la Fontaine, within walking distance of the Seine and the Bois de Boulogne. The hotel is small and functional, but standards of comfort and service are high. Flowers on the facade add an appealing note. *4 rue Bastien-Lepage, 16e, tel. 42–88–89–85. 23 rooms with bath or shower. AE, MC, V.*

Montmartre **Family.** A few minutes' walk from the Tuileries Gardens will
and Central get you to this small two-star hotel near the Madeleine. It was
Moderate entirely renovated in 1988, but the rooms have kept their stylish '30s look. There's no restaurant, but breakfast and snacks can be served in your room. Service is exceptionally friendly. *35 rue Cambon, 1er, tel. 42–61–54–84. 24 rooms and 1 suite with bath. AE, MC, V.*

Inexpensive **Le Laumière.** Though it's located some ways from downtown, the low rates of this two-star hotel, close to the tumbling Buttes-Chaumont park, are hard to resist. Most rooms are functional only, but some of the larger ones overlook the garden. The staff is exceptionally helpful. There's no restaurant, but breakfast is available until midday. *4 rue Petit, 19e, tel. 42–06–10–77. 54 rooms, 39 with bath or shower. AE, DC, MC, V.*

Place des Vosges. A loyal American clientele swears by this historic little hotel, located on a charming street just off the exquisite square of the same name. The grand entrance hall is decorated in Louis XIII style; some of the rooms, however, are little more than functional, and a number of the smaller ones fall into the inexpensive category. There's no restaurant, but there's a welcoming little breakfast room. *12 rue de Birague, 4e, tel. 42–72–60–46. 11 rooms with bath or shower. AE, DC, MC, V.*

Regyn's Montmartre. Despite small rooms (all recently renovated), this small, owner-run hotel in Montmartre's place des Abbesses is rapidly gaining an enviable reputation for simple but stylish accommodation. A predominantly young clientele and a correspondingly relaxed atmosphere have made the hotel very popular. Try for one of the rooms on the upper floors for great views over the city. *18 pl. des Abbesses, 18e, tel. 42–54–45–21. 22 rooms with bath or shower. DC, MC, V.*

Résidence Alhambra. This hotel is on the edge of the historical Marais quarter and is conveniently close to five Métro lines. The Alhambra's gleaming white exterior and flower-filled window boxes provide a bright spot in an otherwise drab neighborhood. The interior has been redecorated, and some improvements include fresh pastel shades in the smallish guest rooms, marble-topped breakfast tables, and a room lobby filled with plants and leather armchairs. Most rooms have color TV, unusual for hotels in this price range. *11 bis rue de Malte, 11e, tel. 47–00–35–52. 50 rooms, most with bath or shower. MC, V.*

Sévigné. Located in the up-and-coming Marais district and convenient to the St-Paul Métro station and the place des Vosges, this hotel remains a good bet for quality low-budget accommodations. The hotel is clean and well-run, and the staff is personable. Extensive renovation a few years back resulted in a mirror-lined lobby, new breakfast room, and a shower or bath in every room. Rooms facing rue Malher are quieter, but those facing busy rue St-Antoine offer a view of the church of St-Paul-St-Louis. *2 rue Malher, 4e, tel. 42–72–76–17. 30 rooms with shower or bath. No credit cards.*

Budget **Lille.** You won't find a less expensive base for exploring the Louvre than this hotel, located just a short distance from the Cour Carrée. The hotel hasn't received a face-lift in years, but then neither have the prices. The decor is somewhat shabby, but it's the epitome of Vieux Paris, and the money you save by staying here can come in handy if you indulge in a shopping spree along the nearby Rue de Rivoli or Forum des Halles. *8 rue du Pélican, 1er, tel. 42–33–33–42. 14 rooms, some with shower. No credit cards.*

The Arts

The monthly magazine *Passion* (in English) and the weekly magazines *Pariscope*, *L'Officiel des Spectacles*, and *7 à Paris* give detailed entertainment listings. The best place to buy tickets is at the place of performance. Otherwise, try hotels, travel agencies (try **Paris-Vision** at 214 rue de Rivoli), and special ticket counters (in the **FNAC** stores at 26 av. de Wagram, near the Arc de Triomphe and the Forum des Halles). Half-price tickets for same-day theater performances are available at the ticket stand at the west side of the Madeleine church.

Theater There is no Parisian equivalent to Broadway or the West End, although a number of theaters line the grand boulevards between Opéra and République. Shows are mostly in French; classical drama is at the distinguished **Comédie Française** (by Palais-Royal). A completely different charm is to be found in the tiny **Théâtre de la Huchette,** near St-Michel, where Ionesco's short modern plays make a deliberately ridiculous mess of the French language.

Concerts The principal venues for classical music are the **Salle Pleyel** (252 rue du Faubourg St-Honoré), near the Arc de Triomphe, and the new **Opéra de la Bastille**. You can also attend one of the many inexpensive organ or chamber music concerts in churches throughout the city.

Opera The **Opéra** itself is a splendid building, and, with Rudolf Nureyev as artistic director, its dance program has reached new heights. Getting a ticket for an opera or ballet performance is not easy, though, and requires either luck, much preplanning, or a well-connected hotel receptionist. The **Opéra Comique** (the French term for opera with spoken dialogue), close by in the rue Favart, is more accessible. The new **Opéra de la Bastille** opened in 1989 and stages both traditional opera and symphony concerts.

Film There are hundreds of movie theaters in Paris and some of them, especially in principal tourist areas such as the Champs-Elysées and the boulevard des Italiens near the Opéra, run English films marked "V.O." *(version originale*—i.e., not dubbed). Admission is around 35–45 frs, with reduced rates on Monday. Movie fanatics should check out the **Centre Pompidou** and **Musée du Cinéma** at Trocadéro, where old and rare films are often screened.

Nightlife

Cabaret This is what Paris is supposed to be all about. Its nightclubs are household names—more so abroad than in France, it would seem, judging by the hefty percentage of foreigners present at most shows. Prices range from 200 frs (basic admission plus one drink) up to 650 frs (dinner included). For 350–450 frs, you can get a good seat plus half a bottle of champagne.

The **Crazy Horse** (12 av. George-V, tel. 47–23–32–32) is one of the field leaders in pretty women and dance routines: It features lots of humor and a lot less clothes. The **Moulin Rouge** (place Blanche, tel. 46–06–00–19) is an old favorite at the foot of Montmartre. Nearby is the **Folies-Bergère** (32 rue Richer, tel. 42–46–77–11), not as it once was but still renowned for its glitter and vocal numbers. The **Lido** (116 bis av. des Champs-Elysées, tel. 40–76–56–10) is all razzle-dazzle.

Bars and Nightclubs Upscale nightclubs are usually private, so unless you have a friend who is a member, forget it. A good bet, though, for drinking and dancing the night away, is the **Club 79** (79 av. des Champs-Elysées). For a more leisurely evening in an atmosphere that is part bar and part gentlemen's club, try an old haunt of Hemingway, Fitzgerald, and Gertrude Stein: **Harry's Bar** (5 rue Danou), a cozy wood-paneled spot for Americans, journalists, and sportsmen.

Jazz Clubs The Latin Quarter is a good place to track down Paris jazz, and the doyen of clubs is the **Caveau de la Huchette** (5 rue de la Huchette), where you can hear Dixieland in a hectic, smoke-filled atmosphere. **Le Slow Club** (130 rue de Rivoli), another favorite, tries to resurrect the style of early Bourbon street, and nearly succeeds.

Rock Clubs **Le Sunset** (60 rue des Lombards) is a small, whitewashed cellar with first-rate live music and a clientele that's there to listen. **New Morning** (7 rue des Petites Ecuries) is a top spot for visiting American musicians and good French bands.

Discos **Club Zed** (2 rue des Anglais off blvd. St.-Germain), is the best place for rock and roll. **Memphis** (3 impasse Bonne-Nouvelle) boasts some impressive lighting and video gadgetry.

Ile de France

The area surrounding Paris is called the Ile (island) de France, reflecting the role it has played over the centuries as the economic, political, and religious center of the country. For many visitors to Paris, it is the first taste of French provincial life, with its slower pace and fierce devotion to the soil.

Although parts of the area are fighting a losing battle to resist the encroaching capital, you can still see the countryside that was the inspiration for the Impressionists and other 19th-century painters and is home to a wealth of architecture dating to the Middle Ages. The most famous buildings are Chartres—one of the most beautiful of French cathedrals—and Versailles, the monumental château of Louis XIV, the Sun King.

Before the completion of Versailles, king and court resided in the delightful château of St-Germain-en-Laye, west of Paris. This is within easy day-trip range from Paris, as are the châteaux of Vaux-le-Vicomte, Rambouillet, and Fontainebleau, and the newest Disney venture, Euro Disney.

Getting Around

The attractions below can all be reached easily from Paris by car and by regular suburban train services. But you might find it convenient to group some of them together: Versailles, Rambouillet, and Chartres are all on the Paris–Chartres train line; Fontainebleau and Barbizon are within a few miles of each other.

By Train Three lines connect Paris with Versailles; on each, the trip takes about 30 minutes. Best for the château is RER C2 (Express métro line) to Versailles Rive Gauche station. Trains from Gare St-Lazare go to Versailles Rive Droite. Trains from Gare Montparnasse go to Versailles Chantiers and then on to Rambouillet and Chartres. Fontainebleau is served by 20 trains a day from Gare de Lyon; buses for Barbizon leave from in front of the main post office in Fontainebleau. The RER-A line will take you to Euro Disneyland (journey time: about 40 minutes).

Tourist Information

Barbizon (41 rue Grande, tel. 60–66–41–87).
Chartres (Pl. de la Cathédrale, tel. 37–21–50–00).
Euro Disney (Euro Disney S.C.A., Central Reservations Office, Box 105 F77777, Marne-la-Vallée, Cedex 4 France, tel. 49–41–49–10).
Fontainebleau (31 pl. Napoléon-Bonaparte, tel. 64–22–25–68).
Rambouillet (8 pl. de la Libération, tel. 34–83–21–21).
Versailles (7 rue des Réservoirs, tel. 39–50–36–22).

Exploring the Ile de France

Versailles **Versailles** is the location of one of the world's grandest palaces and one of France's most popular attractions. Wide, tree-lined avenues, broader than the Champs-Elysées and bordered with massive 17th-century mansions, lead directly to the Sun King's château. From the imposing place d'Armes in front of the château, you enter the Cour des Ministres, a sprawling cobbled forecourt. Right in the middle, the statue of Louis XIV stands triumphant, surveying the town that he built from scratch to house those of the 20,000 noblemen, servants, and hangers-on who weren't lucky enough to get one of the 3,000 beds in the château.

The building of the château in its entirety took 50 years. Hills were flattened, marshes drained, forests transplanted, and water for the magnificent fountains was channeled from the Seine several miles away. Visit the **Grands Appartements,** the six salons that made up the royal living quarters, and the famous **Galerie des Glaces** (Hall of Mirrors). Both can be visited without a guide, but you can get a cassette in English. There are also guided tours of the **petits appartements,** where the royal family and friends lived in relative intimacy, and the miniature opera house—one of the first oval rooms in France, built on the *aile nord* (north wing) for Louis XV in 1770. *Grands Appartements and Galerie des Glaces. Admission: 30 frs adults, 15 frs students and seniors citizens. Open Tues.–Sun. 9–7.*

The château's vast grounds are masterpieces of formal landscaping. At one end of the Petit Canal, which crosses the Grand Canal at right angles, is the **Grand Trianon,** a scaled-down pleasure palace built in the 1680s. The **Petit Trianon,** nearby, is a sumptuously furnished 18th-century mansion, commissioned by Louis XVI for Marie-Antoinette, who would flee here to avoid the stuffy atmosphere of the court. Nearby, she built the village, complete with dairy and mill, where she and her companions would dress as shepherdesses and lead a make-believe bucolic life. *Château grounds. Admission free. Open 8:30–dusk. Grand Trianon. Admission: 16 frs adults, 8 frs children and senior citizens. Open 9:45–noon and 2–5. Petit Trianon. Admission: 11 frs adults, 6 frs children and senior citizens. Open 2–5. Joint ticket: 20 frs adults, 10 frs children and senior citizens.*

Rambouillet Just a little more than 20 kilometers (12 miles) southwest of Versailles is the small town of **Rambouillet,** home of a château, adjoining park, and 13,770 hectares (34,000 acres) of forest. Since 1897, the château has been a summer residence of the French president; today, it is also used as a site for internation-

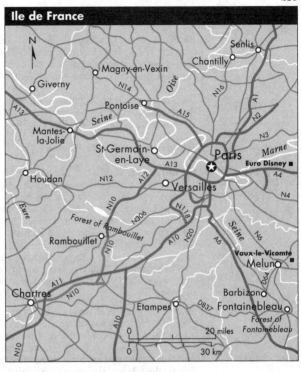

Ile de France

al summits. You can visit the château only when the president is not in residence—fortunately, he's not there often.

French kings have lived in the château since it was built in 1375. Highlights include the **Appartements d'Assemblée,** decorated with finely detailed wood paneling, and Napoleon's bathroom, with its Pompeii-inspired frescoes. The park stretches way behind the château. Beyond the **Jardin d'Eau** (Water Garden) lies the English-style garden and the **Laiterie de la Reine** (Marie-Antoinette's Dairy). This was another of her attempts to "get back to nature." *Château. Admission: 27 frs. Open Apr.–Sept., Wed.–Mon. 10–noon and 2–6; Oct.–Mar., 10–noon and 2–5. Park. Admission free. Open sunrise–sunset. Marie-Antoinette's Dairy. Admission 12 frs. Open same hours as Château; closes at 4 in winter.*

Chartres Long before you arrive you will see **Chartres's** famous cathedral towering over the plain of the Beauce, France's granary. The attractive old town, steeped in religious history and dating to before the Roman conquest, is still laced with winding medieval streets.

Today's Gothic cathedral, **Notre-Dame de Chartres,** is the sixth Christian church to have been built on the site; despite a series of fires, it has remained virtually the same since the 12th century. The **Royal Portal** on the main facade, presenting "the life and triumph of the Savior," is one of the finest examples of Romanesque sculpture in the country. Inside, the 12th- and 13th-century rose windows come alive even in dull weather, thanks to the deep Chartres blue of the stained glass: Its formula remains a mystery to this day. *Cathedral tours available: Ask at the Maison des Clercs, 18 rue du Cloître Notre-Dame.*

Since the rest of the tour is on another side of Paris, return to the capital to continue (*see* Getting Around in Ile de France, *above*).

Fontainebleau In the early 16th century, the flamboyant Francis I transformed the medieval hunting lodge of **Fontainebleau** into a magnificent Renaissance palace. His successor, Henry II, covered the palace with his initials, woven into the *D* for his mistress, Diane de Poitiers. When he died, his queen, Catherine de' Medici, carried out further alterations, later extended under Louis XIV. Napoleon preferred the relative intimacy of Fontainebleau to the grandeur of Versailles. Before he was exiled to Elba, he bade farewell to his Old Guard in the courtyard now known as the **Cour des Adieux** (Farewell Court). The emperor also harangued his troops from the **Horseshoe Staircase.** Ask the curator to let you see the **Cour Ovale** (Oval Court), the oldest and perhaps most interesting courtyard. It stands on the site of the original 12th-century fortified building, but only the keep remains today.

The **Grands Appartements** (royal suites and ballroom) are the main attractions of any visit to the château. The **Galerie de François I** is really a covered bridge (built 1528–30) looking out over the Cour de la Fontaine. The overall effect inside the Galerie—and throughout Fontainebleau—is one of classical harmony and proportion, combining to create a sense of Renaissance lightness and order. Francis I appreciated the Italian Renaissance, and the ballroom is decorated with frescoes by Primaticcio (1504–70) and his pupil, Niccolò dell'Abbate. If you're there on a weekday, you will also be able to join a guided tour of the Petits Appartements, used by Napoleon and Josephine. *Pl. du Gal-de-Gaulle, tel. 64–22–27–40. Admission: 25 frs, 12 frs under 25 and Sun., under 18 free. Open 9:30–12:30 and 2–5. Closed Tues. and holidays.*

The huge **Forest of Fontainebleau** is a favorite spot for walkers, horseback riders, and climbers. The French Alpine club started using the famous *rochers* (outcrops) for training back in 1910 and still climb the best known: Plutus and Gargantua. There are more than 144 kilometers (90 miles) of paths, so before you go, invest in a Touring Club map at the tourist office. One of the best views in the forest is from the **Hauteurs de la Solle,** within easy walking distance of Fontainebleau itself.

Barbizon The **Rochers des Demoiselles,** just south of the town, are also good for an afternoon stroll. The **Gorges d'Apremont,** which offer the best views of the rocks, are located near **Barbizon,** on the edge of the forest, 10 kilometers (6 miles) northwest of Fontainebleau. This delightful little village is scarcely more than a main street lined with restaurants and boutiques, but a group of landscape painters put it on the map in the mid-19th century. Théodore Rousseau and Jean-François Millet both had their studios here. Sculptor Henri Chapu's bronze medallion, sealed to one of the famous sandstone rocks in the forest nearby, pays homage to the two leaders of what became known as the Barbizon group.

Drop in at the **Ancienne Auberge du Père Ganne** (Père Ganne's Inn), where most of the landscape artists ate and drank, while in Barbizon. They painted on every available surface, and even now you can see some originals on the walls and in the buffet. Today, the back room is devoted to modern landscape artists. *Rue Grande, tel. 60–66–46–73. Admission free. Guided visits mid-Mar.–Oct., Wed.–Mon. 9:45–6; Nov.–mid-Mar., Fri. 2–6, weekends 10–6.*

Next to the church, in a barn that Rousseau used as a studio, you'll find the **Musée de l'Ecole de Barbizon** (Barbizon School Museum), containing documents of the village as it was in the 19th century as well as a few original works by Rousseau, Diaz, Troyon, and Charles Jacque. *55 rue Grande, tel. 60–66–22–38. Admission: 10 frs adults, children free. Open Apr.–Sept., Mon. and Wed.–Fri. 10:30–12:30 and 2–6, weekends 2–6; Oct.–Mar., Mon. and Wed.–Fri. 10:30–12:30 and 2–5, weekends 2–5.*

Euro Disney Now you can get a dose of American pop culture in between visits to the Louvre and the Left Bank. On April 12, 1992, the **Euro Disney** complex opened in Marne-la-Vallée, just 32 kilometers (20 miles) east of Paris. The complex is divided into several areas, including **Euro Disneyland,** the pay-as-you-enter theme park that is the main reason for coming here. Occupying 136 acres, Euro Disneyland is less than half a mile across and ringed by a railroad with whistling steam engines. Although smaller than its U.S. counterparts, Euro Disneyland was built with great attention paid to the tiniest detail. Smack in the middle of the park is the soaring Sleeping Beauty Castle, which is surrounded by a plaza from which you can enter the four "lands" of Disney: **Frontierland, Adventureland, Fantasyland,** and **Discoveryland.** In addition, Main Street U.S.A. connects the castle to Euro Disneyland's entrance, under the pointed pink domes of the Disneyland Hotel. *Admission to Euro Disneyland: 225 frs adults, 150 frs children under 12; 2-day Passport 425 frs adults, 285 frs children; 3-day Passport 565 frs adults, 375 frs children. Open Apr.–mid-June, weekdays 9–7, weekends 9–midnight; mid-June–Aug., daily 9–midnight; Sept.–Oct., weekdays 9–7, weekends 9–9; Nov.–Mar., weekdays 10–5, weekends 10–7.*

There are six hotels in the 4,800-acre Euro Disney complex, all part of a section called the **Euro Disney Resort,** just outside the theme park. The resort also comprises parking lots, a train station, and the Festival Disney entertainment center, with restaurants, a theater, dance clubs, shops, a post office, and a tourist office. Cheaper accommodations—log cabins and campsites—are available at Camp Davy Crockett, but it is located farther away from the theme park.

Future plans at Euro Disney call for a second theme park, convention center, new golf course, new campsite, more hotels, and film studios.

Dining and Lodging

For details and price-category definitions, *see* Dining and Lodging in Staying in France.

Barbizon **Le Relais.** The delicious specialties—particularly the beef and
Dining the game (in season)—are served in large portions and there is a good choice of fixed-price menus. The Relais is spacious, with walls covered with paintings and hunting trophies, and there is a big open fire. The owner is proud of the large terrace where

you can eat in the shade of lime and chestnut trees. *2 av. Charles de Gaulle, tel. 60–66–40–28. Weekend reservations required. MC, V. Closed Tues., Wed., Aug. 20–Sept. 5, first half Jan. Inexpensive.*

Lodging **Auberge des Alouettes.** This delightful 19th-century inn is set on 8,000 square meters (2 acres) of grounds. The interior has been redecorated in '30s style, but many rooms still have their original oak beams. The restaurant, with a large open terrace, features nouvelle cuisine in sizable portions. *4 rue Antoine Barye, tel. 60–66–41–98. 22 rooms with bath or shower. Facilities: restaurant, tennis, parking. Reservations required for restaurant. AE, DC, MC, V. Inexpensive.*

Chartres **Buisson Ardent.** Set in an attractive old oak-beamed building
Dining within sight of the cathedral's south portal, Buisson Ardent is a popular restaurant providing inexpensive fixed-price menus (especially good on weekdays) and a choice of imaginative à la carte dishes with delicious sauces. The wine list is comprehensive. *10 rue au Lait, tel. 16/37–34–04–66. Reservations advised. AE, DC, MC, V. Closed Sun. evenings. Inexpensive.*

Dining and Lodging **La Poste.** This comfortable, traditional hotel—smarter these days but still with a folksy charm to its rambling corridors and faded bedroom wallpaper—is good value and, above all, brilliantly situated between the station and the cathedral. The spacious dining room offers a choice of set menus, two of which fall in our budget category; the à la carte offerings are inventive but expensive. *3 rue du Général-Koenig, tel. 16/37–21–04–27. 60 rooms, some with shower. AE, DC, MC, V. Budget.*

Lodging **Grand Monarque.** The Monarque is an 18th-century coaching inn that has had a recent face-lift: 11 rooms were added in 1988 in a separate turn-of-the-century building overlooking a small garden, and the entrance hall was completely renovated. The rooms have the level of comfort and consistency you would expect from a Best Western. It also has an excellent reasonably priced restaurant. *22 pl. des Epars, tel. 16/37–21–00–72. 57 rooms, 52 with bath or shower. Facilities: restaurant. AE, DC, MC, V. Moderate.*

Euro Disney **Euro Disneyland** is peppered with places to eat, ranging from
Dining snack bars and fast-food joints to full-service restaurants—all with a distinguishing theme. In addition, all Disney hotels have restaurants that are open to the public. But since these are outside the theme park, it is not recommended that you waste time traveling to them for lunch. Be aware that only the hotel restaurants serve alcoholic beverages; Disney's no-alcohol standard is maintained throughout the theme park. Eateries serve nonstop as long as the park is open. *AE, DC, MC, V accepted at sit-down restaurants; no credit cards at others. Reservations advised for sit-down restaurants. Counter-service restaurants: Budget–Inexpensive; sit-down restaurants: Inexpensive–Moderate.*

Fontainebleau **Le Dauphin.** Prices are reasonable in this homey, rustic restau-
Dining rant located near the town hall and just five minutes from the château. Specialties include snails, *confit de canard* (duck preserve), and a variety of homemade desserts. *24 rue Grande, tel. 64–22–27–04. Reservations advised, especially on Sun. MC, V. Closed Tues. evening, Wed., Feb., and Sept. 1–8. Inexpensive.*

Lodging **Londres.** The balconies of this tranquil, family-style hotel look out over the palace and the Cour des Adieux; the 19th-century facade is preserved by government order. Inside, the decor is dominated by the Louis XV–style furniture. *1 pl. Général de Gaulle, tel. 64–22–20–21. 22 rooms, most with bath or shower. Facilities: restaurant, tea room, bar, parking. AE, DC, MC, V. Closed Dec. 20–Jan. 31. Inexpensive.*

Rambouillet **La Poste.** Traditional, unpretentious cooking is the attraction
Dining of this former coaching inn, close to the château. Until 1988, it could seat only 36 people, but a new upstairs dining room has been opened, doubling the capacity. The service is good, as is the selection of inexpensive fixed-price menus, even on Sunday. *101 rue du Général-de-Gaulle, tel. 34–83–03–01. Reservations advised. AE, MC, V. Inexpensive.*

Versailles **Quai nºl.** Fish enthusiasts don't have to spend a fortune in Ver-
Dining sailles, as a visit to this atmospheric restaurant—awash in wood and brass and decked out in seafaring paraphernalia—will underline. Smoked salmon is the house specialty, and *crême brûlée* the pick of the desserts. *1 av. de St-Cloud, tel. 39–50–42–26. Reservations advised. DC, MC, V. Closed Sun. evening and Mon. Moderate.*

Londres. This is the place for lunch after a weary, foot-slogging visit to the château. Take a seat on the leafy terrace overlooking the esplanade and order langoustine in a vermouth sauce, or rib of beef with marrow. *7 rue Colbert, tel. 39–50–16–79. Reservations advised. MC, V. Closed Mon. and Jan.–Feb. Inexpensive.*

Potager du Roy. There is excellent value in this restaurant run by Philippe Letourneur, former colleague of Gerard Vié (chef at Versaille's famous Trois Marches restaurant). The cuisine gets better each year, yet the prices remain reasonable. It is hardly surprising that this bistro and the enclosed terrace are often crowded and that reservations are a must. *1 rue du Maréchal-Joffre, tel. 39–50–35–34. Reservations required. MC, V. Closed Sun., Mon. Inexpensive.*

Normandy

Jutting out into the Channel, Normandy probably has more connections with the English-speaking world than does any other part of France. The association continues until this day. Visitors flock to Normandy not only to see historic monuments; they also come simply to relax amid the rich countryside with its apple orchards, lush meadows, and sandy beaches.

The historic city of Rouen, capital of Upper Normandy, is full of churches, well-preserved buildings, and museums. Normandy is also recognized as one of France's finest gastronomic regions; try some of the excellent cheeses washed down with local cider, the apple brandy (Calvados), or the wide range of seafood dishes.

Getting Around

Trains run hourly from Paris (Gare St-Lazare) to Rouen (journey time 70 minutes). Three trains go daily from Rouen to Bayeux: allow at least 2½ hours, including an obligatory change at Caen.

Tourist Information

Rouen (25 pl. de la Cathédrale, tel. 35–71–41–77).

Exploring Roeun and Bayeux

Numbers in the margin correspond to points of interest on the Rouen map.

Rouen Rouen, the capital of Upper Normandy, has a remarkable
❶ number of historic churches, from the city's **Cathédrale Notre-Dame,** dating from the 12th century, to the modern, fishshaped
❷ **Eglise Jeanne d'Arc** on the old market square, where Joan of Arc was burned at the stake in 1431. The tourist office organizes a guided tour leaving from the place de la Cathédrale and
❸ visiting the city's main churches, the **Palais de Justice,** and the lively old quarter around the rue du Gros-Horloge, where you can see the giant Renaissance clock that was built in 1527. The most noteworthy churches are located on the right bank, around the old quarter, and can be visited on foot. Try to visit
❹ ❺ **Eglise St-Maclou,** with its five-gabled facade; **Abbaye St-Ouen,**
❻ a beautifully proportioned 14th-century abbey; and the **Eglise St-Godard,** with well-preserved stained-glass windows.

One ticket will get you into several of Rouen's best museums,
❼ notably the **Musée des Beaux Arts** (Fine Arts Museum), near Eglise St-Godard (on Square Vedral). This specializes in 17th- and 19th-century French paintings, with a particular emphasis on artists who lived and worked locally. There is an outstanding collection of macabre paintings by Romantic painter Géricault.
❽ Nearby museums include the **Musée Le Secq des Tournelles** (rue Jacques Villon, in the Eglise St-Laurent), which has an unusu-
❾ al collection of wrought iron; the **Musée de la Céramique** (rue Faucon), which now houses Rouen's porcelain collections; and
❿ the **Musée du Gros-Horloge** (rue du Gros-Horloge), where you can study the mechanism of the Renaissance clock that gives its name to the museum. *Museums. Admission: 15 frs. Open Thurs.–Mon. 10–noon and 2–6, Wed. 2–6.*

Bayeux **Bayeux,** a few miles inland from the D-Day beaches, was the first French town freed by the Allies in June 1944. But it is known primarily as the home of **La Tapisserie de la Reine Mathilde** (known to us as the Bayeux Tapestry), which tells the epic story of William's conquest of England in 1066. It is on show at the **Centre Culturel Guillaume le Conquérant** (William the Conqueror Cultural Center). *Rue St-Exupère. Admission: 26 frs adults, 13 frs students. Open June–Sept., daily 9–7; Oct.–May, daily 9:30–12:30 and 2–7. Closed Dec. 25, Jan. 1.*

The new **Musée de la Bataille de Normandie** (Museum of the Battle of Normandy) traces the history of the Allied advance against the Germans in 1944. It overlooks the British Military Cemetery. *Blvd. Général-Fabian-Ware. Admission: 18 frs adults, 10 frs students. Open June–Aug., daily 9–7; Sept.–mid-Oct. and mid-Mar.–May, daily 9:30–12:30 and 2:30–6:30; mid-Oct.–mid-Mar., daily 10–12:30 and 2–6.*

Dining and Lodging

For details and price-category definitions, *see* Dining and Lodging in Staying in France.

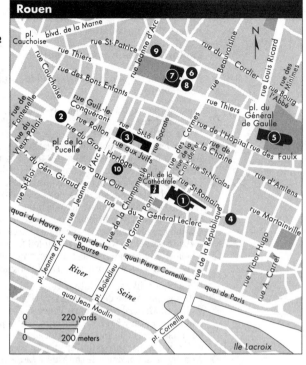

Rouen

Bayeux **Lion d'Or.** Flower-filled balconies and a courtyard full of palm
Lodging trees adorn this '30s property in the center of Bayeux. The
rooms are all well equipped and the recently redecorated restaurant serves Norman specialties. *71 rue St-Jean, tel. 31–92–
06–90. 28 rooms with bath or shower. Facilities: indoor garage.
AE, DC, MC, V. Closed mid-Dec.–mid-Jan. Moderate.*
Notre-Dame. It's difficult to find a better setting for a night in
Bayeux than the Notre-Dame, on a charming cobbled street
leading to the west front of the cathedral. You can sit outside on
the terrace and drink in the scene with your evening aperitif.
Rooms and cuisine are no more than average, and the place attracts the occasional horde of coach-bound tourists. But with
rooms starting at 115 francs, a lunchtime plat du jour for under
50 francs, and a set dinner menu at 80 francs, you can't complain. *44 rue des Cuisiniers, tel. 31–92–87–24. 24 rooms, some
with shower. Facilities: restaurant (closed Sun. evening and
Mon.). DC, MC, V. Closed mid-Oct.–mid-Apr. Budget.*

Rouen **Vieux Logis.** This tiny restaurant near the Hôtel de Ville, with
Dining elegant 18th-century-style furnishings, is the pride and joy of
jolly Joseph Guillou. He treats visitors to a 70-franc menu that
includes wine and coffee, and goes down as the best value meal
in Rouen. *5 rue Joyeuse, tel. 35–71–55–30. Reservations required. No credit cards. Budget.*

Lodging **Hôtel de Dieppe.** A newly renovated 19th-century hotel opposite the train station, Hôtel de Dieppe offers two types of room:
modern and period-style. The buffet-style breakfast is substantial—unlike most in France—and the popular restaurant
serves a range of grilled meats, as well as *canard au sang* (duck

cooked in its own blood). *Pl. Bernard-Tissot, tel. 35–71–96–00.
40 rooms with bath or shower. Facilities: restaurant. AE, DC,
MC, V. Moderate.*
Québec. No frills here, but this straightforward town hotel is
inexpensive and central—just five minutes from the cathedral
as you head toward the Seine. Rooms are small. *18 rue de Québec, 76000, tel. 35–70–09–38. 38 rooms, some with bath or
shower. AE, MC, V. Closed Christmas and New Year's. Budget.*

Burgundy and Lyon

For a region whose powerful medieval dukes held sway over
large tracts of Western Europe and whose current image is
closely allied to its expensive wine, Burgundy is a place of surprisingly rustic, quiet charm.

The heart of Burgundy consists of the dark, brooding Morvan
Forest. Dijon is the region's only city and retains something of
its medieval opulence. Its present reputation is essentially gastronomic, however; top-class restaurants abound, and local "industries" involve the production of mustard, *cassis* (black-
currant liqueur), snails, and—of course—wine. The vineyards
extending down toward the ancient town of Beaune are among
the world's most distinguished and picturesque.

The vines continue to flourish as you head south along the
Saône Valley, through the Mâconnais and Beaujolais, toward
Lyon, one of France's most appealing cities. The combination of
frenzied modernity and unhurried *joie de vivre* give Lyon a
sense of balance. The only danger is a temptation to overin-
dulge in its rich and robust cuisine.

Burgundy's winters are cold, its summers hot. The ideal times
to come are late May, when the countryside is in flower, and
September or October, for the wine harvest.

Getting Around

TGV trains make the 95-minute run from Paris (Gare de Lyon)
to Dijon every two hours. More traditional locomotives chug
from Dijon to Beaune (journey-time 20 minutes) every 1½
hours or so. Six trains daily connect Beaune to Lyon, two hours
away.

Tourist Information

Beaune (Rue de l'Hôtel-Dieu, tel. 80–22–24–51).
Dijon (29 pl. Darcy, tel. 80–43–42–12).
Lyon (Pl. Bellecoeur, tel. 78–42–25–75).

Exploring Burgundy and Lyon

Dijon **Dijon** is capital of both Burgundy and gastronomy. Visit its restaurants and the **Palais des Ducs** (Ducal Palace), testimony to
bygone splendor and the setting for one of France's leading art
museums (Admission: 12 frs. Open Wed.–Mon. 10–6). The
tombs of Philip the Bold and John the Fearless head a rich collection of medieval objects and Renaissance furniture. Outstanding features of the city's old churches include the stained
glass of **Notre-Dame,** the austere interior of the **cathedral of**

St-Bénigne, and the chunky Renaissance facade of **St-Michel.** Don't miss the exuberant 15th-century gateway at the **Chartreuse de Champmol**—all that remains of a former charterhouse—or the adjoining **Puits de Moïse,** a "well" with six large, compellingly realistic medieval statues on a hexagonal base.

Beaune The **Hospices** (or Hôtel-Dieu) **de Beaune** owns some of the finest vineyards in the region yet was founded in 1443 as a hospital. Its medical history is retraced in a **museum** that also features Roger van der Weyden's medieval Flemish masterpiece *The Last Judgment,* plus a collection of tapestries, though a better series (late 15th century, relating the *Life of the Virgin*) hangs in Beaune's main church, the **Collégiale Notre-Dame,** which dates from 1120. *Hospices de Beaune. Admission: 28 frs adults, 14 frs children. Open daily 9–11:30 and 2–5:30.*

The history of local wines can be explored at the **Musée du Vin de Bourgogne,** housed in a mansion built in the 15th and 16th centuries (Admission: 10 frs. Open Apr.–Oct., daily 9–noon and 1:30–6; Nov.–Mar., daily 10–noon and 2–5:30). The place to drink the stuff is in the candlelit cellars of the **Marché aux Vins** (wine market), on rue Nicolas Rolin, where you can taste as much as you please for 45 frs.

Lyon In recent years, **Lyon** has solidified its role as one of Europe's leading commercial centers, thanks to France's policy of decentralization and the TGV train that puts Paris at virtual commuter distance (two hours). Much of the city has an appropriate air of untroubled prosperity, and you will have plenty of choices when it comes to good eating.

The clifftop silhouette of **Notre-Dame de Fourvière** is the city's most striking symbol: an exotic mish-mash of styles with an interior that's pure decorative overkill. Climb the Fourvière heights for the view instead and then go to the nearby Roman remains. *Théâtres Romains. Admission free. Open Mar.–Oct., 8–noon and 2–5, Sat. 9–noon and 3–6, Sun. 3–6; Nov.–Feb., weekdays 8–noon and 2–5.*

The pick of Lyon's museums is the **Musée des Beaux-Arts** (open Wed.–Mon. 11–6). It houses sculpture, classical relics, and an extensive collection of Old Masters and Impressionists. Don't miss local artist Louis Janmot's 19th-century mystical cycle *The Poem of the Soul,* 18 canvases and 16 drawings that took nearly 50 years to complete. *Admission free. Open Wed.–Sun. 10:30–6.*

Dining and Lodging

For details and price-category definitions, *see* Dining and Lodging in Staying in France.

Beaune **L'Ecusson.** Despite its unprepossessing exterior, L'Ecusson is
Dining a comfortable, friendly, thick-carpeted restaurant, with four fixed-price menus offering outstanding value. For around 200 frs, you can have rabbit terrine with tarragon followed by leg of duck in oxtail sauce, then cheese, and dessert. *2 rue du Lieutenant-Dupuis, tel. 80–22–83–08. Reservations advised. AE, DC, MC, V. Closed Sun., mid-Feb.–mid-Mar. Inexpensive.*

Dijon **Toison d'Or.** A collection of superbly restored 16th-century
Dining buildings belonging to the Burgundian Company of Wine-

tasters forms the backdrop to this fine restaurant, which features a small wine museum in the cellar. Toison d'Or is lavishly furnished and quaint (candlelight *de rigueur* in the evening). The food is increasingly sophisticated. Try the langoustines with ginger and the nougat and honey dessert. *18 rue Ste-Anne, tel. 80–30–73–52. Reservations accepted. Jacket required. AE, DC, MC, V. Closed Sat. lunch, Sun., part of Feb., most of Aug., and public holidays. Moderate.*

Lodging **Central Urbis.** This central, old-established hotel has benefited from recent modernization: Its sound-proofed, air-conditioned rooms offer a degree of comfort in excess of their price. The adjoining grill room, the Central Grill Rôtisserie, offers a good alternative to the gastronomic sophistication that is difficult to avoid elsewhere in Dijon. *3 pl. Grangier, 21000, tel. 80–30–44–00. 90 rooms with bath. AE, DC, MC, V. Restaurant closed Sun. Inexpensive.*

Lyon
Dining **A Ma Vigne.** Here is a restaurant that's popular with tourists; it provides straightforward meals as a break from too much gourmet Lyonnais dining. French fries, *moules* (mussels), roast ham, and tripe lead the menu. Locals appreciate this, too, so get there early, especially at lunchtime. *23 rue Jean-Larrivé, tel. 78–60–46–31. Reservations not necessary. MC, V. Closed Sun., Aug. Inexpensive.*

Bouchon de Fourvière. This new, wood-paneled restaurant with a charming view over the Saône River, has won rave reviews for its spinach salad with chicken liver, black pudding with apple, and stewed rabbit with pasta. Two excellent value set menus, and a good choice of inexpensive local wines (mainly Côte du Rhône), make this an address to remember. *9 rue de la Quarantaine, Quai Fulchiron, tel. 72–41–85–02. Reservations advised. AE, MC, V. Closed Sun. and Aug. Budget.*

Lodging **Globe & Cécil.** You won't beat this strangely named hotel for value and convenience in downtown Lyon: It lies just off Place Bellecour (Lyon's largest and most central square) in the heart of the city's shopping district, halfway between the rivers Saône and Rhône and a mere five-minute walk from historic Old Lyon at the foot of Fourvière hill. Rooms are functional, the modern decor sober and tasteful. Ask for a quieter room at the back of the hotel. *21 rue Gasparin, tel 78–42–58–95. 63 rooms, 48 with bath or shower. AE, DC, MC, V. Inexpensive.*

Loire Valley

The Loire is the longest river in France, rising near Le Puy in the east of the Massif Central and pursuing a broad northwest curve on its 1,000-kilometer (620-mile) course to the Atlantic Ocean near Nantes. The region traditionally referred to as the Loire Valley—château country—is the 225-kilometer (140-mile) stretch between Orléans, 113 kilometers (70 miles) south of Paris and Angers, 96 kilometers (60 miles) from the Atlantic coast. Thanks to its mild climate, soft light, and lush meadowland, this area is known as the Garden of France. Its leading actor—the wide, meandering Loire—offers two distinct faces: fast-flowing and spectacular in spring, sluggish and sandy in summer.

The Loire Valley's golden age came under Francis I (1515–47), France's flamboyant contemporary of England's Henry VIII.

He hired Renaissance craftsmen from Italy and hobnobbed with the aging Leonardo da Vinci, his guest at Amboise. His salamander emblem is to be seen in many châteaux, including Chambord, the mightiest of them, begun in 1519.

The best months to visit are June to October, though the weather can sometimes be hot and sticky in midsummer. Nature in the region is at its best in late spring and early fall, when there are fewer crowds. In peak season (especially August), it is essential to have your accommodations reserved.

Getting Around

Trains leave Paris (Gare d'Austerlitz) for Blois every couple of hours. The journey lasts 1½–2 hours. About eight trains daily connect Blois to Amboise, 20 minutes away, stopping near Chaumont (alight at Onzain Station). Frequent buses link Blois to Chambord and Cheverny; hiring a bike is a good alternative here, since distances are short and the terrain undemanding.

Tourist Information

Blois (3 av. du Docteur Jean-Laigret, tel. 54–74–06–49).

Exploring Blois and Amboise

Blois **Blois** is the most attractive of the major Loire towns, with its tumbling alleyways and its château. The **château** is a mixture of four different styles: Feudal (13th century); Gothic-Renaissance transition (circa 1500); Renaissance (circa 1520); and Classical (circa 1635). *Admission: 25 frs. Open May–Aug., daily 9–6:30; Sept.–Apr., daily 9–noon and 2–5.*

Blois makes an ideal launching pad for a visit to the châteaux of Chambord and Cheverny. **Chambord** (begun 1519) is 20 kilometers (11 miles) east of Blois along D33, near Bracieux. It stands in splendid isolation in a vast forest and game park. There's another forest on the roof: 365 chimneys and turrets, representing architectural self-indulgence at its least squeamish. Grandeur or a mere 440-room folly? Judge for yourself, and don't miss the superb spiral staircase or the chance to saunter over the rooftop terrace. *Admission: 30 frs adults, 9 frs children. Open July–Aug., daily 9:30–6:30; Sept.–June, daily 9:30–11:45 and 2–sunset.*

A pleasant 20 kilometers (12 miles) through the forest leads you southwest to **Cheverny.** This white, symmetrical château in the disciplined Classical style (built 1620–34) has ornate painted and gilded paneling on its walls and ceilings. Hunting buffs will thrill at the sight of the antlers of 2,000 hapless stags in the Trophy Room. Hordes of hungry hounds lounge around outside dreaming of their next kill. *Admission: 28 frs adults, 17 frs students and senior citizens. Open mid-June–mid-Sept., daily 9–6:30; mid-Sept.–mid-June, daily 9:30–noon and 2:30–5.*

About 20 kilometers (12 miles) south of Blois stands the sturdy château of **Chaumont,** built between 1465 and 1510—well before Benjamin Franklin became a regular visitor. There is a magnificent Loire panorama from the terrace, and the stables—where thoroughbreds dined like royalty—show the importance attached to fine horses, for hunting or just prestige. *Admission: 26 frs adults, 13 frs students and senior citizens.*

*Open Apr.–Sept., daily 9:30–12:30 and 2–4:30; Oct.–Mar.,
daily 9:30–12:30 and 2–3:30.*

Amboise   Downstream (westward) another 16 kilometers (10 miles) lies
the bustling town of **Amboise,** whose **château,** with charming
grounds, a rich interior, and excellent views over the river
from the battlements, dates from 1500. It wasn't always so
peaceful: In 1560, more than 1,000 Protestant "conspirators"
were hanged from these battlements during the Wars of Religion. *Admission: 30 frs adults, 12 frs children. Open July–
Aug., daily 9–6:30; Sept.–June, daily 9–noon and 2–5.*

The nearby **Clos-Lucé,** a 15th-century brick manor house, was
the last home of Leonardo da Vinci, who was invited to stay
here by Francis I. Da Vinci died here in 1519, and his engineering genius is illustrated by models based on his plans and
sketches. *Admission: 32 frs adults, 20 frs students and senior
citizens. Same hours as château, but open till 6:30 in winter.
Closed. Jan.*

Dining and Lodging

For details and price-category definitions, *see* Dining and
Lodging in Staying in France.

Blois   **Bocca d'Or.** The old 14th-century stone vaults at this restau-
Dining   rant, in the heart of Blois, provide a historical atmosphere that
contrasts with its nouvelle cuisine, though both are refined.
Fish, shellfish, and poultry figure prominently, and the wine
list is comprehensive. *15 rue Haute, tel. 54–78–04–74. Reservations advised. AE, MC, V. Closed Sun., Mon. lunch; late
Jan.–Mar. 5. Moderate.*
Noë. The pastel dining room at the "Noah," a half-mile uptown
from the château, is usually full of locals—always a good sign.
They come to enjoy such inexpensive house specialties as chick-
en liver, duckling, and carp in a wine sauce. There are set
menus at 80–120 francs. *10 bis av. de Vendôme. tel. 54–74–22–
26. Reservations advised. MC, V. Closed Sat. lunch, Tues. evenings, and Sun. evenings in winter. Inexpensive.*

Lodging   **Anne de Bretagne.** An unpretentious hotel without a restaurant, Anne de Bretagne is conveniently situated on a broad avenue close to the tourist office and château. Parking is less of a
headache here than it can be in the narrow streets of old Blois,
but you may feel cheated of some of the atmosphere. *31 av. du
Dr. Jean-Laigret, tel. 54–78–05–38. 29 rooms, some with bath
or shower. AE, DC, MC, V. Closed mid-Feb.–early Mar. Inexpensive.*

Chambord   **Hôtel St-Michel.** Considering its location right across from the
Lodging   château, the St-Michel offers good value. Some of its rooms af-
★   ford splendid views of the château, its lawns, and the forest
backdrop, as does the conveniently situated terrace, an ideal
place for summer morning coffee before the tourist hordes arrive. *41250 Chambord, tel. 54–20–31–31. 38 rooms, some with
bath or shower. Facilities: restaurant, tennis court, parking.
MC, V. Closed Nov. 12–Dec. 19. Inexpensive.*

The Riviera

Few places in the world have the same pull on the imagination as France's fabled Riviera, the Mediterranean coastline stretching from St-Tropez in the west to Menton on the Italian border. Cooled by the Mediterranean in the summer and warmed by it in winter, the climate is almost always pleasant. Avoid the area in July and August, however—unless you love crowds. To see the Riviera at its best, plan your trip in the spring or fall, particularly in May or September.

The Riviera is a land of contrasts. While the coastal resorts seem to live exclusively for the tourist trade and have often been ruined by high-rise blocks, the hinterlands remain relatively untarnished. The little villages perched high on the hills behind medieval ramparts seem to belong to another century.

Artists, attracted by the light, have played a considerable role in popular conceptions of the Riviera, and their presence is reflected in the number of modern art museums. Wining and dining are special treats on the Riviera, especially if you are fond of garlic and olive oil. *Bouillabaisse*, a spicy fish stew, is the most popular regional specialty.

The tiny principality of Monaco, which lies between Nice and Menton, is included in this section despite the fact that it is a sovereign state. Although Monaco has its own army and police force, its language, food, and way of life are French. Its famous casino, the highly visible royal Grimaldi family, and the wealth of jetsetters, chic fashions, and opulent yachts all ensure that it maintains its reputation as a "golden ghetto."

Getting Around

By Train Six TGV trains daily make the 6- to 7-hour run from Paris (Gare de Lyon) to the Riviera, stopping at Cannes and Nice. Frequent local trains connect Nice to Monaco and Menton. Grasse is a 50-minute bus ride from Cannes.

Tourist Information

Cannes (Palais des Congrès, La Croisette, tel. 93–39–24–53).
Grasse (3 pl. Foux, tel. 93–36–03–56).
Menton (Palais de l'Europe, tel. 93–57–57–00).
Monaco (2a blvd. des Moulins, tel. 93–30–87–01).
Nice (Av. Thiers, tel. 93–87–07–07; 5 av. Gustave-V, tel. 93–87–60–60).

Exploring the Riviera

Cannes In 1834, a chance event was to change the lifestyle of **Cannes** forever. Lord Brougham, Britain's lord chancellor, was en route to Nice when an outbreak of cholera forced the authorities to freeze all travel to prevent the disease from spreading. Trapped in Cannes, he fell in love with the place and built himself a house there as an annual refuge from the British winter. The English aristocracy, czars, kings, and princes soon caught on, and Cannes became a community for the international elite. Grand palace hotels were built to cater to them, and Cannes came to symbolize dignified luxury. Today, Cannes is also synonymous with the **International Film Festival.**

The Riviera

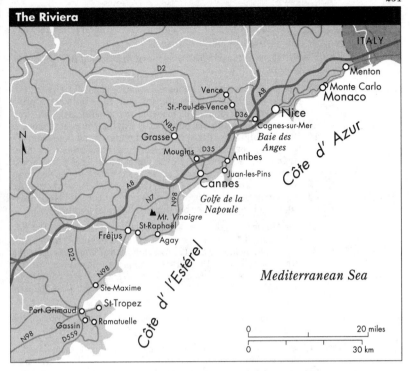

Cannes is for relaxing—strolling along the seafront on the **Croisette** and getting tanned on the beaches. Almost all the beaches are private, but that doesn't mean you can't use them, only that you must pay for the privilege. The Croisette offers splendid views of the **Napoule Bay.** Only a few steps inland is the old town, known as the **Suquet,** with its steep, cobbled streets and its 12th-century watchtower.

Grasse is perched in the hills behind Cannes. Follow your nose to the town that claims to be the perfume capital of the world. A good proportion of its 40,000 inhabitants work at distilling and extracting scent from the tons of roses, lavender, and jasmine produced here every year. The various perfumiers are only too happy to guide visitors around their fragrant establishments. Fragonard is the best known (20 blvd. Fragonard, tel. 93–36–44–65). The old town is attractive, with its narrow alleys and massive, somber **cathedral.** Three of the paintings inside the cathedral are by Rubens and one is by Fragonard, who lived here for many years.

Nice With its population of 400,000, its own university, new congress hall, and nearby science park, **Nice** is the undisputed capital of the Riviera. Founded by the Greeks as Nikaia, it has lived through several civilizations and was attached to France only in 1860. It consequently boasts a profusion of Greek, Italian, British, and French styles. Tourism may not be the main business of Nice, but it is a deservedly popular center with much to offer. The double blessing of climate and geography puts its beaches within an hour-and-a-half's drive of the nearest ski resorts. There is an eclectic mixture of old and new architecture, an opera house, museums, flourishing markets, and regular concerts and festivals, including the Mardi Gras festival and the Battle of Flowers.

Numbers in the margin correspond to points of interest on the Nice map.

❶ The **place Masséna** is the logical starting point for an exploration of Nice. This fine square was built in 1815 to celebrate a local hero: one of Napoleon's most successful generals. The **❷** **Promenade des Anglais,** built by the English community here in **❸** 1824, is only a short stroll past the fountains and the **Jardin Albert Iᵉʳ**. It now carries heavy traffic but still forms a splendid strand between town and sea. The narrow streets in the old town are the prettiest part of Nice: Take the rue de l'Opéra to **❹ ❺** see **St-François-de-Paule** church (1750) and the **opera house.** At **❻** the northern extremity of the old town lies the vast **place Garibaldi** —all yellow-ocher buildings and formal fountains.

❼ The **Musée Chagall** is on the boulevard de Cimiez, near the Roman ruins. The museum was built in 1972 to house the Chagall collection, including the 17 huge canvases of *The Message of the Bible*, which took 13 years to complete. *Admission: 20 frs adults, 10 frs students and senior citizens. Open July–Sept., Wed.–Mon. 10–7; Oct.–June, Wed.–Mon. 10–12:30 and 2–5:30.*

Numbers in the margin correspond to points of interest on the Monaco map.

Monaco Sixteen kilometers (10 miles) along the coast from Nice is **Monaco.** For more than a century Monaco's livelihood was cen- **❶** tered in its splendid copper-roof **casino.** The oldest section dates from 1878 and was conceived by Charles Garnier, architect of the Paris opera house. It's as elaborately ornate as anyone could wish, bristling with turrets and gold filigree, and masses of interior frescoes and bas-reliefs. There are lovely sea views from the terrace, and the gardens out front are meticulously tended. The main activity is in the American Room, where beneath the gilt-edged ceiling busloads of tourists feed the one-armed bandits. *Pl. du Casino, tel. 93–50–69–31. Persons under 21 not admitted. Admission for American Room free. Open daily 10 AM–4 AM. Closed May 1.*

❷ The **Musée National des Automates et Poupées d' Autrefois** (Museum of Dolls and Automatons) has a compelling collection of 18th- and 19th-century dolls and mechanical figures, the latter shamelessly showing off their complex inner workings. It's magically set in a 19-century seaside villa (designed by Garnier). *17 av. Princesse-Grace, tel. 93–30–91–26. Admission: 26 frs adults, 13 frs children. Open daily 10–12:15 and 2:30–6:30.*

Monaco Town, the principality's old quarter, has many vaulted passageways and exudes an almost tangible medieval feel. The **❸** magnificent **Palais du Prince** (Prince's Palace), a grandiose Italianate structure with a Moorish tower, was largely rebuilt in the last century. Here, since 1297, the Grimaldi dynasty has lived and ruled. The spectacle of the **Changing of the Guard** occurs each morning at 11:55; inside, guided tours take visitors through the state apartments and a wing containing the **Palace Archives** and **Musée Napoléon** (Napoleonic Museum). *Pl. du Palais, tel. 93–25–18–31. Palace open July–Sept., daily 9:30–*

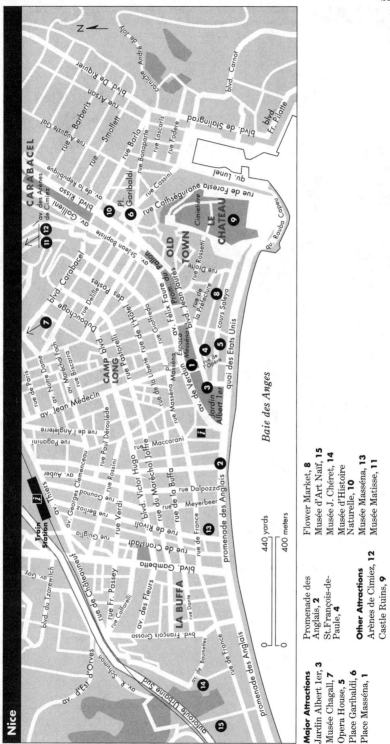

Nice

Major Attractions
Jardin Albert 1er, **3**
Musée Chagall, **7**
Opera House, **5**
Place Garibaldi, **6**
Place Masséna, **1**

Promenade des
Anglais, **2**
St.François-de-
Paule, **4**

Other Attractions
Arènes de Cimiez, **12**
Castle Ruins, **9**

Flower Market, **8**
Musée d'Art Naïf, **15**
Musée J. Chéret, **14**
Musée d'Histoire
Naturelle, **10**
Musée Masséna, **13**
Musée Matisse, **11**

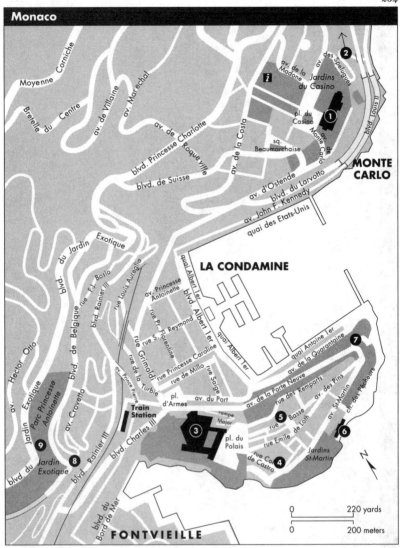

Monaco

Casino, **1**

Cathedral, **4**

Fort Antoine
Theater, **7**

Jardin Exotique, **8**

Musée Historial des
Princes de Monaco, **5**

Musée National des
Automates et Poupées
d'Autrefois, **2**

Musée
Océanographique, **6**

Museum of Prehistoric
Anthropology, **9**

Palais du Prince, **3**

12:30 and 2–6:30. Admission: 34 frs. Musée Napoléon and Palace Archives open year-round, Tues.–Sun. Admission: 18 frs adults, 9 frs children.

4 Monaco's **cathedral** (4 rue Colonel Bellando de Castro) is a late 19th-century neo-Romanesque confection in which Philadelphia-born Princess Grace lies in splendor along with past members of the Grimaldi dynasty. Nearby is the **Musée Historial des Princes de Monaco** (Waxworks Museum), a Monégasque Madame Tussauds, with none-too-realistic wax figures stiffly portraying various episodes in the Grimaldi history. The waxworks may not convince, but the rue Basse is wonderfully atmospheric. *27 rue Basse, tel. 93–30–39–05. Admission: 22 frs. Open May–Sept., daily 9–8; Oct.–Dec., daily 10:30–5:30; Jan.–Apr., daily 9–6:30.*

6 Next to the **St-Martin Gardens**—which contain an evocative bronze monument in memory of Prince Albert I (Prince Rainier's great-grandfather, the one in the sou'wester and flying oil skins, benignly guiding a ship's wheel)—is the **Musée Océanographique** (Oceanography Museum and Aquarium). This museum is also an internationally renowned research institute founded by the very Prince Albert who is remembered outside for being an eminent marine biologist in his day; the well-known underwater explorer Jacques Cousteau is the present director. The aquarium is the undisputed highlight, however, where a collection of the world's fish and crustacea live out their lives in public, some colorful, some drab, some the stuff nightmares are made of. *Av. St-Martin, tel. 93–30–15–14. Admission: 50 frs adults, 25 frs children. Open Sept.–June, daily 9:30–7; July and Aug., daily 9–9.*

7 Before heading back inland, take a short stroll to the eastern tip of the rock, to the **Fort Antoine Theater** (av. de la Quarantaine, tel. 93–30–19–21), a converted 18th-century fortress that certainly looks a lot prettier now than it would have in more warlike times, covered as it is in ivy and flowering myrtle and thyme. In the summer, this is an open-air theater seating 350.

8 The Moneghetti area is the setting for the **Jardin Exotique** (Tropical Garden), where 600 varieties of cacti and succulents cling to the rock face, their improbable shapes and sometimes violent coloring a further testimony to the fact that Mother Nature will try anything once. Your ticket also allows you to explore the **caves,** next to the gardens, and to visit the **Museum of Prehistoric Anthropology,** adjacent. *Blvd. du Jardin Exotique, tel. 93–30–33–65. Admission: 30 frs adults, 20 frs senior citizens, 15 frs children. Open Oct.–May, daily 9–5:30; June–Sept., daily 9–7.*

Menton **Menton** also once belonged to the Grimaldis and, like Nice, was attached to France only in 1860. Because of its popularity among British visitors, the western side of the town was developed at the turn of the century to cater to the influx of the rich and famous, with spacious avenues, first-class hotels, and the inevitable casino. The eastern side of town long remained the domain of the local fishermen but has more recently been developed to cater to the needs of tourists. A large marina was built and the **Sablettes,** once a tiny beach, has been artificially extended.

Down by the harbor stands a small 17th-century fort, where Jean Cocteau, the artist, writer, and filmmaker, once worked. It now houses the **Musée Jean Cocteau,** with a collection of his work. *111 quai Napoléon. Admission free. Open mid-June–mid-Sept., Wed.–Sun. 10–noon and 3–6; mid-Sept.–mid-June, 10–noon and 2–6.*

Dining and Lodging

For details and price-category definitions, *see* Dining and Lodging in Staying in France.

Cannes
Dining

Au Bec Fin. A devoted band of regulars will attest to the quality of this family-run restaurant near the train station. Don't look for a carefully staged decor: It's the spirited local clientele and the homey food that distinguish this cheerful bistro. The fixed-price menus are a fantastic value at 75 or 95 francs; try the fish cooked with fennel or the *salade niçoise. 12 rue du 24-Août, tel. 93–38–35–86. Reservations advised. Dress: casual. AE, DC, MC, V. Closed Sat. dinner, Sun., and Christmas-late Jan. Budget.*

Lodging

Mondial. A three-minute walk from the beach takes you to this six-story hotel, a haven for the traveler seeking solid, unpretentious lodging in a town that leans more to tinsel. Many guest rooms offer sea views. There's no restaurant. *77 rue d'Antibes, 06400, tel. 93–68–70–00. No credit cards. Closed Nov. Moderate.*

Bristol. Despite its name—recalling that of one of Paris's leading palace-hotels—the Bristol offers an intimate, wallet-friendly contrast to the big names lurking nearby on La Croisette. Prices start at around 170 frs, but be prepared to go a bit higher if you fancy one of the 10 (quieter) rooms with a balcony at the back of the building. The beach, train station, and Palais des Festivals are all within a three-minute walk. *14 rue Hoche, tel. 93–39–10–66. 19 rooms, 15 with bath or shower. AE, MC, V. Closed Dec.–mid-Jan. Budget.*

Grasse
Lodging

Panorama. The excellent views of the Massif d'Estérel and right across to Cannes are the vindication of this hotel's name. It is modern and well run and has ample parking. Most rooms have good views, but there is no restaurant. *2 pl. du Cours, tel. 93–36–80–80. 36 rooms with bath. MC, V. Inexpensive.*

Menton
Lodging

Chez Mireille-l'Ermitage. Best known for its restaurant, this elegant yet cozy hotel stands on the promenade du Soleil, overlooking the beach. Each room has its own style and all are different, although many have good views. The restaurant is a favorite for local specialties: *bourride* (fish soup) and bouillabaisse, salmon, and bass fillets. *30 av. Carnot, tel. 93–35–77–23. 21 rooms with bath or shower. AE, DC, MC, V. Restaurant closed Mon. evening, Tues., mid-Nov–mid-Apr. Moderate.*

Monaco
Dining

Polpetta. This popular trattoria is close enough to the Italian border to pass for the real thing. It's excellent value for the money, with delicious home cooking to boot. *2 rue Paradis, tel. 93–50–67–84. Reservations required in high season. MC, V. Closed Sat. lunch, Tues., Feb. 15–Mar. 15, Oct. 15–30. Moderate.*

Port. Harbor views from the terrace and top-notch Italian food make the Port a good choice. A large, varied menu includes shrimp, pastas, lasagna, fettuccine, fish risotto, and veal with ham and cheese. *Qui Albert 1er, tel. 93–50–77–21. Reservations advised. Dress: casual. AE, DC, MC, V. Closed Mon. and Nov. Moderate.*

Lodging **Alexandra.** Shades of the Belle Epoque linger on in this com-
★ fortable hotel's spacious lobby and airy guest rooms. Tan and rose colors dominate the newer rooms. If you're willing to do without a private bath, this place sneaks into the Inexpensive category. The friendly proprietress, Madame Larouquie, makes foreign visitors feel right at home. *35 blvd. Princesse-Charlotte, 98000, tel. 93–50–63–13. 55 rooms, 46 with bath. AE, DC, MC, V. Moderate*

Balmoral. Despite the name, there's nothing even vaguely Scottish about this somewhat old-fashioned hotel overlooking the harbor. Rooms are a reasonable size, if blandly decorated; many have balconies. *12 av. de la Costa, tel. 93–50–62–37. 75 rooms with bath or shower, half with air-conditioning. Facilities: restaurant. AE, DC, MC, V. Restaurant closed Nov. Moderate.*

France. The modest hotel France, near the train station, can't begin to compete with the opulence of some of the others listed here, but it's one of the cheapest around and worth a look if you are on a tight budget. *6 rue de La Turbie, tel. 93–30–24–64. 26 rooms, 18 with bath or shower. DC, MC, V. Inexpensive.*

Nice **La Mérenda.** This noisy bistro lies in the heart of the old town,
Dining and its down-to-earth Italo-Provençal food is tremendously good value. The Giustis, who run it, refuse to install a telephone, so go early to be sure of getting a table. House specials include pasta with *pistou* (a garlic-and-basil sauce) and succulent tripe. *4 rue de la Terrasse. No reservations. Dress: casual. No credit cards. Closed Sat., Sun., Mon., Feb., and Aug. Moderate.*

Lodging **La Mer.** This small hotel is handily situated on place Masséna, close to the old town and seafront. Rooms are spartan (and carpets sometimes frayed), but all have a minibar and represent good value. Ask for a room away from the square to be sure of a quiet night. *4 pl. Masséna, 06000, tel. 93–92–09–10. 12 rooms with bath or shower. No credit cards. Inexpensive.*

Little Palace. Monsieur and Madame Loridan run the closest thing to a country-house hotel in Nice. The old-fashioned decor, the jumble of bric-a-brac, and the heavy wooden furniture lend an Old World air; some may say it's like stepping onto a film set. *9 av. Baquis, 06000, tel. 93–88–70–49. 36 rooms, 31 with bath. MC, V. Closed Nov. Inexpensive.*

9 Germany

While a visit to reunited Germany provides a unique opportunity to see the stark differences between East and West, the experience won't come cheap. The reunification in 1990 was an efficient, orderly affair, but the rebuilding of East Germany since then has caused a jump in inflation. Germany did not suffer the recession felt in so many other western countries in the early 1990s, but it did have to grapple with a sluggish economy. Travelers to Germany will find this reflected in higher prices, particularly throughout the service industries. Nevertheless, it's still possible for the budget traveler to enjoy a visit to Europe's powerhouse. Competition for tourist trade is, in fact, quite keen in the big cities—as long as you steer away from big hotels and ritzy restaurants.

The economic imbalance between East and West is considerable. In the more prosperous western part of Germany, the taxi line outside major train stations is reminiscent of the assembly line of the Mercedes-Benz factory. Top-flight restaurants in Munich (München) and Frankfurt turn customers away every night. Electronics shops are full of expensive gadgets geared to the spoiled child or pampered business executive. In the eastern part of the country, however, Germans still earn only half of the salaries their fellow countrymen in the west make, though some basic costs of living are much lower, too. Eastern German shops are less numerous and elegant, but they are already filled with the sort of material goods that were unobtainable under the Communist regime.

Germans tend to rise very early and are hammering away at the building site by 7 AM or seated at the office desk by 8 AM, but they take their leisure time just as seriously. Annual vacations of up to six weeks are the norm, and secular and religious festivals occupy another 12 days. Every town and village, and many city neighborhoods, manage at least one "fest" a year, when the beer barrels are rolled out and sausages are thrown on the grill. The seasons have their own festivities: Carnivals (Fasching) herald the end of winter, countless beer gardens open up with the first warm rays of sunshine, fall is celebrated with the Munich Oktoberfest, and Advent brings Christkindlmarkt, colorful pre-Christmas markets held in town and city squares.

The great outdoors have always been an important escape hatch for the Germans, and *Lebensraum* (living space) is even more highly prized in the era of high technology and pressurized urban life. Germany does its best to meet the needs of its hardworking inhabitants. A Bavarian mountain inn, the glow of its lights reflected on the blanket of snow outside, may be only a short drive from Munich. The busy industrial city of Stuttgart lies at the gateway to the Black Forest (Schwarzwald), the popular region of spas, hiking trails, and its tempting cake. Berlin is surrounded by its own lakes and green parklands. The Green Party is a political expression of this feeling for the outdoors and nature.

Essential Information

Before You Go

When to Go The main tourist season in Germany runs from May to late October, when the weather is naturally at its best. In addition to many tourist events, this period has hundreds of folk festivals. The winter sports season in the Bavarian Alps runs from Christmas to mid-March. Prices everywhere are generally higher during the summer, so you may find considerable advantages in visiting out of season. Most resorts offer out-of-season (*Zwischensaison*) and "edge-of-season" (*Nebensaison*) rates, and tourist offices can provide lists of hotels offering special low-price inclusive weekly packages (*Pauschalangebote*). Similarly, many winter resorts offer lower rates for the periods immediately before and after the Christmas and New Year high season (*Weisse Wochen*, or "white weeks"). The weeks of December up to Christmas are often colorful in many towns, when the traditional Christkindl market fairs take place.

The major cities, especially Munich and Berlin, are active year-round. Avoid Leipzig around the first weeks in March and September; the trade fair commandeers all accommodations and prices soar.

Climate Germany's climate is generally temperate. Winters vary from mild and damp to very cold and bright. Particularly chilly regions include the Baltic coast, the Alps, the Harz Mountains, and the Black and Bavarian forests. Summers are usually sunny and warm, though be prepared for a few cloudy and wet days. In Alpine regions, spring often comes late, with snow flurries well into April. Fall is sometimes spectacular in the south: warm and soothing.

The following are the average daily maximum and minimum temperatures for Munich.

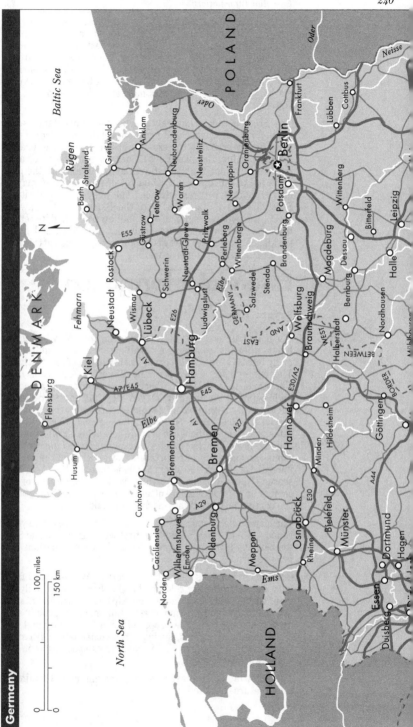

Germany

Baltic Sea

POLAND

Oder

Neisse

Frankfurt

Lübben

Cottbus

Anklam

Greifswald

Rügen

Barth Stralsund

Neubrandenburg

Oranienburg

Berlin

Neustrelitz

Teterow

Waren

Neuruppin

Potsdam

Wittenberg

Leipzig

E55

Güstrow

Pritzwalk

Brandenburg

Magdeburg

Bitterfeld

Rostock

Schwerin

Neustadt-Gleve

Perleberg

Wittenberge

Dessau

Halle

Neustadt

Wismar

Ludwigslust

Elbe

GERMANY

Salzwedel

Stendal

Bernburg

Nordhausen

E26

Lübeck

Hamburg

EAST

AND

Wolfsburg

Braunschweig

WEST

Fehmarn

Kiel

A7/E45

A1

Hannover

E30/A2

Halberstadt

Göttingen

BETWEEN

Flensburg

Elbe

E45

Minden

Hildesheim

BORDER

Husum

Bremerhaven

Bremen

A27

Göttingen

Cuxhaven

A29

Osnabrück

E30

Minden

Bielefeld

Münster

A44

Dortmund

Wilhelmshaven

Oldenburg

Meppen

Rheine

Hagen

Caroliensiel

Emden

Ems

Essen

Norden

Duisberg

HOLLAND

North Sea

DENMARK

N

100 miles

150 km

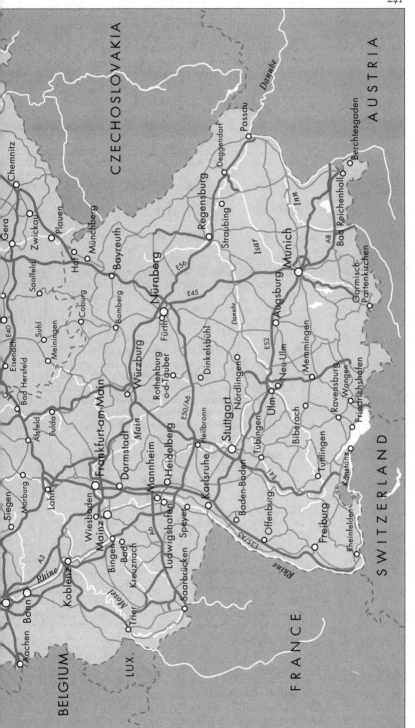

Jan.	35F	1C	May	64F	18C	Sept.	67F	20C
	23	– 5		45	7		48	9
Feb.	38F	3C	June	70F	21C	Oct.	56F	13C
	23	– 5		51	11		40	4
Mar.	48F	9C	July	74F	23C	Nov.	44F	7C
	30	– 1		55	13		33	0
Apr.	56F	14C	Aug.	73F	23C	Dec.	36F	2C
	38	3		54	12		26	– 3

The following are the average daily maximum and minimum temperatures for Berlin.

Jan.	35F	1C	May	66F	19C	Sept.	68F	20C
	26	– 3		47	8		50	10
Feb.	37F	3C	June	72F	22C	Oct.	56F	13C
	26	– 3		53	12		42	6
Mar.	46F	8C	July	75F	24C	Nov.	45F	7C
	31	0		57	14		36	2
Apr.	56F	14C	Aug.	74F	23C	Dec.	38F	3C
	39	4		56	13		29	– 1

Currency The unit of currency in Germany is the deutsche mark, written as DM and generally referred to as the mark. It is divided into 100 pfennig. There are bills of 5 (rare), 10, 20, 50, 100, 200, 500, and 1,000 marks and coins of 1, 2, 5, 10, and 50 pf and 1, 2, and 5 marks. At press time (summer 1992), the mark stood at DM 1.4 to the dollar and DM 2.93 to the pound sterling.

The cost of living is still much lower in the former GDR (German Democratic Republic), where most people earn considerably less than their western colleagues doing the same jobs, and some of these lower costs benefit tourists—for example, on public transportation, in cafés and beer restaurants, and in simple accommodations such as country inns and private guest houses. But a growing number of places that cater specifically to visitors are now charging western rates.

Major credit cards are widely accepted in Germany, though not universally so. You can buy a seat on a Lufthansa flight with a credit card but not on a German train, for example.

What It Will Cost The early 1990s has seen inflation creeping up (at press time, the annual rate of inflation was more than 4%), primarily because of the cost of financing the rejuvenation and integration of former Communist East Germany. For example, a "reunification" tax has been levied on basic commodities such as gas, and telephone charges have risen. There were further modest increases in fares for most forms of public transportation.

The most expensive areas to visit are the major cities, notably Düsseldorf, Hamburg, and Munich. Out-of-the-way rural regions, such as north and east Bavaria, the Saarland on the French border, and many parts of eastern Germany, offer the lowest prices.

Sample Prices Cup of coffee in a café, DM 3.50, in a stand-up snack bar DM 1.80; mug of beer in a beer hall, DM 3, a bottle of beer from a supermarket, DM 1.50; soft drink, DM 2; ham sandwich, DM 3; 2-mile taxi ride, DM 8.

Visas To enter the new Germany, only passports are required of visitors from the United States, Canada, and the United Kingdom, although U.S. citizens must obtain a visa if they plan to stay longer than three months.

Customs From the beginning of 1993 and the start of a single, unrestricted market within the European Community (EC), there will no longer be any restrictions on importing items duty-free for citizens of the 12 member countries traveling among EC countries.

If you are entering Germany as a citizen of a country that does not belong to the EC, you may import duty-free: (1) 200 cigarettes or 50 cigars or 250 grams of tobacco; plus (2) 1 liter of spirits more than 22% proof or 2 liters of spirits less than 22% proof, and 2 liters of still wine; plus (3) 50 grams of perfume and ¼ liter of toilet water; plus (4) other goods to the value of DM 115.

Tobacco and alcohol allowances are for visitors aged 17 and over. Other items intended for personal use may be imported and exported freely. There are no restrictions on the import and export of German currency.

Language Many people under age 40 speak some English, although the level of understanding varies considerably. English is not as widely understood in eastern parts of the country, where before the collapse of communism Russian was the first foreign language taught in many schools.

Germans who speak some English will take every opportunity to practice what they know, and they are delighted when someone makes an effort—no matter how elementary—to speak their language.

Getting Around

By Train Despite reunification, the two publicly owned train networks of the former two Germanies were still operating independently in 1992, but the merger should be complete in 1993. The western Deutsches Bundesbahn (DB) is developing a new high-speed service capable of traveling at 250 kph (156 mph), with half its 27,000 kilometers (16,800 miles) of track electrified. The smaller eastern sector (the Reichsbahn) still has one foot in the steam age, but a multimillion-deutsche mark investment program will bring much-needed improvements in equipment, tracks, and service.

All major cities in western Germany are linked by fast Intercity services with first- and second-class cars and some by the new super **Intercity Express (ICE)** train service. New track is being laid for the ICE, and top speeds of up to 250 kph (155 mph) have already been achieved on the Hamburg–Frankfurt–Munich route. Fares are higher on ICE routes. Railroad links have been increased between western and eastern Germany, particularly to Berlin, but journeys on many eastern sections are slower than in the west because of older track and rolling stock. An 826-kilometer (512-mile) trip from Hamburg to Munich through the old West Germany takes 7 hours, while a 605-kilometer (375-mile) ride from Berlin to Munich takes 9½ hours. All long-distance routes have restaurant cars, and Intercity overnight trains have sleeper cars. Slower long-distance trains also operate between western cities (Inter-Regio), while E-trains provide shorter-distance services. A DM 6 surcharge (DM 10 on first class) is made regardless of distance on all Intercity journeys, but seat reservations are free. Bikes are not permitted on Intercity services.

New routes have opened up linking Hamburg, Frankfurt, and Munich with Berlin, Dresden, Erfurt, Leipzig, Magdeburg, and Rostock. The Reichsbahn runs train classifications similar to the DB. Many trains have first- and second-class cars, and longer-distance routes provide dining cars or buffet facilities. Since fewer people in the east have cars, trains are more heavily used and seat reservations are advisable for long journeys.

Fares   The DB offers a broad range of fares and inclusive tickets, from family rovers to a **Senior Citizen** card. But probably the best and most flexible deal for the foreign visitor is the German **Rail Pass.** It's available to all non-German residents and, most important, is valid for the entire country on both train networks. The Rail Pass can be bought for 5 days ($160), 10 days ($240), or 15 days ($300). These rates are for second-class travel, but first-class rates are also available. A German **Rail Twin Pass** gives a 10% discount on these rates when two people travel together. A German **Rail Youth Pass** (second class only) for travelers aged 12–26 costs $110, $145, and $180 for the same periods. The Rail Pass can be bought anywhere outside Germany, but the prices quoted here are available only in the United States. An added bonus permits you to "spend" your Rail Pass one day at a time over a period of a month, regardless of the length of your pass. The Rail Pass is also valid on all buses operated by the DB, as well as on tour routes along the Romantic and Castle roads served by Deutschen Touring, or DTG (contact DTG, Am Römerhof 17, 6000 Frankfurt, for reservations). It includes free rides on the Rhine and Mosel rivers, with cruises operated by the Köln-Düsseldorfer (KD) Line between Mainz and Cologne (Köln) and Koblenz and Cochem, as well as free admission to the Transportation Museum in Nürnberg (Lessingstrasse 6).

By Bus   Long-distance bus services in Germany are part of the Europe-wide Europabus network. Services are neither as frequent nor as comprehensive as those on the rail system, so make reservations. Be careful in selecting the service you travel on: All Europabus services have a bilingual hostess and offer small luxuries that you won't find on the more basic, though still comfortable, regular services. For details and reservations, contact **Deutsche Touring Gesellschaft** (Am Römerhof 17, 6000 Frankfurt/Main 90, tel. 069/79030). Reservations can also be made at any of the Deutsche Touring offices in Cologne, Hanover, Hamburg, Munich, Nuremberg (Nürnberg), and Wuppertal and at travel agents.

Rural bus services are operated by local municipalities and some private firms, as well as by Deutsche Bundesbahn (the west German railway) and the post office. Services are variable, however, even when there is no other means to reach your destination by public transportation.

By Plane   Germany's national airline, **Lufthansa,** serves all major cities. **LTU International Airways** (in the United States, tel. 800/888–0200; in Germany, tel. 0211/410941) has connections between Düsseldorf and Munich and between Frankfurt and Munich (summer only). Other airlines—for example, **British Airways** and **Aero Lloyd**—operate between Berlin and Munich, Frankfurt and Düsseldorf. Regular fares are high, but you can save up to 40% with Flieg und Spar ("fly and save") specials; several restrictions apply, such as a DM 100 penalty for changing flights. Contact Lufthansa at Frankfurt International Airport (6000 Frankfurt 65, tel. 069/6961; in the United States at 750 Lexington Ave., New York, NY 10022, tel. 718/895–1277 or 800/645–3880; in Great Britain at 23–26 Piccadilly, London W1V 0EJ, tel. 071/355–4994 or 071/408–0442).

By Boat For a country with such a small coastline, Germany is a surprisingly nautical nation: You can cruise rivers and lakes throughout the country. The biggest fleet, and most of the biggest boats, too, belongs to the Cologne-based KD line, the Köln-Düsseldorf Rheinschiffahrt. It operates services on the rivers Rhine, Moselle, and Main. For details, write **KD River Cruises of Europe** (Rhine Cruise Agency, 170 Hamilton Ave., White Plains, NY 10601) or **KD German Rhine Line** (Frankenwerft 15, 5000 Köln 1).

Services on the 160-kilometer (100-mile) stretch of the Danube (Donau) between the spectacular Kelheim gorge and Passau on the Austrian border are operated by **Donauschiffahrt Wurm & Köck** (Höllgasse 26, D-8390 Passau). The company has daily summer cruises on the Rivers Danube, Inn, and Ilz, which meet at Passau. Bodensee (Lake Constance), the largest lake in Germany, located at the meeting point of Germany, Austria, and Switzerland, has up to 40 ships crisscrossing it in summer. Write **Deutsche Bundesbahn**, Bodensee-Schiffsbetriebe, Hafenstrasse 6, D-7750 Konstanz.

By Bicycle Bicycles can be rented at more than 280 train stations throughout Germany. The basic cost is DM 6 per day with a valid train ticket; otherwise it's DM 10. Two marks extra per day gets you a bike with gears. You can pick up a bike at one station and return it to another, provided the station is on the list of those renting bikes. Bavaria has the greatest number of stations offering this service. There is a small charge for taking a bike on the train; Intercity and Intercity Express (ICE) trains do not carry bikes. Most cities also have bike-rental companies, usually priced about DM 15 per day or DM 60–DM 70 a week.

Staying in Germany

Telephones Telephone lines between western and eastern Germany are now much improved after an initial period of difficulty following reunification. All but the more remote eastern regions can be reached by direct dialing; placing calls to a few rural districts might still require the assistance of an operator. There is now a single country code—49—for both eastern and western Germany. This was formerly the code of West Germany only.

Since reunification, all phones in the east and west use the same coins: 10 pf, DM 1, and DM 5 for long-distance calls. A local call costs 30 pf and lasts six minutes. For all self-dial calls, lift the receiver, put the coins into the machine, and dial.

If you have no change or need to make a lengthy overseas call, go to the local post office, where there are usually public booths; the counter clerk gets you a line, and you pay him or her afterward.

Mail Airmail letters to the United States and Canada cost DM 1.65; postcards cost 80 pf. Airmail letters to the United Kingdom cost DM 1; postcards cost 60 pf.

You can arrange to have mail sent to you in care of any German post office; have the envelope marked "Postlagernd." This service is free. Hotels will hold mail for visitors who have reservations; envelopes should indicate the date of expected arrival.

Shopping German goods carry a 14% value-added tax (VAT). You can
VAT Refunds claim this back either as you leave the country or once you've returned home. When you make a purchase, ask the shopkeeper for a form known as an "Ausfuhr-Abnehmerbescheinigung"; he or she will help you fill it out. As you leave the country, give the form, plus the goods and receipts, to German customs. It will give you an official export certificate or stamp. You then send the form back to the shop, and it will send the refund.

Opening and **Banks.** Times vary from state to state and city to city, but
Closing Times banks are generally open weekdays from 8:30 or 9 to 3 or 4 (5 or 6 on Thursday). Some banks close from 12:30 to 1:30. Branches at airports and main train stations open as early as 6:30 AM and close as late as 10:30 PM.

Museums. Museums are generally open Tuesday to Sunday 9–5. Some close for an hour or more at lunch, and some are open on Monday. Many stay open until 9 on Thursdays.

Shops. Times vary, but shops are generally open weekdays from 8:30 or 9 until 6:30 PM and Saturdays until 1 or 2 PM. On the first Saturday of each month, many larger shops and department stores in Germany are open until 6. In 1989, several cities introduced late shopping hours on Thursdays. Large stores then stay open until 8:30 PM.

National Holidays January 1; January 6 (Epiphany); April 9 (Good Friday); April 12 (Easter Monday); May 1; May 20 (Ascension); May 31 (Pentecost Monday); June 10 (Corpus Christi, south Germany only); October 3 (German Unity Day); November 1 (All Saints' Day); November 17 (Day of Prayer and Repentance); December 24–26.

Dining It's hard to generalize about German food beyond saying that standards are high and portions are large. Beer restaurants in Bavaria, *Apfelwein* taverns in Frankfurt, and *Kneipen*—the pub on the corner cum local café—in Berlin nearly always offer best value and atmosphere. But throughout the country you'll find *Gaststätten* and/or *Gasthöfe*—local inns—where atmosphere and regional specialties are always available.

In larger towns and cities throughout the country, Germans like to nibble at roadside or market snack stalls, called *Imbisse*. Hot sausages, spicy meatballs (*Fleischpflanzerl*), meatloaf topped with a fried egg (*Leberkäs*), in the south, and sauerkraut are the traditional favorites. But foods eaten on the hoof are creeping in, too: french fries, pizzas, gyros, and hamburgers. For late breakfasts or good-value lunches, try the restaurants of the main department stores across the country: Hertie, Karstadt, Kaufhof.

The most famous German specialty is sausage. Everyone has heard of frankfurters, but if you're in Munich, try *Weisswurst*, a delicate white sausage traditionally eaten only between midnight and noon. Nürnberg's sausage favorite is the *Nürnberger Bratwurst;* its fame is such that you'll find restaurants all over Germany serving it. Look for the "Bratwurststube" sign. Dumplings (*Knödel*) can also be found throughout the country, though their natural home is probably Bavaria; farther north, potatoes often take their place.

The natural accompaniment to German food is either beer or wine. Munich is the beer capital of Germany, though there's no part of the country where you won't find the amber nectar. Say "Helles" or Export if you want light beer; "Dunkles" if you want dark beer. In Bavaria, try the sour but refreshing beer brewed from wheat, called *Weissbier*. Germany is a major wine-producing country, also, and much of it is of superlative quality. You will probably be happy with the house wine in most restaurants or with one of those earthenware pitchers of cold Moselle wine. If you want something more expensive, remember that all wines are graded in one of three basic categories: *Tafelwein* (table wine); *Qualitätswein* (fine wines); and *Qualitätswein mit Prädikat* (top-quality wines).

Mealtimes Breakfast, served anytime from 6:30 to 10, is often a substantial meal, with cold meats, cheeses, rolls, and fruit. Lunch is served from around 11:30 (especially in rural areas) to around 2; dinner is generally from 6 until 9:30 PM, or earlier in some quiet country areas. Lunch tends to be the main meal, a fact reflected in the almost universal appearance of a lunchtime *Tageskarte*, or suggested menu; try it if you want maximum nourishment for minimum outlay. This doesn't mean that dinner is a rushed or skimpy affair, however; the Germans have too high a regard for food for any meal to be underrated.

Ratings Prices are per person and include a first course, main course, dessert, and tip and tax. Best bets are indicated by a star ★.

The following chart gives price ranges for restaurants in the western part of Germany. Food prices in the five new states in eastern Germany generally fit in the Budget and Inexpensive categories, although in the bigger cities many of the better quality restaurants are already starting to mimic "western" rates and a few are very expensive. Bills in simple restaurants in country areas of the eastern region will, however, still come well below DM 35.

Category	Major Cities and Resorts	Other Areas
Moderate	DM 50–DM 75	DM 35–DM 55
Inexpensive	DM 30–DM 50	DM 20–DM 35
Budget	DM 20–DM 30	under DM 20

Lodging The standard of German hotels is generally excellent. Prices are highest in big cities, where there are fewer budget options to choose from.

In addition to hotels proper, the country also has numerous *Gasthöfe* or *Gasthäuser* (country inns); pensions or *Fremdenheime* (guest houses); and, at the lowest end of the scale, *Zimmer*, meaning, quite simply, rooms, normally in private houses. Look for the sign "Zimmer frei" or "zu vermieten," meaning "for rent." A red sign reading "besetzt" means there are no vacancies.

Lists of hotels are available from the German National Tourist Office (Beethovenstr. 69, 6000 Frankfurt/Main 1, tel. 069/

75720), and from all regional and local tourist offices. Tourist offices will also make reservations for you—they charge a nominal fee—but may have difficulty doing so after 4 PM in peak season and on weekends. A reservations service is also operated by the German National Tourist Office (Allgemeine Deutsche Zimmer-reservierung, Cornelius-str. 34, 6000 Frankfurt/Main 1, tel. 069/740–767).

Most hotels have restaurants, but those describing themselves as *Garni* will provide breakfast only.

Tourist accommodations in eastern Germany are beginning to blossom under free enterprise after the straitjacket of state monopoly, although the choice and facilities are still far behind the western half of the country. Accommodations remain tight at the top- and middle-quality levels, so if you want to stay in good hotels in eastern Germany, book well in advance. The real boom in lodgings has been at the inexpensive end of the market, where thousands of beds are now available for the adventurous traveler. For relatively few marks every village can now provide somewhere for the tourist to put his or her head and perhaps offer a simple but wholesome evening meal. Many guest houses have sprung up under the enterprising stewardship of housewives eager to supplement the family income. For a list of approved addresses, consult the local tourist office.

Castle Hotels   Some of the simpler establishments connected with this hotel association lack a little in the way of comfort and have very basic furnishing, but most can be delightful, with antiques, imposing interiors, and out-of-the-way locations setting the tone. Prices are mostly moderate. Ask the German National Tourist Office or your travel agent for the "Castle Hotels in Germany" brochure. It details a series of good-value packages, most for stays of four to six nights.

Ringhotels   This association groups 130 individually owned and managed hotels in the medium price range. Many are situated in the countryside or in pretty villages. Package deals of 2–3 days are available. Contact **Ringhotels,** Belfortstrasse 8, 8000 Munich 80, tel. 089/482720.

Rentals   Apartments and hotel homes, most accommodating from two to eight guests, can be rented throughout Germany. Rates are low, with reductions for longer stays. Charges for gas and electricity, and sometimes water, are usually added to the bill. There is normally an extra charge for linen, but not if you bring your own. Local and regional tourist offices have lists of apartments in their areas; otherwise contact the **German National Tourist Office** (*see* Lodging in Staying in Germany, *above*).

Farm Vacations   Taking an *Urlaub auf dem Bauernhof,* as the Germans put it, has increased dramatically in popularity over the past four or five years. Almost every regional tourist office has listings of farms by area offering bed and breakfast, apartments, or whole farmhouses to rent. Alternatively, write the **German Agricultural Association** (DLG), Zimmerweg 16, D-6000 Frankfurt/Main. It produces an annual listing of more than 1,500 farms, all of them inspected and graded, that offer accommodations. The brochure costs DM 7.50.

Camping   There are 2,600 campsites in Germany, about 1,600 of which are listed by the **German Camping Club** (DCC), Mandlstrasse 28, D-8000, Munich 40. For details of camping facilities in eastern

Germany, where facilities are neither common nor modern, contact **Camping and Caravanverband** (Postfach 105, 1080 Berlin). The German National Tourist Office also publishes an annually updated listing of sites. Most are open from May through October, with about 400 staying open year-round. They tend to become crowded during the summer, so it's always worthwhile to make reservations a day or two ahead. Prices range from DM 10 to DM 15 per night for two adults, a car, and trailer (less for tents). If you want to camp away from an official site, you must get permission beforehand; if you can't find the owner, ask the police. You're allowed to spend no more than one night in parking lots on roadsides and in city parking lots if you're in a camper, and you may not set up any camping equipment.

Youth Hostels   Germany's youth hostels—*Jugendherberge*—are probably the most efficient and up-to-date in Europe. There are 600 in all, many located in castles, adding a touch of romance to otherwise utilitarian accommodations. There's an age limit of 27 in Bavaria; elsewhere, there are no restrictions, though those under 20 take preference if space is limited. You'll need an International Youth Hostel card to stay in a German youth hostel; write **American Youth Hostels Association** (Box 37613, Washington, DC 20013) or **Canadian Hostelling Association** (333 River Rd., Ottawa, Ontario K1L 8H9). In Great Britain, contact the **Youth Hostels Association** (22 Southampton St., London WC2). The International Youth Hostel card can also be obtained from the **Deutsches Jugendherbergswerk Hauptverband** (Bismarckstr. 8, D-4930 Detmold, tel. 05231/74010), which provides a complete list of German hostels for DM 6.50.

Hostels must be reserved well in advance for midsummer, especially in eastern Germany. Bookings for hostels in the new German states (former East Germany) of Saxony, Thuringia, Saxony-Anhalt, Brandenburg, and Mecklenburg can be made directly through **Jugendtourist** (Alexanderplatz 5, 1026 Berlin).

Ratings   Service charges and taxes are included in all quoted room rates. Similarly, breakfast is usually, but not always, included, so check before you book in. Rates are often surprisingly flexible in German hotels, varying considerably according to demand. Major hotels in cities often have lower rates on weekends or other periods when business is quiet. If you're lucky, you can find reductions of up to 60%. Prices are for two people in a double room. Best bets are indicated by a star ★.

The following chart is for lodgings throughout Germany. Generally, accommodations in eastern Germany are less expensive than in western Germany.

Category	Major Cities or Resorts	Other Areas
Moderate	DM 120–DM 180	DM 100–DM 120
Inexpensive	DM 100–DM 120	DM 80–DM 100
Budget	under DM 100	under DM 80

Tipping   The Germans are as punctilious about tipping as they are about most facets of life in their well-regulated country. Overtipping is as frowned upon as not tipping at all, though the kind of abuse you risk in some countries for undertipping is virtually unknown here. Nonetheless, tips are expected, if not exactly demanded. Follow these simple rules and you won't go wrong.

In restaurants, service is usually included (under the heading *Bedienung*, at the bottom of the check), and it is customary to round out the check to the next mark or two, a practice also commonplace in cafés, beer halls, and bars. For taxi drivers, also round out to the next mark or two: for DM 11.20, make it DM 12; for DM 11.80, make it DM 13. Railway and airport porters (if you can find any) have their own scale of charges, but round out the requested amount to the next mark.

Munich

Arriving and Departing

By Plane Munich's new Franz Josef Strauss (FJS) Airport, named after a former state premier, opened in May, 1992. It is 28 kilometers (17½ miles) northeast of the city center.

Between the Airport and Downtown The S8 suburban train line links FJS Airport with the city's main train station (Hauptbahnhof). Trains depart in both directions every 20 minutes from 3:55 AM to 12:55 AM daily. Intermediate stops are made at Ostbahnhof (good for hotels located east of the River Isar) and city center stations such as Marienplatz. The 38-minute trip costs DM 8 if you purchase a multi-use strip ticket (*see* Getting Around, *below*) and use 8 strips; otherwise an ordinary one-way ticket is DM 10 per person. A tip for families: Up to five people (maximum of two adults) can travel to or from the airport for only DM 16 by buying a Tageskarte (*see* Getting Around, *below*). This is particularly advantageous if you are arriving in Munich, because you can continue to use the Tageskarte in the city for the rest of the day. The only restriction is that you cannot use this special day ticket before 9 AM weekdays.

An express bus also links the airport and Hauptbahnhof, departing in both directions every 20 minutes. The trip takes about 40 minutes and costs DM 7.

By Train All long-distance services arrive at and depart from the main train station, the Hauptbahnhof. Trains to and from destinations in the Bavarian Alps use the adjoining Starnbergerbahnhof. For information on train times, tel. 089/19419; English is spoken by most information office staff. For tickets and information, go to the station or to the ABR travel agency right by the station on Bahnhofplatz.

By Bus Munich has no central bus station. Long-distance buses arrive at and depart from the north side of the train station on Arnulfstrasse. A taxi stand is 20 yards away.

Getting Around

Downtown Munich is only about one mile square, so it can easily be explored on foot. Other areas—Schwabing, Nymphenburg, the Olympic Park—are best reached on the efficient and comprehensive public transportation network. It incorporates buses, streetcars, subways (U-Bahn), and suburban trains (S-

Bahn). Tickets are good for the entire network, and you can break your trip as many times as you like using just one ticket, provided you travel in one direction only and within a given time limit. If you plan to make only a few trips, buy strip tickets (Streifenkarten)—blue for adults, red for children. Adults get 10 strips for DM 10; children the same number for DM 8. For adults, short rides that span up to 4 stations cost 1 strip; trips spanning more than 4 stations cost 2 strips. Children pay 1 strip per ride. All tickets must be validated by time-punching them in the automatic machines at station entrances and on all buses and streetcars. The best buy is the Tageskarte. Up to two adults and three children can use this excellent-value ticket for unlimited journeys between 9 AM and the end of the day's service (about 2 AM). It costs DM 8 for the inner zone, which covers central Munich. A Tageskarte for the entire system, extending to the Starnbergersee and Ammersee lakes, costs DM 16. Holders of a Eurail Pass, a Youth Pass, an Inter-Rail Card, or a DB Tourist Card travel free on all S-Bahn trains.

Important Addresses and Numbers

Tourist Information
The address to write to for information in advance of your visit is Fremdenverkehrsamt München, Postfach, 8000 München 1. This address also deals with lodging questions and bookings. Two other offices provide on-the-spot advice: at the Hauptbahnhof (tel. 089/239–1256), daily between 8 AM and 10 PM, and at the corner of Rindermarkt and Pettenbeckstrasse, behind Marienplatz (tel. 089/239–1272), open weekdays between 9:30 AM and 6 PM.

Consulates
U.S. Consulate General (Königinstrasse 5, tel. 089/28881). **British Consulate General** (Bürkleinstr. 10, tel. 089/211090). **Canadian Consulate** (Tal 29, tel. 089/222–661).

Emergencies
Police (tel. 110). **Ambulance** and **emergency medical attention** (tel. 089/558661). **Dentist** (tel. 089/723–3093).

Exploring Munich

Germans in other parts of the country sometimes refer to Munich as the nation's "secret capital." This sly compliment may reflect the importance of Munich—it's the number-one tourist destination in Germany, as well as the most attractive major German city—but there's nothing "secret" about the way Münchners make this brave claim. Indeed, the noise with which the people of Munich trumpet the attractions of their city could be dismissed as so much Bavarian bombast were it not for the fact that it is so enthusiastically endorsed by others. Flamboyant, easygoing Munich, city of beer and Baroque, is starkly different from the sometimes stiff Prussian influences to be found in Berlin, the gritty industrial drive of Hamburg, or the hard-headed commercial instincts of high-rise Frankfurt. This is a city to visit for its good-natured and relaxed charm—*Gemütlichkeit,* they call it here—and for its beer halls, its museums, its malls, its parks, and its palaces.

Munich is a crazy mix of high culture (witness its world-class opera house and art galleries) and wild abandon (witness the vulgar frivolity of the Oktoberfest). Its citizenry seems determined to perpetuate the lifestyle of 19th-century king Ludwig I, the Bavarian ruler who brought so much international prestige to his home city after declaring: "I want to make out of Munich a town which does such credit to Germany that nobody knows Germany unless he has seen Munich." He kept his promise with an architectural and artistic renaissance—before abdicating because of a wild romance with a Spanish dancing girl, Lola Montez.

The Historic Heart *Numbers in the margin correspond to points of interest on the Munich map.*

❶ Begin your tour of Munich at the **Hauptbahnhof,** the main train station and an important orientation point. The city tourist office is here, too, ready with information and maps. Cross the street and you're at the start of a kilometer (½ mile) of pedestrian shopping malls, the first being Schützenstrasse. Facing you are **Hertie,** Munich's leading department store, and ❷ **Karlsplatz** square, known locally as *Stachus.* The huge, domed building on your left is the late-19th-century **Justizpalast** (Palace of Justice). It's one of Germany's finest examples of *Gründerzeit*, the 19th-century versions of Medieval and Renaissance architectural styles.

Head down into the pedestrian underpass—it's another extensive shopping area—to reach the other side and one of the ❸ original city gates, **Karlstor.** The city's two principal shopping streets—**Neuhauserstrasse** and **Kaufingerstrasse**—stretch away from it on the other side. Two of the city's major churches ❹ ❺ are here, too: the **Bürgersaal** and the **Michaelskirche.** The latter is one of the most magnificent Renaissance churches in Germany, a spacious and handsome structure decorated throughout in plain white stucco. It was built for the Jesuits in the late 16th century and is closely modeled on their church of the Gesù in Rome. The intention was to provide a large preaching space, hence the somewhat barnlike atmosphere. Ludwig II is buried here; his tomb is in the crypt. The large neoclassical tomb in the north transept is the resting place of Eugène de Beauharnais, Napoleon's stepson. The highly decorated Rococo interior of the Bürgersaal makes a startling contrast with the simplicity of the Michaelskirche.

A block past the Michaelskirche to your left is Munich's late- ❻ 15th-century cathedral, the **Frauenkirche,** or Church of Our Lady. Towering above it are two onion-shaped domes, symbols of the city (perhaps because they resemble brimming beer mugs, cynics claim). They were added in 1525 after the body of the church had been completed. Step inside and you'll be amazed at the stark simplicity of the church. This is partly the result of the construction that followed the severe bombing in World War II. The crypt houses the tombs of numerous Wittelsbachs, the family that ruled Bavaria for seven centuries until forced to abdicate in 1918. The cathedral will be closed in 1993 for the costliest structural repairs in its history. It is due to reopen in early 1994 for celebrations marking the 500th anniversary of its consecration.

❼ From the Frauenkirche, walk to the **Marienplatz** square, the heart of the city, surrounded by shops, restaurants, and cafés. It takes its name from the 300-year-old gilded statue of the Virgin in the center. When it was taken down to be cleaned in 1960, workmen found a small casket containing a splinter of wood said to have come from the cross of Christ. The square is domi- ❽ nated by the 19th-century **Neues Rathaus,** the new town hall,

built in the fussy, turreted style so loved by Ludwig II. The
(9) Altes Rathaus, or old town hall, a medieval building of great
charm, sits, as if forgotten, in a corner of the square. At 11 AM
and 9 PM daily (plus May–October, 5 PM), the **Glockenspiel,** or
chiming clock, in the central tower of the town hall, swings into
action. Two tiers of dancing and jousting figures perform their
ritual display. It can be worthwhile scheduling your day to
catch the clock. Immediately after the war, an American soldier donated some paint to help restore the battered figures
and was rewarded with a ride on one of the knight's horses,
high above the cheering crowds.

Heading south down Rosenstrasse to Sendlingerstrasse, you
(10) come to the **Asamkirche** on your right. Some consider the
Asamkirche a preposterously overdecorated jewel box; others
consider it one of Europe's finest late-Baroque churches. One
thing is certain: If you have any interest in church architecture,
this is a place you shouldn't miss. It was built around 1730 by
the Asam brothers—Cosmas Damian and Egid Quirin—next
door to their home, the Asamhaus. They dedicated it to St.
John Nepomuk, a 14th-century Bohemian monk who was
drowned in the Danube. Pause before you go in to see the
charming statue of angels carrying him to heaven from the
rocky riverbank. Inside, there is a riot of decoration: frescoes,
statuary, rich rosy marbles, billowing clouds of stucco, and
gilding everywhere. The decorative elements and the architecture merge to create a sense of seamless movement and color.

(11) Go back to Marienplatz and turn right for the **Viktualienmarkt,**
the food market. Open-air stalls sell cheese, wine, sausages,
fruit, and flowers. Fortified with Bavarian sausage and sauer-
(12) kraut, plunge into local history with a visit to the **Residenz,**
home of the Wittelsbachs from the 16th century to their en-
forced abdication at the end of World War I. From Max-Joseph-
Platz you'll enter the great palace, with its glittering
Schatzkammer, or treasury, and glorious Rococo theater, designed by court architect François Cuvilliès. Also facing the
(13) square is the stern neoclassical portico of the **Nationaltheater,**
built at the beginning of the 19th century and twice destroyed.
*Residenz and Schatzkammer, Max-Joseph-Platz 3. Admission
to each: DM 3.50, children free. Open Tues.–Sun. 10–4:30 PM.
Cuvilliès Theater admission: DM 2, children free. Open Mon.–
Sat. 2–5, Sun. 10–5.*

(14) To the north of the Residenz is the **Hofgarten,** the palace gardens. Two sides of the gardens are bordered by sturdy arcades
designed by Leo von Klenze, whose work for the Wittelsbachs
in the 19th century helped transform the face of the city. Dominating the east side of the Hofgarten is the refurbished copper
dome of Bavaria's former Army Museum, destroyed in World
War II and now incorporated into a new state government chancellery.

Odeonsplatz itself is dominated by two striking buildings. One
(15) is the **Theatinerkirche,** built for the Theatine monks in the mid-
17th century, though its handsome facade, with twin eye-
catching domes, was added only in the following century.
Despite its Italian influences, the interior, like that of the
Michaelskirche, is austerely white. The other notable building
(16) here is the **Feldherrnhalle,** an open loggia built by Ludwig I and
modeled on the Loggia dei Lanzi in Florence. Next to it is the

Alte Pinakothek, **20**
Altes Rathaus, **9**
Asamkirche, **10**
Bürgersaal, **4**
Englischer Garten, **18**
Feldherrnhalle, **16**
Frauenkirche, **6**
Hauptbahnhof, **1**
Haus der Kunst, **19**
Hofgarten, **14**
Karlsplatz, **2**
Karlstor, **3**
Marienplatz, **7**
Michaelskirche, **5**
Nationaltheater, **13**
Neue Pinakothek, **21**
Neues Rathaus, **8**
Residenz, **12**
Siegestor, **17**
Theatinerkirche, **15**
Viktualienmarkt, **11**

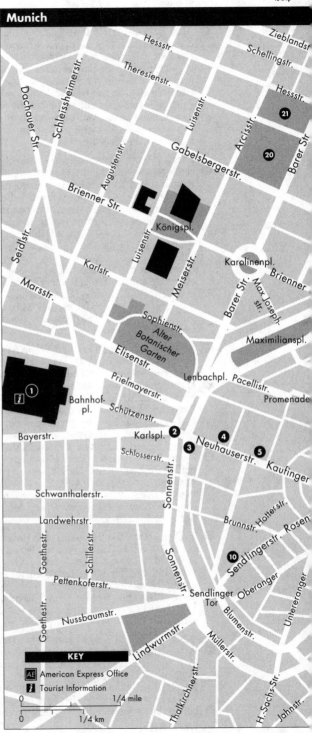

Munich

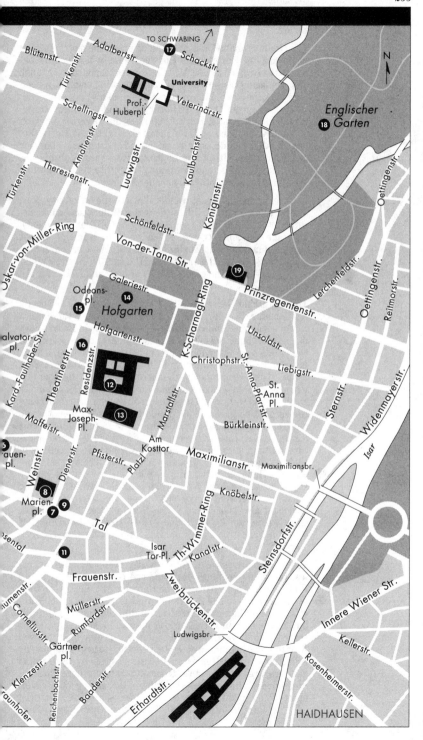

TO SCHWABING

17

Schackstr.

Blütenstr.

Türkenstr.

Adalbertstr.

Schackstr.

University

Schellingstr.

Prof.-Huberpl.

Veterinärstr.

Amalienstr.

N

Englischer

18 Garten

Türkenstr.

Theresienstr.

Ludwigstr.

Kaulbachstr.

Königinstr.

Oettingenstr.

Schönfeldstr.

Oskar-von-Miller-Ring

Von-der-Tann Str.

Lerchenfeldstr.

Oettingenstr.

Reitmorstr.

Galeriestr.

Prinzregentenstr.

19

Odeons-pl.

14

15

Hofgarten

Hofgartenstr.

K.-Scharnagl-Ring

Unsoldstr.

Liebigstr.

Sternstr.

alvator-pl.

Kard.-Faulhaber-Str.

Theatinerstr.

Residenzstr.

16

Christophstr.

St.-Anna-Pfarrstr.

St. Anna Pl.

Widenmayerstr.

12

Marstallstr.

Maffeistr.

Max-Joseph-Pl.

13

Am Kosttor

Bürkleinstr.

Isar

3

auen-pl.

Weinstr.

Dienerstr.

Pfisterstr.

Platzl

Maximilianstr.

Maximiliansbr.

8

Marien-pl.

7 **9**

Tal

Knöbelstr.

Th.-Wimmer-Ring

Steinsdorfstr.

11

Isar Tor-Pl.

Kanalstr.

Frauenstr.

Zweibrückenstr.

Innere Wiener Str.

umenstr.

Müllerstr.

Rumfordstr.

Ludwigsbr.

Kellerstr.

Corneliusstr.

Gärtner-pl.

Rosenheimerstr.

Klenzestr.

Reichenbachstr.

Baaderstr.

Erhardtstr.

aunhofer

HAIDHAUSEN

sental

site of Hitler's unsuccessful *putsch* of 1923, later a key Nazi shrine.

The Feldherrnhalle looks north along one of the most imposing boulevards in Europe, the **Ludwigstrasse,** which in turn becomes the **Leopoldstrasse.** Von Klenze was responsible for much of it, replacing the jumble of old buildings that originally stood here with the clean, high-windowed lines of his restrained Italianate buildings. The state library and the university are located along it, while, halfway up it, is the **Siegestor,** or Arch of Victory, modeled on the Arch of Constantine in Rome. Beyond it is **Schwabing,** once a student and artist quarter but now much glossier, with a mix of bars, discos (*see* Nightlife, *below*), trendy cafés, and boutiques. Nightlife centers around Wedekindplatz, near the Münchener Freiheit subway station.

Back on Leopoldstrasse, wander down to the university, turn on to Professor-Huber-Platz (he was a Munich academic executed by the Nazis for his support of an anti-Hitler movement), and take Veterinärstrasse. It leads you to Munich's largest park, the magnificent **Englischer Garten.** You can rent a bike (tel. 089/397016) at the entrance to the park on summer weekends (May–Oct). The cost is DM 5 per hour and DM 15 for the day.

The Englischer Garten, 4½ kilometers (3 miles) long and over a ½ kilometer (¼ mile) wide, was laid out by Count Rumford, a refugee from the American War of Independence. He was born in England, but it wasn't his English ancestry that determined the park's name as much as its open, informal nature, a style favored by 18th-century English aristocrats. You can rent boats, visit beer gardens—the most famous is at the foot of a Chinese Pagoda—ride your bike (or ski in winter), or simply stroll around. Ludwig II used to love to wander incognito along the serpentine paths. What would he say today, now that so much of the park has been taken over by Munich's nudists? This is no misprint. Late-20th-century Germans have embraced nature worship with almost pagan fervor, and large sections of the park have been designated nudist areas. The biggest is behind the **Haus der Kunst,** Munich's leading modern art gallery and a surviving example of Third Reich architecture. The building underwent major renovations in 1992. Part of the basement also houses one of the city's most exclusive discos, the PI. *Haus der Kunst, Prinzregentenstr. 1. Admission: DM 3.50 adults, 50 pf children; Sun. and holidays free. Open Tues.–Sun. 9–4:30, also Thurs. 7 PM–9 PM.*

You'll find more culture in Munich's two leading picture galleries, the Alte (meaning "old") and the Neue (meaning "new") Pinakothek. They are located on Barerstrasse, just to the west of the university. The **Alte Pinakothek** is not only the repository of some of the world's most celebrated Old Master paintings but an architectural treasure in its own right, though much scarred from wartime bomb damage. It was built by von Klenze at the beginning of the 19th century to house Ludwig I's collections. Early Renaissance works, especially by German painters, are the museum's strongest point, but there are some magnificently heroic works by Rubens, too, among much else of outstanding quality. *Barerstr. 27. Admission: DM 4, adults, 50 pf children; free Sun. and holidays. Open Tues.–Sun. 9–4:30; also Tues. and Thurs. 7 PM–9 PM.*

㉑ The **Neue Pinakothek** was another of Ludwig I's projects, built to house his "modern" collections, meaning, of course, 19th-century works. The building was destroyed during World War II, and today's museum opened in 1981. The low, brick structure—some have compared it with a Florentine palazzo—is an unparalleled environment in which to see one of the finest collections of 19th-century European paintings and sculpture in the world. *Barerstr. 29. Admission: DM 4 adults, 50 pf children; free Sun. and holidays. Open Tues.–Sun. 9–4:30; also Tues. 7PM–9 PM. Take the No. 18 streetcar from Karlsplatz for both the Alte and Neue Pinakothek.*

There are two trips you can take to attractions just out of the city center. One is to the **Olympic Park,** a 10-minute U-Bahn ride (U3); the other is to Nymphenburg, 6 kilometers (4 miles) northwest and reached by the U1 subway to Rotkreuzplatz, then the No. 12 streetcar.

Suburban Attractions **Schloss Nymphenburg** was the summer palace of the Wittelsbachs. The oldest parts date from 1664, but construction continued for more than 100 years, the bulk of the work being undertaken in the reign of Max Emmanuel between 1680 and 1730. The gardens, a mixture of formal French *parterres* (trim, ankle-high hedges and gravel walks) and English parkland, were landscaped over the same period. The interiors are exceptional, especially the Banqueting Hall, a Rococo masterpiece in green and gold. Make a point of seeing the Schönheits Galerie, the **Gallery of Beauties.** It contains more than 100 portraits of women who had caught the eye of Ludwig I; duchesses rub shoulders with butchers' daughters. Among them is Lola Montez. Seek out the **Amalienburg,** or Hunting Lodge, on the grounds. It was built by Cuvilliès, architect of the Residenz Theater in Munich. That the lodge was designed for hunting of the indoor variety can easily be guessed by the sumptuous silver and blue stucco and the atmosphere of courtly high life. The palace also contains the **Marstallmuseum** (the Museum of Royal Carriages), containing a sleigh that belonged to Ludwig II, among the opulently decorated vehicles, and, on the floor above, the **Nymphenburger Porzellan,** with examples of the porcelain produced here between 1747 and the 1920s. *Schloss Nymphenburg. Combined ticket to all Nymphenburg attractions: DM 6. Combined ticket to Schloss, Gallery of Beauties, Amalienburg, and Marstallmuseum: DM 4.50. Botanic gardens: DM 1.50. Children under 15 free. Open Apr.–Sept., Tues.–Sun. 9–12:30 and 1:30–5; Oct.–Mar., Tues.–Sun. 10–12:30 and 1:30–4. Amalienburg and gardens open daily.*

Perhaps the most controversial buildings in Munich are the circus tent–shaped roofs of the **Olympic Park.** Built for the 1972 Olympics, the park, with its undulating, transparent tile roofs and modern housing blocks, represented a revolutionary marriage of technology and visual daring when first unveiled. Sports fans might like to join the crowds in the Olympic stadium when the local soccer team, Bayern Munich, has a home game. Call 089/30613577 for information and tickets. There's an amazing view of the stadium, the Olympic Park, and the city from the Olympic tower. An elevator speeds you to the top in seconds. *Admission: DM 5 adults; DM 2.50 children; combined tower and park tour (until 5 PM) DM 8 adults, DM 4 children. Open mid-Apr.–mid-Oct., daily 8 AM–midnight; mid-Oct.–mid-Apr., daily 9 AM–midnight.*

Off the Beaten Track

Even though the Olympic Tower is higher, romantics say the best view of Munich and the Alps is from the top of the **Alte Peter** church tower (DM 2 adults, 50 pf children); it's just off Marienplatz. Check that a white disk is hanging on the wall outside the entrance: It means that visibility is good. There are 302 steps to climb to the top. For the most inexpensive sightseeing tour of the center, take a No. 19 streetcar from outside the train station at Bahnhofplatz and ride it to **Wienerplatz**, itself located in Haidhausen, one of Munich's most interesting areas. On a fine day, join the chess players at their open-air boards in Schwabing's **Münchener Freiheit** square. On a rainy day, pack your swimsuit and splash around in the Art Nouveau setting of the **Müllersches Volksbad** pool; it's located on the corner of the Ludwigsbrücke, one of the bridges over the Isar.

Shopping

Gift Ideas   Munich is a city of beer, and beer mugs and coasters make an obvious gift to take home. There are many specialist shops in downtown Munich, but **Ludwig Mory,** located in the town hall on Marienplatz, is about the best. Munich is also the home of the famous Nymphenburg porcelain factory; its major outlet is on Odeonsplatz. You can also buy direct from the factory located on the half-moon–shaped road—Schlossrondell—in front of Nymphenburg Palace. *Tel. 089/172439. Salesroom open weekdays 8:30–noon and 12:30–5.*

Shopping Districts   From Odeonsplatz you are poised to plunge into the heart of the huge pedestrian mall that runs through the center of town. The first street you come to, **Theatinerstrasse,** is also one of the most expensive. In fact, it has only one serious rival in the money-no-object stakes: **Maximilianstrasse,** the first street to your left as you head down Theatinerstrasse. Both are lined with elegant shops selling desirable German fashions and other high-priced goods from around the world. Leading off to the right of Theatinerstrasse is **Maffeistrasse,** where **Loden-Frey** has Bavaria's most complete collection of traditional wear, from green "loden" coats to Lederhosen. Maffeistrasse runs parallel to Munich's principal shopping streets: **Kaufingerstrasse** and **Neuhauserstrasse,** the one an extension of the other.

Department Stores   All the city's major department stores—other than **Hertie** (*see* Exploring, *above*)—are along Maffeistrasse, Kaufingerstrasse, and Neuhauserstrasse. **Kaufhof** and **Karstadt-Oberpollinger** are probably the best. Both have large departments stocking Bavarian arts and crafts, as well as clothing, household goods, jewelry, and other accessories.

Antiques   Antique hunters should make for **Karlstrasse, Ottostrasse, Türkenstrasse,** and **Westenriederstrasse.** Also try the open-air Auer Dult fairs held on Mariahilfplatz at the end of April, July, and October (streetcar No. 25).

Dining

Münchners love to eat just as much as they love their beer, and the range of food is as varied and rich as the local breweries' output. Some of Europe's best chefs are to be found here, purveyors of French nouvelle cuisine in some of the most noted—

and pricey—restaurants in Germany. But these restaurants are mainly for the gourmet. For those in search of the local cuisine, the path leads to Munich's tried-and-true wood-paneled, flagstone beer restaurants and halls where the food is as sturdy as the large measure of beer that comes to your table almost automatically. Try the *Weisswurst* (white veal sausages with herbs), brought to your table in a tureen of boiling water to keep them fresh and hot. They are served with a sweet mustard and pretzels and are a breakfast or midmorning favorite. Equally good is *Leberkäs*, wedges of piping-hot meat loaf with a fried egg on top and pan-fried potatoes.

For details and price-category definitions, *see* Dining in Staying in Germany.

Moderate **Grüne Gans.** This small, chummy restaurant near Viktualienmarkt is popular with local entertainers, whose photographs clutter the walls. International fare with regional German influences dominates the menu, although there are a few Chinese dishes. Try the chervil cream soup, followed by calves' kidneys in tarragon sauce. *Am Einlass 5, tel. 089/266228. Reservations required. MC. Closed lunch and Sat.*

★ **Nürnberger Bratwurst Glöckl.** This is about the most authentic old-time Bavarian sausage restaurant in Munich, and it's always crowded. Wobbly chairs, pitch-black wooden paneling, tin plates, monosyllabic waitresses, and, downstairs, some seriously Teutonic-looking characters establish an unbeatable mood. If you want undiluted atmosphere, try for a table downstairs; if you want to hear yourself speak, go for one upstairs. The menu is limited, with *Nürnberger Wurst*—finger-size short supply, is served straight from wooden barrels. The restaurant is right by the Frauenkirche—the entrance is set back from the street and can be hard to spot—and makes an ideal lunchtime layover. *Frauenplatz 9, tel. 089/220385. Reservations advised. No credit cards. Closed Sun. and public holidays.*

Seehaus am Englischen Garten. Diners in this Bavarian country house-style restaurant, decorated with plenty of chunky pine wood, can sit at tables set on a chestnut tree-shaded terrace during the warmer months. The location is one of the city's prettiest, in the Englischer Garten park beside the lake where the locals row boats in summer and ice skate in winter. The menu ranges from the substantial Bavarian pork and dumplings to fish dishes such as lobster and octopus. It's a 10-minute walk from Münchener Freiheit subway (U3/U6) in Schwabing. *Kleinhesselohe 3, tel. 089/381-6130. Reservations advised. AE, DC, MC, V.*

Spöckmeier. This rambling Bavarian beer restaurant, only 50 yards from Marienplatz, is spread over three floors and is a firm favorite with the locals. They are famous for their homemade Weisswurst, but the daily changing menu also offers more than two dozen solid main course dishes and a choice of four draft beers. The house *eintopf* (a rich broth of noodles and pork) is a meal in itself. *Rosenstr. 9, tel. 089/268-088. Reservations not necessary. AE, DC, MC, V.*

Weinhaus Neuner. Originally a seminary, this early 18th-century building houses Munich's oldest surviving wine hostelry. There is a timeless atmosphere in the high-ceilinged dining rooms lined with dark oak paneling. Regional dishes are prepared with flair. Look for the herb-filled pork fillets with noodles, and veal with Morchela mushroom sauce. *Herzogs-*

pitalstr. 8, tel. 089/260–3954. Reservations required. AE, DC, MC, V. Closed Sat. lunch, Sun., and holidays.

Inexpensive **Donisl.** The two-story galleried interior of this centuries-old beer hall bustles with activity from early morning until midnight. During Fasching, Donisl is open all night serving weissbier and Weisswurst to the fancy-dress-ball crowds. In summer, tables spill outside in front of the Rathaus on Marienplatz. Regulars on the menu include *Schweinshaxe* (pig's knuckle) and roast pork and dumplings. Traditional music is performed from 5 PM. *Weinstr. 1, tel. 089/220184. No reservations. AE, DC, MC, V.*

Dürnbräu. A fountain plays outside this picturesque old Bavarian inn. Inside, the mood is crowded and noisy. Expect to share a table; your fellow diners will range from millionaires to students. The food is resolutely traditional. Try the cream of spinach soup and the boiled beef. *Dürnbräugasse 2, tel. 089/222195. Reservations advised. AE, DC, MC, V.*

Franziskaner. Vaulted archways, cavernous rooms interspersed with intimate dining areas, bold blue frescoes on the walls, and long wooden tables create a spick-and-span medieval atmosphere. Aside from the late-morning Weisswurst, look out for *Ochsenfleisch* (boiled ox meat) and dumplings. *Perusastr. 5, tel. 089/645548. No reservations. No credit cards.*

★ **Haxnbauer.** This is about the most sophisticated of the beer restaurants. There's the usual series of interlinking rooms—some large, some small—and the usual sturdy/pretty Bavarian decoration. But there is much greater emphasis on the food than in other similar places. Try Leberkäs or *Schweinshaxe,* pig's knuckle. *Münzstr. 2, tel. 089/221922. Reservations advised. MC, V.*

Hofbräuhaus. The heavy stone vaults of the Hofbräuhaus contain the most famous of the city's beer restaurants. Crowds of singing, shouting, swaying beer drinkers fill the cavernous, smoky hall. Picking their way past the tables are hefty waitresses in traditional garb bearing frothing steins. The menu is strictly solid Bavarian. If you're not here solely to drink, try the more subdued upstairs restaurant, where the service is not so brusque and less beer gets spilled. It's located between Marienplatz and Maximillianstrasse. *Platzl 9, tel. 089/221676. No reservations. No credit cards.*

Hundskugel. This is Munich's oldest tavern, with a history stretching back to 1440. The food is surprisingly good. If *Spanferkel*—roast suckling pig—is on the menu, make a point of ordering it. This is simple Bavarian fare at its best. *Hotterstr. 18, tel. 089/264272. Reservations advised. No credit cards. Closed Sun.*

Noodles. The airy vaulted cellars furnished with long, lumpy wooden tables may be reminiscent of the beer-swilling Hofbräuhaus nearby, but you won't find chunky cuts of pork or heavyweight dumplings here. Instead, Noodles serves up an unexpected menu of Italian pasta dishes in generous portions. Look out for the spaghetti calimari and the selection of ice creams. This upscale address caters to the late-night swingers who spill out from area discos. *Maximilianstr. 21, tel. 089/229295. Reservations advised weekends. No lunch. No credit cards.*

★ **Pfälzer Weinprobierstube.** A warren of stone-vaulted rooms of various sizes, wooden tables, glittering candles, dirndl-clad waitresses, and a vast range of wines add up to an experience as close to your picture of timeless Germany as you're likely to get. The food is reliable rather than spectacular. Local specialties predominate. *Residenzstr. 1, tel. 089/225628. No reservations. No credit cards.*

Zum Brez'n. A hostelry bedecked in the blue-and-white checked colors of the Bavarian flag. The eating and drinking are spread over three floors and cater to a broad clientele—from local business lunchers to hungry night owls emerging from Schwabing's bars and discos looking for a bite at 2 AM. Brez'n offers a big all-day menu of traditional roasts, to be washed down with a choice of three draft beers. *Leopoldstrasse 72, tel. 089/390092. Reservations not necessary. No credit cards.*

Budget **Bella Italia.** The four branches of this Italian restaurant offer the same excellent, no-frills value, which makes them very popular, especially among students. The extensive menu of pasta dishes, priced under DM10, range from spaghetti bolognaise to cannelloni; there are also pizzas. Beer and wine prices are lower than elsewhere in Munich. *Sendlingerstr. 66 (near Karlsplatz); Hohenzollernplatz 8; Leopoldstr. 44; Türkenstr. 50, tel. 089/280739. No reservations. No credit cards.*

Buxs. If you've had your fill of schnitzel and roast pork and dumplings, head to this self-service restaurant catering to vegetarians. Both the food and the beer are produced organically. A daily changing menu includes pastas and a huge salad selection. You can make a light meal of the Gorgonzola soup, or stop in for coffee and cake made with fresh fruit and nuts. *Frauenstr. 9, tel. 089/229-482. No reservations. No dinner Sat., closed Sun. No credit cards.*

Hannenstube. The heavy, polished pine setting might lead you to suspect more Bavarian fare, but the large and very varied menu encompasses dishes from every European country: try a dish from Greece or Finland, or stick to the German offering, Bavarian roast. The product of the north German brewery for which the restaurant was named is the foaming house specialty. *Pannerstr. 1, tel. 089/220-774. Closed Sun. and holidays. AE, DC, MC, V.*

Nordsee Buffet. Seafood is the specialty in this excellent, bustling stand-up cafe, where a large selection of fresh fish—from plaice to king prawns—is flown in daily. One of best deals is from the bouillabaisse pot which simmers away behind the counter in the main window. In summer, customers take their meals outside and sit at tables in the adjacent beer garden. *Am Viktualienmarkt, no phone. No reservations. Open weekdays until 6:30 PM, no dinner Sat., closed Sun. and holidays. No credit cards.*

Nudelbrett. Located on the cobbled passage beside the Alt Peter church, this place is especially popular with families: children 12 and under pay only DM 8.50 for a big plate of spaghetti bolognaise, garlic bread, and ice cream. Adults also pick up good deals on a limited menu which concentrates on pasta, salads, and ice cream. The house wine is also good value. *Rindermarkt 6, tel. 089/260-8681. Reservations not necessary. AE, DC, MC, V.*

Oberpollinger Karstadt. One of the best values in town is found next to the Karlstor city gate at Karlsplatz, at this newly renovated department store self-service restaurant. Aside from such hot dishes as sausages with sauerkraut and Greek gyros, there is also a gourmet delicatessen snack bar serving oysters and lobster and a Japanese hot food counter. A three-course traditional Bavarian lunch costs less than DM 20; mugs of freshly brewed coffee cost DM 2.50; late risers can buy a Continental breakfast for DM 4.50. *Neuhauserstr. 44, tel. 089/ 290230. No reservations. Open weekdays 9:15 AM–6, Sat. 9:15–2. No credit cards.*

Lodging

Make reservations well in advance and be prepared for higher-than-average rates. Though Munich has a vast number of hotels in all price ranges, most are full year-round; this is a major trade and convention city, as well as a prime tourist destination. If you plan to visit during the "fashion weeks" (Mode Wochen) in March and September or during the Oktoberfest at the end of September, make reservations at least several months in advance. Munich's tourist offices will handle only written or personal requests for reservations assistance. Write to: Fremdenverkehrsamt, Postfach, 8000 Munich 1, fax 089/ 2391313. Your best bet for finding a room if you haven't reserved is the tourist office at the Hauptbahnhof, by the Bayerstasse entrance. The staff will charge a small fee.

The closer to the city center you stay, the higher the price. Consider staying in a suburban hotel and taking the U-Bahn or S-Bahn into town. Rates are much more reasonable, and a 15-minute train ride is no obstacle to serious sightseeing. Check out the city tourist office "Key to Munich" packages. These include reduced-rate hotel reservations, sightseeing tours, theater visits, and low-cost travel on the U- and S-Bahn. Write to the tourist office (*see* Important Addresses and Numbers in Munich, *above*).

For details and price-category definitions, *see* Lodging in Staying in Germany.

Moderate   **Adria.** A modern and comfortable hotel, the Adria is located on the edge of Munich's museum quarter, in the attractive Lehel district, a short walk from the Isar River and the Englischer Garten. There's no restaurant, but there's a large and bright breakfast room. *Liebigstr. 8, tel. 089/293081. 51 rooms with bath. AE, DC, MC, V. Closed Dec. 24–Jan. 6.*
Arosa. This plain, well-worn but friendly lodging in the old town is just a 5-minute walk to Marienplatz. If you're driving, make sure you reserve a spot in the hotel garage; parking in the area is difficult. Munich's oldest pub, the Hundskugel, is right down the street. *Hotterstr. 2, tel. 089/267087. 77 rooms, some with bath. Facilities: restaurant, bar, garage. AE, DC, MC, V.*
Bauer. If the rustic Bavarian style of pinewood, blue-and-white check, and red geraniums appeals to you, you'll feel at home at the Bauer. Following the closure of Munich's Riem Airport, the surroundings of this modern hotel on the city's eastern rim are now quiet. It's accessible by suburban train (S6), but it's more convenient for those traveling by car. *Münchnerstr. 6, tel. 089/90980. 103 rooms with bath. Facilities: restaurant, terrace café, sauna, indoor pool. AE, DC, MC, V.*
Gästehaus am Englischer Garten. Despite the slightly basic rooms, you need to reserve well in advance to be sure of getting one in this converted, 200-year-old watermill. The hotel, complete with ivy-clad walls and shutter-framed windows, stands right on the edge of the Englischer Garten, no more than a five-

minute walk from the bars and shops of Schwabing. Be sure to ask for a room in the main building; the modern annex down the road is cheaper but charmless. There's no restaurant, but in summer, breakfast is served on the terrace. *Liebergesellstr. 8, tel. 089/392034. 34 rooms, some with bath. No credit cards.*

★ **Könign Elizabeth.** Housed in a 19th-century neoclassical building, which was completely restored and opened for the first time as a hotel in 1989, the Elizabeth is modern and bright, with an emphasis on pink decor. The restaurant offers Hungarian specialties. The Elizabeth is a 15-minute streetcar ride northwest of the city center en route to Nymphenburg. *Leonrodstr. 79, tel. 089/126860. 80 rooms with bath. Facilities: bar, beer garden, sauna, solarium, and keep-fit equipment. AE, DC, MC, V.*

Mayer. It's a 25-minute train ride from the city center, but this family-run hotel offers comforts and facilities that would cost twice as much in town. The style and furnishings are typical Bavarian country "rustic"; plenty of pine and green and red checkered fabrics. Owner/chef Rainer Radach was a student of Eckhart Witzigmann, one of Germany's most noted gourmet experts. The Mayer is a 10-minute walk, or short taxi ride, from Germering station, on the S5 suburban line, eight stops west of the Hauptbahnhof. *Augsburgerstr. 45, 8034 Germering, tel. 089/840–1515. 56 rooms with bath. Facilities: restaurant, indoor pool. AE, MC.*

Inexpensive **Am Markt.** Although tucked away in a corner of the colorful Viktualienmarkt in the heart of the old town, this old-fashioned hotel has long ceased to be a secret. Its central location and slightly seedy charm make up for the lack of luxury. It's very popular, so book well in advance. Parking in the area is a problem. *Heiliggeistr. 6, tel. 089/225014. 28 rooms, some with bath. No credit cards.*

Gröbner. If you like being close to the action, check yourself into the bed-and-breakfast—it's located on one of the old town side streets around the corner from Germany's most boisterous and famous beer hall, the Hofbräuhaus. The convenient location and the friendly service provided by the owners make up for the lack of luxury in the no-frills rooms. *Herrnstr. 44, tel. 089/293–939. 30 rooms without bath. No credit cards.*

★ **Monopteros.** There are few better deals in Munich than this little hotel. It's located just south of the Englischer Garten, with a tram stop for the 10-minute ride to downtown right by the door. The rooms may be basic, but the excellent service, warm welcome, and great location more than compensate. There's no restaurant. *Oettingenstr. 35, tel. 089/292348. 11 rooms, 3 with shower. No credit cards.*

Pension Beck. One of the best-located, budget-priced hostelries in Munich, the Beck is located between the Haus der Kunst art gallery and Deutsches Museum. Streetcar No. 18 stops outside. Mrs. Beck runs this rambling family pension with a matronly touch, and her sometimes abrasive exterior belies a heart of gold. *Thierschstr. 36, tel. 089/225768. 50 rooms, most with bath. No credit cards.*

Peter im Park. Through this pleasant hotel in Pasing has a quiet, rural location amid tall conifer trees and greenery, it is only a short walk and a 10-minute S-bahn train ride to downtown. Many of the Scandinavian-style rooms have bathrooms, but those without are cheaper. *Neufeldstr. 20, tel. 089/881–356. 30 rooms with bath. AE, V.*

Zur Post. The Post is a comfortable family-run hostelry in the western district of Pasing, not far from Nymphenburg Palace and park. The rooms have Bavarian country-style furnishings and decor with lots of pine woodwork. The location is convenient to both the train and the streetcar routes to town. Traditional Bavarian food is served in the restaurant. *Bodenseestr. 4, tel. 089/886–772. 30 rooms with bath. Facilities: restaurant. No credit cards.*

Budget   **Armin.** Budget-conscious families will appreciate the Armin, a bed-and-breakfast just one tram (No. 20/27) stop from the main train station. Accommodations are simple but clean, and there is a washing machine and drier available to guests. *Augustenstr. 5, tel. 089/593–197. 20 rooms. Facilities: laundry, guest lounge. No credit cards.*

Braunauer Hof. This cheerful old inn, close to the town center and the Viktualienmarket, has a few small rooms above the busy beer bar where local office workers meet for good, budget-priced lunches. Accommodations are a bit cramped and worn, but solid. *Frauenstr. 40, tel. 089/223–613. 17 rooms without bath. No credit cards.*

Jugend-Gästehaus. this excellently serviced modern lodging of the German Youth Hostels Association is five minutes by foot from the Thalkirchen U-bahn station, 15 minutes from the city center. Accommodations range from double rooms (DM 50, without bath) to three- and four-bed rooms to segregated dormitories, with shared bathrooms on each floor. *Miesingstr. 4, tel. 089/723–6550. 340 beds, 34 double rooms.*

Pension Diana. Located in an 18th-century building in the jumble of winding old-town streets, the Diana is only a few steps from the pedestrianized city center (closest U-bahn/S-bahn station: Karlsplatz), with its many historic sights, including the twin-domed cathedral. It offers plainly furnished double and multibed rooms. *Altheimer Eck 15, tel. 089/2603107. No private baths. No credit cards.*

Strigl. A bed-and-breakfast located in a century-old terraced house in the fashionable district of Schwabing, the Strigl is just a short walk from the No. 18 tram stop at Elizabethplatz. The pension is run by a young family, one of whom speaks English. The style of the rooms is turn-of-the-century, with rug-covered hardwood floors. Be forewarned: It's on the second floor and there is no elevator. *Elisabethstr. 11, tel. 089/271–3444. 10 rooms with sinks share 2 baths. No credit cards.*

The Arts

Details of concerts and theater performances are available from the *Vorschau* or *Monatsprogramm* booklets obtainable at most hotel reception desks. Some hotels will make ticket reservations; otherwise use one of the ticket agencies in the city center: **Hieber Max** (Liebfrauenstr. 1, tel. 089/226571) or the **Residenz Bücherstube** (Residenzstr. 1, tel. 089/220868), concert tickets only. You can also book tickets at the two kiosks on the concourse below Marienplatz.

Concerts   Munich's Philharmonic Orchestra entertains in Germany's biggest concert hall, the **Gasteig Cultural Center.** Tickets can be bought directly at the box office (the Gasteig center is on Rosenheimerstrasse, on a hill above the Ludwigsbrücke Bridge). The Bavarian Radio Orchestra performs Sunday concerts here. In summer, concerts are held at two Munich palaces, **Nymphenburg** and **Schleissheim,** and in the open-air interior courtyard of the **Residenz.**

Opera Munich's **Bavarian State Opera** company is world-famous, and tickets for major productions in its permanent home, the State Opera House, are difficult to obtain. Book far in advance for the annual opera festival held in July and August; contact the tourist office for the schedule of performances and ticket prices. The opera house box office (Maximilianstr. 11, tel. 089/221316) takes reservations one week in advance only. It's open weekdays 10:30–1 and 3:30–5:30, Saturday 10–12:30.

Dance The ballet company of the Bavarian State Opera performs at the **State Opera House.** Ballet productions are also staged at the attractive late-19th-century **Gärtnerplatz Theater** (tel. 089/201–6767).

Film Munich has an annual film festival, usually held in June. English-language films are shown regularly at the Europa film theater in the **Atlantik Palast** (Schwantalerstr. 2–6), **Cinema** (Nymphenburgerstr. 31), the **Film Museum** (St. Jakobs Platz), and the **Museum Lichtspiele** (Ludwigsbrücke).

Theater There are two state theater companies, one of which concentrates on the classics. More than 20 other theater companies (some of them performing in basements) are to be found throughout the city. An English-speaking company called the **Company** (tel. 089/343827) presents four productions a year.

Nightlife

Bars, Cabaret, Nightclubs Although it lacks the racy reputation of Hamburg, Munich has something for just about all tastes. For spicy striptease, explore the train station district (Schillerstrasse, for example) or the neighborhood of the famous Hofbräuhaus (Am Platzl).

Jazz The best jazz can be heard at the **Allotria** (Oscar-von-Miller Ring 3), the **Unterfahrt** (Kirchenstr. 96), and the **Podium** (Wagnerstr. 1). Or try **Jenny's Place in the Blue Note** (Moosacherstr. 24, tel. 089/351–0520), named for an English singer who settled in Munich.

Discos Disco bars abound in the side streets surrounding Münchener Freiheit in Schwabing, especially on Occamstrasse. More upscale are **Nachtcafe** (Maximiliansplatz 5), open all night on weekends, and **P1** (adjoining the Haus der Kunst, Prinzregentenstr. 1).

For Singles Every Munich bar is singles territory. Three you might like to try are **Schumann's** (Maximilianstr. 36) anytime after the curtain comes down at the nearby opera house; **Alter Simpl** (Türkenstr. 57) but not before midnight; and **Harry's New York Bar** (Falkenturmstr. 9), which offers an escape from the German bar scene *and* serves genuine Irish Guinness. For the student, beards, and pipe scene, try **Bunte Vogel** in Schwabing (Herzogstr. 44), which also features an unusual collection of table lamps.

Frankfurt

Arriving and Departing

By Plane   Frankfurt airport, the busiest in mainland Europe, is about 10 kilometers (6 miles) southwest of the city.

Between the Airport and Downtown   There are several ways to get into town. Two suburban (S-Bahn) lines connect the airport and the center. The S-14 runs between the Hauptwache station and the airport, and the S-15 from the main train station, the Hauptbahnhof. The S-14 runs every 20 minutes and takes 15 minutes; the S-15 leaves every 10 minutes and takes 11 minutes. The trip costs DM 3.70 (DM 5 in rush hour, 6:30–8:30 AM and 4–6:30 PM. Intercity trains also stop at Frankfurt airport train station on hourly direct runs to Cologne, Dortmund, Hamburg, and Munich. A No. 61 bus runs from the airport to the Südbahnhof station in Sachsenhausen, where there is access to the U-Bahn (subway) lines U-1 and U-3; the fare is DM 3.70 (DM 5 during rush hours). Taxi fare from the airport to downtown is DM 35. By rented car, follow the signs to Frankfurt ("Stadtmitte") via the B-43 main road.

By Train   Frankfurt's main train station, the Hauptbahnhof, and the airport station are directly linked with all parts of the country by fast Euro-City and Intercity services and by the high-speed Intercity Express trains. For train information, tel. 069/19419. For tickets and general information, go directly to the station or to the DER travel office at the Hauptbahnhof.

By Bus   Long-distance buses connect Frankfurt with more than 200 European cities. Buses leave from the south side of the Hauptbahnhof. Tickets and information are available from **Deutsche Touring GmbH** (Am Römerhof 17, tel. 069/79030).

Getting Around

By Public Transportation   A combination of subway and suburban train, streetcar, and bus services provides speedy transportation. Tickets cover travel on the complete network, which is divided into tariff zones. A single ticket for travel within the city costs DM 1.90 (DM 2.60 during rush hour). A multijourney strip ticket costs DM 9. Each trip you make is paid for when you cancel a strip in the automatic machines found on buses, streetcars, and subways. A day ticket (for use during one calendar day) offers unlimited journeys in the inner zone for DM 5. Buy all tickets at newspaper kiosks or from blue automatic dispensing machines. For further information or assistance, call 069/269463.

Important Addresses and Numbers

Tourist Information   There are three city information offices. One is at the Hauptbahnhof, across from platform 23 (tel. 069/212–8849). It's open Monday–Saturday 8 AM–10 PM (November–March until 9 PM), Sunday and holidays 9:30 AM–8 PM. The other is in the town hall in the old town at Römerberg 27 (tel. 069/21238708). It's open weekdays 9 AM–7 PM (November–March until 6 PM), weekends and holidays 9:30 AM–6 PM. Both offices will help you find accommodations. A third information office (tel. 069/690–6211) is in the airport Arrival Hall B, daily 8 AM–9 PM. The DER Deutsches Reisebüro, Arrival Hall B6, can also help you find rooms. Open daily 8 AM–9 PM (tel. 069/693071). For information in advance of your trip, contact the **Verkehrsamt Frankfurt/ Main** (Kaiserstrasse 52, 6000 Frankfurt, tel. 069/212–38800).

Consulates U.S. (Seismayerstrasse 21, tel. 069/75350). U.K. (Bockenheimer Landstrasse 42, tel. 069/170–0020).

Emergencies Police (tel. 110). **Doctor or Ambulance** (tel. 069/112). **Dentist** (tel. 069/660–7271).

Exploring Frankfurt

Numbers in the margin correspond to points of interest on the Frankfurt map.

At first glance, Frankfurt-am-Main doesn't seem to have much to offer the tourist. Virtually flattened by bombs during the war, it now bristles with skyscrapers, the visible sign of the city's role as Germany's financial capital. Yet the inquisitive and discerning visitor will find many remnants of Frankfurt's illustrious past (besides being well placed for excursions to other historic cities, such as Heidelberg and Würzburg, and within easy reach of the Rhine).

Originally a Roman settlement, Frankfurt was later one of Charlemagne's two capitals (the other being Aachen). Still later, it was for centuries the site of the election and coronation of the emperors of that unwieldy entity, the Holy Roman Empire, which was the forerunner of a united Germany. It was also the birthplace of the poet and dramatist Goethe (1749–1832). The house in which he was born is one of many restored and reconstructed old buildings that inject a flavor of bygone days into the center of this busy modern city.

Although the true center of Frankfurt is its ancient **Römerberg Square,** where the election of Holy Roman emperors was traditionally proclaimed and celebrated, this tour of the city begins
❶ slightly to the north, at the **Hauptwache,** an 18th-century guardhouse that today serves a more peaceful purpose as a café. The lower ground floor houses Interpress, an information office that assists young visitors, including finding moderately priced accommodations. *Open weekdays 10–6, Sat. 10–1.*

❷ Head south along Kornmarkt, passing on the left the **Katerinenkirche** (Church of St. Catherine), the historic center of Frankfurt Protestantism, in whose 17th-century font Goethe was baptized. After crossing Berlinerstrasse, and still heading
❸ south, you'll pass the **Paulskirche** (Church of St. Paul). It was here that the first all-German parliament convened in 1848, and the church is therefore an important symbol of German unity and democracy. Continue down Buchgasse and within a few minutes you're on the north bank of the river **Main.** Turn left toward the great iron bridge known as the **Eiserner Steg** and at the **Rententurm,** one of the city's medieval gates, bear left
❹ again and you'll arrive at the massive **Römerberg,** center of Frankfurt civic life over the centuries. In the center of the square stands the 16th-century **Fountain of Justitia** (Justice): At the coronation of Emperor Matthias in 1612, wine instead of water spouted from the stonework. The crush of people was so great, however, that the Germans have not repeated the trick since.

Frankfurt

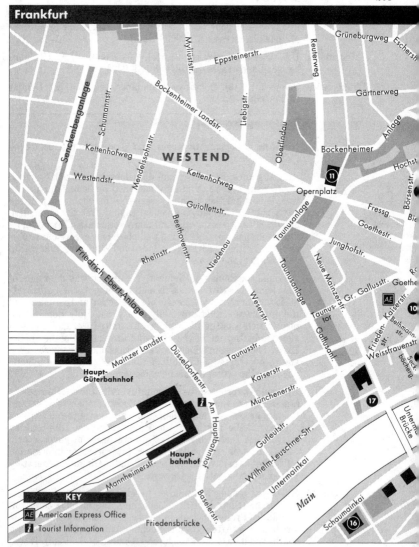

Alte Brücke, **14**
Alte Oper, **11**
Börse, **12**
Goethehaus und
Goethemuseum, **10**
Hauptwache, **1**
Jewish Museum, **17**
Kaiserdom, **6**

Karmeliterkirche, **9**
Katerinenkirche, **2**
Kuhhirtenturm, **15**
Leonhardskirche, **8**
Museum of Modern
Art, **13**
Nikolaikirche, **7**
Paulskirche, **3**
Römer, **5**
Römerberg, **4**
Städelsches
Kunstinstitut und
Städtische Galerie, **16**

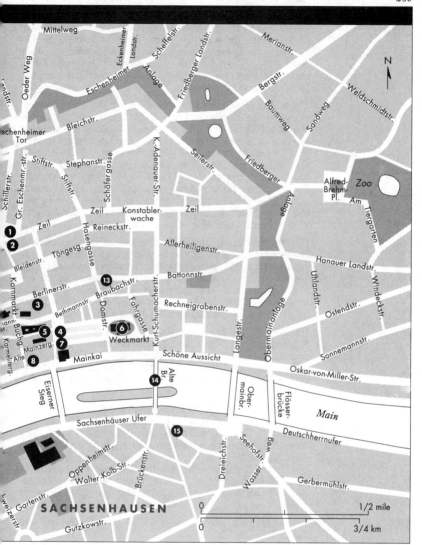

⑤ Compared with many city halls, Frankfurt's **Römer** is a modest affair, with a gabled Gothic facade. It occupies most of one side of the square and is actually three patrician houses (the Alt-Limpurg, the Römer—from which it takes its name—and the Löwenstein). The mercantile-minded Frankfurt burghers used the complex not only for political and ceremonial purposes, but for trade fairs and commerce.

The most important events to take place in the Römer, however, were the elections of the Holy Roman emperors. The **Kaisersaal** (Imperial Hall) was last used in 1792 to celebrate the election of Emperor Francis II, who was later forced to abdicate by arch-egomaniac Napoleon Bonaparte. (A 16-year-old Goethe smuggled himself into the banquet celebrating the coronation of Emperor Joseph II in 1765 by posing as a waiter.) Today, visitors can see the impressive full-length 19th-century portraits of the 52 emperors of the Holy Roman Empire that line the walls of the banqueting hall. *Admission: DM 1 adults, 25 pf children. Open Mon.–Sat. 9–5, Sun. 10–4.*

Charlemagne's son, Ludwig the Pious, established a church on the present site of the Römerberg in AD 850. His church was replaced by a much grander Gothic structure, one used for im-
⑥ perial coronations; it became known as the **Kaiserdom,** the Imperial Cathedral. The cathedral suffered only superficial damage during World War II, and it still contains most of its original treasures, including a fine 15th-century altar.

On the south side of the square stands the 13th-century
⑦ **Nikolaikirche** (St. Nicholas's Church). It's worth trying to time your visit to the square to coincide with the chimes of the glockenspiel carillon, which ring out three times a day. *Carillon chimes daily at 9, noon, and 5. Nikolaikirche open Mon–Sat. 10–5.*

From the Römerberg, stroll south toward the river, but turn
⑧ right this time, past the riverside **Leonhardskirche** (St. Leonhard's Church), which has a fine 13th-century porch and a beautifully carved circa 1500 Bavarian altar, then into the nar-
⑨ row Karmelitergasse to the **Karmeliterkirche** (Carmelite Church and Monastery). Within its quiet cloisters is the largest religious fresco north of the Alps, a 16th-century representation of the birth and death of Christ. *Admission free. Cloisters open weekdays 8–4.*

⑩ From here, it's only a short way to the **Goethehaus und Goethemuseum** (Goethe's House and Museum). It was here that the poet was born in 1749, and though the house was destroyed by Allied bombing, it has been carefully restored and is furnished with pieces from Goethe's time, some belonging to his family. The adjoining museum contains a permanent collection of manuscripts, paintings, and memorabilia documenting the life and times of Germany's most outstanding poet. *Grosser Hirschgraben 23, tel. 069/282824. Admission: DM 3 adults, DM 1.50 children. Open Apr.–Sept., Mon.–Sat. 9–6, Sun. 10–1; Oct.–Mar., Mon.–Sat. 9–4, Sun. 10–1.*

From the Goethehaus, retrace your steps to the Hauptwache via Rossmarkt. From there, take a window-shopping stroll past the elegant boutiques of Goethestrasse, which ends at Opernplatz and Frankfurt's reconstructed opera house, the
⑪ **Alte Oper.** Wealthy Frankfurt businessmen gave generously for the construction of the opera house during the 1870s

(provided they were given priority for the best seats), and Kaiser Wilhelm I traveled from Berlin for the gala opening in 1880. Bombed in 1944, the opera house remained in ruins for many years while controversy raged over its reconstruction. The new building, in the classical proportions and style of the original, was finally opened in 1981.

If you have a camera, position yourself between the arches of the opera house entrance and frame a striking shot of the skyscrapers of Frankfurt's financial world, which rise in striking contrast before you. Cross busy Opernplatz, head down Grosse Bockenheimer Strasse (known locally as Fressgasse—literally "Food Street"—because of its abundance of gourmet shops and restaurants), turn left into Börsenstrasse, and you'll hit the center of the financial district. Just around the corner from Fressgasse is the Frankfurt **Börse,** Germany's leading stock exchange and financial powerhouse. It was founded by Frankfurt merchants in 1558 to establish some order in their often chaotic dealings. Today's dealings can also be quite hectic; see for yourself by slipping into the visitors' gallery. *Admission free. Gallery open weekdays 11:30–1:30.*

From the Börse, turn right into Schillerstrasse, and within two minutes you're back at the Hauptwache. Here begins Frankfurt's main shopping street, the **Zeil,** which claims the highest turnover per square yard of stores in all Germany. Resist if you can the temptations that shriek from the shop windows on both sides of this crowded pedestrian zone and head eastward to the nearby point where it is crossed by Hasengasse. Turn right into Hasengasse and you'll see the striking wedge form of Frankfurt's newest museum rising straight ahead of you. The **Museum of Modern Art** opened in June 1991 and contains an important collection of works by such artists as Sia Armanjani, Joseph Beuys, Walter de Maria, and Andy Warhol. *Domstr. 10, tel. 069/21238818. Admission free. Open Tues.–Sun. 8 AM–10 PM.*

Across the Main lies the district of **Sachsenhausen.** It's said that Charlemagne arrived here with a group of Saxon families during the 8th century and formed a settlement on the banks of the Main. It was an important bridgehead for the crusader Knights of the Teutonic Order and, in 1318, officially became part of Frankfurt. Cross to Sachsenhausen over the **Alte Brücke.** Along the bank to your left you'll see the 15th-century **Kuhhirtenturm,** the only remaining part of Sachsenhausen's original fortifications. The composer Paul Hindemith lived and worked in the tower from 1923 to 1927.

The district still has a medieval air, with narrow back alleys and quiet squares that have escaped the destructive tread of the city developer. Here you'll find Frankfurt's famous *Ebbelwei* taverns. Look for a green pine wreath over the entrance to tell passersby that a freshly pressed—and alcoholic—apple wine or cider is on tap. You can eat well in these little inns, too.

No fewer than seven top-ranking museums line the Sachsenhausen side of the Main, on **Schaumainkai** (locally known as the **Museumsufer** or Museum Bank). These range from exhibitions of art and architecture to the German Film Museum. The **Städelsches Kunstinstitut und Städtische Galerie** (Städel Art Institute and Municipal Gallery) has one of the most significant art collections in Germany, with fine examples of Flemish, German, and Italian Old Masters, plus a sprinkling of French Impressionists. *Schaumainkai 63. Admission: DM 3 adults, DM 1.50 children, free on Sun. and public holidays. Open Tues.–Sun. 10–5, Wed. until 8.*

Across the river from this impressive lineup of museums is Frankfurt's **Jewish Museum** (cross the Untermain Bridge to reach it). The fine city mansion houses a permanent exhibit tracing the history of Frankfurt's Jewish community; its library is Germany's main registry for Jewish history. *Untermainkai 14–15, tel. 069/21235000. Admission free. Open Tues.–Sun. 10–5.*

Dining

Several Frankfurt restaurants close for the school summer vacation break, a six-week period that falls between mid-June and mid-September. Always check to avoid disappointment.

For details and price-category definitions, *see* Dining in Staying in Germany.

Moderate **Bistrot 77.** Mainly Alsatian specialties are served at this bright, ★ light, and cheerful French restaurant in Sachsenhausen. *Ziegelhüttenweg 1–3, tel. 069/614040. Reservations accepted. AE, DC, MC, V. Closed Sat. lunch, Sun., and mid-June–mid-July.*

Börsenkeller. Solid Germanic food, with just a hint of French style, is served here to fortify the business community from the nearby stock exchange (*Börse* means "money market"). Steaks are a specialty. *Schillerstr. 11, tel. 069/281115. Reservations accepted. AE, DC, MC, V. Closed Sat. dinner and Sun.*

Casa Nova. The inviting exterior is fully matched by the cozy interior of this superior Italian restaurant, in an attractive Sachsenhausen house. Fish is prepared with imagination and skill, and if the pasta proves too plentiful, half-portions are willingly served. *Stresemannallee 38, tel. 069/632473. Weekend reservations required. MC. Closed Sat. and 2 weeks in Aug.*

Zur Müllerin. The *müllerin* (miller's wife) is Lieselotte Müller, who has been running this restaurant for 35 years. Her regulars are artists and actors from the nearby theaters; you'll find expressions of appreciation for the cooking skills of their beloved müllerin decorating the restaurant walls. *Weissfrauenstr. 18, tel. 069/285182. Reservations not necessary. No credit cards. Closed for lunch on Sat. and Sun.*

Inexpensive **Knoblauch.** Knoblauch is German for "garlic," and that's the staple of many of the imaginative dishes served in this fashionable Frankfurt haunt. The oysters in garlic sauce have made the place famous. The clientele is young and arty, drawn not only by the menu that changes daily but by the vernissages that take place regularly in the small art gallery on the premises. *Staufenstr. 39, tel. 069/722828. Reservations not necessary. MC.*

★ **Zum Gemalten Haus.** This is the real thing, a traditional wine tavern in the heart of Sachsenhausen. Its name means "At the Painted House," a reference to the frescoes that cover the place inside and out. In the summer and on fine spring and autumn days, the courtyard is the place to be (the inner rooms can get a bit crowded). But if you can't at first find a place at one of the bench-lined long tables, order an apple cider and hang around until someone leaves: It's worth the wait. *Schweizerstr. 67, tel. 069/614559. Reservations not necessary. No credit cards. Closed Mon. and Tues.*

Zum Rad. This 19th-century apple-cider tavern serves inexpensive but tasty local dishes in the picturesque village of Seckbach on the outskirts of Frankfurt (take subway line No. 4 to Seckbacher Landstrasse and then bus Nos. 43 or 12). In summer, the tree-shaded courtyard is a delight. *Leonhardtsgasse 2, tel. 069/479128. Reservations not necessary. No credit cards. Opens 4 PM. Closed Tues.*

Zum Schwarzen Stern. This is a colorful beer restaurant in the heart of the historic quarter. Schnitzel with mushrooms in cream sauce or roast hare in red wine are two examples of the solid and tasty local menu, washed down with good beer. It's a favorite haunt of newlyweds who come out of the Registry Office opposite. *Römerberg 6, tel. 069/281979. Reservations not necessary. No credit cards. Open daily but closed 3–6 PM.*

Budget   **Cafe GegenwART.** The accent on art is quite deliberate—regularly changing exhibitions by local artists decorate the walls of this friendly, noisy café-restaurant. It's frequented by a young crowd, and in the summer diners spill out onto the pavement, where Riviera-style tables brighten up the city scene. There's a French touch about the menu, too—the tomato fondue is a dream. *Berger Str. 6, tel. 069/4970544. Reservations advised. No credit cards. Open daily.*

Grossenwahn. If you're in the neighborhood on a Sunday morning, stop here for a brunch washed down with Rheingau Sekt, perhaps in the garden if the weather is agreeable. Indoors, the walls are covered with modern paintings. For a late meal, this is also the place. *Lehnaustr. 97, tel. 069/599356. Reservations advised. MC, V. No lunch weekdays.*

Pelikan. Inexpensive but imaginative dishes from a daily-changing menu are served up here on finely decked tables draped in pink table linen to a clientele which draws heavily from the nearby university. Vegetarians will find that their choices are numerous. In summer, a boulevard terrace opens for business. *Jordanstr. 19, tel. 069/701287. Reservations advised. No credit cards. Closed Sat. lunch and Sun.*

Zitadells. You won't find cheaper steaks anywhere else in Frankfurt, and they come with sauces to rival those in much more expensive restaurants. You'll have to fight for seating though, at the rough pub-style tables, where you can stake your claim by ordering one of their excellent beers. *Falltorstr. 6, tel. 069/458668. MC, V. No lunch, closed weekends.*

Lodging

For details and price-category definitions, *see* Lodging in Staying in Germany.

Moderate   **Arcade.** This modern hotel is situated on the north bank of the Main river, just five minutes' walk from the train station. The rooms are furnished basically, though all have TV, and two are specially equipped for disabled guests. *Speicherstr. 3–5, tel. 069/273030. 200 rooms with bath. Facilities: restaurant, bar. AE, DC, MC, V.*

Liebig. A comfortable, family-run hotel, the Liebig has spacious, high-ceiling rooms and a friendly feel. Be sure to ask for a room at the back—they're much quieter. The Weinstube restaurant serves an excellent Hessen wine. *Liebigstr. 45, tel. 069/*

*727551. 20 rooms with bath. Facilities: restaurant, garage. DC,
MC, V.*

★ **Maingau.** This excellent-value hotel is in the city's Sachsenhausen district, within easy reach of the downtown area and
just a stone's throw from the lively Altstadt quarter, with its
cheery apple-cider taverns. The rooms are spartanly furnished, though clean and comfortable, and some even have TV.
*Schifferstr. 38–40, tel. 069/617001. 100 rooms with bath. Facili-
ties: restaurant, garage. AE, MC.*

Neue Kräme. This small, friendly hotel is located on a quiet pedestrians-only street right in the downtown area. The rooms
are basic, but all have TV and minibar. There's no restaurant,
but drinks and snacks are available. *Neue Kräme 23, tel. 069/
284046. 21 rooms with bath. AE, DC, MC, V.*

Inexpensive **Am Zoo.** This hotel provides modest but comfortable accommodations in Frankfurt's east end and, as the name suggests, is
near the city's famous big zoo. *Alfred-Brehm-Platz 6, tel. 069/
490771. 85 rooms with bath. Facilities: restaurant. AE, DC,
MC, V. Closed Christmas.*

Pension Uebe. This one occupies the top three floors of an office
building on a street favored with some excellent restaurants.
The elevator stops at the fourth floor, though by walking up
just one extra flight of steps, you'll find yourself on the top
floor, whose rooms are cozily and atmospherically set under
the inclined eaves. *Grüneburgweg 3, tel. 069/591209. 18 rooms
with bath. AE, DC, MC, V.*

Budget **Pension Uebe.** Try for one of the mansard rooms in this friendly, centrally located pension—they are snug and furnished in
hessian farmhouse style, with rocking chairs and basketwork
crafts. Chandeliers lend a touch of luxury to some of the larger
rooms on the lower floors. *Grüneburgweg 3, tel. 069/591209. 19
rooms, 17 with bath. Facilities: parking. AE, DC, MC, V.*

Waldhotel "Hensel's Felsenkeller." Helmut Braun's traditional
old hotel has the woods that ring Frankfurt as its backyard, yet
the city center is just a 15-minute tram ride away (the nearest
stop is a three-minute walk away from the hotel). Rooms are
quite basic, but there are plans to modernize them to add more
comfort. *Buchrainerstr. 95, tel. 069/652086. 14 rooms, 7 with
bath. Facilities: restaurant, parking. MC.*

Hamburg

Arriving and Departing

By Plane Hamburg's international airport, Fuhlsbüttel, is 11 kilometers
(7 miles) northwest of the city. Lufthansa flights connect Hamburg with all other major German cities.

Between the A bus service between Hamburg's central bus station and the
Airport and airport (stopping also at the hotels Atlantic and Plaza and the
Downtown Schauspielhaus Theater) operates daily at 20-minute intervals
between 5:15 AM and 9:30 PM. The first bus leaves the airport
for the city at 6:30 AM. It takes about 25 minutes. One-way fare,
including luggage, is DM 8. There is also an "Airport Express"
bus, No. 110, which runs between the airport and the Ohlsdorf
S-Bahn (suburban line) and U-Bahn (subway) station. The fare
is DM 2.80. Taxi fare from the airport to the downtown area is
about DM 25. By rented car, follow the signs to "Stadtmitte"

(Downtown), which appear immediately outside the airport area.

By Train Hamburg is a terminus for mainline services to northern Germany; trains to Schleswig-Holstein and Scandinavia also stop here. There are two principal stations: the main train station (Hauptbahnhof) and Hamburg-Altona. Euro-City and Intercity services connect Hamburg with all German cities and the European rail network. For train information, tel. 040/19419.

By Bus Hamburg's bus station, the Zentral-Omnibus-Bahnhof, is in Adenauerallee, behind the Hauptbahnhof. For tickets and information, contact the **Deutsche Touring Gesellschaft** (Am Römerhof 17, 6000 Frankfurt/Main, tel. 069/79030).

Getting Around

By Public Transportation The comprehensive city and suburban transportation system includes a subway network (U-Bahn), which connects efficiently with S-Bahn (suburban) lines, and an exemplary bus service. Tickets cover travel by all three, as well as by harbor ferry. A ticket costs DM 2.10 (DM 3.20 for travel outside the inner city) and can be bought at the automatic machines found in all stations and most bus stops. A day's ticket permitting unlimited travel in the entire Hamburg urban area from 9 AM costs DM 6.50 (DM 11.50 for a family ticket); a three-day ticket costs DM 18. The all-night buses (Nos. 600–640) tour the downtown area, leaving the Rathausmarkt and the Hauptbahnhof every hour. Information can be obtained from the **Hamburg Passenger Transport Board** (HHV), Steinstrasse 1, tel. 040/322911.

Important Addresses and Numbers

Tourist Information The principal Hamburg tourist office is at Bieberhaus, Hachmannplatz, next to the Hauptbahnhof. It's open weekdays 7:30–6, Saturday 8–3 (tel. 040/30051244). There's also a tourist information center inside the Hauptbahnhof itself (open daily 7 AM–11 PM, tel. 040/30051230) and in the arrivals hall of Hamburg Airport (open daily from 8 AM to 11 PM, tel. 040/30051240). Other tourist offices can be found in the Hanse-Viertel shopping arcade (tel. 040/30051220; open weekdays 10–6:30, Sat. 10–3:30, Sun. 11–3) and at the Landungsbrücken (tel. 040/30051200; open Mar.–Oct., daily 9–6; Nov.–Feb., daily 10–5). All centers will reserve hotel accommodations.

Consulates U.S. (Alsterufer 27, 1 (tel. 040/411710). U.K. (Hervestehuder Weg 8a, tel. 040/446071).

Emergencies Police (tel. 110). Doctor (tel. 040/228022). Dentist (tel. 11500). Ambulance (tel. 112).

Exploring Hamburg

The comparison that Germans like to draw between Hamburg and Venice is—like all such comparisons with the *Serenissima*—somewhat exaggerated. Nevertheless, Hamburg is, like Venice, a city on water: the great river Elbe, which flows into the North Sea; the small river Alster, which has been dammed to form two lakes, the Binnenalster and Aussenalster; and many canals. Once a leading member of the Hanseatic League of cities, which dominated trade on the North Sea and the Baltic during the Middle Ages, Hamburg is still a major

port, with 33 individual docks and 500 berths for oceangoing
vessels.

Apart from its aquatic aspects, the most striking thing about
Hamburg is its contradictions. Within the remaining traces of
its old city walls, Hamburg combines the seamiest, steamiest
streets of dockland Europe with the sleekest avenues to be
found anywhere between Biarritz and Stockholm. During
World War II and afterward, Hamburg was wrecked from
without and within—by fire, then by Allied bombing raids,
and finally by philistine town planners, who tore down some of
the remaining old buildings to make way for modernistic glass-
and-steel boxes. The result is a city that is, in parts, ugly, but
still a fascinating mixture of old and new.

It is also a city in which escaping the urban bustle is relatively
easy, since it contains more than 800 kilometers (500 miles) of
riverside and country paths within its boundaries. The following itinerary includes a few detours, some by boat, which will
enhance your enjoyment of Hamburg.

*Numbers in the margin correspond to points of interest on the
Hamburg map.*

1 Hamburg's main train station, the **Hauptbahnhof,** is not only
the start of the city tour but very much part of it. It's not often
you are tempted to linger at a train station, but this is an exception. Originally built in 1906 and modernized since, it has a
remarkable spaciousness and sweep, accentuated by a 148-
meter-wide (160-yard-wide) glazed roof, the largest unsup-
ported roof in Germany. Gather city travel guides and maps
from the city tourist office here and ride one stop on the S-Bahn
(suburban railroad) to the Dammtor station. Compare this Art
Nouveau–style building with the one you've just left. You'll
find splendid examples of Germany's version of Art Nouveau,
the *Jugendstil,* throughout your tour of Hamburg.

The Dammtor station brings you out near Theodor-Heuss-
Platz in **Wallringpark,** a stretch of parkland that runs for more
than a kilometer alongside what was once the western defense
2 wall of the city. The first two sections of the park—the **Alter
3** **Botanischer Garten** (Old Botanical Garden) and the **Planten un
Blomen**—have lots to attract the attention of gardeners and
flower lovers. In summer, the evening sky over the Planten un
Blomen lake is lighted up by the colored waters of its fountain,
dancing what the locals romantically call a "water ballet."

The section of the park known as **Grosse Wallanlagen**—to the
southwest—is interrupted abruptly by the northern edge of
the **St. Pauli** district and its most famous—or infamous—thor-
4 oughfare, the **Reeperbahn** (*see* Nightlife, *below*). Unlike other
business sections of Hamburg, this industrious quarter works
around the clock; although it may seem quiet as you stroll down
its tawdry length in broad daylight, any male tourist who stops
at one of its bars will discover that many of the girls who work
this strip are on a day shift.

If it's a Sunday morning, join the late revelers and the early
5 joggers and dog-walkers for breakfast at the **Fischmarkt** (fish
market), down at the Elbe riverside between the St. Pauli
Landungsbrücken (the piers where the excursion boats tie up)
and Grosse Elbstrasse. The citizens of Hamburg like to breakfast on pickled herring, but if that's not to your taste, there's

much more than fish for sale, and the nearby bars are already open. *The fish market is held every Sun., 5 AM–9:30 AM, starting an hour later in winter.*

6 The nearby **Landungsbrücken** is the start of the many boat trips of the harbor that are offered throughout the year.

Along the north bank of the Elbe is one of the finest walks Hamburg has to offer. The walk is a long one, about 13 kilometers (8 miles) from the St. Pauli Landungsbrücken to the **7** attractive waterside area of **Blankenese,** and that's only three-quarters of the route. But there are S-Bahn stations and bus stops along the way, to give you a speedy return to the downtown area. Do, however, try to reach Blankenese, even if you have to catch an S-Bahn train from downtown to Blankenese station and walk down to the riverbank from there.

Blankenese is another of Hamburg's surprises—a city suburb that has the character of a fishing village. If you've walked all the way from St. Pauli, you may not be able to face the 58 flights of stairs (nearly 5,000 individual steps) that crisscross through Blankenese between its heights and the river. But by all means attempt an exploratory prowl through some of the tiny lanes, lined with the retirement retreats of Hamburg's sea captains and the cottages of the fishermen who once toiled here.

A ferry connects Blankenese with Hamburg's St. Pauli, although the S-Bahn ride back to the city is much quicker. Back at St. Pauli, resume your tour at the riverside and head back toward the downtown area through the park at the side of the east of Helgolander Allee. At the eastern end of the park **8** stands the **Bismarckdenkmal** (Bismarck Memorial)—an imposing statue of the Prussian "Iron Chancellor," the guiding spirit of the 19th-century unification of Germany. Cross the square **9** ahead of you and make for the **Museum für Hamburgische Geschichte** at Holstenwall 24. This fascinating display of Hamburg's history has a feature of great interest to American descendants of German immigrants, who can arrange to have called up from the microfilm files information about any ancestors who set out for the New World from Hamburg. Alternating collections close as an extensive renovation continues. *Holstenwall 24, tel. 040/35042360. Admission: DM 3 adults, 70 pf. children. Open Tues.–Sun. 10–5.*

Cross Holstenwall to Peterstrasse, where you'll find a group of finely restored, 18th-century half-timbered houses. Turn right down Neanderstrasse and cross Ost-West-Strasse to Hamburg's principal Protestant church, the **Michaeliskirche** (St. **10** Michael's Church), the finest Baroque church in northern Germany. Twice in its history, this well-loved 17th-century church has given the people of Hamburg protection—during the Thirty Years' War and again in World War II. The Michaeliskirche is undergoing extensive renovation and will be closed until at least August 1993.

From the Michaeliskirche, return to Ost-West-Strasse, turn right, then left down Brunnenstrasse to Wexstrasse. Follow Wexstrasse to Grosse Bleichen, cross the Bleichenbrücke and Adolphsbrücke (Bleichen and Adolph bridges), over two of Hamburg's canals (known as the Fleete), turn left into Alter- **11** wall, and you'll come to the **Rathausmarkt,** the town hall square. The designers of the square deliberately set out to create a northern version of the Piazza San Marco in Venice and, to

Hamburg

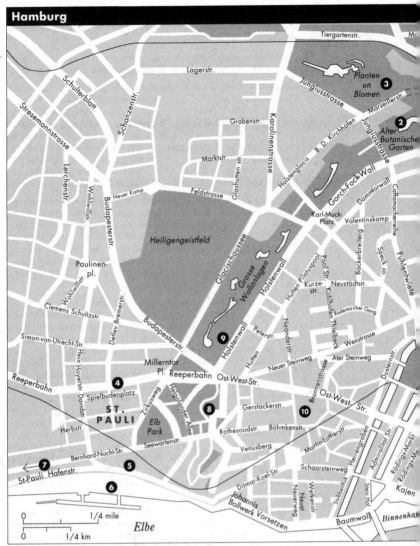

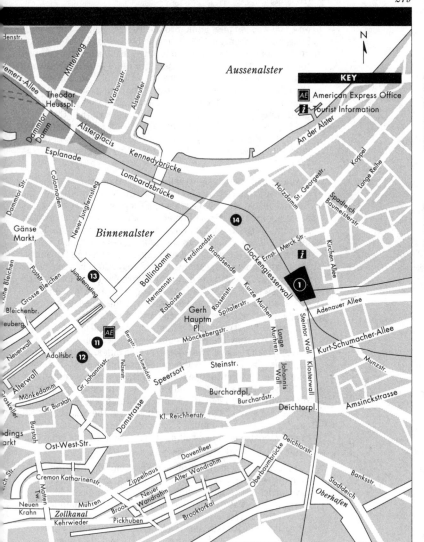

Aussenalster

KEY

AE American Express Office

ℹ️ Tourist Information

Binnenalster

Gänse Markt.

Theodor Heusspl.

Dammtor Damm

Alsterglacis

Esplanade

Kennedybrücke

Lombardsbrücke

Colonnaden

Neuer Jungfernstieg

Ballindamm

Ferdinandstr.

Brandsende

Glockengiesserwall

Ernst Merck Str.

Holzdamm

An der Alster

St. Georgstr.

Lange Reihe

Koppel

Spaaldeich

Baumeisterstr.

Kirchen Allee

14

1

Adenauer Allee

Kurt-Schumacher-Allee

Munzstr.

13

11

12

Jungfernstieg

Hermannstr.

Raboisen

Gerh Hauptm Pl.

Rossenstr.

Spitalerstr.

Mönckebergstr.

Kurze Muhren

Lange Muhren

Johannis Wall

Steintor Wall

Klosterwall

Postslr.

Grosse Bleichen

Bleichenbr.

euberg

Neuerwall

Adolfsbr.

AE

Bergstr.

Schmiedstr.

Felzestr.

Gr. Johannisstr.

Speersort

Steinstr.

Burchardpl.

Burchardstr.

Deichtorpl.

Amsinckstrasse

Alterwall

Mönkedamm

Gr. Burstah

Domstrasse

Kl. Reichhenstr.

Ost-West-Str.

Burstah

Cremon

Katharinenstr.

Dovenfleet

Alter Wandrahm

Oberbaumbrücke

Deichtorstr.

Bankssstr.

Stadtdeich

Oberhafen

Neuen Krahn

Matten Tw.

Mühren

Zollkanal

Kehrwieder

Brook

Neuer Wandrahm

Pickhuben

Brooktorkai

Zippelhaus

Bleichen

Grasskeller

Mitlelweg

Warburgstr.

Alsteruler

Dammtor Str.

⑫ a certain extent, succeeded. The 100-year-old **Rathaus** is built on 4,000 wooden piles sunk into the marshy ground beneath. It is the home not only of the city council but of the Hamburg state government, for Hamburg is one of Germany's federal, semiautonomous states. The sheer opulence of its interior is hard to beat. It has 647 rooms, 6 more than Buckingham Palace. Although visitors can tour only the state rooms, the tapestries, huge staircases, glittering chandeliers, coffered ceilings, and gilt-framed portraits convey forcefully the wealth of the city in the last century and give a rich insight into bombastic municipal taste. *Marktplatz. Admission: DM 1. Guided tours in English weekdays every half hour 10:15–3:15, weekends 10:15–1:15.*

If you've had enough sightseeing by this time, you've ended up at the right place, for an arcade at the western edge of the Rathausmarkt signals the start of Europe's largest undercover shopping area, nearly a kilometer of airy arcades, cool in summer and warm in winter, bursting with color and life. Three hundred shops, from cheap souvenir stores to expensive fashion boutiques, are crammed into this consumer-age labyrinth. There are expensive restaurants and cozy cafés, and one of the rare opportunities in Germany (or anywhere) to eat lobster and sip good wine at a fast-food outlet. It's easy to get lost here, but all the arcades lead at some point to the wide, seasidelike prom-
⑬ enade, the **Jungfernstieg,** which borders Hamburg's two artificial lakes, the **Binnenalster** and the **Aussenalster.** Although called lakes, they are really dammed-up sections of the Alster River, which rises only 56 kilometers (35 miles) away in Schleswig Holstein. The river was originally dammed up at the beginning of the 13th century to form a millrace before it spilled into the Elbe. The original muddy dam wall is today the elegant Jungfernstieg promenade. From the Jungfernstieg, you can take a boat tour of the two Alster lakes and the canals beyond, passing some of Hamburg's most ostentatious homes, with their extensive grounds rolling down to the water's edge (the locals call it "Millionaires' Coast").

Hamburg has its share of millionaires, enriched by the city's thriving commerce and industry. But they, in turn, can claim to have enriched the artistic life of Hamburg. For example, it was a group of wealthy merchants who, in 1817, founded the Kunstverein, from which grew Hamburg's famous Kunsthalle
⑭ collection. The **Kunsthalle** is well placed at the end of our Hamburg tour, next to the Hauptbahnhof, and its collection of paintings is one of Germany's finest. You'll find works by practically all the great northern European masters from the 14th to the 20th century, as well as by such painters as Goya, Tiepolo, and Canaletto. For many visitors, the highlight of the entire collection is the *Grabow Altarpiece*, painted in 1379 by an artist known only as Master Bertram; the central scene is the Crucifixion, but numerous side panels depict the story of man from Genesis to the Nativity. *1 Glockengiesserwall, tel. 040/248251. Admission: DM 4 adults, DM 1 children. Open Tues.–Sun. 10–5.*

Dining

For details and price-category definitions, *see* Dining in Staying in Germany.

Moderate **Ahrberg.** Located on the river in Blankenese, the Ahrberg has a
★ pleasant terrace for summer dining, and, for a warm retreat on
cooler days, a cozy, wood-paneled dining room. The menu features a range of traditional German dishes and seafood specialties—often served together. Try the shrimp and potato soup
and fresh carp in season. *Strandweg 33, tel. 040/860438. Reservations advised. AE, DC, MC.*

★ **Le Château.** Visitors to this traditional French restaurant, located in a modernized, 19th-century mansion in fashionable
Pöseldorf, can enjoy cuisine prepared by a former chef at Maxim's in Paris—for a fraction of the price. *Milchstr. 19, tel. 040/
444200. Reservations advised. AE, DC, MC, V. Closed Sat.
and Sun. lunch.*

Marktplatz. It takes some finding in the suburb of Nienstedten,
but it's well worth the search. The restaurant is in a traditional
old farmhouse, and the menu matches its authentic rustic style.
*Nienstedtener Marktplatz 21, tel. 040/829848. Reservations
advised on weekends. AE, DC, MC. Closed Mon.*

Tre Fontane. At this fine Italian restaurant, the lady of the
house prepares all the dishes herself, and she and her husband
are happy to advise guests on the specials of the day. Be prepared for big portions. *Mundsburger Damm 45, tel. 040/
223193. Reservations advised. No credit cards. Closed Tues.*

Inexpensive **Atnali.** This is one of Hamburg's oldest and most popular Turkish restaurants. It is friendly and comfortable and offers a very
reasonable and extensive menu. It stays open late—until 2 AM.
*Rutschbahn 11, tel. 040/410–3810. Reservations advised. AE,
DC, MC, V.*

Avocado. This popular, modern restaurant offers excellent value and an imaginative menu. Try the salmon in Chablis.
*Kanalstr. 9, tel. 040/220–4599. Reservations required. No
credit cards. Dinner only. Closed Sun.*

Budget **Filmhaus.** This favorite of local journalists and artists, in a municipal film center in the working-class district of Altona, has
good daily specials. The cuisine is Italian and German: the various fish soups are particularly worth trying, as is the sliced
beef and mushrooms in cream sauce. The atmosphere is light
and modern, despite the old furniture. *Friedensallee 7, tel.
040/39–34–67. No reservations. No credit cards.*

Max und Konsorten. This cheap, cheerful, always crowded restaurant serves traditional German fare such as *leberkaese* (a
sort of German pâté) with some Indian specialties. Try the
mussels in pepper sauce or the spicy chicken breast. Located
near the main train station in Hamburg, Max und Konsorten
has a dark woody atmosphere created by old tables and side-
boards. *Spadenteich 7, tel. 040/42–56–17. No reservations. No
credit cards.*

Opitz. North of the city center in the Eppendorf district is
Opitz, a turn-of-the-century restaurant with old marble-top ta-
bles and serving hearty German fare and Hamburg specialties.
Several varieties of Hamburg's ubiquitous pickled herring are
served at Opitz: Try the *labskaus*, marinated beef cooked with
egg and served with pickled herring and roast potatoes.
*Eppendorferlandstr. 165, tel. 040/47–65–98. No reservations.
No credit cards. No lunch Sat.*

Lodging

For details and price-category definitions, *see* Lodging in Staying in Germany.

Moderate **Baseler Hof.** Centrally located near the inner lake and the State Opera House, this hotel offers friendly and efficient service and neatly furnished rooms. There is no charge for children under 10 sharing a room with parents. *Esplanade 11, tel. 040/ 359060. 160 rooms, most with bath. Facilities: restaurant, meeting rooms. AE, DC, MC, V.*

Steen's. This is a small, intimate hotel decorated in a light, airy Scandinavian style. It is conveniently located, close to the main train station. Guests enjoy breakfast in a pleasant garden. *Holzdamm 43, tel. 040/244642. 11 rooms with bath. AE, MC.*

Wedina. This is a somewhat old-fashioned but comfortable hotel. It has a bar, pool, sauna, and garden but no restaurant. *Gurlittstr. 23, tel. 040/243011. 23 rooms, most with bath. AE, DC, MC, V. Closed Dec. 18–Jan. 1.*

Inexpensive **Alameda.** The Alameda offers guests good, basic accommodations. All rooms feature TV, radio, and minibar. *Colonnaden 45, tel. 040/344290. 18 rooms with shower. AE, DC, MC, V.*

Metro Merkur. Centrally located near Hamburg's main train station, the recently renovated Metro Merkur is a convenient, functional hotel. There is no restaurant, but the bar offers a selection of evening snacks and warm dishes. *Bremer Reihe 12–14, tel. 040/247266. 100 rooms, most with bath. AE, DC, MC, V.*

Budget **Hotel Kieler Hof.** Run by a helpful Hamburg family, the Kieler Hof is a few minutes from the main train station (Hauptbahnhof). *Bremer Reihe 15, 2000 Hamburg 1; tel. 040/24–30–24. 30 rooms with bath. Facilities: breakfast. No credit cards.*

Hotel Terminus. Located in a 19th-century row house near the main train station (Hauptbahnhof), the Hotel Terminus is a small, old-style hotel with accommodations that are spartan, but clean. *Steindamm 5, 2000 Hamburg 1; tel. 040/280–3144. 18 rooms. Facilities: breakfast. No credit cards.*

Hotel Zentrum. This fully renovated, 100-year-old hotel is run by a lively East Prussian family. The rooms are starkly decorated but comfortable. Located just a few minutes from the main train station (Hauptbahnhof), the Hotel Zentrum's rooms can be loud: Ask for a room facing the courtyard. *Bremer Reihe 23, 2000 Hamburg 1; tel. 040/280–2528. 15 rooms, 7 with bath. Facilities: breakfast. No credit cards.*

Nightlife

Few visitors can resist taking a look at the **Reeperbahn,** if only by day. At night, however, from 10 onward, the place really shakes itself into life, and *everything* is for sale. Among the Reeperbahn's even rougher side streets, the most notorious is the Grosse Freiheit, which means "Great Freedom." A stroll through this small alley, where the attractions are on display behind plate glass, will either tempt you to stay or send you straight back to your hotel. Three of the leading clubs on the Grosse Freiheit are the **Colibri** (No. 34, tel. 040/313233), the **Safari** (No. 24, tel. 040/315400), and the **Salambo** (No. 11, tel. 040/315622).

The Reeperbahn area is not just a red-light district, however. Side streets are rapidly filling up with a mixture of yuppie bars, restaurants, and theaters that complement the seamen's bars and sex shops. The **Hans-Albers-Platz** is a center of this revival, where the stylish bar La Paloma provides contrast to the Hans-Albers-Ecke, an old sailors' bar. The **Theater Schmidt** (Spielbudenplatz 24, tel. 040/314804) offers variety shows most evenings to a packed house.

A few tips for visiting the Reeperbahn: Avoid going alone; demand a price list whenever you drink (legally, it has to be on display), and pay as soon as you're served; if you have trouble, threaten to call the cops. If that doesn't work—call the cops.

The Rhine

None of Europe's many rivers is so redolent of history and legend as the Rhine. For the Romans, who established forts and colonies along its western banks, the Rhine was the frontier between civilization and the barbaric German tribes. Roman artifacts can be seen in museums throughout the region. The Romans also introduced viticulture—a legacy that survives in the countless vineyards along the riverbanks—and later, Christianity. Throughout the Middle Ages, the river's importance as a trade artery made it the focus of sharp, often violent, conflict between princes, noblemen, and archbishops. Many of the picturesque castles that crown its banks were the homes of robber barons who held up passing ships and barges and exacted heavy tolls to finance even grander fortifications.

For poets and composers, the Rhine—or *"Vater* (Father) *Rhein,"* as the Germans call it—has been an endless source of inspiration. As legend has it, the Lorelei, a treacherous, craggy rock, was home to a beautiful and bewitching maiden who lured sailors to a watery grave. Wagner based four of his epic operas on the lives of the medieval Nibelungs, said to have inhabited the rocky banks. To travel the Rhine by boat, especially in autumn, when the rising mists enshroud the castles high above, is to understand the place the river occupies in the German imagination.

The Rhine does not belong to Germany alone. Its 1,312-kilometer (820-mile) journey takes it from deep within the Alps through Switzerland and Germany, into the Netherlands, and out into the North Sea. But it is in Germany—especially the stretch between Mainz and Köln (Cologne) known as the Middle Rhine—that the riverside scenery is most spectacular. This is the "typical" Rhine: a land of steep and thickly wooded hills, terraced vineyards, tiny villages hugging the banks, and a succession of brooding castles.

A ten-hour steamer trip between Mainz and Köln will give you a taste of this fabled region. But in order really to experience it, you will need to spend several days in the area. A town such as Koblenz provides a convenient base for excursions up and down the river and into the lovely Moselle Valley.

Getting Around

By Train   One of the best ways to visit the Rhineland in very limited time is to take the scenic train journey from Mainz to Köln along the western banks of the river. The views are spectacular, and the entire trip takes less than two hours. Choose an Intercity (IC) train for its wide viewing windows. If you're traveling north toward Köln, make sure you get a window seat on the right-hand side. Better still, sit in the restaurant car where you can enjoy a meal or beverage while you watch the scenery unfold. Contact **German National Railways** in Frankfurt, Reisedienst, Friedrich-Ebert-Anlage 43, tel. 069/2651, or get details at any big train station travel office.

By Boat Passenger ships traveling up and down the Rhine and its tributaries offer a pleasant and relaxing way to see the region. **Köln-Düsseldorfer Steamship Company (KD)** operates a fleet of ships that travel daily between Düsseldorf and Frankfurt, from Easter to late October. They also offer cruises along the entire length of the Rhine. Passengers have a choice of buying an excursion ticket or a ticket to a single destination. For information about services, write to Frankenwerft 15,5000 Köln 1, or tel. 0221/208–8318. This company also offers trips up the Mosel as far as Trier. From March through November, **Hebel-Line** (tel. 06742/2420) offers a scenic cruise of the Lorelei Valley; night cruises feature music and dancing. For information about Neckar River excursions, contact **Neckar Personen Schiffahrt** in Stuttgart (tel. 0711/541073 or 0711/541074).

By Bicycle Another enjoyable and inexpensive way to see the country is by bicycle. Tourist offices in all the larger towns will provide information and route maps. German Railways offers bikes for hire at numerous stations. For information, tel. 069/2651 or ask for the "Bikes for Rent" (*"Fahrrad am Bahnhof"*) brochure at any station. You can also take advantage of the myriad *Wanderwegen* (walking paths) running throughout the region. These are marked with signs depicting red or green grapes. Contact local tourist offices for information.

Tourist Information

Koblenz (Fremden Verkehrsamt, Hauptbahnhof, tel. 0261/31304 and Fremdenverkehrsverband Rheinland-Pfalz, Löhrstrasse 103, tel. 0261/31079).
Köln (Verkehrsamt, Unter Fettenhennen 19, tel. 0221/221–3345).
Mainz (Verkehrsverein, Bahnhofstrasse 15, tel. 06131/233741).

Exploring the Rhine

Köln **Köln** (Cologne) is the largest city on the Rhine, marking the northernmost point of the river's scenic stretch before it becomes a truly industrial waterway through the Ruhr Valley. It's a very old city—first settled by the Romans in 38 BC—and today is a vibrant, zestful Rhineland center, with a very active cultural life and a business and commercial infrastructure that supports trade fairs year-round. It derives its name from the Latin Colonia Claudia Ara Agrippinensium, the title given to it by the Roman emperor Claudius in honor of his wife, Julia Agrippina, who was born there. The Franks and Merovingians followed the Romans before Charlemagne restored the city's fortunes in the 9th century, appointing its first archbishop and ensuring its ecclesiastical prominence for centuries.

By the Middle Ages, Köln was the largest city north of the Alps, and, as a member of the powerful Hanseatic League, it was more important commercially than either London or Paris.

Ninety percent of the city was destroyed in World War II, and in the rush to rebuild it many mistakes were made. But although today's Köln lacks the aesthetic unity of many other rebuilt German cities, the heart of the Altstadt (Old Town), with its streets that follow the line of the medieval city walls, has great charm, and at night it throbs with life.

Towering over the old town is the extraordinary Gothic cathedral, the **Kölner Dom,** dedicated to Sts. Peter and Mary. It's comparable to the best French cathedrals; a visit to it may prove a highlight of your trip to Germany. What you'll see is one of the purest expressions of the Gothic spirit in Europe. Spend some time admiring the outside of the building (you can walk almost all the way around it). Notice that there are practically no major horizontal lines—all the accents of the building are vertical. It may come as a disappointment to learn that the cathedral, begun in 1248, was not completed until 1880. Console yourself with the knowledge that it was still built to original plans. At 157 meters (515 feet) high, the two west towers of the cathedral were by far the tallest structures in the world when they were finished (they are still the tallest in a church). The length of the building is 143 meters (470 feet); the width of the nave is 45 meters (147 feet); and the highest part of the interior is 42½ meters (140 feet).

The cathedral was built to house what were believed to be the relics of the Magi, the three kings or wise men who paid homage to the infant Jesus. Today the relics are kept just behind the altar, in the same enormous gold-and-silver **reliquary** in which they were originally displayed. The other great treasure of the cathedral is the **Gero Cross,** a monumental oak crucifixion dating from 975. Impressive for its simple grace, it's in the last chapel on the left as you face the altar.

Other highlights to admire are the stained-glass windows, some of which date from the 13th century; the 15th-century altar painting; and the early 14th-century high altar with its surrounding arcades of glistening white figures and its intricate choir screens. The choir stalls, carved from oak around 1310, are the largest in Germany, seating 104 people. There are more treasures to be seen in the **Dom Schatzkammer,** the cathedral treasury, including the silver shrine of Archbishop Engelbert, who was stabbed to death in 1225. *Admission: DM 2 adults, DM 1 children. Open Mon.–Sat. 9–5:30, Sun. 12:30–4:30.*

Outside again, you have the choice of either more culture or commerce. Köln's **shopping district** begins at nearby **Wallrafplatz,** and a recommended shopping tour will take you down Hohestrasse, Schildergasse, Neumarkt, Mittelstrasse, Hohenzollernring, Ehrenstrasse, Breitestrasse, Tunisstrasse, Minoritenstrasse, and then back to Wallrafplatz.

Grouped around the cathedral is a collection of superb museums. If your priority is painting, try the ultramodern **Wallraf-Richartz-Museum** and **Museum Ludwig** complex (which includes the Philharmonic concert hall beneath its vast roof). Together, they form the largest art collection in the Rhineland. The Wallraf-Richartz-Museum contains pictures spanning the years 1300 to 1900, with Dutch and Flemish schools particularly well represented (Rubens, who spent his youth in Köln, has a place of honor, but there are also outstanding works by Rembrandt, Van Dyck, and Frans Hals). The Museum Ludwig is devoted exclusively to 20th-century art; its Picasso collection is outstanding. *Bischofsgartenstr. 1. Admission: DM 3 adults, DM 1.50 children. Open Tues.–Sun. 10–5, Thurs. 10–8.*

Opposite the cathedral is the **Römisch-Germanisches Museum,** built from 1970 to 1974 around the famous Dionysus mosaic that was uncovered at the site during the construction of an air-raid shelter in 1941. The huge mosaic, more than 91½ meters (100 yards) square, once covered the dining-room floor of a wealthy Roman trader's villa. Its millions of tiny earthenware and glass tiles depict some of the adventures of Dionysius, the Greek god of wine and, to the Romans, the object of a widespread and sinister religious cult. The pillared 1st-century tomb of Lucius Publicius, a prominent Roman officer, some stone Roman coffins, and a series of memorial tablets are among the museum's other exhibits. Bordering the museum on the south is a restored 82½-meter (90-yard) stretch of the old Roman harbor road. *Roncallipl. 4. Admission: DM 3 adults, DM 1.50 children. Open Tues.–Fri. and weekends 10–5, Wed. and Thurs. 10–8.*

Now head south to the nearby **Alter Markt** and its **Altes Rathaus,** the oldest town hall in Germany (if you don't count the fact that the building was entirely rebuilt after the war). The square has a handsome assembly of buildings—the oldest dating from 1135—in a range of styles. There was a seat of local government here in Roman times, and directly below the current Rathaus are the remains of the Roman city governor's headquarters, the Praetorium. Go inside to see the 14th-century **Hansa Saal,** whose tall Gothic windows and barrel-vaulted wood ceiling are potent expressions of medieval civic pride. The figures of the prophets, standing on pedestals at one end, are all from the early 15th century. Ranging along the south wall are nine additional statues, the so-called *Nine Good Heroes,* carved in 1360. Charlemagne and King Arthur are among them. *Altes Rathaus, Alter Markt. Admission: DM 2 adults, DM 1 children. Open weekdays 8:30–4:45, Sat. 10–2. Praetorium. Open Tues.–Sun. 10–5.*

Now head across Unter Käster toward the river and one of the most outstanding of Köln's 12 Romanesque churches, the **Gross St. Martin.** Its massive 13th-century tower, with distinctive corner turrets and an imposing central spire, is another landmark of Köln. The church was built on the riverside site of a Roman granary.

Gross St. Martin is the parish church of Köln's colorful old city, the **Martinsviertel,** an attractive combination of reconstructed, high-gabled medieval buildings, winding alleys, and tastefully designed modern apartments and business quarters. Head here at night—the place comes to vibrant life at sunset.

To complete your daytime Köln tour, however, leave the Martinsviertel along Martinsstrasse and turn right into Gürzenichstrasse, passing the crenellated Gothic-style Gürzenich civic reception/concert hall. Take a left turn into Hohestrasse and another right turn into Cäcilienstrasse. At No. 29, you'll find the 12th-century St. Cäcilien church, and within its cool, well-lit interior one of the world's finest museums of medieval Christian art, the **Schnütgen Museum.** The museum is named after the cathedral capitular Alexander Schnütgen, who bequeathed his collection of religious art to the city in 1906. Enlarged considerably over the years, the collection was moved to St. Cäcilien in 1956. Although the main emphasis of the museum falls on early and medieval sacred art, the collection also covers the Renaissance and Baroque periods. *Cäcilienstr. 29, tel. 0221/2310. Admission: DM 5 adults, DM 2.50 children. Open Tues.–Sun. 10–5, every first Mon. in month 10–8. Guided tours on Sun. at 11.*

A few steps away is the expansive **Neumarkt** square, at whose western end is one of Köln's finest Romanesque basilicas, **St. Aposteln.** The Neumarkt was an early trading center; the church was built in the 11th century amid the hustle and bustle of a daily market. Today, its weighty east front, surmounted by two graceful hexagonal towers and the more traditional four-sided west steeple, dominates a very different scene, a green city park lined with elegant shops and offices. Inside the church, a modest rectangular nave gives way to a perfect cloverleaf-shape choir, the most harmonious of the three to be found in Köln.

Koblenz In the heart of the Middle Rhine region, at the confluence of the Rhine and Moselle rivers, lies the city of **Koblenz,** the area's cultural and administrative center and the meeting place of the two great wine-producing districts. It is also one of the most important traffic points along the Rhine. Here you are ideally placed to sample and compare the light, fruity Moselle wines and the headier Rhine varieties. The city's **Weindorf** area, just south of the **Pfaffendorfer Bridge,** has a wide selection of taverns, where you can try the wines in traditional Römer glasses, with their symbolic amber and green bowls.

The city of Koblenz began as a Roman camp—Confluentes—more than 2,000 years ago. The vaults beneath **St. Florin Church** contain an interesting assortment of Roman remains. In the 12th and 13th centuries, the city was controlled by the archbishop-electors of Trier, and a host of fine churches and castles were built.

A good place to begin your tour of Koblenz is the **Deutches Eck,** or "Corner of Germany," the tip of the sharp peninsula separating the Rhine and Moselle rivers. In the 12th century, the Knights of the Teutonic Order established their center here. The towering equestrian statue of Kaiser Wilhelm that once stood here was destroyed by Allied bombs during World War II, but the base remains as a monument to German unity. On summer evenings, concerts are held in the nearby **Blumenhof Garden.** Most of the city's historic churches are also within walking distance of the Deutsches Eck. The **Liebfrauenkirche** (Church of Our Lady), completed in the 13th century, incorporates Romanesque, late Gothic, and Baroque elements. **St. Florin,** a Romanesque church built around 1100, was remodeled in the Gothic style in the 14th century. Gothic windows and a vaulted ceiling were added in the 17th century. The city's most important church, **St. Kastor,** also combines Romanesque and Gothic elements and features some unusual altar tombs and rare Gothic wall paintings.

Although the city lost 85% of its buildings during wartime air raids, some of the old buildings survived and others have been built in complementary styles. Much of the **Old Town** of Koblenz is now a pedestrian district, and an attractive area for a leisurely stroll. Many of the ancient cellars beneath the houses have been rediscovered and now serve as wine bars and jazz clubs.

Koblenz also offers an assortment of castles and palaces. The former residence of the archbishop of Trier now houses the city administrative offices. The original 18th-century building was demolished during the war; today only the interior staircase remains. Across the river, on the Rhine's east bank, towers the city's most spectacular castle, the **Ehrenbreitstein.** The fortifications of this vast structure date to the 1100s, although the bulk of it was built much later, in the 16th and 17th centuries. To reach the fortress, take the cable car (*Sesselbahn*) or, if you're in shape, try walking up. The view alone is worth the trip. On the second Saturday in August, a magnificent fireworks display, "The Rhine Aflame," is presented here. The fortress contains two museums: the **Landesmuseum,** tracing the industrial and technological development of the Rhine Valley (among the displays are a reconstructed 19th-century tobacco factory and a pewter works), and the **Rheinmuseum,** which follows the history of the fishing and shipping industries on the Rhine. *Admission to museums free. Open mid-Mar.–first Sun. in Nov., 9–12:30 and 1–5.*

Art enthusiasts won't want to leave Koblenz without visiting the **Mittelrhein Museum** for a look at Rhenish art and artifacts from the Middle Ages to the present day. *15 Florinsmarkt. Admission free. Open Tues.–Sat. 10–1 and 2:30–5:30; Sun. 10–1.*

Mainz On the west side of the Rhine, south of Koblenz, stands the city of **Mainz,** an old university town that's the capital of the Rhineland-Palatinate state. During Roman times, Mainz was a camp called Moguntiacum. Later it was the seat of the powerful archbishops of Mainz. But it is perhaps best known as the city in which, around 1450, printing pioneer Johannes Gutenberg established his first movable press. (He's such an important figure in Mainz that he has his own festival, Johannisnacht, celebrated in mid-June.) He is commemorated by a monument and square bearing his name and a museum containing his press and one of his Bibles. *Liebfrauenplatz 5. Admission free. Open Tues.–Sat. 10–5, Sun. and holidays 10–1. Closed Jan.*

Today, Mainz is a bustling, modern city of nearly 200,000 inhabitants. Although it was heavily bombed during World War II, many of the buildings have been faithfully reconstructed, and the city retains much of its historic charm. On **Gutenbergplatz** in the **Old Town** stand two fine Baroque churches, **Seminary Church** and **St. Ignatius.** The Gothic church of **St. Stephen** features six windows by the French artist Marc Chagall. The city's **Dom** (cathedral) is one of the finest Romanesque churches in Germany. The Old Town also boasts the country's oldest Renaissance fountain—the **Marktbrunnen**—and the **Dativius-Victor-Bogen Arch,** dating to Roman times. The **Römisch-Germanisches Museum,** in the **Kurfürstliches Schloss,** contains a notable collection of archaeological finds. *Rheinstr. Admission free. Open Tues.–Sun. 10–6.*

Dining and Lodging

When it comes to cuisine, the Rhineland offers a number of regional specialties. Be sure to sample the wide variety of sausages available, the goose and duck dishes from the Ahr Valley, and Rhineland *Sauerbraten*—accepted by many as the most succulent of pot roasts. Hotels in the Rhineland range from simple little inns to magnificent castle hotels. Many smaller towns have only small hotels and guest houses, some of which close during the winter months. During the peak summer season and in early autumn—wine festival time—accommodations are scarce, so it is advisable to reserve well in advance.

For details and price-category definitions, *see* Dining and Lodging in Staying in Germany.

Koblenz
Dining

Weinhaus Hubertus. This restaurant, named for the patron saint of hunting, lives up to its sporting image. Its decor is 17th-century rustic, its specialty, fresh game in season. Guests enjoy generous portions and a congenial atmosphere. *Florinsmarkt 6, tel. 0261/31177. Reservations advised. No credit cards. Moderate.*

Lodging

Kleiner Riesen. The Kleiner Riesen was one of the oldest hostelries in Koblenz, with a tradition stretching back three centuries. When it was destroyed in World War II, the owners converted their riverside home into a new Kleiner Riesen—new, but with much of the old tradition of excellent service very much in evidence. Ask for a room with a Rhine view. *Kaiserin-Augusta-Anlagen 18, tel. 0261/32077. 27 rooms with bath. Facilities: restaurant, parking. AE, DC, MC, V. Moderate.*

Hotel Hoegg. Built in the shadow of the mighty Ehrenbreitstein fortress, the Hoegg is convenient for sightseeing on both sides of the Rhine. Rooms with views of the fortress are quieter. *Hofstrasse 282, Ehrenbreitstein, tel. 0261/73629. 55 rooms with shower. AE, MC. Budget.*

Zum schwarzen Baren. This traditional old hotel, on the outskirts of the city, is on the high side of the budget category, but it's well worth the extra D-Marks and 15-minute bus trip to and from the city center. Rooms are small but comfortable and individually furnished. The ground-floor restaurant is one of the best in Koblenz. *Koblenzer Strasse 35, Moselweiss, tel. 0261/460-2700. 13 rooms with bath. AE, DC, MC, V. Budget.*

Köln
Dining
★

Gaststätte Früh am Dom. For real down-home German food, there are few places to compare with this time-honored former brewery. Bold frescoes on the vaulted ceilings establish the mood. Such dishes as Hamchen provide an authentically Teutonic experience. The beer garden is delightful for summer dining. *Am Hof 12–14, tel. 0221/236618. Reservations advised. No credit cards. Moderate.*

★ **Weinhaus im Waldfisch.** The black-and-white gabled facade of this 400-year-old restaurant signals that here, too, you'll come face-to-face with no-holds-barred traditional specialties in a time-honored atmosphere. Try *Himmel und Erde* (a mixture of potatoes, onions, and apples) and any of the wide range of wines. The restaurant is tucked away between the Heumarkt (Haymarket) and the river. *Salzgasse 13, tel. 0221/219575. Reservations advised. DC, MC. Closed weekends and holidays. Moderate.*

Alt Köln. You won't find pork knuckle outside Bavaria that comes bigger or cheaper than in this bustling, friendly tavern-restaurant in the shadow of the cathedral. If pork is not your fancy, then there's a menu crammed with Rhineland specialties (fish roulade, for instance), and the beer is the best local Kölsch. *Trenkgasse 7-9, tel. 0221/134678. No credit cards. Budget.*

Brauerei Zur Malzmühle. The beer is brewed on the premises in this typical Koln Kölsch pub. You can eat for under DM 10, at rough-scrubbed tables and in the noisy company of local traders who flock here from all corners of the old town at lunchtime and early evening. *Heumarkt 6, tel. 0221/210117. No credit cards. Budget.*

Zum Treppchen. One of Köln's oldest hostelries (it dates back to 1656), the Treppchen clings to tradition, serving the same dishes that have been served here for centuries. The smoked eel was a favorite among Rhineland fishermen when the Treppchen began business, and its roast beef is just as great-great-grandfather liked it. In summer, you can enjoy your meal on the terrace. *Kirchstr. 15, tel. 0221/392179. MC. Budget.*

Lodging **Alstadt.** Located close by the river in the old town, this is the ★ place for charm and low rates. Each room is furnished differently, and the service is impeccable—both welcoming and efficient. There's no restaurant. *Salzgasse 7, tel. 0221/234187. 28 rooms with bath. Facilities: sauna. AE, DC, MC, V. Closed Christmas. Moderate.*

Im Kupferkessel. This friendly, family-run hotel is in the center of the city, a short walk from all the major sights. Rooms are small but are equipped with televisions and minibars. *Probsteigasse 4-6, tel. 0221/135338. 13 rooms, 6 with bath. MC. Budget.*

Flandrischer Hof. To squeeze into the budget bracket here you'll have to accept one of the smaller rooms, but it will be as comfortable and as well-appointed as the others. What the rooms lack in space is compensated for in the public rooms, where a log fire crackles in the open hearth of the lounge in winter. The city's pedestrian-only shopping area begins at the end of the street, and the city center is a 10-minute walk away. *Flandrische Str. 3-5, tel. 0221/252095. 63 rooms with bath. Facilities: bar, parking. AE, DC, MC, V. Budget.*

Haus Ingeborg. This solid, friendly, family-run pension-hotel is 4 miles from the city, in the Porz-Weinheide suburb, but regular bus service stops nearby. Rooms at the front overlook a busy road, so try for a quieter, though more expensive, one at the back. All rooms have their own refrigerator. *Grengeier Mauspfad 79, tel. 02203/62043. 33 rooms with bath. Facilities: table-tennis, garden, parking. AE, DC, MC, V. Budget.*

Im Stapelhauschen. Cheaper rooms in this narrow, 13th-century, gabled house are small and don't share the Rhine view enjoyed by the larger and more expensive doubles, but the location—in the old city's former fish market—couldn't be better for the price. The ground-floor tavern-restaurant is a snug retreat from the city bustle, and the food is excellent. *Fischmarkt 1-3, tel. 0221/213043. 35 rooms, 15 with bath. MC, V. Budget.*

Mainz **Rats und Zunftstuben Heilig Geist.** Although the decor is pre-
Dining dominantly modern, this popular restaurant also incorporates some Roman remains and offers a traditional atmosphere. The cuisine is hearty German fare. *Rentengasse 2, tel. 06131/225757. Reservations required. AE, DC, MC, V. Moderate.*

Lodging **Hotel-Restaurant Am Lerchenberg.** The location isn't ideal—some 4 miles from the city center—but there's a bus stop right outside the door and open countryside only short steps away. Family-run, the hotel is friendly, comfortable, and peaceful. *Hindemithstr. 5, tel. 06131/73001. 53 rooms with bath. Facili-*

*ties: restaurant, sauna, solarium, fitness room. AE, DC, MC,
V. Moderate.*

The Black Forest

Only a century ago, the Black Forest (Schwarzwald) was one of
the wildest stretches of countryside in Europe. It had earned
its somber name because of the impenetrable stretches of dark
forest that clothed the mountains and shielded small communities from the outside world. Today, it's a friendly, hospitable
region, still extensively forested but with large, open valleys
and stretches of verdant farmland. Among the trailblazing
tourists of the adventurous 19th century was Mark Twain, who
wrote enthusiastically about the natural beauty of the region.
The deep hot springs first discovered by the Romans were rediscovered, and small forgotten villages became wealthy spas.
Hikers treasured the lonely trails that cut through the forests
and rolling uplands, skiers opened the world's first lift on the
slopes of the region's highest mountain, and horseback riders
cut bridle paths through the tangle of narrow river valleys.

The Black Forest is the southernmost German wine region and
the custodian of some of the country's best traditional foods.
(Black Forest smoked ham and Black Forest cake are world-
famous.) It retains its vibrant clock-making tradition, and local
wood-carvers haven't yet died out. Best of all, though, it's still
possible to stay overnight in a Black Forest farmhouse and eat a
breakfast hearty enough to last the day, all for the price of an
indifferent meal at a restaurant in, say, Munich or Frankfurt.

Getting Around

Today the Black Forest is easily accessible from all parts of the
country. A main north-south train line follows the Rhine Valley, carrying Euro-City and Intercity trains that call at hourly
intervals at Freiburg and Baden-Baden, connecting those two
centers directly with Frankfurt and many other German cities.
Local lines connect most Black Forest towns, and two local
east-west services, the Black Forest Railway and the Höllental
Railway, are spectacular scenic runs. The nearest airports are
at Stuttgart and the Swiss border city of Basel, just 64 kilometers (40 miles) from Freiburg.

Tourist Information

Baden-Baden (Augustaplatz 8, tel. 07221/275200).
Freiburg (Rotteckring 14, tel. 0761/368–9090).

Exploring the Black Forest

The regional tourist authority has worked out a series of scenic
routes covering virtually every attraction the visitor is likely to
want to see (obtainable from the **Fremdenverkehrsverband,**
Bertoldstr. 45, 7800 Freiburg, tel. 0761/31317). Routes are basically intended for the motorist, but most points can be
reached by train or bus. The following itinerary is accessible by
all means of transportation and takes in parts of the Black Forest High Road, Low Road, Spa Road, Wine Road, and Clock
Road.

Perched on the western slopes of the Black Forest, **Freiburg** was founded as a free market town in the 12th century. It was badly bombed in World War II. Towering over the rebuilt, medieval streets of the city is its most famous landmark, the cathedral, or **Münster.** The cathedral took three centuries to build and has one of the finest spires in the world. April through October, English-language walking tours of the old town include an explanation of the Münster's numerous architectural styles. Tours are led daily, except Tuesdays, at 10 AM and last two hours. *Admission: DM 6 adults, DM 3 children. (Contact tourist office; see above.)*

Try to visit Freiburg on a Friday, which is market day. The square in front of the cathedral then becomes a mass of color and movement, while a fitting backdrop is provided by **Kaufhaus,** the 16th-century market house.

From Freiburg, head north to fashionable **Baden-Baden,** idyllically set in a wooded valley of the northern Black Forest. The town sits on top of extensive underground hot springs that gave the city its name (*Bad*, German for "spa"). The Romans first exploited the springs, which were then rediscovered by wealthy 19th-century travelers. By the end of the 19th century, there was scarcely a crowned head of Europe who had not dipped into the healing waters of Baden-Baden. The town became the unofficial summer residence of numerous royal and titled families, and they left their imprint in the form of palatial houses that grace its tree-lined avenues.

One of the grand buildings of Baden-Baden's Belle Epoque is the pillared **Kurhaus,** home of Germany's first casino, which opened its doors to the world's gamblers in 1853. Entrance costs a modest DM 5, though visitors are required to sign a declaration that they enter with sufficient funds to settle subsequent debts! *Jacket and tie required. Passport necessary as proof of identity. Open Sun.–Fri. 2 PM–2 AM, Sat. 2 PM–3 AM. Daily tours (DM 3) from Apr.–Sept., daily 9:30–noon; Oct.–Mar., 10–noon.*

If jackets and ties are customary attire at the casino, no clothes at all are de rigueur at Baden-Baden's famous Roman baths, the **Friedrichsbad.** You "take the waters" here just as the Romans did nearly 2,000 years ago—nude. *Römerplatz 1, tel. 07221/275920. Admission: DM 38. Children under 16 not admitted. Open Mon.–Sat. 9 AM–10 PM.*

The remains of the Roman baths that lie beneath the Friedrichsbad can be visited from April through October. *Admission: DM 2.*

The attractions of the Friedrichsbad are rivaled by the neighboring **Caracalla baths,** opened in 1985. The huge, modern complex has five indoor pools, two outdoor ones, numerous whirlpools, a solarium, and what is described as a "sauna landscape"—you look out through windows at the countryside while steaming. *Römerplatz 11, tel. 07221/275940. Admission: DM 18 for 2 hours. Open daily 8 AM–10 PM.*

Dining and Lodging

For details and price-category definitions, *see* Dining and Lodging in Staying in Germany.

Baden-Baden
Dining

Gasthaus zur Traube. Regional specialties, such as smoked bacon and homemade noodles, take pride of place in this cozy inn, south of the city center in the Neuweier district. If you like the food, you can also spend the night in one of the 18 neatly furnished rooms. *Mauerbergstr. 107, tel. 07223/57216. Reservations not essential. AE, DC, MC, V. Closed Wed. Moderate.*

Bratwurstglöckle. Hunt out the large bronze bell—the *Glöckle*—that hangs outside this traditional beer and wine tavern. It signals good food and drink at reasonable prices. *Steinstr. 7, tel. 07221/2968. Dress: informal. No credit cards. Budget.*

Löwenbräukeller. This Bavarian-style restaurant with a small, tree-shaded beer garden serves only one beer—Munich's famous Löwenbräu—along with a wide selection of Baden wines. The food is simple and filling, with regional specialties predominating. *Gernsbacherstr. 9, tel. 07221/22311. No reservations. Dress: informal. No credit cards. Budget.*

Waldhorn. Set in a villagelike suburb (Oberbeuern) on the edge of the forest, this old inn offers garden charcoal grills every evening in summer—regional dishes prepared with flair. *Beuernerstr. 54, tel. 07221/72288. No reservations. Dress: informal. AE, DC, MC, V. Closed Mon., 1st week of Mar. Budget.*

Lodging

Deutscher Kaiser-Etol. This centrally located old, established hotel, a few minutes' stroll from the Kurhaus, offers homey and individually styled rooms at comfortable prices in an otherwise expensive town. All the double rooms have balconies on a quiet street off one of the main thoroughfares. *Merkurstr. 9, tel. 07221/2700. 44 rooms with bath. Facilities: restaurant (closed Sun. dinner), bar, bicycle hire. AE, DC, MC, V. Moderate.*

Hotel am Markt. The Bogner family has run this historic, 250-year-old hotel for more than 30 years. It's friendly, popular, and right in the center of town. *Marktplatz 17–18, tel. 07221/22747. 27 rooms, 9 with bath or shower. Facilities: restaurant, terrace. AE, DC, MC, V. Inexpensive.*

Hotel Greiner. This new hotel stands in its own grounds at the end of Baden-Baden's stately Lichtentaler Allee. Ask for one of the larger double rooms with balcony. *Lichtentaler Allee 88, tel. 07221/71135. 18 rooms with shower. Facilities: garden, parking. Closed mid-Nov.–mid-Dec. AE, DC, MC, V. Budget.*

Hotel Lohr. In summer flower boxes spill scarlet geraniums down the plain front of Mike Brandau's squat, city-villa hotel, giving the exterior a festive air. Rooms are small and quiet, and each has a television and minibar, unusual luxuries in this price range. The Kurhaus and casino are a minute's walk away. *Adlerstr. 2, tel. 07221/26204. 30 rooms, 26 with bath. MC. Budget.*

Hotel Sonne. Sonne means sun in English, an appropriate name for a hotel that soaks up the sunshine on the wooded slopes outside Baden Baden, at the start of the Schwarzwaldhochstrasse route through the Black Forest. The hotel is attractive, and typical of the Black Forest with flower-smothered wood balconies running along its snow-white facade. *Geroldsauerstr. 145, tel. 07221/7412. 18 rooms with bath. Facilities: restaurant, garden, parking. MC, V. Budget.*

Restaurant/Pension La Sila. This eaved, half-timbered house is one of the prettiest in Baden-Baden. The rooms are simply but comfortably furnished, and the Italian in-house restaurant is very good value. *Fremersbergstr. 23, tel. 07221/22642. 13* *rooms with bath or shower. Facilities: restaurant, garden, parking. No credit cards. Moderate.*

Freiburg
Dining

Enoteca. Three dining possibilities are now offered by the refurbished and recently reopened Enoteca. Lunch is served in the crowded, friendly bistro, while dinner is a more leisurely affair in the adjacent restaurant, where subdued lighting glistens on honey-colored paneling. Late-night diners can get light meals at the Enoteca bar, which is open until 1:30 AM. Proprietor Manfred Schmitz is a respected local wine connoisseur as well as an accomplished chef, and he can be relied on to recommend just the right vintage to accompany such specialties as veal roulade with gorgonzola. *Schwabentorplatz, tel. 0761/ 30751. Restaurant reservations advised. AE, DC, MC, V. Closed Sun. Moderate.*

Ratskeller. In the shadow of the cathedral, the popular Ratskeller has a typical Black Forest ambience (lots of wood paneling and beams), which is matched by a menu of mostly traditional dishes (roasts and rich sauces). *Münsterplatz 11, tel. 0761/37530. Reservations advised. AE, DC, MC, V. Closed Sun. dinner, Mon. Moderate.*

Zum Roten Bären. The Red Bear claims to be the oldest inn in Germany (it was first mentioned in official documents in 1091). It's the archetypal German history-book inn, with a traditional menu to match. Request Swabian *Spätzle* (a delicious variety of noodle) with everything. *Oberlinden 12, tel. 0761/36913. Reservations advised. AE, DC, MC, V. Moderate.*

Lodging

Gasthaus und Pension Hirschen. This charming converted farmhouse has been in the possession of the Winterhalter family for four centuries, and today's Winterhalters take as much care in making their guests feel at home as did their ancestors. The pension is in the village of Wittnau, a 10-minute drive or 15-minute bus trip from Freiburg, but the disadvantages of its distance from the city are more than offset by its peaceful location amid open countryside, a walker's paradise. *Schönberg 11, 7801 Wittnau, tel. 0761/402137. 20 rooms, most with bath. Facilities: restaurant, bowling alley, parking. No credit cards. Moderate.*

Rappen Hotel. You'll sleep like a pampered farmhouse guest here, in brightly painted rustic beds, beneath soft feather quilts. It's as quiet as a country village, too: The Rappen is in the center of the traffic-free old city. In the countrified but comfortable restaurant, patrons have the choice of more than 200 regional wines. *Am Münsterplatz 13, tel. 0761/31353. 20 rooms, most with bath. Facilities: bar-restaurant, terrace. AE, DC, MC, V. Moderate.*

Pforzheim
Dining

Silberburg. This is a rustic restaurant offering classic and regional cooking at bargain prices. For best value, ask to see the *Tagesempfehlungen*—the chef's daily recommendations. *Dietlingerstr. 27, tel. 07231/41159. Reservations necessary. No credit cards. Closed Mon., Tues. lunch, and 3 weeks in Aug.*

Titisee
Lodging

Romantik Hotel Adler Post. This hotel is in the Neustadt district of Titisee, about 4½ kilometers (3 miles) from the lake. The solid old building has been in the possession of the Ketterer family for nearly 140 years. The guest rooms are comfortably and traditionally furnished. The hotel's restaurant, the Rôtisserie zum Postillon, is noted for its regional cuisine. *Hauptstr. 16, tel. 07651/5066. 32 rooms with bath. Facilities: pool, sauna, solarium, game room, library. AE, DC, MC, V. Moderate.*

Berlin

Berlin is now a united metropolis—again the largest in continental Europe—and only two small sections of the Wall have been left in place to remind visitors and residents alike of the hideous barrier that divided the city for nearly 30 years. Old habits die hard, however, and it will be a long time before Germans and even Berliners themselves can get accustomed to regarding Berlin as one entity with one identity. You'll still hear Berliners in the western, more prosperous half talking about "those over there" when referring to people in the still down-at-the-heels eastern part. All restrictions on travel within and beyond the city have, of course, disappeared, and the sense of newly won freedom hangs almost tangibly in the air. But there's still a strong feeling of passing from one world into another when crossing the scar that marks the line where the wall once stood. It's not just the very visible differences between the glitter of West Berlin and the relative shabbiness of the east. Somehow the historical heritage of a long-divided city permeates the place and penetrates the consciousness of every visitor. You'll almost certainly arrive in and depart from the western part of Berlin, but just as surely your steps will lead you into the east. On the way, ponder the miracle that made this easy access to a onetime fortress of communism possible.

Arriving and Departing

By Plane **Tegel Airport** is centrally located, only 7 kilometers (4 miles) from downtown. Airlines flying to Tegel include Delta, TWA, Air France, British Airways, Lufthansa, Euro-Berlin, and some charter specialists. Because of increased air traffic at Tegel following unification, the former military airfield at **Tempelhof** (even closer to downtown) is being used more and more. East Berlin's **Schönefeld** airport is about 24 kilometers (15 miles) outside the downtown area. For information on arrival and departure times at Tegel, call 030/41011; for Schönefeld, call 030/672–4031.

Between the Airports and Downtown The No. 9 bus runs every ten minutes between Tegel airport and downtown. The journey takes 30 minutes and the fare is DM 3. A taxi fare will cost about DM 20. If you've rented a car at the airport, follow signs for the "Stadtautobahn" highway.

A shuttle bus leaves Schönefeld airport every 10–15 minutes for the nearby S-Bahn train station. S-Bahn trains leave every 20 minutes for the Friedrichstrasse station. The trip takes about 30 minutes, and you can get off at whatever stop is nearest your hotel. The fare by bus or subway is DM 3 and covers travel throughout Berlin. Taxis are usually available at the stops from Ostbahnhof onward. You can also take a taxi from the airport; the fare to your hotel will be about DM 30–DM 35, and the trip will take about 40 minutes. By car, follow the signs for "Stadtzentrum Berlin."

By Train There are six major rail routes to Berlin from the western half of the country (from Hamburg, Hannover, Köln, Frankfurt, Munich, and Nürnberg), and the network is set to expand to make the rest of eastern Germany more accessible. Traveling time to and from Berlin is being progressively cut as the system in eastern Germany becomes modernized and streamlined to meet western standards. For the latest information on routes, tel. 030/19419 or 030/31102116, or enquire at the local main train station if you are in western Germany, where you will also get details of reduced fare rates. Three people or more can often travel at discounted group rates. The West Berlin terminus for all lines is the main train station (Bahnhof Zoo).

International trains headed directly for East Berlin arrive at Friedrichstrasse or the Ostbahnhof. Train information: tel. 030/49541 for international trains, 030/49531 for domestic services.

By Bus Long-distance bus services link Berlin with numerous western German and other western European cities. For travel details, if you're in Berlin, call the main bus station (Messedam, tel. 030/301–8028), or if you're in western Germany, inquire at the local tourist office.

Getting Around

By Public Transportation Berlin is surprisingly large, and only the center can comfortably be explored on foot. Fortunately, the city is blessed with excellent public transportation, a combination of U-Bahn (subway) and S-Bahn (metropolitan train) lines, bus services, and even a ferry across the Wannsee lake. The eight U-Bahn lines alone have 116 stations. An all-night bus service (the buses are marked by the letter N next to their number) is also in operation. For DM 3 you can buy a ticket that covers travel on the entire system for 2 hours. A multiple ticket, valid for four trips, costs DM 10.40. Or, you can pay DM 12 for a 24-hour ticket that allows unlimited use (except on the Wannsee Lake ferries). Information can be obtained from the office of the city transport authority, the Berliner Verkehrsbetriebe (BVG) at Hardenbergplatz, in front of the Bahnhof Zoo, or by calling 030/216–5088.

Buses and streetcars in East Berlin are often crowded, and route maps, posted at each stop (marked H or HH), are not particularly clear to the uninitiated. The fare structure now covers both parts of Berlin, although cheap, subsidized tickets are still sold to East Berlin residents. Don't be tempted to buy one if you're traveling in East Berlin—the fine is quite heavy if unauthorized travelers are found in possession of tickets reserved for East Berliners. (It's difficult anyway, because East Berliners normally have to show their identity documents in order to take advantage of the special offer.) The fares in East Berlin are the same as those in the west.

Important Addresses and Numbers

Tourist Information The main tourist office, **Verkehrsamt Berlin,** is at the Europa Center (Budapesterstr., tel. 030/262–6031). It's open daily 7:30 AM–10:30 PM. There are other offices at the main hall of **Tegel airport** (tel. 030/4101–3145, open daily 8 AM–11 PM); the **Bahnhof Zoo** (the main train station, tel. 030/313–9063, open daily 8 AM–11 PM); and at the former border crossing point **Dreilinden** (tel. 030/803–9057, open daily 8 AM–11 PM). Accommodations can be reserved at all offices, which also issue a free English-language information brochure, "Berlin Turns On." Pretravel information on Berlin can be obtained by writing to the Verkehrsamt Berlin (Europa Center, D-1000 Berlin 30).

The main office of the tourist office in East Berlin is at Alexanderplatz 5 (tel. 030/242–4675, 242–4512). It's open weekdays 8–8, Saturday 9–6.

Consulates U.S. (Clayallee 170, tel. 030/832–4087). **Canada** (Europa-Center, tel. 030/261–1161). **U.K.** (Uhlandstr. 7/8, tel. 030/309–5292).

Emergencies **Police** (tel. 030/110). **Ambulance and emergency medical attention** (tel. 030/310031). **Dentist** (tel. 030/1141).

Exploring Berlin

Visiting Berlin is a bittersweet experience, as so many of the triumphs and tragedies of the past are tied up with the bustling present. The result can be either dispiriting or exhilarating. And by European standards, Berlin isn't that old: Köln was more than 1,000 years old when Berlin was born from the fusion of two tiny settlements on islands in the Spree River. Although already a royal residence in the 15th century, Berlin really came into its own three centuries later, under the rule of King Friedrich II—Frederick the Great—whose liberal reforms and artistic patronage led the way as the city developed into a major cultural capital.

The events of the 20th century would have crushed the spirit of most other cities. Hitler destroyed the city's reputation for tolerance and plunged Berlin headlong into the war that led to the wholesale destruction of monuments and houses. And after World War II, Berlin was still to face the bitter division of the city and the construction of the infamous wall in 1961. But a storm of political events, beginning in 1989, brought the downfall of the Communist regime; the establishment of democracy in the east; and finally, in October 1990, the unification of Berlin and of all Germany. Now you can travel from one end of Berlin to the other and in and out of the long-isolated city as easily as you would in any other Western metropolis. You'll still notice the scars left by the infamous wall, however, and contrasts between the prosperous western half of the city and the run-down east are still very visible.

Numbers in the margin correspond to points of interest on the West Berlin map.

West Berlin The **Kurfürstendamm,** or Ku'damm as the Berliners call it, is one of Europe's busiest thoroughfares, throbbing with activity
❶ day and night. At its eastern end is the **Kaiser Wilhelm Gedächtniskirche** (Kaiser Wilhelm Memorial Church Tower). This landmark has come to symbolize not only West Berlin, but the futile destructiveness of war. The shell of the tower is all that remains of the church that was built at the end of the 19th century and dedicated to the memory of Kaiser Wilhelm. Inside is a historical exhibition of the devastation of World War II. *Admission free. Open Tues.–Sat. 10–6, Sun. 11–6.*

❷ Cross Budapesterstrasse to enter the **Zoologischer Garten,** Berlin's zoo. It has the world's largest variety of individual types of fauna along with a fascinating aquarium. *Admission: DM 9 adults, DM 5 children. Open daily from 9–7 PM or to dusk in winter.*

Double back to the Kurfürstendamm to catch bus No. 129 to Kemperplatz. Among the buildings that comprise the

West Berlin

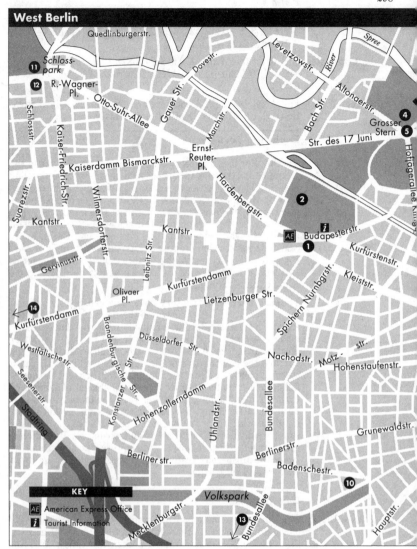

KEY

AE American Express Office

i Tourist Information

Ägyptisches Museum, **12**

Brandenburger Tor, **7**

Checkpoint Charlie Museum, **8**

Englischer Garten, **4**

Gemäldegalerie, **13**

Grunewald, **14**

Kaiser Wilhelm Gedächtniskirche, **1**

Kreuzberg, **9**

Kulturforum, **3**

Rathaus Schöneberg, **10**

Schloss Charlottenburg, **11**

Siegessäule (Victory Column), **5**

Soviet Victory Memorial, **6**

Zoologischer Garten, **2**

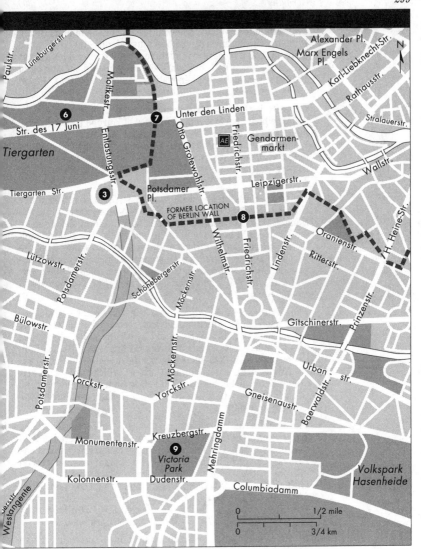

Alexander Pl.

Marx Engels Pl.

Karl-Liebknecht-Str.

Rathausstr.

Stralauerstr.

Wallstr.

Paulstr.

Lüneburgerstr.

Moltkestr.

Entlastungsstr.

Str. des 17 Juni

Tiergarten

Tiergarten Str.

Unter den Linden

Otto Grotewohlstr.

Friedrichstr.

Gendarmenmarkt

Leipzigerstr.

Potsdamer Pl.

FORMER LOCATION OF BERLIN WALL

Wilhelmstr.

Friedrichstr.

Lindenstr.

Oranienstr.

Ritterstr.

H. Heine-Str.

Lützowstr.

Potsdamerstr.

Schöneberaerstr.

Möckernstr.

Gitschinerstr.

Prinzenstr.

Bülowstr.

Urban - str.

Baerwaldstr.

Yorckstr.

Möckernstr.

Yorckstr.

Gneisenaustr.

Monumentenstr.

Kreuzbergstr.

Mehringdamm

Victoria Park

Kolonnenstr.

Dudenstr.

Columbiadamm

Volkspark Hasenheide

Messstr.

Westangente

| 0 | | | 1/2 mile |
| 0 | | | 3/4 km |

❸ Kulturforum (Cultural Forum) on the large square is the **Philharmonie** (Philharmonic Hall), home of the famous Berlin Philharmonic orchestra, whose musical director is Claudio Abbado. You'll recognize it by its roof, which resembles a great wave. The main hall, built in 1963, reopened in the spring of 1992 after an ambitious renovation. *Matthäkirchstr. 1. Ticket office open weekdays 3:30–6 and weekends 11–2.*

Opposite is the **Kunstgewerbemuseum** (Museum of Decorative Arts), which displays arts and crafts of Europe from the Middle Ages to the present day. Among its treasures is the Welfenschatz (Guelph Treasure), a collection of 16th-century gold and silver plate from Nürnberg. *Tiergartenstr. 6, tel. 030/ 266–2911. Admission: DM 4 adults, DM 2 children. Open Tues.–Fri. 9–5, weekends 10–5.*

Leave the museum and walk south past the mid-19th-century church of St. Matthaeus to the **Neue Nationalgalerie** (New National Gallery), a modern glass-and-steel building designed by Mies van der Rohe and built in the mid-1960s. The gallery's collection consists of paintings, sculpture, and drawings from the 19th and 20th centuries, with an accent on works by the Impressionists. *Potsdamerstr. 50, tel. 030/266–2666. Admission: DM 4 adults, DM 2 children. Open Tues.–Fri. 9–5, weekends 10–5.*

The Kulturforum is adjacent to the 255-hectare (630-acre) **Tiergarten Park,** which has at last recovered from the war, when it was not only ripped apart by bombs and artillery, but was stripped of its woods by desperate, freezing Berliners in the bitter cold of 1945–46. In the northern section of the park is **❹** the **Englischer Garten** (English Garden), which borders the riverside **Bellevue Schloss,** a small palace built for Frederick the Great's brother: It is now the official Berlin residence of the German president.

The column in the center of a large traffic circle in the **❺** Tiergarten is the **Siegessäule** (Victory Column), erected in 1873 to commemorate four Prussian military campaigns against the French. The granite and sandstone monument originally stood in front of the Reichstag (parliament), which was burned by Hitler's men in 1933. Climb the 285 steps to its 65-meter (210-foot) summit and you'll be rewarded with a fine view of both West Berlin and East Berlin. *Admission: DM 1.20 adults, 70 pf children. Open Apr. 1–Oct. 31, Mon. 1–6, Tues.–Sun. 9–6.*

At the base of the Siegessäule, go east down the wide Strasse des 17 Juni (June 17th Street), named in memory of the day, in 1953, when 50,000 East Germans staged an uprising that was **❻** put down by force. On the left, you'll pass the **Soviet Victory Memorial,** a semicircular colonnade topped with a statue of a Russian soldier and flanked by what are said to be the first Soviet tanks to have fought their way into Berlin in 1945.

❼ Ahead of you is **Brandenburger Tor** (Brandenburg Gate), built in 1788 as a victory arch for triumphant Prussian armies. The horse-drawn chariot atop the arch was reerected after the war. The monumental gate was cut off from West Berlin by the Wall, and it became a focal point of celebrations marking the unification of Berlin and of all Germany. It was here that German politicians formally sealed unification.

The wall that for so long isolated the Brandenburger Tor is no more, but the history of the hideous frontier fortification can be followed in the museum that arose at its most famous crossing point. Checkpoint Charlie, as it was known, disappeared along with the wall, but the **Checkpoint Charlie Museum** is still there. You can walk to the museum by following Friedrichstrasse south for about a mile, but it's easier to call a cab. *Friedrichstr. 44, tel. 030/251–4569. Admission free. Open daily 9–9.*

Find the nearby Kochstrasse U-Bahn station and go two stops south on the U-6 line to Mehringdamm. Head for Kreuzbergstrasse. Just on the left is the 62-meter (200-foot) **Kreuzberg,** West Berlin's highest natural hill. (There are higher hills made of the rubble gathered from the bombed-out ruins of the city when reconstruction began in 1945.) On the sheltered southern slopes of the Kreuzberg is a vineyard that produces some of Germany's rarest wines: They are served only at official Berlin functions.

Bordering Kreuzberg to the west is the Schöneberg district, where you'll find the seat of the city and state government of Berlin, the **Rathaus Schöneberg,** the former West Berlin city hall. (In 1991 the city administration moved back to the Rote Rathaus in Berlin Mitte.) In the belfry of the Rathaus is a replica of the Liberty Bell, donated to Berliners in 1950 by the United States and rung every day at noon. In a room at the base of the tower are stored 17 million American signatures expressing solidarity with West Berlin, some, no doubt, inspired by President Kennedy's famous "Ich bin ein Berliner" speech, which he made here in 1963. *The tower is open to visitors Wed. and Sun. only, 10–4.*

Take the U-Bahn north one stop from Rathaus Schöneberg station and change to the U-7 line for eight stops, to Richard-Wagner-Platz station. From the station, walk left for about 465 meters (500 yards) to the handsome **Schloss Charlottenburg** (Charlottenburg Palace). Built at the end of the 17th century by King Frederick I for his wife, Queen Sophie Charlotte, the palace was progressively enlarged for later royal residents. Frederick the Great's suite of rooms can be visited; in one glass cupboard, you'll see the coronation crown he inherited from his father—stripped of jewels by the ascetic son, who gave the most valuable diamonds and pearls to his wife. *Luisenplatz. Admission: DM 6 adults, DM 2 children. Open Tues.–Sun. 10–5, Thurs. 10–8.*

Opposite the palace is the **Ägyptisches Museum** (Egyptian Museum), home of perhaps the world's best-known portrait sculpture, the beautiful Nefertiti. The 3,300-year-old Egyptian queen is the centerpiece of a fascinating collection of Egyptology that includes one of the finest preserved mummies outside Cairo. *Schlosstr. 70. Admission: DM 4 adults, DM 2 children. Open Mon.–Thurs. 9–5, weekends 10–5. Closed Fri.*

Take U-Bahn line U-7 back toward Schöneberg until Fehrbelliner Platz, where you change to line U-2 southwest for five stops to Dahlem-Dorf station. This is the stop for the magnificent **Dahlem museums,** chief of which is West Berlin's leading picture gallery, the **Gemäldegalerie.** The collection includes many works by the great European masters, with 26 Rembrandts and 14 by Rubens. Or is it 25 Rembrandts? *The Man in the Golden Hat,* until recently attributed to Rembrandt, has now been ascribed to one of the great Dutch master's pupils. Does it really matter? Maybe not to the public, which still sees it as a masterpiece, but it could affect the value of the painting by a million or two. *Arnimallee 23/27. Admission: DM 4 adults, DM 2 children. Open Tues.–Fri. 9–5, weekends 10–5.*

14 No visit to West Berlin is complete without an outing to the city's outdoor playground, the **Grunewald** park. Bordering the Dahlem district to the west, the park is a vast green space, with meadows, woodlands, and lakes. There are a string of 60 lakes within Berlin's boundaries; some are kilometers long, others are no more than ponds. The total length of their shorelines—if stretched out in one long line—is 209½ kilometers (130 miles), longer than Germany's Baltic Coast. There's even space for nudist beaches on the banks of the Wannsee lake, while in winter a downhill ski run and even a ski jump operate on the modest slopes of the Teufelsberg hill.

East Berlin The infamous Wall is now gone, but the spirit of division remains in a city that was physically split for 28 years. The stately buildings of the city's past are not as overwhelmed by new high-rise construction as in West Berlin, but East Berlin's postwar architectural blunders are just as monumental in their own way. These will be obvious—along with the sad shabbiness of years of neglect—as you explore the side streets together with the main thoroughfares.

Numbers in the margin correspond to points of interest on the East Berlin map.

15 For a sense of déjà vu, enter the eastern part of Berlin at **Checkpoint Charlie,** the most famous crossing point between the two Berlins during the Cold War and the setting of numerous spy novels and films. At this point both ends of Friedrichstrasse—east and west—are lined with attractive new shops and trendy restaurants. Turn right onto Mohrenstrasse and you'll arrive at **Gendarmenmarkt** (formely the Platz der Akademie), with its beautifully reconstructed **16** **Schauspielhaus**—built in 1818, and now the city's main concert hall—and the twin **German** (on the south, undergoing restoration) and **French cathedrals.** In the latter, you'll find the **17** **Huguenot Museum,** which has some interesting collections of the history and art of the French Protestant Huguenots who took refuge in Germany after being expelled from Catholic France in 1685. *Gendarmenmarkt. Admission: DM2 adults, DM1 children. Tues., Wed., Sat. 10–5, Thurs. 10–6, Sun. 11:30–5.*

18 Continue east along the Französischer Strasse and turn left into Hedwigskirchgasse to reach Bebelplatz. The peculiar round shape of **St. Hedwigs Kathedrale** (St. Hedwig's Cathedral) calls to mind Rome's Pantheon. The tiny street named Hinter der Katholischen Kirche (Behind the Catholic Church) is a reminder that though Berlin was very much a Protestant city, St. Hedwig's was built (about 1747) for Catholics.

19 Walk north across Bebelplatz to Unter den Linden, the elegant central thoroughfare of Old Berlin. On your right is the **Deutsche Staatsoper,** the great opera house of Berlin, now with an entirely new interior. Just after Oberwallstrasse is the former crown prince's palace, the **Palais Unter den Linden,** now restored and used to house official government visitors.

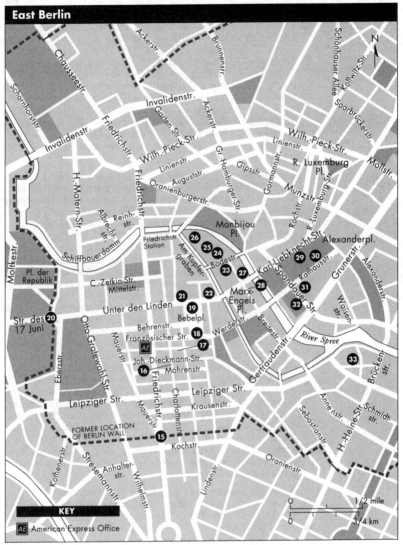

East Berlin

KEY

AE American Express Office

Altes Museum, **23**

Berliner Dom, **27**

Bodemuseum, **26**

Brandenburger Tor, **20**

Checkpoint Charlie, **15**

Deutsche
Staatsoper, **19**

Deutsches Historisches
Museum, **22**

Huguenot Museum, **17**

Humboldt
University, **21**

Marienkirche, **29**

Märkisches
Museum, **33**

Nationalgalerie, **24**

Nikolaikirche, **32**

Palast der
Republik, **28**

Pergamon Museum, **25**

Rathaus, **31**

Schauspielhaus, **16**

St. Hedwigs
Kathedrale, **18**

TV Tower, **30**

Look back down the street to the western sector and you'll see ⑳ the monumental **Brandenburger Tor** (Brandenburg Gate), its chariot-and-horses sculpture now turned to face the east. Cross Unter den Linden and look into the courtyard of ㉑ **Humboldt University:** It was built as a palace for the brother of Friedrich II of Prussia in 1810, and became a university in 1810, and today is one of Germany's largest universities. Marx and Engels were its two most famous students. Beyond the war memorial, ㉒ housed in a onetime arsenal (1695–1705) is the **Deutsches Historisches Museum** (German Historical Museum), which traces events from 1789 to the present. *Unter den Linden 2. Admission: DM 4 adults, DM 2 children. Open Thurs.–Tues. 10–6.*

Turning left along the Spree canal (along Am Zeughaus and Am Kupfergraben) will bring you to East Berlin's museum complex, at the northern end of what is known as **Museumsinsel** (Museum Island). The first of the Big Four that you'll encoun- ㉓ ter is the **Altes Museum** (entrance on Lustgarten), an austere neoclassical building just to the north of Marx-Engels-Platz. The collections here include postwar art from some of Germany's most prominent artists and numerous etchings and draw- ㉔ ings from the Old Masters. Next comes the **Nationalgalerie,** on Bodestrasse, which features 19th- and 20th-century painting ㉕ and sculpture. The **Pergamon Museum,** on Am Kupfergraben, is one of Europe's greatest museums. Its name derives from the museum's principal exhibit and the city's number-one at- traction, the **Pergamon Altar,** a monumental Greek altar dating from 180 BC that occupies an entire city block. Almost as im- pressive is the **Babylonian Processional Way.** The Pergamon Museum also houses vast Egyptian, early Christian, and Byz- antine collections, plus a fine array of sculpture from the 12th ㉖ to the 18th centuries. To the north is the **Bodemuseum** (also on Am Kupfergraben, but with its entrance on Monbijoubrücke), with an outstanding collection of early Christian, Byzantine, and Egyptian art, as well as exhibits of Italian Old Master paintings. *Admission to each museum: DM 4 adults, DM 2 children. Museum complex open Wed.–Sun. 10–6; closed Mon. and Tues. (except Pergamon Museum, whose Pergamon Altar and architectural rooms open 9–6).*

From the museum complex, follow the Spree canal south to ㉗ Unter den Linden and the vast and impressive **Berliner Dom** (Berlin cathedral). The hideous modern building in bronze mir- ㉘ rored glass opposite is the **Palast der Republik** (Palace of the Republic), a postwar monument to socialist progress that also housed restaurants, a theater, and a dance hall. Since 1991 the Palast has been closed down while the politicians argue about whether it should be torn down or used for other purposes. It formerly housed the Volkskammer, the East German People's Chamber (parliament).

Cross Spandauer Strasse diagonally for a closer look at the ㉙ 13th-century **Marienkirche** (Church of St. Mary), especially noting its late-Gothic *Dance of Death* fresco. You are now at the ㉚ lower end of Alexanderplatz. Just ahead is the massive **TV tow- er,** a Berlin landmark. A focal point for shopping is the **Kaufhof department store** (formerly the Centrum), alongside the Hotel Stadt Berlin, at the very top of the plaza.

㉛ The area adjacent to the **Rathaus** (so-called Rotes Rathaus)— itself somewhat of a marvel for its red-brick design and the frieze depicting scenes from the city's history—has been hand-somely rebuilt. In the fall of 1991 the city administration and seat of the governing mayor were transferred from Schöneberg back to the Rotes Rathaus, renewing its prewar function.

③② Nikolaikirche (on Spandauer Strasse), dating from about 1200, is Berlin's oldest building. It was heavily damaged in the war, but has been beautifully restored and is now a museum. The quarter surrounding the church is filled with delightful shops, cafés, and restaurants. Wander back down Muhlendamm into the area around the Breitestrasse—there are some lovely old buildings here—and on over to the **Fischerinsel** area. The throbbing heart of Old Berlin of 750 years ago, Fischerinsel retains a tangible medieval flavor.

③③ Nearby is the **Märkisches Museum** (Museum of Cultural History), which has an amusing section devoted to automaphones—"self-playing" musical instruments, demonstrated Sundays 10–12 and Wednesdays 3–4. Live bears—the city's symbol—are in a pit next to the museum. *Am Köllnischen Park 5. Admission: DM 2 adults, DM 1 children. Open Wed.–Sun. 10–6.*

Shopping

Berlin is a city of alluring stores and boutiques. Despite the new capital's cosmopolitan gloss, prices are generally lower than in cities like Munich and Hamburg.

Fine **porcelain** is still produced at the former Royal Prussian Porcelain Factory, now called **Staaliche Porzellan Manufactur,** or KPM. This delicate, handmade, hand-painted china is sold at KPM's store at Kurfürstendamm 26A (tel. 030/881–1802), but it may be more fun to visit the factory salesroom at Wegelystrasse 1. It also sells seconds at reduced prices. If you long to have the Egyptian Queen Nefertiti on your mantlepiece at home, try the **Gipsformerei der Staatlichen Museen Preussicher Kulturbesitz** (Sophie-Charlotte-Str. 17, tel. 030/321–7011, open weekdays 9–4). It sells plaster casts of this and other treasures from the city's museums.

Shopping Districts The liveliest and most famous shopping area in West Berlin is the **Kurfürstendamm** and its side streets, especially between **Breitscheidplatz** and **Oliver Platz.** The **Europa Center** at Breitscheidplatz encompasses more than 100 stores, cafés, and restaurants—this is not a place to bargain-hunt, though! Running east from Breitscheidplatz is **Tauenzientstrasse,** another shopping street. At the end of it is Berlin's most celebrated department store, **KaDeWe.** Elegant malls include the **Gloria Galerie** (opposite the Wertheim department store on Ku'damm) and the **Uhland-Passage** (connecting Uhlandstrasse and Fasanenstrasse). In both, you'll find leading name stores as well as cafés and restaurants.

For trendier clothes, try the boutiques along **Bleibtreustrasse.** One of the more avant-garde fashion boutiques is **Durchbruch** (Schlutterstr. 54), around the corner. The name means "breakthrough," and the store lives up to its name by selling six different designers' outrageous styles. Less trendy and much less expensive is the mall, **Wilmersdorferstrasse,** where price-conscious Berliners do their shopping. It's packed on weekends.

East Berlin's chief shopping areas are along the Friedrichstrasse, Unter den Linden, and in the area around Alexanderplatz. The Palast and Grand hotels have small shopping malls. A number of smaller stores have sprung up in and around the Nikolai quarter; under the Communist regime, all were supplied from the same central sources, but they make fun places to shop for trinkets.

Department Stores The classiest department store in Berlin is **KaDeWe,** the Kaufhaus des Western (Department Store of the West, as it's modestly known in English), at Wittenbergplatz. The biggest department store in Europe, the KaDeWe is a grand-scale emporium in modern guise. Be sure to check out the food department, which occupies the whole sixth floor. The other main department store downtown is **Wertheim** on Ku'damm. Neither as big nor as attractive as the KaDeWe, Wertheim nonetheless offers a large selection of fine wares.

The main department store in East Berlin is **Kaufhof** (formerly Centrum), at the north end of Alexanderplatz. Under the old regime, you could find ridiculously cheap subsidized prices. Now it is filled with mainly Western-made products, superior, of course, but the prices are higher.

Antiques On Saturdays and Sundays from 10 to 5, the colorful and lively antiques and handicrafts fair on Strasse des 17 Juni swings into action. Don't expect to pick up any bargains—or to have the place to yourself. Not far from Wittenbergplatz is **Keithstrasse,** a street given over to antiques stores. Eisenacherstrasse, Fuggerstrasse, Kalckreuthstrasse, Motzstrasse, and Nollendorfstrasse—all close to Nollendorfplatz—have many antiques stores of varying quality. Another good street for antiques is **Suarezstrasse,** between Kantstrasse and Bismarckstrasse.

In East Berlin, antiques are sold in the Metropol and Palast hotels in the Nikolai quarter and in the restored Husemannstrasse. Some private stores along the stretch of Friedichstrasse north of the Spree Bridge offer old books and prints.

Dining

Dining in Berlin can mean sophisticated nouvelle creations in upscale restaurants with linen tablecloths and hand-painted porcelain plates or hearty local specialties in atmospheric and inexpensive inns: The range is as vast as the city. Specialties include *Eisbein mit Sauerkraut,* knuckle of pork with pickled cabbage; *Rouladen,* rolled stuffed beef; *Spanferkel,* suckling pig; *Berliner Schüsselsülze,* potted meat in aspic; *Schlachteplatte,* mixed grill; *Hackepeter,* ground beef; and *Kartoffelpuffer,* fried potato cakes. *Bockwurst* is a chubby frankfurter that's served in a variety of ways and sold in restaurants and at Bockwurst stands all over the city. *Schlesisches Himmerlreich* is roast goose or pork served with potato dumplings in rich gravy. *Königsberger Klopse* consists of meatballs, herring, and capers—it tastes much better than it sounds.

East Germany's former ties to the Eastern Bloc persist in restaurants featuring the national cuisine of those other one-time socialist states, although such exotica as Japanese, Chinese, Indonesian, and French food is now appearing. Wines and spirits imported from those other countries can be quite good; try Hungarian, Yugoslav, and Bulgarian wines (the whites are lighter), and Polish and Russian vodkas.

For details and price-category definitions, *see* Dining in Staying in Germany.

West Berlin **Alt-Nürnberg.** Step into the tavernlike interior and you could
Moderate be in Bavaria: The waitresses even wear dirndls. The Bavarian colors of blue and white are everywhere, and such Bavarian culinary delights as *Schweinshaxe* (knuckle of pork) are well represented on the menu. If you prefer to eat in the Prussian style, the calves' liver *Berliner Art* is recommended. *Europa Center, tel. 030/261–4397. Reservations advised. AE, DC, MC, V.*

★ **Blockhaus Nikolskoe.** Prussian King Wilhelm III built this Russian-style wooden lodge for his daughter Charlotte, wife of Russia's Czar Nicholas I. It's located in the southwest of the city, on the eastern edge of Glienicke Park. In summer, you can eat on the open terrace overlooking the Havel River. In character with its history and appearance, the Blockhaus features game dishes. *Nikolskoer Weg, tel. 030/805–2914. Reservations advised. AE, DC, MC, V.*

Forsthaus Paulsborn. Game is the specialty in this former woodsman's home deep in the Grunewald Forest. You dine here as the forester did—from an oak table in a great dining room and under the baleful eye of hunting trophies on the wall. Apart from game, the menu extends to various German and international dishes. *Am Grunewaldsee, tel. 030/813–8010. Reservations advised on weekends. AE, DC, MC, V. Closed Mon., dinner in winter (Oct.–Mar.).*

Hecker's Deele. You could find yourself seated in one of the antique church pews that complete the oak-beamed interior of this restaurant that features Westphalian dishes. The *Westfälische Schlachtplatte* (a variety of meats) will set you up for a whole day's sightseeing—the Ku'damm is right outside. *Grolmannstr. 35, tel. 030/88901. No reservations. AE, DC, MC, V.*

Mundart Restaurant. Too many cooks don't spoil the broth (and certainly not the excellent fish soup) at this popular restaurant in the Kreuzberg district. Five chefs are at work in the spacious kitchen. Fortunately, they all agree on the day's specials, and you can follow their advice with impunity. *Muskauerstr. 33/34, tel. 030/612–2061. No reservations. No credit cards. Closed lunch, Mon., and Tues.*

Inexpensive **Alt-Berliner Weissbierstube.** A visit to the Berlin Museum (a permanent historical exhibition on Berlin) must include a stop at this pub-style restaurant in the museum building. There's a buffet packed with Berlin specialties, and a jazz band plays on Sunday morning after 10. *Berlin Museum, Lindenstr. 14, tel. 030/251–0121. Reservations advised, particularly evenings. No credit cards. Closed Mon.*

Thürnagel. Here is a vegetarian restaurant where it's not only healthy to eat but fun. The seitan in sherry sauce or the tempeh curry are good enough to convert a seasoned carnivore. *Gneisenaustr. 57, tel. 030/691–4800. Reservations advised. No credit cards. Dinner only.*

Budget **Deichgraf.** Yuppies and blue-collar workers rub shoulders in this traditional restaurant in West Berlin's Wedding district. Specialties include sliced beef in mushroom and cream sauce. The large beer garden is popular in the summer. *Nordufer 10, tel. 030/453–7613. Reservations not necessary. No credit cards.*

Max und Moritz. You can feast on traditional Berlin fare at this typical, old-style Kreuzberg restaurant complete with dark-wood paneling and a smoky, casual atmosphere. Try the *Könicksberger Klopse* (meatballs with capers in cream sauce). *Oranienstr. 162, tel. 030/614–1045. Reservations accepted. No credit cards.*

Orpheus. This Kreuzberg bar-restaurant owes its popularity to its friendly service and diverse menu, which includes pizza and salads as well as typical local meat dishes. Dinner is served until 2 AM. *Katzbachstr. 17, tel. 030/ 785–7734. Reservations not necessary. No credit cards.*

East Berlin **Französischer Hof.** Not for the infirm or those who are afraid of
Moderate heights, this restaurant is tucked away below the cupola of the French Cathedral, the church that sits in classical splendor on one side of the beautiful Gendarmenmarkt. The restaurant, which runs a circular course around the base of the cupola, is approached by a long, winding staircase—fine for working up an appetite but certainly not recommended for the faint-hearted. The reward at the top of the stairs is a table in one of Berlin's most original and attractive restaurants. The menu is as short as the stairway is long, but there's an impressive wine list. *Gendarmenmarkt, tel. 030/229–3969. Reservations strongly advised (the frustration of being turned away after that climb could spoil anyone's day). No credit cards.*

Ratskeller. This is actually two restaurants in one—a wine and a beer cellar, both vast, atmospheric, and extremely popular. The menus are limited, but offer good, solid Berlin fare. The beer cellar is guaranteed to be packed at main dining hours, and attempts at reservations may be ignored (locals simply line up and wait). *Rathausstr. 15–18, in basement of the City Hall, tel. 030/212–5301. Reservations advised. No credit cards.*

Sofia. Bulgarian and Russian specialties are the basis of the imaginative menu offered at this popular, central restaurant, a few paces from Potsdamer Platz. The Bulgarian wines are particularly recommended. *Leipziger Strasse 46, tel. 030/229–1533 or 030/229–1831. Reservations advised. No credit cards.*

Zur Rippe. This famous eating place near Alexanderplatz serves wholesome food in an intimate setting with oak paneling and ceramic tiles. Specialties include the Märkische cheese platter and herring casserole. *Poststr. 17, tel. 030/217–3235. Reservations not necessary. No credit cards.*

Inexpensive **Alt-Cöllner Schankstuben.** A charming and genuine old Berlin house is the setting for this conglomerate of no fewer than four tiny restaurants, all of which provide exceptionally friendly service. *Friedrichsgracht 50, 030/212–5972. No reservations. No credit cards.*

★ **Zur Letzten Instanz.** Established in 1525, this place combines the charming atmosphere of Old-World Berlin with a limited (but tasty) choice of dishes. Napoleon is said to have sat alongside the tiled stove in the front room. Mikhail Gorbachev enjoyed a beer here during a visit to Berlin in 1989. The emphasis here is on beer, both in the recipes and in the mug. Service can be erratic, though engagingly friendly. *Waisenstr. 14–16, tel. 030/212–5528. Reservations required for both lunch and dinner. No credit cards.*

Budget **Vineta.** Known among insiders as one of Berlin's least expensive restaurants, Vineta cooks up traditional German fare for prices below DM 10. The food is good but don't expect much in the way of ambience: the restaurant is housed in a typically bland 1950s-style East German building, and furnishings are Spartan. *Vinetastr., at the Pankow/Vinetastr. subway station, No phone. Reservations not accepted. No credit cards.*

Lodging

Berlin lost all its grand old luxury hotels in the bombing during World War II; though some were rebuilt, many of the best hotels today are modern. Although they lack little in service and comfort, you may find some short on atmosphere. Eager for hard currency, the East German government built several elegant luxury hotels in East Berlin, all of which are very expensive. If you're seeking something more moderate, the better choice may be West Berlin, where there are large numbers of good-value pensions and small hotels, many of them in older buildings with some character. In East Berlin, however, the hostels run by the Evangelical Lutheran church offer outstanding value for your money.

There are no longer any restrictions on who can stay where in East Berlin, as there were in the past. In West Berlin, business conventions year-round and the influx of summer tourists mean that you should make reservations well in advance. If you arrive without reservations, consult the board at Tegel Airport that shows hotels with vacancies or go to the tourist office.

For details and price-category definitions, *see* Lodging in Staying in Germany.

West Berlin **Alpenland.** Situated near the fashionable Ku'damm, this small
Moderate hotel offers comfort and quiet in a central location. Most rooms have private bathrooms. The Swiss chalet–style restaurant downstairs serves wholesome German food. Advance room reservations are necessary. *Carmerstr. 8, tel. 030/312–3970 or 030/312–4898. 45 rooms, most with bath. Facilities: restaurant. No credit cards.*

Casino Hotel. The owner of the Casino is Bavarian, so his restaurant serves south German specialties. The hotel itself is a former Prussian military barracks but bears little evidence of its former role: The rooms are large and comfortable and well equipped. The hotel is located in the Charlottenburg district. *Königin-Elisabeth-Str. 47a, tel. 030/303090. 24 rooms with bath. AE, DC, MC, V.*

Hotel Gotland. Opened in 1987, the Gotland has modern rooms equipped with showers, radio, and cable TV. A breakfast buffet is included in the rates. The 20 rooms book up quickly, so be sure to make your reservations ahead of time. *Franzstr. 23, tel. 030/771–5016 or 030/771–5017. 20 rooms with bath. Facilities: garage. No credit cards.*

Hotel Pension "Tegel City." This tiny establishment is in northwest Berlin, just 10 minutes from Tegel Airport, but the heart of the city is easily accessible from the nearby Tegel U–bahn station. Rooms are homey and comfortably furnished, with showers as well as radio and TV. *Berliner Str. 9, tel. 030/433–4004. 8 rooms with bath. No credit cards.*

★ **Ravenna.** This small, friendly hotel is located in the Steglitz district, close to the Botanical Garden and the Dahlen Museum. All the rooms are well equipped, but suite 111B is a bargain: It includes a large living room and kitchen for the rate of only DM 200. *Grunewaldstr. 8–9, tel. 030/792–8031. 45 rooms with bath or shower. AE, DC, MC, V.*

Riehmers Hofgarten. Located in the interesting Kreuzberg district, this hotel, in a late-19th-century building, is a short walk from the Kreuzberg hill and has fast connections to the center of town. The high-ceilinged rooms are elegantly furnished. *Yorckstr. 83, tel. 030/781011. 21 rooms with bath or shower. AE, DC, MC, V.*

Inexpensive **Centrum Pension Berlin.** This small, no-frills pension is conveniently located in downtown West Berlin. Rooms are simply furnished and have no baths, only washbasins with hot and cold running water. Breakfast is available for an extra charge. *Kantstr. 31, tel. 030/316153. 7 rooms without bath. No credit cards.*

Econtel. Families are well cared for at this hotel that's situated within walking distance of Charlottenburg Palace. Lone travelers also appreciate the touches in the single rooms, which come with a trouser press and hair dryer. *Sommeringstr. 24, tel. 030/346610. 205 rooms with bath or shower. Facilities: snack bar. No credit cards.*

Hotel Transit. This large, nondescript hotel is located in the lively, colorful Kreuzberg district. Rooms are blandly furnished but are equipped with TVs and minibars. The Yorckstrasse S-Bahn station is just a short walk away. *Hagelberger Str. 53–54, Kreuzberg, tel. 030/785–5051. 50 rooms, some with bath. AE, DC, MC, V.*

Budget **Haus Schliebner Pension.** The Wall used to cut through northern Berlin just a couple of blocks from this tiny pension. Today the whole city is freely and easily accessible from the nearby S-bahn station. Rooms are simply furnished and have washbasins but no showers. *Dannenwalder Weg 95, tel. 030/416–7997. 7 rooms without bath. No credit cards.*

Pension 22. Tucked away in the beautiful outlying district of Kladow, this little pension is ideal for those who like to escape the noise and bustle of the central city. Rooms are comfortable and pleasingly decorated; some are equipped with showers. Bus 37, which stops nearby, can take you to and from the city center. *Schambachweg 22, tel. 030/365–5230. 6 rooms, some with bath. No credit cards.*

Pension Elton. The city is at your doorstep when you stay in this cozy pension located in the heart of West Berlin. You'll get a modest, comfortable room and breakfast for a very reasonable price. *Pariser Str. 9, tel. 030/883–6155 or 030/883–6156. 9 rooms, some with bath. Facilties: elevator. No credit cards.*

East Berlin **Adria.** This hotel tends to be fully booked well in advance, attesting to its less expensive prices rather than to any particular
Moderate charm. The rooms in back are quieter, if you have any choice. *Friedrichstr. 134, tel. 030/280–5105. 67 rooms, 10 with bath. Facilities: restaurant, dance/bar, hairdresser. No credit cards.*

Hotel Merkur. This small hotel is in central East Berlin's Prenzlauer Berg district. Service is friendly and the rooms are comfortable, equipped with extras such as minibar, telephone, radio, and TV. *Wilhelm-Pieck-Str. 156, tel. 030/282–8297. 17 rooms, some with bath. No credit cards.*

Hotel Pension Neues Tor. Before the Wall was torn down, this little pension sat in the shadow of a Communist city checkpoint. Today the checkpoint is defunct, and the Neues Tor is conveniently close to several East Berlin museums. The atmosphere is friendly, and basic rooms come equipped with radio and TV.

Breakfast is included in the rates. *Invalidenstr. 102, tel. 030/282–3859. 7 rooms, some with bath. No credit cards.*

Newa. This older hotel, popular because of its affordability, is just a 10-minute streetcar ride away from the downtown area. Rooms in the back are quieter. At press time, the hotel was undergoing major renovations, scheduled to be completed by September 1993; call ahead to check on its status. *Invalidenstr. 115, tel. 030/282–5461. 57 rooms, most with bath. No credit cards.*

Pension Rosenthal. Rooms in this pension are neatly furnished but hardly luxurious; most have private baths or showers and come with radio, TV, and phone. Complimentary breakfast is served every morning. *Friedrich-Engels-Str. 88, tel. 030/482–4408. 10 rooms, most with bath. Facilities: room service, garage space. No credit cards.*

Inexpensive **Hospiz am Bahnhof Friedrichstrasse.** For reasons of both price and convenience, this Evangelical church-run hostel tends to be heavily booked months in advance. It appeals to families, so the public rooms are not always restful. *Albrechstr. 8, tel. 030/282–5396. 110 rooms, some with bath. Facilities: restaurant. No credit cards.*

Hospiz Auguststrasse. Another church-run hostel, this one has comfortable rooms and a particularly friendly staff. It's about a 10-minute streetcar ride to the downtown sights. Only breakfast is served. *Auguststr. 82, tel. 030/282–5321. 70 rooms, some with bath. No credit cards.*

Budget **Gästehaus Waldowstrasse.** This huge establishment is somewhat off the beaten track in Hellersdorf—hardly one of Berlin's more romantic districts—and connected with downtown East Berlin by local buses. With only the most basic furnishings and decor, this hotel is no lap of luxury—functional would describe it best. *Waldowstr. 47, tel. 030/527–7497. 170 rooms, none with baths. Facilities: conference room, children's play area, bowling, parking lot. AE, V.*

Pension "Monika." Rooms here are simple, but they do have radio and TV. The pension is in a historic building in northern Berlin's Weissensee district. Breakfast costs an extra DM 5. *Schräger Weg 26, tel. 030/949–4502. 3 rooms without bath. No credit cards.*

The Arts

West Berlin Today's Berlin has a tough task in trying to live up to the reputation it gained from the film *Cabaret*, but if nightlife is a little toned down since the '20s, the arts still flourish. Apart from the many hotels that book seats, there are numerous ticket agencies, including **Europa-Center** (Tauentzienstrasse 9, tel. 030/261–7051); **Theaterkasse Centrum** (Meinekestrasse 25, tel. 030/882–7611); and at any of the Top Ticket branches (in all major stores, such as Hertie, Wertheim, and KaDeWe).

The Berlin Philharmonic, one of the world's leading orchestras, performs in the **Philharmonie** (Matthaikirchstrasse 1, tel. 030/254880). It plays a leading role in the annual festival months of August, September, and October. The **Deutsche Oper** (Opera House, Bismarckstrasse 35), by the U-Bahn stop of the same name, is the home of the opera and ballet companies. Tickets are hard to obtain, but call 030/34381 for information.

West Berlin is still Germany's drag-show capital, as you'll see if you go to **Chez Nous** (Marburgerstrasse 14). It's essential to book (tel. 030/213–1810). The girls are for real next door (No. 15) at the **Scotch Club 13.**

East Berlin The quality of opera and classical concerts in East Berlin is impressively high. Tickets are available at the separate box offices, either in advance or an hour before the performance. Tickets are also sold at the central tourist office of the Reisebüro (Alexanderplatz 5), at the ticket offices in the Palast and Grand hotels, or from your hotel service desk. Check the monthly publication *Wohin in Berlin?*

Concerts **Schauspielhaus** (Gendarmenmarkt, tel. 030/227–2156).

Opera and Ballet **Deutsche Staatsoper** (Unter den Linden 7, tel. 030/200–472); **Komische Oper** (Behrenstrasse 55–57, tel. 030/229–2555); **Metropol Theater** (Friedrichstrasse 101, tel. 030/208–2215).

Nightlife

West Berlin Nightlife in West Berlin is no halfhearted affair. It starts late (from 9 PM) and runs until breakfast. Almost 50 bars (*Kneipen*) have live music of one kind or another, and there are numerous small cabaret clubs and discos. The heart of this nocturnal scene is the Kurfürstendamm, but some of the best bar discos are to be found at Nollendorfplatz in Charlottenburg. Try the **Metropol** (Nollendorfplatz 5, tel. 030/216–1020).

Berlin is a major center for jazz in Europe. If you're visiting in the fall, call the tourist office for details of the annual international Jazz Fest. Throughout the year a variety of jazz groups appear at the **Eierschale** (Egg Shell, Podbielskiallee 50, tel. 030/832–7097; evenings after 8:30).

East Berlin The nightlife here is more modest than in West Berlin—but the prices are less extravagant, too. Music in the hotels is generally live; clubs have discos with DJs. For nightclubs with music and atmosphere, try one of the following: **Club Metropol** (in the Metropol Hotel); **Panorama Bar** (atop the Hotel Stadt Berlin); **Hafenbar** (Chauseestrasse 20); **Checkpoint Null** (Leipziger Strasse 55); **Jojo** (Wilhelm-Pieck-Strasse 216).

Saxony and Thuringia

Saxony and Thuringia—the very sound of those names conjures up images of kingdoms and forest legends, of cultural riches and booming industrial enterprises. The reality after 40 years of communism is markedly less glamorous. Isolated from the West for decades, these two regions in eastern Germany are today struggling to make the transition from state-planned economies to a free-market system. Slowly, progress is being made, thanks to massive injections of cash from the federal government and the arrival of foreign and western German investors. But many people have been made jobless in the process. In January 1992, the opening up of the "Stasi" secret police files revealed the full horror and extent of former East Germany's monitoring of its citizens' lives. Closely tied politically and economically to the former Soviet Union for 45 years, many eastern Germans remain uncomfortable with their newly won freedoms and uncertain about the future. In Saxony, though, people seem happy enough with their new "Freistaat Sachsen"

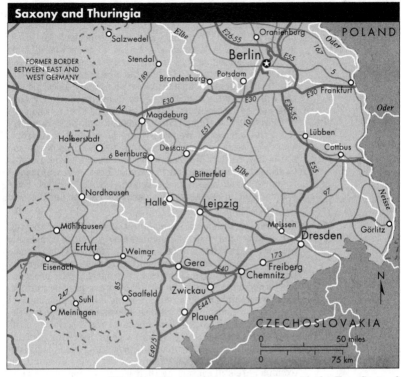

Saxony and Thuringia

title, something they share in common with the Free State of Bavaria.

Dresden was once the capital of the kingdom of Saxony, and no city could be prouder of its history. The sculpture of August the Strong atop his horse was back in its original place many years before East Berlin, remembering its Prussian past, removed the statue of Frederick the Great from its hiding place and put it back on show again on the Unter den Linden in the late 1970s. Even in its darker post-war moments, the glory of Saxony was never completely extinguished. Dresden is again a magnet for millions of visitors from around the world, eager to view its cultural treasures.

Since German reunification, Saxony has thrown open its doors to visitors. Tourists are proudly conducted around the world-famous porcelain factory in Meissen. In Colditz, a small town southeast of Leipzig, foreigners are courteously shown the town's forbidding castle, which during World War II housed captured Allied officers.

Thuringia's fame, it is sometimes said, begins and ends with its vast green forests, an unfair assessment given its many other historical facets and the fact that for centuries it was the home of dozens of kingdoms. Back in the 14th century, Thuringia was known as the Rynestig or Rennsteig (literally, fast trail), when it attracted traders from the dark forested depths of the Thuringian Wald (Woods) to the prospering towns of Erfurt (today the state capital), Eisenach, and Weimar, then already 600 years old. It was in Weimar that the privy councillor and poet,

Johann Wolfgang von Goethe, was inspired by the pristine beauties of the 168 kilometers (104 miles) of the Rennsteig in 1777 to write that "tranquility crowns all its peaks." Goethe enjoyed his time in Weimar—he stayed 57 years—as did his friend and contemporary Friedrich von Schiller, professor and poet, who taught history in Jena but preferred Weimar's cultured atmosphere in which to live with his family. Local historians will tell you that a pilgrimage to Weimar was as obligatory a part of the 19th-century European's Grand Tour as a sojourn in Florence. The Hungarian composer Franz Liszt regularly spent the summer in Weimar, where he conducted the royal court's orchestra and championed the works of his friend and son-in-law, Richard Wagner, who was born in Leipzig. But it is Goethe who reigns supreme in Weimar. His face graces many a monument, and his sayings adorn the town's libraries. Even Weimar's picturesque riverside park, the Park an der Ilm, was planned by him.

The transportation and communications systems of the two halves of a country so long divided have yet to be completely integrated, and that will take time. The former East German tourism ministry and tourist boards are being taken over by German authorities, and the resultant bureaucratic problems are formidable. Former state-run hotels are passing into private ownership, and hundreds are being built to accommodate the surge of tourists and business travelers who followed the opening of the frontiers. The upheaval reaches down to the smallest concerns of everyday life, with prices rising to match those in the west. As this process of price adjustment is still under way, it is difficult to accurately predict costs. Museums, for example, are still converting their old admission charges into the new deutsche mark currency. Opening hours of museums and other attractions are subject to change during renovation. Existing businesses may close, or new ones open, without notice. Telephone exchanges in eastern Germany are also being expanded, and the numbers are being altered at a frustrating rate.

We have given addresses, telephone numbers, and other logistical details based on the best available information, but remember that changes are taking place at a furious pace in everything from postal codes to street and even city names. We suggest that you contact the German National Tourist Office for the latest information, or phone ahead to confirm information locally.

Getting Around

By Train In Saxony and Thuringia, there are generally two types of trains: fast, shown as D in the timetables, and regular/local services indicated with an E. But the Euro-City and Intercity services of the German Federal Railways, the Deutsches Bundesbahn, are being progressively incorporated into the system in eastern Germany. The fast categories have varying supplementary fares; local trains do not. Most trains have first- and second-class cars, and many nowadays have either dining or buffet cars. On long-distance trains, first- and second-class sleeping compartments and couchettes are available. It is advisable to make advance reservations at major stations or through travel agents, as trains are popular and they are often full. Railway buffs will want to ride the narrow-gauge lines in the mountainous south.

By Bus and Streetcar Within Saxony and Thuringia, most areas are accessible by bus, but service is infrequent and serves chiefly to connect with rail lines. Check schedules carefully. In Dresden and Weimar, public transport in the form of buses and streetcars is cheap and efficient.

Tourist Information

Dresden (Box 201, Pragerstr. 10–11, tel. 0351/495–5025). A museum card good for one day and covering admission to all museums in the Staatlichen Kunstsammlungen, including the museums at the Albertinum and the Zwinger, is available at the participating institutions. The card costs DM 8 for adults, DM 4 for children.
Weimar (Box 647, Markstr. 4, tel. 03643/2173).

Exploring Dresden

Dresden, superbly located on the banks of the river Elbe, suffered appalling damage during World War II but has been lovingly rebuilt. Now that the eastern half of Germany is part of the Federal Republic, the city has become a magnet for tourists. Dresden is a compact city, easy to explore. Italianate influences are everywhere, most pronounced in the glorious Rococo and Baroque buildings in pastel shades of yellow and green. Although many of Dresden's architectural and cultural treasures were destroyed during a fateful night of British bombing in 1945, some gems still remain.

The **Semper Opera House,** at Theaterplatz in the center of Dresden, is a mecca for music lovers. Named after its architect, Gottfried Semper, the hall has premiered Wagner's *The Flying Dutchman* and *Tannhäuser* (conducted by the composer) and nine operas of Richard Strauss, including *The Rosenkavalier*. Dating from 1871–78 (the first building by Semper burned down in 1869), the opera house fell victim to the 1945 bombings, but fortunately Semper's architectural drawings had been preserved, so it was rebuilt on the same lines and reopened with much pomp in 1985. At concert intermissions, guests often mingle on the high-up balconies, which have breathtaking views of the city. Tickets are in great demand at the Semper (tel. 0351/4954882065); try booking through your travel agent before you go or ask at your hotel. As a last resort, line up at the Abendkasse (Evening Box Office) half an hour before the performance begins—a limited number of tickets are always available.

From Theaterplatz, stroll down the Sophienstrasse to the largely 18th-century **Zwinger** palace complex, which remains one of the city's cultural wonders in the heart of the Altstadt. Completely enclosing a central courtyard of lawns and pools, the complex consists of six linked pavilions decorated with a riot of garlands, nymphs, and other Baroque ornamentation and sculpture, all created under the direction of Matthaus Daniel Pöppelmann. At press time (summer 1992), restoration work was still in progress on part of the palace.

As a result, the world-renowned **Sempergalerie collection** of Old Master paintings, among them works by Dürer, Holbein the Younger, Rembrandt, Vermeer, Raphael, Correggio, and Canaletto, has been on temporary display at the **Albertinum** (*see below*). But other treasures, including the Porzellansammlung (Porcelain Collection)—famous for its Meissen pieces—Zoological Museum, and salon displaying marvelous old scientific instruments (Mathematisch-Physikalischer Salon), remain on view at the palace. Although the Sempergalerie was slated to reopen in November 1992, it is recommended that you call the Zwinger (tel. 0351/4840119) for the latest information. *Porzellansammlung admission: DM 3 adults, DM 1.50 children. Open Mon.–Thurs. and weekends 9–5. Mathematisch-Physikalischer Salon admission: DM 3 adults, DM 1.50 children. Open Fri.–Wed. 9:30–5. Zoological Museum admission: DM 1.05 adults, 50 pf children. Open daily 9–4.*

After leaving the Zwinger, head eastward along Ernst-Thälmann-Strasse and turn into the **Neumarkt** (New Market), which is, despite its name, the historic heart of old Dresden. The ruined shell on the right is all that remains of the mighty Baroque **Frauenkirche,** once Germany's greatest Protestant church, after the bombing raids of February 1945. Its jagged, precariously tilting walls had been left as a memorial, a poignant reminder of the evils of war. However, it was announced in 1992 that reconstruction would begin in 1993. The church will reopen in 2000.

Behind the Frauenkirche looms Dresden's leading art museum, the **Albertinum.** This large, imperial-style building gets its name from Saxony's King Albert, who between 1884 and 1887 converted a royal arsenal into a convenient setting for the treasures he and his forebears had collected. It is on the upper story of the Albertinum that the Sempergalerie's priceless collection of Old Master paintings has been on view pending completion of restoration work at the Zwinger (*see above*).

Permanent exhibits at the Albertinum include the **Gemäldegalerie Alte Meister/Neue Meister** displaying outstanding 19th- and 20th-century European pictures that include French Impressionist and Post-Impressionist works and Caspar David Friedrich's haunting *Das Kreuz im Gebirge.*

Despite the rich array of paintings, it is the **Grüne Gewölbe** (Green Vault) that invariably attracts most attention. Named after a green room in the palace of August the Strong, this part of the Albertinum (entered from Georg-Treu-Platz) contains an exquisite collection of unique objects d'art fashioned from gold, silver, ivory, amber, and other precious and semiprecious materials. Among them is the world's biggest "green" diamond, 41 carats in weight, and a dazzling group of tiny, gem-studded figures, some of which can be admired only through a magnifying glass. Somewhat larger and less delicate is the drinking bowl of Ivan the Terrible, perhaps the most sensational of the treasures to be found in this extraordinary museum. Next door is the **Skulpturensammlung** (Sculpture Collection), which includes ancient Egyptian and classical objects and Italian Mannerist works. *Tel. 0351/495–3056. Sempergalerie collection admission: DM 5 adults, DM 2.50 children. Open Tues., Thurs.–Sun. 9–5, Wed. 9–6. Gemäldegalerie Alte Meister/Neue Meister admission: DM 5 adults, DM 2.50 children. Open Tues., Thurs.–Sun. 9–5, Wed. 9–6. Grüne Gewölbe and Skulpturensammlung admission: DM 5 adults, DM 2.50 children. Open Fri.–Tues. 9–5, Wed. 9–6.*

The southern exit of the Albertinum, at Augustus-Strasse, brings you back to the Neumarkt and leads you to another former royal building now serving as a museum, the 16th-century **Johanneum,** once the royal stables. Instead of horses, the Johanneum now houses the Vekehrsmuseum (Transport Museum), a collection of historical vehicles, including vintage automobiles and engines. *Augustusstr. 1., tel. 0351/495-3002. Admission: DM 4 adults, DM 2 children. Admission half-price on Fri. Open Tues.–Sun. 10–5.*

On the outside wall of the Johanneum is a prime example of Meissen porcelain art: a 102-meter-long (335-foot-long) painting on Meissen tiles of a royal procession. More than 100 members of the royal Saxon house of Wettin, half of them on horseback, are depicted on the giant jigsaw made up of 25,000 porcelain tiles, painted from 1904 to 1907.

Follow this unusual procession to the end and you arrive at the former royal palace, the **Herzogschloss,** where major restoration work will continue until the mid-1990s behind the fine Renaissance facade. Rooms now in use host historical exhibitions. The main gate of the palace, the Georgentor, has acquired its original appearance, complete with an enormous statue of the fully armed Saxon Count George. *Sophienstr., tel. 0351/495-3110. Admission: DM 5 adults, DM 2.50 children. Open Mon., Tues., Fri.–Sun. 9–5, Thurs. 9–6.*

Standing next to the Herzogschloss is the **Katholische Hofkirche,** also known as the Cathedral of St. Trinitas, Saxony's largest church. The son of August the Strong, Frederick Augustus II (ruled 1733–63) brought architects and builders from Italy to construct this Catholic church, consecrated in 1754, in a city that had been the first large center of Lutheranism. In the cathedral's crypt are the tombs of 49 Saxon rulers and a precious vessel containing the heart of August the Strong.

Moving away from the treasures near the river, along the St. Petersburger Strasse, make a left into Lingnerplatz. The **Deutsches Hygiene-Museum** (German Health Museum) reflects Dresden's important role in the history of medicine. The most famous object is a glass model of a human, which caused a sensation when it was first displayed in 1930. *Lingnerplatz 1, tel. 0351/48460. Admission: DM 3 adults, DM 1.50 children. Open Tues.–Sun. 9–5.*

Two fine examples of Baroque architecture, both designed by Pöppelmann, general designer of the Zwinger palace, are within easy reach from Dresden. Take bus No. 85 from Schillerplatz to the chinoiserie-bedecked **Schloss Pillnitz** (tel. 0351/39325), once the summer residence of the Saxon court and situated in a huge park on the Elbe that embodies both Baroque and English landscape styles. The complex consists of two major palaces—the Wasserpalais (admission: DM 3 adults, DM 1.50 children; open Tues.–Sun. 9:30–5:30) and the Bergpalais (DM 3 adults, DM 1.50 children; open Wed.–Mon. 9:30–5:30)—both housing arts and crafts collections. An imposing hunting lodge built in the 17th century and later renovated and enlarged by Pöppelmann in the Baroque style, **Schloss Moritzburg** (tel. 297/439) displays a decorative arts collection (much of the furniture is original to the building) and hunting trophies (admission: DM 3 adults, DM 1 children; open May–Oct., Tues.–Sun. 10–5; shorter hours Nov.–Apr.) Once used by the Saxon royal family,

Moritzburg is now the site of outdoor concerts in summer. You can get there by taking the Grossenhein bus from the main train station in Dresden.

Exploring Weimar

Weimar, wedged between Erfurt and Jena and southwest of Leipzig, sits prettily on the Ilm River between the Ettersberg and Vogtland hills, and has a place in German political and cultural history out of all proportion to its size (population 63,000). Its civic history, not long by German standards, began as late as 1410, but by the early 19th century Weimar had become one of Europe's most important cultural centers, where Goethe and Schiller were neighbors, Carl Maria von Weber wrote some of his best music, and Liszt was director of music, presenting the first performance of Wagner's *Lohengrin*. Walter Gropius founded his Staatliche Bauhaus design school in Weimar in 1919, and it was there in 1919–20 that the German National Assembly drew up the constitution of the Weimar Republic. After the collapse of the ill-fated Weimar government, a shadow was cast over the unsuspecting city when Hitler chose it as the site for the first national congress of his new Nazi Party, and later built—or forced prisoners to build for him—the notorious Buchenwald concentration camp on the outskirts of Weimar.

Weimar's greatness is bound up with the activity of the widowed Countess Anna Amalia, who in the late 18th century set about attracting cultural figures to enrich the glittering court her Saxon forebears had set up in the town. Goethe, who served the Countess as a councillor, advising on financial matters and town design, was one of them; Schiller was another.

In front of the National Theater on **Theaterplatz** a statue of the famous pair, showing Goethe with a patronizing hand on the shoulder of the younger Schiller, commemorates them. The present theater, alas, is not the Baroque building where the two men produced some of their leading works. That was demolished in 1907 when it became too small to accommodate the increasing number of visitors to Weimar. The theater that replaced it was bombed in World War II and rebuilt in its present form in 1948. It reopened with a performance of Goethe's *Faust*, which was written in Weimar.

Adjacent to the National Theater is the Baroque **Wittumspalais**, once the home of Countess Anna Amalia. In the exquisite drawing room where her soirees were held, you find the original cherrywood table at which company sat. In the east wing is a small museum that is a fascinating memorial to her cultural gatherings. *Theaterpl. 9. Admission: DM 3 adults, DM 2 children. Open Mar.–Oct., Tues.–Sun. 9–noon and 1–5; Nov.–Feb., Tues.–Sun. 9–noon and 1–4.*

Goethe spent 57 years in Weimar, 47 years in the house that has since become a shrine for millions of visitors. **Goethehaus** is two blocks south of Theaterplatz on a street called Frauenplan. The museum it contains is testimony not only to the great man's literary might but also his interest in the sciences, particularly medicine, and his administrative skills (and frustrations) as Weimar's exchequer. Here you find the desk at which Goethe stood to write (he liked to work standing up), his own paintings (he was an accomplished watercolorist), and the modest bed on which he died. *Frauenplan 1, tel. 03643/64386. Admission: DM*

5 adults, DM 3 children. Open Mar.–Oct., Tues.–Sun. 9–5; Nov.–Feb., Tues.–Sun. 9–4.

On a tree-shaded square around the corner from Goethe's house is Schiller's green-shuttered home, **Schillerhaus,** in which he and his family spent a happy, all-too-brief three years (Schiller died there in 1805). The poet and playwright's study, dominated by the desk where he probably completed *William Tell*, is tucked up underneath the mansard roof. Much of the remaining furniture and the collection of books were added later, although they all date from around Schiller's time. *Neugasse 2, tel. 03643/62041. Admission: DM 5 adults, DM 2.55 children. Open Mar.–Oct., Wed.–Mon. 9–5; Nov.–Feb., Wed.–Mon. 9–4.*

Another historic house worth visiting is found on the **Marktplatz,** the central town square. It was the home of the painter Lucas Cranach the Elder, who lived there during his last years, 1552–53. Its wide, imposing facade, richly decorated, bears the coat of arms of the Cranach family. In its ground floor it now houses a private modern art gallery open to the public.

Around the corner and to the left is Weimar's 16th-century castle, the **Stadtschloss,** with its restored classical staircase, festival hall, and falcon gallery. The castle houses an impressive art collection, including several fine paintings by Cranach the Elder and many early 20th-century works by such artists as Böcklin, Liebermann, and Beckmann. *Burgplatz. Admission: DM 4.50 adults, DM 2.50 children. Open Mar.–Oct., Tues.–Sun. 10–6; Nov.–Feb., Tues.–Sun. 10–4.*

In Weimar's old, reconstructed town center stands the Late Gothic **Herderkirche,** with its large winged altarpiece started by Lucas Cranach the Elder and finished by his son in 1555. Nearby in Jakobstrasse you'll spot the Baroque facade of the **Kirms-Krackow** house, at press time (summer 1992) closed for restoration.

A short walk south, past Goethehaus and across Wieland Platz, brings you to the cemetery, **Historischer Friedhof** (Historic Cemetery), where Goethe and Schiller are buried. Their tombs are in the classical-style chapel. The Goethe-Schiller vault can be visited daily (except Tuesday) 9–1 and 2–5; winter 9–1 and 2–4.

On the other side of the Ilm, amid meadowlike parkland, is Goethe's beloved **Gartenhaus** (Garden House), where he wrote much poetry and began his masterpiece *Iphigenie auf Tauris* (admission: DM 3 adults, DM 2 children; open daily 9–noon and 1–5, winter 9–noon, 1–4). Goethe is said to have felt very close to nature here, and you can soak up the same rural atmosphere today on footpaths along the peaceful little river, where time seems to have stood still. Just across the river from the Gartenhaus is a generous German tribute to another literary giant, William Shakespeare, a 1904 statue that depicts him jauntily at ease on a marble plinth, looking remarkably at home in his foreign surroundings.

Just south of the city (take the No. 1 bus from Goetheplatz) is the lovely 18th-century **Schloss Belvedere,** now housing a museum of Baroque art but once a hunting and pleasure castle. The formal gardens were in part laid out according to Goethe's concepts. *Tel. 03643/661831. Admission: DM 1.50 adults, 50 pf children. Open Mar.–Oct., Tues.–Sun. 10–6. Closed Nov.– Feb.*

North of Weimar, in the Ettersberg Hills, is a blighted patch of land that contrasts cruelly with the verdant countryside that so inspired Goethe: **Buchenwald,** where, from 1937 to 1945, 65,000 men, women, and children from 35 countries met their deaths through disease, starvation, and gruesome medical experiments. Each is commemorated today by a small stone placed on the outlines of the former barracks (no longer existing), and by a massive memorial tower. A free bus to Buchenwald leaves from Weimar's main train station. Also leaving from the station are bus tours of the camp organized by the Weimar tourist information office. The buses depart hourly from 9 to 4 daily; the cost is 50 pf for adults, 25 pf for children. *Campsite admission free. Open Tues.–Sun. 8:45–4:30.*

Dining and Lodging

Many of the best restaurants in Saxony and Thuringia are to be found in the larger hotels. You can expect hearty food in both regions. Roast beef, venison, and wild boar are often on Saxon menus, and in the Vogtland you'll find *Kaninchentopf* (rabbit stew). In Thuringia, regional specialties include *Thüringer Rehbraten* (roast venison); roast mutton served in a delicate cream sauce; tasty grilled Thuringian sausages; *Thüringer Sauerbraten mit Klössen* (roast corned beef with dumplings); *Börenschinken* (cured ham); and roast mutton shepherd-style, with beans and vegetables. The light Meissner Wein, wine from the Meissen region, is splendid.

The choice of hotels in Saxony and Thuringia remains limited, and although private householders may now rent rooms, these are also hard to come by, as the demand is far greater than the supply. Contact the local tourist information offices for names of bed-and-breakfasts. Very few inexpensive hotels exist in Weimar. Your best bet is to arrange a private room through the local tourist office. Room prices range from DM 40 to DM 60 in Weimar and are even less in outlying districts. Do not, however, expect too much in the way of comfort or luxury.

For details and price-category definitions, *see* Dining and Lodging in Staying in Germany.

Dresden
Dining

Blockhaus. Situated just across the river from the Zwinger Palace, this restaurant offers a prime location and reasonably priced, high-quality local food. If you're coming for lunch, arrive early to avoid the midday rush. *Neustadtemarkt 19, tel. 0351/53630. Reservations recommended. No credit cards. Moderate.*

Kügelnhaus. A combination grill/coffee shop/restaurant/beer cellar, Kügelnhaus is extremely popular, so either get there early or reserve your table in advance. You'll find the usual hefty local dishes but prepared with a deft touch. *Hauptstr., tel. 0351/52791. Reservations advised. No credit cards. Moderate.*

Sekundogenitur. This famous complex consisting of a restaurant, several bars, a wine cellar, and a bistro, now connected to the Dresdner Hof hotel complex, is situated right on the banks of the Elbe. There is outside dining when the weather permits. The Wiener schnitzel is excellent. *Brühlsche Terrasse, tel.*

0351/495–1772 or 48410. Reservations advised. No credit cards. Closed Sun., Mon. Moderate.

"Trompeter." This historic restaurant serves traditional local cuisine in a friendly atmosphere. To get here from the center of town, take Streetcar 11 in the direction of Buhlau. *Bautzener Land Str. 83, tel. 0351/36123. Reservations recommended. AE, MC, V. Moderate.*

Narren Häuschen ("7-Schwaben"). Traditional menus offer wholesome food in this restaurant. Friendly, attentive service adds to the typically convivial atmoshpere. *An der Augustus Brucke, Grosse Meissner Str., tel. 0351/55502. Reservations recommended. No credit cards. Inexpensive.*

"D-100." This atmospheric pub-restaurant is a popular haunt of late-nighters. The food is very reasonably priced, but warm meals are served only after 10 PM; cold snacks and sandwiches are served from 8 PM. It's a short walk from the Platz der Einheit. *Alan Str. 100, no phone. Reservations not necessary. No credit cards. Budget.*

Lodging **Astoria.** A half mile away from the city center but close to the Dresden Zoo (take bus No. 72 from the main train station), the Astoria is a modern five-story hotel with a garden terrace. The staff is pleasant, but the decor hardly fancy—minimalist would describe it best. *Strehlener Platz 2, tel. 0351/471–5171. 82 rooms, most without bath. Facilities: restaurant, bar, shop. AE, DC, MC, V. Moderate.*

Interhotel Prager Strasse. This modern complex of two hotels, the **Konigstein** and **Lilienstein,** is named for the two promontories overlooking the Elbe River south of the city. Rooms are modern if unexciting; the favored rooms overlook the Prager Strasse, although the back rooms are slightly quieter. *Prager Str., tel. 0351/48–460 or 0351/48–560. 300 rooms with bath. Facilities: 3 restaurants, sauna, garage. AE, DC, MC, V. Moderate.*

Hotel Artushof. The staff is helpful and the atmosphere pleasant in this small city hotel, but don't expect any extra amenities. Just east of the Alstadt, the Artushof is only a few blocks away from the cultural heart of the city. *Fetscher Str. 30, tel. 0351/459–3496. 9 rooms without bath. No credit cards. Budget.*

Hotel Stadt Rendsburg. Rooms in this modest-size hotel are comfortable but hardly luxurious. The hotel is located on a relatively quiet city street on the north side of the Elbe River. *Kamenzer Str. 1, tel. 0351/51551. 22 rooms with bath, 2 suites. Budget.*

Weimar **Elephantenkeller.** In the ancient cellar restaurant of the Ele-
Dining phant hotel, you'll dine on traditional Thuringian cuisine in surroundings that haven't changed much since Goethe's day. Try the *Weimarer Zwiebelmarkt* soup, an onion soup made with pork-knuckle stock. *Markt 19, tel. 03643/61471. Reservations advised. AE, DC, MC, V. Moderate.*

Ratskeller. This historic restaurant is located in the cellar of Stadthaus (City House), a Renaissance building dating back to the 17th century. The wholesome regional fare includes grilled sausages with sauerkraut and onions, and Thuringian onion soup. *Markt 10, tel. 03643/64142. Reservations not necessary. AE, DC, MC, V. Moderate.*

Felsenkeller. In this warm, rustic, country-style restaurant and drinking establishment in the Gasthaus Brauere, a variety of warm dishes is offered at prices between DM 5 and DM 30. The beer is brewed on the premises. *Humboldtstr. 37, tel.*

03643/61941. Reservations not necessary. No credit cards. Inexpensive.

Gastmahl des Meeres. Centrally located, this restaurant offers a wide range of fish dishes, as well as meat. It has fast service and friendly waiters but tends to get crowded between 1 and 2 PM, so it's best to arrive early for lunch. *Herder Platz 16, tel. 03643/4521. No reservations. No credit cards. Inexpensive.*

Lodging **Russischerhof.** This charming hotel built in 1805 was modernized and expanded in 1989. The pleasing rooms are attractively furnished, each equipped with bath, shower, TV, and radio. *Goethe Platz 2, tel. 03643/62331. 85 rooms with bath. Facilities: 2 restaurants, bar, beer cellar, garage. AE, DC, MC, V. Moderate.*

10 Great Britain

Great Britain can be an expensive destination for a vacation, but with very careful planning and forethought it can be considered fairly reasonable. One of the reasons for the high costs in Britain is the unfavorable exchange rate of the dollar against the pound. It would be a very good idea, if you are able to plan far enough ahead, to buy your sterling when a favorable rate shows its head above the parapet.

To make a trip work at a reasonable cost, here are two very important strategies: Book as many lodgings as far ahead as you possibly can. Hotel space will be the biggest component of your travel costs. Believe us, you can mortgage your soul at British hotels. They are among the highest priced in the world and far too often do not give true value for the exorbitant sums they charge. If you manage to find reasonable places and book most of them ahead, then you already have one foot up in controlling your vacation costs. Keep the B&B scene well to the forefront of your mind when searching for lodgings. B&Bs offer the best value for money and will give you a glimpse of the life of the natives. The second saving point is to invest in either a Eurail Card or a BritRail Pass before you leave home. The economy in travel costs and in freedom of movement the passes can represent is enormous.

Great Britain is an ideal holiday destination for anyone with a feeling for the past. Here you'll find soaring medieval cathedrals, tributes to the faith of the churchmen and craftsmen who built them, but terribly heavy financial burdens for their descendents; grand country mansions of the aristocracy, filled with treasures, among them paintings, furniture, and tapestries, and set in elegantly landscaped grounds; grim fortified castles, their gray stone walls still fronting a dangerous world; and endless gardens, rich with lilies and roses, tended by gen-

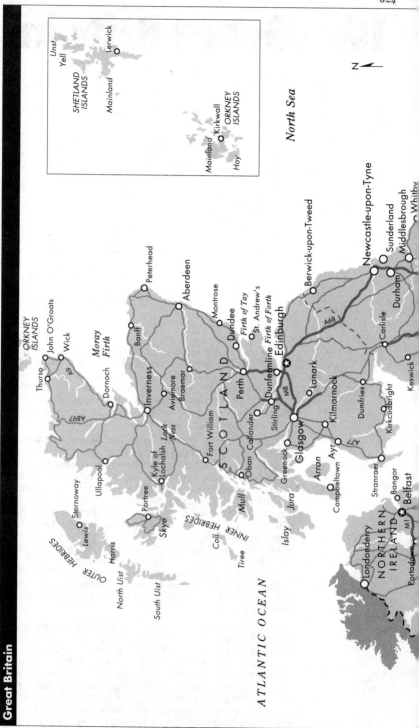

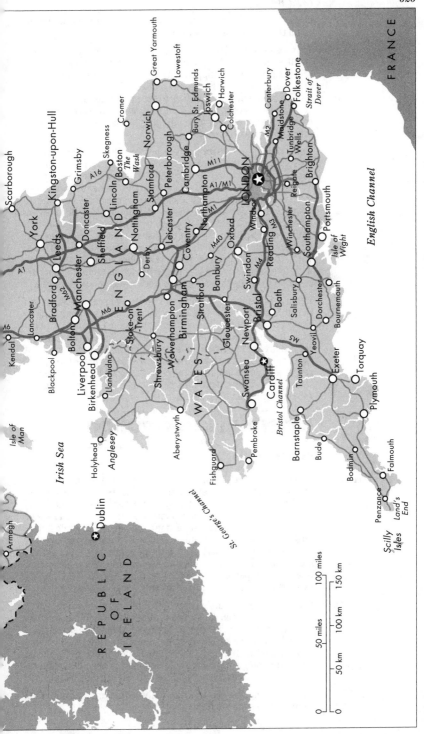

erations of dedicated gardeners who spend more time and money on the plants than they do on their houses.

All these can be visited by everyone, either free or for only a small entrance fee. Make sure, though, before you start on your trip, that you are equipped with as many membership tickets as you can get, from English Heritage, National Trust, and so on. The saving in entrance fees to the properties under the control of these groups can be significant. Most cathedrals are free, though even they are beginning to charge for entrance to offset their vast expenses.

But Britain is not just one huge historic theme park. Many of its most profound pleasures are to be found in wandering through the changing countryside, at any season of the year. Taking a bus for a few hours deep into the open spaces outside a main town can reveal much about the essence of the land and its people. A short ride, for instance, from York, will take you through long stretches of wild, heather-covered moorland, ablaze with color in the fall, or past the steep, sheep-covered mountainsides of the Dales, cut by deep valleys and scattered with stone-built hamlets. If you take a bus from Stratford, you will find a secret world of villages hidden in orchards and surrounded by fields that have been worked for hundreds of years.

If you are centering your trip on London, you can see almost all that it has to offer for free. The city's museums are starting to charge for entry, but the costs of admission are unlikely to become too burdensome. Try the theater ticket booth in Leicester Square for cut-price tickets, not for the sellout shows, but for some good ruuners-up. And you will be surprised, too, how reasonably priced many of the concerts are when you compare them with similar tickets back home—even after taking the rate of exchange into account.

Essential Information

Before You Go

When to Go The main tourist season runs from mid-April to mid-October. In recent years, however, parts of the winter—especially December—have been almost as busy. Winter is also the height of London's theater, ballet, and opera season. Springtime reveals the countryside at its most verdant and beautiful, while fall offers soft vistas of muted, golden color. September and October are the months to visit the northern moorlands and Scottish highlands, while June is best for Wales and the Lake District. Most British people take their vacations during July and August, when costs are high and accommodations at a premium.

Climate On the whole, Britain's climate is a temperate one, although summers have been fairly hot in recent years. Wherever you are, and whatever the season, be prepared for sudden changes. What begins as a brilliant, sunny day often turns into a damp and dismal one by lunchtime. Take an umbrella and raincoat wherever you go, particularly in Scotland, where the temperatures are somewhat cooler and the rainfall more plentiful.

The following are the average daily maximum and minimum temperatures for London.

Jan.	43F	6C	May	62F	17C	Sept.	65F	19C
	36	2		47	8		52	11
Feb.	44F	7C	June	69F	20C	Oct.	58F	14C
	36	2		53	12		46	8
Mar.	50F	10C	July	71F	22C	Nov.	50F	10C
	38	3		56	13		42	6
Apr.	56F	13C	Aug.	71F	22C	Dec.	45F	7C
	42	6		56	13		38	3

Currency The British unit of currency is the pound sterling, divided into 100 pence (p). Bills are issued in denominations of 5, 10, 20, and 50 pounds (£). Coins are £1, 50p, 20p, 10p (the same as the old two-shilling piece, still in circulation), 5p (a new, tiny one), 2p, and 1p. Scottish banks issue Scottish currency, of which all coins and notes—with the exception of the £1 notes—are accepted in England. At press time (summer 1992), the exchange rate was approximately $1.99 to the pound.

Credit cards and traveler's checks are widely accepted in Britain, and many banks, hotels, and shops offer currency-exchange facilities. You will probably lose from 1¢ to 4¢ on the dollar, however, depending on where you change them; banks offer the best rates. In London and other big cities, bureaux de change abound, but it definitely pays to shop around: They usually have a minimum charge of £1 and often a great deal more.

What It Will Cost In general, transportation in Britain is expensive in comparison with other countries. You would be well advised to take advantage of the many reductions and special fares available on trains, buses, and subways. Always ask about these when buying your ticket. Gasoline prices are about the same as those on the Continent.

London now ranks with Tokyo as one of the world's most expensive hotel capitals. Finding budget accommodations—especially during July and August—can be difficult. Many London hotels offer special off-season (October–March) rates, however. Dining out, even in moderate restaurants, can be startlingly expensive, but a large number of pubs offer excellent food at reasonable prices, and fast-food facilities are widespread. Many ethnic restaurants also tend to be better value for your money.

Remember that the gulf between prices in the capital and outside is wide. Take advantage of one ubiquitous bargain: Nearly all state-owned museums are free to visitors. Be prepared to pay a value-added tax (VAT) of 17½% on almost everything you buy; in most cases it is added to the advertised price.

Sample Prices For London: cup of coffee, 80p; pint of beer, £1.40; glass of wine, £1.40; soda, 60p; 1-mile taxi ride, £2.50; ham sandwich, £1.75.

Customs on Arrival There are two levels of duty-free allowance for people entering the United Kingdom: one, for goods bought outside the European Community (EC) or for goods bought in a duty-free shop within the EC; two, for goods bought in an EC country but not in a duty-free shop.

In the first category, you may import duty-free 200 cigarettes or 100 cigarillos or 50 cigars or 250 grams of tobacco *(Note:* If you live outside Europe, these allowances are doubled), plus 1 liter of alcoholic drinks over 22% volume or 2 liters of alcoholic drinks not over 22% volume or fortified or sparkling wine, plus 2 liters of still table wine, plus 50 grams of perfume, plus 9 fluid ounces of toilet water, plus other goods to the value of £32. In the second category, you may import duty-free 300 cigarettes or 150 cigarillos or 75 cigars or 400 grams of tobacco, plus 1½ liters of alcoholic drinks over 22% volume or 3 liters of alcoholic drinks not over 22% volume or fortified or sparkling wine, plus 3 liters of still table wine, plus 75 grams of perfume, plus 13 fluid ounces of toilet water, plus other goods to the value of £420.

In addition, no animals or pets of any kind may be brought into the United Kingdom without a six-month quarantine.

Getting Around

By Train Despite severe financial restrictions and frequent complaints from commuters, Britain offers one of the fastest, safest, and most comfortable rail services in the world. All trains are run by the state-owned **British Rail.**

The country's principal—and most efficient—service is the InterCity network, linking London with every major city in the country. The most modern trains travel up to 125 mph and offer comfortable, air-conditioned cars, with restaurant or buffet facilities. Local train services are not quite as reliable, particularly around congested city centers such as London. In general, seat reservations are not necessary except during peak vacation periods and on popular medium- and long-distance routes. Reserving a standard-class seat costs £1.

Fares British Rail fares are expensive. However, the network does offer a wide range of ticket reductions, and these can make a tremendous difference. The information office in each station is generally the most reliable source of information. Information and tickets can also be obtained from British Rail Travel Centers within the larger train stations and from travel agents displaying the British Rail logo.

One of the best bargains available to overseas visitors is the **BritRail Pass** or the **BritRail Youth Pass,** the U.K. equivalent of the Eurail ticket. It provides unlimited travel over the entire British Rail network (and associated ferry and bus routes) for periods of 8, 14, or 22 days, or one month. The cost of a **BritRail standard ticket** for 8 days is $209; for 15 days, $319; for 22 days, $399; and for a month, $465. The **Youth Pass,** for those aged 16 to 25, provides unlimited second-class travel and costs $169 for 8 days, $255 for 15 days, $319 for 22 days, and $375 for 1 month. The **Senior Citizen Standard Pass** entitles pasengers over 60 to unlimited first-class travel. It costs $189 for 8 days, $289 for 15 days, $359 for 22 days, and $419 for 1 month. These passes can be purchased only outside Britain, either in the United States, before you leave, or in one of 46 other countries. British Rail has its own information offices in New York, Los Angeles, Chicago, Dallas, Vancouver, and Toronto. The quoted prices are in U.S. dollars. Canadian tickets are slightly higher.

If you are planning to travel only short distances, be sure to buy inexpensive same-day return tickets. These cost only slightly more than ordinary one-way, standard-class tickets but can be used only after 9:30 AM and on weekends. Other special offers are regional **Rover** tickets, giving unlimited travel within local areas, and **Saver** returns, allowing greatly reduced round-trip travel during off-peak periods. For information about routes and fares, contact the **British Travel Centre** (12 Regent Street, London SW1Y 4PQ, tel. 071/730–3400). Also inquire at main rail stations for details about reduced-price tickets to specific destinations.

By Plane For a comparatively small country, Britain offers an extensive network of internal air routes. These are run by about a dozen different airlines. Hourly shuttle services operate every day between London and Glasgow, Edinburgh, Belfast, and Manchester. Seats are available on a no-reservations basis, and you can generally check in about half an hour before flight departure time. Keep in mind, however, that Britain's internal air services are not as competitive as those in the United States. And with modern, fast trains and relatively short distances, it is often much cheaper—and not much more time-consuming—to travel by train.

By Bus Buses provide the most economical form of public transportation in Britain. Prices are invariably half that of train tickets, and the network is just as extensive. In recent years, both short- and long-distance buses have improved immeasurably in speed, comfort, and frequency. There is one important semantic difference to keep in mind when discussing bus travel in Britain. Buses (either double- or single-decker) are generally part of the local transportation system in towns and cities and make frequent stops. Coaches, on the other hand, are comparable to American Greyhound buses and are used only for long-distance travel.

National Express offers the largest number of routes of any coach operator in Britain. It also offers a variety of discount tickets, including the **BritExpress Card** for overseas visitors, which covers all the National Express and Scottish Citylink services. This ticket entitles you to one-third off standard fares for any number of trips made during 30 consecutive days on services throughout England and Wales and selected services in Scotland. You can buy it from travel agents in the United States; in London, at the Victoria Coach Station, Buckingham Palace Road, SW1 9TP; or at main train stations in Edinburgh and Glasgow. Information about all services—including bargain fares and special Rover and Explorer tickets—can be obtained from the National Express Information Office at Victoria Coach Station (tel. 071/730–0202) or from **Scottish Omnibuses** (Duke St., Galashiels TD1 1QA, tel. 0896/58484).

The bus companies of Britain have been denationalized for some years now, and they often duplicate routes. However, they almost all offer *Rover* or *Explorer* tickets to their areas, which can be a significant savings.

By Boat Britain offers more than 2,400 kilometers (1,500 miles) of navigable inland waterways—rivers, lakes, canals, locks, and loughs—for leisure travel. Particular regions, such as the Norfolk Broads in East Anglia, the Severn Valley in the West Country, and the sea lochs and canals of Scotland, are especially popular among the nautically minded. Although there are no regularly scheduled waterborne services, hundreds of yachts, canal boats, and motor cruises are available throughout the year. The **British Tourist Authority's** booklet "U.K. Waterway

Holidays" is a good source of information. You can also contact the **Inland Waterways Association** (114 Regents Park Road, London NW1 8UQ, tel. 071/586–2510) or the **British Waterways Board** (Melbury House, Melbury Terr., London NW1 6JX, tel. 071/262–6711).

By Bicycle Cycling provides an excellent way to see the countryside, and most towns—including London—offer bike-rental facilities. Any bike shop or tourist information center should be able to direct you to the nearest rental firm. Rental fees generally run from £15 per day, plus a fairly large deposit, though this can often be put on your credit card. If you're planning a tour and would like information on rental shops and special holidays for cyclists, contact a British Tourist Authority office in the United States before you leave home. Another source for maps and lists of cycle-rental shops is the **Cyclists' Touring Club** (Cotterell House, 69 Meadowrow, Godalming, Surrey GU7 3HS, tel. 0483/417217). Except on InterCity 125 trains and selected London services, British Rail will carry bicycles free of charge.

On Foot Many organizations conduct group walking holidays during the summer months. These are especially popular in the Welsh mountains, the Lake District, Dartmoor, and Exmoor. Details are available from the British Tourist Authority. **The Countryside Commission** (John Dower House, Crescent Place, Cheltenham Glos., GL50 3LR, tel. 0242/521381) also has many useful publications and information about national trails.

Staying in Great Britain

Telephones For years, both foreign tourists and the British themselves have cursed the country's inefficient and antiquated phone system. The recent privatization of British Telecom has brought little improvement, though the system is gradually being modernized. Making a phone call in Britain—especially from a public booth—remains a frustrating experience at best.

Local Calls Public telephones are plentiful in British cities, especially London, although you will ordinarily find a high proportion out of order. Other than on the street, the best place to find a bank of pay phones is in a hotel or large post office. As part of Telecom's modernization efforts, the distinctive red phone booths are gradually being replaced by generic glass and steel cubicles, but the red boxes still remain in a lot of the country. The workings of coin-operated telephones vary, but there are usually intructions in each unit. The oldest kind takes only 10p coins; the new ones take 10p, 20p, 50p, and £1 coins. A Phonecard is also available; it comes in denominations of 10, 20, 40, and 100 units and can be bought in a number of retail outlets. Cardphones are clearly marked with a special green insignia, and they will not accept coins.

A local call during the peak period (9 AM–1 PM) costs 20p for three minutes. Five minutes to the United States, weekday peak, will cost £3.15. Each large city or region in Britain has its own numerical prefix, which is used only when you are dialing from outside the city. In provincial areas, the dialing codes for nearby towns are often posted in the booth, and some even list international codes.

Many British exchanges are being modernized, with an extra digit added to increase the amount of numbers available. We have kept as up-to-date with the new numbers as possible, but these changes are ongoing.

London's 01 prefix was replaced by two three-digit prefixes: 071 for inner London and 081 for outer London. You do not need to dial either if calling from inside the same zone, but you must dial 081 from an 071 number, and vice versa.

International Calls The cheapest way to make an overseas call is to dial it yourself. But be sure to have plenty of coins or Phonecards close at hand. After you have inserted the coins or card, dial 010, the international code, then the country code—for the United States, it is 1—followed by the area code and local number. To make a collect or other operator-assisted call, dial 155.

Operators and For information anywhere in Britain, dial either 142 or 192. For
Information the operator, dial 100.

Mail Airmail letters to the United States and Canada cost 39p; post-
Postal Rates cards, 33p; aerograms, 34p. Letters and postcards to Europe weighing up to 20 grams cost 29p (24p to EC-member countries). Letters within the United Kingdom: first-class, 24p; second-class and postcards, 18p. These rates will have increased by early 1993.

Receiving Mail If you're uncertain where you'll be staying, you can arrange to have your mail sent to American Express, 6 Haymarket, London SW1Y 4BS. The service is free to cardholders; all others pay a small fee. You can also collect letters at London's main post office. Ask to have them sent to Poste Restante, Main Post Office, London. The point of collection is King Edward Building, King Edward Street, London EC1A 1AA. Hours are Monday, Tuesday, Thursday, and Friday 8 AM–7 PM; Wednesday 8:30 AM–7 PM; and Saturday 9 AM–12:30 PM. You'll need your passport or other official form of identification.

Shopping Foreign visitors can avoid Britain's crippling 17½% value-
VAT Refunds added tax (VAT) by taking advantage of a variety of special refund and export schemes. The easiest and most common way of getting a refund is the Over-the-Counter method. To qualify for this, you must buy goods worth £50 or more (stores vary; if you are from the EC, it can be as much as £420). The shopkeeper will attach a special paper—Form VAT 407—to the invoice, and upon leaving the United Kingdom, you present the goods, form, and invoice to the customs officer. Allow plenty of time to do this at the airport. There are often long lines. The form is then returned to the store, and the refund forwarded to you, minus a small service charge. The Direct Export method is another option. With this method, you are also issued Form VAT 407, but your purchases are sent home separately, and upon returning home, you must have the form certified by customs or a notary public. You then return the form to the store, and your money is refunded.

Opening and **Banks.** Banks are open weekdays 9:30–3:30. Some have ex-
Closing Times tended hours on Thursday evenings, and a few are open on Saturday mornings.

Museums. Museum hours vary considerably from one part of the country to another. In large cities, most open on weekdays 10–5; many are also open on Sunday afternoons. The majority close one day a week. Holiday closings vary, so be sure to check individual listings. Be sure, also, to double-check the opening times of historic houses, especially if the visit involves a difficult trip.

Shops. Usual business hours are Monday–Saturday 9–5:30. Outside the main centers, most shops observe an early closing day once a week, often Wednesday or Thursday; they close at 1 PM and do not reopen until the following morning. In small villages, many also close for lunch. In large cities—especially London—department stores stay open for late-night shopping (usually until 7:30 or 8) one day midweek. Apart from some newsstands and small food stores, almost all shops are closed on Sunday.

National Holidays England and Wales: January 1; April 9 (Good Friday); April 12 (Easter Monday); May 3 (May Day); May 31 (Spring Bank Holiday); August 30 (Summer Bank Holiday); December 25, 26. Scotland: January 1, 2; April 9; May 3, 31; August 30, December 25, 26.

Guided Tours **Guide Friday** is one of Britain's leading guided tour operators. They have tours of all the towns we list outside London, Bath, Cambridge, Edinburgh, Oxford, Stratford-upon-Avon, Windsor, and York. Prices vary with the complexity of the route, but they are usually £4 or £4.50 for an adult, £1 for children, and £3.50 for a senior citizen. More than a million visitors take tours, which are an excellent way of seeing the sights in a short time. If you buy a Great British Cities ticket, you can take in five cities for £19, including London. Guide Friday telephone numbers are: Bath, 0225/444102; Cambridge, 0223/62444; Edinburgh, 031/556–2244; Stratford, 0789/294466; Windsor, 0753/855755; and York, 0904/645151.

Dining Until relatively recently, British food was condemned the world over for its plainness and mediocrity. But nowadays the problem is not so much bad food as expensive food. The best of traditional British cooking is solid and straightforward and dependent on top-quality, fresh materials, such as succulent spring beef and seasonal vegetables. The worst consists of heavy, starchy foods, overboiled and deep-fat fried, and vegetables boiled to within an inch of their lives.

Mealtimes These vary somewhat, depending on the region of the country you are visiting. But in general, breakfast is served between 7:30 and 9 and lunch between noon and 2. Tea—an essential and respected part of British tradition and often a meal in itself—is generally served between 4:30 and 5:30. Dinner or supper is served between 7:30 and 9:30, sometimes earlier, but rarely later outside the metropolitan areas. High tea, at about 6, replaces dinner in some areas, and in large cities, after-theater suppers are often available.

Dress Jacket and tie are suggested for the more formal restaurants in the top-price categories, but, in general, casual chic or informal dress is acceptable in most establishments.

Ratings Prices quoted here are per person and include a first course, a main course, and dessert, but not wine or service. Best bets are indicated by a star ★.

Category	Cost
Moderate	£20–£30
Inexpensive	£15–£20
Budget	under £15

Lodging Britain offers a wide variety of accommodations, ranging from enormous, top-quality, top-price hotels to simple, intimate farmhouses and guest houses.

Hotels Expensive is practically the rule in Britain. You can pay an arm and a leg for a night's lodging if you don't check the prices in advance. We have included some hotels within a moderate price range among our selections: These tend to be guest houses masquerading under the name "hotel," but none the worse for that. You have to make a decision. Do you want to pay through the nose for a night's oblivion in fancy, overpriced surroundings, or would you rather spend your money while conscious. You will find that guest houses and B&Bs offer you the best value around.

A useful budget tip is to be sure to ask for a hotel's weekend rates. They often reduce their rates by as much as a half on weekends, when their business guests have gone home to their families, leaving the hotels with many empty rooms. That way you can stay at a notable hotel in splendid comfort that you would not otherwise even contemplate.

Bed-and-Breakfasts B&Bs and their slightly snootier cousins, guest houses, are, generally speaking, private houses that take in guests. The heaviest concentrations of them in Britain are in the resorts where the Brits normally take their holidays: Brighton, Blackpool, Penzance, but they are to be found everywhere in lesser numbers. Many of them are in big Victorian houses, built before the days of family planning, when there were bedrooms for rafts of children.

Many of our selections have only half the number of baths and showers than bedrooms, or even less. All of these places will have communal bathrooms, and you can greatly reduce your expenditure by going for a room without bath. All rooms will almost certainly have a washbasin. You should work out the room-to-bath ratio. Three or four rooms to a bath is acceptable, six or more probably isn't.

B&Bs, as their name tells you, will provide breakfast, often far better than you will get in a full-fledged hotel.

All tourist offices have lists of B&Bs and guest houses, and the central organizations produce national lists. The English Tourist Board has an annual *Hotels and Guesthouses of England*, Wales does a *Bed and Breakfast* guide, Scotland's is called *Hotels and Guest Houses*.

Farmhouses Such accommodations have become increasingly popular in recent years. Farmhouses rarely offer professional hotel standards, but they have a special appeal: the rustic, rural experience. Prices are generally very reasonable. Ask for the British Tourist Authority booklets "Farmhouse Vacations" and "Stay on a Farm." A car is vital for a successful farmhouse stay.

Holiday Cottages Furnished apartments, houses, cottages, and trailers are available for weekly rental in all areas of the country. These vary from quaint, cleverly converted farmhouses to brand-new buildings set in scenic surroundings. For families and large groups, they offer the best value-for-money accommodations. Lists of rental properties are available free of charge from the British Tourist Authority. Discounts of up to 50% apply during the off-season (October to March).

University Housing In larger cities and in some towns, certain universities offer their residence halls to paying vacationers. The facilities available are usually compact sleeping units, and they can be rented on a nightly basis. For information, contact the **British Universities Accommodation Consortium** (Box 773, University Park, Nottingham NG7 2RD, tel. 0602/504571).

Youth Hostels There are more than 350 youth hostels throughout England, Wales, and Scotland. They range from very basic to very good. Many are located in remote and beautiful areas; others can be found on the outskirts of large cities. Despite the name, there is no age restriction. The accommodations are inexpensive and generally reliable and usually include cooking facilities. For additional information, contact the **YHA Headquarters** (Trevelyan House, 8 St. Stephen's Hill, St. Albans, Hertfordshire AL1 2DY, tel. 0727/55215).

Camping Britain offers an abundance of campsites. Some are large and well equipped; others are merely small farmers' fields, offering primitive facilities. For information, contact the British Travel Authority in the United States or the **Camping and Caravan Club, Ltd.** (Greenfields House, Westwood Way, Coventry CV4 8JH, tel. 0203/694995).

Ratings Prices are for two people in a double room and include all taxes. Best bets are indicated by a star ★.

Category	London	Other Areas
Moderate	£55–£100	£50–£70
Inexpensive	£40–£55	£35–£50
Budget	under £40	under £35

Tipping Some restaurants and most hotels add a service charge of 10%–15% to the bill. Check if this has been done. In this case you are not expected to tip. If no service charge is indicated, add 10% to your total bill. Taxi drivers should also get 10%. You are not expected to tip theater or cinema ushers, elevator operators, or bartenders in pubs. Hairdressers and barbers should receive 10%–15%.

London

Arriving and Departing

By Plane International flights to London arrive at either Heathrow Airport, 19.4 kilometers (12 miles) west of London, or at Gatwick Airport, 40.3 kilometers (25 miles) south of the capital. Most—but not all—flights from the United States go to Heathrow, while Gatwick generally serves European destinations, often with charter flights.

Between the Airport and Downtown The Piccadilly Line serves Heathrow (all terminals) with a direct Underground (subway) link. The 40-minute ride costs £2.50 at press time. Three special buses also serve Heathrow: A1 leaves every 30 minutes for Victoria Station; A2 goes to Euston Station every 30 minutes and takes 80 minutes; night bus N97 runs hourly from midnight to 5 AM into central London. The one-way cost is £5.

From Gatwick, the quickest way to London is the nonstop rail Gatwick Express, costing (at press time) £7 one-way and taking 30 minutes to reach Victoria Station. Regular bus services are provided by Greenline Coaches, including the Flightline 777 to Victoria Station. This takes about 70 minutes and costs £6 one-way.

Cars and taxis drive into London on the M4; the trip can take more than an hour, depending on traffic. The taxi fare is about £25. If you are driving from Gatwick, take M23 and then A23 to central London. The taxi fare is about £35.

By Train London is served by no fewer than 15 train stations, so be absolutely certain of the station for your departure or arrival. All have Underground stations either in the train station or within a few minutes' walk from it, and most are served by several bus routes. British Rail controls all major services. The principal routes that connect London to other major towns and cities are on an InterCity network; unlike its European counterparts, British Rail makes no extra charge for the use of this express service network.

Seats can be reserved by phone only with a credit card. You can, of course, apply in person to any British Rail Travel Centre or directly to the station from which you depart. Below is a list of the major London rail stations and the areas they serve.

Charing Cross (tel. 071/928–5100) serves southeast England, including Canterbury, Margate, Dover/Folkestone.
Euston/St. Pancras (tel. 071/387–7070) serves East Anglia, Essex, the Northeast, the Northwest, and North Wales, including Coventry, Stratford-upon-Avon, Birmingham, Manchester, Liverpool, Windermere, Glasgow, and Inverness.
King's Cross (tel. 071/278–2477) serves the east Midlands; the Northeast, including York, Leeds, and Newcastle; and north and east Scotland, including Edinburgh and Aberdeen.
Liverpool Street (tel. 071/928–5100) serves Essex and East Anglia.
Paddington (tel. 071/262–6767) serves the south Midlands, west and south Wales, and the west country, including Reading, Bath, Bristol, Oxford, Cardiff, Swansea, Exeter, Plymouth, and Penzance.
Victoria (tel. 071/928–5100) serves southern England, including Gatwick Airport, Brighton, Dover/Folkestone (from May), and the south coast.
Waterloo (tel. 071/928–5100) serves the southwestern United Kingdom, including Salisbury, Bournemouth, Portsmouth, Southampton, Isle of Wight, Jersey, and Guernsey.

Fares There is a wide, bewildering range of "savers" and other ticket bargains. Unfortunately, ticket clerks cannot always be relied on to know which type best suits your needs, so be sure to ask at the information office first. **Cheap Day Returns** are best if you're returning to London the same day, and many family and other discount railcards are available. You can hear a recorded summary of timetable and fare information to many InterCity destinations by dialing the appropriate "dial and listen" numbers listed under British Rail in the telephone book.

By Bus The **National Express** coach service has routes to over 1,000 major towns and cities in the United Kingdom. It's considerably cheaper than the train, although the trips usually take longer. National Express offers two types of service: an ordinary service, which makes frequent stops for refreshment breaks, and a Rapide service, which has hostess and refreshment facilities on board. Day returns are available on both, but booking is advised on the Rapide service. National Express coaches leave Victoria Coach Station (Buckingham Palace Rd.) at regular intervals, depending on the destination. For travel information, dial 071/730–0202. For reservations with a credit card, dial 071/730–3499.

Getting Around

By Underground Known as "the tube," London's extensive Underground system is by far the most widely used form of city transportation. Trains run both beneath and above ground out into the suburbs, and all stations are clearly marked with the London Underground circular symbol. (A "subway" sign refers to an under-the-street crossing.) Trains are all one class; smoking is *not* allowed on board or in the stations.

There are ten basic lines—all named—plus the East London line, which runs from Shoreditch and Whitechapel across the Thames south to New Cross, and the Docklands Light Railway, which runs from Stratford in London's East End to Greenwich, with an extension to the Royal Docks to be completed. The Central, District, Northern, Metropolitan, and Piccadilly lines all have branches, so be sure to note which branch is needed for your particular distination. Electronic platform signs tell you the final stop and route of the next train, and some signs also indicate how many minutes you'll have to wait for the train to arrive.

From Monday to Saturday, trains begin running around 5:30 AM; the last services leave central London between midnight and 12:30 AM. On Sundays, trains start two hours later and finish about an hour earlier. The frequency of trains depends on the route and the time of day, but normally you should not have to wait more than 10 minutes in central areas.

A pocket map of the entire tube network is available free from most Underground ticket counters. There should also be a large map on the wall of each platform—though often these are defaced beyond recognition.

Fares For both buses and tube fares, London is divided into six concentric zones; the fare goes up the farther afield you travel. Ask at Underground ticket counters for the London Transport (LT) booklet "Tickets," which gives details of all the various ticket options and bargains for the tube; after some experimenting, you'll soon know which ticket best serves your particular needs. Till then, here is a brief summary of the major ticket categories, but note that these prices are subject to increases.

Singles and Returns. For one trip between any two stations, you can buy an ordinary single for travel anytime on the day of issue; if you're coming back on the same route the same day, then an ordinary return costs twice the single fare. Singles vary in price from 70p in the central zone to £2.30 for a six-zone journey—not a good option for the sightseer who wants to make several journeys.

Cheap Day Return. Issued weekdays after 9:30 AM and anytime on weekends, these are basically good for one return journey within the six zones.

One-Day Off-Peak Travelcards. These allow unrestricted travel on the tube, most buses, and British Rail trains in the Greater London zones and are valid weekdays after 9:30 AM, weekends, and all public holidays. They cannot be used on airbuses, night buses, Route 128, for special services, or on tours and excursions. The price is £2.30–£3.10.

Visitor's Travelcard. These are the best bet for visitors, but they must be bought before leaving home and are available both in the United States and Canada. They are valid for periods of one, three, four, or seven days ($6, $18, $23, $40) and can be used on the tube and virtually all buses and British Rail services in London. This card also includes a set of money-saving discounts to many of London's top attractions. Apply to travel agents or to BritRail Travel International.

For more information, there are **LT Travel Information Centres** at the following tube stations: Euston, *open Sat.–Thurs. 7:15–6, Fri. to 7:30;* King's Cross, *open Sat.–Thurs. 8:15–6, Fri. to 7:30;* Oxford Circus, *open Mon.–Sat. 8:15–6;* Piccadilly Circus, *open Mon.–Sun. 8:15–6;* Victoria, *open Mon.–Sun. 8:15–9:30;* and Heathrow, *open Mon.–Sun. (to 9 or 10 PM in Terminals 1 and 2).* For information on all London bus and tube times, fares, etc., dial 071/222–1234; the line is operated 24 hours.

By Bus London's bus system now consists of the bright red double- and single-deckers, plus, in the outer zones, other buses of various colors. Destinations are displayed on the front and back, with the bus number on the front, back, and side. By no means do all buses run the full length of their route at all times, so always check the termination point before boarding, preferably with the conductor or driver. Many buses are still operated with a conductor whom you pay after finding a seat, but there is now a move to one-man buses, in which you pay the driver upon boarding.

Buses stop only at clearly indicated stops. Main stops—at which the bus *should* stop automatically—have a plain white background with a red LT symbol on it. There are also request stops with red signs, a white symbol, and the word "Request" added; at these you must hail the bus to make it stop. Smoking is not allowed on any bus. Although you can see much of the town from a bus, *don't* take one if you want to get anywhere in a hurry; traffic often slows travel to a crawl, and during peak times you may find yourself waiting at least 20 minutes for a bus and not being able to get on it once it arrives. If you intend to go by bus, ask at a Travel Information Centre for a free London Wide Bus Map.

Fares Single fares start at 50p for short distances (70p in the central zone). Travelcards are good for tube, bus, and British Rail trains in the Greater London Zones. There are also a number of bus passes available for daily, weekly, and monthly use, and prices vary according to zones. A photograph is required for weekly or monthly bus passes; this also applies to children and older children who may need a child-rate photocard to avoid paying the adult rate.

By Boat The **Thamesline Riverbus** operates between Chelsea and Greenwich, with seven stops between. For information, call 071/512–0555.

Important Addresses and Numbers

Tourist Information The main **London Tourist Information Centre** at Victoria Station Forecourt provides details about London and the rest of Britain, including general information; tickets for tube and bus; theater, concert, and tour bookings; and accommodations. Telephone information service: 071/730–3488. Open Apr.–Oct., daily 9–8:30; rest of the year, Mon.–Sat. 9–7, Sun. 9–5.

Other information centers are located in **Harrods** (Brompton Rd., SW1 7XL) and **Selfridges** (Oxford St., W1A 2LR) and are open store hours only; at **Tower of London** (West Gate, EC3W 4AB), open summer months only; and **Heathrow Airport** (Terminals 1, 2, and 3). The **City of London Information Centre** (St. Paul's Churchyard, EC4M 8BX, tel. 071/606–3030) has information on sights and events in the City. Open May–Oct., daily 9:30–5; Nov.–Apr., weekdays 9:30–5, Sat. 9:30–12:30.

The **British Travel Centre** (12 Regent St., SW1Y 4PQ, tel. 071/730–3400) provides details about travel, accommodations, and entertainment for the whole of Britain. Open weekdays 9–6:30 and weekends 10–4.

Embassies and Consulates **American Embassy** (24 Grosvenor Sq., W1A, 1AE, tel. 071/499–9000). Located inside the embassy is the **American Aid Society,** a charity set up to help Americans in distress. Dial the embassy number and ask for extension 570 or 571.

Canadian High Commission (Canada House, Trafalgar Sq., London SW1 Y 5BJ, tel. 071/629–9492).

Emergencies For police, fire brigade, or ambulance, dial 999.

The following **hospitals** have 24-hour emergency rooms: **Guys** (St. Thomas St., SE1, tel. 071/955–5000); **Royal Free** (Pond St., Hampstead, NW3, tel. 071/794–0500); **St. Bartholomew's** (West Smithfield, EC1, tel. 071/601–8888); **St. Thomas's** (Lambeth Palace Rd., SE1, tel. 071/928–9292); **University College** (Gower St., W1, tel. 071/387–9300); **Westminster** (Dean Ryle St., Horseferry Rd., SW1, tel. 071/828–9811, adults only).

Credit Cards Should your credit cards be lost or stolen, here are some numbers to dial for assistance: **Access (MasterCard)** (tel. 0702/352244 or 352255); **American Express** (tel. 071/222–9633, 24 hours, or 0273/696933 8–6 only for credit cards, tel. 0800/521313 for traveler's checks); **Barclaycard (Visa)** (tel. 0604/230230); **Diners Club** (tel. 0252/516261).

Exploring London

Traditionally London has been divided between the City, to the east, where its banking and commercial interests lie, and Westminster to the west, the seat of the royal court and of government. In these two areas stand the Tower of London and St. Paul's Cathedral, Westminster Abbey and the Houses of Parliament, Buckingham Palace, and the older royal palace of St. James's. Other parts of London worth exploring include Covent Garden, where a former fruit and flower market has been converted into a lively shopping and entertainment center Hyde Park and Kensington Gardens, which cut a great swathe of green parkland across the city center; the museum district of South Kensington; the South Bank Arts Complex; and Hayward Gallery. The views from the gallery are stunning—to the west are the Houses of Parliament and Big Ben, to the east the dome of St. Paul's is just visible on London's changing skyline. The key to London is a simple one. Explore for yourself off the beaten track. Use your feet, and when you're tired, take to the bus or the Underground. And look around you, for London's centuries of history and its vibrant daily life are revealed as much in the individual streets and houses of the city as in its grand national monuments and galleries.

Numbers in the margin correspond to points of interest on the London map.

Westminster **Westminster** is the royal backyard—the traditional center of the royal court and of government. Here, within a kilometer or so of each other, are virtually all London's most celebrated buildings (St. Paul's Cathedral and the Tower of London excepted), and there is a strong feeling of history all around you. Generations of kings and queens and their offspring have lived here since the end of the 11th century, in no less than four palaces, three of which (Buckingham, St. James's, and Westminster) still stand.

❶ Start at **Trafalgar Square,** which is on the site of the former Royal Mews. Both the square's name and its present appearance date from about 1830. A statue of Lord Nelson, victor over the French in 1805 at the Battle of Trafalgar, at which he lost his life, stands atop a column. Lions guard the base of the column, which is decorated with four bronze panels depicting naval battles against France and cast from French cannons captured by Nelson. The bronze equestrian statue on the south side of the square is of the unhappy Charles I; he is looking down Whitehall toward the spot where he was executed in 1649.

❷ In the **National Gallery,** which occupies the long neoclassical building on the north side of the square, is a comprehensive collection of paintings, with works from virtually every famous artist and school from the 14th to the 19th century. The gallery is especially strong on Flemish and Dutch masters, Rubens and Rembrandt among them, and on Italian Renaissance works. The recently completed Sainsbury Wing houses the early Renaissance collection. *Trafalgar Sq., tel. 071/839–3321; 071/839–3526 (recorded information). Admission free. Open Mon.–Sat. 10–6, Sun. 2–6; June–Aug., Wed. until 8.*

❸ Around the corner, at the foot of Charing Cross Road, is a second major art collection, the **National Portrait Gallery,** which contains portraits of well-known (and not so well-known) Britons, including monarchs, statesmen, and writers. *2 St. Martin's Pl., tel. 071/930–1552. Admission free. Open weekdays 10–5, Sat. 10–6, Sun. 2–6.*

❹ The Gallery's entrance is opposite the distinctive neoclassical church of **St. Martin-in-the-Fields,** built in about 1730. Regular lunchtime music recitals are held here.

London

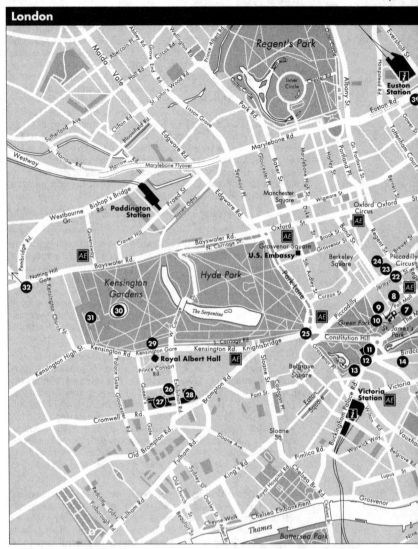

Admiralty Arch, **5**

Albert Memorial, **29**

Bank of England, **45**

Banqueting House, **20**

Barbican, **42**

British Museum, **38**

Buckingham Palace, **11**

Cabinet War Rooms, **15**

Carlton House Terrace, **6**

Cenotaph, **19**

Clarence House, **10**

Covent Garden, **33**

Guildhall, **43**

Horse Guards Parade, **21**

Hyde Park Corner, **25**

Jewish Museum, **39**

Kensington Palace, **31**

Lancaster House, **9**

Leadenhall Market, **48**

Lloyd's of London, **49**

London Transport Museum, **35**

Mansion House, **47**

Museum of London, **41**

Museum of Mankind, **24**

National Gallery, **2**

National Portrait Gallery, **3**

Natural History Museum, **27**

Palace of Westminster, **17**

Parliament Square, **16**

Portobello Road, **32**

Queen's Gallery, **12**

Round Pond, **30**

Royal Academy, **23**

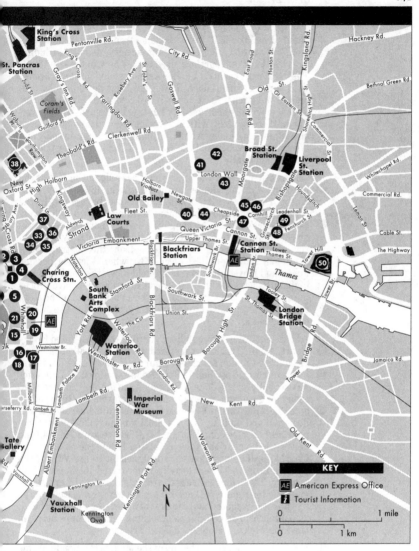

⑤ Admiralty Arch guards the entrance to **The Mall,** the great ceremonial way that leads alongside **St. James's Park** to Buckingham Palace. The Mall takes its name from a game called "pell mell," a version of croquet that society people, including Charles II and his courtiers, used to play here in the late 1600s. The park, one of central London's smallest and most attractive, with superbly maintained flowerbeds, was developed by successive monarchs, most recently by George IV in the 1820s, having originally been used for hunting by Henry VIII. Join office workers relaxing with a lunchtime sandwich, or stroll here on a summer's evening when the illuminated fountains play and Westminster Abbey and the Houses of Parliament beyond the trees are floodlit.

On the other side of the Mall, you'll pass along the foot of the **⑥** imposing **Carlton House Terrace,** built in 1827–32 by John Nash. A right turn up Marlborough Road brings you to the complex of royal and government buildings known collectively **⑦** as **St. James's Palace.** Although the earliest parts of this lovely brick building date from the 1530s, it had a relatively short career as the center of royal affairs, from the destruction of Whitehall Palace in 1698 until 1837, when Victoria became queen and moved the royal household down the road to Buckingham Palace. A number of royal functionaries have offices here, however, and various court functions are held in the state rooms. Foreign ambassadors are still accredited to the "Court of St. James's."

At the end of Marlborough Road, beyond the open-sided **Friary ⑧ Court,** turn left along **Cleveland Row,** and walk past **York House,** the London home of the duke and duchess of Kent. An- **⑨** other left turn into **Stable Yard Road** takes you to **Lancaster House,** built for the duke of York by Nash in the 1820s and used today for government receptions and conferences. On the other **⑩** side of Stable Yard is **Clarence House,** so called because it was designed and built by Nash in 1825 for the duke of Clarence, who later became King William IV. It was restored in 1949 and is now the home of the Queen Mother. Inside the palace is the **Chapel Royal,** said to have been designed for Henry VIII by the painter Holbein; it was heavily redecorated in the mid-19th century. The ceiling still has the initials H and A, intertwined, standing for Henry VIII and his second wife, Anne Boleyn, the mother of Elizabeth I and the first of his wives to lose her head. The public can attend Sunday morning services here between the first week of October and Good Friday.

⑪ Buckingham Palace, at the end of the Mall, is the London home of the queen and the administrative hub of the entire royal family. When the queen is in residence (on weekdays except in January, August, September, and part of June), the royal standard flies over the east front. Inside there are dozens of splendid state rooms used on such formal occasions as banquets for visiting heads of state. The private apartments of Queen Elizabeth and Prince Philip are in the north wing. Behind the palace lie some 40 acres of private gardens, a haven for wildlife in the midst of the capital.

The ceremony of the **Changing of the Guard** takes place in front of the palace at 11:30 daily, April through July, and on alternate days during the rest of the year. It's advisable to arrive early; the Queen Victoria Memorial in the middle of the traffic round-about provides a grandstand view.

Buckingham Palace is not open to the public. The former chapel, bombed during World War II and rebuilt in 1961, has been converted into the **Queen's Gallery,** however, where regular exhibitions are drawn from the vast royal art collections. *Buckingham Palace Rd., tel. 071/799-2331. Admission: £2 adults, £1 children, £1.50 senior citizens. Open Tues.–Sat. 10:30–4:30, Sun. 2–4:30; closed between exhibitions.*

Just along Buckingham Palace Road from the Queen's Gallery is the **Royal Mews,** where some of the queen's horses are stabled and the elaborately gilded state coaches are on view. *Tel. 071/ 799-2331. Admission: £1.30 adults, 70p children, £1 senior citizens. Open Wed. and Thurs. 2–4; closed during state occasions involving royal carriage processions and during Royal Ascot week (June).*

Birdcage Walk, so called because it was once the site of the royal aviaries, runs along the south side of St. James's Park, past the **Wellington Barracks.** These are the regimental headquarters of the Guards Division, the elite troops that traditionally guard the sovereign and mount the guard at Buckingham Palace. The **Guards Museum** relates the history of the Guards from the 1660s to the present; paintings of battle scenes, uniforms, and a cat o'nine tails are among the items on display. *Tel. 071/930-4466, ext. 3430. Admission: £2 adults, £1 children under 16 and senior citizens. Open Sat.–Thurs. 10–4.*

The **Cabinet War Rooms,** between the Foreign Office and the Home Office, are the underground offices used by the British High Command during World War II. Among the rooms on display are the Prime Minister's Room, from which Winston Churchill made many of his inspiring wartime broadcasts, and the Transatlantic Telephone Room, from which he spoke directly to President Roosevelt in the White House. *Clive Steps, King Charles St., tel. 071/930-6961. Admission: £3.60 adults, £1.80 children under 16, £2.70 senior citizens. Open daily 10–5:15.*

Parliament Square is flanked, on the river side, by the Palace of Westminster. Among the statues of statesmen long since dead are those of Churchill, Abraham Lincoln, and Oliver Cromwell, the Lord Protector of England during the country's sole, brief republican period (1648–60).

The **Palace of Westminster** was the monarch's main residence from the 11th century until 1512, when the court moved to the newly built Whitehall Palace. The only part of the original building to have survived, however, is **Westminster Hall,** which has a fine hammer-beam roof. The rest was destroyed in a disastrous fire in 1834 and was rebuilt in the newly popular mock-medieval Gothic style with ornate interior decorations. The architect, Augustus Pugin, provided many delightful touches, such as Gothic umbrella stands. In addition to Westminster Hall, which is used only on rare ceremonial occasions, the palace contains the debating chambers and committee rooms of the two Houses of Parliament—the Commons (whose members are elected) and the Lords (whose members are appointed or inherit their seats). There are no tours of the palace, but the public is admitted to the Public Gallery of each House; expect to wait in line for several hours (the line for the Lords is generally much shorter than that for the Commons).

The most famous features of the palace are its towers. At the south end is the 104-meter (336-foot) **Victoria Tower** (currently undergoing restoration). At the other end is **St. Stephen's Tower,** better known, but inaccurately so, as Big Ben. That name properly belongs to the 13-ton bell in the tower on which the hours are struck; Big Ben himself was Sir Benjamin Hall, commissioner of works when the bell was installed in the 1850s. A light shines from the top of the tower during a night sitting of Parliament.

⑱ Westminster Abbey is the most ancient of London's great churches and the most important, for it is here that Britain's monarchs are crowned. It is unusual for a church of this size and national importance not to be a cathedral. The abbey dates largely from the 13th and 14th centuries, although **Henry VII's Chapel,** an exquisite example of the heavily decorated late Gothic style, was not built until the early 1600s, and the twin towers over the west entrance are an 18th-century addition. There is much to see inside, including the memorial to Winston Churchill; the tomb of the Unknown Warrior, a nameless World War I soldier buried in earth brought with his corpse from France; and Poets' Corner, where some of the country's finest writers are commemorated. Behind the high altar are the royal tombs, including those of Queen Elizabeth I, Mary Queen of Scots, and Henry V. In the Chapel of Edward the Confessor stands the Coronation Chair. Among the royal weddings that have taken place here are those of the present queen and most recently, in 1986, the duke and duchess of York.

It is all too easy to forget, swamped by the crowds trying to see the abbey's sights, that this is a place of worship. Early morning is a good moment to catch something of the building's atmosphere. Better still, take time to attend a service. *Broad Sanctuary, tel. 071/222–5152. Admission to the nave is free, to Poets' Corner and Royal Chapels, £3 adults, £1.50 children, students, and senior citizens (Royal Chapels, free Wed. 6–7:45 PM). Open weekdays 9–4, Sat. 9–2 and 3:45–5; Sun. all day for services only; museum and cloisters open Sun.; closed weekdays to visitors during services; Royal Chapels closed Sun. No photography except Mon. evening.*

The Norman **Undercroft,** off the original monastic cloisters, houses a small museum with exhibits on the abbey's history. In the **Pyx Chamber** next door are fine examples of silver vessels and other treasures. The nearby **Chapter House** was where the English Parliament first met. *Tel. 071/222–5152. Joint admission: £1.80 adults, £1 students and senior citizens, 40p children. Open daily 10:30–1:45.*

⑲ From Parliament Square, walk up **Parliament Street** and **Whitehall** (this is a single street—its name changes), past government offices, toward Trafalgar Square. The **Cenotaph,** in the middle of the road, is the national memorial to the dead of both world wars. On the left is the entrance to **Downing Street,** an unassuming row of 18th-century houses. The prime minister's office is at No. 10 (he has a private apartment on the top floor). The chancellor of the exchequer, the finance minister, occupies No. 11.

⑳ On the right side of Whitehall is the **Banqueting House,** built by the architect Inigo Jones in 1625 for court entertainments. This is the only part of Whitehall Palace, the monarch's principal residence in the 16th and 17th centuries, that was not burned down in 1698. It has a magnificent ceiling by Rubens, and outside there is an inscription that marks the window through which King Charles I stepped to his execution. *Tel. 071/930–4179. Admission: £2 adults, £1.50 students and senior citizens, £1.35 children. Open Tues.–Sat. 10–5, Sun. 2–5.*

㉑ Opposite is the entrance to **Horse Guards Parade,** the former tilt yard of Whitehall Palace. This is the site of the annual ceremony of Trooping the Colour, when the queen takes the salute in the great military parade that marks her official birthday on the second Saturday in June (her real one is on April 21). There is also a daily guard-changing ceremony outside the guard house, at 11 AM (10 on Sunday).

St. James's and Mayfair After such a concentrated dose of grand, historical buildings, it's time to explore two of London's elegant shopping areas. Start by walking west from Piccadilly Circus along **Piccadilly,** which contains a mixture of airline offices, shops (including **Hatchards,** the booksellers, and **Fortnum and Mason,** the queen's grocer), and academic societies.

㉒ **St. James's Church** was designed by the 17th-century architect Christopher Wren and contains beautiful wood carvings by Grinling Gibbons.

Jermyn Street, south of Piccadilly, is famous for upscale shops selling costly shirts, ties, and sweaters. **Paxton & Whitfield** sells an extraordinary variety of cheeses. Shops along **Duke Street** and **Bury Street** specialize in paintings, the former in Old Masters, the latter in early English watercolors. Don't be put off by the exclusive appearance of these establishments—anyone is free to enter, and there is no obligation to buy. **King Street** is home to **Christie's,** the fine art auctioneer, and to **Spink and Son,** renowned for Oriental art.

On the north side of Piccadilly, **Burlington House** contains the offices of many learned societies and the headquarters of the ㉓ **Royal Academy.** The RA, as it is generally known, stages major visiting art exhibitions. The best known is the Summer Exhibition (May–Aug.), featuring works by living British artists.

Burlington Arcade, beside the RA, is a covered walkway with tiny shops selling primarily jewelry and craft goods, such as woolens. Built in 1819, it was the first shopping precinct in the country, and it retains something of its original atmosphere. A uniformed beadle is on duty to ensure that no one runs, whistles, or sings here.

㉔ The **Museum of Mankind,** behind the RA, contains the British Museum's ethnographic collection, though this will shortly be transferred to the British Museum when the British Library moves to its new premises in St. Pancras. There are displays on the South Seas, the Arctic, and other regions of the world. *6 Burlington Gardens, tel. 071/437–2224. Admission free. Open Mon.–Sat. 10–5, Sun. 2:30–6.*

There are three special shopping streets in this section of Mayfair, each with its own specialties. **Savile Row** is the home of gentlemen's tailors. Nearby **Cork Street** has many dealers in modern and classical art. **Bond Street** (divided into two parts, Old and New, though both are some 300 years old) is the classiest shopping street in London, the home of haute couture, with such famous names as **Gucci, Hermès,** and **St. Laurent,** and costly jewelry from such shops as **Asprey, Tiffany,** and **Cartier.**

Some of the original 18th-century houses survive on the west side of **Berkeley Square.** Farther along is **Curzon Street,** which runs along the northern edge of **Shepherd Market,** a maze of narrow streets full of antiques shops, restaurants, and pubs that retain something of a village atmosphere.

Hyde Park and Beyond
㉕ A great expanse of green parkland begins at **Hyde Park Corner** and cuts right across the center of London. **Hyde Park,** which covers about 137 hectares (340 acres), was originally a royal hunting ground, while **Kensington Gardens,** which adjoins it to the west, started life as part of the royal Kensington Palace. These two parks contain many fine trees and are a haven for wildlife. The sandy track that runs along the south edge of the parks has been a fashionable riding trail for centuries. Though it's called **Rotten Row,** there's nothing rotten about it. The name derives from *route du roi* ("the King's Way")—the route William III and Queen Mary took from their home at Kensington Palace to the court at St. James's. There is boating and swimming in the **Serpentine,** the S-shaped lake formed by damming a stream that used to flow here. Refreshments can be had at the Serpentine bars, buffet, and restaurant complex, and the **Serpentine Gallery** holds temporary exhibitions of modern art (tel. 071/402-6075).

㉖ Leave the park at **Exhibition Road** and visit three of London's major museums. The **Science Museum** is the leading national collection of science and technology, with extensive hands-on exhibits on outer space, astronomy, computers, transportation, and medicine. *Tel. 071/938-8000; 071/938-8123 (recorded information). Admission: £3.50 adults, £.75 children under 15 and senior citizens. Open Mon.–Sat. 10–6, Sun. 11–6.*

㉗ The **Natural History Museum** is housed in an ornate late-Victorian building with striking modern additions. As in the Science Museum, its displays on topics such as human biology and evolution are designed to challenge visitors to think for themselves. *Cromwell Rd., tel. 071/938-9123; 042/692-7654 (recorded information). Admission: £3.50 adults, £1.75 children under 15 and senior citizens; free weekdays 4:30–6. Open Mon.–Sat. 10–6, Sun. 2:30–6.*

㉘ The **Victoria and Albert Museum** (or V & A) originated in the 19th century as a museum of decorative art and has extensive collections of costumes, paintings, jewelry, and crafts from every part of the globe. The collections from India, China, and the Islamic world are especially strong. *Cromwell Rd., tel. 071/938-8500; 071/938-8441 (recorded information). Suggested voluntary contribution: £3.50 adults, £1.75 children. Open Mon.–Sat. 10–5:50, Sun. 2:30–5:50.*

㉙ Back in Kensington Gardens, the **Albert Memorial** commemorates Queen Victoria's much-loved husband, Prince Albert, who died in 1861 at the age of 42. The monument, itself the epitome of high Victorian taste, commemorates the many socially uplifting projects of the prince, among them the Great Exhibition of 1851, whose catalog he is holding. The Memorial, which has been badly eroded by pollution, is currently being restored.

From the **Flower Walk,** behind the Albert Memorial, carefully planted so that flowers are in bloom virtually throughout the year, strike out across Kensington Gardens to the **Round Pond,** a favorite place for children to sail toy boats.

③ **Kensington Palace,** across from the Round Pond, has been a royal home since the late 17th century—and is one still, for the prince and princess of Wales and Princess Margaret. From the outside it looks less like a palace than a country house, which it was until William III bought it in 1689. Inside, however, are state rooms on a grand scale, mostly created in the early 18th century. Such distinguished architects as Wren, Hawksmoor, Vanbrugh, and William Kent were all employed here. Queen Victoria lived at Kensington Palace as a child, and several rooms are furnished as they were during her time. The public part of the palace also contains an exhibition of court dress. *Tel. 071/937–9561. Admission: £3.75 adults, £2.80 students and senior citizens, £2.50 children. Open Mon.–Sat. 9–5, Sun. 1–5.*

North of Kensington Gardens are two lively districts, **Bayswater** and **Notting Hill,** both full of restaurants and cafés where young people gather. The best-known attraction in this area is **③** **Portobello Road,** where the lively antiques and bric-a-brac market is held each Saturday (arrive early in the morning for the best bargains). The street is also full of regular antiques shops that are open most weekdays.

Covent Garden You could easily spend a half day exploring the block of streets **③** north of the Strand known as **Covent Garden.** The heart of the area is a former wholesale fruit and vegetable market, established in 1656. The market moved to more modern and accessible premises only in 1974. The Victorian **Market Building** is now a vibrant shopping center, with numerous boutiques, crafts shops, and cafés. On the south side of the market building is the lively and much less formal **Jubilee open-air market,** where artists and craftspeople sell their wares at stalls.

The atmosphere in Covent Garden is friendly and informal. Look for the open-air entertainers performing under the porti- **③** co of **St. Paul's Church**—you can enjoy an excellent show for the price of a few coins thrown in the hat that's passed among the onlookers. The church, entered from Bedford Street, is known as the Actors' Church, and inside are numerous memorials to theater people. The **Royal Opera House** and the **Theatre Royal Drury Lane,** two of London's oldest theaters, are close by.

For interesting specialty shops, head north of the Market Building. Shops on **Long Acre** sell maps, art books, and glass; shops on **Neal Street** sell clothes, pottery, jewelry, and goods from the Far East.

③ The collection of vehicles at the **London Transport Museum** includes a steam locomotive, a tram, a subway car, and an Underground train simulator. Visitors are encouraged to operate many of the vehicles. The shop sells T-shirts, books, souvenirs, and current and historic London Transport posters. *The Piazza (southeast corner), tel. 071/379–6344. Admission: £3 adults, £1.50 children 5–16 and senior citizens, children under 5 free. Open daily 10–5:15.*

③ The **Theatre Museum** contains a comprehensive collection of material on the history of the English theater—not merely the classic drama but also opera, music hall, pantomime, and musical comedy. Scripts, playbills, costumes, and props are displayed; there is even a re-creation of a dressing room filled with memorabilia of former stars. *Russell St., tel. 071/836–7891. Admission: £2.50 adults, £1.50 children under 14, students, and senior citizens. Open Tues.–Sun. 11–7.*

㉛ On **Bow Street** is the **Royal Opera House,** home of the Royal Ballet and the Royal Opera Company. The plush interior captures the richness of Victorian England.

Bloomsbury **Bloomsbury** is a semiresidential district to the north of Covent Garden that contains some spacious and elegant 17th- and 18th-century squares. It could claim to be the intellectual center of London, since both the British Museum and the University of London are found here. The area also gave its name to the Bloomsbury Group, a clique of writers and painters who thrived here in the early 20th century. The antiquarian and specialist bookshops, publishing houses, restaurants, and pubs frequented by the local literati add to the academic-cum-bohemian ambience of the area.

㉜ The **British Museum** houses a vast and priceless collection of treasures, including Egyptian, Greek, and Roman antiquities; Renaissance jewelry; pottery; coins; glass; and drawings from virtually every European school since the 15th century. It's best to pick out one section that particularly interests you—to try to see everything would be an overwhelming and exhausting task. Some of the highlights are the **Elgin Marbles,** sculptures that formerly decorated the Parthenon in Athens; the **Rosetta Stone,** which helped archaeologists to interpret Egyptian script; a copy of the **Magna Carta,** the charter signed by King John in 1215 to which is ascribed the origins of English liberty; and the **Mildenhall treasure,** a cache of Roman silver found in East Anglia in 1842. *Great Russell St., tel. 071/636–1555; 071/580–1788 (recorded information). Admission free; guided tours of museum's highlights, £5. Open Mon.–Sat. 10–5, Sun. 2:30–6.*

㉝ The **Jewish Museum** has a small but interesting collection of antiquities illustrating Judaism, Jewish life, and history. There are also audiovisual programs on Jewish festivals and ceremonies. *Woburn House, Upper Woburn Pl., tel. 071/388–4525. Admission free. Open Tues.–Thurs. (and Fri. in summer) 10–4, Sun. (and Fri. in winter) 10–12:45.*

The City The **City,** the traditional commercial center of London, is the most ancient part of the capital, having been the site of the great Roman city of Londinium. Since those days, the City has been built and rebuilt several times. The wooden buildings of the medieval City were destroyed in the Great Fire of 1666. There were further waves of reconstruction in the 19th century, and then again after World War II, to repair the devastation wrought by air attacks. The 1980s have seen the construction of many mammoth office developments, some undistinguished, others incorporating adventurous and exciting ideas.

Throughout all these changes, the City has retained its unique identity and character. The lord mayor and Corporation of London are still responsible for the government of the City, as they have been for many centuries. Commerce remains the lifeblood of the City, which is a world financial center rivaled only by New York, Tokyo, and Zurich. The biggest change has been in the City's population. Until the first half of the 19th century, many of the merchants and traders who worked in the City lived there, too. Today, despite its huge daytime population, scarcely 8,000 people live in the 274 hectares (677 acres) of the City. Try, therefore, to explore the City on a weekday morning or afternoon. On weekends its streets are deserted, and many of the shops and restaurants, even some of the churches, are closed.

40 Following the Great Fire, **St. Paul's Cathedral** was rebuilt by Sir Christopher Wren, the architect who was also responsible for designing 50 City parish churches to replace those lost in the Great Fire. St. Paul's is Wren's greatest work. Fittingly, he is buried in the crypt, under the simple epitaph composed by his son: "Reader, if you seek his monument, look around you." The cathedral has been the site of many famous state occasions, including the funeral of Winston Churchill in 1965 and the marriage of the prince and princess of Wales in 1981. There is much fine painting and craftsmanship—the choir stalls are by the great 17th-century wood carver Grinling Gibbons—but overall the atmosphere is somewhat austere and remote. The cathedral contains many monuments and tombs. Among those commemorated are George Washington; the essayist and lexicographer Samuel Johnson; and two military heroes—Nelson, victor over the French at Trafalgar in 1805, and Wellington, who defeated the French on land at Waterloo 10 years later. In the ambulatory (the area behind the high altar) is the American Chapel, a memorial to the 28,000 U.S. citizens stationed in Britain during World War II who lost their lives while on active service.

The greatest architectural glory of the cathedral is the dome. This consists of three distinct elements: an outer, timber-framed dome covered with lead; an interior dome built of brick and decorated with frescoes of the life of St. Paul by the 18th-century artist Sir James Thornhill; and, in between, a brick cone that supports and strengthens both. There is a good view of the church from the **Whispering Gallery,** high up in the inner dome. The gallery is so called because of its remarkable acoustics, whereby words whispered on one side can be clearly heard on the other, 35 meters (112 feet) away. Above this gallery are two others, both external, from which there are fine views over the City and beyond. *Tel. 071/248–2705. Admission to cathedral free (donation requested); Ambulatory (American Chapel), Crypt, and Treasury: £2 adults, £1 children; to galleries: £2 adults, £1 children. Tours of the cathedral weekdays at 11, 11:30, 2, and 2:30, £4 adults, £2 children. Cathedral open Mon.–Sat. 7:30–6, Sun. 8–6; the Ambulatory, Crypt, and Galleries weekdays 10–4:15, Sat. 11–4:15.*

A short walk north of the cathedral, to **London Wall,** so called because it follows the line of the wall that surrounded the Roman settlement, brings you to the **Museum of London.** Its displays enable you to get a real sense of what it was like to live in London at different periods of history, from Roman times to the present day. Among the highlights are the Lord Mayor's Ceremonial Coach, an imaginative reconstruction of the Great Fire, and the Cheapside Hoard, jewelry hidden during an outbreak of plague in the 17th century and never recovered by its owner. A new gallery devoted to the 18th century was opened in 1989. The 20th-century exhibits include a Woolworth's counter and elevators from Selfridges; both stores were founded by Americans and had an immense impact on the life of Londoners. *London Wall, tel. 071/600–3699. Admission £3 adults, £1.50 under 18 and senior citizens. Open Tues.–Sat. 10–6, Sun. 2–6.*

42 The **Barbican** is a vast residential complex and arts center built by the City of London. It takes its name from the watchtower that stood here during the Middle Ages, just outside the City walls. The arts center contains a concert hall, where the London Symphony Orchestra is based, two theaters, an art gallery, a cinema, and several cafés and restaurants. The theaters are the London home of the Royal Shakespeare Company.

43 On the south side of London Wall stands **Guildhall,** the much reconstructed home of the Corporation of London; the lord mayor of London is elected here each year with ancient ceremony. *King St., tel. 071/606–3030. Admission free. Open weekdays 10–5.*

Now walk south to **Cheapside.** This was the chief marketplace of medieval London (the word *ceap* meant "market"), as the street names hereabouts indicate: Milk Street, Ironmonger Lane, etc. Despite rebuilding, many of the streets still run on the **44** medieval pattern. The church of **St. Mary-le-Bow** in Cheapside was rebuilt by Christopher Wren after the Great Fire; it was built again after being bombed during World War II. It is said that to be a true Cockney, you must be born within the sound of Bow bells.

A short walk east along Cheapside brings you to a seven-way **45** intersection. The **Bank of England,** which regulates much of Britain's financial life, is the large windowless building on the left. At the northern side of the intersection, at right angles to **46** the bank, is the **Royal Exchange,** originally built in the 1560s as a trading hall for merchants. The present building, opened in 1844 and the third on the site, is now occupied by the **London International Financial Futures Exchange.** You can watch the hectic trading from the Visitors' Gallery. *Tel. 071/623–0444. Admission free. Visitors' Gallery open weekdays 11:30–1:45.*

The third major building at this intersection, on its south side, **47** is the **Mansion House,** the official residence of the lord mayor of London.

Continue east along **Cornhill,** site of a Roman basilica and of a medieval grain market. Turn right into Gracechurch Street **48** and then left into **Leadenhall Market.** There has been a market here since the 14th century; the present building dates from 1881.

Just behind the market is one of the most striking pieces of contemporary **49** City architecture: the headquarters of **Lloyd's of London,** built by the modernist architect Richard Rogers. Its main feature is a 62-meter-high (200-foot-high) barrel vault made of sparkling glass. The underwriters of Lloyd's provide insurance for everything imaginable, from oil rigs to a pianist's fingers. An exhibit traces the history of Lloyd's from the 17th century. *1 Lime St., tel. 071/623–7100, ext. 6210 or 5786. Admission free. Open weekdays 10–2:30.*

50 From here it's a short walk east to the **Tower of London,** one of London's most famous sights and one of its most crowded, too.

Come as early in the day as possible and head for the Crown Jewels so you can see them before the crowds arrive.

The tower served the monarchs of medieval England as both fortress and palace. Every British sovereign from William the Conqueror in the 11th century to Henry VIII in the 16th lived here, and it remains a royal palace, in name at least. The **History Gallery,** south of the White Tower, is a walk-through display designed to answer questions about the inhabitants of the tower and its evolution over the centuries.

The **White Tower** is the oldest and also the most conspicuous building in the entire complex. Inside, the **Chapel of St. John** is one of the few unaltered parts. A structure of great simplicity, it is almost entirely lacking in ornamentation. The **Royal Armories,** England's national collection of arms and armor, occupies the rest of the White Tower. Armor of the 16th and 17th centuries forms the centerpiece of the displays, including pieces belonging to Henry VIII and Charles I.

Among other buildings worth seeing is the **Bloody Tower.** This name has been traced back only to 1571; it was originally known as the Garden Tower. Sir Walter Raleigh was held prisoner here, in relatively comfortable circumstances, between 1603 and 1616, during which time he wrote his *History of the World;* his rooms are furnished much as they were during his imprisonment. The little princes in the tower—the boy king Edward V and his brother Richard, duke of York, supposedly murdered on the orders of Gloucester, later crowned Richard III—certainly lived in the Bloody Tower, and may well have died here, too. Another bloody death is alleged to have occurred in the **Wakefield Tower,** when Henry VI was murdered in 1471 during England's medieval civil war, the Wars of the Roses. It was a rare honor to be beheaded in private inside the tower; most people were executed outside, on **Tower Hill,** where the crowds could get a much better view. Important prisoners were held in the **Beauchamp Tower;** the walls are covered with graffiti and inscriptions carved by prisoners.

The **Crown Jewels,** housed in the **Jewel House,** are a breathtakingly beautiful collection of regalia, precious stones, gold, and silver. The Royal Scepter contains the largest cut diamond in the world. The Imperial State Crown, made for the 1838 coronation of Queen Victoria, contains some 3,000 precious stones, largely diamonds and pearls. Look for the ravens whose presence at the tower is traditional. It is said that if they leave, the tower will fall and England will lose her greatness. *Tower Hill, tel. 071/709–0765. Admission: £6 adults, £4.50 students and senior citizens, £3.70 children under 16, family ticket £17. Reduced admission charges apply during Feb. when the Jewel House is closed. Small additional admission charge to the Fusiliers Museum only. Open Mar.–Oct., Mon.–Sat. 9:30–5, Sun. 2–5; Nov.–Feb., Mon.–Sat. 9:30–4.*

Yeoman Warder guides conduct tours daily from the Middle Tower, no charge, but a tip is always appreciated. Subject to weather and availability of guides, tours are conducted about every 30 minutes until 3:30 in summer, 2:30 in winter.

Off the Beaten Track

Greenwich   The historical and maritime attractions at **Greenwich,** on the
Thames, some 8 kilometers (5 miles) east of central London,
make it an ideal place for a day out. You can get to Greenwich by
riverboat from Westminster and Tower Bridge piers, by
ThamesLine's high-speed river buses, or by train from Charing
Cross station. You can also take the Docklands Light Railway
from Tower Gateway to Island Gardens and walk a short distance along a pedestrian tunnel under the river.

Visit the **National Maritime Museum,** a treasure house of paintings; maps; models; sextants; and, best of all, ships from all
ages, including the ornate royal barges. *Romney Rd., tel. 081/
858–4422. Joint admission with the Royal Observatory: £3.25
adults, £2.25 children and senior citizens. Open late Mar.–late
Oct., Mon.–Sat. 10–6, Sun. 2–6; late Oct.–late Mar., Mon.–
Sat. 10–5, Sun. 2–5.*

Two ships now in dry dock are the glorious 19th-century clipper
ship *Cutty Sark* and the tiny *Gipsy Moth IV,* which Sir Francis
Chichester sailed single-handed around the world in 1966.
*Cutty Sark, King William Walk, tel. 081/858–3445. Admis-
sion: £3 adults, £2 children under 16 and senior citizens. Open
late Mar.–Sept., Mon.–Sat. 10–5:30, Sun. noon–5:30; Oct.–
Mar., Mon.–Sat. 10–4:30, Sun. noon–4:30. Gipsy Moth IV,
King William Walk, tel. 081/853–3589. Admission: 50p adults,
30p children and senior citizens. Open Apr.–Oct., Mon.–Sat.
10–5:30, Sun. noon–5:30.*

The **Royal Naval College** was built in 1694 as a home, or hospital, for old sailors. You can see the magnificent **Painted Hall,**
where Nelson's body lay in state following the Battle of Trafalgar, and the College Chapel. *Tel. 081/858–2154. Admission
free. Open Fri.–Wed. 2:30–4:30.*

Behind the museum and the college is **Greenwich Park,** originally a royal hunting ground and today an attractive place in
which to wander and relax. On top of the hill is the **Old Royal
Observatory,** founded in 1675, where original telescopes and
other astronomical instruments are on display. The prime meridian—zero degrees longitude—runs through the courtyard
of the observatory. *Greenwich Park, tel. 081/858–4422. Joint
admission with National Maritime Museum: £3.25 adults,
£2.25 children and senior citizens. Open Apr.–Oct., Mon.–Sat.
10–6, Sun. 2–6; Nov.–Mar., Mon.–Sat. 10–5, Sun. 2–5.*

Shopping

Shopping is one of London's great pleasures, but you have to
know where and when to go to pick up a bargain. In January
and June, when retailers clear the racks ready for next season's
ranges, you'll find most goods in most shops on sale. Reductions
typically start at 10% and go up to 75%.

Shopping Districts   Certain areas can't be beat, but strictly for window shopping,
since they harbor London's highest price tags. These include
Bond Street, where the big-name jewelers and couturiers are
(plus **Fenwick's** fashion store, where prices are reasonable),
and **Piccadilly,** with its beautiful **Arcades** and the food hall at
Fortnum & Mason.

Up **Regent Street,** find **Hamleys** toy store, almost bigger than F.A.O. Schwarz, and **Liberty,** not inexpensive, but possibly the city's most appealing department store, with famous fabrics and a bazaar atmosphere. **Oxford Street** is packed with bargains and office workers. **John Lewis** ("never knowingly undersold") and rather staid **Selfridges** are two department stores worth checking out. **Marks & Spencer** is where all British people buy their underwear (and sweaters)—an essential stop.

Though his suits may be made in Savile Row, the English gentleman comes to **St. James's** for the rest of his outfit, which includes shoes, shirts, silk ties, hats, and all manner of accessories. The prices mirror the quality.

Knightsbridge, dominated by **Harrods,** also boasts many fine boutiques on **Beauchamp Place, Walton Street** and **Sloane Street,** and **Harvey Nichols,** an excellent fashion store, where there's a permanent sale department.

Chelsea includes the famous, now tired, **King' Road** and borders **South Kensington,** where **Brompton Cross** is good for designer items of all categories. **Kensington Church Street** is full of exquisite, expensive antiques, while **Kensington High Street** has a good array of mid-priced clothes.

Over at **Covent Garden,** you'll find crafts, clothes, and ephemera of all sorts in a lively knot of streets around the **Piazza,** where the street entertainment's free—central London's best value.

Markets Street markets are one aspect of London life not to be missed, especially if you're watching the pennies. Here are some of the more interesting markets:

Bermondsey. Arrive as early as possible for the best treasure— or junk. *Tower Bridge Rd., SE1. Open Fri. 4:30 AM–noon. Take the tube to London Bridge and walk or take the No. 15 or 25 bus to Aldgate and then a No. 42 bus over Tower Bridge to Bermondsey Square.*
Camden Lock. This is just the place for an unusual and inexpensive gift; it's also a picturesque place to wander around. There's an open-air antiques market on weekends, but it gets horribly crowded. *Chalk Farm Rd., NW1. Open Tues.–Sun. 9:30–5:30. Take the tube or the No. 24 or 29 bus to Camden Town.*
Camden Passage. The rows of little antiques shops are a good hunting ground for silverware and jewelry. Saturday is the day for stalls; shops are open the rest of the week. *Islington, N1. Open Wed.–Sat. 8:30–3. Take the tube or No. 19 or 38 bus to the Angel.*
Petticoat Lane. Look for good-quality, budget-priced leather goods, dazzling knitwear, and bargain-price fashions, plus cameras, videos, and stereos at budget prices. *Middlesex St., E1. Open Sun. 9–2. Take the tube to Liverpool Street, Aldgate, or Aldgate East.*
Portobello Market. Saturday is the best day to search the stalls for not-quite-bargain-priced silverware, curios, porcelain, and jewelry. It's always crowded, with an authentic hustle-and-bustle atmosphere, and firmly on the tourist route. *Portobello Rd., W11. Open Fri. 5–3, Sat. 8–5. Take the tube or No. 52 bus to Notting Hill Gate or Ladbroke Grove or No. 15 bus to Kensington Park Road.*

Dining

For details and price-category definitions, *see* Dining in Staying in Great Britain.

Bloomsbury
Moderate

The Museum Street Café. Not really a café, but a small restaurant serving a limited menu of perfect, fresh, plainly cooked, but always fashionable food in the evenings; hearty soups and creative sandwiches, like Stilton on homemade walnut bread, at lunchtime. Smoking is not permitted here. *47 Museum St., tel. 071/405-3211. Reservations required for dinner. No credit cards. Closed weekends, public holidays.*

Inexpensive

The Agra. This Indian restaurant is popular with media folk for its good value and wide choice of meat and vegetarian curries. Overhead fans, low lighting, and attentive waiters add a touch of class. *135-137 Whitfield St., tel. 071/387-8833. Reservations advised for dinner. AE, DC, MC, V. Closed Dec. 25.*

The Hermitage. A favorited haunt of University of London staff and students, this unpretentious, welcoming French bistro/restaurant is fine for a herb tea or coffee and croissant in between meals (newspapers and cats provided), or a full three courses of home-style, filling French food. *19 Leigh St., tel. 071/387-8034. Reservations advised for lunch. MC, V. Closed weekend dinner, Christmas.*

Budget

The North Sea Fish Restaurant. Only freshly caught fish is served in this popular haunt. It's a bit tricky to find—three blocks south of St. Pancras station, down Judd Street. Recommended are the seafood platter and Dover sole. You can eat in or take out. *7-8 Leigh St., tel. 071/387-5892. Reservations advised. AE, DC, MC, V. Closed Sun., holidays, 10 days at Christmas.*

Chelsea
Moderate

Gavvers. This is the down-market branch of the Gavroche empire, located two blocks below Sloane Square. The set menus at £15 for lunch and £28 for dinner offer simpler versions of the Roux brothers' classic French dishes. The place is rather cramped and noisy but full of character. *61-63 Lower Sloane St., tel. 071/730-4772. Reservations essential. AE, DC, MC, V. Closed Sat. lunch, Sun.*

PJ's Bar and Grill. This is a very friendly place fitted with polo memorabilia on white walls, wooden floorboards, and stained glass windows. Large amounts of all-American staples like soft-shell crab, gumbo, steak and salads are offered, accompanied by any cocktail ever invented, mixed by expert bartenders. *52 Fulham Rd., tel. 071/581-0025. Reservations advised weekends. AE, DC, MC, V. Closed Christmas.*

Inexpensive

Henry J. Bean's. Hamburgers and Tex-Mex food are served to American oldies music. There's American-bar decor: The walls are covered with newspapers and other ephemera. *195-197 King's Rd., tel. 071/352-9255. No reservations. No credit cards. Closed Dec. 25, 26, 31.*

Budget

Chelsea Kitchen. This café opened in the '60s to feed the crowds of hungry people searching for hot, filling, and inexpensive food. Expect nothing more fancy than pasta, omelets, salads, stews, and casseroles. The menu changes every day. *98 King's Rd., tel. 071/589-1330. No credit cards. Closed Christmas.*

The City
Moderate

Sweetings. City gents stand in line to lunch at this tiny, basic Victorian restaurant close to the remains of a Roman temple.

The service is Old World courteous; the fish, cheese, and puddings are comforting and well prepared. *39 Queen Victoria St., tel. 071/248–3062. No reservations. No credit cards. Open weekdays for lunch only; closed Christmas, holidays.*

Quality Chop House. This trendy place housed in a converted Victorian café serves generous portions of exquisitely cooked, grease-free "caff" food, like homemade veal sausages with onion gravy and creamed potato. You may have to share one of the tables for six. *94 Farringdon Rd., tel. 071/837–5093. Reservations advised. No credit cards. Closed Sun., Mon. dinner, Sat. lunch, Christmas.*

Covent Garden
Moderate
★

Bertorelli's. Opposite the stage door of the Royal Opera House, Bertorelli's is a favorite with opera goers. Chic, postmodern decor complements the traditional Italian food—try the hot mushroom and garlic salad and whatever is the fresh fish of the day. *44a Floral St., tel. 071/836–3969. Reservations advised. AE, DC, MC, V. Closed Sun., Dec. 25.*

Inexpensive
★

Café des Amis du Vin. This genuinely Gallic place in a tiny lane off Long Acre is split into three establishments, the affordable parts being the wine-bar basement and the ground-floor café, both of which also have the lively atmospheres. Seafood ragout is a perennial favorite on a menu of regional dishes supplemented by daily specials. *11–14 Hanover Pl., tel 071/379–3444. AE, DC, MC, V. Closed Sun., Christmas.*

Joe Allen. This basement restaurant behind the Strand Palace Hotel follows the style of its New York counterpart. It's a great place to spot stage or screen stars. The barbecued ribs and Caesar salad are a real treat. There's a pianist after 9 PM, if you can hear through the surrounding decibels. *13 Exeter St., tel. 071/ 836–0651. Reservations required. No credit cards. Closed Christmas.*

Budget

Diana's Diner. Diana has moved elsewhere, and this superior café is now Italian-run, but still serves enormous portions of well-cooked, homey food—roast chicken, stuffed baked potatoes, pasta, and risotto. It's very popular with local workers and residents, so it's always full. *39 Endell St., tel. 071/240– 0272. No credit cards. Closed after 7 PM, Sun. dinner.*

Food for Thought. This is a simple downstairs vegetarian restaurant, with seats for only 50, so there's almost always a waiting line. The menu—stir fries, casseroles, salads, and dessert—changes daily, and each dish is freshly made. No alcohol is served here. *31 Neal St., tel. 071/836–0239. No reservations. No credit cards. Closed Sun., Sat. after 4:30 PM, weekdays after 8 PM, 2 weeks at Christmas, holidays.*

Rock & Sole Plaice. The horrible pun announces exactly what is served here—fish in the British fashion, dipped in batter and deep-fried. Everything here is very fresh, and the central location makes it useful for the very hungry. Try banana fritters for dessert. *47 Endell St., tel. 071/836–3785. No credit cards. Closed Sun., Christmas.*

Kensington
Moderate

Bombay Brasserie. Here's one of London's most fashionable and stylish Indian restaurants. The fine menu, drawn from different regions, includes *Bombay thali* (small bowls of vegetables or meat), Kashmiri lamb, and Goan fish curry. The Sunday lunch buffet is particularly popular. Try for a table in the conservatory. *Courtfield Close, Courtfield Rd., tel. 071/370–4040. Reservations required for dinner. AE, DC, MC, V. Closed Christmas.*

★ **Lou Pescadou.** A boating theme predominates at this Provençal restaurant—there are pictures of boats, boats as lamps, and so on. Fish is the specialty: Try the *petite bouillabaisse* (fish soup) or red mullet poached in tarragon sauce. *241 Old Brompton Rd., tel: 071/370-1057. No reservations. AE, DC, MC, V. Closed Aug., Dec. 25.*

★ **Wodka.** This small, modern Polish restaurant in a quiet backstreet serves stylish food to a fashionable group and often has the relaxed atmosphere of a dinner party. Try herring blinis, roast duck with figs and port, and the several flavored vodkas. *12 St Albans Grove W8, tel. 071/937-6513. Reservations advised. AE, DC, MC, V. Closed weekend lunch, Dec. 25-26.*

Knightsbridge
Moderate

Caravela. This traditional Portuguese restaurant on the lower ground floor is surprisingly reasonably priced for such a swanky street. Most evenings, live music accompanies your *caldo verde* (cabbage soup) and charbroiled lamb in wine sauce. *39 Beauchamp Pl., tel. 071/581-2366. AE, DC, MC, V. Closed Sun. lunch, Christmas, Easter.*

Grill St. Quentin. This is a popular French spot just five blocks west of Harrods. Choose from a selection of fresh meat from Scotland or fish, which is then cooked on an open grill. The set lunch at £12 is excellent value for shoppers. *2 Yeoman's Row, tel. 071/583-8377. Reservations advised. AE, DC, MC, V. Closed Sun.*

Inexpensive

Luba's Bistro. Luba's, with its long wooden tables, plain decor, and authentic Russian cooking, has been popular for decades. This is where to find your favorite culinary clichés—chicken Kiev and beef Stroganoff. *6 Yeoman's Row, tel. 071/589-2950. MC, V. Closed Sun., public holidays.*

Stockpot. Speedy service is the mark of this large, jolly restaurant full of young people and middle-aged shoppers. The food is filling and wholesome; try the homemade soups, the Lancashire hot pot, or the apple crumble. Breakfast is also served Monday–Saturday. *6 Basil St., tel. 071/589-8627. Reservations accepted. No credit cards. Closed Dec. 25, New Year's Day.*

Mayfair
Moderate

Pizzeria Condotti. Run by the cartoonist Enzo Apicella, this spot has walls lined with cartoons and modern paintings. The pizzas are first-class, thin-crusted in the Italian style, with the usual toppings. Alternatives are various salads like the *insalata Condotti* (mixed leaves with mozzarella and avocado). *4 Mill St., tel. 071/499-1308. No reservations. AE, DC, MC, V. Closed Sun., holidays, Dec. 25, 26.*

Smollensky's Balloon. This American-style bar/restaurant is a favorite among families and has a children's Sunday lunch. The menu has a few weekly specials, but your best bet is steak, which comes in a choice of cuts and sauces accompanied by lots of good, thin fries. *1 Dover St., tel. 071/491-1199. AE, DC, MC, V. Closed Christmas.*

Inexpensive

The Chicago Pizza Pie Factory. Huge pizzas with salad and garlic bread are served at reasonable prices in this bright basement spot. These pies are American-style with a thick chewy base and a somewhat limited choice of toppings; try the American sausage and mushroom. There's also a cocktail bar, rock music, and videos. *17 Hanover Sq., tel. 071/629-2669. Reservations advised for lunch. No credit cards. Closed Dec. 25, 26.*

Down Mexico Way. This atmospheric place is decorated with beautiful Spanish ceramic tiles and serves better-than-the-average Mexican food for London. Try fish in almond-chili sauce with spiced spinach, and avoid evenings if you want a quiet night out. *25 Swallow St., tel. 071/437-9895. Reservations advised evenings. AE, MC, V. Closed Christmas.*

L'Artiste Muscle. With two cramped floors of France in picturesque Shepherd Market, this place is eccentric, but well-loved and good value. Steak, baked potatoes, and salad are always available. The daily specials, of things like beouf bourguignonne, come heaped on large plates. You can sit outside in summer. *1 Shepherd Market, tel. 071/493-6150. AE, MC, V. Closed Sun. lunch, Christmas.*

Notting Hill Gate
Moderate
★

L'Artiste Assoiffé. The parrots Stanley and Sally will amuse you in the bar of this eccentric Victorian house before you escape to eat in the can-can room or the merry-go-round room to the accompaniment of operatic music. Pop stars, actors, and royals come here for the unique atmosphere and the French food: fillet of steak caramelized with Dijon mustard and spinach pancakes with nuts and cheese. *122 Kensington Park Rd., tel. 071/727-4714. Reservations required. AE, DC, MC, V. Closed Sun., holidays; no lunch weekdays.*

192. Upstairs is a noisy wine bar, downstairs a relaxed restaurant serving up-to-the-minute combinations of fresh ingredients, like a warm salad of duck marinated in Thai spices and lime or a saffron seafood risotto. Choosing two or three first courses instead of an entrée keeps the check reasonable. *192 Kensington Park Rd., tel. 071/229-0482. Reservations advised. AE, MC, V. Closed Mon. lunch, public holidays.*

Inexpensive

Hollands. London's only Filipino wine bar, this is a relaxed and friendly place with a bar downstairs and a restaurant area and rooftop conservatory (lovely in summer) upstairs. The food is anglicized Filipino (stirfried squid with ginger) or wine bar staples (steak, taramosalata). *6 Portland Rd., W11, tel. 071/229-3130. Dress: casual. Reservations advised for restaurant. AE, MC, V. Closed Christmas.*

Tootsies. Some of London's best burgers are cheerfully served in a dark restaurant brightened by vintage advertisements and vintage rock music. Big salads, BLTs, chicken, and chili are also on offer; pies and ice cream are the choices for dessert. *120 Holland Park Ave., tel. 071/229-8567. MC, V. Closed Christmas.*

Soho
Moderate

Chiang Mai. The interior is modeled on a traditional Thai stilt house. The food is delicious and spicy, all easy to order from an English menu. Try a *Tom Yum* (hot-and-sour soup) or a *Pad Kra Prow* (beef, pork, or chicken with fresh Thai basil and chili). *48 Frith St., tel. 071/437-7444. Reservations advised. AE, MC, V. Closed Sun. and holidays.*

Fung Shing. This comfortable, mint-green restaurant is a cut above the Chinatown crowd in service, ambience, and food. The usual offerings are supplemented here by unusual dishes like fried intestines (nicer than it sounds!) and the delicious salt-baked chicken. *15 Lisle St., tel. 071/437-1539. AE, DC, MC, V. Closed Christmas.*

Soho Soho. You can't miss this lively place, which is located on a corner and apparently built of glass. The ground floor is a café/bar with a rotisserie at the rear (upstairs is a formal restaurant), serving flavorful Provençal-influenced food to match the decor. Omelets, charcuterie, and cheeses supplement dishes like wild mushroom risotto with shaved Parmesan. *11–13 Frith St., tel. 071/494–3491. AE, DC, MC, V. Closed Sun., Christmas.*

Inexpensive **Deal's West.** This restaurant is part-owned by Viscount Linley, but you'd never guess the royal connection from the party atmosphere and big, no-nonsense helpings in this wood-beamed diner. Choose salads, ribs, and burgers or Thai-influenced dishes, like the "DIY Deals," where you cook strips of marinated meat on your own personal hot brick. *14–16 Fouberts Pl., tel. 071/287–1050. Reservations advised. AE, DC, MC, V. Closed Sun. dinner, Christmas.*

Poon's. A popular Chinese restaurant (there are long lines in the evening), Poon's specializes in wind-dried meats. There are two other Poon's, but this one is the cheapest and most authentic. *4 Leicester St., tel. 071/437–1528. Reservations required. Closed Sun., Dec. 25, 26.*

Budget **Pollo.** Are you a hip club animal or a fashion student? If you are, then come to the Soho Italina institution and stand on line for great pasta and people-watching. Otherwise come for lunch, when it's a little calmer, and stick to soup, pasta, or risotto—the meat dishes aren't so reliable. *20 Old Compton St., tel. 071/734–5917. No credit cards. Closed Sun., public holidays.*

St. James's **Café Fish.** This bustling restaurant has a wonderful selection of
Moderate fish, from trout and halibut to turbot and shark, arranged on the menu according to cooking method—*meunière*, steamed, broiled, or baked. Other dishes include fresh seafood straight out of a Paris brasserie; smoked fish pâté and crusty bread are included in the cover, and there's often a pianist. *39 Panton St., tel. 071/930–3999. Reservations advised. AE, DC, MC, V. Closed Sat. lunch, Sun, Christmas.*

Inexpensive **The Fountain.** At the back of Fortnum & Mason's famous store is this elegant and very English restaurant serving light meals, sandwiches, ice cream, cakes, and tea. Welsh rarebit, Fortnum's game pie, or filet steak are typical offerings, and the place is licenced, so you can have a glass of wine with your meal. *181 Piccadilly, tel. 071/734–4938. Reservations accepted for dinner. AE, DC, MC, V. Closed Sun., public holidays.*

Lodging

Although British hotels traditionally included breakfast in their nightly tariff, this is not to be taken for granted these days. Although lodging in London is expensive, money may often be saved by staying outside the center of town. For details and price-category definitions, *see* Lodging in Staying in Great Britain.

Bayswater **Camelot.** This affordable hotel, recently refurbished and ex-
Moderate tended, has beautifully decorated rooms. The breakfast room
★ has a large open fireplace with wooden trestle tables and a polished wood floor. *45–47 Norfolk Sq., W2 1RX, tel. 071/723–9118. 43 rooms, 33 with bath or shower. Facilities: lounge, free in-house videos. MC, V.*

Inexpensive **Norfolk Court.** This is a modest, fairly spartan, but pleasant Regency hotel near Paddington Station. Some rooms have French windows and balconies overlooking the square. *20 Norfolk Sq., W2 1RS, tel. 071/723–4963. 50 rooms, 9 with bath. MC.*

Bloomsbury **Academy.** Convenient to the British Museum and area shops,
Moderate the Academy is in a Georgian building and has a bar, library/
lounge, and patio garden. *17–21 Gower St., WC1E 6HG, tel.
071/631–4115. 32 rooms, 24 with bath. AE, DC, MC, V.*

Morgan. This charming family-run hotel in an 18th-century terrace house has rooms that are small and comfortably furnished,
but friendly and cheerful. The tiny paneled breakfast room is
straight out of a doll's house. The back rooms overlook the British Museum. *24 Bloomsbury St., WC1B 3QJ, tel. 071/636–
3735. 14 rooms with shower. No credit cards.*

Whitehall. The imposing entrance is promising, and the interi-
or lives up to the expectations. Arched windows in the lobby, a
bar leading onto a patio, and a pleasantly disheveled garden are
characterful, and everything here is clean and inviting. *2–5
Montague St., WC1B 5BU, tel. 071/580–5871. 80 rooms, 20 with
bath. Facilities: bar, restaurant. AE, DC, MC, V.*

Inexpensive **Ridgemount.** The kindly owners, Mr. and Mrs. Rees, make you
feel at home in this tiny hotel by the British Museum. There's a
homey, cluttered feel in the public areas and some bedrooms
overlook a leafy garden. *65 Gower St., WC1E 6HJ, tel. 071/636–
1141. 15 rooms, none with bath. Facilities: lounge. No credit
cards.*

Ruskin. Immediately opposite the British Museum, the family-
owned, well-run, and very popular Ruskin is both pleasant and
quiet—all front windows are double-glazed. Bedrooms are
clean, though nondescript; back ones overlook a pretty garden.
*23–24 Montague St., WC1B 5BN, tel. 071/636–7388. 35 rooms,
7 with shower. Facilities: lounge. AE, DC, MC, V.*

St Margaret's. This guest house on a tree-lined Georgian street
conveniently close to Russell Square has been run for many
years by a friendly Italian family. You'll find spacious rooms,
the back ones with a garden view. *24 Bedford Pl., WC1B 5JL,
tel. 071/636–4277. 64 rooms, 45 with bath. Facilities: 2 lounges.
No credit cards.*

Budget **Central Club.** Since this YMCA underwent a major face-lift,
only the three- and four-bedrooms fit into this category, but an
excellent location, the facilities, and standards make it worth
the bit extra. There's free access to the sports center with large
pool and gymnasium, and aerobics, yoga, and martial arts
classes are included in the rate. Nobody under 18 years old admitted. *16–22 Great Russell St., WC1B 3LR, tel. 071/636–7512
(ask for reservations manager). 104 rooms, 25 shared bathrooms. Facilities: sports center, coffee shop, laundry, hairdresser. No credit cards.*

John Adams Hall. This group of Georgian houses has been converted into student accommodations that are available at bargain rates during school vacations. There is nothing luxurious
here, but it's a short walk to the British Museum and Euston
Station is across the street. *15–23 Endleigh St., WC1H 0DH,
tel. 071/387–4086 or 4796. 148 rooms (126 are singles), 28
shared bathrooms. No credit cards.*

Passfield Hall. This is another Georgian conversion around the
corner from John Adams Hall (*see above*) and similar in all respects—rooms are simple, the location is convenient, and it's
open only during student breaks. *1 Endsleigh Pl., WC1H 0PW,
tel. 071/387–7743 or 071/387–3584. 144 rooms (100 are single),
36 shared bathrooms. No credit cards.*

Chelsea and Kensington
Moderate

The Gore. Owned by the Hazlitt's people (*see* West End, *below*), this mansion-size town house by the Albert Hall just scrapes into this price range, but is so unique, welcoming, and comfortable, it's worth it. All rooms are scattered with antiques and covered in prints and etchings, while some more expensive ones are utterly over the top, with Tudor-style wood paneling and a four-poster bed, for instance. Bistrot 190 downstairs is one of London's best brasseries. *189 Queen's Gate, SW7 5EX, tel. 071/584–6601. 54 rooms, all with bath. AE, DC, MC, V.*

Inexpensive

Abbey House. Standards are high and the rooms unusually spacious in this hotel in a fine residential block near Kensington Palace and Gardens. *11 Vicarage Gate, W8 4AG, tel. 071/727–2594. 15 rooms, none with bath. Facilities: orthopedic beds. No credit cards.*

The Gate Hotel. This tiny bed-and-breakfast at the top of the famous Portobello Road is friendly, quirky, and clean and has a fair share of devoted fans. Stairs are steep, but bedrooms are spacious and equipped with refrigerators; a massive cooked breakfast is served in the pub across the road. *6 Portobello Rd., W11 3DG, tel. 071/221–2403. 8 rooms, 5 with bath/shower. No credit cards.*

Vicarage Hotel. This genteel establishment, run by the same husband-wife team for the past 25 years, has high standards of cleanliness. Bedrooms are traditional and comfortable with solid English furniture. It attracts many repeat visitors from the United States and welcomes single travelers. *10 Vicarage Gate, W8 4AG, tel. 071/229–4030. 20 rooms, none with bath. Facilities: small TV lounge. No credit cards.*

Budget

Holland Park Independent Hostel. In this Edwardian house in an upscale neighborhood, everything is friendly and relaxed, which is just as well, since guests sleep in dormitories and share a kitchen. Unlike many hostels, there is no curfew or lockout; rates are rock bottom. *31 Holland Park Gardens, W14, tel. 071/602–3369. 15 dormitory rooms (60 beds), 4 shared bathrooms. No credit cards.*

King George VI Memorial Hostel. This historic Jacobean mansion, plus its modern extension is in one of London's prettiest small parks. The setting and very low rates are the draw, since this hostel has dormitory rooms. There is an 11 PM curfew and 10 AM–5 PM lockout. *Holland House, Holland Walk, W8 7QU, tel. 071/937–0748. 13 dormitory rooms (186 beds), 1 double room, 38 bathrooms. No credit cards.*

Hampstead and Regent's Park
Moderate

Swiss Cottage Hotel. A charming, family-run hotel, formerly a retirement home, stuffed with antiques and reproductions and staffed with very pleasant people. Bedrooms are freshly decorated in Victorian style, well-sized, and comfortable. There's a restaurant, a cozy lounge, and a welcoming bar that opens onto the patio garden. It's about a 20-minute ride to the West End from here. *4 Adamson Rd., NW3 3HP, tel. 071/722–2281. 80 rooms, all with bath. AE, DC, MC, V.*

Inexpensive

La Gaffe. In Hamstead, these converted shepherd's cottages are very quaint, if very small. Bedrooms in this friendly, eccentric, Italian-run hotel are minute, but they're spotless and come complete with TV and phone. Downstairs is a wine bar/café that is popular with locals that serves as the hotel lounge. *107–111 Heath St., NW 3 6SS, tel. 071/435–8965. 14 rooms, all with shower. AE, MC, V.*

Budget **Primrose Hill B&B.** Members of this small B&B agency believe "traveling shouldn't be a ripoff," and invite guests into their beautiful homes at reasonable rates to prove it. All houses are in and around Primrose Hill and Hampstead, and guests receive a key. Booking well ahead is essential; phone or write for more details. *Gail O'Farrell, 14 Edis St., NW1 8LG, tel. 071/722–6869. Around 15 rooms with varying facilities. No credit cards.*

Regents College. As the name suggests, this is off-duty student accommodation that enjoys an ideal setting right in the middle of Regent's Park. The location is the only luxury though— rooms are mostly dormitory style, some with bunk beds, and there are eight showers per bathroom. Rooms are only available during school vacations. *Inner Circle, Regent's Park, NW1 4NS, tel. 071/487–7483. 82 rooms, 9 shower rooms, 5 bathrooms. No credit cards.*

Knightsbridge and Victoria **Basil Street.** Women guests here are granted automatic membership in the ladies' organization called "Parrot Club." Family-run for some 75 years, this is a gracious Edwardian hotel on a quiet street around the corner from Harrods. Everywhere are antiques, polished wooden floors, and Oriental carpets. Only the smallest rooms without bathrooms fit this category. *Basil St., SW3 1AH, tel. 071/581–3311. 96 rooms, 72 with bath. Facilities: 2 restaurants, wine bar, lounge, ladies' club. AE, DC, MC, V.*

Moderate

Claverley. Located on a quiet, tree-lined street, the Claverley offers friendly, attractive surroundings, some four-poster beds, and the wealthy world of Knightsbridge shopping, just around the corner. *13–14 Beaufort Gdns., SW3 1PS, tel. 071/589–8541. 36 rooms, all with bath. AE, V.*

Ebury Court. This small, old-fashioned, country house–style hotel is near Victoria Station. The rooms are small, with chintz and antique furniture to give them extra character. The reception area, lounge, and restaurant have all been recently renovated and some new guest rooms were added—ask the rate, since this varies considerably. *26 Ebury St., SW1W 0LU, tel. 071/730–8147. 42 rooms, 18 with bath. Facilities: restaurant, club with bar and lounge (membership fee payable). DC, MC, V.*

Londonwide **London Homestead Services.** This family-run business offers bed and breakfast in private homes, most of which are in quiet residential areas and provide first-floor bedrooms with shared bathrooms. Rates get higher the closer you get to central London, but all hosts provide you with a key and all homes have been evaluated by LHS staff. Minimum stay is three nights. Phone or write for more details. *Coombe Wood Rd., Kingston-upon-Thames, Surrey KT2 7JY, tel. 081/949–4455. About 500 rooms with varying facilities. MC, V.*

Inexpensive

Pimlico **Dolphin Square.** This unique Art Deco quadrangle on the Thames five minutes from Westminster offers peaceful, modern, self-catering apartments, from studio size with kitchenette up to two-bedroom. A large swimming pool, several squash courts, and a tennis court are at your disposal and you have a very stylish brasserie and bar in house. *Dolphin Sq. SW1V 3LX, tel. 071/834–9134. 152 apartments, all with bath. AE, DC, MC, V.*

Moderate

West End **Bryanston Court.** Three 18th-century houses have been converted into a traditional English family-run hotel with open

Moderate

fires and comfortable armchairs; the bedrooms are more contemporary. *56–60 Great Cumberland Pl., W1H 7FD, tel. 071/ 262–3141. 56 rooms with bath or shower. Facilities: restaurant, bar, lounge, satellite TV. AE, DC, MC, V.*

Durrants. A hotel since the late 18th century, Durrants is at the top end of moderate and a little shabby, too, but the location—in the heart of the West End just by the Wallace collection—is unbeatable. Decor is Olde English wood paneling with motel-like bedrooms, but everything is clean and comfortable. *George St., W1H 6BH, tel. 071/935–8131. 96 rooms, 85 with bath. Facilities: restaurant, bar, lounges. AE, MC, V.*

Edward Lear. The former home of Edward Lear, the artist and writer of nonsense verse, this hotel has an imposing entrance leading to a black-and-white tiled lobby. Ask for one of the quieter rooms at the rear. The breakfast room has huge French windows. *28–30 Seymour St., W1H 5WD, tel. 071/402–5401. 32 rooms, 12 with bath or shower. V.*

Fielding Hotel. Tucked away in a quiet alley in Covent Garden, this small hotel is adored by its regulars. The atmosphere is homey and welcoming; bedrooms are all different and, though some are very small, comfortable. There are rather a lot of stairs in this labyrinthine conversion and no elevator. *4 Broad Court, Bow St., WC2B 5QZ, tel. 071/836–8305. 26 rooms, 1 with bath, 23 with shower. Facilities: bar, breakfast room. AE, DC, MC, V.*

Hazlitt's. It's an open secret that this, Soho's only hotel, is a unique place. Disarmingly friendly, full of antiques and character, Hazlitt's trademarks are its thousands of framed prints obscuring the walls and the Victorian claw-foot bath in every bathroom. Each room is different and all are heavily booked. Rooms here are at the top of this price range. *6 Frith St., W1V 5TZ, tel. 071/434–1771. 23 rooms, all with bath. AE, DC, MC, V.*

The Arts

For a list of events in the London arts scene, visit a newsstand or bookstore to pick up the weekly magazine: *Time Out.* The city's evening paper, the *Evening Standard*, carries listings, as do the major Sunday papers; the daily *Independent* and *Guardian;* and, on Friday, *The Times.*

Theater London's theater life can broadly be divided into three categories: the government-subsidized national companies; the commercial, or "West End," theaters; and the fringe.

The main national companies are the **National Theatre** (NT) and the **Royal Shakespeare Company** (RSC). Each has its own custom-designed facilities, in the South Bank arts complex and in the Barbican Arts Centre, respectively. Each presents a variety of plays by writers of all nationalities, ranging from the classics of Shakespeare and his contemporaries to specially commissioned modern works. Box office: NT, tel. 071/928–2252; RSC, tel. 071/638–8891.

The West End theaters largely stage musicals, comedies, whodunits, and revivals of lighter plays of the 19th and 20th centuries, often starring television celebrities. Occasionally there are more serious productions, including successful productions transferred from the subsidized theaters, such as RSC's *Les Liasons Dangereuses* and *Les Misérables.*

The two dozen or so established fringe theaters, scattered around central London and the immediate outskirts, frequently present some of London's most intriguing productions, if you're prepared to overlook occasional rough staging and uncomfortable seating. Fringe tickets are considerably less expensive than West End ones.

Most theaters have an evening performance at 7:30 or 8 daily, except Sunday, and a matinee twice a week (Wednesday or Thursday and Saturday). Expect to pay from £6 for a seat in the upper balcony to at least £20 for a good seat in the stalls (orchestra) or dress circle (mezzanine)—more for musicals. Tickets may be booked in person at the theater box office; over the phone by credit card; or through ticket agents, such as **First Call** (tel. 081/741–9999). In addition, the ticket booth in Leicester Square sells half-price tickets on the day of performance for about 45 theaters; there is a small service charge. Beware of unscrupulous ticket agents who sell tickets at four or five times their box-office price (a small service charge is legitimate) and scalpers, who stand outside theaters offering tickets for the next performance. It's worth asking at the box office on the night of the performance—there will always be around 20 "returns" and nearly all theaters keep a row of "house seats" for emergencies or to sell at the last minute.

Concerts Ticket prices for symphony orchestra concerts are still relatively moderate—between £5 and £15, although you can expect to pay more to hear big-name artists on tour. If you can't book in advance, arrive half an hour before the performance for a chance at returns.

The London Symphony Orchestra is in residence at the **Barbican Arts Centre** (tel. 071/638–8891), although other top symphony and chamber orchestras also perform here. The **South Bank arts complex** (tel. 071/928–8800), which includes the **Royal Festival Hall** and the **Queen Elizabeth Hall,** is another major venue for choral, symphony, and chamber concerts. For less expensive concert going, try the **Royal Albert Hall** (tel. 071/589–8212) during the summer Promenade season; special tickets for standing room are available at the hall on the night of performance. **The Wigmore Hall** (tel. 071/935–2141) is a small auditorium, ideal for recitals. Inexpensive lunchtime concerts take place all over the city in smaller halls and churches, often featuring string quartets, singers, jazz ensembles, and gospel choirs. **St. John's, Smith Square** (tel. 071/222–1061), a converted Queen Anne church, is one of the more popular venues. It has a handy crypt cafeteria.

Opera The **Royal Opera House** ranks alongside the New York Met. Prices range from £8.50 (in the upper balconies, from which only a tiny portion of the stage is visible) to £392 for a box in the Grand Tier. Bookings are best made at the box office (tel. 071/240–1066). The **Coliseum** (tel. 071/836–3161) is the home of the English National Opera Company; productions are staged in English and are often innovative and exciting. The prices, which range from £6.50 to £43, are much cheaper than those of the Royal Opera House.

Ballet The Royal Opera House also hosts the **Royal Ballet.** The prices are slightly more reasonable than for the opera, but be sure to book well ahead. The **English National Ballet** and visiting companies perform at the Coliseum from time to time, especially during the summer. **Sadler's Wells Theatre** (tel. 071/278–8916) hosts regional ballet and international modern dance troupes. Prices here are reasonable.

Film Most West End cinemas are in the area around Leicester Square and Piccadilly Circus. Tickets run from £4 to £7.50. Matinees and Monday evenings are cheaper. Cinema clubs screen a wide range of films: classics, Continental, underground, rare, or underestimated masterpieces. A temporary membership fee is usually about £1. One of the best-value clubs is the **National Film Theatre** (tel. 071/928–3232), part of the South Bank arts complex.

Nightlife

London's night spots are legion, and there is only space here to list a few of the best known. For up-to-the-minute listings, buy *Time Out*.

Jazz **Bass Clef** (85 Coronet St., tel. 071/729–2476), situated in an out-of-the-way warehouse on the northern edge of the City, (the nearest tube is Old Street), offers some of the best live jazz in town and a mainly vegetarian menu. **Ronnie Scott's** (47 Frith St., tel. 071/439–0747) is the legendary Soho jazz club where a host of international performers have played.

Nightclubs **Legends** (29 Old Burlington St., tel. 071/437–9933) has an impressive high-tech interior; a large choice of cocktails is served at the upstairs bar, while the downstairs area is graced with a large cool dance floor and central bar. Glitzy **Stringfellows** (16 Upper St. Martin's Lane, tel. 071/240–5534) has an Art Deco upstairs restaurant, mirrored walls, and a dazzling light show in the downstairs dance floor.
The Limelight (136 Shaftesbury Ave., tel. 071/434–0572), in a converted church, is one of London's enduringly popular night spots, with lots of one-nighter shows and special events. Liveliest on the weekend.

Casinos By law, you must apply in person for membership in a gaming house; in many cases, clubs prefer an applicant's membership to be proposed by an existing member. Approval usually takes about two days.

Crockford's (30 Curzon St., tel. 071/493–7771) is a civilized and unflashy 150-year-old club with a large international clientele; American roulette, punto banco, and blackjack are played.
Sportsman Club (3 Tottenham Court Rd., tel. 071/637–5464) is one of the few gaming houses in London to have a dice table as well as punto banco, American roulette, and blackjack.

Discos **Camden Palace** (1A Camden High St., tel. 071/387–0428) is perennially popular with both London and visiting youth. This multi-tier dance hall features different theme nights, three bars, and a colorful light show. American-style food is served.
The Hippodrome (Cranbourn St., tel. 071/437–4311) is a hugely popular and lavish disco with an exciting sound-and-laser light system, live bands and dancing acts, video screen, bars, and restaurant.

Rock **Dingwalls** (Camden Lock, Chalk Farm Rd., tel. 071/267–4967) is a very popular dance venue where a good selection of live bands play everything from rock to jazz every night of the week.

The Rock Garden (67 The Piazza, Covent Garden, tel. 071/240–3961) is famous for encouraging younger talent; Talking Heads, U2, and The Smiths are among those who played here while still virtually unknown. Music is in the standing-room-only basement, so eat first in the American restaurant upstairs.

The Marquee (105 Charing Cross Rd., tel. 071/437–6603), Soho's original rock club, is now in new premises; at least two live bands perform every night.

Cabaret The best comedy in town can be found in the small, crowded basement of the **Comedy Store** (28A Leicester Sq., tel. 071/839–6665). There are two shows, at 8 and midnight on Friday and Saturday, at 8 only Tuesday to Thursday.

Madame Jo Jo's (8 Brewer St., tel. 071/734–2473) is possibly the most fun of any London cabaret, with its outrageous, glittering drag shows. The place is luxurious, and civilized. There are two shows, at 12:15 and 1:15 AM, and the food and drinks are reasonably priced.

Windsor to Stratford

The towns covered in this section can all be visited on a day-trip basis—with the possible exception of Stratford-upon-Avon. British Rail seem determined to make this—one of England's leading tourist destinations—as difficult to reach as possible. Windsor, Oxford, and Bath, however, are great for a day's jaunt. The InterCity trains are Britain's pride and joy. You can reach Bath from London, for example, in just an hour and ten minutes.

These excursions will allow you to explore historic townships, such as Windsor, where the castle is still regularly used by the royal family; Oxford, home of the nation's oldest university; and Shakespeare's birthplace at Stratford-upon-Avon. Traveling south, you come to Bath, whose 18th-century streets recall an age more elegant than our own.

Getting Around

By Train Suburban services run from London (Waterloo and Paddington stations) to Windsor. Regular fast trains run from Paddington to Oxford and Bath, and less frequent and slower services requiring at least one change, to Stratford. For information, call 071/262–6767. An alternative route to Stratford is from London's Euston Station to Coventry, from which Guide Friday operates bus connections (summer four times daily, winter three times daily); telephone 0789–294466 for details.

By Bus Regular long-distance services leave from Victoria Coach Station. For information, call 071/730–0202. The **Badgerline** bus company in Bath has a series of **trails** that connect walking trails with bus routes to make a super budget way of exploring the countryside.

Tourist Information

Bath (The Colonnades, 11–13 Bath St., tel. 0225/462831).
Oxford (St. Aldate's, opposite the town hall, tel. 0865/726871).
Stratford (Bridgefoot, next to the canal bridge, tel. 0789/293127).
Windsor (Central Station, tel. 0753/852010).

Exploring Windsor to Stratford

Windsor **Windsor,** some 40 kilometers (25 miles) west of London, has been a royal citadel since the days of William the Conqueror in the 11th century. In the 14th century, Edward III revamped the old castle, building the Norman gateway, the great round tower, and new apartments. Almost every monarch since then has added new buildings or improved existing ones; over the centuries, the medieval fortification has been transformed into the lavish royal palace the visitor sees today. Windsor Castle remains a favorite spot of Queen Elizabeth and Prince Philip; they spend most weekends here, and there is a grand celebration with all the family at Christmas. Naturally, the royal family's private apartments are closed to the public, but you can see the State Apartments, where visiting heads of state are sometimes entertained.

The following are some of the highlights of the castle: **St. George's Chapel,** more than 71 meters (230 feet) long with two tiers of great windows and hundreds of gargoyles, buttresses, and pinnacles, is one of the noblest buildings in England. Inside, above the choir stalls, hang the banners, swords, and helmets of the Knights of the Order of the Garter, the most senior Order of Chivalry. The many monarchs buried in the chapel include Henry VIII and George VI, father of the present queen. The **State Apartments** indicate the magnificence of the queen's art collection; here hang paintings by such masters as Rubens, Van Dyck, and Holbein; drawings by Leonardo da Vinci; and Gobelin tapestries, among many other treasures. There are splendid views across to Windsor Great Park, the remains of a former royal hunting forest. Make time to view **Queen Mary's Dolls' House,** a charming toy country house with every detail complete, including electricity, running water, and miniature books on the library shelves. It was designed in 1921 by the architect Sir Edwin Lutyens for the present queen's grandmother. *Windsor Castle, tel. 0753/868286. Admission: Precincts—free; State Apartments—£4 adults, £1.50 children, £2.50 senior citizens; Dolls' House and Carriages, each—£1.50 adults, 70p children, £1.30 senior citizens. Opening times are extremely complicated and subject to change. We recommend that you check before visiting.*

After seeing the castle, stroll around the town and enjoy the shops; antiques are sold in cobbled Church Lane and Queen Charlotte Street. Opposite the castle, the **Royalty and Empire Exhibition,** in part of the central station, re-creates in waxworks the arrival at the station of Queen Victoria to celebrate her Diamond Jubilee in 1897; the scene is incredibly lifelike. *Thames St., tel. 0753/857837. Admission: £3.95 adults, £2.80 children under 16, £2.95 senior citizens. Open Apr.–Oct., daily 9:30–5:30, Nov.–Mar., daily 9:30–4:30.*

A short walk over the river brings you to **Eton,** Windsor Castle's equally historic neighbor and home of the famous public school. (In Britain, so-called "public" schools are private and charge fees.) Classes still take place in the distinctive redbrick Tudor-style buildings; the oldest buildings are grouped around a quadrangle called School Yard. The **Museum of Eton Life** has displays on the school's history, and a guided tour is also available. *Brewhouse Yard, tel. 0753/863593. Admission: £2.20 adults, £1.50 children; £3 or £4.50 adults, £2.50 or £4.50 chil-*

dren (rates vary with length of tour). Open daily during term 2–4:30, 10:30–4:30 on school holidays. Guided tours Mar.–Oct., daily at 2:15 and 3:15.

Numbers in the margin correspond to points of interest on the Oxford map.

Oxford Continue along A423 north to **Oxford.** The surest way to absorb Oxford's unique blend of history and scholarliness is to wander around the tiny alleys that link the honey-colored stone buildings topped by elegant "dreaming" spires, exploring the colleges where the undergraduates live and work. Oxford University, like Cambridge University, is not a single building but a collection of 35 independent colleges; many of their magnificent chapels and dining halls are open to visitors—times are displayed at the entrance lodges. **Magdalen College** (pronounced "maudlin") is one of the most impressive, with more than 500-year-old cloisters and lawns leading down to a deer park and the river Cherwell. **St. Edmund Hall,** the next college up the High Street, has one of the smallest and most picturesque quadrangles, with an old well in the center. **Christ Church,** on St. Aldate's, has the largest quadrangle, known as Tom Quad; hanging in the medieval dining hall are portraits of former pupils, including John Wesley, William Penn, and no fewer than 14 prime ministers. The doors between the inner and outer quadrangles of **Balliol College,** on Broad Street, still bear the scorch marks from the flames that burned Archbishop Cranmer and Bishops Latimer and Ridley at the stake in 1555 for their Protestant beliefs.

The **Oxford Story** on Broad Street is a dramatic multimedia presentation of the university's 800-year history, in which visitors travel through depictions of college life. *Broad St., tel. 0865/728822. Admission: £3.75 adults, £2.50 children, £3.25 senior citizens, £11 family ticket. Open daily, 9:30–5.*

Also on Broad Street is the **Sheldonian Theatre,** which St. Paul's architect Christopher Wren designed to look like a semicircular Roman amphitheater; it's one of his earliest works. Graduation ceremonies are held here. *Broad St., tel. 0865/277299. Admission: 50p adults, 25p children. Open Mon.–Sat. 10–12:45 and 2–4:45; closes at 3:45 Dec.–Feb.*

The **Ashmolean Museum,** which you encounter by turning right out of Broad Street into Magdalen Street, then taking the first left, is Britain's oldest public museum, holding priceless collections of Egyptian, Greek, and Roman artifacts; Michelangelo drawings; and European silverware. *Beaumont St., tel. 0865/278000. Admission free. Open Tues.–Sat. 10–4, Sun. 2–4.*

For a relaxing walk, make for the banks of the river Cherwell, either through the University Parks area or through Magdalen College to Addison's Walk, and watch the undergraduates idly punting a summer's afternoon away. Or rent one of these narrow flat-bottom boats yourself. But be warned: Navigating is more difficult than it looks!

Blenheim Palace, about 13 kilometers (8 miles) north of Oxford on the A34 (Woodstock Road), is a vast mansion in neoclassical style built in the early 18th century by the architect Sir John Vanbrugh; it stands in 1,012 hectares (2,500 acres) of beautiful gardens landscaped later in the 18th century by "Capability" Brown, perhaps the most famous of all English landscape gar-

Oxford

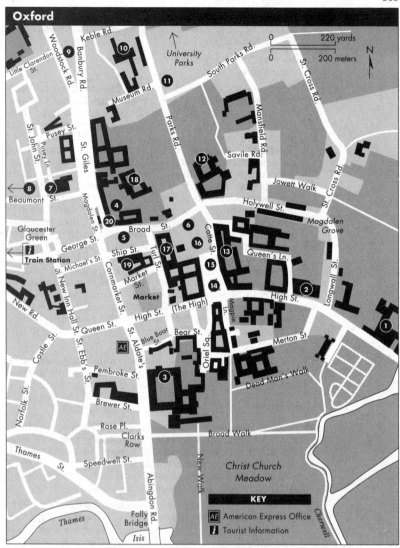

0 — 220 yards
0 — 200 meters

N

University Parks

KEY

AE American Express Office

i Tourist Information

Major Attractions
Ashmolean Museum, **7**
Balliol College, **4**
Christ Church, **3**
Magdalen College, **1**
Oxford Story, **5**
St. Edmund Hall, **2**
Sheldonian Theatre, **6**

Other Attractions
All Souls College, **13**
Bodleian Library, **16**
Exeter College, **17**
Jesus College, **19**
Keble College, **10**
Radcliffe Camera, **15**
St. Giles' Church, **9**
St. Mary Magdalen
Church, **20**

Trinity College, **18**
University Church
(St. Mary's), **14**
University
Museum, **11**
Wadham College, **12**
Worcester College, **8**

deners. The house was built by the soldier and statesman John Churchill, first duke of Marlborough, on land given to him by Queen Anne and with money voted him by Parliament on behalf of a "grateful nation" as a reward for his crushing defeat of the French at the Battle of Blenheim in 1704. The house is filled with fine paintings, tapestries, and furniture. Winston Churchill, a descendant of Marlborough, was born in the palace; some of his paintings are on display, and there is an exhibition devoted to his life. *Woodstock, tel. 0993/811325. Admission: £6 adults, £3 children under 15, £4.50 senior citizens. Open mid-Mar.–Oct., 10:30–4:45. Grounds open all year 9–5. Restaurant and cafeteria.*

Sir Winston Churchill (1874–1965) is buried in the nearby village of **Bladon.** His grave in the small tree-lined churchyard is all the more touching for its simplicity.

Stratford-upon-Avon Even without its most famous son, **Stratford-upon-Avon** would be worth visiting. The town's timbered buildings bear witness to its prosperity in the 16th century, when it was a thriving craft and trading center, and attractive 18th-century buildings are also of note.

Numbers in the margin correspond to points of interest on the Stratford-upon-Avon map.

The main places of Shakespearean interest are run by the **Shakespeare Birthplace Trust.** They all have similar opening times (Mar.–Oct., weekdays 9:30–5:30, Sun. 10–5:30; Nov.–Mar., weekdays 9:30–4, Sun. 10:30 (or 1:30)–4) and you can get an inclusive ticket for them all—£6.50 adults, £3 children—or pay separate entry fees if you want to visit only one or two. The **Shakespeare Centre** and **Shakespeare's Birthplace** contain the costumes used in the BBC's dramatization of the plays and an exhibition of the playwright's life and work. *Henley St., tel. 0789/204016. A Shakespeare Birthplace Trust property.*

Two very different attractions reveal something of the times in which Shakespeare lived. Originally a farmhouse, the girlhood home of Shakespeare's mother, **Mary Arden's House,** is now an extensive museum of farming and country life. It was built in the 16th century and many of the original outbuildings are intact, together with a 600-nesting-hole dovecote. *Wilmcote (4.8 km [3 mi] northwest of Stratford, off A34 and A422), tel. 0789/204016. Also reachable by train in a few minutes from Stratford. A Shakespeare Birthplace Trust property.*

A complete contrast is **Hall's Croft,** a fine Tudor town house that was the home of Shakespeare's daughter Susanna and her doctor husband; it is furnished in the decor of the day, and the doctor's dispensary and consulting room can also be seen. *Old Town, tel. 0780/292107. A Shakespeare Birthplace Trust property.*

The **Royal Shakespeare Theatre** occupies a perfect position on the banks of the Avon—try to see a performance if you can. The company (always referred to as the RSC) performs several Shakespeare plays each season, as well as plays by a wide variety of other playwrights, between March and January. Beside the main theater there is the smaller **Swan,** modeled on an Elizabethan theater, providing a very exciting auditorium for in-the-round staging, and a new auditorium for experimental productions, **The Other Place.** It's best to book well in advance for

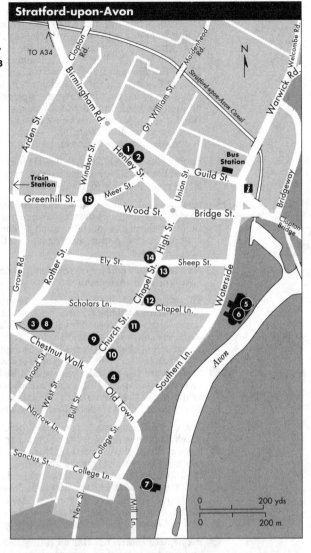

Major Attractions

Anne Hathaway's
Cottage, **8**

Hall's Croft, **4**

Holy Trinity Church, **7**

Mary Arden's House, **3**

Royal Shakespeare
Theatre, **5**

Shakespeare Centre, **1**

Shakespeare's
Birthplace, **2**

Swan, **6**

Other Attractions

American
Fountain, **15**

Grammar School and
Guildhall, **10**

Guild Chapel, **11**

Harvard House, **14**

Shakespeare
Institute, **9**

Town Hall, **13**

RSC productions, but tickets for the day of performance are always available, and it is also worth asking if there are any returns. *Programs are available starting in February from the Royal Shakespeare Theatre, Stratford-upon-Avon, Warwickshire CV37 6BB, tel. 0789/205301.*

⑦ It is in **Holy Trinity Church,** close to the Royal Shakespeare Theatre, that Shakespeare and his wife are buried.

⑧ **Anne Hathaway's Cottage,** in Shottery on the edge of the town, is the early home of the playwright's wife. *Tel. 0789/292100. Admission: £2 adults, 90p children. Shakespeare Trust opening times.*

Bath   Bath is a perfect 18th-century city, perhaps the best preserved in all Britain, it is a compact place, easy to explore on foot; the museums, elegant shops, and terraces of magnificent town houses are all close to each other.

Numbers in the margin correspond to points of interest on the Bath map.

It was the Romans who first took the waters at Bath, building a temple in honor of their goddess Minerva and a sophisticated series of baths to make full use of the curative hot springs. To this day, these springs gush from the earth at a constant temperature of 115.7°F (46.5°C). In the **Roman Baths Museum,** underneath the 18th-century Pump Room, you can see the excavated remains of almost the entire baths complex. *Abbey Churchyard, tel. 0225/461111. Admission: £3.60 adults, £1.70 children. Combined ticket for Roman Baths and Costume Museum: £4.40 adults, £2.20 children. Open Mar.–Oct., daily 9–6 (July–Aug. 9–7); Nov.–Feb., Mon.–Sat. 9–5, Sun. 10–5.*

➋ Next to the Pump Room is the **Abbey,** built in the 15th century. There are superb fan-vaulted ceilings in the nave.

In the 18th century, Bath became the fashionable center for taking the waters. The architect John Wood created a harmonious city from the mellow local stone, building beautifully executed terraces, crescents, and villas. The heart of Georgian **➌** Bath is the perfectly proportioned **Circus** and the Royal Cres- **➍** cent. On the corner, **No. 1 Royal Crescent** is furnished as it might have been when Beau Nash, the master of ceremonies and arbiter of 18th-century Bath society, lived in the city. *Tel. 0225/428126. Admission: £3 adults, £2 children and senior citizens. Open Mar.–Oct., Tues.–Sun. 11–5; Nov.–Dec., weekends 11–4.*

➎ Also near the Circus are the **Assembly Rooms,** frequently mentioned by Jane Austen in her novels of early 19th-century life. This neoclassical villa now houses a Museum of Costume, which was lavishly redesigned and opened in mid-1990. *Bennett St., tel. 0225/461111, ext. 2789. Admission: £2.30 adults, £1.30 children. Opening times are slightly later than at the Roman Baths Museum.*

Across the Avon, in an elegant 18th-century building, is the **➏** **Holburne Museum and Crafts Study Centre,** which houses a superb collection of 17th- and 18th-century fine art and decorative arts. There are also works by 20th-century craftsmen in the study center. *Great Pulteney St., tel. 0225/466669. Admission: £2 adults, £1 children, £1.50 senior citizens, family tickets £5. Open Easter–Oct., Mon.–Sat. 11–5, Sun. 2:30–6; Nov.–mid-Dec. and mid-Feb.–Easter, Tues.–Sat. 11–5, Sun. 2:30–6.*

Dining and Lodging

For details and price-category definitions, *see* Dining and Lodging in Staying in Great Britain.

Bath   **Tarts.** A good spot near the abbey for a meal and a break from
Dining   sightseeing. In a network of cellar rooms, you can choose from a regularly changing menu or daily specials. The desserts are rich and delicious, and the wine list has some excellent values. *8*

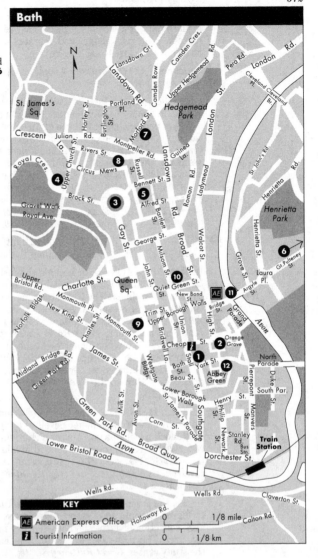

Major Attractions
Abbey, **2**
Assembly Rooms, **5**
Circus, **3**
Holburne Museum and Crafts Study Center, **6**
No. 1 Royal Crescent, **4**
Roman Baths Museum, **1**

Other Attractions
Camden Works Museum, **7**
Carriage Museum, **8**
Octagon and National Center of Photography, **10**
Pulteney Bridge, **11**
Sally Lunn's, **12**
Theatre Royal, **9**

KEY

AE American Express Office
i Tourist Information

0   1/8 mile
0   1/8 km

Pierrepont Pl., tel. 0225/330280. MC, V. Closed Sun. Moderate.

Number Five. A great spot for summer eating, this winebar/restaurant has a courtyard with a fountain. It serves delicious buffet food—try the pigeon breast or monkfish. 5 Argyle St., tel. 0225/444499. No credit cards. Inexpensive.

Theatre Vaults. These busy stone cellars house a very handy restaurant that serves light meals at lunchtime and early evening or full-scale dinner menus later. Try the rack of lamb or spinach lasagne. Sawclose, tel. 0225/442265. AE, DC, MC, V. Closed Sun. Inexpensive.

Lodging **Paradise House.** This worthwhile B&B is about a 10-minute, uphill walk from the center of town. Its upstairs windows have great views over the city. Cheerfully decorated in a cool blue and white, this 1720 house has been restored and has open fires in winter and a garden in summer. A full breakfast is on offer. All rooms have TV. *88 Holloway, BA2 4PX, tel. 0225/317723. 9 rooms, 6 with bath or shower. MC, V. Moderate.*

Pratt's. Just a few minutes' walk from the center of town and the main sights, Pratt's is a fine Georgian house. Once the home of novelist Sir Walter Scott, it is now a comfortable hotel with an innovative restaurant. *South Parade, BA2 4AB, tel. 0225/ 46041. 46 rooms with bath. Facilities: restaurant, parking nearby. AE, MC, V. Moderate.*

The Tasburgh Hotel. This refurbished Victorian house, surrounded by gardens with beautiful views over the Avon Valley, has tastefully furnished rooms complete with every modern comfort. It's situated a mile from city center. *Warminster Rd., tel. 0225/425096. 14 rooms, 10 with bath. Facilities: extensive gardens, fishing and mooring rights. AE, DC, MC, V. Moderate.*

Oxford	
Dining	**Fifteen North Parade.** Just outside the city center, this is an intimate, stylish restaurant with cane furniture and plants. The menu changes regularly and may feature steamed breast of chicken with morel mousse, served with truffle noodles, or pot-roast pheasant. *15 North Parade, tel. 0865/513773. Reservations advised. MC, V. Closed Sun. evening. Moderate.*

Oxford

Dining **Fifteen North Parade.** Just outside the city center, this is an intimate, stylish restaurant with cane furniture and plants. The menu changes regularly and may feature steamed breast of chicken with morel mousse, served with truffle noodles, or pot-roast pheasant. *15 North Parade, tel. 0865/513773. Reservations advised. MC, V. Closed Sun. evening. Moderate.*

Munchy Munchy. A daily changing menu of spicy Malaysian dishes and a good selection of fresh fruit and vegetables make this a refreshing and popular spot. The surroundings are unpretentious and the prices are reasonable. *6 Park End St., tel. 0865/245710. Reservations accepted. No credit cards. Inexpensive.*

The Trout. This ivy-covered medieval pub, on the northern edge of Oxford, is a wonderful spot for a summer bar lunch. There are peacocks by the stream, and a tasty selection of both hot and cold dishes is available. Indoors is a beamed restaurant. *Godstow, tel. 0865/54485. No food Sun. evening, except barbecue on summer Sun. evenings. Budget.*

Lodging **Cotswold House.** This popular B&B lies in the north of town, on the main A423 Banbury road. Inside the stone building the comfortable rooms are furnished with lovely old oak furniture and TVs. Don't confuse it with the much more pricey Cotswold Lodge. *363 Banbury Rd., OX3 7SP, tel. 0865/310558. 6 rooms with bath. No credit cards. Moderate.*

Highfield House. This comfortable guest house lies about 1½ miles from the center of town but is on a good bus route. It is close to the attrative old village of Iffley. The house stands on its own grounds; the rooms have TVs and tea/cofffee-making facilities. *91 Rosehill, OX4 4HT, tel. 0789/774083. 6 rooms, 5 with bath. No credit cards. Moderate.*

Pickwicks. Pickwicks is located ¼ mile east of the town center, off the main A420, the London road. This quietly run inn, situated on a corner in its own garden, features standard rooms with TVs and tea/coffee-making facilities. Evening meals are available on request. *17 London Rd., OX3 7SP, tel. 0865/ 750487. 14 rooms, 10 with bath or shower. MC, V. Moderate.*

Stratford

Dining **Box Tree Restaurant.** In the Royal Shakespeare Theatre, this elegant restaurant overlooks the river and is a favored spot for pre- and post-theater dining. Specialties include noisettes of lamb Box Tree and poached Scotch beef fillet. *Waterside, tel.*

0789/293226. Reservations required. Jacket and tie required. AE, MC, V. Moderate.

The River Terrace. For less expensive fare at the theater, this spot provides informal meals and light refreshments. Hot dishes include lasagna and shepherd's pie, and there are also salads, cakes, and sandwiches. *Waterside, tel. 0789/293226. No reservations. No credit cards. Inexpensive.*

The Slug and Lettuce. Don't let the name put you off. This is a pine-paneled pub that serves excellent meals; the long-standing favorites are chicken breast baked in avocado and garlic, and salmon escalope. *38 Guild St., tel. 0789/299700. Reservations accepted. MC, V. Inexpensive.*

Vintner's Wine Bar. This bar and restaurant, just up the hill from the theater, has an imaginative menu that changes regularly. You order before sitting down and the food is delivered to your table, so stake a claim for a seat first. Before a performance the place gets very busy indeed. *5 Sheep St., tel. 0789/297259. MC, V. Budget.*

Lodging **Arden Hotel.** Next to the theater, these recently refurbished 18th-century town houses have been successfully converted into a comfortable Old World hotel with beamed bedrooms. *44 Waterside, CV37 6BA, tel. 0789/294949. 65 rooms with bath. Facilities: garden. AE, DC, MC, V. Moderate.*

Caterham House. Built in 1830, this landmark building is in the center of town, close to the theater. Its rooms are individually decorated in early 19th-century style, featuring brass bedsteads and antiques. *58 Rother St., CV37 6LT, tel. 0789/267309. 14 rooms, 2 with bath. MC, V. Closed Christmas week. Moderate.*

Penryn House. This lodging is coveniently located halfway between the theater and Anne Hathaway's cottage and within easy walk of both. The comfortably furnished rooms have TV, hairdryers, and tea/coffee-making facilities. *126 Alcester Rd., CV37 0DP, tel. 0789/293718. 7 rooms, 5 with bath or shower. MC, V. Inexpensive.*

Windsor and Eton **Amamona's.** This is one of England's few South American res-
Dining taurants. It offers unusual specialties and a good-value set menu. *4 Church La., Windsor, tel. 0753/858331. MC, V. Closed Sun. evening and Mon. Moderate.*

The Courtyard. The idyllic setting, near the river and castle, make this a pleasant spot for light lunches and teas. *8 King George Pl., tel. 0753/858338. Open daily 11:30–5. Budget.*

The Dôme. Proximity to the castle, reasonable prices, and a varied French menu are reasons for having lunch here. Croque-monsieur, charcuterie, pâté, and salads, among other dishes, are available. *5 Thames St., tel. 0753/864405. MC, V. Budget.*

Lodging **Ye Harte and Garter.** Originally two Tudor taverns, this hotel was rebuilt during the last century. It is in a busy position immediately opposite the castle. *21 High St., Windsor, SL4 1LR, tel. 0753/863426. 50 rooms, 44 with bath or shower. AE, DC, MC, V. Moderate.*

Cambridge

Cambridge, home of England's second-oldest university, is an ideal place to explore. Students began studying here in the late 13th century, and virtually every generation since then has produced fine buildings, often by the most distinguished architects of their day. The result is a compact gallery of the best of English architecture. There is also good shopping in the city, as well as relaxing riverside walks.

Getting Around

By Train Fast, hourly trains from London's Liverpool Street Station take 90 minutes to Cambridge; there's somewhat slower service from London's King's Cross Station. For information, call 071/928–5100. Cambridge is an easy day trip from London by train. It can be a long day, too, as the last train back leaves just before 11 PM.

By Bus There are seven buses daily from Victoria Coach Station that take just under two hours. Tel. 071/730–0202.

Tourist Information

Cambridge (Wheeler St., off King's Parade, tel. 0223/322640).

Exploring Cambridge

The university is in the very heart of **Cambridge.** It consists of a number of colleges, each of which is a separate institution with its own distinct character and traditions. Undergraduates join an individual college and are taught by dons attached to the college, who are known as "fellows." Each college is built around a series of courts, or quadrangles; because students and fellows live in these courts, access is sometimes restricted, especially during examination weeks in early summer. Visitors are not normally allowed into college buildings other than chapels and halls.

Cambridge is very much a walker's town. In fact, the colleges lie so they can only be visited on foot. The station is quite close to the center of town. The only trouble is that Cambridge, a fenland city, can be very rainy. Take an umbrella and wear strong shoes.

Numbers in the margin correspond to points of interest on the Cambridge map.

① **King's College,** off King's Parade, is possibly the best known of all the colleges. Its chapel, started by Henry VI in 1446, is a masterpiece of late Gothic architecture, with a great fan-vaulted roof supported only by a tracery of soaring side columns. Behind the altar hangs Rubens's painting *Adoration of the Magi.* Every Christmas Eve the college choir sings the Festival of Nine Lessons and Carols, which is broadcast all over the world.

King's runs down to the "Backs," the tree-shaded grounds on the banks of the river Cam, which is the background of many of the colleges. From King's make your way along the river and **② ③** through the narrow lanes past **Clare College** and **Trinity Hall** to **④** **Trinity.** This is the largest college, established by Henry VIII

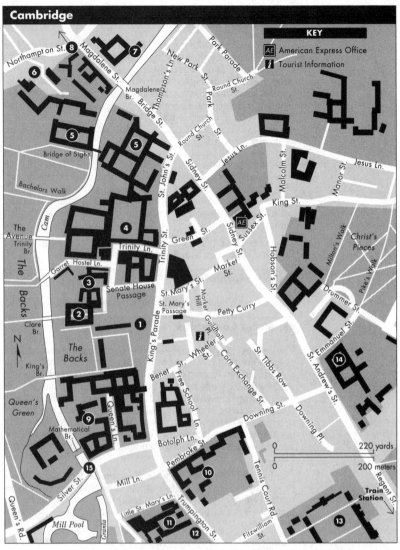

Cambridge

KEY

AE American Express Office

i Tourist Information

Clare College, **2**

Downing College, **13**

Emmanuel College, **14**

Fitzwilliam Museum, **12**

Kettle's Yard, **8**

King's College, **1**

Magdalene College, **7**

Merton Hall, **6**

Pembroke College, **10**

Peterhouse, **11**

Queen's College, **9**

St. John's, **5**

Silver Street Bridge, **15**

Trinity, **4**

Trinity Hall, **3**

in 1546. It has a handsome 17th-century Great Court, around which are the chapel, hall, gates, and a library by Christopher Wren. In the massive gate house is Great Tom, a large clock that strikes each hour with high and low notes. Prince Charles was an undergraduate here during the late 1960s.

❺ Beyond Trinity lies **St. John's,** the second-largest college. The white crenellations of the enormous mock-Gothic **New Building** of 1825 have earned it the nickname "the wedding cake." It is reached across a facsimile of the Bridge of Sighs in Venice. Be-
❻ hind St. John's is the oldest house in Cambridge, the 12th-century **Merton Hall.**

Across **Magdalene** (pronounced "maudlin") **Bridge** you come to
❼ **Magdalene College,** with its pretty redbrick courts. The **Pepys Library** contains the 17th-century diarist's own books and desk. *Admission free. Open Oct.–Mar., daily 2:30–3:30; Apr.–Sept., daily 11:30–12:30 and 2:30–3:30.*

❽ Beyond Magdalene is **Kettle's Yard.** This was originally the home of Jim Ede, a connoisseur of 20th-century art. Here he displayed his collections to the public; a gallery extension now houses temporary exhibits. *Castle St., tel. 0223/352124. Admission free. House open Tues.–Sun. 2–4; gallery open Tues.–Sat. 12:30–5:30 (Thurs. to 7), Sun. 2–5:30.*

Returning the way you've just come, along the Backs from
❾ King's, you'll see **Queen's College,** where Isaac Newton's **Mathematical Bridge** crosses the river. This arched wooden structure was originally held together by gravitational force; when it was taken apart to see how Newton did it, no one could reconstruct it without using nails.

❿ Back from the river, on Trumpington Street, sits **Pembroke College,** which contains some 14th-century buildings and a
⓫ chapel by Wren, and **Peterhouse,** the oldest college, dating from
⓬ 1281. Next to Peterhouse is the **Fitzwilliam Museum,** which contains outstanding art collections (including paintings by Constable) and antiquities (especially from ancient Egypt). *Trumpington St., tel. 0223/332900. Admission free. Open Tues.–Sat. 10–5, Sun. 2:15–5.*

⓭ Other colleges worth visiting include **Downing College,** which has a unique collection of neoclassical buildings dating from
⓮ about 1800, and **Emmanuel College,** whose chapel and colonnade are by Christopher Wren. Emmanuel's spacious gardens have a pretty duck pond with several unusual breeds. Among the portraits of famous Emmanuel men hanging in the hall is one of John Harvard, founder of Harvard University.

⓯ If you have time, hire a punt at **Silver Street Bridge** or at **Magdalene Bridge** and navigate down past St. John's or upstream to **Grantchester,** the pretty village made famous by the Edwardian poet Rupert Brooke. On a sunny day, there's no better way to absorb Cambridge's unique atmosphere—somehow you will seem to have all the time in the world.

Dining and Lodging

For details and price-category definitions, *see* Dining and Lodging in Staying in Great Britain.

Cambridge **Charlie Chan.** This is one of Cambridge's more exotic spots.
Dining The Chinese food is popular with undergrads, so there's a

good-value set meal for around £20 for two. Downstairs is casual, upstairs fancier. Dancing Thursday to Saturday. *14 Regent St., tel. 0223/61763. Reservations advised. AE. Moderate.*

Three Horseshoes. This is an early 19th-century thatched cottage, with a recently added conservatory. A pub restaurant serves beautifully prepared grilled fish, and the conservatory menu offers traditional English fare and seafood, also beautifully presented. *Madingley, tel. 0954/210221 (3 mi outside Cambridge). AE, DC, MC, V. Moderate.*

Twenty-Two. This intimate restaurant occupies a modest house a half-mile from the city center. The proprietor cooks the set dinner. Fish and game are the specialties. *22 Chesterton Rd., tel. 0223/351880. Reservations advised. MC, V. Closed Sun. and Mon. Moderate.*

Hobbs Pavilion. This friendly creperie near the colleges is located in a former cricket pavilion (you can sometimes watch a game of cricket on the grounds). The menu is a wide selection of savory and sweet crepes, which makes an ideal lunch. *Parker's Piece, Park Terr., tel. 0223/67480. No credit cards. Closed Sun., Mon. and mid-Aug.–mid-Sept. Budget.*

Lodging **Arundel House.** This hotel occupies a converted terrace of Victorian houses overlooking the river. The recently redecorated bedrooms are comfortably furnished with locally made mahogany furniture. *53 Chesterton Rd., CB4 3AN, tel. 0223/67701. 88 rooms, 78 with bath. Facilities: restaurant, bar, videos, garden. AE, DC, MC, V. Moderate.*

Centennial Hotel. The Centennial is conveniently located opposite the Botanical Gardens on the south side of town, near the station. All rooms have TV and tea/coffee-making facilities. There's an excellent restaurant serving steaks and Aylesbury duckling with black cherry and brandy sauce. *63–71 Hills Rd., CB2 1PG, tel. 0223/314652. 26 rooms with bath. Facilities: restaurant, TV. AE, DC, MC, V. Moderate.*

York

Once England's second city, the ancient town of York has survived the ravages of time, war, and industrialization to remain one of northern Europe's few preserved walled cities. It was King George VI, father of the present queen, who once remarked that the history of York is the history of England. Even in a brief visit to the city, you can see evidence of life from every era since the Romans, not only in museums but in the very streets and houses. On a more contemporary note, the city also boasts one of the most fashionable shopping centers in this part of the country.

York is surrounded by some of the grandest countryside England has to offer. A fertile plain dotted with ancient abbeys and grand aristocratic mansions leads westward to the hidden valleys and jagged, windswept tops of the Yorkshire Dales and northward to the brooding mass of the North York Moors. This is a land quite different from the south of England—it's friendlier, emptier, and less aggressively materialistic. No visitor to Britain should overlook it.

Getting Around

By Train Regular fast trains run from London's King's Cross Station to York. The trip takes two hours. For information, call 071/278–2477. York can be visited as a day trip from London, but only if you are prepared to make an early start. The last train leaves York at 9:40 in the evening.

By Bus Regular long-distance buses leave from Victoria Coach Station. The trip takes 4½ hours. For information, call 071/730–0202.

Tourist Information

There is a tourist information office at De Grey Rooms (Exhibition Square, North Yorkshire Y01 2HB, tel. 0904/621756) and one at the York railway station (tel. 0904/643700).

Exploring York

Numbers in the margin correspond to points of interest on the York map.

❶ York's greatest glory is the **Minster,** the largest Gothic church in England and one of the greatest in Europe. Take time to gaze at the soaring columns and intricate tracery of the 14th-century nave, the choir screen portraying the kings of England, and the rose window that commemorates the marriage of Henry VII and Elizabeth of York. Visit the exquisite 13th-century **Chapter House** and the Roman and Saxon remains in the **Undercroft Museum and Treasury.** Climb the 275 steps of the **Central Tower** for an unrivaled view of the city and the countryside beyond. *York Minster Undercroft Museum and Treasury, Chapter House, and Central Tower, tel. 0904/624426. Admission: Undercroft £1.50 adults, 60p children, £1.20 senior citizens, family ticket £4; Chapter House 60p adults, 30p children; Central Tower £1.50 adults, 70p children. Open Mon.–Sat. 10–6, Sun. 1–6 (summer till 7).*

❷ At the **Jorvik Viking Centre,** south of the Minster through tiny medieval streets, you can take another journey into history—traveling in little "time cars" back to the sights, sounds, and even the smells of a Viking street, which archaeologists have re-created in astonishing detail. *Coppergate, tel. 0904/643211. Admission: £3.50 adults, £1.75 children. Open Apr.–Oct., daily 9–7; Nov.–Mar., daily 9–5.*

Walk south down Castlegate and onto Tower Street, where
❸ you'll find the **Castle Museum,** housed in an 18th-century prison. It has a series of realistic period displays that bring the past to life. Highlights include a Victorian street scene, an 18th-century dining room, and a moorland farmer's cottage. Don't miss the Coppergate Helmet, one of only three Anglo-Saxon helmets ever found. *Clifford St., tel. 0904/653611. Admission: £3.35 adults, £2.35 children and senior citizens, family ticket £9.40. Open Apr.–Oct., Mon.–Sat. 9:30–5:30, Sun. 10–5:30; Nov.–Mar., Mon.–Sat. 9:30–4, Sun. 10–4.*

Even more than the wealth of museums, it is the streets and city walls that bring the city's past to life. A walk along the **walls,** most of which date from the 13th century, though with extensive restoration, provides delightful views across roof-

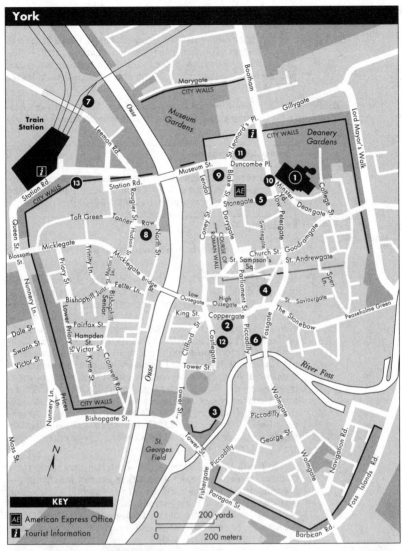

York

KEY

🄰🄴 American Express Office

🄸 Tourist Information

Major Attractions:
Castle Museum, **3**
Jorvik Viking Centre, **2**
Merchant Adventurers' Hall, **6**
Minster, **1**
National Railway Museum, **7**
Shambles, **4**
Stonegate, **5**

Other Attractions:
All Saints, **8**
Assembly Rooms, **9**
Cholera Burial Ground, **13**
St-Michael-le-Belfry, **10**
Theater Royal, **11**
York Story (Heritage Center), **12**

tops and gardens and the Minster itself. The narrow paved path winds between various fortified gates where the old roads ran out of the city.

④ Within the walls, the narrow streets still follow the complex medieval pattern. The **Shambles,** in the heart of this walled city, is a well-preserved example; the half-timbered shops and houses have such large overhangs that you can practically reach
⑤ from one second-floor window to another. **Stonegate** is a narrow pedestrian street of 18th-century (and earlier) shops and courts. Along a narrow passage off Stonegate, at 52A, you will find the remains of a 12th-century Norman stone house—one of the very few surviving in England.

⑥ The **Merchant Adventurers' Hall** is a superb medieval building (1357–68) built and owned by one of the richest medieval guilds; it contains the largest timber-framed hall in York. *Fossgate, tel. 0904/654818. Admission: £1.80 adults, 50p children under 15, £1.50 senior citizens. Open Easter–Aug., daily 9:30–5; Sept.–Easter, Mon.–Sat. 9:30–3.*

⑦ One very different attraction is the **National Railway Museum,** just outside the city walls, by the train station. This houses Britain's national collection of railway locomotives, including such giants of the steam era as *Mallard,* holder of the world speed record for a steam engine (126 mph), early rolling stock, and pioneer diesel and electric locomotives. *Leeman Rd., tel. 0904/621261. Admission: £3.30 adults, £1.65 children under 16, £2.10 senior citizens, £8 family ticket. Open Mon.–Sat. 10–6, Sun. 11–6.*

Dining and Lodging

For details and price-category definitions, *see* Dining and Lodging in Staying in Great Britain.

York **Freshneys.** Fish is the name of the game here—salmon, lemon
Dining and Dover sole, local fresh trout, and, when available, lobster. *Galtres Hotel, Petergate, tel. 0904/622478. Reservations advised. MC, V. Moderate.*

Giovanni's Restaurant. Delicious pasta, veal, and beef dishes are served with Italian wine in this typical small Italian restaurant. It's close to the Minster. *Goodramgate, tel. 0904/623539. Reservations advised. AE, MC, V. Closed Sun. and Mon. Moderate.*

19 Grape Lane. This tall, narrow, crowded restaurant offers simple, delicious dishes. Try the hare with mushrooms, or the Yorkshire treacle tart. There are good-value light lunches. *19 Grape La., tel. 0904/636366. Reservations essential. MC, V. Closed Sun. and Mon. Moderate.*

Four Seasons. These two 15th-century beamed houses were converted into a restaurant/café and have been used as such for 60 years. Some of the rooms still have timbered ceilings and stone floors. This is a good spot to taste Yorkshire cooking and offers excellent value light lunches. *45 Goodramgate, tel. 0904/633767. MC, V. Open daily 10–10. Inexpensive.*

The Hole in the Wall. A large pub near the Minster, The Hole in the Wall has beams, exposed stone, prints, plates, and all the trappings of a well-established watering hole. The bar food comes in generous helpings, and the beer is locally brewed. *High Petergate, tel. 0904/634468. No food Sat. evening. Budget.*

Lodging **Savages.** A comfortable, small hotel on a tree-lined road near the city center, Savages has a reputation for attentive service. *15 St. Peter's Grove, YO3 6AQ, tel. 0904/610818. 18 rooms with bath. Facilities: garden, baby-sitting service. AE, DC, MC, V. Moderate.*

Acer House. The station and town center are withing easy walking distance from this pleasant, small hotel on the southeast side of the city. The rooms are recently redecorated, and all have tea/coffee-making facilities. Meals are available. *52 Scarcroft Hill, The Mount, YO2 1DE, tel. 0904/653839. 6 rooms, all with bath or shower. MC, V. Moderate.*

Wheatlands Lodge Hotel. This small hotel–guest house with a reputation for warm Yorkshire hospitality occupies a handsome 19th-century bay-windowed house. The rooms are simple but of a high standard. *77–85 Scarcroft Rd., YO2 1DB, tel. 0904/654318. 32 rooms, most with bath. MC, V. Inexpensive.*

Edinburgh

Scotland and England *are* different—and let no Englishman tell you otherwise. Although the two nations have been united in a single state since 1707, Scotland retains its own marked political and social character, with, for instance, legal and educational systems quite distinct from those of England. And by virtue of its commanding geographic position, on top of a long-dead volcano, and the survival of a large number of outstanding buildings carrying echoes of the nation's history, Edinburgh proudly ranks among the world's greatest capital cities.

Getting Around

By Train Regular fast trains run from London's King's Cross Station to Edinburgh Waverley; the fastest journey time is about 4½ hours. For information in London, call 071/278–2477; in Edinburgh, 031/557–3000.

By Bus Regular services are operated by **Citylink Coaches** (071/636–1921 and 031/556–5717) and **Caledonian Express Stagecoach** (071/930–5781 and 0738/33481) between Victoria Coach Station, London, and St. Andrew Square bus station, Edinburgh. The journey takes approximately eight to nine hours. Both **Lothian Region Transport** (deep-red-and-white buses) and **S.M.T.** (green buses) operate tours in and around Edinburgh. For information, call 031/220–4111 (Lothian) or 031/556–2515 (S.M.T). Tickets allowing unlimited travel on city buses for various periods are also available.

Tourist Information

City Information (3 Princes Street, tel. 031/557–1700) is the main tourist center for Edinburgh. There is also a **tourist information desk** at the airport (tel. 031/333–2167). The **Scottish Travel Centre** (14 South St. Andrew Street, tel. 031/557–5522, individuals only) offers a travel service for those going beyond Edinburgh.

Exploring Edinburgh

The key to understanding Edinburgh is to make the distinction between the Old and New Towns. Until the 18th century, the city was confined to the rocky crag on which its castle stands, straggling between the fortress at one end and the royal residence, the Palace of Holyroodhouse, at the other. In the 18th century, during a civilizing time of expansion known as the "Scottish Enlightenment," the city fathers fostered the construction of another Edinburgh, one a little to the north. This is the New Town, whose elegant squares, classical facades, wide streets, and harmonious proportions remain largely intact and lived-in today.

Numbers in the margin correspond to points of interest on the Edinburgh map.

The Royal Mile
❶ **Edinburgh Castle,** the brooding symbol of Scotland's capital and the nation's martial past, dominates the city center. The castle's attractions include the city's oldest building—the 11th-century **St. Margaret's Chapel;** the **Crown Room,** where the Regalia of Scotland are displayed; **Old Parliament Hall;** and **Queen Mary's Apartments,** where Mary, Queen of Scots, gave birth to the future King James VI of Scotland (who later became James I of England). In addition, there are excellent views. *Tel. 031/225–9847. Admission: £3.40 adults, £1.70 children and senior citizens, £8.50 families. Open Apr.–Sept., Mon.–Sat. 9:30–5:05, Sun. 11–5:05; Oct.–Mar., Mon.–Sat. 9:30–4:20, Sun. 12:30–3:35.*

❷ The **Royal Mile,** the backbone of the Old Town, starts immediately below the **Castle Esplanade,** the wide parade ground that hosts the annual Edinburgh Military Tattoo—a grand military display staged during a citywide festival every summer (*see* below). The Royal Mile consists of a number of streets, running into each other—**Castlehill, Lawnmarket, High Street,** and **Canongate**—leading downhill to the Palace of Holyroodhouse, home to the Royal Family when they visit Edinburgh. Tackle this walk in leisurely style; the many original Old Town "closes," narrow alleyways enclosed by high tenement buildings, are rewarding to explore and give a real sense of the former life of the city.

❸ In Lawnmarket, the six-story tenement known as **Gladstone's Land** dates from 1620. It has a typical arcaded front and first-floor entrance and is furnished in the style of a merchant's house of the time; there are magnificent painted ceilings. *747B Lawnmarket, tel. 031/226–5856. Admission: £2 adults, £1 children and senior citizens. Open Apr.–Oct., Mon.–Sat. 10–5, Sun. 2–5.*

❹ Close by is **Lady Stair's House,** a town dwelling of 1622 that now recalls Scotland's literary heritage with exhibits on Sir Walter Scott, Robert Louis Stevenson, and Robert Burns. *Lady Stair's Close, Lawnmarket, tel. 031/225–2424, ext. 6593. Admission free. Open May–Sept., Mon.–Sat. 10–6; Oct.–Apr., Mon.–Sat. 10–5, Sun. 2–5 during the festival.*

A heart shape set in the cobbles of the High Street marks the
❺ site of the **Tolbooth,** the center of city life until it was demol-
❻ ished in 1817. Nearby stands the **High Kirk of St. Giles,** Edinburgh's cathedral; parts of the church date from the 12th century, the choir from the 15th. *High St. Admission free. Open Mon.–Sat. 9–7, Sun. for services.*

❼ Farther down High Street you'll see **John Knox's House.** Its traditional connections with Scotland's celebrated religious re-

384

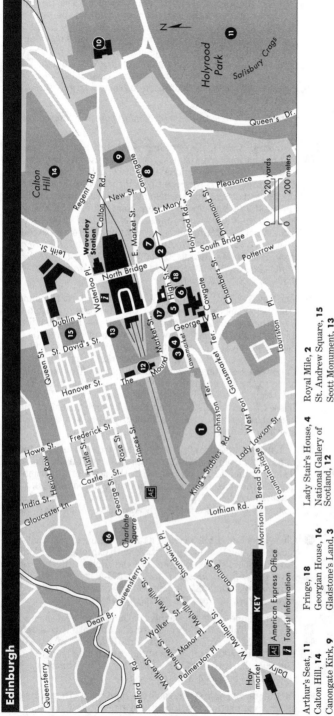

Edinburgh

Arthur's Seat, **11**
Calton Hill, **14**
Canongate Kirk, **9**
Edinburgh Castle, **1**
Edinburgh
International Festival
Office, **17**

Fringe, **18**
Georgian House, **16**
Gladstone's Land, **3**
High Kirk of
St. Giles, **6**
Huntly House, **8**
John Knox's House, **7**

Lady Stair's House, **4**
National Gallery of
Scotland, **12**
Palace of
Holyroodhouse, **10**

Royal Mile, **2**
St. Andrew Square, **15**
Scott Monument, **13**
Tolbooth, **5**

KEY

AE American Express Office

i Tourist Information

former are tenuous, but it is said to be the only 15th-century house surviving in Scotland and gives a flavor of life in the Old Town during Knox's time. *45 High St., tel. 031/556–2647. Admission: £1.50 adults, 75p children, £1.25 senior citizens. Open Mon.–Sat. 10–5.*

⑧ Canongate was formerly an independent burgh, or trading community, outside the city walls of Edinburgh. **Huntly House,** built in 1570, is a museum featuring Edinburgh history and social life. *142 Canongate, tel. 031/225–2424, ext. 6689. Admission free. Open June–Sept., Mon.–Sat. 10–6; Oct.–May, Mon.–Sat. 10–5, Sun. 2–5 during the festival.*

⑨ Some notable Scots are buried in the graveyard of the **Canongate Kirk** nearby, including the economist Adam Smith and the poet Robert Fergusson.

⑩ The **Palace of Holyroodhouse,** still the Royal Family's official residence in Scotland, was founded by King James IV at the end of the 15th century and was extensively remodeled by Charles II in 1671. The state apartments, with their collections of tapestries and paintings, can be visited. *Tel. 031/556–7371. Admission: £2.50 adults, £1.30 children, £2 senior citizens, £6.50 family ticket. Open Apr.–Oct., Mon.–Sat. 9:30–5:15, Sun. 10:30–4:30; end Oct.–Mar., Mon.–Sat. 9:30–3:45; closed during royal and state visits. (The palace will be closed for renovation Nov. 1992–mid-Feb. 1993.)*

⑪ The open grounds of **Holyrood Park** enclose Edinburgh's distinctive originally volcanic minimountain, **Arthur's Seat,** with steep slopes and miniature crags.

In 1767, the competition to design the New Town was won by a young and unknown architect, James Craig. His plan was for a grid of three east–west streets, balanced at each end by a grand square. The plan survives today, despite all commercial pressures. Princes, George, and Queen streets are the main thoroughfares, with St. Andrew Square at one end and Charlotte Square at the other.

⑫ The **National Gallery of Scotland,** on the Mound, the street that joins the Old and New Towns, contains works by the Old Masters and the French Impressionists and has a good selection of Scottish paintings. *Tel. 031/556–8921. Admission free; charge for special exhibitions. Open Mon.–Sat. 10–5, Sun. 2–5. Print Room, weekdays 10–12:30 and 2–4:30 by arrangement.*

⑬ To the east along Princes Street is the unmistakable soaring Gothic spire of the 62-meter- (200-foot-) high **Scott Monument,** built in the 1840s to commemorate the celebrated novelist of Scots history. There is a statue of Sir Walter and his dog within. The views from the top are well worth the 287-step climb. *Tel. 031/225–2424. Admission: 60p. Open Apr.–Sept., Mon.–Sat. 9–6; Oct.–Mar. Mon.–Sat. 9–3.*

⑭ There are more splendid views from **Calton Hill:** north across the Firth (or estuary) of Forth to the Lomond Hills of Fife and to the Pentland Hills that enfold the city from the south. Among the various monuments on Calton Hill are a partial reproduction of the **Parthenon,** in Athens, begun in 1824 but left incomplete because the money ran out; the **Nelson Monument;** and the **Royal Observatory.**

⑮ Make your way to **St. Andrew Square,** then along George Street, where there is a wide choice of shops, and on to **Charlotte Square,** whose north side was designed by the great Scottish classical architect Robert Adam. The rooms of the elegant

⑯ **Georgian House** are furnished to show the domestic arrangements of a prosperous late-18th-century Edinburgh family. *7 Charlotte Sq., tel. 031/225–2160. Admission: £2.40 adults, £1.20 children and senior citizens. Open Apr.–Oct., Mon.–Sat. 10–4:30, Sun. 2–4:30.*

Finally, a word about the **Edinburgh International Festival,** the annual celebration of music, dance, and drama that the city stages each summer (the 1993 dates are Aug. 15–Sept. 4), featuring international artists of the highest caliber. The **Festival Fringe,** the unruly child of the official festival, spills out of halls and theaters all over town, offering visitors a cornucopia of theatrical and musical events of all kinds—some so weird that they defy description. While the official festival is the place to see top-flight performances by established artists, at a Fringe event you may catch a new star, or a new art form, or a controversial new play in the making. Or then again, you may not; it's very much up to luck. Advance information, programs, and

⑰ ticket sales for the festival are available from the **Edinburgh International Festival Office,** 21 Market St. (tel. 031/226–4001);

⑱ for the **Fringe,** from 180 High St. (tel. 031/226–5257/5259).

Dining and Lodging

For details and price-category definitions, *see* Dining and Lodging in Staying in Great Britain.

Dining **L'Auberge.** An established restaurant, L'Auberge is comfortably old-fashioned and now has a new chef who has worked in Atlanta. The French-style cuisine uses the best Scottish ingredients. Try the brill with oysters or the tender venison. *56–58 St. Mary's St., tel. 031/556–5888. Reservations advised. AE, DC, MC, V. Moderate.*

Cousteau's. Enjoy fresh fish and seafood in a traditional dining room with cane furniture and an open fire in winter. The house specialty is the hot seafood platter, but the menu also features a few meat dishes. There's an oyster bar as well. *Hill Street North Lane, tel. 031/226–3355. Reservations advised. AE, DC, MC, V. Moderate.*

Jackson's Restaurant. Intimate and candlelit in a historic Old Town close, Jackson's offers good Scots fare. Aberdeen Angus steaks and Border lamb are excellent; there are vegetarian and seafood specialties, too. *2 Jackson Close, High St., tel. 031/ 225–1793. Reservations advised. MC, V. Closed for lunch Sat. and Sun. Moderate.*

Martin's. This is a good spot for imaginative vegetarian dishes and fresh seafood. Try the succulent halibut in a nettle sauce or pink sea trout cooked with seaweed. There's a good-value set lunch. *70 Rose St., tel 031/225–3106. Reservations required. AE, DC, MC, V. Open lunch Tues.–Fri., dinner Tues.–Sat. Moderate.*

Henderson's Salad Table. This friendly place claims to be the city's original vegetarian restaurant, long before such places became fashionable. Try the vegetarian haggis! *94 Hanover St., tel. 031/225–2131. Reservations accepted. AE, DC, MC, V. Inexpensive.*

Howie's. Howie's is a simple, neighborhood bistro, unlicensed, so you have to take your own bottle. The steaks are tender Aberdeen beef, and the clientele's lively. *75 St. Leonard's St., tel. 031/668–2917. MC, V. Open lunch Tues.–Fri. and Sun., dinner Tues.–Fri. Inexpensive.*

Guildford Arms. This is one of the hundreds of Edinburgh pubs that serve acceptable bar food. It is decorated in molded plaster, mahogany, gilt, and velvet. There is bar food as well as more substantial fare such as steaks and steamed fish. *West Register St., tel. 032/556–4312. Bar open daily, restaurant closed Sun. Budget.*

Jolly Judge. This atmospheric pub, in an old tenement, is in one of the oldest parts of town, just off the Royal Mile. There is basic bar food, with curries and lasagne, too. Beamed ceilings and a collection of foreign banknotes make this a pleasant place to eat. *James Court (beside 495 Lawnmarket), tel. 031/225–2669. No main meals Sun. lunch. Budget.*

Lodging **The Albany Hotel.** Three fine 18th-century houses with many original features have been carefully converted into a comfortable city-center hotel. There's a good restaurant in the basement. *39 Albany St., EH1 3QY, tel. 031/556–0397. 20 rooms with bath. AE, DC, MC. Moderate.*

Brunswick. This owner-run, Georgian guest house, convenient to the city center, has a friendly atmosphere and pleasant bedrooms, all with TV and tea/coffee-making facilities. *7 Brunswick St., EH7 5JB, tel. 031/556–1238. 10 rooms with shower. Closed Dec.–Feb. No credit cards. Moderate.*

Bruntisfield Hotel. All the rooms have their own style and character, with the lavish use of floral patterns and antiques. *68–74 Bruntisfield Pl., EH10 4HH, tel. 031/229–1393. 53 rooms with bath. AE, DC, MC, V. Moderate.*

Dorstan Private Hotel. A Victorian villa in a quiet area, the Dorstan has fully modernized rooms decorated in bright, country-cottage colors. *7 Priestfield Rd., EH16 5HJ, tel. 031/ 667–6721. 12 rooms, 9 with bath. No credit cards. Inexpensive.*

Salisbury Guest House. Another successful 18th-century building conversion, this quiet hotel is situated in a pleasant area. It's a good value and has a convenient location for city sightseeing. *45 Salisbury Rd., EH16 5AA, tel. 031/667–1264. 13 rooms, 8 with bath. No credit cards. Inexpensive.*

11 Greece

For centuries, Greece was a country of few material resources, poverty was borne with dignity, and a tradition of offering hospitality to strangers was upheld. Attitudes may have changed a bit as the Greek standard of living approaches that of other European Community countries, but the budget traveler is still made to feel welcome, particularly in out-of-the-way places in the countryside and on the islands.

You cannot travel far across the land here without meeting the sea or far across the sea without meeting one of its roughly 2,000 islands. About the size of New York State, Greece has 15,019 kilometers (9,387 miles) of coastline, more than any other country of its size in the world. The sea is everywhere, not on three sides only but at every turn, reaching through the shoreline like a probing hand. The land itself is stunning, dotted with cypress groves, vineyards, and olive trees, carved into gentle bays or dramatic coves with startling white sand, rolling hills, and rugged mountain ranges that plunge straight into the sea. This natural beauty and the sharp, clear light of sun and sea, combined with plentiful archaeological treasures, make Greece one of the world's most inviting countries.

Poetry, music, architecture, politics, medicine, law—all had their Western birth here in Greece centuries ago, alongside the great heroes of mythology who still seem to haunt this sun-drenched land. Among the great mountains of mainland Greece are the cloud-capped peak of Mount Olympus, fabled home of the Greek gods, and Mount Parnassus, favorite haunt of the sun-god Apollo and the nine Muses, goddesses of poetry and science. The remains of the ancient past—the Acropolis and the Parthenon, the temples of Delphi, the Tombs of the Kings in Mycenae—and a later procession of Byzantine churches,

Crusader castles and fortresses, and Turkish mosques are spread throughout the countryside.

Of the hundreds of islands and islets scattered across the Aegean Sea in the east and the Ionian Sea in the west, fewer than 200 are still inhabited. This world of the farmer and seafarer has largely been replaced by the world of the tourist. More than 8 million holiday makers visit Greece each year, almost as many as the entire native population; in fact, tourism has overtaken shipping as the most important element in the nation's economy. On some of the islands, the impact of the annual influx of visitors has meant the building of a new Greece, more or less in their image. But traditionalism survives: Now, pubs and bars stand next door to *ouzeries*, discos are as popular as *kafeneia*, and pizza and hamburger joints compete with *tavernas;* once-idyllic beaches have become overcrowded and noisy, and fishing harbors have become flotilla sailing centers. Prices rose steeply after Greece joined the European Community in 1981, and the simplicity and hardships of a peasant economy have largely disappeared from the islands' way of life.

Although mass tourism has taken over the main centers, it is still possible to strike out and find your own place among the smaller islands and the miles of beautiful mainland coastline. Except for some difficulty in finding accommodations (Greek families on vacation tend to fill the hotels in out-of-the-way places during high summer), this is the ideal way to see traditional Greece. Those who come only to worship the classical Greeks and gaze at their temples, seeing nothing but the glory that was, miss today's Greece. If you explore this fascinating country with open eyes, you'll enjoy it in all its forms: its slumbering cafés and buzzing tavernas; its elaborate religious rituals; its stark, bright beauty; and the generosity, curiosity, and kindness of its people.

Essential Information

Before You Go

When to Go Although the tourist season runs from May to October, the heat can be unpleasant in July and August, particularly in Athens. On the islands, a brisk northwesterly wind, the *meltemi*, can make life more comfortable. If you want to move about the country and avoid all the other tourists, the ideal months are May, June, and September. The winter months tend to be damp and cold virtually everywhere.

The following are the average daily maximum and minimum temperatures for Athens.

Jan.	55F	13C	May	77F	25C	Sept.	84F	29C
	44	6		61	16		67	19
Feb.	57F	14C	June	86F	30C	Oct.	75F	24C
	44	6		68	20		60	16
Mar.	60F	16C	July	92F	33C	Nov.	66F	19C
	46	8		73	23		53	12
Apr.	68F	20C	Aug.	92F	33C	Dec.	58F	15C
	52	11		73	23		47	8

Greece

BULGARIA

MACEDONIA

ALBANIA

Stavróupoli
Sidirókastro
Séres
Philippi
Eleftheroúpoli
Amfipoli
Kilkis
Kava
Edessa
Florina
Gianítsa
Thessaloniki
Alexandria
Kastoria
Thérmi
Néa
Apolonia
Ptolemaïda
Veria
E90
Polygyros
Ormylia
Vatopec
Kozani
Katerini
Iviríc
Siatista
Mount
Gulf of
Thermaikos
Dafni
Athos
Kónitsa
Grevena
Olympus
Kerkira
Delvináki
Elassóna
Kalithéa
Corfu
Métsovo
Tirnavos
Palioúri
Gulf of Kassandra
Igoumenítsa
Ioanina
Kalambaka
Agia
Paramythia
Trikala
Larissa
Parga
Arta
Karditsa
Volos
SPORADE
Aliki
Stavros
Farsala
Skiathos
Preveza
Almiros
Lefkas
Karpenissi
Lamia
Skópelos
Skyros
Vassiliki
Agrinio
Orhomenós
ÉVIA
Kymi
Kephalonia
Ithaki
Itea
Delphi
Nefpaktos
Livadia
Halkida
Lixouri
Sami
Messolongi
Galaxidi
Thebes
Patras
Gulf of Corinth
Kárystos
Diakofto
Megara
Athens
Killini
Corinth
Piraeus
Loutra
Nemea
Egina
Voula
Lavrio
Kéa
Zákynthos
Amalias
Argos
Poros
Sounio
Zákynthos
Pyrgos
Olympia
Náfplio
Ermioni
Kythnos
Kaiafas
Tripoli
Toló
Andritsena
Ydra
Kyparissia
PELOPONNESE
Spetses
Serifos
Ionian Sea
Messíni
Sparta
Leonidio
Gargaliani
Kalamata
Mystras
Geraki
Mirtoan
Pilos
Kyparíssi
Sea
Methoni
Koroni
Skala
Areopoli
Gythio
Monemvassia
Milos
Agía Pelagia
Kythira
Kythira
Mediterranean Sea
Haniá
0   100 miles
0   300 km
CRETE
N

Black Sea

THRACE

TURKEY

Kastaniés

Xanthi

Didymótiho

E90

Avdira

Mákri

Alexandróupoli

Thassos

Samothrace

Sea of
Marmara

Límnos

Troy

Lesvos

Mytilini

Plomari

TURKEY

Aegean Sea

Hios

Hios

Mésta

Pyrga

Izmir (Smyrna)

Andros

Andros

Ephesus

Sámos

Sámos

Ikaria

Pythagorio

Tinos

Agios
Kirykos

moupoli

Tinos

Syros

Mykonos

Pátmos

Delos

Paros

Leros

Bodrum
(Halicarnassus)

Naxos

Kos

Kos

CYCLADES

Amorgós

Ios

Astypalea

Nissyros

Symi

Thira

Tilos

Kámiros

Rhodes

Santorini

Anafi

DODECANESE

Halki

Lindos

Rhodes

Sea of Crete

Kárpathos

Iraklio

Mallia

Knossos

Kassos

Phaestos

Ierapetra

Currency The Greek monetary unit is the drachma (dr.). Bank notes are in denominations of 50, 100, 500, 1,000, and 5,000 dr.; coins, 1, 2, 5, 10, 20, and 50. At press time (summer 1992), there were approximately 193 dr. to the US dollar and 335 dr. to the pound sterling. Daily exchange rates are prominently displayed in banks. You'll get a better exchange rate at banks than from hotels or stores.

What It Will Cost Inflation in Greece is high—just under 20% a year—and fluctuations in currency make it impossible to do accurate budgeting long in advance, so keep an eye on the exchange rates before your vacation. On the whole, Greece offers good value compared with many other European countries. The values are especially good for modest hotels and restaurants, transportation, and entertainment.

There are few regional price differences for hotels and restaurants. A modest hotel in a small town will charge only slightly lower rates than a modest hotel in Athens, with the same range of amenities. The same is true of restaurants. The spread of tourism has made Rhodes, Corfu, and Crete as affordable as many other islands. Car rentals are expensive in Greece, but taxis are inexpensive even for long-distance runs.

Sample Prices At a central-city café, you can expect to pay about 400 dr. to 600 dr. for a cup of coffee or a bottle of beer, 200 dr. to 400 dr. for a soft drink, and around 500 dr. for a toasted cheese sandwich. These prices can, of course, vary considerably from one place to another. A 1½-kilometer (1-mile) taxi ride costs about 400 dr.

Customs on Arrival You may take in 200 cigarettes or 50 cigars or ¼ pound of smoking tobacco; 1 liter of alcohol, or 2 liters of wine; and gifts up to a total value of 5,000 dr. There's no duty on articles for personal use. Foreign bank notes in excess of $1,000 (about £560) must be declared for re-export. There are no restrictions on traveler's checks. Foreign visitors may take in 100,000 dr. in Greek currency and export up to 20,000 dr. plus $1,000 in foreign currencies. Larger amounts may be exported, depending on your export declaration on arrival.

Language English is widely spoken in hotels and elsewhere, especially by young people, and even in out-of-the-way places someone is always happy to lend a helping hand.

In this guide, names are given in the Roman alphabet according to the Greek pronunciation except when there is a familiar English form, such as "Athens."

Getting Around

By Bicycle Jeeps, dune buggies, pedal cycles, mopeds, and motorcycles can be rented on the islands. Use extreme caution. Crash helmets are not usually available, and injuries are common.

By Train Trains, although slow, are cheap and convenient, offering spectacular scenery on the route north to Thessaloniki and south to Mycenae. The main line runs north from Athens to Yugoslavia. It divides into three lines at Thessaloniki. The main line continues on to Yugoslavia, a second line goes east to the Turkish border and Istanbul, and a third line heads northeast to Bulgaria. The Peloponnese in the south is served by a narrow-gauge line dividing at Corinth into the Mycenae–Argos section and the Patra–Olympic–Kalamata section.

By Plane **Olympic Airways** (Syngrou 96, Athens, tel. 01/961–6161) has service between Athens and most towns and islands. Thessaloniki is also linked to the main islands, and there are many interisland connections.

By Bus Travel by bus is inexpensive, usually comfortable, and relatively fast. The journey from Athens to Thessaloniki, for example, takes roughly the same amount of time as the slow train, though the express covers the distance 1¼ hours faster. In the Peloponnese, however, buses are much faster than trains. Bus information and timetables are available at tourist information offices throughout Greece. Make reservations at least one day before your planned trip. Railway-operated buses leave from the main railway station in Athens. All other buses leave from one of two bus stations: Liossiou 260—for central and eastern Greece and Evvia; Kifissou 100—for the Peloponnese and northwestern Greece.

By Boat There are frequent ferries and more expensive hydrofoils from Piraeus, the port of Athens, to the central and southern Aegean islands and Crete. Nearby islands are also served by hydrofoils and ferries from Rafina, east of Athens. Ships to other islands sail from ports nearer to them. Connections from Athens/Piraeus to the main island groups are good, connections from main islands to smaller ones within a group less so, and services between islands of different groups or areas—such as Rhodes and Crete—are less frequent. Travel agents and shipping offices in Athens and Piraeus and in the main towns on the islands have details. Buy your tickets two or three days in advance, especially if you are traveling in summer or taking a car. Reserve or confirm your return journey or continuation soon after you arrive.

Timetables change very frequently, and boats may be delayed by weather conditions, so your itinerary should allow for some flexibility.

Staying in Greece

Telephones Most curbside kiosks have pay telephones for local calls only.
Local Calls You pay the man inside the booth after the call.

International Calls The easiest way to make and pay for international and long-distance calls is to go to a Telecommunications Office (OTE), usually located in the center of towns and villages. There are several branches in Athens. There are also a few special telephone booths (distinguished by their orange band) for international and long-distance calls. Calls to the United States and Canada cost 1,367 dr. for a three-minute-minimum station-to-station connection and 1,793 dr. for a three-minute-minimum person-to-person connection, plus 425 dr. for each additional minute or part of a minute. Hotels tend to add a hefty service charge for long-distance calls.

Operators and Information There are English-speaking operators on the International Exchange. Ask your hotel reception desk or an employee at the OTE for help in reaching one.

Mail
Postal Rates
Airmail letters or postcards for delivery within Europe cost 80 dr. for 20 grams and 140 dr. for 50 grams; outside Europe the cost is 100 dr. for 20 grams and 170 dr. for 50 grams.

Receiving Mail
You can have your mail sent to Poste Restante, Aeolou 100, Athens (take your passport to pick up your mail), or to American Express, Syntagma Square 2, Athens. For holders of American Express cards or traveler's checks, there is no charge for the service. Others pay 300 dr. for each pick-up.

Shopping
VAT Refunds
Prices quoted in shops include the VAT. There are no VAT refunds.

Bargaining
Prices in large stores are fixed. Bargaining may take place in small owner-managed souvenir and handicrafts shops. In flea markets, bargaining is expected.

Opening and Closing Times
The government has freed opening hours for shops and businesses under its program to liberalize the economy. As a result, office and shopping hours can vary considerably and may also change according to the season. Check with your hotel for up-to-the-minute information on opening and closing times. Below is a rough guide:

Banks. Banks are open weekdays 8–2:30; closed weekends and public holidays.

Museums. Most major museums are open 8:30–3; some smaller ones close earlier. Generally, museums are closed on Monday, with shorter hours on Sunday and public holidays. During the summer, major museums may be open daily. Archaeological sites usually open at 8:30 and close at sunset during the summer, at 3 during the winter. Hours vary from one site to another and often change without notice; always check with tourist offices or travel agencies before visiting. *See* Exploring for hours, which were correct at press time (spring 1992) but may change by summer.

Shops. Most shops are open weekdays from 8–5: some smaller ones close at 2:30. Some are open different hours on alternate days: Tuesday, Thursday, and Friday, 8–1:30 and 5–8; Monday, Wednesday, and Saturday, 8–2:30.

National Holidays
January 1; January 6 (Epiphany); February 18 (Shrove Monday); March 1 (Clean Monday); March 25 (Independence); April 16 (Good Friday); April 18 (Easter Sunday); April 19 (Easter Monday); May 1 (Labor Day); May 27 (Pentecost); August 15 (Assumption); October 28 (Ochi Day); December 25–26.

Dining
Greek cuisine cannot be compared to that of France, and few visitors would come to Greece for its food alone. You'll certainly be able to find a delicious and inexpensive meal, but don't look in hotel restaurants, where the menus usually consist of bland, unimaginative international fare (although it's only here that you will find a reasonably priced fixed menu). The principal elements of Greek cuisine are such vegetables as eggplants, tomatoes, and olives, fresh and inventively combined with lots of olive oil and such seasonings as lemon juice, garlic, basil, and oregano. While meat dishes are limited (veal, lamb, and chicken being the most common), fish is often the better, though more expensive choice, particularly on the coast. Your best bet is to look for tavernas and *estiatoria* (restaurants) and choose the one frequented by the most Greeks. The *estiatorio* serves oven-baked dishes, precooked and left to stand, while tavernas

offer similar fare plus grilled meats and fish. The decor of both types of establishment may range from simple to sophisticated, with prices to match.

Traditional fast-food in Greece consists of the *giro* (slices of grilled meat with tomato and onions in pita bread), *souvlaki* (shish kebab), and pastries filled with a variety of stuffings (spinach, cheese, or meat)—but hamburgers and pizzas can now be found even on the smaller islands.

Mealtimes Lunch in Greek restaurants is served from 12:30 until 3. Dinner begins at about 9 and is served until 1 in Athens and until midnight outside Athens.

Precautions Tap water is safe to drink everywhere, but it is often heavily chlorinated. Excellent bottled mineral water, such as *Loutraki*, is available.

Dress Throughout the Greek islands you can dress informally for dinner, even at Expensive restaurants; in Athens, you may want to wear a jacket and tie at some of the top-price restaurants.

Ratings Prices are per person and include a first course, main course, and dessert (generally fruit and cheese or a sticky Asian pastry such as baklava). They do not include drinks or the 12%–15% service charge. Best bets are indicated by a star ★.

Category	Athens/Thessaloniki	Other Areas
Moderate	3,000 dr.–5,000 dr.	2,000 dr.–4,000 dr.
Inexpensive	1,500–3,000 dr.	1,500–2,000 dr.
Budget	under 1,500	under 1,500

Lodging Most accommodations are in standard hotels, sometimes called motels. There are a number of "village" complexes, especially at the beaches, and as part of some hotels. On islands and at beach resorts, large hotels are complemented by family-run pensions and guest houses—usually clean, bright, and recently built—and self-catering apartment and bungalow complexes. In a very few places, there are state-organized "traditional settlements"—fine old houses with guest accommodations.

Greek hotels are classified as Deluxe, A, B, C, etc. For the budget traveler, a class-C Greek hotel usually offers the best value. In this guide, hotels are classified according to price: Moderate, Inexpensive, and Budget. If a hotel is air-conditioned, this is indicated. All have been built or completely renovated during the past 20 years, and some have private baths.

Prices quoted by hotels usually include service, local taxes, and VAT. Some may also include breakfast. Prices quoted are for double occupancy. Single occupancy is slightly less. The official price should be posted on the back of the door or inside a closet.

Ratings Prices quoted are for a double room in high season, including taxes and service, but not breakfast. Rates are the same throughout the country for each category. Best bets are indicated by a star ★.

Category	All Areas
Moderate	10,000 dr.–15,000 dr.
Inexpensive	7,000–10,000 dr.
Budget	under 7,000

Tipping There are no absolute rules for tipping. In restaurants, cafés, and tavernas, in addition to the 15% service charge, you should leave a tip for the waiter of around 10% in the better restaurants and between 5% and 10% in cheaper tavernas. This should be left on the table for your waiter and not on the plate, where it will be taken by the head waiter. In hotels, tip porters 50 dr. or 100 dr. per bag for carrying your luggage. Taxi drivers don't expect tips, but Greeks usually give something, especially to round off the fare or if the driver has been especially helpful.

Athens

Arriving and Departing

By Plane Most visitors arrive by air at Helleniko Airport. All Olympic Airways flights, both international and domestic, use the Western terminal next to the ocean. All other flights arrive and depart from the Eastern terminal on the opposite side of the airport.

Between the Airport and Downtown A blue-and-yellow coach service connects the two air terminals, Syntagma Square, the bus and train stations, and Piraeus. The coaches run every 20 minutes from 6 AM until midnight (fare: 160 dr.) and every 90 minutes from midnight until 6 AM (fare: 200 dr.). A taxi to the center of Athens costs about 1,200 dr.

By Train Athens has two railway stations, side by side, not far from Omonia Square. International trains from the north arrive at, and depart from, Stathmos Larissis, and trains from the Peloponnese use the marvelously ornate and old-fashioned Stathmos Peloponnisos next door.

By Bus Greek buses arrive at the Athens bus station at 100 Kifissou. International buses drop their passengers off on the street, usually in the Omonia or Syntagma Square areas or at Stathmos Larissis.

By Ship Except for cruise ships, few passenger ships from other countries call at Piraeus, the port of Athens, 10 kilometers (6 miles) from Athens' center. If you do dock at Piraeus, you can take the metro right into Omonia Square. The trip takes 20 minutes and costs 75 dr. Alternatively, you can take a taxi, which may well take longer due to traffic and will cost a great deal more, around 1,000 dr.

Getting Around

Many of the sights you'll want to see, and most of the hotels, cafés, and restaurants, are within a fairly small central area. It's easy to walk everywhere.

By Metro An electric (partially underground) railway runs from Piraeus to Omonia Square and then on to Kifissia. It is not useful for getting around the central area. The standard fare is 75 dr. or 100 dr., depending on the distance. There are no special fares or day tickets for visitors, and there is, as yet, no public transport map.

By Bus The fare on blue buses and the roomier yellow trolley buses is 75 dr. Tickets should be purchased beforehand at one of the yellow kiosks, or from booths at one of the terminals. Buses run from the center to all suburbs and suburban beaches until about midnight. For suburbs beyond central Kifissia, you have to change at Kifissia. Attica has an efficient bus network. Most buses, including those for Sounion, leave from the KTEL terminal, Platia Aigyptiou on Mavromateon, at the corner of Patission and Alexandras avenues.

Important Addresses and Numbers

Tourist Information There are **Greek National Tourist Offices** at Karageorgi Servias 2, in the bank, tel. 01/322–2545; at East Helleniko Airport, tel. 01/970–2395; at Stadiou 4, tel. 01/322–1459; at Ermou 1, inside the General Bank building, tel. 01/325–2267; and at Piraeus, NTOG Building, Marina Zeus, tel. 01/413–5716.

Embassies **U.S.** (Vasilissis Sofias 91, tel. 01/721–2951); **Canadian** (Gennadiou 4, tel. 01/723–9511); **U.K.** (Ploutarchou 1, tel. 01/723–6211).

Emergencies **Police:** Tourist Police (tel. 171); Traffic Police (tel. 01/523–0111); and City Police (tel. 100). **Ambulance** (tel. 166). **Doctors:** Top hotels usually have one on staff; any hotel will call one for you. You can also call your embassy. **Dentist:** Ask your hotel or embassy.

Exploring Athens

Athens is essentially a village that outgrew itself, spreading out from the original settlement at the foot of the Acropolis. Back in 1834, when it became the capital of modern Greece, the city had a population of 20,000. Now it houses more than a third of the Greek population—around 4 million. A modern concrete city has engulfed the old village and now sprawls for 388 square kilometers (150 square miles), covering almost all the surrounding plain from the sea to the encircling mountains.

The city is very crowded, very dusty, and overwhelmingly hot during the summer. It also has an appalling air-pollution problem, caused mainly by traffic fumes; in an attempt to lessen the congestion, it is forbidden to drive private cars in central Athens on alternate workdays. Despite the smog, heat, and dust, Athens is an experience not to be missed. It has a tangible vibrancy that makes it one of the most exciting cities in Europe, and the sprawling cement has failed to overwhelm the few striking and astonishing reminders of ancient Athens.

The central area of modern Athens is small, stretching from the Acropolis to Mount Lycabettos, with its small white church on top. The layout is simple: Three parallel streets—Stadiou, Venizelou, and Academias—link two main squares—Syntagma and Omonia. Do wander off this beaten tourist track to catch some of the real flavor of living Athens. Seeing the Athenian butchers in the central market near Monastiraki sleeping on their cold, marble slabs during the heat of the afternoon siesta may give you more of a feel for the city than seeing hundreds of fallen pillars.

Numbers in the margin correspond to points of interest on the Athens map.

The Historic Heart
❶ At the center of modern Athens is **Syntagma (Constitution) Square.** It has several leading hotels, airline and travel offices, and numerous cafés. Along one side of the square stands the
❷ **Parliament Building,** completed in 1838 as the royal palace for the new monarchy. In front of the palace, you can watch the changing of the vividly costumed **Evzone guard** at the Tomb of the Unknown Soldier. Amalias Avenue, leading out of Syntagma, will take you to the **National Gardens,** a large oasis in the vast sprawl of this largely concrete city.

Across the street, at the far end of the National Gardens, you
❸ will see the columns of the once-huge **Temple of Olympian Zeus.** This famous temple was begun in the 6th century BC, and, when it was finally completed 700 years later, it exceeded in magnitude all other temples in Greece. It was destroyed during the invasion of the Goths in the 4th century, and today only the towering sun-browned columns remain. *Admission: 400 dr. Open Apr.–Oct., Tues.–Sun. 8:30–3.*

❹ To the right stands **Hadrian's Arch,** built at the same time as the temple by the Roman emperor. It consists of a Roman archway, with a Greek superstructure of Corinthian pilasters. Visiting heads of state are officially welcomed here.

About three-quarters of a kilometer (a half mile) east, down
❺ Leoforos Olgas Avenue, you'll come to the marble **stadium** built for the first modern Olympic Games in 1896; it is a blindingly white, marble reconstruction of the ancient Roman stadium of Athens and can seat 70,000 spectators.

From Hadrian's Arch, take the avenue to the right, Dionysiou
❻ Areopagitou, a few blocks west to the **Theater of Dionysos,** built during the 6th century BC. Here the famous ancient dramas and comedies were originally performed in conjunction with bacchanalian feasts. *Tel. 01/323–6665. Admission: 400 dr. Open Apr.–Oct., Tues.–Sun. 8:30–3.*

A little higher up, on the right, you'll see the massive back wall
❼ of the much better preserved **Theater of Herodes Atticus,** built by the Romans during the 2nd century AD. Here, on pine-scented summer evenings, the **Athens Festival** takes place. It includes opera, ballet, drama, and concerts (*see* The Arts, below). *Tel. 01/321–0219. It is not otherwise open to the public.*

❽ Beyond the theater, a steep, zigzag path leads to the **Acropolis.** Though the Sacred Rock had been a center of worship for 5,000 years, the Athenians built this complex during the 5th century BC to commemorate the Greek naval victory at Salamis over the Persians. It is now undergoing conservation as part of an ambitious 20-year rescue plan launched with international support in 1983 by Greek architects. The first ruins you'll see are the **Propylaea,** the monumental gateway that led worshipers from the temporal world into the spiritual world of the sanctuary; now only the columns of Pentelic marble and a fragment of stone ceiling remain. Above, to the right, stands the graceful **Temple of Wingless Victory** (or Athena Nike), so called because the sculptor depicted the goddess of victory without her wings in order to prevent her from flying away. The elegant and architecturally complex **Erechtheion temple,** most sacred of the shrines of the Acropolis and later turned into a harem by the Turks, has now emerged from extensive repair work. Dull, heavy copies of the infinitely more beautiful Caryatids (draped maidens) now support the roof. The Acropolis Museum houses five of the six originals, their faces much damaged by acid rain. The sixth is in the British Museum in London.

9 The **Parthenon** dominates the Acropolis and indeed the Athens skyline. Designed by Ictinus, with Phidias as master sculptor, it is the largest Doric temple ever built and the most architecturally sophisticated. Even with hordes of tourists wandering around the ruins, you can still feel a sense of wonder. It was completed in 438 BC. The architectural decorations were originally picked out in vivid red and blue paint, and the roof was of marble tiles, but time and neglect have given the marble pillars their golden-white shine, and the beauty of the building is all the more stark and striking. The British Museum houses the largest remaining part of the original 162-meter (523-foot) frieze (the Elgin Marbles). The building has 17 fluted columns along each side and 8 at the ends, and these lean slightly inward and bulge to cleverly counterbalance the natural optical distortion. The Parthenon has had a checkered history: It was made into a brothel by the Romans, a church by the Christians, and a mosque by the Turks. The Turks also stored gunpowder in the Propylaea, and when this was hit by a Venetian bombardment in 1687, a fire raged for two days and 28 columns were blown out, leaving the Parthenon in its present condition. *Tel. 01/321–0219. Admission: 1,500 dr., joint ticket to Acropolis and museum. Open weekdays 8–7, weekends and holidays 8:30–3.*

10 The **Acropolis Museum,** just below the Parthenon, contains some superb sculptures from the Acropolis, including the Caryatids and a large collection of colored *kore* (statues of women dedicated by worshipers to the goddess Athena, patron of the ancient city). *Tel. 01/323–6665. Admission: 1,500 dr., joint ticket to the Acropolis. Open weekdays 8–7, weekends and holidays 8:30–3.*

On the rocky outcrop facing the Acropolis, St. Paul preached to the Athenians; the road leading down between it and the hill of Pnyx is called Agiou Pavlou (St. Paul). To the right stands the
11 **Agora,** which means "marketplace," the civic center and focal point of community life in ancient Athens. The sprawling confusion of stones, slabs, and foundations is dominated by the
12 best-preserved temple in Greece, the **Hephestaion** (often wrongly referred to as the Theseion), built during the 5th century BC. Nearby, the impressive Stoa of Attalus II, reconstructed by the American School of Classical Studies in Athens with the help of the Rockefeller Foundation, houses the
13 **Museum of the Agora Excavations.** *Tel. 01/321–0185. Admission: 800 dr. Open Tues.–Sun. 8:30–3.*

Next to the Agora you'll find the **Plaka,** almost all that's left of 19th-century Athens. During the 1950s and '60s, the area became garish with neon as nightclubs moved in and residents moved out. Renovation in recent years has restored the Plaka, and it is again lined with attractive red-tile-roof houses and the vine-shaded courtyards of open-air tavernas and bars.

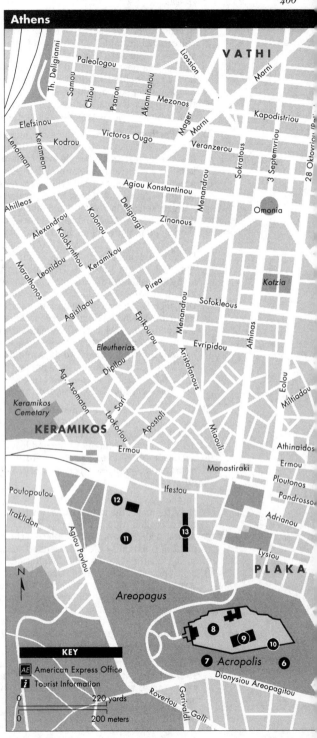

Athens

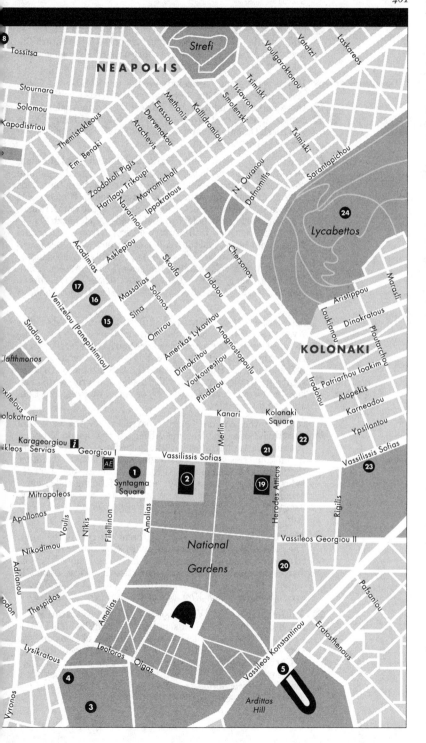

Strefi

NEAPOLIS

Tossitsa
Stournara
Solomou
Kapodistriou

Themistokleous
Em. Benaki
Arachevis
Dervenakou
Eressou
Methonis
Kallidromiou

Zoodoho1i Pigis
Harilaou Trikoupi
Mavromichali
Navarinou
Ippokratous

Voulgaroktonou
Vatatzi
Laskareos
Tsimiski
Issavron
Smolenski

N. Ouranou
Dafnomilis
Tsimiski
Sarantapichou

Acadimias
Asklepiou
Massalias
Sina
Skoufa
Solonos
Omirou
Didotou
Chersonos

Lycabettos

24

17
16
15

Venizelou (Panepistimiou)
Stadiou
lafthmonos

Amerikas Lykavitou
Dimokritou
Voukourestiou
Pindarou
Anagnostopoulu

KOLONAKI

Aristippou
Loukianou
Dinokratous
Ploutarchou
Patriarhou Ioakim
Iraodiou
Alopekis
Karneadou
Ypsilantou
Marasli

xileous
olokotroni
Karageorgiou
ikleos Servias

Georgiou I
AE

Kanari
Merlin

Kolonaki
Square

22

21

Vassilissis Sofias

23

Vassilissis Sofias

1
Syntagma
Square

2

19

Mitropoleos
Apollonos
Nikodimou
Adrianou
odon
Thespidos

Vouls
Nikis
Filellinon
Amalias

Herodes Atticus

Rigilis

Vassileos Georgiou II

National

Gardens

20

Lysikratous

Amalias
Leoforos Olgas

Vyronos

4

3

Vassileos Konstantinou
Eratosthenous
Patsaniou

5

Ardittos
Hill

Below the Plaka, in Cathedral Square, stands a charming 12th-
⑭ century Byzantine church known as the "Old" or **"Little Cathedral,"** nestled below the vast structure of the 19th-century **Cathedral of Athens.** From here, a short walk up Mitropoleos will
take you back to Syntagma.

Downtown Athens If you walk along Venizelou Avenue (also known as Panepistimiou Avenue) from the square, you will pass, on the right,
⑮ three imposing buildings in Classical style: the **Academy,** the
⑯ ⑰ **Senate House of the University,** and the **National Library.** When
you reach **Omonia Square,** a bedlam of touts and tourists, you
are in the heart of downtown Athens.

⑱ Try to spare time to see the **National Archaeological Museum.**
Despite being somewhat off the tourist route, a good 10-minute
walk north of Omonia Square, it is well worth the detour. This
is by far the most important museum in Athens. It houses one
of the most exciting collections of antiquity in the world, including sensational archaeological finds made by Heinrich Schliemann at Mycenae, a 16th-century BC fresco from the Akrotiri
ruins on Santorini, and the 6½-foot-tall bronze sculpture *Poseidon,* an original work of circa 470 BC, possibly by the sculptor
Kalamis, which was found in the sea off Cape Artemision in
1928. *Tossitsa 1, off 28 Oktovriou, tel. 01/821–7717. Admission: 1,500 dr. Open weekdays 8–7, weekends and holidays
8:30–3.*

Alternatively, from Syntagma you can take Vassilissis Sofias
Avenue along the edge of the National Gardens to reach the
⑲ **Evzone Guards' barracks.** From here you have several options.
If you continue farther along Vassilissis Sofias, it will eventually take you to the Hilton Hotel and the U.S. Embassy. Or, turn
⑳ right onto Herodes Atticus, which leads to the **Presidential Palace,** the former royal palace, now occupied by President Constantine Karamanlis.

Opposite the Evzone Guards' barracks, on the corner of
㉑ Vassilissis Sofias and Herodes Atticus, is the **Benaki Museum,**
with an eclectic and interesting hodgepodge of objects from different countries and periods, ranging from ancient sculpture
through Byzantine pieces, Ottoman ceramics, and Chinese
jades to modern paintings. There is also a fabulous collection of
genuine Greek national costumes, folk art, and embroidery.
*Koumbari 1, tel. 01/361–1617. Admission: 400 dr. Open Wed.–
Mon. 8:30–2.*

㉒ The **Museum of Cycladic Art** is up the next street to the right.
The collection spans 5,000 years, with 230 exhibits of the Cycladic civilization (3,000–2,000 BC), including many of the slim
marble figurines that so fascinated artists like Picasso and Mo-
digliani. *Neofytou Douka 4, tel. 01/722–8321. Admission: 200
dr., free on Sat. Open Mon. and Wed.–Fri. 10–4, Sat. 10–3.*

㉓ A little farther along Vassilissis Sofias is the **Byzantine Museum,** housed in an 1848 mansion that was built by an eccentric
French aristocrat. It has a unique collection of icons and the
very beautiful 14th-century Byzantine embroidery of the body
of Christ in gold, silver, yellow, and green. Sculptural fragments provide an excellent introduction to Byzantine architecture. *Vassilissis Sofias 22, tel. 01/721–1027. Admission: 1,000
dr. Open Tues.–Sun. 8:30–3.*

Kolonaki, the chic shopping district and one of the most fashionable residential areas, occupies the lower slopes of **Mount Lycabettos** and is only a 10-minute walk northeast of Syntagma; it's worth a stroll around if you enjoy window-shopping and people-watching. Three times the height of the Acropolis, Lycabettos can be reached by funicular railway from the top of Ploutarchou Street (the No. 23 bus from Kolonaki Square will drop you at the station; fare: 300 dr. round-trip). The view from the top—pollution permitting—is the finest in Athens. You can see all Athens, Attica, the harbor, and the islands of Aegina and Poros laid out before you.

Shopping

Gift Ideas Better tourist shops sell copies of traditional Greek jewelry, silver filigree, enamel, Skyrian pottery, onyx ashtrays and dishes, woven bags, attractive rugs (including *flokates*—shaggy wool rugs, often brightly colored), good leather items, and furs. Furs made from scraps are inexpensive. Some museums sell replicas of small items that are in their collections. Other shops sell dried fruit, packaged pistachios, and canned olives.

Shopping Areas The central shopping area lies between Syntagma and Omonia. The **Syntagma** area has good jewelers, shoe shops, and handicrafts and souvenir shops, especially along **Voukourestiou.** **Stadiou Street** is the best bet for men's clothing. Go to **Mitropoleos** for rugs and souvenirs. Ermou runs west to **Monastiraki,** a crowded market area popular with Athenians. Below the cathedral, **Pandrossou** has antiques, sandals (an especially good buy), and inexpensive souvenirs.

Flea Market The flea market, based on **Pandrossou** and **Ifestou streets,** operates on Sunday mornings and sells almost anything: secondhand clothes, daggers, cooking pots and pans, old books, guitars, *bouzouki* (stringed instruments), old furniture and carpets, and backgammon sets. Pontians—Greeks who lived in the former Soviet Union—sell Russian caviar, vodka, and table linen. However little it costs, you should haggle. Ifestou Street, where the coppersmiths have their shops, is more interesting on a weekday—and you can pick up copper wine jugs, candlesticks, cooking ware, etc., for next to nothing.

Dining

Be adventurous and go looking for the places that have at least half a dozen tables occupied by Athenians—they're discerning customers.

Moderate **Apotsos.** A famous ouzerie, close to Syntagma Square but hidden away down an arcade, this is an echoing barn of a place—truly Athenian in atmosphere. Politicians, journalists, and artists gather here at lunchtime. As well as ouzo, wine and beer are served, along with dishes of *mezedes* (snacks for nibbling)—though three or four of these will add up to a substantial meal. The walls are decorated with old advertisements; the tabletops are of well-worn marble. *Venizelou 10, tel. 01/363-7046. Reservations not necessary. No credit cards. Lunch only (11:30–4).*

Dionyssos. Located on top of Mount Lycabettos, this restaurant has a sweeping view of Athens and Piraeus, down to the sea. Take the funicular railway from the top of Ploutarchou

Street, in Kolonaki. In addition to the restaurant, which serves Continental and Greek cuisine, there is a cafeteria and patisserie, open from the earliest to the latest cablecar run (check the time of the last one!). *Mount Lycabettos, tel. 01/722–6374. Reservations not necessary. AE, DC, V.*

Ideal. This old Athenian restaurant, which opened in 1922, has been refurbished and still attracts Athenians of all ages, as well as students from the nearby university. It has an extensive menu featuring high-quality Greek and Continental dishes. *Venizelou 46, tel. 01/361–4604. Reservations not necessary. DC.*

★ **Kostoyannis.** If you're looking for authenticity, this is the place to go. One of the oldest and most popular tavernas in the area, located behind the Archaeological Museum, it has an impressively wide range of Greek dishes—including excellent shrimp and crab salads, stuffed mussels, rabbit *stifado* (a stew with onions), and fried brains. *Zaimi 37, tel. 01/821–2496. Reservations advised in summer. AE, DC, MC, V. Dinner only. Closed Sun.*

Inexpensive **Delphi Restaurant.** Very popular with businesspeople wanting a quick, cheap meal, this restaurant serves excellent Greek and international food and is always crowded. It may be a little touristy and service can be slow, but the food is worth the wait. The front part of the restaurant is rustic, while the back-room decor is more refined. *Nikis 13, tel. 01/323–4869. No reservations. AE, DC. Closed Sun.*

Eden. This macrobiotic restaurant, in a converted old Plaka villa, serves superb vegetable pies and spinach burgers in yogurt sauce—a delightful experience for those who are tired of seeing lamb roasted on a spit at every corner. You can sit outside at wrought-iron tables on a rooftop terrace. *Flessa 3, tel. 01/324–8858. Reservations not necessary. AE, DC. Closed Tues.*

O Platanos. Set in a picturesque corner of the Plaka, this is one of the oldest tavernas in the area. It has a shady garden for outdoor dining. There's no music, so prices are low. Although it's extremely friendly, not much English is spoken. *Diogenous 4, tel. 01/322–0666. Reservations not necessary. AE, DC, MC, V.*

Sintrivani. This pleasant restaurant just off Syntagma Square has a small, shady garden beyond the main dining room. It is patronized mostly by tourists, but the food remains unmistakably Greek. The egg-and-lemon soup is delicious, and fish dishes are modestly priced. Service is always friendly. *Philhellinon 5, tel. 01/323–8862. Reservations not necessary. No credit cards.*

Budget **Athinaikon.** An old, established ouzerie close to Omonia Square, it's always crowded with Athenians at lunchtime. The variety and quality of the food more than compensate for brusque service. Mussels are a specialty, along with grilled green peppers and spicy meatballs. *Themistocles 2, no tel. No reservations. AE, DC, MC, V.*

Cafe Abyssinia. Northern Greek cooking is featured at this cheerful, crowded restaurant near the Monastiraki flea market. *Kinetou 7, tel. 01/321–7047. Reservations not necessary. No credit cards. No dinner.*

Kentrikon. Popular with journalists from nearby newspaper offices, this cavernous restaurant is a cool refuge in summer. The menu is varied, with a good range of modestly priced meat dishes and simple but delicious salads. *Kolokotronis 3, inside* *arcade, tel. 01/323–2482. Reservations not necessary. No credit cards.*

Levka. This is one of the last old-fashioned tavernas in central Athens, hidden away behind high green doors. Its garden is packed in warm weather. Try lamb cutlets in summer and pork in lemon sauce in winter. Salads are hearty, and the wine is dispensed from a huge barrel in the courtyard. *Mavromichali 121, tel. 01/361–4038. Reservations not necessary. No credit cards.*

Nea Olympia. This is another favorite eating place in the Omonia district for lawyers and businessmen looking for a quick meal at a modest price. The wood-panel surroundings are spacious, and all the traditional Greek dishes are on offer, from *dolmadakia* (stuffed vine leaves) to moussaka and *tzatziki* (yogurt-and-cucumber dip spiked with garlic). *Benaki 3, tel. 01/321–7972. Reservations not necessary. No credit cards.*

Lodging

Since Athens is the starting point for so many travelers, its hotels are very full, and it's always advisable to reserve a room in advance. Which type of hotel you choose is really a matter of personal taste. Basically, the style of hotels in Athens can be divided into two neat brackets—traditional and modern—and these can be found both in the center of town, around Omonia and Syntagma Squares, and near the U.S. Embassy. For details and price-category definitions, *see* Lodging in Staying in Greece.

Moderate **Athens Gate Hotel.** This hotel looks across the busy Amalias Avenue to the Arch of Hadrian. Front rooms have the view, but also the traffic noise; back rooms are quiet and look out toward the Acropolis. The hotel is conveniently located between the center of town and the Acropolis. The restaurant is only mediocre, but it serves a good, American-style buffet breakfast. *Syngrou 10, tel. 01/923–8302/9. 106 rooms with bath. Facilities: restaurant, roof garden, air-conditioning. AE, DC, MC, V.*

Hotel La Mirage. This large but friendly hotel makes the most of its proximity to Omonia Square, with a comfortable lounge— with satellite TV—overlooking the fountain. Rooms are well fitted with double-glazed windows to keep out noise, and the restaurant offers good-value meals. *M. Kotopouli 3, tel. 01/523–4071. 200 rooms with bath or shower. Facilities: restaurant, air-conditioning, bar. No credit cards.*

Ilissia Hotel. This small, but rather shabby, friendly hotel is located near the Hilton, in an area where there are many good restaurants and night spots. Generally, it could use a good spring-cleaning, but the location makes up for its dowdy appearance. *Mihalakopoulou 25, tel. 01/724–4051. 90 rooms with bath. Facilities: restaurant, air-conditioning. AE, DC, MC, V.*

Plaka Hotel. This family-owned hotel, conveniently located for sight-seeing and shopping, was fully renovated in 1989. The roof garden offers a spectacular view across the red-tile roofs of the region extending from the old Plaka district to the Acropolis temples. Most rooms have balconies; fifth- and sixth-floor rooms are best to escape street noise. The buffet breakfast is recommended. *Kapnikareas and Mitropoleos 7, tel. 01/322–2096. 57 rooms with bath or shower. Facilities: restaurant, air-conditioning. AE, DC, MC, V.*

Inexpensive **Aphrodite Hotel.** This is near Syntagma and perfectly comfortable. With all the facilities of other, more costly hotels, it offers excellent value for the money. Don't be put off by its cold-looking entrance. *Apollonos 21, tel. 01/323–4357/9. 84 rooms with bath. Facilities: bar, roof garden. AE, DC, MC, V.*

Attalos Hotel. The market area, where the Attalos is located, is full of life and color by day, but deserted at night. The hotel is pleasant and well run and has an exceptionally fine view of the Acropolis and Mount Lycabettos. Try to get a room on the 5th or 6th floor, where the street noise is less. *Athinas 29, tel. 01/ 321–801/3. 80 rooms with bath. Facilities: bar, roof garden. AE, DC, MC, V.*

★ **Austria.** This small, unpretentious hotel is on Filopappou Hill, opposite the Acropolis, ideal as a base for wandering around the heart of ancient Athens. It has no restaurant and is at the top of the inexpensive category, but is well worth considering. *Mouson 7, tel. 01/923–5151. 40 rooms with bath. AE, DC, MC, V.*

Hotel Lycabettus. This small, well-run hotel is centrally located in a pedestrian precinct just around the corner from Voukourestiou Street and opposite Jimmy's, a coffee shop popular with diplomats and journalists. The hotel's friendly staff offers helpful advice about travel arrangements. *Valaoritou 6, tel. 01/363–3514. 24 rooms with shower. Facilities: bar, airconditioning. AE, DC, MC, V.*

Hotel Nefeli. This small, family-run hotel in the old Plaka district is a favorite with regular visitors to Athens. Its neatly furnished rooms look out onto banks of potted geraniums, and service is attentive. *Iperidou 16, tel. 01/322–8044. 18 rooms with shower. AE, DC, MC, V.*

Phoebus Hotel. This hotel in a traditional Plaka house has so many regular visitors it resembles a club. Ask for a top-floor room so you can make use of a spacious terrace looking across to the Acropolis. The comfortable breakfast room includes a small lending library. *Peta 12, tel. 01/322–0142. 23 rooms with shower. AE, DC, MC, V.*

Budget **Exarcheion Hotel.** If you want a taste of alternative Athens, this hotel's location is perfect; it's just off colorful Exarcheia Square and near the bars and tavernas of Strefi hill. Most rooms have balconies, and there's a superb view across Athens from the rooftop bar. *Themistocleous 5, tel. 01/360–1256. 62 rooms with bath or shower. No credit cards.*

Imperial Hotel. A thoroughly old-fashioned Athenian hotel, the Imperial has large, spotless rooms, with a convivial atmosphere and balconies overlooking the Cathedral Square at the edge of the Plaka district. Room rates are reduced for stays of more than two nights. *Mitropoleos 46, tel. 01/322–7617. 25 rooms, most with shower. No credit cards.*

Museum Hotel. At this friendly and efficiently run hotel just behind the National Archaeological Museum in a middle-class residential area, you're likely to meet a distinguished archaeologist at breakfast in the cheerful café-bar. All rooms have balconies; choose one on the fifth floor to avoid street noise. *Bouboulinas 16, tel. 01/360–5611. 60 rooms with shower. AE, DC, MC, V.*

Omonia Hotel. This huge but welcoming hotel overlooking the bustle of Omonia Square is a convenient landing place between trips to the islands and is just one minute from the metro to Piraeus. Rooms are spacious, with balconies and picture windows. *Omonia Sq. and Tritis Septemvriou, tel. 01/523–7211. 270 rooms with bath. Facilities: restaurant, café-bar. V.*

The Arts

The **Athens Festival** runs from late June through September and includes concerts, recitals, opera, ballet, folk dancing, and drama. Performances are in various locations, including the open-air theater of Herodes Atticus at the foot of the Acropolis, nearby Philopappou Hill, and Mount Lycabettos. Tickets are available a few days before the performance from the festival box office in the arcade at Stadiou 4 (tel. 01/322–1459). Admission ranges from 1,500 dr. to 10,000 dr.

For those who are disappointed with the daytime view of the Acropolis, the **son-et-lumière** shows bring history to life. Performances are given nightly from April to October, in English, at 9:15 (the time is subject to change), and admission is 1,000 dr. The entrance is on Dionysiou Areopagitou, opposite the Acropolis, and from your seat on the top of Philopappou Hill, you watch the changing lighting of the monuments.

Cultural activity in the winter has improved enormously with the opening in 1991 of the **Athens Concert Hall** (tel. 01/322–1549), with two auditoriums equipped with state-of-the-art acoustics. Daily listings are published year-round in *The Athens News* and weekly listings in *This Week in Athens*, both available in hotels. **The Athenian** lists concerts, exhibitions, and showings of films in English.

Opera The **Lyriki Skini Opera Company** has a winter season and a small—not very good—ballet season at the Olympia Theater (Akademias 59, tel. 01/361–2461). The best seats cost about 3,000 dr.

Films Almost all cinemas now show foreign films, usually managing to show the latest Hollywood offerings within a week or so of their New York and London openings. *The Athens News* lists them in English. Downtown cinemas are the most comfortable. Try the **Embassy** in Kolonaki (Patriarchou Ioachim 5, tel. 01/722–0903) or the **Apollon** (tel. 01/323–6811) on Stadiou, just off Syntagma Square for new American films and the **Cinema Thission** (Pavlou 7, tel. 01/347–0980) for American and European classics.

Mycenae

Legend and history meet in Mycenae, where Agamemnon, Elektra, and Orestes played out their grim family tragedy. This city dominated the entire area from the 14th to the 12th century BC, and may even have conquered Minoan Crete. According to Greek mythology, Paris, son of the king of Troy, abducted the beautiful Helen, wife of Menelaus, the king of Sparta. Agamemnon, the king of Mycenae, was Menelaus's brother. This led to the Trojan War in which Troy was defeated. The story of the war is told in Homer's *Iliad*. Following Heinrich Schliemann's discoveries of gold-filled graves and a royal palace during excavations in 1874, Mycenae has become a world-class archaeological site and, of all the sites in the Peloponnese, is most worthy of a visit.

Getting Around

The quickest way to reach Mycenae is by taking a bus for Argos or Nafplio and getting off at the Mycenae village turnoff. The train via Corinth offers an enjoyable, if slower, ride. Nafplio is the best place to stay; a local bus will take you there.

Exploring Mycenae

Mycenae, 48 kilometers (25 miles) from Corinth, was the fabulous stronghold of the Achaean kings of the 13th century BC. Destroyed in 468 BC, it was forgotten until 1874 when German archaeologist Heinrich Schliemann, who discovered the ruins of ancient Troy, uncovered the remains of this ancient fortress city. Mycenae was the seat of the doomed House of Atreus—of King Agamemnon and his wife, Clytemnestra, sister of Helen of Troy, and of their tragic children, Orestes and Elektra. When Schliemann uncovered six shaft graves (so named because the kings were buried standing up) of the royal circle, he was certain that one was the tomb of Agamemnon. The gold masks and diadems, daggers, jewelry, and other treasures found in the graves are now in the Athens Archaeological Museum; the new local museum is dedicated to archaeological studies. Along with the graves, you'll find the astounding bee-hive tombs built into the hillsides outside the reconstructed wall, the **Lion Gate,** dating to 1250 BC, and the castle ruins crowning the bleak hill, all remnants of the first great civilization in continental Europe. The tombs, the acropolis, the palace, and the museum can all be explored for the cost of admission. *Tel. 0751/66–585. Admission: 1,000 dr. Open weekdays 8–7, weekends and holidays 8:30–3.*

Farther on is **Nafplio,** a picturesque town below the Venetian fortifications. Modern Greece's first king lived for a year or two within the walls of the higher fortress when Nafplio was capital of Greece. His courtiers had to climb 999 steps to reach him; you can still climb the long staircase or drive up to the fortress. The **Venetian naval arsenal** on the town square houses a museum crowded with Mycenaean finds. *Tel. 0752/27–502. Admission: 400 dr. Open Tues.–Sun. 8:30–3.*

Dining and Lodging

Nafplio
Dining

Savouras. Fresh seafood is served in this unpretentious taverna overlooking the bay; it is generally regarded as one of the best fish restaurants in the area. *Akti Miaouli, no telephone. Reservations not necessary. No credit cards. Inexpensive.*

Lodging
★

Agamemnon. Located on the waterfront, this hotel has a large, cool lobby overhung with vines, a superb spot from which to watch the action. The double rooms have marble terraces overlooking the water. *Akti Miaouli 3, tel. 0752/28–021. 40 rooms with bath. Facilities: restaurant, roof garden, pool. DC. Moderate.*

Dioscuri. Located high up beneath the castle in the old town, with a fine view across the Nafplion gulf, this family-run hotel is cool and quiet. *Zigomala 7, tel. 0752/28–550. 50 rooms with shower. No credit cards. Inexpensive.*

Mainland Greece

The dramatic rocky heights of mainland Greece provide an appropriate setting for man's attempt to approach divinity. The ancient Greeks placed their gods on snowcapped Mount Olympus and chose the precipitous slopes of Parnassus, "the navel of the universe," as the site for Delphi, the most important religious center of the ancient world. In fact, many of mainland Greece's most memorable sights are closely connected with religion—including the remarkable Byzantine churches of Thessaloniki. Of course, there are remains of palaces and cities, but these do not have the impact of the great religious centers.

In this land of lonely mountain villages, narrow defiles, and dark woods, bands of *klephts* (a cross between brigands and guerrillas) earned their place in folk history and song during the long centuries of Turkish rule. The women of Souli, one of the mountain strongholds of the klephts, threw themselves dancing and singing over a cliff rather than be captured by the Turks. In these same mountains during the German occupation of Greece during World War II, guerrilla bands descended to the valleys and plains to assault the occupying army and drive it from their land.

Farmers have flourished since Greece joined the European Community, and few villages, even those tucked away in the hills, are still poor and isolated. Despite the arrival of video clubs and discos, the traditional way of life still survives. This is a beautiful area to explore. The mainland Greeks see fewer tourists and have more time for those they do see, hotels are unlikely to be full, and the sights—steep, wooded mountains, cypress trees like candles, narrow gorges, the soaring monasteries of Meteora—are beautiful.

Getting Around

A one-day trip to Delphi is rushed; two days will give you more leisure time. Take the train or bus to Thessaloniki. In September, during the Thessaloniki International Trade Fair, there are no hotel rooms to be had; make reservations well in advance.

Tourist Information

In **Delphi,** visit the New Delphi Tourist Office on Frederikis, open daily 9–7 (tel. 0265/82–900); the Tourist Police is at Pavlou and Frederikis 25. In **Thessaloniki,** visit the Greek National Tourist Office (Metropoleos 34, tel. 031/271–888); here, the Tourist Police is at Egnatia 10.

Exploring Mainland Greece

The ancient Greeks believed that **Delphi** was the center of the universe because two eagles released by the gods at opposite ends of Earth met here. For hundreds of years, the worship of Apollo and the pronouncements of the Oracle here made Delphi the most important religious center of the ancient world. As you walk up the Sacred Way to the **Temple of Apollo,** the **theater,** and the **stadium** that make up the **Sanctuary of Apollo,** you'll see Mount Parnassus above; silver-green olive trees below; and, in the distance, the blue Gulf of Itea. This is one of the most rugged and lonely sites in Greece, and one of the most striking; if you can get to the site in the early morning or evening, avoiding the busloads of tourists, you will feel the power and beauty of the place. You may even see an eagle or two. First excavated in 1892, most of the ruins date from the 5th to the 3rd century BC. *Tel. 0265/82–313. Admission (includes Delphi Museum): 1,000 dr. Open Apr.–Oct., weekdays 8–7, weekends and holidays 8:30–3; Nov.–Mar., daily 8–5.*

Don't miss the famous bronze charioteer (early 5th century BC) in the **Delphi Museum.** Other interesting and beautiful works of art here include the column of the dancers (or Caryatids), 4th century BC; a statue of Antinous, Emperor Hadrian's lover; and the stone representing the navel of the earth. Don't miss the delicate ivory statuettes and the bull made out of silver leaf; both are in an air-conditioned inner gallery. *Tel. 0265/82–313. Admission: joint ticket 1,000 dr. Open Apr.–Oct., Mon. 12:30–7, Tues.–Fri. 8–7, weekends and holidays 8:30–3; Nov.–Mar., daily 8–5.*

Thessaloniki, the birthplace of Aristotle, is Greece's second-largest city, its second port after Piraeus, and the capital of northern Greece.

Although Thessaloniki still has some remains from the Roman period, the city is best known for its fine Byzantine churches. The city is compact enough for you to see the main sights on foot. Start at the 15th-century grayish **White Tower,** landmark and symbol of Thessaloniki, previously named "Tower of Blood," referring to its use as a prison. Now it houses a museum, with an exhibition on the history and art of Byzantine Thessaloniki, including pottery, mosaics, and ecclesiastical objects. *Tel. 031/267–832. Admission: 300 dr. Open Wed.–Mon. 2:45–9.*

Then walk up Pavlou Mela toward Tsimiski, the elegant tree-lined shopping street, and cut across to the green-domed basilica-style church of **Aghia Sophia,** which dates from the 8th century and has beautifully preserved mosaics.

Walk up Egnatia, which traces the original Roman road leading from the Adriatic to the Bosphorous. You will pass the **Roman Agora** (town center) and come to **Agios Dimitrios,** the principal church and the largest in Greece. Though it is only a replica of the original church that burned down in 1917, it is adorned with many 8th-century mosaics that were in the original building. Follow Aghiou Dimitriou to **Agios Georgios,** a rotunda built by Roman emperor Galerius as his tomb during the 4th century AD. His successor, Constantine the Great, the first Christian emperor, turned it into a church.

Return to Egnatia and the **Arch of the Emperor Galerius,** built shortly prior to the rotunda to commemorate the Roman victories of Emperor Galerius over forces in Persia, Armenia, and Asia Minor. A short walk downhill toward the sea wall will bring you to the **Archaeological Museum.** Among its many beautiful objects are a huge bronze vase and a delicate, gold myrtle wreath from Deryeni, as well as gold artifacts from recent excavations of the royal tombs of Vergina, including an 11-kilogram gold casket standing on lions' feet that contains bones thought to be those of Philip II, father of Alexander the Great.

Tel. 031/830–583. Admission: 1,000 dr. Open Mon. 12:30–7, Tues.–Fri. 8–7, weekends and holidays 8:30–3.

Dining and Lodging

For details and price-category definitions, *see* Dining and Lodging in Staying in Greece.

Delphi
Dining

Taverna Pan. Decorated with local folk art and weavings, this taverna offers fixed-price meals as well as à la carte Greek specialties. *Isaia St., tel. 0265/82–473. Reservations not necessary. No credit cards. Budget.*

Lodging
★

Acropole. This friendly, family-run hotel has a garden and a spectacular view of a bare mountainside and a sea of olive groves. *Philhellinon 13, tel. 0265/82–676. 30 rooms with shower. Facilities: garden, breakfast room, bar, TV lounge. DC, MC, V. Inexpensive.*

Hermès. This small hotel is built on a hillside in a quiet part of the main street. It is perfectly adequate for a night's sleep and has good views from its top-story bedrooms. The lobby is decorated with local weavings. *Vas. Pavlou and Frederikis 29, tel. 0265/82–318. 24 rooms with bath. No credit cards. Closed Nov.–Feb. Budget.*

Thessaloniki
Dining

Ta Nissia. This very bright, clean restaurant, with tiled floor and wooden tables, is excellent for fresh seafood, especially mussels. The *mezedes* (hors d'oeuvres) are particularly unusual and tasty. *Koromila 13, tel. 031/285–991. Reservations advised. DC. No lunch. Moderate.*

Olympia Naoussa. This traditional restaurant close to the waterfront offers delicious old-style Greek cuisine. Try *vrasto* (pot au feu) or *spanakorizi* (spinach with rice). *Vassiliou Constantinou 33, tel. 031/272–563. No credit cards. No dinner. Inexpensive.*

Lodging

ABC. This large hotel is centrally located, near the museum and the landmark White Tower. It offers the comforts of a more expensive hotel, with color TV in some rooms. *Agelaki 41, tel. 031/265–421. 110 rooms with bath. Facilities: restaurant, bar, coffee shop, air-conditioning. AE, DC, MC, V. Moderate.*

Pella. This quiet hotel close to the former military-governor's mansion was renovated recently and offers small but spotless rooms. *Ion Dragoumi 65, tel. 031/542–221. 40 rooms with shower. DC, MC, V. Inexpensive.*

The Greek Islands

The islands of the Aegean have colorful legends of their own— the Minotaur in Crete; the lost continent of Atlantis, which some believe was Santorini; and the Colossus of Rhodes, to name a few. Each island has its own personality. Mykonos has windmills, dazzling whitewashed buildings, hundreds of tiny churches and chapels on golden hillsides, and small fishing harbors. Visitors to volcanic Santorini sail into what was once a vast volcanic crater and anchor near the island's forbidding cliffs. Crete, with its jagged mountain peaks, olive orchards, and vineyards, contains the remains of the Minoan civilization. In Rhodes, a bustling modern town surrounds a walled town with a medieval castle.

Getting Around

The simplest way to visit the Aegean Islands is by ferry from Piraeus, the port of Athens. There is also frequent air service from Athens, but most flights are fully booked year-round. It's vital to book well in advance and to confirm and reconfirm in order to be sure of your seat. (See Getting Around, By Boat, at the beginning of this chapter.)

Tourist Information

There are **Greek National Tourist Organization** offices on **Crete,** at Kriari 40, Hania (tel. 0821/26–426), and at Xanthoulidou 1, Iraklio (tel. 081/228–203); on **Rhodes,** at Archbishop Makarios and Papagou 5, Rhodes (tel. 0241/23–655).

Exploring the Greek Islands

Cruise ships and car ferries to Mykonos leave from Piraeus or Rafina. As you sail to Mykonos, you will be able to see one of the great sights of Greece: the Temple of Poseidon looming on a hilltop at the edge of Cape Sounion, about two hours from the mainland.

Mykonos is the name of the island and also of its chief village—a colorful maze of narrow, paved streets lined with whitewashed houses, many with bright blue doors and shutters. Every morning, women scrub the sidewalks and streets in front of their homes, undaunted by the many donkeys that pass by each day. During the 1960s, the bohemian jet set discovered Mykonos, and most of the old houses along the waterfront are now restaurants, nightclubs, bars, and discos, all blaring loud music until the early morning; a quiet café or taverna is hard to find. Mykonos is still a favorite anchorage with the international yacht set, as well as being *the* holiday destination for the young, lively, and liberated—finding yourself alone on any of its beaches is unlikely.

A half hour by boat from Mykonos and its 20th-century holiday pleasures is the ancient isle of **Delos,** the legendary sanctuary of Apollo. Its **Terrace of the Lions,** a remarkable group of five large sculptures from the 7th century BC, is a must. Worth seeing, too, are some of the houses of the Roman period, with their fine floor mosaics. The best of these mosaics are in a museum, the **House of Dionysos.** *Tel. 0289/22–259. Admission (including fee to the site): 1,000 dr. Open Tues.–Sun. 8:30–3.*

The large island of **Rhodes,** 170 kilometers (105 miles) southeast of Mykonos, is 11.2 kilometers (7 miles) off the coast of Turkey. The northern end of the island is one of Greece's major vacation centers, and the town of Rhodes is full of the trappings of tourism, mainly evident in the pubs and bars that cater to the large Western European market. The island as a whole is not particularly beautiful—most of the pine and cedar woods that covered its hilly center were destroyed by fire in 1987 and 1988—but it has fine beaches and an excellent climate. The town of Rhodes has an attractive harbor with fortifications; the gigantic bronze statue of the Colossus of Rhodes is supposed to have straddled the entrance. The old walled city, near the harbor, was built by crusaders—the Knights Hospitaller of St. John—who ruled the island from 1310 until they were

The Greek Islands

Athens
Piraeus
Voula
Cape Sounion
Ydra
Kythnos
Kéa
Syros
Serifos
Milos
Andros
Andros
Tinos
Mykonos
Mykonos
Delos
Paros
Naxos
Ios
Santorini Thira
Acrotiri
Anafi
Aegean Sea
Ikaria
Agios Kirykos
Pátmos
CYCLADES
Amorgós
Astypalea
Sea of Crete
Sámos
Sámos
Pythagorio
Leros
Kos
Kos
Nissyros
DODECANESE
Tilos
Halki
Kárpathos
Kassos
Ephesus
Bodrum (Halicarnassus)
Symi
Rhodes
Kámiros
Lindos
Rhodes

N

Haniá
Iraklio
Mallia
Elounda
CRETE
Knossos
Agios Nikolaos
Phaestos
Ierapetra

0   50 miles
0   75 miles

defeated by the Turks in 1522. Within its fine medieval walls, on the Street of the Knights, stands the **Knights' Hospital,** now the Archaeological Museum, housing two statues of Aphrodite. *Tel. 0241/27–657. Admission: 600 dr. Open Tues.–Sun. 8:30–3.*

Another museum that deserves your attention is the restored and moated medieval **Palace of the Grand Masters.** Destroyed in 1856 by a gunpowder explosion, the palace was renovated by the Italians as a summer retreat for Mussolini. It is especially noted for its splendid Roman and early Christian floor mosaics. *Tel. 0241/27–657. Admission: 800 dr. Open Tues.–Sun. 8:30–3.*

To get the best overall view of the walled city, including the surviving Turkish buildings, go to one of the flower-filled parks that surround it. Try to see the son et lumière—English-language performances are held on Sunday evening.

Many attractive souvenir and handicrafts shops in the old town sell decorative Rhodian pottery, local embroidery, and relatively inexpensive jewelry.

Crete, situated in the south Aegean and Greece's largest island, was the center of Europe's earliest civilization, the Minoan, which flourished from about 2000 BC to 1200 BC. It was struck a mortal blow by a devastating volcanic eruption on the neighboring island of Santorini (Thera) in about 1450 BC.

The most important Minoan remains are to be seen in the **Archaeological Museum of Heraklion** in Iraklio, Crete's largest city. The museum houses many Minoan treasures, including some highly sophisticated frescoes and elegant ceramics depicting Minoan life. *Xanthoulidou St., tel. 081/226–092. Admission: 1,000 dr. Open Mon. 12:30–7, Tues.–Sat. 8–7, Sun. and holidays 8–6.*

Not far from Iraklio is the partly reconstructed **Palace of Knossos,** which will also give you a feeling for the Minoan world. Note the simple throne room, which contains the oldest throne in Europe, and the bathrooms with their efficient plumbing. The palace was the setting for the legend of the Minotaur, a monstrous offspring of Queen Pasiphae and a bull confined to the Labyrinth under the palace. *Tel. 081/231–940. Admission: 1,000 dr. Open Apr.–Oct., Mon.–Sat. 8–7, Sun. and holidays 8–6; Nov.–Mar., daily 8–5.*

Crete belonged to Venice from 1210 to 1669, at which time it was conquered by the Turks. The island did not become part of Greece until early in this century. The **Venetian ramparts** that withstood a 24-year Turkish siege still surround Iraklio. In addition to archaeological treasures, Crete can boast beautiful mountain scenery and a large number of beach resorts along the north coast. One is **Mallia,** which contains the remains of another Minoan palace and has good sandy beaches. Two other beach resorts, **Agios Nikolaos** and the nearby **Elounda,** are east of Iraklio. The south coast offers good, quieter beaches for those who want to get away from it all.

The best way to approach **Santorini** is to sail into its harbor, once the vast crater of its volcano, and dock beneath its black and red cliffs. In some parts, the cliffs rise nearly 310 meters (1,000 feet) above the sea. The play of light across them can produce strange color effects. The white houses and churches of the main town, Thira, cling to the rim in dazzling white contrast to the somber cliffs.

Most passenger ferries now use the new port, Athinios, where visitors are met by buses, taxis, and a gaggle of small-hotel owners hawking rooms. The bus ride into Thira takes about a half hour, and from there you can make connections to other towns on the island. Despite being packed with visitors in the summer, the tiny town is charming and has spectacular views. It has the usual souvenir and handicrafts shops and several reasonably priced jewelry shops. Be sure to try the local white wines. The volcanic soil produces a unique range of flavors from light and dry to rich and aromatic.

The island's volcano erupted during the 15th century BC, destroying its Minoan civilization. At **Acrotiri,** on the south end of Santorini, the remains of a Minoan city buried by lava are being excavated. The site, believed by some to be part of the legendary Atlantis, is open to the public. *Tel. 0286/81–366. Admission: 1,000 dr. Open Tues.–Fri. 8:30–3, weekends and holidays 9:30–2:30.*

At **Ancient Thira,** a clifftop on the east coast of the island, a well-preserved ancient town includes a theater and agora, houses, fortifications, and ancient tombs. *Tel. 0286/22–217. Admission free. Open Tues.–Sun. 8:30–3.*

For an enjoyable but slightly unnerving excursion, take the short boat trip to the island's still-active small offshore volcanoes called the **Kamenes** or Burnt Islands. You can descend into a small crater, hot and smelling of sulfur, and swim in the nearby water that has been warmed by the volcano.

Dining and Lodging

For details and price-category definitions, *see* Dining and Lodging in Staying in Greece.

Crete Iraklio has many moderately priced open-air restaurants in the
Dining central area around Platia Venizelou and Platia Daedelou. The island is known for its fine local wine, fresh seafood, and fresh local produce, which is available year-round.

Minos Taverna. This is one of the many outdoor restaurants near the Venetian fountain. Lamb, fresh seafood, and yogurt dishes make this one of the island's most popular restaurants. Service is prompt and attentive. *Daedelou 10, tel. 081/281–263. Reservations not necessary. No credit cards. Moderate.*

Taverna Faros. Located near the new port in Iraklio, this is an excellent, inexpensive choice for a Greek fish supper. The distinct fisherman's ambience is created by fishnet drapes, conch shells, and razor clams on the walls. *Tel. 081/423–233. Reservations not necessary. No credit cards. Inexpensive.*

Lodging **Mediterranean.** This is another comfortable hotel in the center
★ of Iraklio and 4.8 kilometers (3 miles) from the beach. It's priced at the top of its category. *Smyrnis 1, tel. 081/289–331. 55 rooms with bath. Facilities: restaurant, roof garden, partially air-conditioned. AE, MC, V. Moderate.*

Rea. This comfortable hotel in Ahgios Nicolaos offers outdoor dining and a roof garden with a spectacular view across the Mirabello Gulf. *Marathonas and Milatou 10, tel. 0841/28–321. 110 rooms with bath. Facilities: indoor and outdoor restaurants, bar, roof garden. AE, DC, MC, V. Moderate.*

Atrion. This family-run hotel frequented by Dutch and Scandinavian tourists is located in a quiet residential street close to the Historical Museum and the bus station for western Crete. *K. Paleologou 9, tel. 081/229–225. 50 rooms with shower. Facilities: bar, air-conditioning. AE, DC, MC, V. Budget.*

Mykonos **Pilafas.** This friendly taverna just behind the waterfront is pa-
Dining tronized by locals as well as tourists. It offers good grilled dishes and salads. Ask for directions at any waterfront café. *No reservations. No credit cards. Inexpensive.*

Lodging **Kamari.** This new family-run hotel is located 4 kilometers (2½
★ miles) from Mykonos town, between two sheltered sandy beaches, each a five-minute walk away. *Platy Gialos, tel. 0289/ 23–424. 35 rooms with bath. Facilities: breakfast room, bar, transport to town. AE, DC, MC, V. Moderate.*

Kouneni Hotel. This is a comfortable family-run hotel in the town center, and it's quieter than most. It is set in a cool green garden, a rarity on Mykonos. Rooms are fairly large; the slightly shabby, but cozy lounge has a tiled floor. *Tria Pigadia, tel. 0289/22–301. 20 rooms with bath. No credit cards. Inexpensive.*

Rhodes **Kabo n' Toro Taverna.** You can't go wrong at this tiny restau-
Dining rant, which is one of the best in the town of Rhodes and possibly on the entire island. *Omilou and Parado Sts., tel. 0241/36–182. Reservations not necessary. No credit cards. Moderate.*

Ta Kiopia. Located in the village of Tris, this unusual restaurant offers farmhouse cooking in a traditional Rhodian house.

Tel. 0241/91–824. Reservations required. No credit cards. Moderate.

Vlachos. A traditional taverna close to the medieval harbor, it's popular with the islanders as well as tourists. *Michali Petridi 20, tel. 0241/63–287. DC, MC, V. Budget.*

Lodging **Marie Rodos.** This hotel is conveniently located on the beach but is only a few minutes' walk from the city center. A wide choice of water sports is available. *Kos 7, tel. 0241/30–577. Facilities: restaurant, sauna. AE, DC, MC, V. Moderate.*

Spartalis. Many rooms in this simple but lively hotel near the city's port have balconies overlooking the bay. *Plastira 2, tel. 0241/24–371/2. 70 rooms with bath. AE, DC, MC, V. Moderate.*

Hermes. Another family-run hotel close to the port. Ask for a room with a view across the bay to the Turkish coast. *Plastira 7, tel. 0241/27–677. 30 rooms with shower. No credit cards. Inexpensive.*

Santorini **Camille Stefani.** This is one of the island's best restaurants, *Dining* where you can enjoy seafood, Greek and Continental cuisine, and the local wines. A taste of the mellow Santorini Lava red wine, a product of the volcanic ash, is a must! *Main St., Thira, tel. 0286/22–265. Reservations advised. AE, MC, V. Moderate.*

Lodging **Matina.** Close to the beach at Kamari, this pleasant family-run hotel is set among vineyards. *Tel. 0286/31–491. 27 rooms with shower. Facilities: bar. AE, DC, MC, V. Moderate.*

Panorama. Recently renovated, this family-run hotel in the center of Fira, the island's main town, has a fine view across the bay to the dormant volcano. *Tel. 0286/22–479. 24 rooms with shower. Facilities: bar, restaurant. AE, DC, MC, V. Moderate.*

12 Holland

The innate common sense of the Dutch people assures that, no matter how sophisticated their cities seem to be at first glance, you always will find a choice of practically outfitted, quality hotels and restaurants at affordable prices, often in the same neighborhood with the five-star establishments. This is, after all, a land of traders that has a long tradition of welcoming both lowly sailors and ship's captains.

Following World War II, tourist posters of Holland featured windmills, tulips, canals, and girls wearing lacy caps and clogs. Nearly five decades later, although these picturesque images are still to be found, certainly, there is far more to this tiny country than just these clichés. Remember, too, that this is the land of such creative geniuses as the painters Rembrandt, Hals, and Vermeer, and the philosophers Descartes, Erasmus, and Spinoza.

Holland, known widely and more correctly as the Netherlands, is one of Europe's smallest countries. It is also one of the world's most densely populated nations, with a population of around 15 million occupying a land area that is less than half the size of Maine—40,145 square kilometers (15,500 square miles), almost half of which has been reclaimed by the industrious Dutch from the North Sea. The nation's history has been dominated by continual resistance to two forces of invasion: the sea and successive foreign armies. Over the centuries, the Romans, Franks, Burgundians, Austrians, Spanish, English, French, and Germans have all tried to win and hold Holland, but none has succeeded for long. These endless struggles against nature and enemies have molded the Dutch into a determined and independent nation, yet a remarkably tolerant one that is often at the forefront of many liberal social reforms

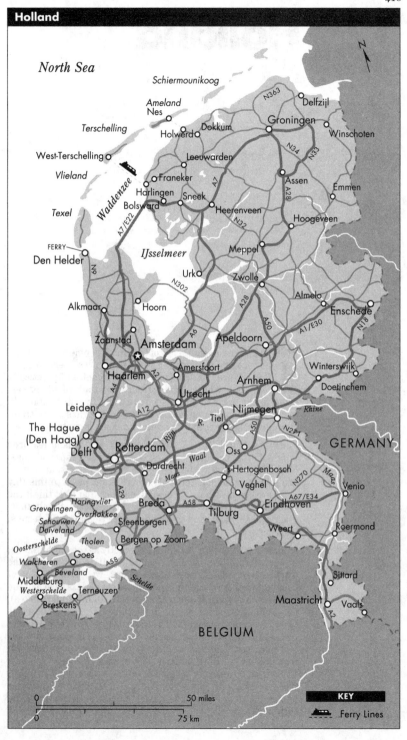

Holland

North Sea

Schiermounikoog

Ameland
Nes

Terschelling

Holwerd   Dokkum   Groningen   Delfzijl

West-Terschelling

Winschoten

Vlieland

Leeuwarden

N363

Franeker

N34   N33

Texel

Harlingen   Sneek   Assen   Emmen

Bolsward   Heerenveen

A7

Waddenzee

A7/E22

Hoogeveen

N32

FERRY

IJsselmeer

Den Helder

Meppel

N9

N302   Urk   Zwolle

Alkmaar   Hoorn   Almelo

A28   Enschede

Zaanstad   A50   A1/E30   N18

Amsterdam   Apeldoorn

A6

Haarlem   Amersfoort   Winterswijk

A2   Arnhem   Doetinchem

A4   Utrecht

Leiden   A12   Nijmegen   *Rhine*

The Hague   *R.* Tiel   A50   N2?1

(Den Haag)   *Rijn*   GERMANY

Delft   Rotterdam   Oss

Dordrecht   Waal   s-Hertogenbosch   N270

Maes   Veghel   A67/E34   Venlo

Grevelingen   *Haringvliet*   Breda   A58   Tilburg   Eindhoven

Schouwen/   *Overflakkee*   Steenbergen   Weert   Roermond

Duiveland   A29

Oosterschelde   *Tholen*   Bergen op Zoom

Walcheren   Goes   A58

Beveland

Middelburg   Sittard

Westerschelde   Terneuzen

Breskens   Maastricht   Vaals

Schelde   A2

BELGIUM

| 0 | | 50 miles |
| 0 | | 75 km |

KEY
Ferry Lines

and attitudes. Religious and political freedom are an essential part of Dutch life.

Holland's eventful history and the great cultural energy of its people have created an abundance of historic towns and buildings and filled its many museums with great works of art. The Dutch revere their past and have gone to great lengths to preserve their heritage. They have sensitively converted many of the gabled houses into hotels, restaurants, and museums. They also have a progressive approach to the creation of new design and architecture, as well as to the development of efficient services, railroads, roads, and amenities for the traveler.

Amsterdam's medieval Nieuwe Kerk, both a church and a cultural center, embodies the Dutch spirit of practicality and social responsibility. It is also a sign of Amsterdam's cultural prominence. The city is now as famous for its jazz, modern art, and ballet as it is for its Rembrandts and Van Goghs.

The Hague, sedate and refined, presents a contrast to Amsterdam's vitality and progressiveness. As can be expected in a city that is the national seat of government as well as home to the International Court of Justice, diplomacy and ceremony color the lives of all residents, from Queen Beatrix, ambassadors, and parliamentarians downward.

In landscape as in food, Holland is not as flat as it seems. Certainly low-lying Zeeland lives with the sea and on the sea—its oysters and mussels are world-famous. And versatile North Holland is not restricted to sand dunes, bulb fields, and melancholy seascapes. (Just inland from Bergen-aan-Zee, deep woods and moorland encircle the village of Bergen, once an artists' enclave.) In and across the southern provinces of Holland, bulb fields and windmills abound, but so do nature reserves, inland lakes, lush lowland, and rolling hills.

The Dutch themselves reflect a number of contrasts. They are hospitable to visiting strangers, yet fiercely independent if their values are challenged by outsiders. They are dedicated to democracy, yet enjoy being one of the world's few remaining popular monarchies. Their ideals of social behavior are, perhaps, best described by two of their own words: *netjes* (polite, friendly, and respectable) and *gezellig* (cozy, comfortable, and enjoying oneself).

Essential Information

Before You Go

When to Go The prime tourist season in Holland runs from April through October and peaks during school vacation periods (Easter, July, and August), when hotels may impose a 20% surcharge. Dutch bulb fields bloom from early April to the end of May—not surprisingly, the hotels tend to fill up then, too. June is the ideal time to catch the warm weather and miss the crowds, but every region of the Netherlands has its season. Delft is luminous after a winter storm, and fall in the Utrecht countryside can be as dramatic as in New England. Bargain rates are most likely to be found in winter, though weekend rates at business-oriented hotels are often a good deal in any season.

Climate Summers are generally warm, but beware of sudden showers and blustery coastal winds. Winters are chilly and wet but are not without clear days. After a cloudburst, notice the watery quality of light that inspired Vermeer and other great Dutch painters.

The following are the average daily maximum and minimum temperatures for Amsterdam.

Jan.	40F	4C	May	61F	16C	Sept.	65F	18C
	34	1		50	10		56	13
Feb.	41F	5C	June	65F	18C	Oct.	56F	13C
	34	1		56	13		49	9
Mar.	47F	8C	July	70F	21C	Nov.	47F	8C
	38	3		59	15		41	5
Apr.	52F	11C	Aug.	68F	20C	Dec.	41F	5C
	43	6		59	15		36	2

Currency The unit of currency in Holland is the *guilder*, written as NLG (for Netherlands guilder), Fl., or simply F. (from the centuries-old term for the coinage, *florin*). Each guilder is divided into 100 cents. Bills are in denominations of 1,000, 250, 100, 50, 25, and 10 guilders. Coins are 5, 2.5, and 1 guilder and 25, 10, and 5 cents. Be careful not to confuse the 2.5- and 1-guilder coins and the 5-guilder and 5-cent coins. Bills have a code of raised dots that can be identified by touch; this is for the blind.

At press time (summer 1992), the exchange rate for the guilder was Fl. 1.50 to the U.S. dollar and Fl. 3.29 to the pound sterling.

Most major credit cards are accepted in hotels, restaurants, and shops, but check first; not all establishments accept all cards.

What It Will Cost Holland is a prosperous country with a high standard of living, so overall costs are similar to those in other northern European countries. Prices for hotels and other services in major cities are 10%–20% above those in rural areas. Amsterdam and The Hague are the most expensive. Hotel and restaurant service charges and the 18.5% value-added tax (VAT) are usually included in the prices quoted.

The cost of eating varies widely in Holland, from a snack in a bar or a modest restaurant offering a *dagschotel* (day special), or "tourist menu" at around Fl. 20 to the considerable expense of gourmet cuisine. A traditional Dutch breakfast is occasionally included in the overnight hotel price.

One cost advantage Holland has over other European countries is that because it is so small, traveling around is inexpensive—especially if you use the many price-saving transportation deals available. The **Leisure Card,** for example, is a comprehensive discount card that provides significant reductions on rail travel, car rentals, hotels, tours, entertainment, and shopping. Valid for a year, it costs Fl. 25 and is available from the Netherlands Board of Tourism (NBT) or main train stations and local information offices (VVV).

Sample Prices Half-bottle of wine, Fl. 25; glass of beer, Fl. 3; cup of coffee, Fl. 2.50; ham and cheese sandwich, Fl. 5; 1-mile taxi ride, Fl. 5.

Museums The **Museumkaart,** which can be purchased from museums, provides a year's free or reduced admission to 350 museums. It costs Fl. 40, or Fl. 15 if you're under 26. A photo and passport are required for purchase. If your time is limited, you might want to check the list; not all museums participate.

Customs on Arrival For travelers arriving from a country that is not a member of the European Community (EC) or those coming from an EC country who have bought goods in a duty-free shop, the allowances are (1) 200 cigarettes or 50 cigars or 100 cigarillos or 250 grams of tobacco, (2) 1 liter of alcohol more than 22% by volume or 2 liters of liqueur wine or 2 liters of sparkling wine, (3) 50 grams of perfume or 25 centiliters of toilet water, and (4) other goods to the value of Fl. 125.

For travelers arriving from an EC country, the allowances for goods, provided they were not bought in a duty-free shop, are (1) 300 cigarettes or 75 cigars or 400 grams of tobacco, (2) 1½ liters of alcohol more than 22% by volume or 3 liters of alcohol less than 22% by volume or 3 liters of sparkling wine or 3 liters of liqueur wine and 5 liters of nonsparkling wine, (3) 75 grams of perfume and 38 centiliters of toilet water, and (4) other goods to the value of Fl. 910.

All personal items are considered duty-free, provided you take them with you when you leave Holland. Tobacco and alcohol allowances are for those 17 and older. There are no restrictions on the import and export of Dutch currency.

Language Dutch is a difficult language for foreigners, but luckily the Dutch are fine linguists, so almost everyone speaks at least some English, especially in larger cities and tourist centers.

Getting Around

By Train Fast, frequent, and comfortable trains operate throughout the country. All trains have first- and second-class cars, and many intercity trains have buffet or dining-car services. Intercity trains run every 30 minutes and regular trains run to the smaller towns at least once an hour. Sometimes one train contains two separate sections that divide during the trip, so be sure you are in the correct section for your destination.

Fares The best value in the Netherlands is the **Rail Pass,** a ticket for unlimited train travel; you can buy one for one or seven days, with no reductions for children. A second-class day pass costs Fl. 51; a seven-day pass costs Fl. 118. If you buy a Rail Pass, for a small additional charge you can also get a **Link Rover,** which is good for unlimited travel on all public transportation. Your passport may be needed when you purchase these tickets.

If you are also traveling through Belgium and Luxembourg, the five-day **Benelux Tourrail** card is the best bet. It allows for unlimited travel and is valid for any five days within a period of 17 consecutive days. It costs about Fl. 156 first class or Fl. 104 second class. **Dagtochtkaartjes** are special combined tickets covering train, boat, and bus trips. Using the Leisure Card (*see* What it Will Cost, *above*) is another option. Ask about these fares at railway information bureaus or local tourist offices. **The Netherlands Board of Tourism's** (NBT) offices abroad have information on train services, as do overseas offices of Netherlands Railways (*see* Before You Go in Chapter 1).

By Bus Holland has an excellent bus network between towns that are not connected by rail and also within towns. Bus excursions can be booked on the spot and at local VVV offices. In major cities, the best buy is a **strippenkaart** ticket (Fl. 9.75), which can be used for all bus, tram, and metro services. Each card has 15 strips, which are canceled by the driver as you enter the buses, or by the stamping machine at each door of the trams. More than one person can travel on a strippenkaart—it just gets used up more quickly. A strippenkaart with 45 strips is available for Fl. 28. You can buy it at train stations, post offices, and some VVV offices, or in Amsterdam at the GVB (national bus system) ticket office in the plaza in front of the central railway station. A two-day **dagkaart,** a travel-anywhere ticket, covers all urban bus/streetcar routes and costs Fl. 12.60; three days, Fl. 15.60.

By Bicycle   Holland is a "cyclist-friendly" country with specially designated cycle paths, signs, and picnic areas. Bikes can usually be rented at train stations in most cities and towns, and Dutch trains are "cycle-friendly," too, with extra spacious entryways designed to accommodate bicycles (as well as wheelchairs). You will need an extra ticket for the bike, however. The basic cost is Fl. 14 round-trip to anywhere in the country; the price goes up to Fl. 22.50 during the busy summer months. Rental costs for bicycles are around Fl. 8 per day or from Fl. 22.50 per week, plus a deposit of Fl. 50–Fl. 200. Advice on rentals and routes is available from offices of The Netherlands Board of Tourism in North America or in Holland, or from local VVV offices; cycling packages can be booked at the larger offices.

Staying in Holland

Telephones   The telephone system in Holland is excellent and reliable. All
Local Calls   towns and cities have area codes that are to be used only when you are calling from outside the area. Pay phones take 25¢, Fl. 1, and Fl. 2.50 coins. Local calls cost 25¢ per minute. Increasingly, public phone booths are being converted to a credit-card payment system (for Dutch phone subscribers only), which may necessitate either a search for a coin phone or a long wait at the booth, or both.

International Calls   Direct-dial international calls can be made from post offices, but not from a phone booth without a credit card issued by PTT, the Dutch telephone service. Lower rates are charged from 7 PM to 10 AM weekdays, and from 7 PM Friday to 10 AM Monday. The average cost per minute to the U.S. is Fl. 2.60 (Fl. 2.30 nights and weekends). Think twice about making international calls from your hotel room because high service charges may double or triple the cost over and above the already doubled or tripled rates that are charged for calls from Europe to North America.

Operators   In Holland, dial 06/022911 to reach **ATT USA Direct;** tel. 06/0229116 to reach **Bell Canada.** To telephone elsewhere internationally, call 06–0410 for an English-speaking operator; to call within Holland, dial the same number.

Mail   The Dutch post office is as efficient as the telephone network.
Postal Rates   Airmail letters to the United States cost Fl. 1.30 for the first 10 grams; postcards cost 75¢; aerograms cost Fl. 1. Airmail letters to the United Kingdom cost 75¢ for the first 20 grams; postcards cost 55¢; aerograms cost 65¢.

Receiving Mail   If you're uncertain where you'll be staying, have mail sent to Poste Restante, GPO, in major cities along your route, or to American Express offices, where a small charge will be made on collection.

Shopping   Purchases of goods in one single store in one single day amount-
VAT Refunds   ing to Fl. 300 or more qualify for a value-added tax (VAT) refund of 18.5%, which can be claimed at the airport or main border crossing when you leave Holland, or by mail. Ask the salesperson for a VAT refund form when you buy anything that may qualify.

Bargaining   The prices in most shops are fixed, but you can try to bargain for items in any of the open-air markets.

Opening and   **Banks.** Banks are open weekdays from 9 to 4. You can also
Closing Times   change money at GWK bureaux de change at major railway stations and Schiphol Airport, which are open Monday–Saturday 8–8 and Sunday 10–4. GWK offices in major cities or at border checkpoints are open 24 hours.

Museums. Most major museums now close on Monday, but not all, so check with local VVV offices. In rural areas, some museums close or operate shorter hours during winter. Usual hours are 10–5.

Shops. In general, shops are open weekdays from 8:30 or 9 to 5:30 or 6, but outside the cities, some close for lunch. Department stores and most shops, especially in shopping plazas (in The Hague and Amsterdam) do not open until 1 PM on Monday, and a few close one afternoon a week on whichever day they choose. Late-night shopping usually can be done until 9 PM on Thursday or Friday.

National Holidays   January 1; April 11–12 (Easter); April 30 (Queen's Day; shops are open unless it falls on Sunday); May 5 (Liberation); May 9 (Ascension); June 7 (Pentecost); December 25–26.

Dining   Of the many earthly pleasures the Dutch indulge, eating probably heads the list. There is a wide variety of cuisines from traditional Dutch to Indonesian—the influence of the former Dutch colony.

Breakfast tends to be hearty and substantial—traditionally including several varieties of bread, butter, jam, ham, cheese, boiled eggs, juice, and steaming coffee or tea. Dutch specialties for later meals include *erwtensoep*, a rich, thick pea soup with pieces of tangy sausage or pigs' knuckles, and *hutspot*, a meat, carrot, and potato stew; both are usually served only during winter. *Haring* (herring) is particularly popular, especially the "new herring" caught between May and September and served in brine, garnished with onions. If Dutch food begins to pall, try an Indonesian restaurant, where the chief dish is *rijsttafel*, a meal made up of 20 or more small dishes, many of which are hot and spicy.

The indigenous Dutch liquor is potent and warming *jenever* (gin), both "old" and "new." Dutch liqueurs and beers are also popular.

Eating places range from snack bars, fast-food outlets, and modest local cafés to gourmet restaurants of international repute. Of special note are the "brown cafés," traditional pubs of great character that normally offer snack-type meals.

Mealtimes The Dutch tend to eat dinner around 6 or 7 PM, especially in the country and smaller cities, so many restaurants close at about 10 PM and accept final orders at 9. In larger cities dining hours vary, and some restaurants stay open until midnight.

Dress Casual dress is acceptable. In general, Holland is a somewhat formal country, so when in doubt, it's better to dress up.

Ratings Prices are per person including three courses (appetizer, main course, and dessert), service, and sales tax but not drinks. For budget travelers, many restaurants offer a tourist menu at an officially controlled price, currently Fl. 20. Best bets are indicated by a star ★.

Category	Amsterdam	Other Areas
Moderate	Fl. 35–Fl. 50	Fl. 30–Fl. 40
Inexpensive	Fl. 25–Fl. 35	Fl. 25–Fl. 30
Budget	under Fl. 25	under Fl. 25

Lodging Holland offers a wide range of accommodations encompassing, at the less expensive end of the spectrum, traditional, small-town hotels and family-run guest houses. For young or adventurous travelers, the provinces abound with modest hostels, camping grounds, and rural bungalows. Travelers with modest budgets may prefer to stay in friendly bed-and-breakfast establishments; these are in short supply and need to be booked on the spot at local VVV offices.

Hotels Dutch hotels are generally clean, if not spotless, no matter how modest their facilities, and service is normally courteous and efficient. There are many moderate and inexpensive hotels, most of which are relatively small. In the provinces the range of accommodations is more limited, but there are pleasant, inexpensive family-run hotels that are usually centrally located and offer a friendly atmosphere. Some have good—if modest—dining facilities. English is spoken or understood almost everywhere. Hotels usually quote room prices for double occupancy, and rates often include breakfast, service charges, and VAT.

To book hotels in advance, you can use the free **National Reservation Center** (Box 404, 2260 KA Leidschendam, tel. 070/3202500, fax 070/3202611). Alternatively, for a small fee, VVV offices can usually make reservations at short notice. Bookings must be made in person, however.

Ratings Prices are for two people sharing a double room. Best bets are indicated by a star ★.

Category	Amsterdam	Other Areas
Moderate	Fl. 200–Fl. 300	Fl. 150–Fl. 200
Inexpensive	Fl. 150–Fl. 200	Fl. 100–Fl. 150
Budget	under Fl. 150	under Fl. 100

Tipping Hotels and restaurants almost always include 15% service and VAT in their charges. Give a doorman 50¢ to Fl. 1 for calling a cab. The official minimum for porters in train stations is Fl.

2.50 a bag. Hat-check attendants expect at least 25¢, and washroom attendants get 50¢.

Amsterdam

Arriving and Departing

By Plane Most international flights arrive at Amsterdam's Schiphol Airport, one of Europe's finest. Immigration and customs formalities on arrival are relaxed, with no forms to be completed.

Between the Airport and Downtown The best transportation between the airport and the city center is the direct rail link to the central station, where you can get a tram to your hotel. The train runs every 10 to 15 minutes throughout the day and takes about half an hour. Second-class fare is Fl. 5.

By Train The city has excellent rail connections with the rest of Europe. Fast services link it to Paris, Brussels, Luxembourg, and Cologne. **Centraal Station** is conveniently located in the center of town.

Getting Around

By Bus, Tram, and Metro A zonal fare system is used. Tickets (starting at Fl. 2) are bought from automatic dispensers on the metro or from the drivers on trams and buses; or buy a money-saving **strippenkaart** (*see* Getting Around, By Bus, *above*). Even simpler is the two-day **dagkaart,** which covers all city routes for Fl. 12.60. These discount tickets can be obtained from the main GVB ticket office in front of Centraal Station, along with route maps of the public transportation system. Recently introduced water buses in the city center also have day cards. The **Canalbus,** which travels between the central station and the Rijksmuseum, is Fl. 12.50.

By Bicycle Rental bikes are readily available for around Fl. 7.50 per day with a Fl. 100–Fl. 200 deposit. Bikes are an excellent and inexpensive way to explore the city. Several rental companies are close to the central station, or ask at the VVV offices for details.

By Boat The **Museum Boat** which makes seven stops near major museums, is Fl. 15 for adults, Fl. 13 for children.

On Foot Amsterdam is a small, congested city of narrow streets, which makes it ideal for exploring on foot. The VVV issues seven excellent guides that detail walking tours around the center. The best are "The Jordaan," a stroll through the lively canalside district, and "Jewish Amsterdam," a walk past the symbolic remains of Jewish housing and old synagogues.

Important Addresses and Numbers

Tourist Information There are two **VVV** offices: one across from the central station in the Old Dutch Coffee House (Stationsplein 10, tel. 020/6266444), and the other at Leidsestraat 106. The VVV reserves for accommodations, tours, and entertainment, but reservations must be made in person. The Stationsplein office is open Easter–September, daily 9 AM–11 PM; October–Easter, daily 9–5.

Consulates U.S. (Museumsplein 19, tel. 020/6790321). **Canadian** (7 Sophia-laan, The Hague, tel. 070/3614111). **U.K.** (Koningslaan 44, tel. 020/6764343).

Emergencies The general number for emergencies is 06–11, but note direct numbers. **Police** (tel. 020/6222222); **Ambulance** (tel. 020/5555555); **Doctor Academisch Medisch Centrum** (Meibergdreef 9, tel. 020/5669111). **Central Medical Service** (tel. 020/6642111) will give you names of pharmacists and dentists as well as doctors. **Dentist Practice AOC** (W.G. Plein 167, tel. 020/6161234) is also open on weekends.

Exploring Amsterdam

Amsterdam is a gem of a city for the tourist. Small and densely packed with fine buildings, many dating from the 17th century or earlier, it is easily explored on foot or by bike. The old heart of the city consists of canals, with narrow streets radiating out like the spokes of a wheel. The hub of this wheel and the most convenient point to begin sightseeing is the central station. Across the street, in the same building as the Old Dutch Coffee House, is a VVV tourist information office that offers helpful tourist advice.

Amsterdam's key points of interest can be covered within two or three days, with each walking itinerary taking in one or two of the important museums and galleries. The following exploration of the city center can be broken up into several sessions.

Around the Dam *Numbers in the margin correspond to points of interest on the Amsterdam map.*

❶ Start at the **Centraal Station** (Central Station). Designed by P. J.H. Cuijpers and built in 1885, it is a good example of Dutch architecture at its most flamboyant. The street directly in front of the station square is Prins Hendrikkade. To the left, a good
❷ vantage point for viewing the station, is **St. Nicolaaskerk** (Church of St. Nicholas), consecrated in 1888. Of interest are the baroque altar with its revolving tabernacle, the swinging pulpit that can be stowed out of sight, and the upstairs gallery.

Around the corner from St. Nicolaaskerk, facing the harbor, is
❸ the **Schreierstoren** (Weeping or Criers' Tower), where seafarers used to say good-bye to their women before setting off to sea. The tower was erected in 1487, and a tablet marks the point from which Henrik (aka Henry) Hudson set sail on the *Half Moon* on April 4, 1609, on a voyage that took him to what is now New York and the river that still bears his name. Today the Weeping Tower is used as a combined reception and exhibition center, which includes a maritime bookshop.

Three blocks to the southwest along the Oudezijds Voor-
❹ burgwal is the **Amstelkring Museum,** whose facade carries the inscription "Ons Lieve Heer Op Solder" ("Our Dear Lord in the Attic"). In 1578, Amsterdam embraced Protestantism and outlawed the church of Rome. So great was the tolerance of the municipal authorities, however, that secret Catholic chapels were allowed to exist; at one time there were 62 in Amsterdam alone. One such chapel was established in the attics of these three neighboring canalside houses, built around 1661. The lower floors were used as ordinary dwellings, while services were held in the attics regularly until 1888, the year St. Nicolaaskerk was consecrated for Catholic worship. *Oudezijds*

Voorburgwal 49, tel. 020/246604. Admission: Fl. 4. Open Mon.–Sat. 10–5, Sun. 1–5.

⑤ Just beyond, you can see the **Oude Kerk,** the city's oldest church. Built during the 14th century but badly damaged by iconoclasts after the Reformation, the church still retains its original bell tower and a few remarkable stained-glass windows. From the tower, there is a typical view of old Amsterdam stretching from St. Nicolaaskerk to medieval gables and, if your eyesight is good, to glimpses of negotiations between a prostitute and a prospective client immediately below! *Admission free. Open Apr.–Oct., Mon.–Sat. 11–5, Sun. 1:30–5; Nov.–Mar., Mon.–Sat. 1–3, Sun. 1:30–3. Tower open June–Sept., Mon. and Thurs. 2–5, Tues. and Wed. 11–2.*

This area, bordered by Amsterdam's two oldest canals (Oudezijds Voorburgwal and Oudezijds Achterburgwal), is the heart of the *rosse buurt,* the red-light district. In the windows at canal level, women in sheer lingerie slouch, stare, or do their nails. Drawn red curtains above suggest a brisker trade. Although the area can be shocking, with its sex shops and porn shows, it is generally safe, but midnight walks down dark side streets are not advised. If you do decide to explore the area, take care; purse snatching is common.

⑥ Return to the Damrak and continue to the **Dam,** the broadest square in the old section of the town. It was here that the fishermen used to come to sell their catch. Today it is circled with shops and people, and bisected with traffic; it is also a popular center for outdoor performers. At one side of the square you will notice a simple monument to Dutch victims of World War II. Eleven urns contain soil from the 11 provinces of Holland, while a 12th contains soil from the former Dutch East Indies, now Indonesia.

⑦ In a corner of the square is the **Nieuwe Kerk** (New Church). A huge Gothic church, it was gradually expanded until 1540, when it reached its present size. Gutted by fire in 1645, it was reconstructed in an imposing Renaissance style, as interpreted by strict Calvinists. The superb oak pulpit, the 14th-century nave, the stained-glass windows, and the great organ (1645) are all shown to great effect on national holidays, when the church is bedecked with flowers. As befits Holland's national church, the Nieuwe Kerk is the site of all inaugurations (as the Dutch call their coronations), including that of Queen Beatrix in 1980. But in democratic Dutch spirit, the church is also used as a meeting place and is the home of a lively café, temporary exhibitions, and concerts. *Open daily 11–5. Closed Jan. and Feb.*

⑧ Dominating Dam Square is the **Koninklijk Paleis** (Royal Palace), or **Dam Palace,** a vast, well-proportioned structure on Dam Square that was completed in 1655. It is built on 13,659 pilings sunk into the marshy soil. The great pedimental sculptures are an allegorical representation of Amsterdam surrounded by Neptune and mythological sea creatures.

⑨ From behind the palace, Raadhuisstraat leads west across three canals to the **Westermarkt** and the **Westerkerk** (West Church), built in 1631. The church's 85-meter (275-foot) tower is the highest in the city. It also features an outstanding carillon (set of bells). Rembrandt and his son Titus are buried in the

Amstelkring
Museum, **4**
Amsterdam Historisch
Museum, **12**
Anne Frank Huis, **10**
Begijnhof, **13**
Centraal Station, **1**
Concertgebouw, **27**
Dam, **6**
Dokwerker, **22**
Flower Market, **16**
Golden Bend, **17**
Joods Historisch
Museum, **23**
Jordaan, **28**
Koninklijk Paleis, **8**
Leidseplein, **14**
Muntplein, **15**
Museum Het
Rembrandthuis, **19**
Nederlands Theater
Instituut, **18**
Nieuwe Kerk, **7**
Noorderkerk, **11**
Oude Kerk, **5**
Portuguese
Synagogue, **21**
Rijksmuseum, **24**
Rijksmuseum Vincent
van Gogh, **25**
Schreierstoren, **3**
St. Nicolaaskerk, **2**
Stedelijk Museum, **26**
Town Hall-Muziek-
theater, **20**
Westermarkt, **9**

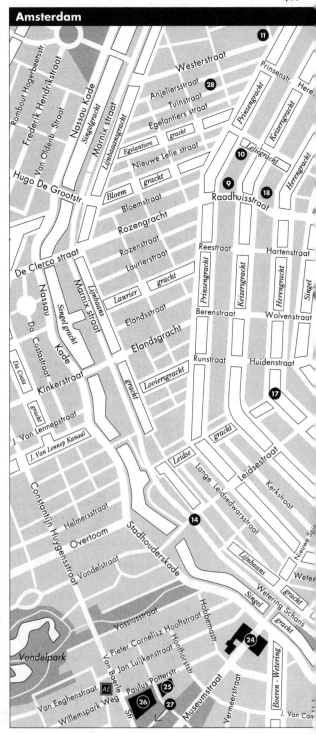

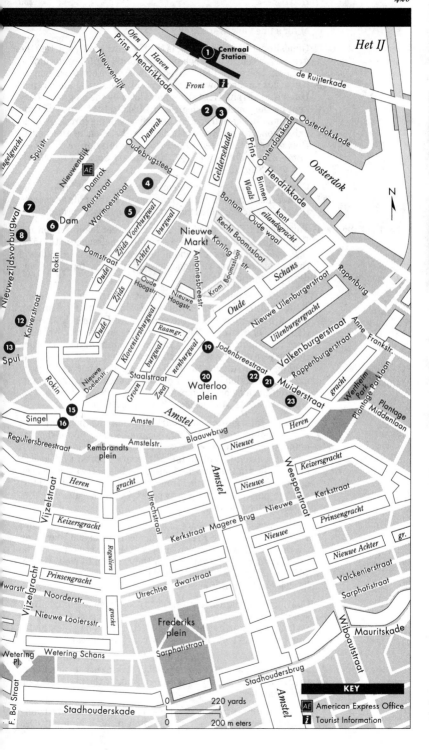

Het IJ

Centraal Station

de Ruijterkade

Front

Ofen

Haven

Prins Hendrikkade

Nieuwendijk

Damrak

Oudebrugsteeg

Geldersekade

Oosterdokskade

Oosterdok

Prins Hendrikkade

Binnen Kant

Waals

Bantam

eilandsgracht

Oude waal

Recht Boomssloot

Schans

Rapenburg

N

Nieuwendijk

Damrak

Beursstraat

Warmoesstraat

Zijds Voorburgwal

Achter burgwal

Nieuwe Markt

Koning str.

Antoniesbreestr.

Krom Boomssloot str.

Oude

Nieuwe Uilenburgerstraat

Uilenburgergracht

Valkenburgerstraat

Anne Frankstr.

Rapenburgergracht

Dam

Rokin

Damstraat

Oude

Zijds

Achter

Oude Hoogstr.

Nieuwe Hoogstr.

Kloveniersburgwal

Raamgr.

burgwal

nenburgwal

Jodenbreestraat

Muiderstraat

gracht

Wertheim Park

Plantage Parklaan

Plantage Middenlaan

Nieuwezijdsvoorburgwal

Kalverstraat

Spui

Rokin

Nieuwe Doelenstr.

Staalstraat

Groen

Zwa

Waterloo plein

Amstel

Amstel

Heren

Singel

Reguliersbreestraat

Rembrandts plein

Amstelstr.

Blaauwbrug

Nieuwe

Nieuwe

Nieuwe

Weesperstraat

Keizersgracht

Kerkstraat

Prinsengracht

gr.

Vijzelstraat

Heren

gracht

Utrechtstraat

Amstel

Kerkstraat Magere Brug

Nieuwe

Nieuwe Achter

Valckenierstraat

Keizersgracht

Reguliers

Sarphatistraat

Prinsengracht

Noorderstr.

Utrechtse dwarstraat

warstr.

Vijzelgracht

gracht

Nieuwe Looiersstr.

Frederiks plein

Sarphatistraat

Mauritskade

Wetering Pl.

Wetering Schans

0   220 yards

0   200 meters

Stadhouderskade

Sarphatistraat

Stadhoudersbrug

Amstel

Wibautstraat

Stadhouderskade

F. Bol Straat

KEY

Aᴱ American Express Office

𝒊 Tourist Information

church. During the summer, you can climb to the top of the tower for a fine view over the city.

Opposite, at Westermarkt 6, is the house where Descartes, the great 17th-century French philosopher ("Cogito, ergo sum"— "I think, therefore I am") lived in 1634. Another more famous house lies farther down Prinsengracht. This is the **Anne Frank Huis** (Anne Frank House), immortalized by the poignant diary kept by the young Jewish girl from 1942 to 1944, when she and her family hid here from the German occupying forces. A small exhibition on the Holocaust can also be seen in the house. *Prinsengracht 263, tel. 020/6264533. Admission: Fl. 6. Open June–Aug., Mon.–Sat. 9–7, Sun. 10–7; Sept.–May, Mon.– Sat. 9–5, Sun. 10–5.*

Continuing across the Prinsengracht, you'll reach the **Noorderkerk,** built in 1623. In the square in front of the church, the Noorderplein, a bird market, is held every Saturday.

South of the Dam Turn down Kalverstraat, a shopping street leading from the Royal Palace. You will notice a striking Renaissance gate (1581) that guards a series of tranquil inner courtyards. In medieval times, this area was an island devoted to piety. Today the bordering canals are filled in.

The medieval doorway just around the corner in St. Luciensteeg leads to the former Burgerweeshuis (City Orphanage), once a nunnery but now the **Amsterdam Historisch Museum** (Museum of History). The museum traces the city's history from its origins as a fishing village through the 17th-century Golden Age of material and artistic wealth to the decline of the trading empire during the 18th century. The engrossing story unfolds through a display of old maps, documents, and paintings, often aided by a commentary in English. *Kalverstraat 92, tel. 020/5231822. Admission: Fl. 5. Open daily 11–5.*

A small passageway and courtyard link the museum with the **Begijnhof,** an enchanting, enclosed square of almshouses founded in 1346. The *beguines* were women who chose to lead a form of convent life, often taking the vow of chastity. The last beguine died in 1974 and her house, No. 26, has been preserved as she left it. No. 34, dating from the 15th century, is the oldest and the only one to keep its wooden Gothic facade. *Tel. 020/ 6235554. Open weekdays 11–4.*

In the center of the square is a church given to Amsterdam's English and Scottish Presbyterians more than 300 years ago. On the church wall and also in the chancel are tributes to the Pilgrim Fathers who sailed from Delftshaven to New York in 1620. Opposite the church is another of the city's secret Catholic chapels, built in 1671.

Continuing along Kalverstraat, you soon come to Spui, a lively square in the heart of the university area. It was a center for student rallies in revolutionary 1968. Now it is a center for bookstores and bars, including the cozy "brown cafés."

Beyond is the Singel Canal and, following the tram tracks, Leidsestraat, an important shopping street that terminates in the **Leidseplein,** a lively square that is one of the night-life centers of the city.

If you continue straight along Kalverstraat instead of turning at Spui, you'll soon reach the **Muntplein,** with its **Munttoren**

(Mint Tower, built in 1620), a graceful structure whose clock and bells still seem to mirror the Golden Age. Beginning at the ⑯ Muntplein is the floating **flower market** on the Singel Canal. *Open Mon.–Sat. 9:30–5.*

From the Singel, take Leidsestraat to the Herengracht, the city's most prestigious "Gentlemen's Canal." The stretch of ca⑰ nal from here to Huidenstraat is named The **Golden Bend** for its sumptuous patrician houses with double staircases and grand entrances. Seventeenth-century merchants moved here from the Amstel River to escape the disadvantageous byproducts of their wealth: the noisy warehouses, the unpleasant smells from the breweries, and the risk of fire in the sugar refineries. These houses display the full range of Amsterdam facades: from neck, bell, and step gables to grander Louis XIV–style houses with elaborate cornices and frescoed ceilings. In particular, look at Nos. 364–370, as well as No. 380, with its sculpted angels and Louis XIV facade; Nos. 390 and 392 display neck-shaped gables surmounted by statues of a couple in matching 17th-century garb. These houses are best seen from the east side of the canal. For more gables, turn down Wolvenstraat into the Keizersgracht, the Emperor's Canal. Walk northward toward Westerkerk and the Anne Frank Huis (*see above*).

⑱ Along Herengracht, parallel to the Westerkerk, is the **Nederlands Theater Instituut.** This theater museum is a dynamic find on such a genteel canal. Two frescoed Louis XIV–style merchants' houses form the backdrop for a history of the circus, opera, musicals, and drama. Miniature theaters and videos of stage productions are just two entertaining features. During the summer, the large garden is open for buffet lunches. *Herengracht 168. Admission: Fl. 5. Open Tues.–Sun. 11–5.*

Jewish Amsterdam   Take the Museumboat or the metro from the central station to Waterlooplein and walk east to Jodenbreestraat. This is the heart of **Jodenbuurt,** the old Jewish district and an important area to all Amsterdammers. The original settlers here were wealthy Sephardic Jews from Spain and Portugal, later followed by poorer Ashkenazic refugees from Germany and Poland. At the turn of the century, this was a thriving community of Jewish diamond polishers, dyers, and merchants. During World War II, the corner of Jodenbreestraat marked the end of the *Joodse wijk* (Jewish neighborhood), by then an imposed ghetto. Although the character of the area was largely destroyed by highway construction in 1965, and more recently by construction of both the metro and the Town Hall–Muziektheater complex, neighboring Muiderstraat has retained much of the original atmosphere. Notice the gateways decorated with pelicans, symbolizing great love; according to legend, the pelican will feed her starving young with her own blood.

From 1639 to 1658, Rembrandt lived at Jodenbreestraat No. 4, ⑲ now the **Museum Het Rembrandthuis** (Rembrandt's House). For more than 20 years, the ground floor was used by the artist as living quarters; the sunny upper floor was his studio. It is fascinating to visit, both as a record of life in 17th-century Amsterdam and as a sketch of Holland's most illustrious artist. It contains a superb collection of his etchings and engravings. From St. Antonies Sluis bridge, just by the house, there is a canal view that has barely changed since Rembrandt's time. *Jodenbreestraat 4–6, tel. 020/6249486. Admission: Fl. 4. Open Mon.–Sat. 10–5, Sun. 1–5.*

After visiting Rembrandt's House, walk back to the canal and go left to pass the Waterlooplein flea market. Ahead of you is ⑳ the Amsterdam **Town Hall–Muziektheater** complex, which presents an intriguing combination of bureaucracy and art. Amsterdammers come to the Town Hall section of the building by day to obtain driving licenses, to pick up welfare payments, and to be married. They return by night to the rounded part of the building facing the river to see opera and ballet by Holland's well-known performing companies. Feel free to wander into Town Hall (there are some interesting sculptures and other displays to see). Opera and ballet fans can go on a tour of the Muziektheater, which takes you around the dressing rooms, dance studios, and even the wig department. *Amstel 3. Tel. 020/5518100. Cost: Fl. 8.50. Guided tours every Wed. and Sat. at 4.*

㉑ Facing the Muziektheater is the 17th-century **Portuguese Synagogue.** As one of Amsterdam's four neighboring synagogues, it was part of the largest Jewish religious complex in Europe. The austere interior is still intact, even if the building itself is marooned on a traffic island. *Open May–Oct., Sun.–Fri. 10–4; Nov.–Apr. Mon.–Thurs. 10–4, Fri. 10–2.*

Jonas Daniel Meijerplein is a square behind the Portuguese ㉒ Synagogue. In the center is a statue of the **Dokwerker** (Dockworker), a profession that has played a significant part in the city's history. The statue commemorates the 1942 strike by which Amsterdam dockworkers expressed their solidarity with persecuted Jews. A memorial march is held every year on February 25.

㉓ On the other side of the square is the intriguing **Joods Historisch Museum** (Jewish History Museum), set in a complex of three ancient synagogues. These synagogues once served a population of 100,000 Jews, which shrank to less than 10,000 after 1945. The new museum, founded by American and Dutch Jews, displays religious treasures in a clear cultural and historical context. Since the synagogues lost most of their treasures in the war, their architecture and history are more compelling than the individual exhibits. *Jonas Daniël Meijerplein 2–4, tel. 020/6269945. Admission: Fl. 7. Open daily 11–5.*

Instead of returning on foot, you can catch the Museum Boat from the Muziektheater to the central station or to a destination near your hotel. If you feel like a breath of fresh air, stroll along Nieuwe Herengracht, once known as the "Jewish Gentlemen's Canal." In Rembrandt's day, there were views of distant windjammers sailing into port, but today the canal is oddly deserted.

The Museum Quarter By crossing the bridge beyond the Leidseplein and walking a short distance to the left on Stadshouderskade, you'll find three of the most distinguished museums in Holland—the Rijksmuseum, the Stedelijk Museum, and the Rijksmuseum ㉔ Vincent van Gogh. Of the three, the **Rijksmuseum,** easily recognized by its towers, is the most important, so be sure to allow adequate time to explore it. It was founded in 1808, but the current, rather lavish, building dates from 1885. The museum contains significant collections of furniture, textiles, ceramics, sculpture, and prints, as well as Italian, Flemish, and Spanish paintings, many of which are of the highest quality. But the museum's fame rests on its unrivaled collection of 16th- and

17th-century Dutch masters. Of Rembrandt's masterpieces, make a point of seeing *The Nightwatch*, concealed during World War II in caves in Maastricht. The painting was misnamed because of its dull layers of varnish; in reality it depicts the Civil Guard in daylight. Also worth searching out are Jan Steen's family portraits, Frans Hals's drunken scenes, Van Ruysdael's romantic but menacing landscapes, and Vermeer's glimpses of everyday life bathed in his usual pale light. *Stadhouderskade 42, tel. 020/6732121. Admission: Fl. 6.50. Open Tues.–Sat. 10–5, Sun. 1–5.*

㉕ A few blocks beyond is the **Rijksmuseum Vincent van Gogh.** This museum contains the world's largest collection of the artist's works—200 paintings and 500 drawings—as well as works by some 50 other painters of the period. *Paulus Potterstraat 7, tel. 020/5705200. Admission: Fl. 10. Open Tues.–Sat. 10–5, Sun. 1–5; Easter–Sept. 21, additional hours Mon. 10–5.*

㉖ Next door is the **Stedelijk Museum** (Municipal Museum), with its austere neoclassical facade designed to counterbalance the Rijksmuseum's neo-Gothic turrets. The museum has a stimulating collection of modern art and ever-changing displays of contemporary art. Before viewing the works of Cézanne, Chagall, Kandinsky, and Mondrian, check the list of temporary exhibitions in Room 1. Museum policy is to trace the development of the artist rather than merely to show a few masterpieces. Don't forget the museum's restaurant overlooking a garden filled with modern sculptures. *Paulus Potterstraat 13, tel. 020/5732911. Admission: Fl. 7. Open daily 11–5.*

㉗ Diagonally opposite the Stedelijk Museum, at the end of the broad Museumplein, is the **Concertgebouw,** home of the country's foremost orchestra, the world-renowned Concertgebouworkest. Many visiting orchestras also perform here. The building has two auditoriums, the smaller of which is used for chamber music and recitals. A block or two in the opposite direction is **Vondelpark,** an elongated rectangle of paths, lakes, and pleasant shady trees. A monument honors the 17th-century epic poet Joost van den Vondel, for whom the park is named. From Wednesday to Sunday during the summer, free concerts and plays are performed in the park.

The Jordaan One old part of Amsterdam that is certainly worth exploring is
㉘ the **Jordaan,** the area bordered by Herengracht, Lijnbaansgracht, Brouwersgracht, and Raadhuisstraat. The canals and side streets here are all named for flowers and plants. Indeed, at one time, when this was the French quarter of the city, the area was known as *le jardin* (the garden), a name that over the years has become Jordaan. The best time to explore this area is on a Sunday morning, when there are few cars and people about, or in the evening. This part of the town has attracted many artists and is something of a bohemian quarter, where rundown buildings are being renovated and converted into restaurants, antiques shops, boutiques, and galleries.

Off the Beaten Track

Beer lovers—or anyone with an interest in the production of a world-class product—will want to take time to visit the **Heinekenontvangstgebouw,** formerly the Heineken Brewery. The guided weekday tours (year-round 9:30 and 11, additional summer tours at 1 and 2:30) take in a slide presentation, the old brewery stables, and, of course, include free beer at the end of the tour. *Van der Helstraat. Admission: Fl. 2. Children under 18 not admitted.*

Shopping

Serious shoppers should buy the VVV's four excellent shopping guides to markets, art and antiques shops, boutiques, and department stores (Fl. 10).

Gift Ideas **Diamonds.** Since the 17th century, "Amsterdam cut" has been synonymous with perfection in the quality of diamonds. There is a cluster of diamond houses on the Rokin. Alternatively, try **Van Moppes Diamonds.** *Albert Cuypstraat 2–6, tel. 020/6761242. Open daily 9–5.*

Porcelain. The Dutch have been producing Delft, Makkum, and other fine porcelain for centuries. Try the **Focke and Meltzer** store situated near the Rijksmuseum (P.C. Hooftstraat 65–67, tel. 020/6231944).

Shopping Districts Amsterdam's chief shopping districts, which have largely been turned into pedestrianized areas, are the **Leidsestraat, Kalverstraat,** and **Nieuwendijk. Rokin,** somber and sedate, houses a cluster of boutiques and renowned antiques shops. By contrast, some of the **Nieuwe Spiegelstraat**'s old curiosity shops sell a more inexpensive range. For trendy small boutiques and unusual crafts shops, locals browse through the Jordaan. When leaving Holland, remember that Schiphol Airport is Europe's best tax-free shopping center.

Department Stores **De Bijenkorf** (Dam Square), the city's number-one department store, is excellent for contemporary fashions and furnishings. Running a close second is **Vroom and Dreesman** (Kalverstraat 201), with well-stocked departments carrying all manner of goods.

Markets There is a lively open-air **flea market** on Waterlooplein around the Musiektheater (Mon.–Sat. 9:30–4). For antiques, especially silver and toys, visit the **Sunday Waterlooplein Market** during the summer. You can also try the **Antiekmarkt de Looier** (Elandsgracht 109. Open Sun.–Wed. 11–5, Thurs. 11–9). During the summer, art lovers can buy etchings, drawings, and watercolors at the Sunday **art markets** on Thorbeckeplein and the Spui.

Dining

Amsterdammers are less creatures of habit than are the Dutch in general. Even so, set menus and early dinners are preferred by these health-conscious citizens. For travelers on a diet or budget, the blue-and-white "Tourist Menu" sign guarantees an economical (Fl. 20) yet imaginative set menu created by the head chef. For traditionalists, the "Nederlands Dis" soup tureen sign is a promise of regional recipes and seasonal ingredients. "You can eat in any language" is the city's proud boast, so when Dutch restaurants are closed, Indonesian, Chinese, and Turkish restaurants are often open. Between meals, you can follow your nose to the nearest herring cart or drop into a cozy brown café for coffee and an apple tart. For details and price-category definitions, *see* Dining in Staying in Holland.

Moderate **China Treasure.** Given the Dutch fascination with Indonesian cooking, it can be a task to find traditional Chinese cuisine. China Treasure is a fine choice that is also conveniently located near Dam Square. The dim sum lunch is popular. *N.Z. Voorburgwal 115, tel. 020/6260915. Reservations accepted. AE, DC, MC, V.*

★ **De Orient.** Excellent Indonesian food is just minutes away from major museums and the Concertgebouw. Complementing the rijsttafel are excellent *loempia* (egg rolls) and soups. Every Wednesday night there is a rijsttafel buffet. *Van Baerlestraat 21, tel. 020/6734958. Reservations required. AE, DC, MC, V.*

Oesterbar. As its name suggests, the Oyster Bar specializes in seafood, some of which eyes you from the tank. The downstairs bistro offers relatively inexpensive dining, while upstairs, presentation and price are somewhat higher. Salmon and trout are the specialties, and the oysters themselves make a good, if expensive, first course. *Leidseplein 10, tel. 020/6232988. Reservations advised. AE, DC.*

Sea Palace. The Sea Palace is an appropriate establishment for a city built on canals—it's a huge, floating Chinese restaurant. The Cantonese menu is of only modest quality, but the surroundings make up for it. A special children's menu is also available. *Oosterdokskade (near the central station), tel. 020/6264777. Reservations accepted. No credit cards.*

Speciaal. Although set in the Jordaan area, this Indonesian restaurant is slightly off the beaten track. From the outside, the Speciaal looks very mundane, but inside, the soothing Indonesian prints, raffia work, and bamboo curtains create an intimate atmosphere. Along with the usual rijsttafel, chicken, fish, and egg dishes provide tasty variants on a sweet-and-sour theme. *Nieuwe Leliestraat 142, tel. 020/6249706. Reservations accepted. AE, MC, V.*

Inexpensive **Haesje Claes.** Traditional Dutch food is served here in a traditional Dutch environment, with prices that are easy on the wallet; it sounds like a tourist's dream and, in ways, it is. There's a cozy feeling here and a relaxed simplicity. Menu choices can be as basic as liver and onions or as elaborate as filet of salmon with lobster sauce. There is a tourist menu. *Spuistraat 273–275, tel. 020/6249998. Reservations accepted. AE, DC, MC, V. Closed Sun. lunch.*

Oud Holland. This restaurant is in a convenient location for a night on the town—not far from the Leidseplein, yet just far enough from the red-light district. Oud Holland is one of the few Amsterdam restaurants to offer a tourist menu. A typical three-course meal is a game pâté followed by pork in cream sherry sauce and an apple pancake for dessert. A children's menu is also available. The heated terrace opens at 5 PM for restaurant guests. *NZ Voorburgwal 105, tel. 020/6246848. Reservations accepted. AE, DC, MC, V.*

Pancake Bakery. Here is a chance to try a traditionally Dutch way of keeping eating costs down. The name of the game is pancakes—for every course including dessert, for which the topping can be ice cream, fruit, or liqueur. The Pancake Bakery is not far from Anne Frank Huis. *Prinsengracht 191, tel. 020/6251333. No reservations. No credit cards.*

Budget **Blauwe Hollander.** The name is a bit of nonsense (it means Blue Dutchman), but the pricing strategy is not. This is a simple, straightforward sort of eatery, located near the Leidseplein entertainment area. There's always a daily special as well as a variety of other meat-and-potato sort of choices. The no-frills decor is traditional Dutch. *Leidsekruisstraat 28, no phone. Closed lunch. No credit cards.*

De Keuken van 1870. You absolutely, positively can't get cheaper than this. Day menus are Fl. 10 and à la carte selections are only a few guilders more. The choices on any given night may be spare ribs, fried liver, or even jugged hare with peaches and cranberry, and every plate comes complete with vegetables and potato. The decor, if it can be called decor, is simple (like the soup kitchen this Keuken once was), but you come here for good eats, not ambience. *Spuistraat 4, tel. 020/6238965. AE, DC, MC, V.*

Hotel School Amsterdam. This is the ideal choice for those who say they have champagne tastes and a beer budget. You'll have to be willing to let would-be chefs and apprentice sauciers practice their skills, but you can dine on selections such as rable de lievre à la poivandre or salmon grille au romaine for no more than you might pay elsewhere for a simple plate of chopped steak. Menus change weekly at the school's two dining rooms. *70 Elandsgracht and 175 Elandsstraat, tel. 020/623-84-28. Closed Mon. at Elandsgracht location; closed Fri. at Elandsstraat location. No credit cards.*

Lodging

Accommodations are tight from Easter to summer, so early booking is advised if you wish to secure a popular hotel. The other snag is parking: Amsterdam is a pedestrian's paradise but a driver's nightmare. Since few hotels have parking lots, cars are best abandoned in a multistory parking ramp for the duration of your stay. Most tourists prefer to stay inside the concentric ring of canals. This area, the quiet museum quarter, is a convenient choice for the Rijksmuseum yet is near enough to the Vondelpark for light jogging. More atmospheric lodgings can be found in the historic canalside neighborhood with its gabled merchants' houses. For details and price-category definitions, *see* Lodging in Staying in Holland.

Moderate **Ambassade.** With its beautiful canalside location, its Louis
★ XV–style decoration, and its Oriental carpets, the Ambassade seems more like a stately home than a hotel. Service is attentive and room prices include breakfast. For other meals, the neighborhood has a good choice of restaurants for eating out. *Herengracht 341, tel. 020/6262333. 46 rooms with bath. AE, MC, V.*

Atlas Hotel. Renowned for its friendly atmosphere, this small hotel has moderate-size rooms decorated in Art Nouveau style. It's also very handy for Museumsplein, whose major museums are within easy walking distance. *Van Eeghenstraat 64, tel. 020/6766336. 22 rooms with bath. Facilities: bar, restaurant. AE, DC, MC, V.*

Het Canal House. The American owners of this canalside hotel also opt to put antiques rather than televisions in the rooms. Spacious rooms overlook the canal or the illuminated garden. A hearty Dutch breakfast comes with the room. *Keizergracht 148, tel. 020/6225182. 26 rooms with bath or shower. AE.*

RHO Hotel. Just off Dam Square, at the head of the street that is Amsterdam's equivalent of Off Broadway, this hotel is housed in a building once used by Holland's foremost gold company. The lobby, bar, and breakfast room occupy a chamber built originally as a theater in 1908. The rooms are cheerful, modern, and attractively furnished in contemporary style. *Nes 11–23, tel. 020/6207826. 80 rooms with bath. Facilities: parking. AE, DC, MC, V.*

Inexpensive **Agora.** Near the Singel flower market, this small hotel reflects
★ the cheerful bustle. The rooms are light and spacious, some decorated with vintage furniture; the best overlook the canal or the university. Recently refurbished, this 18th-century house has a considerate staff, and a relaxed neighborhood ensures the hotel's popularity. Book well in advance. *Singel 462, tel. 020/ 6272200. 14 rooms with bath or shower. No credit cards.*

Amsterdam Classic Hotel. In a building that once was a distillery has been created an attractive, though somewhat stark, small hotel near Dam Square. The rooms are bright and spacious and furnished in light colors for an open, airy feeling. *Gravenstraat 14–16, tel. 020/6233716. 33 rooms with bath. AE, DC, MC, V.*

Hotel Seven Bridges. Named for the scene beyond its front steps, this small canal-house hotel offers clean, simple rooms with private bathrooms (also small but clean). The Rembrandtsplein is nearby. *Reguliersgracht 31, tel. 020/6231329. 6 rooms with bath. No credit cards.*

Singel Hotel. There's a bright, contemporary look to this little canal-house hotel that belies the traditional exterior and could easily compete with higher-priced establishments for the caliber of its decor. Rooms seem to be tucked into every possible corner of the building, and as a result they vary greatly in size and arrangement. Located just behind the Round Church (now used as a concert hall and business meeting center), this hotel is within easy walking distance of both Dam Square and the central station. *Singel 13–17, tel. 020/6263108. 22 rooms with bath. AE, DC, MC, V.*

Budget **De La Haye.** There is a convivial mood in this simple little canal house hotel, located not far from the Leidseplein. Rooms are simple but clean and fresh; more than half have private showers. *Leidsegracht 114, tel. 020/6244044. 12 rooms with bath. AE, DC, MC, V.*

Hotel Hoksbergen. This no-nonsense canal-house hotel, neither stylish nor dowdy, offers a comfortable room at a comfortable price. The location, near both Dam Square and central station, is another plus. *Singel 301, tel. 020/6266043. 14 rooms with bath. AE, DC, MC, V.*

Hotel van Haalen. In this friendly family hotel, the husband built the platform beds himself and the cheerful wife personally welcomes her guests. Fittingly, though the city that has gone mad for Art Deco in recent years, the van Haalen still feels like a Dutch country hotel. Knick-knacks and kerosene-style hanging lamps make the bar-breakfast room a cozy place to begin and end a day of sightseeing. *Prinsengracht 520, tel. 020/ 624334. 10 rooms with bath. No credit cards.*

The Arts

The arts flourish in tolerant and cosmopolitan Amsterdam. The best sources of information about performances are the monthly publications *City Life* (in English) and *Uit Krant* (in Dutch) and the biweekly *What's On in Amsterdam*, which can be obtained from the VVV office, where you can secure tickets for the more popular events. Tickets must be booked in person from Monday to Saturday, 10 to 4. You also can book at the **Amsterdam Uit Buro** (Stadsschouwburg, Leidseplein 26, tel. 020/62112111).

Classical Music Classical music is featured at the **Concertgebouw** (Concertgebouwplein 2–6), home of one of Europe's finest orchestras. A smaller auditorium in the same building is used for chamber music, recitals, and even jam sessions. While ticket prices for international orchestras are fairly high, most concerts are good value and the Wednesday lunchtime concerts are free. The box office is open from 9:30 to 7; you can make telephone bookings (020/6718345) from 10 to 3.

Opera and Ballet The Dutch national ballet and opera companies are housed in the new **Muziektheater** on Waterlooplein. Guest companies from foreign countries perform there during the three-week Holland Festival in June.

Theater **Stalhouderij Theater** (1e Bloemdwarsstraat 4, tel. 020/6262282). An international cast performs a wide range of English-language plays in a former stable in the Jordaan. For experimental theater and colorful cabaret in Dutch, catch the shows at **Felix Meritis House** (Keizersgracht 324, tel. 020/6231311).

Film The largest concentration of movie theaters is around Leidseplein and near Muntplein. Most foreign films are subtitled rather than dubbed, which makes Amsterdam a great place to catch up on movies you missed at home. The **City 1–7** theater near Leidseplein is the biggest (seven screens), but the Art Deco–era **Tuschinski** on Reguliersbreestraat is the most beautiful cinema house.

Nightlife

Amsterdam has a wide variety of discos, bars, and exotic shows. The more respectable—and expensive—after-dark activities are in and around Leidseplein, Rembrandtsplein, and Thorbeckeplein; fleshier productions are on Oudezijds Achterburgwal. Names and locations change from year to year, but most bars and clubs are open every night from 5 PM to 2 AM or 4 AM. On weeknights, very few clubs charge admission, though the more lively ones sometimes ask for a "club membership" fee of Fl. 20 or more. Drink prices are for the most part not exorbitant. It is wise to steer clear of the area behind the central station at night.

Bars The **Bamboo Bar** (Lange Leidsedwarsstraat) is informal, expensive, relaxing, and typically international. It boasts good jazz and blues around the longest bar in Amsterdam.

Jazz Clubs Set in a converted warehouse, the **BIMhuis** is currently the most fashionable jazz club. Ticket holders can sit in the adjoining BIMcafé and enjoy a magical view across Oude Schans to the port (Oude Schans 173–177, tel. 020/6271255. Open Thurs.–Sat. from 9 PM). If you long for good Dixieland jazz, go to **Joseph Lam Jazz Club** (Van Diemenstraat 8, tel. 020/6228086); it's only open on Saturdays.

Rock Clubs **Maloe Melo** (Lijnbaansgracht 160) caters to the slightly older-than-teenage crowd.

Discos Mostly only hidden in cellars around the Leidseplein, the discos fill up after midnight. The **Cruise Inn** (Zeeburgerdijk 271, tel.

020/6927188) is the place to go for '50s and '60s music and dance. **Escape Disco Theatre** (Rembrandtsplein 11, tel. 020/6221111) is a current hot spot. **Mazzo** (Rozengracht 114, tel. 020/267500) uses dramatic lighting and slick videos to attract student poseurs, would-be musicians, and artists.

Casinos Blackjack, roulette, and slot machines have come lately—but not lightly—to the thrifty Dutch. Now everyone wants to play. The newest and most elegant venue, **Holland Casino** (Max Euweplein 62, tel. 020/6201006), just off Leidseplein, opened in 1991. You'll need your passport to get in; the minimum age is 18.

Historic Holland

This circular itinerary can be followed either clockwise or counterclockwise, but whichever way you decide to follow it, you'll be sure to see some of Holland's most characteristic sights. There are the historic towns of Leiden and Utrecht and the major museums in Haarlem; in between these towns, you'll see some of Holland's windmill-dotted landscape and pass through centers of tulip growing and cheese production.

Getting Around

All the towns on the following itinerary can be reached by bus or train. From Amsterdam there are, for example, three direct trains per hour to Haarlem, Leiden, and Utrecht. Check with the VVV office in Amsterdam for help in planning your trip, or inquire at the central station.

Tourist Information

Apeldoorn (Stationsplein 6, tel. 055/788421).
Gouda (Markt 27, tel. 01820/13666).
Haarlem (Stationsplein 1, tel. 023/319059).
Leiden (Stationsplein 210, tel. 071/146846).
Utrecht (Vredenburg 90, tel. 030/314132).
Zandvoort (Schoolplein 1, tel. 02507/17947).

Exploring Historic Holland

Apeldoorn Ninety kilometers (56 miles) southeast of Amsterdam is Apeldoorn, where the main attraction is the **Rijksmuseum Paleis Het Loo.** This former royal palace was built during the late 17th century for Willem III and has been beautifully restored to illustrate the domestic surroundings enjoyed by the House of Orange for more than three centuries. The museum, which is housed in the stables, has a fascinating collection of royal memorabilia, including cars and carriages, furniture and photographs, silver and ceramics. The formal gardens and the surrounding parkland offer attractive walks. *Tel. 055/212244. Admission Fl. 5. Open Tues.–Sun. 10–5.*

Utrecht West of Apeldoorn, 72 kilometers (44 miles), is the city of **Utrecht.** The high gabled houses of the Nieuwegracht, the canals with their water gates, the 13th-century wharves and storage cellars of the Oudegracht, and the superb churches and museums are just some of the key attractions, most of which are situated around the main cathedral square. The **Domkerk** is a late-Gothic cathedral containing a series of fine stained-glass windows. The Domtoren (bell tower) opposite the building was connected to the cathedral until a hurricane hit in 1674. The bell tower is the tallest in the country, and it has 456 steep steps that lead to a magnificent view. A guide is essential in the labyrinth of steps and passageways. *Domplein. Admission free to cathedral; Fl. 1.50 to Domtoren. Open May–Sept., daily 10–5; Oct.–Apr., weekends 1–5.*

Not far from the cathedral is the merry **Nationaal Museum van Speelklok tot Pierement** (Musical Clocks Museum), devoted solely to music machines—from music boxes to street organs and even musical chairs. During the guided tour, music students play some of the instruments. The museum is housed in Utrecht's oldest parish church. *Buurkerkhof 10. Admission: Fl. 6. Open Tues.–Sat. 11–5, Sun. 1–5.*

Behind the museum is **Pieterskerk,** the country's oldest Romanesque church, built in 1048. The grandeur of the city's churches reflects the fact that Utrecht was Holland's religious center during the Middle Ages. Most churches are open during the summer and a church concert is held almost every day.

Walk south out of Domplein, down Lange Nieuwstraat. Halfway down is the **Rijksmuseum Het Catharijneconvent.** In addition to its collection of holy relics and vestments, this museum contains the country's largest display of religious art and history. *Nieuwe Gracht 63. Admission: Fl. 3.50. Open Tues.–Fri. 10–5, weekends 11–5.*

There are more museums to be explored on Agnietenstraat, which crosses Lange Nieuwstraat. The **Centraal Museum** houses a rich collection of contemporary art and other city exhibits. Amid the clutter is an original Viking ship (discovered in 1930) and a 17th-century dollhouse complete with period furniture, porcelain, and miniature old masters. *Agnietenstraat 1. Admission: Fl. 2.75. Open Tues.–Sat. 10–5, Sun. 1–5.*

An important part of the Centraal Museum's collection is a house that is located just a few blocks away; it is known as the **Rietveld Schröder House.** Designed in 1924 by the architect Gerrit Rietveld working with Truus Schröder, this is considered to be the architectural pinnacle of the style known as De Stijl (The Style). The use of primary colors (red, yellow, blue) and black and white, and the definition of the interior space are unique and innovative even today. The experience of the house is, as one art historian phrased it, "like wandering into a Mondrian painting." The house was completely restored to its original condition in 1987. Allow 15 minutes to walk to the house; there is a guided tour through the rooms. *Prins Hendrikiaan 50, tel. 030/517926. Admission: Fl. 9. Open Tues.–Sun. 12:30–5.*

Gouda West of Utrecht, 36 kilometers (22 miles) along the A12, you'll come to **Gouda,** famous for its cheese. Try to be there on a Thursday morning in July or August, when the cheese market, centered around the **Waag,** or Weigh House, is held.

By the side of the market square is **Sint Janskerk** (Church of St. John); what you see today was built during the 16th century. It has the longest nave in the country, and 70 glorious stained-glass windows, the oldest of which dates from 1555. Around the corner from the cathedral is the Catharina Gasthuis, now the

Stedelijk Museum Het Catharina Gasthuis, the municipal museum. *Oosthaven 9, Achter de Kerk 14. Admission: Fl. 3. Open Mon.–Sat. 10–5, Sun. 1–5.*

Leiden North of Gouda is the ancient city of **Leiden,** renowned for its spirit of religious and intellectual tolerance and known for its university and royal connections. Start at the **Lakenhal,** built in 1639 for the city's cloth merchants and now an art gallery, cloth, and antiques museum. Pride of place in the collection goes to the 16th- and 17th-century Dutch paintings, with works by Steen; Dou; Rembrandt; and, above all, Lucas van Leyden's *Last Judgment*—the first great Renaissance painting in what is now the Netherlands. Other rooms are devoted to furniture and to the history of Leiden's medieval guilds: the drapers, tailors, and brewers. *Oude Singel 32. Admission: Fl. 3. Open Tues.–Sat. 10–5, Sun. 1–5.*

Near the Lakenhal is the **Molenmuseum De Valk** (Windmill Museum), housed in an original windmill, built in 1747, which was worked by 10 generations of millers until 1964. The seven floors still contain the original workings, an old forge, washrooms, and living quarters. On summer Saturdays, the mill turns—but for pleasure, not business. *2e Binnenvesstgracht 1a. Admission: Fl. 3. Open Tues.–Sat. 10–5, Sun. 1–5.*

Crossing the canal and walking into narrow, bustling Breestraat, you'll come to the imposing **St. Pieterskerk,** with its memories of the Pilgrim Fathers who worshiped here and of their spiritual leader, John Robinson, who is buried here. A narrow street by the **Persijnhofje** almhouse, dating from 1683, takes you downhill, across the gracious Rapenburg Canal. In Leiden, as in most old Dutch towns, the aristocracy continues to live in the center. The tree-lined canal is crossed by triple-arched bridges and bordered by stately 18th-century houses, including the prince's current home.

Continuing on, you find the **Academie** (university) and the **Hortus Botanicus** gardens. The university was founded by William the Silent as a reward to Leiden for its victory against the Spanish in the 1573–74 siege. During the war, the dikes were opened and the countryside flooded so that the rescuing navy could sail right up to the city walls. Members of the royal family generally attend Leiden's university, a tradition maintained by the present crown prince. Founded in 1587, these botanical gardens are among the oldest in the world. The highlights are a faithful reconstruction of a 16th-century garden, the herb garden, the colorful orangery, and the ancient trees. *Rapenburg 73. Admission: Fl. 1.50. Open Apr.–Oct., weekdays 9–4:30, weekends 10:30–3; Nov.–Mar., weekdays 9–4:30, Sun. 10:30–3.*

Follow Keiserstraat out of Rapenburg and turn left into Boisotkade. On your left is the **Pilgrim Fathers Documentatie Centrum.** This tiny museum contains photocopies of documents and maps related to the Pilgrims during their stay in Leiden, before they went to Delftshaven on the first stage of their arduous voyage to the New World. *Vliet 45. Admission free. Open weekdays 9:30–4:30.*

Haarlem With its secret inner courtyards and pointed gables, **Haarlem** can resemble a 17th-century canvas, even one painted by Frans Hals, the city's greatest painter. The area around the **Grote Markt,** the market square, provides an architectural stroll through the 17th and 18th centuries. Some of the facades are adorned with such homilies as "The body's sickness is a cure for the soul." Haarlem's religious faith can also be sensed in any of its 20 almshouses. The **Stadhuis** (Town Hall) was once a hunting lodge. Nearby is the **Vleeshal,** or meat market, which has an especially fine gabled front. This dates from the early 1600s and is now used as an art gallery and a museum of local history. *Lepelstraat. Admission free. Open Mon.–Sat. 10–5, Sun. 1–5.*

Across from the Vleeshal is the **Grote Kerk,** dedicated to St. Bavo. The church, built between 1400 and 1550, houses one of Europe's most famous organs. This massive instrument has 5,000 pipes, and both Mozart and Handel played on it. It is still used for concerts, and an annual organ festival is held here in July. Make your way down Damstraat, behind the Grote Kerk, and turn left at the **Waag** (Weigh House). On the left is the **Teylers Museum,** which claims to be the oldest museum in the country. It was founded by a wealthy merchant in 1778 as a museum of science and the arts; it now houses a fine collection of The Hague school of painting as well as a collection of drawings and sketches by Michelangelo, Raphael, and other non-Dutch masters. Since the canvases in this building are lit by natural light, try to see the museum on a sunny day. *Spaarne 16. Admission: Fl. 4. Open Tues.–Sat. 10–5, Sun. 1–5.*

Follow the Binnen Spaarn and turn right into Kampervest and then Gasthuisvest. On your right, in Groot Heiligland, you'll find the **Frans Hals Museum.** This museum, in what used to be a 17th-century hospice, contains a marvelous collection of the artist's work; his paintings of the guilds of Haarlem are particularly noteworthy. The museum also has works by Hals's contemporaries. *Groot Heiligland 62. Admission: Fl. 4.50. Open Mon.–Sat. 11–5, Sun. 1–5.*

Dining and Lodging

In towns such as Apeldoorn and Gouda are bed-and-breakfast accommodations, booked through the VVV office, an interesting choice for overnight visitors. Rooms in Utrecht are often in short supply, so book in advance or immediately upon arrival. For details and price-category definitions, *see* Dining and Lodging in Staying in Holland.

Apeldoorn
Lodging

Hotel Berg en Bos. If it were not for the flags and small covered entry, you might mistake this hotel on a quiet side street for a private house. You may feel that it is when you stay there as well. While the rooms are not particularly large, they are neat, clean, and bright. There is also a homey lounge. *Aquamarijnstraat 58, tel. 055/552352. 15 rooms with bath. MC, V. Budget.*
Hotel Pension Astra. As you might expect in a quiet residential city such as Apeldoorn, family-owned pensions abound. The Astra is just off the main road from the city center, the railway station, and Palace Het Loo. The rooms are tidy though not large, and have small private shower-baths. *Bas Backerlaan 12–14, tel. 055/223021. 26 rooms with bath. AE, DC, MC, V. Budget.*

Leiden
Dining

Oudt Leiden Pannekoekenhuijsje. This Old Dutch restaurant is in fact two contrasting restaurants run by the same management, from the same kitchen. One is famous for its roast meats and seafood specialties; the other is a pancake house that serves hearty *pannekochen* (pancakes) on huge plates. *Steen-*

straat 51, tel. 071/13344. Reservations advised. AE, DC, MC. Closed Sat. lunch and Sun. Moderate.

Lodging   **Hotel De Doelen.** This small hotel is situated in a characteristic patrician house. The spartan decor is in keeping with the character of the 15th-century house, but the 11 rooms are comfortable and much sought after. *Rapenburg 2, tel. 071/120527. 9 rooms with bath. AE, DC, MC, V. Moderate.*

Dining and Lodging   **Nieuw Minerva.** This family-run hotel is a conversion of eight
★   15th-century buildings. While the original part of the hotel is decorated in Old Dutch style, the newer part is better equipped but has slightly less character. Many of the rooms overlook a quiet tributary of the Rhine. The restaurant caters to most tastes and pockets. The excellent three-course tourist menu offers separate fish, meat, and vegetarian menus. A monthly menu is served with four or six courses of one own's choice. Delicacies are also found on the à la carte menu. *Boommarkt 23, tel. 071/126358. 40 rooms, 30 with bath or shower. Facilities: restaurant. AE, DC, MC, V. Moderate.*

Utrecht   **Het Draeckje.** This typical Dutch restaurant is set in a vaulted
Dining   cellar on Utrecht's loveliest canal. It offers a seasonal Dutch menu at reasonable prices. Coffee is accompanied by the local spicy biscuits. *Oudegracht 114–120, tel. 030/321999. Reservations advised on weekends. AE, DC, MC. Closed Sun. Moderate.*

Polman's With its lofty ceilings and early 20th-century fixtures, Polman's has been a grand cafe since long before *grande cafés* became the rage in Holland. The Art Deco decor is part of the joy of eating here. By choosing carefully from the menu, it is possible to limit the damage to your pocketbook. *Keistraat 2, tel. 030/313368. No credit cards. Moderate.*

Town Castle Oudaen/"Between Heaven and Earth." In medieval times Utrecht's Oudegracht (Old Canal) was lined with many "town castles" such as this one, and some would say that along with the Dom Tower, this is one of the finest examples of medieval architecture in Utrecht. As a restaurant it is a curious place. You may be confused by the clublike atmosphere as you enter, but you'll find the dining room on the second floor (which may be why it is called "Between Heaven and Earth"). Another unique feature of the Oudaen is that they brew their own beer in the basement and, in addition to serving it on tap, use it as an ingredient in many of their dishes. *Oudegracht 99, tel. 030/311864. Reservations accepted. AE, DC, MC, V. Closed lunch (except public house). Moderate.*

Lodging   **Malie.** The Malie hotel is on a quiet leafy street, a five-minute walk from the old center. This small, friendly hotel has an attractive breakfast room overlooking the garden and terrace. *Maliestraat 2–4, tel. 030/316424. 30 rooms with bath or shower. Facilities: bar, breakfast room. AE, DC, MC, V. Moderate.*

Hotel Ouwi. A friendly host is often the secret of an enjoyable visit to a city. You will find one here, along with a convenient neighborhood location just off a main bus route to the town center. Rooms are tidy and, while they vary in size, all are fairly roomy. *F. C. Dondersstraat 12, tel. 030/716303. 18 rooms with bath. Budget.*

Zandvoort   **Hotel Faber.** This small family hotel is not far from the beach or
Lodging   the railway station (this is the end of the line from Amsterdam). Neat, tidy, and friendly, it is a good budget choice if you are

visiting nearby Haarlem, and is especially desirable in summer, when reservations may be difficult to come by. *Kostverlornstraat 13–15, tel. 02507/12825. 34 rooms with bath. AE, MC, V. Budget.*

The Hague, Delft, and Rotterdam

Within this itinerary you can visit the Netherlands' most dignified and spacious city—the royal, diplomatic, and governmental seat of Den Haag (in English, better known as The Hague)—and its close neighbor, the leading North Sea beach resort of Scheveningen. Also nearby are Delft, a historic city with many canals and ancient buildings, and the energetic and thoroughly modern international port city of Rotterdam. It is known to the Dutch as "Manhattan on the Maas," both for its office towers and its cultural attractions.

Getting Around

The Hague and Delft are each about 60 kilometers (37½ miles) southwest of Amsterdam and can be reached within less than an hour by fast and frequent trains. The heart of both towns is compact enough to be explored on foot. Scheveningen is reached from The Hague's center by bus or tram. Travelers will find public transportation more convenient than driving because of severe parking problems at the resort. The RET Metro is an easy-to-use option for getting around Rotterdam. There are two lines, blue and red (north–south and east–west), and they cross in the heart of the business district at a major transfer center, which connects one line to the other.

Tourist Information

Delft (Markt 85, tel. 015/126100).
The Hague (Babylon Center, Koningin Julianaplein 30, next to the central station, tel. 070/3546200).
Rotterdam (Coolsingel 67, in Centraal Station, tel. 06/34034065).
Scheveningen (Gevers Deynootweg 126, tel. 070/3546200).

If you're planning to spend a few days in The Hague or Rotterdam, ask for the *VVV* brochure on city events and entertainment. Tickets for concerts and other entertainment can be reserved in person at the VVV office.

Exploring The Hague, Delft, and Rotterdam

The Hague   During the 17th century, when Dutch maritime power was at its zenith, **The Hague** was known as "The Whispering Gallery of Europe" because it was thought to be the secret manipulator of European politics. Although the Golden Age is over, The Hague remains a powerful world diplomatic capital, quietly boastful of its royal connections. It also is the seat of government for the Netherlands.

Its heart is the **Hofvijver** reflecting pool and the complex of gracious **Parliament Buildings** reflected in it. At the center of it all is the **Ridderzaal** (Knight's Hall). Inside are vast beams spanning a width of 18 meters (59 feet), flags, and stained-glass windows. A sense of history pervades the 13th-century great hall. It is now used mainly for ceremonies: Every year the queen's gilded coach brings her here to open Parliament. The two government chambers sit separately in buildings on either side of the Ridderzaal and can be visited by guided tour only when Parliament is not in session. Tours in English are conducted by Stichting Bezoekerscentrum Binnenhof (tel. 070/3646144), located just to the right of the Ridderzaal. Groups should book in advance. *Binnenhof 8a. Open Mon.–Sat. 10–4. Cost: Fl. 4.*

On the far side of the **Binnenhof,** the inner court of the Parliament complex, is a small, well-proportioned Dutch Renaissance building called the **Mauritshuis,** one of the finest small art museums in the world. This diminutive 17th-century palace contains a feast of art from the same period, including six Rembrandts; of these the most powerful is *The Anatomy Lesson of Dr. Tulp,* a theatrical work depicting a gruesome dissection of the lower arm. Also featured are Vermeer's celebrated *Girl Wearing a Turban* and his masterpiece, the glistening *View of Delft,* moodily emerging from a cloudburst. *Korte Vijverberg 8. Admission: Fl. 6.50. Open Tues.–Sat. 10–5, Sun. 11–5.*

Outside the Mauritshuis, follow the Korte Vijverberg past the reflecting pool, which is bordered by patrician houses with revamped 18th- and 19th-century facades, a sign of the area's continuing popularity with the local aristocracy. Only the presence of huge ducks ruffles the surface of this stately lake.

Turn right at Lange Vijverberg and walk a short way until you come to Lange Voorhout, a large L-shaped boulevard. During the last century, horse-drawn trams clattered along its cobbles and deposited dignitaries outside the various palaces. Apart from the trams, not much has changed. Diplomats still eat in the historic Hotel des Indes. For more than 100 years, Hotel des Indes has hosted ambassadors and kings, dancers and spies. Memories of famous guests remain in the form of Emperor Haile Selassie's gold chair and the ballerina Anna Pavlova's silver candlesticks. Pavlova and the spy Mata Hari both have suites named for them. No. 34 once belonged to William I, the first king of the Netherlands, but later it became the royal library; it is now the **Supreme Court.** With its clumsy skewed gable, the headquarters of the Dutch Red Cross at No. 6 seems out of place on this stately avenue. A few doors down, at the corner of Parkstraat, is The Hague's oldest church, the **Kloosterkerk,** built in 1400 and once used by the Black Friars. During the spring, the adjoining square is covered with yellow and purple crocuses; on Thursdays during the summer, it is the scene of a colorful antiques market.

Take the Kneuterdijk road back toward the Hofvijver reflecting pool. After pausing at the Plaats Square, pass under the arch to visit the **Gevangenpoort,** the 14th-century prison gate. A prison for many centuries, today it is a museum of instruments of torture. *Buitenhof 33. Admission: Fl. 4. Open weekdays 10–4, weekends (summer only) 1–4.*

A second route is farther out but within walking distance of the center. North of Lange Voorhout is the **Panorama Mesdag,** a 122-meter (400-foot) painting-in-the-round that shows the nearby seaside town of Scheveningen as it looked in 1880. Housed in a specially designed building, the painting encircles you. Hendrik Mesdag was a late-19th-century marine painter, and his calming seascape is painted in the typically melancholic colors of The Hague School. Mesdag was assisted by his wife, who painted much of the fishing village, and by a friend, who painted the sky and dunes. *Zeestraat 65b, tel. 070/3642563. Admission: Fl. 4. Open Mon.–Sat. 10–5, Sun. noon–5.*

Just around the corner in Laan van Meerdervoort is the painter's home, now transformed into the **Rijksmuseum H.W. Mesdag.** Paintings by Mesdag and members of The Hague School are hung beside those of Corot, Courbet, and Rousseau. These delicate landscapes represent one of the finest collections of Barbizon School painting outside France. *Laan van Meerdervoort 7f. Admission: Fl. 3.50. Open Tues.–Sat. 10–5, Sun. 1–5.*

The **Vredespaleis** (Peace Palace), near Laan van Meerdervoort, is a monument to world peace through negotiation. Following the first peace conference at The Hague in 1899, the Scottish-American millionaire Andrew Carnegie donated $1.5 million for the construction of a building to house a proposed international court. The Dutch government donated the grounds, and other nations offered furnishings and decorations. Although it still looks like a dull multinational bank, the building has been improved by such gifts as Japanese wall hangings, a Danish fountain, and a grand staircase presented by The Hague. Today the **International Court of Justice,** consisting of 15 jurists, has its seat here. There are guided tours when the court is not in session. *Carnegieplein 2, tel. 070/3469680. Admission: Fl. 3. Open weekdays 10–noon and 2–4.*

The nearby **Haags Gemeentemuseum** (Municipal Art Museum) is the home of the largest collection of Mondrians in the world plus two vast collections of musical instruments—European and non-European. The building itself is also fascinating. It was built in 1935 and is an example of the International Movement in modern architecture. *Stadhouderslaan 41. Admission: Fl. 6. Open Tues.–Sun. 11–5.*

The Hague is a city of parks, the biggest of which is the **Zorgvliet,** separating city from countryside. Opposite the park is the **Omniversum,** described as Europe's first space theater. It is housed in a cylindrical building with a 23-meter (75-foot) dome that acts as a screen for the projection of 6–10 daily video presentations of outer space and oceanic voyages. *President Kennedylaan 5, tel. 070/3545454 for reservations and show times. Admission: Fl. 14. Open Tues.–Thurs. 11–4, Fri.–Sun. 11–9.*

Between The Hague and Scheveningen is **Madurodam,** a miniature Holland where the country's important buildings and facilities are duplicated at a scale of 1/52 of what its life-size counterpart would be. None of the details has been forgotten, from the harbor, with its lighthouse and quayside cranes, to the hand-carved furniture in the gabled houses. Son-et-lumière (sound-and-light) shows are planned for the summer months. *Haringkade 17, tel. 070/3553900. Admission: Fl. 11 adults, Fl. 6 children. Open end of March–May, 9 AM–10:30 PM; June–Aug., 9 AM–11 PM; Sept., 9 AM–9:30 PM; Oct.–beg. of Jan., 9–6.*

Scheveningen is adjacent to The Hague along the North Sea coast. A fishing village since the 14th century, it became popular as a beach resort during the last century, when the grand

Kurhaus Hotel was built, which still is a focal point of this beach community.

The beach itself, protected from tidal erosion by stone jetties, slopes gently into the North Sea in front of a high promenade whose function is to protect the boulevard and everything behind it from winter storms. The surface of the beach is fine sand, and you can bicycle or walk for miles to the north.

At the turn of the century, the **Kurhaus Hotel** stood alone at the center of the beach as a fashionable and aristocratic resort. After being in decline for a long time, it was restored and reopened, having added a casino among its new attractions. There is a painted ceiling over the large central court and buffet restaurant.

Part of the new design around the Kurhaus area includes the Golfbad, a surf pool complete with artificial waves. **The Pier,** completed in 1962, stretches 372 meters (1,200 feet) into the sea. Its four circular end buildings provide a sun terrace and restaurant, a 43-meter- (141-foot-) high observation tower, an amusement center with children's play area, and an underwater panorama. At 11 on summer evenings, the Pier is the scene of dramatic fireworks displays.

Delft Thirteen kilometers (8 miles) along the A13 from The Hague, you'll enter **Delft.** There is probably no town in the Netherlands that is more intimate, more attractive, or more traditional than this mini-metropolis, whose famous blue-and-white earthenware is popular throughout the world. Compact and easy to explore, despite its web of canals, Delft is best discovered on foot—although canal boat excursions are available April through October, as are horse-drawn trams that leave from the marketplace. Every street is lined with attractive medieval Gothic and Renaissance houses that bear such names as Wijnhaus (Wine House) and Boter Brug (Butter Bridge).

In the marketplace, the only lively spot in this tranquil town, is the **Nieuwe Kerk** (New Church), built during the 14th century, with its piercing Gothic spire 93 meters (300 feet) high, a magnificent carillon of 48 bells, and the tomb of William the Silent. Beneath this grotesque black marble sarcophagus is a crypt containing the remains of members of the Orange-Nassau line, including all members of the royal family since King William I ascended the throne during the mid-16th century. *Admission: Fl. 2. Tower: Fl. 3.25. Open May–Sept., Tues.–Sat. 10–4:30, also Mon. 10–4:30 in midsummer.*

Walk around the right side of the Nieuwe Kerk, then left at the back and along the Vrouwenregt canal for a few steps before taking another left turn into Voldergracht. To the left, the backs of the houses rise straight from the water as you stroll to the end of the street, which is marked by the sculptured animal heads and outdoor stairs of the old **Meat Market** on the right. Cross the Wijnhaven and turn left along its far side to the Koornmarkt, a stately canal spanned by a high, arching bridge that is one of the hallmarks of Delft.

Turn right at the Peperstraat to reach the **Oude Delft canal,** the city's oldest waterway. A few blocks farther along the canal is the **Prinsenhof,** formerly the Convent of St. Agatha, founded in 1400. The chapel inside dates from 1471; its interior is remarkable for the wooden statues under the vaulting ribs. Today the

Prinsenhof is a museum that tells the story of the liberation of the Netherlands after 80 years of Spanish occupation (1568–1648). For Dutch royalists, the spot is significant for the assassination of Prince William of Orange in 1584; the bullet holes can still be seen in the wall. *St. Agathaplein 1. Admission: Fl. 3.50. Open Tues.–Sat. 10–5, Sun. 1–5.*

Across the Oude Delft canal is the **Oude Kerk** (Old Church), a vast Gothic monument of the 13th century. Its beautiful tower, surmounted by a brick spire, leans somewhat alarmingly. *Oudegracht. Admission: Fl. 2. Open Apr.–Nov. 10–5.*

Beyond the Prinsenhof on the same side of the Oude Delft canal is the **Lambert van Meerten Museum,** a mansion whose timbered rooms are filled with the country's most complete collection of old Dutch tiles as well as Delft pottery. *Oude Delft 199. Admission: Fl. 3.50. Open Tues.–Sat. 10–5, Sun. 1–5. Also Mon. 1–5 in summer.*

While in Delft, you will want to see the famous local specialty — Delftware. Decorated porcelain was brought to Holland from China on East India Company ships and was so much in demand that Dutch potters felt their livelihood was being threatened. They therefore set about creating pottery to rival Chinese porcelain. There are only two manufacturers that still make hand-painted Delftware: **De Delftse Pauw** and the more famous "Royal" **De Porceleyne Fles.** *De Delftse Pauw: Delftweg 133, tel. 015/124920. Admission free. Open Apr.–mid–Oct., daily 9–4; mid–Oct.–Mar., weekdays 9–4, weekends 11–1. De Porceleyne Fles: Rotterdamsweg 196, tel. 015/560234. Admission free. Open Apr.–Oct., Mon.–Sat. 9–5, Sun. 10–4; Nov.–Mar., weekdays 9–5, Sat. 10–4.*

Rotterdam Thirteen kilometers (8 miles) farther along A13 is **Rotterdam,** one of the few thoroughly modern cities in the Netherlands and the site of the world's largest and busiest port. Art lovers know Rotterdam for its extensive and outstanding collection of art; philosophers recall it as the city of Erasmus. It is a major stop on the rock 'n' roll concert circuit, and its soccer team is well known. Rotterdam is lively and full of surprises.

The biggest surprise in Rotterdam is the remarkable 30-mile-long **Europoort,** which handles more than 250 million tons of cargo every year and more ships than any other port in the world. It is the delta for three of Europe's most important rivers (the Rhine, the Waal, and the Meuse/Maas) and a seemingly endless corridor of piers, warehouses, tank facilities, and efficiency. You can get to the piers at Willemsplein by tram or Metro (blue line to the Leuvehaven station) from the central station. A 1¼-hour harbor tour illuminates Rotterdam's vital role in world trade.

As an alternative to the boat tour, you also can survey the harbor from the vantage point of the **Euromast** observation tower. Get there via the Metro red line to Dijkszicht. *Parkhaven 20, tel. 010/4364811. Admission: Fl. 13. Open mid-Mar.–mid-Oct., daily 10–5; mid-Oct.–mid-Mar., daily 10–6. Jan.–Feb., weekends only.*

After the harbor tour, walk down the boulevard past the Metro station into Leuvehaven. On your right as you stroll along the inner harbor is **IMAX Rotterdam,** a gigantic theater in which films are projected onto a screen six stories high. There are earphones for English translation. *Leuvehaven 77, tel. 06/ 4048844. Admission: Fl. 13. Shows Tues.–Sun. 1, 2, 3, 7, 8, and 9. Mon. also during holiday periods.*

Past the theater is a hodgepodge of cranes, barges, steamships, and old shipbuilding machines, even a steam-operated grain elevator. What looks at quick glance to be a sort of maritime junkyard is in fact a work in progress: Volunteers are working daily to restore these vessels and machines. The whole operation is an open-air museum of shipbuilding, shipping, and communications that is part of the **Prins Hendrick Maritime Museum,** housed in a large gray building at the head of the quay. Also moored in this inner harbor adjacent to the museum is the historic 19th-century Royal Dutch Navy warship *De Buffel.* Within the museum are exhibits devoted to the history and activity of the great port outside. *Leuvehaven 1, tel. 06/ 4132680. Open Tues.–Sat. 10–5, Sun. 11–5.*

From the nearby Churchillplein Metro station, take the red line toward Marconiplein to the first stop at Eendrachtsplein, where you will walk along the canal toward the park. As a welcome contrast to the industrial might of the Europoort and Holland's maritime history, the **Boymans–van Beuningen Museum** is an impressive refresher course in Western European art history. The collection includes paintings by many famous master painters, Dutch and otherwise, from the 14th century to the present day. There is an Old Arts section that includes the work of Brueghel, Bosch, and Rembrandt and a renowned print gallery with works by artists as varied as Dürer and Cézanne. Dali and Magritte mix with the Impressionists in the Modern Arts collection. *Mathenesserlaan 18–20, tel. 06/4419400. Admission: Fl. 3. Open Tues.–Sat. 10–5, Sun. 11–5.*

Dining and Lodging

For details and price-category definitions, *see* Dining and Lodging in Staying in Holland.

Delft
Dining and Lodging

Les Compagnons/Den Dulk. With three locations within a block of each other, this is a true family affair: The children operate the small, comfortable hotel on the market square; their father runs the small neighboring brasserie; and Mama has the well-stocked deli adjacent to them. You can't beat the location, directly on the historic market square. Rooms are bright and spiffy, and guests are given a discount for dinner at Dad's restaurant, which faces a canal and offers such temptations as cranberry pâté with Cumberland sauce. *Markt 61–65/ Voldersgracht 17–18, tel. 015/140102. 13 rooms with bath. Closed lunch. AE, DC, MC, V. Inexpensive–Budget.*

Lodging

Hotel Leeuwenbrug. This is a traditional Dutch family-style hotel on one of the prettiest canals in Delft. There are two buildings, one more traditional and simpler, with smaller, cheaper rooms; the annex is more contemporary and businesslike. Everyone enjoys breakfast overlooking the canal, however, and rooms on the top floor of the annex overlook the city. *Koornmarkt 16, tel. 015/147741. 38 rooms with bath. Facilities: parking. AE, DC, MC, V. Moderate.*

Hotel De Kok. Conveniently near the railway station, this tidy little hotel is cozy and inviting. Rooms are spacious and bright and offer the sort of amenities you'd expect in a much larger hotel. There's a family-style lounge and, in summer, a garden terrace for guests. *Houttuinen 15, tel. 015/122125. 14 rooms with bath. AE, DC, MC, V. Inexpensive.*

Dining **Rumours.** The decor in this trendy, small restaurant on one of the main canals of Delft evokes the spirit of the Caribbean with its wicker furniture, ceiling fans, and aqua color scheme. The chef is American, although the menu is decidedly French-influenced. *Oude Delft 76, tel. 015/158689. AE, DC, MC, V. Inexpensive.*

The Hague **'t Goude Hooft.** The foundations of the building on the old vege-
Dining table market square date from the early 15th century, and town records show that ever since the 14th century there has been a tavern of essentially the same name on the very same spot. When the restaurant's promotions say that The Hague was built around it, it can be taken as truth. As might be expected, the ambience is totally Old Dutch; the menu, too, is traditional. There is a grand terrace café on the square in the summer months. *Groenmarkt 13, tel. 070/3469713. Reservations accepted. AE, DC, MC, V. Moderate–Inexpensive.*

Lodging **Hotel Petit.** Not far from the Peace Palace and the Gemeente-museum, this tidy little family hotel has spacious, bright, and attractive rooms equipped with tub and shower. *Groot Hertoginnelaan 42, tel. 070/3465500. 18 rooms with bath. Facilities: parking. No credit cards. Inexpensive–Moderate.*

Dining and Lodging **Hotel City.** This small hotel near the Scheviningen beach has a sparkle and brightness that can be attributed as much to its cheerful owners as to its sunny seaside location. The hotel is divided among several buildings, and the small restaurant has a bar and a sidewalk terrace. *Renvaanstraat 1–3/17–23, tel. 070/3557923. 35 rooms with bath. Facilities: restaurant. No credit cards. Inexpensive.*

Rotterdam **La Gondola.** Mick Jagger, Gloria Estefan, and other rock su-
Dining perstars eat here when they are in town, as proved by the photographs that adorn the entry to this small and spiffy Italian restaurant on a side street between Coolsingel boulevard and the Lijnbaan shopping promenade. The menu is an uncomplicated array of Italian specialties, including pizzas. *Kruiskade 6, tel. 010/4114284. Reservations advised. AE, DC, MC, V. Lunch weekdays only. Inexpensive.*

Lodging **Hotel van Walsum.** With typically Dutch regularity, the gregarious owner of this small hotel redecorates and refurbishes his rooms. Everything from the bath tiles to the bedspreads is redone in whatever that year's colors and textures happen to be. *Mathenessarlaan 199–201, tel. 010/4364410. 26 rooms with bath. Facilities: lounge, private bar, parking elevator. No credit cards. Inexpensive.*

Dining and Lodging **Intell.** Not the least of the attractions of the Hotel Intell are its views of Rotterdam harbor—from the rooms, the restaurant, and even from the fully equipped rooftop health club that includes an 8-by-4-meter swimming pool. This is a busy, cheerful, modern hotel located adjacent to the IMAX super theater and near both the maritime museum and the Spido harbor tour pier. Named Le Papillon, the Intell's restaurant is a lively, intimate dining room with the best view in the house—if not the best view in Rotterdam! The menu is traditional Continental, offering such standbys as sole Picasso and beef stroganoff. Both the Metro and tram stop outside the door. *Leuvehaven 80,* *tel. 010/4134139. 150 rooms with bath. Facilities: parking, bar, restaurant, health club, sauna, pool. AE, DC, MC, V. Moderate.*

13 Hungary

Even under the reformist but now discredited communist regime, Hungary's stores were full of food and the latest fashions, and Hungarians enjoyed what they called "the happiest barracks in the bloc." Today, as the nation rebuilds in the spirit of freedom, comfortable accommodations, pleasant restaurants, and attractive shops are more plentiful than ever—and most prices remain below Western Europeans levels.

Nonetheless, Hungary's rush to modernize has not obliterated evidence of its past. Amenities are relatively modern, but the abundant Habsburg architecture creates an aura of faded charm. Walk through the quiet back streets of Budapest on a foggy autumn morning, or survey the majestic Danube from the city's Castle Hill on a summer day, and you'll quickly sense the sweep of Hungary's tumultuous history at the crossroads of Central Europe.

Hungarians struggled against foreign occupation for centuries: the Turks in the 17th century, the Habsburgs in 1848, and the Soviet Union in 1956. In the '60s and '70s, Hungarian Communist party leader János Kádár opened trade relations with the West and relaxed travel restrictions, giving Hungarians a taste of what life was like in the rest of Europe.

Because Hungary is a small, agriculturally oriented country, visitors are often surprised by its grandeur and Old World charm, especially in the capital, Budapest, which bustles with life as never before. Hungarians like to complain about their economic problems, but they spare visitors bureaucratic hassles at the border and airport. Entry is easy and quick for westerners, most of whom no longer need visas. Gone are the days

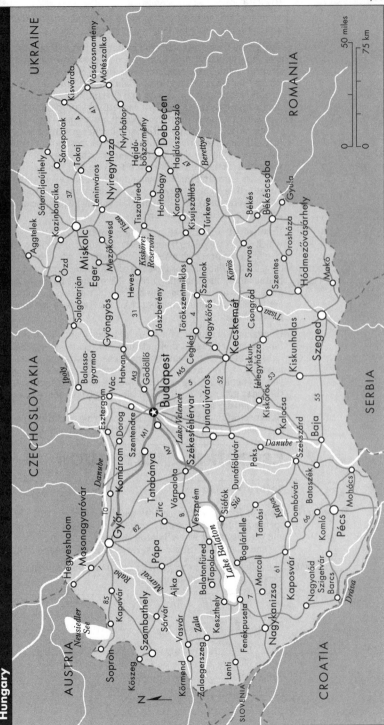

Hungary

when visitors were forced to make daily currency exchanges and to register with local police on arrival.

Two rivers cross the country. The famous Duna (Danube) flows from the west through Budapest on its way to the southern frontier, while the smaller Tisza flows from the northeast across the Nagyalföld (Great Plain). What Hungary lacks in size, it makes up for in beauty and charm. Western Hungary is dominated by the largest lake in Central Europe, Lake Balaton. Although some overdevelopment has blighted its splendor, its shores are still lined with Baroque villages, relaxing spas, magnificent vineyards, and shaded garden restaurants serving the catch of the day. In eastern Hungary, the Nagyalföld offers visitors a chance to explore the folklore and customs of the Magyars (the Hungarians' name for themselves and their language). It is an area of spicy food, strong wine, and the proud *csikós* (horsemen). The unspoiled towns of the provincial areas are rich in history and culture.

However, it is Budapest, a city of more than 2 million people, which draws travelers from all over the world. The hills of Buda rise from the brackish waters of the Danube, which bisects the city; on the flatlands of Pest are an imposing array of hotels, restaurants, and shopping areas. Throughout Hungary, comfortable accommodations can be found for comparatively modest prices, and there's an impressive network of inexpensive guest houses.

Hungarians are known for their hospitality and love talking to foreigners, although their strange language, which has no links to other European tongues, can be a problem. Today, however, everyone seems to be learning English, especially young people. Trying out a few words of German will delight the older generation. But what all Hungarians share is a deep love of music, and the calendar is star-studded with it, from Budapest's famous opera to its annual spring music festival and the serenades of gypsy violinists during evening meals.

Essential Information

Before You Go

When to Go Many of Hungary's major fairs and festivals take place in the spring and fall. During July and August, Budapest can be hot and the resorts at Lake Balaton crowded, so spring (May) and the end of summer (September) are the ideal times to visit.

Climate The following are average daily maximum and minimum temperatures for Budapest.

Jan.	34F	1C	May	72F	22C	Sept.	73F	23C
	25	– 4		52	11		54	12
Feb.	39F	4C	June	79F	26C	Oct.	61F	16C
	28	– 2		59	15		45	7
Mar.	50F	10C	July	82F	28C	Nov.	46F	8C
	36	2		61	16		37	3
Apr.	63F	17C	Aug.	81F	27C	Dec.	39F	4C
	45	7		61	16		30	– 1

Currency The unit of currency is the forint (Ft.), divided into 100 fillérs (f.). There are bills of 20, 50, 100, 500, 1,000, and 5,000 forints and coins of 1, 2, 5, 10, and 20 forints and 10, 20, and 50 fillérs. The tourist exchange rate was approximately 60 to the dollar and 100 to the pound sterling at press time (summer 1992). Note that official exchange rates are adjusted at frequent intervals.

Hungary does not require you to change a certain sum of money for each day of your stay. Exchange money as you need it at banks, hotels, or travel offices, but take care not to change too much, because although in theory you can change back 50% of the original sum when you leave (up to U.S. $100), it may prove difficult in practice—at least until the forint becomes convertible.

Most credit cards are accepted, though don't rely on them in smaller towns or less expensive accommodations and restaurants. Eurocheque holders can cash personal checks in all banks and in most hotels. American Express, which now has a full-service office in Budapest (V Deák Ferenc utca 10, tel. 361/1374–394, 361/2510–010, or 361/2515–500), also dispenses cash to its cardholders.

There is still a black market in hard currency, but changing money on the street is illegal and the bank rate almost always comes close. Stick with official exchange offices.

What It Will Cost Rates in Budapest's quality hotels are modest by Western standards. Even though the introduction of value-added tax (VAT) in 1988 has increased many of the prices in the service industry by up to 25%, and the annual inflation rate is 36% and going up, enjoyable vacations with all the trimmings remain less expensive than in nearby Western cities like Vienna.

Sample Prices Cup of coffee, 60 Ft.; bottle of beer, 50 Ft.–75 Ft.; soft drinks, 20 Ft.–50 Ft.; ham sandwich, 100 Ft.; 1-mile taxi ride, 50 Ft.; museum admission, 100 Ft.

Visas Only a valid passport is required of U.S., British, and Canadian citizens. For additional information, contact the Hungarian Embassy in the United States (3910 Shoemaker St., NW, Washington, DC 20008, tel. 202/362–6730) or Canada (7 Delaware Ave., Ottawa KP2 OZ2, Ontario, tel. 613/234–8316), or the Hungarian Consulate in London (35b Eaton Pl., London SW1 8BY, tel. 071/235–2664).

Customs Objects for personal use may be imported freely. If you are
On Arrival over 16, you may also bring in 250 grams of tobacco, plus 2 liters of wine, 1 liter of spirits, and 250 grams of perfume. A 30% customs charge is made on gifts valued in Hungary at more than 10,000 Ft.

On Departure Take care when you leave Hungary that you have the right documentation for exporting goods. Keep receipts of any items bought from Konsumtourist, Intertourist, or Képcsarnok Vállalat. A special permit is needed for works of art valued at more than 1,000 Ft.

Language Hungarian (Magyar) tends to look and sound intimidating to everyone at first because it is a non-Indo-European language. However, most people in the tourist trade, from bus drivers to waiters, speak some English or German.

Getting Around

By Train Travel by train from Budapest to other large cities or to Lake Balaton is cheap and efficient. Remember to take *gyorsvonat* (express trains) and not *személyvonat* (locals), which are extremely slow. A *helyjegy* (seat reservation), which costs 50 Ft. and is sold up to 60 days in advance, is advisable for all express trains, especially for weekend travel in summer. It is also worth paying a little extra for first-class tickets.

Fares Unlimited-travel tickets for 7 or 10 days are inexpensive—2,000 Ft. and 2,500 Ft., respectively. All students with a valid I.D. receive 50% off. InterRail cards are available for those under 26, and the Rail Europe Senior Travel Pass entitles senior citizens to a 30% reduction on all trains. Snacks and drinks can be purchased on all express trains, but the supply often runs out, especially in summer, so pack a lunch just in case. For more rail travel information, contact the **MÁV Passenger Service** (Andrássy útja 35, Budapest VI, tel. 361/1228–049).

By Bus Long-distance buses link Budapest with many cities in Eastern and Western Europe. Services to the eastern part of the country leave from Népstadion station (tel. 361/1187–315). Buses to the west and south leave from the main Volán bus station at Erzsébet tér in the Inner City (tel. 361/1172–966). Although inexpensive, they tend to be crowded, so reserve your seat.

By Boat Hungary is well equipped with nautical transport, and Budapest is situated on a major international waterway—the Danube. Vienna is five hours away by hydrofoil, and many Hungarian resorts are accessible by hydrofoil or boat. For information about excursions or pleasure cruises, contact **MAHART Landing Stage** (Vigadó tér 1, Budapest V, tel. 361/1181–223) or **IBUSZ** (Hungarian Travel Bureau; Tanács körút 3/C, Budapest VII, tel. 361/1423–140 or 361/1211–007).

By Bicycle A land of rolling hills and flat plains, Hungary lends itself to bicycling. The larger train stations around Lake Balaton rent bicycles for about 100 Ft. a day. For information about renting in Budapest, contact **Tourinform** (Sütő utca 2, tel. 361/1179–800). **HUNTOURS** provides guided bicycle tours (Retek utca 34, tel. 361/1152–403).

Staying in Hungary

Telephones Pay phones use 5-Ft. coins—the cost of a three-minute local
Local Calls call. Most towns in Hungary can be dialed directly—dial 06 and wait for the buzzing tone, then dial the local number.

International Calls Direct calls to foreign countries can be made from Budapest and all major provincial towns only by using the red push-button telephones, or from hotels and post offices, and by dialing 00 and waiting for the international dialing tone. The phones take 5-, 10-, and 20-Ft. coins.

Operators International calls can be made through the operator by dialing 09; for operator-assisted calls within Hungary, dial 01. Be patient: The telephone system is antiquated, especially in the countryside.

Information Dial 361/1172–200 for information in English.

Mail Stamps can be bought from tobacco shops as well as post offices. The post offices at the Keleti (East) and Nyugati (West) train stations are open 24 hours.

Postal Rates An airmail postcard to the United States, the United Kingdom, and the rest of Western Europe costs 25 Ft., and an airmail letter costs from 30 Ft. Postcards to the United Kingdom and the rest of Western Europe cost 15 Ft., letters 20 Ft.

Receiving Mail A poste restante service, for general delivery, is available in Budapest. The address is Magyar Posta, H-1052 Budapest, Petőfi Sándor utca 17–19.

Opening and Closing Times **Banks.** Hours are weekdays 8–1.

Museums. Most are open daily from 10 to 6 and are closed on Mondays.

Shops. They're open weekdays 10–6, Saturday 9–1. Many shops stay open until 8 on Thursday.

National Holidays January 1; March 15 (Anniversary of 1848 Revolution); April 11 and 12 (Easter and Easter Monday); May 1 (Labor Day); August 20 (St. Stephen's and Constitution Day); October 23 (1956 Revolution Day); December 25 and 26.

Dining There are plenty of good, affordably priced restaurants offering a variety of Hungarian dishes. Meats, rich sauces, and creamy desserts predominate, but salads can be found, even out of season. There are self-service restaurants *(önkiszolgáló étterem)*, snack bars *(bistró* or *étel bár)*, buffets *(büfé)*, cafés *(eszpresszó)*, and bars *(drink-bár)*. The pastry shops *(cukrászda)* are also worth a try.

In almost all restaurants, an inexpensive fixed-price lunch, called a *menü*, is available. It costs as little as 250 Ft and includes soup or salad, an entrée, and a dessert.

Mealtimes Hungarians eat early—you risk off-hand service and cold food after 9 PM. Lunch, the main meal for many, is served from noon to 2.

Dress At most moderately priced and inexpensive restaurants, casual but neat dress is acceptable.

Ratings Prices are per person and include a first course, main course, and dessert, but no wine or tip. Prices in Budapest tend to be a good 30% higher than elsewhere in Hungary. Best bets are indicated by a star ★.

Category	All Areas
Moderate	600 Ft.–1,000 Ft.
Inexpensive	400 Ft.–600 Ft.
Budget	under 400 Ft.

Lodging There are few expensive hotels outside Budapest, but the moderately priced hotels are generally comfortable and well-run, although single rooms with baths are scarce. Inexpensive establishments—more numerous every year as Hungarians convert unused rooms or second apartments into rental units for tourists—seldom have private baths, but plumbing is adequate almost everywhere.

Hotels

Rentals Apartments in Budapest and cottages at Lake Balaton are available. Rates and reservations can be obtained from tourist offices in Hungary and abroad. A Budapest apartment might cost 15,000 Ft. a week, while a luxury cottage for two on Lake Balaton costs around 35,000 Ft. a week. Bookings can be made in Budapest at the **IBUSZ** on Petőfi tér 3 (tel. 361/1185–707), which is open 24 hours a day, or through IBUSZ offices in the United States and Great Britain. (*See* Government Tourist Offices in Chapter 1.)

Guest Houses Also called pensions, these offer simple accommodations—well suited to young people on a budget. Some offer simple breakfast facilities. Arrangements can be made through local tourist offices or travel agents abroad.

In the provinces it is safe to accept rooms that you are offered directly: They will almost always be clean and in a relatively good neighborhood, and the prospective landlord will probably not cheat you. *Szoba kiadó* (or the German *Zimmer frei*) means "Room to Rent." The rate per night for a double room in Budapest or at Lake Balaton is around 2,000 Ft., which includes the use of a bathroom but not breakfast. Reservations and referrals can also be made by any tourist office, and if you go that route, you have someone to complain to if things don't work out.

Camping The 140 campsites in Hungary are open from May through September. Rates are 500 Ft.–600 Ft. a day. There's a small charge for hot water and electricity plus an accommodations fee of 25 Ft.–75 Ft. per person per night. Children get a 50% reduction. Camping is forbidden except in appointed areas. Reservations can be made through travel agencies or through the **Hungarian Camping and Caravanning Club** (Budapest IX, Kálvin tér 9, tel. 361/1177–208).

Ratings The following price categories are in forints for a double room with bath and breakfast during the peak season (June through August); rates are even lower off-season (in Budapest, September through March; at Lake Balaton, in May and September) and in the countryside, sometimes less than 1,500 Ft. for two. For single rooms with bath, count on about 80% of the double-room rate. Best bets are indicated by a star ★.

Category	Budapest	Balaton
Moderate	4,500–8,500 Ft.	3,500–7,000 Ft.
Inexpensive	3,000–4,500 Ft.	2,000–3,000 Ft.
Budget	1,500–3,000 Ft.	under 2,000 Ft.

During peak season, full board may be compulsory at the Lake Balaton hotels.

Tipping Four decades of socialism didn't alter the Hungarian habit of tipping generously. Cloakroom and gas-pump attendants, hairdressers, waiters, and taxi drivers all expect tips. At least 10% should be added to a restaurant bill or taxi fare. If a gypsy band plays exclusively for your table, you can leave 100 Ft. in the plate discreetly provided for that purpose.

Budapest

Arriving and Departing

By Plane Hungary's international airport, **Ferihegy,** is about 22 kilometers (14 miles) southeast of the city. All **Malév** and **Lufthansa** flights operate from the new Terminal 2 (tel. 361/1578–768 or 361/1578–477); other airlines use Terminal 1 (tel. 361/1572–122). For same-day flight information, call the airport authority (tel. 361/1577–155). The staff takes its time to answer calls, and may not be cordial; be prepared.

Between the Airport and Downtown Buses to and from Erzsébet tér station (Platform 1) in downtown Budapest leave every half hour from 5 AM to 9 PM. The trip takes 30–40 minutes (longer in rush hours) and costs either 100 Ft. or 200 Ft., depending on which terminal you use. The modern minivans of the fast, friendly, and reliable Airport Shuttle service (tel. 361/1578–993) transport you to any destination in Budapest, door to door, for 400 Ft., even less than the least expensive taxi—and most employees speak English. At the airport, buy tickets in the arrivals hall near baggage claim; for your return trip, just call ahead for a pick-up. A taxi ride to the center of Budapest should cost no more than 800 Ft., and take about the same time. Avoid drivers who offer their services before you are out of the arrivals lounge.

By Train There are three main train stations in Budapest: Keleti (East), Nyugati (West), and Déli (South). Trains from Vienna usually operate from the Keleti station, while those to the Balaton depart from the Déli.

By Bus Most buses to Budapest from the western region of Hungary, including those from Vienna, arrive at **Erzsébet tér** station.

Getting Around

Budapest is best explored on foot. The maps provided by tourist offices are not very detailed, so arm yourself with one from any of the bookshops in Váci utca or from downtown stationery shops.

By Public Transportation The public transportation system—a metro (subway), buses, streetcars, and trolleybuses—is cheap, efficient, and simple to use but closes down around midnight. However, certain trams and buses run on a limited schedule all night. A day ticket *(napijegy)* costs 60 Ft. and allows unlimited travel on all services within the city limits. You can also buy tickets for single rides for 18 Ft. from metro stations or tobacco shops. You can travel on all trams, buses, and on the subway with this ticket, but you can't change lines.

Bus, streetcar, and trolleybus tickets must be canceled on board—watch how other passengers do it. Don't get caught without a ticket: Spot checks are frequent, and you can be fined several hundred forints.

By Boat In summer a regular boat service links the north and south of the city, stopping at points on both banks, including Margit-sziget (Margaret Island). From May to September boats leave from the quay at Vigadó tér on 1½-hour cruises between the Árpád and Petőfi bridges. The trip, organized by

MAHART, runs three times a day and costs around 200 Ft. (tel. 361/1181–223).

Important Addresses and Numbers

<table>
<tr>
<td>Tourist
Information</td>
<td>Tourinform (Sütő utca 2, tel. 361/1179–800) is open daily 8–8. IBUSZ Accommodation Office (Petőfi tér 3, tel. 361/1185–707) is open 24 hours. Budapest Tourist (Roosevelt tér 5, tel. 361/1173–555) is also helpful. Budapest Week, a new English-language newspaper that mixes politics and culture, lists upcoming concerts and foreign-language films; it's sold in hotels and book stores.</td>
</tr>
<tr>
<td>Embassies</td>
<td>U.S. Szabadság tér 12, Budapest V, tel. 361/1126–450). Canadian Budakeszi út 32, Budapest II, tel. 361/1767–711). U.K. Harmincad utca 6, Budapest V, tel. 361/1182–888).</td>
</tr>
<tr>
<td>Emergencies</td>
<td>Police (tel. 07). Ambulance (tel. 04). Doctor: Ask your hotel or embassy for recommendations. U.S. and Canadian visitors are advised to take out full medical insurance. U.K. visitors are covered for emergencies and essential treatment.</td>
</tr>
</table>

Exploring Budapest

Budapest, situated on both banks of the Danube, unites the colorful hills of Buda and the wide boulevards of Pest. Though it was the site of a Roman outpost in the 1st century, the city was not actually created until 1873, when the towns of Obuda, Pest, and Buda were joined. The cultural, political, intellectual, and commercial heart of the nation beats in Budapest; for the 20% of the nation's population who live in the capital, anywhere else is simply "the country."

Much of the charm of a visit to Budapest lies in unexpected glimpses into shadowy courtyards and in long vistas down sunlit cobbled streets. Although some 30,000 buildings were destroyed during World War II and in 1956, the past lingers on in the often crumbling architectural details of the antique structures that remain and in the memories and lifestyles of Budapest's citizens.

The principal sights of the city fall roughly into three areas, each of which can be comfortably covered on foot. The Budapest hills are best explored by public transportation. Note that street names are always being changed to purge all reminders of the Communist regime. If the street you're looking for seems to have disappeared, ask any local—though he or she may well be as bewildered as you are.

Numbers in the margin correspond to points of interest on the Budapest map.

① ② Take a bus (No. 16 from **Erzsébet tér**) to **Dísz tér,** at the foot of **Várhegy** (Castle Hill), where the painstaking work of reconstruction has been in progress since World War II. Having made their final stand in the Royal Palace itself, the Nazis left behind them a blackened wasteland. Under the rubble, archaeologists discovered the medieval foundations of the palace of King Matthias Corvinus, who, in the 15th century, presided over one of the most splendid courts in Europe.

③ The **Királyi Palota** (Palace), now a vast museum complex and cultural center, can be reached on foot from Dísz tér—it is one block south—or by funicular railway *(Sikló)* from Clark Adám tér. The northern wing of the building is devoted to the **Magyar Újkori Történeti Múzeum** (Museum of Modern Hungarian History). The central block houses the **Magyar Nemzeti Galléria** (Hungarian National Gallery), exhibiting a wide range of Hungarian fine art, from medieval paintings to modern sculpture. Names to look for are Munkácsy, a 19th-century Romantic painter, and Csontváry, an early Surrealist whom Picasso much admired. *Dísz tér 17. Museum of Modern Hungarian History: tel. 361/1757–533. Admission: 10 Ft. adults, 5 Ft. children. Hungarian National Gallery: tel. 316/1755–567. Admission: 20 Ft. adults, 10 Ft. children, free on Sat. Open Apr.– Oct., Tues.–Sun. 10–6; Nov.–Mar., Tues.–Sun. 10–4; closed Mon.*

The southern block contains the **Budapesti Történeti Múzeum** (Budapest History Museum). Down in the cellars are the original medieval vaults of the palace, portraits of King Matthias and his second wife, Beatrice of Aragon, and many late-14th-century statues that probably adorned the Renaissance palace. *Buda Castle Palace, Szt. György tér 2, tel. 361/1757–533, ext. 253. Same admission and hours as Hungarian National Gallery (above). Choral concerts Sun. at 11:30 (except July– Aug.).*

❹ The **Mátyás templom** (Matthias Church), northeast of Dísz tér, with its distinctive patterned roof, dates from the 13th century. Built as a mosque by the occupying Turks, it was destroyed and reconstructed in the 19th century, only to be bombed during World War II. Only the south porch is from the original structure. The Habsburg emperors were crowned kings of Hungary here, including Charles IV in 1916. High mass is celebrated every Sunday at 10 AM with an orchestra and choir.

❺ The turn-of-the-century **Halászbástya** (Fishermen's Bastion) is on your left as you leave the church. It was built as a lookout tower to protect what was once a thriving fishing settlement. Its neo-Romanesque columns and arches frame views over the city and river. Near the church, in Hess András tér, are remains of the oldest church on Castle Hill, built by Dominican friars in the 13th century. These have now been tastefully integrated into the modern Hilton hotel.

The town houses lining the streets of the Castle District are largely occupied by offices, restaurants, and diplomatic residences, but the house where Beethoven stayed in 1800 is now
❻ the **Zenetörténeti Múzeum** (Museum of Music History). *Táncsics Mihály utca 7, tel. 361/1759–011. Admission: 15 Ft. Open Wed.–Sun. 10–6, Mon. 4–9.*

❼ The remains of a **medieval synagogue** are also in the neighborhood and open to the public. On display are a number of objects relating to the Jewish community, including religious inscriptions, frescoes, and tombstones dating from the 15th century. *Táncsics Mihály utca 26. Admission: 15 Ft. Open Apr.–Oct., Tues.–Fri. 10–4, weekends 10–6.*

❽ The **Hadtörténeti Múzeum** (War History Museum) is at the far end of Castle Hill. The collection includes uniforms and regalia, many belonging to the Hungarian generals who took part in the abortive uprising against Austrian rule in 1848. Other exhibits trace the military history of Hungary from the original Magyar conquest in the 9th century through the period of Ottoman rule

Belvárosi plébánia templom, **12**
Dísz tér, **2**
Erzsébet tér, **1**
Hadtörténeti Múzeum, **8**
Halászbástya, **5**
Királyi Palota, **3**
Március 15 tér, **11**
Mátyás templom, **4**
Medieval Synagogue, **7**
Mezögazdasági Múzeum, **21**
Millennium Monument, **18**
Mücsarnok, **20**
Néprajzi Múzeum, **15**
Parliament, **14**
Roosevelt tér, **9**
State Opera House, **17**
Szépmüvészeti Múzeum, **19**
Szt. István Bazilika, **16**
Váci utca, **13**
Vigadó tér, **10**
Zenetörténeti Múzeum, **6**

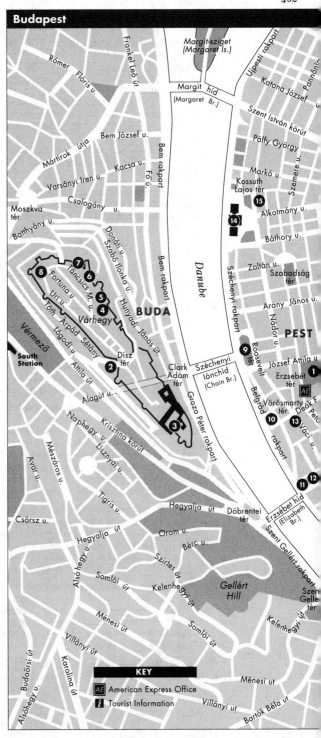

Budapest

KEY

AE American Express Office

i Tourist Information

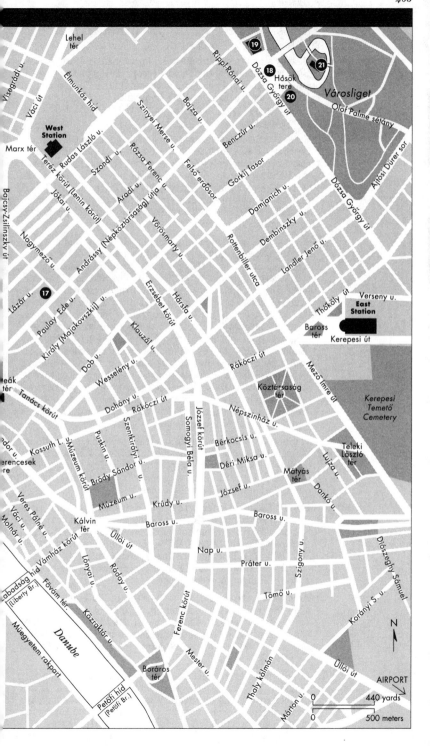

Lehel tér

Visegrádi u.

Váci út

Élmunkás híd

Rippl-Rónai u.

19

Dózsa György út

18 Hősök tere **20**

21

Városliget

Olof Palme sétány

Szinyei Merse u.

Bajza u.

Benczúr u.

West Station

Rudas László u.

Teréz körút (Lenin körút)

Marx tér

Szondi u.

Rózsa Ferenc u.

Felső erdősor

Gorkij fasor

Aradi u.

Damjanich u.

Altosi Dürer sor

Jókai u.

Bajcsy-Zsilinszky út

Nagymező u.

Andrássy (Népköztársaság) útja

Vörösmarty u.

Dembinszky

Rottenbiller utca

Landler Jenő u.

Dózsa György út

Lázár u.

17

Paulay Ede u.

Erzsébet körút

Hársfa u.

Thököly út

Verseny u.

East Station

Király (Majakovszkij) u.

Klauzál u.

Baross tér

Kerepesi út

Dob u.

Wesselényi u.

eák tér

Tanács körút

Dohány u.

Rákóczi út

Rákóczi út

Köztársaság tér

Mező Imre út

Kerepesi Temető Cemetery

Puskin u.

Szenkirályi u.

József körút

Somogyi Béla u.

Népszinház u.

Kossuth L.

Múzeum körút

andor u.

Bródy Sándor u.

Bérkocsis u.

erencsek re

Déri Miksa u.

Teleki László tér

Veres Pálné u.

Múzeum u.

Krúdy u.

József u.

Mátyás tér

Luiza u.

Dankó u.

Váci u.

Molnár u.

Kálvin tér

Baross u.

Baross u.

Diószeghy Sámuel

Liberty Br.)

Vámház körút

Üllői út

Lónyai u.

Nap u.

Práter u.

Szigony u.

Korányi S. u.

Ráday u.

Fővám tér

Közraktár u.

Müegyetem rakpart

Danube

N

Boráros tér

Ferenc körút

Mester u.

Tömő u.

Üllői út

AIRPORT

Petőfi híd (Petőfi Br.)

Thaly Kálmán

Márton u.

0   440 yards

0   500 meters

and right to the middle of this century. *Tóth Árpád sétány 40, tel. 361/1569–522 or 361/1569–770. Admission: 15 Ft. Open Tues.–Sat. 9–5, Sun. 10–6.*

Nearby stands a monument to Abdurrahman, the last pasha of Buda, commander of the Turkish troops in Hungary, who died, sword in hand, in 1686. For a good view of the Vérmező (Blood Meadow) and the surrounding Buda hills, stroll the length of Tóth Árpád sétány, along the rampart that defended Castle Hill to the west.

The Heart of the City Cross the **Széchenyi lánchíd** (Chain Bridge) from Clark Adám tér to reach **Roosevelt tér** in Pest, with the 19th-century neoclassical Academy of Sciences on your left. Pest fans out from the **Belváros** (Inner City), which is bounded by the **Kiskörút** (Little Circular Road). The **Nagykörút** (Grand Circular Road) describes a wider semicircle from the Margaret Bridge to Petőfi Bridge. To your right, an elegant promenade, the **Korzó,** runs south along the river.

❿ A square called **Vigadó tér** is dominated by the Danube view and Vigadó concert hall, built in a Romantic mix of Byzantine, Moorish, and Romanesque styles, with Hungarian motifs thrown in for good measure. Liszt, Brahms, and Bartók all performed here. Completely destroyed during World War II, it has ⓫ been rebuilt in its original style. Another square, **Március 15 tér,** commemorates the 1848 struggle for independence from the Habsburgs with a statue of the poet Petőfi Sándor, who died later in the uprising. Every March 15, the national holiday commemorating the revolution, the square is packed with patriotic Hungarians. Behind the square is the 12th-century ⓬ **Belvárosi plébánia templom** (Inner City Parish Church), the oldest in Pest. The church has been redone in a variety of western architectural styles; even Turkish influences, such as the Muslim prayer niche, remain. Liszt, who lived only a few yards away, often played the organ here.

⓭ Parallel to the Korzó, Pest's riverside promenade, lies Budapest's most upscale shopping street, **Váci utca. Vörösmarty tér,** a handsome square in the heart of the Inner City, is a good spot to sit and relax. Street musicians and sidewalk cafés make it one of the liveliest places in Budapest.

⓮ North of Roosevelt tér is the riverfront's most striking landmark, the imposing neo-Gothic **Parliament,** now minus the red star on top (open for tours only; call IBUSZ, tel. 361/1185–707, Budapest Tourist, tel. 361/1173–555, or Omnibusz Travel, tel. 361/1172–511). To its left sits an expressive statue of József Attila (1905–37), who, in spite of his early death, became known as one of Hungary's greatest poets.

⓯ Across from the Parliament is the **Néprajzi Múzeum** (Museum of Ethnography), with exhibits depicting folk traditions and such social customs as Hungarian costume and folklore. There is a particularly interesting collection from Oceania. *Kossuth Lajos tér 12, tel. 361/1326–340. Admission: 10 Ft. Open Tues.–Sun. 10–6.*

⓰ Dark and massive, the 19th-century **Szt. István Bazilika** (St. Stephen's Basilica) is one of the chief landmarks of Pest. It was planned early in the 19th century as a neoclassical building, but was in the neo-Renaissance style by the time it was completed more than 50 years later. During World War II, the most precious documents from the Municipal Archives were placed in the cellar of the basilica—one of the few available bombproof sites.

Andrássy útja runs 3.2 kilometers (2 miles) from the basilica to ⑰ **Hősök tere** (Heroes' Square). On the left is the **State Opera House,** with its statues of the Muses in the second-floor corner niches. Completed in 1884, it was the crowning achievement of architect Miklós Ybl. It has been restored to its original ornate glory—particularly inside—and has been spared attempts at modernization. There are no performances in summer.

Városliget Park In the center of Heroes' Square stands the 36.5-meter (118-⑱ foot) **Millennium Monument,** begun in 1896 to commemorate the 1,000th anniversary of the Magyar Conquest. Statues of Prince Árpád and six other founders of the Magyar nation occupy the base of the monument, while Hungary's greatest rulers and princes are between the columns on either side.

⑲ The **Szépművészeti Múzeum** (Fine Arts Museum) stands on one side of the square. Egyptian, Greek, and Roman artifacts dominate an entire section of the museum, and the collection of ceramics includes many rare pieces. The institution's largely unknown Spanish collection, which includes many works by El Greco and a magnificent painting by Velásquez, is considered the best of its kind outside Spain. *Dózsa György út 41, tel. 361/ 1429–759. Admission: 20 Ft. Open Tues.–Sat. 10–6, Sun. 10–6; closed Jan.–Mar.*

⑳ The **Műcsarnok** (Art Gallery), on the other side of the square, usually houses visiting exhibitions of contemporary Hungarian and international art but is closed for renovation until 1994.

The **Városliget** (City Park) extends beyond the square; on the left as you enter it are the zoo, state circus, amusement park, and outdoor swimming pool of the Széchenyi mineral baths. On ㉑ the right is the **Mezőgazdasági Múzeum** (Agricultural Museum), housed in a number of buildings representing different styles of Hungarian architecture—again a part of the Millennium Exhibition of 1896. *Széchenyi sziget, Városliget XIV, tel. 361/1423–011. Admission: 15 Ft. Open Tues.–Sat. 10–5, Sun. 10–6.*

On the shores of the artificial lake stands the statue of George Washington, erected in 1906 from donations by Hungarians living in the United States. The **Olaf Palme sétány** (walk) is a pleasant route through the park.

Off the Beaten Track

A *libegő* (chair lift) will take you to the highest point in Budapest, **Jánoshegy** (János Hill), where you can climb a lookout tower for the best view of the city. *Take bus No. 158 from Moszkva tér to the last stop, Zugligeti út. Admission: 20 Ft. Open May 15–Sept. 15, daily 9–5.*

For another good view, make the strenuous climb up the staircase that ascends the high cliff overlooking the Danube at the Buda end of the Szabadság Bridge. This will lead you to **Gellért-hegy** (Gellert Hill), named for an 11th-century bishop who was hurled to his death here by some pagan Magyars. During the Middle Ages the hill was associated with witches; nowadays there is a towering memorial to the liberation of Budapest by the Red Army.

Shopping

You'll find plenty of folk art and souvenir shops, foreign-language bookshops, and classical record shops in or around **Váci utca,** but a visit to some of the smaller, more typically Hungarian shops on **Erzsébet** and **Teréz boulevards** and to the modern **Skála-Coop** department store near the Nyugati train station may prove more interesting.

The **central market hall** at IX Vámhaz körút 1–3 is closed for rebuilding, but the **flea market** *(ecseri piac)* some way out on Nagykorösi utca 156 (take bus No. 58 from Boráros tér) stocks antiques, clothes, lamps, and such relics of the former Soviet empire as Red Army caps, Lenin statues, and Gorbachev dolls.

Dining

Private restaurateurs are breathing excitement into the Budapest dining scene. You can choose among Chinese, Mexican, Italian, French, and Czech cuisines—there are even two vegetarian restaurants. Or you can stick to solid, traditional Hungarian fare as served in dozens of little restaurants scattered throughout the center of town, where you'll find Transylvanian folk art on the walls, linens with folk patterns on the tables, gypsy music in the air, and lots of heavy wood furniture; and where a mere 200 Ft. will buy you a bowl of goulash or a platterful of hearty hot food. For price-category definitions, *see* Dining in Staying in Hungary.

Moderate **Fórum Grill.** Anyone with a touch of homesickness will enjoy
★ this spot in the Fórum Hotel. The salad bar is fresh and the pizza tasty, and there are even real cheeseburgers and a nonsmoking section. Enjoy the courteous service, and ask about the daily specials. *V Apáczai Csere János utca 12–14, tel. 361/1179–111. AE, DC, MC, V.*

Kisbuda Gyöngye. This is the reincarnation of a venerable Budapest favorite that fell victim to foreign buyers. The longtime management, now at a new address, has made their establishment better than ever with art deco furniture and pink tablecloths; a violin-piano duo with a repertoire favoring Mozart set a romantic mood. Try the chicken Cumberland (grilled boneless breasts marinated in basil and spices) or the fresh trout smothered in a cream sauce nutted with mushrooms and capers. *Kenyeres utca 34, tel. 361/1686–402. Reservations advised 2 days ahead. AE. Closed Sun.*

Kispipa. The street outside, a lane full of crumbling old buildings, makes this restaurant's gleaming brass fixtures, stylish art deco chairs, and convivial crowd seem that much more polished. On the extensive menu, the game dishes stand out. *VII Akácfa utca 38, tel. 361/1422–587. Reservations advised. No credit cards.*

Inexpensive **Bohémtanya.** There's always a wait for a table at this lively hangout, but it pays to be patient. The reward: heaping plates of stuffed cabbage, fried pork chops filled with goose liver, and other Hungarian specialties. *VI Paulay Ede utca 6, tel. 361/ 1221–453. Reservations advised. No credit cards.*

Felafel Number One. This bright, modern spot, all mirrors,

You've Let Your Imagination Go, Now Get Up And Follow Your Dreams.

For The Vacation You're Dreaming Of, Call
American Express®Travel Agency At 1-800-YES-AMEX.*

American Express will send more than your imagination soaring. We'll
fly you, sail you, drive you to any Fodor's destination and beyond.
Because American Express believes the best vacations happen
from Europe to the Orient, Walt Disney®World to Hawaii
and everywhere in between.

For dependable service, expert advice, and value wherever
your dreams take you, call on American Express. After all,
the best traveling companion
is a trustworthy friend.

AMERICAN EXPRESS · Travel Agency

It's easy to recognize a good place when you see one.

American Express Cardmembers have been doing it for years.

The secret? Instead of just relying on what they see in the window, they look at the door. If there's an American Express Blue Box on it, they know they've found an establishment that cares about high standards.

Whether it's a place to eat, to sleep, to shop, or simply meet, they know they will be warmly welcomed.

So much so, they're rarely taken in by anything else.

Always a good sign.

white tile, and light paneling, serves pita bread with plenty of fresh vegetables and salads to stuff into it—not always easy to find in these parts. *V Paulay Ede utca 53, no phone. No reservations. Dress: casual. No credit cards. Closed weekends.*

McDonald's. Nowadays golden arches are all over town—but not one will you see in this dazzling Baroque and Belle Epoque spot in the old railroad station, possibly the world's most beautiful fast-food outlet. Only the smell tells you that yes, Virginia, this is the real thing. *VI Teréz krt. 52, next to Nyugati station, 361/132–5970. Dress: casual. No reservations. No credit cards.*

Ristorante Giuseppe Pizzeria. Take a table by the big picture window and watch the world go by on the busy sidewalk outside while you sit amid posters of Italy and eat your pizza—the only thing they sell here, cooked in ovens before your eyes. *XIII Szent István krt. 20, no phone. Dress: casual. No reservations. No credit cards.*

Szerb. Down a sawdust-covered stairway, this lively cellar serves grilled meats on a skewer and other Serbian dishes for a song, along with giant pitchers of beer. *V Nagy Ignác utca 16, tel. 361/1111–858. Reservations advised. No credit cards.*

Vegetárium Etterem. This oasis in a land of avid meat-eaters feels like something straight out of California, with its bleached-wood floors, modern posters, plethora of plants, and soft guitar music, and the menu is positively exotic for Hungary: brown rice and vegetables, tempura, and fresh salads, all lovingly prepared. *V Cukor utca 3, tel. 1383–710. Dress: casual. No reservations. No credit cards.*

Lodging

Forty million tourists came to Hungary last year, and the boom has encouraged hotel building; yet there is sometimes a shortage of rooms, especially in summer.

If you arrive without a reservation, go to the IBUSZ travel office at Petőfi tér (tel. 361/1185–707) or to one of the tourist offices at any of the train stations or at the airport. For details and price-category definitions, *see* Lodging in Staying in Hungary.

Moderate **Astoria.** Revolutionaries and intellectuals once gathered in the marble-and-gilt Art Deco lobby here. Recent renovations have not obscured its charm, but have meant the addition of other comforts—most notably soundproofing, essential since the Astoria is located at the city's busiest intersection. *V Kossuth Lajos utca 19, tel. 361/1173–411, fax 361/1186–798. 198 rooms with bath or shower. Facilities: nightclub, café, beer hall. AE, DC, MC, V.*

Centrál. Relive history—stay in this hotel, well situated in a leafy diplomatic quarter, as visiting Communist dignitaries once did. The architecture and furnishings are straight out of the 1950s. *XIV Munkácsy utca 5–7, tel. 361/1212–000, fax 361/1212–008. 42 rooms with bath. Facilities: restaurant. AE, DC, MC, V.*

Ifjúság. The hotel is somewhat spartan, but you can't fault the location near Margaret Island. Ask for a room with a view, and you won't be sorry. *II Zivatar utca 3, tel. 361/1154–260. 100 rooms, most without bath. Facilities: restaurant. AE, DC, MC, V.*

Liget. It's luxurious, it's postmodern, and with two major museums nearby, it's ideal for art lovers. Városliget, the city park, is a few steps away, and offers respite from traffic and noise. *XIV Aréna út 106, tel. 361/1113–205 or 361/1317–159, fax 361/ 1317–153. 55 rooms with bath. Facilities: coffee shop, bar, sauna. AE, DC, MC, V.*

Nemzeti. The baby-blue Baroque facade stands out in this dingy neighborhood, which turns seedy after dark. The homey atmosphere is the real draw. *VIII József Körút 4, tel. 361/1339–160, fax 361/1140–019. 76 rooms, most with bath. Facilities: restaurant, brasserie. AE, DC, MC, V.*

Inexpensive **Citadella.** Built into a fortress on top of a hill overlooking the city this small property is charming outside but militantly '60s-socialist inside, with its bare linoleum floors, cotlike beds, and bare walls. But it's airy, it's spotless, and the views are splendid. *XI Citadella sétány, tel. 361/166–5794. 15 rooms, 10 with shower. No credit cards.*

Korona Penzió. This typical Hungarian guest-house is in a quiet, tasteful residential area on the hill called Sas-hegy. Rooms are a bit cold, but bedspreads with a folkloric motif and inexpensive rugs on the floors add a homey note, and the management is friendly. *XI Sasadi út 127, tel. 361/186–2460. 15 rooms and 3 apartments, all with shower. No credit cards.*

Kulturinnov. One wing of what looks like a Gothic castle now houses basic budget accommodations. Rooms are clean, and the neighborhood, the luxurious Castle District, is quite pleasant. *I Szentháromság tér 6, tel. 361/1550–122 or 361/1751–651, fax 361/1751–886. 17 rooms, some with 3 or 4 beds, not all with bath or shower. Facilities: snack bar, reading room. AE.*

Park. This establishment, fresh from a major renovation, is centrally located across the street from Keleti station. The poet Allen Ginsberg once stayed here, and it has always been popular with young people. *VIII Baross tér 10, tel. 361/113–1420. 155 rooms, 40 with bath. Facilities: restaurant. AE, DC, MC, V.*

The Arts

Hotels and tourist offices will provide you with a copy of the monthly publication *Programme*, which contains details of all cultural events in the city. The newspaper *Budapest Week* lists upcoming events in English; look for it in hotels and bookshops. Tickets are available from your hotel desk, the **Central Booking Agency** (Vörösmarty tér, tel. 361/1176–222), or from **Budapest Tourist** (Roosevelt tér 5, tel. 361/1173–555).

There are two opera houses, for which dress can be informal. Concerts are given all year at the **Academy of Music** on Liszt F. tér, the **Vigadó** on Vigadó tér and at the **Old Academy of Music** on Vörösmarty út. Displays of Hungarian folk dancing are held at the **Cultural Center** on Corvin tér.

Arts festivals fill the calendar beginning in early spring. The season's first, the **Spring Art Festival** (Mar.), showcases Hungary's best opera, music, theater, and dance as well as visiting foreign artists. It's followed by the annual **Jazz Festival** (Apr.), and after the opera season ends, by the **Summer Opera Festival** (July–Aug.) at the open-air theater on Margit-sziget. Information and tickets are available from the Central Booking Agency, above.

Nightlife

Budapest is a lively city by night. Establishments stay open late and Western European–style *drink-bárs* have sprung up all over the city.

Nightclubs Many of the nightclubs are attached to the luxury hotels. Beware of the inflated prices. Admission starts at 150 Ft. Drinks cost from 200 Ft. to 500 Ft.

Ballantine's Club. The atmosphere is hushed and British; billiards and chess are the games. *VI Andrássy út 19, tel. 361/ 1227–896. Open weekdays 10 AM–5 AM, weekends 5 PM–5 AM.*

Casanova offers music and dancing in an attractive building where the great lover is said to have spent the night. *II Batthyány tér, tel. 361/1358–320. Open 10 PM–4 AM.*

Duna-bár Boat sails up and down the river with dancing and disco music on board. *15 Apaza út, next to the Hotel Fórum, on the Pest side, tel. 361/1170–803. Open noon–3 and 6 PM–midnight.*

Pierrot is an elegant café and piano bar well suited for secret rendezvous. *I Fortuna utca 14, tel. 361/1756–971. Open 5 PM–1 AM. No credit cards.*

Cabarets **Horoszkóp,** in the Buda-Penta Hotel, is the favorite among Budapest's younger set. Floor shows begin at 11 PM. *I Krisztina körút 41–43, tel. 361/1566–333. Open 10 PM–4 AM.*

Maxim's, in the Hotel Emke, offers a Parisian-style variety show, complete with leggy chorus girls, at top prices. *VII Akácfa utca 3, tel. 361/1420–145. Open 8 PM–3 AM.*

Discos The university colleges organize the best discos in town. Try the **ELTE Club** (Eötvös Loránd) in the Inner City, on the corner of Károlyi Mihály utca and Irányi utca. Admission and drink prices are reasonable. Bring some student I.D.

Excursion from Budapest: Szentendre

About 40 kilometers (25 miles) north of Budapest, the Danube abandons its eastward course and turns abruptly south toward the capital, cutting through the Börzsöny and Visegrád hills. This area is called the Danube Bend and includes the Baroque town of Szentendre, about 19 kilometers (12 miles) north of Budapest. Szentendre, nowadays a flourishing artists' colony with a lively Mediterranean atmosphere, was first settled by Serbs and Greeks fleeing the advancing Turks in the 14th and 17th centuries. There is a Greek Orthodox church in the main square and a Serbian Orthodox cathedral on the hill. The narrow cobbled streets are lined with cheerfully painted houses. There are regular connections to Budapest by boat and hydrofoil—the most pleasant way to get around. You can also get there by bus and by HÉV commuter rail, departing from the Batthyány tér metro; the fare is 48 Ft.

Tourist Information Contact Dunatours (Bacsó part 6, on the quay, tel. 26/11–311) for details on this area.

Exploring Szentendre Heading north from Budapest look on your right for the reconstructed remains of **Aquincum,** capital of the Roman province of Pannonia. Careful excavations have unearthed a varied selection of artifacts and mosaics, and have given a tantalizing inkling of what life was like on the northern fringes of the Roman Empire.

Part of the town's artistic reputation can be traced to the life and work of the ceramic artist Margit Kovács, whose work blended Hungarian folk art traditions with motifs from modern art. The **Margit Kovács Pottery Museum,** devoted to her work, is housed in a small 18th-century merchant's house with an attractive courtyard. *Vastag György utca 1, tel. 26/10–244. Admission: 50 Ft. Open daily 9–7.*

A short bus ride from the train station the **Szabadtéri Néprajzi Múzeum** (Open-Air Ethnographical Museum), where a collection of buildings has been designed to show Hungarian peasant life and folk architecture in the 19th century. *Szabadság Forrás út, tel. 26/12–304. Admission: 50 Ft. Open Apr.–Oct., daily 10–5.*

Dining   For details and price-category definitions, *see* Dining and Lodging in Staying in Hungary.

Angyal Borozó. This wine bar, also a restaurant, serves hefty portions of Hungarian food. *Alkotmány utca 4 (no telephone). No reservations or credit cards accepted. Moderate.*
Rab Ráby. Fish soup and fresh grilled trout are the specialties in this popular restaurant with wood beams and equestrian decorations. *Péter Pál utca 1, tel. 26/10–819. Reservations advised in summer. No credit cards. Moderate.*

Lodging   **Bükkös Panzió.** Impeccably clean, this stylishly modernized old house is on a small canal just a few minutes' walk from the town center. *Bükkös part 16, tel. 26/12–021. 16 rooms with bath. Facilities: restaurant. No credit cards. Moderate.*

Lake Balaton

Lake Balaton, the largest lake in Central Europe, stretches 80 kilometers (50 miles) across western Hungary. It is within easy reach of Budapest by any means of transportation. Sometimes known as the nation's playground, it goes some way toward making up for Hungary's much-lamented lack of coastline. On its hilly northern shore, ideal for growing grapes, is **Balatonfüred,** the country's oldest and most famous spa town.

The national park on the Tihany Peninsula is just to the south, and regular boat service links Tihany and Balatonfüred with Siófok on the southern shore. This shore is not as attractive as the northern one—being flatter and more crowded with resorts, cottages, and high-rise hotels once used as Communist trade-union retreats. Still, it is worth visiting for its shallower, warmer waters, which make it a better choice for swimming than other locations.

A circular tour taking in Veszprém, Balatonfüred, and Tihany could be managed in a day, but two days, with a night in Tihany or Balatonfüred, would be more relaxed.

The region is crowded in July and August, so visit at any other time if you can.

Getting Around

Trains from Budapest serve all the resorts on the northern shore; a separate line links the resorts of the southern shore. Road 71 runs along the northern shore; M7 covers the southern. Buses connect most resorts. Regular ferries link the major ones. On summer weekends, traffic can be heavy and driving slow around the lake. Book bus and train tickets in advance then. In winter, note that schedules are curtailed, so check before making plans.

Tourist Information

Balatonfüred (Balatontourist, Blaha L. utca 5, tel. 86/42–822). **Tihany** (Balatontourist, Kossuth utca 20, tel. 86/48–512). **Veszprém** (Balatontourist, Münnich F. tér 3, tel. 80/13–750).

Exploring Lake Balaton

Hilly **Veszprém** is the center of cultural life in the Balaton region. **Várhegy** (Castle Hill) is the most attractive part of town, north of Szabadság tér. **Hősök Kapuja** (Heroes' Gate), at the entrance to the Castle, houses a small exhibit on Hungary's history. Just past the gate and down a little alley to the left, is the **Tűztorony** (Fire Tower); note that the lower level is medieval while the upper stories are Baroque. There is a good view of the town and surrounding area from the balcony. *Exhibit admission: 10 Ft. Open May–Oct., Tues.–Sun. 10–6.*

Tolbuhin út, the only street in the castle area, leads to a small square in front of the **Bishop's Palace** and **Cathedral;** outdoor concerts are held here in the summer. Tolbuhin út continues past the square up to a terrace erected on the north staircase of the castle. Stand beside the modern statues of St. Stephen and his queen, Gizella, for a far-reaching view of the old quarter of town.

Balatonfüred, a spa and resort with good beaches, is about 15 kilometers (9 miles) from Veszprém. It is also one of the finest wine-growing areas of Hungary. Above the main square, where medicinal waters bubble up under a colonnaded pavilion, the hillsides are thick with vines.

A seven-minute boat trip takes you from Balatonfüred to the **Tihany Peninsula,** a national park rich in rare flora and fauna and an ideal place for strolling. From the ferry port, follow green markers to the springs (Oroszkút) or red ones to the top of **Csúcs-hegy,** a hill from which there is a good view of the lake.

The village of **Tihany,** with its famous **abbey,** is on the eastern shore. The abbey building houses a **museum** with exhibits related to the Balaton area. Also worth a look are the pink angels floating on the ceiling of the abbey church, and the abbey organ, on which recitals are given in summer. *Batthyány utca 80, tel. 80/48–405. Admission: 20 Ft. Open Tues.–Sun. 10–6.*

Dining and Lodging

ABC convenience stores make picnics on the beach cheap and easy. And, although hotels can be expensive, it's relatively easy to line up rooms in private homes, which fall in the inexpensive and budget price categories. For details and definitions, *see* Dining and Lodging in Staying in Hungary.

Balatonfüred **Tölgyfa Csárda.** This restaurant on a hillside away from the
Dining beach takes its name from the large oak tree nearby. Although it's one of the most expensive dining options in town, with a menu and decor worthy of a first-class establishment even in

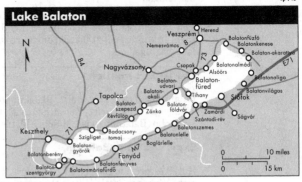

Lake Balaton

Budapest, it's not difficult to keep the tab in the moderate range. There's Gypsy music and a nice view. *Meleghegy út, tel. 86/43-036. Reservations advised. Dress: casual. No credit cards. Closed Nov.-Mar. Moderate.*

Halászkert Etterem. This beachfront restaurant, whose name translates as "Fisherman's Garden," is famous for its grilled Balaton pike perch, cooked over an open flame, among other reasonably priced fish dishes. There's an outdoor dance floor. *Széchenyi 2, off Jókai Mór utca, tel. 86/43-039. Reservations advised for dinner July-Aug. Dress: casual. AE, DC, MC, V. Closed Dec.-Feb. Inexpensive.*

Lodging **Arany Csillag.** Once a castle and later the headquarters for the
★ local Soviet garrison, this hotel is well-worn but atmospheric, and the rooms are spotless. It's a good choice if you've had enough of Hungary's more modern accommodations. Ten minutes from the beach, it's one of the best buys in Balaton. *Balatonfüred 8231, tel. 86/43-466. 40 rooms, none with bath. Facilities: restaurant. No credit cards. Closed Dec.-Mar. Inexpensive.*

Tihany **Halásztánya.** The relaxed atmosphere and gypsy music in the
Dining evening help contribute to the popularity of the Halásztánya, which specializes in fish. *Visszhang utca 11, no tel. No reservations. Closed Nov.-Mar. Moderate.*

Pál Csárda. Two thatched-roof cottages make up this simple restaurant, where cold fruit soup and fish stew are the specialties. You can eat in the garden, which is decorated with gourds and strands of peppers, from which paprika is made. *Visszhang utca 19, no tel. No reservations. Dress: casual. No credit cards. Closed Dec.-Mar. Moderate.*

Lodging **Kolostor.** The cozy, wood-panel rooms are built into an attic above a restaurant in the heart of Tihany village. *Kossuth út, tel. 86/48-408. 7 rooms with bath. Facilities: breakfast room. No credit cards. Moderate.*

Park. Lush landscaped gardens surround this stately mansion at the water's edge. Inside, it's all understated elegance; rooms have balconies, views, and crisp sheets embroidered with the names of former Communist-party bosses. *Fürdötelepi út 1, tel. 86/48-611. 26 rooms with bath. Facilities: restaurant, private beach. AE, DC, MC, V. Summer, Expensive; fall-spring, Moderate.*

Veszprém **Betyácsárda.** Mock country weddings are performed at this
Dining folkloric dinner-theater—touristy but fun, and easily accessi-

ble by bus from Veszprém. The audience joins in the celebration dances, and the Hungarian food is as spirited as the atmosphere. The bill covers the meal, dancing, and music. *Nemesvamos, 8 km (5 mi) from Veszprém, tel. 80/650-87. Reservations advised. Dress: casual. DC. Closed Nov.-Easter. Moderate.*

Tüztorony Sörkluh. At this restaurant on the winding cobblestone street leading to the castle you can order game specialties such as venison soup and veal stew. Try the cherry strudel for dessert. *Vár utca, no tel. No reservations. Dress: casual. No credit cards. Moderate.*

★ **Vadásztanya.** The Vadásztanya is just a little southwest of the town center, but worth the trip if you want to experience the old-fashioned charm of a small provincial Hungarian restaurant. The decor could be called "cozy traditional," and the fish and game specialties are perennial favorites. *József Attila utca 22, tel. 80/12-495. No reservations. No credit cards. Moderate.*

Lodging **Vezprém.** This modern, comfortable hotel in the center of town now has a fresh paint job and pleasant new furniture. *Budapesti utca 6, tel. 80/12-345. Facilities: restaurant. No credit cards. Moderate.*

14 Ireland

With its informal, unpretentious way of life, Ireland is an ideal destination for the budget traveler. Indeed, some of its best attractions—including its unspoiled scenery and unpolluted coast—are available for free. Ruined abbeys, medieval castles, and prehistoric remains are freely accessible, as are most of Dublin's galleries and museums. By staying in affordable bed-and-breakfasts, visitors can come to know firsthand the Irish and their way of life. Nightlife in Ireland consists of a visit to the local pub where, for the price of a few drinks, you can enjoy performances by traditional musicians or take part in a sing-song.

Ireland, one of the westernmost countries in Europe, is a small island on which you are never more than an hour's drive from the sea. It's actually two countries in one. The northeast corner of the island, Northern Ireland, remains a part of the United Kingdom, while the Republic, with a population of only 3½ million, has been independent since 1921.

The Republic of Ireland is virtually free from the "troubles" that dominate Northern Ireland. Over the past few years, millions of pounds have been spent upgrading tourist facilities, but the attractions of Ireland as a vacation destination remain the same as ever: those of a small, friendly country with a mild climate and a relaxed pace of life, where simple pleasures are found in its scenery, its historical heritage, its sporting opportunities, and the informal hospitality of its loquacious inhabitants.

Dublin, the capital, is a thriving modern city. It's a strikingly elegant city, too, a fact of which the Dubliners are well aware. Trinity College, Dublin Castle, and the magnificent public buildings and distinctive Georgian squares of the city have all been restored, allowing the elegance of 18th-century Dublin to emerge again after centuries of neglect.

The pace of life outside Dublin is even more relaxed. When a local was asked for the Irish-language equivalent of *mañana*, the reply came that there is no word in Irish to convey quite the same sense of urgency. An exaggeration, of course, but the farther you travel from the metropolis, the more you will be inclined to linger. Apart from such sporting attractions as championship golf, horse racing, deep-sea fishing, and angling, the thing to do in Ireland is to take it easy, and look around you.

The lakes of Killarney—a chain of deep-blue lakes—surrounded by romantic, boulder-strewn mountains are justifiably the country's most famous attractions. The nearby Ring of Kerry provides the motorist with a day-long tour through lush coastal vegetation. Galway is a compact, attractive city with a lively atmosphere.

Throughout the country, there are prehistoric and early Christian remains to be discovered. You can also seek out the places made famous by James Joyce, William Butler Yeats, John Millington Synge, and other well-known writers and gain a new insight into the land and the people who inspired them.

Essential Information

Before You Go

When to Go The main tourist season runs from June to mid-September. The attractions of Ireland are not as dependent on the weather as those in most other northern European countries, and the scenery is just as attractive in the off-peak times of fall and spring. Accommodations are more economical in winter, although some of the smaller attractions are closed from October to March. In all seasons the visitor can expect to encounter rain.

Climate Winters are mild though wet; summers can be warm and sunny, but there's always the risk of a sudden shower. No one ever went to Ireland for a suntan.

The following are the average daily maximum and minimum temperatures for Dublin.

Jan.	46F	8C	May	60F	15C	Sept.	63F	17C
	34	1		43	6		48	9
Feb.	47F	8C	June	65F	18C	Oct.	57F	14C
	35	2		48	9		43	6
Mar.	51F	11C	July	67F	19C	Nov.	51F	11C
	37	3		52	11		39	4
Apr.	55F	13C	Aug.	67F	19C	Dec.	47F	8C
	39	4		51	11		37	3

Currency The unit of currency in Ireland is the pound, or punt (pronounced "poont"), written as IR£ to avoid confusion with the pound sterling. The currency is divided into the same denominations as in Britain, with IR£1 divided into 100 pence (written *p*). There is likely to be some variance in the rates of exchange between Ireland and the United Kingdom (which includes Northern Ireland). This usually favors the visitor. Change

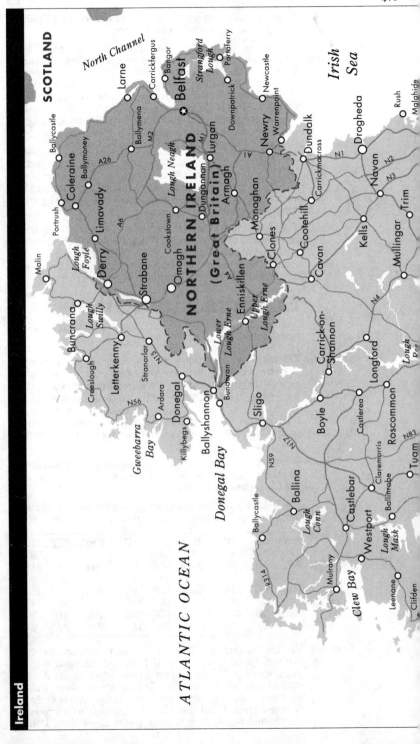

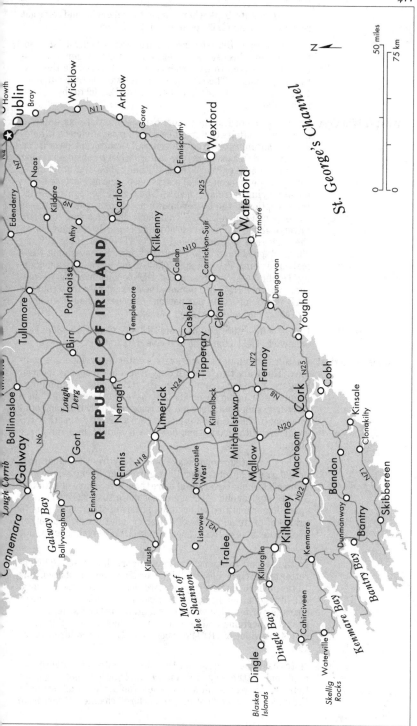

U.K. pounds at a bank when you get to Ireland (pound coins not accepted); change Irish pounds before you leave.

U.S. dollars and British currency are accepted only in large hotels and shops licensed as bureaux de change. In general, visitors are expected to use Irish currency. Banks give the best rate of exchange. The rate of exchange at press time (summer 1992) was IR£.70 to the U.S. dollar and IR£1.09 to the British pound sterling.

What It Will Cost Dublin is one of Europe's most expensive cities—an unfortunate state of affairs that manifests itself most obviously in hotel and restaurant rates. You can generally keep costs lower if you visit Ireland on a package tour. Alternatively, consider staying in a guest house or one of the multitude of bed-and-breakfasts; they provide an economical and atmospheric option (*see* Lodging in Staying in Ireland, *below*). The rest of the country—with the exception of the better-known hotels and restaurants—is less expensive than Dublin. That the Irish themselves complain bitterly about the high cost of living is partly attributable to the high rate of value-added tax (VAT)—a stinging 23% on "luxury" goods and 10% on other items. Some sample costs make the point. For instance, while a double room in a moderate Dublin hotel will cost about IR£75, with breakfast sometimes another IR£7 per person, the current rate for a country B&B is around IR£14 per person. A modest small-town hotel will charge around 1R£18 per person.

Sample Prices Cup of coffee, 60p; pint of beer, IR£1.85; Coca-Cola, 80p; ham sandwich, IR£1.30; 1-mile taxi ride, IR£3.50.

Customs on Arrival Customs regulations for travelers entering Ireland are complex. There are two levels of duty-free allowance: one for passengers arriving from other EC (European Community) countries bringing in goods that *not* been bought in a duty-free shop and a second for residents of European countries not in the EC and for passengers arriving from other EC countries with goods that *have* been bought in a duty-free shop.

In the first category you may import duty-free: 300 cigarettes or 400 grams of tobacco or 150 cigarillos or 75 cigars; plus 1½ liters of alcoholic beverage of more than 22% volume or a total of 3 liters of alcoholic beverage of not more than 22% volume or sparkling or fortified wines, plus 4 liters of other wine; plus 75 grams of perfume and ⅜ of a liter of toilet water; plus other goods to a value of IR£302 per person (IR£77 for children under 15).

In the second category you may import duty-free: 200 cigarettes or 100 cigarillos or 50 cigars or 250 grams of tobacco; plus 1 liter of alcoholic beverage of more than 22% volume or a total of 2 liters of alcoholic beverage of not more than 22% volume or sparkling or fortified wine, plus 2 liters of other wine; plus 50 grams of perfume and ¼ of a liter of toilet water; plus other goods to a value of IR£34 per person (IR£17 for children under 15).

Note that in both categories the tobacco and alcohol allowances apply only to those aged 17 and older. If you have nothing more than the duty-free allowance when you arrive, walk straight through the green "nothing to declare" channel. If you have more than your duty-free allowance, however, you must go into the red channel and declare the goods you are bringing in.

Visitors may import any quantity of currency, whether foreign or Irish, and nonresidents may export any amount of foreign currency, provided it was declared on arrival. Otherwise you may export no more than IR£100, in denominations no larger than IR£20, and no more than the equivalent of IR£500 in foreign currency.

Language Officially, the Irish language is the first language of the Republic, but the everyday language of the majority of Irish people is English. Except for the northwest, where many signs are not translated, most signs in the country are written in Irish with an English translation underneath. There is one important exception to this rule, with which all visitors should familiarize themselves: *Fir* and *mná* translate respectively into "men" and "women." The *Gaelteacht*—areas in which Irish *is* the everyday language of most people—comprises only 6% of the land, and all its inhabitants are, in any case, bilingual.

Getting Around

By Train **Iarnód Eireann** (Irish Rail) and **Bus Eireann** (Irish Bus) are independent components of the state-owned public transportation company **Coras Iompair Eireann** (CIE). The rail network, although much cut back in the past 25 years, is still extensive, with main routes radiating from Dublin to Cork, Galway, Limerick, Tralee, Killarney, Westport, and Sligo; there is also a line for the north and Belfast. All trains are diesel; cars on principal expresses have air-conditioning. There are two classes on many trains—Super Standard (first class) and Standard (second class). Dining cars are carried on main expresses. There are no sleeping cars.

Speeds are slow in comparison with those of other European trains. Dublin, however, now has a modern commuter train—the DART—running south from the suburb of Howth through the city to Bray on the Wicklow coast, with various stops along the way.

Fares For the strictly independent traveler, the 15-day **Rambler** ticket gives unlimited travel by train and bus and is an excellent value at IR£110. It can be purchased from any city bus terminal or train-station ticket office and is valid for travel on any 15 days in a 30-day period. There is an eight-day **Rambler** ticket (rail and bus) for IR£75, valid for any 8 days in a 15-day period. One- and four-day round-trip train tickets are also available at discounted rates. The **Overlander** ticket includes travel in Northern Ireland via rail, bus, and Ulsterbus; it costs IR£115 for 15 days.

By Bus The provincial bus system operated by Bus Eireann is widespread—more so than the train system—although service can be infrequent in remote areas. But the routes cover the entire country and are often linked to the train services (*see* By Train, *above*) for details of combined train and bus discount tickets.

By Bicycle Biking can be a great way to get around Ireland. Details of bicycle rentals are available from the Irish Tourist Board. Rates average IR£7.50 per day or IR£35 per week. You must pay a IR£30 deposit. Be sure to make reservations, especially in July and August. If you rent a bike in the Republic, you may *not* take it into Northern Ireland; nor may you take a bike rented in Northern Ireland into the Republic.

Staying in Ireland

Telephones
Local Calls There are pay phones in all post offices and most hotels and bars, as well as in street booths. Local calls cost 20p for three minutes, calls within Ireland cost about 50p for three minutes, and calls to Britain cost about IR£1.75 for three minutes. Rates go down by about a third after 6 PM and all day Saturday and Sunday.

International Calls For calls to the United States and Canada, dial 161 followed by the area code. For calls to the United Kingdom, dial 03 followed by the number. Don't make international calls from your hotel room unless absolutely necessary. Most hotels add a 200–300% surcharge to calls.

Mail
Postal Rates Airmail rates to the United States, Canada, and the Commonwealth are 52p for the first 10 grams, air letters 45p, and postcards 38p. Letters to Britain and continental Europe cost 32p, postcards 28p.

Receiving Mail A general delivery service is operated free of charge from Dublin's General Post Office at O'Connell St., Dublin 1, tel. 01/728888.

Shopping
VAT Refunds Visitors from outside Europe can take advantage of the "cashback" system on value-added tax (VAT) if their purchases total more than IR£50. A cash-back voucher must be filled out by the retailer at the point of sale. The visitor pays the total gross price, including VAT, and receives green and yellow copies of the invoice; both must be retained. These copies are presented to and stamped by customs, as you leave the country. Take the stamped form along to the cashier, and the VAT will be refunded.

Opening and Closing Times **Banks.** Banks are open weekdays 10–12:30 and 1:30–3, and until 5 on selected days.

Museums. Museums are usually open weekdays 10–5, Saturday 10–1, Sunday 2–5. Always make a point of checking, however, as hours can change unexpectedly.

Shops. Shops are open Monday–Saturday 9–5:30, closing earlier on Wednesday, Thursday, or Saturday, depending on the locality.

National Holidays January 1; March 17 (St. Patrick's Day); April 9 (Good Friday); April 12 (Easter Monday); June 7 (Whit Monday); August 2 (August Monday); and December 25, 26. If you're planning a visit at Easter, remember that theaters and cinemas are closed for the last three days of the preceding week.

Dining When it comes to food, Ireland has some of the best raw materials in the world: prime beef, locally raised lamb and pork, free-range poultry, game in season, abundant fresh seafood, and locally grown seasonal vegetables. Despite the near-legendary awfulness of much Irish cooking in the recent past, times are definitely changing, and a new generation of chefs is beginning to take greater advantage of this abundance of magnificent produce. In almost all corners of the country, you'll find a substantial choice of restaurants, many in hotels, serving fresh local food that is imaginatively prepared and served.

If your tastes run toward traditional Irish dishes, there are still a few old-fashioned restaurants serving substantial portions of excellent, if plain, home cooking. Look for boiled bacon and cabbage, Irish stew, and *colcannon* (cooked potatoes diced and fried in butter with onions and either cabbage or leeks and covered in thick cream just before serving). The best bet for daytime meals is "pub grub"—a choice of soup and soda bread, two or three hot dishes of the day, salad platters, or sandwiches. Most bars serve food, and a growing number offer coffee and tea as an alternative to alcohol. Guinness, a dark beer, or "stout," brewed with malt, is the Irish national drink. Even if you never go out for a drink at home, you should visit at least one or two pubs in Ireland. The pub is one of the pillars of Irish society, worth visiting as much for entertainment and conversation as for drinking.

To help travelers on a budget, more than 360 restaurants participate in a *tourist menu* program. Three-course meals are offered at set prices ranging from about IR£7 to IR£14. The Irish Tourist Board's *Tourist Menu* leaflet (50p) gives full details. Most places limit the availability of this menu to lunchtime and early evening.

Mealtimes Breakfast is served between 8 and 10—earlier by special request only—and is a substantial meal of cereal, bacon, eggs, sausage, and toast. Lunch is eaten between 12:30 and 2. Having enjoyed a hearty breakfast, however, most visitors tend to have a light lunch and to eat their main meal in the evening. The old tradition of "high tea" taken around 5, followed by a light snack before bed, is still encountered in many Irish homes, including many bed-and-breakfasts. Elsewhere, however, it is generally assumed that you'll be eating between 7 and 9:30 and that this will be your main meal of the day.

Dress Casual dress is acceptable.

Ratings Prices are per person and include a first course, a main course, and dessert, but no wine or tip. Sales tax at 10% is included in all Irish restaurant bills. A tip of 10% is adequate.

Category	Cost
Moderate	IR£16–IR£28
Inexpensive	IR£12–IR£16
Budget	under IR£12

Lodging Accommodations in Ireland range all the way from deluxe castles and renovated stately homes to thatched cottages and farmhouses to humble B&Bs. Standards everywhere are high, and they continue to rise. Pressure on hotel space reaches a peak between June and September, but it's a good idea to make reservations in advance at any time of the year. Rooms can be reserved directly from the United States; ask your travel agent for details. The Irish Tourist Board's Central Reservations Service (14 Upper O'Connell St., Dublin 1, tel. 01/747733) can make reservations, as can local tourist board offices.

The Irish Tourist Board (ITB) has an official grading system and publishes a detailed price list of all approved accommodations, including hotels, guest houses, farmhouses, B&Bs, and hostels. No hotel may exceed this price without special authorization from the ITB; prices must also be displayed in every room. Don't hesitate to complain either to the manager or to the ITB, or both, if prices exceed this maximum.

In general, hotels charge per person. In most cases (but not all, especially in more expensive places), the price includes a full breakfast. VAT is included, but some hotels—again, usually the more expensive ones—add a 10–15% service charge. This should be mentioned in their price list. In Moderate and Inexpensive hotels, be sure to specify whether you want a private bath or shower; the latter is cheaper. Off-season (October–May) prices are reduced by as much as 25%.

Guest Houses Some smaller hotels are graded as guest houses. To qualify, they must have at least five bedrooms. A few may have restaurants; those that do not will often provide evening meals by arrangement. Few will have a bar. Otherwise these rooms can be as comfortable as those of a regular hotel, and in major cities they offer very good value for the money, compared with the inexpensive hotels.

Bed-and-Breakfasts Bed-and-breakfast means just that. The bed can vary from a four-poster in the wing of a castle to a feather bed in a whitewashed farmhouse or the spare bedroom of a modern cottage. Rates are generally around IR£14 per person, though these can vary significantly. Although many larger B&Bs offer rooms with bath or shower, in some you'll have to use the bathroom in the hall and, in many cases, pay 50p–IR£1 extra for the privilege.

B&B accommodations can be booked for that night at local tourist information offices for a nominal fee. Most travelers do not bother booking a B&B in advance. They are so plentiful that it's often more fun to leave the decision open. But you should check in by at least 6 PM to obtain the best choice of rooms. Many B&Bs offer reductions for stays longer than two nights.

Hostels **An Oige** (The Irish Youth Hostels Association, 39 Mountjoy Sq., Dublin 1, tel. 01/363111) has a chain of 40 hostels. You must have an International Youth Hostel card to stay at one. All have a curfew and are closed 10 AM–5 PM. Charges for adults are IR£6 per night in city hostels and around IR£4 in rural ones.

About 100 other hostels are linked together in the **Association of Independent Hostels.** These are friendly, easy-going places with no curfew and no daytime closing rules. Most have private double rooms for around IR£6.50 per person per night, and dormitory accommodations for about IR£5. Self-catering kitchens and hot showers are usually available. For a list of locations and facilities, write to Patrick O'Donnell, Dooey Hostel, Glencolumcille, Co. Donegal (tel. 073/30130).

Rentals In nearly 30 locations around Ireland, there are clusters of cottages for rent. The majority are built in traditional styles, but have central heating and all other conveniences. The average rent for a three-bedroom cottage equipped for six adults is around IR£250 in midseason; be sure to make reservations well in advance. The ITB's booklet "Self Catering" (IR£2) has full details.

Camping There are a variety of beautifully sited campgrounds and trailer parks, but be prepared for wet weather! The ITB publishes a useful booklet "Caravan and Camping Guide" (IR£1.50).

Ratings Prices are for two people in a double room, based on high season (June to September) rates.

Category	Cost
Moderate	IR£70–IR£100
Inexpensive	IR£50–IR£70
Budget	under IR£50

Tipping Other than in upscale hotels and restaurants, the Irish are not really used to being tipped. Some hotels and restaurants will add a service charge of about 12% to your bill, so tipping isn't necessary unless you've received particularly good service.

Tip taxi drivers about 10% of the fare if the taxi has been using its meter. For longer journeys, where the fare is agreed in advance, a tip will not be expected unless some kind of commentary (solicited or not) has been provided. In luxury hotels, porters and bellhops will expect IR£1; elsewhere, 50p is adequate. Hairdressers normally expect a tip of about IR£1. You don't tip in pubs, but if there is waiter service in a bar or hotel lounge, leave about 20p.

Dublin

Arriving and Departing

By Plane All flights arrive at Dublin's Collinstown Airport, 10 kilometers (6 miles) north of town. For information on arrival and departure times, call individual airlines.

Between the Airport and Downtown Buses leave every 20 minutes from outside the Arrivals door for the central bus station in downtown Dublin. The ride takes about 30 minutes, depending on the traffic, and the fare is IR£2.50. A taxi ride into town will cost from IR£6 to IR£12, depending on the location of your hotel.

By Train There are three main stations. Heuston Station (at Kingsbridge) is the departure point for the south and southwest; Connolly Station (at Amiens Street), for Belfast, the east coast, and the west; Pearse Station (on Westland Row), for Bray and connections via Dun Laoghaire to the Liverpool/Holyhead ferries. Tel. 01/366222 for information.

By Bus The central bus station, Busaras, is at Store Street near the Custom House. Some buses terminate near Connolly Bridge. Tel. 01/734222 for information on city services (Dublin Bus); tel. 01/366111 for express buses and provincial services (Bus Eireann).

Getting Around

Dublin is small as capital cities go—the downtown area is positively compact—and the best way to see the city and soak in the full flavor is on foot.

By Train An electric train commuter service, DART (Dublin Area Rapid Transport), serves the suburbs out to Howth, on the north side of the city, and to Bray, County Wicklow, on the south side. Fares are about the same as for buses. Street-direction signs to

DART stations read Staisiun/Station. The **Irish Rail** office is at 35 Lower Abbey Street; for rail inquiries, tel. 01/366222.

By Bus Most city buses originate in or pass through the area of O'Connell Street and O'Connell Bridge. If the destination board indicates "An Lar," that means that the bus is going to the city's central area. Timetables (IR£2) are available from the **Dublin Bus** office (59 Upper O'Connell St., tel. 01/720000) and give details of all routes, times of operation, and price codes. The minimum fare is 55p.

Important Addresses and Numbers

Tourist Information There is a tourist information office in the entrance hall of the **Irish Tourist Board** headquarters (Baggot Street Bridge, tel. 01/765871); open weekdays 9–5. More conveniently located is the office at 14 Upper O'Connell St., tel. 01/747733; open weekdays 9–5:30, Saturday 9–1. There is also an office at the airport, tel. 01/376387. From mid-June to September, there is an office at the Ferryport, Dun Laoghaire, tel. 01/280–6984.

Embassies U.S. (42 Elgin Rd., Ballsbridge, tel. 01/688–8777). **Canadian** (65 St. Stephen's Green, tel. 01/781988). **U.K.** (33 Merrion Rd., tel. 01/269–5211).

Emergencies **Police** (tel. 999), **Ambulance** (tel. 999), **Doctor** (tel. 01/537951 or 01/767273), **Dentist** (tel. 01/679–4311).

Travel Agencies **American Express** (116 Grafton St., tel. 01/772874). **Thomas Cook** (118 Grafton St., tel. 01/771721).

Exploring Dublin

Numbers in the margin correspond to points of interest on the Dublin map.

Dublin is a small city with a population of just over 1 million. For all that, it has a distinctly cosmopolitan air, one that complements happily the individuality of the city and the courtesy and friendliness of its inhabitants. Originally a Viking settlement, Dublin is situated on the banks of the river Liffey. The Liffey divides the city north and south, with the more lively and fashionable spots, such as the Grafton Street shopping area, to be found on the south side. Most of the city's historically interesting buildings date from the 18th century, and, although many of its finer Georgian buildings disappeared in the overenthusiastic redevelopment of the '70s, enough remain, mainly south of the river, to recall the elegant Dublin of the past. The slums romanticized by writers Sean O'Casey and Brendan Behan have virtually been eradicated, but literary Dublin can still be recaptured by those who want to follow the footsteps of Leopold Bloom's progress, as described in James Joyce's *Ulysses*. And Trinity College, alma mater of Oliver Goldsmith, Jonathan Swift, and Samuel Beckett, among others, still provides a haven of tranquillity.

Dubliners are a talkative, self-confident people, eager to have visitors enjoy the pleasures of their city. You can meet a lively cross section of people in the city's numerous bars, probably the best places to sample the famous wit of the only city to have produced three winners of the Nobel Prize for Literature: William Butler Yeats, George Bernard Shaw, and Samuel Beckett.

O'Connell Begin your tour of Dublin at **O'Connell Bridge,** the city's most
Street central landmark. Look closely and you will notice a strange
❶ feature: The bridge is wider than it is long. The north side of
O'Connell Bridge is dominated by an elaborate memorial to
Daniel O'Connell, "The Liberator," erected as a tribute to the
great 19th-century orator's achievement in securing Catholic
Emancipation in 1829. Today **O'Connell Street** is the city's main
shopping area, though it seems decidedly parochial to anyone
accustomed to Fifth Avenue or Rodeo Drive. Turn left just before the General Post Office and take a look at Henry Street.
This pedestrians-only shopping area leads to the colorful
Moore Street Market, where street vendors recall their most famous ancestor, Molly Malone, by singing their wares—mainly
flowers—in the traditional Dublin style.

❷ The **General Post Office,** known as the GPO, occupies a special
place in Irish history. It was from the portico of its handsome
classical facade that Padraig Pearse read the Proclamation of
the Republic on Easter Monday, 1916. You can still see the
scars of bullets on its pillars from the fighting that ensued. The
GPO remains the focal point for political rallies and demonstrations even today and is used as a viewing stand for VIPs during
the annual St. Patrick's Day Parade.

❸ **The Gresham Hotel,** opposite the GPO, has played a part in
Dublin's history since 1817, although, along with the entire
O'Connell Street area, it is less fashionable now than it was
during the last century. Just north of the Gresham is the Irish
Tourist Board information office; drop in for a free street map,
shopping guides, and information on all aspects of Dublin tourism. Opposite is the main office of Bus Eireann, which can supply bus timetables and information on excursions.

❹ At the top of O'Connell Street is the **Rotunda,** the first materni-
ty hospital in Europe, opened in 1755. Not much remains of the
once-elegant Rotunda Assembly Rooms, a famous haunt of
fashionable Dubliners until the middle of the last century. The
Gate Theater, housed in an extension of the Rotunda Assembly
Rooms, however, continues to attract crowds to its fine repertoire of classic Irish and European drama. The theater was
founded by the late Micheál MacLiammoir in 1928.

❺ Beyond the Rotunda, you will have a fine vista of **Parnell
Square,** one of Dublin's earliest Georgian squares. You will notice immediately that the first-floor windows of these elegant
brick-face buildings are much larger than the others and that it
is easy to look in from street level. This is more than simply the
result of the architect's desire to achieve perfect proportions on
the facades: These rooms were designed as reception rooms,
and fashionable hostesses liked passersby to be able to peer in
and admire the distinguished guests at their luxurious, candlelit receptions.

Charlemont House, whose impressive Palladian facade domi-
❻ nates the top of Parnell Square, now houses the **Hugh Lane Municipal Gallery of Modern Art.** Sir Hugh Lane, a nephew of
Lady Gregory, who was Yeats's curious, high-minded aristocratic patron, was a keen collector of Impressionist paintings.
The gallery also contains some interesting works by Irish artists, including Yeats's brother Jack. *Parnell Sq. Admission
free. Open Tues.–Sat. 9:30–6, Sun. 11–5.*

Abbey Theatre, **9**
Archbishop Marsh's
Library, **23**
Brown Thomas, **20**
Christ Church
Cathedral, **25**
City Hall, **27**
Civic Museum, **22**
Custom House, **34**
Dublin Castle, **26**
Dublin Writers
Museum, **7**
Four Courts, **33**
Genealogical Office, **18**
General Post Office, **2**
Gresham Hotel, **3**
Guinness Brewery, **29**
Halfpenny Bridge, **35**
Hugh Lane Municipal
Gallery of Modern
Art, **6**
Irish Whiskey
Corner, **32**
Kilkenny Design
Workshops, **12**
Leinster House, **15**
Merrion Square, **13**
National Gallery, **14**
National Library, **17**
National Museum, **16**
O'Connell Bridge, **1**
Parliament House, **10**
Parnell Square, **5**
Phoenix Park, **30**
Powerscourt Town
House, **21**
Rotunda, **4**
Royal Hospital
Kilmainham, **36**
Royal Irish
Academy, **19**
St. Mary's Pro
Cathedral, **8**
St. Michan's, **31**
St. Patrick's
Cathedral, **24**
Temple Bar, **28**
Trinity College, **11**

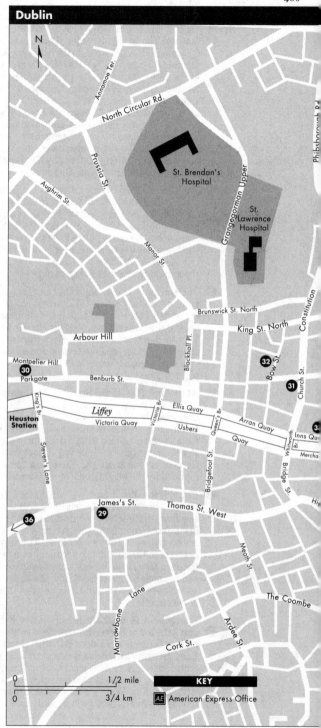

Dublin

N

North Circular Rd.

St. Brendan's
Hospital

St.
Lawrence
Hospital

Annamoe ter.

Prussia St.

Aughrim St.

Manor St.

Grangegorman Upper

Phibsborough Rd.

Brunswick St. North

King St. North

Constitution

Arbour Hill

Blackhall Pl.

Bow St.

Church St.

32

31

Montpelier Hill

30
Parkgate

Benburb St.

Ellis Quay

Arran Quay

Liffey

Heuston
Station

Victoria Quay

Ushers

Quay

Inns Qu

Merchant

King's Br.

Steven's Lane

Victoria Br.

Queen's Br.

Bridgefoot St.

Whitworth Br.

James's St.

Thomas St. West

29

36

Meath St.

High

The Coombe

Marrowbone

Lane

Ardee St.

Cork St.

0   1/2 mile

0   3/4 km

KEY

AE American Express Office

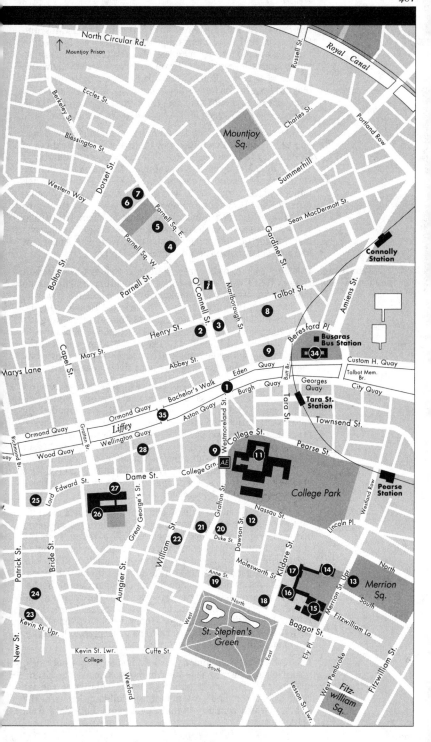

The Parnell Square area is rich in literary associations, which **7** are explained and illustrated in the **Dublin Writers Museum.** Opened in 1991 in two carefully restored 18th-century buildings, paintings, letters, manuscripts, and photographs relating to James Joyce, Sean O'Casey, George Bernard Shaw, W. B. Yeats, Brendan Behan, and others are on permanent display. There are also temporary exhibitions, lectures, and readings, as well as a bookshop. *18–19 Parnell Sq. N, tel. 727810. Admission: IR£2. Open Mon.–Sat. 10–5, Sun. 2–6.*

Return to O'Connell Street, where a sign on the left will lead **8** you to **St. Mary's Pro Cathedral,** the main Catholic church of Dublin. Try to catch the famous Palestrina Choir on Sunday at 11 AM. John McCormack is one of many famous voices to have **9** sung with this exquisite ensemble. The **Abbey Theatre,** a brick building dating from 1966, was given a much-needed new facade in 1991. It has some noteworthy portraits and mementos in the foyer. Seats are usually available at about IR£10, and with luck you may just have a wonderful evening. The luck element, unfortunately, must be stressed, since the Abbey has had both financial and artistic problems lately.

Trinity and It is only a short walk across O'Connell Bridge to **Parliament**
Stephen's Green **House.** Today this stately early 18th-century building is no
10 more than a branch of the Bank of Ireland; originally, however, it housed the Irish Parliament. The original House of Lords, with its fine coffered ceiling and 1,233-piece Waterford glass chandelier, is open to the public during banking hours (weekdays 10–12:30 and 1:30–3). It's also worth taking a look at the main banking hall, whose judicial character—it was previously the Court of Requests—has been sensitively maintained.

11 Across the road is the facade of **Trinity College,** whose memorably atmospheric campus is a must for every visitor. Trinity College, Dublin (familiarly known as TCD) was founded by Elizabeth I in 1591 and offered a free education to Catholics—provided that they accepted the Protestant faith. As a legacy of this condition, right up until 1966, Catholics who wished to study at Trinity had to obtain a dispensation from their bishop or face excommunication. Today more than 70% of Trinity's students are Catholics, a clear indication of how far away those days seem to today's generation.

The facade, built between 1755 and 1759, consists of a magnificent portico with Corinthian columns. The design is repeated on the interior, so the view from outside the gates and from the quadrangle inside is the same. On the sweeping lawn in front of the facade are statues of two of the university's illustrious alumni—statesman Edward Burke and poet Oliver Goldsmith. Other famous students include the philosopher George Berkeley, who gave his name to the San Francisco area campus of the University of California; Jonathan Swift; Thomas Moore; Oscar Wilde; John Millington Synge; Henry Grattan; Wolfe Tone; Robert Emmet; Bram Stoker; Edward Carson; Douglas Hyde; and Samuel Beckett.

The 18th-century building on the left, just inside the entrance, is the chapel. There's an identical building opposite, the Examination Hall. The oldest buildings are the library in the far right-hand corner and a row of redbrick buildings known as the Rubrics, which contain student apartments; both date from 1712.

Ireland's largest collection of books and manuscripts is housed in **Trinity College Library.** There are more than 2½ million volumes gathering dust here; about half a mile of new shelving has to be added every year to keep pace with acquisitions. The library is entered through the library shop. Its principal treasure is the **Book of Kells,** a beautifully illuminated manuscript of the Gospels dating from the 8th century. Because of the beauty and the fame of the Book of Kells, at peak hours you may have to wait in line to enter the library; it's less busy early in the day. Apart from the many treasures it contains, the aptly named Long Room is impressive in itself, stretching for 65 meters (209 feet). Originally it had a flat plaster ceiling, but the perennial need for more shelving resulted in a decision to raise the level of the roof and add the barrel-vaulted ceiling and the gallery bookcases. *Admission: IR£1.75. Open weekdays 9:30–4:45, Sat. 9:30–12:45.*

A breath of fresh air will be welcome after the library, so, when you're done admiring the award-winning modern architecture of the New Library and the Arts Building, pass through the gate to the sports grounds—rugby fields on your left, cricket on your right. Leave Trinity by the Lincoln Place Gate—a handy "back door."

Shoppers will find a detour along Nassau Street in order here. As well as being well endowed with bookstores, it contains the ⑫ **Kilkenny Design Workshops,** which, besides selling the best in contemporary Irish design for the home, also holds regular exhibits of exciting new work by Irish craftsmen. *Open Mon.–Sat. 9–5.*

⑬ Nassau Street will lead you into **Merrion Square,** past a distinctive corner house that was the home of Oscar Wilde's parents. Merrion Square is one of the most pleasant in Dublin. Its flower gardens are well worth a visit in the summer months. Note the brightly colored front doors and the intricate fanlights above them—a distinctive feature of Dublin's domestic architecture.

⑭ The **National Gallery** is the first in a series of important buildings on the west side of the square. It is one of Europe's most agreeable and compact galleries, with more than 2,000 works on view, including a major collection of Irish landscape painting, 17th-century French works, paintings from the Italian and Spanish schools, and a collection of Dutch masters. *Merrion Sq. Admission free. Open weekdays 10–5, Sat. 10–1, Sun. 2–5.*

⑮ Next door is **Leinster House,** seat of the Irish Parliament. This imposing 18th-century building has two facades: Its Merrion Square facade is designed in the style of a country house, while the other facade, in Kildare Street, is in the style of a town house. Visitors may be shown the house when the Dail (pronounced "Doyle"), the Irish Parliament, is not in session.

Stephen's Green, as it is always called by Dubliners, suffered more from the planning blight of the philistine '60s than did its neighbor, Merrion Square. An exception is the magnificent **Shelbourne Hotel,** which dominates the north side of the green. It is still as fashionable—and as expensive—as ever.

Time Out Budget-conscious visitors should put on their finery and try afternoon tea in the elegant splendor of the Shelbourne's **Lord**

Mayor's Room. You can experience its old-fashioned luxury for around IR£7.50 (including sandwiches and cakes) per head.

Around the corner on Kildare Street, the town-house facade of

⑯ Leinster House is flanked by the **National Museum** and the

⑰ **National Library,** each featuring a massive colonnaded rotunda entrance built in 1890. The museum (Admission: free. Open Tues.–Sat. 10–5, Sun. 2–5) houses a remarkable collection of Irish treasures from 6000 BC to the present, including the Tara Brooch, the Ardagh Chalice, and the Cross of Cong. Every major figure in modern Irish literature, from James Joyce onward, studied in the National Library at some point. In addition to a comprehensive collection of Irish authors, it contains extensive newspaper archives. *Kildare St. Admission free, except for certain exhibits. Open Mon. 10–9, Tues.–Wed. 2–9, Thurs.–Fri. 10–5, Sat. 10–1.*

⑱ The **Genealogical Office**—the starting point for ancestor-tracing—also incorporates the **Heraldic Museum,** which features displays of flags, coins, stamps, silver, and family crests that highlight the uses and development of heraldry in Ireland. *2 Kildare St. Genealogical Office. Open weekdays 10–5. Heraldic Museum. Admission free. Open weekdays 10–12:30 and 2:30–4. Guided tours Mar.–Oct., cost IR£1.*

⑲ The **Royal Irish Academy,** on Dawson Street, is the country's leading learned society; it has many important manuscripts in its unmodernized 18th-century library (open Mon.–Fri. 9:30–5:15). Just below the academy is **Mansion House,** the official residence of the Lord Mayor of Dublin. Its Round Room was the location of the first assembly of the Dail Eireann—the Irish Parliament—in January 1919. It is now used mainly for exhibitions.

Grafton Street, which runs between Stephen's Green and Trini-

⑳ ty College, is a magnet for shoppers. Check out **Brown Thomas,** Ireland's most elegant and old-fashioned department store; it has an extremely good selection of sporting goods and Waterford crystal—an odd combination. Many of the more stylish boutiques are just off the main pedestrians-only areas, so be

㉑ sure to poke around likely corners. Don't miss the **Powerscourt Town House,** an imaginative shopping arcade installed in and around the covered courtyard of an impressive 18th-century

㉒ building. Nearby is the **Civic Museum,** which contains drawings, models, maps of Dublin, and other civic memorabilia. *58 S. William St. Admission free. Open Tues.–Sat. 10–6, Sun. 11–4.*

A short walk from Stephen's Green will bring you to one of the

㉓ smaller and more unusual gems of old Dublin, **Archbishop Marsh's Library.** It was built in 1701, and access is through a tiny but charming cottage garden. Its interior has been unchanged for more than 300 years and still contains "cages" into which scholars who wanted to peruse rare books were locked. (The cages were to discourage students who, often impecunious, may have been tempted to make the books their own.) *St. Patrick's Close. Open Wed.–Fri. 10:30–12:30 and 2–4, Mon. 2–4, Sat. 10:30–12:30.*

㉔ Opposite, on Patrick Street, is **St. Patrick's Cathedral.** Legend has it that St. Patrick baptized many converts at a well on the site of the cathedral in the 5th century. The building dates from

1190 and is mainly early English in style. At 93 meters (300 feet), it is the longest church in the country. Its history has not always been happy. In the 17th century, Oliver Cromwell, dour ruler of England and no friend of the Irish, had his troops stable their horses in the cathedral. It wasn't until the 19th century that restoration work to repair the damage was put in hand. St. Patrick's is the national cathedral of the Protestant Church of Ireland and has had many illustrious deans. The most famous was Jonathan Swift, author of *Gulliver's Travels*, who held office from 1713 to 1745. Swift's tomb is in the south aisle, and Dean Swift's corner at the top of the north transept contains his pulpit, his writing table and chair, his portrait, and his death mask. Memorials to many other celebrated figures from Ireland's past line the walls of St. Patrick's.

㉕ St. Patrick's originally stood outside the walls of Dublin. Its close neighbor, **Christ Church Cathedral** (Christ Church Rd.), on the other hand, stood just within the walls and belonged to the See of Dublin. It is for this reason that the city has two cathedrals so close to each other. Christ Church was founded in 1172 by Strongbow, a Norman baron and conqueror of Dublin for the English crown, and it took 50 years to build. Strongbow himself is buried in the cathedral beneath an impressive effigy. The vast and sturdy **crypt** is Dublin's oldest surviving structure and should not be missed.

㉖ Signs in the Christ Church area will lead you to **Dublin Castle.** Guided tours of the lavishly furnished state apartments are offered every half hour and provide one of the most enjoyable sightseeing experiences in town. Only fragments of the original 13th-century building survive; the elegant castle you see today is essentially an 18th-century building. The state apartments were formerly the residence of the English viceroys—the monarch's representative in Ireland—and are now used by the president of Ireland to entertain visiting heads of state. The state apartments are closed when in official use, so phone first to check. *Off Lord Edward St., tel. 01/777129. Admission: IR£2.50. Open weekdays 10–12:15 and 2–5, weekends 2–5.*

㉗ Step into the **City Hall** on Dame Street to admire the combination of grand classical ornament and understated Georgian simplicity in its circular main hall. It also contains a good example of the kind of gently curving Georgian staircase that is a typical feature of most large town houses in Dublin.

㉘ Between Dame Street and the river Liffey is a new semipedestrianized area known as **Temple Bar,** which should interest anyone who wants to discover "young Dublin." The area is chock-full of small, imaginative shops; innovative art galleries; and inexpensive restaurants.

㉙ The **Guinness Brewery,** founded by Arthur Guinness in 1759, dominates the area to the west of Christ Church, covering 60 acres. Guinness is proud of its brewery and invites visitors to attend a 30-minute film shown in a converted hops store next door to the brewery itself. After the film, you can sample the famous black beverage. *Guinness Museum and Visitors' Center, James's St. Admission free. Open weekdays 10–3.*

Phoenix Park Across the Liffey is **Phoenix Park,** 7,122 square kilometers
and the Liffey (1,760 acres) of green open space. Though the park is open to
㉚ all, it has only two residents: the president of Ireland and the

American ambassador. The park is dominated by a 64 meter-high (205-foot) obelisk, a tribute to the first duke of Wellington. Sunday is the best time to visit: Games of cricket, soccer, polo, baseball, hurling—a combination of lacrosse, baseball, and field hockey—or Irish football will be in progress.

Returning to the city's central area along the north bank of the Liffey, you pass through a fairly run-down section that's scheduled for major redevelopment. A diversion up Church Street to **③ St. Michan's** will be relished by those with a macabre turn of mind. Open coffins in the vaults beneath the church reveal mummified bodies, some more than 900 years old. The sexton, who can be found at the church gate on weekdays, will guide you around the church and crypt.

㉜ Irish Whiskey Corner is just behind St. Michan's. A 90-year-old warehouse has been converted into a museum to introduce visitors to the pleasures of Irish whiskey. There's an audiovisual show and free tasting. *Bow St., tel. 01/725566. Admission: IR£2. Tours weekdays at 3:30, or by appointment.*

The Liffey has two of Dublin's most famous landmarks, both of them the work of 18th-century architect James Gandon and **㉝** both among the city's finest buildings. The first is the **Four Courts,** surmounted by a massive copper-covered dome, giving it a distinctive profile. It is the seat of the High Court of Justice of Ireland. The building was completed between 1786 and 1802, then gutted in the Civil War of the '20s; it has since been painstakingly restored. You will recognize the same architect's hand **㉞** in the **Custom House,** farther down the Liffey. Its graceful dome rises above a central portico, itself linked by arcades to the pavilions at either end. Behind this useful and elegant landmark is an altogether more workaday structure, the central bus station, known as Busaras.

Midway between Gandon's two masterpieces is the Metal **㉟** Bridge, otherwise known as the **Halfpenny Bridge,** so called because, until early in this century, a toll of a half-penny was charged to cross it. The poet W. B. Yeats was one among many Dubliners who found this too high a price to pay—more a matter of principle than of finance—and so made the detour via O'Connell Bridge. Today no such high-minded concern need prevent you from marching out to the middle of the bridge to admire the view up and down the Liffey as it wends its way through the city.

㊱ The **Royal Hospital Kilmainham** is a short ride by taxi or bus from the center; it's well worth the trip. The hospital is considered the most important 17th-century building in Ireland and has recently been renovated. It was completed in 1684 as a hospice—the original meaning of the term "hospital"—for veteran soldiers. Note especially the chapel with its magnificent Baroque ceiling. It also houses the **Irish Museum of Modern Art,** which opened in 1991. Parts of the old building, used as a national cultural center, are occasionally closed to the public. *District of Kilmainham, tel. 01/718666. Guided tours: Sun. noon–5 and holidays 2–5; cost IR£2. Exhibitions: open Tues.–Sat. 2–5.*

Devotees of James Joyce may wish to take the DART train south to **Sandycove,** about 8 kilometers (5 miles) out of the city center. It was here, in a Martello tower (a circular fortification built by the British as a defense against possible invasion by

Napoleon at the beginning of the 19th century), that the maverick Irish genius lived for some months in 1904. It now houses the **Joyce Museum.** *Sandycove Coast. Admission: IR£1.20 adults, 60p children. Open Apr.–Oct., Mon.–Sat. 10–1 and 2–5, Sun. 2:30–6. Also by appointment, tel. 01/280–8571.*

Shopping

Although the rest of the country is well supplied with crafts shops, Dublin is the place to seek out more specialized items—antiques, traditional sportswear, haute couture, designer ceramics, books and prints, silverware and jewelry, and designer handknits.

Shopping Districts The most sophisticated shopping area is around **Grafton Street:** Its delis stock Irish whiskey marmalade, Irish lakeside wholegrain mustard, whole handmade cheeses, and sides of smoked salmon or trout. The new **St. Stephen's Green Center** contains 70 stores, large and small, in a vast Moorish-style glass-roof building on the Grafton Street corner. **Molesworth** and **Dawson Streets** are the places to browse for antiques; **Nassau** and **Dawson Streets,** for books; the smaller cross side streets for jewelry, art galleries, and old prints.

Department Stores The shops north of the river tend to be less expensive and less design-conscious; chain stores and lackluster department stores make up the bulk of them. The **ILAC Shopping Center,** on Henry Street, is worth a look, however. **Switzers** and **Brown Thomas** are Grafton Street's main department stores; the latter is Dublin's most elegantly decorated department store, with many international fashion labels on sale. **Arnotts,** on Henry Street, is Dublin's largest department store and has a good range of cut crystal. Visit **Kilkenny Design Workshops** on Nassau Street for the best selection of Irish designs for the home. Nearby, the **House of Ireland** has an abundance of traditional gifts and souvenirs.

Tweeds and Woolens Ready-made tweeds for men can be found at **Kevin and Howlin,** on Nassau Street, and at **Cleo Ltd.,** on Kildare Street. The **Blarney Woollen Mills,** on Nassau Street, has a good selection of tweed, linen, and woolen sweaters in all price ranges. The **Woolen Mills,** at Halfpenny Bridge, has a good selection of handknits and other woolen sweaters at competitive prices.

Dining

The restaurant scene in Dublin has improved beyond recognition in recent years. Though no one is ever likely to confuse the place with, say, Paris, the days of chewy boiled meats and soggy, tasteless vegetables are long gone. Food still tends to be substantial rather than subtle, but more and more restaurants are at last taking advantage of the magnificent livestock and fish that Ireland has in such abundance. For details and price-category definitions, *see* Dining in Staying in Ireland.

Moderate **Dobbin's Wine Bistro.** Though Dobbin's aims at a French identity, with its red-and-white gingham tablecloths and sawdust-strewn slate floor, the cooking here is international and imaginative, with an emphasis on fresh Irish produce. Specialties are phyllo pastry with pepper and seafood filling, paupiettes of salmon and sole with spinach and dill sauce, and Szechuan boned crispy duckling with fresh peaches. *Stephen's La., tel. 01/764670. Reservations advised. AE, DC, MC, V. Closed Sun.*

Latchfords. The clientele here has long been loyal to this restaurant's type of hearty meat dishes. Specialties are fillets, sirloins, and T-bones of prime Irish beef, prepared in 15 different ways. Try Gaelic steak, with a sauce of Irish whiskey, onions, mushrooms, and cream, or Surf 'n' Turf, an eight-ounce fillet accompanied by Dublin Bay prawns. The restaurant is located in the labyrinthine basement of two Georgian town houses and is furnished with wood-top tables and burgundy drapes and carpets. *99–100 Lower Baggot St., tel. 01/760784. Reservations advised. AE, DC, MC, V. Closed weekends lunch.*

Le Caprice. This Italian restaurant, situated right in the city center, features white linen-covered tables amid lots of bric-a-brac and busy decorations. The place also has a real party atmosphere later in the evening when the pianist is in the right mood. The menu includes traditional Continental dishes such as prawn cocktail, deep fried scampi, and roast duckling a l'orange, as well as an interesting selection of authentic Italian dishes including pasta and veal. *12 St. Andrew's St., tel. 01/679–4050. Reservations accepted. AE, DC, MC, V. Dinner only.*

Inexpensive **Bad Ass Café.** Definitely one of Dublin's loudest restaurants, this barnlike place, situated in the trendy Temple Bar area, between the Central Bank and the Halfpenny Bridge, is always a fun place to eat. American-style fast food—burgers, chili, and pizzas—and the pounding rock music attract a lively crowd, both the young and the young at heart. Look out for the old-fashioned cash shuttles whizzing around the ceiling! *9–11 Crown Alley, tel. 01/712596. Reservations for large parties recommended. AE, MC, V. Closed Jan. 1, Good Friday, and Dec. 25–26.*

Corncucopia Wholefoods. This vegetarian restaurant above a health-food shop provides good value for the money. The seating consists of bar stools at high, narrow glass-top tables. It's popular with student types from nearby Trinity College. The menu includes red lentil soup, avocado quiche, vegetarian spring roll, and vegetarian curry—all of them regular favorites. *19 Wicklow St., tel. 01/777583. No reservations. No credit cards. Closed Sun.*

Da Vicenza. Watching the pizza dough being kneaded, rolled, topped off, and thrust into the brick oven will probably influence your menu choice here. The pizzas are indeed excellent, but the restaurant also offers interesting pasta combinations, and fish and steak. Dark blue blinds and drapery against natural stone and wood are the background for a venue that is popular with all age groups. *133 Upper Leeson St., tel. 01/609906. Reservations advised. AE, DC, MC, V.*

Pasta Pasta. This small, bright, and unpretentiously pretty Italian eatery serves combinations of pasta shapes and sauces plus a few Italian specials—medallions of pork *à la funghi, escalope milanesa*—against a background of muted jazz-rock. It's an excellent value. *27 Exchequer St., tel. 01/679–2565. Reservations advised for groups over 6 and on weekends. MC, V. Closed Sun.*

Rudyards. One of the first restaurants to open in the Temple Bar area (Dublin's "left bank"), this is an informal but stylish place in a narrow three-story building. The rooms are decorated in an austere art nouveau style, with bare wooden tables and bentwood chairs, paper napkins, and a hint of elegance in the mirrors and framed posters. The food, by contrast, is light; typical dishes include smoked salmon eclairs and canneloni with spinach and cheese stuffing. There is live jazz most weekends. *15–16 Crown Alley, tel. 01/710864. No reservations. AE, DC, MC, V. Closed Sun.*

Budget **Bewley's.** This famous chain of coffeehouses is essential to Dublin's social fabric. Recent refurbishment restored the original turn-of-century style, with dark mahogany trim, stained-glass windows, and bentwood chairs, and put the motherly waitresses back into traditional black dresses with white aprons and headbands. Variations on the traditional Irish breakfast (eggs, bacon, sausage, black-and-white pudding, tomatoes, and mushrooms) are the thing to eat here—at any hour of the day. Other specialties include Bewley's 11 blends of tea and 15 blends of coffee, as well as home-baked scones, buns, and pastries. *Westmoreland St., Grafton St., South Great George's St., and suburban branches, tel. 01/776761 (head office). Open daily 8–6. No reservations. AE, DC, MC, V.*

Burdock's. In the heart of Viking Dublin, next door to the Lord Edward pub. Dublin's most famous fish and chipper sticks to the traditional method of frying in beef drippings over a coal fire. Waiting in line is all part of the fun. As your meal should be eaten as soon as possible, the favored seating is on the steps of St. Patrick's Cathedral. *Werburgh St., tel. 01/540306. Dinner only. Closed Tues. and Sun. No credit cards.*

Captain America. A surprise awaits you here at the top of a flight of stairs on fashionable Grafton Street. The collection of outrageous Americana strewn throughout is dominated by a replica of the Statue of Liberty that visibly shudders at the loud rock music. A wide selection of hamburgers graces the menu, plus beef tacos, burritos, enchiladas, and chili. *Grafton Court, Grafton St., tel. 01/715266. No reservations. AE, DC, MC, V.*

Gallagher's Boxty House. This highly original Irish eatery has a charming country ambience with antique pine furniture complementing the dark green decor. Boxty is a traditional Irish potato bread or cake that is served here as a pancake thin enough to wrap around savory fillings such as bacon and cabbage, chicken with leeks, and smoked fish. Follow these with brown bread and Bailey's ice cream or the superb bread and butter pudding. *20 Temple Bar, tel. 01/772762. No reservations. V. Closed Christmas and Good Friday.*

Pub Food All the pubs listed here serve food at lunchtime; some also have food in the early evening. They form an important part of the dining scene in Dublin and make a pleasant and informal alternative to a restaurant meal. In general, a one-course meal should not cost much more than IR£4–IR£5, but a full meal will put you in the lower range of the Moderate category. In general, credit cards are not accepted.

Barry Fitzgerald's. Salads and a freshly cooked house special are available in the upstairs bar at lunch on weekdays. Pretheater dinners are served in the early evening. *90 Marlboro St., tel. 01/774082.*

Davy Byrne's. James Joyce immortalized Davy Byrne's in *Ulysses.* Nowadays it's more akin to a cocktail bar than a Dublin pub, but it's good for fresh and smoked salmon, salads, and a hot daily special. Food is available at lunchtime and in the early evening. *21 Duke St., tel. 01/711298.*

Kitty O'Shea's. Kitty O'Shea's cleverly, if a little artificially, re-creates the atmosphere of old Dublin. *23–25 Grand Canal St., tel. 01/609965. Reservations accepted for lunch and Sun. brunch.*

Lord Edward Bar. With its Old World ambience, the Lord Edward Bar serves a wide range of salads and a hot dish of the day at lunchtime only. *23 Christ Church Pl., tel. 01/542158.*

Old Stand. Located conveniently close to Grafton Street, the Old Stand offers grilled food, including steaks. *37 Exchequer St., tel. 01/770821.*

Lodging

Although only a few major hotels have opened in Dublin in the past few years, considerable investment in redevelopment, updating of facilities, and refurbishing of some of the older establishments is taking place. As in most major cities, there is a shortage of mid-range accommodations. For value-for-the-money, try one of the registered guest houses; in most respects they are indistinguishable from small hotels. Most economical of all is the bed-and-breakfast. Both guest houses and B&Bs tend to be located in suburban areas—generally a 10-minute bus ride from the center of the city. This is not in itself a great drawback, and savings can be significant.

The Irish Tourist Board (14 Upper O'Connell St.) publishes a comprehensive booklet, "Guest Accommodation" (IR£4), that covers all approved possibilities in Dublin and the rest of the country, from the grandest hotel to the humblest B&B. The office can usually help if you find yourself without reservations.

There is a VAT of 10% on hotel charges, which should be included in the quoted price. A service charge of 12–15% is also included and listed separately in the bills of top-grade hotels; elsewhere, check to see if the service is included. If it's not, a tip of between 10% and 15% is customary—if you think the service is worth it. For details and price-category definitions, *see* Lodging in Staying in Ireland.

Moderate **Ariel Guest House.** This is Dublin's leading guest house, just a ★ block away from the elegant Berkeley Court and a 10-minute walk from Stephen's Green. The lobby lounge and restaurant of this Victorian villa are furnished with leather and mahogany heirlooms, as are most of their spacious bedrooms, 13 of which were added to the house in 1991. This is a good bet if you're in town for a leisurely, relaxing holiday. *52 Lansdowne Rd., tel. 01/685512. 28 rooms with bath. Facilities: restaurant (wine license only), lounge, parking. AE, MC, V. Closed Dec. 21–Jan. 31.*

Ashling. This family-run hotel sits on the edge of the river Liffey, close to Heuston Station. Some may find that the Ashling's relentlessly bright modern decor verges on the garish. It has a faithful following, however, not least because of its proximity to Phoenix Park and its friendly staff. The center of town is a brisk 10–15 minute walk away, taking in many famed landmarks en route. *Parkgate St., Kingsbridge, tel. 01/772324. 56 rooms with bath. AE, DC, MC, V.*

Clarence. You'll find the Clarence either charmingly old-fashioned or just plain dowdy; it's all a matter of taste. Most of its Edwardian interior is dominated by oak-paneled walls and solid leather sofas and chairs. The restaurant and lobby have been prettified by fake Art Deco drapes and cane chairs. The bedrooms are small and functional: no frills here. Its central Liffey-side location is relentlessly urban. Beware of early-morning traffic noise in the front bedrooms. It remains an excellent place to meet a cross section of Dubliners and mildly eccentric provincials. *6–7 Wellington Quay, tel. 01/776178. 67 rooms with bath. Facilities: restaurant. AE, DC, MC, V.*

Leeson Court. Two 18th-century terraced houses have been combined to form this recently opened hotel, which is close to St. Stephen's Green. The small bedrooms are all cheerfully decorated in matching colors, with thick carpeting and stained-wood furnishings. The tiled bathrooms are surprisingly spacious. In spite of double-glazing, there is some daytime traffic noise. The conservatory at the back of the hotel faces a pleasant patio and beer garden. The basement nightclub is fully soundproofed from the rest of the building. *26–27 Lower Leeson St., Dublin 2, tel. 01/763380. 20 rooms. Facilities: bar, nightclub, restaurant. AE, DC, MC, V.*

Royal Dublin. This new (1991) centrally located Best Western hotel is just within the moderate category if you choose a "standard" room. Its modern facade dominates the top end of busy O'Connell Street. The interior incorporates part of a building that dates from 1752, providing an elegant and relaxing lounge area and restaurant. In contrast, Raffles Bar is a lively spot with a busy local trade. The rooms, decorated in pleasant pastel shades, are exceptionally well-appointed by Dublin standards for this price range, and have floor-to-ceiling windows. *40 Upper O'Connell St., tel. 01/733666. 120 rooms with bath. AE, DC, MC, V.*

Inexpensive   **Abrae Court Guest House.** This is a typical, large early-Victorian house in the highly respectable suburb of Rathgar. It's a 10-minute bus ride to the center of Dublin. There are six bedrooms in the main house; the rest are in a carefully designed period-style annex with ornate stucco ceilings. All are furnished with Irish carpets and handcrafted Irish furniture. The restaurant is open for evening meals. *9 Zion Rd., Rathgar, tel. 01/979944. 14 rooms with bath. Facilities: restaurant (wine license only). AE, DC, MC, V.*

Clifton Court. This is one of Dublin's centralmost hotels, on the banks of the Liffey just below O'Connell Bridge—but don't get any romantic ideas about the views. A four-lane traffic artery runs between the tall narrow building and the river, and most of the rooms overlook an internal service area. There is a busy bar on the ground floor, and a busy restaurant in the basement. Rooms are small but well equipped for the price range. *O'Connell Bridge, Dublin 1, tel. 01/743535. 20 rooms, 13 with bath. AE, DC, MC, V.*

Kilronan House. This guest house, a five-minute walk from St. Stephen's Green, is a favorite with vacationers. The large, late-19th-century terraced house is well-converted, and the decor and furnishings are updated each year by the Murray family, who have run the place for the past 30 years. The bedrooms are pleasantly furnished with plush carpeting and pastel colored walls. *70 Adelaide Rd., Dublin 2, tel. 01/755266. 12 rooms. Closed Dec.23–Jan. 1. No credit cards.*

★ **Maples House.** According to the ITB's complex grading system, Maples House is a guest house; to the rest of the world, however, it is definitely a small hotel. The lobby of this Edwardian house is decked out with oil paintings, Waterford crystal chandeliers, and a discreetly modern carpet, and is dominated by a vast mirror-topped Victorian rococo sideboard that sets the tone for the ornate decor of the public rooms. The bedrooms are small but adequate, lacking the rococo splendor of the rest of the building. *Iona Rd., Glasnevin, tel. 01/303049. 21 rooms with bath. Facilities: grill restaurant and bar. AE, DC, MC, V. Closed Dec. 25, 26.*

Budget **Dublin International Youth Hostel.** Housed in a converted convent, it offers dormitory accommodations (up to 25 persons per room) and a few four-bed rooms. This is a spartan, inexpensive (around IR£6 per night) alternative to hotels; nonmembers of the international youth hosteling organization can stay for a small extra charge. The hostel is located north of Parnell Square, near the Mater Hospital. *51 Mountjoy St., Dublin 1, tel. 01/301766. 500 beds. No credit cards.*

The Gate. Its location atop O'Connell Street opposite the Gate Theatre gives this hotel its name. Its raison d'etre is a large, ground-floor nightclub-cum-disco, which is open on weekends. This need not bother residents, who have their own small but attractive lounge and restaurant at the top of the stairs. Rooms are plainly decorated and some overlook the busy life of Parnell Street. *80–81 Parnell St., Dublin 1, tel. 01/745253. 20 rooms, 18 with bath. AE, DC, MC, V.*

Kelly's. A small canopied door at street level labeled "Kelly's" is the only indication of this hotel that occupies the upper floors of a rambling old building. The tiny bar and the dining room are over-decorated in that mish-mash of styles with which veterans of budget European hotels will be only too familiar. Rooms vary in size and are furnished with only the basics (no TV or phone), the plumbing gurgles at night, but the staff is friendly and helpful, and its central location (between Trinity College and Dublin Castle) makes an excellent touring base. *26 S. Great George's St., Dublin 2, tel. 01/779277. 23 rooms, 19 with bath. AE, DC, MC, V.*

Kinlay House. This holiday hostel is an exception in that it has most of its beds in private rooms and only one dormitory. It is ideally located, a 5-minute walk from the gates of Trinity College on the edge of the buzzing Temple Bar area. Prices rise in relation to your privacy, peaking at IR£16.50 (including Continental breakfast) for a single room. There are 8 twin-bed rooms, and over 20 four- and six-bed rooms, some with private bathrooms. Tour groups and sports clubs take block bookings in winter, and in summer it is a favorite stopover for backpackers. Book well in advance to be sure of a place. *2–12 Lord Edward St., Dublin 2, tel. 01/679–6644. MC, V.*

Mount Herbert Guest House. Located close to the swank luxury hotels in the tree-lined inner suburb of Ballsbridge, a 10-minute bus ride from Dublin's center of town, the Mount Herbert is popular with budget-minded American visitors in the high season. Bedrooms are small, but all have 10-channel TV and hair dryers. There is no bar on the premises, but there are plenty to choose from nearby. *7 Herbert Rd., Ballsbridge, tel. 01/684321. 88 rooms, 77 with bath. Facilities: restaurant (wine license only). AE, DC, MC, V.*

519 M.P.H.

190 M.P.H.

75 M.P.H.

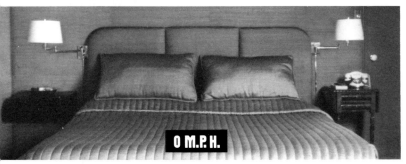

0 M.P.H.

WE LET YOU SEE EUROPE AT YOUR OWN PACE.

Regardless of your personal speed limits, Rail Europe offers everything to get you over, around and through anywhere you want in Europe. For more information, call your travel agent or **1-800-4-EURAIL.**

Rail Europe

MCI brings Europe and America closer together.

Call the U.S. for less with MCI CALL USA.

It's easy and affordable to call home when you use MCI CALL USA!

- Less expensive than calling through hotel operators
- Available from over 65 countries and locations worldwide
- You're connected to English-speaking MCI® Operators
- Even call 800 numbers in the U.S.

Call the U.S. for less from these European locations.

Dial the toll-free access number for the country you're calling from. Give the U.S. MCI Operator the number you're calling and the method of payment: MCI Card, U.S. local phone company card, Telecom Canada Card or collect. Your call will be completed!

Austria	022-903-012	Hungary	00*800-01411	Poland	0*-01-04-800-222
Belgium	078-11-00-12	Ireland	1800-551-001	Portugal	05-017-1234
Czechoslovakia	00-42-000112	Italy	172-1022	San Marino	172-1022
Denmark	8001-0022	Liechtenstein	155-0222	Spain	900-99-0014
Finland	9800-102-80	Luxembourg	0800-0112	Sweden	020-795-922
France	19*-00-19	Monaco	19*-00-19	Switzerland	155-0222
Germany	0130-0012	Netherlands	06*-022-91-22	United Kingdom	0800-89-0222
Greece	00-800-1211	Norway	050-12912	Vatican City	172-1022

* Wait for 2nd dial tone. Collect calls not accepted on MCI CALL USA calls to 800 numbers

Call 1-800-444-4444 in the U.S. to apply for your MCI Card® now!

The Arts

The fortnightly magazine *In Dublin* contains comprehensive details of upcoming events, including ticket availability. In peak season, consult the free ITB leaflet "Events of the Week."

Theaters Ireland has a rich theatrical tradition. The **Abbey Theatre,** Marlborough Street, is the home of Ireland's national theater company, its name forever associated with J. M. Synge, William Butler Yeats, and Sean O'Casey. The **Peacock Theatre** is the Abbey's more experimental small stage. The **Gate Theatre,** Parnell Square, is an intimate spot for modern drama and plays by Irish writers. The **Gaiety Theatre,** South King Street, features musical comedy, opera, drama, and revues. The **Olympia Theatre,** Dame Street, has seasons of comedy, vaudeville, and ballet. The **Project Arts Centre,** East Essex Street, is an established fringe theater. The new **National Concert Hall,** in Earlsfort Terrace, just off Stephen's Green, is the place to go for classical concerts.

Nightlife

Dublin does not have sophisticated nightclubs in the international sense. Instead, there is a choice of discos (often billed as nightclubs) and cabarets, catering mainly to visitors. There is also a very animated bar-pub scene—some places with live music and folksinging. No visit to this genial city will be complete without spending at least one evening exploring them.

Discos **New Annabels** (Mespil Rd., tel. 01/605222) is a popular late-evening spot; so is **The Pink Elephant** (S. Frederick St., tel. 01/775876).

Cabarets The following all offer Irish cabaret, designed to give visitors a taste of Irish entertainment: **Braemor Rooms** (Churchtown, tel. 01/988664); **Burlington Hotel** (Upper Leeson St., tel. 01/605222, open May–Oct.); **Jury's Hotel** (Ballsbridge, tel. 01/605000, open May–mid Oct.); **Abbey Tavern** (Howth, Co. Dublin, tel. 01/390307).

Pubs Check advertisements in evening papers for "sessions" of folk, ballad, Irish traditional, or jazz music. The **Brazen Head** (20 Lower Bridge St., tel. 01/779549)—Dublin's oldest pub, dating from 1688—and **O'Donoghue's** (15 Merrion Row, tel. 01/607194) feature some form of musical entertainment on most nights. Several of Dublin's centrally located pubs are noted for their character and ambience; they're usually at their liveliest from 5 to 7 PM and again from 10. The **Bailey** (2 Duke St.) is mentioned in *Ulysses* (under its original name, Burton's) and retains something of its Edwardian character, while **William Ryan's** (28 Parkgate St.) is a beautifully preserved Victorian gem. **Henry Grattan** (47–48 Lower Baggot St.) is popular with the business and sporting crowd; **O'Neill's Lounge Bar** (37 Pearse St.) is always busy with students and faculty from nearby Trinity College; and the **Palace Bar** (21 Fleet St.) is a journalists' haunt. You can eavesdrop on Dublin's social elite and their hangers-on at the expensive **Horseshoe Bar** in the Shelbourne Hotel or bask in the theatrical atmosphere of **Neary's** (Chatham St.)

For details on pubs serving food, *see* Dining in Staying in Ireland.

Cork

Many visitors find that Cork is closer to their idea of Ireland than the bustling capital city, Dublin. You'll be amazed at the difference in accent only 254 kilometers (158 miles) down the road, and you'll appreciate the slower and friendlier way of life. Cork is the base for an excursion to the famous Blarney Stone, and it is also well worth taking a trip down its magnificent harbor to visit the port of Cobh.

Getting Around

By Train The terminus at Cork is Kent Station. There are direct services from Dublin and Tralee and a suburban line to Cobh (tel. 021/504422 for information).

By Bus The main bus terminus in Cork is at Parnell Place (tel. 021/504422).

By Bicycle Bicycles can be rented from **D.M.D. Cycles** (3 Washington St., Cork, tel. 021/271529).

Guided Tours

CIE operates a number of trips from Parnell Place in Cork (tel. 021/273251).

Tourist Information

Tourist House (Grand Parade, Cork, tel. 021/273251).

Exploring Cork

Cork is the major metropolis of the south, and, with a population of about 138,000, the second largest city in Ireland. In the center of Cork, the Lee divides in two, giving the city a profusion of picturesque quays and bridges. The name Cork derives from the Irish *corcaigh*, meaning a marshy place. The city received its first charter in 1185 and grew rapidly in the 17th and 18th centuries with the expansion of its butter trade.

The main business and shopping center of Cork lies on the island created by the two diverging channels of the Lee, and most places of interest are within walking distance of the center. **Patrick Street** is the focal point of Cork. Here, you will find the city's most famous statue, that of **Father Theobald Mathew** (1790–1861), who led a nationwide temperance crusade, no small feat in a country as fond of a drink (or two) as this one. In the hilly area to the north of Patrick Street is the famous 120-foot **Shandon Steeple**, the bell tower of **St. Anne's Church**. It is shaped like a pepper pot and houses the bells immortalized in the song "The Bells of Shandon." Visitors can climb the tower; read the inscriptions on the bells; and, on request, have them rung over Cork.

Patrick Street is the main shopping area of Cork, and here you will find the city's two major department stores, **Roches** and **Cash's.** Cash's has a good selection of Waterford crystal. The liveliest place in town to shop is just off Patrick Street, to the west, near the city center parking lot, in the pedestrians-only **Paul Street** area. The **House of James** stocks the best in modern

Irish design, including tableware, ceramics, knitwear, hand-woven tweeds, and high fashion. The **Donegal Shop** next door specializes in made-to-order tweed suits and rain wear. At the top of Paul Street is the **Crawford Art Gallery,** which has an excellent collection of 18th- and 19th-century prints and modern arts. *Emmet Place, tel. 021/273377. Admission free. Open weekdays 10–5, Sat. 9–1.*

One of Cork's most famous sons was William Penn (1644–1718), founder of the Pennsylvania colony. He is only one of thousands who sailed from Cork's port, the Cove of Cork on Great Island, 24 kilometers (15 miles) down the harbor. **Cobh,** as it is known nowadays, can be reached by train from Kent Station, and the trip provides excellent views of the magnificent harbor. Cobh is an attractive hilly town dominated by its 19th-century **cathedral.** It was the first and last European port of call for transatlantic liners, one of which was the ill-fated *Titanic.* Cobh has other associations with shipwrecks: It was from here that destroyers were sent out in May 1915 to search for survivors of the *Lusitania,* torpedoed by a German submarine with the loss of 1,198 lives. Cobh's maritime past and its links with emigration will be documented in a new IR£2 million heritage center known as **The Queenstown Project,** due to open in the town's old railway station in early 1993. *Tel. 021/273251 for details.*

Fota Island, midway between Cork and Cobh, and accessible by rail, is a recent and very welcome addition to Cork's tourist attractions. The Royal Zoological Society has created a 238-square-kilometer (70-acre) wildlife park here. *Tel. 021/812555. Admission: IR£2.50 adults, IR£1.25 children and senior citizens. Car park: IR£1.25 per car. Open mid-Mar.–Sept., Tues.–Sat. 11–6, Sun. 1–6.*

Most visitors to Cork want to kiss the famous **Blarney Stone** in the hope of acquiring the "gift of gab." Blarney itself, 8 kilometers (5 miles) from Cork City, can be reached by the regular bus service from Parnell Bus Station. All that is left of **Blarney Castle** is its ruined central keep containing the celebrated stone. This is set in the battlements, and to kiss it, you must lie on the walk within the walls, lean your head back, and touch the stone with your lips. Nobody knows how the tradition originated, but Elizabeth I is credited with giving the word *blarney* to the language when, commenting on the unfulfilled promises of Cormac MacCarthy, Lord Blarney of the time, she remarked, "This is all Blarney; what he says, he never means." Adjoining the castle is a first-rate crafts shop. *Tel. 021/385252. Admission: IR£2.50 adults, IR£1.50 senior citizens, IR£1 children. Open Mon.–Sat. 9 to sundown, Sun. 9:30–5:30; winter, 9:30–sundown.*

Dining and Lodging

For details and price-category definitions, *see* Dining and Lodging in Staying in Ireland.

Cork
Dining

Jacques. You will find this little place on a side street behind the Imperial Hotel to be an inexpensive self-service restaurant at lunch time, and a more pricey, more intimate restaurant in the evenings. The owner-chef is famed for her imaginative use of Clonakilty black pudding (a local specialty related to the French *boudin* sausage), and her insistence on fresh local produce. She also served vegetarian and gluten-free dishes. *9*

Phoenix St., off Pembroke St., tel. 021/277387. Open Mon. 9–5, Tues.–Sat. 9–10:30. Reservations evenings only. AE, DC, MC, V. Budget (lunch), Moderate (dinner).

Oyster Tavern. This delightfully old-fashioned bar–restaurant has changed little during the past 30 years. *Market Lane, off Patrick St., tel. 021/272716. MC, V. Moderate.*

The Gallery Cafe. The food here is prepared by a team from Balleymaloe, one of Ireland's most famous country house hotels, and is the freshest and most elegant budget food in town, served amid statues and prints from the municipal art collection. *Crawford Gallery, Emmet Pl., tel. 021/274415. Open Mon., Tues., and Sat. 10:30–5:30; Wed.–Fri. 10:30–9:30. No credit cards. Inexpensive.*

Halpin's. This is a popular self-service restaurant at lunchtime; at night the atmosphere is more intimate. It serves generous salads, curries, and pizzas. *Cook St., MC, V. Inexpensive.*

The Huguenot. Situated in the fashionable Paul Street area, this is an atmospheric spot to enjoy unpretentious French cooking. The dark, high-ceilinged room is dominated by an elaborately carved mahogany fireplace, and additional seating is provided on a balustraded mezzanine. Lunchtime specials supplement the bistro-style menu, which is served continuously from 12:30. *French Church St., tel. 021/273357. Reservations advised. AE, DC, MC, V. Closed Sun. Inexpensive.*

Beechers Inn. This tiny bar in a narrow alley off Patrick Street turns into a bustling restaurant at lunchtime, serving homemade soup, seafood sandwiches, and a selection of hot specials. *Faulkeners La., Patrick St., tel. 01/273144. No credit cards. Budget.*

The Long Valley. Resist the familiar neighborhood fast-food fare and try this extraordinary, mildly eccentric bar, which is just across from the General Post Office. Nip in for one of their amazing "doorstep" sandwiches, the meat freshly cut before your eyes from vast hunks of home-baked ham or hot salt beef. *Winthrop St., tel. 021/272144. No reservations. No credit cards. Budget.*

Lodging **Arbutus Lodge.** This exceptionally comfortable hotel has an
★ outstanding restaurant and panoramic views of the city and the river. *Middle Glanmire Rd., Montenotte, tel. 021/501237. 20 rooms with bath. AE, DC, MC, V. Closed 1 week at Christmas. Moderate.*

Moore's. Good for its central location on a quiet part of the riverbank, the hotel has a fine reputation for friendliness and personal attention. *Morrison's Island, tel. 021/271291. 36 rooms, most with bath. MC, V. Moderate.*

Lotamore House. A five-minute bus ride from town is a small drawback in return for a well-equipped room in a Georgian manor situated in its own grounds overlooking the River Lee. *Tivoli., tel. 021/822344. 20 rooms with bath. AE, MC, V. Inexpensive.*

★ **Victoria Lodge.** Originally built in the early 20th century as a Capuchin monastery, this exceptionally well-appointed B&B is located a five-minute drive from the town center; it is also on several bus routes. The rooms are simple but comfortable, with views over the lodge's own grounds. Breakfast is served in the spacious old refectory. *Victoria Cross, tel. 021/542233. 32 rooms with bath. Facilities: TV lounge. MC. V. Inexpensive.*

Gabriel House. Convenient for both bus and train stations, this well-run Victorian guest house offers well-equipped rooms and boasts many satisfied customers. *Summerhill, St. Luke's., tel. 021/500333. 20 rooms with bath. AE, DC, MC, V. Budget.*

Sheila's Cork Tourist Hotel. One of the easy-going chain of Independent Hostels with no petty rules, this is a popular economy stopover for backpackers. *Wellington Rd., tel. 021/343531. 100 beds in dormitories, 20 in double rooms. Budget.*

Glenvera House. A Victorian town house, the Glenvera is just three minutes from the bus and train stations. *Wellington Rd., tel. 021/502030. 34 rooms. All rooms have showers, toilets, and televisions. No credit cards. Budget.*

Killarney

Killarney is undoubtedly the most scenic and beautiful part of Ireland, where mountains and lakes combine with luxuriant vegetation to create unforgettable vistas: a deep blue sky reflected in the blue waters of the chain of lakes, surrounded by giant tangles of dark green foliage. Seasoned travelers have been captivated by Killarney ever since it was first "discovered" in the late 18th-century, and many visitors return year after year to relax in the balmy mountain air.

Getting Around

By Bus   Buses offer a more flexible service than do trains; details are available from local tourist information offices.

By Bicycle   You can rent bicycles from **O'Callaghan Bros.** (College St., Killarney, tel. 064/31465), **D. O'Neill** (Plunkett St., Killarney, tel. 064/315900).

Tourist Information

All tourist information offices are open weekdays 9–6, Sat. 9–1.

Killarney (Town Hall, tel. 064/31633).
Shannon Airport (tel. 061/61664).

Exploring Killarney

Killarney itself is an undistinguished market town, well developed to handle the tourist trade that flourishes here in the peak season. To find the famous scenery, you must head out of town toward the lakes that lie in a valley running south between the mountains. Part of Killarney's lake district is within **Killarney National Park.** At the heart of the park is the 40,470-square-kilometer (10,000-acre) **Muckross Estate** (open Easter–May and Sept.–Oct., daily 8–7; June–Aug., daily 9–5). Cars are not allowed in the estate, so if you don't want to walk, rent a bicycle in town or take a trip in a jaunting car—a small two-wheeled horse-drawn cart. At the center of the estate is **Muckross House,** a 19th-century manor that contains a folk museum and visitor center. *Tel. 064/31440. Admission: IR£2 adults, IR£1 children. Open Sept.–Oct., daily 9–6; Nov.–mid-Mar., daily 11–5; July and Aug., daily 9–7.*

To get an idea of the splendor of the lakes and streams—of the massive glacial sandstone and limestone rocks and lush vegetation that characterize the Killarney district—take one of the day-long tours of the **Gap of Dunloe, the Upper Lake, Long**

Range, Middle and **Lower lakes,** and **Ross Castle.** The central section, the Gap of Dunloe, is not suitable for cars, but horses and jaunting cars are available at **Kate Kearney's Cottage,** which marks the entrance to the gap.

The **Ring of Kerry** will add about 176 kilometers (110 miles) to your trip, but in good weather it provides a pleasant experience. All Killarney-based tour operators offer day trips of the Ring by coach or minibus. **Kenmare** is a small market town 34 kilometers (21 miles) from Killarney at the head of Kenmare Bay. Across the water, as you drive out along the Iveragh Peninsula, will be views of the gray-blue mountain ranges of the Beara Peninsula. **Sneem,** on the estuary of the river Ardsheelaun, is one of the prettiest villages in Ireland, although its English-style central green makes it an exception among Irish villages. Beyond the next village, Caherdaniel, is **Derrynane House,** home of the 19th-century politician and patriot Daniel O'Connell, "The Liberator," and completed by him in 1825. It still contains much of its original furniture. *Tel. 0667/ 5113. Admission: IR£1 adults, 30p children and senior citizens. Open mid-June–Sept., daily 10–1 and 2–7; Oct.–mid-June, Tues.–Sat. 10–1, Sun. 2–5.*

The village of **Waterville** is famous as an angling center; it also has a fine sandy beach and a championship golf course. Offshore, protruding in conical shapes from the Atlantic, are the **Skellig Rocks,** which contain the cells of early Christian monks. Beyond Cahirciveen, you are on the other side of the Ring, with views across Dingle Bay to the rugged peaks of the Dingle Peninsula. At the head of the bay is **Killorglin,** which has a three-day stint of unbridled merrymaking the first weekend in August, known as Puck Fair.

If time and the weather are on your side, take an organized day-tour by coach or minibus, or an overnight trip on the regular bus service (July and August only) from Killarney to the **Dingle Peninsula**—one of the wildest and least spoiled regions of Ireland—taking in the **Connor Pass, Mount Brandon, the Gallarus Oratory,** and stopping at **Dunquin** to hear some of Ireland's best traditional musicians. For an adventure off the beaten path, arrange for a boat ride to the **Blasket Islands** and spend a few blissful hours wandering along the cliffs.

Dining and Lodging

For details and price-category definitions, *see* Dining and Lodging in Staying in Ireland.

Dingle Beginish. The best of several small but sophisticated restau-
Dining rants in town, this relaxing place serves local meat and seafood in a generous version of nouvelle cuisine. *Green St., tel. 066/ 51588. AE, DC, MC, V. Closed Mon. and Nov. 1–Mar. Moderate.*

The Islandman. This place is a combination of bar, bookshop, café, and restaurant furnished in simple art-nouveau style. Snacks and light meals are served all day; the more serious dinner menu is worth lingering over. *Main St., tel. 066/51803. AE, DC, MC, V. Budget–Inexpensive (dinner).*

Lodging Benner's. This busy town-center hotel has been beautifully restored with country-pine antique furniture in all bedrooms.

Main St., tel. 066/51638. 25 rooms with bath. Facilities: 2 bars, restaurant. AE, DC, MC, V. Moderate.

The Alpine. This modern three-story guest house just outside Dingle town (a three-minute walk) is a better bet than most of the B&Bs in town; it has good ocean views from the front rooms. *Tel. 066/51250. 14 rooms with bath. No credit cards. Closed Dec.–Feb. Budget.*

Killarney **Foley's.** This popular eatery specializes in seafood, steaks, and
Dining Kerry mountain lamb. *23 High St., tel. 064/31217. AE, DC,*
★ *MC, V. Moderate.*
★ **Gaby's.** For simple and fresh seafood, Gaby's can't be beat. *17 High St., tel. 064/32519. AE, DC, MC, V. Closed Sun. (except for dinner in July and Aug.), Mon. lunch, and Dec.–mid-Mar. Moderate.*

The Strawberry Tree. A young and enthusiastic team of chefs prepares an imaginative nouvelle-cuisine influenced menu from the freshest local ingredients, in this intimate, relaxing town-center restaurant. *24 Plunkett St., tel. 064/32688. Open 12:30– 3:30 and 6:30–10:30. AE, DC, MC, V. Moderate.*

West End House. Hearty meat-eaters will be well satisfied with the steak or Kerry lamb cooked on an open charcoal grill at this friendly, informal wine bar-restaurant. *Lower New St., tel. 064/32271. Open noon–4 and 6–11, closed Sun. AE, MC, V. Inexpensive.*

An Sugan. Even if you would not consider staying in a hostel, you'll find this one's restaurant a friendly and informal place to fill up on warming bistro-style food. *Lewis Rd., tel. 064/33104. Open 6–9, closed Mon. Budget.*

Sheila's. This reliable, family-run restaurant has been feeding visitors of Killarney for over 30 years. Brightly lit and simply furnished with pine tables and red paper mats, the menu has a good selection of traditional Irish dishes, as well as international favorites like burgers and pizzas. *75 High St., tel. 064/31270. MC, V. Budget.*

Lodging **Arbutus.** Newly refurbished and centrally located, the Arbutus benefits from a lively bar and an Old World atmosphere. *College St., tel. 064/31037. 35 rooms with bath. AE, DC, MC, V. Moderate.*

East Avenue. This centrally located mock-timber building offers better comfort and cleanliness than many older hotels nearby. *East Ave., tel. 064/32522. 25 rooms with bath. AE, DC, MC, V. Inexpensive.*

Kathleen's Country House. Situated on the Tralee Road 2 kilometers (1 mile) outside town, this is an imaginatively designed modern guest house with spacious, prettily decorated rooms. The owner-manager, Kathleen, maintains exacting standards of comfort and cleanliness. *Tralee Rd., tel. 064/ 32810. 15 rooms with bath. Restaurant (dinner only). No credit cards. Inexpensive.*

Aghadoe House. This establishment is generally considered the Hilton of the Irish Youth Hostel Association's properties. The glorious Victorian-Gothic mansion in its own lakeside grounds is something of a tourist attraction in itself, and the views are better than in all but the most expensive hotels. *Aghadoe, tel. 064/31240. 220 dormitory beds. V. Budget.*

An Sugan. A long-established member of the chain of Independent Hostels, this is the liveliest of the town center hostels, although, like all of them, it is small and rather cramped. The friendly restaurant, which often has live music, makes up for the lack of elbow room. *Lewis Rd., tel. 064/33104. 18 dormitory beds. No credit cards. Budget.*

Linden House. This family-run guest house is located in a functional 1960s suburban home, a two-minute walk from the town center. The quietest rooms are in the back. *New Rd., tel. 064/31379. 20 rooms with bath. Restaurant (dinner only). V. Budget.*

The Northwest

This route from Galway to Westport and Sligo takes you through the rugged landscape of Connemara to the fabled Yeats country in the northwest, passing some of the wildest and loneliest parts of Ireland. Galway still has a number of Irish-speaking residents, who contribute to its lively arts scene.

Getting Around

By Train Trains to Galway, Westport, and Sligo operate from Dublin's Heuston or Connolly (Sligo) stations. There is no train service north of Sligo.

By Bus Travel within the area is more flexible by bus; details are available from local tourist information offices.

By Bicycle You can rent bikes from **Salthill Rentals** (Galway City, tel. 091/22085), **John Mannion** (Railway View, Clifden, tel. 095/21160), or **Gerry Conway** (Wine St., Sligo, tel. 071/61240).

Tourist Information

All are open weekdays 9–6, Sat. 9–1.

Galway (off Eyre Sq., tel. 091/63081).
Sligo (Temple St., tel. 071/61201).
Westport (The Mall, tel. 098/25711).

Exploring the Northwest

Galway City is the gateway to the ancient province of Connacht, the most westerly seaboard in Europe. Galway City was well established even before the Normans arrived in the 13th century, rebuilding the city walls and turning the little town into a flourishing port. Later its waterfront was frequented by Spanish grandees and traders. The salmon fishing in the river Corrib, which flows through the lower part of the town, is unsurpassed. In early summer, you can stand on the **Weir Bridge** beside the town's cathedral and watch thousands of salmon as they leap and twist through the narrow access to the inner lakes. **Lynch's Castle** in Shop Street, now a bank, is a good example of a 16th-century fortified house—fortified because the neighboring Irish tribes persistently raided Galway City, whose commercial life excluded them. Nowadays the liveliest part of town is around the area between **Eyre Square** (the town's center) and **Spanish Arch.** Galway is a compact city, best explored on foot.

Galway has a lively and informal arts scene, particularly in mid-August during its annual Arts Festival. It is the home base of the **Druid Theatre;** if the group is performing, a visit to the tiny auditorium is highly recommended.

On the west bank of the Corrib estuary, just outside of the Galway town walls, is the **Claddagh,** said to be the oldest fishing village in Ireland. **Salthill Promenade,** with its lively seaside amenities, is the traditional place "to sit and watch the moon rise over Claddagh, and see the sun go down on Galway Bay"—in the words of the city's most famous song.

Westport is a quiet, mainly 18th-century town overlooking Clew Bay—a wide expanse of water studded with nearly 400 islands. The distinctive silhouette of **Croagpatrick,** a 775-meter mountain, dominates the town. Today some 25,000 pilgrims climb it on the last Sunday in July in honor of St. Patrick, who is believed to have spent 40 days fasting on its summit in AD 441. Whether he did or not, the climb is an exhilarating experience and can be completed in about three hours; it should be attempted only in good weather, however.

County Sligo is noted for its seaside resorts, the famous golf course at Rosse's Point (just outside Sligo Town), and its links with Ireland's most famous 20th-century poet, William Butler Yeats, who is buried just north of **Sligo Town** at Drumcliffe. An important collection of paintings by the poet's brother, Jack B. Yeats, can be seen in the **Sligo Museum** (Stephen St., tel. 071/ 42212), which also has displays on the folk life of the area. Take a boat from Sligo up to **Lough Gill** and see the **Lake Isle of Innisfree** and other places immortalized in the poetry of W. B. Yeats. His grave is found beneath the slopes of Ben Bulben, just north of the town. Nearby is **Lissadell House,** a substantial mansion dating from 1830 that features prominently in his writings. It was the home of Constance Gore-Booth, later Countess Markeviecz, who took part in the 1916 uprising. *Tel. 071/63150. Admission: IR£1.50 adults, 50p children. Open May–Sept., Mon.–Sat. 2:25–5:15.*

Dining and Lodging

For details and price-category definitions, *see* Dining and Lodging in Staying in Ireland.

Galway City
Dining

Malt House. This is a cheerful, relaxing pub-restaurant hidden away in a shopping arcade. *Olde Malte Arcade, High St., tel. 091/67866. AE, MC, V. Closed Dec. 24–30. Moderate.*

Noctan's. This excellent, small French restaurant is situated above a popular pub. *17 Cross St., tel. 091/66172. MC, V. Dinner only. Closed Sun.–Mon. Moderate.*

Rabbitts. Just off Eyre Square opposite the railway station you will find this long-established, family-run restaurant adjoining a bar. It serves good steaks, local seafood, and traditional Irish dishes. *23–25 Forster St., tel. 091/66490. Open 12:30–2:30 and 6:30–10:30. AE, DC, MC, V. Inexpensive.*

The Brasserie. The decor and ambience here are French café-style, but the food is predominantly American—ribs, pizzas, tacos, and burgers. *Middle St., tel. 091/61610. Closed Sun. and holidays. AE, DC, MC, V. Budget.*

Conlon's. Opposite the General Post office, this place serves the freshest fish at the lowest prices. Upstairs is a take-out counter and downstairs a café serving oysters, chowder, and a selection of fresh fish with chips or salad. *Eglinton St., tel. 091/62268. No credit cards. Budget.*

Lodging **Ardilaun House.** This hotel is set in pleasant grounds midway between Galway City and the seaside suburb of Salthill. *Taylors Hill, tel. 091/21433. 91 rooms with bath. AE, DC, MC, V. Moderate.*

Anno Santo. This is a small family-run hotel with rooms in a modern annex adjoining the original bungalow. It is about 300 meters (320 yards) from the sea on a residential road in the seaside suburb, Salthill. *Threadneedle Rd., Salthill, tel. 091/ 23011. 14 rooms with bath. AE, DC, MC, V. Inexpensive.*

The Skeffington. This Victorian landmark on the west side of Eyre Square has been fully modernized, but the rooms still retain a certain period charm. *28 Eyre Sq., tel. 091/63173. 22 rooms with bath. AE, MC, V. Inexpensive.*

The Banba. All the rock-bottom hotels in Galway are clustered along the seafront in Salthill. This one is preferable because it does not have a nightclub, so your sleep is less likely to be disturbed. *Upper Salthill., tel. 091/21944. 29 rooms, 2 with bath. V. Budget.*

Sligo Town **Reflections.** Located in the center of town, Reflections is a mod-
Dining ern restaurant. *Gratten St., tel. 071/43828. MC, V. Moderate.*

Lodging **Ballincar House.** Just outside of town, this converted country house with gardens serves excellent food. *Rosses Point Rd., tel. 071/45361. 20 rooms with bath. Facilities: squash, tennis, sauna, solarium. AE, DC, MC, V. Closed Dec. 23–Jan. 12. Moderate.*

Sligo Park. This is a modern two-story building, set in spacious grounds. *Pearse Rd., tel. 071/60291. 60 rooms with bath. AE, DC, MC, V. Moderate.*

Southern. This solid, four-story, 19th-century hotel is set in its own pretty gardens. *Lord Edward St., tel. 071/62101. 50 rooms, most with bath. AE, DC, MC, V. Inexpensive.*

Westport **Asgard.** The Asgard is a pub with award-winning food in both
Dining its bar and second-floor restaurant. *The Quay, tel. 098/25319. AE. Inexpensive.*

Quay Cottage. This tiny waterside cottage is a wine bar-cum-restaurant crammed with nautical bric-a-brac and specializing in simple dishes of the freshest seafood. *The Quay, tel. 098/ 26412. AE, V. Inexpensive.*

Lodging **Old Railway.** A delightful Victorian hotel in the town center, the Old Railway has been fully refurbished with no loss of character. *The Mall, tel. 098/25166. 20 rooms with bath. Facilities: 2 restaurants, 2 bars, fishing. AE, DC, MC, V. Moderate.*

Clew Bay. Built in the 1960s, this is an unassuming and well-run town center hotel with friendly, helpful staff. *James St., tel. 098/25438. 27 rooms with bath. AE, DC, MC, V. Inexpensive.*

15   Italy

taly has great art, historic cities, dazzling landscapes, delectable food and wines and, of course, the many curious charms of the Italians themselves. The country is also a real challenge to the budget-conscious tourist, because the days of laughably low-price hotels and inexpensive meals are gone forever. Italy's higher standard of living has brought an increase in the cost of living as well, and it is at present one of the most expensive countries in Europe.

You will have to spend more than ever before on dining and lodging, and you will probably have to settle for fewer creature comforts in order to stay within your budget. Still, it costs nothing to walk through the twisting streets of Rome, Venice, or Florence, past ancient palaces and time-honored churches, and it costs little to admire some of the world's greatest art in sumptuous settings. This Mediterranean country has profoundly contributed to the Western way of life, and has produced some of the world's greatest thinkers, writers, politicians, saints, and artists. Impressive traces of their lives and works can still be seen in the great buildings and lovely countryside.

The whole of Italy is one vast attraction, but the triangle of its most-visited cities—Rome (Roma), Florence (Firenze), and Venice (Venezia)—gives a good idea of the great variety to be found here. In Rome and Florence, especially, you can feel the uninterrupted flow of the ages, from the Classical era of the ancient Romans to the bustle and throb of contemporary life carried on in centuries-old settings. Venice, by contrast, seems suspended in time, the same today as it was when it held sway over the eastern Mediterranean and the Orient. Each of these cities presents a different aspect of the Italian character: the

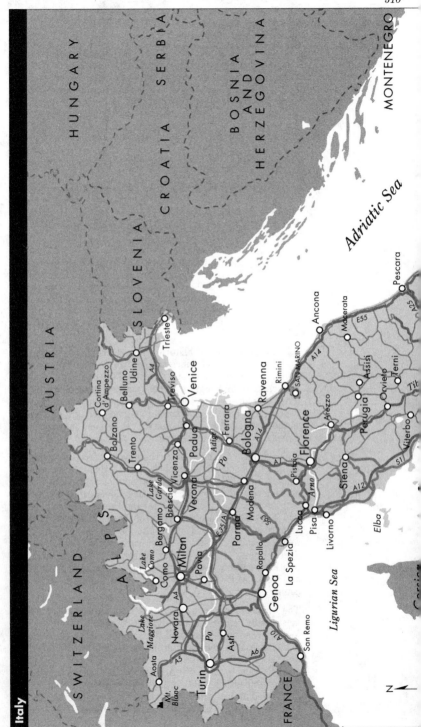

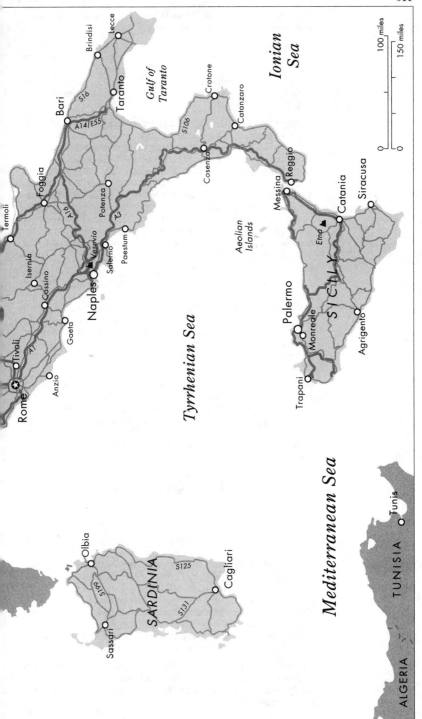

Baroque exuberance of Rome, Florence's serene stylishness, and the dreamy sensuality of Venice.

The uninhibited Italian lifestyle can be entertaining or irritating, depending on how you look at it. Rarely do things run like clockwork here; you are more likely to encounter unexplained delays and incomprehensible complications. Relax: There's usually something you can smile about even in the darkest circumstances.

Trying to soak in Italy's rich artistic heritage is a great challenge to tourists. The country's many museums and churches draw hordes of visitors, all wanting to see the same thing at the same time. From May through September, the Sistine Chapel, Michelangelo's *David*, St. Mark's Square, and other key sights are more often than not swamped by mobs of fellow tourists. Try to see the highlights at off-peak times in the day. Off-season travel has significant advantages for the budget tourist. Not only are there fewer people competing for elbow room at the major sights, but costs may be lower, especially for value-conscious prepaid package tours and for special off-season discount plans offered locally.

Even in the major tourist cities, Italians generally take a friendly interest in their visitors. Only the most blasé waiters and salespeople will be less than courteous and helpful. However, the persistent attention Italian males pay to foreign females can be oppressive and annoying. If you're not interested, the best tactic is to ignore them. But do not ignore matters of personal security; in particular, always be on guard against pickpockets and purse snatchers in Rome and in Naples. Small cities and towns are usually safe.

Making the most of your time in Italy doesn't mean rushing through it. To gain a rich appreciation, don't try to see everything all at once. Do what you really want to do, and if that means skipping a museum to sit at a pretty café, enjoying the sunshine and a cappuccino, you're getting into the Italian spirit. Art—and life—are to be enjoyed, and the Italians can show you how.

Essential Information

Before You Go

When to Go The main tourist season in Italy runs from mid-April to the end of September. The best months for sightseeing are April, May, June, September, and October, when the weather is generally pleasant and not too hot. Foreign tourists crowd the major cities at Easter, when Italians flock to resorts and the countryside. Avoid traveling in August, when the heat can be oppressive and when vacationing Italians cram roads, trains, and planes, as well as beach and mountain resorts. Especially around the August 15 holiday, such cities as Rome and Milan are deserted, and many restaurants and shops close.

The hottest months are July and August, when brief afternoon thunderstorms are common in inland areas. Winters are relatively mild in most places on the tourist circuit, but there are always some rainy spells.

Although low-season rates do not apply at hotels in Rome, Florence, and Milan, you can save on hotel accommodations in Venice and in some summer resorts during their low seasons—the winter, early spring, and late-autumn months. Tourist boards and hotel associations in Florence and Venice often offer bargain packages during the winter that include special hotel rates and discounts in restaurants, shops, and museums. If business is slow, even hotels in Rome, Florence, and Milan may be willing to negotiate lower rates.

Climate The following are average daily maximum and minimum temperatures for Rome.

Jan.	52F	11C	May	74F	23C	Sept.	79F	26C
	40	5		56	13		62	17
Feb.	55F	13C	June	82F	28C	Oct.	71F	22C
	42	6		63	17		55	13
Mar.	59F	15C	July	87F	30C	Nov.	61F	16C
	45	7		67	20		49	9
Apr.	66F	19C	Aug.	86F	30C	Dec.	55F	13C
	50	10		67	20		44	6

The following are average daily maximum and minimum temperatures for Milan.

Jan.	40F	5C	May	74F	23C	Sept.	75F	24C
	32	0		57	14		61	16
Feb.	46F	8C	June	80F	27C	Oct.	63F	17C
	35	2		63	17		52	11
Mar.	56F	13C	July	84F	29C	Nov.	51F	10C
	43	6		67	20		43	6
Apr.	65F	18C	Aug.	82F	28C	Dec.	43F	6C
	49	9		66	16		35	2

Currency The unit of currency in Italy is the lira (plural, lire). There are bills of 1,000, 2,000, 5,000, 10,000, 50,000, and 100,000 lire; coins are worth 10, 20, 50, 100, 200, and 500 lire. At press time (summer 1992), the exchange rate was about 1,400 lire to the dollar and 2,200 lire to the pound sterling. Sooner or later the zeros will be lopped off the lire in order to simplify money dealings and life in general. The long-heralded move has not yet been made, but it seems imminent. If and when it does come to pass, 5,000 lire would become 5 lire, 50 lire would become 50 centesimi. Both old and new values would be in effect until people became accustomed to the new system.

While the present system continues, especially when your purchases run into hundreds of thousands of lire, beware of being shortchanged, a dodge that is practiced at ticket windows and cashiers' desks, as well as in shops and banks. *Always count your change before you leave the counter.*

Always carry some smaller-denomination bills for sundry purchases; you're less likely to be shortchanged, and you won't have to face the eye-rolling dismay of cashiers chronically short of change.

Credit cards are generally accepted in shops and hotels, but may not be welcome in restaurants, so always look for those little signs in the window or ask when you enter to avoid embarrassing situations. When you wish to leave a tip beyond the 15% service charge (*see* Staying in Italy, Tipping, *below*) that is usually included with your bill, leave it in cash rather than adding it to the credit card slip.

What It Will Cost Rome and Florence, and, especially, Milan and Venice are the more expensive Italian cities to visit. Taxes are usually included in hotel bills; a cover charge appears as a separate item in restaurant checks, as does the service charge, usually about 15%, if added. Admission to state-owned museums is free to those under 18 and those over 60.

Sample Prices A cup of espresso consumed while standing at a bar costs from 800 lire to 1,200 lire, triple that for table service. A bottle of beer costs from 2,000 lire to 3,500 lire, a soft drink costs about 1,800 lire. A *tramezzino* (small sandwich) costs about 1,800 lire, a more substantial one about 3,000. You will pay about 8,000 lire for a short taxi ride in Rome, less in Florence, more in Milan. Admission to a major museum is about 10,000 lire; a three-hour sightseeing tour, about 36,000 lire.

Customs on Arrival Two still cameras and one movie camera can be brought in duty-free. Travelers arriving in Italy from an EC (European Community) country are allowed, duty-free, a total of 300 cigarettes (*or* 150 cigarillos *or* 75 cigars), 3 liters of still wine plus 1½ liters of spirits over 22% volume (or 3 liters if under 22%— or 3 more liters of table wine), and 90 milliliters of perfume and 375 milliliters of toiletwater if duty and taxes have been paid on them at the time of purchase. Visitors traveling directly from non-European countries are allowed 400 cigarettes and cigars or tobacco not exceeding 500 grams, ¾ liter of spirits, and 2 liters of still wine. Not more than 2 million lire in Italian bank notes may be taken into or out of the country.

Language Italy is accustomed to English-speaking tourists, and in major cities you will find that many people speak at least a little English. In smaller hotels and restaurants, a smattering of Italian comes in handy.

Getting Around

By Train The fastest trains on the FS (Ferrovie dello Stato), the state-owned railroad, are the *intercity* trains, for which you pay a supplement and for which seat reservations may be required (and are always advisable). *Espresso* trains usually make more stops and are a little slower. *Diretto* and *locale* are slowest of all. You can buy tickets and make seat reservations at travel agencies displaying the FS symbol, avoiding long lines at station ticket windows, up to two months in advance. Tickets for stops within a 100-km (62-mi) range can be purchased at any *tabacchi* (tobacconist's shop). There is a refreshment service on all long-distance trains. Tap water on trains is not drinkable. Carry compact bags for easy overhead storage. Trains are very crowded at holiday times; always reserve.

By Plane **Alitalia** and domestic affiliate **ATI,** plus several privately owned companies, provide service throughout Italy. Alitalia offers several discount fares; inquire at travel agencies or at Alitalia agencies in major cities.

By Bus An extensive network of bus routes provides service throughout Italy. A timetable of routes of interest to tourists is published by **ANAC** (Piazza Esquilino 29, Rome) and distributed by travel agencies.

By Boat Ferries connect the mainland with all the major islands. Lake ferries connect the towns on the shores of the Italian lakes: Como, Maggiore, and Garda.

Staying in Italy

Telephones Pay phones take either 100- or 200-lire coins, a *gettone* (token),
Local Calls or magnetic card. Some older phones take only tokens, which you insert in the slot before picking up the receiver; dial, and when your party answers, push the little knob on the slot to release the token and complete the connection. Tokens can be purchased from the token machine or from the cashier of the store, bar, or other facility where the phone is located. Local calls cost 200 lire for nine minutes. For *teleselezione* (long-distance direct dialing), place several coins in the slot; unused coins are returned when you push the large yellow knob. Buy magnetic cards at tobacconists.

International Calls Since hotels tend to add exorbitant service charges for long-distance and international calls, it's best to go to the "Telefoni" telephone exchange, where the operator assigns you a booth, can help place your call, and will collect payment when you have finished. Telephone exchanges (usually marked *SIP* or, in Rome, *ASST)* are found in all cities. The cheaper and easier option, however, will be to use your AT&T or MCI calling card. For AT&T, dial access number 172–1011; and for MCI, dial access number 172–1022. An English-speaking operator will then ask for your calling card number and proceed to connect you through to the United States.

Operators and For Europe and the Mediterranean area, dial 15; for interconti-
Information nental service, dial 170.

Mail The Italian mail system is notoriously erratic and often excruciatingly slow. Allow up to 21 days for mail to and from the United States and Canada, almost as much to and from the United Kingdom, and much longer for postcards.

Postal Rates Airmail letters to the United States cost 1,100 lire for up to 20 grams; postcards with a short greeting and signature cost 950 lire, but cost letter rate if the message is lengthy. Airmail letters to the United Kingdom cost 750 lire, postcards 650 lire.

Receiving Mail You can have mail sent to American Express offices or to Italian post offices, marked "Fermo Posta" and addressed to you c/o Palazzo delle Poste, with the name of the city in which you will pick it up. In either case you must show your passport and pay a small fee.

Shopping Most shops now have *prezzi fissi* (fixed prices), but you may be
Bargaining able to get a discount on a large purchase. Always bargain with a street vendor or at a market (except for food).

Opening and **Banks.** Banks are open weekdays 8:30–1:30 and from 2:45 to
Closing Times 3:45.

Churches. Churches are usually open from early morning to noon or 12:30, when they close for about two hours or more, opening again in the afternoon until about 7 PM.

Museums. National museums are usually open until 2 and closed on Monday, but there are many exceptions. Other museums have entirely different hours, which may vary according to season. Archaeological sites are usually closed on Monday. At all museums and sites, ticket offices close an hour or so before official closing time. Always check with the local tourist office for current hours.

Shops. Shops are open, with individual variations, from 9 to 1 and from 3:30 or 4 to 7 or 7:30. They are open from Monday through Saturday, but close for a half-day during the week; for example, in Rome most shops (except food shops) are closed on Monday morning or Saturday afternoon in July and August. Some tourist-oriented shops are open all day, every day, as in Venice.

National Holidays January 1; January 6 (Epiphany); April 12 (Easter Monday); April 25 (Liberation Day); May 1 (May Day); June 2 (Republic Day); August 15 (the religious feast of the Assumption, known as Ferragosto, when cities are literally deserted and most restaurants and shops are closed); November 1 (All Saints Day); December 8 (Immaculate Conception); December 25 and 26.

Dining Generally speaking, a *ristorante* pays more attention to decor, service, and menu than does a *trattoria*, which is simpler and often family-run. An *osteria* used to be a lowly tavern, though now the term may be used to designate a chic and expensive eatery. A *tavola calda* offers hot dishes and snacks, with seating. A *rosticceria* has the same, to take out.

The menu is always posted in the window or just inside the door of an eating establishment. Check to see what is offered, and note the charges for *coperto* (cover) and *servizio* (service), which will increase your check. A *menu turistico* includes taxes and service, but beverages are extra. When ordering, remember that seafood is usually pricey and that anything marked "s.q." (according to quantity) or "al hg." or "all 'etto" (both referring to weight in hectograms) will invariably be expensive. To keep meal costs down, forego fruit or dessert, which you can pick up at a street market or local bakery for a better price. At lunchtime look for coffee bars with food counters selling cold or toasted sandwiches, or go to one of the ubiquitous pizza counters.

Mealtimes Lunch hour in Rome lasts from 1 to 3, dinner from 8 to 10. Service begins and ends a half-hour earlier in Florence and Venice, later in the south. Practically all restaurants close one day a week; some close for winter or summer vacation.

Precautions Tap water is safe in large cities and almost everywhere else unless noted *Non Potabile*. Bottled mineral water is available everywhere, *gassata* (with bubbles) or *non gassata* (without). If you prefer tap water, ask for *acqua semplice*, a move that also means a lower restaurant check.

Dress Casual attire is acceptable.

Ratings Prices are per person and include first course, main course, dessert or fruit, and house wine, where available. Best bets are indicated by a star ★.

Category	Rome, Milan*	Other Areas
Moderate	35,000–55,000 lire	28,000–35,000 lire
Inexpensive	28,000–34,000 lire	20,000–27,000 lire
Budget	under 28,000 lire	under 20,000 lire

Note that restaurant prices in Venice are slightly higher than those in Rome and Milan; in small cities prices are usually lower.

Lodging Italy, and especially the main tourist capitals of Rome, Florence, and Venice, offers a good choice of accommodations, but affordable hotels usually do not offer the amenities of comparably priced lodgings in other European capitals or the United States. They do, however, generally offer very clean accommodations. Inexpensive and budget hotels can be spartan, with basic furnishings and shower and toilets down the hall (Showers may be the drain-in-the-floor type guaranteed to flood the bathroom). Hotels in the moderate, inexpensive, and budget categories are to some extent interchangeable, in that a room without bath in a superior category costs about the same as a room without bath in a lower one. Affordable hotels can often accommodate three or four people in a room, which makes the amount you pay per person a real bargain. Taxes and service are included in the room rate. Breakfast is an extra charge, and you can decline to take breakfast in the hotel, though the desk may not be happy about it; make this clear when booking or checking in. Air-conditioning, if available at all, is sure to be an extra charge. In older hotels, room quality may be uneven; if you don't like the room you're given, ask for another. This applies to noise, too; some front rooms are bigger and have views but get street noise. Major cities have hotel reservation service booths in the rail stations.

Hotels Italian hotels are officially classified from five-star (deluxe) to one-star (bed-and-breakfasts and small inns). Prices are established officially and a rate card on the back of the door of your room or inside the closet door tells you exactly what you will pay for that particular room. Any variations should be cause for complaint and should be reported to the local tourist office. The **Family Hotels** group (Via Faenza 77, 50123 Firenze, tel. 055/217975, fax 055/210101) includes small, independent, family-run hotels with affordable rates in many locations, including the major tourist cities. In Rome and elsewhere, institutions run by religious orders take paying guests—couples and families as well as single men and women. Some require that guests take half-board, and all have a nightly curfew, but otherwise no rules apply. Costs are low, accommodtions spotless, the atmosphere quiet and very cordial. For information, inquire at tourist-information offices.

Camping Italy has a wide selection of campgrounds, and the Italians themselves are taking to camping by the thousands, which means that beach or mountain sites will be crammed in July and August. It's best to avoid these peak months and to send for the (necessary) camping license (15,000 lire) from the **Federazione Italiana del Campeggio,** Casella Postale 649, 50100 Firenze.

Ratings The following price categories are determined by the cost of two people in a double room. Best bets are indicated by a star

★. As with restaurant prices, the cost of hotels in Venice is slightly more than those shown here.

Category	Rome, Milan	Other Areas
Moderate	100,000–125,000 lire	90,000–120,000 lire
Inexpensive	65,000–100,000 lire	60,000–90,000 lire
Budget	under 65,000 lire	under 60,000 lire

Tipping In restaurants, a 15% service charge is usually added to the total, but it doesn't all go to the waiter. In large cities and resorts it is customary to give the waiter a 5% tip in addition to the service charge made on the check.

Charges for service are included in all hotel bills, but smaller tips to staff members are appreciated. In general, chambermaids should be given about 1,000 lire per day, 3,000 lire–4,000 lire per week.

Taxi drivers are happy with 5%. Porters at railroad stations and airports charge a fixed rate per suitcase; tip an additional 500 lire per person, more if the porter is very helpful. Tip guides about 2,000 lire per person for a half-day tour, more if they are very good.

Rome

Arriving and Departing

By Plane Rome's principal airport is at Fiumicino, 29 kilometers (18 miles) from the city. Though its official name is Leonardo da Vinci Airport, everybody calls it Fiumicino. For flight information, tel. 06/65951. The smaller military airport of Ciampino is on the edge of Rome and is used as an alternative by international and domestic lines, especially for charter flights.

Between the Airport and Downtown The express-train link between Leonardo da Vinci Airport and the Ostiense railway station in downtown Rome offers frequent departures from both ends. The ride takes about 30 minutes. The fare is 5,000 lire. At the Ostiense station you can get a bus or take the *metro* (subway). The fastest way to get to Termini station or thereabouts is to take Metro Line B; follow the signs at the Ostiense station to the Piramide station of the metro. *See* Getting Around by Metro, *below*.

Ciampino is connected with the Anagnina station of the Metro Line A by bus.

By Train Termini station is Rome's main train terminal, while Tiburtina and Ostiense stations are used principally by commuters. For train information, try the English-speaking personnel at the Information Office in Termini, or at any travel agency. Tickets and seats can be reserved and purchased at travel agencies bearing the FS (Ferrovie dello Stato) emblem. Short-distance tickets are also sold by tobacconists.

By Bus There is no central bus station in Rome; long-distance and suburban buses terminate either near Termini station or near strategically located metro stops.

Getting Around

The best way to see Rome is to choose an area or a sight that you particularly want to see, reach it by bus or Metro (subway), then explore the area on foot, following one of our itineraries or improvising one to suit your mood and interests. Wear comfortable, sturdy shoes, preferably with thick rubber soles to cushion you against the cobblestones. Heed our advice on security, and try to avoid the noise and polluted air of heavily trafficked streets, taking parallel byways wherever possible.

You can buy transportation route maps at newsstands and at ATAC information and ticket booths.

By Metro The subway, or Metro, provides the easiest and fastest way to get around. The Metro opens at 5:30 AM, and the last train leaves each terminal at 11:30 PM. Line A runs from the eastern part of the city to Termini station and past Piazza di Spagna and Piazzale Flaminio to Ottaviano, near St. Peter's and the Vatican Museums. Line B serves Termini, the Colosseum, and the Piramide station (air terminal). The fare is 800 lire. There are change booths and/or ticket machines on station mezzanines; it's best to buy single tickets or books of 5 or 10 ahead of time at newsstands and tobacco shops. A daily tourist ticket known as a **BIG** is good on buses as well, costs 2,800 lire, and is sold at ATAC ticket booths.

By Bus Orange ATAC (tel. 06/4695–4444) city buses (and two streetcar lines) run from about 6 AM to midnight, with skeleton *notturno* services on main lines throughout the night. The fare is 800 lire, and tickets are valid on all ATAC lines for 90 minutes; you must buy your ticket before boarding. They are sold singly or in books of five or 10 to tobacco shops and newsstands. Weekly tourist tickets cost 10,000 lire and are sold at ATAC booths. When entering a bus, remember to board at the rear and exit at the middle.

By Bicycle Bikes provide a pleasant means of getting around when traffic isn't heavy. There are bike-rental shops at Via di Porta Castello 43, near St. Peter's, and at Piazza Navona 69, next to Bar Navona. Rental concessions are at the Piazza di Spagna and Piazza del Popolo Metro stops, and at Largo San Silvestro and Largo Argentina. There are also two in Villa Borghese, at Viale della Pineta and Viale del Bambino on the Pincio.

By Moped You can rent a moped or scooter and mandatory helmet at **Scoot-a-Long** (Via Cavour 302, tel. 06/678–0206) or **St. Peter Moto** (Via di Porta Castello 43, tel. 06/687–5714).

Important Addresses and Numbers

Tourist Information The main **EPT** (Rome Provincial Tourist) office is at Via Parigi 5 (tel. 06/488–3748, open Mon.–Sat. 9–1:30 and 2–7). There are also EPT booths at Termini station and Leonardo da Vinci Airport. A booth on the main floor of the **ENIT** (National Tourist Board) building at Via Marghera 2 (tel. 06/497–1222, open weekdays 9–1, Wed. also 4–6) can provide information on destinations in Italy outside Rome.

Consulates U.S. (Via Veneto 121, tel. 06/46741). **Canadian** (Via Zara 30, tel. 06/440–3082). **U.K.** (Via Venti Settembre 80a, tel. 06/482–5441).

Emergencies **Police** (tel. 06/4686); **Carabinieri** (tel. 06/112); **Ambulance** (tel. 06/5100 Red Cross). **Doctor:** Call your consulate, the private **Salvator Mundi Hospital** (tel. 06/586041), or the **American Hospital** (tel. 06/22551), which has English-speaking staff members, for a recommendation.

Exploring Rome

Antiquity is taken for granted in Rome, where successive ages have piled the present on top of the past—building, layering, and overlapping their own particular segments of Rome's 2,500 years of history to form a remarkably varied urban complex. Most of the city's major sights are located in a fairly small area known as the *centro*, or center. At its heart lies ancient Rome, where the Forum and Colosseum stand. It was around this core that the other sections of the city grew up through the ages: medieval Rome, which covered the horn of land that pushes the Tiber toward the Vatican and extended across the river into Trastevere; and Renaissance Rome, which was erected upon medieval foundations and extended as far as the Vatican, creating beautiful villas on what was then the outskirts of the city.

The layout of the center is highly irregular, but several landmarks serve as orientation points: the Colosseum, the Pantheon and Piazza Navona, St. Peter's, the Spanish Steps, and Villa Borghese. You'll need a good map to find your way around; newsstands offer a wide choice. Energetic sightseers will walk a lot, a much more pleasant way to see the city now that some traffic has been barred from the center during the day; others might choose to take buses or the Metro. The important thing is to relax and enjoy Rome, taking time to savor its pleasures. If you are in Rome during a hot spell, do as the Romans do: Start out early in the morning, have a light lunch and a long siesta during the hottest hours, then resume sightseeing in the late afternoon and end your evening with a leisurely meal outdoors, refreshed by cold Frascati wine and the *ponentino*, the cool evening breeze.

Ancient Rome *Numbers in the margin correspond to points of interest on the Rome map.*

❶ Start your first tour at the city's center, in **Piazza Venezia.** Behind the enormous marble monument honoring the first king of
❷ unified Italy, Victor Emmanuel II, stands the **Campidoglio** (Capitol Square) on the Capitoline Hill. The majestic ramp and beautifully proportioned piazza are Michelangelo's handiwork, as are the three palaces. The **Palazzo Senatorio** at the center is still the ceremonial seat of Rome's city hall; it was built over the Tabularium, where ancient Rome's state archives were kept.

❸ The palaces flanking the Palazzo Senatorio contain the **Capitoline Museums.** On the left, the **Museo Capitolino** holds some fine classical sculptures, including the *Dying Gaul*, the *Capitoline Venus*, and a fascinating series of portrait busts of ancient
❹ philosophers and emperors. In the courtyard of the **Palazzo dei Conservatori** on the right of the piazza, you can use the mammoth fragments of a colossal statue of the emperor Constantine as amusing props for snapshots. Inside you will find splendidly frescoed salons, as well as sculptures and paintings. *Piazza del Campidoglio, tel. 06/671–02071. Admission: 8,000 lire. Open Apr.–Sept., Tues. 9–1:30, 5–8; Wed.–Fri. 9–1:30; Sat. 9–1:30,*

7:30–11:30; Sun. 9–1. Oct.–Mar., Tues. and Sat. 9–1:30, 5–8; Wed.–Fri. 9–1:30; Sun. 9–1.

5 The Campidoglio is also the site of the very old **Aracoeli** church, which you can reach by way of the stairs on the far side of the Museo Capitolino. Stop in to see the medieval pavement; the Renaissance gilded ceiling that commemorates the victory of Lepanto; some Pinturicchio frescoes; and a much-revered wooden statue of the Holy Child. The Campidoglio gardens offer a splendid view of Roman antiquity, extending from the Palatine Hill on the right and across the original Roman Forum to Via dei Fori Imperiali on the left, beyond which stretch the Imperial Fora that were built when the city outgrew the original one.

6 In the valley directly below, the **Roman Forum,** once only a marshy hollow, became the political, commercial, and social center of Rome, studded with public meeting halls, shops, and temples. As Rome declined, these monuments lost their importance and eventually were destroyed by fire or the invasions of barbarians. Rubble accumulated, much of it was carted off by medieval home-builders as construction material, and the site reverted to marshy pastureland; sporadic excavations began at the end of the 19th century.

You don't really have to try to make sense of the mass of marble fragments scattered over the area of the Roman Forum. Just consider that 2,000 years ago this was the center of the then-known world. Wander down the Via Sacra and climb the Palatine Hill, where the emperors had their palaces and where 16th-century cardinals strolled in elaborate Italian gardens. From the belvedere you have a good view of the Circus Maximus. *Entrances on Via dei Fori Imperiali, Piazza Santa Maria Nova and Via di San Gregorio, tel. 06/679–0333. Admission: 10,000 lire. Open Apr.–Sept., Mon., Wed.–Sat. 9–6, Tues., Sun. 9–1; Oct.–Mar., Mon., Wed.–Sat. 9–3, Tues., Sun. 9–1.*

Leave the Forum from the exit at Piazza Santa Maria Nova, **7** near the Arch of Titus, and head for the **Colosseum,** inaugurated in AD 80 with a program of games and shows that lasted 100 days. On opening day alone, 5,000 wild animals perished in the arena. The Colosseum could hold more than 50,000 spectators; it was faced with marble, decorated with stuccos, and had an ingenious system of awnings to provide shade. Try to see it both in daytime and at night, when yellow floodlights make it a magical sight. The Colosseum, by the way, takes its name from a colossal, 36-meter (115-foot) statue of Nero that stood nearby. You must pay a fee to explore the upper levels, where you can also see a dusty scale model of the arena as it was in its heyday. *Piazza del Colosseo, tel. 06/700–4261. Admission: 6,000 lire to upper levels. Open Mon., Tues., and Thurs.–Sat. 9–one hour before sunset; Sun. and Wed. 9–1.*

8 Stroll past the **Arch of Constantine.** The reliefs depict Constantine's victory over Maxentius at the Milvian Bridge. Just before this battle in AD 312, Constantine had a vision of a cross in the heavens and heard the words, "In this sign thou shalt conquer." The victory led not only to the construction of this majestic marble arch but, more important, was a turning point in the history of Christianity: Soon afterward a grateful Con-

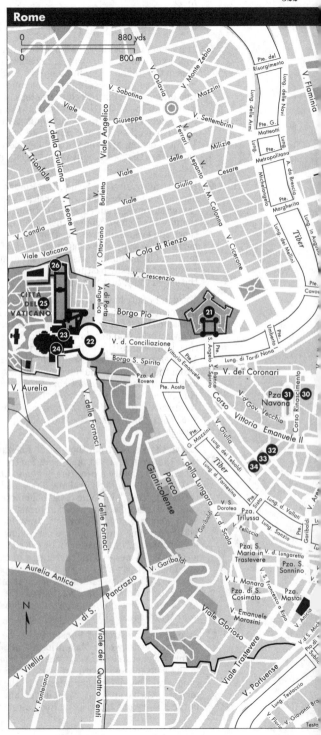

Rome

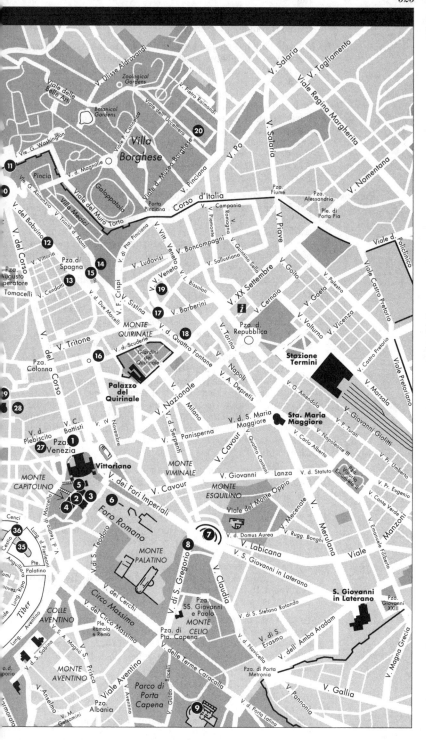

stantine decreed that it was a lawful religion and should be tolerated throughout the empire.

⑨ A fairly long but pleasant walk takes you to the **Baths of Caracalla,** which numbered among ancient Rome's most beautiful and luxurious, inaugurated by Caracalla in 217 and used until the 6th century. An ancient version of a swank athletic club, the baths were open to the public; citizens could bathe, socialize, and exercise in huge pools and richly decorated halls and libraries, now towering ruins. The open-air opera performances that take place here today can be an exciting experience, especially *Aïda,* but take a wrap in case the night is cool. *Via delle Terme di Caracalla. Admission: 6,000 lire. Open Apr.–Sept., Tues.–Sat. 9–6, Sun. and Mon. 9–1; Oct.–Mar., Tues.–Sat. 9–3, Sun.–Mon. 9–1.*

Piazzas and Fountains **Piazza del Popolo** is one of Rome's most vast and airy squares, but for many years it was just an exceptionally beautiful parking lot with a 3,000-year-old obelisk in the middle. Now most traffic and parking has been barred, and the piazza is open to **⑩** strollers. The church of **Santa Maria del Popolo** over in the corner of the piazza near the arch stands out more, now that it has **⑪** been cleaned, and is rich in art, including two stunning Caravaggios in the chapel to the left of the main altar.

⑫ If you're interested in antiques, stroll along **Via del Babuino.** If window-shopping suits your fancy, take Via del Corso and turn **⑬** into **Via Condotti,** Rome's most elegant and expensive shopping street. Here you can ogle fabulous jewelry, designer fashions, and accessories in the windows of Buccellati, Ferragamo, Valentino, Gucci, and Bulgari. The more-than-200-year-old **Antico Caffè Greco** is a Roman institution, the haunt of writers, artists, and well-groomed ladies toting Gucci shopping bags. With its small marble-topped tables and velour settees, it's a nostalgic sort of place—Goethe, Byron, and Liszt were regulars here, and even Buffalo Bill stopped in when his road show came to town. Whatever you have here should be ordered at the bar, because table service is very expensive.*Via Condotti 86. Closed Sun.*

Via Condotti gives you a head-on view of the Spanish Steps in **⑭** **Piazza di Spagna,** and of the church of **Trinità dei Monti.** In the center of the piazza is Bernini's **Fountain of the Barcaccia** (Old Boat), around which Romans and tourists cool themselves on **⑮** hot summer nights. The 200-year-old **Spanish Steps,** named for the Spanish Embassy to the Holy See, opposite the American Express office, is a popular rendezvous, especially for the young people who throng this area. On weekend afternoons, Via del Corso is packed wall-to-wall with teenagers, and the nearby McDonald's is a mob scene. In contrast, **Babington's Tea Room,** to the left of the Spanish Steps, is a stylish institution that caters to an upscale clientele.

To the right of the Spanish steps is the **Keats and Shelley Memorial House.** Once the home of these romantic poets, it's now a museum. *Piazza di Spagna 26, tel. 06/678–4235. Admission: 4,000 lire. Open June–Sept., weekdays 9–1 and 3–6; Oct.–May, weekdays 9–1 and 2:30–5:30.*

Head for Via del Tritone and cross this heavily trafficked shopping street into narrow Via della Stamperia, which leads to the **⑯** **Fountain of Trevi,** a spectacular fantasy of mythical sea creatures and cascades of splashing water. Legend has it that visitors must toss a coin into the fountain to ensure their return to Rome, but you'll have to force your way past crowds of tourists and aggressive souvenir vendors to do so. The fountain as you see it was completed in the mid-1700s, but there had been a drinking fountain on the site for centuries. Pope Urban VIII almost sparked a revolt when he slapped a tax on wine to cover the expenses of having the fountain repaired.

⑰ At the top of Via del Tritone, **Piazza Barberini** boasts two fountains by Bernini: the jaunty **Triton** in the middle of the square and the **Fountain of the Bees** at the corner of Via Veneto. Decorated with the heraldic Barberini bees, this shell-shaped fountain bears an inscription that was immediately regarded as an unlucky omen by the superstitious Romans, for it erroneously stated that the fountain had been erected in the 22nd year of the reign of Pope Urban VIII, who had commissioned it, while in fact the 21st anniversary of his election was still some weeks away. The wrong numeral was hurriedly erased, but to no avail: Urban died eight days before the beginning of his 22nd year as pontiff.

⑱ A few steps up Via delle Quattro Fontane is **Palazzo Barberini,** Rome's most splendid 17th-century palace, now surrounded by rather unkempt gardens and occupied in part by the **Galleria Nazionale di Arte Antica.** Visit the latter to see Raphael's *Fornarina,* many other good paintings, some lavishly frescoed ceilings, and a charming suite of rooms decorated in 1782 on the occasion of the marriage of a Barberini heiress. *Via delle Quattro Fontane 13, tel. 06/481-4591. Admission: 6,000 lire. Open Mon.-Sat. 9-2, Sun. 9-1.*

⑲ One of Rome's oddest sights is the **crypt** of the **Church of Santa Maria della Concezione** on Via Veneto, just above the Fountain of the Bees. In four chapels under the main church, the skeletons and scattered bones of some 4,000 dead Capuchin monks are arranged in decorative motifs, a macabre practice peculiar to the bizarre Baroque Age. *Via Veneto 27, tel. 06/462850. Admission free, but a donation is encouraged. Open daily 9-noon and 3-6.*

The lower reaches of Via Veneto are quiet and sedate, but at the intersection with Via Bissolati, otherwise known as "Airline Row," the avenue comes to life. The big white palace on the right is the U.S. Embassy, and the even bigger white palace beyond it is the luxurious **Hotel Excelsior.** Together with Doney's next door and the Café de Paris across the street, the Excelsior was a landmark of La Dolce Vita, that effervescent period during the 1950s when movie stars, playboys, and exiled royalty played hide-and-seek with press agents and *paparazzi,* ducking in and out of nightclubs and hotel rooms along the Via Veneto. The atmosphere of the street is considerably more sober now, and its cafés cater more to tourists and expensive pickups than to barefoot cinema *contesse.*

Via Veneto ends at **Porta Pinciana,** a gate in the 12-mile stretch of defensive walls built by Emperor Aurelian in the 3rd century; 400 years later, when the Goths got too close for comfort, Belisarius reinforced the gate with two massive towers. Beyond is **Villa Borghese,** the most famous of Rome's parks, studded with tall pines that are gradually dying off as pollution and age take their toll. Inside the park, strike off to the right to-
⑳ ward the **Galleria Borghese,** a pleasure palace created by Car-

dinal Scipione Borghese in 1613 as a showcase for his fabulous sculpture collection. In the throes of structural repairs for several years, the now-public gallery is, at press time, only partially open to visitors. It's still worth a visit to see the seductive reclining statue of Pauline Borghese by Canova, and some extraordinary works by Bernini, among them the unforgettable *Apollo and Daphne*, in which marble is transformed into flesh and foliage. With restorations dragging on, probably into 1993, a few of the best works, including Caravaggio's, have been moved downstairs from the picture gallery, which is now closed. *During reconstruction the entrance is on Via Raimondi, reached from Via Pinciana. Via Pinciana (Piazzale Museo Borghese–Villa Borghese), tel. 06/858577. Admission free for the duration of the renovations. Open Mon.–Sat. 9–1:30, Sun. 9–1.*

Castel Sant'Angelo, St. Peter's, Vatican Museums
㉑

Ponte Sant'Angelo, the ancient bridge across the Tiber in front of Castel Sant'Angelo, is decorated with lovely Baroque angels designed by Bernini and offers fine views of the castle and of St. Peter's in the distance. **Castel Sant'Angelo,** a formidable fortress, was originally built as the tomb of Emperor Hadrian in the 2nd century AD. In its early days, it looked much like the **Augusteo,** or Tomb of Augustus, which still stands more or less in its original form across the river. Hadrian's Tomb was incorporated into the town walls and served as a military stronghold during the barbarian invasions. According to legend it got its present name in the 6th century, when Pope Gregory the Great, passing by in a religious procession, saw an angel with a sword appear above the ramparts to signal the end of the plague that was raging. Enlarged and fortified, the castle became a refuge for the popes, who fled to it along the **Passetto,** an arcaded passageway that links it with the Vatican. Inside the castle you see ancient corridors, medieval cells and Renaissance salons, a museum of antique weapons, courtyards piled with stone cannonballs, and terraces with great views of the city. There's a pleasant bar with outdoor tables on one level. The highest terrace of all, under the newly restored bronze statue of the legendary angel, is the one from which Puccini's heroine, Tosca, threw herself. *Lungotevere Castello 50, tel. 06/ 687–5036. Admission: 8,000 lire. Open Oct.–Mar., Tues.–Sat. 9–1, Sun. 9–noon, Mon. 2–7. From Apr.–Sept. hours vary but are usually Mon.–Sat. 9–7.*

Via della Conciliazione, the broad avenue leading to St. Peter's Basilica, was created by Mussolini's architects by razing blocks of old houses. This opened up a vista of the basilica, giving the eye time to adjust to its mammoth dimensions, and thereby spoiling the effect Bernini sought when he enclosed his vast square (which is really oval) in the embrace of huge quadruple colonnades. In **Piazza San Pietro** (St. Peter's Square), which has held up to 400,000 people at one time, look for the stone disks in the pavement halfway between the fountains and the obelisk. From these points the colonnades seem to be formed of a single row of columns all the way around.

When you enter Piazza San Pietro (completed in 1667), you are entering Vatican territory. Since the Lateran Treaty of 1929, **Vatican City** has been an independent and sovereign state, which covers about 44 hectares (108 acres) and is surrounded by thick, high walls. Its gates are watched over by the Swiss Guards, who still wear the colorful dress uniforms designed by

Michelangelo. Sovereign of this little state is John Paul II, 264th Pope of the Roman Catholic Church. At noon on Sunday, ❷❸ the Pope appears at his third-floor study window in the **Vatican Palace,** to the right of the basilica, to bless the crowd in the square. (Note: Entry to St. Peter's and the Vatican Museums is barred to those wearing shorts, miniskirts, sleeveless T-shirts, and otherwise revealing clothing. Women should carry scarves to cover bare shoulders and upper arms or wear blouses that come to the elbow. Men should dress modestly, in slacks and shirts.)

❷❹ **St. Peter's Basilica** is one of Rome's most impressive sights. It takes a while to absorb the sheer magnificence of it, however, and its rich decoration may not be to everyone's taste. Its size alone is overwhelming, and the basilica is best appreciated when providing the lustrous background for ecclesiastical cere-monies thronged with the faithful. The original basilica was built in the early 4th century AD by the emperor Constantine, over an earlier shrine that supposedly marked the burial place of St. Peter. After more than a thousand years, the old basilica was so decrepit it had to be torn down. The task of building a new, much larger one took almost 200 years and employed the architectural genius of Alberti, Bramante, Raphael, Peruzzi, Antonio Sangallo the Younger, and Michelangelo, who died be-fore the dome he had planned could be completed. Finally, in 1626, St. Peter's Basilica was finished.

The basilica is full of extraordinary works of art. Among the most famous is Michelangelo's *Pietà* (1498), seen in the first chapel on the right just as you enter from the square. Michelan-gelo has four *Pietàs* to his credit. The earliest and best known can be seen here. Two others are in Florence, and the fourth, the *Rondanini Pietà,* is in Milan.

At the end of the central aisle is the bronze statue of **St. Peter,** its foot worn by centuries of reverent kisses. Above the altar in the apse is the *Chair of St. Peter,* a bronze monument created by Bernini as a sort of combined throne and reliquary for a sim-ple wood-and-ivory chair once believed to have belonged to St. Peter. An even more celebrated work is the bronze *baldacchino* (canopy) over the papal altar, which Bernini made with metal stripped from the portico of the Pantheon at the order of Pope Urban VIII, one of the powerful Roman Barberini family. His practice of plundering ancient monuments for material to im-plement his grandiose schemes inspired the famous quip, *"Quod non fecerunt barbari, fecerunt Barberini"* ("What the barbarians didn't do, the Barberini did").

As you stroll up and down the aisles and transepts, observe the fine mosaic copies of famous paintings above the altars, the monumental tombs and statues, and the fine stucco work. Stop at the **Treasury** (Historical Museum), which contains some priceless liturgical objects, and take the elevator up to the roof of the basilica. From here you can climb a short interior stair-case to the base of the dome for an overhead view of the interior of the basilica. Only if you are in good shape should you attempt the strenuous climb up the narrow, one-way stairs to the balco-ny of the lantern atop the dome, where the view embraces the Vatican Gardens as well as all of Rome.

The entrance to the **Crypt of St. Peter's** is in one of the huge piers at the crossing. It's best to leave this visit for last, as the crypt's only exit takes you outside the church. The crypt contains chapels and the tombs of many popes. It occupies the area of the original basilica, over the **grottoes,** where evidence of what may be St. Peter's burial place has been found. You can book special tours of the grottoes. *St. Peter's Basilica, tel. 06/ 698–4466. Open daily 7–7. Treasury (Museo Storico-Artistico): entrance in Sacristy. Admission: 3,000 lire. Open Apr.–Sept., daily 9–6:30; Oct.–Mar., daily 9–5:30. Roof and Dome: entrance between Gregorian Chapel and right transept. Admission: 5,000 lire, including use of elevator to roof, 4,000 lire if you climb the spiral ramp on foot. Open Apr.–Aug., daily 8–6; Sept.–Mar., daily 8–5. Crypt (Tombs of the Popes): entrance alternates among the piers at the crossing. Admission: free. Open Apr.–Sept., daily 7–6; Oct.–Mar., daily 7–5. Grottoes: Apply several days in advance to Ufficio Scavi, left beyond the Arco delle Campane entrance to the Vatican, left of the basilica, tel. 06/698–5318. Admission: 8,000 lire for 2-hour guided visit, 5,000 lire with tape cassette. Ufficio Scavi office hours: Mon.–Sat. 9–noon and 2–5; closed Sun. and religious holidays.*

For many visitors, a **papal audience** is the highlight of a trip to Rome. The Pope holds mass audiences on Wednesday morning; during most of the year they take place in a modern audience hall (capacity 7,000) off the left-hand colonnade. In spring and fall they may be held in **St. Peter's Square,** and sometimes at the papal residence at **Castel Gandolfo.** *You can pick up free tickets from 4–6 PM at the North American College, Via dell 'Umiltà 30 (tel. 06/678–9184), or apply to the Papal Prefecture (Prefettura), which you reach through the Bronze Door in the right-hand colonnade, tel. 06/698–4466. Open Mon.–Tues. and Thurs.–Sat. 9–1, Wed. 9–shortly before audience commences.*

㉕ Guided minibus tours through the **Vatican Gardens** show you some attractive landscaping, a few historical monuments, and the Vatican mosaic school, which produced the mosaics decorating St. Peter's. These tours give you a different perspective on the basilica itself. From March through October, you can choose a garden tour that includes the Sistine Chapel, which you would otherwise see as part of a tour of the Vatican Museums. *Tickets at information office, on the left side of St. Peter's Square, tel. 06/698–4466. Open Mon.–Sat. 8:30–7. Garden tour cost: 15,000 lire. Available Mon., Tues., Fri., and Sat. Garden and Sistine Chapel tour cost: 27,000, including admission to Vatican Museums. Available Mar.–Oct., Mon. and Thurs. All tours begin at 10 AM.*

From the information office in St. Peter's Square you can take a shuttle bus (cost: 2,000 lire) direct to the Vatican Museums. This operates every morning, except Wednesday and Sunday, and saves you the 15-minute walk that goes left from the square and continues along the Vatican walls.

㉖ The collections in the **Vatican Museums** cover nearly 8 kilometers (5 miles) of displays. If you have time, allow at least half a day for Castel Sant'Angelo and St. Peter's and another half-day for the museums. Posters at the museum entrance plot out a choice of four color-coded itineraries; the shortest takes about 90 minutes, the longest more than four hours, depending on your rate of progress. All include the **Sistine Chapel.**

In 1508, Pope Julius II commissioned Michelangelo to fresco the more than 930 square meters (10,000 square feet) of the chapel's ceiling. For four years Michelangelo dedicated himself to painting over fresh plaster, and the result was his masterpiece. The cleaning operations, now completed, have revealed its original and surprisingly brilliant colors.

You can try to avoid the tour groups by going early or late, allowing yourself enough time before the closing hour. In peak season, the crowds definitely detract from your appreciation of this outstanding artistic achievement. Buy an illustrated guide or rent a taped commentary in order to make sense of the figures on the ceiling. A pair of binoculars helps.

The Vatican collections are so rich that unless you are an expert in art history, you will probably want only to skim the surface, concentrating on a few pieces that strike your fancy. If you really want to see the museums thoroughly, you will have to come back again and again. Some of the highlights that might be of interest on your first tour include the *Laocoön*, the *Belvedere Torso*, and the *Apollo Belvedere*, which inspired Michelangelo. The Raphael Rooms are decorated with masterful frescoes, and there are more Raphaels in the Picture Gallery *(Pinacoteca)*. At the Quattro Cancelli, near the entrance to the Picture Gallery, a rather spartan cafeteria provides basic nonalcoholic refreshments. *Viale Vaticano, tel. 06/698-3333. Admission: 10,000 lire, free on last Sun. of the month. Open Easter period and July–Sept., weekdays 8:45–5, Sat. 8:45–2; Oct.–June, Mon.–Sat. 8:45–1. Ticket office closes 60 minutes before museums close. Closed Sun., except last Sun. of the month, and on religious holidays.*

Old Rome   Take Via del Plebiscito from Piazza Venezia to the huge **Church**
㉗ **of the Gesù.** This paragon of Baroque style is the tangible symbol of the power of the Jesuits, who were a major force in the Counter-Reformation in Europe. Encrusted with gold and precious marbles, the Gesù has a fantastically painted ceiling that flows down over the pillars, merging with painted stucco figures to complete the three-dimensional illusion.

㉘ On your way to the Pantheon you will pass **Santa Maria Sopra Minerva,** a Gothic church built over a Roman temple. Inside there are some beautiful frescoes by Filippo Lippi; outside there is a charming elephant by Bernini with an obelisk on its back.

Originally built in 27 BC by Augustus's general Agrippa and re-
㉙ built by Hadrian in the 2nd century AD, the **Pantheon** is one of Rome's most perfect, best-preserved, and perhaps least appreciated ancient monuments. Romans and tourists alike pay little attention to it, and on summer evenings it serves mainly as a backdrop for all the action in the square in front. It represents a fantastic feat of construction, however. The huge columns of the portico and the original bronze doors form the entrance to a majestic hall covered by the largest dome of its kind ever built, wider even than that of St. Peter's. In ancient times the entire interior was encrusted with rich decorations of gilt bronze and marble, plundered by later emperors and popes. *Piazza della Rotonda. Open Oct.–June, Mon.–Sat. 9–5, Sun. 9–1; July–Sept., daily 9–6.*

㉚ Stop in at the church of **San Luigi dei Francesi** on Via della Dogana Vecchia to see the three paintings by Caravaggio in the last chapel on the left; have a few hundred-lire coins handy for the light machine. The clergy of San Luigi considered the artist's roistering and unruly lifestyle scandalous enough, but his realistic treatment of sacred subjects was just too much for them. They rejected his first version of the altarpiece and weren't particularly happy with the other two works either. Thanks to the intercession of Caravaggio's patron, an influential cardinal, they were persuaded to keep them—a lucky thing, since they are now recognized to be among the artist's finest paintings. *Open Fri.–Wed. 7:30–12:30 and 3:30–7, Thurs. 7:30–12:30.*

31 Just beyond San Luigi is **Piazza Navona,** an elongated 17th-century piazza that traces the oval form of the underlying Circus of Diocletian. At the center, Bernini's lively **Fountain of the Four Rivers** is a showpiece. The four statues represent rivers in the four corners of the world: the Nile, with its face covered in allusion to its then unknown source; the Ganges; the Danube; and the River Plate, with its hand raised. And here we have to give the lie to the legend that this was Bernini's mischievous dig at Borromini's design of the facade of the church of **Sant'Agnese in Agone,** from which the statue seems to be shrinking in horror. The fountain was created in 1651; work on the church's facade began some time later. The piazza dozes in the morning, when little groups of pensioners sun themselves on the stone benches and children pedal tricycles around the big fountain. In the late afternoon the sidewalk cafés fill up for the aperitif hour, and in the evening, especially in good weather, the piazza comes to life with a throng of street artists, vendors, tourists, and Romans out for their evening *passeggiata* (promenade). A good many of them stop at the **Tre Scalini** café (Piazza Navona 30) to treat themselves to a *tartufo,* a chocolate ice-cream specialty that was invented here. You may want to do the same, but order it at the counter, since table service is expensive at this and all cafés on the piazza.

32 Across Corso Vittorio is **Campo dei Fiori** (Field of Flowers), the site of a crowded and colorful daily morning market. The hooded bronze figure brooding over the piazza is philosopher Giordano Bruno, who was burned at the stake here for heresy.

33 The adjacent **Piazza Farnese,** with fountains made of Egyptian granite basins from the Baths of Caracalla, is an airy setting for

34 the **Palazzo Farnese,** now the French Embassy, one of the most beautiful of Rome's many Renaissance palaces. There are several others in the immediate area: **Palazzo Spada,** a Wedgwood kind of palace encrusted with stuccos and statues; **Palazzo della Cancelleria,** a massive building that is now the Papal Chancellery, one of the many Vatican-owned buildings in Rome that enjoy extraterritorial privileges; and the fine old palaces along Via Giulia.

The area is one for browsing, through antiques shops and through streets where daily life takes place in a timeworn setting. Stroll along Via Arenula into a rather gloomy part of Rome bounded by Piazza Campitelli and Lungotevere Cenci, the ancient Jewish ghetto. Among the most interesting sights here are the pretty **Fountain of the Tartarughe** (Turtles) on Piazza Mattei, the **Via Portico d'Ottavia,** with medieval inscriptions and friezes on the old buildings, and the **Teatro di Marcello,** a theater built by Julius Caesar to hold 20,000 spectators.

③⑤ A pleasant place to end your walk is on **Tiberina Island.** To get
③⑥ there, walk across the ancient **Fabricio Bridge,** built in 62 BC,
the oldest bridge in the city.

Ostia Antica   Make an excursion to **Ostia Antica,** the well-preserved ancient
Roman port city near the sea, just as rewarding as an excursion
to Pompeii. Pick up the pamphlet-guide at the Rome EPT office
(Via Parigi 5). There is regular train service from the Ostiense
station (Piramide Metro stop). *Via dei Romagnoli, Ostia
Antica, tel. 06/565–1405. Admission: 8,000 lire. Open daily
9–2 hrs. before sunset.*

Shopping

Shopping is part of the fun of being in Rome, no matter what
your budget. The best buys are leather goods of all kinds, from
gloves to handbags and wallets to jackets; silk goods; and high-
quality knitwear. Shops are closed on Sunday and on Monday
morning; in July and August, they close on Saturday afternoon
as well.

Prints   A well-trained eye will spot some worthy old prints and minor
antiques in the city's fascinating little shops. For prints,
browse among the stalls at **Piazza Fontanella Borghese;** at
Casali, Piazza della Rotonda 81a, at the Pantheon; and **Tanca,**
Salita de' Crescenzi 10, also near the Pantheon.

Boutiques   Lower-price fashions may be found on display at shops on **Via
Frattina, Via del Corso, Via Ottaviano** (near St. Peter's), and
around **San Giovanni in Laterano.**

Shopping Districts   In addition to those mentioned, Romans themselves do much of
their shopping along **Via Cola di Rienzo** and **Via Nazionale.**

Religious Articles   These abound in the shops around St. Peter's, on **Via di Porta
Angelica** and **Via della Conciliazione,** and in the souvenir shops
tucked away on the roof and at the crypt exit in St. Peter's itself.

Department Stores   You'll find a fairly broad selection of women's, men's, and children's fashions and accessories at the **Rinascente** stores on Piazza Colonna and at Piazza Fiume and at the **Coin** department
store on Piazzale Appio near San Giovanni in Laterano. The
UPIM and **Standa** chains have shops all over the city that offer
medium-quality, low-price goods. The **Croff** chain features
housewares.

Food and Flea   The open-air markets at **Piazza Vittorio** and **Campo dei Fiori**
Markets   are colorful sights. The flea market held at **Porta Portese** on
Sunday morning is stocked mainly with new or second-hand
clothing. If you go, beware of pickpockets and purse snatchers.

Dining

There are plenty of fine restaurants in Rome serving various
Italian regional cuisines and international specialties with a
flourish of linen and silver, as well as a whopping *conto* (check)
at the end. If you want family-style cooking and prices, try a
trattoria, a usually smallish and unassuming, often family-run
place. Fast-food places and Chinese restaurants are prolif-
erating in Rome; very few can be recommended. Fixed-price
tourist menus can be scanty and unimaginative. The lunch hour
in Rome lasts from about 1 to 3 PM, dinner from 8 or 8:30 to

about 10:30, though some restaurants stay open much later. Romans love to eat out, so most restaurants, especially inexpensive and budget places, are jammed on weekend evenings. To get a table you have to arrive 15–20 minutes before normal dining hours. During August many restaurants close for vacation.

For details and price-category definitions, *see* Dining in Staying in Italy.

Moderate

La Campana. An inconspicuous trattoria off Via della Scrofa, this has a long tradition of hospitality—there has been an inn on this spot since the 15th century. Now it's a classic Roman eating place, with friendly but businesslike waiters and a menu that offers Roman specialties such as *vignarola* (sautéed fava beans, peas, and artichokes), rigatoni with prosciutto and tomato sauce, and *olivette di vitello* (tiny veal rolls, served with mashed potatoes). *Vicolo della Campana 18, tel. 06/686–7820. Dinner reservations advised. AE, V. Closed Mon. and Aug.*

Colline Emiliane. Located near Piazza Barberini, the Colline Emiliane is an unassuming trattoria offering exceptionally good food: light homemade pastas, a very special chicken broth, and meats ranging from pot roast to *giambonetto di vitella* (roast veal) and *cotoletta alla bolognese* (veal cutlet with cheese and tomato sauce). *Via degli Avignonesi 22, tel. 06/481–7538. Reservations advised. No credit cards. Closed Fri.*

★ **Mario.** This Tuscan trattoria in the center of Rome's shopping district has been run by Mario for 30 years. Hearty Tuscan specialties, such as *pappardelle alla lepre* (noodles with hare sauce) and *coniglio* (rabbit), are featured on the menu. Try *panzanella* (Tuscan bread salad with tomatoes) and the house Chianti. *Via della Vite 55, tel. 06/678–3818. Dinner reservations advised. AE, DC, MC, V. Closed Sun. and Aug.*

Orso 80. A bustling trattoria located in Old Rome, near Piazza Navona, it is known for a fabulous antipasto table. The egg pasta is freshly made, and the *bucatini all'amatriciana* (thick spaghetti with a tangy tomato and bacon sauce) is a classic Roman pasta. For dessert, try the ricotta cake, a Roman specialty. *Via dell'Orso 33, tel. 06/686–4904. Reservations advised. AE, DC, MC, V. Closed Mon. and Aug. 10–20.*

Pierluigi. Pierluigi, in the heart of Old Rome, is a longtime favorite. On busy evenings it's almost impossible to find a table, so make sure you reserve well in advance. Seafood predominates—but can be pricey; instead, try traditional Roman dishes such as *orecchiette con broccoli* (disk-shaped pasta with greens) or just simple spaghetti. In warm weather ask for a table in the piazza. *Piazza dei Ricci 144, tel. 06/686–1302. Reservations advised. AE. Closed Mon. and 2 weeks in Aug.*

La Rampa. It's right behind the American Express office on Piazza Mignanelli, off Piazza di Spagna, and it has colorful marketplace decor. The house antipasto is a specialty, as is *frittura alla Rampa* (deep-fried vegetables and mozzarella). Get there early to get a table. *Piazza Mignanelli 18, tel. 06/678–2621. No reservations. No credit cards. Closed Sun., Mon. lunch, and Aug.*

Inexpensive

★ **Abruzzi.** This simple trattoria off Piazza Santi Apostoli near Piazza Venezia specializes in regional cooking of the Abruzzi, a mountainous region southeast of Rome. Specialties include *tonnarelli Abruzzi* (square-cut pasta with mushrooms, peas, and ham) and *abbacchio* (roast lamb). *Via del Vaccaro 1, tel. 06/679–3897. Lunch reservations advised. V. Closed Sat and Aug.*

Fratelli Menghi. A neighborhood trattoria that has been in the same family as long as anyone can remember, Fratelli Menghi produces typical Roman fare. There's usually a thick, hearty soup such as minestrone, *pasta e ceci* (with chick peas), and other standbys including *involtini* (meat roulades). *Via Flaminia 57, tel. 06/320–0803. No reservations. No credit cards. Closed Sun.*

Hostaria Farnese. This is a tiny trattoria between Campo dei Fiori and Piazza Farnese, in the heart of Old Rome. Papa serves, Mamma cooks, and depending on what they've picked up at the Campo dei Fiori market, you may find rigatoni with tuna and basil, spaghetti with vegetable sauce, *spezzatino* (stew), and other homey specialties. *Via dei Baullari 109, tel. 06/654–1595. Reservations advised. AE, V. Closed Thurs.*

Pallaro. No confusing menus to deal with in this simple trattoria near Campo dei Fiori; the set menu, changed nightly, begins with antipasto, and by the time you get through pasta and a meat course you may not have room for the homemade desserts. The house wine is worth the extra lire. At these prices, Pallaro is often booked solid. *Largo del Pallaro 14, tel. 06/654–1488. Reservations advised. No credit cards. Closed Mon.*

Pollarola. Located near Piazza Navona and Campo dei Fiori, this typical Roman trattoria has flowers (artificial) on the tables and an antique Roman column embedded in the rear wall, evidence of its historic site. You can eat outdoors in fair weather. Try a pasta specialty such as *fettuccine al gorgonzola* (noodles with creamy gorgonzola sauce) and a mixed plate from the temptingly fresh array of antipasti. The house wine, white or red, is good. *Piazza della Pollarola 24 (Campo dei Fiori), tel. 06/654–1654. Reservations advised for groups. AE, V. Closed Sun.*

Tavernetta. Its central location, between Trevi Fountain and the Spanish Steps, is convenient, and the economical tourist menu makes this a reliable place for a simple but satisfying meal. If you order à la carte your check will be in the moderate range. *Via del Nazareno 3, tel. 06/679–3124. Reservations advised in evening. AE, DC, MC, V. Closed Mon. and Aug.*

Budget **Baffetto.** Rome's best-known pizzeria is ultra-plain and very popular. You may have to wait for seating at one of the paper-covered tables, and you'll probably have to share it. *Bruschetta* (toast with olive oil) and *crostini* (mozzarella toast) are the only variations on the pizza theme. *Via del Governo Vecchio 114, tel. 06/686–1617. No reservations. No credit cards. Closed lunch, Sun., and Aug.*

Birreria della Scala. Crowded in the evening, this restaurant and music club in Trastevere is a favorite among young Americans and Romans. It's a bargain, with everything on the menu priced less than 11,000 lire and no cover charge for the live music from 8 to 10 PM. The salads are especially good. *Piazza della Scala 58, tel. 06/580–3763. Reservations advised. AE, DC, V. Closed Wed.*

Birreria Tempera. This old-fashioned beer hall near Piazza Venezia is very busy at lunchtime. There's a good selection of salads and cold cuts, as well as pasta and daily specials. *Via San Marcello 19, tel. 06/678–6203. No reservations. No credit cards. Closed Sun. and Aug.*

Cottini. On a corner of Piazza Santa Maria Maggiore, this reliable cafeteria-style restaurant annexed to a large coffee bar offers everything from salads to main courses and tempting desserts from the in-house bakery. *Via Merulana 287, tel. 06/ 474–0768. No reservations. No credit cards. Closed Mon.*

L'Insalata Ricca. An informal place near Piazza Navona, it specializes in salads and basic pastas. No smoking here. If it's packed, as is often the case, try its sister restaurant, with the same name, at Piazza Pasquino 72 (closed Mon.). *Largo dei Chiavari 85, tel. 06/654–3656. Reservations advised in evening. No credit cards. Closed Wed.*

Da Lucia. This family-run trattoria in Trastevere makes room for everyone by overflowing into the street in fair weather; you may have to wait for a table otherwise. The food is homey Roman. There are no menus, and the waiters recite the day's specials. But don't worry, they speak a little English. *Vicolo del Mattonato 2, tel. 06/580–3601. Reservations not necessary. No credit cards. Closed Mon.*

La Sagrestia. Centrally located near the Pantheon, this tavern serves pizza, bean dishes, and 15 types of pasta. *Via del Seminario 89, tel. 06/679–7581. Reservations not necessary. AE, DC, V. Closed Wed.*

Lodging

The list below covers mostly those hotels that are within walking distance of at least some sights and that are handy to public transportation. Rooms facing the street get traffic noise throughout the night, and few hotels in the lower categories have double glazing. Ask for a quiet room, or bring earplugs. Generally, rooms without bath in inexpensive hotels cost as little as rooms in budget hotels and may offer more amenities.

We strongly recommend that you always make reservations in advance. Should you find yourself in the city without reservations, however, contact one of the following EPT offices: at Leonardo da Vinci Airport (tel. 06/601–1255); Termini train station (tel. 06/487–1270); or the main information office at Via Parigi 5 (tel. 06/488–3748), which is near Piazza della Repubblica. Students can try the **Centro Turistico Studentesco (CTS)** bureau (tel. 06/457–9254) at Termini station or the main office, a 10-minute walk away, at Via Genova 16 (tel. 06/46791).

For details and price-category definitions, *see* Lodging in Staying in Italy.

Moderate **Lunetta.** Located near Campo dei Fiori in the heart of Old Rome, this hotel has a drab entrance but spacious, even attractive rooms, a big plus at these rates. *Piazza del Paradiso 68, tel. 06/686–1080. 34 rooms, 18 with bath. No credit cards.*

★ **Margutta.** Centrally located near the Spanish Steps and Piazza del Popolo, this small hotel has an unassuming lobby but bright, attractive bedrooms and modern baths. *Via Laurina 34, tel. 06/322–3674. 24 rooms with bath. AE, DC, MC, V.*

Santa Prisca. This is a basic hotel in the Aventine neighborhood, adjacent to the Testaccio quarter's plentiful trattorie. It's run by nuns, and everything is clean and orderly. Meals are available. *Largo Manlio Gelsomini 25, tel. 06/575–0009. 45 rooms with shower. Facilities: restaurant, garden. No credit cards.*

Smeraldo. Near Largo Argentina, on a narrow byway in Old

Roma, Smeraldo offers basic but clean and functional accommodations. About half the rooms have small private baths. *Vicolo dei Chiodaroli 9, tel. 06/687–5929, fax 06/654–5495. 35 rooms, 18 with bath. AE, MC, V.*

Suisse. The mood in the Suisse's public rooms may be old-fashioned—the check-in desk is distinctly drab—but the bedrooms, while small, are cheerful enough. Some rooms face the (fairly) quiet courtyard. There's an upstairs breakfast room, but no restaurant. *Via Gregoriana 56, tel. 06/678–3649. 28 rooms, 14 with bath. No credit cards.*

Inexpensive **Abruzzi.** Rooms in this central hotel are tiny and dark, but almost all have a view of the Pantheon and its café-filled square, a Roman rendezvous in all seasons. The noise continues past midnight in summer, but that view is worth the aggravation. Bring earplugs. *Piazza della Rotonda 69, tel. 06/679–2021. 25 rooms without bath. No credit cards.*

Alemandi. A few yards from the Vatican Museum entrance, this family-run hotel has a homey atmosphere, comfortable public rooms, and a terrace. *Via Tunisi 8, tel. 06/314–457. 29 rooms, 22 with bath. AE, MC, V.*

Coronet. A small, comfortable hotel in an enviable location: it is in the 17th-century Palazzo Doria on central Via del Corso. High-ceiling rooms are large and well furnished, and many have baths that are not new but clean and in good condition. Rooms on the palazzo courtyard are quieter. Hallways are worn, but the breakfast room is cheery. *Piazza Grazioli 5, tel. 06/679–2341. 13 rooms, 3 with bath. AE, MC, V.*

Parlamento. In the heart of Rome's elegant shopping district, this small, well-kept hotel refurbished one floor in 1992. It has a rooftop terrace and a friendly management. *Via delle Convertite 5, tel. 06/678–7880. 22 rooms, 14 with bath. No credit cards.*

Pomezia. On a side street near Campo dei Fiori, Pomezia occupies two floors of an old building. One floor has been renovated, and rooms have new baths and good lighting; the other floor is drab, but rooms on both floors cost the same. *Via dei Chiavari 12, tel. 06/686–1371. 22 rooms, 12 with bath. No credit cards.*

Teti. This small hotel near Termini station is clean and fresh-looking but austere. Rooms have firm beds and ample closets; all rooms have sinks and some have compact toilet/shower units. *Via Principe Amedeo 76, tel. 06/482–5240. 11 rooms, 8 with bath. No credit cards.*

Budget **Fiorella.** This tiny hotel on Via del Babuino, a once-bohemian street of artists in the heart of Rome near the Spanish Steps, is quiet and simply furnished. Its cordial owner is always ready to attend your needs. *Via del Babuino 196, tel. 06/361–0597. 8 rooms without bath. No credit cards.*

Fraterna Domus. This religious establishment is recommended by the Vatican Information Office and it has a central location, between Piazza Navona and the Tiber. It offers good value; all rooms have private bath and the 30,000-lire per-person rate includes breakfast. Full- and half-board terms are also offered. There is an 11 PM curfew. *Via di Monte Brianzo 62, tel. 06/654–2727. 20 rooms with bath. No credit cards.*

Licia. Although the train-station area is run-down, this little hotel is a safe bet. It's managed by the mother of the owner of the Teti (*see above*), and it's clean and has basic furnishings. It is located halfway between the station and Santa Maria Maggiore. *Via Principe Amedeo 76, tel. 06/482–5293. 10 rooms without bath. No credit cards.*

Zurigo. Part of a double-barrel operation that includes the Nautilus hotel, this clean, well-run hotel is in a solid residential building near the Vatican, in a neighborhood that offers a range of eating places and shops. The reception staff speaks English. *Via Germanico 198, tel. 06/372–0139. 13 rooms, 5 with shower. No credit cards.*

The Arts

Pick up a copy of the *Carnet di Roma* at EPT tourist offices; issued monthly, it's free and has an exhaustive listing of scheduled events and shows. The bi-weekly booklet *Un Ospite a Roma*, free at some hotels and at EPT offices, is another source of information. Tickets for opera, concerts, and ballet are sold at box offices only, just a few days before performances.

Opera The **Teatro dell'Opera** is on Via del Viminale (tel. 06/6759–5725 for information in English; tel. 06/6759–5721 to book tickets in English); its summer season at the **Baths of Caracalla** from May through August is famous for spectacular performances amid the Roman ruins. Tickets are on sale at the opera box office or at the box office at Caracalla (*see* Exploring Rome, *above*).

Concerts The main concert hall is the **Accademia di Santa Cecilia** (Via della Conciliazione 4, tel. 06/654–1044). The Santa Cecilia Symphony Orchestra has a summer season of concerts. For tickets to rock or pop concerts, try **Orbis** (Piazza Esquilino 37, tel. 06/482–7903).

Film The only English-language movie theater in Rome is the **Pasquino** (Vicolo del Piede, just off Piazza Santa Maria in Trastevere, tel. 06/580–3622). The program is listed in Rome daily newspapers.

Nightlife

Rome's "in" nightspots change like the flavor of the month, and many fade into oblivion after a brief moment of glory. The best source for an up-to-date list is the weekly entertainment guide, "Trovaroma," published each Thursday in the Italian daily *La Repubblica*.

Bars Informal wine bars are popular with young Romans. Near the Pantheon is **Spiriti** (Via Sant'Eustachio 5, tel. 06/689–2499). Another current favorite near the Pantheon, a hub of after-dark activity, is **Antico Caffè della Pace** (Via della Pace 3, tel. 06/686–1216), open evenings only, until very late. **Birreria Marconi** (Via di Santa Prassede 9c, tel. 06/486636), near Santa Maria Maggiore, is a beer-hall pizzeria.

Discos and There's deafening disco music for an under-30s crowd at the
Nightclubs **Tatum** (entrance at Via Luciani 52, tel. 06/322–1251). Special events such as beauty pageants and theme parties are a feature, and there's a restaurant on the premises. **Casanova** (Piazza Rondanini 36, tel. 06/654–7314), in the Pantheon area, where much of the late-night crowd hangs out, offers disco music and often has theme nights and sometimes cabaret. Sports personalities and other celebrities are attracted to **Veleno** (Via Sardegna 27, tel. 06/493583), one of the few places in Rome to offer black dance music, including disco, rap, funk, and soul.

Florence

Arriving and Departing

By Plane The nearest, medium-size airport is the Galileo Galilei Airport at Pisa (tel. 050/28088), connected with Florence by train direct from the airport to the Santa Maria Novella Station. Service is hourly throughout the day and takes about 60 minutes. Some domestic and a few European flights use Florence's Peretola Airport (tel. 055/373498), connected by bus to the downtown area.

By Train The main train station is Santa Maria Novella Station, abbreviated SMN on signs. There is an Azienda Trasporti Autolinee Fiorentine (ATAF) city bus information booth across the street from the station (and also at Piazza del Duomo 57/r). Inside the station is an Informazioni Turistiche Alberghiere (ITA) hotel association booth, where you can get hotel information and bookings.

By Bus The SITA bus terminal is on Via Santa Caterina da Siena, near Santa Maria Novella train station. The CAP bus terminal is at Via Nazionale 13, also near the station.

Getting Around

On Foot You can see most of Florence's major sights on foot, as they are packed into a relatively small area in the city center. Don't plan on using a car; most of the center is off limits, and ATAF buses will take you where you want to go. Wear comfortable shoes, wander to your heart's content, and don't worry about finding your way around. There are so many landmarks that you cannot get lost for long. The system of street numbers is unusual, with commercial addresses written with a red "r" to distinguish them from residential addresses (32/r might be next to or even a block away from plain 32).

By Bus ATAF city buses run from about 5:15 AM to 1 AM. Buy tickets before you board the bus; they are on sale singly or in books of five at many tobacco shops and newsstands. The cost is 1,000 lire for a ticket good for 60 minutes on all lines, 1,300 lire for 120 minutes. An all-day ticket (*turistico*) costs 5,000 lire.

By Bicycle You can rent a bicycle at **Ciao e Basta**, on Via Alamanni (tel. 055/256555), on the stairway side of the train station; at **Costa dei Magnoli 24** (tel. 055/234–2726); and at city concessions in several locations, including Piazza della Stazione, Piazza Pitti, and Fortezza da Basso.

By Moped For a moped, go to **Alinari** (Via Guelfa 85/r, tel. 055/280500), **Motorent** (Via San Zenobi 9/r, tel. 055/490113), or to **Ciao e Basta** (*see* By Bicycle, *above*).

Important Addresses and Numbers

Tourist Information The municipal tourist office is at Via Cavour 1/r (tel. 055/276–0382; open 8:30–7). The **Azienda Promozione Turistica (APT)** tourist board has its headquarters and an information office at Via Manzoni 16 (tel. 055/23320; open Mon.–Sat. 8:30–1:30). There is an information office next to the train station and another near Piazza della Signoria, at Chiasso dei Baroncelli 17/r (tel. 055/230–2124).

Consulates **U.S.** (Lungarno Vespucci 38, tel. 055/298276). **U.K.** (Lungarno Corsini 2, tel. 055/284133).

Emergencies **Police** (tel. 113). **Ambulance** (tel. 055/212222). **Doctor:** Call your consulate for recommendations, or call the **Tourist Medical Service** (tel. 055/475411), associated with IAMAT, for English-speaking medical assistance 24 hours a day.

Exploring Florence

Founded by Julius Caesar, Florence has the familiar grid pattern common to all Roman colonies. Except for the major monuments, which are appropriately imposing, the buildings are low and unpretentious. It is a small, compact city of ocher and gray stone and pale plaster; its narrow streets open unexpectedly into spacious squares populated by strollers and pigeons. At its best, it has a gracious and elegant air, though it can at times be a nightmare of mass tourism. Plan, if you can, to visit Florence in late fall, early spring, or even in winter, to avoid the crowds.

A visit to Florence is a visit to the living museum of the Italian Renaissance. The Renaissance began right here in Florence, and the city bears witness to the proud spirit and unparalleled genius of its artists and artisans. In fact, there is so much to see that it is best to savor a small part rather than attempt to absorb it all in a muddled vision.

Numbers in the margin correspond to points of interest on the Florence map.

Piazza del Duomo and Piazza della Signoria
The best place to begin a tour of Florence is **Piazza del Duomo,** where the cathedral, bell tower, and baptistry stand in the rather cramped square. The lofty **cathedral of Santa Maria del Fiore** is one of the longest in the world. Begun by master sculptor and architect Arnolfo di Cambio in 1296, its construction took 140 years to complete. Gothic architecture predominates; the facade was added in the 1870s but is based on Tuscan Gothic models. Inside, the church is cool and austere, a fine example of the architecture of the period. Among the sparse decorations, take a good look at the frescoes of equestrian monuments on the left wall; the one on the right is by Paolo Uccello, the one on the left by Andrea del Castagno. The dome frescoes by Vasari have been hidden by the scaffolding put up some years ago in order to study a plan for restoring the dome itself, Brunelleschi's greatest architectural and technical achievement. It was also the inspiration of such later domes as Michelangelo's dome for St. Peter's in Rome and even the Capitol in Washington. You can climb to the cupola gallery, 463 fatiguing steps up between the two skins of the double dome, for a fine view of Florence and the surrounding hills. *Dome entrance is in the left aisle of cathedral. Admission: 4,000 lire. Open Mon.–Sat. 10–5. Cathedral open Mon.–Sat. 10–5, Sun. 2:30–5.*

❷ Next to the cathedral is Giotto's 14th-century **bell tower,** richly decorated with colored marble and fine sculptures (the originals are in the Museo dell'Opera del Duomo). The 414-step climb to the top is less strenuous than that to the cupola. *Piazza del Duomo. Admission: 4,000 lire. Open Mar.–Oct., daily 9–7; Nov.–Feb., daily 9–5.*

③ In front of the cathedral is the **baptistry** (open Mon.–Sat. 1–6, Sun. 9–1), one of the city's oldest and most beloved edifices, where, since the 11th century, Florentines have baptized their children. A gleaming copy of the most famous of the baptistry's three portals has been installed facing the cathedral, where Ghiberti's doors (dubbed "The Gate of Paradise" by Michelan-
④ gelo) stood. The originals have been removed to the **Museo dell'Opera del Duomo** (Cathedral Museum). The museum contains some superb sculptures by Donatello and Luca della Robbia—especially their *cantorie*, or choir decorations—as well as an unfinished *Pietà* by Michelangelo, which was intended for his own tomb. *Piazza del Duomo 9, tel. 055/230–2885. Admission: 4,000 lire. Open Mar.–Oct., daily 9–7:30; Nov.–Feb., daily 9–5:30.*

⑤ Stroll down fashionable Via Calzaiuoli to the church of **Orsanmichele,** for centuries an odd combination of first-floor church and second-floor wheat granary. The statues in the niches on the exterior constitute an anthology of the work of eminent Renaissance sculptors, including Donatello, Ghiberti, and Verrocchio, while the tabernacle inside is an extraordinary piece by Andrea Orcagna.

Continuing another two blocks along Via Calzaiuoli you'll come upon **Piazza della Signoria,** the heart of Florence, and the city's largest square. During the long and controversial process of replacing the paving stones over the past few years, well-preserved remnants of Roman and medieval Florence came to light and were thoroughly examined and photographed before being buried again and covered with the new paving. In the center of the square a slab marks the spot where in 1497 Savonarola—the Ayatollah Khomeini of the Middle Ages—induced the Florentines to burn their pictures, books, musical instruments, and other worldly objects—and where a year later he was hanged and then burned at the stake as a heretic. The square, the **Neptune Fountain** by Ammanati, and the surrounding cafés are popular gathering places for Florentines and for tourists who come to admire the massive **Palazzo della Signoria** (better
⑥ known as the **Palazzo Vecchio**), the copy of Michelangelo's *David* on its steps, and the frescoes and artworks in its impressive salons. *Piazza della Signoria, tel. 055/276–8465. Admission: 8,000 lire; Sun. free. Open weekdays 9–7, Sun. 8–1.*

⑦ If you'd like to do a little shopping, make a brief detour off Piazza della Signoria to the **Loggia del Mercato Nuovo** on Via Calimala. It's crammed with souvenirs and straw and leather goods at reasonable prices; bargaining is acceptable here. *Open Mon.–Sat. 8–7 (closed Mon. AM).*

⑧ If time is limited, this is your chance to visit the **Uffizi Gallery,** which houses Italy's most important collection of paintings. (Try to see it at a leisurely pace, though—it's too good to rush through!) The Uffizi Palace was built to house the administrative offices of the Medicis, onetime rulers of the city. Later their fabulous art collection was arranged in the Uffizi Gallery on the top floor, which was opened to the public in the 17th century—making this the world's first public gallery of modern times. The emphasis is on Italian art of the Gothic and Renaissance periods. Make sure you see the works by Giotto, and look for the Botticellis in Rooms X–XIV, Michelangelo's *Holy Family* in Room XXV, and the works by Raphael next door. In addition to its art treasures, the gallery offers a magnificent

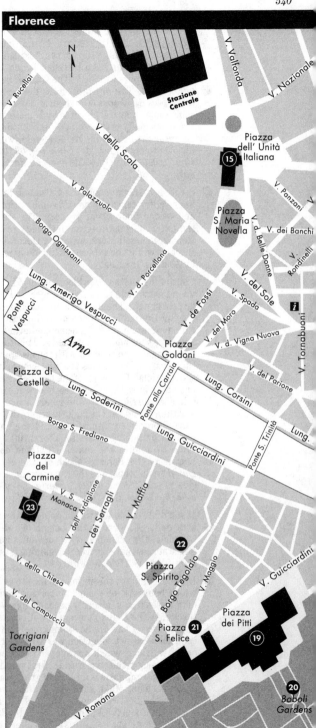

Florence

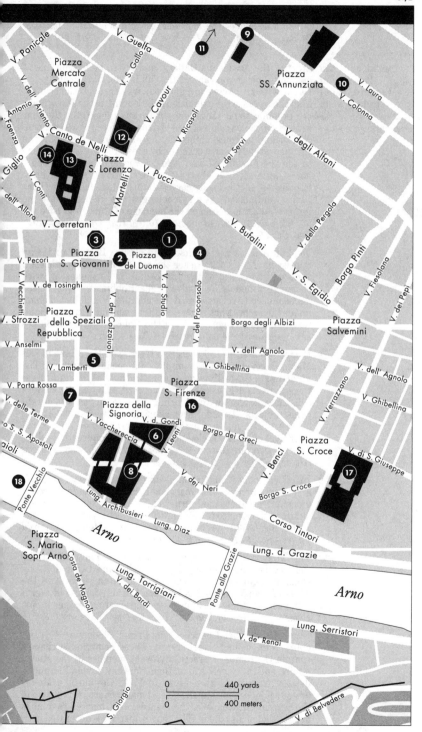

V. Panicale

Piazza Mercato Centrale

V. Guelfa

V. S. Gallo

V. dell' Ariento

V. Antonio

V. Faenza

Canto de Nelli

Giglio

V. Conti

dell' Alloro

9

11

Piazza SS. Annunziata

10

V. Laura

V. Colonna

V. Cavour

V. Ricasoli

V. dei Servi

V. degli Alfani

12

14 **13**

Piazza S. Lorenzo

V. Martelli

V. Pucci

V. della Pergola

V. Cerretani

3

1

4

Piazza S. Giovanni **2** Piazza del Duomo

V. Bufalini

V. S. Egidio

Borgo Pinti

V. Fiesolana

V. dei Pepi

V. Pecori

V. de Tosinghi

V. d. Studio

V. del Proconsolo

Borgo degli Albizi

Piazza Salvemini

V. Vecchietti

V. Strozzi

Piazza della Repubblica

V. della Spezieri

V. dei Calzaiuoli

V. dell' Agnolo

V. Anselmi

5

V. Lamberti

V. Ghibellina

V. dell' Agnolo

V. Ghibellina

V. Porta Rossa

7

Piazza S. Firenze

V. Verrazzano

V. delle Terme

o S. S. Apostoli

Piazza della Signoria

16

V. Vacchereccia

V. d. Gondi

6

V. Leoni

Borgo dei Greci

Piazza S. Croce

V. di S. Giuseppe

17

aioli

18

8

V. dei Neri

V. Benci

Borgo S. Croce

Ponte Vecchio

Lung. Archibusieri

Lung. Diaz

Corso Tintori

Piazza S. Maria Sopr' Arno

Arno

Lung. d. Grazie

Costa de Magnoli

Lung. Torrigiani

V. dei Bardi

Ponte alle Grazie

Arno

Lung. Serristori

V. de' Renai

S. Giorgio

0		440 yards
0		400 meters

V. di Belvedere

close-up view of Palazzo Vecchio's tower from the little coffee bar at the end of the corridor. *Loggiato Uffizi 6, tel. 055/ 218341. Admission: 10,000 lire. Open Tues.–Sat. 9–7, Sun. 9–1.*

Accademia, San Marco, San Lorenzo, Santa Maria Novella
⑨

Start at the **Accademia Gallery,** and try to be first in line at opening time so you can get the full impact of Michelangelo's *David* without having to fight your way through the crowds. Skip the works in the exhibition halls leading to the *David;* they are of minor importance and you'll gain a length on the tour groups. Michelangelo's statue is a tour de force of artistic conception and technical ability, for he was using a piece of stone that had already been worked on by a lesser sculptor. Take time to see the forceful *Slaves,* also by Michelangelo; the rough-hewn, unfinished surfaces contrast dramatically with the highly polished, meticulously carved *David.* Michelangelo left the *Slaves* "unfinished" as a symbolic gesture, to accentuate the figures' struggle to escape the bondage of stone. *Via Ricasoli 60, tel. 055/214375. Admission: 10,000 lire. Open Tues.–Sat. 9–2, Sun. 9–1.*

You can make a detour down Via Cesare Battisti to Piazza Santissima Annunziata to see the arcade of the **Ospedale degli Innocenti** (Hospital of the Innocents) by Brunelleschi, with charming roundels by Andrea della Robbia, and the **Museo Archeologico** (Archaeological Museum) on Via della Colonna, under the arch. It has some fine Etruscan and Roman antiquities, and a pretty garden. *Via della Colonna 36, tel. 055/247–8641. Admission: 6,000 lire. Open Tues.–Sat. 9–2, Sun. 9–1.*

⑪ Retrace your steps to Piazza San Marco and the **Museo di San Marco,** housed in a 15th-century Dominican monastery. The unfortunate Savonarola meditated on the sins of the Florentines here, and Fra Angelico decorated many of the austere cells and corridors with his brilliantly colored frescoes of religious subjects. (Look for his masterpiece, *The Annunciation.*) Together with many of his paintings arranged on the ground floor, just off the little cloister, they form an interesting collection. *Piazza San Marco 1, tel. 055/210741. Admission: 6,000 lire. Open Tues.–Sat. 9–2, Sun. 9–1.*

⑫ Lined with shops, Via Cavour leads to **Palazzo Medici Riccardi,** a massive Renaissance mansion housing Benozzo Gozzoli's glorious frescoes of the Journey of the Magi, a spectacular cavalcade with Lorenzo the Magnificent on a charger. *Via Cavour 1, tel. 055/27601. Admission free. Open Mon.–Tues. and Thurs.–Sat. 9–12:30 and 3–5, Sun. 9–noon.*

⑬ Turn right here to the elegant **Church of San Lorenzo,** with its Old Sacristy designed by Brunelleschi, and two pulpits by Donatello. Rounding the church, you'll find yourself in the midst of the sprawling **San Lorenzo Market,** dealing in everything and anything, including some interesting leather items. *Piazza San Lorenzo, Via dell'Ariento. Open Tues.–Sat. 8–7.*

⑭ Enter the **Medici Chapels** from Piazza Madonna degli Aldobrandini, behind San Lorenzo. These remarkable chapels contain the tombs of practically every member of the Medici family, and there were a lot of them, for they guided Florence's destiny from the 15th century to 1737. Cosimo I, a Medici whose acumen made him the richest man in Europe, is buried in the crypt of the Chapel of the Princes, and Donatello's tomb is next to that of his patron. The chapel upstairs is decorated in an eye-dazzling array of colored marble. In Michelangelo's New Sacristy, his tombs of Giuliano and Lorenzo de' Medici bear the justly famed statues of *Dawn* and *Dusk*, and *Night* and *Day*. *Piazza Madonna degli Aldobrandini, tel. 055/213206. Admission: 8,500 lire. Open Tues.–Sat. 9–2, Sun. 9–1.*

You can take either Via Panzani or Via del Melarancio to the large square next to the massive church of **Santa Maria Novella,** a handsome building in the Tuscan version of Gothic style. See it from the other end of Piazza Santa Maria Novella for the best view of its facade. Inside are some famous paintings, especially Masaccio's *Trinity,* a Giotto crucifix in the sacristy, and Ghirlandaio's frescoes in the apse. *Piazza Santa Maria Novella, tel. 055/210113. Open Mon.–Sat. 7–11:30 and 3:30–6, Sun. 3:30–6.*

Next door to the church is the entrance to the **cloisters,** worth a visit for their serene atmosphere and the restored Paolo Uccello frescoes. *Piazza Santa Maria Novella 19, tel. 055/282187. Admission: 4,000 lire. Open Mon.–Thurs., Sat. 9–2, Sun. 8–1.*

Only a few blocks behind Piazza della Signoria is the **Bargello,** a fortresslike palace that served as residence of Florence's chief magistrate in medieval times, and later as a prison. Don't be put off by its grim look, for it now houses Florence's **Museo Nazionale** (National Museum), a treasure house of Italian Renaissance sculpture—it is to Renaissance sculpture what the Uffizi is to Renaissance painting. In a historically and visually interesting setting, it displays masterpieces by Donatello, Verrocchio, Michelangelo, and many other major sculptors, so don't shortchange yourself on time. *Via del Proconsolo 4, tel. 055/210801. Admission: 6,000 lire. Open Tues.–Sat. 9–2, Sun. 9–1.*

From Piazza San Firenze follow Via degli Anguillara or Borgo dei Greci toward Piazza Santa Croce. En route you'll pass close by **Vivoli,** which dispenses what many consider the best ice cream in Florence. (It's at Via Isole delle Stinche 7/r, on a little side street, the second left off Via degli Anguillara as you head toward Santa Croce.)

The mighty church of **Santa Croce** was begun in 1294; inside, Giotto's frescoes brighten two chapels and monumental tombs of Michelangelo, Galileo, Machiavelli, and other Renaissance luminaries line the walls. In the adjacent museum, you can see what remains of a Giotto crucifix, irreparably damaged by a flood in 1966, when water rose to 16 feet in parts of the church. The **Pazzi Chapel** in the cloister is an architectural gem by Brunelleschi. *Piazza Santa Croce, tel. 055/244619. Church open Mon.–Sat. 7–12:30 and 3–6:30, Sun. 3–6. Opera di Santa Croce (Museum and Pazzi Chapel), tel. 055/244619. Admission: 3,000 lire. Open Mar.–Sept., Thurs.–Tues. 10–12:30 and 2:30–6:30; Oct.–Feb., Thurs.–Tues. 10–12:30 and 3–5.*

The monastery of Santa Croce harbors a leather-working school and showroom, with entrances at Via San Giuseppe 5/r and Piazza Santa Croce 16. The entire Santa Croce area is known for its leather factories and inconspicuous shops selling gold and silver jewelry at prices much lower than those of the elegant jewelers near the Ponte Vecchio.

Ponte Vecchio, Oltrarno The **Ponte Vecchio,** Florence's oldest bridge, is the second bridge you'll encounter as you walk along the river toward the center. It seems to be just another street lined with goldsmiths' shops until you get to the middle and catch a glimpse of the Arno flowing below. Spared during World War II by the retreating Germans (who blew up every other bridge in the city), it also survived the 1966 flood. It leads into the **Oltrarno district,** which has its own charm and still preserves much of the atmosphere of oldtime Florence, full of fascinating craft workshops.

But for the moment you should head straight down Via Guicciardini to **Palazzo Pitti,** a 15th-century extravaganza that the Medicis acquired from the Pitti family shortly after the latter had gone deeply into debt to build it. Its long facade on the immense piazza was designed by Brunelleschi: Solid and severe, it looks like a Roman aqueduct turned into a palace. The palace houses several museums: One displays the fabulous Medici collection of objects in silver and gold; another is the **Gallery of Modern Art.** The most famous museum, though, is the **Palatine Gallery,** with an extraordinary collection of paintings, many hung frame-to-frame in a clear case of artistic overkill. Some are high up in dark corners, so try to go on a bright day. *Piazza dei Pitti, tel. 055/210323. Gallery of Modern Art. Admission: 4,000 lire. Palatine Gallery. Admission: 8,000 lire. Silver Museum. Admission: 6,000 lire (includes admission to the Porcelain Museum and Historical Costume Gallery). All open Tues.–Sat. 9–2, Sun. 9–1.*

Take time for a refreshing stroll in the **Boboli Gardens** behind Palazzo Pitti, a typical Italian garden laid out in 1550 for Cosimo Medici's wife, Eleanor of Toledo. *Piazza dei Pitti, tel. 055/213440. Admission free. Open Tues.–Sun. Apr., May, and Sept., 9–6:30; June–Aug., 9–7:30; Oct. and Mar.–Apr., 9–5:30; Nov.–Feb., 9–4:30.*

In the far corner of Piazza dei Pitti, poets Elizabeth Barrett and Robert Browning lived in the **Casa Guidi,** facing the smaller Piazza San Felice. *Piazza San Felice 8, tel. 055/284393. Admission free. Open by appointment.*

The church of **Santo Spirito** is important as one of Brunelleschi's finest architectural creations, and it contains some superb paintings, including a Filippino Lippi *Madonna.* Santo Spirito is the hub of a colorful neighborhood of artisans and intellectuals. An **outdoor market** enlivens the square every morning except Sunday; in the afternoon, pigeons, pet owners, and pensioners take over. The area is definitely on an upward trend, with new cafés, restaurants, and upscale shops opening every day.

Walk down Via Sant'Agostino and Via Santa Monaca to the church of **Santa Maria del Carmine,** of no architectural interest but of immense significance in the history of Renaissance art. It contains the celebrated frescoes painted by Masaccio in the **Brancacci Chapel,** unveiled not long ago after a lengthy and meticulous restoration. The chapel was a classroom for such artistic giants as Botticelli, Leonardo da Vinci, Michelangelo, and Raphael, since they all came to study Masaccio's realistic use of light and perspective and his creation of space and depth. *Piazza del Carmine, tel. 055/212331. Admission: 5,000 lire. Open Mon. and Wed.–Sat. 10–5, Sun. 1–5.*

Take the No. 13 bus from the train station or cathedral up to Piazzale Michelangelo, then walk along Viale dei Colli and climb to **San Miniato al Monte,** a charming green-and-white marble Romanesque church full of artistic riches.

Shopping

Florence offers top quality for your money in leather goods, linens and upholstery fabrics, gold and silver jewelry, and cameos. Straw goods, gilded-wood trays and frames, hand-printed paper desk accessories, and ceramic objects make good inexpensive gifts. Many shops offer fine old prints.

Department Stores UPIM, in Piazza della Repubblica and various other locations, has inexpensive goods of all types.

Markets The big food market at **Piazza del Mercato Centrale** is open in the morning (Mon.–Sat.) and is worth a visit. The **San Lorenzo market** on Piazza San Lorenzo and Via dell'Ariento is a fine place to browse for buys in leather goods and souvenirs (open Tues. and Sat. 8–7; also Sun. in summer). The **Mercato Nuovo,** Via Calimala, which is sometimes called the **Mercato del Porcellino** because of the famous bronze statue of a boar at one side, is packed with stalls selling souvenirs and straw goods (open Tues.–Sat. 8–7; closed Sun. and Mon. morning in winter). There's a colorful neighborhood market at **Sant'Ambrogio,** Piazza Ghiberti (open Mon.–Sat. morning), and a permanent flea market at **Piazza Ciompi** (open Mon.–Sat. 9–1 and 4–7, Sun. 9–1 in summer).

Dining

Mealtimes in Florence are 12:30–2 and 7:30–9 or later. Many Moderate and Inexpensive places are small, and you may have to share a table. Reservations are always advisable; to find a table at inexpensive places, get there early.

For details and price-category definitions, *see* Dining in Staying in Italy.

Moderate **Buca Mario.** Visitors can expect to share a table at this characteristically unadorned *buca* (downstairs trattoria), whose menu includes such hearty down-to-earth Tuscan food as homemade *pappardelle* (noodles) and *stracotto* (beef stew with beans). It's near Santa Maria Novella. *Piazza Ottaviani 16/r, tel. 055/214179. Reservations advised in evening. AE, DC, MC, V. Closed Thurs. lunch and Wed. and Aug.*
Cavallini. It makes sense that this restaurant, with its outdoor café, is touristy, since it's situated right on Piazza della Signoria. But it is also consistently good, and it's open on Sunday. The cooking is pure Tuscan, with broad pappardelle noodles, bean soup, and grilled meat on the menu. *Via della Farina 6/r, tel. 055/215818. Reservations advised, especially for outdoor tables. AE, DC, MC, V. Closed Tues. eve., Wed., and Aug. 1–22.*
Il Fagioli. This typical Florentine trattoria near Santa Croce has a simple decor and a menu in which such local dishes as *ribollita* (vegetable-and-bread soup) and involtini predominate. *Corso Tintori 47/r, tel. 055/244285. Reservations advised. No credit cards. Closed weekends, Aug., and Christmas Day.*
Leo. Located in the Santa Croce area, Leo caters to tourists (especially at lunch) and locals in an attractive setting of vaulted ceilings and dark Tuscan-style wooden chairs. Order the daily specials here and the *crostini Pier Capponi* (toast rounds with a savory topping). *Via Torta 7/r, tel. 055/210829.*

Dinner reservations advised. AE, DC, MC, V. Closed Mon. and mid-July–mid-Aug.

Mario da Ganino. Highly informal, rustic, and cheerful, this trattoria greets you with a taste of mortadella, and offers homemade pastas and *gnudoni* (ravioli without pasta), plus a heavenly cheesecake for dessert. It's tiny, seating only 35, double that in summer at outdoor tables. *Piazza dei Cimatori 4/r, tel. 055/214125. Reservations advised. AE, DC. Closed Sun. and Aug. 15–25.*

Inexpensive **Acqua al Due.** At this tiny, popular restaurant near the Bargello you can make a meal of pasta and find a really good hamburger. *Via dell'Acqua 2/r, tel. 055/284170. No reservations. AE, MC, V. Closed Mon. and Tues.*

★ **Angiolino.** You won't regret taking a meal at this bustling little trattoria. Glowing with authentic atmosphere, Angiolino offers such Tuscan specialties as *ribollita* (minestrone) and juicy *bistecca alla fiorentina* (T-bone steak basted in olive oil and black pepper). The bistecca will push the bill up into the Moderate range. *Via Santo Spirito 36/r, tel. 055/239–8976. Reservations advised in the evening. No credit cards. Closed Sun. dinner, Mon., and last 3 weeks in July.*

Caminetto. Try the *maccheroni alla maremmana* (pasta with sausages, tomato, and black olives) or *pappa al pomodoro* (tomato-and-bread soup). The rustic Caminentto is handy for a quick lunch before or after visiting the cathedral. *Via dello Studio 34/r, tel. 055/296274. Dinner reservations advised. No credit cards. Closed Tues., Wed., and July.*

Del Carmine. This typical neighborhood trattoria is a favorite discovery of tourists out to see the Masaccio frescoes in the church across the square. *Piazza del Carmine 18/r, tel. 055/218601. Reservations advised. AE, DC, MC, V. Closed Sun.*

Za-Za. Informal but trendy, this trattoria near the San Lorenzo market serves classic Florentine food, including the vegetable-and-bread minestrone known as *ribollita. Piazza del Mercato Centrale 16/r, tel. 055/215411. Reservations advised. AE, DC, MC, V. Closed Sat. evening, Sun.*

Budget **Casa del Vin Santo.** It's a bustling combination restaurant–pizzeria–tavola calda, it's in the heart of town, and it's a good bet for a quick meal. *Via Porta Rossa 17/r, tel. 055/216995. No reservations. AE, MC, V. Closed Wed.*

Mario. Clean and classic, this family-run trattoria on a corner of Piazza del Mercato Centrale near San Lorenzo offers genuine Florentine cooking and good house wine. *Via Rosina (Piazza del Mercato Centrale). No phone. No credit cards. No dinner. Closed Sun.*

Nuti. On a central street where there are plenty of other budget alternatives, Nuti is an old favorite, with minimal decor and good pizza, soups, and pasta. It's open all day until 1 AM. *Via Borgo San Lorenzo 22, tel. 055/210145. No reservations. No credit cards. Closed Mon.*

Lodging

What with mass tourism and trade fairs, rooms are at a premium in Florence for most of the year. Make reservations well in advance. If you arrive without a reservation, the ITA office in the railway station (open 8:20 AM–9 PM) can help you, but there may be a long line. Now that most traffic is banned in the downtown area, hotel rooms are quieter. Local traffic and motorcycles can still be bothersome, however, so check the decibel level before you settle in.

For details and price-category definitions, *see* Lodging in Staying in Italy. Keep in mind that rooms without bath in inexpensive hotels can be had at budget rates. Hotels may require that guests take breakfast, priced disproportionately high. Be sure you understand the all-inclusive rate, or try to get by with paying for your room only.

Moderate **Apollo.** One of two hostelries run by the same owner (*see* Tony's Inn, *below*), it is bright and cheery and handy to the station and most sights. Rooms are distributed on two floors, and all have photos by proprietor-photographer Lelli on the walls. *Via Faenza 77, tel. 055/284119, fax 055/210101. 15 rooms with bath. No credit cards.*

Bellettini. This central hotel occupies two floors of an old but well-kept building near the Church of San Lorenzo, handy to inexpensive eating places. Rooms are ample, with Venetian or Tuscan decor, and bathrooms are modern. *Via dei Conti 7, tel. 055/213561, fax 055/283551. 27 rooms, 23 with bath. Facilities: bar, lounge. AE, DC, MC, V.*

Liana. Located in a residential neighborhood, this small hotel is within walking distance of most sights. It's a dignified 19th-century town house with pleasant rooms overlooking the garden and bright new baths. *Via Vittorio Alfieri 18, tel. 055/245303., fax 055/234-4596. 26 rooms, 23 with bath. Facilities: parking lot, garden. AE, MC, V.*

Nuova Italia. This pleasant place close to the train station is run by an English-speaking family. There are lots of paintings on the walls, well-furnished rooms with bath, and low rates for this category, inclusive of breakfast. *Via Faenza 26, tel. 055/287508, fax 055/210941. 20 rooms with bath. AE, DC, MC, V.*

Rigatti. Furnished with antiques and located on the top two floors of a building between Palazzo Vecchio and Santa Croce, the Rigatti has views of the Arno from a tiny front terrace. *Lungarno Diaz 2, tel. 055/213022. 28 rooms, 14 with bath. No credit cards.*

Inexpensive **Alessandra.** Only a block from the Ponte Vecchio, the Alessandra is clean and well kept, with large rooms and a friendly, English-speaking staff. *Borgo Santi Apostoli 17, tel. 055/283438, fax 055/210619. 25 rooms, 18 with bath. MC, V.*

Ausonia. A cordial sister team runs this tiny hotel near the train station. Many rooms have private bath; those without are budget values. Special winter rates make it even more affordable. *Via Nazionale 24, tel. 055/496547, fax 055/496324. 20 rooms, 11 with bath. AE, MC, V.*

Tony's Inn. High-ceiling rooms in an 18th-century building near the train station are bright with enlargements of the owner's photos. Some rooms have 18th-century decor, and many can accommodate an extra bed. Two rooms have balconies. *Via Faenza 77, tel. 055/217975, fax 055/210101. 23 rooms, 20 with bath. AE, MC, V.*

Budget **Accademia.** Near the train station and within walking distance of most sights, this is a simply furnished but comfortable family-run hotel. Guests mingle in the homey living room and large breakfast room. *Via Faenza 7, tel. 055/293451. 16 rooms, 9 with bath. V.*

Globus. The Globus has a handy location between the train station and the San Lorenzo market, where there are plenty of inexpensive eating places. There is a small, homey lounge. Rooms without bath are a bargain. *Via Sant'Antonino 24, tel. 055/ 211062. 21 rooms, 3 with bath. No credit cards.*

Mary. Located on a parklike square, the Mary is near the station and the San Marco museum. Rooms are simply furnished, and there are stairs to climb, but the proprietor couldn't be nicer (regulars say staying here is like staying at a friend's home). Rates are low, even for rooms with private baths. *Piazza Indipendenza 5, tel. 055/496310. 12 rooms, 9 with bath. No credit cards.*

The Arts

For a list of events, pick up a "Florence Concierge Information" booklet from your hotel desk, or the monthly information bulletin published by the **Comune Aperto** city information office (Via Cavour 1/r).

Music and Ballet Most major musical events are staged at the **Teatro Comunale** (Corso Italia 16, tel. 055/277–9236). The box office (closed Mon.) is open from 9 to 1, and a half-hour before performances. It's best to order your tickets by mail, however, as they're difficult to come by at the last minute. You can also order concert and ballet tickets through **Universalturismo** (Via degli Speziali 7/r, tel. 055/217241). **Amici della Musica** (Friends of Music) puts on a series of concerts at the **Teatro della Pergola** (box office, Via della Pergola 10r, tel. 055/247–9651). For program information, contact the Amici della Musica directly at Via Sirtori 49 (tel. 055/608420).

Film English-language films are shown at the **Cinema Astro,** on Piazza San Simone near Santa Croce. There are two shows every evening, Tuesday through Sunday. It closes in July.

Nightlife

Other than strolling and hanging out in the cathedral square, Piazza della Signoria, and Piazzale Michelangelo, there's not much to do in Florence at night. Discos cost about 15,000 lire for entrance and a first drink. The most popular with a young international crowd are **Yab Yum** (Via Sassetti 5/r, tel. 055/ 282018) and **Space Electronic** (Via Palazzuolo 37, tel. 055/239– 3082). There are several beer halls, including **Be-Bop** (Via dei Servi 76/r), **Il Boccale** (Borgo Santi Apostoli 33/r), and **Nuti** (Via Borgo San Lorenzo 22), which stay open late.

Tuscany

Tuscany is a blend of rugged hills, fertile valleys, and long, sandy beaches that curve along the west coast of central Italy and fringe the pine-forested coastal plain of the Maremma. The gentle, cypress-studded green hills may seem familiar: Leonardo and Raphael often painted them in the backgrounds of their masterpieces. To most people, Tuscan art means Florence, but the other cities and towns of the region contain gems of art and architecture—the artists of the Middle Ages and the Renaissance took their work where they found it. Come to Tuscany to enjoy its unchanged and gracious atmosphere of good living, and, above all, its unparalleled artistic treasures, many still in their original settings in tiny old churches and patrician palaces.

Getting Around

By Train The main train network connects Florence with Pisa, while a secondary line goes from Prato to the coast via Lucca.

By Bus The entire region is crisscrossed by bus lines, good alternatives to trains, especially for reaching Siena. Use local buses to tour the many pretty hill towns around Siena, such as San Gimignano, and then take a train or bus from Siena to Arezzo, where you can get back onto the main Rome–Florence train line.

Guided Tours

American Express (Via Guicciardini 49/r, tel. 055/278751) operates one-day excursions to Siena and San Gimignano out of Florence.

Tourist Information

Lucca (Via Vittorio Veneto 40, tel. 0583/493639; Piazza Guidiccione 2, tel.. 0583/41205).
Pisa (Piazza del Duomo, tel. 050/560464).
Siena (Via di Città 43, tel. 0577/42209; Piazza del Campo 56, tel. 0577/280551).

Exploring Tuscany

Lucca Less than 90 minutes from Florence by train or bus is **Lucca,** Puccini's hometown and a city well-loved by sightseers who appreciate the careful upkeep of its medieval look. Though it hasn't the number of hotels and other tourist trappings that, say, Pisa does, for that very reason it's a pleasant alternative. You can easily make an excursion to Pisa from here by either train or bus—it's only 22 kilometers (14 miles) away. First enjoy the views of the city and countryside from the tree-planted 16th-century ramparts that encircle Lucca. Then explore the city's marvelously elaborate Romanesque churches, fronted with tiers and rows of columns, and looking suspiciously like oversize marble wedding cakes.

From vast **Piazza Napoleone,** a swing around the Old Town will take you past the 11th-century **Duomo** on Piazza San Martino, with its 15th-century tomb of Ilaria del Carretto by Jacopo della Quercia. Don't neglect a ramble through the **Piazza del Mercato,** which preserves the oval form of the Roman amphitheater over which it was built, or the three surrounding streets that are filled with atmosphere: **Via Battisti, Via Fillungo,** and **Via Guinigi.** In addition to the Duomo, Lucca has two other fine churches. **San Frediano** (Piazza San Frediano) is graced with an austere facade ornamented by 13th-century mosaic decoration. Inside, see the exquisite reliefs by Jacopo della Quercia in the last chapel on the left. **San Michele in Foro** (Piazza San Michele) is an exceptional example of the Pisan Romanesque style and decorative flair peculiar to Lucca: Note its facade, a marriage of arches and columns crowned by a statue of St. Michael.

Pisa **Pisa** is a dull, overcommercialized place, though even skeptics have to admit that the **Torre Pendente** (Leaning Tower) really is one of the world's more amazing sights. Theories vary as to whether the now-famous list is due to shifting foundations or to an amazing architectural feat by Bonanno Pisano (the first of three architects to work on the tower). A 294-step staircase spirals its way up. If you want a two-foot marble imitation of the Leaning Tower, perhaps even illuminated from within, this is your chance to grab one! *Campo dei Miracoli.*

Pisa has two other fine buildings, and, conveniently enough, they're next to the Leaning Tower. The **baptistery** was begun in 1153 but not completed until 1400, the Pisano family doing most of its decoration. Test out the excellent acoustics (occasionally the guard will slam the great doors shut and then sing a few notes—the resulting echo is very impressive, and costly, too, since he'll expect a tip). *Piazza del Duomo, in the Campo dei Miracoli. Open daily 9–sunset.*

Pisa's **Duomo** is elegantly simple, its facade decorated with geometric and animal shapes. The cavernous interior is supported by a series of 68 columns, while the pulpit is a fine example of Giovanni Pisano's work. Be sure to note the suspended lamp that hangs across from the pulpit; known as Galileo's Lamp, it's said to have inspired his theories on pendular motion. *Piazza del Duomo. Open daily 8–12:45 and 3–sunset.*

From Pisa you can take a train to Florence, where you can get a bus or train for the 60-minute trip to Siena. SITA buses are more convenient than the train, however, because you have to take a local bus from the Siena train station up to the town. SITA deposits passengers within walking distance of the sights.

Siena **Siena** is one of Italy's best-preserved medieval towns, rich both in works of art and in expensive antique shops. The famous **Palio** is held here, a breakneck, 90-second horse race that takes place twice each year in the Piazza del Campo, on July 2 and August 16. Built on three hills, Siena is not an easy town to explore, for everything you'll want to see is either up or down a steep hill or stairway. But it is worth every ounce of effort. Siena really gives you an idea of what the Middle Ages must have been like: dark stone palaces, low dwellings, and narrow streets opening out into airy squares.

Siena was a center of learning and art during the Middle Ages, and almost all the public buildings and churches in the town have enough artistic or historical merit to be worth visiting. Unlike most churches, Siena's **Duomo** has a mixture of religious and civic symbols ornamenting both its interior and exterior. The cathedral museum in the unfinished transept contains some fine works of art, notably a celebrated *Maestà* by Duccio di Buoninsegna. The animated frescoes of papal history in the Piccolomini Library (with an entrance off the left aisle of the cathedral) are credited to Pinturicchio and are worth seeking out. *Piazza del Duomo. Cathedral Museum. Admission: 4,000 lire. Open mid-Mar.–Oct., daily 9–7:30; Nov.–mid-Mar., daily 9–1:30. Library. Admission: 1,500 lire. Open mid-Mar.–Oct., daily 9–7:30; Nov.–mid-Mar., daily 10–1 and 2:30–5.*

Nearby, the fan-shaped **Piazza del Campo** is Siena's main center of activity, with 11 streets leading into it. Farsighted planning has preserved it as a medieval showpiece, containing the

13th-century **Palazzo Pubblico** (City Hall) and the **Torre del Mangia** (Bell Tower). Try to visit both these buildings, the former for Lorenzetti's frescoes on the effects of good and bad government, the latter for the wonderful view (you'll have to climb 503 steps to reach it, however). *Piazza del Campo, tel. 0577/ 292111. Bell Tower. Admission: 4,000 lire. Open Apr.–Sept., Mon.–Sat. 9:30–7:30; Oct.–Mar., Mon.–Sat. 9:30–1:30, Sun. 9:30–1. Palazzo Pubblico (Civic Museum). Admission: 5,500 lire. Open Apr.–Oct., Mon.–Sat. 9:30–7:30, Sun. 9:30–1:30; Nov.–Mar., daily 9:30–1:30.*

From Siena make an excursion to **San Gimignano,** about a half hour by bus. It is perhaps the most delightful of the Tuscan medieval hill towns with their timeless charm. There were once 79 tall towers here, symbols of power for the wealthy families of the Middle Ages. Thirteen are still standing, giving the town its unique skyline. The bus stops just outside the town gates, from which you can stroll down the main street to the picturesque Piazza della Cisterna.

Just around the corner is the church of the **Collegiata.** Its walls, and those of its chapel dedicated to Santa Fina, are decorated with radiant frescoes. From the steps of the church you can observe the town's countless crows as they circle the tall towers. In the pretty courtyard on the right as you descend the church stairs, there's a shop selling Tuscan and Deruta ceramics, which you'll also find in other shops along the Via San Giovanni. The excellent San Gimignano wine could be another souvenir of your visit; it's sold in gift cartons from just about every shop in town.

Dining and Lodging

For details and price-category definitions, *see* Dining and Lodging in Staying in Italy.

Lucca **Il Giglio.** Off vast Piazza Napoleone, Il Giglio has a quiet, turn-
Dining of-the-century charm and a dignified atmosphere. In the summer the tables outdoors have a less formal air. The menu is classic: *crostini* (savory Tuscan chicken liver, anchovy, and caper paste on small pieces of toast), *stracotto* (braised beef with mushrooms), and seafood, as well. *Piazza del Giglio 3, tel. 0583/ 44058. Dinner reservations advised. AE, DC, MC, V. Closed Tues. dinner and Wed. Moderate.*
Giulio. Although it was recently renovated and enlarged, this classic trattoria hasn't changed its menu (a trove of local dishes) or its prices. *Via delle Conce 47, tel. 0583/55948. Reservations advised. No credit cards. Closed Sun. and Mon. Inexpensive.*

Lodging **Universo.** There's plenty of genteel, Old World charm here to
★ please those looking for the atmosphere of times past. During renovation completed in 1992, rooms were modernized and endowed with TV, fridge-bars, and sparkling new baths. *Piazza del Giglio 1, tel. 0583/493678. 60 rooms with bath. V. Moderate.*
Ilaria. This small, family-run hotel sits in a pretty location on a minuscule canal within easy walking distance of the main sights. The rooms are smallish but fresh and functional. *Via del Fosso 20, tel. 0583/47558. 17 rooms, most with bath. AE, DC, MC, V. Inexpensive.*

Pisa **Bruno.** A country-inn look, with beamed ceilings and soft
Dining lights, makes Bruno a pleasant place to lunch on classic Tuscan

dishes, from *zuppa alla pisana* (vegetable soup) to *baccalà con porri* (cod with leeks). It's just outside the old city walls and only a short walk from the bell tower and cathedral. *Via Luigi Bianchi 12, tel. 050/560818. Reservations advised. AE, DC, MC, V. Closed Mon. dinner, Tues., Aug. 5–15. Moderate.*

Spartaco. Centrally located on the station square, Spartaco has the solid look of the well-established trattoria that it is, with contemporary white chairs contrasting with terra-cotta-tiled walls and some fine antique pieces. It's large, and seating doubles in the summer when tables are set out on the square. Specialties include a cocktail of ravioli in different colors and grilled fish, along with the usual Tuscan dishes. *Piazza Vittorio Emanuele 22, tel. 050/20457. Reservations accepted. AE, DC, MC, V. Closed Sun. Moderate.*

Lodging **Terminus Plaza.** Conveniently located near the train station but across town from the famous tower, this is a basic commercial hotel. Ask for a quiet room away from the street. *Via Colombo 45, tel. 050/500303, fax 050/502148. 52 rooms, most with bath. AE, DC, MC, V. Moderate.*

Ariston. You couldn't ask for anything closer to the tower—it's practically outside the door of this smallish, simply furnished hotel. *Via Maffi 42, tel. 050/561834, fax 050/561891. 33 rooms, 23 with bath. DC, MC, V. Inexpensive.*

San Gimignano **Bel Soggiorno.** Bel Soggiorno is attached to a small hotel. It has
Dining fine views, refectory tables set with linen and candles, and leather-covered chairs. Specialties are *pappardelle alla lepre* (egg noodles with hare sauce) and herbed grilled meat. Order carefully to keep your check within moderate range. *Via San Giovanni 89, tel. 0577/940375. Reservations advised. AE, DC, MC, V. Closed Mon. and Jan. 7–Feb. 7. Moderate.*

Delle Catene. This is one of the little trattorie in San Gimignano's byways, off the main street, where you can eat well at moderate prices. It's run by a trio of young hosts who oversee a menu offering typical Tuscan food: *ribollita* (thick minestrone) and pork roasted with wine. *Via Mainardi 18, tel. 0577/984966. Reservations advised. AE, DC, MC, V. Closed Wed. Moderate.*

Stella. Farm-fresh vegetables and the owner's own olive oil are part of the fare at this simple trattoria. *Via San Matteo 77, tel. 0577/940444. No reservations. AE, DC, MC, V. Closed Wed. and Jan. 6–Feb. 15. Inexpensive.*

Siena **Tullio Tre Cristi.** This historic trattoria is off Via dei Rossi,
Dining which is off Via Banchi di Sopra. Try *spaghetti alle briciole*, a poor-man's pasta, with bread crumbs, tomato, and garlic. *Vicolo di Provenzano 1, tel. 0577/280608. No reservations. AE, DC, MC, V. Closed Sun. evening, Mon., and Jan. Moderate.*

La Grotta del Gallo Nero. At this wine cellar off Piazza del Campo, Chianti is king, and you can make a meal of *crostini* (toast with liver pâté) and local cheese. There are hot dishes, too. *Via del Porrione 65, tel. 0577/220446. No reservations. No credit cards. Closed Sun. Inexpensive.*

★ **La Torre.** The kitchen and dining room of this family-run trattoria a few blocks from the Mangia Tower are in full view of each other. Try the homemade *pici*, the local pasta, and soups. The *arista* (roast pork) is redolent of herbs. *Via Salicotto 7, tel. 0577/287548. No reservations. No credit cards. Closed Thurs. and Aug. 14–31. Inexpensive.*

Le Tre Campane. Boasting a convenient location between Piazza del Campo and the Duomo, this small trattoria displays the colorful banners of Siena's 17 districts. Popular with the locals, it specializes in Tuscan fare and a *trittico* (trio) of pastas. *Piazzetta Bonelli, tel. 0577/286091. Reservations advised. No credit cards. Closed Tues. and Jan.–Feb. Inexpensive.*

Lodging **Duomo.** This simply furnished hotel is in the heart of Siena, in the Contrada della Pantera, one of the districts that competes for the Palio. The Duomo occupies one floor of a large *palazzo. Via Stalloreggi 38, tel. 0557/289088, fax 0577/43043. 22 rooms, 18 with bath. AE, MC, V. Moderate.*

Chiusarelli. Near the SITA bus stop and within walking distance of Piazza del Campo, this is an undistinguished commercial hotel, but it's clean and quiet. *Viale Curtatone 9, tel. 0577/ 280562, fax 0577/271177. 50 rooms with bath. MC, V. Inexpensive.*

Lea. In a residential neighborhood separated by a ravine from the medieval center, Lea is an 18th-century villa with garden, transformed into an intimate family-run hotel. *Viale XXIV Maggio 10, tel. 0577/283207. 13 rooms with bath. No credit cards. Inexpensive.*

Tre Donzelle. This hotel in the heart of Siena, off Piazza del Campo, has an unbeatable location that makes you feel a part of Sienese life. Tre Donzelle has basic modern furnishings; rooms without bath are a bargain. *Via delle Donzelle 5, tel. 0577/ 280358. 27 rooms, 7 with bath. No credit cards. Budget.*

Milan

Arriving and Departing

As Lombardy's capital and the most important financial and commercial center in northern Italy, Milan is well connected with Rome and Florence by fast and frequent rail and air service, though the latter is often delayed in winter by heavy fog.

By Plane Linate Airport, 11 kilometers (7 miles) outside Milan, handles mainly domestic and European flights (tel. 02/7485–2200). Malpensa, 50 kilometers (30 miles) from the city, handles intercontinental flights (tel. 02/7485–2200).

Between the Airport and Downtown Buses connect both airports with Milan, stopping at the central station and at the Porta Garibaldi station. Fare from Linate is 2,500 lire on the special airport bus or 1,000 lire on municipal bus no. 73 (to Piazza San Babila); from Malpensa 8,000 lire.

By Train The main train terminal is the central station in Piazzale Duca d'Aosta (tel. 02/67500). Several smaller stations handle commuter trains. There are several fast Intercity trains daily between Rome and Milan, stopping in Florence. A nonstop Intercity leaves from Rome or Milan morning and evening, taking about four hours to go between the two cities.

Getting Around

By Subway Milan's subway network, the Metropolitana, is modern, fast, and easy to use. "MM" signs mark Metropolitana stations. There are at present two lines, with another scheduled to open soon. The ATM (city transport authority) has an information office on the mezzanine of the Duomo Metro station (tel. 02/ 875495). Tickets are sold at newsstands at every stop, and in ticket machines *for exact change only.* The fare is 1,000 lire, and the subway runs from 6:20 AM to midnight.

By Bus and Buy tickets at newsstands, tobacco shops, and bars. Fare is
Streetcar 1,000 lire. One ticket is valid for 75 minutes on all surface lines, and one subway trip. Daily tickets valid for 24 hours on all public transportation lines are on sale at the Duomo Metro station ATM Information Office, and at Stazione Centrale Metro station.

Tourist Information

APT information offices (Via Marconi 1, tel. 02/809662; Central Station, tel. 02/669–0432). **Municipal Information Office** (Galleria Vittorio Emanuele at the corner of Piazza della Scala, tel. 02/870545).

Exploring Milan

Numbers in the margin correspond to points of interest on the Milan map.

The center of Milan is the Piazza del Duomo. The massive
① **Duomo** is one of the largest churches in the world, a mountain of marble fretted with statues, spires, and flying buttresses. The interior is a more solemn Italian Gothic. Take the elevator or walk up 158 steps to the roof, from which—if it's a clear day—you can see over the city to the Lombard plain and the Alps beyond, all through an amazing array of spires and statues. The **Madonnina,** a gleaming gilt statue on the highest spire, is a Milan landmark. *Entrance to elevator and stairway outside the cathedral, to the right. Admission: stairs, 3,000 lire; elevator, 5,000 lire. Open Mar.–Oct., daily 9–5:45; Nov.– Feb. 9–4:15.*

Outside the cathedral to the right is the elegant, glass-roofed
② **Galleria,** where the Milanese and visitors stroll, window-shop, and sip pricey cappuccinos at trendy cafés. At the other end of
③ the Galleria is **Piazza della Scala,** with Milan's city hall on one
④ side and **Teatro alla Scala,** the world-famous opera house, opposite.

Via Verdi, flanking the opera house, leads to Via Brera, where
⑤ the **Pinacoteca di Brera** houses one of Italy's great collections of paintings. Most are of a religious nature, confiscated in the 19th century when many religious orders were suppressed and their churches closed. *Via Brera 28, tel. 02/864–63501. Admission: 8,000 lire. Open Tues. and Thurs.–Sat. 9–1:30, Wed. 9– 1:30 and 3–5:30, Sun. 9–12:30. (Hours may vary; check locally.)*

After an eyeful of artworks by Mantegna, Raphael, and many other Italian masters, stop at the pleasant café open to Brera visitors (just inside the entrance to the gallery), or explore the Brera neighborhood, dotted with art galleries, chic little restaurants, and such offbeat cafés as the **Jamaica** (Via Brera 26),
⑥ once a bohemian hangout. Take Via dei Fiori Chiari in front of the Brera and keep going in the same direction to the moated
⑦ **Castello Sforzesco,** a somewhat sinister 19th-century reconstruction of the imposing 15th-century fortress built by the Sforzas, who succeeded the Viscontis as lords of Milan in the 15th century. It now houses wide-ranging collections of sculp-

Milan

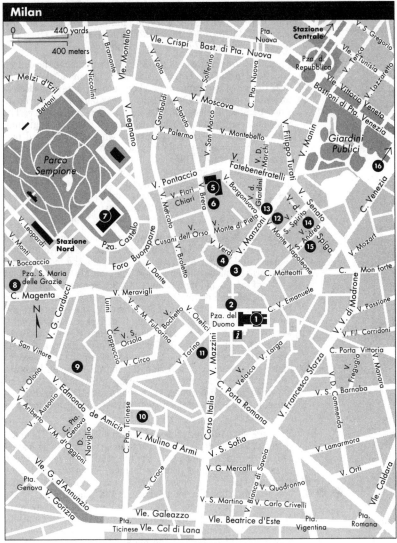

0 440 yards
400 meters

Vle. Crispi · Bast. di Pta. Nuova

Pta. Nuova

Stazione Centrale

Pza. d. Repubblica

V. Melzi d'Eril

V. Bertani

V. Bramante

V. Montello

V. Niccolini

V. Volta

V. Solferino

V. Moscova

C. Pta. Nuova

V. Filippo Turati

V. Mann

Vle. Vittoria Veneto

Bastioni di Pta. Venezia

V. Legnano

V. Garibaldi

V. Statuto

V. Palermo

V. San Marco

V. Montebello

V. d. Marchi

Giardini Publici

Parco Sempione

V. Fatebenefratelli

V. Pontaccio

V. Borgonuovo

V. Giardini

V. d. Senato

C. Venezia

V. Mozart

Mon forte

V. Fiori Chiari

Brera

V. Mercato

Monte di Pieta

V. Manzoni

V. S. Spirito

V. Monte Napoleone

V. Andrea Spiga

Stazione Nord

Pza. Castello

Cusani dell'Orso

V. Verdi

V. Broletto

V. Leopardi

V. Monti

V. Boccaccio

Foro Buonaparte

V. Dante

Pza. S. Maria delle Grazie

C. Magenta

V. Meravigli

V. G. Carducci

Luini

V. S.M. Fulcorina

V. Bochetto

V. Orefici

Pza. del Duomo

C. V. Emanuele

C. Matteotti

C.

V. di Modrone

V. Passione

V. S. Orsola

Cappuccio

V. Circo

V. Torino

V. Mazzini

V. Velasca

V. Larga

V. Fil. Corridoni

V. San Vittore

V. Olona

V. Edmondo de Amicis

Corso Italia

C. Porta Romana

C. Porta Vittoria

C. Francesco Sforza

V. S. Commenda

V. Freguglia

V. S. Barnaba

V. Manara

V. Ariberto

V. Ausonio

V. M. d'Oggiono

C. Pta. Genova

D. Naviglio

V. Pta. Ticinese

V. Mulino d'Armi

S. Croce

V. S. Sofia

V. G. Mercalli

Bianca di Savoia

V. Quadronno

V. Lamarmora

V. Orti

Vle. Caldara

Pta. Genova

V. G. d'Annunzio

V. Gorizia

Vle. Galeazzo

Pta. Ticinese

Vle. Col di Lana

Vle. Beatrice d'Este

V. S. Martino

V. Carlo Crivelli

Pta. Vigentina

Pta. Romana

Castello Sforzesco, **7**

Corso Buenos Aires, **16**

Duomo, **1**

Galleria, **2**

Jamaica, **6**

Piazza della Scala, **3**

Pinacoteca di Brera, **5**

San Lorenzo Maggiore, **10**

San Satiro, **11**

Santa Maria delle Grazie, **8**

Sant'Ambrogio, **9**

Teatro alla Scala, **4**

Via Manzoni, **13**

Via Monte Napoleone, **12**

Via Sant'Andrea, **15**

Via della Spiga, **14**

tures, antiques, and ceramics, including Michelangelo's *Rondanini Pietà*, his last work, left unfinished at his death. *Piazza Castello, tel. 02/6236 ext. 3947. Admission free. Open daily 9:30–5:30; closed last Tues. of month.*

From the vast residence of the Sforzas it's not far to the church of **Santa Maria delle Grazie.** Although portions of the church were designed by Bramante, it plays second fiddle to the **Refectory** next door, where, over a three-year period, Leonardo da Vinci painted his megafamous fresco, *The Last Supper.* The fresco has suffered more than its share of disaster, beginning with the experiments of the artist, who used untested pigments that soon began to deteriorate. *The Last Supper* is now a mere shadow of its former self, despite meticulous restoration that proceeds at a snail's pace. To save what is left, visitors are limited in time and number, and you may have to wait in line to get a glimpse of this world-famous work. *Piazza Santa Maria delle Grazie 2, tel. 02/498–7588. Admission: 10,000 lire. Open Tues.–Sun. 9–1:15. (Hours may vary; check locally.)*

If you are interested in medieval architecture, go to see the medieval church of **Sant'Ambrogio** (Piazza Sant'Ambrogio). Consecrated by St. Ambrose in AD 387, it's the model for all Lombard Romanesque churches, and contains some ancient works of art, including a remarkable 9th-century altar in precious metals and enamels, and some 5th-century mosaics. On December 7, the feast day of St. Ambrose, the streets around the church are the scene of a lively flea market. Another noteworthy church is **San Lorenzo Maggiore** (Corso di Porta Ticinese), with 16 ancient Roman columns in front and some 4th-century mosaics in the Chapel of St. Aquilinus. Closer to Piazza del Duomo on Via Torino, the church of **San Satiro** is another architectural gem in which Bramante's perfect command of proportion and perspective, a characteristic of the Renaissance, made a small interior seem extraordinarily spacious and airy.

The **Peck** shops are only a few steps from San Satiro. The main store, at Via Spadari 9, is Italy's premiere gourmet delicatessen, and a satellite shop at Via Cantu 3 offers an array of snacks to eat on the premises. But for fashion, Milan's most elegant shopping streets are beyond the Duomo—**Via Monte Napoleone, Via Manzoni, Via della Spiga,** and **Via Sant' Andrea.** Prices are stratospheric, so for bargains you'll have to go elsewhere. Make your way to **Corso Buenos Aires,** near the central station, which has hundreds more shops and accessible prices, too. You may also want to take in the huge outdoor market on **Viale Papiniano,** not far south of San Lorenzo Maggiore, if your visit includes a Tuesday or Saturday morning.

Dining

For details and price-category definitions, *see* Dining in Staying in Italy.

Moderate **Antica Trattoria della Pesa.** This quintessential Milanese neighborhood restaurant near Porta Garibaldi has aged dark-wood paneling and white tablecloths. Waiters take their time, but they eventually will provide the traditional *osso buco* (braised veal shank) with risotto on the side. *Viale Pasubio 10, tel. 02/655–5741. Reservations advised. No credit cards. Closed Sun.*
Dina e Pierino. This busy and friendly trattoria in the Brera

district has tables outdoors in fair weather and an inside dining room done in early 1900s style. The menu features Tuscan cuisine, including antipasto, *gnocchi* (potato dumplings) with butter and sage, and *panna cotta* (a delicate milk pudding) for dessert. *Via Marsala 2, tel. 02/659–9488. Reservations advised. No credit cards. Closed Mon. and Aug.*

La Frittata. Near Sant'Ambrogio and the Porta Nuova station, this small restaurant and pizzeria stays open late. The kitchen provides Tuscan-style home cooking, as well as good economical pizzas. *Viale Papiniano 43, tel. 02/402643. Reservations accepted. AE, MC, V. Closed Tues. and Aug.*

Trattoria Milanese. This trattoria on a narrow street near the main post office has simple decor and informal service and offers Milanese food such as minestrone and *cotoletta alla milanese* (breaded veal cutlet). *Via Santa Marta 11, tel. 02/873–8886. Reservations advised. No credit cards. Closed Tues., and Aug.*

Inexpensive **La Bruschetta.** A winning partnership of Tuscans and Neapolitans runs this tiny, busy, and first-class pizzeria near the Duomo. It features the obligatory wood-burning stove, so you can watch your pizza being cooked, though there are plenty of other dishes to choose from as well—try the *spaghetti alle cozze e vongole* (spaghetti with clams and mussels). *Piazza Beccaria 12, tel. 02/802494. Reservations advised, but service is so fast you don't have to wait long. No credit cards. Closed Mon., 3 weeks in Aug.*

Margherita. An old-fashioned wood-burning oven turns out good pizzas amid an otherwise high-tech ambience: Margherita looks vaguely like the Pompidou Center in Paris, with huge pastel-color tubing. *Via Giovanni del Muro 5, tel. 02/805–3939. Reservations advised. MC, V. Closed Sun.*

La Piazzetta. A popular lunch spot in the Brera quarter, it's usually crowded with journalists, actors, and politicians. There's a salad bar, but you'll find hot dishes, too, such as the typically Milanese *ossobuco con risotto* (braised veal shanks with white wine and tomato). *Via Solferino 25, tel. 02/659–1076. No reservations. No credit cards. Closed Sun., Easter, and Aug.*

Taverna Moriggi. This dusky, wood-paneled wine bar near the stock exchange serves a fixed-price lunch for about 25,000 lire, and cold cuts and cheeses in the evening. *Via Moriggi 8, tel. 02/864–50880. No reservations. No credit cards. Closed Sat. lunch and Sun.*

Budget **Flash.** This is one of countless *paninoteche* (sandwich bars) where the Milanese eat economically. Here sandwiches are made in a tempting variety, and pizza and soup are served, as well. *Via Bergamini 1, no phone. No credit cards. Closed Sun.*

★ **Grand'Italia.** Big and busy, it's crowded at lunchtime with those who work in the Corso Garibaldi–Brera district. They stop in for a satisfying one-dish meal, whether that's pizza, *focaccia* (freshly baked flat bread) with sandwich fillings, or a fixed-price lunch. The mood changes in the evening: Pizza is still available, but a full meal can be costly. *Via Palermo 5, tel. 02/877–759. Reservations accepted. MC, V. Closed Tues., Sat. lunch, Aug.*

★ **Magenta.** Founded in 1908, Bar Magenta is a monument to Art Nouveau and is a Milanese classic. From late morning to 2 AM you can find thick, made-to-order *panini* (sandwiches) and other light snacks. At lunchtime it's a favorite with models and other fashion folk. *Via Carducci 13 at Corso Magenta, tel. 02/ 805–3808. No credit cards. Closed Mon.*

★ **Panino Giusto.** Some consider the sandwiches here the best in Milan. Try the Madeira, made with pâté, creamy Caprino cheese and port wine. *Corso Garibaldi 125, no phone. No credit cards.*

San Tomaso. An old beer hall in the Brera district, San Tomaso has a self-service lunch with made-to-order salads, cheese platters, and cold cuts. It's very busy at lunchtime but quieter for supper. *Via San Tomaso 5, tel. 02/874510. No credit cards. Closed Sun.*

Spaghetteria. This restaurant in the Brera district is open only in the evening and offers an amazing number of pasta dishes. *Assaggini* means "samples," and if you order it you'll be able to taste several types of pasta for one low price. *Via Solferino 3, tel. 02/872735. No reservations. AE, MC, V. Closed Mon.*

Lodging

Make reservations well in advance, particularly when trade fairs are on, which can be most of the year except for August (when many hotels close) and mid-December to mid-January. March and October are months with the highest concentration of fairs, and it's virtually impossible to find a room at this time. Should you arrive without reservations, there's a booking service at Via Palestro 24 (tel. 02/782072).

For details and price-category definitions, *see* Lodging in Staying in Italy.

Moderate **Antica Locanda Solferino.** Make reservations well in advance
★ for this one: The rooms are few, and provide excellent value. The building is 19th century, but the rooms have been recently redecorated with delightful peasant-print bedspreads, bedside tables draped with lace-edge cloths, attractive dried-flower arrangements on the tables, and 19th-century prints on the walls. *Via Castelfidardo 2, tel. 02/657–0129, fax 02/656460. 11 rooms with bath. No credit cards. Closed 10 days mid-Aug. and another 10 days at Christmas.*

Città Studi. This hotel is near the university and Piazzale Susa, some distance from the center, which you can reach by bus. It is functionally furnished in modern style. Most rooms have private showers; the few without showers are a bargain. *Via Saldini 24, tel. 02/744666, fax 02/713122. 45 rooms, 38 with bath. AE, MC, V.*

London. A 10-minute walk from the cathedral, the London is clean, with large rooms but cramped bathrooms. The friendly staff speaks English. *Via Rovello 3, tel. 02/720–20166, fax 02/ 805–7037. 29 rooms with bath. Closed Aug. and Dec. 23–Jan. 3. MC, V.*

Inexpensive **La Pace.** Located near the Piazzale Loreto Metro station, La Pace has 19th-century-style furnishings, modern bedrooms, and a tiny garden. *Via Alfredo Catalani 69, tel. 02/261–7900, fax 02/621–12091. 20 rooms with bath. MC, V.*

San Francisco. This hotel near the Piazzale Piola Metro station is modern in style with functional furnishings, TV, and telephone in the rooms. It is family-owned and managed and has one of Milan's "secret" inner gardens. *Viale Lombardia 55, tel. 02/236–1009, fax 02/266–80377. 33 rooms, 31 with bath. MC, V.*

Budget **Johnny.** You have to ask for one of the lower-price rooms here to get budget rates. It is a commercial hotel adjacent to the big Fiera di Milano exposition grounds and near the Metro. *Via Prati 6, tel. 02/341812. 31 rooms, 23 with bath. No credit cards. Closed Aug. and Dec. 22–Jan. 2.*

Rovello. Accommodations here are simple and spanking clean, with warm terra-cotta tile floors and plain white walls. It's a favorite with younger travelers and American fashion models. Expect to pay in advance. *Via Rovello 18A, tel. 02/864396. 12 rooms, 10 with bath. AE, DC, MC, V.*

Valley. Close to the Central Station and Metro lines, the Valley is clean and conveniently located. The rooms are simply furnished, some of the staff speak English, and doubles with bath are available. *Via Soperga 19, tel. 02/669–2777. 21 rooms. No credit cards.*

The Arts

The most famous spectacle in Milan is the one at **La Scala,** which presents some of the world's most impressive operatic productions. The house is invariably sold out in advance; ask at your hotel whether tickets can be found for you. You can book in advance by mail or fax (0039–2–8879297). You can also book tickets at CIT travel agencies elsewhere in Italy and in foreign countries, but no more than 10 days before the performance. The opera season begins early in December and ends in May. The concert season runs from May to the end of June and from September through November. There is a brief ballet season in September. Programs are available at principal travel agencies and tourist information offices in Italy and abroad. *Box Office, Teatro alla Scala, Piazza della Scala, tel. 02/809126. Open daily noon–7, noon–8:15 on performance days. Closed national holidays and July 28–Aug. 28.*

Venice

Arriving and Departing

By Plane Marco Polo International Airport is situated about 10 kilometers (6 miles) northeast of the city on the mainland. For flight information, tel. 041/661262.

Between the Airport and Downtown ATVO buses make the 25-minute trip in to Piazzale Roma, going through the city's unappealing outlying regions; the cost is around 5,000 lire. From Piazzale Roma visitors will most likely have to take a local to *vaporetto* (water bus) to their hotel (*see* Getting Around, *below*). The Cooperative San Marco motor launch is only slightly more costly (15,000 lire) and presents a far more attractive introduction to the city; it runs direct from the airport, dropping passengers across the lagoon at Piazza San Marco. (It works on a limited schedule in winter.)

By Train Make sure your train goes all the way to Santa Lucia train station in Venice's northeast corner; some trains leave passengers at the Mestre station on the mainland, from which you must connect with a local to Santa Lucia. The APT information booth (open daily 8–8) and the baggage depot in the station are usually festooned with long lines of tourists. If you need a hotel room, go to the AVA hotel association desk (open daily 9–9); there are others at the airport and at the city garage at Piazzale

Roma. The deposit (10,000–30,000 lire, depending on the hotel category) is discounted on your hotel bill. Vaporetto landing stages are directly outside the station. *Make sure you know how to get to your hotel before you arrive.* You will probably have to walk some distance from the landing stage nearest your hotel; for this reason, try to obtain a map of Venice before arrival, and travel with a luggage cart—porters are hard to find.

Getting Around

First-time visitors find that getting around Venice presents some unusual problems: the complexity of its layout (the city is made up of more than 100 islands linked by bridges); the bewildering unfamiliarity of waterborne transportation; the illogical house numbering system and duplication of street names in its six districts; and the necessity of walking whether you enjoy it or not. It's essential to have a good map showing all street names and water bus routes; buy the most detailed one you can find at any newsstand.

By Vaporetto ACTV water buses run the length of the Grand Canal and circle the city. There are several lines, some of which connect Venice with the major and minor islands in the lagoon; Line 1 is the Grand Canal local. Timetables are posted on all landing stages, where ticket booths are located (open early morning–9 PM). Buy single tickets or books of 10. The fare is 2,200 lire on most lines, 3,300 lire for the Line 2 express between the train station, Rialto, San Marco, and the Lido. Stamp your ticket in the machine on the landing stage. A daily tourist ticket costs 12,000 lire. Vaporetti run every 10 minutes or so during the day; Lines 1 and 2 run every hour between midnight and dawn. Landing stages are clearly marked with name and line number and serve boats going in both directions.

By Traghetto Few tourists know about the two-man gondolas that ferry people across the Grand Canal at various fixed points. It's the cheapest and shortest gondola ride in Venice, and it can save a lot of walking. The fare is 500 lire, which you hand to one of the gondoliers when you get on. Look for "Traghetto" signs.

By Gondola Don't leave Venice without treating yourself to a gondola ride, preferably in the quiet of the evening when the churning traffic on the canals has died down, the palace windows are illuminated, and the only sounds are the muted splashes of the gondolier's oar. Make sure he understands that you want to see the *rii*, or smaller canals, as well as the Grand Canal. They're supposed to charge a fixed minimum rate of about 70,000 lire for 50 minutes, but in practice they ask for 90,000 lire–120,000 lire for a 30- to 40-minute ride. Come to terms with your gondolier *before* stepping into his boat.

On Foot This is the only way to reach many parts of Venice, so wear comfortable shoes. Invest in a good map that names all the streets, and count on getting lost more than once.

Important Addresses and Numbers

Tourist Information The main Venice **APT Tourist Office** (tel. 041/522–6356) is at Calle Ascensione 71C, just off Piazza San Marco, under the arcade in the far left corner opposite the basilica. Open Mon.–Sat., Nov.–Mar., 8:30–1:30; Apr.–Oct., 8:30–7:30. There are APT information booths at the Santa Lucia station (tel. 041/

715016); in the bus terminal at Piazzale Roma (tel. 041/522–7402), open summer only; at Marco Polo airport; and at Tronchetto parking lot.

Consulates   **U.K.** (Campo della Carità 1051, Dorsoduro, tel. 041/522–7207). **U.S.** (The nearest U.S. Consulate is in Milan, at Largo Donegani 1, tel. 02/652841).

Emergencies   **Police** (tel. 113). **Ambulance** (tel. 041/523–0000). **Doctor:** Try the emergency room at Venice's hospital (tel. 041/523–0000), or call the British Consulate (*see above*) and ask for recommendations.

Exploring Venice

Venice—La Serenissima, the Most Serene—is disorienting in its complexity, an extraordinary labyrinth of narrow streets and waterways, opening now and again onto some airy square or broad canal. The majority of its magnificent palazzi are slowly crumbling, yet somehow in Venice the shabby and the derelict create an effect of supreme beauty and charm, rather than one of horrible urban decay. The place is romantic, especially at night when the lights from the vaporetti and the stars overhead pick out the gargoyles and arches of the centuries-old facades. For hundreds of years Venice was the unrivaled mistress of trade between Europe and the Orient, and the staunch bulwark of Christendom against the tide of Turkish expansion. Though the power and glory of its days as a wealthy city-republic are gone, the art and exotic aura remain.

To enjoy the city, you will have to come to terms with the crowds, which take over from May through September. Hot and sultry in the summer, Venice is much more welcoming in early spring and late fall. Romantics like it in the winter when prices are much lower, the streets are deserted (well, nearly), and the sea mists impart a haunting melancholy to the *campi* (squares) and canals. Piazza San Marco (St. Mark's Square), the pulse of Venice, is crowded with people and pigeons no matter what time of year. But after joining with the crowds to visit the Basilica di San Marco and the Doge's Palace, strike out on your own and just follow where your feet take you—you won't be disappointed.

Numbers in the margin correspond to points of interest on the Venice map.

Piazza San Marco   Even the pigeons have to fight for space on **Piazza San Marco,**
and the Accademia   and pedestrian traffic jams clog the surrounding byways. De-
① spite the crowds and because it is the most famous piazza in Venice, San Marco is the logical starting place of each of our various itineraries. Pick up pamphlets at the **APT Information Office** in the far left corner of Piazza San Marco, opposite the basilica. The information office is in the wing built by order of Napoleon to complete the much earlier buildings on either side of the square, enclosing it to form what he called "the most
② beautiful drawing room in all of Europe." Upstairs is the **Museo Correr,** with eclectic collections of historical objects and a picture gallery of fine 15th-century paintings. *Piazza San Marco, Ala Napoleonica, tel. 041/522–5625. Admission: 5,000 lire. Open daily 9–4.*

③ The **Basilica di San Marco** (St. Mark's Cathedral) was begun in the 11th century to hold the relics of St. Mark the Evangelist,

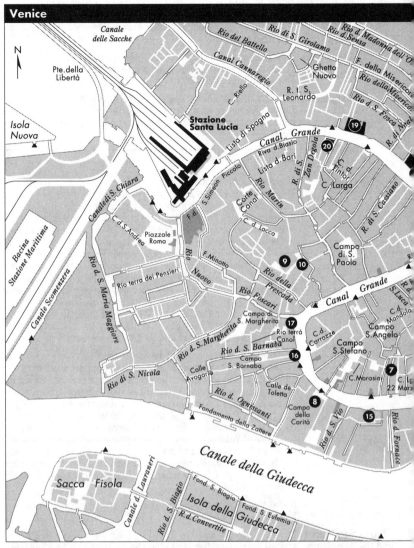

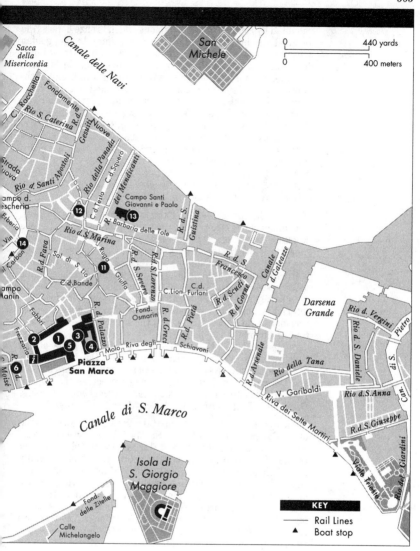

Sacca della Misericordia

Canale delle Navi

San Michele

0   440 yards
0   400 meters

Rio S. Caterina

Fondamente

Gesuiti

Rio d. Santi Apostoli

Strada Nuova

Rio della Panada

C.d. Squero

dei Mendicanti

Campo d. Pescheria

C.d. Testa

Campo Santi Giovanni e Paolo

❶❷

R. di Barbaria delle Tole

Erberia

Rio d. S. Marina

Ruga Giuffa

R. d. S. Giustina

V. ...

Erberia

R. d. Fava

Sal. di S. Lio

C.d. Bande

❶❶

R. d. S. Lorenzo

R. d. S. Severo

C. Lion

C.d. Furlani

R. d. S. Francesco

R. d. Scudi

R. d. Corno

Canale d. Galeazze

Darsena Grande

Rio d. Vergini

Fabbri

R. d. Palazzo

Fond. Osmarin

R. d. Greci

R. d. Pietà

Rio d. S. Daniele

Pietro

Frezzaria

❷ ❶ ❸
❺ ❹

Molo

Riva degli

Schiavoni

R. d. Arsenale

Rio della Tana

V. Garibaldi

di S.

❻

R. d. Moise

Piazza San Marco

Rio d. S. Anna

Can.

Riva dei Sette Martiri

R.d. S. Giuseppe

Canale di S. Marco

Isola di S. Giorgio Maggiore

Viale Trieste

R. d. Giardini

Fond. delle Zitelle

Calle Michelangelo

KEY

—— Rail Lines
▲ Boat stop

the city's patron saint, and its richly decorated facade is surmounted by copies of the four famous gilded bronze horses (the
originals are in the basilica's upstairs museum). Inside, golden
mosaics sheathe walls and domes, lending an extraordinarily exotic aura, half Christian church, half Middle Eastern
mosque. Be sure to see the **Pala d'Oro**, an eye-filling 10th-
century altarpiece in gold and silver, studded with precious
gems and enamels. From the atrium, climb the steep stairway
to the museum: The bronze horses alone are worth the effort.
*The Basilica is open from early morning, but tourist visits are
allowed Mon.–Sat. 9:30–5:30, Sun. 2:30–5:30. No admission
to those wearing shorts or other revealing clothing. Pala d'Oro
and Treasury. Admission: 2,000 lire. Open Apr.–Sept., Mon.–
Sat. 9:30–5:30, Sun. 2–5:30. Oct.–Mar., Mon.–Sat. 10–4,
Sun. 1:45–4. Gallery and Museum. Admission: 2,000 lire.
Open Apr.–Sept., daily 9:30–5:30; Oct.–Mar., daily 10–4.*

❹ Next to St. Mark's is the **Palazzo Ducale** (Doge's Palace),
which, during Venice's prime, was the epicenter of the Serene
Republic's great empire. More than just a palace, it was a combination White House, Senate, Supreme Court, torture chamber, and prison. The building's exterior is striking; the lower
stories consist of two rows of fragile-seeming arches, while
above rests a massive pink-and-white marble wall whose solidi-
ty is barely interrupted by its six great Gothic windows. The
interior is a maze of vast halls, monumental staircases, secret
corridors, state apartments, and the sinister prison cells and
torture chamber. The palace is filled with frescoes, paintings,
carvings, and a few examples of statuary by some of the
Renaissance's greatest artists. Don't miss the famous view
from the balcony, overlooking the piazza and St. Mark's Basin
and the church of San Giorgio Maggiore across the lagoon.
*Piazzetta San Marco, tel. 041/522–4951. Admission: 8,000 lire.
Open Apr.–Sept., daily 8:30–7; Oct.–Mar., daily 9–4.*

❺ For a pigeon's-eye view of Venice take the elevator up to the top
of the **Campanile di San Marco** (St. Mark's bell tower) in Piazza
San Marco, a reconstruction of the 1,000-year-old tower that
collapsed one morning in 1912, practically without warning.
Fifteenth-century clerics found guilty of immoral acts were
suspended in wooden cages from the tower, sometimes to live
on bread and water for as long as a year, sometimes to die of
starvation and exposure. (Look for them in Carpaccio's paintings of the square that hang in the Accademia.) *Piazza San
Marco, tel. 041/522–4064. Admission: 3,000 lire. Open Apr.–
Oct., daily 9:30–7:30; Nov.–Mar. 10–4.*

One last landmark on the square is the *Caffè Florian*, a great
place to nurse a Campari or a cappuccino. Unfortunately, the
pleasure of relaxing amid so much history does not come cheap,
either inside or outside, and there's an extra charge (about $3)
if you're served when the orchestra is playing. If you succeed in
denying yourself this pleasure, head west out of San Marco
(with the facade of the basilica to your back), making your way
❻ past **San Moisè**'s elaborate Baroque facade and by the American Express office, on to Calle Larga 22 Marzo. Continue on to
❼ the church of **Santa Maria del Giglio**, behind the **Gritti Palace**
hotel. Across the bridge behind the church, **Piazzesi** on
Campiello Feltrina is famous for its handprinted paper and
desk accessories.

Join the stream of pedestrians crossing the Grand Canal on the
❽ wooden **Accademia Bridge,** and head straight on for the **Galleria dell'Accademia** (Academy of Fine Arts), Venice's most important picture gallery and a must for art lovers. Try to spend at least an hour viewing this remarkable collection of Venetian art, which is attractively displayed and well lighted. Works range from 14th-century Gothic and Bellini's 15th-century oils to the Golden Age of the 16th century, represented by Titian, including his last work, the *Pietà;* Tintoretto, including his *Virgin of the Treasures* and *Miracles of St. Mark;* and Veronese. *Campo della Carità, tel. 041/522–2247. Admission: 8,000 lire. Open Mon.–Sat. 9–2, Sun. 9–1.*

Consulting your map, make your way through Calle Contarini, Calle Toletta, and Campo San Barnaba to Rio Terrà Canal, where **Mondonovo** ranks as one of the city's most interesting mask shops (Venetians, who originated Italy's most splendid carnival, love masks of all kinds, from gilded lions to painted sun faces and sinister death's heads). Just around the corner is Campo Santa Margherita, which has a homey feel.

Continue past Campo San Pantalon to Campo San Rocco, just beside the immense church of the Frari. In the 1500s, Tintoret-
❾ to embellished the **Scuola di San Rocco** with more than 50 canvases; they are an impressive sight, dark paintings aglow with figures hurtling dramatically through space amid flashes of light and color. The *Crucifixion* in the Albergo (the room just off the great hall) is held to be his masterpiece. *Campo di San Rocco. Admission: 6,000 lire. Open weekdays 10–1 and 3:30–6:30, weekends 10–4.*

The church of Santa Maria Gloriosa dei Frari (known simply as
❿ the **Frari**) is one of Venice's most important churches, a vast soaring Gothic building of brick. Since it is the principal church of the Franciscans, its design is suitably austere to reflect that order's vows of poverty, though paradoxically it contains a number of the most sumptuous pictures in any Venetian church. Chief among them are the magnificent Titian altarpieces, notably the immense *Assumption of the Virgin* over the main altar. Titian was buried here at the ripe old age of 88, the only one of 70,000 plague victims to be given a personal church burial. *Campo dei Frari. Admission: 1,000-lire donation "for lighting expenses."*

San Zanipolo and Backtracking once again to Piazza San Marco, go to the arch
the Rialto under the Torre dell'Orologio (Clock Tower) and head northeast into the **Mercerie,** one of Venice's busiest streets and, with the **Frezzeria** and **Calle Fabbri,** part of the shopping area that extends across the Grand Canal into the **Rialto district.** At Campo San Zulian, turn right into Calle Guerra and Calle delle
⓫ Bande to the graceful white marble church of **Santa Maria Formosa;** it's situated right on a lively square (of the same name) with a few sidewalk cafés and a small vegetable market on weekday mornings.

Use your map to follow Calle Borgoloco into Campo San Marina, where you turn right, cross the little canal, and take Calle
⓬ Castelli to **Santa Maria dei Miracoli** (Calle Castelli). Perfectly proportioned and sheathed in marble, this late-15th-century building embodies all the classical serenity of the early Renaissance. The interior is decorated with marble reliefs by the church's architect, Pietro Lombardo, and his son Tullio.

Retrace your steps along Calle Castelli and cross the bridge
into Calle delle Erbe, following signs for "SS. Giovanni e
Paolo." The massive Dominican church of Santi Giovanni e
⑬ Paolo—**San Zanipolo,** as it's known in the slurred Venetian dialect—is the rival of the Franciscan Frari. The church is a kind
of pantheon of the doges (25 are buried here), and contains a
wealth of artworks. Outside in the campo stands Verrocchio's
equestrian statue of Colleoni, who fought for the Venetian
cause in the mid-1400s.

Cross the canal in front of the church and continue along Calle
Larga Giacinto Gallina, crossing a pair of bridges to Campiello
Santa Maria Nova. Take Salizzada San Canciano to Salizzada
San Giovanni Crisostomo to find yourself once again in the
⑭ mainstream of pedestrians winding their way to the **Rialto
Bridge.** Street stalls hung with scarves and gondolier's hats
signal that you are entering the heart of Venice's shopping district. Cross over the bridge, and you'll find yourself in the market district. Try to visit the Rialto market when it's in full
swing, every morning except Sunday, with fruit and vegetable
vendors hawking their wares in a colorful and noisy jumble of
sights and sounds. Not far beyond is the fish market, where
you'll probably find sea creatures you've never seen before (and
possibly won't want to see again). A left turn into Ruga Vecchia
San Giovanni and Rughetta del Ravano will bring you face to
face with scores of shops: At **La Scialuppa** (Calle Saoneri 2695)
you'll find hand-carved wooden models of gondolas and their
graceful oar locks known as *forcole.*

The Grand Canal Just off Piazzetta di San Marco (the square in front of the
Doge's Palace) you can catch Vaporetto Line 1 at either the San
Marco or San Zaccaria landing stages (on Riva degli Schiavoni),
to set off on a boat tour along the **Grand Canal.** Serving as
Venice's main thoroughfare, the canal winds in the shape of an
"S" for more than 3½ kilometers (2 miles) through the heart of
the city, past some 200 Gothic-Renaissance palaces. Until boat
traffic was restricted in 1992, this was the route taken by
vaporetti, gondolas, water taxis, mail boats, police boats, fire
boats, ambulance boats, barges carrying provisions and building materials, bridal boats, and funeral boats. Now all non-
public traffic has been rerouted to limit the erosive action of
waves caused by the boats. Your vaporetto tour provides a
ringside view of Venice's beautiful, opulent palaces and a peek
into the side streets and tiny canals where the Venetians go
about their daily business. *Vaporetto Line 1. Cost: 2,200 lire.*

Departing from the San Marco landing, this tour passes first
the **Galleria dell'Accademia,** with its fine collection of 14th- to
⑮ 18th-century Venetian paintings (*see above*), then the **Peggy
Guggenheim Museum,** in the late heiress's Palazzo Venier dei
Leoni, which usually has excellent exhibitions. *Entrance:
Calle del Cristo, tel. 041/520–6288. Admission: 7,000 lire, free
on Sat. Open Apr.–Oct., Sun., Mon., Wed.–Fri. noon–6, Sat.
6–9 PM.*

⑯ Next you see the **Ca' Rezzonico,** built in 1680 and now a museum
⑰ with Venetian paintings and furniture, and the **Ca' Foscari,** a
15th-century Gothic building that was once the home of Doge
Foscari, who was unwillingly deposed and died the following
⑱ day. Today it's part of Venice's university. **Ca' d'Oro,** farther
along, is the most flowery palace on the canal; it now houses the
⑲ Galleria Franchetti. The **Palazzo Vendramin Calergi** is a Ren-

aissance building where Wagner died in 1883. It's also the winter home of the municipal casino. The **Fondaco dei Turchi** was an original Byzantine "house-warehouse" of a rich Venetian merchant, but the building has suffered some remodeling during the past 100 years.

Shopping

Glass Venetian glass is as famous as the city's gondolas, and almost every shop window displays it. There's a lot of cheap glass for sale; if you want something better, window shop at the top showrooms—**Venini** (Piazzetta dei Leoncini 314), **Pauly** (Calle dell' Ascensione 72, opposite the APT information office), **Salviati** (Piazza San Marco 78 and 110), **Cenedese** (Piazza San Marco 139), and **Isola** (Campo San Moisè and Mercerie 723)—and then look for similar pieces at lower-price shops between San Marco and the Rialto market. On the island of Murano, where prices are generally no lower than in Venice, **Domus** (Fondamenta dei Vetrai) has a good selection.

Shopping District The main shopping area extends from Piazza San Marco through the Mercerie and Calle Fabbri toward the Rialto.

Department Stores The **Coin** store (off Campo San Bartolomeo) specializes in fashion and accessories. **Standa** has stores on Campo San Luca and Strada Nuova, where you can pick up medium-price goods of all kinds.

Dining

Venetian restaurants are more expensive than those in Florence or Rome; figure on spending about 10,000 lire to 15,000 lire more for the same sort of meal. Many *trattorie* have inexpensive fixed-price menus, providing adequate if uninspired food for the money. There are also plenty of sandwich bars and *pizzerie* and the typically Venetian wine bars, where you can order wine by the glass and snack on tidbits offered at the counter. In *trattorie*, save by ordering *acqua semplice* (tap water) instead of bottled mineral water and by choosing *vino sfuso* (a carafe of house wine) rather than bottled wine. City specialties include pasta e fagioli; risotto and all kinds of seafood; and the delicious *fegato alla veneziana*, thin strips of liver cooked with onions, served with grilled *polenta*, cornmeal cakes.

For details and price-category definitions, *see* Dining in Staying in Italy.

Moderate ★ **L'Incontro.** This trattoria near San Barnaba, handily situated about halfway between the Accademia Gallery and the Frari church, has won a faithful clientele of locals and visitors by offering generous portions, friendly service, and reasonable prices. *Rio Terrà Canal 3062/a, tel. 041/522–2404. Reservations advised. MC, V. Closed Mon.*

Alle Lanternine. This friendly place in the Cannaregio quarter is especially nice in summer, when you dine outdoors. The menu offers a variety of fish and meat dishes and pizza, too. *Campiello della Chiesa 2134, tel. 041/721679. Reservations advised. AE, DC, MC, V. Closed Thurs.*

Al Tucano. This neighborhood trattoria conveniently close to St. Mark's is one of the rare reliable places to eat in the vicinity at affordable prices. It also serves pizza. *Ruga Giuffa 4835, tel. 041/520–0811. No reservations. No credit cards. Closed Thurs.*

Inexpensive **Ai Cugnai.** A bevy of efficient ladies runs this popular neigh-
★ borhood tavern near the Accademia. The limited menu offers
Venetian specialties. *Calle Nuova Sant'Agnese 857, tel. 041/
528–9238. Reservations advised in evening. No credit cards.
Closed Mon. and Jan.*

Al Milion. This bistro is behind San Giovanni Crisostomo. Be
prepared to choose quickly from the handwritten menu: Lingering is not encouraged. *Campo San Giovanni Crisostomo,
tel. 041/522–9302. No reservations. No credit cards. Closed
Wed.*

Paradiso Perduto. Popular with young people, this informal
wine bar in the Cannaregio quarter serves hot meals and is one
of few such places in Venice to stay open late. Live music is featured on Monday evening. The menu changes daily, but pizza is
served every day. *Fondamenta Misericordia 2540, tel. 041/
720581. No reservations. No credit cards. Closed Tues.*

San Trovaso. A wide choice of Venetian dishes and pizzas, reliable house wines, and economical fixed-price menus make this
busy tavern near the Accademia Gallery a good value.
*Fondamenta Priuli 1016 (Dorsoduro), tel. 041/520–3703. Res-
ervations advised. AE, DC, MC, V. Closed Mon.*

Da Silvio. The large garden and reasonable prices attract a lively young crowd. Be prepared to relax and enjoy your surroundings, because service can be slow. *Calle San Pantalon 3748
(Dorsoduro), tel. 041/520–5833. No reservations. MC. Closed
Sun.*

Budget **Boldrin.** This cafeteria-style restaurant offers home cooking
and a selection of pasta and meat dishes in a friendly atmosphere. It's near San Giovanni Crisostomo. *Salizzada San
Canciano 5550, tel. 041/523–7859. No credit cards. No dinner.
Closed Sun.*

Sottoprova. In the Castello district, off the beaten track, this
trattoria offers typical Venetian cooking and is popular with locals, especially in summer, when there are tables outdoors.
The fixed-price menu is an exceptional value. *Via Garibaldi
1698, tel. 041/520–6493. Reservations advised. AE, MC, V.
Closed Tues.*

★ **Vino Vino.** This is an informal annex of the upscale Antico Martini around the corner. A limited choice of reasonably priced
dishes is available at mealtimes, and snacks are served
throughout the day, 10 AM–1 AM. The wine list is impressive.
*Calle del Cafetier 2007/A (San Fantin), tel. 041/523–7027. No
reservations. AE, DC, MC, V. Closed Tues.*

Lodging

Venice is made up almost entirely of time-worn buildings, so it
stands to reason that the majority of hotels are in renovated
palaces. Renovations in most affordable hotels do not include
the installation of elevators, so you will probably have to climb
stairs. You are likely to find the rooms cramped and the furnishings simple. Inexpensive and budget hotels are essentially
in the same one-star official category, the key distinction being
whether you have a private bath (usually a shower) or not—
doubles with bath fall into the inexpensive category, doubles
without bath are budget. If you have not reserved your room,
go to the AVA office at the train station, airport, or Piazzale
Roma (*see* Arriving by Train, *above*). You can save considerably

during low season, especially with winter packages (Venezia d'Inverno) that include low hotel rates and museum discounts. The main tourist season runs from mid-March through October, December 20 to New Year's Day, and the two-week Carnival period in mid-February. Make reservations well in advance at all times, but especially for these periods.

Moderate ★ **Alboretti.** This small hotel is simply but attractively furnished, and, despite its size and central location, it has a little garden courtyard off the breakfast room and a lounge upstairs from the tiny lobby and bar area. There is no elevator. Together with its moderately priced restaurant, it represents real value. *Rio Terrà Foscari (Rio Terrà Sant'Agnese) 884, tel. 041/523–0058, fax 041/521–0158. 19 rooms with bath or shower. AE, MC, V.*

Bucintoro. This small, family-run hotel is right on the lagoon near the Arsenale, where the real *Bucintoro*, Venice's official and elaborate ceremonial boat, is kept. Every room has a water view, and rooms without private bath are a bargain. *Riva degli Schiavoni 2135, tel. 041/522–3240, fax 041/523–5224. 28 rooms, 18 with bath. No credit cards.*

Paganelli. This pleasant, comfortable, well-run hotel is on the waterfront, and has an annex on Campo San Zaccaria, near San Marco. Rooms are decorated in traditional Venetian style; some of the costlier ones have air-conditioning. *Riva degli Schiavoni 4182 and Campo San Zaccaria 4687, tel. 041/522–4324, fax 041/523–9267. 22 rooms, 19 with bath. AE, MC, V.*

Inexpensive **Caneva.** One of the larger inexpensive hotels, it has its own quiet courtyard, and rooms on one side overlook a canal. It is located between San Marco and the Rialto. *Calle Rio della Fava 5515, on calle to right of church of Fava, tel. 041/522–8118. 23 rooms, 10 with bath. No credit cards.*

Silva. This small hotel off Campo Santa Maria Formosa close to San Marco is on a quiet canal. Low rates include breakfast; some rooms can accommodate an extra bed. *Fondamenta del Remedio 4423, tel. 041/522–7643. 25 rooms, 5 with bath. No credit cards.*

Tintoretto. This popular little hotel is off Strada Nuova, near the church of Santa Fosca and the Ca' d'Oro landing stage. *Campiello della Chiesa 2316, tel. 041/721522. 20 rooms, 10 with bath. MC, V. Closed Jan.*

Budget **Casa de Stefani.** Guests gather in a homey sitting room at this small hostelry near the university and off Campo San Barnaba. Some rooms have frescoed ceilings, but furnishings are otherwise basic. It is a few steps from one of the two-man gondolas that ferries you across the Grand Canal. *Calle del Traghetto 2786, tel. 041/522–3337. 17 rooms, 7 with bath. No credit cards.*

Al Piave. You get clean, basic accommodations here, plus the convenience of being centrally located, near San Marco and Santa Maria Formosa. *Ruga Giuffa 4840, tel. 041/528–5174. 12 rooms without bath. AE, MC, V.*

Riva. This recently refurbished hotel close to San Marco is located at the junction of three canals. *Ponte dell'Angelo 5310, tel. 041/522–7034. 12 rooms, 10 with bath. No credit cards. Closed mid-Nov.–Feb. 1, except 2 weeks at Christmas.*

The Arts

For a program of events, pick up the free "Guest in Venice" booklet at the APT tourist office in Piazza San Marco, or at most hotel desks. Your hotel may also be able to get you tickets for some events.

Concerts A **Vivaldi Festival** is held in September, and concerts are held year-round in the city's churches; contact the **Kele e Teo Agency** (Piazza San Marco 4930, tel. 041/520–8722), which supplies tickets for many of the city's musical events.

Opera The opera season at **Teatro La Fenice** (Campo San Fantin, tel. 041/521–0161) runs from December to May. The box office is open September to July, Monday–Saturday 9:30–12:30 and 4–6.

Nightlife

You won't find much in the way of organized nightlife in this city. The **Martini Scala Club** (Calle della Veste, near Teatro La Fenice, tel. 041/522–4121) is an elegant piano bar with late-night restaurant. The bars of the top hotels stay open as long as their customers keep on drinking. **El Souk** disco (Calle Contrarini 1056, near the Accademia, tel. 041/520–0371) draws a fairly sophisticated young crowd. **Ai Speci** (Calle Specchieri 648, tel. 041/520–9088) is an intimate American-style bar.

Campania

As to be expected in a region where extremes of wealth and poverty meet, the traveler in Campania (the region of Naples, Capri, and the Amalfi coast, among other sights) can find the level of comfort that suits his or her pocket. Between the slums of Naples and the villas of Capri, a variety of dining and accommodations options present themselves. On the whole, though, restaurants offer better value for your money than hotels. In Naples budget hotels tend to be on the sleazy side, but simple restaurants and pizzerias offer some of the best cooking available in the Italian south.

Once a cultural capital that rivaled Paris for its brillance and refinement, today's Napoli (Naples) is afflicted by acute urban decay and chronic delinquency that ranges from nefarious Mafia activities to bag-snatching perpetrated by thieves on scooters; though few visitors ever experience these directly they cast a certain notoriety over this otherwise sunny, active city. But what really characterizes Naples—for other Italians as much as for tourists—is the combination of exuberance and cynicism in the local people, who have evolved a way of life that almost makes Naples a city foreign to Italians, with laws and customs all its own.

For those who would rather skip the stress of Naples, there are other practical bases. Transport connections are good, and none of Campania's attractions is remote, from classical ruins by the acre to gorgeous scenery, all bathed in plenty of hot sun.

Sorrento is touristy but has some fine old hotels and beautiful views; it's a good base for a leisurely excursion to Pompeii. Capri is a pint-size paradise, though sometimes too crowded for comfort, while the Amalfi coast, which runs from Sorrento to Salerno, has some enchanting towns and spectacular scenery. A word of warning: out-of-season travelers, who find prices considerably reduced in resorts such as Capri and the towns of the Amalfi coast, also find many establishments closed during winter.

Getting Around

By Plane There are several daily flights between Rome and Naples's Capodichino Airport (tel. 081/780–5763), 7 kilometers (4 miles) north of the downtown area. Bus no. 14 connects the airport with the center of town. During the summer months there's a direct helicopter service between Capodichino, Capri, and Ischia; for information, tel. 081/789–6273 or 081/584–1481.

By Train A great number of trains run between Rome and Naples every day; Intercity trains make the journey in less than two hours. The central station (tel. 081/553–4188) is at Piazza Garibaldi, but there are several smaller stations, also serving a network of suburban lines that connect the city with points of interest in Campania. The most useful line for excursions outside Naples is the **Circumvesuviana** (tel. 081/779–2444), which leaves from Piazza Garibaldi and takes in Ercolano (Herculaneum), Pompeii, and Sorrento. Other lines are the **Ferrovia Cumana** (tel. 081/551–3328) and the **Circumflegrea** (tel. 081/551–3328), both of which leave from the station in Piazza Montesanto.

By Subway The **Metropolitana** subway system can save hours of aggravation crossing the traffic-clogged city center. Be warned that service ends at 11 PM.

By Bus Neapolitan buses and trams are unpredictable and often crowded, but they are convenient when walking becomes a chore or you need to travel between the station and the ferry-and-hydrofoil port. Useful services for this route are nos. 1 (tram) and 150 (bus). Tickets (800 lire) must be bought from ticket kiosks or tobacconists before boarding; punch them after you board.

Buses for the Amalfi coast leave from Naples, Salerno, and Sorrento. The trip can be unbearably slow in high season, but the cliff-hugging route is never dull. SITA buses leave Naples from Corso Arnaldo Lucci, beside the station, and from Via Pisanelli (tel. 081/552–2176), near Piazza Municipio. SITA buses from Salerno leave from Piazza Concordia, 100 meters straight out of the station, by the seafront. Tickets (5,000 lire to Sorrento, 3,000 lire to Amalfi) can be bought at the nearby office (tel. 089/791660). Departures are every hour or half-hour. From Sorrento, SITA buses leave from outside the train station (hourly to Amalfi, 3,200 lire). For more detailed bus information, call the offices at Sorrento (tel. 081/878–1115) or Amalfi (tel. 089/871016).

By Boat Boats and hydrofoils for the islands, the Sorrento peninsula, and the Amalfi coast leave from the Molo Beverello, near Naples's Piazza Municipio. **Caremar** (tel. 081/551–3882) and **Lauro** (tel. 081/551–3236) operate a frequent passenger and car ferry service, while hydrofoils of the **Caremar** and **Alilauro** (tel. 081/761–1004) lines leave from both Molo Beverello and the hydrofoil station at Mergellina pier, from which **SNAV** (tel. 081/761–2348) also operates.

Tourist Information

Capri (Marina Grande pier, tel. 081/837–0634; and Piazza Umberto I, Capri town, tel. 081/837–0686).
Naples. EPT Information Offices (Piazza dei Martiri 58, tel. 081/405311; central station, tel. 081/268779; Mergellina station, tel. 081/761–2102; and Capodichino Airport, tel. 081/780–5761). AAST Information Office (Piazza del Gesù, tel. 081/552–3328).
Sorrento (Via De Maio 35, tel. 081/878–2104).

Exploring Campania

Naples Founded by the Greeks, **Naples** became a playground of the Romans and was ruled thereafter by a succession of foreign dynasties, all of which left traces of their cultures in the city and its environs. The most splendid of these rulers were the Bourbons, who were responsible for much of what you will want to see in Naples, starting with the 17th-century **Palazzo Reale** (Royal Palace), still furnished in the lavish Baroque style that suited them so well. *Piazza Plebiscito, tel. 081/413888. Admission: 6,000 lire. Open Apr.–Oct., Mon.–Sat. 9–7:30, Sun. 9–1; Nov.–Mar., Mon.–Sat. 9–2, Sun. 9–1.*

Across the way is the massive stone **Castel Nuovo,** which was built by the city's Aragon rulers in the 13th century; it's not open to the public. Walk up Via Toledo, the name of which changes to Via Roma, keeping an eye on the antics of the Neapolitans, whose daily lives are overwrought with theatricality—they all seem to be actors in their own human comedy. Make a detour to the right off Via Toledo to see the oddly faceted stone facade and elaborate Baroque interior of the church of the **Gesù** (Via Benedetto Croce) and, directly opposite, the church of **Santa Chiara,** built in the early 1300s in Provençal Gothic style. A favorite Neapolitan song celebrates the quiet beauty of its cloister, decorated in delicate floral tiles.

Another detour off Via Roma, to the left this time, takes you from **Piazza Dante** to the Montesanto funicular, which ascends to the Vomero hill, where you can see the bastions of **Castel Sant'Elmo** and visit the museum in the **Certosa di San Martino,** a Carthusian monastery restored in the 17th century. It contains an eclectic collection of Neapolitan landscape paintings, royal carriages, and *presepi* (Christmas crèches). Check out the view from the balcony off room No. 25. *Certosa di San Martino, tel. 081/578–1769. Admission: 6,000 lire. Open Tues.–Sat. 9–2, Sun. 9–1.*

Return to Piazza Dante and follow Via Pessina (an extension of Via Roma) to the **Museo Archeologico Nazionale.** Dusty and unkempt, the museum undergoes perpetual renovations, but it holds one of the world's great collections of antiquities. Greek and Roman sculptures, vividly colored mosaics, countless objects from Pompeii and Herculaneum, and an equestrian statue of the Roman emperor Nerva are all worth seeing. *Piazza Museo, tel. 081/440166. Admission: 8,000 lire. Open May–Sept., Mon.–Sat. 9–7:30, Sun. 9–1; Oct.–Apr., Mon.–Sat. 9–2, Sun. 9–1.*

About a mile north on the same road (reachable by bus), you'll come to the **Museo di Capodimonte,** housed in an 18th-century palace built by Bourbon king Charles III, and surrounded by a

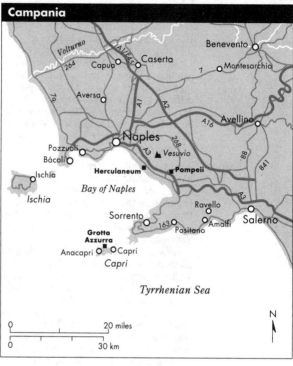

Campania

vast park that must have been lovely when it was better cared
for. In the picture gallery are some fine Renaissance paintings;
climb the stairs to the terrace for a magnificent view of Naples
and the bay. Downstairs you can visit the State Apartments
and see the extensive collection of porcelain, much of it produced in the Bourbons' own factory right here on the grounds.
*Parco di Capodimonte, tel. 081/744–1307. Admission: 8,000
lire. Tues.–Sat. 9–2, Sun. 9–1.*

Herculaneum **Herculaneum** (Ercolano) lies 14 kilometers (9 miles) southeast
of Naples. Reputed to have been founded by the legendary
Hercules, the elite Roman resort was devastated by the same
volcanic eruption that buried Pompeii in AD 79. Recent excavations have revealed that many died on the shore in an attempt to
escape, as a slow-moving mud slide embalmed the entire town by
covering it with an 11-meter-deep (35-foot-deep) blanket of volcanic ash and ooze. While that may have been unfortunate for
Herculaneum's residents, it was fortunate for us. Herculaneum
has been marvelously preserved for nearly two millennia! *Corso
Ercolano, tel. 081/739–0963. Admission: 8,000 lire. Open daily
9–one hour before sunset.*

Pompeii **Pompeii,** a larger community 8 kilometers (5 miles) farther to
the east, lost even more residents. An estimated 2,000 of them
perished on that fateful August day. The ancient city of Pompeii was much larger than Herculaneum, and excavations have
progressed to a much greater extent (though the remains are
not as well preserved, due to some 18th-century scavenging for
museum-quality artworks, most of which you are able to see at
Naples's Museo Archeologico Nazionale; *see above).* This pros-

perous Roman city had an extensive forum, lavish baths and temples, and patrician villas richly decorated with frescoes. It's worth buying a detailed guide of the site in order to give meaning and understanding to the ruins and their importance. Be sure to see the **Villa dei Misteri,** whose frescoes are in mint condition. Perhaps that is a slight exaggeration, but the paintings are so rich with detail and depth of color that one finds it difficult to believe that they are 1,900 years old. Have lots of small change handy to tip the guards at the more important houses so they will unlock the gates for you. *Pompeii Scavi, tel. 081/861-0744. Admission: 10,000 lire. Open daily 9–one hour before sunset.*

Sorrento Another 28 kilometers (18 miles) southwest is **Sorrento,** in the not-too-distant past a small, genteel resort for a fashionable elite. Now the town has spread out along the crest of its fabled cliffs. Once this was an area full of secret haunts for the few tourists who came for the beauty of this coastline, but it has now been discovered by the purveyors of package tours. In Sorrento's case, however, the change is not as grim as it sounds, since nothing can dim the delights of the marvelous climate and view of the Bay of Naples. For the best views go to the **Villa Comunale,** near the old church of **San Francesco** (in itself worth a visit), or to the terrace behind the **Museo Correale.** The museum, an attractive 18th-century villa, houses an interesting collection of decorative arts (furniture, china, and so on) and paintings of the Neapolitan school. *Via Capasso. Admission: 5,000 lire; gardens only, 2,000 lire. Open Oct.–Mar., Mon. and Wed.–Sat. 9:30–12:30 and 3–5, Sun. 9–12:30; Apr.–Sept., Mon. and Wed.–Sat. 9:30–12:30 and 5–7, Sun. 9–12:30.*

Capri Sorrento makes a convenient jumping-off spot for a boat trip to **Capri.** No matter how many day-trippers crowd onto the island, no matter how touristy certain sections have become, Capri remains one of Italy's loveliest places. Incoming visitors disembark at Marina Grande, from which excursion boats leave for trips around the island and also for the **Grotta Azzurra** (Blue Grotto). Be warned that the latter must rank as one of the country's all-time great rip-offs: Motorboat, rowboat, and grotto admissions are charged separately, and if there's a line of boats waiting, you'll have little time to enjoy the grotto's marvelous colors.

A cog railway or bus service takes you up to the town of Capri, where you can stroll through the **Piazzetta,** a choice place from which to watch the action and window-shop expensive boutiques on your way to the **Gardens of Augustus,** which have gorgeous views. The town of Capri is deliberately commercial and self-consciously picturesque. To get away from the crowds, hike to **Villa Jovis,** one of the many villas that Roman Emperor Tiberius built on the island, at the end of a lane that climbs steeply uphill. The walk takes about 45 minutes, with pretty views all the way and a final spectacular vista of the entire Bay of Naples and part of the Gulf of Salerno. *Via Tiberio. Admission: 4,000 lire. Open daily 9–one hour before sunset.*

Or take the bus to **Anacapri** and look for the little church of **San Michele,** off Via Orlandi, where a magnificent handpainted majolica tile floor shows you an 18th-century vision of the Garden of Eden. *Admission: 2,000 lire. Open Easter–Nov., Mon.–Sat. 10–6, Sun. 10–2.*

From Piazza della Vittoria, picturesque Via Capodimonte leads to **Villa San Michele,** the charming former home of Swedish scientist-author Axel Munthe, now open to the public. *Via Axel Munthe. Admission: 4,000 lire. Open Apr.–Sept., daily 9–6; Oct.–Mar., daily 10:30–3:30.*

Amalfi and Positano From Sorrento, the coastal drive down to the resort town of Amalfi provides some of the most dramatic and beautiful scenery you'll find in all of Italy. Hourly buses ply the twisting clifftop road between Sorrento and Salerno. **Positano**'s jumble of pastel houses, topped by whitewashed cupolas, cling to the mountainside above the sea. The exhaustingly vertical town—the prettiest along this stretch of coast—attracts a sophisticated group of visitors and summer residents who find that its relaxed atmosphere more than compensates for the sheer effort of moving about its streets, most of which are stairways. This former fishing village now reaps the rewards of tourism and commercialized fashion; practically every other shop displays locally made casual wear. The beach is the town's focal point, with a little promenade and a multitude of café-restaurants.

Amalfi itself is a charming maze of covered alleys and narrow byways straggling up the steep mountainside. The piazza just below the cathedral forms the town's heart—a colorful assortment of pottery stalls, cafés, and postcard shops grouped around a venerable old fountain. The cathedral's exterior is its most impressive feature, so there's no need to climb all those stairs unless you really want to.

Ravello Do not miss **Ravello,** 16 kilometers (10 miles) north of Amalfi, to which it's linked by an hourly bus, a 30-minute journey (board at the main bus-park on the oceanfront). Ravello is not actually on the coast, but on a high mountain bluff overlooking the sea. The road up to the village is a series of switchbacks, and the village itself clings precariously to the mountain spur. The village flourished during the 13th century and then fell into a tranquillity that has remained unchanged for the past six centuries. The center of the town is **Piazza Vescovado,** with its cathedral, founded in 1087 and recently restored. Note its fine bronze 12th-century door, and, just inside on the left, the pulpit with mosaics telling the story of Jonah and the whale. Look to the right as well and you will see another pulpit with fantastic carved animals.

To the right of the cathedral is the entrance to the 11th-century **Villa Rufolo.** The composer Richard Wagner once stayed in Ravello, and there is a Wagner festival every summer on the villa's garden terrace. There is a moorish cloister with interlacing pointed arches, beautiful gardens, an 11th-century tower, and a belvedere with a fine view of the coast.

Across the square from the cathedral is a lovely walk leading to the Villa Cimbrone. At the entrance to the villa complex is a small cloister that looks medieval but was actually built in 1917, with two bas-reliefs: one representing nine Norman warriors, the other illustrating the seven deadly sins. Then, the long avenue leads through peaceful gardens scattered with grottoes, small temples, and statues emphasizing a contemplative silence to a belvedere and terrace where, on a clear day, the view stretches out over the Mediterranean Sea.

Dining and Lodging

It is not hard to find good, cheap dining spots in Campania, although the smaller, trendier resorts cater to a more upscale crowd—in other words, the Amalfi coast towns and the islands make demands on your pocket. But even here, in summer especially, bargain fixed-price menus can be found. Everywhere else, pizzerias and trattorie abound, and often the plainer they are the better the fare.

With accommodations, the main problem is finding space in the high season, so call ahead. Most of the budget hotels in Naples and Salerno are located in the station areas; they tend to be dingy, if generally clean. In Naples, lodgings in the market zone around Piazza del Mercato south and west of the station are not recommended, although you might want to visit the area to lap up local color (hang onto your handbag!). Outside the towns it is always worth asking at the tourist offices for lodging with families, who often set aside rooms for tourists in summer. Out of season, prices drop considerably in those establishments that remain open.

For details and price-category definitions, *see* Dining and Lodging in Staying in Italy.

Amalfi
Dining

La Caravella. Tucked away under some arches lining the coast road, the Caravella has a nondescript entrance but pleasant interior decorated in a medley of colors and paintings of old Amalfi. It's small and intimate, and proprietor Antonio describes the cuisine as "*sfiziosa*" (taste-tempting). Specialties include *scialatelli* (homemade pasta with shellfish sauce) and *pesce al limone* (fresh fish with lemon sauce). *Via M. Camera 12, tel. 089/871029. Reservations advised. AE, V. Closed Tues. and Nov. 10–30. Moderate.*

Lodging

Proto. The Proto, off the main Via Lorenzo d'Amalfi, offers some of the cheapest accommodations in this otherwise expensive resort. One of the few budget-price establishments that stay open all year, it requires guests to take full board in July and August. But it makes an ideal base for a family—clean, with large, multiple-bed rooms. Be sure to book ahead during high season. *Via Genova, tel. 089/871003. 18 rooms, 5 with bath. Facilities: restaurant. No credit cards. Budget.*

Capri
Dining

La Capannina. Only a few steps away from Capri's social center, the Piazzetta, La Capannina has a delightful vine-hung courtyard for summer dining and a reputation as one of the island's best eating places. Antipasto features fried ravioli and eggplant stuffed with ricotta, and house specialties include chicken, scaloppine and a refreshing, homemade lemon liqueur. *Via Botteghe 14, tel. 081/837–0732. Reservations advised. AE, V. Closed Wed. (except during Aug.) and Nov.–mid-Mar. Moderate.*

Da Gemma. One of Capri's favorite places for a homey atmosphere and a good meal, Da Gemma features *pappardelle all'aragosta* (egg noodles with lobster sauce) and *fritto misto*. If you're budgeting, don't order fish that you pay for by weight; it's always expensive. You can have pizza as a starter in the evening. *Via Madre Serafina 6, tel. 081/837–0461. Reservations advised. AE, DC, MC, V. Closed Mon. and Nov. Moderate.*

★ **Al Grottino.** This small family-run restaurant, with a handy location near the Piazzetta, sports autographed photographs of celebrity customers. House specialties are gnocchi with mozzarella and *linguine con gamberini* (pasta with shrimp sauce). *Via Longano 27, tel. 081/837-0584. Dinner reservations advised. AE, DC, MC, V. Closed Tues. and Nov. 3-Mar. 20. Moderate.*

Lodging **Villa Sarah.** Just a 10-minute walk from the Piazzetta, the Sarah is a whitewashed Mediterranean villa with bright, simply furnished rooms. There's a garden and small bar, but no restaurant. *Via Tiberio 3/A, tel. 081/837-7817. 20 rooms with bath. AE. Closed Nov.-Mar. Moderate.*

La Tosca. The Tosca is a tranquil haven from Capri's bustle and hard sell, a 10-minute walk from the center of town but only 20 minutes from the beach at Marina Piccola. The shady garden setting is pleasant, and all rooms are bright and airy—to enjoy the sea views, choose one with an attached bathroom. Book ahead for high season. *Via Birago, tel. 081/837—0989. 12 rooms, 6 with bath. No credit cards. Closed Jan. and Feb. Budget.*

Villa Eva. A couple of kilometers outside Anacapri, Villa Eva is convenient to the beach and the Blue Grotto. Its large garden makes it ideal for families, which are welcomed by the friendly couple who run the place. Each bedroom is refreshingly different, and much of the solid rustic furniture was built by the artist-proprietor. It's open year-round—come in winter and you'll find fire on the hearth. To get here, take the Blue Grotto bus from Anacapri, or phone ahead to be picked up. *Via La Fabbrica 8, Anacapri, tel. 081/837-2040. 18 rooms, 5 with bath. No credit cards. Budget.*

Naples **La Bersagliera.** This restaurant has been making tourists hap-
Dining py for years, with a great location on the Santa Lucia waterfront, cheerful waiters, mandolin music, and good spaghetti *alla disgraziata* (with tomatoes, capers, and black olives) and *mozzarella in carrozza* (cheese fried in batter). *Borgo Marinaro 10, tel. 081/764-6016. Reservations advised. No credit cards. Closed Tues. Moderate.*

★ **Ciro a Santa Brigida.** Centrally located off Via Toledo near the Castel Nuovo, this no-frills place is a favorite with businesspeople, artists, and journalists. Tables are arranged on two levels, and the decor is classic trattoria. This is the place to try traditional Neapolitan *sartù di riso* (a rich rice dish with meat and peas) and *melanzane* (eggplant) *alla parmigiana* or *scaloppe alla Ciro*, with prosciutto and mozzarella. There's pizza, too. *Via Santa Brigida 71, tel. 081/552-4072. Reservations advised. AE, DC, MC, V. Closed Sun. and Aug. Moderate.*

Brandi. Where better to sample a pizza than at Brandi's, where a plaque on the wall commemorates the invention here, in 1889, of the famous pizza Margherita, named in honor of Queen Margherita di Savoia. Although Brandi offers a range of toppings, it would be a shame to miss the authentic article, the plain mozzarella-and-tomato *pizza Margherita*, to find out how it should be done. Popular with Neapolitans, Brandi also offers a more expensive, three-course menu. *Salita Sant'Anna di Palazzo 1, off Via Chiaia, tel. 081/416928. Reservations advised on weekends. AE. Closed Mon. Budget.*

Lodging **Cavour.** Located in the rundown Stazione Centrale area, on the square in front of the main train station, it's handy for anyone wanting to use Naples as a touring base. The hotel is gradually being renovated and can offer clean, comfortable rooms, as well as a restaurant. Those on the courtyard are quieter. *Piazza Garibaldi 32, tel. 081/283122, fax 081/264306. 105 rooms, most with bath. AE, DC, MC, V. Moderate.*

San Pietro. Just off Corso Umberto, at the Piazza Garibaldi end, the San Pietro is comfortable if rather gloomy. It's clean enough and convenient to the station and the market area. The rooms are old-fashioned, but the hotel's size ensures you will almost always find space here. *Via San Pietro ad Aram 18, tel. 081/286040, fax 081/553-5914. 54 rooms, 20 with bath. Facilities: bar. AE, DC, MC, V. Inexpensive.*

Casanova. One of a wide selection of cheap hotels around Piazza Garibaldi and convenient to the station, the Casanova is cleaner than most in the area and has a relaxed and friendly management. Rooms are small and spartan but quiet, a big plus in Naples. The house dog, Zeus, enjoys a certain fame among the traveling fraternity. *Via Venezia 2, tel. 081/268287, fax 081/554-3768. 18 rooms, most with baths. AE, DC, MC, V. Budget.*

Positano
Dining

Capurale. Among all the popular restaurants on the beach promenade, Capurale (just around the corner) has the best food and lowest prices. Tables are set under vines on a breezy sidewalk in the summer, upstairs and indoors in winter. Spaghetti con melanzane and *crêpes al formaggio* (cheese-filled crepes) are good choices here. *Via Marina, tel. 089/875374. Reservations advised for outdoor tables. No credit cards. Closed Nov. 3–Mar. Moderate.*

Lodging

Palazzo Murat. The location is perfect, in the heart of town, near the beachside promenade, but set within a walled garden. The old wing is a historic palazzo, with tall windows and wrought-iron balconies; the newer wing is a whitewashed Mediterranean building with arches and terraces. Guests can relax in antique-strewn lounges or on the charming vine-draped patio. *Via dei Mulini 23, tel. 089/875177, fax 089/811419. 28 rooms with bath. AE, DC, MC, V. Closed Nov. 5–Mar. Moderate.*

Italia. This tiny pensione is more a private house, really—but the vista from its windows and balconies keeps you from feeling cramped. Rooms are small, but there's a large *salone* overgrown with plants and flowers framing the view. Signora Durso, who runs the place, fusses over her guests, whom she provides with an indoor cooking area. *Via Pasitea 137, tel. 089/875024. 5 rooms, 2 with bath. No credit cards. Budget.*

Santa Caterina. There is more to this newly refurbished hotel than meets the eye. Rooms descend the steep slope on three levels, and each has a generous balcony or terrace that makes the most of the exquisite view of the town and seashore. On street level (the top floor) is an excellent fish restaurant, a favorite with locals. The beach is quite a hike—but that's Positano. *Via Pasitea 113, tel. 089/811513. 12 rooms, 6 with bath. Facilities: bar, restaurant. AE, DC, MC, V. Budget.*

Ravello
Lodging

Villa Amore. This family-run pensione, a 10-minute walk from the main Piazza Vescovado, is tidy and comfortable, and most rooms have exhilarating views. There's a garden and an air of utter tranquility, particularly at dusk, when the valley is tinged purple by glorious sunsets. Furnishings are modest but modern. Full board is available and may be required in summer. Book ahead if possible. *Via Santa Chiara, tel. 089/857135.*

15 rooms, 8 with bath. Facilities: bar, restaurant, garden. MC, V. Inexpensive.

Sorrento
Dining

Antica Trattoria. This is a homey, hospitable place with a garden for summer dining. The specialties of the house are a classic *pennette al profumo di bosco* (pasta with a creamy mushroom and ham sauce), fish (which can be expensive), and melanzane alla parmigiana. *Via Giuliani 33, tel. 081/807–1082. Dinner reservations advised. No credit cards. Closed Mon., Jan. 10–Feb. 10. Moderate.*

La Belle Époque. Occupying a 19th-century villa perched on the edge of the vine-covered gorge of the Mulini, this is an elegant veranda restaurant. Try the *scialatelli Belle Époque* (homemade pasta with mozzarella and eggplant). *Via Fuorimura 7, tel. 081/878–1216. Reservations advised. AE, DC, MC, V. Closed Mon. Moderate.*

★ **Parrucchiano.** One of the town's best and oldest, Parrucchiano features greenhouse-style dining rooms dripping with vines and dotted with plants. Among the antipasti, try the *panzarotti* (pastry crust filled with mozzarella and tomato), and for a main course, the *scalloppe alla sorrentina*, again with mozzarella and tomato. *Corso Italia 71, tel. 081/878–1321. Reservations advised. V. Closed Wed. from Nov. to May. Moderate.*

Lodging
★

Bellevue Syrene. A palatial villa in a garden overlooking the sea, the Syrene features solid, old-fashioned comforts, along with plenty of charm and antique paintings. *Piazza della Vittoria 5, tel. 081/878–1024. 50 rooms with bath. AE, DC, MC, V. Moderate.*

Eden. Eden occupies a fairly quiet but central location, with a garden and a pool. The bedrooms are bright but undistinguished; the lounge and lobby have more character. It's an unpretentious but friendly hotel, with some smaller rooms in the Inexpensive category. *Via Correale 25, tel. 081/878–1909, fax 081/807–2016. 60 rooms with bath. AE, V. Closed Nov.–Feb. Moderate.*

Linda. With the *Mara*, this pensione is the only budget accommodation open all year. Bland but clean, it's just above the bus and railway station. *Via degli Aranci 125, tel. 081/878–2916. 10 rooms, 8 with bath. No credit cards. Budget.*

Mara. Small and friendly, this pensione is near the museum, in a modern block just up from the bus and train station. The rooms—doubles only—are functional; and some have a balcony. *Via Rota 5, tel. 081/878–3665. 14 rooms, 10 with bath. Facilities: restaurant, bar. No credit cards. Budget.*

16 Luxembourg

uxembourg is going through the greatest period of prosperity in its 1,000-plus-year history, and the plethora of construction sites, roadworks, and upscale renovations offers visible evidence. But the budget traveler can find a great deal of history, atmosphere, and good country cooking despite the cosmopolitan metamorphosis taking place all around, and the best Luxembourg has to offer can be easily attained on foot.

One of the smallest countries in the United Nations, Luxembourg measures only 2,587 square kilometers (999 square miles), less than the size of Rhode Island. It is dwarfed by its neighbors—Germany, Belgium, and France—yet from its history of invasion, occupation, and siege, you might think those square miles were built over solid gold. In fact, it was Luxembourg's very defenses against centuries of attack that rendered it all the more desirable: From AD 963, when Siegfried founded a castle on the high promontory of the Bock, the once-grander duchy encased itself in layer upon layer of fortifications until by the mid-19th century, its very invulnerability was considered a threat to those not commanding its thick stone walls. After successive invasions by Burgundians, Habsburgs, the French, the Spanish, the Dutch, and the Austrians, Luxembourg was ultimately dismantled in the name of peace, its neutrality guaranteed by the 1867 Treaty of London, its function reduced to that of a buffer zone. What remains of its walls, while impressive, is only a reminder of what was one of the strongholds of Europe—the "Gibraltar of the North."

Nowadays Luxembourg is besieged again, this time by bankers and Eurocrats. Its Boulevard Royal bristles with international banks—enough to rival Switzerland—and, just outside the old city, a new colony has been seeded, populated by *fonctionnaires* for the European Community, the heir to the Common

Market. Fiercely protecting its share of the expanding bureaucracy from competitive co-capitals Strasbourg and Brussels, Luxembourg digs its heels in once again, vying not only for political autonomy but for its new-found prosperity and clout. Thus the national motto takes on new meaning: *Mir wëlle bleiwe wat mir sin*, or "We want to stay what we are"—nowadays, a powerful, viable Grand-Duchy in the heart of modern Europe.

Essential Information

Before You Go

When to Go The main tourist season in Luxembourg is the same as in Belgium—early May to late September. But temperatures in Luxembourg tend to be cooler than those in Belgium, particularly in the hilly north, where there is frequently snow in winter.

Climate In general, temperatures in Luxembourg are moderate. It does drizzle frequently, however, so be sure to bring a raincoat.

The following are the average daily maximum and minimum temperatures for Luxembourg.

Jan.	37F	3C	May	65F	18C	Sept.	66F	19C
	29	-1		46	8		50	10
Feb.	40F	4C	June	70F	21C	Oct.	56F	13C
	31	-1		52	11		43	6
Mar.	49F	10C	July	73F	23C	Nov.	44F	7C
	35	1		55	13		37	3
Apr.	57F	14C	Aug.	71F	22C	Dec.	39F	4C
	40	4		54	12		32	0

Currency In Luxembourg, as in Belgium, the unit of currency is the franc. Luxembourg issues its own currency in bills of 100, 500, and 1,000 francs and coins of 1, 5, 20, and 50 francs. Belgian currency can be used freely in Luxembourg, and the two currencies have exactly the same value. However, Luxembourg currency is not valid in Belgium. At press time (summer 1992), the exchange rate was 33 fr. L. to the U.S. dollar, 28 fr. L. to the Canadian dollar, and 60 fr. L. to the pound sterling.

What It Will Cost Luxembourg is a developed and sophisticated country with a high standard and cost of living. Luxembourg City is an international banking center, and a number of European institutions are based there, a fact that tends to push prices slightly higher in the capital than in the countryside.

Sample Prices Cup of coffee, 50 fr. L.; glass of beer, 40 fr. L.; movie ticket, 170 fr. L.; 3-mile taxi ride, 500 fr. L.

Customs on Arrival For information on customs regulations, *see* Customs on Arrival in Belgium.

Language Native Luxembourgers speak three languages fluently: Luxembourgish (best described as a dialect of German), German, and French. Many also speak English.

Staying in Luxembourg

Telephones You can find public phones both on the street and in city post offices. A local call costs about 5 fr. L. (slightly more from restaurants and gas stations). The cheapest way to make an international call is to dial direct from a public phone; in a post office, you may be required to make a deposit before the call. For operator-assisted calls, dial 0010.

Mail Airmail postcards and letters weighing less than 20 grams cost *Postal Rates* 22 fr. L. to the United States. Letters and postcards to the United Kingdom cost 14 fr. L.

Receiving Mail If you are uncertain where you'll be staying, have your mail sent in care of American Express (6/8 rue Origer, 2269 Luxembourg).

Shopping Purchases of goods for export may qualify for a sales tax (TVA) *Sales Tax Refunds* refund of 12%. Ask the shop to fill out a refund form. You must then have the form stamped by customs officers on leaving either Luxembourg, Belgium, or Holland.

Opening and **Banks.** Banks generally are open weekdays 8:30–noon and **Closing Times** 1:30–4:30, though more and more remain open through the lunch hour.

Museums. Opening hours vary, so check individual listings. Many close on Monday, and most also close for lunch between noon and 2.

Shops. Large city department stores and shops are generally open weekdays, except Monday morning, and Saturday 9–noon and 2–6. A few small family businesses are open Sunday morning from 8 to noon.

National Holidays January 1; February 22–23 (Carnival); April 12 (Easter Monday); May 1 (May Day); May 20 (Ascension); May 31 (Pentecost Monday); June 23 (National Day); August 15 (Assumption); November 1 (All Saints' Day); November 2 (All Souls Day); December 25, 26.

Dining Restaurants in Luxembourg offer their best deals at lunch, when you can find a *plat du jour* (one-course special) or *menu* (two or three courses included in price) at bargain rates. Pizzerias offer an excellent and popular source of cheap food, with pasta, risotti, and wood-oven pizzas making a full meal. Light lunches—easy on the stomach if not always the wallet—can be found in chic pastry shops, where you point to the dishes in the display case (a slice of *pâté en croute*, an egg salad, a few small casseroles to be heated), then take your number upstairs to the *salon de consommation*, where your drink order will be taken and your meal served.

Mealtimes Most hotels serve breakfast until 10. Lunch hours are noon–2, sometimes extending until 3. Long accustomed to the Continental style of dining heavily at midday, business-conscious Luxembourgers now eat their main meal in the evening between 7 and 10.

Lodging Most hotels in the capital are relatively modern and vary from
Hotels the international style, mainly near the airport, to family-run establishments in town. As Luxembourg City is an important business center, many of its hotels offer reduced rates on weekends, particularly out of season.

Youth Hostels Inexpensive youth hostels are plentiful in Luxembourg. They are often set in ancient fortresses and castles. For information, contact **Centrale des Auberges de Jeunesse** (18 pl. d'Armes, L-1136, Luxembourg, tel. 25588).

Camping The Grand Duchy is probably the best-organized country in Europe for camping. It offers some 120 sites, all with full amenities and most with scenic views. Information is available from the **Fédération Luxembourgeoise de Camping et de Caravaning** (31 rte. d'Esch, L-4450 Belvaux, tel. 591274). You can also get a brochure at the National Tourist Office.

Tipping In Luxembourg hotels and restaurants, taxes and service charges are included in the overall bill and it is not necessary to leave more. If you wish to, round off the sum to the nearest 50 fr.L. or 100 fr.L. Bellhops and doormen should receive between 50 fr.L. and 100 fr.L., depending on the grade of the hotel. At the movies, tip the usher 20 fr.L. if you are seated personally. In theaters, tip about 20 fr.L. for checking your coat, and the same to the program seller. In public washrooms the attendant will usually expect between 5 fr.L. and 10 fr.L. Taxi drivers expect a tip; add about 15% to the amount on the meter.

Luxembourg City

Arriving and Departing

By Plane All international flights arrive at Luxembourg's Findel Airport, 6 kilometers (4 miles) from the city.

Between the Bus No. 9 leaves the airport at regular intervals for Luxem-
Airport and bourg's main bus depot, located just beside the train station.
Downtown Bus Nos. 2, 4, 11, and 12 go to the city center. Individual tickets cost 30 fr.L. A taxi will cost you about 600 fr.L. If you are driving, follow the signs for the Centre Ville (city center).

Getting Around

One of the best transportation options in Luxembourg is the **Oeko-Carnet,** a block of five one-day tickets good for unlimited transportation on trains and buses throughout the country. Cards are on sale, for 480 fr.L., at Gare Centrale (the main train station) in Luxembourg City, or at Aldringen Center, located underground in front of the central post office.

By Bus Luxembourg City has a highly efficient bus service. The blue-and-yellow buses outside the city train station will take you all around the city and also to some of the outlying areas. Get details about services at the information counter in the station arrivals hall. Fares are low, but the best bet is to buy a 10-ride ticket (240 fr.L.), available from banks or from the bus station in the Aldringen Center. Other buses, connecting Luxembourg City with towns throughout the country, leave from Gare Centrale.

By Train Luxembourg is served by frequent direct trains from Paris and Brussels. From Paris, travel time is about four hours; from Brussels, just under three hours. From Amsterdam, the journey is via Brussels and takes about six hours. There are connections from most German cities via Koblenz. Outside Luxembourg City, three major train routes extend north, south, and west into the Moselle Valley. For all train information, phone 492424. All service is from Gare Centrale in place de la Gare.

By Bicycle Bicycling is a popular sport in Luxembourg, and it is an excellent way to see the city and outlying regions. A new brochure, "Cycling Tracks," is available from the Luxembourg National Tourist Office, Box 1001, L-1010 Luxembourg. Bikes can be rented in Luxembourg City at **Luxembourg DELTA** (8 Bisserwee), from March 30 through October 31; in Reisdorf, Diekirch, and Echternach, rent bikes at the tourist office (**Syndicat d'Initiative**). Maps are available from the tourist office.

Important Addresses and Numbers

Tourist The main **Office Nationale du Tourisme (ONT)** in Luxembourg
Information City (Aerogare [Air Terminal] bus depot, place de la Gare, tel. 481199) is open daily (except Sunday in winter) 9–noon and 2–6:30 (July–mid-Sept., 9–7:30). The Luxembourg City tourist office (place d'Armes, tel. 222809) is open mid-Sept.–mid-June, Mon.–Sat. 9–1 and 2–6; mid-June–mid-Sept., weekdays 9–7, Sat. 9–1 and 2–7, Sun. 10–noon and 2–6.

Embassies U.S. (22 blvd. Emmanuel Servais, tel. 460123). **U.K.** (14 blvd. F. D. Roosevelt, tel. 29864). **Canada:** The Brussels embassy (ave. de Tervuren 2, 1040 Brussels, tel. 00322/7356040) covers Luxembourg.

Emergencies **Police, Ambulance, Doctor, Dentist** (tel. 012). **Pharmacies** in Luxembourg stay open nights on a rotation system. Signs listing late-night facilities are posted outside each pharmacy.

Exploring Luxembourg City

Numbers in the margin correspond to points of interest on the Luxembourg City map.

This walk takes you through Luxembourg City's maze of ancient military fortifications, now transformed into peaceful paths. Begin at Gare Centrale, in the southern section of the city. As you head right from the station toward the city center along avenue de la Gare, you will pass through a bustling shopping district.

❶ Take the **Passerelle Viaduct,** a 19th-century road bridge that links the station with the valley of the Petrusse. The Petrusse is more of a brook than a river and is now contained by concrete, but the valley has become a singularly beautiful park. From here you'll see the rocky ledges—partly natural, partly manmade—on which the city is perched.

At the town end of the Passerelle, on the right, is the
❷ **Monument de la Solidarité Nationale** (National Monument to Luxembourg Unity). Despite its modern design, the monument doesn't look out of place: It appears to be just another broken tower on top of the rocks.

Follow the road along the remains of the old city fortifications,
❸ known as the **Citadelle du St-Esprit** (Citadel of the Holy Spirit). This 17th-century citadel was built by Vauban, the French military engineer, on the site of a former monastery. Ahead of you are the three spires of the cathedral.

Retrace your steps along the old city fortifications, cross boule-
❹ vard F. D. Roosevelt, and continue on to the **place de la Constitution,** marked by the war memorial, a striking gilt *Gëlle Fra,* or Golden Woman. Here you'll find the entrance to the ancient military tunnels carved into the rocky **Bock** or **Petrusse** fortifications. During the many phases of the fortress's construction, the rock itself was hollowed out to form a honeycomb of passages running for nearly 24 kilometers (15 miles) below the town. These were used both for storage and as a place of refuge when the city was under attack. Two sections of the passages, known as the **Casemates,** are open to the public. These sections contain former barracks, cavernous abattoirs, bakeries, and a deep well. *Admission: 50 fr.L. adults, 30 fr.L. children. Open July–Sept.*

Take rue de l'ancien Athénée alongside the former Jesuit college, now the National Library. In rue Notre-Dame to your
❺ right is the main entrance to the **Cathédrale Notre-Dame,** originally the 17th-century Jesuit church, with its Baroque organ gallery and crypt. The roof of the main tower was rebuilt after a fire in 1985. *Open daily 8–noon and 2–7; crypt open only by request.*

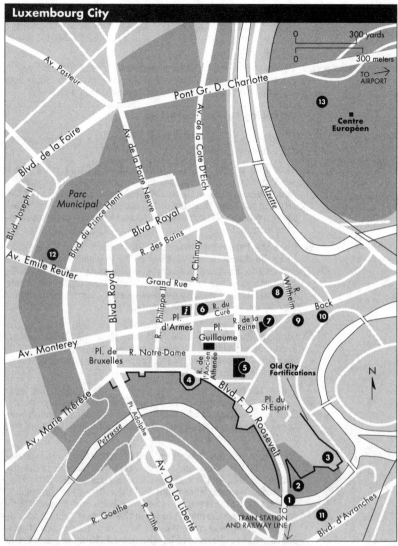

Luxembourg City

TO AIRPORT

Centre Européen

Opposite the cathedral lies the place Guillaume, known locally as the Knuedler, a name derived from the girdle worn by Franciscan monks who once had a monastery on the site. On market days (Wednesday and Saturday mornings) the square is noisy and colorful.

The lively place d'Armes, with its cafés and restaurants, lies just beyond the place Guillaume. Open-air concerts are held every evening in summer. The town tourist office is located on the square, and on rue du Curé there is a small museum, **Maquette,** that houses models of the fortress at various stages of its construction: It provides a fascinating glimpse of the historical city. *Admission: 40 fr.L. adults, 20 fr.L. children. Open July–Aug. only, 10–12:30 and 2–6.*

From place Guillaume, rue de la Reine leads to the **Grand Ducal Palace,** currently closed for renovations (the duke works and resides temporarily in the Villa Vauban, in the municipal park).

Behind the palace is the oldest part of town, the Marché-aux-Poissons, site of the old fish market and originally the crossing point of two Roman roads. Now a quiet square, it comes alive on Easter Monday with the quaint, if obscure, Emais'chen Festival in which lovers exchange terra-cotta bird whistles and everyone indulges in *thüringer* (the standard local sausage) and the ubiquitous *gromperekichelcher* (fried potato patties).

On the left is the **Musée de l'Etat** (State Museum), set in an attractive row of 16th-century houses. The museum contains an eclectic collection of exhibits from the Stone Age to the Space Age, encompassing humble village crafts and fine arts. The Gallo-Roman collection features a fascinating assortment of small treasures—toga buckles, miniature deities—unearthed along the ancient routes that crisscrossed Luxembourg in the first centuries AD. Dramatic views over the ramparts compensate for the slightly confusing museum route. The museum now houses the spectacular Bentinck-Thyssen collection of 15th- to 19th-century art, including works by Breughel, Rembrandt, Canaletto, and other masters. *Admission free. Open Tues.–Fri. 10–4:45, Sat. 2–5:45, Sun. 10–11:45 and 2–5:45.*

At the bottom of rue Wiltheim is the gate of the **Trois Tours** (Three Towers), the oldest of which was built around 1050. During the French Revolution, the guillotine was set up in these towers. From here you can clearly see the source of Luxembourg's strength as a fortress.

To the left is the **Bock** promontory, the site of the earliest castle (AD 963) and always the duchy's most fortified point. From the Bock, steep cliffs plunge downward to the Alzette Valley. The Bock also has a series of passages similar to the Petrusse Casemates. *Admission: 50 fr.L. adults, 30 fr.L. children. Open Mar.–Oct., daily 10–5.*

The scenic ramparts of the Bock's **Corniche** provide a view over the lower town, known as the Grund. Many of the houses on the right were refuges, used in times of danger by nobles and churchmen from the surrounding area. The massive towers on the far side of the valley date to the Wenceslas fortifications, which, in 1390, extended the protected area, and the block-like *casernes* (barracks) were built in the 17th century by the French.

At the ruined fortifications of the Citadelle du St-Ésprit, take the elevator down to the Grund, and turn right on leaving the tunnel. As you follow the Petrusse Valley below the cliffs, you'll see two signs marking the high-water points of two devastating floods; that's why the Petrusse has been tamed with locks and concrete today. Turn right into the green Petrusse Valley park. On the left, the little **chapel of St-Quirin** is built into the rock near the Passerelle Viaduct. At Pont Adolphe, walk back up to city level and you are suddenly face-to-face with the 20th century. The boulevard Royal, once the main moat of the fortress, is now Luxembourg's Wall Street, packed with the famous names of the international banking scene.

From here you can either take avenue de la Liberté, an important shopping street, toward the station or head back into town, perhaps to the Grand Rue shopping area. Or if you want to extend your tour, take avenue Emile Reuter to the municipal park and **Villa Vauban,** the Duke's temporary lodging during palace renovations. Portions of its permanent collection of Dutch and Flemish paintings may be seen at the Musée de l'Etat.

Walk up boulevard Royal to rond-point Robert Schuman, named for one of the founders of the European Common Market, and cross the Pont Grande Duchesse Charlotte (with stunning views of the valley) to **Plateau Kirchberg,** a moonscape of modern architecture housing the European Court of Justice and various branches of the European Community. The most prominent structure—at 23 stories, Luxembourg's only skyscraper—is home to the secretariat of the European Parliament.

Shopping

Luxembourg City has two main shopping areas: the **Grand-Rue** and the **avenue de la Gare.** Jewelry and designer fashions are particularly well represented in the Grand-Rue. There are a few small department stores near the train station, but most of the stores in this area are specialty shops: Hi-fi equipment is considerably cheaper here than in neighboring countries. Luxembourg chocolates, called *knippercher,* are popular purchases, available from the best pastry shops. Luxembourg's most famous product is Villeroy and Boch porcelain, available in most gift shops here. Feast your eyes at the glossy main shop, located at rue du Fossé 2, then buy at the excellent second-quality factory outlet (rue Rollingergrund 330); the outlet will not ship, so weigh your purchases carefully.

Dining

French *cuisine bourgeoise*—steak, pork chops, veal with mushrooms, all served in generous portions, with heaps of *frites* (french fries) on the side—dominates local menus. Yet this tiny country has its own earthy specialties, fresh off the farm: *judd mat gardebohn'en* (salted pork with fava beans); *Eslecker ham* or *jambon d'Ardennes* (pearly-pink raw-smoked ham served cold with pickled onions); *choucroute* (sauerkraut); *treipen* (blood pudding); and batter-fried *merlan* (whiting). A few restaurants still feature them, though nowadays you're as likely to find Chinese, Thai, Japanese, Indian, and—leading the ethnic selection by several laps—Italian.

Dress Stylish, casual dress is generally acceptable in most restaurants, but when in doubt, err on the formal side. In expensive French restaurants, formal dress is taken for granted.

Ratings Prices quoted here are per person and include a first course, main course, and dessert, but not wine. Best bets are indicated by a star ★.

Category	All Areas
Moderate	600–1,200 fr.L.
Inexpensive	400–600 fr.L.
Budget	under 400 fr.L.

Moderate **Kamakura.** If heavy Western cuisine palls, take the elevator from the Citadelle du St-Esprit to the up-and-coming Grund and try this chic Japanese restaurant. A number of fixed-price menus offer a variety of delicate, nouvelle-accented dishes, artfully presented and graciously served. A la carte specialties, considerably more expensive, include impeccably fresh sashimi (raw fish) and light tempura vegetables. *2–4 rue Munster, tel. 470604. Reservations accepted. AE, DC, MC, V. Closed Sun.*

★ **Mousel's Cantine.** Directly adjoining the great Mousel brewery (there are beer taps that feed from tanks within), this fresh, comfortable café serves up heaping platters of local specialties—braised and grilled ham, sausage, *gardebohn'en* (fava beans), sauerkraut, and fried potatoes—to be washed down with crockery steins of creamy *Gezwickelte Béier* (unfiltered beer). The front café is brighter, with sanded tabletops, but the tiny fluorescent-lit dining room has windows into the brewery. *46 montée de Clausen, tel. 470198. Reservations advised. MC, V. Closed Sun.*

★ **La Trattoria dei Quattro.** Despite an undesirable location—on one of the sleazier back streets around the avenue de la Gare shopping area—this restaurant merits the trip off the beaten track. It's set in a 150-year-old town house with an impressive carved wooden ceiling and fireplace. Excellent homemade pastas include *maccheroni alla Sarda* (sauced with tomato, onion, tuna, and fennel seeds) and *bucatini alla melanzani e funghi* (with eggplant and mushrooms). *64 rue Fort-neipperg, tel. 490039. Reservations accepted. AE, DC, MC, V. Closed lunchtime weekends.*

Inexpensive **Ancre d'Or.** This tidy, friendly brasserie, just off the place
★ Guillaume, serves a wide variety of old-time Luxembourgish specialties as well as good *cuisine bourgeoise*. Try their *judd mat gardebohn'en*, *kuddelfleck* (breaded tripe), or *treipen* (rich blood sausages served with red cabbage and onion sauce). The apple tart (Luxembourgish style, with custard base) is homemade. Portions are generous, service friendly, and the clientele local. *23 rue du Fossé, tel. 472973. Reservations advised at lunch. MC, V. Closed Sun.*

Ems. Directly across the street from the train station, this lively diner-equivalent (vinyl booths, posted specials) draws a loyal clientele for its vast portions of *moules* (mussels) in a rich wine-and-garlic broth, accompanied by *frites* (french fries) and a bottle of sharp, cold *Auxerrois* or *Rivaner* (local white wines). For dessert, try one of the huge ice-cream specialties. Food is served until 1 AM. *30 pl. de la Gare, tel. 487799. Reservations not necessary. DC, MC, V.*

Budget **Taverne Bit.** With sanded tabletops and dark-wood banquettes, this is a cozy and very local pub, where you can drink a *clensch* (stein) of draft Bitburger beer (from just across the German border) and have a plate of sausage with good potato salad, a plate of cold ham, or *kachkes*, the pungent local cheese spread, served with baked potatoes. *43 allée Scheffer, tel. 460751. Reservations not necessary. No credit cards. Closed Sat. PM, Sun.*

Lodging

Hotels in Luxembourg City are located in three main areas: the town center, the station area, and the area close to the airport. By far the largest number are around the station. Most hotels are modern, but a warm welcome and high standards compensate for the relative lack of character.

Ratings Price categories are determined by the cost of a double room (Continental breakfast is sometimes included in the room price). Best bets are indicated by a star ★.

Category	Cost
Moderate	2,500–3,500 fr.L.
Inexpensive	1,700–2,500 fr.L.
Budget	under 1,700 fr.L.

Moderate **Auberge du Coin.** At the edge of a quiet, dignified residential
★ area but within easy reach of the station and the old town, this pleasant hotel was completely renovated in 1989 in pure "new Luxembourg" style—stone and terra-cotta floors, wood-framed double windows, polished oak, Persian rugs, and tropical plants. Rooms are freshly furnished in bright knotty pine with new tile baths. There's a lovely French restaurant and a comfortable oak-and-stone bar as well. Prices are at the high end of this category; the nine-room matching annex down the street, which has no elevator, costs slightly less. *2 blvd. de la Petrusse, tel. 402101. 23 rooms with bath. Facilities: restaurant, bar. AE, DC, MC, V.*

Empire. Slick, freshly decorated, simple, and aimed at single businesspeople (there are only three double rooms), this station hotel offers all comforts and a few bargain no-bath rooms (though all have toilets). Both a pizzeria and a French restaurant adjoin. *34 pl. de la Gare, tel. 485252. 27 rooms with bath. Facilities: restaurant, pizzeria, bar. AE, DC, MC, V.*

★ **Italia.** This is a valuable and remarkably inexpensive find in the *gare* area: a former private apartment converted into hotel rooms, some with plaster details and cabinetry left behind. Rooms are solid and freshly furnished, all with private tiled bathrooms. The somewhat pricey restaurant downstairs is one of the city's better Italian eateries. *15–17 rue d'Anvers, tel. 486626. 20 rooms with bath. Facilities: restaurant, bar, garden. AE, DC, MC, V.*

Nobilis. Built new in 1980 on the busy avenue de la Gare and decorated in heavy wood and earth tones, this is a welcoming, relatively quiet property with business-class comforts. Despite double-glazed windows in front, back rooms (over the parking area) are considerably quieter, and cost only 100 fr.L. more. *47 av. de la Gare, tel. 494971. 44 rooms with bath. Facilities: restaurant, coffee shop, bar. AE, DC, MC, V.*

Inexpensive **Bristol.** Though on a street near the train station that is lined with strip joints and flophouses (as well as legitimate shops and restaurants), this modest hotel offers comfortable, secure lodging and fresh decor. The lobby/bar is warm and familial, and baths are newly refurbished. A few bathless rooms on the first and fourth floors go for bargain rates. *11 rue de Strasbourg, tel. 485830. 30 rooms, 22 with shower/toilet. Facilities: bar for guests only. AE, DC, MC, V.*

Dauphin. Another low-priced option, this modern hotel offers plain, clean rooms with splashy '60s decor—daisy prints, linoleum—and private baths. Back rooms avoid heavy street noise. *42 av. de la Gare, tel. 488282. 36 rooms with bath. Facilities: breakfast room. AE, DC, MC, V.*

Budget **Auberge de Jeunesse Mansfeld.** Considerably more palatable than some of the unlisted flophouses by the train station, this youth hostel looks like a U.S. campus dorm. There are rooms with 8–20 beds as well as recently refurnished doubles with sinks. Breakfast is included in room price, but sheets must be rented at 100 fr.L. *2 rue du fort Olisy, tel. 26889. 312 beds, showers downstairs. Facilities: restaurant, bar. MC, V.*

★ **Carlton.** In this vast 1918 hotel, buffered from the rue de Strasbourg scene by a rank of stores and opening onto a quiet inner court, budget travelers will find roomy, quiet quarters. The beveled glass, oak parquet, and terrazzo floors are original—but so are the toilets, all located down the hall. Each room has antique beds, floral-print comforters, and a sink; wood floors, despite creaks, are white-glove clean. *9 rue de Strasbourg, tel. 484802. 50 rooms without toilet. Facilities: breakfast room, bar. No credit cards.*

17 Malta

For years, travelers to Malta and its two sister islands, Gozo and Comino, have enjoyed uncrowded and moderately priced seaside hotels and colorful taverns. The sunny climate finds many tourists spread out across the islands' white sandy beaches, and the festive and hospitable residents happily welcome tourists.

For those interested in history and archaeology, tiny Malta—with only 28 kilometers (17 miles) between its two farthest points—displays the remains of a long and eventful history. Among the most fascinating ruins are Neolithic temples and stone megaliths left by prehistoric inhabitants. In AD 60, St. Paul, shipwrecked here, converted the people to Christianity. Other less welcome visitors, attracted by Malta's strategic position, conquered and ruled. These include the Phoenicians, Carthaginians, and Romans.

The Knights of the Order of St. John of Jerusalem arrived here in 1530 after they had been driven from their stronghold on the island of Rhodes by the Ottoman emperor Suleiman the Magnificent. In 1565, with only a handful of men, the Knights held Malta against the Ottoman Turks in a dramatic and bloody siege. They ruled the islands until Napoleon arrived in 1798 and left massive fortifications, rich architecture, and the city of Valletta, Malta's capital.

The British drove the French out in 1800 and gave the island the distinctive British feel that it still retains. In 1942, during World War II, King George VI awarded the Maltese people the George Cross for their courage in withstanding repeated German and Italian attacks, especially from the air. Malta gained independence from Britain in 1964 and was declared a republic within the Commonwealth in 1974. On December 2–3,

Malta

Mediterranean Sea

1989, the island hosted the first Bush-Gorbachev summit, marking the beginning of improved relations between the two superpowers.

Essential Information

Before You Go

When to Go The archipelago is a year-round delight, but May through October is the time of the main tourist season. April and May are the months for spring freshness; the summer months can be very hot though sometimes tempered by sea breezes. August is just too hot for touring. If you visit in the winter, you'll find the climate pleasant and mild, but you may encounter sudden rainstorms.

Climate The following are the average daily maximum and minimum temperatures for Valletta.

Jan.	58F	14C	May	71F	22C	Sept.	81F	27C
	50	10		61	16		71	22
Feb.	59F	15C	June	79F	26C	Oct.	75F	24C
	51	10		67	19		66	19
Mar.	61F	16C	July	84F	29C	Nov.	67F	20C
	52	11		72	22		60	16
Apr.	65F	18C	Aug.	85F	29C	Dec.	61F	16C
	56	13		73	23		54	12

Currency The unit of currency is the Maltese lira (Lm), also sometimes referred to as the pound. It's divided into 100 cents, and the cents are divided into 10 mils; but in recent years the mils have dropped out of circulation. There are Lm 20, Lm 10, Lm 5, and Lm 2 bills; coins—1¢, 2¢, 5¢, 10¢, 25¢, 50¢, and Lm 1—are bronze and silver. At press time (summer 1992), the exchange rate was Lm .31 to the dollar and Lm .57 to the pound sterling.

What It Will Cost Malta is one of the cheapest holiday destinations in Europe, though with the rapid tourist development, prices are inevitably rising. Prices tend to be uniform across the island, except in Valletta, the capital, where they are slightly higher.

Sample Prices Cup of coffee, 25¢ (Maltese); bottle of beer, 25¢; Coca-Cola, 15¢.

Customs on Arrival You may bring into Malta, duty-free, 200 cigarettes, one bottle of liquor, one bottle of wine, and one bottle of perfume. You may bring in up to Lm 50 in currency.

Language The spelling of many Maltese words can be bewildering. Fortunately, both Maltese and English are the official languages on the island, so you shouldn't experience any problems. Italian is widely spoken, too.

Getting Around

By Bus Most routes throughout the island are via Valletta, which facilitates travel out of the capital but makes cross-country trips a bit longer. Public transportation is very inexpensive. Though some of the old green buses show their age, they are usually on time and are not crowded.

By Boat Daily car/passenger ferries operate year-round from Cirkewwa to Mġarr on Gozo. Telephone 243964 or 556016 for details. The crossing from Marfa to Mġarr in Gozo lasts 25 minutes, with departures every hour in summer and every two hours in winter. The round-trip fare is Lm 1 adults, 50¢ children. There is also one service daily from Pietà to Gozo, leaving in the morning and taking an hour and 15 minutes each way. The fare from Mġarr (passenger plus car) is Lm 3.50. A ferry service links the tourist resort town of Sliema to Valletta.

By Taxi There are plenty of metered taxis available and fares are reasonable compared with those in other European countries. Be sure the meter is switched on when your trip starts, or bargain first. Tip the driver 10%.

Staying in Malta

Telephones There is direct dialing to most parts of the world from Malta. The best place to make calls is either from your hotel or from the Overseas Telephone Division of Telemalta at St. George's, Qawra, St. Paul's Bay, Sliema, Valletta, and Luqa Airport. The international dialing access code is 00.

Mail Airmail letters to the United States cost 14¢; postcards cost 12¢. Airmail letters to the United Kingdom cost 10¢; postcards 10¢.

Opening and Closing Times Banks. Banks are open weekdays 8:30–12:30, Saturday 8:30–noon. Summer hours are weekdays 8–noon, Saturday 8–11:30. Banks in tourist areas are also open in the afternoon.

Museums. Most museums run by the Museums Department are open mid-June through September, daily 8–2; October through mid-June, daily 8:30–5; closed holidays. Other museums' hours may vary slightly, so check locally.

Shops. Shops are open Monday–Saturday 9–1 and 4–7.

National Holidays January 1; February 10 (St. Paul's shipwreck); March 19 (St. Joseph's Day); March 31 (Freedom Day); April 9 (Good Friday); May 1 (Workers' Day); June 7 (Sette Giugno); June 29 (Sts. Peter and Paul); August 15 (Assumption, or Santa Marija); September 8 (Our Lady of Victories); September 21 (Independence Day); December 8 (Immaculate Conception); December 13 (Republic Day); December 25.

Dining There is a good choice of restaurants, ranging from expensive hotel restaurants to fast-food hamburger joints. Local specialties include *torta tal-lampuki* (dorado fish pie), *dentici* (sea bream), and tuna. *Minestra* is the local variant of minestrone soup, and the *timpana* (baked macaroni and meat) is filling. Rabbit, stewed or fried, is a national dish. Accompany your meal with the locally produced wine: *Marsovin* comes in red, white, or rosé; *lachryma vitis*, in red or white—try sampling the house wines, too. Maltese beers are excellent; highly popular are Cisk Lager and Hop Leaf.

Precautions The water in Malta is safe to drink, with the only drawback being its salty taste: Many prefer bottled mineral water.

Dress A jacket and tie are suggested for higher-priced restaurants. Otherwise, casual dress is acceptable.

Ratings Prices are for a three-course meal, not including wine, sales tax, and tip. Best bets are indicated by a star ★.

Category	Cost*
Moderate	Lm 5–Lm 7.50
Inexpensive	Lm 3–Lm 5
Budget	under Lm 3

A 10% sales tax is charged on meals eaten in all but the most informal restaurants.

Lodging Malta has a variety of lodgings, from deluxe modern hotels to modest guest houses. There are also self-contained complexes geared mainly to package tours.

Ratings Prices are for two people sharing a double room.

Category	Cost
Moderate	Lm 12–Lm 22
Inexpensive	Lm 6–Lm 12
Budget	under Lm 6

Tipping A tip of 10% is expected when a service charge is not included.

Valletta

Arriving and Departing

By Plane   There are no direct flights from the United States, but several airlines, including **Air Malta,** fly from London, Paris, Frankfurt, Athens, and Rome to Luqa Airport, 6 kilometers (4 miles) south of Valletta.

Between the   There is a local bus service that passes through the town of
Airport and   Luqa on its way to Valletta, with a stop in front of the airport.
Downtown   It operates every 10 or 15 minutes from 6 AM to 11 PM; the trip takes about 30 minutes, and the fare is about 10¢.

Important Addresses and Numbers

Tourist   **Gozo** (Mġarr Harbor, tel. 553343).
Information   **St. Julian's Bay** (Balluta Bay, tel. 342671 or 342672).
Sliema (Bisazza St., tel. 313409).
Valletta (1 City Gate Arcade, tel. 237747; Luqa Airport, tel. 239915; or 280 Republic St., tel. 224444 or 228282).

Embassies   **U.S. Development House** (St. Anne St., Floriana, tel. 243653). **British High Commission** (7 St. Anne St., Floriana, tel. 233134).

Emergencies   **Hospital:** St. Luke's (Gwardamangia, tel. 241251) or Craig Hospital (Gozo, tel. 561600). **Police** (tel. 191). **Ambulance** (tel. 196). **Fire Brigade** (tel. 199).

Exploring Valletta

The minicity of Valletta, with ornate palaces and museums, protected by massive honey-colored fortifications, was built by the Knights of the Order of St. John who occupied the island from 1530 to 1798.

The main entrance to the city is through the arched **City Gate** (where all bus routes end), which leads onto Republic Street, the spine of the city and the main shopping street. From Republic Street, other streets are laid out on a grid pattern. Some streets are stepped. Houses along the narrow streets have overhanging wooden balconies, which foreign artists visiting the island love to paint.

Valletta's small size makes it ideal to explore on foot. Before setting out along Republic Street, stop at the tourist information office for maps, brochures, and a copy of *What's On.* On your left is the Auberge de Provence (the hostel of the knights from Provence), which now houses the **National Museum of Archaeology.** Its collection includes finds from Malta's many prehistoric sites—Tarxien, Hagar Qim, and the Hypogeum at Paola. You'll see pottery, statuettes, temple carvings, and, on the upper floor, finds from Punic and Roman tombs. *Republic St., tel. 225577. Admission: 15¢. Open mid-June–Sept., daily 8–2; Oct.–mid-June, daily 8:30–5; closed holidays.*

From Republic Street, turn right at the Inter-Flora kiosk and head to St. John's Square. Dominating the square (where an open-air market is held) is **St. John's co-Cathedral.** This was the Order of St. John's own church, completed in 1578. It is by far Malta's most important treasure. A side chapel was given to each national group of knights, who decorated it in their own distinctive way. The cathedral **museum** includes the oratory in which hangs *The Beheading of St. John,* the masterpiece painted by Caravaggio when he was staying on Malta in 1608. In the museum, you'll find a rich collection of Flemish tapestries based on drawings by Poussin and Rubens, antique embroidered vestments, and illuminated manuscripts. Keep your ticket, since you can use it to get into the cathedral at Mdina. *St. John's Sq. Museum admission: 50¢. Open weekdays 9:30–noon and 3–5:30.*

While in St. John's Square, visit the **Government Craft Center,** which has a wide range of traditional, handmade goods. *Open weekdays 9–7, Sat. 9–1 and 4–7.*

Continue along Republic Street to the **Grand Master's Palace,** where Malta's parliament sits. You can walk through the shady courtyards. Inside, friezes in the sumptuously decorated state apartments depict scenes from the history of the Knights. There is also a gallery with Gobelin tapestries. At the back of the building is the **Armoury of the Knights,** with displays of arms and armor down through the ages. *Republic St. Admission: 15¢. Open mid-June–Sept., daily 8–2; Oct.–mid-June, 8:30–5; closed holidays.*

Another building from the days of the Knights of Malta is the order's library, now the **National Library,** which stands on Republic Square. There are some outdoor cafés here, where you can dine beneath a statue of Queen Victoria. On Old Theatre Street, you can see the elegant **Manoel Theatre.** Built in 1731, it is said to be Europe's oldest theater still in operation.

Return to Republic Street and continue to Fort St. Elmo and the War Museum. **Fort St. Elmo** was built by the Knights to defend the harbor. Though completely destroyed during the siege of 1565, it was rebuilt by succeeding military leaders. Today part of the fort houses the **War Museum,** with its collection of armaments largely related to Malta's role in World War II. Here you can see an Italian E-boat and the Gladiator *Faith,* one of three Gloster Gladiator biplanes that defended the island. The other two, *Hope* and *Charity,* were shot down in the air battles of 1942–44. *St. Elmo. Admission: 15¢. Open mid-June–Sept., daily 8–2; Oct.–mid-June, daily 8:30–5; closed holidays.*

Continue along the seawall to the **Hospital of the Order** at the end of Merchants Street. This gracious building has been converted into the Mediterranean Conference Center. For an excellent introduction to the island, see the "Malta Experience," a multimedia presentation on the history of Malta that is given here six times a day. *Admission: $2.*

Continue along the seawall and climb up to the **Upper Barrakka Gardens.** Once part of the city's defenses, they're now a pleasant area from which to watch the comings and goings in the Grand Harbour.

Then walk down to Merchants Street, which is dominated by an open-air market. Here, the hagglers among you can snap up some terrific bargains. Next, cut along South Street, across Republic Street, to the **National Museum of Fine Art.** The former 18th-century palace has paintings from the 16th century to the present day, including works by Tintoretto, Preti, and Tiepolo, as well as local artists. *South St., tel. 225769. Admission: 15¢. Open mid-June–Sept., daily 8–2; Oct.–mid-June, daily 8:30–5; closed holidays.*

Dining

For details and price-category definitions, *see* Dining in Staying in Malta.

Moderate **Pappagallo.** This restaurant in Valletta is popular with locals
★ and visitors alike. Traditional Maltese food is featured, and the bustling atmosphere is warm and friendly. *Melita St., tel. 236195. Reservations advised. AE, DC, MC, V. Closed Mar.*

Scalini. An attractive cellar restaurant with walls of Malta's golden limestone, it features seafood and Italian-style pastas. The fixed-price menu is a good value. *32 South St., tel. 246221. Dress: casual. Reservations advised. AE, DC, MC, V.*

Inexpensive **British.** Cozy and informal with a terrace overlooking Grand Harbour, this festive eatery is known for quick service and generous portions. Some noteworthy Maltese dishes include octopus and stewed rabbit. *267 St. Ursula St., tel. 236019 or 224730. Reservations not necessary. MC, V.*

Pizzeria Bologna. A street-level annex of the good restaurant upstairs, and beside the Grand Master's Palace, it serves delicious pizzas with an interesting choice of ingredients. *59 Republic St., tel. 238014. Open until 9 in the evening.*

Budget **Galea Sluta.** Just inside the City Gate, this place is convenient for grabbing a quick snack before starting your tour of Valletta. It's especially known for its sweets. *City Gate, Republic St., tel. 225386. No reservations. No credit cards.*

La Veneziana. This newly opened restaurant, close to museums and the main bus terminus, serves a wide variety of dishes including *Mangia Beve*, a rich and delicious "vice-cream." *29/30 Melita St., tel. 222513. No reservations. No credit cards.*

Lodging

For details and price-category definitions, *see* Lodging in Staying in Malta.

Moderate **Castille.** For a touch of old Malta, stay at the Castille in what used to be a 16th-century palazzo. This is a gracious, comfortable, Old World hotel with a friendly, relaxed ambience. It has an ideal central location, close to the museums and the bus terminus. There's a good rooftop restaurant with an excellent fixed-price menu offering several choices. A pianist plays most evenings during dinner, and the views across the harbor are stunning. *St. Paul St., tel. 243677 or 243678. 35 rooms with bath. Facilities: coffee shop-bar, sun terrace. AE.*

Osborne. Centrally located in Valletta, it has spacious rooms and undistinguished decor. Spend a few minutes in the rooftop lounge and enjoy the view. *South St., tel. 232120 or 232128. 50 rooms with bath. Facilities: restaurant. AE, DC, MC, V.*

Inexpensive **Belmont.** An inexpensive but clean and functional hotel, it's close to the Sliema–St. Julian's seafront. *Mrabat St., St. Julian's, tel. 313077. 25 rooms with bath. Facilities: restaurant. No credit cards.*

Budget **British Hotel.** This is an old family hotel with a panoramic view of Malta's main seaport, Grand Harbour, and its restaurant specializes in Maltese dishes. Try stewed rabbit and octopus. In winter, pick a sunny day so you can lunch on the terrace. *267 St. Ursula St., Valletta, tel. 236019 or 224730, fax 239711. 30 rooms with bath. MC, V.*

Seacliff Hotel. Just across the road from the Sliema sea promenade and Independence Garden, this is the place from which to watch the Maltese take their evening stroll in summer. *225 Tower Rd., Sliema, tel. 330313. MC, V.*

18 Norway

Most visitors traveling to Norway for the first time usually have two preconceived notions: The temperature is cold year-round, and price levels are sky-high. They will be pleasantly surprised on both counts. The Gulf Stream makes the coastal waters ice-free all year. Winters do without the famous wind-chill factor, and summers are bearably warm with never-ending summer nights. Norway does not seem quite as expensive as it did a few years ago, because low inflation and increased competition in the tourist industry have kept prices stable. And there are many ways to beat the high costs.

Norway has some of the most remote and dramatic scenery in Europe. Along the west coast, deep fjords knife into steep mountain ranges. Inland, cross-country ski trails follow frozen trout streams and downhill trails careen through forests whose floors teem with wildflowers and berries during the summer. In older villages, wooden houses spill down toward docks where Viking ships—and later, whaling vessels—once were moored. Today the maritime horizon is dominated by tankers and derricks, for oil is now Norway's economic lifeblood. Fishing and timber, however, still provide many Norwegians with a staple income.

Inhabited since 1700 BC, Norway is today considered a peaceful nation. This was hardly so during the Viking period (the 9th and 10th centuries AD), when, apart from vicious infighting at home, the Vikings were marauding as far afield as Seville and Iceland. This fierce fighting spirit remained, despite Norway's subsequent centuries of subjugation by the Danes and Swedes. Independence came early this century but was put to the test during World War II, when the Germans occupied the country.

Norway

0 — 200 miles
0 — 300 km

ATLANTIC OCEAN

North Cape

Vardø
Vadsø
Hammerfest
Kirkenes
Alta
Masi
Tromsø

FINLAND

Norwegian Sea

Bardu
Narvik

Vestfjorden

Bodø Fauske
Saltdal

Arctic Circle

Umbukta
Mo-i-Rana
Sandnessjøen
Møsjøen
Brønnøysund

SWEDEN

E6

Vikna
Namsos

Gulf of Bothnia

Steinkjer

Trondheim
Meråker
Støren

Kristiansund N.

70 Oppdal
Røros
Tynset

Ålesund

9

Dombås
Otta

Nord fjord

Koppang

Florø

Jostedalsbreen

Rena

Lillehammer

Sognafjord

Lake
Mjøsa
Hamar
Eidsvoll

Voss E16

Bergen

40

Hardangerfjord

Hønefoss
Kongsberg
Drammen
Larvik

★ Oslo

Oslofjord

Sarpsborg
Fredrikstad

Haugesund

11

Baltic Sea

Stavanger
Sandnes
Evje
Grimstad
Arendal
Porsgrunn

Mandal Kristiansand S.

Skagerrak

Kattegat

Norwegian Resistance fighters rose to the challenge, eventually squashing Nazi efforts to develop atomic weapons.

The foundations for modern Norwegian culture were laid in the 19th century, during the period of union with Sweden, which lasted until 1905. Oslo blossomed at this time, and Norway produced its three greatest men of arts and letters: composer Edvard Grieg (1843–1907), dramatist Henrik Ibsen (1828–1906), and painter Edvard Munch (1863–1944). The polar explorers Roald Amundsen and Fridtjof Nansen also lived during this period.

All other facts aside, Norway is most famous for its fjords, which were formed during an ice age a million years ago. The ice cap burrowed deep into existing mountain-bound riverbeds, creating enormous pressure. There was less pressure along the coast, so the entrances to most fjords are shallow, about 155 meters (508 feet), while inland depths reach 1,240 meters (4,067 feet). Although Norway's entire coastline is riddled with fjords, the most breathtaking sights are on the west coast between Stavanger and Trondheim.

Essential Information

Before You Go

When to Go Cross-country skiing was born in Norway, and the country remains an important winter sports center. While much of the terrain is dark and impassable through the winter, you can cross-country or downhill ski within Oslo's city limits. February and early March are good skiing months, and hotel rooms are plentiful then. Avoid late March and April, when sleet, rain, and countless thaws and refreezings may ruin the good skiing snow and leave the roads—and spirits—in bad shape. Bear in mind that the country virtually closes down for the five-day Easter holidays, when Norwegians make their annual migration to the mountains. If you plan to visit at this time, reserve well in advance. Hotels are more crowded and expensive during this period, but some offer discounts during the two weeks before Easter—which is a good time for skiing.

Summers are generally mild. Then there's the famous midnight sun: Even in the "southern" city of Oslo, night seems more like twilight around midnight, and dawn comes by 2 AM. The weather can be fickle, however, and rain gear and sturdy waterproof shoes are recommended even during the summer. The best times to avoid crowds in museums and on ferries are May and September; Norwegians themselves are on vacation in July and the first part of August.

Climate The following are the average daily maximum and minimum temperatures for Oslo.

Jan.	28F	− 2C	**May**	61F	16C	**Sept.**	60F	16C
	19	− 7		43	6		46	8
Feb.	30F	− 1C	**June**	68F	20C	**Oct.**	48F	9C
	19	− 7		50	10		38	3
Mar.	39F	4C	**July**	72F	22C	**Nov.**	38F	3C
	25	− 4		55	13		31	− 1
Apr.	50F	10C	**Aug.**	70F	21C	**Dec.**	32F	0C
	34	1		53	12		25	− 4

Currency The unit of currency in Norway is the krone, written as Kr. on price tags but officially written as NOK. It is divided into 100 øre. Bills of NOK 50, 100, 500, and 1,000 are in general use. Coins are 50 øre and 1, 5, and 10 kroner. Credit cards are accepted in most hotels, stores, restaurants, and many gas stations and garages, but generally not in smaller shops and inns in rural areas. Banks charge per transaction, so it is more economical to change larger amounts of money or traveler's checks. The exchange rate at press time (summer 1992) was NOK 5.73 to the dollar and NOK 11.1 to the pound sterling.

What It Will Cost Norway has a high standard—and cost—of living, but there are ways of saving money by taking advantage of some special offers for accommodations and travel during the tourist season and on weekends throughout the year.

The **Oslo Card**—valid for one, two, or three days—entitles you to free admission to museums and galleries and unlimited travel on vehicles operated by the Oslo Transport system and the Norwegian Railways commuter trains within the city limits. Adults get a 30% discount on trains to and from Oslo, free parking, and discounts at various stores, cinemas, and sports centers. You can get the card at Oslo's tourist information offices (*see* Important Addresses and Numbers in Oslo, *below*). A one-day card costs NOK 95 adults, NOK 45 children; two days NOK 140 adults, NOK 65 children; three days NOK 170 adults, NOK 80 children.

Hotels in larger towns have special weekend and summer rates from late June to early August, and some chains have their own discount schemes—see Norway's annual accommodation guide. Discounts in rural hotels are offered to guests staying several days; meals are then included in the rate. Meals are generally expensive, so take hotel breakfast when it's offered. Alcohol is very expensive and is sold only during strictly regulated hours.

Sample Prices Cup of coffee, NOK 12–NOK 18; bottle of beer, NOK 40–NOK 45; soft drink, NOK 20–NOK 25; ham sandwich, NOK 40; 1-mile taxi ride, NOK 40 (for night rates, add 15%).

Customs on Arrival Residents of non-European countries who are over 16 may import duty-free into Norway 400 cigarettes or 500 grams of other tobacco goods, souvenirs, and gifts to the value of NOK 3,500. Residents of European countries who are over 16 may import 200 cigarettes or 250 grams of tobacco or cigars, a small amount of perfume or eau de cologne, and goods to the value of NOK 1,200. Anyone over 20 may bring in 1 liter of wine and 1 liter of liquor or 2 liters of wine and beer.

Language In larger cities, on public transportation, and in most commercial establishments, people speak English. Younger Norwegians generally speak it well; English is the main foreign language taught in schools, and movies and cable TV reinforce its popularity.

There are two official forms of the Norwegian language plus many dialects, so don't be disappointed if you've studied it but find that you can't understand everyone. Typical of Scandinavian languages, Norwegian's additional vowels—æ, ø, and å—come at the end of the alphabet. Remember this when you're using alphabetical listings.

Getting Around

By Train Norwegian trains are punctual and comfortable, and most routes are scenic. They fan out from Oslo and leave the coasts (except in the south) to buses and ferries. Some express trains have observation cars; the Oslo–Bergen route has a dining car, while all other long-distance routes have buffet cars. Reservations are required on all express (*ekspresstog*) and some fast (*hurtigtog*) services. The Oslo–Bergen route is superbly scenic, while the Oslo–Trondheim–Bodø route takes you within the Arctic Circle. The trains leave Oslo from Sentralstasjon (Oslo S or Central Station) on Jernbanetorget (at the beginning of Karl Johans gate).

Fares Apart from the Europe-wide passes (EurailPass and Inter-Rail), a special Scandinavian pass called **Nordturist** allows unlimited travel in Norway, Sweden, Denmark, and Finland for 21 days. The cost is NOK 1,775 (second class) or NOK 2,365 (first class), and the ticket is available through **NSB Travel,** the Norwegian State Railway (21–24 Cockspur St., London SW1Y 5DA, tel. 071/930–6666). In the U.S., contact ScanAm, 933 Highway 23, Pompton Plains, NJ 07444, tel. 201/835–7070 or 800/545–2204. Credit-card payments are accepted. A 30-day **Youth Pass** is also available for 12–26 year olds at a cost of NOK 3,450 (second class). Minifares during off-peak times are also available but must be booked 24 hours in advance.

By Plane The remoteness of so much of Norway means that air travel is a necessity for many inhabitants. The main Scandinavian airline, **SAS,** operates a network, along with **Braathens SAFE** and **Widerøe.** Fares are high, but the time saved makes it attractive if you are in a hurry. For longer distances, flying can be cheaper than driving a rented car and paying for gas and incidentals. Inquire about "Visit Norway" passes, which give you relatively cheap domestic-flight coupons (usually good only for summer travel). Norwegian airlines can be contacted at the following addresses: **SAS** (Oslo City, Stenersgate 1A, 0184 Oslo, tel. 02/170020); **Braathens SAFE AS** (Haakon VII's gate 2, 0161 Oslo, tel. 02/834470); **Norsk Air** (Gardermoen Airport, Akershus, tel. 06/978220); and **Widerøes Flyveselskap AS** (Mustads vei 1, 0283 Oslo, tel. 02/736500).

By Bus The Norwegian bus network makes up for some of the limitations of the country's train system, and several of the routes are particularly scenic. For example, the north Norway bus service, starting at Fauske (on the train line to Bodø), goes right up to Kirkenes on the Russian-Norwegian border, covering the 1,000 kilometers (625 miles) within four days. Long-distance bus routes also connect Norway with all its Scandinavian neighbors. Most buses leave from Bussterminalen (Galleri Oslo, Schweigaardsgate 10, tel. 02/170166), close to Oslo Central Station.

By Ferry Norway's long, fjord-indented coastline is served by an intricate and essential network of ferries and passenger ships. A wide choice of services is available, from simple hops across fjords (saving many miles of traveling) and excursions among the thousands of islands to luxury cruises and long journeys the entire length of the coast. Most ferries carry cars. Reservations are required on ferry journeys of more than one day but are not needed for simple fjord crossings. Many ferries are small and have room for only a few cars, so book ahead if possible; this will allow you to drive onto the ferry ahead of the cars that are waiting in line. Fares and exact times of departures depend on the season and availability of ships. The main Norwegian travel office, Nortra (*see below*) has the most accurate information, or contact the Norway Information Center (*see* Important Addresses and Numbers, *below*).

One of the world's great sea voyages is a mail-and-passenger service called the Hurtigrute, which runs up the Norwegian coast from Bergen to Kirkenes, well above the Arctic Circle. For information about the Hurtigrute, contact the Bergen Line, 505 Fifth Avenue, New York, NY 10017, tel. 212/986–2711, or the Tromsø Main Office, tel. 083/86088.

Nortra (Norwegian Travel Association), Postboks 499, Sentrum, 0105 Oslo, tel. 02/427044, will answer your queries about long-distance travel.

Staying in Norway

Telephones Norway's phone system is one of the world's most expensive, so try to make calls when rates are reduced (5 PM–8 AM weekdays and all day on weekends). Also, avoid using room phones in hotels unless you're willing to pay a hefty service charge. In public booths, place coins in the phone before dialing. Unused coins are returned. The largest coins accepted are NOK 10, with most older phones taking only NOK 1 or NOK 5 coins, so make sure you have enough small change. The minimum deposit is NOK 2.

Local Calls The cost of calls within Norway varies according to distance: Within Oslo, the cost goes up according to the amount of time used after the three-minute flat fee. Check the Oslo phone book for dialing information. Oslo's code is 02, needed only when dialing from outside Oslo.

In 1993, telephone numbers throughout Norway will change from six digits to eight digits.

International Calls To call North America, dial 095–1, then the area code and number. For the United Kingdom, dial 095–44, then the area code (minus the first 0) and number.

Operators and Information For local information, dial 0180. For international information, dial 0181.

Mail Letters and postcards to the United States cost NOK 5.20 for
Postal Rates the first 20 grams. For the United Kingdom, the rate is NOK 4.20 for the first 20 grams.

Receiving Mail Have letters marked "poste restante" after the name of the town, with the last name underlined. The service is free, and letters are directed to the nearest main post office. American Express offices (Winge—the agent for American Express—is located at Karl Johans gate 35, tel. 02/412030) will also hold mail (nonmembers pay a small charge on collection).

Shopping
VAT Refunds
Much of the 16.7% Norwegian value-added tax (VAT) will be refunded to visitors who spend more than NOK 300 in any single store. Ask for a special tax-free check and show your passport. All purchases must be presented together with the tax-free check at the tax-free counter at ports, on ferries destined for abroad, and at airports and border posts. The VAT will be refunded, minus a service charge. General information about the tax-free system is available by calling tel. 02/249901.

Opening and Closing Times
Banks. Banks are open weekdays 8:30–3:30; summer hours are 8:15–3. (All post offices change money.)

Museums. Museums are usually open Tuesday to Sunday 10–3 or 4. Many, but not all, are closed on Monday.

Shops. Though times vary, most shops are open weekdays 9 or 10–5 (Thursday until 7) and Saturday 9–1 or 2. Shopping malls are often open until 8 on weeknights.

National Holidays
January 1; April 9–12 (Easter); May 1 (Labor Day); May 17 (Constitution Day); May 20 (Ascension); May 30–31 (Pentecost); December 25–26.

Dining
The Norwegians depend on protein and carbohydrates to outlast the fierce winters. Breakfast is usually a large buffet of smoked fish, cheeses, sausage, cold meats, and whole-grain breads washed down with tea, good coffee, or milk. Lunch is often similar to breakfast, or the famous, but not very filling, *smørbrød* open sandwich. Restaurant and hotel dinners are usually three-course meals, often starting with soup and ending with fresh fruit and berries. The main course may be salmon, trout, or other fish; alternatives can include lamb or pork, reindeer, or even ptarmigan. Remember that the most expensive part of eating is drinking (*see* What It Will Cost in Before You Go, *above*) and that alcohol is not served on Sunday in most areas except Oslo and a handful of other regions. One consolation is the quality of the water, which is still among the purest in the world despite the growing problem of acid rain.

Mealtimes
Lunch is from noon to 3 at restaurants featuring a *koldtbord*, the famous Scandinavian buffet. Few Scandinavians ever partake of this, except when dining at mountain resorts. Most Scandinavians bring their own lunchboxes, consisting of open-face sandwiches. (Some hotels let guests pack their own lunches.) Dinner has traditionally been early, but in hotels and major restaurants it is now more often from 6 to 10. Some rural places still serve dinner from 4 to 7, however.

Dress
Neat casual dress is acceptable in most places.

Ratings
Prices are per person and include a first course, main course, and dessert, without wine or tip. Outside the major cities, prices are considerably less. Service is always included (*see* Tipping, *below*). Best bets are indicated by a star ★.

Category	Oslo
Moderate	NOK 125–NOK 300
Inexpensive	NOK 85–NOK 125
Budget	under NOK 85

Lodging Accommodations in Norway are usually spotless, and smaller
Hotels establishments are often family-run. Service is thoughtful and
considerate, right down to blackout curtains to block out the
midnight sun. Passes are available for discounts in hotels. The
Scandinavia Bonus Pass, costing approximately NOK 60 (about
$10) and also valid in Denmark, Sweden, and Finland, gives dis-
counts of 15% to 40% in many hotels during the summer (June
15–August 20). In addition, children under 15 stay in their parents' room at no extra charge. For full details, write to **Inter
Nor Hotels** (Sommerservice, Postboks 150, 4891 Grimstad,
Norway). Other chains' addresses are listed in Norway's accommodations guide, free from any tourist office. **Nordturist**
passes (*see* Getting Around By Train, *above*) also offer discounts of about 40% in nearly 100 top hotels.

Camping Camping is a popular way of keeping down costs. There are
more than 1,400 authorized campsites in the country, many set
in spectacular surroundings. Prices vary according to the facilities provided: A family with a car and tent can expect to pay
about NOK 100 per night. Some campsites have log cabins
available from about NOK 250 per night. The *Camping Norway*
guide is available from tourist offices, or go to NAF (the Norwegian Automobile Association), Storgatan 2, 0155 Oslo, tel.
02/341400.

Youth Hostels There are about 90 youth hostels in Norway; some are schools
or farms doing extra summer duty. You must be a member of
the Youth Hostel Association (YHA) to stay in the hostels, but
there are no age restrictions. For a full list, write to **Norske
Vandrerhjem (NoVa)** (Dronningensgate 26, 0154 Oslo, tel. 02/
421410).

International YHA guides are available to members in the
United Kingdom and North America. (Despite the name, there
are no age restrictions for YHA membership.) In the United
States, contact **American Youth Hostels Inc.** (National Offices,
Box 37613, Washington, DC 20013–7613, tel. 202/783–6161). In
Canada, contact **Canadian Hostelling Association** (1600 James
Naismith Dr., Suite 608, Gloucester, Ont. V1B 5N4, tel. 613/
748–5638).

Rentals Norwegians escape to mountain cabins whenever they have a
chance. Stay in one for a week or two and you'll see why—magnificent scenery; pure air; edible wild berries; and the chance
to hike, fish, or cross-country ski. For full details of this most
popular of Norwegian vacations, which includes accommodations in rented cabins, farms, or private homes, write to Den
Norske Hytteformidling A.S., Box 3404, Bjølsen, 0406 Oslo,
tel. 02/356710. The brochure *Norsk Hytteferie* can be requested
from tourist offices. An unusual alternative is to rent a *rorbu*
(fisherman's dwelling) in the northerly Lofoten Islands. For information, contact Lofoten Reiselivslag, Box 210, N-8301
Svolvær, tel. 88/71053.

Ratings   Prices are summer rates and are for two people in a double room with bath and include breakfast, service, and all taxes. Best bets are indicated by a star ★.

Category	Oslo	Other Areas
Moderate	NOK 500–NOK 700	NOK 450–NOK 600
Inexpensive	NOK 400–NOK 500	NOK 350–NOK 450
Budget	under NOK 400	under NOK 350

Tipping   In Norway, a 10%–12% service charge is generally added to bills at hotels and restaurants. If you have had exceptional service, then give an additional 5% tip. It is not the custom to tip taxi drivers unless they help with luggage; porters at airports have set fees per bag, but the carts are free. If a doorman hails a taxi for you, you can give NOK 5. On sightseeing tours, tip the guide NOK 10–NOK 15 if you are satisfied. Tip with local currency only; it is nearly impossible to exchange foreign coins. Even bills in small amounts present problems because of the transaction charge (usually NOK 20).

Oslo

Arriving and Departing

By Plane   Most international flights go to Fornebu Airport on the edge of the fjord, about 20 minutes west of Oslo. Charter flights usually go to Gardermoen Airport, about 50 minutes north of Oslo.

Between the Airport and Downtown   Buses from Fornebu to Oslo Central Station leave every 15 minutes (7:30 AM–11:30 PM) and run every half hour on weekends; the fare is NOK 30. Alternatively, take bus No. 31 from Jernbanetorget, marked "Snarøya." The fare is NOK 15; the bus makes a round-trip once hourly. Buses meet flights to Gardermoen and take passengers to Oslo Central Station; the fare is NOK 60.

By Train   Trains on international or domestic long-distance and express routes arrive at Oslo Central Station. Suburban trains depart from Oslo Central Station, Stortinget, and National Theater Station.

Getting Around

By Public Transportation   The best way to get around Oslo is by using the **Oslo Card** (*see* What It Will Cost in Before You Go, *above*), which offers unlimited travel for one, two, or three days on all Oslo's public transportation systems—bus, T-bane (the subway), streetcar, and even local ferries. You can buy the Oslo Card at Oslo tourist offices, from hotels, travel agents in Oslo, and larger stores (*see* Important Addresses and Numbers, *below*).

If you are using public transportation only occasionally, you can get tickets (adults NOK 15, children NOK 7.50) at bus and subway stops. For NOK 30, the **Tourist Ticket** gives 24 hours' unlimited travel on any means of public transportation, including the summer ferries to Bygdøy. The **Flexikort** gives you eight subway, bus, or streetcar rides for NOK 100, including transfers.

Important Addresses and Numbers

Tourist Information The **Oslo Tourist Information Office** (tel. 02/830050) is located at the **Norway Information Center,** Vestbaneplassen 1, tel. 02/839100. Open weekdays 9–4, weekends 9–3; September–May, closed on weekends. **Oslo Central Station,** tel. 02/171124. Open May 1–October 15, Monday–Sunday 8 AM–11 PM (call for winter hours). **Trafikanten,** Oslo Central Station, tel. 02/177030. Open daily 7 AM–8 PM.

Embassies U.S. (Drammensveien 18, tel. 02/448550). **Canadian** (Oscarsgate 20, tel. 02/466955). U.K. (Thos. Heftyesgate 8, tel. 02/552400).

Emergencies **Police** (Grønlandsleiret 44, tel. 02/669050, 24-hour service). **Ambulance:** 24-hour service (tel. 02/117070). **Dentist** (Oslo Kommunale Tannlegevakt, Tøyen Center, Kolstadsgate 18, Oslo 6, tel. 02/674846). Emergency treatment, weekdays 8 PM–11 PM, weekends and holidays 11 AM–2 PM.

Post Office The main post office is located at Dronningensgate 15. The **Telegraph Office** is at Kongensgate 21.

Exploring Oslo

Oslo is a small capital city, with a population of just less than half a million. The downtown area is compact, but the geographic limits of Oslo spread out to include forests, fjords, and mountains, which give the city a pristine airiness that complements its urban amenities. Oslo has an excellent public transportation network. Explore downtown on foot, enjoying its jazz clubs and museums, then venture beyond via bus, streetcar, or train.

Numbers in the margin correspond to points of interest on the Oslo map.

Oslo's main street, **Karl Johans gate,** runs right through the center of town, from Oslo Central Station uphill to the Royal Palace. Half its length is closed to traffic, and it is in this section that you will find many of the city's shops and outdoor cafés.

① Start at the **Slottet** (Royal Palace), the king's residence (not open to the public). The palace was built during the early 19th-century neoclassical style and is as sober, sturdy, and unpretentious as the Norwegian character. The surrounding park is open to the public. Time your visit to coincide with the changing of the guard (daily at 1:30). When the king is in residence (signaled by a red flag), the Royal Guard strikes up the band.

② Walk down Karl Johans gate to the old **Universitet** (University), which is made up of the three big buildings on your left. The main hall of the university is decorated with murals by Edvard Munch (1863–1944), Norway's most famous artist. The hall (*aula*) is open only during July. The Nobel Peace Prize is presented there each year on December 10. *Admission to hall free. Open July, weekdays noon–2.*

③ Behind the University is the **Nasjonalgalleriet** (National Gallery), Norway's largest public gallery. It has a small but high-quality selection of paintings by European artists, but of particular interest is the collection of works by Norwegian artists. Edvard Munch is represented here, but most of his

Oslo

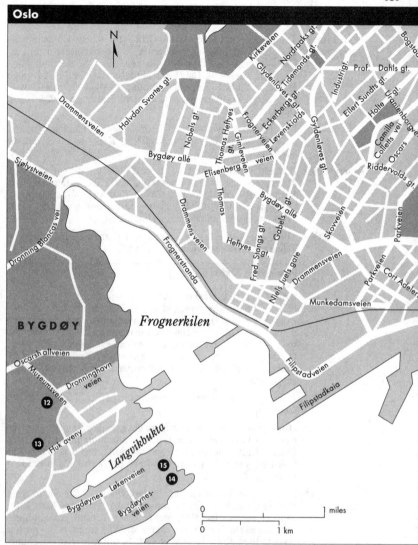

Aker Brygge and harbor, **10**
Akershus Castle, **8**
Contemporary Art Museum, **9**
Domkirken, **7**
Framhuset, **15**
Historisk Museum, **4**
Kon-Tiki Museum, **14**
Nasjonalgalleriet, **3**

Nationaltheatret, **5**
Norsk Folkemuseum, **12**
Rådhuset, **11**
Slottet, **1**
Storting, **6**
Tøyen, **16**
Universitet, **2**
Vikingskiphuset, **13**

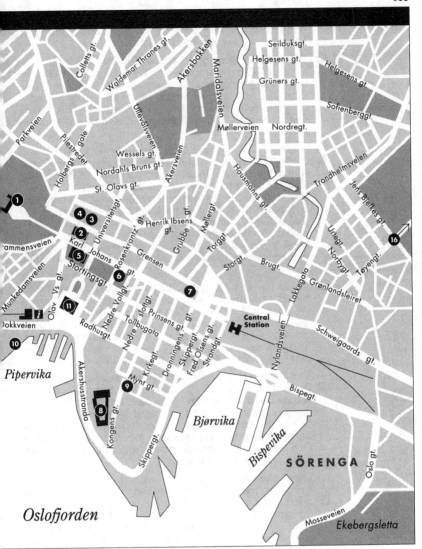

work is in the Munch Museum (*see below*), east of the center. *Universitetgaten 13. Admission free. Open Mon., Wed., Fri. 10–4, Thurs. 10–8, Sat. and Sun. 11–3.*

❹ The **Historisk Museum** (Historical Museum) is in back of the National Gallery. It features displays of daily life and art from the Viking period, including treasures recovered from Viking ships. The Ethnographic Section houses a collection related to the great polar explorer Roald Amundsen, the first man to reach the South Pole. *Frederiksgate 2. Admission free. Open Tues.–Sun. 11–3.*

Return to Karl Johans gate and cross over for a closer look at ❺ the **Nationaltheatret,** watched over by the statues of Bjørnstjerne Bjørnson and Henrik Ibsen. Bjørnson was the nationalist poet who wrote Norway's anthem. Internationally lauded playwright Ibsen wrote *Peer Gynt* (he personally requested Edvard Grieg's musical accompaniment), *A Doll's House,* and *Hedda Gabler,* among others. He worried that his plays, packed with allegory, myth, and sociological and emotional angst, might not have appeal outside Norway. Instead, they were universally recognized and changed the face of modern theater.

❻ At the far (eastern) end of the pond is the **Storting** (Parliament), a bow-fronted yellow-brick building stretched across the block. It is open to visitors when Parliament is not in session (mid-June through August): A guided tour takes visitors around the frescoed interior and into the debating chamber. *Karl Johans gate 22, tel. 02/313050. Admission free. Open July–Aug., Mon.–Sat. Guided tours at 11, 12, and 1.*

Karl Johans gate is closed to traffic near the staid, bronze-door ❼ **Domkirken** (Cathedral). The much-renovated cathedral, consecrated in 1697, is modest by the standards of some other European capital cities, but the interior is rich with treasures, such as the Baroque carved wooden altarpiece and pulpit. The ceiling frescoes by Hugo Lous Mohr were done after World War II. Behind the cathedral is an area of arcades, small restaurants, and street musicians.

Facing the cathedral, turn right at Kirkegata. Three blocks down, turn right onto Rådhusgate and then almost immediate-❽ ly left onto Kongens gate. This takes you to **Akershus Castle** on the harbor. The castle was built during the Middle Ages but restored in 1527 by Christian IV of Denmark—Denmark then ruled Norway—after it was damaged by fire; he then laid out the present city of Oslo (naming it Christiania after himself) around his new residence. Oslo's street plan still follows his design. Some rooms are open for guided tours, and the grounds form a park around the castle. The grounds also house the **Forsvarsmuseet** and **Hjemmefrontsmuseum** (Norwegian Defense and Resistance museums). Both give you a feel for the Norwegian fighting spirit throughout history and especially during the German occupation, when the Nazis set up headquarters on this site and had a number of patriots executed within its walls. *Akershus Castle and Museums. Entrance from Festningsplassen, tel. 02/412521. Admission: NOK 10 adults, NOK 5 children. Guided tours of the castle, May–Sept., Mon.–Sat. 11, 1, and 3, Sun. 1 and 3. Museums open weekdays 10–4, Sun. 12:30–4.*

Just behind Akershus Castle, in the direction of Oslo Central
9 Station, is the **Contemporary Art Museum,** housed in the Bank
of Norway's old building. *Bankplassen 4, tel. 02/335820. Admission free. Open Tues.–Fri. 11–7, Sat.–Sun. 11–4.*

10 Continue along the waterfront toward the central **harbor**—the
heart of Oslo and head of the fjord. Shops and cafés stay open
late at **Aker Brygge,** the new quayside shopping and cultural
center, with a theater, cinemas, and galleries among the shops,
restaurants, and cafés. You don't have to buy anything—just
sit amid the fountains and statues and watch the portside activities.

11 The large redbrick **Rådhuset** (City Hall) is here: Note the
friezes in the courtyard, depicting scenes from Norwegian
folklore, then go inside and see murals depicting daily life in
Norway, historical events, and Resistance activities. You can
set your watch by the astronomical clock in the inner courtyard. *Admission: NOK 15 adults, NOK 5 children. Open Mon.–
Sat. 9–3:30, Thurs. 9–7. Tours several times daily.*

The **Norway Information Center** is on the right side across the
street when facing the harbor. From nearby Pipervika Bay,
you can board a ferry in the summertime for the seven-minute
crossing of the fjord to the **Bygdøy** peninsula, where there is a
complex of seafaring museums. *Ferries run Apr.–Sept., at 15
past and 15 to each hour.*

The first ferry stop is Dronningen. From here, walk up a well-
12 marked road to the **Norsk Folkemuseum** (Open Air Museum), a
large park where historic farmhouses, some of them centuries
old, have been collected from all over the country and reassem-
bled. A whole section of 19th-century Oslo was moved here, as
was a 12th-century wooden stave church. There are displays of
weaving and sheepshearing on Sunday, and throughout the
park there are guides in period costume. *Museumsveien. Admission: NOK 35. Open daily 11–5.*

Around the corner (signs will lead you) is the second museum.
13 The **Vikingskiphuset** (Viking Ship Museum) contains 9th-cen-
tury ships recovered from the fjord, where they had been ritu-
ally sunk while carrying the mortal remains of Viking kings
and queens to the next world. Also on display are the treasures
and jewelry that accompanied the royal bodies on their last voyage. The ornate craftsmanship evident in the ships and jewelry
dispels any notion that the Vikings were skilled only in looting
and pillaging. *Huk aveny. Admission: NOK 15 adults, NOK 7
children. Open Nov.–Mar., daily 11–3; Apr. and Oct., daily
11–4; May–Aug., daily 10–6; Sept., daily 11–5.*

Reboard the ferry or follow signs for the 20-minute walk to the
14 **Kon-Tiki Museum,** where the *Kon-Tiki* raft and the reed boat
RA II are on view. Thor Heyerdahl made no concessions to the
modern world when he used these boats to cross the Pacific
(Kon-Tiki) and the Atlantic *(RA II). Admission: NOK 15
adults, NOK 8 children. Open Oct.–Mar., daily 10:30–4; Apr.–
May 15 and Sept., daily 10:30–5; May 16–Aug., daily 10–6.*

Directly across from the Kon-Tiki Museum is a large triangular
15 building, the **Framhuset.** This museum is devoted to the polar
ship *Fram,* the sturdy wooden vessel that belonged to bipolar
explorer Fridtjof Nansen. (It was also used by Amundsen.) In
1893 Nansen led an expedition that reached latitude 86°14′N,

the most northerly latitude to have been reached at that time. The book *Farthest North* tells his story. (Active in Russian famine-relief work, Nansen received a Nobel Peace Prize in 1922.) You can board the ship and imagine yourself in one of the tiny berths, while outside a force-nine gale is blowing and the temperature is dozens of degrees below freezing. *Admission: NOK 15 adults, NOK 8 children. Open Mar.–Apr., daily 11–2:45; May 1–15, daily 11–4:45; May 16–Sept., daily 10–5:45; Oct., daily 11–2:45; Nov., Sat.–Sun. 11–2:45.*

16 Back at City Hall, board bus No. 29 to **Tøyen,** the area northeast of Oslo, where you'll find the **Munch-Museet** (Munch Museum). In 1940, four years before his death, Munch bequeathed much of his work to the city of Oslo; the museum opened in 1963, the centennial of his birth. Although only a fraction of its 22,000 items—books, paintings, drawings, prints, sculptures, and letters—are on display, you can still get a sense of the tortured expressionism that was to have such an effect on European painting. *Tøyengaten 53. Admission: NOK 30 adults, NOK 10 children. Open June–Sept. 15, Tues.–Sat. 10–6, Sun. noon–6; Sept. 16–May, Tues.–Sat. 10–4, Sun. noon–6.*

Excursions from Oslo

An interesting day trip from Oslo is a visit to the old cobalt works at **Åmot i Modum** (Blaafarveværket). There's always a special exhibition of paintings by any one of Scandinavia's leading artists, in addition to the permanent collection of cobalt glass and porcelain. The children's farm and the old-fashioned country store at nearby Haugfossen are also popular attractions. *Cobalt works: open May–Sept., tel. 03/784900.*

Beyond Oslo, trips might include a visit to **Lillehammer,** designated as the site of the 1994 Winter Olympics, and home of **Maihaugen De Sandvigske Samlinger,** one of the largest open-air museums in northern Europe (tel. 062/50135). Lillehammer is at the top of the long finger of **Lake Mjøsa** and is reached by train from Oslo Central Station in about two hours. A paddle steamer, **D/S *Skibladner,*** travels the length of the lake (six hours each way) during the summer, making several stops. At the southern tip of the lake is **Eidsvoll,** where the Norwegians announced their new constitution in 1814, marking the end to centuries of domination by Denmark. There are limitless possibilities for outdoor activities in the Lake Mjøsa region, all within easy reach of Oslo.

Shopping

Gift Ideas Since prices here are controlled, Oslo is the obvious place to do your shopping. In addition, the selection is widest here: Pewter, silver, enamelware, crystal, sheepskin, leather, and knitwear are all appealing samples of Norwegian craftsmanship.

Shopping Districts Many of the larger stores are located in the area between the Storting and the cathedral; much of this area is for pedestrians only. The **Basarhallene,** at the back of the cathedral, is an art and handicrafts boutique center. Oslo's newest shopping area is **Aker Brygge** (once a shipbuilding wharf). Located right on the waterfront, it is a complex of stalls, offices, and garden cafés. Check out Bogstadveien/Hegdehaugsveien, which runs from Majorstua to Parkveien. This street offers a good selection of stores and has plenty of places to rest your tired feet and quench your thirst. Shops stay open until 5 PM (Thursday to 7 PM).

Department Stores and Malls Oslo's department stores, **Steen & Strøm** and **Christiania Glasmagasin,** are both in the shopping district near the cathedral. **Paléet** on Karl Johans gate is a new, elegant addition to Oslo's main street, with 40 shops and 10 restaurants.

Food and Flea Markets Every Saturday during spring, summer, and fall, there is a flea market at Vestkanttorget, two blocks away from Frogner Park. Check the papers for local flea markets.

Dining

For details and price-category definitions, *see* Dining in Staying in Norway. Best bets are indicated by a star ★.

Moderate **Brasserie Costa.** Costa is a trendy, continental restaurant and bar with excellent pasta dishes that cost less in the bar. *Klingenberggate 4, tel. 02/424130. Reservations necessary. AE, DC, MC, V.*

D/S Louise. This casual restaurant in a maritime setting is part of the Aker Brygge shopping/entertainment complex. *Stranden 3, tel. 02/830060. Reservations accepted. AE, DC, MC, V.*

Gamle Raadhus. The "old city hall," Oslo's oldest restaurant, is located in a building dating from 1641. Specialties include mussels and fresh shrimp. *Nedre Slottsgate 1, tel. 02/420107. Reservations advised. AE, DC, MC, V. Closed Sun.*

Kastanjen. The short menu at this neighborhood restaurant changes often and features all seasonal ingredients. The three-course fixed-price dinner is an excellent value. *Bygdøy Allé 18, tel. 02/434467. Reservations recommended. AE, DC, MC, V. Closed Sun.*

Stefan. The top-floor restaurant at the Stefan Hotel has the best lunch buffet in Oslo, with smoked, marinated, and pickled salmon; smoked reindeer; hot dishes; and homemade caramel pudding. The restaurant is nonlicensed. *Stefan Hotel, Rosenkrantz' gate 1, tel. 02/429250. Lunch reservations required. AE, DC, MC, V.*

★ **Theatercafeen.** This Oslo institution is the last Viennese-style café in northern Europe and is a favorite with the literary and entertainment crowd. The daily menu is a good value. Save room for dessert, which the pastry chef also makes for Norway's royal family. *Hotel Continental, Stortingsgata 24/26, tel. 02/419060. Reservations required. AE, DC, MC, V.*

Inexpensive **Albin Upp.** This cozy wine and snack bar is in a farmer's reno-
★ vated cottage, located in a residential district about a 10-minute streetcar ride from town—catch the No. 1. Contemporary art is on display downstairs. *Briskebyveien 42, tel. 02/557192. No reservations. No credit cards. Lunch only. Closed weekends.*

Clodion Art Café. This crowded New York–style place serves breakfast, lunch, and dinner; the fare is mainly sandwiches and snacks. *Bygdøy Allé 63, tel. 02/449726. No reservations. MC.*

Felix. This recently renovated day and night spot has marble-top tables and black café chairs, which create an informal atmosphere. Felix serves light meals and has extended opening hours. There's live music on weekends. *Drammensveien 30, tel. 02/442650. No reservations. AE, DC, MC, V.*

Lorry. This informal, funky restaurant was established in 1887 and still has its original interior. Lorry serves up standard Norwegian food in a good atmosphere that's also a bit out of the ordinary. *Parkveien 12, tel. 02/696904. No reservations. AE, DC, MC, V.*

Nye Kaffistova. This cafeteria serves Norwegian "country-style" cooking at rock-bottom prices. *Rosenkrantz' gate 8, tel. 02/429974. No reservations. No credit cards.*

Onkel Oswald. This trendy hangout is in Homansbyren, a popular area. Breakfast, lunch, and dinner are served in an informal atmosphere. *Hegdehaugsveien 34, tel. 02/690535. No reservations. No credit cards.*

Recepten. Recepten is a nostalgic '50s-inspired café in an old drugstore. Try the dish of the day. The Elgen Club, with varied music, is downstairs. *Prinsensgate 22, tel. 02/426500. No reservations. No credit cards. Opens at 6 PM Sun.–Fri.; Sat. 11 AM.*

Vegeta. Next to the Nationaltheatret bus and streetcar station, this is a popular spot for hot and cold vegetarian meals and salads. It is a nonsmoking restaurant. The all-you-can-eat specials offer top value. *Munkedamsveien 3B, tel. 02/834232. No reservations. No credit cards.*

Budget **Cruise Kafé.** Looking for hard-to-find music? Cruise Kafé is a quiet café during the day and a rock café at night. The Cruise Burgers are famous; the dish of the day is about NOK 50. *Aker Brygge 1, tel. 02/836430. No reservations. AE, DC, MC, V.*

Eilefs Landhandleri. This is an untraditional restaurant made to look like an old-fashioned country store. The popular dishes start at NOK 23. There's live music from 10 PM. *Kristian IVs gate 1, tel. 02/425347. No reservations. AE, DC, MC, V.*

Olsens's Café. Located on Bogstadveien, this sunny yellow bohemian-style café has dishes that cost from NOK 24 (there's a good quiche Lorraine). Keep yourself occupied with the many newspapers and backgammon and chess boards. *Bogstadveien 8 (entrance at Holtegata), tel. 02/463965. No reservations. No credit cards.*

Pasta Caruso. This is a takeout place that serves excellent homemade pasta and sauces. There's a tiny bar area for eating. *Bygdøy Allé 3 (entrance at Frognerveien), tel. 02/445544. No reservations. No credit cards.*

Tiffani. Tiffani is a two-story café with a basement and fireplace, plus friendly, good service. There's a variety of good homemade dishes served at breakfast, lunch, and dinner. *Behrensgate 2, tel. 02/434039. No reservations. No credit cards.*

Lodging

The tourist office's accommodations bureaus (open daily 8 AM–11 PM) in Oslo Central Station can help you find rooms in hotels, pensions, and private homes. You must apply in person and pay a fee of NOK 20 (NOK 10 children) plus 10% of the room rate, which will be refunded when you check in. For details and price-category definitions, *see* Lodging in Staying in Norway.

Moderate **Bondeheimen.** The most Norwegian hotel in town has modern, comfortable rooms and a staff that wears national costumes. *Rosenkrantz' gate 8, tel. 02/429530. 76 rooms with bath or shower. AE, DC, MC, V.*

Cecil Hotel. Built in 1989, just off Stortingsgata right in the heart of town, this bed-and-breakfast–only hotel is a good value for the money. *Stortingsgata 8, tel. 02/427000. 112 rooms with bath. AE, DC, MC, V.*

Europa. This centrally located modern hotel is a moderately priced alternative to its expensive next-door neighbor, the SAS Scandinavia Hotel. The rooms are comfortable (all have color TV), and there are special reductions for children. *St. Olavs gate 31, tel. 02/209990. 150 rooms with bath. AE, DC, MC, V.*

Majorstuen Hotel. Located in busy Majorstuen, a bustling business residential area, with easy access to the city and vicinity, this small, intimate hotel has a warm and friendly atmosphere and inviting rooms. *Bogstadveien 64, tel. 02/693495. 40 rooms with bath. Facilities: restaurant, pub. AE, DC, MC, V.*

Stefan. The service is cheerful and accommodating in this hotel in the center of Oslo. One of its main attractions is the popular restaurant on the top floor, with Oslo's best lunch; buffet and early-bird specials feature traditional Norwegian dishes. *Rosenkrantz' gate 1, tel. 02/429250. 130 rooms with bath or shower. Facilities: restaurant. AE, DC, MC, V.*

Vika Atrium. This new, modern hotel is centrally located near City Hall and Aker Brygge. A restaurant serves breakfast, lunch, dinner, and a set à la carte menu that is served throughout the day. *Munkedamsveien 45, tel. 02/833300. 132 rooms with bath. Facilities: restaurant. AE, DC, MC, V.*

Inexpensive **Astoria.** This nicely renovated bed-and-breakfast–style hotel is located in the center of Oslo. *Dronningensgate 21, tel. 02/420010. 132 rooms with bath. Facilities: breakfast room. AE, DC, MC, V.*

Coch's Pensjonat. Centrally located near the Royal Castle, Coch's is within walking distance of most of Oslo's attractions. Rooms are simple and clean with bathrooms and kitchenettes. Note that prices are cheaper for rooms with three to four beds. *Parkveien 25, tel. 02/604836. 70 rooms with bath. V.*

Gyldenløve. Centrally located at Bogstadveien, this bed-and-breakfast hotel—renovated in 1992—offers quality at a reasonable price and 160 well-equipped rooms with all conveniences. *Bogstadveien 20, tel. 02/601090. 160 rooms with bath or shower. AE, DC, MC, V.*

Munch Hotel. This bed-and-breakfast hotel has large but rather basic rooms. It's a 10-minute walk from downtown. *Munchs gate 5, tel. 02/424275. 180 rooms with shower. AE, DC, MC, V.*

Ritz. A little less grand than some of the others that share its name, this Ritz is about seven minutes from downtown by streetcar. *Fr. Stangs gate, tel. 02/443960. 42 rooms, some with bath. AE, DC, MC, V.*

Budget **Ellingsens Pensjonat.** Ellingsens is centrally located, and very simple; no breakfast is served. *Holtegate 25, tel. 02/600359. 20 rooms without bath. No credit cards.*

Oslo Vandrerhjem, Haraldsheim. Located close to public transport, this is a clean, well-run hostel for members of IYHF. Breakfast is served. *Haraldsheimveien 4, tel. 02/222965. 270 rooms. No credit cards.*

Oslo Vandrerhjem, Pan. Easily accessible to public transportation, these hostel accommodations are good but are only open June 1–August 20. *Sognsveien 218, tel. 02/237640. 119 rooms. No credit cards.*

The Arts

Considering the size of the city, Oslo has a surprisingly good artistic life. Consult the "Oslo Guide" or "Oslo This Week" for details. Winter is *the* cultural season, with the **Nationaltheatret** featuring modern plays (all in Norwegian), classics, and a good sampling of Ibsen. **Det Norske Teatret** (Kristian IVs gate 8), one of Europe's most modern theater complexes, features musicals and plays.

Oslo's modern **Konserthuset** (Concert Hall), at Munkedamsveien 14, is the home of the Oslo Philharmonic, famous for its recordings of Tchaikovsky's symphonies. A smaller hall in the same building is the setting for performances of chamber music and—in summer only—folk dancing, held Monday and Thursday at 9 in July and August. In addition to the **Museum of Contemporary Art,** there's a good modern collection at the **Henie-Onstad Kunstsenter** (Art Center) at Høvikodden. This center specializes in 20th-century art and was a gift from the Norwegian Olympic skater Sonja Henie and her husband, shipowner Niels Onstad. The center is open Tuesday–Friday 9–9, Saturday–Monday 11–5.

Nightlife

Oslo used to be a place where the sidewalks rolled up at 8. Now Karl Johansgate is a lively place into the wee hours. There are loads of music cafés and clubs, as well as more conventional night spots. A few good ones are **Barock** (Universitetsgate 26, tel. 02/334216), **Cruise Kafé** (Aker Brygge 1, tel. 02/836430), **Rockefeller** (Torggata 16—entrance from Mariboes gate, tel. 02/203232), and **LIPP** (Olav Vs gate 2, tel. 02/414400). Why not go to a movie? All films are screened in the original language with Norwegian subtitles. Tickets cost NOK 40.

Stavanger and Vicinity

In the area around the southwestern city of Stavanger, whaling has given way to canneries, lumber, paper production, and petrochemicals. Yet its natural beauty has not been greatly marred, and you'll find rocky headlands and stretches of forest (fjord country does not begin until north of Stavanger).

Getting Around

By Plane   There are daily airplane departures to and from Oslo and other major Norwegian towns, as well as international flights. The airport bus departs frequently to the hotels in the center of town (it's approximately a 20-minute ride).

By Train   The best train service is the Sørland line, which leaves Oslo Central Station and goes all the way to Stavanger. The Oslo–Drammen stretch is an engineering feat and features Norway's longest tunnel, an 11-kilometer (7-mile) construction through sheer rock.

By Bus   Express buses from Oslo travel to Stavanger, and there's also local service. For details on fares and schedules, check with the Stavanger Tourist Office or the main one in Oslo (*see* Important Addresses and Numbers in Oslo, *above*).

The Stavanger Card. When checking into your hotel, ask for this card, which offers discounts on a variety of services, such as sightseeing, museums, shows, sports activities, and some bus and boat services.

Tourist Information

Stavanger (Stavanger Kulturhus, Sølvberget, tel. 04/535100).

Exploring Stavanger

Stavanger is believed to date back to the 8th century. The Anglo-Norman **St. Svithuns Cathedral,** next to the central market, was established in 1125 by the bishop of Winchester in England. Traditionally a fishing and shipping center, Stavanger's main source of income before World War II was the sardine industry. These days, Stavanger is the oil capital of Norway. It is a prosperous town with modern shops and malls, but has managed to retain the quaint atmosphere of yesteryear in the old sections in the center of town, where there are narrow, cobbled lanes and clapboard houses at odd angles.

Ledaal is a fine patrician mansion where the king resides when he's visiting Stavanger and that is part of the **Stavanger Museum.** It houses relics from the area and a special maritime display. An ultramodern concert hall and arts center opened in Stavanger during the mid-'80s. Also of interest is **Viste Cave** outside the city. It is said to be 6,000 years old. Nearby **Ullandhaug** is a reconstructed Iron Age farm. The **Canning Museum** is a reconstructed sardine factory dating from 1890 to 1920; here you'll get a lesson in the production of sardines and fish conserves.

The Norwegian Emigration Center is a center for genealogy, family research, and contact between Norway and the Norwegians who emigrated to America. *Bergjelandsgate 30, tel. 04/ 501267. Open weekdays 9–3.*

The **Ryfylke fjords** north and east of Stavanger form the southern end of the fjord country. The city is a good base for exploring this region, with a "white fleet" of low-slung seabuses making daily excurions into even the most distant fjords. Trips to Prekestolen and Månafossen are recommended.

Dining and Lodging

For details and price-category definitions, *see* Dining and Lodging in Staying in Norway.

Stavanger **Skagen.** This restored wharf house specializes in seafood, plus
Dining it has lots of atmosphere. *Skagenkaien, tel. 04/526190. Reservations advised. AE, DC, MC, V. Moderate.*
City Bistro. This is a very nice bistro with good service and tasty food. *Madlaveien 18–20, tel. 04/533181. No reservations. AE, DC, MC, V. Moderate–Inexpensive.*
Tante Molla. Tante Molla is a friendly café combined with an art gallery. *Salvågergate 10, tel. 04/534999. No reservations. No credit cards. Inexpensive.*

Lodging **Commandør.** This small and basic hotel offers clean and comfortable accommodations. *Valberg gate 9, tel. 04/528000. 40 rooms with bath. AE, DC, MC, V. Moderate.*

Mælands Gjestgiveri. Centrally located, this charming bed-and-breakfast–style hotel is a gem. The building is 120 years old, and newly renovated. There's a café on the premises. *N. Holmegate 2, tel. 04/523821. 17 rooms. Facilities: café. AE, DC, MC, V. Moderate–Inexpensive.*

Bergen and Vicinity

Bergen is Norway's second-largest city. To get there, you pass through the Telemark area, midway between Oslo and Bergen. This region is characterized by steep valleys, pine forests, lakes, and fast-flowing rivers that are full of trout. Bergen is also the gateway to the fabled land of the fjords.

Getting Around

By Plane Flesland Airport is located about 40 miles from the Bergen town center. There is good airport bus service to the downtown area.

By Train The Oslo–Bergen train route passes through forests, mountains, and fjords and is the most spectacular in Norway.

By Bus Contact the Bergen Tourist Information Office (*see below*) about express or local bus service to and from Bergen.

Bybilletten. When checking into your hotel, ask for this card, which offers discounts on buses, ferries, car rentals, theaters, and more.

Tourist Information

Bergen (Slottsgate 1, tel. 05/313860; Torvalmenningen, tel. 05/321480).

Exploring Bergen

Bergen is Norway's second-largest city, with a population of 215,000. Before oil brought an influx of foreigners to Stavanger, it was the most international of the country's cities, having been an important trading and military center when Oslo was an obscure village. Bergen was a member of the medieval Hanseatic League and offered an ice-free harbor and convenient trading location on the west coast. Natives of Bergen still think of Oslo as a dour provincial town.

Despite numerous fires in its past, much of medieval Bergen has remained. Seven surrounding mountains set off the weathered wooden houses, cobbled streets, and Hanseatic-era warehouses of the **Bryggen** (harbor area). Founded in 1070, the town was first called Bjørgvin.

The best way to get a feel for Bergen's medieval trading heyday is to visit the **Hanseatic Museum** on the Bryggen. One of the oldest and best-preserved of Bergen's wooden buildings, it is furnished in 16th-century style. The guided tour is excellent. *Admission: NOK 15 adults, NOK 8 children. Open June–Aug., daily 10–5; May, Sept., daily 11–2; Oct.–Apr., Mon., Wed., Fri., Sun. 11–2.*

On the western end of the Vågen is the **Rosenkrantz Tower,** part of the **Bergenhus,** the 13th-century fortress guarding the harbor entrance. The tower and fortress were destroyed during World War II, but were meticulously restored during the '60s and are now rich with furnishings and household items from the 16th century. *Admission: NOK 10 adults, NOK 5 children. Open mid-May–mid-Sept., daily 10–4; mid-Sept.–mid-May, Sun. 12–3, or upon request.*

Across the Vågen is the **Nordnes peninsula,** where you can look back toward the city and the mountainous backdrop. Save time to meander through the winding back streets, intersected by broad *almenninger* (wide avenues built as protection against fires). For the best view of Bergen and its surroundings, take the funicular from the corner of Lille Øvregate and Vetrlidsalmenning. It climbs 310 meters (1,016 feet) to the top of **Fløyen,** one of the seven mountains guarding this ancient port.

Troldhaugen manor on Nordås Lake, once home to Edvard Grieg, is now a museum and includes a new chamber music hall. Recitals are held each Wednesday and Sunday at 8 PM from late June through early August. *Hopsvegen, Bergen, tel. 05/911791. Admission: NOK 15 adults, NOK 8 children. Open May–Sept., daily 10:30–5:30.*

Excursions from Bergen

Lysøen Island Ole Bull was one of Norway's favorite musicians, and he passed many a violin-playing hour on **Lysøen Island,** the site of what was his villa. It is now a national monument, donated to Norway by his American granddaughter. Apart from Ole Bull memorabilia, there are 13 kilometers (8 miles) of nature trails. Ferries to Lysøen leave Bergen from Buena pier (Sørstraumen), 26 kilometers (16 miles) south of the center. Round-trip fare is NOK 25 adults, NOK 10 children. *Admission to villa (tel. 05/309077): NOK 20 adults, NOK 5 children. Open mid-May–early Sept., Mon.–Sat. 12–4, Sun. 11–5.*

Bergen is the start of fjord cruises of all descriptions. Crossing fjords is a necessary as well as a scenic way to travel in Norway. Hardangerfjord, Sognefjord, and Nordfjord are three of the deepest and most popular fjords. Details on cruises can be obtained from the Bergen Tourist Information Office.

Dining and Lodging

For details and price-category definitions, *see* Dining and Lodging in Staying in Norway. Best bets are indicated by a star ★.

Bergen **Banco Rotto.** This beautiful Art Deco building, formerly a
Dining bank, is now a reasonably priced restaurant. There's a club and
★ piano bar later at night. *Vågsalmenningen, tel. 05/327520. Reservations required. AE, DC, MC, V. Open 11–5. Moderate.*
Enhjørningen (Unicorn). One of Bergen's most popular seafood restaurants, Unicorn is located in an old Hanseatic warehouse. *Bryggen, tel. 05/327919. Reservations required. AE, DC, MC, V. Moderate.*
Madam Felle. Located at Bryggen, Madam Felle is *the* place to be on a sunny summer day. The restaurant serves very enjoyable light meals and snacks. *Bryggen, tel. 05/543000. No reservations. AE, DC, MC, V. Moderate.*
Michelangelo. A restaurant with Italian food and lots of atmosphere, Michelangelo serves up great pasta specialities.

Neumannsgate 25, tel. 05/900825. Reservations required on weekends. AE, DC, MC, V. Moderate.

Ervingen. Boasting a panorama view of the market and the harbor, Ervingen serves tasty homemade Norwegian food for breakfast, lunch, and dinner. *Toregaarden 2, Strandkaien, tel. 05/323030. No reservations. No credit cards. Budget.*

Lodging **Augustin.** This small but excellent hotel in the center of town has been recently restored to its original late–Art Nouveau character, complete with period furniture in the lobby. *C. Sundtsgate 24, tel. 05/230025. 38 rooms with bath. AE, DC, MC, V. Moderate.*

Bryggen Orion. Facing the harbor in the center of town, the recently renovated (1991) hotel is surrounded by Bergen's most famous sights. *Bradbenken 3, tel. 05/318080. 229 rooms with bath. Facilities: restaurant, bar, nightclub. AE, DC, MC, V. Moderate.*

Myklebust Pensjonat. This tiny, popular, family-run lodge has a quiet, central location. *Rosenbergsgate 19, tel. 05/901670. 6 double rooms, 2 with private bath. No credit cards. Inexpensive.*

Private accommodations are available as well, and range in price from NOK 145–NOK 170 for a single room; NOK 235–NOK 300 for a double. Apply in person at the Bergen Tourist Information Office.

Above Bergen: The Far North

The northern part of Norway is best known as the Land of the Midnight Sun. This area is enormous: A trip from Tromsø to Nordkapp (North Cape), the northernmost mainland point in Norway and Europe, is 464 kilometers (280 miles). The far north is ideal for anyone eager to hike, climb, fish, bird watch, and observe the *Same* (Lapp) culture. The Lofoten Islands present the grand face of the "Lofoten Wall"—a rocky, 96-kilometer-long (60-mile-long) massif surrounded by sea and broken into six pieces. Svolvær, the port, has a thriving summer artists' colony. It is also known for winter cod fishing. To get there, board a ferry from Skutvik.

Cheaper accommodations are the rule in the North, whether you stay in a cabin, campsite, guest house, or *rorbu*—fishermen's huts in the islands that are available for rent outside the January to April fishing season. These days, many *rorbuer* are built to be motels.

Getting Around

By Ship One of the best ways to travel in northern Norway is the **Hurtigrute,** or coastal steamer, which begins in Bergen and turns around 2,000 nautical kilometers (1,250 miles) later at Kirkenes. Many steamers run this route, so you can put in at any of the ports for any length of time and pick up the next one coming through: Major tourist offices have schedules and reservations are essential (*see* Important Addresses and Numbers in Oslo, *above*, and Getting Around by Ferry, *above*).

By Train Bodø is the last stop on the train route from Oslo via Trondheim.

By Bus The northern part of Norway has a well-developed bus network. To get all the way to Nordkapp and the Land of the Midnight Sun, you must travel by bus (the last train connection is Fauske).

Tourist Information

Bodø (Sjøgata 21, tel. 081/26000).
Tromsø (Storgata 61, tel. 083/10000).
Trondheim (Kongensgate 7 [entrance from Torvet, the marketplace], tel. 071/511466).

Exploring the Far North

Trondheim sits at the southern end of Norway's widest fjord, Trondheimfjord, and was founded in 977 by the Viking King Olav Tryggvason as the first capital of Norway. This waterbound city is the third largest in the country and is the traditional coronation place of Norwegian royalty. Scandinavia's largest medieval building, **Nidaros Cathedral,** started in 1320 but not completed until about 70 years ago, is here. For centuries it served as a goal for religious pilgrims. There is a historic fish market that is worth seeing. Scandinavia's two largest wooden buildings are in Trondheim. One is the rococo **Stiftsgården,** a royal palace built in 1774 (the other is a student dormitory) that houses the crown jewels.

There is much to do in the Trondheim area as well. **Stiklestad,** an historic battlefield in the town of Verdel, is worth a visit in summer for the outdoor medieval plays that are staged there. The Music History Museum in **Ringve** (also called the Ringve Museum) has unique collections that have achieved renown worldwide. **Munkholmen Fortress** is an old convent and prison island situated close to the harbor, and can be reached by boat from Ravnkloa, Trondheim's fish market. **Roros** is an old mining town that's now on UNESCO's preservation list. There's good skiing and hiking in **Oppdal.**

After Trondheim, the country thins into a vertebral cord of land hugging the border with Sweden and hunching over the top of Finland. **Bodø** is the first major town above the Polar Circle. As the northern terminus of the Nordland railway, Bodø is bathed in midnight sun from early June to mid-July. For those who want boat excursions to **coastal bird colonies** (the Væren Islands), Bodø is the best base. The city was bombed by the Germans in 1940. The stunning, contemporary **Bodø Cathedral,** its spire separated from the main building, was built after the war. Inside are rich, modern tapestries; outside is a war memorial. The **Nordland County Museum** depicts the life of the Lapps *(Same),* as well as regional history. *Prinsengate 116, tel. 081/26128. Admission: NOK 10 adults, NOK 2 children. Open weekdays 9–3, Sat. 10–3, Sun. 12–3.*

If you've never seen a real **maelstrom**—a furious natural whirlpool—inquire at the tourist office (*see* Tourist Information, *above*) about **Saltstraumen.** Bodø is considered a gateway to the Lofoten and Vesterålen islands; the tourist office will make the necessary arrangements.

Tromsø dubs itself "the Paris of the North" for the nightlife inspired by the midnight sun. Looming over this remote arctic university town are 1,860-meter (6,100-foot) peaks with permanent snowcaps. Tromsø trails off into the islands: Half the town lives offshore. Its population is about 50,000. Be sure to see the spectacular **Arctic Church,** with its eastern wall made entirely of stained glass, across the long stretch of **Tromsø bridge.** Coated in aluminum, its triangular peaks make a bizarre mirror for the midnight sun.

Be sure to walk around old Tromsø (along the waterfront) and to visit the **Tromsø Museum,** which concentrates on science, the Lapp people, and northern churches. *Strandveien via No. 21 bus. Admission: NOK 10 adults, NOK 5 children. Open Sept.– May, daily 9–6 (Wed. also 7–10 PM).*

Dining and Lodging

For details and price-category definitions, *see* Dining and Lodging in Staying in Norway.

Bodø **Turisthytta.** This mountaintop lodge (accessible by taxi) is a
Dining fine place to eat if you want to bask in the midnight sun. There is a good range of dishes, from snacks and open-faced sandwiches to fresh fish. *Turisthytta, tel. 081/83300. Reservations advised. No credit cards. Moderate.*

Løvold's Kafeteria. Experience the view of the harbor while enjoying a traditional Norwegian meal and homemade pastries. *Tollbugate 9, tel. 081/20261. No reservations. No credit cards. Inexpensive.*

Lodging **Norrøna.** This bed-and-breakfast–style establishment is comfortable, with the location just as grand as that of the SAS Royal next door. *Storgata 4, tel. 081/25550. 150 rooms with bath or shower. AE, DC, V. Moderate.*

Bodø Gjestegård. Centrally located near the railroad station, this is a convenient place to stay. *Storgate 90, tel. 081/20402. 14 rooms. No credit cards. Inexpensive.*

Tromsø **Arctandria.** For seafood lovers. Arctandria serves excellent
Dining northern Norwegian food. On the ground floor at the same address is Vertshuset Skarven, a very popular pub and café. *Strandtorget 1, 1st floor, tel. 083/10101. Reservations required. AE, DC, MC, V. Moderate.*

Saga. Situated on a pretty town square, the Saga combines its central location with the staff's expertise. Its restaurant has affordable, hearty meals, and the rooms—although somewhat basic—are quiet and comfortable. *Richard Withs Plass 2, tel. 083/81180. 52 rooms with bath. Facilities: restaurant, cafeteria. AE, DC, MC, V. Moderate.*

Lodging **Tromsø Rainbow Hotel.** This cozy bed-and-breakfast–style hotel is located in the center of town. Newly renovated, it's equipped with a breakfast room. There's a restaurant across the street. *Grønnegate 50, tel. 083/87520. 46 rooms with bath. Facilities: breakfast room. AE, DC, MC, V. Moderate.*

Trondheim **Benito.** This very popular restaurant serves both Italian and
Dining Norwegian food, with great prices and good atmosphere. *Vår Fruegate 4, tel. 07/526422. No reservations. AE, DC, MC, V. Moderate.*

Tavern på Sverresborg. Outside the city, at the open-air Folk Museum, this restaurant serves Norwegian specialties.

Sverresborg, tel. 07/520932. No reservations. No credit cards. Moderate.

Cafe Prinsenhjørnet. This café is a popular meeting place with hearty food at reasonable prices. *Kongensgate 30, tel. 07/ 530650. No reservations. AE, DC, MC, V. Budget.*

Lodging **Ambassadeur.** Take in the panoramic view from the roof terrace of this first-rate modern hotel, located about 93 meters (101 yards) from the market square. The deep blue waters of the Trondheimsfjord reflect the dramatic and irregular coastline. Most rooms in the Ambassadeur have fireplaces, and some have balconies. *Elvegate 18, tel. 07/527050. 34 rooms with bath. Facilities: restaurant, bar. AE, DC, MC, V. Moderate.*

Gildevangen. Centrally located in the heart of town, Gildevangen has comfortable rooms and a special children's playroom. *Søndregate 22B, tel. 07/528340. 74 rooms with bath. Facilities: restaurant. AE, DC, MC, V. Moderate.*

Singsaker Sommerhotell. This dormitory becomes a comfortable hotel every summer. *Singsaker, tel. 07/520092. 104 rooms with bath. Facilities: restaurant, sauna. AE, MC, V. Inexpensive.*

19 Poland

Three years after the revolution of 1989, Poland offers the budget traveler more than ever before. Despite rampant inflation and price hikes, the lifting of state controls on charges for accommodation and other services has made life much easier for the foreign visitor, and now country-wide there is a far greater range of lodging and dining options.

Poland is a land rich in natural beauty and contrasts. Its landscape varies from rolling plains with slow-moving rivers, broad fields, and scattered villages to lakes, forests, and marshes in the north and jagged mountains in the south. This makes available a variety of low-cost touring possibilities. Every one of the major cities, with the exception of Cracow and Łódź, had to be rebuilt after the destruction of World War II. Particularly fine restoration work has been done on Warsaw's Old Town and in Gdańsk on the Baltic coast.

Poland never did fit into the mold of a Communist country. Through more than 40 years of Communist rule, a majority of the people remained devoutly Catholic. Both rural and urban life remain centered on the home and family, where old traditions are diligently upheld. Four-fifths of the country's farmland has remained privately owned, and since 1990 a major privatization drive has been under way in the rest of the economy.

Poland's geographic position between Germany and Russia has determined its history of almost continual war and struggle for independence since the late 18th century. More than 40 years of Communist rule left Poland in a serious economic crisis, and although Poland now has a non-Communist government, no one has simple answers to the country's complicated political and economic problems.

In spite of all this, the Polish people continue to be resilient, resourceful, and hopeful. Poles openly welcome visitors; their uninhibited sense of hospitality makes them eager to please their guests. It is easy to make friends here and to exchange views with strangers on trains and buses. Poles have a passionate interest in all things Western, from current affairs to the arts, clothes, and music.

Essential Information

Before You Go

When to Go The official tourist season runs from May through September. The best times for sightseeing are late spring and early fall. Major cultural events usually take place in the cities during the fall. The early spring is often wet and windy.

Below are the average daily maximum and minimum temperatures for Warsaw.

Jan.	32F	0C	May	67F	20C	Sept.	66F	19C
	22	−6		48	9		49	10
Feb.	32F	0C	June	73F	23C	Oct.	55F	13C
	21	−6		54	12		41	5
Mar.	42F	6C	July	75F	24C	Nov.	42F	6C
	28	−2		58	16		33	1
Apr.	53F	12C	Aug.	73F	23C	Dec.	35F	2C
	37	3		56	14		28	−3

Currency The monetary unit in Poland is the złoty (zł). There are notes of 10, 20, 50, 100, 200, 500, 1,000, 2,000, 5,000, 10,000 20,000, 50,000, 100,000, 200,000, 500,000, and 1,000,000 złotys, and coins of 1, 2, 5, 10, 20, 50, and 100 złotys (rarely seen). At press time (summer 1992), the bank exchange rate was about zł 11,750 to the U.S. dollar and zł 19,800 to the pound sterling. Since spring 1989, the złoty has been legally exchangeable at a free market rate in both banks (*Bank Narodowy* and *Pekao*) and private exchange bureau (*Kantor wymiany walut*), which sometimes offer slightly better rates than do the banks; kantor rates also vary, so it's worth shopping around. If you run out of złotys, you will find that Polish taxi drivers, waiters, and porters will usually accept dollars or any other Western currency. Money exchanged into złotys can be reconverted upon leaving the country.

Credit Cards American Express, Diners Club, MasterCard, and Visa are accepted in all Orbis hotels, in the better restaurants and nightclubs, and for other Orbis services. In small cafés and shops, credit cards may not be accepted.

What It Will Cost At press time (summer 1992), it was still illegal to import or export złotys. This may change if the new Polish government goes through with plans to make the złoty fully convertible on the international market. Still, don't buy more złotys than you need, or you will have to go to the trouble of changing them back at the end of your trip.

Poland is now one of the more expensive countries of Eastern Europe, and inflation is still high by Western standards, despite the reforms of 1990. Prices are highest in the big cities,

Poland

Baltic Sea

especially in Warsaw. The more you stray off the tourist track, the cheaper your vacation will be. The cost difference can sometimes be enormous. What you save in money, however, you may lose in quality of service.

Sample Prices   A cup of coffee, zł 4,000–15,000; a bottle of beer, zł 8,000–25,000; a soft drink, zł 5,000–20,000; a ham sandwich, zł 10,000–20,000; 1-mile taxi ride, zł 10,000.

Museums   Admission fees to museums and other attractions are also rising in line with inflation, and seem ever-changing. At press time (spring 1992), fees ranged from zł 1,000 to zł 5,000. Note that most museums offer free admission one day a week (usually Wednesday).

Visas U.S. citizens are no longer required to obtain visas for entry to Poland; British and Canadian citizens and citizens of other countries that have not yet abolished visas for Poles must pay the equivalent of $35 (more for multiple-entry visas). Apply at any Orbis office (the official Polish tourist agency), an affiliated travel agent, or from the Polish Consulate General in any country. Each visitor must complete three visa application forms and provide two photographs. Allow about two weeks for processing. Visas are issued for 90 days but can be extended in Poland, if necessary, either through the local county police headquarters or through Orbis.

You can contact the **Polish Consulate General** at the following addresses: **In the United States:** 233 Madison Ave., New York, NY 10016 (tel. 212/391–0844); 1530 North Lake Shore Dr., Chicago, IL 60610 (tel. 312/337–8166); 2224 Wyoming Ave., Washington DC 20008 (tel. 202/234–2501). **In Canada:** 1500 Pine Ave., Montreal, Quebec H3G (tel. 514/937–9481); 2603 Lakeshore Blvd. W., Toronto, Ont. M8V 1G5 (tel. 416/252–5471). **In the United Kingdom:** 73 New Cavendish St., London W1 (tel. 071/636–4533).

Customs on Arrival Persons over 17 may bring in duty-free: personal belongings, including musical instruments, typewriter, radio, 2 cameras with 24 rolls of film; up to 250 cigarettes or 50 cigars and 1 liter each of wine and spirits; and goods to the value of $200. Any amount of foreign currency may be brought in but must be declared on arrival.

Language Most older Poles know German; the younger generation usually knows some English. In the big cities you will find people who speak English, especially in hotels, but you may have difficulty in the provinces and countryside.

Getting Around

By Train Poland's PKP railway network is extensive and inexpensive. Most trains have first- and second-class accommodations, but Western visitors usually prefer to travel first-class; second-class is reasonably comfortable on intercity and express trains but can be cramped and uncomfortable on slow trains. You should arrive at the station well before departure time. The fastest trains are intercity and express trains, which require reservations. Some Orbis offices furnish information, reservations, and tickets. Overnight trains have first- and second-class sleeping cars and second-class couchettes. Most long-distance trains carry buffets, but the quality of the food is unpredictable and you may want to bring your own.

Fares Fares vary according to the speed at which a train travels: It is twice as expensive to travel on an express as on a stopping train. Note that your ticket is valid only for the day or days specified when you buy it; getting a refund is complicated, so it is best to plan carefully. Since a return ticket costs exactly twice the one-way fare, you may prefer to put off purchase until your plans are definite.

By Plane **LOT,** Poland's national airline, operates daily flights linking five main cities. Fares begin at about $60 round-trip and can be paid for in złotys. Tickets and information are available from LOT or Orbis offices. All flights booked through Orbis in the United Kingdom carry a discount, but it is cheaper to pay in local currency in Poland. Be sure to book well in advance, especially for the summer season.

By Bus Express bus services link all main cities as well as smaller towns and villages off the rail network. Buses are crowded; expresses buses are more expensive than trains, but local buses are inexpensive. PKS bus stations are usually located near railway stations. Tickets and information are best obtained from Orbis. Warsaw's central bus terminal is on aleje Jerozolimskie.

Staying in Poland

Telephones Public phone booths take tokens: zł 600 for local calls and zł
Local Calls 2,000 for long-distance calls, which must be made from special booths, usually situated in post offices. Place a token in the groove on the side or top of the phone, lift the receiver, and dial the number. Push the token into the machine when the call is answered.

International Calls Post offices and first-class hotels have assigned booths, at which you pay after the completion of your call. To place an international call, dial 901; for domestic long-distance calls, dial 900. There's a heavy surcharge on calls made from hotel rooms.

Information For general information (including international codes), tel. 913.

Mail Airmail letters to the United States cost zł 2,700; postcards,
Postal Rates zł 2,200. Letters to the United Kingdom or Europe cost zł 2,400; postcards, zł 1,900. Post offices are open 8 AM–8 PM (except weekends). At least one post office is open 24 hours in every major city. In Warsaw the post office is located at ulica Świętokrzyska 31.

Opening and **Banks.** Banks are open weekdays 8 AM–3 PM or 6 PM.
Closing Times
Museums. Museum opening hours vary greatly, but they are generally open Tuesday–Sunday 9–5.

Shops. Food shops are open weekdays 7 AM–7 PM, Saturday 7 AM–1 PM. Other stores are open weekdays 11 AM–7 PM and Saturday 9 AM–1 PM; closed Sunday.

National Holidays January 1; April 11 (Easter); May 1 (Labor Day); May 3 (Constitution Day); June 18 (Corpus Christi); August 15 (Feast of the Assumption); November 1 (Remembrance); November 11 (rebirth of Polish state, 1918); December 25, 26.

Dining Polish food and drink are basically Slavic with Baltic overtones. There is a heavy emphasis on soups and meat (especially pork) as well as freshwater fish. Much use is made of cream, and pastries are rich and often delectable.

The most popular soup is *barszcz* (known to many Americans as borscht), a clear beet soup often served with such Polish favorites as sausage, cabbage, potatoes, sour cream, coarse rye bread, and beer. Other dishes include *pierogi* (a kind of ravioli), which may be stuffed with savory or sweet fillings; *gołąbki*, cabbage leaves stuffed with minced meat; *bigos*, sauerkraut with meat and mushrooms; and *flaki*, a select dish of tripe, served boiled or fried. Polish beer is good; vodka is a specialty and is often downed before, with, and after meals.

There is an ever-widening selection of eating places, although—at least in the cities—the top end of the price range is currently better served than the lower end. The *bary mleczne* (milk bars) selling cheap and healthy dairy and vegetable dishes are fast disappearing, replaced by the ubiquitous pizza parlor. However, if you look hard, you can still find one or two good, low-budget traditional eating places in most towns. As elsewhere in Central Europe, cafés are a way of life in Poland and are often stocked with delicious pastries and ice creams; they also have savory snacks at reasonable prices.

Mealtimes At home, Poles eat late lunches and late suppers; the former is their main meal. Many restaurants, however, close around 9 PM. Most hotel restaurants serve the evening meal until 10:30.

Precautions Tap water is unsafe, so ask for mineral water. Beware of meat dishes served in cheap snack bars. Avoid the food on trains.

Dress Although Poles tend to dress less formally than many Westerners, casual but neat dress is appropriate in most of the restaurants listed below.

Ratings Prices are for one person and include three courses and service but no drinks. Best bets are indicated by a star ★.

Category	Warsaw	Other Areas
Moderate	zł 70,000–120,000	zł 50,000–70,000
Inexpensive	zł 35,000–70,000	zł 25,000–50,000
Budget	under zł 35,000	under zł 25,000

Lodging
Hotels Orbis hotels are usually very expensive (not to say overpriced) in cities and major tourist spots. But in more out-of-the-way places—if you don't mind a room without a private bath—these hotels can be inexpensive. The standards of municipally owned hotels vary greatly, but some are very good, and you can occasionally find a real bargain. *Dom Turysty* hotels, run or licensed by the Polish Tourist Association, are usually unpretentiously comfortable but often have only a limited number of single and double rooms. *Gromada,* the cooperative, runs an excellent network of comfortable and inexpensive hotels with a reputation for good food.

Remember that in many holiday resorts (Zakopane, Cracow, the Baltic coast) off-season prices can be as little as half those charged in full season.

Hostels The Polish Youth Hostels Association operates hostels at budget rate, zł 10,000–zł 25,000 per night; in addition, hostels are open to people of all ages. Information is available from your local branch of the International Youth Hostel Association.

Roadside Inns A number of roadside inns, often very attractive, offer inexpensive food and a few guest rooms at moderate rates.

Private Accommodations Rooms can be arranged either in advance through Orbis or on the spot at the local tourist information office. Villas, lodges, rooms, or houses are available, and the prices are often negotiable. Rates vary from about $6 for a room to more than $150 for a villa.

Ratings The following chart is based on a rate for two people in a double room, with bath or shower and breakfast. These prices are in U.S. dollars. Best bets are indicated by a star ★.

Category	Cost
Moderate	$50–$90
Inexpensive	$25–$50
Budget	under $25

Tipping Waiters get a standard 10% of the bill. Hotel porters and doormen should get about zł 10,000. In Warsaw and other big towns frequented by foreign tourists, waiters also often expect a tip to help find you a table. If you choose to tip in foreign currency (readily accepted), remember that $1 is about an hour's wage.

Warsaw

Arriving and Departing

By Plane All international flights arrive at Warsaw's Okęcie Airport (Port Lotniczy) just southwest of the city. Terminal 1 serves international flights from the West; Terminal 2 serves domestic and East European flights. For flight information, contact the airlines, or call the airport at tel. 022/46–96–70 or 022/46–11–43.

Between the Airport and Downtown LOT operates a regular bus service into Warsaw. Otherwise the 175 bus leaves every 10 minutes from the international terminal. The trip takes about 15 minutes and the fare is zł 2,000; after 11 PM, it is raised to zł 4,000.

By Train Trains to and from Western Europe arrive at Dworzec Centralny on aleje Jerozolimskie in the center of town. For tickets and information, contact Orbis.

By Car There are seven main access routes to Warsaw, all leading to the center of the city. Drivers heading to or from the West will use the E8 or E12 highways.

Getting Around

By Tram and Bus These are often crowded, but they are the cheapest way of getting around. Trams and buses cost zł 2,000; express buses cost zł 3,000. The bus fare goes up to zł 4,000 between 11 PM and 5:30 AM. Tickets must be bought in advance from **Ruch** newsstands. You must cancel your own ticket in a machine on the tram or bus when you get on; watch others do it.

Important Addresses and Numbers

Tourist Information The **Center for Tourist Information** is open 24 hours; it is located at plac Zamkowy 1, tel. 022/27–00–00. **Orbis** offices in Warsaw include: ulica Bracka 16, tel. 022/26–02–71; and ulica Marszałkowska 142, tel. 022/27–80–31 or 022/27–36–73.

Embassies U.S. (aleje Ujazdowskie 29–31, tel. 022/628–30–41). **Canadian** (ulica Matejki 1/5, tel. 022/29–80–51). **U.K.** (aleje Róż 1, tel. 022/628–10–01). **U.K. Consulate** (ulica Wawelska 14, tel. 022/25–30–31).

Emergencies **Police** (tel. 997). **Ambulance** (tel. 998). **Doctor** (tel. 998 or call your embassy).

Travel Agencies **Thomas Cook**, ul. Nowy Świat 64, tel. 022/26–47–29.

Guided Tours

Bus tours of the city depart in the morning and afternoon from the major hotels. **Orbis** also has half-day excursions into the surrounding countryside. These usually include a meal and some form of traditional entertainment. Check for details with your hotel, the Orbis office, or a tourist information office.

Exploring Warsaw

At the end of World War II, Warsaw lay in ruins, a victim of systematic Nazi destruction. Only one-third of its prewar population survived the horrors of German occupation. The experience has left its mark on the city and is visible everywhere in the memorial plaques describing mass executions of civilians and in the bullet holes on the facades of buildings.

Against all the odds, Warsaw's survivors have rebuilt their historic city. The old districts have been painstakingly reconstructed according to old prints and paintings, including those of Belotto and Canaletto from the 18th century. The result, a city of warm pastel colors, is remarkable.

Surrounding the old districts, however, is the modern Warsaw, built since the war in utilitarian Socialist-Realist style. Whether you like it or not is your business, but it is worth noting as a testimony to one approach to urban life. The sights of Warsaw are all relatively close to each other, making most attractions accessible by foot.

Numbers in the margin correspond to points of interest on the Warsaw map.

The Old Town
❶ A walking tour of the old historic district takes about two hours. Begin in the heart of the city at **plac Zamkowy** (Castle Square), where you will see a slender column supporting the **statue of Zygmunt (Sigismund) III Vasa,** the king who made Warsaw his capital in the early 17th century. It is the city's oldest monument and, symbolically, the first to be rebuilt after
❷ the wartime devastation. Dominating the square is the **Royal Castle.** Restoring the interior was a herculean task, requiring workers to relearn traditional skills, match ancient woods and fabrics, and even reopen abandoned quarries to find just the right kind of stone. A visit is worthwhile, despite the crowds. *Tel. 022/635–39–95. Admission: zł 30,000 adults, zł 15,000 children. Open Tues.–Sat. 10–2:30, Sun. 9–2:30.*

Enter the narrow streets of the **Old Town** (Stare Miasto), with its colorful medieval houses, cobblestone alleys, uneven roofs, and wrought-iron grillwork. On your right as you proceed
❸ along ulica Świętojańska is the **Cathedral of St. John,** the oldest church in Warsaw, dating back to the 14th century. Several Pol-
❹ ish kings were crowned here. Soon you will reach the **Old Market Square** (Rynek Starego Miasta), the charming and intimate center of the old town. The old town hall, which once stood in the middle, was pulled down in the 19th century. It was not replaced, and today the square is full of open-air cafés, tubs of flowering plants, and the inevitable artists displaying their talents for the tourists. At night the brightly lighted Rynek (marketplace) is the place to go for good food and atmosphere.

Continue along ulica Nowomiejska until you get to the imposing
❺ redbrick **Barbican,** a fine example of a 16th-century defensive

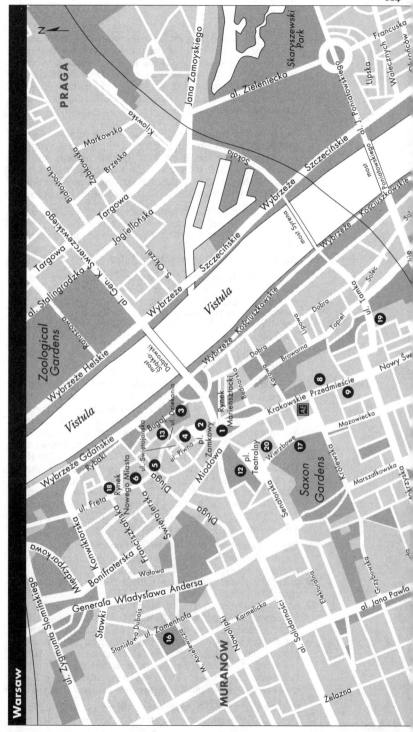

Warsaw

635

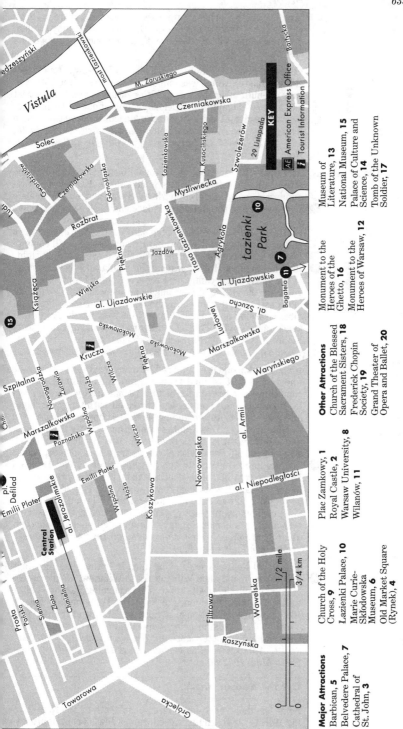

KEY

AE American Express Office

i Tourist Information

Major Attractions

Barbican, **5**
Belvedere Palace, **7**
Cathedral of St. John, **3**

Church of the Holy Cross, **9**
Łazienki Palace, **10**
Marie Curie-Skłodowska Museum, **6**
Old Market Square (Rynek), **4**

Plac Zamkowy, **1**
Royal Castle, **2**
Warsaw University, **8**
Wilanów, **11**

Other Attractions

Church of the Blessed Sacrament Sisters, **18**
Frederick Chopin Society, **19**
Grand Theater of Opera and Ballet, **20**

Monument to the Heroes of the Ghetto, **16**
Monument to the Heroes of Warsaw, **12**

Museum of Literature, **13**
National Museum, **15**
Palace of Culture and Science, **14**
Tomb of the Unknown Soldier, **17**

fortification. From here you can see the partially restored town wall that was built to enclose the Old Town, and enjoy a splendid view of the Vistula River, with the district of Praga on its east bank.

Follow the street called ulica Freta to Warsaw's **New Town** (Nowe Miasto), which was founded at the turn of the 15th century. Rebuilt after the war in 18th-century style, this district has a more elegant and spacious feeling about it. Of interest ❻ here is the **Marie Curie-Skłodowska Museum,** where the woman who discovered radium and polonium was born. *Ul. Freta 16, tel. 022/31–80–92. Admission: zł 2,000. Open Tues.–Sun. 10–5.*

The Royal Way All towns with kings had their Royal Routes; the one in Warsaw stretched south from Castle Square down Krakowskie Przedmieście, curving through Nowy Świat and on along aleje ❼ Ujazdowskie to the **Belvedere Palace** and Łazienki Park. Some of Warsaw's finest churches and palaces are found along this route, as well as the names of famous Poles. A few blocks south of plac Zamkowy on Krakowskie Przedmieście, you'll come to ❽ **Warsaw University** on your left. Farther down, on your right, ❾ the **Church of the Holy Cross** contains a pillar in which the heart of the great Polish composer Frédéric Chopin is entombed. As you pass the statue of Nicolaus Copernicus, Poland's most famous astronomer, you enter the busy Nowy Świat thoroughfare. Crossing aleje Jerozolimskie, on your left is the **former headquarters of the Polish Communist party,** a large solid gray building typical of the Socialist-Realist architectural style, which now houses banks and Poland's new stock exchange.

Aleje Ujazdowskie is considered by many locals to be Warsaw's finest street. It is lined with magnificent buildings and has something of a French flavor to it. A hundred years ago, this fashionable *corso* (avenue) was thronged with fancy carriages and riders eager to see and be seen. It is now a favorite with Sunday strollers. Down at its southern end, before the name inexplicably changes to Belwederska, the French-style landscaped **Łazienki Park,** with pavilions and a royal palace, stands ❿ in refreshing contrast to the bustling streets. The **Łazienki Palace,** a gem of Polish neoclassicism, was the private residence of Stanisław August Poniatowski, last king of Poland. It overlooks a lake stocked with huge carp. At the impressionistic Chopin monument nearby, you can stop for a well-deserved rest and, on summer Sundays, listen to an open-air concert. *Tel. 022/21–62–41. Admission: zł 14,000 adults, zł 8,000 children. Open Tues.–Sat. 9:30–3.*

The Royal Route extends along ulica Belwederska, ulica Jana ⑪ Sobieskiego, and aleja Wilanowska to **Wilanów,** 10 kilometers (6 miles) from the town center. This charming Baroque palace was the summer residence of King Jan III Sobieski, who, in 1683, stopped the Ottoman advance on Europe at the Battle of Vienna. The palace interior is open and houses antique furniture and a fine poster museum. *Ul. Wiertnicza l, tel. 022/42–81–01. Admission: zł 20,000 adults, zł 10,000 children. Open Wed.–Mon. 10–2:30.*

Off the Beaten Track

Some 3 million Polish Jews were put to death by the Nazis during World War II, ending the enormous Jewish contribution to

Polish culture, tradition, and achievement. A simple monument to the **Heroes of the Warsaw Ghetto,** a slab of dark granite with a bronze bas relief, stands on ulica Zamenhofa in the Muranów district, the historic heart of the old prewar Warsaw Jewish district and ghetto under the Nazi regime. The Warsaw Ghetto uprising that broke out in April 1943 was put down with unbelievable ferocity, and the Muranów district was flattened. Today there are only bleak gray apartment blocks here.

With ironic humor, Warsaw locals tell you that the best vantage point from which to admire their city is atop the 37-story **Palace of Culture and Science.** Why? Because it is the only point from which you can't see the Palace of Culture and Science. This wedding-cake-style skyscraper was a personal gift from Stalin. Although it is disliked by Poles as a symbol of Soviet domination, it does afford a panoramic view and is the best example in Warsaw of 1950s "Socialist Gothic" architecture. *Plac Defilad, tel. 022/20–02–11 ext. 2777. Admission: zł 10,000. Open daily 9–5.*

Shopping

The most fashionable shopping streets, Nowy Świat and Chmielna, are lined with elegant boutiques that are good for window-shopping—but if you want bargains, look elsewhere. Polish leather goods are of high quality and often substantially cheaper than those sold in the West; large specialty stores (for example at Marszałkowska 83) are the best places to look. *Cepelia* stores (Marszałkowska 99, Nowy Świat 35) have a wide range of reasonably priced traditional handicrafts, such as hand-woven wool rugs, tapestries, amber jewelry, and carved-wood kitchenware. Polish crystal and glass are good buys; try the specialty store at Piękna 26–34. State-owned department stores, **Junior** and **Centralne Domy Towarowe,** still survive in somewhat altered form on ulica Marszałkowska opposite the Palace of Culture and Science.

For the more adventurous there is a flea market, **Bazar Róży-ckiego,** on ulica Targowa 55, where you can find almost anything. Another market is now open daily at Stadion Dzięsieciolecia (Rondo Waszyngtona); here, visitors from all over Eastern Europe gather to sell their wares, often very cheaply—although you should inspect purchases carefully. There is also a Sunday flea market at the Skra sports stadium (ul. Wawelska).

Dining

A large number of Warsaw restaurants are to be found in and around the Old Town. The setting is atmospheric, but the food here may well be overpriced, so it is worth investigating what is available in other parts of town. Remember that in inexpensive and budget restaurants it is unlikely that English will be spoken; take along a dictionary to help with the menu. For details and price-category definitions, *see* Dining in Staying in Poland.

Moderate **Kamienne Schodki.** This intimate, candlelit restaurant is lo-
★ cated in one of the Market Square's medieval houses. Its main specialty is duck; also try the pastries. *Rynek Starego Miasta 26, tel. 022/31–08–22. Reservations advised. No credit cards.*
Pod Samsonem. This small restaurant, decorated in wood, has a

smoke-filled Warsaw atmosphere and friendly waitresses. The fish and pierogi are good when available. *Ul. Freta 3/5, tel. 022/ 31–17–88. Reservations accepted. No credit cards.*

Staropolska. Fish dishes and old-fashioned Polish cuisine are the specialties. Portions are on the small side. *Krakowskie Przedmiéscie 8, tel. 022/26–90–70. Reservations advised. No credit cards. Open until 5 AM.*

Inexpensive **Mesa.** This second-floor fish restaurant has informal waitress service and is usually busy at lunchtime. *Al. Wyzwolenia 18, tel. 022/628–44–50. No reservations. No credit cards.*

★ **Pod Retmanem.** Wood trestle tables and folk decoration provide the backdrop here for a solid, traditional meal. *Ul. Bednarska 9, tel. 022/26–87–58. Reservations accepted. No credit cards.*

Budget **Bar Kubuś.** This small, self-service bar just off Nowy Świat is spotless and serves excellent food to a faithful clientele. *Ul. Ordynacka 13, no tel. No reservations. No credit cards.*

Lodging

There is no off-season for tourism in Warsaw, and although five new hotels are currently under construction there is a great shortage of hotel beds that is expected to continue until the mid-1990s. It is therefore difficult to find accommodations at the middle and lower end of the price range; book early. Private accommodations are sometimes cheaper and are available through the Center for Tourist Information. For details and price-category definitions, *see* Lodging in Staying in Poland.

Moderate **Dom Chłopa.** Built in the 1960s by the Gromada Peasants' Co-operative, this hotel offers clean, cheerful, and reasonably priced accommodations in the center of Warsaw. *Plac Powstańców Warszawy 2, tel. 022/27–49–43, telex 022/86–67–01. 160 rooms. Facilities: restaurant. AE, DC, MC, V.*

M.D.M. This socialist-realist hotel run by the municipal authorities is on the main shopping thoroughfare and is clean, if shabby. *Plac Konstytucji 1, tel. 022/21–41–76, telex 022/81–48–71. 153 rooms, ⅓ with bath. Facilities: restaurant. AE, DC, MC, V.*

Metropol. Built during the 1960s, this clean, modern hotel is located right in the center of town. It's a good value for the money. The rooms have recently been renovated. *Al. Jerozolimskie 45, tel. 022/21–43–54, fax 022/628–66–22. 175 rooms with bath. Facilities: restaurant, café. AE, DC, MC, V.*

Polonia. The Art Nouveau Polonia was the only Warsaw hotel to survive the Second World War intact–although renovation in the 1970s removed many of the original features. The hotel is central, comfortable, and has a friendly staff. *Al. Jerozolimskie 45, tel. 022/628–72–41, fax 022/628–66–22. 234 rooms, most with bath. Facilities: restaurant. AE, DC, MC, V.*

Inexpensive **Dom Nauczyciela.** Run by the union of schoolteachers, this ho-
★ tel down by the banks of the Vistula has comfortable if slightly drab rooms and is easily accessible from the city center. *Wybrzeże Kościuszkowskie 31, tel. 022/625–26–00. 216 rooms, ⅓ with bath. Facilities: self-service restaurant. No credit cards.*

Dom Turysty. Run by the Polish Tourist Association until recently, this hotel has just been renovated and is now cheerfully furnished. *Krakowskie Przedmieście 4–6, tel. 022/26–26–25.*

*63 rooms, some with bath. Facilities: self-service restaurant.
AE, DC, MC, V.*

Pensjonat Biała Dalia. This small, privately owned pension in
Konstancin Jeziorno 24-kilometers (15 miles) from the center of
Warsaw stands in a beautifully kept garden. The rooms are ele-
gantly furnished, clean, and comfortable. *Ul. Sobieskiego 24,
Konstancin Jeziorno, tel. 022/56–33–70. 5 rooms with bath.
Facilities: restaurant. No credit cards.*

Budget   **Druh.** This 1960s-era, five-story hotel (with no elevator) in
Warsaw's Ochota district belongs to the Boy Scouts' Association. It has a limited number of single and double rooms, which
are clean, if Spartan. *Ul. Niemcewicza 17, tel. 022/659–00–11,
telex 022/81–23–08. 40 rooms. Facilities: self-service restaurant. No credit cards.*

Gromada Camp Site. Open May–October, this camp site offers
accommodation in wood chalets (bedding provided); it is five
minutes by bus from the center of town. *Ul. Zwirki i Wigury
3–5, tel. 022/25–43–91. 60 chalets. Facilities: cafeteria. No
credit cards.*

Uniwersytecki. Taken over by the University of Warsaw in 1990
from the Central Committee of the Communist Party, this hotel gives priority to guests of the university, but there are usually a few rooms available for other visitors. *Ul. Belwederska
26–30, tel. 022/41–93–58. 90 rooms. Facilities: café-bar. No
credit cards.*

The Arts

For information, buy the newspaper *Życie Warszawy* or *Gazeta
Wyborcza* at Ruch newsstands. Tickets can be ordered by your
Orbis hotel receptionist, through the tourist information center (pl. Zamkowy 1, tel. 022/27–00–00), or at the ticket office on
ulica Marszałkowska 104. Note that in the last hour before a
performance most theaters and concert halls sell *wejsciowka*
(entry tickets) for as little as zł 1,000, which entitle you to take
any empty seat or sit on the floor.

Theaters   There are 17 theaters in Warsaw, attesting to the popularity of
this art form, but none offers English performances. **Teatr
Narodowy,** opened in 1764 and the oldest in Poland, is on plac
Teatralny. **Teatr Polski Kameralny** (Foksal 16) has a small stage
and is thus more intimate. **Współczesny** (Mokotowska 13) shows
contemporary works.

Concerts   **The National Philharmonic** puts on the best concerts. The hall
is on ulica Sienkiewicza 12. In the summer, free Chopin con-
certs take place both at the Chopin monument in **Łazienki Park**
and each Sunday at **Żelazowa Wola,** the composer's birthplace,
58 kilometers (36 miles) outside Warsaw.

Opera   **Teatr Wielki** (plac Teatralny) hosts the Grand Theater of Opera
and Ballet. It has a superb operatic stage—one of the largest in
Europe.

Film   Almost all non-Polish films are shown in their original versions,
but check before you buy your tickets. Of interest on a rainy
day is the fact that many cinemas have all-day programs.

Nightlife

Cabaret The Victoria, Forum, Grand, Europejski, and Marriott hotels all have nightclubs that are popular with Westerners. The acts vary, so check listings in the press. These clubs also present striptease and jazz. The most famous cabaret is **Pod Egidą** on Nowy Świat, renowned for its risqué political satire.

Bars Gwiazdeczka (Piwna 42) is a noisy, hip, upscale joint, popular with chic young Warsovians.

Jazz Clubs Akwarium (ul. Emilii Platter) and **Wanda Warska's Modern Music Club** (Stare Miasto) are popular jazz clubs. Jazz musicians are booked frequently at the major hotels, too.

Discos Apart from the hotels, the most popular discos are **Hybrydy** (ul. Złota 7) and **Stodoła** (ul. Batorego 2).

Cafés Warsaw is filled with cafés *(kawiarnie)*, which move outdoors in the summer. They are popular meeting places and usually serve delicious coffee and pastries in the best Central European style.

Ambassador is an elegant and brightly lit café with a tree-lined terrace for summer visitors. *Ul. Matejki 4.*
Le Petit Trianon is a tiny, intimate 18th-century French-style restaurant and café. It is difficult to find a seat, but worth it once you do. *Ul. Piwna 40.*
Telimena is a small corner café with an art gallery on the ground floor. *Krakowskie Przedmieście 27.*
Trou Madame has a secluded setting in Łazienki Park.
Ujazdowska is elegant and spacious in a 19th-century French-style house. *Al. Ujazdowskie 47.*

Cracow and Environs

Cracow (Kraków), seat of Poland's oldest university and once the capital of the country (before losing the honor to Warsaw in 1611), is one of the few Polish cities that escaped devastation during World War II. Hitler's armies were driven out before they had a chance to destroy it. Today Cracow's fine ramparts, towers, facades, and churches, illustrating seven centuries of Polish architecture, make it a major attraction for visitors. Its location—about 270 kilometers (160 miles) south of Warsaw—also makes it a good base for hiking and skiing trips in the mountains of southern Poland.

Also within exploring range from Cracow are the famous Polish shrine to the Virgin Mary at Częstochowa, and, at Auschwitz (Oświęcim), the grim reminder of man's capacity for inhumanity.

Getting Around

Trains link Cracow with most major destinations in Poland; the station is in the city center near the Old Town, on ulica Pawia. The bus station is nearby.

Tourist Information

Cracow (ulica Pawia 8, tel. 012/22–04–71).

Częstochowa (aleje Najświętszej Marii Panny 37/39, tel. 833/ 467–55).

Exploring Cracow

Numbers in the margin correspond to points of interest on the Cracow map.

Cracow's old city is ringed by a park called the **Planty.** The park replaced the old walls of the town, which were torn down in the mid-19th century. Begin your tour at **St. Florian's Gate,** which leads to the old town. The gate is guarded by an imposing 15th-century fortress called the **Barbican.** Enter the city, passing along ulica Floriańska, the beginning of the Royal Route through the town, where you should not pass up the chance to stop for refreshments at Cracow's most famous café, **Jama Michalikowa** (Ul. Floriańska 8).

Ulica Floriańska leads to the **Rynek Główny** (main market), one of the largest and finest Renaissance squares in Europe. The calm of this spacious square, with its pigeons and flower stalls, is interrupted every hour by four short bugle calls drifting down from the spire of the Church of the Virgin Mary. The plaintive notes recall a centuries-old tradition in memory of a trumpeter whose throat was pierced by a well-aimed enemy arrow as he was warning his fellow citizens of an impending Tartar attack. The square Gothic **Kościół Mariacki** (Church of the Virgin Mary) contains a 15th-century wooden altarpiece—the largest in the world—carved by Wit Stwosz. The faces of the saints are reputedly those of Cracovian burghers. In the center of the square stands a covered market called **Sukiennice** (Cloth Hall), built in the 14th century but remodeled during the Renaissance. The ground floor is still in business, selling trinkets and folk art souvenirs. *Open Mon.–Sat. 10–6, Sun. 10–5.*

From the Main Market, turn down ulica Św. Anny to No. 8, the **Collegium Maius,** the oldest building of the famous **Jagiellonian University** (founded 1364). Its pride is the Italian-style arcaded courtyard. Inside is a museum where you can see the Copernicus globe, the first on which the American continents were shown, as well as astronomy instruments belonging to Cracow's most famous graduate. *Admission free. Courtyard open Mon.–Sat. 8–6. Museum shown by appointment only, 10– noon.*

Backtracking on ulica Grodzka will lead you to the **Wawel Castle and Cathedral.** This impressive complex of Gothic and Renaissance buildings stands on fortifications dating as far back as the 8th century. Inside the castle is a museum with an exotic collection of Oriental tents that were captured from the Turks at the battle of Vienna in 1683 and rare 16th-century Flemish tapestries. Wawel Cathedral is where, until the 18th century, Polish kings were crowned and buried. Until 1978, the cathedral was the principal church of the see of Archbishop Karol Wojtyla, now known as Pope John Paul II. *Ul. Grodzka, tel. 012/22–51– 55. Castle. Admission: zł 30,000 adults, zł 15,000 children. Open Tues., Thurs., Sat., Sun. 10–3, Wed. and Fri. noon–6. Cathedral Museum. Admission: zł 3,000. Open Tues.–Sun. 10–3.*

About 50 kilometers (30 miles) west of Cracow is Oświęcim, better known by its German name, **Auschwitz.** Here 4 million

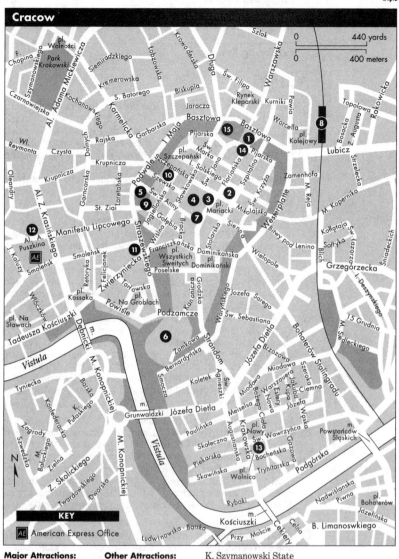

Cracow

0 — 440 yards
0 — 400 meters

Major Attractions:
Jagiellonian
University, **5**
Kosciót Mariacki, **3**
Rynek Glówny, **2**
St. Florian's Gate, **1**
Sukiennice, **4**
Wawel Castle and
Cathedral, **6**

Other Attractions:
Barbican, **14**
Central Station, **8**
Czártoryski
Museum, **15**
Ethnographic
Museum, **13**
Helena Modrzejewska
Stary Theater, **10**
Jagiellonian
University Museum, **9**

K. Szymanowski State
Philharmonic Hall, **11**
National Museum, **12**
St. Adalbert
Romanesque
Church, **7**

KEY

AE American Express Office

victims, mostly Jews, were executed by the Nazis in the Ausch-witz and Birkenau concentration camps. Auschwitz is now a museum, with restored crematoria and barracks housing dra-matic displays of Nazi atrocities. The buildings at Birkenau, a 15-minute walk away, have been left just as they were found in 1945 by the Soviet Army. Oświęcim itself is an industrial town with good connections from Cracow; buses and trains leave Cracow approximately every hour, and signs in Oświęcim di-rect visitors to the camp. *Auschwitz: admission free. Open Mar. and Nov., Tues.–Sun. 8–4; Apr. and Oct., Tues.–Sun. 8–5; May and Sept., daily 8–6; June–Aug., daily 8–7; Dec.– Feb., Tues.–Sun. 8–3. Birkenau: open all times.*

Wieliczka, about 8 kilometers (5 miles) southeast of Cracow, is the oldest salt mine in Europe, in operation since the end of the 13th century. It is famous for its magnificent underground chapel hewn in crystal rock, the **Chapel of the Blessed Kinga.** *Wieliczka Mines. Admission: zł 2,000. Open Apr.–Oct. 8–6; Nov.–Mar. 8–4. Guided tours only.*

Częstochowa, 120 kilometers (70 miles) from Cracow and reached by regular trains and buses, is the home of the holiest shrine in a country that is more than 90% Catholic. Inside the 14th-century **Pauline monastery** on Jasna Góra (Light Hill) is the famous *Black Madonna,* a painting of Our Lady of Częst-ochowa attributed by legend to St. Luke. It was here that an invading Swedish army was halted in 1655 and finally driven out of the country. About 25 miles southwest of Cracow is the little town of **Wadowice,** birthplace of Pope John Paul II. *Wadowice Museum. Admission: zł 20,000 adults, zł 10,000 children. Open Tues.–Sat. 10–3, Sun. 10–5.*

Dining and Lodging

For details and price-category definitions, *see* Dining and Lodging in Staying in Poland.

Cracow Dining
★

Balaton. Sitting on benches at trestle tables, you can sample good Hungarian cuisine in this popular folksy restaurant. *Ul. Grodzka 37, tel. 012/22–04–69. Reservations accepted. AE, DC, MC, V. Moderate.*

Kurza Stopka. This crowded restaurant has a limited range of dishes, but the food is good and service friendly. *Plac Wszystkich Świętych 9, tel. 012/22–91–96. No reservations. No credit cards. Inexpensive.*

Tunis Bar. This busy, self-service bar offers delicious Tunisian dishes, which are slightly exotic for Cracow. *Plac Domin-ikański 1. No reservations. No credit cards. Budget.*

Lodging

Dom Turysty. This 1960s-era hotel stands opposite the Planty park, facing the walls of the Bernadine convent. The accommo-dation is standard but comfortable. *Westerplatte 15, tel. 012/ 22–95–66. 129 rooms, ½ with bath. Facilities: self-service res-taurant. No credit cards. Moderate.*

Hotel Pollera. This 19th-century hotel on the edge of the Old Town has recently had a face-lift after being restored to private ownership. It is well located, and the management is keen to create a family atmosphere. *Ul Szpitalna 40, tel. 012/22–10– 44. 77 rooms, ½ with bath. Facilities: restaurant. No credit cards. Moderate.*

Europejski. This small, older hotel overlooking the Planty park has seen better days, so make sure you see your room before you accept it. *Ul. Lubicz 5, tel. 012/22–09–11. 55 rooms, some with bath. No credit cards. Inexpensive.*

Warszawski. This late-19th-century hotel opposite the main railway station has seen better days, although it is clean and the location central. Take breakfast in the café next door. *Ul. Pawia 6, tel. 012/22–06–22. No facilities. No credit cards. Inexpensive.*

Krakowianka. This hotel is somewhat the worse for wear and has only three-person rooms (one double), but it offers acceptable low-budget accommodation in the Old Town. *Żywiecka Boczna 2, tel. 012/66–41–91. 25 rooms. No credit cards. Budget.*

Częstochowa
Lodging

Centralny. The Centralny makes a good base for exploring the Pauline monastery, and since most of the other guests are pilgrims, the atmosphere is an interesting mixture of piety and good fun. *Ul. Piłsudskiego 9, tel. 833/440–67. 62 rooms, most with bath or shower. No credit cards. Inexpensive.*

Gdańsk and the North

In contrast to Cracow and the south, Poland north of Warsaw is the land of medieval castles and châteaus, dense forests and lakes, and beaches along the Baltic coast. Rail services in the region are good, although you may prefer going straight to Gdańsk and making excursions from there.

Getting Around

Gdańsk is a major transportation hub, with an airport just outside town (and good bus connections to downtown) and major road and rail connections with the rest of the country.

Tourist Information

Gdańsk (Ul. Heweliusza 8, tel. 058/31–03–38; Orbis, pl. Górskiego 1, tel. 058/31–49–44).
Ostróda (Orbis, ul. Czarnieckiego 10, tel. 889–82/35–57).
Płock (Ul. Tuńska 4, tel. 824/226–00; Orbis, al. Jachowa 47, tel. 824/229–89).
Toruń (Ul. Kopernika 27, tel. 856/272–99; Orbis, ul. Żeglarska 31, tel. 856/261–30).

Exploring Gdańsk and the North

Płock is a day trip from Warsaw by PKS bus. Once you get through Płock's industrial area, you'll find a lovely medieval city that was, for a short time, capital of Poland. Worth seeing are the 12th-century cathedral, where two Polish kings are buried, and the dramatic 14th-century Teutonic castle. Continue through Włocławek to Toruń, where an overnight stay is recommended.

Toruń, birthplace of Nicolaus Copernicus, is also within easy reach (three hours) of Warsaw by train. It is an interesting medieval city that grew wealthy due to its location on the north-south trading route along the Vistula. Its old town district is a remarkably successful blend of Gothic buildings—churches, town hall, and burghers' homes—with Renaissance and Baroque patricians' houses. The Town Hall's Tower (1274)

Gdańsk and the North

is the oldest town hall building in Poland. Don't leave without trying some of Toruń's famous gingerbread and honey cakes.

North from Toruń lie some of the oldest towns, castles, and churches in Poland. You should not miss **Malbork,** on the main rail route from Warsaw to Gdańsk (be sure your train stops there). This huge castle, 58 kilometers (36 miles) from Gdańsk, was one of the most powerful strongholds in medieval Europe. From 1308 to 1457, it was the residence of the Grand Masters of the Teutonic Order. The Teutonic Knights were a thorn in Poland's side until their defeat at the battle of Grunwald in 1410. Inside Malbork castle is a museum with beautiful examples of amber—including lumps as large as melons and pieces containing perfect specimens of prehistoric insects. *tel. 850/06-33-64. Open Tues.-Sat. 10-3, Sun. 10-5. Admission: zł 20,000 adults, zł 10,000 children.*

Gdańsk, once the free city of Danzig, is another of Poland's beautifully restored towns, displaying a rich heritage of Gothic, Renaissance, and Mannerist architecture. This is where the first shots of World War II were fired and where the free trade union Solidarity was born after strikes in 1980. The city's old town has a wonderful collection of historic town houses and narrow streets. The splendid Długa and Długi Targ streets (best for shopping) form the axis of the city and are good starting points for walks into other districts. The evocative **Solidarity Monument** outside the Lenin shipyards was erected in honor of workers killed there by the regime during strikes in 1970. The nearby town of **Sopot** is Poland's most popular seaside resort.

Most of the small towns in the scenic Mazurian lake district southeast of Gdańsk can be reached by public transport if you are persistent and have plenty of time to spare. The area is rich in nature and wildlife, as well as in places of historical interest. The medieval town of **Olsztyn,** once administered and fortified by Copernicus, is well worth a visit, as is **Olsztynek,** where the **Museum of Folk Buildings** has a collection of timber buildings from different parts of the country. They include a small Mazurian thatch-roofed church, an inn, a mill, a forge, old windmills, and thatched cottages, some of which have been furnished period-style. *Tel. 889/19–24–64. Admission: zł 25,000 adults, zł 10,000 children. Open May–Sept., Tues.–Sun. 9–4; closed Mon.*

Both Olsztyn and Olsztynek can be reached by PKS bus from Warsaw or Gdańsk.

Dining and Lodging

For details and price-category definitions, *see* Dining and Lodging in Staying in Poland.

Gdańsk **Kaszubska.** The specialties here come from Kashubia. Smoked
Dining fish dishes are highly recommended. *Ul. Kartuska 76, tel. 058/*
★ *32–06–02. Reservations advised. AE, DC, MC, V. Moderate.*

Pod Wieżą. This restaurant has a reputation for good meat dishes and generous portions. *Piwna 51, tel. 058/31–39–24. Reservations advised. AE, DC, MC, V. Moderate.*

Jantar. This centrally located restaurant has a wide selection on the menu and friendly service. *Ul. Długi Targ 19, tel. 058/ 31–13–93. Reservations accepted. AE, DC, MC, V. Inexpensive.*

Karczma Michał. This dockside restaurant serves generous helpings of good food in a bustling, cheerful atmosphere. *Ul. Jana z Kolna 8, tel. 058/31–05–35. No reservations. No credit cards. Budget.*

Lodging **Jantar.** This small hotel is picturesquely situated in the heart of the Old Town—which largely compensates for the slightly shabby furnishings. *Ul. Długi Targ 19, tel. 058/31–27—16. 42 rooms, ½ with bath. Facilities: restaurant. AE, DC, MC, V. Moderate.*

★ **Maryla.** This pension near Sopot's wooded northern beach offers homely comforts and is near public transport to Gdańsk. *Ul. Sępia 22, Sopot, tel. 058/51–00–34. 16 rooms with bath. No credit cards. Moderate.*

Dom Turysty PTTK. This sea-view tourist hotel is clean and comfortable with easy transport links to Gdańsk. *Ul. Zamkowa Góra 25, Sopot, tel. 058/51–80–11. 150 rooms, most with bath. Facilities: restaurant. AE, DC, MC, V. Inexpensive.*

Sopot. With easy access to the Sopot beach, and on main bus and trolley-bus routes into Gdańsk, this hotel offers comfortable accommodation in three pavilions set in wooded grounds. *Ul. Haffnera 81–85, tel. 058/51–57–51. 120 rooms, most with bath. No credit cards. Inexpensive.*

Piast. Attractively sited by the beach and woods of Gdańsk's northern Jelitkowo district, this small single-story hotel is a peaceful retreat from the bustle of the city center. *Ul. Piastowska 199–201, tel. 058/53–09–28. 68 rooms, most with bath. No credit cards. Budget.*

Zabianka. Situated between Gdańsk and Sopot, this small hotel is near transport routes. *Ul. Dickmana 15, tel. 058/52–27–72, 26 rooms, most with bath. No credit cards. Budget.*

Olsztyn
Lodging

Orbis may be able to locate private rooms for you. Otherwise, there is the **Orbis Novotel** *(Ul. Sielska 4A, tel. 889/27–60–81), which is expensive.*

Toruń
Dining

Polonia. The Art Nouveau decor in this hotel restaurant has a certain faded charm, and the food is plain and wholesome. *Plac Teatralny 5, tel. 856/230–28. Moderate.*

Zajazd Staropolski. This restaurant features excellent meat dishes and soups in a restored 17th-century interior. *Ul. Żeglarska 10/14, tel. 856/260–60. Reservations advised. Moderate.*

Wodnik. This large café along the banks of the Vistula is very popular with locals. *Blwd. Filadelfijski, tel. 856/287–55. No credit cards. Inexpensive.*

Lodging

Kosmos. A functional 1960s hotel, Kosmos is beginning to show signs of wear and tear. It is situated near the river, in the city center. *Ul. Portowa 2, tel. 856/270–85. 180 rooms, most with bath or shower. AE, DC, MC, V. Moderate.*

★ **Zajazd Staropolski.** This Gromada hotel in a converted Renaissance granary has been recently redecorated and is homely and comfortable. *Ul. Żeglarska 10–14, tel. 856/260–60. 36 rooms with bath. AE, DC, MC, V. Inexpensive.*

20 Portugal

First-time visitors to Portugal are often surprised by the relatively low cost of travel throughout the country. Although prices have been on the rise here for several years, especially in Lisbon, transportation, dining, and lodging rates remain among the lowest in Europe. Budget travelers in Portugal can indulge in the "good life" that is all too often prohibitively expensive in other European countries: Superb alfresco meals, fine wines, and comfortable accommodations in country inns and *pousadas* (small, government-owned accommodations, some of historic importance) at nearly giveaway prices are a reality in Portugal. Café and restaurant meals, in particular, represent excellent values, and you should find the food fresh from the sea or market and prepared in portions so huge that you may consider ordering a *meia dose* (half-portion) or sharing an entrée with your companion.

Given its long Atlantic coastline, it isn't surprising that Portugal has been a maritime nation for most of its history. The valor of its seamen is well known; from the charting of the Azores archipelago in 1427 to the discovery of Japan in 1542, Portuguese explorers unlocked the major sea routes to southern Africa, India, the Far East, and the Americas. To commemorate this great era of exploration, a period that reached its height in the 15th century under the influence of Prince Henry the Navigator, the years 1988 to 2000 have been set aside for various celebrations throughout the country.

Despite its sailors' worldly adventures, Portugal itself has remained relatively undiscovered. Although it shares the Iberian Peninsula with Spain, it attracts far fewer visitors—a strange fact, because Portugal has much to recommend it to tourists: fine beaches, beautiful castles, charming fishing villages, excellent restaurants, and colorful folk traditions.

Portugal

0   50 miles

0   50 km

N

ATLANTIC OCEAN

Minho

Valença

Viana do Castelo

Barcelos

Póvoa de Varzim

Vila do Conde

Oporto

Espinho

Albergaria-a-Velha

Aveiro

Mealhada

Mira

Figueira da Foz

Lima

Serra do Gerês N103

N101

Braga

Guimarães

Amarante

Penafiel

Tâmega

Chaves

Bragança

Mirandela

N15

Vila Real

Douro

Lamego

Moimenta da Beira

Mogadouro

Sabor

Duoro

Oliveira dos Azeméis

Douro

S. Pedro do Sul

Vouga

Viseu

Pinhel

Sta. Comba Dão

Mondego

Cantanhede

Coimbra

Arganil

Serra da Estrêla

Guarda

Covilhã

Fundão

Penamacor

E1/A1

Pombal

N110

Zêzere

Serra da Gardunha

N233

Leiria

Nazaré

Alcobaça

Caldas da Rainha

Óbidos

Batalha

Sra. do Aire

Ourém

Tomar

Fátima

Proença-a-Nova

Castelo Branco

N109

Abrantes

Nisa

N118

Tagus

S P A I N

Torres Novas

Aveiras de Cima

Torres Vedras

Mafra

Tejo

Santarém

Ponte de Sor

Portalegre

Sintra

Cascais

Estoril

N8

Vila Franca de Xira

Sorraia

Avis

Arraiolos

Estremoz

Elvas

Lisbon

N10

Montemor-o-Novo

Sra. de Ossa

Vila Viçosa

Guadiana

Seixal

Setúbal

A2

Cabo Espichel

Sado

Alcácer do Sal

N2

Evora

Reguengos

Ferreira do Alentejo

Moura

E1

Sines

Cabo de Sines

Santiago do Cacem

Beja

Serpa

Odemira

Ourique

Castro Verde

N122

Mértola

Chança

Mira

Monchique

N120

Almodovar

Guadiana

Vila do Bispo

Portimão

Lagos

Cabo de S. Vicente

N125

A L G A R V E

Albufeira

S. Bráz

Faro

Olhão

Tavira

Vila Real de S. António

About the size of Indiana, Portugal is so small that its main attractions can be seen during a short visit; at the country's widest point the distance between the Atlantic and Spain is a mere 240 kilometers (150 miles). Short distances don't mean monotony, however, for this narrow coastal strip of land has more geographic and climatic variations than virtually any other nation in Western Europe.

Although Portugal has seen numerous divisions in modern times, the country has traditionally been divided into six historic provinces. Most visitors head for the low-lying plains of the southern Algarve or the region around the Lisbon/Estoril coast, but as traditional tourist destinations become more crowded, adventurous travelers are trekking in other directions. The northern and central provinces—Minho, Beiras, and Trás-os-Montes—are largely unspoiled, full of tiny villages and splendid scenery. Getting around by public transportation is easy, too, and some of the views you'll get from the trains are among the most spectacular in Europe.

Observant visitors are likely to notice other differences between Portugal's northern and southern regions and people. The northern character is decidedly more Celtic, while in the south, Moorish ancestry is apparent. But throughout the country, the Portuguese people are welcoming wherever you meet them.

For the purposes of this guide, we have concentrated our Exploring sections on the southern part of the country—the section most frequented by foreign visitors—including Lisbon—Portugal's sophisticated capital—and the Algarve.

Essential Information

Before You Go

When to Go The tourist season runs from spring through autumn, but some parts of the country—especially the Algarve, which boasts 3,000 hours of sunshine annually—are balmy even in winter. Hotel prices are greatly reduced between November and February, except in Lisbon where business visitors keep prices uniformly high throughout the year.

Climate Since Portugal's entire coast is on the Atlantic Ocean, the country's climate is temperate year-round. Portugal rarely suffers the extremes of heat that Mediterranean countries do. Even in August, the hottest month, the Algarve is the only region where the midday heat may be uncomfortable, but most travelers go there to swim and soak up the sun. What rain there is falls from November to March; December and January can be chilly outside the Algarve, and very wet to the north, but there is no snow except in the mountains of the Serra da Estrêla in the northeast. The almond blossoms and vivid wildflowers that cover the countryside start to bloom early in February. The dry months, June–September, can turn much of the landscape the tawny color of a lion's hide, but there is always a breeze in the evening in Lisbon, as well as along the Estoril coast west of the capital.

The following are the average daily maximum and minimum temperatures for Lisbon.

Jan.	57F	14C	May	71F	21C	Sept.	79F	26C
	46	8		55	13		62	17
Feb.	59F	15C	June	77F	25C	Oct.	72F	22C
	47	8		60	15		58	14
Mar.	63F	17C	July	81F	27C	Nov.	63F	17C
	50	10		63	17		52	11
Apr.	67F	20C	Aug.	82F	28C	Dec.	58F	15C
	53	12		63	17		47	9

Currency The unit of currency in Portugal is the *escudo*, which can be divided into 100 centavos. Escudos come in bills of 100$00, 500$00, 1,000$00, 5,000$00, and 10,000$00. (In Portugal the dollar sign stands between the escudo and the centavo.) Coins come in 1$00, 2$50, 5$00, 10$00, 20$00, 50$00, 100$00, and 200$00. Newly minted 1$00, 5$00, and 10$00 yellow-colored coins can be confused for older coins still in circulation, so make sure you know exactly what you're spending.

At press time (summer 1992), the exchange rate was 112$00 to the U.S. dollar and 255$00 to the pound sterling. Owing to the complications of dealing in millions of escudos, 1,000$00 is always called a *conto*, so 10,000$00 is referred to as 10 contos. Credit cards are accepted in all the larger shops and restaurants, as well as in hotels; however, better exchange rates are obtained in banks and *cambios* (exchange offices). Short-changing is rare, but, as in every country, restaurant bills should be checked. Change in post offices and railway booking offices should also be counted. Shopkeepers are usually honest.

What It Will Cost While the cost of hotels and restaurants in Portugal is still reasonable, inflation is pushing prices up to levels approaching those found in the more affluent countries in northern Europe. Some of Portugal's best food bargains are to be enjoyed in its many simple seaside restaurants. The most expensive areas are Lisbon, the Algarve, and the tourist resort areas along the Tagus estuary. The least expensive areas are country towns, which all have reasonably priced hotels and *pensões*, or pensions, as well as numerous café-type restaurants. A sales, or value-added, tax (called IVA) of 8% is imposed on hotel and restaurant bills.

Sample Prices Cup of coffee, 80$00; bottle of beer, 110$00; soft drink, 150$00; bottle of house wine, 650$00; ham sandwich, 175$00; 1-mile taxi ride, 300$00; city bus ride, 125$00; museum entrance, 200$00.

Customs on Arrival Non–European-Community (EC) visitors over age 17 are allowed to bring the following items into Portugal duty-free: 200 cigarettes or 250 grams of tobacco, 1 liter of liquor (over 22% volume) or 2 liters (under 22% volume), 2 liters of wine, 100 ml of perfume, and a reasonable amount of personal effects (camera, binoculars, etc). There is no limit on money brought into the country. However, no more than 100,000$00 in Portuguese currency or the equivalent of 500,000$00 in foreign currency may be taken out without proof that an equal amount or more was brought into Portugal. Computerized customs services make random and often thorough checks on arrival.

Language Portuguese is easy to read by anyone with even slight knowledge of a Latin language, but it is difficult to pronounce and understand (most people speak quickly and elliptically). However, you will find that in the larger cities and major resorts many people, especially the young, speak English and, occasionally, French. In the country, people are so friendly and eager to be helpful that visitors can usually make themselves understood in sign language.

Getting Around

By Train The Portuguese railway system is surprisingly extensive for such a small country, and ticket prices are very reasonable. Trains are clean and leave on time, but there are few express runs except between Lisbon and Oporto. These take just over three hours for the 210-mile journey. Most trains have first- and second-class compartments; suburban lines around Lisbon have a single class. Tickets should be bought, and seats reserved if desired, at the stations or through travel agents, two or three days in advance. Advance reservations are essential on Lisbon–Oporto express trains. Timetables are mostly the same on Saturday and Sunday as on weekdays, except on suburban lines. **Wasteels–Expresso** (Ave. António Augusto Aguiar 88, 1000 Lisbon, tel. 01/579180) is reliable for all local and international train tickets and reservations.

Special **tourist passes** can be obtained through travel agents or at main train stations. These are valid for periods of 7, 14, or 21 days for first- and second-class travel on any domestic train service; mileage is unlimited. At press time (summer 1992), the cost was 15,200$00 for 7 days; 24,200$00 for 14 days; and 34,600$00 for 21 days. Child passes cost exactly half those amounts.

International trains to Madrid, Paris, and other parts of Europe depart from the Santa Apolonia Station in Lisbon and Campanhã in Oporto.

By Bus The nationalized bus company, **Rodoviaria Nacional,** has passenger terminals in Lisbon (Ave. Casal Ribeiro 18, tel. 01/577715), with regular bus services throughout Portugal. Several private companies offer luxury service between major cities. For information and reservations in Lisbon, contact the main tourist office (*see* Important Addresses and Numbers *in Lisbon, below*) or **Mundial Turismo** (Ave. António Augusto de Aguiar 90–A, tel. 01/563521). Most long-distance buses have toilet facilities, and the fares are often cheaper than for trains.

By Boat Ferries across the river Tagus leave from Praça do Comércio, Cais do Sodré, and Belém. From June to September, a two-hour boat excursion leaves the ferry station at Praça do Comércio in Lisbon daily at 2:30 PM for Paço d'Arcos. The price is 2,500$00. There are also cruises to Cascais; details from **Transtejo** (Terreiro do Paço, tel. 01/875058).

Boat trips on the river Douro (Oporto) are organized from May to October by **Porto Ferreira** (Rua da Cavalhosa, 19, Vila Nova de Gaia, Oporto). They leave every day on the hour, except Saturday afternoon and Sunday.

By Bicycle **Tip Tours** (Ave. Costa Pinto 91-A, 2750 Cascais, tel. 01/2865150) rents out bicycles by the day or half day. **Cycle Portugal** (Roatan Charter, Box 877, San Antonio, FL 34266, USA, tel. 800/282–8932 or, in Portugal, tel. 01/4533759) offers bicycle tours throughout the country with accommodations in first-class hotels. Each tour is accompanied by a guide, a mechanic, and a van for luggage.

Staying in Portugal

Telephones Pay phones take 10$00, 20$00, and 50$00 coins; 10$00 is the minimum payment for short local calls (some pay phones may not accept the newly minted yellow-colored coins). Some specially marked pay phones will accept plastic phone cards, which can be purchased at post offices and most tobacconist shops. Long-distance calls cost less from 8 PM to 7 AM. All telephone calls are more expensive when made from a hotel, so it is wise to make international calls from a post office, where you will be assigned a private booth. Collect calls can also be made from post offices, and some telephone booths accept international calls.

Mail Postal rates, both domestic and foreign, increase twice a year. Country post offices close for lunch and at 6 PM on weekdays; they are not open on weekends. Main post offices in towns are open weekdays 8:30 to 6 with no midday closings. In Lisbon, the post office in the Praça dos Restauradores is open daily until 10 PM.

Receiving Mail Mail can be sent in care of American Express Star (Ave. Sidonio Pais 4, 1000 Lisbon, tel. 01/539841); there is no service charge. Main post offices also accept poste restante letters.

Shopping Bargaining is not common in city stores or shops, but it is sometimes possible in flea markets, antiques shops, and outdoor markets that sell fruit, vegetables, and household goods. The **Centro de Turismo Artesanato** (Rua Castilho 61, 1200 Lisbon) will ship goods abroad even if they were not bought in Portugal. By air to the United States, parcels take about three weeks; by sea, two months.

IVA Refunds IVA is included in the price of goods, but the tax on items over a certain value can be reclaimed, although the methods are time-consuming. For Americans and other non-EC residents, the tax paid on individual items costing more than 10,000$00 can be reclaimed on presentation of receipts to special departments in airports (in Lisbon, near Gate 23). For British citizens and other EC visitors, a more complicated procedure must be followed, which involves claiming the tax refund from customs officials when returning home; tax may be reclaimed on items worth more than 53,000$00. Shops specializing in IVA-refund purchases are clearly marked throughout the country, and shop assistants can help with the forms.

Opening and Closing Times **Banks.** Banks are open weekdays 8:30 to 3 PM; they do not close for lunch. There are automatic currency-exchange machines in Lisbon in the Praça dos Restauradores and in major cities.

Museums. Museums are usually open 10–12:30 and 2–5. Most close on Sunday afternoon, and they are all closed on Monday. Most palaces close on Tuesday.

Shops. Shops are open weekdays 9–1 and 3–7, Saturdays 9–1. Shopping malls and supermarkets in Lisbon and other cities remain open until 10 PM or midnight and are often open on Sunday.

National Holidays January 1; February 23 (Carnival, Shrove Tuesday); April 9 (Good Friday); April 25 (Anniversary of the Revolution); May 1 (Labor Day); June 10 (National Day); June 18 (Corpus Christi); August 15 (Assumption); October 5 (Day of the Republic); November 1 (All Saints Day); December 1 (Independence Day); December 8 (Immaculate Conception); December 25.

Dining Eating is taken quite seriously in Portugal, and, not surprisingly, seafood is a staple. Freshly caught lobster, crab, shrimp, tuna, sole, and squid are prepared in innumerable ways, but if you want to sample a little bit of everything, try *caldeirada*, a piquant stew made with whatever is freshest from the sea. In the Algarve, *cataplana* is a must: It's a mouth-watering mixture of clams, ham, tomatoes, onions, garlic, and herbs, named for the dish in which it is cooked. There are some excellent local wines, and in modest restaurants even the *vinho da casa* (house wine) is usually very good. Water is generally safe, but visitors may want to drink bottled water—*sem gas* for still, *com gas* for fizzy—from one of the many excellent Portuguese spas.

Mealtimes Lunch usually begins around 1 PM; dinner is served at about 8 PM.

Dress and Jacket and tie are advised for the most expensive restaurants in
Reservations Lisbon, but otherwise casual dress is acceptable. Unless noted, reservations are not necessary.

Ratings Prices are per person, without alcohol. Taxes and service are usually included, but a tip of 5%–10% is always appreciated. All restaurants must post a menu with current prices in a window facing the street. Best bets are indicated by a star ★.

Category	All Areas
Moderate	3,000$00–5,000$00
Inexpensive	1,500$00–3,000$00
Budget	under 1,500$00

Lodging Visitors have a wide choice of lodging in Portugal, which offers some of the lowest rates in Europe for accommodations. Hotels are graded from one to five stars, as are the smaller inns called *estalagems*, which usually provide breakfast only. *Pensões* go up to four stars and often include meals. The state-subsidized *pousadas*, most of which are situated in castles, old monasteries, or have been built where there is a particularly fine view, are five-star luxury properties. *Residencias* (between a pensõe and a hotel) are located in most towns and larger villages; most rooms have private baths or showers, and breakfast is usually included in the charge. They are a good value, around 3,000$00–5,000$00, but usually they have only a few rooms from which to choose. Therefore, we don't review many residencias under Lodging, below.

A recent innovation is *Turismo de Habitacão* (Country House Tourism), in which private homeowners all over the country offer visitors a room and breakfast (and sometimes provide dinner on request). This is an excellent way to experience life on a country estate or in a small village. Details are available from Avenida António Augusto Aguiar 86, 1000 Lisbon, tel. 01/575015.

Tourist offices can help visitors with hotel or other reservations and will provide lists of the local hostelries without charge. Few international chains have hotels in Portugal.

Camping Camping has become increasingly popular in Portugal in recent years, and there are now more than 100 campsites throughout the country offering a wide range of facilities. The best equipped have markets, swimming pools, and tennis courts. For additional information, contact **Federação Portuguesa de Campismo** (Ave. 5 Outubro 15-3, 1000 Lisbon, tel. 01/523308).

Ratings Prices are for two people in a double room, based on high-season rates. Highly recommended lodgings are indicated by a star ★.

Category	All Areas
Moderate	14,000$00–20,000$00
Inexpensive	8,000$00–14,000$00
Budget	under 8,000$00

Tipping In Portugal, modest tips are usually expected by those who render services. Service is included in bills at hotels and most restaurants. Otherwise tip 5%–10% on restaurant bills, except at inexpensive establishments, where you may just leave any coins given in change. Taxi drivers get 10%; cinema and theater ushers who seat you, 20$00 to 50$00; train and airport porters, 100$00 per bag; service-station attendants, 10$00–20$00 for gas, 20$00–50$00 for checking tires and cleaning windshields; hairdressers, around 10%.

Lisbon

Arriving and Departing

By Plane Lisbon's Portela Airport (tel. 01/802060) is only about 20 minutes from the city by taxi. The airport is small, but has been recently modernized.

Between the Airport and Downtown There is a special bus service from the airport into the city center called the *Linha Verde* (Green Line), but taxis here are so much cheaper than in other European capitals that visitors would be wise to take a taxi straight to their destination. The cost into Lisbon is about 800$00, and to Estoril or Sintra, 4,500$00. There are no trains or subways between the airport and the city.

By Train International trains from Paris and Madrid arrive at Santa Apolonia Station (tel. 01/876025), in the center of the city. There is a tourist office at the station and plenty of taxis and porters.

Getting Around

Lisbon is a hilly city, and the sidewalks are paved with cobblestones, so walking can be tiring, even when you're wearing comfortable shoes. Fortunately, Lisbon's tram service is one of the best in Europe and buses go all over the city. A **Tourist Pass** for unlimited rides on the tram or bus costs 1,550$00 for a week or 1,100$00 for four days; it can be purchased at the Cais do Sodré Station and other terminals. Books of 20 discount tickets are also available.

By Tram and Bus Buses and trams operate from 6 AM to 1 AM. Try tram routes 13, 24, 28, 29, and 30 for an inexpensive tour of the city; buses nos. 52 and 53 cross the Tagus bridge. Many of the buses are double-deckers, affording an exceptional view of the city's architecture, which includes a remarkable number of Art Nouveau buildings. There's a flat fare of 125$00 per journey.

By Subway The subway, called the Metropolitano, operates from 6:30 AM to 1 AM; it is modern and efficient but covers a limited route. You're unlikely to use it, but if you do—watch out for pickpockets during rush hour.

By Taxi Taxis here are among the cheapest in Europe—even the tightest budget can allow for a few taxi rides around Lisbon. There are ranks in the main squares, and you can hail a cruising vehicle, though this can be difficult late at night. Taxis take up to four passengers at no extra charge. Rates start at 130$00.

Important Addresses and Numbers

Tourist Information The main Lisbon tourist office (tel. 01/3463643) is located in the Palacio Foz, Praça dos Restauradores, at the Baixa end of the Avenida da Liberdade, the main artery of the city; open Mon.– Sat. 9–8, Sun. 10–6. The tourist office at Lisbon airport (tel. 01/893689) is open daily 9–midnight, and the office at Avenida António Augusto Aguiar 86 (tel. 01/575086) is open daily 9–6.

Embassies **U.S.** (Av. Forças Armadas, tel. 01/726–6600); **Canadian** (Av. da Liberdade 144-3, tel. 01/3474892); **U.K.** (Rua S. Domingos à Lapa 37, tel. 01/3961191).

Emergencies **SOS Emergencies** (tel. 115). **Police** (tel. 01/3466141). **Ambulance** (tel. 01/301–7777). **Fire Brigade** (tel. 01/606060). **Doctor:** British Hospital (Rua Saraiva de Carvalho 49, tel. 01/602020; night: 01/603785). You can also contact native English-speaking doctors at tel. 01/554113 (Lisbon) and tel. 01/2845317 (Cascais).

Exploring Lisbon

North of the river Tagus estuary, spread out over a string of hills, Portugal's capital presents unending treats for the eye. Its wide boulevards are bordered by black-and-white mosaic sidewalks made up of tiny cobblestones called *calçada*. Modern, pastel-colored apartment blocks vie for attention with Art Nouveau houses faced with decorative tiles. Winding, hilly streets provide scores of *miradouros*, natural vantage points that offer spectacular views of the bay.

Lisbon is not a city that is easily explored on foot. The steep inclines of many streets present a tough challenge to the casual tourist, and visitors are often surprised to find that, because of the hills, places that appear to be close to one another on a map are actually on different levels. Yet the effort is worthwhile— judicious use of trams, a funicular railway, and the majestic city-center elevator make walking tours enjoyable even on the hottest summer day.

With a population of around a million, Lisbon is a small capital by European standards. Its center stretches north from the spacious Praça do Comércio, one of the largest riverside squares in Europe, to the Rossio, a smaller square lined by shops and sidewalk cafés. This district is known as the Baixa

(Low District), and it is one of the earliest examples of town planning on a large scale. The grid of parallel streets between the two squares was built after an earthquake and tidal wave destroyed much of the city in 1755.

The Alfama, the old Moorish quarter that survived the earthquake, lies just to the east of the Baixa, while Belém, where many of the royal palaces and museums are situated, is about 3.2 kilometers (2 miles) to the west.

Numbers in the margin correspond to points of interest on the Lisbon map.

Castelo de São The Moors, who imposed their rule on most of the southern
Jorge and the Iberian Peninsula during the 8th century, left their mark on
Alfama Lisbon in many ways. The most visible examples are undoubtedly the imposing castle, set on one of the city's highest hills; and the Alfama, a district of narrow, twisting streets that wind their way up toward the castle. The best way to tour this area of Lisbon is to take a taxi—they're plentiful and cheap—to the castle and walk down; otherwise you'll have little energy left for sightseeing. Several trams also run to the Alfama: take the No. 28 from Rua Conceicão in the Baixa or the No. 12 from Largo Martim Monez, northwest of Rossio.

1 Although the **Castelo de São Jorge** (St. George's Castle) is Moorish in construction, it stands on the site of a fortification used by the Visigoths in the 5th century. Today its idyllic atmosphere is shattered only by the shrieks of the many peacocks that strut through the grounds, a well-tended area that is also home to swans, turkeys, ducks, ravens, and other birds. The castle walls enclose an Arabian palace that formed the residence of the kings of Portugal until the 16th century; there is also a small village lived in by artists and craftspeople. Panoramic views of Lisbon can be seen from the castle walls, but visitors should take care, since the uneven, slippery surfaces have barely been touched for centuries. *Admission free. Open Apr.–Sept., daily 9–9; Oct.–Mar., daily 9–7.*

2 After leaving the castle by its impressive gate, wander down through the warren of streets that make up the **Alfama.** This jumble of whitewashed houses, with their flower-laden balconies and red-tile roofs, managed to survive devastating earthquakes because it rests on foundations of dense bedrock. The Alfama district is a notorious place for getting lost in, but it's relatively compact and you'll keep coming upon the same main squares and streets. Find your way to the Largo Rodrigues de Freitas, a street to the east of the castle, then take a look at the **3** **Museu da Marioneta** (Puppet Museum) at No. 19A (Admission: 200$00. Open Tues.–Sun. 11–1 and 3–6). From there head south along the Rua de São Tome to the Largo das Portas do **4** Sol, where you'll find the **Museu de Artes Decorativas** (Museum of Decorative Arts) in the Fundaçaõ Ricardo Espirito Santo (Admission: 500$00. Open Tues.–Sat. 10–1 and 2:30–5). More than 20 workshops teach rare handicrafts, including bookbinding, ormulu, carving, and cabinetmaking.

Head southwest past the Largo de Santa Luzia along the Rua do Limoeiro, which eventually becomes the Rua Augusto Rosa. **5** This route takes you past the **Sé** (cathedral), which is also worth a visit. Built in the 12th century, the Sé has an austere Romanesque interior; its extremely thick walls bear witness to the

Lisbon

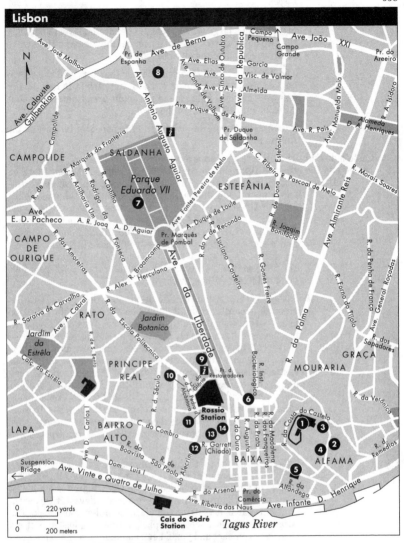

Alfama, **2**

Castelo de São
Jorge, **1**

Elevador da Glória, **9**

Elevador de Santa
Justa, **14**

Gulbenkian
Foundation, **8**

Igreja do Carmo, **13**

Igreja de São
Roque, **11**

Instituto do Vinho do
Porto, **10**

Largo do Chiado, **12**

Museu de Artes
Decorativas, **4**

Museu da Marioneta, **3**

Parque
Eduardo VII, **7**

Rossio, **6**

Sé, **5**

fact that it also served as a fortress. *Largo da Sé. Admission free. Open daily 8:30–noon and 2–6.*

Continue northwest from the cathedral along the Rua de Santo António da Sé, turn left along the Rua da Conceiçao, then right and north up the Rua Augusta. A 10-minute stroll along this street takes you through the **Baixa**, which is also one of Lisbon's main shopping and banking districts. Semipedestrianized, this old-fashioned area boasts a small crafts market, some of the best shoe shops in Europe, and a host of delicatessens selling anything from game birds to *queijo da serra*—a delicious mountain cheese from the Serra da Estrela range north of Lisbon.

Avenida da Liberdade Rua Augusta leads into the **Rossio**, Lisbon's principal square, which in turn opens on its northwestern end into the Praça dos ⑥ Restauradores. This can be considered the beginning of modern Lisbon, for here the broad, tree-lined **Avenida da Liberdade** (sometimes known as the Portuguese Champs-Élysées) begins its northwesterly ascent, and ends just over 1.6 kilometers ⑦ (1 mile) away at the **Parque Eduardo VII** (Edward VII Park).

A leisurely stroll from the Praça dos Restauradores to the park takes about 45 minutes. As you make your way up the Liberdade, you'll find several cafés at its southern end serving coffee and cool drinks. Most notable is the open-air *esplanada* (café), which faces the main post office on the right. You'll also pass through a pleasant mixture of ornate 19th-century architecture and Art Deco buildings from the '30s—a marked contrast to the cool, green atmosphere of the park itself. Rare flowers, trees, and shrubs thrive in the *estufa fria* (cold greenhouse) and the *estufa quente* (hot greenhouse). *Parque Eduardo VII. Admission: 60$00. Open winter, daily 9–5; summer, daily 9–6.*

Turn right from the park and head north along the Avenida António Augusto de Aguiar. A 15-minute walk will bring you to the busy Praça de Espanha, to the right of which, in the Parque ⑧ de Palhava, is the renowned **Gulbenkian Foundation,** a cultural trust. The foundation's art center houses treasures that were collected by Armenian oil magnate Calouste Gulbenkian and donated to the people of Portugal. The collection includes superb examples of Greek and Roman coins, Persian carpets, Chinese porcelain, and paintings by such Old Masters as Rembrandt and Rubens. *Ave. de Berna 45, tel. 01/7935139. Admission: 200$00, free Sun. Open June–Sept., Tues., Thurs., Fri., and Sun. 10–5; Wed. and Sat. 2–7:30; Oct.–May, Tues.–Sun. 10–5; closed Mon. year-round.*

The complex also houses a good modern art museum (same times and price as the main museum) and two concert halls where music and ballet festivals are held during the winter and spring. Modestly priced tickets are available at the box office (tel. 01/774167), thanks to subsidies from the Gulbenkian Foundation.

Bairro Alto Lisbon's **Bairro Alto** (High District) is largely made up of 18th- and 19th-century buildings that house an intriguing mixture of restaurants, theaters, nightclubs, churches, bars, and antiques shops. The best way to start a tour of this area is via the ⑨ **Elevador da Glória** (funicular railway), located on the western side of Avenida da Liberdade by the Praça dos Restauradores. The trip takes about a minute and drops passengers at the São

Pedro de Alcãntara miradouro, a viewpoint that looks toward the castle and the Alfama (Cost: 30$00. Open 5 AM–midnight).

⑩ Across the street from the miradouro is the **Instituto do Vinho do Porto** (Port Wine Institute), where, in its cozy, clublike lounge, visitors can sample from more than 100 brands of Portugal's most famous beverage—from the extra-dry white varieties to the older, ruby-red vintages. *Rua S. Pedro de Alcãntara 45, tel. 01/3423307. Admission free. Prices of tastings vary, starting at 100$00. Open Mon.–Sat. 10–10.*

From the institute, turn right and walk down Rua da Misericórdia. On your left is the Largo Trindade Coelho, site of the
⑪ highly decorative **Igreja de São Roque** (Church of São Roque). The church (open daily 8:30–6) is best known for the flamboyant 18th-century **Capela de São João Baptista** (Chapel of St. John the Baptist), but it is nonetheless a showpiece in its own right. The precious stones that adorn its walls were imported from Italy. Adjoining the church is the **Museu de Arte Sacra** (Museum of Sacred Art). *Admission: 250$00. Open Tues.–Sun. 10–5.*

Continue south down Rua da Misericórdia until you reach the
⑫ **Largo do Chiado** on your left. The Chiado, once Lisbon's chic shopping district, was badly damaged by a fire in August 1988, but it still houses some of the city's most fashionable department stores. An ambitious building program is restoring the area's former glory.

North of the Chiado, on the Largo do Carmo, lies the partially
⑬ ruined **Igreja do Carmo** (Carmo Church), one of the few older structures in the area to have survived the 1755 earthquake. Today open-air orchestral concerts are held beneath its majestic archways during the summer, and its sacristy houses an **archaeological museum.** *Museu Arqueologico. Largo do Carmo. Admission: 250$00. Open May–Sept., Mon.–Sat. 10–6; Oct.–Apr., Mon.–Sat. 10–1 and 2–5.*

Return directly to the Praça dos Restauradores via the nearby
⑭ **Elevador de Santa Justa** (the Santa Justa elevator), which is enclosed in a Gothic tower created by Raul Mesnier, the Portuguese protégé of Gustave Eiffel. *Cost: 28$00. Open 5 AM–midnight.*

An alternative, though somewhat macabre, route can be taken through the fire ruins. A temporary covered walkway has been built through parts of Rua Garrett and Rua do Carmo, and here visitors can see the disastrous effects of the 1988 fire on what was once the heart of sophisticated Lisbon.

Numbers in the margin correspond with points of interest on the Belém map.

Belém To see the best examples of that uniquely Portuguese, late-Gothic architecture known as Manueline, head for Belém at the far southwestern edge of Lisbon. If you are traveling in a group of three or four, taxis are the cheapest means of transportation; otherwise take a No. 15, 16, or 17 tram from the Praça do Comércio for a more scenic, if bumpier, journey.

⑮ Trams Nos. 15 and 16 stop directly outside the **Mosteiro dos Jerónimos,** Belém's Hieronymite monastery, located in the Praça do Império. This impressive structure was conceived and planned by King Manuel I at the beginning of the 16th century

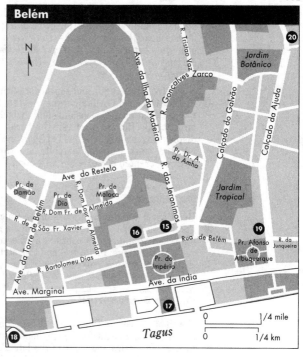

to honor the discoveries of such great explorers as Vasco da Gama, who is buried here. Construction of the monastery began in 1502, and was largely financed by treasures brought back from the so-called *descobrimentos*—the "discoveries" made by the Portuguese in Africa, Asia, and South America. Don't miss the stunning double cloister with its arches and pillars heavily sculpted with marine motifs. *Admission to church free. Closed noon–2. Admission to cloisters: 400$00. Open Oct.–Apr., daily 10–5; May–Sept., daily 10–6:30.*

16 The **Museu de Marinha** (Maritime Museum) is located at the other end of the monastery. Its huge collection reflects Portugal's long seafaring tradition, and exhibitions range from early maps and navigational instruments to entire ships, including the sleek caravels that took Portuguese explorers and traders around the globe. *Admission: 200$00, free Wed. Open Tues.–Sun. 10–5.*

Across from the monastery at the water's edge stands the **17** **Monumento dos Descobrimentos** (Monument to the Discoveries). Built in 1960, this modern tribute to the seafaring explorers stands on what was the departure point of many of their voyages. An interesting mosaic, surrounded by an intricate wave pattern composed of black-and-white cobblestones, lies at the foot of the monument. *Admission for elevator: 225$00. Open Tues.–Sun. 10–5.*

A 15-minute walk west of the monument brings you to the **18** **Torre de Belém** (the Belém Tower), another fine example of Manueline architecture with openwork balconies, loggia, and domed turrets. Although it was built in the early 16th century on an island in the middle of the river Tagus, today the tower stands near the north bank—the river's course has changed over the centuries. *Av. da Torre de Belém and Av. de India. Admission: 250$00. Open Tues.–Sun., 10–6:30 summer, 10–5 winter.*

⑲ Away from the Tagus and southeast of the monastery, on the Praça Afonso de Albuquerque, is the **Museu Nacional do Coches** (National Coach Museum), which houses one of the largest collections of coaches in the world. The oldest vehicle on display was made for Philip II of Spain in the late 16th century, but the most stunning exhibits are three golden Baroque coaches, created in Rome for King John V in 1716. *Admission: summer 400$00, winter 250$00; free Sun. Open summer, Tues.–Sun. 10–1 and 2:30–6:30; winter, Tues.–Sun. 10–1 and 2:30–5:30.*

⑳ Head north of the coach museum on Calçada da Ajuda to the **Palácio da Ajuda** (Ajuda Palace). Once a royal residence, this impressive building now contains a collection of 18th- and 19th-century paintings, furniture, and tapestries. *Largo da Ajuda. Admission: 200$00; free Sun. 10–2. Guided tours arranged on request. Open Thurs.–Tues. 10–5. Closed Wed.*

Off the Beaten Track

North of the city in the suburb of São Domingos de Benfica is one of the most beautiful private houses in the capital. The **Palácio da Fronteira** was built in the late 17th century and contains splendid reception rooms with 18th-century figurative tiles, contemporary furniture, and paintings, but it is the gardens that are unique. A long rectangular water tank is backed by 17th-century tiled panels of heroic-size knights on prancing horses. Stone steps at either side lead to a terraced walk above, between pyramid pavilions roofed with copper-colored tiles. This beautiful conceit is surrounded by a topiary garden, statuary, fountains, and terraces. *Largo de S. Domingos de Benfica 1. Admission to gardens: 300$00; to palace and gardens: 1,000$00. Open Mon.–Sat. for 1-hr. tour, but visitors must arrive between 10:45 and 11 AM.*

Portuguese **bullfighting** is a treat on a summer evening—particularly since the bull is not killed in the ring (although it is killed when the event has finished) but is wrestled to the ground by a group of *forcados* in their traditional red-and-green costumes. The bull, its horns padded, is also fought from horseback in what is a first-class display of the remarkable Portuguese riding skills. The ornate Campo Pequeno (Avenida da República) hosts weekly bullfights from Easter to September, on Sunday afternoons and Thursday evenings. Prices range from 2,000$00 to 8,000$00, depending on the seat.

Shopping

Shopping Districts Fire destroyed much of Lisbon's choicest shopping street in 1988; however, an extensive reconstruction project is well under way. Another important shopping area is in the **Baixa** quarter (between the Rossio and the river Tagus). The blue-and-pink towers of the **Amoreiras,** a huge modern shopping center (open daily 9 AM–11 PM) located on Avenida Engeneiro Duarte Pacheco, dominate the Lisbon skyline.

Flea Markets   A **Feira da Ladra** (flea market) is held on Tuesday morning and all day Saturday in the Largo de Santa Clara behind the Church of São Vicente, near the Alfama district.

Gift Ideas   Fine leather handbags and luggage are sold at **Galeão** (Rua
Leather Goods   Augusto 190) and at **Casa Canada** (Rua Augusta 232). Shoe stores abound in Lisbon, but they may have a limited selection of large sizes (the Portuguese have relatively small feet). Leather gloves can be purchased at a variety of specialty shops on Rua do Carmo and Rua Aurea.

Handicrafts   **Viúva Lamego** (Largo do Intendente 25) has the largest selection of tiles and pottery, while **Fabrica Sant'Ana** (Rua do Alecrim 95), in the Chiado, sells wonderful handpainted ceramics and tiles based on antique patterns. For embroidered goods and baskets, try **Casa Regional da Ilha Verde** (Rua Paiva de Andrade 4) or **Tito Cunha** (Rua Aurea 286). **Casa Quintão** (Rua Ivens 30), probably has the largest selection of *arraiolos* rugs, the traditional, hand-embroidered Portuguese carpets, in town. For fine porcelain, visit **Vista Alegre** (Largo do Chiado 18).

Jewelry and   **Antonio da Silva** (Praça Luis de Camoes 40) at the top of the
Antiques   Chiado, specializes in antique silver and jewelry, as does **Barreto e Goncalves** (Rua das Portas De Santo Antão 17). Most of the antique shops are along the Rua Escola Politecnica, the Rua de São Bento and the Rua de Santa Marta.

Look for characteristic Portuguese gold- and silver-filigree work at **Sarmento** (Rua do Ouro 251).

Dining

For details and price-category definitions, *see* Dining in Staying in Portugal.

Moderate   **Alcântara.** Ranked among the trendier, newer restaurants, this one is smartly decorated with a glorious modernistic design. The menu features traditional Portuguese specialties and a good wine list. *Rua Maria Luisa Holstein 15, tel. 3637176. Reservations necessary. AE, DC, MC, V. Open until 2 AM for dinner only. Closed Tues.*
Comida de Santo. The Brazilian-style food is excellent, and is served in an attractive, bohemian atmosphere. Lively Brazilian music ensures that this restaurant is packed during later hours. *Rua Engenheiro Miguel Pais 39, tel. 01/396-3339. AE, DC, MC, V.*
O Paco. Good steaks, regional food, and folkloric decor attract a literary crowd to this restaurant opposite the Gulbenkian Foundation. *Av. Berna 44, tel. 01/770642. AE, DC, MC, V. Closed Mon.*
Pap' Açorda. This very popular restaurant in the Bairro Alto is housed in a converted bakery. It offers good food and service in a pleasant garden atmosphere. *Rua da Atalaia 57–59, tel. 01/ 3464811. Reservations advised. AE, DC, MC, V. Closed Sat. lunch and Sun.*
Solmar. Located near the Rossio, Lisbon's main square, this large restaurant is best known for its seafood and shellfish, but try the wild boar or venison in season. *Rua Portas de S. Antão 108, tel. 01/346-0010. AE, DC, MC, V.*

Inexpensive **A Quinta.** A menu of Portuguese, Russian, and Hungarian dishes is available at this country-style restaurant that overlooks the Baixa and the Tagus from next to the top of the Santa Justa elevator. *Passarela do Elevador de Santa Justa, at Largo do Carmo, tel. 01/346–5588. AE, DC, MC, V. Closed Sun.*

Cervejaria Trindade. You get good value for your money at this large restaurant, which has a garden and a cave-style wine cellar. *Rua Nova da Trindade 20, tel. 01/342–3506. AE, DC, MC, V.*

Chimarrão. A lively, attractive restaurant near the Roma metro stop, Chimarrão features authentic Brazilian dishes, an extensive salad bar, and a large selection of grilled meats. *Avenida Roma 90 D, tel. 01/800784. MC, V. Closed Sun.*

O Alexandre. This tiny restaurant in Belaem has outdoor tables from which diners, mostly locals, can soak up the superb view of the monastery. The seafood here is served on large platters, so bring your appetite! Try the grilled *peixe espada* (scabbard fish) or one of the more unusual squid or octopus dishes. Note that the restaurant closes at 9:45. *Rue Vieira Portuense 84, Belaem, tel. 01/3634454. No reservations. MC, V. Closed Sat.*

Ribadouro. This bustling basement retaurant, facing the main avenue, fills quickly with locals who come to sample the choice spread of freshly prepared seafood. The surroundings are functional, not fancy, but the layout allows you to watch the chefs preparing crabs and crayfish at the counter. Prices are even more reasonable if you eat at the bar. *Av. di Liberdade 155, tel. 01/549411. Reservations recommended. AE, DC, MC, V.*

Budget **Bonjardim.** Known locally as *Rei dos Frangos* (the King of Chickens), the Bonjardim specializes in the spit-roasted variety. Just off the Restauradores, it gets very crowded at peak hours. *Travesssa S. Antão 11, tel. 01/324389. AE, DC, MC, V.*

Casa Faz Frio. A traditional *adega* (wine cellar) on the edge of the Bairro Alto, this restaurant is decorated with a sea of blue tiles and bunches of garlic suspended from the ceiling. There's a changing menu of Portuguese specialties, and all are good value. *Rua D. Pedro V 96–98, no tel. Reservations not necessary. No credit cards.*

Farah's Tandoori. What appears to be a simple Indian restaurant is really one of the best in Lisbon. The good curries and Indian bread are not to be missed. Two dining floors makes finding a table a manageable task. *Rua de Sant'Ana à Lapa 73, tel. 01/609219. MC, V. Closed Tues.*

Leitaria A Camponeza. The blue-tiled walls in this old-fashioned Baixa *leitaria* (specializing in milk products and pastries) depict bucolic scenes. The coffee, cakes, and sandwiches are all good. *Rua dos Sapateiros 155–157. No credit cards. Closed Sun.*

O Cantinho do Aziz. Hidden in the ring of tiny streets below the castle, this small, family-run Mozambican restaurant offers "Comida Indio-Africana," plenty of rich curried meat and fish dishes served with coconut-flavored rice. The decor is Spartan, but the food comes with a smile. Climb the flight of steps from Poco do Borratem, near Praça da Figueira, to find the entrance. *Rua de S. Lourenço 3–5, tel. 01/876472. Reservations not necessary. No credit cards. Closed Sun.*

Lodging

Lisbon has a good array of accommodations in all price categories, ranging from major international chain hotels to charming
little family-run establishments. During peak season reservations should be made well in advance. For details and price-category definitions, *see* Lodging in Staying in Portugal.

Moderate **Albergaria Senhora do Monte.** The rooms in this unpretentious
★ little hotel, located in the oldest part of town near St. George's
Castle, have terraces that offer some of the loveliest views of
Lisbon, especially at night when the castle and Carmo ruins in
the middle distance are softly illuminated. The top-floor grill
has a picture window. The surrounding neighborhood is quiet,
and parking is available. *Calçada do Monte 39, tel. 01/866002,
fax 01/877783. 28 rooms with bath. Facilities: restaurant, bar,
grill. AE, DC, MC, V.*

Fenix. Located at the top of Avenida da Liberdade, this hotel
has largish guest rooms and a pleasant first-floor lounge. Its
restaurant serves good Portuguese food. *Praça Marquês de
Pombal 8, tel. 01/535121, fax 01/536131. 113 rooms with bath.
Facilities: restaurant. AE, DC, MC, V.*

Florida. This centrally located hotel has a pleasant atmosphere
and is popular with Americans. *Rua Duque de Palmela 32, tel.
01/576145, fax 01/543584. 112 rooms with bath. Facilities: bar.
AE, DC, MC, V.*

★ **Novotel Lisboa.** There's an attentive staff and a quiet, welcoming atmosphere at this pleasant, modern hotel near the U.S.
Embassy. The public rooms are spacious and the guest rooms
attractive. *Av. Jose Malhoa, tel. 01/726–6022, fax 01/726–
6496. 246 rooms with bath. Facilities: pool, garage. AE, MC, V.*

York House. A former 17th-century convent, this residencia is
set in a shady garden, up a long flight of steps, near the Museu
de Arte Antiga (Museum of Ancient Art). It has a good restaurant, and full or half board is available. Book well in advance:
This atmospheric place is small and has a loyal following. *Rua
das Janelas Verdes 32, tel. 01/3962544, fax 01/672793. 54 rooms
with bath. Facilities: restaurant, bar, garden. AE, DC, MC, V.*

Inexpensive **Duas Nacões.** You're paying for the superb location at this
★ *pensão*—right in the heart of the Baixa—rather than for any
particular facilities. The rooms here are comfortable enough,
however, and there is a bar. Try to avoid booking any of the
rooms facing the street—they can be noisy. *Rua da Vitória 41,
tel. 01/3460710. 66 rooms, 42 with bath. Facilities: bar. No credit cards.*

Eduardo VII. An elegant old hotel, the Eduardo is well situated
in the center of the city. The best rooms are in the front, but the
ones in the rear are quieter. The top-floor restaurant has a marvelous view of the city and the Tagus. *Av. Fontes Pereira de
Melo 5, tel. 01/530141, fax 01/53879. 121 rooms with bath. Facilities: restaurant. AE, DC, MC, V.*

Flamingo. Another good value choice near the top of the
Avenida da Liberdade, this hotel has a friendly staff and pleasant guest rooms, though the ones in the front tend to be noisy.
There's a pay parking lot right next door, which is a bonus in
this busy area. *Rua Castilho 41, tel. 01/532191, fax 01/3521216.
39 rooms with bath. Facilities: restaurant, bar, shops. AE, DC,
MC, V.*

Budget **Pensão Arco Bandeira.** It's reasonably quiet at this friendly pensão, despite its location at the bottom of the Rossio. The simple rooms and bathroom down the hall are spotless. *Rua dos Sapateiros 226–4, tel. 01/3423478. 8 rooms. No credit cards.*

Pensão Beira-Minho. The best rooms here have sweeping views over one of Lisbon's busiest squares, Praça da Figueira, so it's a good base for sightseeing in the city center. It's also just across from the Pastelano Sulça, an excellent breakfast spot. *Praça da Figueira, 6–2, tel. 01/3461846. 19 rooms, 12 with bath. No credit cards.*

Pensão Ninho das Aguias. The location is what makes this place special: On the road below the castle, the pensão's attractive garden terrace has superb views over the city center. *Costa do Castelo 74, tel. 01/867000. 16 rooms, 6 with bath. No credit cards.*

Residencial Casa de S. Mamede. Located halfway between the main avenue and Amoreiras shopping center, this attractive, old-fashioned *residencial* is a good value. *Rua da Escola Politecnica 159, tel. 01/3963166. 30 rooms with bath. MC, V.*

The Arts

Two local newspaper supplements provide listings of music, theater, ballet, film, and other entertainment in Lisbon: *Sete*, published on Wednesdays, and *Sabado*, published on Fridays.

Plays are performed in Portuguese at the **Teatro Nacional de D. Maria II** (Praça Dom Pedro IV, tel. 01/322210) year-round except in July, and there are revues at small theaters in the Parque Mayer. Classical music, opera, and ballet are presented in the beautiful **Teatro Nacional de Opera de São Carlos** (Rua Serpa Pinto 9, tel. 01/3465914). Classical music and ballet are also staged from autumn to summer by the **Fundação Calouste Gulbenkian** (Ave. Berna 45, tel. 01/7935139). Of particular interest is the annual Early Music and Baroque Festival held in churches and museums around Lisbon every spring; for details *see* the Gulbenkian Foundation in Exploring Lisbon, *above.* The **Nova Filarmonica,** a recently established national orchestra, performs concerts around the country throughout the year; consult local papers for details.

Nightlife

The most popular night spots in Lisbon are the *adegas tipicas* (wine cellars), where customers dine on Portuguese specialties, drink wine, and listen to *fado* (traditional Portuguese folk music), those haunting melodies unique to Portugal. Most of these establishments are scattered throughout the Alfama and Bairro Alto districts. Try the **Senhor Vinho** (Rua Meio a Lapa 18, tel. 01/672681. Closed Sun.), **Lisboa à Noite** (Rua das Gaveas 69, tel. 01/3468557. Closed Sun.), or the **Machado** (Rua do Norte 91, tel. 01/346–0095. Closed Mon.). The singing starts at 10 PM, and reservations are advised. Lisbon's top spot for live jazz is **The Hot Clube** (Praça da Alegria 39, tel. 01/346–7369. Closed Sun.–Wed.), where sessions don't usually begin until 11 PM.

Discos New discos open and close frequently in Lisbon, and many have high cover charges. Among the more respectable ones are **Ad Lib** (Rua Barata Salgueiro 28–7, tel. 01/561717), **Banana Power** (Rua Cascais 51, tel. 01/3631815), **Stones** (Rua do Olival 1, tel.

01/664545), and **Alcântara-Mar** (Rua da Cozinha Económica 11, tel. 01/649440). The current sensation is **Kremlin** (Rua Escadinhas da Praia 5, tel. 01/665116).

The Portuguese Riviera

Just 32 kilometers (20 miles) west of Lisbon lies a stretch of coastline known as the Portuguese Riviera. Over the years, the casino at Estoril and the beaches, both there and in Cascais, have provided playgrounds for the wealthy, as well as homes for expatriates and exiled European royalty. To the north of these towns lie the lush, green mountains of Sintra and to the northeast, the historic town of Queluz, dominated by its 18th-century rococo palace and formal gardens. Whether you stick to the coast or head for the mountains, you'll find the area is heavily populated with highly varied scenery and attractions.

The villas, châteaus, and luxury *quintas* (country properties) of Sintra contrast notably with Cascais and Estoril, where life revolves around the sea. Beaches here differ both in quality and cleanliness. Some display the blue Council of Europe flag, which signals a high standard of unpolluted water and sands, but others leave much to be desired—be guided by your nose. The waters off Cascais and Estoril are calmer, though sullied as a result of their proximity to the meeting of the sea and Lisbon's Tagus estuary. To the north, around Guincho's rocky promontory and the Praia de Maças coast, the Atlantic Ocean is often windswept and rough but provides good surfing, windsurfing, and scuba diving. The entire region offers comprehensive sports facilities: golf courses, horseback riding, fishing, tennis, squash, swimming, water sports, grand prix racing, mountain climbing, and country walking.

Getting Around

A commuter train leaves every quarter of an hour from Cais do Sodré Station in Lisbon for the trip to Estoril and then to Cascais, four stops farther. The 30-minute-total journey affords splendid sea views as it hugs the shore. A one-way ticket costs 130$00. Trains from Lisbon's Rossio station run every quarter of an hour to Queluz, taking 20 minutes, and on to Sintra, which takes 40 minutes.

Tourist Information

Cascais (Av. Marginal, tel. 01/2868204).
Estoril (Arcadas do Parque, tel. 01/2680113 or 01/2687044).
Sintra (Praça da Republica 3, tel. 01/9231157 or 01/9233919).

Exploring the Portuguese Riviera

Estoril   **Estoril** is filled with grand homes and gardens, and many of its large mansions date from the last century when the resort was a favorite with the European aristocracy. Portugal's jet-set resort is expensive, with little in the way of sights. For those of us who weren't born with a silver spoon in mouth, people-watching is always a satisfying pastime, and one of the best places for it is on the **Tamariz esplanade,** especially from an alfresco restaurant. A palm-studded coastline, plush accommodations, sports facilities, and restaurants are among Estoril's other at-

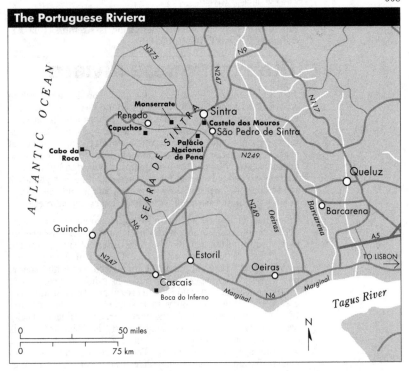

The Portuguese Riviera

tractions, but it is perhaps best known for its **casino,** an excellent gambling hall and night spot that includes a restaurant, bar, theater, and art gallery. A major open-air handicrafts and ceramics fair is held each summer (July–September), and many of the Costa do Sol summer music festival concerts and ballets are staged here (a schedule is available at the tourist office).

Cascais   Cascais lies less than 3.2 kilometers (2 miles) west of Estoril along the train route. A pretty but heavily developed tourist resort, it is packed with shopping centers, restaurants, cinemas, and hotels. The three beaches are small and crowded: even so, there are still some sights worth seeing, including the **Igreja de Nossa Senhora da Assunção** (Church of Our Lady of the Assumption), which contains paintings by Portuguese artist Josefa de Óbidos. *Largo de Igreja. Admission free. Open daily 8–noon and 2–6.*

Less than 2 kilometers (about 1¼ miles) out of the town center, in the direction of Guincho beach, lies the notorious **Boca do Inferno,** or Hell's Mouth. This rugged section of coastline is made up of numerous grottoes; visitors are able to see the full impact of the sea as it pounds into the walkways and viewing platforms. A path leads down to a secluded beach.

Not far from the grottoes, back toward Cascais, is the **Museu Conde de Castro Guimarães** (Museum of the Count of Castro Guimarães), a large, stately home set in spacious grounds. It houses some good paintings, ceramics, furniture, and other items. *Estrada da Boca do Inferno. Admission: 150$00. Open Tues.–Sun. 11–12:30 and 2–5.*

Sintra **Sintra,** full of art, history, and architecture, is one of the country's oldest towns. This is where Portuguese kings and aristocrats formerly had their summer residences. At the center of the **Old Town** near the Hotel Tivoli Sintra stands the 14th-century **Palácio Nacional de Sintra** (Sintra Palace). This twin-chimneyed building, a combination of Moorish and Gothic architectural styles, was once the summer residence of the House of Avis, Portugal's royal lineage. Today it's a museum that houses some fine examples of mozarabic *azulejos* (hand-painted tiles). *Admission: summer 400$00, winter 200$00, free Sun. morning. Open Mon., Tue., and Thurs.–Sun. 10–1 and 2–5.*

If you stand on the steps of the palace and look up toward the Sintra Mountains, you can spot the 8th-century ruins of the **Castelo dos Mouros** (Moors' Castle), which defied hundreds of invaders until it was finally conquered by Dom Afonso Henriques in 1147. For a closer look, follow the steep, partially cobbled road that leads up to the ruins; or, if you're a romantic, rent one of the horse and carriages outside the palace for the trip. From the castle's serrated walls, you can see why its Moorish architects chose the site: The panoramic views falling away on all sides are breathtaking. *Estrada da Pena, tel. 01/9230137. Admission free. Open daily 10–5.*

Farther up the same road you'll reach the **Palácio Nacional de Pena** (the Pena Palace), a Wagnerian-style extravaganza built by the King Consort Ferdinand Saxe-Coburg in 1840. It is a cauldron of clashing styles, from Arabian to Victorian, and was home to the final kings of Portugal, the last of whom went into exile in 1910 after a republican revolt. The nucleus of the palace is a convent commissioned by Dom Fernando, consort to Queen Dona Maria II. The palace is surrounded by a splendid park filled with a lush variety of trees and flowers brought from every corner of the Portuguese empire by Dom Fernando in the 1840s. *Admission for guided tour: summer 400$00, winter 200$00, free Sun. 10–2. Open Tues.–Sun. 10–5.*

Back in downtown Sintra, the **Museu do Brinquedo** (Toy Museum) houses an enjoyable collection of dolls and traditional toys from this region of Portugal. *Largo Latino Coelho 9, tel. 01/9232875, ext. 280. Admission: 200$00. Open Tues.–Sun. 10–12:30 and 2:30–5.*

If you're in the area on the second or fourth Sunday of each month, visit the **Feira de Sintra** (Sintra Fair) in the nearby village of **São Pedro de Sintra,** 2 kilometers (about 1¼ miles) to the south. This is one of the best-known fairs in the country.

Queluz The train back to Lisbon will pass through **Queluz** where, less than half a mile from the train station, you'll be confronted by the magnificent **Palácio Nacional de Queluz** (Queluz Palace). Partially inspired by Versailles, this salmon-pink rococo palace was begun by Dom Pedro III in 1747 and took 40 years to complete. The formal landscaping and waterways that surround it are the work of the French designer Jean-Baptiste Robillon. Restored after a disastrous fire in 1934, the palace is used today for formal banquets, music festivals, and as accommodations for visiting heads of state. In summer, a month-long medieval festival, the **Noites de Queluz** (Queluz Nights), is staged in the gardens, complete with costumed cast and orchestra. Visitors may walk through the elegant state rooms, including the Music Salon, the Hall of the Ambassadors, and the mirrored Throne Room with its crystal chandeliers and gilt trimmings. *Admission: summer 400$00, winter 200$00. Open Mon. and Wed.–Sun. 10–1 and 2–5.*

Dining and Lodging

Budget travelers will find that dining and lodging along the Portuguese Riviera can run into quite a tidy sum—staying in Lisbon while making day trips into the area might be a less expensive alternative. For details and price-category definitions, *see* Dining and Lodging in Staying in Portugal.

Cascais **Beira Mar.** This well-established restaurant located behind the
Dining fish market, has a wide variety of fish and meat dishes. The atmosphere is comfortable and unpretentious. *Rua das Flores 6, tel. 01/4830152. AE, DC, MC, V. Closed Thurs. Moderate.*
Joshua's Shoarma Grill. This very popular Middle Eastern restaurant serves kebabs and other light fare until 2 AM. *Rua Visconde de Luz 19, tel. 01/2843064. Reservations not necessary. Inexpensive.*

Lodging **Hotel Baia.** This modern hotel overlooks the glistening blue water of Cascais bay. The rooms are comfortable and well-appointed; ask for one with a private balcony facing the sea. *Ave. Marginal 2750, tel. 01/281033, fax 01/281095. 114 rooms with bath, 66 with a sea view. Facilities: roof terrace, pool, restaurant, bar. AE, DC, MC, V. Moderate.*

Estoril **The English Bar.** This mock-Tudor-style establishment serves
Dining good international cuisine in friendly, comfortable surroundings. There are good views over the beach to Cascais. *Av. Sabóia, Monte Estoril, tel. 01/4680413. Reservations advised. AE, DC, MC, V. Closed Sun. Moderate.*
Restaurante Frolic. The Frolic is a friendly restaurant/bar next to Hotel Palácio. Try the delectable cakes. *Av. Clotilde, tel. 01/4681219. AE, DC, MC, V. Closed Sun. Inexpensive.*

Lodging **Hotel Lido.** Located on a quiet street set back from the beach, the Lido is justly popular for its good facilities, which include a pool and garden as well as a fine restaurant. *Rua do Alentejo 12, tel. 01/2684123, fax 01/2683665. 62 rooms with bath. Facilities: pool, restaurant, bar, garden, garage. AE, DC, MC, V. Moderate.*

Sintra **Solar São Pedro.** Highly recommended by its habitués, this res-
Dining taurant specializes in French cooking. Its English-speaking host adds to the warm and friendly atmosphere. *Largo da Feira 12, São Pedro de Sintra, tel. 01/9231860. Reservations advised. AE, DC, MC, V. Closed Wed. Moderate.*

The Algarve

The Algarve, Portugal's southernmost holiday resort, encompasses some 240 kilometers (150 miles) of sun-drenched coast below the Serra de Monchique and the Serra do Caldeirão. It is the top destination for foreign visitors to Portugal. During the past two decades, this area, indelibly marked by centuries of Arab occupation, has been heavily developed in an effort to create a playground for international sun worshipers. Well known by Europeans as a holiday center of clean, sandy beaches; championship golf courses; and local color, this section of Portugal is only now being discovered by Americans. Although some parts of the coastline have been seriously overbuilt, there are still plenty of picturesque fishing villages and secluded beaches to leaven the concentration of hotels, casinos, disco nightclubs, and sports facilities.

This itinerary takes you to some of the most interesting and typical towns and villages in the Algarve, starting near the Portuguese border with Spain in the east and ending at the most southwesterly point of the European continent.

Getting Around

There is daily bus and rail service between Lisbon and several towns in the Algarve; the trip takes between four and six hours, depending on your destination. The best places to head are the main towns of Lagos and Faro; from here local rail and bus services serve most of the surrounding villages. Although the road and train do not run right along the immediate coast, it is generally a simple matter to walk to, or catch a bus to, the most popular beachside destinations.

Tourist Information

Local tourist offices can be found in the following towns: **Albufeira** (Rua 5 de Outubro, tel. 089/512144), **Faro** (Airport, tel. 089/818582; Rua da Misericorida 8/12, tel. 089/803604; Rua Ataide de Oliveira 100, tel. 089/803667), **Lagos** (Largo Marquês de Pombal, tel. 082/763031), **Olhão** (Largo da Lagoa, tel. 089/713936), **Portimão** (Largo 1° de Dezembro, tel. 082/22065 or 082/23695), **Praia da Rocha** (Ave. Tomás Cabreira, tel. 082/22290), **Sagres** (Promontório de Sagres, tel. 082/64125), **Silves** (Rua 25 de Abril, tel. 082/442255), **Tavira** (Praça da República, tel. 081/22511), **Vila Real de Santo António** (Praça Marquês de Pombal, tel. 081/44495; Frontier Tourist Post, tel. 081/43272).

Exploring the Algarve

Vila Real de Santo António is the easternmost town of the Algarve; its ferries (and a new suspension bridge) cross the River Guadiana to Ayamonte, the Spanish frontier town. Vila Real is worth noting for its design: Laid out, on a grid, similar to that of Lisbon's Baixa section, it's considered a showcase of 18th-century Portuguese town planning. Aside from this, there's little reason to linger.

Tavira From Vila Real it's 40 minutes west by train to **Tavira,** which many people call the prettiest town in the Algarve. Situated at the mouth of the River Gilão, it is famous for its figs, arcaded streets, a seven-arched Roman bridge, old Moorish defense walls, and interesting churches. There are good sand beaches on nearby **Tavira Island,** which is reached by ferry (summer only) from the town beach. Another 22 kilometers (14 miles) west lies the fishing port and market town of **Olhão.** Founded in the 18th century, Olhão is notable for its North African–style architecture—cube-shaped whitewashed buildings—and the best food markets in the Algarve.

Faro From Olhão it's just 9 kilometers (6 miles) to **Faro,** the provincial capital of the Algarve, located roughly at the center of the coast. When this city was finally taken by Afonso III in 1249, it

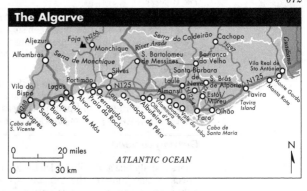

The Algarve

ATLANTIC OCEAN

0   20 miles

0   30 km

N

ended the Arab domination of Portugal, and remnants of the medieval walls and gates that surrounded the city then can still be seen in the older district, the **Cidade Velha.** One of the gates, the **Arco da Vila,** with a white marble statue of St. Thomas Aquinas in a niche at the top, leads to the grand Largo de Sé. The **Gothic cathedral** here has a stunning interior decorated with 17th-century tiles (Admission free. Open weekdays 10–noon, Sat. 5 for service, Sun. 8–1). There are also several fascinating museums in Faro, notably the **Museu do Etnografia Regional** (Algarve Ethnographic Museum) on Rua do Pé da Cruz, with good historical and folkloric displays (Admission: 50$00. Open weekdays 9:30–12:30 and 2–5:30); and the **Museu Maritimo** (Maritime Museum) on Rua Comunidade Lusiada near the yacht basin, next to the Hotel Eva (Admission: 100$00. Open Mon.–Sat. 10–11 and 2:30–4:30). The **Museu Municipal** (Municipal Museum) on Largo Afonso III has a section dedicated to the Roman remains found at Milreu (Admission: 120$00. Open Mon.–Sat. 9–noon and 2–5). There's a large sand beach on Faro Island, the **Praia de Faro,** which is connected to land by road or reached by ferry from the jetty below the old town.

Albufeira   From Faro, regular buses and trains head west to **Albufeira;** there is a shuttle bus between the railroad station and town, 6 kilometers to the south. At one time an attractive fishing village, Albufeira has long since mushroomed into the Algarve's largest and busiest resort, too brash for many. Even the dried-up riverbed has been turned into a parking lot. But with its steep, narrow streets and hundreds of whitewashed houses snuggled on the slopes of nearby hills, Albufeira still has a distinctly Moorish flavor. Its attractions include the lively fish market (held daily); interesting rock formations, caves, and grottoes along the beach; and plenty of nightlife.

Away from the coast, 25 kilometers (16 miles) to the west, is the hill town of **Silves.** Once the Moorish capital of the Algarve, Silves lost its importance after it was almost completely destroyed by the 1755 earthquake. The 12th-century sandstone **fortress,** together with its impressive parapets, was restored in 1835 and still dominates the town. Below the fortress stands the 12th–13th-century **Santa Maria da Sé** (Cathedral of Saint Mary), which was built upon the site of a Moorish mosque. (Admission free. Fortress and church open daily 9–5:30.) The excellent **Museu Arqueologia** features artifacts from prehistoric times through the 17th century. (Admission: 250$00. Open

Mon.–Sat. 10–1 and 2–5.) The **Cruz de Portugal,** a 16th-century limestone cross, stands on the road to Messines.

Portimão   From Silves it's only 10 kilometers (6 miles) to **Portimão,** the most important fishing port in the Algarve. There was a settlement here at the mouth of the river Arade even before the Romans arrived. This is a cheerful, busy town and a good center for shopping. Although the colorful fishing boats now unload their catch at a modern terminal across the river, the open-air restaurants along the quay are a pleasant place to sample the local specialty: charcoal-grilled sardines with chewy fresh bread and red wine. Across the bridge, in the fishing hamlet of **Ferragudo,** are the ruins of a 16th-century castle, and 3 kilometers (about 2 miles) south of Portimão is **Praia da Rocha,** to which there is regular bus service. Now dominated by high-rise apartments and hotels, this was the first resort in the Algarve to be developed; it can still boast of an excellent beach, made all the more interesting by a series of huge, colored rocks that have been worn by sea and wind into strange shapes.

The train and bus route continues west through **Lagos,** a busy fishing port with an attractive harbor and some startling cove beaches in the vicinity that attract a bustling holiday crowd. The 18th-century Baroque **Igreja de Santo António** (Church of Santo António), off Rua General Alberto Silveira, is renowned for its gilt, carved wood, and exuberant decoration. An amusing regional museum is alongside. (Admission 200$00. Open Tues–Sat. 9:30–12:30 and 2–5.) Lagos is the western terminus of the coastal railway that runs from Vila Real de Santo António, connecting with the Lisbon line at Tunes.

Sagres   After Lagos, the terrain along this route becomes more rugged. It is a 40-kilometer (25-mile) journey to the windy headland at **Sagres,** where Prince Henry established his famous school of navigation in the 15th century. The **Compass Rose,** made of stone and earth, in the courtyard of the **Forteleza de Sagres** (Sagres Fortress), was uncovered in this century, but is believed to have been used by Prince Henry in his calculations. The **Graça Chapel** is also located inside the fortress (which is always open), as are Henry's house and his school of navigation—the first of its kind. Both are now used as a youth hostel.

There are spectacular views from here and from **Cabode São Vicente** (Cape São Vicente) 6 kilometers (4 miles) to the west; it's a 90-minute walk. This point, the most southwesterly tip of the European continent, where the landmass juts into the rough waters of the Atlantic, is sometimes called *O Fim do Mundo,* "the end of the world." Admiral Nelson defeated the Spanish off this cape in 1797. The lighthouse at Cape São Vicente is said to have the strongest reflectors in Europe, casting a beam 96 kilometers (60 miles) out to sea; it is open to the public. It seems only appropriate that it was at this breathtaking spot that Christopher Columbus, Vasco da Gama, Ferdinand Magellan, and other great explorers learned their craft 500 years ago.

Dining and Lodging

The accommodations listed below are only some of the many lodging possibilities in Algarve. Budget travelers are likely to be approached by people offering very reasonably priced rooms in private houses throughout Algarve's main towns and resorts. Though you should always ask to see the room before accepting, they are invariably clean and cheerful—even if they are small and share a bathroom. For details and price-category definitions, *see* Dining and Lodging in Staying in Portugal.

Albufeira
Dining
★

A Ruina. A big, rustic restaurant on the beach, built on several levels, this is the place for good views and charcoal-grilled seafood. *Praia dos Pescadores, tel. 089/512094. DC, MC. Moderate.*

Cabaz da Praia. This long-established restaurant has a spectacular view of the main beach, as well as a cliffside terrace for alfresco dining. Try the soufflé omelets (served at lunchtime only). *Praça Miguel Bombarda 7, tel. 089/512137. Reservations recommended. No credit cards. Closed Sat. lunch and Sun. Inexpensive.*

Lodging

Hotel-Apartamento Auramar. This pleasant beachside complex offers 287 well-appointed self-service apartments. *Just outside of town at Praia dos Aveiros, Areias de São João, tel. 089/ 513337, fax 089/513327. 287 units. AE, DC, MC, V. Moderate.*

Hotel da Aldeia. Adjacent to Ouro Beach, 2 kilometers (1¼ miles) east of Albufeira, this pleasant hotel within a large tourist complex is built in the traditional Algarvian style. Most rooms have terraces overlooking the pool and gardens. *Av. Dr. Francisco Sá Carneiro, Areias de São João, tel. 089/ 588861-2, fax 089/588864. 133 rooms with bath. Facilities: restaurant, 2 pools, tennis court, minigolf, health club. AE, MC, V. Moderate.*

Faro
Dining

Restaurante Adega Nova. Traditional Portuguese dishes are served at massive wooden tables at this restaurant that has plenty of atmosphere. *Rua Francisco Barreto 24, tel. 089/ 813433. No credit cards. Moderate.*

Café Aliança. This old-style coffee house, with outdoor seating facing the harbor, serves good snacks and sandwiches as well as full meals. *Rua F. Gomes 7-11, tel. 089/801621. No credit cards. Budget.*

Lodging

Hotel Eva. This well-appointed modern hotel block is located on the main square overlooking the yacht basin. The best rooms overlook the sea, and there's a courtesy bus to the beach. *Av. da República, tel. 089/803354, fax 089/802304. 146 rooms with bath. Facilities: pool, restaurant, disco. AE, DC, MC, V. Moderate.*

Casa de Lumena. This 150-year-old Faro mansion has been tastefully converted into a small hotel. Each room has its own individual ambience. *Praça Alexandre Herculano 27, tel. 089/ 801990, fax 089/804019. 12 rooms with bath. Facilities: restaurant, courtyard bar. AE, DC, MC, V. Inexpensive.*

Lagos
Dining

Dom Sebastião. Portuguese cooking and charcoal-grilled specials and fish are the main attractions at this cheerful restaurant. It has a wide range of Portuguese aged wines. *Rua 25 de Abril 20, tel. 082/62795. Reservations advised. AE, DC, MC, V. Closed Sun. in winter. Moderate.*

Restaurante Piri-Piri. This small restaurant has a menu heavy with Portuguese specialties, including the spicy pork and chicken dishes that give the establishment its name. *Rua Afonso d' Almeida 10, tel. 082/63803. Reservations not necessary. MC, V. Inexpensive.*

Lodging

Pensão Mar Azul. Though this pensão has an excellent central location, rooms facing the street can be noisy in high season.

Accommodations are more than adequate, however—some guest quarters even have a terrace—and there's a comfortable lounge. *Rua 25 de Abril 13-1, tel. 082/769749. 17 rooms, 13 with bath. Budget.*

Portimão **A Lanterna.** This well-run restaurant is located just over the
Dining bridge at Parchal, on the Ferragudo side. Its specialty is duck, but try the exceptional fish soup or smoked fish. *Tel. 082/23948. Reservations advised. MC, V. Closed Sun. Moderate.*

A Vela. A pleasant restaurant decorated in Moorish fashion, A Vela has a spacious open kitchen that produces a varied selection of tasty Portuguese and international specialties. The staff is accommodating. *Rua Dr., Manuel de Almeida 97, tel. 082/ 414016. Reservations advised in summer. AE, DC, MC, V. Closed Sun. Moderate.*

Praia da Rocha **Safari.** This lively Portuguese seafront restaurant has a dis-
Dining tinctly African flavor. Seafood and delicious Angolan recipes are the specialties. *Rua António Feu, tel. 082/415540. Reservations advised. AE, DC, MC, V. Moderate.*

Vila Real de **Caves do Guadiana.** Located in a large, old-fashioned building
Santo António facing the fishing docks, this restaurant is well known for its
Dining seafood and Portuguese specialties. *Av. República 90, tel. 081/ 44498. No reservations. DC, MC. Closed Thurs. Inexpensive.*

21 Romania

Romania is not the easiest destination for tourists, but it has advantages for the budget traveler. Few Romanians earn more than the equivalent of $40 a month, and costs of living are set accordingly. Visitors may tour the country cheaply and without restriction—through the stunning peaks and lush valleys of the Carpathian mountains, on hot Black Sea beaches, around the Moldavian winegrowing region with its many historic monasteries and folk traditions, and through Dracula's Transylvania, where Hungarian and German ethnic minorities maintain their old ways. People come each year from many countries for affordable Black Sea holidays and winter skiing in Sinaia; to view the historic buildings of the capital, Bucharest; or to stay in Europe's largest wetlands preserve, the Danube Delta, where traditional caviar-fishing communities live alongside pelicans and other rare species. Romanians are hospitable, although many regard Western visitors as opportunities to earn inflation-proof hard currency.

The 1989 revolution, which overthrew the Ceauşescu regime, led toward democratic reforms and a capitalist economy but also revealed Romania's shortcomings as Europe's poorest country after Albania. Poor-quality goods and services; shortages of water, heating, and other basic essentials; and waiting in line are the lot of most ordinary Romanians—and your lot, too, if you try to live like one. All visitors should bring a supply of toilet paper to beat shortages; a flashlight for unlighted streets and corridors; and, in summer, insect repellent. Since medical facilities are primitive, it is best to bring along all medicines (including needles and syringes for injections).

It is always easiest and often cheapest to book either a package trip or a prepaid fly-drive tour with accommodation vouchers. These arrangements usually benefit from price discounts and

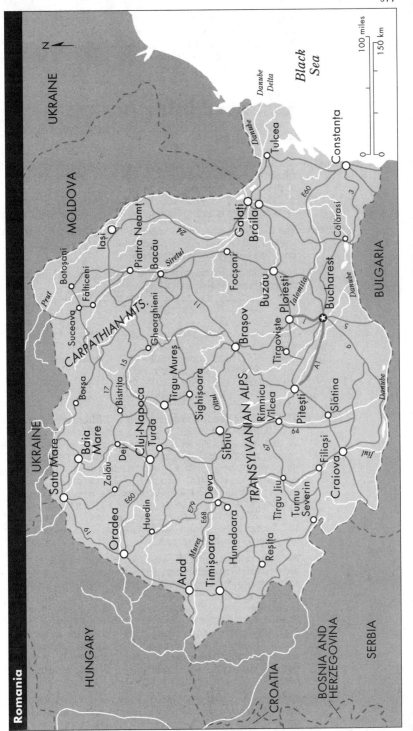

Romania

guarantee at least minimum standards of quality. More intrepid independent travelers need a good phrase book, flexible standards and a flexible itinerary, and a good sense of humor to cope with the rip-offs, frustration, and discomforts most will experience. For many, discovering the numerous areas still untouched by modern ways is well worth the effort.

Essential Information

Before You Go

When to Go   Bucharest, like Paris, is at its best during the spring. The Black Sea resorts open in mid- to late May and close at the end of September. Winter ski resorts in the Carpathians are now well developed and increasingly popular, while the best time for touring the interior is late spring to fall.

Climate   The Romanian climate is temperate and generally free of extremes, but snow as late as April is not unknown, and the lowlands can be very hot in midsummer.

The following are the average daily maximum and minimum temperatures for Bucharest.

Jan.	34F	1C	May	74F	23C	Sept.	78F	25C
	19	- 7		51	10		52	11
Feb.	38F	4C	June	81F	27C	Oct.	65F	18C
	23	- 5		57	14		43	6
Mar.	50F	10C	July	86F	30C	Nov.	49F	10C
	30	- 1		60	16		35	2
Apr.	64F	18C	Aug.	85F	30C	Dec.	39F	4C
	41	5		59	15		26	- 3

Currency   The unit of currency is the *leu* (plural *lei*). There are coins of 1, 3, 5, 10, 20, 50, and 100 lei. Banknotes come in denominations of 50, 100, 500, and 1000 lei. The Romanian currency is expected to continue to drop sharply in value through 1993, causing frequent price rises; costs are therefore best calculated in hard currency. At press time (summer 1992), the exchange rate is 250 lei to the dollar and 400 lei to the pound sterling. The price of a pack of Western cigarettes rose from 150 lei to 200 lei, but because of exchange-rate inflation, the "real" cost remained 77¢. Prices of basic items, artificially low from Communism, are gradually being increased.

Because of high inflation, check on your arrival that low-denomination notes and coins are still in use. There is no longer an obligatory currency exchange, and an increasing number of licensed exchange offices (*casă de schimb*) have been competing to offer rates better than those available on the illegal and risky black market. Retain your exchange receipts, as you may need to prove your money was changed legally. Except for air tickets, by law foreigners must pay in lei, though hard currency is widely accepted. The financial police (*garda financiară*) are useful if you experience difficulty. You may not import or export lei.

Credit Cards   Major credit cards are welcome in a number of major hotels and their restaurants, but are not accepted in most shops and independent restaurants.

What It Will Cost Prices of hotels and restaurants are as expensive as those in Western Europe as far as the independent traveler is concerned. Those with prepaid arrangements, however, enjoy reductions of up to 30% and more.

Sample Prices Museum admission costs about 7¢; a bottle of imported beer in a restaurant around $1; a bottle of good local wine in a top restaurant around $2.50. A one-mile taxi ride will cost around 25¢.

Visas All visitors to Romania must have a visa, obtainable from Romanian embassies abroad or at border stations (for those with prepaid arrangements, the cost of the visa is often included). Send the visa fee (United States, $30; Canada, $40; United Kingdom, £20), a stamped, self-addressed envelope, and your passport to the relevant consulate: in the **United States,** Romanian Consulate, 1067 23rd Street, NW, Washington DC 20008, tel. 202/387–6902; in **Canada,** Romanian Consulate, 111 Peter Street, Suite 530, Toronto, Ontario M5V 2H1, tel. 416/585–5802; in the **United Kingdom,** Consular Section of the Romanian Embassy, 4 Palace Green, London W8, tel. 071/937–9667.

Customs You may bring in 2 cameras, 20 rolls of film, 1 small movie camera, 2 rolls of movie film, a typewriter, binoculars, a radio/tape recorder, 200 cigarettes, 2 liters of liquor and 4 of wine or beer. Gifts up to the value of 2,000 lei are permitted; camping and sports equipment may be imported freely. Declare video cameras and expensive jewelry on arrival.

An old law still forbids any gifts being taken out of Romania except for five paintings from the galleries of the Plastic Artists' Union. However, customs officers won't trouble you over a few small, cheap gift items. Anything of value and any item made before 1965 needs an export license.

Language Romanian sounds appealingly familiar to anyone who speaks a smattering of French, Italian, or Spanish. French is widely spoken and understood in Romanian cities. Romanians involved with the tourist industry, in all hotels and major resorts, speak English.

Getting Around

By Train Romanian Railways (CPR) operates *expres, accelerat, rapide,* and *personal* trains; if possible, avoid the *personal* trains because they are very slow. Trains are inexpensive but are often crowded, with carriages in poor repair. First class is worth the extra cost. A *vagon de dormit* (sleeper) or cheap *cuşeta,* with bunk beds, is available on longer journeys. It is always advisable to buy a seat reservation in advance, but you cannot buy the ticket itself at a train station more than one hour before departure. If your reserved seat is already occupied, it may have been sold twice. If you're in Bucharest, go to the Advance Reserve Office, Strada Brezoianu 10, tel. 0/132644. You will be charged a small commission fee, but it is a less time-consuming process than buying your ticket at the railway station.

By Plane **Tarom** operates daily flights to 15 major cities from Bucharest's Baneasa Airport. During the summer, additional flights link Constanţa with major cities, including Cluj and Iaşi. Be prepared for delays. External flights can be booked at the central reservations office, Strada Brezoianu 10, and at some major hotels. For domestic flights go to Mendeleev 14, tel. 0/594125.

By Bus Bus stations, or *autogara*, are usually located near train stations. Buses are generally crowded and far from luxurious. Tickets are sold at the stations up to two hours before departure.

By Boat Regular passenger services operate on various sections of the Danube; tickets are available at the ports.

Staying in Romania

Telephones All large Romanian towns can be dialed directly, and international direct dialing is slowly being introduced in Bucharest. The system is stretched, and you may have to order and wait a long time for nonlocal calls. It is less expensive to telephone from the post office than from hotels. Post offices have a waiting system whereby you order your call and pay at the counter. When your call is ready, the name of the town or country you are phoning is announced, together with the number of the cabin you should proceed to for your call. Private business services are opening in large towns, offering phone, fax, and telex facilities. Coin-operated telephones at roadsides, airports, and train stations may work only for local calls.

Bucharest's area code is 0. For information dial the relevant area code, then 11515; in Bucharest it is 031 (A–L) and 032 (M–Z). Your hotel's front desk or a phone book will be much more helpful.

Mail The central post office in Bucharest is at Calea Victoriei 37 and is open Monday through Saturday from 7 AM to 8 PM. The telephone section is open at the same times on Sunday as well.

Postal Rates Rates are increasing regularly in line with inflation, so check before you post.

Opening and Closing Times **Banks.** Open weekdays 9 to 12:30 or 1. Licensed exchange (schimb) bureaus are open weekday afternoons and Saturday mornings.

Museums. Museums and art galleries are usually open from 10 to 6, but it's best to check with local tourist offices. Most museums are closed on Monday.

Shops. Shops are generally open Monday–Saturday from 9 or 10 AM to 6 or 8 PM and shut between 1 and 3, though some food shops open earlier.

National Holidays January 1; January 2; April 12 (Easter Monday); May 1; May 25; May 26; December 25.

Dining Shortages have eased and poor standards have now improved sufficiently for the better hotels and restaurants to offer reasonable cuisine and menu choices. Elsewhere, expect poorly cooked dishes based around pork or beef. Vegetables and salads may be canned or pickled. Traditional Romanian main courses are not usually offered, but you might try *gustare*, a platter of hot or cold mixed hors d'oeuvres, or *ciorbă*, a soup stock, slightly spicy and sour. Overcharging is a hazard outside the bigger restaurants with printed menus. You can insist on seeing the prices, but small establishments may genuinely not have a menu prepared for just one or two dishes.

Mealtimes Outside the Black Sea and Carpathian resorts, many restaurants will have stopped serving by 9 PM, although an increasing number have begun staying open until 11 PM or later. Restaurants usually open at midday.

Precautions The far less expensive *bufet expres, lacto vegetarian* snack bars, and *autoservire* cannot be recommended, but excellent creamy cakes are available at the better *cofetarie* (coffee shops). Romanian coffee is served with grounds; instant coffee is called *nes*. You may want to bring your own coffee whitener, as milk is in short supply.

Dress There are no dress rules as such, but Romanians themselves usually wear smart, informal clothes for an expensive evening out. Casual dress is appropriate elsewhere.

Ratings Prices are per person and include first course, main course, and dessert, plus wine and tip. Because high inflation means local prices frequently change, ratings are given in dollars, which remain reasonably constant. But your bill will be in lei. Best bets are indicated by a star ★.

Category	Cost
Moderate	$4–$7
Inexpensive	$3–$4
Budget	under $3

Lodging Prepaid arrangements through travel agencies abroad often benefit from discounted prices. Some schemes, such as fly-drive holidays, give bed-and-breakfast accommodation vouchers (these cannot be bought in Romania). Most places take vouchers. Otherwise, book accommodations directly with hotels, or through tourism agencies. Some agencies deal only with their local areas; those spawned from the formerly monolithic national tourism office (ONT)—the *agenţia de turism*—and from the former youth tourism bureau, now known as the *Compania de Turism pentru Tineret* (CTT), offer nationwide services. Visitors on very tight budgets may want to avoid the cheap, but often cheerless, hotels used by many Romanians. Private citizens come to railway stations and offer spare rooms in their homes, but use discretion and be prepared to bargain. Inexpensive accommodations such as pensions or hostels are almost nonexistent, and student hostels are not available to foreigners.

Hotels The star system of hotel classification is only just being introduced in Romania. Instead, you will encounter Deluxe categories A and B, First-class categories A and B, and so on. Deluxe A is equivalent to five-star or Very Expensive, Deluxe B to four-star or Expensive, first-class A to three-star or Moderate, and first-class B to two-star or Inexpensive. Standards of facilities, including plumbing and hot water, decline rapidly through the categories. Ask at the front desk when hot water will be available. In principle, at least, all hotels leave a certain quota of rooms unoccupied until 8 PM for unexpected foreign visitors.

Rentals A few delightfully rustic cottages may be rented at such ski resorts as Sinaia and Predeal. Details are available from Romanian tourist offices abroad (*see* Important Addresses and Numbers in Bucharest, *below*).

Camping There are more than 100 campsites in Romania; they provide an inexpensive way of exploring the country, but standards vary. The best ones are at Braşov, Cluj, Sibiu, and Suceava, which also offer reasonable bungalow accommodations. They all have clean toilets and showers with hot water at least some of the time. The worst ones—Hunedoară, Iaşi, Moldoviţă—have no running water apart from a natural spring and very unpleasant toilets. Rates vary. Usually campsites are clean and comfortable but are only for use during the summer. Details are available from Romanian tourist offices abroad.

Ratings The following hotel price categories are for two people in a double room. Guests staying in single rooms are charged a supplement. Prices are estimates for high season. Because of inflation, ratings are given according to hard-currency equivalents—but you must pay in lei. (Note that hotels may insist on your buying lei from them to pay your bill, unless you can produce an exchange receipt to prove you changed your money legally.) Best bets are indicated by a star ★.

Category	Cost
Moderate	$35–$60
Inexpensive	$20–$35
Budget	under $20

Tipping A 12% service charge is added to meals at most restaurants. Elsewhere, a 10% tip is welcomed, and is expected by taxi drivers and porters.

Bucharest

Arriving and Departing

By Plane All international flights to Romania land at Bucharest's Otopeni Airport (tel. 0/333137), 16 kilometers (9 miles) north of the city.

Between the Airport and Downtown Buses leave every one to two hours from outside the airport and stop outside the Tarom office, Strada Brezoianu 10. Your hotel can arrange transport by car from the airport. Taxi drivers at the airport seek business aggressively and charge outrageously in dollars. Note that the "official" fare is in lei, and the equivalent of about $5 with tip, so bargain.

By Train There are five main stations in Bucharest, though international lines operate from Gara de Nord (tel. 0/052). For tickets and information, go to the Advance Booking Office (Str. Brezoianu 10, tel. 0/132644).

Getting Around

Bucharest is spacious and sprawling. Though the old heart of the city and the two main arteries running the length of it are best explored on foot, long, wide avenues and vast squares make some form of transportation necessary. New tourist maps are being printed and may be available at tourism agencies and hotels. It is generally very safe on the streets at night, but watch out for vehicles and hidden potholes.

By Subway Three lines of the subway system are now in operation. Tokens are available from kiosks inside stations, and you may travel any distance. The system closes at 1 AM.

By Tram, Bus, and Trolley Bus These are uncomfortable, crowded, and infrequent, but service is extensive. A ticket valid for two trips of any length can be purchased from kiosks near bus stops or from tobacconists; validate your ticket when you board. There are also day and week passes *(abonaments)*, but more expensive *maxi taxis* (minibuses that stop on request) and express buses take fares on board. The system shuts down at midnight.

Important Addresses and Numbers

Tourist Information The main **Romanian National Tourist Office (ONT)** is located at 7 Boulevard General Magheru (tel. 0/145160) and deals with all inquiries related to tourism (open weekdays 8–4). There are ONT offices at Otopeni Airport, open 24 hours, and at the Gara de Nord, open 7:30 AM–3:30 PM. ONT is currently being broken up and privatized, so its office signs in most Romanian towns now read *Agenţia de Turism*. The **Compania de Turism pentru Tineret (CTT)** at 5 Strada Mendeleev (tel. 0/144200) also has branches nationwide.

For information before your trip, write or call **in the United States** (573 Third Avenue, New York, NY 10016, tel. 212/697–6971); **in the United Kingdom** (17 Nottingham Street, London W1M 3RD, tel. 071/224–3692).

Exploring Bucharest

The old story goes that a simple peasant named Bucur settled on the site upon which the city now stands. True or not, the name Bucureşti was first officially used only in 1459, by none other than Vlad Ţepeş, the real-life Dracula (sometimes known as Vlad the Impaler for his bloodthirsty habit of impaling unfortunate victims on wooden stakes). Two centuries later, this citadel on the Dimboviţa (the river that flows through Bucharest) became the capital of Walachia, and after another 200 years, it was named the capital of Romania. The city gradually developed into a place of bustling trade and gracious living, with ornate and varied architecture, landscaped parks, busy, winding streets, and wide boulevards. It became known before the Second World War as the Paris of the Balkans; like Paris, Bucharest is still at its best in the spring, but its past glory is now only hinted at. The high-rise Intercontinental Hotel now dominates the main crossroads at Piaţa Universităţii; northwards, up the main shopping streets of Bulevardul Nicolae Bălcescu, Bulevardul General Magheru, and Bulevardul Ana Ipătescu, only the occasional older building survives. However, along Calea Victoriei, a flavor of Bucharest's grander past can be savored, especially at the former royal palace opposite the Romanian senate (formerly Communist Party headquarters) in Piaţa Revoluţiei. Here, one also sees reminders of the December 1989 revolution, including the slow restoration of the domed National Library, gutted by fire, and bullet holes on walls nearby. Modest, touching monuments to the more than 1,000 people killed in the revolution can be found here, and Piaţa Universităţii has a wall still festooned with protest posters.

South along Calea Victoriei is the busy Lipscani trading district, a remnant of the old city that used to sprawl farther southward before it was bulldozed in Nicolae Ceauşescu's megalomaniacal drive to redevelop the capital. Piaţa Unirii is the hub of his enormously expensive and impractical vision, which involved the forced displacement of thousands of people and the demolition of many houses, churches, and synagogues. Cranes now stand eerily idle above unfinished tower blocks with colonnaded, white marble frontages. They flank a lengthy boulevard leading to the enormous, empty, and unfinished Palace of the People, second in size only to the Pentagon. With such a massive diversion of resources, it is not surprising that Bucharest is potholed and faded, and suffers shortages and erratic services. But happily, the city continues to offer many places of historic interest, as well as cinemas, theaters, concert halls, and an opera house.

Numbers in the margin correspond to points of interest on the Bucharest map.

Historic Bucharest A tour of this city should start at its core, the **Curtea Veche** (old
❶ Princely Court) and the Lipscani District. The Princely Court now houses **Muzeul Curtea Veche-Palatul Voievodal,** a museum exhibiting the remains of the palace built by Vlad Ţepeş during the 15th century. One section of the cellar wall presents the palace's history from the 15th century onward. You can see the rounded river stones used in the early construction, later alternating with red brick, and later still in plain brick. Prisoners were once kept in these cellars, which extend far into the surrounding city; a pair of ancient skulls belonging to two young *boyars* (aristocrats), decapitated at the end of the 17th century, will interest some. *Str. Iuliu Maniu 31. Admission charged. Open Tues.–Sun. 10–6.*

❷ The **Biserica din Curtea Veche** (Curtea Veche Church), beside the Princely Court, was founded during the 16th century and remains an important center of worship in the city. Nearby,
❸ **Hanul lui Manuc** (Manuc's Inn), a renovated 19th-century inn arranged in the traditional Romanian fashion around a courtyard, now houses a hotel and restaurant. Manuc was a wealthy Armenian merchant who died in Russia by poisoning—at the hand of a famous French fortune-teller who, having forecast Manuc's death on a certain day, could not risk ruining her reputation. The 1812 Russian-Turkish Peace Treaty was signed here.

Nearby, **Lipscani** is a bustling area of narrow streets, open stalls, and small artisans' shops that combine to create the atmosphere of a bazaar. At Strada Selari 11–13, you'll find glassblowers hard at work; glassware is sold next door. On
❹ Strada Stavreopolos, a small but exquisite **Biserica Ortodoxă** (Orthodox church) combines late Renaissance and Byzantine styles with elements of the Romanian folk-art style. Go inside to look at the superb wood and stone carving and a richly ornate iconostasis, the painted screen that partitions off the altar. Boxes on either side of the entrance contain votive candles—for the living on the left, for the "sleeping" on the right.

❺ At the end of the street is the **Muzeul Naţional de Istorie** (Romanian History Museum), which contains a vast collection of exhibits from neolithic to modern times. The Treasury, which can be visited and paid for separately, has a startling collection of objects in gold and precious stones—royal crowns, weapons, plates, and jewelry—dating from the 4th millennium BC through the 20th century. Opposite the Treasury is a full-size replica of **Columna Traiană** (Trajan's Column; the original is in Rome), commemorating a Roman victory over Dacia in AD 2. *Calea Victoriei 12. Museum admission charged. Open Tues.– Sun. 10–6.*

Turning north along the Calea Victoriei, you'll pass a military club and academy before reaching the pretty little **Crețulescu Church** on your left. Built in 1722, the church and some of its original frescoes were restored during the 1930s. Immediately north is a massive building, once the royal palace and now the Palace of the Republic. The **Muzeul de Artă al României** (National Art Museum) is housed here, with its fine collection of Romanian art, including works by the world-famous sculptor Brâncuşi. The foreign section has a wonderful Brueghel collection and is well worth a visit. *Str. Stribei Voda 1. Museum admission charged. Open Tues.–Sun. 10–6.*

Opposite the palace, in Piața Revoluției, was the former headquarters of the Romanian Communist party. Before the revolution in December 1989, no one was allowed to walk in front of this building. During the uprising the square was a major site of the fighting that destroyed the National Library, parts of the Palace, and the Cina restaurant next to the **Ateneul Român** (Romanian Athenaeum Concert Hall). The Ateneul, dating from 1888, with its Baroque dome and Greek columns, survived the upheavals and still houses the George Enescu Philharmonic Orchestra.

Follow Calea Victoriei as far as the Piața Victoriei. Opposite is the **Muzeul de Științe Naturale "Grigore Antipa"** (Natural History Museum), with its exceptional butterfly collection and the skeleton of *Dinotherium gigantissimum. Şoseaua Kiseleff 1. Admission charged. Open Tues.–Sun. 10–6.*

Şoseaua Kiseleff, a pleasant tree-lined avenue, brings you to the **Arcul de Triumf**, built in 1922 to commemorate the Allied victory in World War I. Originally constructed of wood and stucco, it was rebuilt during the 1930s and carved by some of Romania's most talented sculptors.

Still farther north lies Herăstrău Park, accommodating the fascinating **Muzeul Satului Romanesc** (Village Museum), as well as Herăstrău Lake. The museum is outstanding, with more than 300 authentic, fully furnished peasants' houses in folk styles taken from all over Romania. *Şoseaua Kiseleff 28. Admission charged. Open daily 10–5.*

Shopping

Gifts and Souvenirs New private shops are beginning to bring extra style and choice to Bucharest, but note the astonishing customs restrictions (*see* Customs in Before You Go, *above)* that prohibit exporting even bric-a-brac. Keep receipts of all purchases, regardless of their legal export status. The **Apollo** gallery, in the National Theater building next to the Intercontinental Hotel, and the galleries in the fascinating **Bazarul Hanul** off Strada Lipscani sell art that you may legally take home with you. Hotel shops stock the best range of cheap souvenirs.

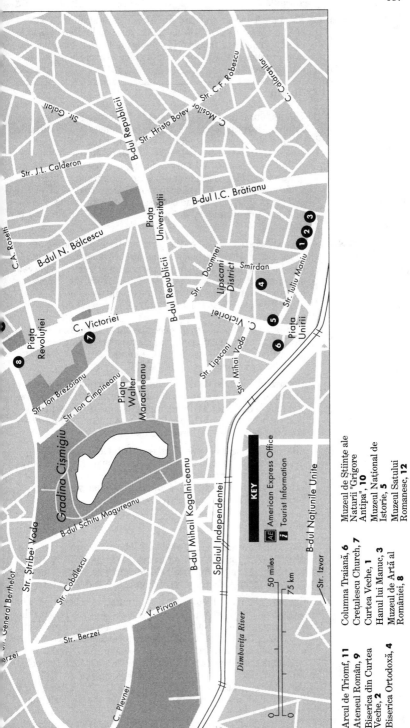

KEY

AE American Express Office

ℹ Tourist Information

50 miles

75 km

Arcul de Triomf, **11**
Ateneul Român, **9**
Biserica din Curtea
Veche, **2**
Biserica Ortodoxă, **4**

Columna Traiană, **6**
Crețulescu Church, **7**
Curtea Veche, **1**
Hanul lui Manuc, **3**
Muzeul de Artă al
României, **8**

Muzeul de Științe ale
Naturii "Grigore
Antipa", **10**
Muzeul Național de
Istorie, **5**
Muzeul Satului
Romanesc, **12**

Market The main food market is in Piaţa Amzei, open seven days a week and best visited during the morning. It sells a limited variety of cheese, fruit, and flowers. If you decide to visit outlying flea markets such as Piaţa Obor, take a guide to avoid being hassled and ripped off.

Dining

The restaurants of the Continental, Minerva, Bucureşti, and Intercontinental hotels are all recommended for a reasonable meal in pleasant surroundings. Some, like the **Balada,** at the top of the Intercontinental, offer a folklore show or live music. Although prices are not unreasonable, it is possible to rack up quite a total: Many restaurants have no menu, and waiters' recommendations can be expensive. Also note that most places will serve wine only by the bottle and not by the glass. For details and price-category definitions, *see* Dining in Staying in Romania.

Moderate **Doina.** Located on one of the main boulevards heading out of town, Doina was once much frequented by elegant promenaders. It has a pretty garden terrace and an attractive wine cellar; make it a point to sample wines from the vineyards inscribed over the door. There's music and dancing in the evenings. *Şoseaua Kiseleff 4, tel. 0/176715. Reservations required. No credit cards.*

★ **Nan Jing.** This is Bucharest's one and only Chinese eatery. It's located in the Hotel Minerva and makes a nice change from the usual Romanian cuisine. *Str. Lt. Lemnea 2–4, tel. 0/506010. Reservations advised. AE, DC, MC, V.*

Inexpensive **Restoratul Victoriei.** Dine in comfortable, turn-of-the-century surroundings in this restaurant just off the main thoroughfare. The food is basic but well prepared and unusually inexpensive. *Pasajul Victoriei, off Calea Victoriei, tel. 0/155147. Reservations in person only. No credit cards.*

Budget **Pik-Nik.** The best of several takeout eateries offering limited in-house dining around the central Amzei market serves burgers and hotdogs of consistent quality. This is a good place for a snack, if not for a night out. *Piaţa Amzei, opposite main market, no tel. No reservations. No credit cards.*

Lodging

Hotels in Bucharest are often heavily booked during the tourist season. If you don't have reservations, the ONT office will be of help in suggesting available alternatives. For details and price-category definitions, *see* Lodging in Staying in Romania.

Moderate **Capitol.** The circa 1900 Capitol is situated in a lively part of town near the Cişmigiu Gardens. In days gone by, it was the stomping ground of Bucharest's mainstream artists and writers. Today the Capitol is fully modernized and offers comfortable rooms and a large restaurant—though the literati have long since moved on. *Calea Victoriei 29, tel. 0/140926. 70 rooms with bath. Facilities: restaurant. No credit cards.*

Parc. Located near Herăstrău Park and the Flora Hotel, the Parc is modern and within easy reach of the airport; many guests stay here before moving on to the Black Sea resorts. There's a good restaurant that provides music every evening.

B-dul Poligrafiei 3, tel. 0/506081. 314 rooms with bath. Facilities: restaurant, pool, sauna, tennis. AE, DC, MC, V.

Budget **Negoiu.** Doubtless this was once a very elegant hotel, but the Negoiu is badly in need of refurbishment. It does offers a clean and comfortable stay. *Str. Ion Cîmpineanu 16, tel. 0/155250. 91 rooms, 72 with bath. No reservations. No credit cards.*

The Arts

You can enjoy Bucharest's lively theater and music life at prices way below those in the West. Tickets can be obtained directly from the theater or hall or from your hotel (for a commission fee). Performances usually begin at 7 PM (6 in winter). **Opera Română** (The Opera House, B-dul Mihail Kogălniceanu 70) has some excellent productions. The **Teatrul de Operetă** (Operetta House) is now located at the **Teatrul National** (National Theater, B-dul N. Bălcescu 2), which also offers serious drama. For lighter entertainment, try the **Teatrul de Comedie** (Comedy Theater, Str. Mandinesti); despite the language barrier, there is often enough spectacle to ensure a very good evening's entertainment. **Teatrul Tăndărică** (The Tandarica Puppet Theater, Calea Victoriei 50), has an international reputation, and the **Teatrul Evreesc de Stat** (State Jewish Theater, Str. Barasch 15), stages Yiddish-language performances. Don't miss the fine folkloric show at the **Rapsodia Română Artistic Ensemble** (Str. Lipscani 53). The **Cinematica Romana** (Str. Eforie 5) runs a daily program of old, undubbed American and English films.

Nightlife

Increasing numbers of bars and restaurants stay open late. Coffee shops, however, are usually closed after 10 PM.

Nightclubs The **Athenée Palace** and **Intercontinental** hotels have nightclubs with floor shows, and many others are popping up as well. **Vox Maris,** opposite the Bulevard hotel, is among several late-night discos. **Şarpele Roşu** (Str. Icoanei Piaţa Galaţi), or "Red Snake," has a pleasant, bohemian atmosphere, with Gypsy bands playing until 3 AM.

Cafés Cafés with outdoor terraces remain a feature of the city. It's worth taking a taxi to **Ficus,** on Strada Radu Beller next to Floreasca Park, for open-air drinks or snacks until dawn.

22   Spain

The Spain that for generations attracted penurious adventure-seekers has disappeared. With the country's admission to the European Community (EC)—formally completed in 1992—life has become as expensive as in most of the peninsula's western European neighbors. Spain still offers great rewards to the intrepid budget traveler, but don't expect to find many deals in the main cities, or in tourist-saturated areas such as the Costa del Sol. Travel to Seville and Barcelona grew especially pricey in 1992, when those cities hosted the International Exposition and the Olympic Games; it remains to be seen whether sometimes astronomical hotel prices will fall back to earth. Trips to lesser-known towns and the countryside in Spain will reward the traveler with lower prices and fewer crowds. The once-common image of Spain as a package-vacation destination suffering from overdevelopment and mass tourism has faded. In its place is a Spain of sophisticated European cities, romantic hilltop villages, and a magnificent Moorish legacy.

If it's beaches you're after, there is the jet-set Costa del Sol in the south, or San Sebastián in the Basque country, formerly the summer capital of Spain. Farther west is the resort city of Santander and La Coruña, a long-standing favorite of British visitors. In the east is the Costa Brava, while to the south, around Alicante, is the Costa Blanca, with its most popular tourist center at Benidorm. Perhaps the number-one tourist attraction in Spain is the Alhambra, in Granada. Following close behind it come the Mosque of Córdoba, and the Alcázar and cathedral of Seville. Àvila is a historic walled town and Madrid, the capital, contains some of the greatest art collections in the world. Toledo, home of El Greco and boasting a cathedral, synagogues, and startling views, is one of Spain's greatest treasures. Finally, Barcelona, capital of Catalunya, has a charm and vitality quite its own.

Essential Information

Before You Go

When to Go The tourist season runs from Easter to mid-October. The best months for sightseeing are May, June, September, and early October, when the weather is usually pleasant and sunny without being unbearably hot. During July and August try to avoid Madrid or the inland cities of Andalusia, where the heat can be stifling and many places close down at 1 PM. If you visit Spain in high summer, the best bet is to head for the coastal resorts or to mountain regions such as the Pyrenees or Picos de Europa. The one exception to Spain's high summer temperatures is the north coast, where the climate is similar to that of northern Europe. The high season, when hotels are significantly more expensive, is usually in summer, although there are exceptions.

Visitors should be aware of the seasonal events that can clog parts of the country, reserving in advance if traveling during peak periods. Easter is always a busy time, especially in Madrid, Barcelona, and the main Andalusian cities of Seville, Córdoba, Granada, Málaga, and the Costa del Sol resorts. July and August, when most Spaniards and other Europeans take their annual vacations, see the heaviest crowds, particularly in coastal resorts. Holiday weekends are naturally busy, and major fiestas, such as Pamplona's bull runnings, make advance booking essential and cause prices to soar. Off-season travel offers fewer crowds and lower rates in many hotels.

Climate The following are the average daily maximum and minimum temperatures for Madrid.

Jan.	47F	9C	May	70F	21C	Sept.	77F	25C
	35	2		50	10		57	14
Feb.	52F	11C	June	80F	27C	Oct.	65F	18C
	36	2		58	15		49	10
Mar.	59F	15C	July	87F	31C	Nov.	55F	13C
	41	5		63	17		42	5
Apr.	65F	18C	Aug.	85F	30C	Dec.	48F	9C
	45	7		63	17		36	2

Currency The unit of currency in Spain is the peseta. There are bills of 500, 1,000, 2,000, 5,000, and 10,000 ptas. Coins are 1 pta., 5, 25, 50, 100, 200, and 500 ptas. The 2- and 10-pta. coins and the old 100-pta. bills are rare but still legal tender. Note that pay phones in Spain won't accept the new, smaller 5- and 25-pta. coins first minted in 1991. At press time (summer 1992), the exchange rate was about 97.5 ptas. to the U.S. dollar and 180 ptas. to the pound sterling.

Credit Cards Most hotels, restaurants, and stores (though not gas stations) accept payment by credit card. Visa is the most widely accepted piece of plastic, followed by MasterCard (called Euro-Card in Spain). More expensive establishments may also take American Express and Diners Club.

Spain

Changing Money The word to look for is "Cambio" (exchange). Most Spanish banks take a 1½% commission, though some less scrupulous places charge more; always check, as rates can vary greatly. To change money in a bank, you need your passport and a lot of patience, because filling out the forms takes time. Hotels offer rates lower than banks, but they rarely make a commission, so you may well break even. Restaurants and stores, with the exception of those catering to the tour bus trade, do not usually accept payment by dollars or traveler's checks.

Currency Regulations Visitors may take any amount of foreign currency in bills or traveler's checks into Spain as well as any amount of pesetas. When leaving Spain, you may take out only 100,000 ptas. per person in Spanish bank notes and foreign currency up to the equivalent of 500,000 ptas, unless you can prove you declared the excess at customs on entering the country.

What It Will Cost Prices rose fast during the first decade of Spain's democracy, and the nation's inflation rate was one of the highest in Europe. By 1991, however, inflation had been curbed and was running at a little over 5%. Generally speaking, the cost of living in Spain is now on a par with that of most other western European countries. Hotels are relatively expensive, sometimes shockingly so, especially in Seville, Barcelona, and Madrid. Dining out generally is not expensive; even with constantly rising prices, inexpensive restaurants abound. Snacks in cafés and bars are moderate to expensive by American standards, and alcohol is generally reasonable, except for cocktails in hotel bars. Trains and long-distance buses are relatively inexpensive. City subways and buses are a very good value.

Taxes A value-added tax known as IVA was introduced in 1986 when Spain joined the EC. IVA is levied at 6% on most goods and services, but a luxury rate of 13% applies to four- and five-star hotels and to car rental. IVA is always included in the purchase price of goods in stores, but for hotels and car rentals, the tax will be added to your bill. Many restaurants include IVA in their menu prices, but plenty—usually the more expensive ones—do not. Large stores, such as the Corte Inglés and Galerías Preciados, operate a tax refund plan for foreign visitors who are not EC nationals; but to qualify for this refund, you need to spend at least 48,000 ptas. in any one store and, in theory, on any one item. There is no airport tax in Spain.

Sample Prices A cup of coffee will cost around 100 ptas., a Coca-Cola 130 ptas., bottled beer 100 ptas.–120 ptas., a small draught beer 80 ptas.–100 ptas., a glass of wine in a bar 60 ptas., an American-style cocktail 300 ptas., a ham sandwich 220 ptas., an ice-cream cone about 100 ptas., a local bus or subway ride 100 ptas.–125 ptas., and a one-mile taxi ride about 350 ptas.

Language In major cities and coastal resorts you should have no trouble finding people who speak English. In such places, reception staff in hotels of three or more stars are required to speak English. Don't expect the man in the street or the bus driver to speak English, although they may.

Visitors may be surprised to find that Spanish is not the principal language of many regions of Spain. The Basques speak Euskera; in Catalunya (Catalonia), where Barcelona is located, you'll hear Catalan; in Galicia, Gallego; and in Valencia, Valenciana. While almost everyone in these regions also speaks Spanish, local radio and TV broadcasts are often in these other languages, as well as road signs, menus, and other printed material you will encounter.

Getting Around

Between cities, your best options are trains and buses—flying is convenient but expensive. Subways in the major cities are generally excellent, city buses a little harder to figure out. In emergencies, taxicabs are still a good deal, although you can get caught in traffic jams where you sit while the meter ticks inexorably on.

By Train   The Spanish railroad system, known usually by its initials RENFE, has greatly improved in recent years. Air-conditioned trains are now widespread but by no means universal. Most overnight trains have first- and second-class sleeping cars and second-class *literas* (couchettes). Dining, buffet, and refreshment services are available on most long-distance trains. There are various types of trains—*talgo*, ELT (electric unit expresses), TER (diesel rail cars), and ordinary *expresos* and *rápidos*. Fares are determined by the kind of train you travel on and not just by the distance traveled. Talgos are by far the quickest, most comfortable, and the most expensive train; *expresos* and *rápidos* are the slowest and cheapest of the long-distance services. In spring 1992, a high-speed train alternately referred to as the TAV (Tren Alto Velocidad) or the AVE began service between Madrid and Seville, reducing travel time between these cities from six to three and a half hours (fares vary, but the AVE can cost almost as much as flying). A few lines, such as the FEVE routes along the north coast from San Sebastián to El Ferrol and on the Costa Blanca around Alicante, do not belong to the national RENFE network, and international rail passes are not valid on these lines.

Ticket Purchase   Tickets can be bought from any station (whether or not it is
and Seat   your point of departure), and from downtown RENFE offices
Reservation   and travel agents displaying the blue and yellow RENFE sign. The latter are often best in the busy holiday season. At stations, buy your advance tickets from the window marked "Largo Recorrido, Venta Anticipada" (Long Distance, Advance Sales). Seat reservation can be made up to 60 days in advance and is obligatory on all the better long-distance services.

Fare Savers   The **RENFE Tourist Card** is an unlimited-kilometers pass, valid for 8, 15, or 22 days' travel, and can be bought by anyone who lives outside Spain. It is available for first- or second-class travel and can be purchased from RENFE's General Representative in Europe (3 Ave. Marceau, 75116 Paris, France, tel. 14/723–52–00); from selected travel agencies and main railroad stations abroad; and within Spain, at RENFE travel offices and the stations of Madrid, Barcelona, Port Bou, and Irún. At press time (spring 1992) the second-class pass cost 11,500 ptas. for 8 days, 18,500 ptas. for 15 days, and 24,000 ptas. for 22 days.

If you plan to travel to other countries in Europe, you may want to invest in a **EurailPass** or a **Eurail FlexiPass** (*see* Getting Around by Train in Chapter 1).

Blue Days *(Días Azules)* leaflets are available from RENFE offices and stations and show those days of the year (approximately 270) when you can travel at reduced rates. Be warned, though, that some of these bargains may apply only to Spaniards or to foreigners officially resident in Spain.

By Plane **Iberia** and its subsidiary **Aviaco** operate a wide network of domestic flights, linking all the main cities and the Balearic Islands. Distances are great and internal airfares still are low by European standards, so plane travel around Spain is well worth considering. Flights from the mainland to the Balearics are heavily booked in summer, and the Madrid–Málaga route is frequently overbooked at Easter and in high season. A frequent shuttle service operates between Madrid and Barcelona. Iberia has its own offices in most major Spanish cities and acts as agent for Aviaco. In Madrid, Iberia headquarters are at Velázquez 130 (tel. 91/585–8585, or call Inforiberia for flight information, tel. 91/411–2545). Flights can also be booked at most travel agencies. For information on other airlines' flights to and within Spain, call the airline itself, or tel. 91/205–8343, 8344, or 8345; for information on flight delays in and out of Madrid, call 91/305–8343.

By Bus Spain has an excellent bus network, but there is no national or nationwide bus company. The network simply consists of numerous private regional bus companies *(empresas)* and there are therefore no comprehensive bus passes. Some of the buses on major routes are now quite luxurious, although this is not always the case in rural areas. Buses tend to be more frequent than trains, are sometimes cheaper, and often allow you to see more of the countryside. On major routes and at holiday times it is advisable to buy your ticket a day or two in advance. Some cities have central bus stations but in many, including Madrid and Barcelona, buses leave from various boarding points. Always check with the local tourist office. Bus stations, unlike train stations, usually provide luggage storage facilities.

Staying in Spain

Telephones Pay phones are supposed to work with coins of 25 and either 50
Local Calls or 100 ptas. (smaller 5- and 25-ptas. coins do not work in the machines). Twenty-five ptas. is the minimum for short local calls. In the older gray phones, place several coins in the slot, or in the groove on top of the phone, lift the receiver, and dial the number. Coins then fall into the machine as needed. In the newer green phones, place several coins in the slot, watch the display unit and feed as needed. These phones take 100-pta. coins. Area codes, necessary when calling another province from within Spain, always begin with a 9 and are different for each province. In Madrid province, the code is 91; in Cantabria, it's 942.

International Calls Calling abroad is best done from the *Telefónica*, a telephone office found in all sizable towns, where an operator assigns you a private booth and collects payment at the end of the call. This is by far the least expensive way of making international calls. You can also call from any pay phone marked *Teléfono Internacional*. These phones are feasible for very short transatlantic calls, but you'll need a large handful of 25-, 50- and 100-ptas. coins. Use 50-pta. (or 100-pta. if the phone takes them) coins initially, then coins of any denomination to prolong your call. Dial 07 for international, wait for the tone to change, then 1 for the United States, or 44 for England, followed by the area code and number. For calls to England, omit the initial 0 from the area code. You can also call abroad from your room in major hotels, but a hefty service charge will be added, even for collect calls.

Operators and   For the operator and information for the city you are in, dial
Information   003; for information for the rest of Spain, 009. If you're in Madrid, dial 008 for Europe; 005 for the rest of the world. From anywhere else in Spain, dial 9198 for Europe and 9191 for the rest of the world.

Mail   To the United States, airmail letters up to 15 grams and post-
Postal Rates   cards each cost 83 ptas. To the United Kingdom and other EC countries, letters up to 20 grams and postcards each cost 45 ptas. To non–EC European countries, letters and postcards up to 20 grams cost 60 ptas. If you wish to expedite your overseas mail, send it *Urgente* for 160 ptas. over the regular airmail cost. Within Spain, letters and postcards each cost 27 ptas.; within a city in Spain, letters and postcards cost 17 ptas. Mailboxes are yellow with red stripes, and the slot marked "Extranjero" is the one for mail going abroad. Buy your stamps *(sellos)* at a post office *(correos)* or in a tobacco shop *(estanco)*.

Receiving Mail   If you're uncertain where you'll be staying, have mail sent to American Express or to the Poste Restante *(Lista de Correos)* of the local post office. To claim your mail, you'll need to show your passport. American Express has a $2 service charge per letter for non-cardholders. The Spanish mail is notoriously slow and not always very efficient.

Shopping   If you purchase goods up to a value of 48,000 ptas. or more in
Sales Tax Refunds   any one store (and in theory this should be on only *one* item), you are entitled to a refund of the IVA tax paid (usually 6% but more in the case of certain luxury goods), provided you leave Spain within three months. You will be given two copies of the sales invoice, which you must present at customs together with the goods as you leave Spain. Once the invoice has been stamped by customs, mail the blue copy back to the store, which will then mail your tax refund to you. If you are leaving via the airports of Madrid, Barcelona, Málaga or Palma de Mallorca, you can get your tax refund immediately from the Banco Exterior de España in the airport. The above does not apply to residents of EC countries, who must claim their IVA refund through customs in their own country. The Corte Inglés and Galerías Preciados department stores operate the above system, but don't be surprised if other stores are unfamiliar with the tax-refund procedure and do not have the necessary forms.

Bargaining   Prices in city stores and produce markets are fixed; bargaining is possible only in flea markets, some antiques stores, and with gypsy vendors, with whom it is *essential*, though you'd do best to turn them down flat as their goods are almost always fake and grossly overpriced.

Opening and   **Banks.** Banks are open Monday through Saturday 8:30–2 from
Closing Times   October to June; during the summer months they are closed on Saturdays.

Museums and churches. Opening times vary. Most are open in the morning, and most museums close one day a week, often Monday.

Post offices. These are usually open weekdays 9–2, but this can vary; check locally.

Stores. Stores are open weekdays from 9 or 10 until 1:30 or 2, then again in the afternoon from around 4 to 7 in winter, and 5 to 8 in summer. In some cities, especially in summer, stores close on Saturday afternoon. The Corte Inglés and Galerías Preciados department stores in major cities are open continuously from 10 to 8, and some stores in tourist resorts also stay open through the siesta.

National Holidays January 1; January 6 (Epiphany); March 19 (St. Joseph); April 8 (Holy Thursday); April 9 (Good Friday); May 1 (May Day); June 10 (Corpus Christi); July 25 (St. James); August 15 (Assumption); October 12 (National Day); November 1 (All Saints' Day); December 6 (Constitution); December 8 (Immaculate Conception); December 25. Other holidays include May 2 (in the province of Madrid) and June 24 (St. John). These holidays are not celebrated in every region; always check locally.

Dining Visitors have a choice of restaurants, tapas bars, and cafés. Restaurants are strictly for lunch and dinner; they do not serve breakfast. Tapas bars are ideal for a glass of wine or beer accompanied by an array of savory tidbits *(tapas)*. Cafés, called *cafeterías*, are basically coffee houses serving snacks, light meals, tapas, pastries, and coffee, tea, and alcoholic drinks. They also serve breakfast and are perfect for afternoon tea.

Mealtimes Mealtimes in Spain are much later than in any other European country. Lunch begins between 1 and 2:30, with 2 being the usual time, and 3 more normal on Sunday. Dinner is usually available from 8:30 onward, but 10 PM is the usual time in the larger cities and resorts. An important point to remember is that lunch is the main meal, not dinner. Tapas bars are busiest between noon and 2 and from 8 PM on. Cafés are usually open from around 8 AM to midnight.

Precautions Tap water is said to be safe to drink in all but the remotest villages (in Madrid, tap water, from the surrounding Guadarrama Mountains, is excellent; in Barcelona, it's safe but tastes terrible). However, most Spaniards drink bottled mineral water; ask for either *agua sin gas* (without bubbles) or *agua con gas* (with). A good paella should be served only at lunchtime and should be prepared to order (usually 30 minutes); beware the all-too-cheap version.

Typical Dishes Paella—a mixture of saffron-flavored rice with seafood, chicken, and vegetables—is Spain's national dish. Gazpacho, a cold soup usually made of crushed garlic, tomatoes, and olive oil, garnished with diced vegetables, is a traditional Andalusian dish and is served mainly in summer. The Basque Country and Galicia are the gourmet regions of Spain, and both serve outstanding fish and seafood. Asturias is famous for its *fabadas* (bean stews), cider, and dairy products; Extremadura for its hams and sausages; and Castile for its roasts, especially *cochinillo* (suckling pig), *cordero asado* (roast lamb), and *perdiz* (partridge). The best wines are those from the Rioja and Penedés regions. Valdepeñas is a pleasant table wine, and most places serve a perfectly acceptable house wine called *vino de la casa*. Sherries from Jerez de la Frontera make fine aperitifs; ask for a *fino* or a *manzanilla;* both are dry. In summer you can try *horchata*, a sweet white drink made from ground nuts, or *granizados de limón* or *de café*, lemon juice or coffee served over crushed ice. *Un café solo* is a small, black, strong coffee, and *café con leche* is espresso diluted with hot milk; weak black American-style coffee is hard to come by.

Dress Casual dress is almost always appropriate; you'll need a jacket and tie for only the most expensive restaurants. However, shorts are often frowned upon in cities.

Ratings Spanish restaurants are officially classified from five forks down to one fork, with most places falling into the two- or three-fork category. In our rating system, prices are per person and include a first course, main course, and dessert, but not wine or tip. Sales tax (IVA) is usually included in the menu price; check the menu for *IVA incluído* or *IVA no incluído*. When it's not included, an additional 6% (13% in the fancier restaurants) will be added to your bill. Most restaurants offer a fixed-price menu called a *menú del día;* however, this is often offered only at lunch, and at dinner tends to be merely a reheated midday offering. This is usually the cheapest way of eating; *à la carte* dining is more expensive. Service charges are never added to your bill; leave around 10%, less in inexpensive restaurants and bars. Major centers such as Madrid, Barcelona, Marbella, and Seville tend to be a bit more expensive. Best bets are indicated by a star ★.

Category	All Areas
Moderate	2,800 ptas.–5,000 ptas.
Inexpensive	1,600 ptas.–2,800 ptas.
Budget	under 1,600 ptas.

Lodging Spain has a wide range of accommodations, including luxury palaces, medieval monasteries, converted 19th-century houses, modern hotels, high rises on the coasts, and inexpensive hostels in family homes. All hotels and hostels are listed with their rates in the annual *Guía de Hoteles* available from bookstores and kiosks for around 500 ptas., or you can see a copy in local tourist offices. Rates are always quoted per room, and not per person. Single occupancy of a double room costs 80% of the normal price. Breakfast is rarely included in the quoted room rate; always check. The quality of rooms, particularly in older properties, can be uneven; always ask to see your room *before* you sign the acceptance slip. If you want a private bathroom in a less expensive hotel, state your preference for shower or bathtub; the latter usually costs more though many hotels have both. Local tourist offices will provide you with a list of accommodations in their region, but they are not allowed to make reservations for you. In Madrid and Barcelona, hotel booking agencies are found at the airports and railroad stations.

Hotels and Hostels Hotels are officially classified from five stars (the highest) to one star, hostels from three stars to one star. Good, inexpensive lodging can be found at hostels, which in Spain are usually family homes converted to provide accommodations (though they are frequently comfortable and modern midsize hotels). If an R appears on the blue hotel or hostel plaque, the hotel is classified as a *residencia*, and full dining services are not provided, though breakfast and cafeteria facilities may be available. A three-star hostel usually equates with a two-star hotel; two- and one-star hostels offer simple, basic accommodations. The main hotel chains are Husa, Iberotel Melia, Sol, and

Tryp, and the state-run *paradores* (tourist hotels). Holiday Inn, InterContinental, and Trusthouse Forte also own some of the best hotels in Madrid, Barcelona, and Seville; only these and the paradores have any special character. The others mostly provide clean, comfortable accommodation in the two- to four-star range. The cost of lodging in Spain varies wildly according to place and season, so you're wise to *always* inquire before booking.

In many hotels rates vary fairly dramatically according to the time of year. The hotel year is divided into *estación alta, media,* and *baja* (high, mid, and low season); high season usually covers the summer and Easter and Christmas periods, plus the major fiestas. IVA is rarely included in the quoted room rates, so be prepared for an additional 6%, or, in the case of luxury four- and five-star hotels, 13%, to be added to your bill. Service charges are never included.

Paradors   There are about 80 state-owned-and-run paradors, many of which are located in magnificent medieval castles or convents or in places of great natural beauty. Most of these fall into the four-star category and are priced accordingly. Most have restaurants that specialize in local regional cuisine and serve a full breakfast. The most popular paradors (Granada's San Francisco parador, for example) are booked far in advance, and many close for a month or two in winter (January or February) for renovations. While the paradors aren't cheap, they're a wonderful treat—and far less expensive than anything comparable in the United States or western Europe.

Camping   There are approximately 530 campsites in Spain, with the highest concentration along the Mediterranean coast. The season runs from April to October, though some sites are open year-round. Sites are listed in the annual publication *Guía de Campings* available from bookstores or local tourist offices, and further details are available from the Spanish National Tourist Office. Reservations for the most popular seaside sites can be made either directly with the site or through camping reservations at: Federación Española de Empresarios de Campings (Príncipe de Vergara 85, 2° Dcha, 28006 Madrid, tel. 91/562–9994).

Ratings   Prices are for two people in a double room and do not include breakfast. Best bets are indicated by a star ★.

Category	Major City	Other Areas
Moderate	8,000–12,000 ptas.	6,000–10,000 ptas.
Inexpensive	4,000–8,000 ptas.	3,500–6,000 ptas.
Budget	under 4,000 ptas.	under 3,500 ptas.

Tipping   Spaniards appreciate being tipped, though the practice is becoming less widespread. Restaurants and hotels are by law not allowed to add a service charge to your bill, though confusingly your bill for both will most likely say *servicios e impuestos incluídos* (service and tax included). Ignore this unhelpful piece of advice, and leave 10% in most restaurants where you have had a full meal; in humbler eating places, bars, and cafés, 5%–10% is enough, or you can round out the bill to the nearest 100 ptas. A cocktail waiter in a hotel will expect at least 30 ptas.

a drink, maybe 50 ptas. in a luxury establishment. Tip taxi drivers about 10% when they use the meter, otherwise *nothing*—they'll have seen to it themselves. Gas-station attendants get no tip for pumping gas, but they get about 50 ptas. for checking tires and oil and cleaning windshields. Train and airport porters usually operate on a fixed rate of about 60 ptas. a bag. Coat-check attendants get 25 ptas., and rest-room attendants get 10 ptas. In top hotels doormen get 100 ptas. for carrying bags to the check-in counter or for hailing taxis, and bellhops get 50 ptas.–100 ptas. for room service or for each bag they carry to your room. In moderate hotels about 50 ptas. is adequate for the same services. Leave your chambermaid about 300 ptas. for a week's stay. There's no need to tip for just a couple of nights. The waiter in your hotel dining room will appreciate 500 ptas. a week.

Madrid

Arriving and Departing

By Plane All international and domestic flights arrive at Madrid's **Barajas Airport** (tel. 91/205–8343/8344/8345; for information on flight delays, in Spanish only, tel. 91/305–8343), 16 kilometers (10 miles) northeast of town just off the N-II Barcelona highway. For information on arrival and departure times, call **Inforiberia** (tel. 91/411–2545) or the airline concerned.

Between the Airport and Downtown Buses leave the national and international terminals every 15 minutes from 5:40 AM to 2 AM for the downtown terminal at Plaza de Colón just off the Paseo de la Castellana. The ride takes about 20 minutes and the fare at press time was 275 ptas. Most city hotels are then only a short taxi ride away. The fastest and most expensive route into town (up to 2,000 ptas. plus tip) is by taxi. Pay what is on the meter plus 300 ptas. surcharge and 50 ptas. for each suitcase.

By Train Madrid has three railroad stations. **Chamartín,** in the northern suburbs beyond the Plaza de Castilla, is the main station, with trains to France, the north, and the northeast (including Barcelona). Most trains to Valencia, Alicante, and Andalusia now leave from here, too, but stop at **Atocha station,** at the southern end of Paseo del Prado on the Glorieta del Emperador Carlos V. Also departing from Atocha, where a new station was built in 1989, are trains to Toledo, Granada, Extremadura, and Lisbon. In 1992, a convenient new metro stop (Atocha RENFE) was opened in Atocha station, connecting it to the city subway system. The old Atocha station, designed by Eiffel and refurbished in 1990–91, was reopened in 1992 as the Madrid terminus for the new high-speed rail service to Seville (AVE). **Norte** (or Príncipe Pío), on Paseo de la Florida, in the west of town below the Plaza de España, is the departure point for Ávila, Segovia, El Escorial, Salamanca, Santiago, La Coruña, and all destinations in Galicia.

For all train information, call RENFE (tel. 91/530–0202, in Spanish only), or go to its offices on the second floor of Torre de Madrid in the Plaza de España, right above the main tourist office (open weekdays 9–3 and 5–7, Sat. 9–3). There's another RENFE office at Barajas Airport in the International Arrivals Hall, or you can purchase tickets at any of the three main stations, or from travel agents displaying the blue and yellow RENFE sign.

By Bus Madrid has no central bus station. The two main bus stations are the **Estación del Sur** (Canarias 17, tel. 91/468–4200), nearest metro Palos de la Frontera, for buses to Toledo, La Mancha, Alicante, and Andalusia; and **Auto-Rés** (Plaza Conde de Casal 6, tel. 91/551–7200), nearest metro Conde de Casal, for buses to Extremadura, Cuenca, Salamanca, Valladolid, Valencia, and Zamora. Auto-Rés has a central ticket and information office at Salud 19 near the Hotel Arosa, just off Gran Vía. Buses to other destinations leave from various points, so check with the tourist office. The Basque country and most of north central Spain is served by Auto Continental (Alenza 20, nearest metro Ríos Rosas, tel. 91/533–0400). For Àvila, Segovia, and La Granja, Empresa La Sepulvedana (tel. 91/230–4800) leaves from Paseo de la Florida 11, next to the Norte station, a few steps from the Norte metro stop. Empresa Herranz (tel. 91/543–3645 or 91/543–8167), serving San Lorenzo de El Escorial and the Valley of the Fallen, departs from the base of Calle Fernandez de los Ríos, a few yards from the Moncloa metro stop. La Veloz (Avda. Mediterraneo 49, tel. 91/409–7602) serves Chinchón.

Getting Around

Madrid is a fairly compact city and most of the main sights can be visited on foot. But if you're staying in one of the modern hotels in the north of town off the Castellana, you may well need to use the bus or subway (metro). The metro is efficient, inexpensive, and easy to use; buses are priced identically but are generally harder to use (an exception may be the buses that run up and down the Castellana, a useful route). As a rough guide, the walk from the Prado to the Royal Palace at a comfortable sightseeing pace but without stopping takes around 30 minutes; from Plaza del Callao on Gran Vía to the Plaza Mayor, it takes about 15 minutes.

By Metro The subway offers the simplest and quickest means of transport and is open from 6 AM to 1:30 AM. Metro maps are available from ticket offices, hotels, and tourist offices. Fares at press time (but expected to rise soon) were 115 ptas. a ride. Savings can be made by buying a *taco* of 10 tickets for 450 ptas., or a tourist card called **Metrotour** that is good for unlimited travel for three or five days. Keep some change (5, 25, 50, and 100 ptas.) handy for the ticket machines, especially after 10 PM; the machines give change and are handy for beating often long lines for tickets.

By Bus City buses are red and run from 6 AM to midnight (though check, as some stop earlier). Again there is a flat-fare system, with each ride costing 115 ptas. The smaller, yellow microbuses also cost 115 ptas. and are slightly faster. Route plans are displayed at bus stops *(paradas)*, and a map of the entire system is available from EMT (Empresa Municipal de Transportes) booths on Plaza de la Cibeles, Callao, or Puerta del Sol. Savings can be made by buying a **Bonobus** (450 ptas.), good for 10 rides, from EMT booths or any branch of the Caja de Ahorros de Madrid.

Important Addresses and Numbers

Tourist The main Madrid tourist office (tel. 91/541–2325) is on the
Information ground floor of the Torre de Madrid in Plaza de España, near
the beginning of Calle de la Princesa, and is open weekdays
9–7, Saturdays 9:30–1:30. Another Madrid Provincial Tourist
Office (Duque de Medinaceli 2, tel. 91/429–4951) is conveniently located on a small street across from the Palace Hotel. The
much less useful municipal tourist office is at Plaza Mayor 3
(tel. 91/266–5477) and is open weekdays 10–1:30 and 4–7, Saturdays 10–1:30. A third office is in the International Arrivals
Hall of Barajas Airport (tel. 91/305–8656) and is open weekdays
8–8, Saturdays 8–1.

Embassies U.S. (Serrano 75, tel. 91/576–3400), **Canadian** (Núñez de Bal-
boa 35, tel. 91/431–4300), **U.K.** (Fernando el Santo 16, tel. 91/
308–0459).

Emergencies **Police:** (National Police, tel. 091; Municipal Police, tel. 092;
Main Police [Policía Nacional] Station, Puerta del Sol 7, tel. 91/
522–0435). To report lost passports, go to Los Madrazos 9 just
off the top of Paseo del Prado. **Ambulance:** tel. 91/734–2554 or
734–2600. **Doctor:** Your hotel reception will contact the nearest
doctor for you. Emergency clinics: **Hospital 12 de Octubre**
(Avda. Córdoba, tel. 91/390–8000) and **La Paz Ciudad Sanitaria**
(Paseo de la Castellana 261, tel. 91/734–3200). English-speaking doctors are available at Conde de Aranda 7 (tel. 91/
435–1595).

Airlines **Iberia** (Princesa 2, tel. 91/585–8159; for flight information, call
Inforiberia, tel. 91/411–2545), **British Airways** (Serrano 60, 5th
floor, tel. 91/431–7575), and **TWA** (Plaza de Colón 2, tel. 91/410–
6007 or 91/410–6010).

Exploring Madrid

*Numbers in the margin correspond to points of interest on the
Madrid map.*

You can walk the following route in a day, or even half a day if
you stop only to visit the Prado and Royal Palace. Two days
should give you time for browsing. Begin in the Plaza Atocha,
more properly known as the Glorieta del Emperador Carlos V,
at the bottom of the Paseo del Prado, and check out what's
❶ showing in the **Reina Sofía Arts Center** opened by Queen Sofía
in 1986. This converted hospital, home of art and sculpture exhibitions and symbol of Madrid's new cultural pride, is fast becoming one of Europe's most dynamic venues—a Madrileño
rival to Paris's Pompidou Center. The center's status as an important art repository rose last year when it acquired from the
Prado Picasso's *Guernica*, the artist's monumental expression
of anguish and outrage at the German bombing of a Basque
town in 1937. The main entrance is on Calle de Santa Isabel 52.
*Tel. 91/467–5062. Admission: 400 ptas. Open daily except
Tues., 10 AM–9 PM.*

Walk up Paseo del Prado to Madrid's number-one sight, the fa-
❷ mous **Prado Museum**, one of the world's most important art galleries. Plan on spending at least 1½ days here, though it will
take at least two full days to view its treasures properly. Brace
yourself for the crowds. The greatest treasures—the Velázquez, Murillo, Zurbarán, El Greco, and Goya galleries—are all

Major Attractions

Other Attractions

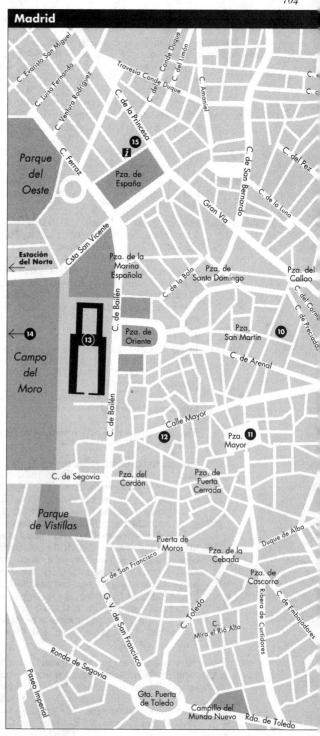

Madrid

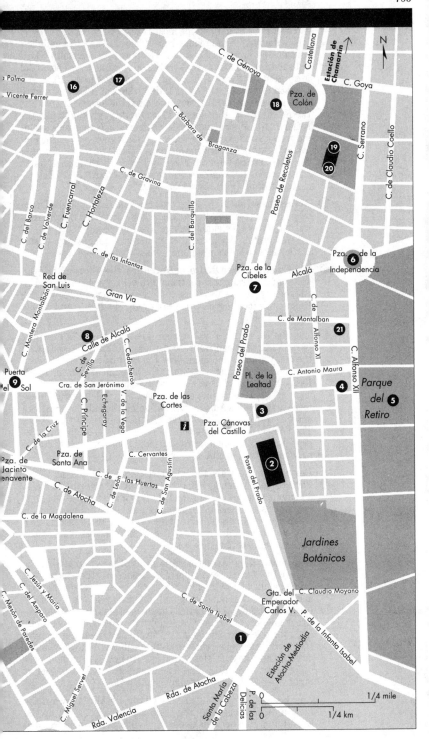

C. de Génova

Castellana

Estación de
Chamartín

N

C. Goya

Pza. de
Colón

18

16   **17**

a Palma

Vicente Ferrer

C. Bárbara de
Braganza

C. de Claudio Coello

C. Serrano

19
20

Paseo de Recoletos

C. de Gravina

C. del Barquillo

C. del Barco

C. de Valverde

C. Fuencarral

C. Hortaleza

C. de las Infantas

Pza. de la
Cibeles

Pza. de la
Independencia

6

Alcalá

Red de
San Luis

Gran Vía

7

C. de Montalban

21

Alfonso XI

C. de

C. Antonio Maura

C. Montera

C. Montalbán

Calle de Alcalá

8

C. de Sevilla

C. Cedaceros

Paseo del Prado

Pl. de la
Lealtad

4

C. Alfonso XII

Parque
del
Retiro

5

Puerta
del Sol

9

Cra. de San Jerónimo

Pza. de las
Cortes

Pza. Cánovas
del Castillo

3

C. de la Cruz

C. Príncipe

Echegaray

V. de la Vega

Pza. de
Santa Ana

C. Cervantes

C. de León

las Huertas

C. de San Agustín

𝑖

2

Pza. de
Jacinto
Benavente

C. de Atocha

C. de la Magdalena

Jardines
Botánicos

C. Jesús y María

C. del Amparo

C. Mesón de Paredes

C. de Santa Isabel

Gta. del
Emperador
Carlos V.

C. Claudio Moyano

P. de la Infanta Isabel

1

Estación de
Atocha-Mediodía

C. Miguel Servet

Rda. de Atocha

Rda. Valencia

Santa María
de la Cabeza

P. de las
Delicias

0   1/4 mile

0   1/4 km

on the upstairs floor. Two of the best works are Velázquez's *Surrender of Breda* and his most famous work, *Las Meninas*, which dominates the room where it hangs. The Goya galleries contain the artist's none-too-flattering royal portraits (Goya believed in painting the truth) his exquisitely beautiful *Marquesa de Santa Cruz*, and his famous *Naked Maja* and *Clothed Maja*, for which the 13th duchess of Alba was said to have posed. Goya's most moving works, the *Second of May* and the *Fusillade of Moncloa* or *Third of May*, vividly depict the sufferings of Madrid patriots at the hands of Napoleon's invading troops in 1808. Before you leave, feast your eyes on the fantastic flights of fancy of Hieronymus Bosch's *Garden of Earthly Delights* and his triptych *The Hay Wagon*, both downstairs on the ground floor. *Paseo del Prado s/n, tel. 91/420–2836. Admission: 400 ptas. Open Tues.–Sat. 9–7, Sun. 9–2.*

❸ Across the street is the **Ritz,** the grand old lady of Madrid's hotels, built in 1910 by Alfonso XIII when he realized that his capital had no hotels elegant enough to accommodate the guests at his wedding in 1906. The Ritz garden is a delightfully aristocratic place to lunch in summer—men always need ties.

❹ The **Casón del Buen Retiro,** entrance on Calle Alfonso XII, is an annex of the Prado that contains 19th-century Spanish art. Until recently, it was also home to Picasso's *Guernica*, now in the Reina Sofía (*see above*). *Open same hours as Prado and visited on same ticket.*

❺ The **Retiro,** once a royal retreat, is today Madrid's prettiest park. Visit the beautiful rose garden, **La Rosaleda,** and enjoy the many statues and fountains. You can hire a carriage, row a boat on **El Estanque,** gaze up at the monumental **statue to Alfonso XII,** one of Spain's least notable kings though you wouldn't think so to judge by its size, or wonder at the **Monument to the Fallen Angel**—Madrid claims the dubious privilege of being the only capital to have a statue dedicated to the Devil. The **Palacio de Velázquez** and the beautiful steel-and-glass **Palacio de Cristal,** built as a tropical plant house in the 19th century, now host art exhibits.

❻ Leaving the Retiro via its northwest corner, you come to the Plaza de la Independencia, dominated by the **Puerta de Alcalá,** a grandiose gateway built in 1779 for Charles III. A customs post once stood beside the gate, as did the old bullring until it was moved to its present site at Ventas in the 1920s. At the turn of the century, the Puerta de Alcalá more or less marked the eastern limits of Madrid.

❼ Continue to the **Plaza de la Cibeles,** one of the great landmarks of the city, at the intersection of its two main arteries, the Castellana and Calle de Alcalá. If you can see it through the roar and fumes of the thundering traffic, the square's center is the **Cibeles Fountain,** the unofficial emblem of Madrid. Cybele, the Greek goddess of fertility, languidly rides her lion-drawn chariot, overlooked by the mighty **Palacio de Comunicaciones,** a splendidly pompous cathedral-like building often jokingly dubbed Our Lady of Communications. In fact, it's the main post office, erected in 1918. The famous goddess looks her best at night when she's illuminated by floodlights.

Now head down the long and busy Calle de Alcalá toward the Puerta del Sol, resisting the temptation to turn right up the Gran Vía, which beckons temptingly with its mile of stores and cafés. Before you reach the Puerta del Sol, art lovers may want ⑧ to step inside the **Real Academia de Bellas Artes** at Alcalá 13. This recently refurbished fine arts gallery boasts an art collection second in Madrid only to the Prado's and features all the great Spanish masters: Velázquez, El Greco, Murillo, Zurbarán, Ribera, and Goya. *Alcalá 13, tel. 91/532–1546. Admission: 200 ptas. Open Tues.–Fri. 9–7; Sat., Sun., and Mon. 9–3.*

⑨ The **Puerta del Sol** is at the very heart of Madrid. Its name means Gate of the Sun, though the old gate disappeared long ago. It's easy to feel you're at the heart of things here—indeed, of all of Spain—for the kilometer distances for the whole nation are measured from the zero marker in front of the Police Headquarters. The square was expertly revamped in 1986 and now accommodates both a copy of **La Mariblanca** (a statue that 250 years ago adorned a fountain here) and, at the bottom of Calle Carmen, the much-loved **statue of the bear and *madroño*** (strawberry tree). The Puerta del Sol is inextricably linked with the history of Madrid and of the nation. Here, half a century ago, a generation of literati gathered in the long-gone cafés to thrash out the burning issues of the day; and if you can cast your thoughts back almost 200 years, you can conjure up the heroic deeds of the patriots' uprising immortalized by Goya in the *Second of May.*

This is a good place to break the tour if you've had enough sightseeing for one day. Head north up Preciados or Montera for some of the busiest and best shopping streets in the city or southeast toward Plaza Santa Ana for tavern-hopping in Old Madrid.

⑩ Art lovers will want to make a detour to the **Convento de las Descalzas Reales** on Plaza Descalzas Reales just above Arenal. It was founded by Juana de Austria, daughter of Charles V, and is still inhabited by nuns. Over the centuries the nuns, daughters of the royal and noble, endowed the convent with an enormous wealth of jewels, religious ornaments, superb Flemish tapestries, and the works of such great masters as Titian and Rubens. A bit off the main tourist track, it's one of Madrid's better-kept secrets. Your ticket includes admission to the nearby, but less interesting, **Convento de la Encarnación.** *Plaza de las Descalzas Reales, tel. 91/248–7404. Admission: 350 ptas. Guided Spanish-language tours only. Open Tues.–Thurs., Sat. 10:30–12:30 and 4–5:30; Fri. 10:30–12:30; Sun. 11–1:30.*

Walk up **Calle Mayor,** the Main Street of Old Madrid, past the shops full of religious statues and satins for bishops' robes, to ⑪ the **Plaza Mayor,** the capital's greatest architectural showpiece. It was built in 1617–19 for Philip III—that's Philip on the horse in the middle. The plaza has witnessed the canonization of saints, burning of heretics, fireworks and bullfights, and is still one of the great gathering places of Madrid.

If you're here in the morning, take a look inside the 19th-century steel-and-glass San Miguel market, a colorful provi-⑫ sions market, before continuing down Calle Mayor to the **Plaza de la Villa.** The square's notable cluster of buildings includes some of the oldest houses in Madrid. The **Casa de la Villa,** the Madrid city hall, was built in 1644 and has also served as the city prison and the mayor's home. Its sumptuous salons are now open to the public on Mondays at 5 PM. The free guided visits are usually in Spanish, but English tours can be arranged with advance notice. An archway joins the Casa de la Villa to the **Casa Cisneros,** a palace built in 1537 for the nephew of Cardinal Cisneros, primate of Spain and infamous inquisitor general. Across the square, the **Torre de Lujanes** is one of the oldest buildings in Madrid. It once imprisoned Francis I of France, archenemy of the Emperor Charles V.

⑬ The last stop on the tour, but Madrid's second most important sight, is the **Royal Palace.** This magnificent granite and limestone residence was begun by Philip V, the first Bourbon king of Spain, who was always homesick for his beloved Versailles, the opulence and splendor of which he did his best to emulate. His efforts were successful, to judge by the 2,800 rooms with their lavish Rococo decorations, precious carpets, porcelain, time pieces, mirrors, and chandeliers. From 1764, when Charles III first moved in, till the coming of the Second Republic and the abdication of Alfonso XIII in 1931, the Royal Palace proved a very stylish abode for Spanish monarchs. Today King Juan Carlos, who lives in the far less ostentatious Zarzuela Palace outside Madrid, uses it only for official state functions. The Palace can be visited only on guided tours, sometimes available in English. Allow 1½–2 hours for a visit. A *visita completa* (full visit), including the Royal Carriage Museum (*see below*), Royal Pharmacy, and other outbuildings, costs 500 ptas.; many visitors opt for the *Salones Oficiales* (State Rooms) ticket at 325 ptas. *Bailén s/n, tel. 91/248–7404. Admission: 500 ptas. for entire complex, 325 ptas. for palace only. Open Mon.–Sat. 9–5:15 (6:15 in winter), Sun. 9–2:15. Closed during frequent official functions.*

⑭ The **Royal Carriage Museum,** which belongs to the palace (and has the same hours) but has a separate entrance on Paseo Vírgen del Puerto, can be visited only on an all-inclusive ticket. One of its highlights is the wedding carriage of Alfonso XIII and his English bride, Victoria Eugenia, granddaughter of Queen Victoria. The carriage was damaged by a bomb thrown at it in the Calle Mayor during the royal wedding procession in 1906; another is the chair that carried the gout-stricken old Emperor Charles V to his retirement at the remote monastery of Yuste.

Shopping

Gift Ideas There are no special regional crafts associated with Madrid itself, but traditional Spanish goods are on sale in many stores. The **Corte Inglés** and **Galerías Preciados** department stores both stock good displays of Lladró porcelain. They also carry fans, but for really superb examples, try the long-established **Casa Diego** in Puerta del Sol. Two stores opposite the Prado on Plaza Cánovas del Castillo, **Artesanía Toledana** and **El Escudo de Toledo,** have a wide selection of souvenirs, especially Toledo swords, inlaid marquetry ware, and pottery. Carefully selected handicrafts from all over Spain—ceramics, furniture, glassware, rugs, embroidery, and more—are sold at **Artespaña** (Plaza de las Cortes 3, Gran Vía 32, and Hermosilla 14), a government-run crafts store.

Antiques The main areas to see are the Plaza de las Cortes, the Carrera San Jerónimo, and the Rastro flea market, along the Ribera de Curtidores and the courtyards just off it.

Shopping Districts	The main shopping area in the heart of Madrid is around the pedestrian streets of **Preciados** and **Montera,** between Puerta del Sol and Plaza Callao on Gran Vía. **Calle Mayor** and the streets to the east of **Plaza Mayor** are lined with fascinating old-fashioned stores straight out of the 19th century.
Department Stores	**El Corte Inglés** is the biggest and most successful Spanish chain store. Its main branch is on Preciados, just off the Puerta del Sol. **Galerías Preciados** is its main rival, with branches on Plaza Callao right off Gran Vía, Calle Arapiles, Goya, corner of Conde de Peñalver, Serrano and Ortega y Gasset. Both stores are open Monday–Saturday 10–8, and neither closes for the siesta.
Flea Markets	**The Rastro,** Madrid's most famous flea market, operates on Sundays from 9 to 2 around the Plaza del Cascorro and the Ribera de Curtidores. A **stamp and coin** market is held on Sunday mornings in the Plaza Mayor, and there's a **secondhand book** market most days on the Cuesta Claudio Moyano near Atocha Station.

Bullfighting

The Madrid bullfighting season runs from March to October. Fights are held on Sunday, and sometimes also on Thursday; starting times vary between 4:30 and 7 PM. The pinnacle of the spectacle may be seen during the three weeks of daily bullfights held during the San Isidro festivals in May. The bullring is at Las Ventas (formally known as the Plaza de Toros Monumental), Alcalá 237 (metro Ventas). You can buy your ticket there shortly before the fight, or, with a 20% surcharge, at the agencies that line Calle Victoria, just off Carrera San Jerónimo and Puerta del Sol.

Dining

For details and price-category definitions, *see* Dining in Staying in Spain.

Moderate	**Armstrong's.** This charming English-owned restaurant opposite the Teatro Zarzuela is bright and modern, with refreshing pink decor, and is quite a change from the usual Madrid scene. Its imaginative menu mixes French and Spanish nouvelle cuisine with English and American favorites, and there's a good choice of salads, brunch on weekends, and a special teatime menu. It stays open unusually late—until 1AM. *Jovellanos 5, tel. 91/522–4230. Reservations advised. AE, DC, MC, V. Closed Sun. evening and Mon.*

Botín. Madrid's oldest and most famous restaurant, just off the Plaza Mayor, has been catering to diners since 1725. Its decor and food are traditionally Castilian. *Cochinillo* (suckling pig) and *cordero asado* (roast lamb) are its specialties. It was a favorite with Hemingway; today it's very touristy and a bit overrated, but fun. Insist on the *cueva* or upstairs dining room. *Cuchilleros 17, tel. 91/266–4217. Reservations advised, especially at night. AE, DC, MC. V.*

Carmencita. Dating to 1850, this charming restaurant is small and intimate, with ceramic wall tiles, brass hat racks, and photos of bullfighters. The menu recounts the famous who have dined here and their life stories. The cuisine is part traditional, part nouvelle with an emphasis on *pasteles* (a kind of mousse) both savory and sweet. *Libertad 16, on the corner of San Marcos in the Chueca area above Gran Vía; tel. 91/531–6612. Reservations advised. V. Closed Sun.*

Casa Ciriaco. In this atmospheric old standby only a few paces from the Plaza Mayor and city hall, the Madrid of 50 years ago lives on. You won't find many foreigners here—just businesspeople and locals enjoying traditional Spanish cooking and delicious *fresones* (strawberries) for dessert. *Mayor 84, tel. 91/248–0620. Reservations accepted. No credit cards. Closed Wed., and Aug.*

★ **Fuente Real.** Dining here is like eating in a turn-of-the-century home. Tucked away between Mayor and Arenal, it's brimming with personal mementos such as antique dolls, Indian figures, and Mexican Christmas decorations. The cuisine is French and Spanish with an emphasis on high-quality meats and crêpes. Try the *pastel de espinacas* (spinach mousse) or *crêpes de puerros* (leeks). *Fuentes 1, tel. 91/247–3036. Reservations not necessary. AE, MC, V. Closed Sun. eve. and Mon.*

La Barraca. A Valencian restaurant with cheerful blue-and-white decor, colorful windowboxes, and ceramic tiles, this is the place to go for a wonderful choice of paellas. Located just off Gran Vía (Alcalá end), behind Loewe, it's popular with businesspeople and foreign visitors. Try the *paella reina* or the *paella de mariscos. Reina 29, tel. 91/532–7154. Reservations advised. AE, DC, MC, V.*

Inexpensive **Bodegon Logroñes.** This charming restaurant is hidden behind a gaudy cafeteria-style bar. Walk to the back of the ground floor bar and dining room and descend into an old wine cellar cheerfully decorated with game trophies. There's a surprisingly fine wine list, and excellent Spanish specialties, with an emphasis on—fittingly—game. Try the excellent *pimientos rellenos de carne* (green peppers stuffed with meat). *Plaza Tirso de Molina 5, tel. 91/369–1137. No credit cards. Reserve for Sun. lunch only. Closed Wed.*

El Club. It's touristy, and its outside terrace is often plagued by thieves and bullfight ticket scalpers, but the food here is good. The terrace, crowded with metal tables in a busy pedestrian alley, is a great place to have a paella, the house special, or the *menú del día. Victoria 4, tel. 91/522–2293. AE, DC, MC, V.*

★ **El Cuchi.** "Hemingway *never* ate here" is the sign that will lure you inside this colorful tavern at the bottom of the Cuchilleros, steps off the Plaza Mayor. A fun-packed experience awaits. The ceilings are plastered with photos of Mexican revolutionaries, huge blackboards announce the menu and list the calories in the irresistible desserts, and home-baked rolls are lowered in baskets from the ceiling to your table. Salads are on the house. This is a place you shouldn't miss. *Cuchilleros 3, tel. 91/266–4424. Reservations advised. AE, DC, MC, V.*

El Luarqués. One of many budget restaurants on this street, El Luarqués is decorated with photos of the port of Luarca on Spain's north coast, and it's always packed with Madrileños who recognize its good value. *Fabada asturiana* (bean and meat stew) and *arroz con leche* (rice pudding) are two of its Asturian specialties. *Ventura de la Vega 16, tel. 91/429–6174. No reservations. No credit cards. Closed Sun. eve., Mon., and Aug.*

Budget **Sanabresa.** You can tell by the clientele what a find this is: a demanding crowd of working men and women and penurious dance students from the nearby flamenco school. The menu is classic Spanish fare, with wholesome meals like the *pechuga villaroy* (breaded roast chicken with white sauce) and paella. If you arrive later than 1:30, you'll wait in line for lunch. *Amor de Díos 12, no phone. No credit cards. Closed Sun. eve. and Aug.*

Zara. Here's one of the finest gastronomic expressions of Madrid's Cuban community, second in size only to Miami's. Low prices and hearty Cuban specialties have made this small restaurant an extremely popular lunch spot—so popular you should plan on getting there before 1:30 for lunch. It's a dim room, without natural light and crowded with tables, but the animated talk of Cuban expatriates gives it great life. *Infantas 5, tel. 91/532-2074. AE, DC, MC, V. Closed weekends and Aug.*

Lodging

Affordable hotels in the midst of all the sights and shops are mostly located in 19th-century houses, a great many of which are now small, inexpensive hostels. It's still possible to find a decent, if tiny, room in one of these for less than $20, but you'll have to hunt for it. The scores of such hostels close to the Puerta del Sol and the Plaza Santa Ana are not listed here—their few rooms are snapped up quickly and are impossible to reserve in advance. You can inquire upon arrival, but be prepared with alternatives, especially during high tourist season.

Most of the newer hotels that conform to American standards of comfort are located in the northern part of town on either side of the Castellana and are a short metro or bus ride from the center. There are hotel reservation desks in the national and international terminals of the airport, and at Chamartín station (tel. 91/315–7894). Or you can contact **La Brújula** (tel. 91/248–9705) on the sixth floor of the Torre de Madrid in Plaza de España, which is open 9–9. It has English-speaking staff and can book hotels all over Spain for a fee of 200 ptas.

For details and price-category definitions, *see* Lodging in Staying in Spain.

Moderate   **Capitol.** If you like being right in the center of things, then this hotel on the Plaza Callao is for you. It's an older hotel, but four floors have been renovated; the rooms on these floors are more comfortable, but also 30% more expensive. There's a well-decorated reception area and a pleasant cafeteria for breakfast. *Gran Vía 41, tel. 91/521-8391, fax 91/247-1238. 145 rooms. AE, DC, V.*

Mayorazgo. This is an older hotel that has yet to be renovated, but it's comfortable as long as you're not seeking all the conveniences of home. Advantages include its friendly, old-fashioned service and its prime location right in the heart of town, tucked away in a quiet back street off Gran Vía that leads down to Plaza de España. *Flor Baja 3, tel. 91/247-2600, fax 91/541-2485. 200 rooms. AE, DC, MC, V.*

Paris. Overlooking the Puerta del Sol, the Paris is a stylish hotel full of old-fashioned appeal. It has an impressive turn-of-the-century lobby and a restaurant where you can dine for around 1,500 ptas. Recently refurbished, the hotel has managed to retain its character while adding modern amenities. *Alcalá 2, tel. 91/521-6496. 114 rooms. MC, V.*

Rex. This is a sister hotel to the Capitol next door, and both belong to the Tryp chain. It's located on the corner of Silva just down from Callao, and the lobby, bar, restaurant, and two floors have been completely refurbished. The unrenovated rooms are considerably cheaper, but you'll be much more comfortable in one of the newer ones. *Gran Vía 43, tel. 91/247–4800, fax 91/247–1238. 147 rooms. AE, DC, V.*

Inexpensive   **Cliper.** This simple hotel offers good value for the cost-conscious traveler. It's tucked away in a side street off the central part of Gran Vía between Callao and Red San Luis. *Chinchilla 6, tel. 91/531–1700. 52 rooms. AE, MC, V.*

★ **Inglés.** The exterior may seem shabby but don't be deterred. The Inglés is a long-standing budget favorite. Its rooms are comfortable, with good facilities, and the location is a real bonus: You're a short walk from the Puerta del Sol one way, and from the Prado the other; inexpensive restaurants and atmospheric bars are right at hand. *Echegaray 10, tel. 91/429–6551, fax 91/420–2423. 58 rooms. AE, DC, MC, V.*

Monaco. Just a few steps from the tiny Plaza de Chueca, the Monaco is an eccentrically opulent delight. The lobby is resplendent with red carpeted stairs, potted plants, brass rails, and mirrors; rooms are similarly ornate, with Louis XIV–style furniture and mirrored walls. The Portuguese owner is very gracious. *Barbieri 5, tel. 91/522–4630. 32 rooms. AE, MC, V.*

Ramón de la Cruz. If you don't mind a longish metro ride from the center of town, this medium-size hotel is a find. The rooms are large, with modern bathrooms, and the lobby is spacious, with stone floors. Given Madrid prices, it's a bargain. *Don Ramón de la Cruz 94, tel. 91/401–7200. 103 rooms. MC, V.*

San Antonio de la Florida. This is a somewhat more inexpensive version of the Florida Norte, beside which it is located. The dark brown rooms are furnished in wood and have oversize beds, but the best thing about them is the view facing the Norte railway station. The second-floor lobby, while far from grand, is homey. *Paseo de la Florida 13, tel. 91/247–1400, fax 91/559–0951. 100 rooms. DC, MC, V.*

Budget   **Lisboa.** Clean, small, and central, the Lisboa has for years been a well-kept secret just off the Plaza de Santa Ana. It offers no frills but it's in a good location on a busy bar and restaurant street. Rooms tend to vary greatly in size and quality. Most of them are sparsely furnished, with tile floors and papered walls, but they are clean and functional. There's a tiny lobby. *Ventura de la Vega 17, tel. 91/429–9894. 22 rooms. AE, DC, MC, V.*

Bars and Cafés

Bars   **The Mesones.** The most traditional and colorful taverns are on Cuchilleros and Cava San Miguel just west of Plaza Mayor, where you'll find a whole array of mesones with names like **Tortilla, Champiñón,** and **Huevo.**

Old Madrid. Wander the narrow streets between Puerta del Sol and Plaza Santa Ana, which are packed with traditional tapas bars. Favorites here are the **Cervecería Alemana,** Plaza Santa Ana 6, a beer hall founded more than 100 years ago by Germans and patronized, inevitably, by Hemingway; **Los Gabrieles,** Echegaray 17, with magnificent ceramic decor; **La Trucha,** Manuel Fernández y González 3, with loads of atmosphere; and **Viva Madrid,** Fernández y González 7, a lovely old bar.

Calle Huertas. Fashionable wine bars with turn-of-the-century decor and chamber or guitar music, often live, line this street. **La Fídula** at No. 57 and **El Hecho** at No. 56 are two of the best.

Plaza Santa Barbara. This area just off Alonso Martínez is packed with fashionable bars and beer halls. Stroll along Santa Teresa, Orellana, Campoamor, or Fernando VI and take your pick. The **Cervecería Santa Barbara** in the plaza itself is one of the most colorful, a popular beer hall with a good range of tapas.

Cafés If you like cafés with an old-fashioned atmosphere, dark wooden counters, brass pumps, and marble-topped tables, try any of the following: **Café Comercial,** Glorieta de Bilbao 7; **Café Gijón,** Paseo de Recoletos 21, a former literary hangout and the most famous of the cafés of old, now one of the many café-terraces that line the Castellana; **Café León,** Alcalá 57, just up from Cibeles; **Café Roma** on Serrano; and **El Espejo,** Paseo de Recoletos 31, with art-nouveau decor and an outdoor terrace in summer.

The Arts

Details of all cultural events are listed in the daily newspaper *El País* or in the weekly *Guía del Ocio.*

Concerts and The main concert hall is the new **Auditorio Nacional de Madrid**
Opera (tel. 91/337–0100), Príncipe de Vergara 136 (metro, Cruz del Royo), which opened at the end of 1988. The old **Teatro Real** (tel. 91/248–1405) on the Plaza de Oriente opposite the Royal Palace is being converted into Madrid's long-needed opera house and may reopen in 1993; inquire at the tourist office.

Zarzuela and Zarzuela, a combination of light opera and dance ideal for non-
Dance Spanish speakers, is held at the **Teatro Nacional Lírico de la Zarzuela,** Jovellanos 4, tel. 91/429–8225. The season runs from October to July.

Theater If language is no problem, check out the fringe theaters in Lavapiés and the **Centro Cultural de la Villa** (tel. 91/575–6080) beneath the Plaza Colón, and the open-air events in the Retiro Park. Other leading theaters—you'll also need reasonable Spanish—include the **Círculo de Bellas Artes,** Marqués de Casa Riera 2, just off Alcalá 42 (tel. 91/531–7700); the **Teatro Español,** Príncipe 25 on Plaza Santa Ana (tel. 91/429–6297) for Spanish classics; and the **Teatro María Guerrero,** Tamayo y Baus 4 (tel. 91/319–4769), home of the Centro Dramático Nacional, for plays by García Lorca. Most theaters have two curtains, at 7 and 10:30 PM, and close on Mondays. Tickets are inexpensive and often easy to come by on the night of performance.

Films Foreign films are mostly dubbed into Spanish, but movies in English are listed in *El País* or *Guía del Ocio* under "V.O.," meaning *versión original.* A dozen or so theaters now show films in English; some of the best bets are **Alphaville** and **Cines Renoir,** both in Martín de los Heros, just off Plaza España, and the **Filmoteca Español** (Santa Isabel 3), a city-run institution where first-rate V.O. films change daily.

Nightlife

Cabaret **Florida Park** (tel. 91/573–7805), in the Retiro Park, offers dinner and a show that often features ballet, Spanish dance, or flamenco and is open Monday to Saturday from 9:30 PM with shows at 10:45 PM. **Berlin** (Costanilla de San Pedro 11, tel. 91/266–2034) opens at 9:30 PM for a dinner that is good by most cabaret standards, followed by a show and dancing until 4 AM. **La Scala** (Rosario Pino 7, tel. 91/571–4411), in the Meliá Castilla hotel, is Madrid's top nightclub, with dinner, dancing, cabaret at 8:30, and a second, less expensive show around midnight. This is the one visited by most night tours.

Flamenco Madrid offers the widest choice of flamenco shows in Spain; some are good, but many are aimed at the tourist trade. Dinner tends to be mediocre and overpriced, but it ensures the best seats; otherwise, opt for the show and a drink *(consumición)* only, usually starting around 11 PM and costing around 3,000 ptas.–3,500 ptas. **Arco de Cuchilleros** (Cuchilleros 7, tel. 91/266–5867), behind the Plaza Mayor, is one of the better, cheaper ones. **Café de Chinitas** (Torija 7, tel. 91/248–5135) and **Corral de la Morería** (Morería 17, tel. 91/265–8446 and 265–1137) are two of the more authentic places where well-known troupes perform. Another choice is **Corral de la Pacheca** (Juan Ramón Jiménez 26, tel. 91/458–1113). **Zambra** (Velázquez 8, tel. 91/435–4928), in the Hotel Wellington, is one of the smartest (jacket and tie essential), with a good show and dinner served into the small hours.

Jazz The leading club of the moment is **Café Central** (Plaza de Angel 10), followed by **Clamores** (Albuquerque 14). Others include **Café Jazz Populart** (Huertas 22) and **El Despertar** (Torrecilla del Leal 18). Excellent jazz frequently comes to Madrid as part of city-hosted seasonal festivals; check the local press for listings and venues.

Casino **Madrid's Casino** (tel. 91/856–1100) is 28 kilometers (17 miles) out at Torrelodones on the N-VI road to La Coruña. *Open 5 PM–4 AM. Free transportation service from Plaza de España 6.*

Madrid Environs

The beauty of the historic cities surrounding Madrid and the role they have played in their country's history rank them among Spain's most worthwhile sights. Ancient Toledo, the former capital, the great palace-monastery of El Escorial, the sturdy medieval walls of Ávila, and the magnificent Plaza Mayor of the old university town of Salamanca all lie within an hour or so from the capital.

It's possible to visit all the town below, with the exception of Salamanca, on day trips from Madrid—either by bus or train, or by organized tour (inquire at any travel agency). But you'll find it far more rewarding to spend a night or two in your destination cities. Long after the day-trippers have gone home, you discover the real charm of these small provincial towns and wander at leisure throughout their medieval streets. In some cases, you'll have to return to Madrid to visit another one of the outlying towns; in others, there's direct service, usually by bus.

Getting There

Trains to Toledo leave from Madrid's Atocha Station (metro: Atocha-RENFE); to Salamanca, from Norte Station (metro: Norte); and to El Escorial and Ávila from Chamartín (metro: Chamartín). Madrid has no central bus station, and buses are generally less popular than trains. La Sepulvedana (Paseo de la Florida 11, near the Norte station, tel. 91/230–4800) serves Ávila; Estación del Sur (Canarias 17, tel. 91/68–4200) has buses to Toledo; Auto-Rés (Plaza Conde de Casal 6, tel. 91/551–7200) serves Salamanca; and Herranz (tel. 91/543–3645) has buses for the Escorial and Valley of the Fallen that depart regularly from Calle Fernándo de los Ríos (metro: Moncloa).

Getting Around

There's a direct train from Madrid, making stops in El Escorial, Ávila, and Salamanca; another line goes to Toledo. Tourist offices can help you with schedules. Toledo's bus station is on the Ronda de Castilla la Mancha (tel. 925/215850) just off the road to Madrid; Ávila's bus station is on Avenida de Madrid (tel. 918/220154); and Salamanca's is at Filiberto Villalobos 73 (tel. 923/236717). Regional train stations are all a bit of a walk from the city centers.

Tourist Information

Ávila (Plaza de la Catedral 4, tel. 918/211387); open weekdays 8–3 and 4–6 (5–7 in summer), Saturday 9–1:30.
El Escorial (Floridablanca 10, tel. 91/8901554); open weekdays 9:45–2:15 and 3–6, Saturday 9:45–1:15.
Salamanca (Gran Vía 41, tel. 923/268571); open weekdays 9:30–2 and 4:30–8, Saturday 9:30–2. There's also an information booth on the Plaza Mayor (market side).
Toledo (Puerta Nueva de Bisagra tel. 925/220843); open weekdays 9–2 and 4–6, Saturday 9:30–1:30.

Exploring the Madrid Environs

The following includes tours of Toledo, El Escorial, the Valley of the Fallen, Ávila, and Salamanca. You'll want to work out the best mode of transportation according to the towns you intend to visit.

By bus or train, the trip to **Toledo** is drab and industrial. But after about 90 minutes of travel, the unforgettable silhouette of Toledo suddenly rises before you, the imposing bulk of the Alcazar and the slender spire of the cathedral dominating the skyline. This former capital, where Moors, Jews, and Christians once lived in harmony, is now a living national monument, depicting all the elements of Spanish civilization in hand-carved, sun-mellowed stone. For a stunning view and to capture the beauty of Toledo as El Greco knew it, begin with a panoramic drive around the Carretera de Circunvalación, crossing over the Alcántara bridge and returning by way of the bridge of San Martín. As you gaze at the city rising like an island in its own bend of the Tagus, reflect how little the city skyline has changed in the four centuries since El Greco painted *Storm Over Toledo*.

Toledo is a small city steeped in history and full of magnificent buildings. It was the capital of Spain under both Moors and Christians until some whim caused Philip II to move his capital to Madrid in 1561. Begin your visit with a drink in one of the many terrace cafés on the central **Plaza Zocodover,** study a map, and try to get your bearings, for a veritable labyrinth confronts you as you try to find your way to Toledo's great treasures. While here, search the square's pastry shops for the typical marzipan candies *(mazapanes)* of Toledo.

Begin your tour with a visit to the 13th-century **Cathedral,** seat of the Cardinal Primate of Spain, and one of the great cathedrals of Spain. Somber but elaborate, it blazes with jeweled chalices, gorgeous ecclesiastical vestments, historic tapestries, some 750 stained-glass windows, and paintings by Tintoretto, Titian, Murillo, El Greco, Velázquez, and Goya. The cathedral has two surprises: a **Mozarabic chapel,** where Mass is still celebrated on Sundays according to an ancient Mozarabic rite handed down from the days of the Visigoths (AD 419–711); and its unique **Transparente,** an extravagent Baroque roof that gives a theatrical glimpse into heaven as the sunlight pours down through a mass of figures and clouds. *Admission: 300 ptas. Open Mon.–Sat. 10:30–1 and 3:30–6 (7 in summer), Sun. 10:30–1:30 and 4–6.*

En route to the real jewel of Toledo, the **Chapel of Santo Tomé,** you'll pass a host of souvenir shops on Calle Santo Tomé, bursting with damascene knives and swords, blue-and-yellow pottery from nearby Talavera, and El Greco reproductions. In the tiny chapel that houses El Greco's masterpiece, *The Burial of the Count of Orgaz,* you can capture the true spirit of the Greek painter who adopted Spain, and in particular Toledo, as his home. Do you recognize the sixth man from the left among the painting's earthly contingent? Or the young boy in the left-hand corner? The first is El Greco himself, the second his son Jorge Manuel—see 1578, the year of his birth, embroidered on his handkerchief. *Admission: 100 ptas. Open daily 10–1:45 and 3:30–5:45 (6:45 in summer).*

Not far away is **El Greco's House,** a replica containing copies of his works. *Tel. 925/224046. Admission: 200 ptas. Open Tues.– Sat. 10–2 and 4–6, Sun. 10–2.*

The splendid **Sinagoga del Tránsito** stands on the corner of Samuel Levi and Reyes Católicos. Commissioned in 1366 by Samuel Levi, chancellor to Pedro the Cruel, the synagogue shows Christian and Moorish as well as Jewish influences in its architecture and decoration—look at the stars of David interspersed with the arms of Castile and León. There's also a small **Sephardic Museum** chronicling the life of Toledo's former Jewish community. *Admission: 200 ptas. Open Tues.–Sat. 10–2 and 3:30–6 (4–7 in summer), Sun. 10–2.*

Another synagogue, the incongruously named **Santa María la Blanca** (it was given as a church to the Knights of Calatrava in 1405), is just along the street. Its history may have been Jewish and Christian, but its architecture is definitely Moorish, for it resembles a mosque with five naves, horseshoe arches, and capitals decorated with texts from the Koran. *Admission: 100 ptas. Open daily 10–1 and 4–6.*

Across the road is **San Juan de los Reyes,** a beautiful Gothic church begun by Ferdinand and Isabella in 1476. Wander around its fine cloisters and don't miss the iron manacles on the outer walls; they were placed there by Christians freed by the Moors. The Catholic Kings originally intended to be buried here, but then their great triumph at Granada in 1492 changed their plans. *Admission: 75 ptas. Open daily 10–2 and 3:30–6 (7 in summer).*

Walk down the hill through the ancient **Cambrón Gate** and your visit to Toledo is over. Should you have more time, however, head for the **Museum of Santa Cruz,** just off the Zocodover, with its splendid El Grecos. *Tel. 925/221036. Admission: 200 ptas. Open Mon. 10–2, 4:30–6:30, Tues.–Sat. 10–6:30, Sun. 10–2.*

Also consider a visit to the **Hospital de Tavera,** outside the walls, where you can see Ribera's amazing *Bearded Woman. Tel. 925/220451. Admission: 250 ptas. Open daily 10:30–1:30 and 3:30–6.*

In the foothills of the Guadarrama Mountains, 50 kilometers (31 miles) to the northwest of Madrid (an easy day-trip by bus or train), and 120 kilometers (74 miles) from Toledo, lies **San Lorenzo de El Escorial,** burial place of Spanish kings and queens. The **Monastery,** built by the religious fanatic Philip II as a memorial to his father, Charles V, is a vast rectangular edifice, conceived and executed with a monotonous magnificence worthy of the Spanish royal necropolis. It was designed by Juan de Herrera, Spain's greatest Renaissance architect. The **Royal Pantheon** contains the tombs of monarchs from Charles V to Alfonso XIII, grandfather of Juan Carlos, and those of their consorts. Only two kings are missing, Philip V, who chose to be buried in his beloved La Granja, and Ferdinand VI, buried in Madrid. In the **Pantheon of the Infantes** rest the 60 royal children who died in infancy, and those queens who bore no heirs. The lavishly bejeweled tomb here belongs to Don Juan, bastard son of Charles V and half brother of Philip II, dashing hero and victor of the Battle of Lepanto. The monastery's other highlights are the magnificent **Library of Philip II,** with 40,000 rare volumes and 2,700 illuminated manuscripts, including the diary of Santa Teresa, and the **Royal Apartments.** Contrast the spartan private apartment of Philip II and the simple bedroom in which he died in 1598 with the beautiful carpets, porcelain, and tapestries with which his less austere successors embellished the rest of his somber monastery-palace. *Tel. 91/890–5905. Admission: 300 ptas. for a partial visit (Pantheon, Royal Apartments, Basilica, and Library), or 500 ptas. for whole complex, including Casita del Príncipe. Open Tues.–Sun. 10–6 (7 in summer). Last entry is 45 mins. before closing time.*

The **Valley of the Fallen** is easily reached by bus from Madrid; many tours to the Escorial include a visit to the Valley of the Fallen. This vast basilica hewn out of sheer granite was built by General Franco between 1940 and 1959 as a monument to the dead of Spain's Civil War of 1936–39. Buried here are 43,000 war dead, José Antonio Primo de Rivera, founder of the Falangists and early martyr of the war, and Franco himself, who died in 1975. A funicular to the top of the monument costs 200 ptas. *Tel. 91/890–5611. Admission: 300 ptas. Open daily 10–7 (6 in winter).*

Ávila, almost 1,240 meters (4,000 feet) above sea level, is the highest provincial capital in Spain. Alfonso VI and his son-in-law, Count Raimundo de Borgoña, rebuilt the town and walls in 1090, bringing it permanently under Christian control. It is these walls, the most complete military installations of their kind in Spain, that give Ávila its special medieval quality.

Thick and solid, with 88 towers tufted with numerous untidy storks' nests, they stretch for 2½ kilometers (1½ miles) around the entire city and make an ideal focus for the start of your visit. For a superb overall view and photo spot, drive out to the **Cuatro Postes,** three-quarters of a kilometer (half a mile) out on the road to Salamanca.

The personality of Santa Teresa the Mystic, to whom the city is dedicated, lives today as vividly as it did in the 16th century. Several religious institutions associated with the life of the saint are open to visitors, the most popular of which is the **Convent of Santa Teresa,** which stands on the site of her birthplace. There's an ornate Baroque chapel, a small gift shop, and a museum with some of her relics: her rosary, books, walking stick, a sole of her sandal, and her finger wearing her wedding ring. *Admission free. Located at Plaza de la Santa, just inside the southern gate. Open daily 8:30–1:30 and 3:30–9.*

Ávila's other ecclesiastical monuments are far older and more rewarding than those that commemorate the saint. The impregnable hulk of the **cathedral** is in many ways more akin to a fortress than a house of God. Though of Romanesque origin— the Romanesque sections are recognizable by their red and white brickwork—it is usually claimed as Spain's first Gothic cathedral. Inside, the ornate alabaster tomb of Cardinal Alonso de Madrigal, a 15th-century bishop whose swarthy complexion earned him the nickname of "El Tostado" (the toasted one) is thought to be the work of Domenico Fancelli, who also sculpted the tomb of Prince Juan in Santo Tomás and the sepulchers of the Catholic Kings in Granada's Royal Chapel. *Tel. 918/211641. Admission free. Cathedral open daily 8–1:30 and 3–7 (5 in winter). Cathedral Museum open daily 10–1:30 and 3–7 (5 in winter). Admission: 100 ptas.*

The **Basilica of San Vicente,** just outside the walls, is one of Ávila's finest Romanesque churches, standing on the spot where St. Vincent and his sisters Sabina and Cristeta were martyred in AD 306. Here, too, Santa Teresa is said to have experienced the vision that told her to reform the Carmelite order. *Admission: 25 ptas. Open Tues.–Sat. 10–1 and 4–6 (7 in summer); Sun. 10:30–2.*

Before continuing to the **Monastery of Santo Tomás,** you can relax in the pleasant **Plaza de Santa Teresa,** with its outdoor cafés and statue of the saint erected for Pope John Paul's visit in 1982. Built between 1482 and 1493 by Ferdinand and Isabella, who used it as a summer palace, the monastery houses the tomb of their only son, Prince Juan—who died at the age of 19 while a student at Salamanca—as well as the tomb of that far less lovable character, the notorious Inquisitor General Tomás de Torquemada. *Admission: monastery free, cloisters 50 ptas., Museum of Oriental Art 50 ptas. Open daily 10–1 and 4–7.*

Farthest from Madrid of the towns we have visited, **Salamanca** is an ancient city, and your first glimpse of it is bound to be unforgettable. Beside the road flows the Tormes River and beyond it rise the old houses of the city and the golden walls, turrets, and domes of the Plateresque cathedrals. "Plateresque" comes from *plata* (silver) and implies that the stone is chiseled and engraved as intricately as that delicate metal. A superb example of this style is the facade of the Dominican **Monastery of San Esteban** (50 ptas.; open daily 9–1 and 4–7), which you'll pass on your way to the cathedrals. The **old cathedral** far outshines its younger sister, the **new cathedral,** in beauty. (The new cathedral's funds ran out during construction—1513–1733—leaving a rather bare interior.) Inside the sturdy Romanesque walls of the old cathedral, built between 1102 and 1160, your attention will be drawn to Nicolás Florentino's stunning altarpiece with 53 brightly painted panels. Don't miss the splendid **cloisters,** which now house a worthwhile collection of religious art, and the **Degree Chapel,** where anxious students sought inspiration on the night before their final exams. *New cathedral free; old cathedral and cloisters 200 ptas. Open daily 10–1:30 and 4–5:30 (9:30–2 and 3:30–7 in summer).*

Founded by Alfonso IX in 1218, **Salamanca University** is to Spain what Oxford University is to England. On its famous **doorway** in the Patio de las Escuelas, a profusion of Plateresque carving surrounds the medallions of Ferdinand and Isabella. See if you can find the famous frog and skull, said to bring good luck to students in their examinations. Inside, the **lecture room** of Fray Luis de León has remained untouched since the days of the great scholar, and the prestigious **Library** boasts some 50,000 parchment and leather-bound volumes. *Tel. 923/294400, ext. 1150. Library admission: 100 ptas. Open Mon.–Sat. 9:30–1:30 and 4:30–6:30, Sun. 10–1.*

Now make for Salamanca's greatest jewel, the elegant 18th-century **Plaza Mayor.** Here you can browse in stores offering typical *charro* jewelry (silver and black flowerheads), head down the steps to the market in search of colorful tapas bars, or simply relax in an outdoor café. In this, the city's crowning glory, and the most exquisite square in Spain, you've found the perfect place to end your tour of Salamanca and Castile.

Dining and Lodging

For details and price-category definitions, *see* Dining and Lodging in Staying in Spain.

Ávila
Dining

El Fogón de Santa Teresa. Traditional Castilian roasts, lamb chops, and trout feature on the menu of this attractive restaurant in the vaults of the Palacio de Valderrábanos. *Alemania 3, tel. 918/211023. AE, DC, MC, V. Moderate.*

★ **El Rastro.** This ancient inn tucked into the city walls is Ávila's most atmospheric place to dine. Local specialties include Ávila's famous veal *(ternera)* and *yemas de Santa Teresa,* a dessert made from candied egg yolks. *Plaza del Rastro 1, tel. 918/211218. AE, DC, MC, V. Moderate.*

El Torreón. Castilian specialties are served in this typical mesón situated in the basement of the old Velada Palace, opposite the cathedral. *Tostado 1, tel. 918/213171. AE, MC, V. Moderate.*

Lodging

Don Carmelo. This functional, modern, and comfortable hotel, close to the station, is Ávila's best moderate bet. *Paseo Don Carmelo 30, tel. 918/228050. 60 rooms. V. Moderate.*

El Escorial
Dining

Mesón de la Cueva. Founded in 1768, this atmospheric mesón has several small, rustic dining rooms. This inn is a must for ambience, and the food is good, too. *San Antón 4, tel. 91/890-1516. Reservations advised on weekends. AE, DC, MC, V. Moderate.*

El Candil. One of the best of the many middle-range restaurants in El Escorial, El Candil is situated above a bar on the corner of Plaza San Lorenzo on the village's main street. In summer you can dine outdoors in the square, a delightful spot. *Reina Victoria 12, tel. 91/890–4103. AE, DC, MC, V. Moderate.*

Cafeteria del Arte. Just a few steps from El Escorial monastery, this restaurant/café is a perfect spot for a light meal or snack. It's part of a complex that includes the much more formal Carillon restaurant and the Hotel Florida. One delightful regional dish is the *chocolate con picatostas* (hot chocolate with toasted bread). *Floridablanca 14, tel. 91/890–1520. No credit cards. Budget.*

Lodging **Miranda Suizo.** Rooms are comfortable in this charming old hotel on the main street, and the hotel café, with its dark wood fittings and marble tables, is right out of the 19th century. *Floridablanca 20, tel. 91/890–4711. 47 rooms. AE, DC, MC, V. Moderate.*

Continental. Many of the rooms in this aging but still-charming hotel on the Plaza de la Catedral have remarkable views of the cathedral. The rooms are large, if somewhat fading. *Plaza de la Catedral 6, tel. 918/211502. 57 rooms. No credit cards. Inexpensive.*

Vasca. Small rooms look out on the bustling Plaza de Santiago in the center of town. The hostel boasts a lounge on each floor, a restaurant serving three meals a day, and outdoor dining in summer. *Plaza de Santiago 11, tel. 91/890–1619. 20 rooms. No credit cards. Inexpensive.*

Las Cancelas. In the heart of the old city, this 14-room hostel—which even has its own elevator—is a good economical choice, although you'll have to share a bathroom. Every room has a view of the street. *Cruz Vieja 6, 918/212249. 14 rooms. No credit cards. Budget.*

Salamanca **Chapeau.** This chic spot carefully offers both meat and fish
Dining carefully roasted in its wood-fired ovens. Try their *pimientos*
★ *rellenos* (stuffed peppers) and orange mousse for dessert. *Gran Vía 20, tel. 923/271833. Reservations advised. AE, DC, MC, V. Closed Sun. in summer. Moderate.*

El Mesón. There's plenty of colorful atmosphere and good traditional Castilian food in this typical mesón just off the Plaza Mayor, beside the Gran Hotel. *Plaza Poeta Iglesias 10, tel. 923/217222. AE, MC, V. Closed Jan. Moderate.*

Río de la Plata. This small, atmospheric restaurant close to El Mesón and the Gran Hotel serves superb *farinato* sausage; it's a great find. *Plaza del Peso 1, tel. 923/219005. No credit cards. Closed Mon., July. Moderate.*

El Bardo. Students and others daily pack this popular Salamanca restaurant, a bustling place with three wood-and-stone dining rooms. Both a regular and a vegetarian *menu del día* are on offer—exceedingly unusual for Spain. Other specialties prepared by the friendly owners include the house salad and a fine *crema de champiñon* (mushroom soup). *Companía 8, tel. 923/219089. No credit cards. Budget.*

Lodging **Castellano III.** Overlooking the Alamedilla Park just a few minutes' walk from the center, this comfortable, modern hotel is considered the best medium-price hotel in town. *San Francisco Javier 2, tel. 923/261611, fax 923/266741. 73 rooms. AE, MC, V. Moderate.*

Condal. A functional but comfortable hotel in a central location just off Calle Azafranal, two minutes from the Plaza Mayor. *Santa Eulalia 2, tel. 923/218400. 70 rooms. AE, DC, MC, V. Inexpensive.*

Tormes. This is a clean, well-kept family hostel with a TV lounge and a central location—a good choice for basic accommodations. *Rua Mayor 20, tel. 923/219683. 12 rooms. No credit cards. Inexpensive.*

Toledo
Dining
★

Asador Adolfo. This restaurant is situated near the cathedral and is well known for its good food (try the superb roast meat and the *pimentos del piquillo rellenos de pescado*) and service. *Calle de la Granada 6, tel. 925/227321. AE, DC, MC, V. Closed Sun. eve. Moderate.*

Casa Aurelio. There are two branches of this popular restaurant, both around the corner from the cathedral. Try the partridge or quail. *Sinagoga 6, tel. 925/221392, and Sinagoga 1, tel. 925/221392. AE, DC, MC, V. Closed Wed. Moderate.*

Los Cuatro Tiempos. The picturesque downstairs bar, decorated with ceramic tiles, is an ideal place for a *fino* and tapas before you head upstairs for a traditional Toledo meal. *Sixto Ramón Parro 7, tel. 925/223782. MC, V. Moderate–Inexpensive.*

Los Arcos. Located off Toledo de Ohio, this attractive modern restaurant offers good-value *menus del día* as well as inexpensive main courses such as roast partridge, and is fast gaining in popularity. *Cordonerías 11, tel. 925/210051. AE, DC, MC, V. Inexpensive.*

Transito. If you're in the mood for some benchmark Castillian specialties—*sopa castellana* and *ternera asada* (roast veal) among them—this large restaurant just a few yards from the Santa Maria la Blanca synagogue, facing Plaza de Barrionuevos, is a popular spot. *Reyes Católicos 7, tel. 925/225623. AE, DC, MC, V. Inexpensive.*

Lodging
★

Alfonso VI. This pleasant modern hotel has Castilian-style decor and is conveniently located in the center of town by the alcázar. *Gen. Moscardó 2, tel. 925/222600, fax 925/214458. 80 rooms. AE, DC, MC, V. Moderate.*

Carlos V. No hotel in town enjoys such a convenient situation as this one, halfway between the Alcazar and the main square. It stands on a delightful square of its own, with an excellent view of the town. The staff is exceptionally friendly, and the Castile-style interior is pleasantly old-fashioned, although slightly faded. *Plaza Horno de los Vizcochos, tel. 925/222100. 55 rooms. AE, MC, V. Moderate.*

María Cristina. You'll pass this comfortable new hotel on your way from Madrid. Located beside the bullring, it opened in 1986 and provides excellent facilities. Its El Abside restaurant is fast gaining in prestige. *Marqués de Mendigorría 1, tel. 925/213202. 65 rooms. AE, V. Moderate.*

Maravilla. This simple but very central old-world hotel just off Plaza Zocodover has a good, old-fashioned restaurant. *Barrio Rey 7, tel. 925/223304. 18 rooms. AE, DC, MC, V. Inexpensive.*

Barcelona

Arriving and Departing

By Plane All international and domestic flights arrive at **El Prat de Llobregat** airport, 14 kilometers (8½ miles) south of Barcelona just off the main highway to Castelldefels and Sitges. For information on arrival and departure times, call the airport (tel. 93/478–5000 or 478–5032) or Iberia information (tel. 93/301–3993).

Between the Airport and Downtown
The airport–city train leaves every 30 minutes between 6:30 AM and 11 PM and reaches the Barcelona Central (Sants) Station in 15 minutes; a new extension now carries you to the Plaça de Catalunya, at the head of the Ramblas, in the heart of the old city. Taxis will then take you to your hotel. A new Aerobus service connects the airport with Plaza Catalunya every 15 minutes between 6:25 AM and 11 PM; pay the driver the fare of 375 ptas. RENFE provides a bus service to the Central Station during the night hours. A cab from the airport to your hotel, including airport and luggage surcharges, will cost about 2,000 ptas.

By Train
The old Terminal (or **França**) Station on Avenida Marquès de l'Argentera reopened in 1992 after major renovations as Barcelona's main long-distance train station. Almost all long-distance trains now arrive and depart from here. The Central (**Sants**) Station on Plaça Paisos Catalans, which was a long-distance station while França was under renovation, is now a suburban train station. Many long-distance trains also stop at the **Passeig de Gràcia** underground station at the junction of Aragó. This station is closer to the Plaça de Catalunya and Ramblas area than Central (Sants), but though tickets and information are available here, luggage carts and taxi ranks are not. Check with tourist offices for current travel information and phone numbers. For RENFE information, call 93/490–0202 (24 hours).

By Bus
Barcelona has no central bus station, but many buses operate from the old Estació Vilanova (or Norte) at the end of Avenida Vilanova. **Juliá,** Ronda Universitat 5, runs buses to Zaragoza and Montserrat; and **Alsina Graëlls,** Ronda Universitat 4, to Lérida and Andorra.

Getting Around

Modern Barcelona above the Plaça de Catalunya is mostly built on a grid system, though there's no helpful numbering system as in the United States. The Old Town from the Plaça de Catalunya to the port is a warren of narrow streets, however, and you'll need a good street map to get around. Most sightseeing can be done on foot—you won't have any other choice in the Gothic Quarter—but you'll need to use the metro or buses to link sightseeing areas.

By Metro
The subway is the fastest way of getting around, as well as the easiest to use. You pay a flat fare, no matter how far you travel, or purchase a **targeta multiviatge,** good for 10 rides. Plans of the system are available from main metro stations or from branches of the Caixa savings bank.

By Bus
City buses run from about 5:30 or 6 AM to 10:30 PM, though some stop earlier. Again, there's a flat-fare system though tickets cost a little more on weekends. Plans of the routes followed are displayed at bus stops. A reduced-rate targeta multiviatge, good for 10 rides, can be purchased at the transport kiosk on Plaça de Catalunya.

By Cable Car and Funicular Montjuïc Funicular is a cog railroad that runs from the junction of Avenida Parallel and Nou de la Rambla to the Miramar Amusement Park on Montjuïc. It runs only when the amusement park is open (11–8:15 in winter, noon–2:45 and 4:30–9:25 in summer). A cable car (*teleféric*) then runs from the amusement park up to Montjuïc Castle (noon–9 daily in summer; winter, weekends only, 11–7:30).

A **Transbordador Aeri Harbor Cable Car** runs from Miramar on Montjuïc across the harbor to the Torre de Jaume I on Barcelona *moll* (jetty), and on to the Torre de Sant Sebastià at the end of Passeig Nacional in Barceloneta. You can board at either stage. The cable car runs from 11:30 AM to 6 PM in winter, 11 AM to 10 PM in summer.

To reach Tibidabo summit, take either bus No. 58 or the Ferrocarrils de la Generalitat train from Plaça de Catalunya to Avenida Tibidabo, then the *tramvía blau* (blue tram) to Peu del Funicular, and the Tibidabo Funicular from there to the Tibidabo Fairground. The funicular runs every half hour from 7:15 AM to 9:45 PM.

By Boat **Golondrinas** harbor boats operate short harbor trips from the Portal de la Pau near the Columbus Monument between 10 AM and 1:30 PM weekends only in winter, daily in summer between 10 AM and 8 PM.

Important Addresses and Numbers

Tourist Information The city's three main tourist offices are at the **Central** (Sants) train station (tel. 93/490–9171; open daily 8–8), the **Palacio de Congresos** (Avda. Maria Cristina, tel. 93/423–3101, ext. 8356; open 10–8 during holidays and business congresses), and in the **Ajuntament** (Plaça Sant Jaume, tel. 93/402–7000, ext. 433; open daily 9–8 during the summer months). In the summer there are tourist offices at **Palau de la Virreina** (Ramblas 99, tel. 93/301–7775; open daily 9:30–9).

Information on the province can be found at Gran Vía 658 (tel. 93/301–7443; open weekdays 9–7, Sat. 9–2) and at the airport (tel. 93/478–4704; open Mon.–Sat. 9:30–8, Sun. 9:30–3).

American Visitors' Bureau (Gran Vía 591 between Rambla de Catalunya and Balmes, 3rd floor, tel. 93/301–0150 or 301–0032).

Consulates **U.S.** (Vía Laietana 33, tel. 93/319–7394, or for after-hour emergencies, 93/237–2505), **Canadian** (Vía Augusta 125, tel. 93/209–0634), **U.K.** (Diagonal 477, tel. 93/419–9044).

Emergencies **Police** (National Police, tel. 091; Municipal Police, tel. 092; Main Police [Policía Nacional] Station, Vía Laietana 43, tel. 93/301–6666). **Ambulance** (tel. 93/329–7766). **Doctor: Hospital Clínico** (Casanova 143, tel. 93/323–1414); **Hospital Evangélico** (Alegre de Dalt 87, tel. 93/219–7100).

Exploring Barcelona

Numbers in the margin correspond to points of interest on the Barcelona map.

Barcelona, capital of Catalonia and Spain's second-largest city, thrives on its business acumen and industrial muscle. Its hard-working citizens are almost militant in their use of their own language—with street names, museum exhibits, newspapers, radio programs, and movies all in Catalan (*see* Language in Essential Information, *above*). Their latest cause for rejoicing is the realization of their long-cherished goal to host the Olympic Games, held in Barcelona in summer 1992 after a massive building program. This thriving metropolis also has a rich history and an abundance of sights. Few places can rival the narrow alleys of its Gothic Quarter for medieval atmosphere, the elegance and distinction of its Modernista Eixample area, or the fantasies of Gaudí's whimsical imagination.

It should take you two full days of sightseeing to complete the following tour. The first part covers the Gothic Quarter, the Picasso Museum, and the Ramblas. The second part takes you to Passeig de Gràcia, the Sagrada Familia, and Montjuïc.

Start on Plaça de la Seu, where on Sunday morning the citizens of Barcelona gather to dance the *Sardana*, a symbol of Catalan **1** pride. Step inside the magnificent Gothic **Cathedral** built between 1298 and 1450, though the spire and Gothic facade were not added until 1892. Highlights are the beautifully carved **choir stalls,** Santa Eulalia's tomb in the crypt, the battlescarred crucifix from Don Juan's galley in the **Lepanto Chapel,** and the cloisters. *Tel. 93/315–1554. Admission free. Open daily 9–1:30 and 4–7:30.*

2 Around the corner at Comtes de Barcelona 10 is the **Frederic Marès Museum,** where you can browse for hours among the miscellany of sculptor-collector Frederic Marès. On display is everything from polychrome crucifixes to hat pins, pipes, and walking sticks. *Admission: 250 ptas. Open Tues.–Sat. 9–2 and 4–7, Sun. 9–2.*

3 The neighboring **Plaça del Rei** embodies the very essence of the Gothic Quarter. Legend has it that after Columbus's first voyage to America, the Catholic Kings received him in the **Saló de Tinell,** a magnificent banqueting hall built in 1362. Other ancient buildings around the square are the **Lieutenant's Palace;** the 14th-century **Chapel of St. Agatha,** built right into the Roman city wall; and the **Padellás Palace,** which houses the City History Museum.

Cross Vía Laietana, walk down Princesa, and turn right into Montcada, where you come to one of Barcelona's most popular **4** attractions, the **Picasso Museum.** Two 15th-century palaces provide a striking setting for the collections donated in 1963 and 1970, first by Picasso's secretary, then by the artist himself. The collection ranges from early childhood sketches done in Málaga to exhibition posters done in Paris shortly before his death. Of particular interest are his Blue Period pictures and his variations on Velázquez's *Las Meninas. Tel. 93/319–6310. Admission: 50 ptas. Open Tues.–Sat. 10–8, Sun. 10–3.*

5 **Santa María del Mar** is one of the loveliest Gothic churches in Barcelona. It was built between 1329 and 1383 in fulfillment of a vow made a century earlier by Jaume I to build a church for the Virgin of the Sailors. Its simple beauty is enhanced by a stunning rose window and magnificent soaring columns. *Open daily 8–1 and 4–7:30.*

Continue up Carrer Argentería, cross Vía Laietana, and walk **6** along Jaume I till you come to **Plaça Sant Jaume,** an impressive square built in the 1840s in the heart of the Gothic Quarter. The two imposing buildings facing each other across the square are very much older. The 15th-century **Ajuntament,** or City Hall, has an impressive black and gold mural (1928) by Josep María Sert (who also painted the murals for New York's Waldorf Astoria) and the famous **Saló de Cent,** from which the Council of One Hundred ruled the city from 1372 to 1714. The **Palau de la Generalitat,** seat of the Catalan Regional Government, is a 15th-century palace open to the public on Sunday mornings only.

Continue along the Carrer Ferrán, with its attractive 19th-century shops and numerous Modernista touches, to the **Plaça Reial.** Here in this splendid, if rather dilapidated, 19th-century square, arcaded houses overlook the wrought-iron **Fountain of the Three Graces** and lampposts designed by a young Gaudí in 1879. Watch out for drug pushers here; the safest and most colorful time to come is on a Sunday morning when crowds gather at the stamp and coin stalls and listen to soap-box orators.

Head to the bottom of Ramblas and take an elevator to the top of the **Columbus Monument** for a breathtaking view over the city. Columbus faces out to sea, overlooking a replica of his own boat, the *Santa María.* (Nearby you can board the cable car that crosses the harbor to Montjuïc.) *Admission: 175 ptas. adults, 75 ptas. children. Open Tues.–Sat. 10–2 and 3:30– 6:30, Sun. 10–7.*

Our next stop is the **Maritime Museum** (Plaça Portal de la Pau 1) housed in the 13th-century Atarazanas Reales, the old Royal Dockyards. The museum is packed with ships, figureheads, nautical paraphernalia, and several early navigation charts, including a map by Amerigo Vespucci, and the 1439 chart of Gabriel de Valseca from Mallorca, the oldest chart in Europe. *Tel. 93/318–3245. Admission: 150 ptas. Open Tues.–Sat. 10–2 and 4–7, Sun. 10–2.*

Turn back up the Ramblas to Nou de la Rambla. At No. 3 is Gaudí's **Palau Güell,** which houses the **Museum of Performing Arts.** Gaudí built this mansion between 1885 and 1890 for his patron, Count Eusebi de Güell, and it's the only one of his houses that is readily open to the public. It makes an intriguing setting for the museum's collection of theatrical memorabilia. *Admission: 100 ptas. Open weekdays 4–8.*

Back to the Ramblas and our next landmark, the **Gran Teatre del Liceu,** on the corner of Sant Pau. Built between 1845 and 1847, the Liceu claims to be the world's oldest opera house. A fairly mundane facade conceals an exquisite interior with ornamental gilt and plush red velvet fittings. Anna Pavlova danced here in 1930, and Maria Callas sang here in 1959. *Tel. 93/318– 9780 or 412–3532. Admission: free. Open for guided visits (some in English) by telephone reservation only.*

This next stretch of the **Ramblas** is the most fascinating. The colorful paving stones on the Plaça de la Boquería were designed by Joan Miró. Glance up at the swirling Modernista dragon and the Art Nouveau street lamps. Then take a look inside the bustling **Boquería Food Market** and the **Casa Antigua Figueras,** an old grocery store on the corner of Petxina, with a splendid mosaic facade.

The **Palau de la Virreina** was built by a viceroy from Peru in 1778. It's recently been converted into a major exhibition cen-

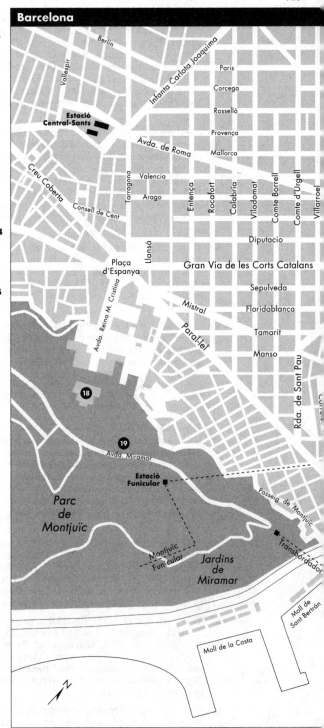

Barcelona

Berlin

Vallespir

Infanta Carlota Joaquima

Paris

Corcega

Rosselló

Estació Central-Sants

Provença

Avda. de Roma

Mallorca

Creu Coberta

Tarragona

Valencia

Entença

Rocafort

Calabria

Viladomat

Comte Borrell

Comte d'Urgell

Villarroel

Consell de Cent

Arago

Diputacio

Llansá

Gran Vía de les Corts Catalans

Plaça d'Espanya

Avda. Reina M. Cristina

Plaça d'Espanya

Sepulveda

Mistral

Floridablanca

Paral·lel

Tamarit

Rda. de Sant Pau

Manso

Currec

18

19

Avda. Miramar

Estació Funicular

Passeig de Montjuïc

Parc de Montjuïc

Montjuïc Funicular

Jardins de Miramar

Transbordador

Moll de Sant Bertrán

Moll de la Costa

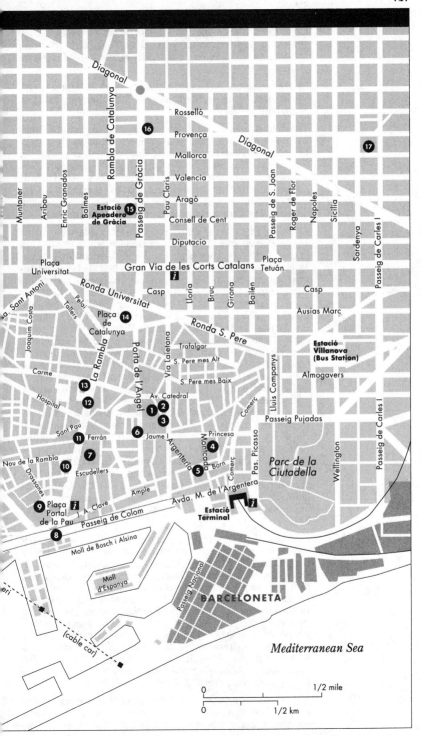

Diagonal

Rambla de Catalunya

Rosselló

Provença

Diagonal

Mallorca

Valencia

16

17

Enric Granados

Aribau

Muntaner

Balmes

Passeig de Gràcia

Pau Claris

Aragó

Passeig de S. Joan

Roger de Flor

Napoles

Sicilia

Sardenya

Passeig de Carles I

Estació
Apeadero
de Gràcia
15

Consell de Cent

Diputacio

Plaça
Tetuán

Plaça
Universitat

Gran Vía de les Corts Catalans
i

Ronda Universitat

Casp

Lloria

Bruc

Girona

Bailén

Casp

Ronda S. Pere

Ausias Marc

a Sant Antoni

Joaquim Costa

Tallers

Pelai

Plaça
de
Catalunya
14

Porta de l'Angel

Via Laietana

Trafalgar

Ronda S. Pere

Estació
Villanova
(Bus Station)

La Rambla

Carme

S. Pere mes Alt

S. Pere mes Baix

Almogavers

Hospital

Sant Pau

13

12

Av. Catedral

1 2

3

Lluis Companys

Passeig de Carles I

Nou de la Rambla

11

Ferràn

7

6

Jaume I

Princesa

Montcada

4

Comerç

Passeig Pujadas

Escudellers

10

Argentería

Born

5

Comerç

Pas. Picasso

Parc de la
Ciutadella

Wellington

Drassanes

9

Plaça
Portal
de la Pau
i

J. A. Clave

Ample

Avda. M. de l'Argentera

Estació
Terminal

i

8

Passeig de Colom

Moll de Bosch i Alsina

Moll
d'Espanya

Passeig Nacional

BARCELONETA

eri

(cable car)

Mediterranean Sea

0   1/2 mile

0   1/2 km

ter, and you should check to see what's showing while you're in town. *Corner of Carme and Rambla de las Flores 99, tel. 93/ 301-7775. Admission: 300 ptas. Open Tues.-Sat. 10-2 and 4:30-9, Sun. 10-2, Mon. 4:30-9. Last entrance 30 mins. before closing.*

On the next block is the 18th-century **Church of Betlem** (Bethlehem) and, opposite, the handsome ocher Baroque **Palau de Moja,** built in 1702.

The final stretch of the Ramblas brings us out onto the busy **⓮ Plaça de Catalunya,** the frantic business center and transport hub of the modern city. The first stage of the tour ends here. You may want to head for the Corte Inglés department store across the square or for any of the stores on the nearby **Porta de l'Angel.** Alternatively, you can relax on the terrace of the ancient **Café Zurich** on the corner of Pelai, or stop at the colorful beer hall, the **Cervecería,** opposite the Hostal Continental.

Above the Plaça de Catalunya you come into modern Barcelona and an elegant area known as the **Eixample,** which was laid out in the late 19th century as part of the city's expansion scheme. Much of the building here was done at the height of the **Modernista** (Modernisme in Catalan) movement, a Spanish and mainly Barcelonian offshoot of Art Nouveau, whose leading exponents were the architects Antoni Gaudí, Domènech i Montaner, and Puig i Cadafalch. The principal thoroughfares of the Eixample are the Rambla de Catalunya and the Passeig de Gràcia, where some of the city's most elegant shops and cafés are found. Modernista houses are one of Barcelona's special drawing cards, so walk up **Passeig de Gràcia** until you come to the **⓯ Manzana de la Discordia,** or Block of Discord, between Consell de Cent and Aragó. Its name is a pun on the word *manzana,* which means both "block" and "apple." The houses here are quite fantastic: The floral **Casa Lleó Morera** at No. 35 is by Domènech i Montaner. The pseudo-Gothic **Casa Amatller** at No. 41 is by Puig i Cadafalch. At No. 43 is Gaudí's **Casa Batlló.** Farther along the street on the right, on the corner of **⓰ Provença,** is Gaudí's **Casa Milà** (Passeig de Gràcia 92), more often known as **La Pedrera** (which, along with Casa Batlló, was dramatically spruced up in conjunction with the 1992 Olympics). Its remarkable curving stone facade with ornamental balconies actually ripples its way around the corner of the block.

Now take the metro at Diagonal directly to Barcelona's most **⓱** eccentric landmark, Gaudí's **Church of the Sagrada Familia** (Holy Family). Far from finished at his untimely death in 1926—the absentminded Gaudí was run over by a tram and died in a pauper's hospital—this striking creation will cause consternation or wonder, shrieks of protest or cries of rapture. In 1936 during the Civil War the citizens of Barcelona loved their crazy temple enough to spare it from the flames that engulfed all their other churches except the cathedral. An elevator takes visitors to the top of one of the towers for a magnificent view of the city. Gaudí is buried in the crypt. *Tel. 93/255-0247. Admission: 350 ptas. Open Sept.-Mar., daily 9-7; Apr.-June, daily 9-8; July-Aug., daily 9-9.*

Way across town to the south, the hill of **Montjuïc** was named for the Jewish community that once lived on its slopes. Montjuïc is home to a castle, an amusement park, several delightful gardens, a model Spanish village, an illuminated fountain, the recently rebuilt Mies van der Rohe Pavilion, and a cluster of museums—all of which could keep you busy for a day or more. This was the principal venue for the 1992 Olympics.

⑱ One of the leading attractions here is the **Museum of Catalan Art** in the Palau Nacional atop a long flight of steps. The collection of Romanesque and Gothic art treasures—medieval frescoes and altarpieces, mostly from small churches and chapels in the Pyrenees—is simply staggering. The building was closed for extensive renovations at press time but was scheduled to open in 1993; ask at the tourist office for current information.

⑲ Nearby is the **Miró Foundation,** a gift from the artist Joan Miró to his native city. One of Barcelona's most exciting contemporary galleries, it has several exhibition areas, many of them devoted to Miró's works. Miró himself now rests in the cemetery on the southern slopes of Montjuïc. *Admission: 400 ptas. Open Tues.–Sat. 11–7 (9:30 on Thurs.), Sun. 10:30–2:30.*

Shopping

Gift Ideas If you're into fashion and jewelry, then you've come to the right place, as Barcelona makes all the headlines on Spain's booming fashion front. **Xavier Roca i Coll,** Sant Pere mes Baix 24, just off Laietana, specializes in silver models of Barcelona's buildings.

Antiques Carrer de la Palla and Banys Nous in the Gothic Quarter are lined with antiques shops where you'll find old maps, books, paintings, and furniture. An **antiques market** is held every Thursday morning in Plaça Nova in front of the cathedral. The **Centre d'Antiquaris,** Passeig de Gràcia 57, has some 75 antiques stores. **Gothsland,** Consell de Cent 331, specializes in Modernista designs.

Shopping Districts Elegant shopping districts are the Passeig de Gràcia, Rambla de Catalunya, and the Diagonal. For more affordable, more old-fashioned, and typically Spanish-style shops, explore the area between Ramblas and Vía Laietana, especially around C. Ferran.

Department Stores **El Corte Inglés** is on the Plaça de Catalunya 14 (tel. 93/302–1212) and at Diagonal 617 (tel. 93/322–4011) near María Cristina metro. **Galerías Preciados** is at Porta de l'Angel 19 just off the Plaça de Catalunya; Diagonal 471 on the Plaça Francesc Macià; and Avenida Meridiana 352. All are open Monday to Saturday 10–8.

Food and Flea Markets The **Boquería** or **Sant Josep Market** on the Ramblas between Carme and Hospital is a superb, colorful food market, held every day except Sunday. **Els Encants,** Barcelona's fascinating Flea Market, is held every Monday, Wednesday, Friday, and Saturday at the end of Dos de Maig on the Plaça Glòries Catalanes. There's an **artists' market** in the Placeta del Pi just off Ramblas and Boquería on Saturday mornings.

Bullfighting

Barcelona has two bullrings, the **Arènes Monumental** on Gran Vía and Carles I, and the smaller, rarely used, **Arènes las Arenas** on the Plaça d'Espanya. Bullfights are held on Sundays between March and October; check the newspaper for details. The official ticket office, where there is no markup on tickets, is

at Muntaner 24 (tel. 93/253–3821) near Gran Vía. There's a
Bullfighting Museum at the Monumental ring, open March–
October, daily 10–1 and 5:30–7.

Bars and Cafés

Cafés and **Zurich** (Plaça de Catalunya 35), on the corner of Pelai, is one of
Tearooms the oldest and most traditional cafés, perfect for watching the
world go by. **The Croissant Show** (Santa Anna 10 just off
Ramblas), is a small coffee and pastry shop, ideal for a quick
mid-morning or afternoon break.

Tapas Bars You'll find these all over town, but two of the most colorful are
Alt Heidelberg (Ronda Universitat 5), with German beer on tap
and German sausages, and the **Cervecería** at the top of
Ramblas, opposite the Hostal Continental.

Cocktail Bars These places are both popular and plentiful everywhere, but
the two best areas are the **Passeig del Born,** which is near the
Picasso Museum and very fashionable with the affluent young,
and the **Eixample,** near Passeig de Gràcia.

Champagne Bars *Xampanyerías,* serving sparkling Catalan *cava,* are popular all
over town and are something of a Barcelona specialty. Try **Brut**
(Trompetas 3), in the Picasso Museum area; **La Cava del Palau**
(Verdaguer i Callis 10), near the Palau de la Música; **La Folie**
(Bailén 169), one of the best; or **La Xampanyería** (Provença
236), on the corner of Enric Granados.

Special Cafés **Els Quatre Gats** (Montsió 5, off Porta de l'Angel) is a reconstruction of the original café that opened in 1897, and a real
Barcelona institution. Literary discussions, jazz, and classical
music recitals take place in this café where Picasso held his first
show, Albéniz and Granados played their piano compositions,
and Ramón Casas painted two of its original murals. **Café
de l'Opera** (Ramblas 74), right opposite the Liceu, is a long-
standing Barcelona tradition, ideal for a coffee or drink at any
time of day.

Dining

For details and price-category definitions, *see* Dining in Staying in Spain.

Moderate **Can Culleretes.** This picturesque old restaurant began life as a
pastry shop in 1786, and it is one of the most atmospheric and
reasonably priced finds in Barcelona. Located on an alleyway
between Ferran and Boquería, its three dining rooms are decorated with photos of visiting celebrities. It serves real Catalan
cooking and is very much a family concern; don't be put off by
the prostitutes outside! *Quintana 5, tel. 93/317–3022. Reservations accepted. AE, MC, V. Closed Sun. eve. and Mon.*
Los Caracoles. Just below the Plaça Reial is Barcelona's most
famous restaurant, which caters to tourists but has real atmosphere. Its walls are hung thick with photos of bullfighters and
visiting celebrities; its specialties are mussels, paella and, of
course, snails (*caracoles*). Don't miss it; it's fun. *Escudellers
14, tel. 93/317–3185. Reservations accepted. AE, DC, MC, V.*
★ **Sete Portes.** With plenty of old-world charm, this delightful restaurant near the waterfront has been going strong since 1836.
The cooking is Catalan, the portions enormous, and specialties
are *paella de pescado* and *zarzuela sete portes* (seafood casse-

role). *Passeig Isabel II 14, tel. 93/319–3046. Reservations advised on weekends. AE, DC, MC, V. Open 1 PM–1 AM.*

★ **Sopeta Una.** Dining in this delightful small restaurant with old-fashioned decor and intimate atmosphere is more like eating in a private home. The menu is in Catalan, all the dishes are Catalan, and the atmosphere is very genteel and middle class. For dessert, try the traditional Catalan *música*—a plate of raisins, almonds, and dried fruit served with a glass of muscatel. It's near the Palau de la Música; don't be put off by the narrow street. *Verdaguer i Callis 6, tel. 93/319–6131. Reservations accepted. V. Closed Sun., and Mon. AM.*

Inexpensive **Agut.** Simple, hearty Catalan fare awaits you in this unpreten-
★ tious restaurant in the lower reaches of the Gothic Quarter. Founded in 1924, its popularity has never waned. There's plenty of wine to wash down the traditional home cooking, but you won't find frills like coffee or liqueurs. *Gignàs 16, tel. 93/315–1709. Reservations not necessary. No credit cards. Closed Sun. eve., Mon., and July.*

Cardoner. Just around the corner from the Agut (so you can check out both before deciding), this restaurant serves *cocina del mercado*—good food at affordable prices. As a result, it is often full to bursting. Try the *cabrito al horno* (roast kid). Its main drawback is the rather gloomy 1970s decor, but the location, a couple of streets up from the port, is convenient to the lively tapas bars along Calle Merce. *Ample 46, tel. 93/315–2260. AE, DC, MC, V. Closed Wed. and Aug.*

Pitarra. Writers, politicians, artists, and intellectuals have crowded this wonderful restaurant since 1890. It's named after the Barcelonan poet Federico Soler, whose pen name was Pitarra, and run today with loving care by brothers Marc and Jaume Roig. The food is a delight: *salmon ahumado* (salmon smoked in the restaurant's own smoker), *jamón de pato* (duck fillets), tuna cooked in a squid ink sauce, and *oca a la catalana* (a regional fowl dish). *Carrer d'Avinyo 56, tel. 93/301–1647. AE, DC, MC, V. Closed Sun.*

Budget **Egipte.** This small, friendly restaurant is hidden away in a very convenient location behind the Boquería Market. Its traditional Catalan home cooking, huge desserts, and swift, personable service all contribute to its popularity and good value. *Jerusalem 12, tel. 93/317–7480. No reservations. No credit cards.*

Lodging

For a city of its size and importance, Barcelona has long been underendowed with hotels. The 1992 Olympic Games, however, brought with them some new hotels—generally of the featureless modern variety—and also spurred the renovation and cleaning up of most of the older ones. Prices also shot up, often outrageously; it remains to be seen whether they will subside now that the festivities are over. Hotels in the Ramblas and Gothic Quarter have plenty of old-world charm, but are less strong on creature comforts; those in the Eixample are mostly '50s or '60s buildings, often recently renovated; and the newest hotels are found out along the Diagonal or beyond, in the residential district of Sarriá. There are hotel reservation desks at the airport and Sants Central Station.

For details and price-category definitions, *see* Lodging in Staying in Spain.

Moderate   **Gran Vía.** Architectural features are the special charm of this 19th-century mansion, close to the main tourist office. The original chapel has been preserved, and you can have breakfast in a hall of mirrors, climb its Modernista staircase, and call from elaborate Belle Epoque phone booths. *Gran Vía 642, tel. 93/318–1900, fax 93/318–9997. 48 rooms. AE, DC, MC, V.*

★   **Oriente.** Barcelona's oldest hotel opened in 1843. Its public rooms are a delight—the ballroom and dining rooms have lost none of their 19th-century magnificence—though the bedrooms have undergone rather featureless renovation. It's located just below the Liceu and its terrace café is the perfect place for a drink. *Ramblas 45, tel. 93/302–2558. 142 rooms. AE, DC, MC, V.*

Inexpensive   **Continental.** Something of a legend among cost-conscious travelers, this comfortable hostel with canopied balconies stands at the top of Ramblas, just below Plaça Catalunya. The rooms are homey and comfortable, the staff is friendly, and the location's ideal. Buffet breakfasts are a plus. *Ramblas 136, tel. 93/301–2508, fax 93/302–7360. 34 rooms. V.*

España. The Domenech i Montaner–designed Modernista interior renders this hotel an amazing bargain for those who put architectural style before comfort. The high-ceilinged downstairs features a breakfast room decorated with mermaids, elaborate woodwork, and an Art Nouveau chimney in the cafeteria. The rooms themselves, however, are very basic, and the nighborhood can be a bit daunting for women walking alone. *San Pau 9, tel. 93/318–1758. 75 rooms. AE, DC, MC, V.*

Paseo de Gracia. This is one of those rare hostales with good quality plain carpets and sturdy wooden furniture adorning the soft-color bedrooms. Add to this the location on the handsomest of Eixample's boulevards, and you have an excellent option, if you want to stay uptown. Half the rooms have superb rooftop terraces, with great views up to Tibidabo. *Passeig de Gracia 102, tel. 93/215–5828. 33 rooms. AE, DC, MC, V.*

★   **Urbis.** This family-run hostel on Barcelona's central parade is popular with businesspeople and Spanish families. Though generally comfortable, room standards can vary, so it's best to check first. Its location close to stores and only a short walk from most major sights is an advantage. *Passeig de Gràcia 23, tel. 93/231–6904, fax 93/447–3742. 61 rooms. AE, DC, MC, V.*

Budget   **Nouvel.** Ideally situated just below Plaça de Catalunya, this hotel blends white marble and dark brown woodwork in its handsome Art Nouveau interior. The rooms are quite basic and none have carpets, so it can be cold in winter. There are larger rooms for families or groups. *Santa Ana 18–20, tel. 93/301–8274. 76 rooms. No credit cards.*

The Arts

To find out what's on in town, look in the daily papers or in the weekly *Guía del Ocio*, available from newsstands all over town. *Actes a la Ciutat* is a weekly list of cultural events published by the Ajuntament and available from its information office on Plaça Sant Jaume.

Concerts   Catalans are great music lovers, and their main concert hall is **Palau de la Música** (Amadeo Vives 1, tel. 93/317–9982). The ticket office is open weekdays 11–1 and 5–8 and Saturdays 5–8. Its Sunday morning concerts are a popular tradition. Tickets are reasonable and can usually be purchased just before the concert.

Opera The **Gran Teatre del Liceu** is one of the world's finest opera houses, considered by some second only to Milan's La Scala. The box office for advance bookings is on Sant Pau 1 (tel. 93/ 318–9122), open weekdays 8–3, Saturdays 9–1. Tickets for same-day performances are on sale in the Ramblas entrance 11–1:30 and 4 PM onward. Tickets are inexpensive by New York or London standards.

Dance You can watch the traditional Catalan Sardana danced in front of the cathedral on Sunday mornings and often on Wednesday evenings, too.

Theater Most theater performances are in Catalan but look out for mime shows, especially if Els Joglars or La Claca, two famous Catalan troupes, are appearing.

Film Most foreign movies are dubbed into Spanish. Try the **Filmoteca** on Travessera de Gràcia 63, on the corner of Tusset, for original English-language films.

Nightlife

Cabaret **Belle Epoque** (Muntaner 246, tel. 93/209–7385) is a beautifully decorated music hall with the most sophisticated shows. **El Mediévolo** (Gran Vía 459, tel. 93/325–3480) has medieval feasts and entertainment; it's all geared to tourists but fun. **Scala Barcelona** (Passeig Sant Joan 47, tel. 93/232–6363) is the city's leading nightclub, with two shows nightly, the first with dinner.

Jazz Clubs Try **Abraxas Jazz Auditorium** (Gelabert 26); **La Cova del Drac** (Tuset 30, just off the Diagonal); and **Zeleste** (Almogávares 122).

Rock Check out **Zeleste** (Almogávares 122). Major concerts are usually held in sports stadiums; keep an eye out for posters.

Flamenco The best place is **El Patio Andaluz** (Aribau 242, tel. 93/209–3378). **El Cordobés** (Ramblas 35, tel. 93/317–6653) is aimed at tour groups but can be fun.

Casino The **Gran Casino de Barcelona** (tel. 93/893–3666), 42 kilometers (26 miles) south in Sant Pere de Ribes, near Sitges, also has a dance hall and some excellent international shows in a 19th-century atmosphere. Jacket and tie essential.

Moorish Spain

Stretching from the dark mountains of the Sierra Morena in the north, west to the plains of the Guadalquivir valley, and south to the mighty snowcapped Sierra Nevada, Andalusia rings with echoes of the Moors. In the kingdom they called Al-Andalus, these Muslim invaders from North Africa dwelt for almost 800 years, from their first conquest of Spanish soil (Gibraltar) in 711 to their expulsion from Granada in 1492. And to this day the cities and landscapes of Andalusia are rich in their legacy. The great Mosque of Córdoba, the magical Alhambra Palace in Granada, and the Giralda tower, landmark of Seville, were the inspired creations of Moorish architects and craftsmen working at the behest of Al-Andalus's Arab emirs. The brilliant white villages with narrow streets and sturdy-walled houses clustered round cool inner patios, the whitewashed facades with heavily grilled windows, and the deep wailing song of Andalusia's flamenco, so reminiscent of the muezzin's call to prayer, all stem from centuries of Moorish occupation.

Getting There

Seville, Córdoba, and Granada all lie on direct train routes from Madrid. Service is frequent from both Chamartín and Atocha stations in Madrid, and includes overnight trains, slower day trains, and express talgos. In addition, the high-speed AVE train connecting Seville and Atocha Station began service in 1992 on an entirely new track; it's very expensive, but has cut traveling time on that route from 5½–6 hours to about 3½ hours. Most bus service from Madrid to Moorish Spain operates out of the Estación del Sur (*see* Madrid Arriving and Departing).

Getting Around

Seville and Córdoba are linked by direct train service. Buses are a better choice between Seville and Granada, and between Córdoba and Granada, as trains are relatively slow and infrequent and often involve a time-consuming change. **Seville**'s bus station (tel. 95/441–7111) is between José María Osborne and Manuel Vazquez Sagastizabal; the city also has a spanking new train station, Santa Justa (tel. 95/441–4111), built in conjunction with the 1992 International Exposition. In **Granada**, the main bus station in Alsina Gräells (Camino de Ronda 97, tel. 958/251358); the train station is at the end of Avenida Andaluces (RENFE office, Reyes Católicos 63, tel. 958/223119). **Córdoba** has no central bus depot, so check at the tourist office for the appropriate company. The long-distance train station is on the Avenida de America (RENFE office, Ronda de los Tejares 10, tel. 957/475884); trains to Seville and Granada run out of the adjacent Estación del Brillante (tel. 957/487446).

Tourist Information

Córdoba (Plaza de Judá Leví, tel. 957/472000, and the much less useful office at Palacio de Congresos y Exposiciones, Torrijos 10, tel. 957/471235).
Granada (Plaza Mariana Pineda 10, tel. 958/226688, and Libreros 2, tel. 958/225990).
Seville (Avd. Constitución 21, tel. 95/422–1404, not far from the cathedral and Archives of the Indies, and the smaller office at Costurero de la Reina, Paseo de las Delícias, tel. 95/423–4465).

Exploring Moorish Spain

Our tour begins in Seville and continues to Córdoba and Granada. Seville and Granada are relatively expensive cities—Seville especially after its hotels and restaurants boosted prices for last year's Expo '92—but Córdoba retains a provincial feel, and, with a few exceptions, prices to match.

The downside to a visit here, especially to Seville, is that petty crime, much of it directed against tourists, is rife. Purse snatching and thefts from cars, frequently when drivers are in them, are depressingly familiar. *Always* keep your car doors *and* trunk locked. *Never* leave any valuables in your car. Leave your passport, traveler's checks, and credit cards in your hotel's safe, *never* in your room. Don't carry expensive cameras or wear jewelry. Take only the minimum amount of cash with you. There comes a point, however—your bag is snatched, for example—when all the precautions in the world will prove inadequate. If you're unlucky, it's an equally depressing fact that the police, again especially in Seville, have adopted a distinctly casual attitude to such thefts, and often combine indifference to beleaguered tourists with rudeness in about equal measure. Frankly, there's little you can do except remain calm.

Numbers in the margin correspond to points of interest on the Seville map.

Seville Lying on the banks of the Guadalquivir, **Seville**—Spain's fourth-largest city and capital of Andalusia—is one of the most beautiful and romantic cities in Europe. Here in this city of the sensuous Carmen and the amorous Don Juan, famed for the spectacle of its Holy Week processions and April Fair, you'll come close to the spiritual heart of Moorish Andalusia. Begin ❶ your visit in the **Cathedral,** begun in 1402, a century and a half after St. Ferdinand delivered Seville from the Moors. This great Gothic edifice, which took just over a century to build, is traditionally described in superlatives. It's the biggest and highest cathedral in Spain, the largest Gothic building in the world, and the world's third-largest church after St. Peter's in Rome and St. Paul's in London. And it boasts the world's largest carved wooden altarpiece. Despite such impressive statistics, the inside can be dark and gloomy, with too many overly ornate Baroque trappings. But seek out the beautiful Virgins by Murillo and Zurbarán, and reflect on the history enshrined in these walls. In a silver urn before the high altar rest the precious relics of Seville's liberator, St. Ferdinand, said to have died from excessive fasting, and down in the crypt are the tombs of his descendants Pedro the Cruel, founder of the Alcázar, and his mistress María de Padilla. But above all, you'll want to pay your respects to Christopher Columbus, whose mortal vestiges are enshrined in a flamboyant mausoleum in the south aisle. Borne aloft by statues representing the four medieval kingdoms of Spain, it's to be hoped the great voyager has found peace at last after the transatlantic quarrels that carried his body from Valladolid to Santo Domingo and from Havana to Seville. *Admission: 300 ptas. Open Mon.–Sat. 11–5, Sun. 2–4. Cathedral also open for Mass.*

Every day the bell that summons the faithful to prayer rings out from a Moorish minaret, relic of the Arab mosque whose admirable tower of Abu Yakoub the Sevillians could not bring themselves to destroy. Topped in 1565–68 by a bell tower and ❷ weather vane and called the **Giralda,** this splendid example of Moorish art is one of the marvels of Seville. In place of steps, a gently sloping ramp climbs to the viewing platform 71 meters (230 feet) above Seville's rooftops. St. Ferdinand is said to have ridden his horse to the top to admire the view of the city he had conquered. Seven centuries later your view of the Golden Tower and shimmering Guadalquivir River will be equally breathtaking. Try, too, to see the Giralda at night when the floodlights cast a new magic on this gem of Islamic art. *Open*

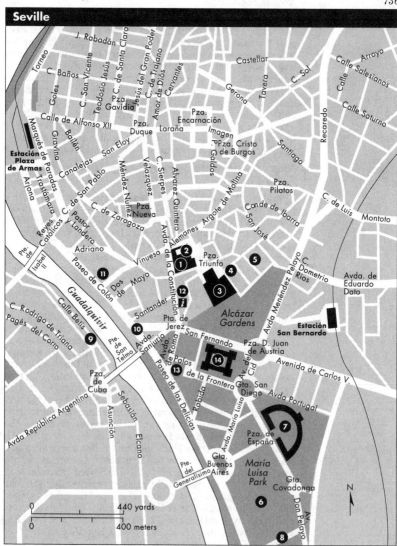

Seville

Major Attractions
Alcázar, **3**
Barrio Santa Cruz, **5**
Calle Betis, **9**
Cathedral, **1**
Giralda, **2**

Golden Tower, **10**
Maestranza
Bullring, **11**
María Luisa Park, **6**
Patio de las
Banderas, **4**
Plaza de America, **8**
Plaza de España, **7**

Other Attractions
Museo Arte
Comtemporaneo, **12**
San Telmo Palace, **13**
Tobacco Factory
(University), **14**

same hours as Cathedral and visited on same ticket. Admission to Giralda only: 200 ptas.

③ The high fortified walls of the **Alcázar** belie the exquisite delicacy of the palace's interior. It was built by Pedro the Cruel—so known because he murdered his stepmother and four of his half-brothers—who lived here with his mistress María de Padilla from 1350 to 1369. Don't mistake this for a genuine Moorish palace, as it was built more than 100 years after the reconquest of Seville; rather, its style is Mudéjar—built by Moorish craftsmen working under orders of a Christian king. The Catholic Kings (Ferdinand and Isabella), whose only son, Prince Juan, was born in the Alcázar in 1478, added a wing to serve as administration center for their New World empire, and Charles V enlarged it further for his marriage celebrations in 1526. Pedro's Mudéjar palace centers around the beautiful **Patio de las Doncellas** (Court of the Damsels) whose name pays tribute to the annual gift of 100 virgins to the Moorish sultans whose palace once stood on the site. Resplendent with the most delicate of lacelike stucco and gleaming azulejo decorations, it is immediately reminiscent of Granada's Alhambra, and is in fact the work of Granada craftsmen. Opening off this are the apartments of María de Padilla, whose hold over her lover, and seemingly her courtiers, too, was so great that they apparently vied with one another to drink her bath water!

The **Alcázar Gardens** are fragrant with jasmine and myrtle, an orange tree said to have been planted by Pedro the Cruel, and a lily pond well stocked with fat, contented goldfish. The end of
④ your visit brings you to the **Patio de las Banderas** for an unrivaled view of the Giralda. *Palace and gardens admission: 600 ptas. Open Tues.–Sat. 10:30–5, Sun. 10–1.*

⑤ The **Barrio Santa Cruz,** with its twisting alleyways, cobbled squares, and whitewashed houses, is a perfect setting for an operetta. Once the home of Seville's Jews, it was much favored by 17th-century noblemen and today boasts some of the most expensive properties in Seville. All the romantic images you've ever had of Spain will come to life here: Every house gleams white or deep ocher yellow; wrought-iron grilles adorn the windows, and every balcony and patio is bedecked with geraniums and petunias. You'll find the most beautiful patio at Callejón del Agua 12. Ancient bars nestle side by side with antiques shops. Don't miss the famous **Casa Román** bar in Plaza de los Venerables Sacerdotes with its ceilings hung thick with some of the best hams in Seville, or the **Hostería del Laurel** next door, where in summer you can dine in one of the loveliest squares in the city. Souvenir and ceramic shops surround the **Plaza Doña Elvira,** where the young of Seville gather to play guitars around the fountain and azulejo benches. And in the **Plaza Alianza,** with its well-stocked antiques shops and **John Fulton gallery** (Fulton is the only American ever to qualify as a full-fledged bullfighter), stop a moment and admire the simplicity of the crucifix on the wall, framed in a profusion of bougainvillea.

⑥ Walk, or better still, hire a horse carriage from the Plaza Virgen de los Reyes, below the Giralda, and visit **María Luisa Park,** whose gardens are a delightful blend of formal design and wild vegetation, shady walkways and sequestered nooks. In the 1920s the park was redesigned to form the site of the 1929 Hispanic-American exhibition, and the impressive villas you

see here today are the fair's remaining pavilions. Visit the mon-
7 umental **Plaza de España,** whose grandiose pavilion of Spain
was the centerpiece of the exhibition. At the opposite end of the
park you can feed the hundreds of white doves that gather
8 round the fountains of the lovely **Plaza de America;** it's a magical spot to while away the sleepy hours of the siesta.

9 An early evening stroll along the **Calle Betis** on the far side of
the Guadalquivir is a delight few foreigners know about. Between the San Telmo and Isabel II bridges, the vista of the
sparkling water, the palm-lined banks, and the silhouette of
10 the **Golden Tower** (built 1220; admission: 25 ptas., open Tues.–
11 Fri. 10–2, weekends 10–1) and the **Maestranza Bullring** (built
1760–63), one of Spain's oldest, is simply stunning.

*Numbers in the margin correspond to points of interest on the
Córdoba map.*

Córdoba   Ancient **Córdoba,** city of the caliphs, is one of Spain's oldest cities and the greatest embodiment of Moorish heritage in all Andalusia. From the 8th to the 11th centuries, the Moorish emirs
and Caliphs of the West held court here, and it became one of
the Western world's greatest centers of art, culture, and learning. Moors, Christians, and Jews lived together in harmony
within its walls. Two of Córdoba's most famous native sons
were Averröes, the great Arab scientist, and Maimónides, the
notable Jewish doctor and philosopher. But above all Córdoba
1 is known for its famous **Mosque** (or Mezquita), one of the finest
built by the Moors. Its founder was Abd ar-Rahman I (756–
788), and it was completed by Al Mansur (976–1002) around the
year 987. As you step inside you'll come face to face with a forest of gleaming pillars of precious marble, jasper, and onyx,
rising to a roof of red-and-white horseshoe arches, one of the
most characteristic traits of Moorish architecture. Not even
the heavy Baroque cathedral that Charles V so mistakenly
built in its midst—and later regretted—can detract from the
overpowering impact and mystery wrought by the art of these
Moorish craftsmen of a thousand years ago. It was indeed a fitting setting for the original copy of the Koran and a bone from
the arm of the Prophet Mohammed, holy relics once housed in
the Mezquita that were responsible for bringing thousands of
pilgrims to its doors in the great years before St. Ferdinand re-
conquered Córdoba for the Christians in 1236. In Moorish
times, the mosque opened onto the **Orange Tree Courtyard,**
where the faithful performed their ablutions before worship-
ing, and the bell tower, which you can climb for a magnificent
view of the city, served as the mosque's minaret. *Tel. 957–
470512. Admission: 400 ptas. Open daily Apr.–Sept., 10–1:30
and 4–7; Oct.–Mar., 10–1:30 and 3:30–5:30.*

Near the mosque, the streets of Torrijos, Cardenal Herrero,
and Deanes are lined with tempting souvenir shops specializing in local handicrafts, especially the filigree silver and em-
bossed leather for which Córdoba is famous. In her niche on
2 Cardenal Herrero, the **Virgin of Lanterns** stands demurely behind a lantern-hung grille, rather like a lovely lady awaiting a
serenade. In a narrow alleyway off to your left is the **Callejón de
las Flores,** its houses decked with hanging flower baskets. Now
3 make your way westward to the old **Judería,** or Jewish quarter.
4 On the **Plaza Judá Leví** you'll find the municipal tourist office. A
few paces down, on Calle Manríquez, is another outstanding patio open to visitors.

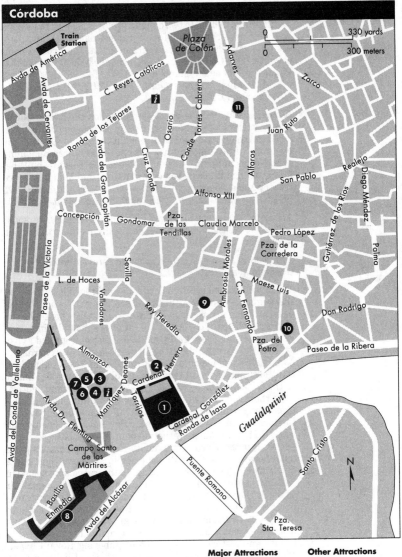

Córdoba

Major Attractions

Judería, **3**
Maimónides Statue, **6**
Mosque, **1**
Museum of
Bullfighting, **5**
Plaza Judá Levi, **4**
Synagogue, **7**
Virgin of Lanterns, **2**

Other Attractions

Alcázar, **8**
Cristo de los
Faroles, **11**
Museo Arqueológico, **9**
Museo de Bellas
Artes, **10**

5 Overlooking the Plaza Maimónides (or Bulas) is the **Museum of Bullfighting,** housed in two delightful old mansions. You'll see a well-displayed collection of memorabilia, paintings, and posters by early 20th-century Córdoban artists, and rooms dedicated to great Córdoban *toreros*—even the hide of the bull that killed the legendary Manolete in 1947. *Tel. 957/472000, ext. 211. Admission: 200 ptas. Open Tues.–Sat. 9:30–1:30 and 5–8 (4–7 in winter); Sun. 9:30–1:30.*

6 A moving **statue** of the great Jewish philosopher **Maimónides** stands in the Plaza Tiberiades. A few paces along Judíos, you
7 come to the only **synagogue** in Andalusia to have survived the expulsion of the Jews in 1492. It's one of only three remaining synagogues in Spain—the other two are in Toledo—built before 1492, and it boasts some fine Hebrew and Mudéjar stucco tracery and a women's gallery. *Tel. 957/298133. Admission: 75 ptas. Open Tues.–Sat. 10–2 and 3:30–5:30, Sun. 10–1:30.*

Across the way is the courtyard of El Zoco, a former Arab souk, with some pleasant shops and stalls, and sometimes a bar open in summer.

Numbers in the margin correspond to points of interest on the Granada map.

Granada The city of **Granada** rises majestically on three hills dwarfed by the mighty snowcapped peaks of the Sierra Nevada, which boasts the highest roads in Europe. Atop one of these hills the pink-gold palace of the Alhambra, at once splendidly imposing yet infinitely delicate, gazes out across the rooftops and gypsy caves of the Sacromonte to the fertile *vega* rich in orchards, tobacco fields, and poplar groves. Granada, the last stronghold of the Moors and the most treasured of all their cities, fell finally to the Catholic Kings in January 1492. For Ferdinand and Isabella their conquest of Granada was the fulfillment of a long-cherished dream to rid Spain of the Infidel, and here they built
1 the flamboyant **Royal Chapel** where they have lain side by side since 1521, later joined by their daughter Juana la Loca. Begin your tour in the nearby Plaza de Bib-Rambla, a pleasant square with flower stalls and outdoor cafés in summer, then pay a
2 quick visit to the huge Renaissance **Cathedral** commissioned in 1521 by Charles V, who thought the Royal Chapel "too small for so much glory" and determined to house his illustrious grandparents somewhere more worthy. But his ambitions came to little, for Granada Cathedral is a grandiose and gloomy monument, not completed until 1714, and is far surpassed in beauty and historic value by the neighboring Royal Chapel, which, despite the great emperor's plans, still houses the tombs of his grandparents and mother. *Tel. 958/229239. Admission to both: 150 ptas. Royal chapel and Cathedral open 10:30–1 and 4–7 (3:30–6 in winter).*

3 The adjacent streets of the **Alcaicería,** the old Arab silk exchange, will prove a haven for souvenir hunters. Here you can find any number of local handicrafts inspired by Granada's Moorish heritage: brass and copperware, green and blue Fajalauza pottery, wooden boxes, tables and chess sets inlaid with mother of pearl, and woven goods from the villages of the Alpujarras in which the colors green, red, and black predominate. Across the Gran Vía de Colón, Granada's main shopping street, the narrow streets begin to wind up the slopes of the
4 **Albaicín,** the old Moorish quarter, which is now a fascinating

Granada

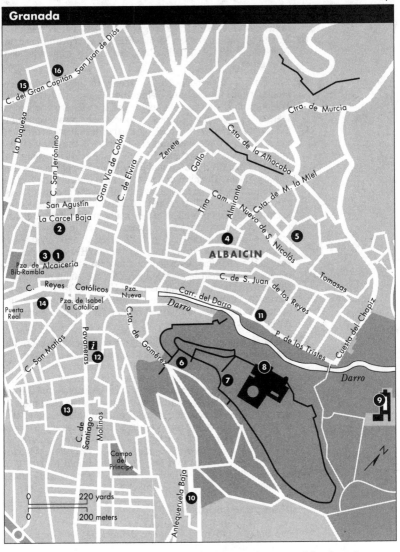

Major Attractions
Albaicín, **4**
Alcaicería, **3**
Alhambra, **8**
Alhambra Precincts, **6**
Cathedral, **2**
Generalife, **9**
Puerta de la Justicia, **7**
Royal Chapel, **1**
San Nicolás Church, **5**

Other Attractions
Casa de los Tiros, **12**
Casa Museo de
Falla, **10**
Corral del Carbón, **14**
Museo
Arqueológico, **11**
San Jerónimo, **15**
San Juan de Diós, **16**
Santo Domingo, **13**

mixture of dilapidated white houses and beautiful *cármenes*, luxurious villas with fragrant gardens. Few visitors find their

⑤ way to the balcony of **San Nicolás Church,** which affords an unforgettable view of the Alhambra, particularly when it is floodlit at night.

⑥ The Cuesta de Gomérez climbs steeply to the **Alhambra precincts,** where the Duke of Wellington planted shady elms and Washington Irving tarried among the gypsies from whom he learned the Moorish legends so evocatively recounted in his

⑦ *Tales of the Alhambra.* Above the **Puerta de la Justicía** the hand of Fatima, her fingers evoking the five laws of the Koran, beckons you inside the mystical Alhambra, the most imposing and infinitely beautiful of all Andalusia's Moorish monuments. The

⑧ history of the **Alhambra** is woven through the centuries. Once inside its famous courts the legends of the Patio of the Lions, the Hall of the Two Sisters, and the murder of the Abencerrajes spring to life in a profusion of lacy walls, frothy stucco, gleaming tiles, and ornate domed ceilings. Here in this realm of myrtles and fountains, festooned arches and mysterious inscriptions, every corner holds its secret. Here the emirs installed their harems, accorded their favorites the most lavish of courts, and bathed in marble baths. In the midst of so much that is delicate the Baroque palace of Charles V would seem an intrusion, heavy and incongruous, were it not for the splendid acoustics that make it a perfect setting for Granada's summer music festival.

⑨ Wisteria, jasmine, and roses line your route to the **Generalife,** the nearby summer palace of the caliphs, where crystal drops shower from slender fountains against a background of stately cypresses. The view of the white, clustered houses of the Albaicín, the Sacromonte riddled with gypsy caves, and the imposing bulk of the Alhambra towering above the tiled roofs of the city will etch on your memory an indelible image of this most beautiful setting and greatest Moorish legacy. *Admission to Alhambra and Generalife, 525 ptas. Free Sun. after 3. Open Sept.–Feb., daily 9–6, Mar.–Oct., daily 9–8. Floodlit visits: Tues., Thurs., and Sat. 10 PM–midnight (8–10 PM in winter). Ticket office closes 45 mins. before closing times above.*

Dining and Lodging

For details and price-category definitions, *see* Dining and Lodging in Staying in Spain.

Córdoba **La Almudaina.** This attractive restaurant is located in a 15th-
Dining century house and former school that overlooks the Alcázar at
★ the entrance to the Judería. It has an Andalusian patio, and the decor and cooking are both typical of Córdoba. *Campo Santo de los Mártires 1, tel. 957/474342. AE, DC, MC, V. Closed Sun. eve. Moderate.*

El Blasón. Under the same management as El Caballo Rojo, this charming restaurant is fast gaining a name for fine food and unbeatable ambience. Located in an old inn with a pleasant tapas patio and a whole array of restaurants upstairs, its specialties include *salmón con naranjas* (salmon in oranges) and *ternera con salsa de alcaparrones* (roast veal in caper sauce). *José Zorrilla 11, tel. 957/480625. AE, DC, MC, V. Moderate.*

El Cardenal. Close to the mosque, beside the Marisa hotel, this restaurant in the heart of Córdoba's tourist center offers a stylish setting for lunch or dinner. A marble staircase with Oriental carpets leads up to the second-floor dining room. Good food and professional service complement the cool, agreeable atmosphere. *Cardenal Herrero 14, tel. 957/480346. AE, DC, MC, V. Closed Sun. eve. and Mon. Moderate.*

★ **El Churrasco.** This atmospheric restaurant with a patio is famous for its grilled meat dishes. Specialties are, of course, *churrasco*, a pork dish in pepper sauce, and an excellent salmorejo. *Romero 16, tel. 957/290819. AE, DC, MC, V. Closed Aug. Moderate.*

Federación de Peñas. You'll find this popular budget restaurant on one of the main thoroughfares of the old town, halfway between the mosque and the Plaza Tendillas. You can eat traditional Spanish fare at one of several outdoor tables in the spacious courtyard, graced with a fountain and surrounded by horseshoe arches, or inside, in a pretty room with dark green cloths and linen. *Conde de Luque 8, tel. 957/475427. MC, V. Inexpensive.*

Mesón El Burladero. Off a small patio at the end of an alley off Deanes, this is a typical mesón, decorated with bullfight posters, stags' heads, stuffed birds, and a boar's head. Try the *menú Manolete*, which includes concoctions such as *revuelto de la casa* (a scrambled egg dish). *Calleja la Hoguera 5, tel. 957/472719. AE, DC, MC, V. Inexpensive.*

Benítez. Located in a residential neighborhood that's a brisk 15-minute walk from the mosque, this large, marble-floored eatery offers even better prices if you eat at the counter. This pleasant spot features a dozen very inexpensive combination plates. *Gran Capitán 25, tel. 957/228365. AE, DC, MC, V. Budget.*

Lodging **El Califa.** This is a small, modern hotel in a reasonably quiet, central location in the heart of the old city. It accepts no tour groups, only individual guests, and is a comfortable place to stay, with the sights and shops close at hand. *Lope de Hoces 14, tel. 957/299400. 67 rooms. MC, V. Moderate.*

Marisa. A charming old Andalusian house whose location in the heart of the old town overlooking the mosque's Patio de los Naranjos is its prime virtue. You'll find the decor quaint and charming, and the rates reasonable. *Cardenal Herrero 6, tel. 957/473142. 28 rooms. DC, V. Moderate.*

Antonio Machado. On a pretty little street above the Mosque, this hostel is typically Moorish, with its small, flower-bedecked interior courtyard, pleasant rooms overlooking the street, and friendly family of proprietors. You'll have to share a bath, however. *Buen Pastor 4, tel. 957/296259. 10 rooms. AE, MC, V. Inexpensive.*

Granada **Alacena de las Monjas.** In the heart of town, by the Casa de los *Dining* Tiros, this restaurant ("The Nun's Closet") specializes in a short menu of regional dishes and wines. Meaty stews are prevalent in winter. If you're in a more adventurous mood, try the *lomos de salmon en salsa de naranja y estagon* (salmon in orange and tarragon sauce). *Plaza Padre Suarez, tel. 958/224028. AE, V. Closed Sun. and Mon. Moderate.*

Sevilla. This is a very atmospheric, colorful restaurant located in the Alcaicería beside the cathedral. There's a superb tapas bar at the entrance, and the dining room is picturesque but rather small and crowded. The menu tends to be tourist-oriented, but try their *sopa Sevillana* (fish soup). *Oficios 12, tel. 958/221223. AE, DC, MC, V. Closed Sun. eve. Moderate.*

★ **El Macasar.** In a small house on Alhambra hill, with extraordinary views over Granada, this restaurant has served exquisitely delicate food with a nouvelle touch since 1991. Normally run-of-the-mill dishes like *sopa obispo* (soup with chicken, duck, and ham) and *pollo campero de frutas* (chicken prepared in fruit) come alive in owner Rosario Lopez Tamayo's five-table dining room. *Aire Alta de San Cecilio 4, on a narrow street below the Alhambra Palace Hotel, tel. 958/227811. No credit cards. Reservations advised weekend evenings. Closed Sun. and Mon. Inexpensive–Moderate.*

Los Manueles. This old inn is one of Granada's long-standing traditions. The walls are decorated with ceramic tiles, and the ceiling is hung with hams. There's lots of atmosphere, good old-fashioned service, and plenty of traditional Granada cooking. *Zaragoza 2, tel. 958/223415. AE, DC, MC, V. Inexpensive.*

Torres Bermejas. A functional, good-value restaurant at the base of the Alhambra hill, this typically Spanish restaurant offers good deals on such standards as paella for two. A fine steak (*solomillo*) will cost you less than $15. The dining room's at the back of the long wooden bar. *Plaza Nueva 6, tel. 958/223116. AE, DC, MC, V. Closed Mon. Budget.*

Lodging **América.** A simple but charming hotel within the Alhambra precincts. It's very popular so you'll need to reserve a room months ahead. The location is magnificent, and guests can linger over breakfast on a delightful patio. *Real de la Alhambra 53, tel. 958/227471. 14 rooms. No credit cards. Open Mar.–Oct. only. Moderate.*

Britz. Housed in a clean, pleasant building, this small hotel is conveniently located at the base of the Alhambra hill and close to downtown attractions—a good, cheap bet all around. *Plaza Nueva y Gomerez 1, tel. 958/223052. 22 rooms. No credit cards. Moderate.*

Juan Miguel. This comfortable, modern hotel right in the center of town opened in 1987. The rooms are well equipped, service is professional, and there's a good restaurant. *Acera del Darro 24, tel. 958/258912. 66 rooms. AE, DC, MC, V. Moderate.*

Inglaterra. Set in a period house just two blocks above the Gran Vía de Colón in the heart of town, this is a hotel that will appeal to those who prefer Old World charm to creature comforts, though accommodations are perfectly adequate for the reasonable rates. *Cetti Meriem 6, tel. 958/221559, fax 958/221586. 40 rooms. V. Inexpensive.*

Navarro Ramos. Perhaps the best deal among the hostales that line the main road up to the Alhambra, this 16-room hotel (6 with private baths) in an old apartment building is very clean, well-maintained, and friendly. The rooms are unusually large and pleasant for this price range. *Cuesta de Gomérez 21, tel. 958/250555. 16 rooms. No credit cards. No reservations. Budget.*

Zacatin. The Zacatin is hidden away in one of the tiny alleys that make up the Alcaiceria, the reconstructed Moorish market that's become a bustling, slightly seedy shopping area in the old city center. Climb up the stairs to this little hideaway to find 12 well-kept rooms (three with bath); eight have balconies that look out into the market. *Ermita 11–1, tel. 958/221155. 12 rooms. No credit cards. No reservations. Budget.*

Seville
Dining

El Bacalao. This popular fish restaurant, opposite the church of Santa Catalina, is in an Andalusian house decorated with ceramic tiles. As its name suggests, the house specialty is *bacalao* (cod); try the *bacalao con arroz* or the *bacalao al pilpil. Plaza Ponce de León 15, tel. 95/421–6670. Reservations advised. AE, DC, MC, V. Closed Sun. and Aug. Moderate.*

Enrique Becerra. This small intimate restaurant in an old Andalusian house just off the Plaza Nueva is well known for its Andalusian cuisine. *Gamazo 2, tel. 95/421–3049. Reservations advised. AE, V. Closed Sun. Moderate.*

La Isla. Located in the center of town between the cathedral and the Convent of La Caridad, La Isla has long been famous for its superb seafood and paella. *Arfe 25, tel. 95/421–5376. AE, DC, MC, V. Closed Mon. and Aug. Moderate.*

★ **La Judería.** This bright, modern restaurant near the Hotel Fernando III is fast gaining recognition for the quality of its Andalusian and international cuisine and for its reasonable prices. Fish dishes from the north of Spain and meat from Ávila are specialties. Try *cordero lechal* (roast baby lamb) or *urta a la roteña* (a fish dish unique to Rota). *Cano y Cueto 13, tel. 95/441–2052. Reservations required. AE, DC, MC, V. Closed Tues. and first 2 weeks in Aug. Moderate.*

★ **Mesón Don Raimundo.** Located in an old convent close to the cathedral, the atmosphere and decor are deliberately Sevillian. Its bar is the perfect place to sample a *fino* and some splendid tapas, and the restaurant, when not catering to tour groups, is one of Seville's most delightful. *Argote de Molina 26, tel. 95/422–3355. Reservations advised. AE, DC, MC, V. Closed Sun. eve. Moderate.*

La Cueva del Pez de Espada. The Swordfish's Cave is a colorful, somewhat tourist-oriented restaurant just off the Plaza Doña Elvira. The tables have bright red cloths, and the white walls are hung with cheerful oil paintings, ceramic tiles, trailing plants, and other typical Sevillian paraphernalia. The service is friendly and helpful, and an English-language menu offers a good choice of traditional Spanish meat and fish dishes. *Rodrigo Caro 18, tel. 95/421–3143. AE, DC, MC, V. Inexpensive.*

Las Escobas. Located a few steps from the Giralda, this atmospheric restaurant with *azulejo* (tile) wainscoting, coffered ceilings, and other classic Andalucian touches, claims to have first opened in 1386. It also counts such illustrious former patrons as Cervantes, Lord Byron, Lope de Vega, and a host of other literary luminaries. Today, it serves inexpensive Sevillian staples such as *gazpacho andaluz* and *pescaito frito sevillano* (fried fish plate). *Alvarez Quintero 62, tel. 95/214479. MC, V. Inexpensive.*

Mesón Castellano. This old Sevillian house opposite the church of San José is an ideal place for lunch after a morning's shopping on Calle Sierpes. Specialties are Castilian meat dishes, at reasonable prices. *Jovellanos 6, tel. 95/421–4128. Open for lunch only. AE, DC, MC, V. Closed Sun. Inexpensive.*

Girarda. A family-run hotel (*see below*) that doubles as a charming, tiny restaurant. *Justin de Neve 8, tel. 95/421–5113. Budget.*

Lodging

Bécquer. This functional, modern hotel with attentive service is convenient for the shopping center and offers comfortable if unexciting accommodations. It's one of the best moderate bets, with a parking garage but no restaurant. *Reyes Católicos 4, tel.*

95/422–8900, fax 95/421–4400. 126 rooms. AE, DC, MC, V. Moderate.

Giralda. Recently modernized and extensively renovated, this is a comfortable, functional hotel with spacious, light rooms decorated in typical Castilian style. Located in a cul-de-sac off Avenida Menéndez Pelayo, it lies on the edge of the old city; rooms on the fifth floor are best. *Sierra Nevada 3, tel. 95/441–6661, fax 95/441–9352. 107 rooms, garage. AE, DC, MC, V. Moderate.*

La Rábida. With lots of delightful 19th-century touches, this is a charming old-fashioned hotel in the center of town. *Castelar 24, tel. 95/422–0960. 87 rooms. Moderate.*

Girarda. One of several very basic family-run hotels in the Barrio Santa Cruz, the Girarda is in an old, Moorish-style building with a colorful interior patio that also serves as a restaurant. Antonia Miranda runs the place in the absence of her bullfighter husband, Pedro Sanchez Martínez. *Justin de Neve 8, tel. 95/421–5113. 5 rooms. No credit cards. Inexpensive.*

Goya. This charming hostel is centrally located near the cathedral and the Barrio Santa Cruz, and has a typically Sevillian lobby with iron grillwork and abundant flowers decorating the covered courtyard. The rooms are large, with only two facing the sometimes noisy street. *Mateos Gagos 31, tel. 95/421–1170. 20 rooms. No credit cards. Inexpensive.*

Internacional. Well maintained and charming, this Old World hotel lies in the narrow streets of the old town near Casa Pilatos. *Aguilas 17, tel. 95/421–3207. 26 rooms. Inexpensive.*

Monreal. In a pedestrian alley in the Barrio Santa Cruz, the Monreal offers a spacious lobby and some large rooms for prices that won't break you. There's a family-run restaurant in the azulejo-decorated lobby, and the rooms (only five with full bath) are well-kept. *Rodrigo Caro 8, tel. 95/421–4166. 22 rooms. No credit cards. Inexpensive.*

Murillo. This picturesque hotel in the heart of the Barrio Santa Cruz was redecorated in 1987. The rooms are simple and small, but the setting is a virtue. You can't reach the hotel by car, but porters with trolleys will fetch your luggage from your taxi. *Lope de Rueda 7, tel. 95/421–6095, fax 95/421–9616. 61 rooms, 30 with bath, 31 with shower. AE, DC, MC, V. Inexpensive.*

The Arts and Nightlife

Granada Flamenco There are several "impromptu" flamenco shows in the caves of the Sacromonte, but these can be dismally bad and little more than tourist rip-offs. Go only if accompanied by a Spanish friend who knows his way around. There are also two regular flamenco clubs that cater largely to tourists and tour groups: **Jardines Neptuno** (tel. 958/252050) and **Reina Mora** (tel. 958/278228). Both can be booked through your hotel.

Seville Flamenco Regular flamenco clubs cater largely to tourists, but their shows are colorful and offer a good introduction for the uninitiated. Try any of the following: **El Arenal** (Rodo 7, tel. 95/421–6492); **Los Gallos** (Plaza Santa Cruz 11, tel. 95/421–6981), a small intimate club in the heart of the Barrio Santa Cruz offering fairly authentic flamenco; and **El Patio Sevillano** (Paseo de Colón, tel. 95/421–4120), which caters largely to tour groups.

Bullfights Corridas take place at the Maestranza bullring on Paseo de Colón, usually on Sundays from Easter to October. The best are during the April Fair. Tickets can be bought in advance from the windows at the ring (one of the oldest and most picturesque in Spain) or from the kiosks in Calle Sierpes (these charge a commission).

Costa del Sol

What were impoverished fishing villages in the 1950s are now retirement villages and package-tour meccas for northern Europeans and Americans. Despite the abuses of this naturally lovely area during the boom years of the 1960s and '70s, and the continuing brashness of the resorts that cater to the package-tour trade, the Costa del Sol has managed to preserve at least some semblance of charm. Behind the hideous concrete monsters—some of which are now being demolished—you'll come across old cottages and villas set in gardens that blossom with jasmine and bougainvillea. The sun still sets over miles of beaches and the lights of small fishing craft still twinkle in the distance. Most of your time should be devoted to indolence—sunbathing and swimming (though not in the polluted Mediterranean; all hotels have pools for this reason). When you need something to do, you can head inland to the historic town of Ronda and the perched white villages of Andalusia. You can also make a day trip to Gibraltar or Tangier.

Getting There

Daily Iberia and Aviaco flights connect Málaga with Madrid and Barcelona. Iberia (tel. 95/213–6126), British Airways, and charter services like Dan Air offer frequent service from London; most other major European cities also have direct air links. You'll have to make connections in Madrid for all flights from the United States. Málaga's airport (tel. 95/223–1169) is 12 kilometers (7 miles) west of the city, but there are city buses every 20 minutes (fare: 80 ptas., 6:20 AM–10:40 PM); the **Portillo** bus company (tel. 95/236–0091) has frequent service to Torremolinos. A useful suburban train serving Málaga, Torremolinos, and Fuengirola also stops at the airport every half hour. From Madrid, Málaga is easily reached by a half dozen rapid trains a day.

Getting Around

Buses are the best way of getting around the Costa del Sol (as well as reaching it from Seville or Granada). Málaga's long-distance station is on the Paseo de los Tilos (tel. 95/235–0061); nearby, on Muelle de Heredía, a smaller station serves suburban destinations. The main bus company is **Portillo** (Córdoba 7, tel. 95/236–0091), serving the Costa del Sol. **Alsina Gräells** (Plaza de Toros Vieja, 95/231–8295) has service to Granada, Córdoba, Seville, and Nerja. In Torremolinos, Fuengirola, and Marbella, buses operate out of Portillo stations. The train station in Málaga (Explanada de la Estación, tel. 95/231–2500) is a 15-minute walk from the town center, across the river. The **RENFE** office (Stracham 2, tel. 95/221–3122) is more convenient for tickets and information.

Tourist Information

The most helpful tourist offices, by far, are in Málaga and Marbella. The Málaga office covers the entire province.

Estepona (Paseo Marítimo Pedro Manrique, tel. 95/280–0913).
Fuengirola (Plaza de España, in the park, tel. 95/247–9500).
Gibraltar (On Cathedral Square, the Piazza, and John Mackintosh Square, tel. 9567/76400).
Málaga (Pasaje de Chinitas 4, tel. 95/221–3445, and at the airport in both national and international terminals).
Marbella (Miguel Cano 1, tel. 95/277–1442).
Nerja (Puerta del Mar, tel. 95/252–1531).
Ronda (Plaza de España 1, tel. 95/287–1272).
Torremolinos (Plaza Pablo Ruiz Picasso, tel. 95/237–1159).

Exploring the Costa del Sol

You'll find it quite easy to get around the well-linked Costa del Sol by public transportation; inquire at helpful local tourist offices if you need assistance. The tour below includes visits to Málaga, Torremolinos, Benalmádena, Fuengirola, Mijas, Marbella, Ronda, Estepona, and Gibraltar. Of those, only Ronda and Mijas are set back from the coast, but both towns are quite accustomed to tourists and easily reached by public transportation from most coastal towns.

Málaga is a busy port city with ancient streets and lovely villas set among exotic foliage, but it has little to recommend it to the overnight visitor. The central Plaza de la Marina, overlooking the port, is a pleasant place for a drink. The main shops are along the Calle Marqués de Larios.

The **Alcazaba** is a fortress begun in the 8th century when Málaga was the most important port of the Moorish kingdom. The ruins of the Roman amphitheater at its entrance were uncovered when the fort was restored. The inner palace dates from the 11th century when, for a short period after the breakup of the Caliphate of the West in Córdoba, it became the residence of the Moorish emirs. Today you'll find the **Archaeological Museum** here and a good collection of Moorish art. *Tel. 95/221–6005. Admission: 20 ptas. Open Tues.–Sat. 10–1:30 and 5–8 (4–7 in winter).*

Energetic souls can climb through the Alcazaba gardens to the summit of **Gibralfaro.** Others can drive by way of Calle Victoria or take the parador minibus that leaves roughly every 1½ hours from near the cathedral on Molina Lario. The Gibralfaro fortifications were built for Yusuf I in the 14th century. The Moors called it Jebelfaro, which means "rock of the lighthouse," after the beacon that stood here to guide ships into the harbor and warn of invasions by pirates. Today the beacon has gone, but there's a small parador that makes a delightful place for a drink or a meal and has some stunning views.

Your first glimpse of **Torremolinos,** the ocean of concrete blocks that form its outskirts, makes it difficult to grasp that as recently as the early 1960s this was an inconsequential fishing village. Today, this grossly overdeveloped resort is a prime example of 20th-century tourism run riot. The town center, with its brash Nogalera Plaza, is full of overpriced bars and restaurants. Much more attractive is the district of La Carihuela,

on

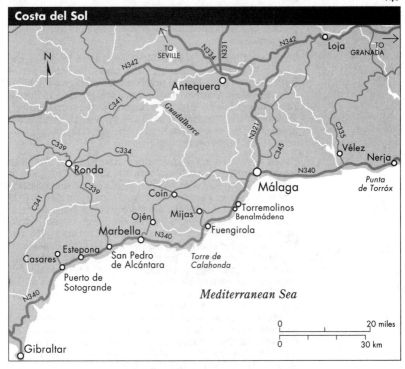

Costa del Sol

farther west, below the Avenida Carlota Alexandra. You'll find some old fishermen's cottages here, a few excellent seafood restaurants, and a traffic-free esplanade for an enjoyable stroll on a summer evening.

West of Torremolinos are the similar but more staid resorts of **Benalmádena** and **Fuengirola,** both retirement havens for British and American senior citizens. Frequent buses from Fuengirola, Marbella, or Málaga will take you up into the mountains to the picturesque—and over-photographed—village of **Mijas.** Though the vast tourist-oriented main square may seem like an extension of the Costa's tawdry bazaar, there are hillside streets of whitewashed houses where you'll discover an authentic village atmosphere that has changed little since the days before the tourist boom of the 1960s. Visit the bullring, the nearby church, and the chapel of Mijas's patroness, the Virgen de la Peña (to the side of the main square), and enjoy shopping for quality gifts and souvenirs.

Marbella is the most fashionable and sedate resort area along the coast. It does have a certain Florida land boom feel to it, but development has been controlled, and Marbella will, let's hope, never turn into another Torremolinos. The town's charming old Moorish quarter may be crowded with up-market boutiques and a modern, T-shirt-and-fudge section along the main drag; but when people speak of Marbella they refer both to the town and to the resorts—some more exclusive than others—stretching 16 kilometers (10 miles) or so on either side of town, between the highway and the beach. If you're vacationing in southern Spain, this is the place to stay. There's championship golf and tennis, fashionable waterfront cafés, and trendy shopping arcades.

The coastal highway outside Marbella, known locally as the Golden Mile, with its mosque, Arab banks, and residence of King Fahd of Saudi Arabia, proclaims the ever-growing influence of wealthy Arabs in this playground of the rich. In **Puerto Banús** (accessible by city buses; inquire at the tourist office), Marbella's plush marina, with its flashy yachts, fashionable people, and expensive restaurants, the glittering parade outshines even St. Tropez in ritzy glamour.

Ronda is reached via a spectacular mountain road from the coast. One of the oldest towns in Spain, and last stronghold of the legendary Andalusian bandits, Ronda's most dramatic feature is its ravine, known as **El Tajo,** which is 279 meters (900 feet) across and divides the old Moorish town from the "new town" of El Mercadillo. Spanning the gorge is the **Puente Nuevo,** an amazing architectural feat built between 1755 and 1793. Its parapet offers dizzying views of the River Guadalevin way below. Countless people have plunged to their death from this bridge, including its own architect, who accidentally fell over while inspecting his work, and numerous victims of the Civil War of 1936–39 who were hurled into the ravine—an episode recounted in Hemingway's *For Whom the Bell Tolls.* Ronda is visited more for its setting, breathtaking views, and ancient houses than for any particular monument. Stroll the old streets of **La Ciudad;** drop in at the historic **Reina Victoria** hotel, built by the English from Gibraltar as a fashionable resting place on their Algeciras to Bobadilla railroad line; and visit the **bullring,** one of the earliest and most beautiful rings in Spain. Here Ronda's most famous native son, Pedro Romero (1754–1839), father of modern bullfighting, is said to have killed 5,600 bulls during his 30-year career; and in the **Bullfighting Museum** you can see posters dating back to the very first fights held in the ring in May 1785. The ring is privately owned now, but three to four fights a year are still held in the summer months. Tickets are exceedingly difficult to come by (tel. 95/287–7977, admission to ring and museum: 175 ptas., open daily 10–6). Above all, don't miss the cliff-top walk and the gardens of the **Alameda del Tajo,** where you can contemplate one of the most dramatic views in all of Andalusia.

Returning to the coast, the next town is **Estepona,** which until recently marked the end of the urban sprawl of the Costa del Sol. Estepona lacks the hideous high rises of Torremolinos and Fuengirola, and set back from the main highway, it's not hard to make out the old fishing village this once was. Wander the streets of the Moorish village, around the central food market and the **Church of San Francisco,** and you'll find a pleasant contrast to the excesses higher up the coast.

Gibraltar

To enter **Gibraltar,** simply walk across the border at La Línea and show your passport. It is also possible to fly into Gibraltar on daily flights from London but, as yet, there are no flights from Spanish airports. There are, however, plenty of bus tours from Spain. **Juliá Tours, Pullmantur,** and many smaller agencies, run daily tours (not Sunday) to Gibraltar from most Costa del Sol resorts. Alternatively, you can take the regular **Portillo** bus to La Línea and walk across the border. In summer, **Portillo** runs an inexpensive daily tour to Gibraltar from Torremolinos bus station. Once you reach Gibraltar the official language is English and the currency is the British pound sterling, though pesetas are also accepted.

The Rock of Gibraltar acquired its name in AD 711 when it was captured by the Moorish chieftain Tarik at the start of the Arab invasion of Spain. It became known as Jebel Tarik (Rock of Tarik), later corrupted to Gibraltar. After successive periods of Moorish and Spanish domination, Gibraltar was captured by an Anglo-Dutch fleet in 1704 and ceded to the British by the Treaty of Utrecht in 1713. This tiny British colony, whose impressive silhouette dominates the straits between Spain and Morocco, is a rock just 5¾ kilometers (3⅝ miles) long, three-quarter kilometers (half a mile) wide, and 425 meters (1,369 feet) high.

On entering Gibraltar you have a choice. You can either plunge straight into exploring Gibraltar town, or opt for a tour around the Rock. Several minibus tours are available, some at the point of entry that crosses the Gibraltar Airport's runway. Inquire at the tourist office for details.

Numbers in the margin correspond to points of interest on the Gibraltar map.

The minibus tour around the Rock is best begun on the eastern side. As you enter Gibraltar, you'll turn left down Devil's Tower Road, and drive as far as **Catalan Bay,** a small fishing village founded by Genoese settlers in the 18th century, and now one of the Rock's most picturesque resorts. The road continues on beneath water catchments that supply the colony's drinking water, to another resort, **Sandy Bay,** and then plunges through the Dudley Ward Tunnel to bring you out at the Rock's most southerly tip, **Europa Point.** The view here is remarkable, across the Straits to the coast of Morocco, 22½ kilometers (14 miles) away. You are standing on what in ancient times was called one of the two Pillars of Hercules. Across the water in Morocco, a mountain between the cities of Ceuta and Tangier formed the second pillar. The Europa Point lighthouse has stood above the meeting point of the Atlantic and the Mediterranean since 1841. Plaques explain the history of the gun installations here, and, nearby on Europa Flats, you can see the **Nuns Well,** an ancient Moorish cistern, and the shrine of **Our Lady of Europe,** venerated by sailors since 1462.

Europa Road winds its way high on the western slopes above **Rosia Bay,** to which Nelson's flagship, HMS *Victory,* was towed after the Battle of Trafalgar in 1805. Aboard were the dead of the battle, who are now buried in Trafalgar Cemetery on the southern edge of town, and the body of Admiral Nelson himself, preserved in a barrel of rum. He was then taken to London for burial.

Europa Road continues to the **casino** (tel. 9567/76666, open daily 10 PM–4 AM) above the Alameda Gardens. Make a sharp right here up Engineer Road to **Jews Gate,** an unbeatable lookout point over the docks and Bay of Gibraltar to Algeciras in Spain. Queens Road leads to **St. Michael's Cave,** a series of underground chambers adorned with stalactites and stalagmites, which provides an admirable setting for concerts, ballet, and

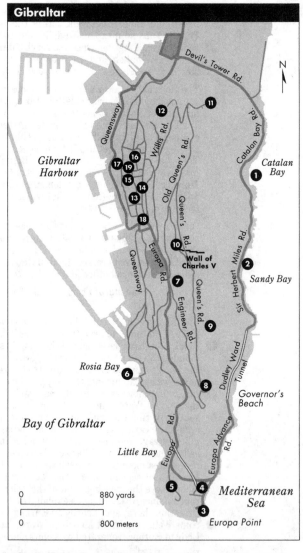

Gibraltar

drama. Sound-and-light shows are held here most days at 11 AM and 4 PM. A skull of Neanderthal Woman (now in the British Museum in London) was found in the caves some eight years *before* the world-famous discovery in Germany's Neander Valley in 1856. *Admission: £1.50. Open daily 10–5:30.*

10 Down Old Queen's Road you'll find the **Apes' Den** near the **Wall of Charles V.** The famous Barbary apes are a breed of cinnamon-colored, tailless monkeys, natives of the Atlas Mountains in Morocco. Legend holds that as long as the apes remain, the British will continue to hold the Rock. Winston Churchill himself issued orders for the maintenance of the ape colony when its numbers began to dwindle during World War II. Today the apes are the responsibility of the British Army, and a special Officer in Charge of Apes is assigned to feed them twice daily at 8 AM and 4 PM.

⓫ Passing beneath the cable car that runs to the Rock's summit, you'll ascend the **Upper Galleries** at the northern end of the Rock. These huge galleries were carved out during the Great Siege of 1779–1783. Here, in 1878, the Governor, Lord Napier of Magdala, entertained ex-President Ulysses S. Grant at a banquet in **St. George's Hall.** From here, the **Holyland Tunnel** leads out to the east side of the Rock above Catalan Bay. *Admission: 70 pence adults, 40 pence children. Open daily 10–5:30.*

⓬ The last stop before the town is at the **Moorish Castle** on Willis Road. Built by the successors of the Moorish invader Tarik, the present **Tower of Homage** was rebuilt by the Moors in 1333. Admiral Rooke hoisted the British flag from its top when he captured the Rock in 1704, and here it has flown ever since. The castle has been closed to the public and can be seen only from the outside.

Willis Road leads steeply down to the colorful, congested town of Gibraltar where the dignified Regency architecture of Britain blends with the shutters, balconies, and patios of southern Spain. Apart from the attraction of shops, restaurants, and pubs on Main Street, you'll want to visit some of the following: **⓭** the **Governor's Residence,** where the ceremonial Changing of the Guard once took place weekly (it now occurs four to five **⓮** times a year; ask at the tourist office); the **Law Courts,** where the famous case of the *Mary Celeste* sailing ship was heard in **⓯** 1872; the Anglican **Cathedral of the Holy Trinity;** the Catholic **⓰ ⓱** **Cathedral of St. Mary the Crowned;** and the **Gibraltar Museum,** whose exhibits recall the history of the Rock throughout the ages. *Gibraltar Museum, Bomb House La., tel. 9567–74289. Admission: £1 adults, 50 pence children. Open Mon.–Sat. 10–6.*

⓲ Finally, the **Nefusot Yehudada Synagogue** on Line Wall Road is worth a look for its inspired architecture, and, if you're inter-**⓳** ested in guns, the **Koehler Gun** in **Casemates Square** at the northern end of Main Street is an impressive example of the type of gun developed during the Great Siege.

Dining and Lodging

For details and price-category definitions, *see* Dining and Lodging in Staying in Spain.

Estepona **Antonio.** Head for the patio of this prize-winning restaurant, if *Dining* you can beat the crowds of locals who flock to the place. Try the ★ *ensalada de pimientos asados* (roast pepper salad) or the *fritura malaguena* (fried fish Malaga style). *Puerto Deportivo, tel. 95/280–1142. Reservations advised. DC, MC, V. Moderate.* **Costa del Sol.** This friendly French bistro offers French and Spanish dishes in an informal setting. French favorites include *bouillabaisse* and duck in orange sauce. It's located on a side street beside the Portillo bus station. *San Roque s/n, tel. 95/ 2801101. AE, MC, V. Closed Mon. lunch and Sun. Inexpensive.*

Lodging **Santa Marta.** This is a small, quiet hotel with just 37 rooms in chalet bungalows set in a large, peaceful garden. Some rooms are a little faded after 30 years, but the tranquil setting is a plus. Good lunches are served by the pool. *Rte. N340, km. 173, tel. 95/278–0716. 37 rooms. AE, MC, V. Open Apr.–Sept. only. Moderate.*

Gibraltar **Country Cottage.** Opposite the Catholic cathedral, this is the
Dining place to go for a taste of Old England. Enjoy steak and kidney pie, Angus steak, and roast beef, by candlelight. *13 Giro's Passage, tel. 9567/70084. Reservations advised. AE, MC, V. Closed Sun. Moderate.*

Ye Olde Rock. A changing menu of hearty pub fare is offered at this colorful spot on McKintosh Square. *Tel. 9567/71804. No credit cards. Budget.*

Lodging **Bristol.** This colonial-style hotel is just off Gibraltar's main street, right in the heart of town. Rooms are large and comfortable, and the tropical garden is a real haven for those guests who want to relax in peaceful isolation. *10 Cathedral Sq., tel. 9567/76800. 60 rooms. AE, DC, MC, V. Moderate.*

Miss Serruya Guest House. Miss Serruya rents four quite luxurious rooms (one of them really a small apartment most) in her renovated 1850 frame house, one of Gibraltar's old aristocratic residences. *92/1A Irish Town, tel. 9567/73220. 4 rooms. No credit cards. Inexpensive.*

Málaga **Antonio Martín.** This is another old Málaga standby, with a
Dining splendid terrace overlooking the ocean, at the beginning of the Paseo Marítimo. It's long been famous for its fresh seafood and paella. Try the local *fritura malagueña. Paseo Marítimo 4, tel. 95/222–2113. Reservations advised. AE, DC, MC, V. Closed Sun. evening. Moderate.*

El Encuentro. The former Cortijo de Manuela has been taken over by new owners, but it retains much the same *cortijo* (country-home) atmosphere as in the past. Ocean fish and delicious Malagueña standbys like *frituras* (fried seafood) are the order of the day. *Plaza de Malagueta 3, tel. 95/222–4139. AE, DC, V. Closed Sun. eve. Moderate.*

Rincon de Mata. This is one of the best of the many restaurants in the pedestrian shopping streets between Calle Larios and Calle Nueva. Its menu is more original than most. In summer, there are tables outside on the sidewalk. *Esparteros 8, tel. 95/222–3135. Reservations not necessary. V. Moderate.*

Rincón de la Catedral. This beautiful restaurant in a beautiful setting directly faces the cathedral. In an atmosphere of elegant wood, rafter-hung ham, and fresh flowers, try specialties such as *brochetas de rape con gambas* (kebabs with angler and prawns) or the relatively expensive *solomillo a la pimienta verde* (pork steak in green pepper sauce). *Canon 7, tel. 95/260–0518. AE, MC, V. Closed Sun. Moderate–Inexpensive.*

La Cancela. This is a colorful restaurant in the center of town, just off Calle Granada. Dine indoors or alfresco. *Denís Belgrano 3, tel. 95/222–3125. Reservations not necessary. AE, DC, MC, V. Closed Wed. Inexpensive.*

Don Jamón. You'll dine on a landing above the bar at Don Jamón, which features a wide offering of traditional Castillian dishes. Try the *conejo a la castellana* (rabbit in sauce), roast chicken, paella, or *morcilla* (blood sausage). Heads of boar and deer and roof-hung hams give the place a hunter ambience. *Strachan 5, tel. 95/222–1343. No credit cards. Budget.*

Lodging **Las Vegas.** In a pleasant part of town, just east of the center, this recently renovated hotel has a dining room overlooking the Paseo Marítimo, an outdoor pool, and a large leafy garden.

Rooms at the back enjoy a good view of the ocean. *Paseo de Sancha 22, tel. 95/221–7712. 100 rooms. AE, DC, MC, V. Moderate.*

Niza. Several friendly lobby rooms greet you at the second-floor entrance of this highly regarded hotel, off one corner of the Plaza Constitucion. The rooms, relatively spacious and well-maintained but a bit faded, include brass beds, wood armoires, and desks. *Larios 2, tel. 95/222–7704. 46 rooms. No credit cards. Reserve ahead in summer. Inexpensive.*

Victoria. This small, recently renovated hostel in an old house just off Calle Larios offers excellent budget accommodations in a convenient central location. *Sancha de Lara 3, tel. 95/222–4223. 13 rooms. AE, V. Inexpensive.*

Chinitas. A giant sign on the Plaza Constitucion points the way to Hostal Chinitas. After climbing a rather gruff set of stairs, you'll find a charming home, hung with pictures and inhabited by a cheerful family. *Pasaje de Chinitas 2–2, tel. 95/221–4683. 4 rooms. No credit cards. Budget.*

Marbella
Dining

La Tricycleta. Located in an old house in the center of town, this English-owned restaurant is a local institution. Have a drink at the downstairs bar, then dine upstairs beside a log fire in winter or outside on the rooftop patio when it's warm. *Buitrago 14, tel. 95/277–7800. Reservations advised in summer. AE, MC, V. Closed Sun. Moderate.*

Meson del Pasaje. A warren of small dining rooms and bars awaits you in this old house just off the Plaza Naranjos. The decor is Victorian, with Spanish touches. The menu features a wide variety of pastas. *Pasaje 5, tel. 95/277–1261. Reservations advised in summer. V. Closed summer lunch. Inexpensive.*

Meson del Pollo. This small, sunny, "house of chicken" illustrates how Marbella, despite tourism, remains truly Spanish. Porcelain lampshades, azulejo tiles, a dozen tables, and the scents of roasting chicken fill this popular lunch spot. Try the *pollo a la sevillana* dinner (roast chicken with squid, fried potatoes, salad, and cider), or sample tapas of octopus or meatballs. *Antonio Martín, across from the El Fuerte Hotel, tel. 95/277–2200. No credit cards. Inexpensive.*

Guerola. At this small restaurant, the food's good, homemade, and inexpensive. Stop for a tapa at the bar. The *gazpacho* is tasty, and so is the *fritura variada* (fried fish assortment). *Padre Enrique Cantos 4, 95/277–0007. No credit cards. Budget.*

Lodging

A number of pleasant small hotels are scattered throughout the old town in Marbella; if you look, you'll find them. Some of them go for as little as $15–$20 a room, but you'll generally pay more for something nice. There are a few reasonably priced, high-rise hotels, popular with those on package tours, only a block from the busy town beach. A hotel pool is a plus.

El Fuerte. This is the best of the few hotels in the center of Marbella, with simple, adequate rooms. It's located in a 1950s-type building in the midst of a large garden with an outdoor pool. *Avda. El Fuerte, tel. 95/277–1500. 146 rooms. AE, DC, V. Moderate.*

Alfil. The recently renovated Alfil, on Marbella's busy main street, is functional, moderately priced, and located right downtown. Rooms at the back are quieter. *Ricardo Soriano 15, tel. 95/277–2350. 41 rooms. V. Moderate–Inexpensive.*

Finlandia. If you're looking for clean, inexpensive accommodations in the heart of town, try this simple white hostel on a quiet residential street. The atmosphere is friendly and informal, with a small bar and TV lounge in the lobby. The large rooms have balconies. *Finlandia s/n, tel. 95/277–0700. 11 rooms. MC, V. Inexpensive.*

Paco. On a quiet and pretty white street above the main road, the Hostal Paco is another good find in the old town (unfortunately, it's closed in winter). Many of the rooms have small balconies on the three-story building front. *Peral 16, tel. 95/277–1200. 25 rooms. No credit cards. Budget–Inexpensive.*

Pilar. This may be the best find in Marbella: a cheerful, relatively large and charming hotel in a central location. The Pilar is run by Dave Bland, a good-natured Englishman, and his Spanish wife, and contains such unexpected surprises as a pool table and a log fire in winter. *Mesoncillo 4, 95/282–9936. 16 rooms. Facilities: bar serving breakfast and lunch. No credit cards. Budget.*

Mijas
Dining

La Reja. This charming restaurant has two dining rooms overlooking the main square of Plaza Virgen de la Peña. There's an atmospheric bar and an inexpensive pizzeria, too. *Caños 9, tel. 95/248–5068. Reservations accepted. AE, DC, MC, V. Closed Mon. Moderate.*

Mirlo Blanco. Here you can sample Basque specialties such as *txangurro* (crab) and *merluza a la vasca* (hake with asparagus, eggs, and clam sauce). *Plaza Constitución 13, tel. 95/248–5700. Reservations accepted. AE, DC, V. Moderate.*

El Horno. You'll have a choice in summer of where to eat: out in the pedestrian alley where you enter, or inside a dining room with spectacular views of the main plaza. There's a wide range of traditional Spanish fare here, more unusual dishes like spaghetti bolognesa, and a variety of sandwiches. *Loscanos 13, tel. 95/248–5097. AE, MC, V. Inexpensive.*

Lodging

Luque. There is no inexpensive lodging in Mijas, but just a few miles away and reachable by hourly bus service connecting Marbella and Mijas, you'll find this serene and charming hotel. The family that runs it keeps the seven rooms spotless, and many of them face out onto the Plaza Andalucía, a small plaza dotted with palm trees. *Plaza Andalucía 4, enter from the main road, Benalmádena, tel. 95/244–8197. 7 rooms. No credit cards. Budget.*

Ronda
Dining

Pedro Romero. Located opposite the bullring, this restaurant is, not surprisingly, packed with colorful taurine decor. Among the traditional regional recipes worth trying is the *sopa de mesón*—the soup of the house. *Virgen de la Paz 18, tel. 95/287–1110. AE, DC, MC, V. Moderate.*

Hermanos Macias. In summer, if you dine on the *terraza* out front, you'll be looking down an alley at the main entrance to the bullring. Inside, there's a dark and moody dining room with a Moorish feel. Service is attentive, and the food is good. *Pedro Romero s/n, tel. 95/287–4238. No credit cards. Inexpensive.*

Mesón Santiago. This typical Andalusian mesón with colorful decor opens for lunch only and has a pleasant outdoor patio. It serves hearty portions of home-cooked food—but be prepared for long waits. *Marina 3, tel. 95/287–1559. MC, V. Open 1–4 PM only. Inexpensive.*

Flores. This very Spanish restaurant, with a large, bare dining room, faces the bullring. *Vírgen de la Paz 9, tel. 95/287–1040. No credit cards. Budget.*

Lodging **Polo.** A cozy, old-fashioned hotel in the center of town, Polo sports a reasonably priced restaurant. The staff is friendly and the rooms simple but comfortable. *Mariano Soubiron 8, tel. 95/287-2447. 33 rooms. AE, DC, V. Moderate.*

La Española. Starkly simple rooms, sometimes a bit cold but clean, are in a building with dramatic views of the rocky and wild countryside upon which Ronda is built. *Jose Aparicio 3, tel. 95/287-1052. 20 rooms. No credit cards. Budget.*

Torremolinos **Casa Guaquin.** Casa Guaquin is widely known as the best sea-
Dining food restaurant in the region. Changing daily catches are served on a seaside patio alongside such menu stalwarts as *coquillas al ajillo* (sea cockles in garlic sauce). *Paseo Maritimo 63, tel. 95/238-4530. AE, V. Closed Thurs. Moderate.*

El Atrio. This small, stylish restaurant is located in the Pueblo Blanco. Its cuisine is predominantly French. In summer, you can dine on the terrace. *Casablanca 9, tel. 95/238-8850. AE, V. Open 8 PM-midnight. Closed Sun. and Dec. Moderate.*

El Roqueo. Owned by a former fisherman, this is one of the locals' favorite Carihuela fish restaurants. Ingredients are always fresh and the prices are very reasonable. *Carmen 35, tel. 95/238-4946. AE, V. Closed Tues. and Nov. Moderate.*

Juan. This is a good place to enjoy seafood in summer, with a sunny outdoor patio facing the sea. The specialties include the great Costa del Sol standbys: *sopa de mariscos* (shellfish soup), *dorada al horno* (oven-roasted giltheads), and *fritura malagueña. Paseo Marítimo 29, La Carihuela, tel. 95/238-5656. AE, DC, MC, V. Moderate.*

Lodging **Tropicana.** Located on the beach at the far end of the Carihuela is this comfortable, relaxing resort hotel. Several good restaurants are nearby. *Trópico 6, tel. 95/238-6600, fax 95/238-0568. 86 rooms. Facilities: pool. AE, DC, MC, V. Moderate.*

Pizarro. If you want to stay right downtown, this modern hotel just off the Plaza Andalucia is a good choice. It's well-maintained and comes with a functional restaurant and bar. It's a 15-minute walk to the beach. *Pasaje Pizarro s/n, tel. 95/238-7167. 49 rooms. No credit cards. Inexpensive-Moderate.*

★ **Miami.** Set in an old Andalusian villa in a shady garden to the west of the Carihuela, this is something of a find amid the ocean of concrete blocks. *Aladino 14, tel. 95/238-5255. 26 rooms. No credit cards. Inexpensive.*

Marloy. Near the Pizarro, the Pensión Marloy offers very cheap rooms that are clean but in need of sprucing-up. The street can be noisy. *Cruz 6, tel. 95/238-7820. 28 rooms. No credit cards. Budget.*

23 Sweden

Less expensive ways of visiting Sweden are available to the traveler who takes the trouble to do a little research. Major hotel chain discounts and packages, youth hostels, special rail passes, and carefully selected restaurants and hotels are among the many ways visitors can substantially cut costs in Sweden. Because of its size—450,707 square kilometers (173,349 square miles), approximately that of California—a visit to Sweden is wisely limited to a region or two. But no matter where you go in this sparsely populated country of vast spaces and pristine forests, unspoiled lakes and churning rivers, jagged coastlines and countless archipelagoes, relieved here and there by fascinating cities and towns, the visit is well worth the price of admission. The distances are considerable, especially by European standards—almost 1,600 kilometers (1,000 miles) as the crow flies, from north to south. The 2,128-kilometer (1,330-mile) train journey from Trelleborg, in the far south, through endless birch forests to Riksgränsen, in the Arctic north, is said to be the world's longest stretch of continuously electrified railroad.

This chapter concentrates on the more densely populated southern part of the country—essentially the area dominated by the two largest cities, Stockholm and Gothenburg—although it also suggests an itinerary through the celebrated Folklore District, where the most distinctly Swedish cultural traditions are faithfully maintained.

The Swedish Tourist Board, which will be phased out by August 1993 to make way for an ambitious, privately supported tourism corporation, has had some difficulty in recent years marketing the country to overseas visitors. But Sweden's image has not kept pace with reality, and that too is expected to change under the new tourism organization. While it is widely

Sweden

N

Norwegian
Sea

Abisko
Kiruna
Suorva
Luleälven
Jokkmokk
Arjeplog
Töre
Tornio
Tärnaby
400
Arvidsjaur
Kalix
E79
Sorsele
95
Luleå
Storuman
Piteå
Lycksele
Umeälven
Skellefteå
342
Strömsund
Åsele
90
92
Åre
Umeå
Östersund
E75
E4
Tännäs
Ljungan
Sundsvall
84
FINLAND
Idre
Hudiksvall
70
Bollnäs
Gulf
Mora
Söderhamn
of
62
Falun
Gävle
Bothnia
80
Klarälven
Borlänge
Avesta
Fagersta
E4
Karlstad
Västerås
Uppsala
E18
Lake
Stockholm
Mellerud
Mälaren
Strömstad
Lake
Örebro
Gulf of Finland
Vänern
Gotska
Uddevalla
Norrköping
Sandön
Trollhättan
Lake
REP.
Vättern
Linköping
Baltic
OF
Gothenburg
Jönköping
ESTONIA
40
Sea
Borås
Visby
Gulf of
Falkenberg
Nässjö
Riga
E66
E6
Värnamo
Gotland
Oskarshamn
Halmstad
Växjö
23
Kalmar
REP. OF
Helsingborg
Öland
LITHUANIA
Malmö
Karlskrona
Kristianstad
DEN.
0   50 miles
Trelleborg
Ystad
0   75 km

NORWAY

accepted that prices in Sweden are higher than in other European countries, recent efforts have been made to bring prices in line, an effort that in part reflects the fact that Sweden has officially applied to join the European Community and is expected to become a member by 1995. For example, Sweden recently decreased its value-added tax (known in Swedish as *Moms*) from 25% to 18%. And a whole generation of restaurateurs with a Continental outlook is introducing affordable dishes utilizing Swedish ingredients. Indeed, those who visit Sweden today will be surprised by the breadth and quality of the cuisine as well as the high standards of lodging. Even the most modest establishments are spotlessly clean, and you will be given a warm welcome (almost certainly in excellent English, too).

Sweden's scenic attractions may not be as spectacular as the Norwegian fjords across the border, but the country offers a varied landscape, with more than 96,000 lakes and a jagged coastline with countless archipelagoes, forests, mountains, and rushing rivers. While Sweden is very much a modern country, it zealously guards its rural heritage. Most city dwellers have access to second homes in the country to which they retreat as often as possible. Traditional arts and crafts are also highly prized.

The cities, too, make the most of their natural settings and are carefully planned, with an emphasis on light and open spaces. Stockholm, one of the most beautiful of European capitals, is the major attraction, though Gothenburg, on the west coast, and Malmö, just across the sound from Denmark, are worthy of short visits as well.

Essential Information

Before You Go

When to Go   The main tourist season runs from June through August, but Sweden needs to extend the season to encourage visitors from abroad. It's disappointing to note how many visitor attractions do not start operating until mid-June and then suddenly restrict their opening times or close down altogether in mid-August, when the Swedes' own vacation season ends and the children return to school. The weather can also be magnificent in the spring and fall, and there are plenty of tourists who would like to do some sightseeing when there are fewer people around.

Sweden virtually shuts up shop for the entire month of July, so avoid planning a business trip at that time. The concentrated nature of the Swedes' own vacation period can sometimes make it difficult to get hotel reservations during July and early August. On the other hand, the big city hotels, which cater mainly to business travelers, reduce their rates drastically in the summer, when their ordinary clients are on vacation. (If you're traveling in winter, the high season for business travel, be forewarned that prices can be very high.) Ask your travel agent about special discount schemes offered by the major hotel groups.

Climate   As in the rest of northern Europe, Sweden's summer weather is unpredictable, but, as a general rule, it is more likely to be rainy on the west coast than on the east. When the sun shines, the climate is usually agreeable; it is rarely unbearably hot. In Stockholm it never really gets dark in midsummer, while in the far north, above the Arctic Circle, the sun doesn't set between the end of May and the middle of July.

The following are the average daily maximum and minimum temperatures for Stockholm.

Jan.	30F	–1C	May	58F	14C	Sept.	60F	15C
	23	–5		43	6		49	9
Feb.	30F	–1C	June	67F	19C	Oct.	49F	9C
	22	–5		51	11		41	5
Mar.	37F	3C	July	71F	22C	Nov.	40F	5C
	26	–4		57	14		34	1
Apr.	47F	8C	Aug.	68F	20C	Dec.	35F	3C
	34	1		55	13		28	–2

Currency   The unit of currency in Sweden is the krona (plural kronor), which is divided into 100 öre and is written as SEK or kr. Coins come in values of 10 or 50 öre and 1 or 5 kronor, while bills come in denominations of 10, 50, 100, 500, and 1,000 SEK. The 10-kronor note is being phased out and replaced by new coins sometime within the next three years. At the same time, a 20-kronor note is being introduced. Traveler's checks and foreign currency can be exchanged at banks all over Sweden and at post offices bearing the NB Exchange sign. At press time (summer 1992), the exchange rate was 5.29 kronor to the dollar and 10.25 kronor to the pound sterling.

What It Will Cost   Sweden is an expensive country. Hotel prices are above the European average, but, as in most countries, the most expensive hotels are found in major cities, such as Stockholm and Gothenburg. Restaurant prices are generally fairly high, but there are bargains to be had: Look for the *dagens rätt* (dish of the day) in many city restaurants. This costs about SEK 50–SEK 65 and can include a main dish, salad, soft drink, bread and butter, and coffee.

Many hotels have special low summer rates and cut costs during weekends in winter. But because of heavy taxes and excise duties, liquor prices are among the highest in Europe. It pays to take in your maximum duty-free allowance. Value-added tax (*Moms*) is imposed on most goods and services at a rate of 25%, with the exception of an 18% "tourist" Moms on hotels, restaurants, and transportation (introduced January 1, 1992). You can avoid most of the tax on goods if you take advantage of the tax-free shopping service offered at more than 13,000 stores throughout the country (*see* Shopping in Staying in Sweden, *below*).

Sample Prices   Cup of coffee, SEK 10–SEK 15; bottle of beer, SEK 30–SEK 40; Coca-Cola, SEK 12–SEK 15; ham sandwich, SEK 25–SEK 35; 1-mile taxi ride, SEK 70 (depending on the taxi company).

Customs on Arrival   You may bring duty-free into Sweden 400 cigarettes or 200 cigarillos or 100 cigars or 500 grams of tobacco. You may also import 1 liter of spirits and 1 liter of wine *or* 2 liters of beer, plus a reasonable amount of perfume and other goods to the value of SEK 600. Residents over the age of 15 of other European countries may bring duty-free into Sweden 200 cigarettes or 100 cigarillos, or 50 cigars or 250 grams of tobacco; visitors aged 20 or more may import 1 liter of spirits, 1 liter of wine, and 2 liters of beer, plus a reasonable amount of perfume, and other goods to the value of SEK 600. There are no limits on the amount of foreign currency that can be imported or exported.

Language   Virtually all Swedes you are likely to meet will speak English, for it is a mandatory subject in all schools and is the main foreign language that Swedish children learn. Some of the older people you meet in the rural areas may not be quite so familiar with English, but you'll soon find someone who can help out. Swedish is one of the Germanic languages and is similar to Danish and Norwegian. Grammatically it is easier than German, although pronunciation can pose some problems. Also, the letters å, ä, and ö rank as separate letters in the Swedish alphabet and come at the end after *Z*. So if you're looking up a Mr. Ängelholm in a Swedish telephone book, you'll find him near the end. Few Swedish place names have anglicized spellings, with the notable exception of Göteborg (Gothenburg).

Getting Around

By Train   Sweden's rail network, mostly electrified, is highly efficient, and trains operate frequently, particularly on the main routes linking Stockholm with Gothenburg and Malmö, on which there is frequent service. First- and second-class cars are provided on all main routes, and sleeping cars are available in both classes on overnight trains. On virtually all long-distance trains, there is a buffet or dining car. Seat reservations are always advisable, and on some trains—indicated with R or IC on the timetable—they are compulsory. Reservations can be made right up to departure time at a cost of SEK 20 per seat (tel. 020/757575).

Fares   On certain trains, listed as "Low price" or "Red" departures, fares are reduced by 50%, so careful planning is necessary to take advantage of the lower prices. Passengers paying low fares cannot make stopovers and the tickets are valid for only 36 hours.

Contact the Swedish rail network for a special pass called the **Nordturistkort** (Nordic Tourist Card), which allows for free rail travel anywhere in Scandinavia. The pass costs SEK 1,680 for second-class train travel and can also be used for free travel or 50% discounts on certain bus and ferry services. The Eurail and InterRail passes are also available from **Statens Jarnvagar** (SJ), the Swedish state railway company. For more information contact any local railway station or SJ (Vasagatan 22, 10551 Stockholm, tel. 020/757575).

By Plane   Sweden's domestic air network is highly developed. Most major cities are served by **SAS** (Scandinavian Airlines) or its domestic partner **Linjeflyg**. From Stockholm, there are services to about 30 points around the country. SAS and Linjeflyg offer cut-rate round-trip "minifares" every day of the week on selected flights, and these fares are available on most services during the peak tourist season, from late June to mid-August. Some even more favorable offers on domestic flights are frequently available from the end of June through early August and during the Christmas and Easter seasons.

By Bus Sweden has an excellent network of express bus services that provides an inexpensive and relatively speedy way of getting around the country. **Swebus,** tel. 031/103285 (Gothenburg) or 08/237190 (Stockholm), offers daily bus services from most major Swedish cities to various parts of Sweden. A number of other private companies operate weekend-only services on additional routes. In the far north of Sweden, post buses delivering mail to remote areas also carry passengers, and provide an offbeat and inexpensive way of seeing the countryside.

By Boat The classic boat trip in Sweden is the four-day journey along the Göta Canal between Gothenburg and Stockholm, operated by **Göta Kanal,** Gothenburg, tel. 031/806315.

By Bicycle Cycling is a popular activity in Sweden, and the country's uncongested roads make it ideal for extended bike tours. Bicycles can be rented throughout the country; inquire at the local tourist information office. Rental costs average around SEK 80 per day or SEK 400 per week. The **Swedish Touring Club** (STF) in Stockholm (tel. 08/790–3100) can give you information about cycling packages that include bike rental, overnight accommodations, and meals. **Cykelfrämjandet** (tel. 08/321680) has an English-language guide to cycling trips.

Staying in Sweden

Telephones Sweden has plenty of pay phones, although they are not found *Local Calls* (as in many other European countries) in post offices. There are, however, special offices marked Tele or Telebutik from which you can make calls. To make calls from a pay phone, you should have SEK 1 and SEK 5 coins available. For a local call, you need two SEK 1 coins.

International Calls These can be made from any pay phone. For calls to the United States and Canada, dial 009, then 1 (the country code), then wait for a second dial tone before dialing the area code and number. When dialing the United Kingdom, omit the initial zero on area codes (for Central London you would dial 009 followed by 44, wait for the second tone, then dial 71 and the local number). Making calls from your hotel room is convenient but can be expensive, so check with the front desk about rates first. You pay the normal rate at Telebutik offices.

Operators and The international exchange number is 0018. Dial 07975 for di-*Information* rectory assistance in Sweden, 0013 for the Nordic Area, and 0019 for foreign inquiries.

Mail Airmail letters and postcards to the United States and Canada *Postal Rates* weighing less than 20 grams cost SEK 5.50. Postcards and letters within Europe cost SEK 4.50.

Receiving Mail If you're uncertain where you will be staying, have your mail sent to Poste Restante, S-101 10 Stockholm. The address for collection is Vasagatan 28–32. A Poste Restante service is also offered by American Express (Birger Jarlsgatan 1, tel. 08/235330).

Shopping Swedish goods have earned an international reputation for elegance and quality, and any visitor to the country should spend some time exploring the many impressive shops and department stores. The midsummer tourist season is as good a time as any to go shopping, for that is when many stores have their annual sales. The best buys are to be found in glassware, stainless steel, pottery and ceramics, leather goods, and textiles. You will find a wide selection of goods available in such major stores as **NK, Åhléns, PUB,** and **Domus,** which have branches all over the country.

High-quality furniture is a Swedish specialty, and it is worthwhile visiting one of the many branches of **IKEA,** a shop usually located on the outskirts of major towns. IKEA's prices are extremely competitive, and the company also operates an export service. For glassware at bargain prices, head for the "Kingdom of Crystal" area (*see* Gothenburg and the Glass Country, *below*). All the major glassworks, including **Orrefors** and **Kosta Boda,** have large factory outlets where you can pick up "seconds" (normally indistinguishable from the perfect product) at only a fraction of the normal retail price. In country areas, look for the local **Hemslöjd** craft centers, featuring high-quality clothing and needlework items.

VAT Refunds   About 13,000 Swedish shops—1,000 in Stockholm alone—participate in the tax-free shopping service for visitors, enabling you to claim a refund on most of the value-added tax (Moms) that you have paid. Shops taking part in the scheme display a distinctive black, blue, and yellow sticker in the window. (Some stores offer the service only on purchases worth more than SEK 200.) Whenever you make a purchase in a participating store, you are given a "tax-free shopping check" equivalent to the tax paid, less a handling charge. This check can be cashed when you leave Sweden, either at the airport or aboard ferries. You should have your passport with you when you make your purchase and when you claim your refund.

Opening and Closing Times   **Banks.** Banks are open weekdays 9:30–3, but some stay open until 5:30 in some larger cities. Banks at Stockholm's Arlanda Airport and Gothenburg's Landvetter Airport open every day, with extended hours. "Forex" currency-exchange offices operate in downtown Stockholm, Gothenburg, and Malmö, also with extended hours.

Museums. Hours vary widely, but museums are typically open weekdays 10–4 or 10–5. Many are also open on weekends but may close on Monday.

Shops. Shops are generally open weekdays 9 or 9:30–6 and Saturday 9–1 or 9–4. Some large department stores stay open until 8 or 10 on certain evenings, and some are also open on Sunday 12–4 in the major cities. Many supermarkets open on Sunday.

National Holidays   January 1; April 9 (Good Friday); April 12 (Easter Monday); May 1 (Labor Day); May 20 (Ascension); May 30, 31 (Pentecost); June 25 (Midsummer's Eve); June 26 (Midsummer's Day); November 6 (All Saints' Day); December 25, 26.

Dining   Swedish cuisine used to be considered somewhat uninteresting, but lately it has become much more cosmopolitan. The inevitable fast-food outlets, such as McDonald's and Burger King, have come on the scene, as well as Clock, the homegrown version. But there is also a good range of more conventional restaurants, including less expensive places where you can pick up a somewhat cheaper lunch or snack. Snacks can also be enjoyed in a *Konditori,* which offers inexpensive sandwiches, pastries, and pies with coffee, tea, or soft drinks. A cross between a café and a coffee shop, the Konditori can be found in every city and town.

Many restaurants all over the country specialize in *Husmanskost*—literally "home cooking"—which is based on traditional Swedish recipes.

Sweden is best known for its *smörgåsbord*, a word whose correct pronunciation defeats non-Swedes. It consists of a tempting buffet of hot and cold dishes, usually with a strong emphasis on seafood, notably herring, prepared in a wide variety of ways. Authentic smörgåsbord can be enjoyed all over the country, but the best is found in the many inns in Skåne, where you can eat as much as you want for about SEK 200. Many Swedish hotels serve a lavish smörgåsbord-style breakfast, often included in the room price. Do justice to your breakfast and you'll probably want to skip lunch!

Mealtimes The Swedes tend to eat early. Restaurants start serving lunch at about 11 AM, and outside the main cities you may find that they close quite early in the evening (often by 9) or may not even open at all for dinner. Don't wait too long to look for someplace to have a meal.

Dress Casual—or casual chic—attire is perfectly acceptable for restaurants in all price categories.

Ratings With the exception of the budget category, prices are per person and include a first course, main course (Swedes tend to skip desserts), and service charge, but no drinks. Service charges and Moms are included in the meal, so there is no need to tip. Restaurants in the budget category tend to offer simpler meals that don't usually include more than a main dish with bread, salad, coffee, and a beverage. Best bets are indicated by a star ★.

Category	Cost
Moderate	SEK 120–SEK 230
Inexpensive	SEK 80–SEK 120
Budget	under SEK 80

Lodging Sweden offers a wide range of accommodations, from simple village rooms and campsites to top-class hotels of the highest international standard. Except at the major hotels in the larger cities that cater mainly to business clientele, rates are fairly reasonable. Prices are normally on a per-room basis and include all taxes and service and usually breakfast. Apart from the more modest inns and the cheapest budget establishments, private baths and showers are now standard features, although it is just as well to double-check when making your reservation. Budget hotels are typically small, family-run establishments offering basic accommodations with access to showers and baths. These hotels generally do not offer any additional facilities. Whatever their size, virtually all Swedish hotels provide scrupulously clean accommodations and courteous service. In Stockholm, there is a hotel reservation office—**Hotellcentralen**—at the central train station and at the Stockholm Tourist Center in the Sweden House. In other areas, local tourist offices will help you with hotel reservations. A number of farms throughout Sweden offer accommodations, normally on a bed-and-breakfast basis, with self-catering facilities for cooking and other meals. A list of farm and cottage accommodations in Sweden is available from most regional tourist offices, or by contacting the **Federation of Swedish Farmers** (tel. 08/787–5000).

Hotels You can get a good idea of the facilities and prices at a particular hotel by consulting the official annual guide, "Hotels in Sweden," obtainable free of charge from the Swedish National Tourist Office. There is a fair selection of hotels in all price categories in every town and city, though major international chains such as Sheraton have made only small inroads in Sweden thus far. The main homegrown chains are SARA, Scandic, and RESO. The Sweden Hotels group has about 100 independently owned hotels and offers a central reservation office. The group also has its own classification scheme—A, B, or C—based on the facilities available at each establishment. CountrySide Sweden is a group of 35 handpicked resort hotels, some of them restored historic manor houses or centuries-old inns. Most have been family-run for generations.

House-Rental Vacations In Sweden, these are popular among other Europeans, particularly the British and Germans. There are about 250 chalet villages with amenities, such as grocery stores, restaurants, saunas, and tennis courts. You can often arrange such accommodations on the spot at local tourist information offices. An alternative is a package, such as the one offered by **Scandinavian Seaways,** which combines a ferry trip from Britain across the North Sea with a stay in a chalet village. Scandinavian Seaways is based in the United Kingdom at Parkeston Quay, Harwich, Essex (tel. 0255/240240). Their number in Gothenburg is 031/650600.

Camping Camping is also popular in Sweden. There are about 750 officially approved sites throughout the country, most located next to the sea or a lake and offering such activities as windsurfing, riding, and tennis. They are generally open between June 1 and September 1, though some are available year round. The Swedish National Tourist Board publishes, in English, an abbreviated list of sites.

Ratings Prices are for two people in a double room, based on summer season rates. Best bets are indicated by a star ★.

Category	Cost
Moderate	SEK 725–SEK 970
Inexpensive	SEK 600–SEK 725
Budget	under SEK 600

Tipping Unlike some countries, Sweden cannot be described as "the land of the outstretched palm"—probably because earnings are relatively high anyway, and hotel and restaurant staff do not depend on their tips for their existence. Taxi drivers do not expect a tip. Usually the fee for checking coats is set between SEK 6 and SEK 10 and is clearly posted on the checkroom counter or wall.

Stockholm

Arriving and Departing

By Plane   All international flights arrive at Arlanda Airport, 40 kilometers (25 miles) north of the city. The airport is linked to Stockholm by a fast freeway. For information on arrival and departure times, call the individual airlines.

Between the Airport and Downtown   Buses leave both the international and domestic terminals every 10–15 minutes, from 7:10 AM to 10:30 PM, and run to the city terminal at Klarabergsviadukten next to the central train station. The bus costs SEK 50 per person.

By Train   All major domestic and international services arrive at Stockholm Central Station on Vasagatan, in the heart of the city. This is also the terminus for local commuter services. For 24-hour train information, tel. 020/757575. At the station there is a ticket and information office where you can make seat or sleeping-car reservations. An automatic ticket-issuing machine is also available. Seat reservations on the regular train cost SEK 20, couchettes SEK 80, and beds SEK 160.

By Bus   Long-distance buses, from such places as Härnösand and Sundsvall, arrive at Norra Bantorget, a few blocks north of the central train station, and all others at Klarabergsviadukten, just beside it. Bus tickets can also be bought at the railroad reservations office.

Getting Around

The most cost-effective way of getting around Stockholm is to use a **Stockholmskortet** (Key to Stockholm) card. Besides giving unlimited transportation on city subway, bus, and rail services, it offers free admission to 50 museums and several sightseeing trips. The card costs SEK 135 for 24 hours, SEK 270 for two days, and SEK 405 for three days. It is available from the tourist center at Sweden House, at Kungsträdgården, and the Hotellcentralen accommodations bureau at the central train station.

Maps and timetables for all city transportation networks are available from the Stockholm Transit Authority (SL) information desks at Norrmalmstorg or Sergels Torg. You can also obtain information by phone (tel. 08/236000).

By Bus and Subway   The Stockholm Transit Authority (SL) operates both the bus and subway systems. Tickets for the two networks are interchangeable.

The subway system, known as T-banan (the *T* stands for tunnel), is the easiest and fastest way of getting around the city. Some of the stations offer permanent art exhibitions. Station entrances are marked with a blue T on a white background. The T-banan has about 100 stations and covers more than 60 route-miles. Trains run frequently between 5 AM and 2 AM.

Individual tickets are available at ticket counters, but it is cheaper to buy a special discount coupon that gives a significant savings compared with buying separate tickets each time you travel. The coupons are available at Pressbyrån newsstands. A one-day ticket for the city center alone, valid on both bus and subway, costs SEK 30. A ticket covering the entire Greater Stockholm area costs SEK 55 for 24 hours or SEK 105 for 72 hours. People under 18 or over 65 pay half price. Also available from the Pressbyrån newsstands are SEK 60 T-banan coupons, good for 15 subway rides.

The Stockholm bus network is one of the world's largest. Services run not only within the central area but also to out-of-town points of interest, such as Waxholm, with its historic fortress, and Gustavsberg, with its well-known porcelain factory. Within Greater Stockholm, buses run throughout the night.

By Train SL operates conventional train services from Stockholm Central Station to a number of nearby points, including Nynäshamn, a departure point for ferries to the island of Gotland. Trains also run from the Slussen station to the fashionable seaside resort of Saltsjöbaden.

Important Addresses and Numbers

Tourist Information The main tourist center is at **Sweden House** (Kungsträdgården, tel. 08/789–2000 or 789–2490). During the peak tourist season (mid-June to mid-August), it is open weekdays 8:30–6; weekends 8–5. Off-season the hours are 9–5 and 9–2, respectively. Besides providing information, it is the main ticket center for sightseeing excursions. There are also information centers at the central train station, in the City Hall (summer only), and in the Kaknäs TV Tower.

Embassies **U.S.** (Strandvägen 101, tel. 08/783–5300). **Canadian** (Tegelbacken 4, tel. 08/237920). **U.K.** (Skarpögatan 6–8, tel. 08/667–0140).

Emergencies **Police** (tel. 08/769–3000; emergencies only: 90000); **Ambulance** (tel. 90000); **Doctor** (Medical Care Information, tel. 08/644–9200)—tourists can get hospital attention in the district where they are staying or can contact the private clinic, **City Akuten** (tel. 08/117102); **Dentist** (tel. 08/654–1117).

Exploring Stockholm

Numbers in the margin correspond to points of interest on the Stockholm map.

Because Stockholm's main attractions are concentrated in a relatively small area, the city itself can be explored in several days. But if you want to take advantage of some of the full-day excursions offered, it is worthwhile to devote a full week to your visit.

The city of Stockholm, built on 14 small islands among open bays and narrow channels, has been dubbed the "Venice of the North." It is a handsome, civilized city, full of parks, squares, and airy boulevards, yet it is also a bustling, modern metropolis. Glass-and-steel skyscrapers abound, but in the center you are never more than five minutes' walk from twisting, medieval streets and waterside walks.

The first written mention of Stockholm dates from 1252, when a powerful regent named Birger Jarl is said to have built a fortified castle here. And it must have been this strategic position, where the calm, fresh waters of Lake Mälaren meet the salty

Baltic Sea, that prompted King Gustav Vasa to take over the city in 1523, and King Gustavus Adolphus to make it the heart of an empire a century later.

During the Thirty Years' War (1618–48), Sweden gained importance as a Baltic trading state, and Stockholm grew commensurately. But by the beginning of the 18th century, Swedish influence had begun to wane, and Stockholm's development had slowed. It did not revive until the Industrial Revolution, when the hub of the city moved north from the Old Town area.

City Hall and the Old Town Anyone in Stockholm with limited time should give priority to a tour of **Gamla Stan** (the Old Town), a labyrinth of narrow, medieval streets, alleys, and quiet squares just south of the city center. Ideally, you should devote an entire day to this district. But before crossing the bridge, pay a visit to the modern-day **❶ City Hall,** constructed in 1923 and now one of the symbols of Stockholm. You'll need an early start, since there is only one guided tour per day, at 10 AM (also at noon on Saturday and Sunday). Lavish mosaics grace the walls of the **Golden Hall,** and the **Prince's Gallery** features a collection of large murals by Prince Eugene, brother of King Gustav V. Take the elevator to the top of the 106-meter (348-foot) tower for a magnificent view of the city. *Admission: SEK 25. Tower open May–Sept., daily 10–3.*

Crossing into the Old Town, the first thing you'll see is the magnificent **❷ Riddarholm Church,** where a host of Swedish kings are buried. *Admission: SEK 10. Open Mon.–Sat. 10–3, Sun. 1–3.*

❸ From there proceed to the **Royal Palace,** preferably by noon, when you can see the colorful changing-of-the-guard ceremony. The smartly dressed guards seem superfluous, since tourists wander at will into the castle courtyard and around the grounds. Several separate attractions are open to the public. Be sure to visit the **Royal Armory,** with its outstanding collection of weaponry and royal regalia. The **Treasury** houses the Swedish crown jewels, including the regalia used for the coronation of King Erik XIV in 1561. You can also visit the **State Apartments,** where the king swears in each successive government. *Admission: SEK 30 for Armory and Treasury; SEK 30 for State Apartments. Armory and Treasury open Mon.–Sat. 10–3, Sun. noon–4. State Apartments open Tues.–Sun. noon–3.*

From the palace, stroll down **Västerlånggatan,** one of two main shopping streets in the Old Town. This is a popular shopping area, brimming with boutiques and antiques shops. Walk down to the Skeppsbron waterfront, then head back toward the center over the Ström bridge, where anglers cast for salmon. If **❹** you feel like a rest, stop off at **Kungsträdgården** and watch the world go by. Originally built as a royal kitchen garden, the property was turned into a public park in 1562. During the summer, entertainment and activities abound, and you can catch a glimpse of local people playing open-air chess with giant chessmen.

Djurgården Be sure to spend at least a day visiting the many attractions on the large island of **Djurgården.** Although it's only a short walk from the city center, the most pleasant way to approach it is by ferry from Skeppsbron, in the Old Town. The ferries drop you off near two of Stockholm's best-known attractions, the Vasa

Stockholm

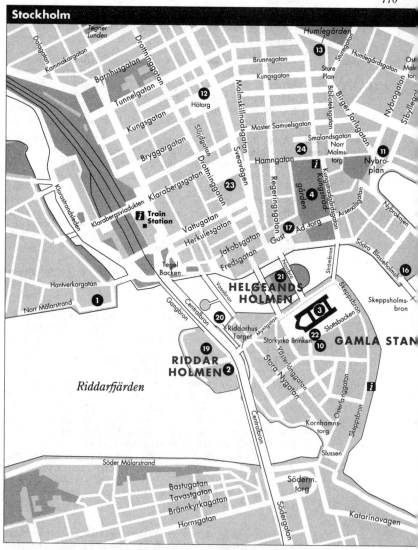

Major Attractions
City Hall, **1**
Gröna Lund Tivoli, **6**
Kungsträdgården, **4**
Museum of National
Antiquities, **9**
Nordic Museum, **8**
Riddarholm Church, **2**
Royal Palace, **3**
Skansen, **7**
Vasamuseet, **5**

Other Attractions
Cathedral, **22**
Concert Hall, **12**
House of Nobles, **20**
Kaknäs TV Tower, **15**
Kulturhuset, **23**
Museum of Far
Eastern Antiquities, **18**
Museum of Modern
Art, **14**
National Museum, **16**

NK, **24**
Parliament, **21**
Prince Eugene's
Waldemarsudde, **25**
Royal Dramatic
Theater, **11**
Royal Library, **13**
Royal Opera House, **17**
Stock Exchange, **10**
Supreme Court, **19**

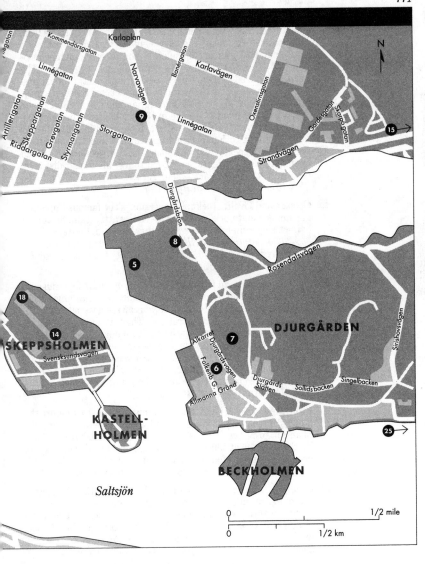

Museum and Gröna Lund Tivoli. (Or you might want to take the reinstated streetcar, which runs along refurbished tracks from Norrmalmstorg, near the city center, to **Prince Eugene's Waldemarsudde,** an art museum in the former summer residence of a Swedish prince, on a peninsula in Djurgården.) The *Vasa,* a restored 17th-century warship, is one of the oldest preserved war vessels in the world and has become Sweden's most popular tourist sight. She sank ignominiously in Stockholm Harbor on her maiden voyage in 1628, reportedly because she was not carrying sufficient ballast. Recovered in 1961, she has been restored to her original appearance and has now been

❺ moved into a spectacular new museum, the **Vasamuseet,** which opened in 1990. It features guided tours, films, and displays. *Galarvarvet, tel. 08/666–4800. Admission: SEK 30 adults, SEK 10 children. Open daily 9:30–7.*

❻ **Gröna Lund Tivoli,** Stockholm's version of the famous Copenhagen amusement park, is a favorite family attraction, featuring hair-raising roller coasters as well as tamer delights. *Tel. 08/ 665–7000. Admission: SEK 30 adults (SEK 40 after 6 PM), SEK 15 children. Open Apr. 25–Sept. 6 (opening hours vary widely; check in daily newspapers).*

❼ Just across the road is **Skansen,** a large, open-air folk museum consisting of 150 reconstructed traditional buildings from Sweden's different regions. Here you can see a variety of handicraft displays and demonstrations. There is also an attractive open-air zoo—with many native Scandinavian species, such as lynxes, wolves, and brown bears—as well as an excellent aquarium. *Tel. 08/663–0500. Admission: May–Aug., SEK 25 adults, SEK 20 group; Sept.–Apr., SEK 18 adults, SEK 13 group. Children free. Open Jan.–Apr. and Sept.–Dec., daily 9–5; May–Aug., daily 9 AM–midnight.*

❽ From the zoo, head back toward the city center. Just before the Djurgård bridge, you come to the **Nordic Museum,** which, like Skansen, provides an insight into the way Swedish people have lived over the past 500 years. The collection includes displays of peasant costumes, folk art, and Lapp culture. *Admission: SEK 30. Open Tues., Wed., Fri. 10–4; Thurs. 10–8; weekends 11–4.*

❾ Once you're back on the "mainland," drop into the **Museum of National Antiquities.** Though its name is uninspiring, it houses some remarkable Viking gold and silver treasures. **The Royal Cabinet of Coin,** located in the same building, boasts the world's largest coin. *Narvavägen 13–17. Admission: SEK 30. Open Tues., Wed., Fri.–Sun. noon–5; Thurs. noon–8.*

Stockholm Environs

The region surrounding Stockholm offers many attractions that can easily be seen on day trips out of the capital. Most sights in the Stockholm environs can be visited inexpensively by using the SL (Stockholm Local Traffic) bus and/or subway system (tel. 08/686–1000) or by taking a boat or ferry. If you have a Stockholmskortet (Key to Stockholm card), you are entitled to free travel on SL's subways and buses, and reduced fares on other means of transportation.

Nearby **Drottningholm Slott,** a Baroque castle whose spectacular gardens were influenced by those at Versailles, can be reached by a combined subway and bus trip. Take the subway

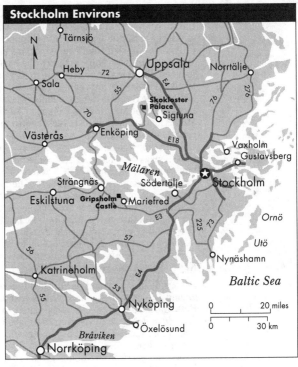

Stockholm Environs

N
Tärnsjö
Heby 72 Uppsala Norrtälje
Sala E4 276
55 Skokloster
Palace 70
Sigtuna
70 Enköping
Västerås E18
Mälaren Vaxholm
Gustavsberg
Strängnäs Södertälje **Stockholm**
Eskilstuna Gripsholm Mariefred
Castle E3 Ornö
57 225 73
56 Utö
Katrineholm Nynäshamn
E4 **Baltic Sea**
55 53
Nyköping 0   20 miles
Öxelösund 0   30 km
Bråviken
Norrköping

to Brommaplan and then Bus 301 to 323. The one-way cost is SEK 24. A more spectacular approach is by ferry, which only costs SEK 60 round-trip. The ferry leaves from in front of city hall in Stockholm.

One "must" is the trip to the majestic 16th-century **Gripsholm Castle,** at Mariefred, on the southern side of Lake Mälaren and about 64 kilometers (40 miles) from Stockholm. Gripsholm, with its drawbridge and four massive round towers, is one of Sweden's most romantic castles. There had been a castle on the site as early as the 1380s, but it was destroyed, and King Gustav Vasa had the present building erected in 1577. Today the castle is best known for housing the Swedish state collection of portraits and is one of the largest galleries in the world, with some 3,400 paintings.

Mariefred can be reached by bus from the Liljeholmen subway stop. The one-way fare is SEK 41. But the most pleasant way of traveling to Gripsholm from Stockholm is on the vintage steamer *Mariefred,* the last coal-fired ship on Lake Mälaren. Departures, between mid-June and late August, are from the city hall, daily except Monday at 10 AM, returning from Mariefred at 4:30. The journey takes 3½ hours each way, and there is a restaurant on board. *Round-trip fare: SEK 150. Tel. 08/669–8850. Admission to castle: SEK 25. Open May–Aug., daily 10–4.*

Another popular boat trip goes to **Skokloster Palace,** about 70 kilometers (44 miles) from Stockholm. Departures are from the city hall bridge (Stadshusbron) daily, except Monday and Friday, between early June and mid-August. The route follows the narrow inlets of Lake Mälaren along the "Royal Waterway" and stops at **Sigtuna,** an ancient trading center. You can get off the boat here; visit the town, which has medieval ruins and an 18th-century town hall; and catch the boat again on the return journey. But it is also worthwhile to stay on board and continue to Skokloster, an impressive palace dating from the 1650s. Built by the Swedish field marshal Carl Gustav Wrangel, it contains many of his trophies from the Thirty Years' War. Other attractions include what is reckoned to be the largest private collection of arms in the world, as well as some magnificent Gobelin tapestries. Next door to the palace is a motor museum that houses Sweden's largest collection of vintage cars and motorcycles. The round-trip boat fare is SEK 145, and there is a restaurant and cafeteria on board. The castle is also reachable via Uppsala by taking the SJ train from Stockholm's Central Station and then a bus to Skokloster—a time-consuming trip but well worth it if you want to take in the sights of Uppsala. The round-trip fare to Uppsala is SEK 120. *Admission to Skokloster Palace: SEK 30 (free with Key to Stockholm card). Open daily 11–4. Admission to motor museum: SEK 25 (free with Key to Stockholm card). Open daily noon–4.*

Lovers of the sea could easily spend an entire week cruising among the 24,000 islands in the **Stockholm archipelago.** The **Båtluffarkortet** (Inter-Skerries Card), available from early June to mid-August, gives you 16 days' unlimited travel on the Waxholm Steamship Company boats, which operate scheduled services throughout the archipelago. The card is on sale in the Excursion Shop at the Sweden House Tourist Center and at the Waxholm Steamship Company terminal at Strömkajen. It costs around SEK 235.

Shopping

Gift Ideas Stockholm is an ideal place to find items that reflect the best in Swedish design and elegance, particularly glass, porcelain, furs, handicrafts, home furnishings, and leather goods. The quality is uniformly high, and you can take advantage of the tax-free shopping service in most stores (*see* Shopping in Staying in Sweden, *above*).

Department Stores The largest is **NK,** on Hamngatan, where you can find just about anything. Other major stores are **PUB,** on Hötorget, and **Åhléns City,** on Klarabergsgatan. All three are open on Sunday.

Shopping Districts The center of Stockholm's shopping activity has shifted from Kungsgatan to Hamngatan, a wide boulevard along which a huge, covered shopping complex called **Gallerian** has been built. The **Old Town** area is best for handicrafts, antiquarian bookshops, and art shops.

Food and Flea Markets One of the biggest flea markets in northern Europe is located in **Skärholmen** shopping center, a 20-minute subway ride from the downtown area. Market hours are weekdays 11–6, Saturday 9–3, Sunday 10–3. Superior food markets can be found on **Ostermalmstorg** and **Hötorget.**

Glassware For the best buys, try **Nordiska Kristall,** on Kungsgatan, or **Rosenthal Studio-Haus,** on Birger Jarlsgatan. The latter operates its own shipping service. **Arioso,** on Västerlånggatan in the Old

Town, is good for modern crystal and ceramics, and **Önske-butiken,** on the corner of Kungsgatan and Sveavägen, specializes in crystal as well as porcelain.

Handicrafts **Stockholms Läns Hemslöjdsförening,** on Drottninggatan, has a wide selection of Swedish folk costumes and handicraft souvenirs from different parts of Sweden.

Dining

Prices quoted here are per person and include a first course, main course, tax, and service, but not wine. For details and price-category descriptions, *see* Dining in Staying in Sweden. Best bets are indicated by a star ★.

Moderate **Bakfickan.** The name means "hip pocket" and is appropriate
★ because this restaurant is tucked around the back of the Opera House complex. It's particularly popular at lunchtime, offering Swedish home cooking and a range of daily dishes. Counter and table service are available. *Operahuset, tel. 08/207745. No reservations. AE, DC, MC, V. Closed Sun.*

Eriks Backficka. An extremely popular dining spot among local residents, this unpretentious eatery serves a wide variety of Swedish dishes. The bustling 120-seat restaurant is located a block from the elegant waterside street Strandvägen, a flight down from street level. *Frederikshovsgatan 4, tel. 08/660–1599. Reservations advised. AE, DC, MC, V. Closed Christmas and weekends in July.*

Gondolen. Suspended under the gangway of the *Katarina* elevator at Slussen, Gondolen offers a magnificent view over the harbor, Lake Mälaren, and the Baltic Sea. The cuisine is international, and a range of fixed-price menus is available. *Slussen, tel. 08/640–2021. Reservations advised. AE, DC, MC, V. Closed Christmas and New Year's Day.*

Markurell's. The two separate restaurants, the Wärdshuset and the Bistro, are conveniently located opposite the central train station. It's a busy establishment serving international cuisine. *Mäster Samuelsgatan 73, tel. 08/211012. Reservations advised. AE, DC, MC, V.*

Sturehof. Centrally located, with an unpretentious, nautical ambience, Sturehof's specialty is its seafood. It also boasts an English-style pub. *Stureplan 2, tel. 08/679–8750. Reservations advised. AE, DC, MC, V. Closed Sat. lunch, Sun., Christmas, New Year's Day, and June 25.*

Inexpensive **Cassi.** This centrally located restaurant specializes in French cuisine at reasonable prices. *Narvavägen 30, tel. 08/661–7461. Reservations not necessary. MC, V. Closed Sat.*

★ **Open Gate.** Located near the Slussen locks, on the south side of Stockholm Harbor, this is a popular, trendy Art Deco Italian-style trattoria. Pasta dishes are the house specialty. *Högbergsgatan 40, tel. 08/643–9776. No reservations. AE, DC, MC, V.*

Örtagården. This all-vegetarian, no-smoking restaurant is located one floor up from the Östermalmshallen market hall. It offers an attractive buffet, with soups, salads, and hot dishes, served in a turn-of-the-century atmosphere. *Nybrogatan 31, tel. 08/662–1728. MC, V. Closed Christmas and New Year's Day.*

Budget **Belvéns Restaurant.** A small, family-run restaurant a block
★ east of Kungliga Humlegården, Belvéns offers a surprisingly wide variety of tasty dishes at low prices. Usually crowded at

dinner, this quaint restaurant has a dozen or so tables with red-and-white checked tablecloths. *Kommendörsgatan 7, tel. 08/ 662–5487 or 08/667–1800. Reservations required. AE, DC, MC, V. Closed Sun. and between Christmas and New Year's Day.*

Lodging

Stockholm has plenty of hotels in most price brackets, although relatively few in the Inexpensive or Budget categories. Many hotels cut their rates in the summer season, however, when business travelers are on vacation. The major hotel chains also have a number of bargain schemes available on weekends throughout the year and daily during the summer.

Almost 50 hotels offer the "Stockholm Package," providing accommodations for one night, costing between SEK 380 and SEK 610 per person, including breakfast and a Stockholms-kortet (Key to Stockholm) card (*see* Getting Around, *above*). Details of the Stockholm Package can be obtained from the **Stockholm Information Service,** Excursion Shop, Box 7542, S-103 93 Stockholm (tel. 08/789–2000 or 08/789–2490). Also, you can call **The Hotel Center** (tel. 08/240880) or reserve the package through travel agents.

If you arrive in Stockholm without a hotel reservation, the **Hotellcentralen** in the central train station will arrange accommodations for you. The office is open daily 8 AM–9 PM, June–September; weekdays 8:30–5 the rest of the year, except for December 20–January 2, when it is open 10–5. There is a reservations office in the Sweden House (*see* Important Addresses and Numbers, *above*) as well. There's a small fee for each reservation. Or phone one of the central reservations offices run by the major hotel groups: RESO (tel. 08/235700), SARA (tel. 08/ 753–7350), Scandic (tel. 08/610–5050), Sweden Hotels (tel. 08/ 204311), or Best Western (tel. 08/300420).

Ratings   Prices quoted here are for two people in a double room. For details and price-category definitions, *see* Lodging in Staying in Sweden.

Moderate   **Birger Jarl.** A short subway ride from the city center, Birger Jarl is a modern, characteristically Scandinavian hotel that opened in 1974. There is no full-service restaurant. *Tulegatan 8, tel. 08/151020. 252 rooms with bath. Facilities: sauna, pool, coffee shop. AE, DC, MC, V. Closed Christmas and New Year's Day.*

City. A large, modern-style hotel built in the 1940s but modernized in 1982–83, City is located near the city center and the Hötorget market. It is owned by the Salvation Army, so alcohol is not served. Breakfast is served in the atrium Winter Garden. *Slöjdgatan 7, tel. 08/222240. 300 rooms with bath. Facilities: restaurant, café, sauna, rooms for disabled guests. AE, DC, MC, V.*

Gamla Stan. A quiet, cozy hotel in the Old Town, the Gamla Stan was recently renovated, and each room is uniquely decorated. Breakfast is included. *Lilla Nygatan 25, tel. 08/244450. 51 rooms with shower. AE, DC, MC, V. Closed between Christmas and New Year's Day.*

Stockholm. This hotel has an unusual location—the upper floors of a downtown office building. The mainly modern decor is offset by traditional Swedish furnishings that help create its family atmosphere. Breakfast is the only meal served. *Norrmalmstorg 1, tel. 08/678–1320. 92 rooms with bath. AE, DC, MC, V. Closed Christmas and New Year's Day.*

Inexpensive **Alexandra.** Although it is in the Södermalm area, to the south of the Old Town, the Alexandra is only five minutes by subway from the city center. It is a small, modern hotel, opened 20 years ago and renovated in 1988. Only breakfast is served. *Magnus Ladulåsgatan 42, tel. 08/840320. 79 rooms with bath. Facilities: sauna, solarium. AE, DC, MC, V. Closed Christmas and New Year's Day.*

Långholmen. This former prison, built in 1724, was converted into a combined hotel and hostel in 1989. It is located on the island of Långholmen, which has popular bathing beaches. The Inn, next door, serves Swedish home cooking, and the wine cellar offers light snacks. *Långholmen, tel. 08/668–0500. 101 rooms with shower. Facilities: mini-golf course and boule court. AE, DC, MC, V.*

Budget **Gustav af Klint.** A "hotel ship" moored at Stadsgården quay, near Slussen subway station, the Gustav af Klint is divided into two sections—a hotel and a hostel. It was refurbished in 1989. There is a cafeteria and restaurant, and you can dine on deck in summer. *Stadsgårdskajen 153, tel. 08/640–4077. 14 cabins with showers. 80 hostel beds. Facilities: restaurant, cafeteria. AE, MC, V. Closed Christmas and New Year's Day.*

Queen's Hotel. Located on Drottninggatan, Stockholm's major shopping street, the family-run Queen's Hotel is a 5–10-minute walk from Stockholm's central train station and interesting sights in the downtown area. The hotel recently added 10 modern hotel rooms, all with showers, telephone, and TV. Breakfast is included. *Drottninggatan 71A, tel. 08/249460. 30 rooms with shower. AE, MC, V. Closed Christmas Day.*

Wasa Park. A clean, family-run hotel, the Wasa Park is convenient for travelers coming into Stockholm from the airport (the airport shuttle bus regularly stops in front of the building before going on to Stockholm's central train station). The hotel is convenient to a subway station and city bus lines. Breakfast is included. *St. Eriks Plan 1, tel. 08/340285. 15 rooms, all with telephones. MC, V.*

The Arts

Stockholm's main theater and concert season runs from September through May or June, so there are not many major performances during the height of the tourist season. But for a list of events, pick up the free booklet "Stockholm This Week," available from hotels and tourist information offices. You can get last-minute tickets to theaters and shows at the cut-price ticket booth on Norrmalmstorg Square. Tickets sold here are priced 25% below box office rates. The booth is open Monday to Friday 11–6 and Saturday 11–4. There is also a **central reservation office** for regular-price tickets (tel. 08/108800).

Concerts During the summer, free concerts are given in many city parks. For information, phone 08/785–8182.

Theater Stockholm has about 20 top-rank theaters, but dramatic productions are unlikely to interest those who don't understand Swedish. A better option is to go to a musical; several city theaters hold regular performances. Plays in English are featured at the **Regina Theater** (Drottninggatan 71A, tel. 08/207000).

Film English and American films predominate, and they are screened with the original soundtrack and Swedish subtitles. Programs are listed in the local evening newspapers, though titles are usually in Swedish. Movie buffs should visit **Filmstaden** (Film City), Mäster Samuelsgatan 25 (tel. 08/840500), where there are 15 cinemas under one roof.

Nightlife

Cabaret Stockholm's biggest nightclub, **Börsen** (Jakobsgatan 6, tel. 08/101600), offers high-quality international cabaret shows. Another popular spot is the **Cabaret Club** (Barnhusgatan 12, tel. 08/110608). Although it can accommodate 450 guests, reservations are advised.

Bars and **Café Opera** (tel. 08/110026) is a popular meeting place for young
Nightclubs and old alike. It has the longest bar in town, plus dining and roulette, and dancing after midnight. Piano bars are also an important part of the Stockholm scene. **Riche** (tel. 08/611–8460) is another popular watering hole in the city center. Try the **Anglais Bar** at the Hotel Anglais (tel. 08/614–1600) or the **Clipper Club** at the Hotel Reisen, Skeppsbron (tel. 08/223260). Not to be forgotten is the recently renovated restaurant/bar **Berns Salon** (Berzelii Park 9, tel. 08/614–0500). Worth a visit is the Red Room, a private dining room on the second floor, where playwright August Strindberg once held court.

Jazz Clubs **Fasching** (Kungsgatan 63, tel. 08/216267) is Stockholm's largest, but another popular spot is **Stampen** (Stora Nygatan 5, tel. 08/205793). Get here in good time if you want a seat, and phone first to be sure the establishment hasn't been reserved for a private party.

Discos **Galaxy** (Strömsborg, tel. 08/215400) is one of the most popular night spots, catering to a variety of musical tastes. There is an outdoor bar and dining area in summer. Others are **Downtown** (Norrlandsgatan 5A, tel. 08/119488) and **Karlsson** (Kungsgatan 65, tel. 08/119298).

Uppsala and the Folklore District

The area of Sweden referred to as the "Folklore District"—essentially the provinces of Dalarna and Värmland—has the merit of being both easily accessible from Stockholm and the best region in which to see something of the country's enduring folk traditions. This itinerary takes you to Dalarna through the ancient city of Uppsala and returns to Stockholm through the Bergslagen region, the heart of the centuries-old Swedish iron industry.

Getting Around

The route can be covered entirely by train. The ride from Stockholm to Uppsala takes only 45 minutes, and the service is fairly frequent.

Tourist Information

Falun (Stora Torget, tel. 023/83637).
Ludvika (Sporthallen, tel. 0240/86050).
Mora (Ångbåtskajen, tel. 0250/26550).
Örebro (Drottninggatan 9, tel. 019/211080).
Rättvik (Torget, tel. 0248/10910).
Uppsala (Fyris Torg, tel. 018/117500 and 018/274800 and at Uppsala Castle in summer).

Exploring Uppsala and the Folklore District

Uppsala is really the cradle of Swedish civilization, so it is well worth spending a day or two exploring it. If you opt for a guided tour, you should first stop by **Gamla Uppsala** (Old Uppsala), which is dominated by three huge burial mounds. During the 5th century AD, Aun, Egil, and Adils, the first Swedish kings, were buried here. Adjoining the burial mounds are a church, the seat of Sweden's first archbishop, built on the site of a former pagan temple, and the Odinsborg restaurant, where you can sample local mead, brewed from a 14th-century recipe.

Back in **Uppsala** itself, your first stop should be the enormous **cathedral,** with its twin towers dominating the city skyline. The cathedral has been the seat of the archbishop of the Swedish church for 700 years, although its present appearance owes much to major restoration work completed during the late 19th century. Make a point of visiting the **Cathedral Museum** in the north tower, which boasts one of Europe's finest collections of ecclesiastical textiles. *Admission free. Open June–Aug., daily 8–8; Sept.–May, daily 8–6. Check weekend opening times locally.*

Nearby, in a strategic position atop a hill, is **Uppsala Castle.** This prepossessing structure was built during the 1540s by King Gustav Vasa. Having broken his ties with the Vatican, the king was eager to show who was actually running the country. He arranged to have the cannons aimed directly at the archbishop's palace. *Open mid-Apr.–Sept. Check times and prices with the local tourist office.*

Uppsala is the site of Scandinavia's oldest university, founded in 1477. Be sure to visit one of its most venerable buildings, the **Gustavianum,** located near the cathedral. Just below the cupola is the anatomical theater, where public dissections of executed convicts were a popular 17th-century tourist attraction. *Admission: SEK 5. Open July–Aug., daily 11–3; Sept.–June, daily noon–3.*

One of Uppsala's most famous sons was Carl von Linné, known as Linnaeus. A professor of botany at the university during the 1740s, he developed a system of plant and animal classification that is still used today. You can visit the **gardens** he designed, as well as his former residence, now a **museum.** *Admission to gardens: free. Open May 1–Aug. 31, daily 9–9. Admission to museum: SEK 10. Open May 18–Sept. 15, Tues.–Sun. 1–4.*

From Uppsala, the route heads northwest through a pleasant agricultural landscape into the province of Dalarna, passing through **Säter,** one of the best-preserved wooden villages in Sweden. This is a pleasant spot in which to just wander around.

Uppsala and the Folklore District

For an overnight stop it is best to head for Falun, Dalarna's provincial capital.

Falun is best known for a huge hole in the ground, referred to as the **"Great Pit."** The hole has been there since 1687, when an abandoned copper mine collapsed. Other mines on the site are still working today. You can take a guided tour down into some of the old shafts and hear the gruesome story of 17th-century miner Fat Mats, whose body was perfectly preserved in brine for 40 years following a cave-in. There is also a museum that tells the story of the local mining industry. *Admission: SEK 40. Open May 1–Aug. 31, daily 10–4:30; Sept. 1–Nov. 15 and Mar. 1–Apr. 30, weekends only 12:30–4:30.*

Just outside Falun, at **Sundborn,** is the former home of Swedish artist Carl Larsson. Here, in an idyllic, lakeside setting, you can see a selection of his paintings, which owe much to local folk-art traditions. His grandchildren and great-grandchildren are on hand to show you around. *Admission: SEK 45. Open May–Sept., Mon.–Sat. 10–5, Sun. 1–5.*

The real center of Dalarna folklore is the area around **Lake Siljan,** by far the largest of the 6,000 lakes in the province. Begin your tour at the attractive lakeside village of **Tällberg,** or at **Mora,** toward the north end of the lake. In the neighboring village of **Rättvik,** hundreds of people wearing traditional costumes arrive in longboats to attend Midsummer church services. Mora itself is best known as the home of the artist Anders Zorn. His house and a museum featuring his paintings are open to the public. *Admission to museum: SEK 15. Admis-*

sion to home: SEK 20. Open Sept. 16–May 14, daily 12–5; May 15–Sept. 15, daily 10–5.

Near Mora is the village of **Nusnäs.** This is the village where the famous, brightly colored **Dalarna wooden horses** are produced. You can visit either of the two workshops where they are made.

Heading south again you'll come to **Ludvika,** an important center of the old Bergslagen mining region. This region stretches from the forests of Värmland in the west to the coastal forges in the east. Ludvika has a notable open-air mining museum, **Gammelgården.** *Check times and prices with the Ludvika Tourist Office.* There is also a **Railway Engine Museum** that features three steam turbine–driven iron-ore engines, the only ones of their kind in the world. *Admission: SEK 10. Open June 1–Aug. 31, daily 10–6.*

Another local attraction is **Luosa Cottage.** The poet Dan Andersson lived here during the early part of the century so he could experience for himself the rigorous life of the local charcoal burners. A music and poetry festival will be held at the cottage and in nearby towns in Andersson's memory, July 24–Aug. 1. *Admission to cottage: SEK 20. Open Tues.–Sun. 11–5.*

Continuing south from Ludvika, you'll come to **Örebro,** a sizable town at the western edge of **Lake Hjälmaren,** which is connected to Lake Mälaren and the sea by the Hjälmare Canal. Örebro received its charter in the 13th century and developed as a trading center for the farmers and miners of the Bergslagen region. Rising from a small island in the Svartån River, right in the center of town, is an imposing **castle,** parts of which date to the 13th century. The castle is now the residence of the regional governor. Guided tours run from mid-June to the end of August. Check with the Örebro tourist office for further information. An added attraction is the excellent restaurant in the castle.

To get a feel for the Örebro of bygone days, wander around the **Wadköping** district, where a number of old houses and craftsmen's workshops have been painstakingly preserved. At the north end of town is **Svampen** (The Mushroom), a water tower rising 59 meters (193 feet) into the air. If you take the elevator to the top, you'll get a magnificent view of the surrounding countryside. There is also a cafeteria and tourist office. *The tower is open Apr. 15–Sept. 15, daily 9–9.*

Direct train service from Örebro back to Stockholm operates at two-hour intervals, and the journey takes just under three hours. You can also take the hourly train to Hallsberg and change there to the frequent Gothenburg–Stockholm service.

Dining and Lodging

For details and price-category definitions, *see* Dining and Lodging in Staying in Sweden. Best bets are indicated by a star ★.

Falun **Hotel Falun.** Located in the center of the city, Hotel Falun is a
Lodging medium-size hotel built in the 1950s. Breakfast is included. *Centrumhuset, Trotzgatan 16, tel. 023/29180. 25 rooms, most with showers. AE, DC, MC, V. Moderate.*
Birgittagården. Run by the Birgitta sisters of Dalarna,

Birgittagården is 13 kilometers (8 miles) east of Falun in a large park in the village of Hosjö. The hotel is very clean, and most rooms in the two-building complex have showers (two rooms have baths). There is a choice of breakfast or all meals. *Uddnäs, Hosjö, tel. 023/32147. 25 rooms, some with bath or shower. Facilities: 3 conference rooms, library, 2 living rooms. No credit cards. Budget.*

Ludvika **Rex.** The Rex is a fairly basic but modern hotel conveniently lo-
Lodging cated near the city center. It was built in 1960. Its restaurant serves breakfast only. *Engelbrektsgatan 9, tel. 0240/13690. 28 rooms, 15 with bath. Facilities: restaurant. AE, DC, MC, V. Closed Christmas and 1 week in summer. Inexpensive.*

Mora **Siljan.** Taking its name from the nearby lake, the largest in
Lodging Dalarna, the Siljan is a popular, small, but modern-style hotel.
★ *Moragatan 6, tel. 0250/13000. 46 rooms, most with bath. Facilities: sauna, disco, restaurant. AE, DC, MC, V. Moderate.*

Örebro **City.** Also built in 1985, City is a modern, centrally located ho-
Lodging tel. It offers special facilities for disabled guests and those suf-
fering from allergies. The restaurant serves "home cooking" at lunchtime and more elaborate, à la carte fare in the evening. *Kungsgatan 24, tel. 019/100200. 113 rooms with bath. Facilities: restaurant. AE, DC, MC, V. Moderate.*

Hotel Ansgar. Centrally located, this is a small, family-run ho-
tel within walking distance of the train station. Some of the rooms have a balcony, kitchen, or pantry. Breakfast is included. *Järnsvägsgatan 10, tel. 019/100429. 27 rooms, some with bath or shower. Facilities: breakfast room. MC, V. Budget.*

Tällberg **Åkerblads.** Located near the shores of Lake Siljan, Åkerblads
Lodging is a real rural Swedish experience. The hotel occupies a typical
★ Dalarna farmstead, parts of which date to the 16th century. It is run by the 14th and 15th generations of the Åkerblad family. A hotel since 1910, it was modernized in 1987. The restaurant serves table d'hôte meals only. *793 03 Tällberg, tel. 0247/50800. 64 rooms, most with bath. Facilities: sauna, Jacuzzi, restaurant, pub-style bar. AE, DC, MC, V. Closed Christmas. Mod-
erate.*

Siljansgården. A renovated Dalarna-style homestead, Siljans-
gården is located 3 kilometers (2 miles) south of Tällberg in a wooded area with a view of Lake Siljan. Cozy and intimate, this hotel is ideal for getting closer to the Dalarna atmosphere. Breakfast and dinner are included. *Sjögattu 36, tel. 0247/50040. 22 rooms and 10 cottages, all with showers. DC, MC, V. Budget.*

Uppsala **Saluhalenbaren.** Located in an enclosed food market called
Dining Saluhalen in downtown Uppsala, this casual restaurant offers a
★ variety of international and Swedish dishes. Menus change dai-
ly. *St. Eriks Torg, tel. 018/122323. Reservations not required. DC, MC, V. Budget.*

Lodging **Grand Hotel Hörnan.** An Old World, medium-size hotel, the Grand Hotel Hörnan is in the city center near the train station. Opened in 1906, it has been refurbished during the past several years. *Bangårdsgatan 1, tel. 018/139380. 37 rooms with bath. AE, MC. Closed July. Moderate.*

Samaritemhet. Operated by the Lutheran Foundation of Good Samaritans, the Samaritemhet is a traditional Swedish guest house located two blocks from the train station. Rooms in the turn-of-the-century part of the building do not have running water; rooms in the modern section have running water and some have showers. Breakfast is included. *Kungsängstorg 4, tel. 018/103400. 30 rooms, some with shower. No credit cards. Budget.*

Gothenburg and the Glass Country

For many visitors traveling to Sweden by ferry, Gothenburg (or Göteborg) is the port of arrival. But those who arrive in Stockholm should not miss making a side trip to this great shipping city and Sweden's scenic western coast. This itinerary combines a western trip with a route through the Glass Country.

Getting Around

As with the previous itinerary, the route can be followed by train. Regular trains for Gothenburg depart from Stockholm's central train station about every hour, and normal travel time is about four hours. Seat reservations are compulsory on most trains to Gothenburg. There are also hourly flights to Gothenburg from Stockholm's Arlanda Airport between 7 AM and 10 PM on weekdays, slightly less frequently on weekends. The trip by air takes 55 minutes.

For getting around the city of Gothenburg itself, the best transportation option for the visitor is the **Göteborgskortet** (Key to Gothenburg) card, similar to the Key to Stockholm card. This entitles the user to free travel on all public transportation, free parking, and free admission to the Liseberg amusement park and all city museums. Prices for the card range from SEK 100 for one day and SEK 225 for three days.

Tourist Information

Gothenburg (Kungsportsplatsen 2, tel. 031/100740).
Växjö (Kronobergsgatan 8, tel. 0470/41410).

Exploring Gothenburg and the Glass Country

Visitors arriving in **Gothenburg** often go straight through the city in their haste to reach their coastal vacation spots, but it is well worth spending a day or two exploring this attractive harbor city. A quayside jungle of cranes and warehouses attests to the city's industrial might, yet within 10 minutes' walk of the waterfront is an elegant, modern city of broad avenues, green parks, and gardens. It is an easy city to explore. Most of the major attractions are within walking distance of each other, and there is an excellent streetcar network. In the summer, you can even take a sightseeing trip on a vintage open-air streetcar.

Gothenburg's development was pioneered mainly by British merchants in the 19th century, when it acquired the nickname "Little London." But a more accurate name would have been "Little Amsterdam," for the city was designed during the 17th century by Dutch architects, who gave it its extensive network of straight streets divided by canals. There is only one major canal today, but you can explore it on one of the popular "Paddan" sightseeing boats. The boats got their nickname, Swedish for toad, because of their short, squat shape, necessary for negotiating the city's 20 low bridges. You embark at the **Paddan terminal** at Kungsportsplatsen. *Fare: SEK 55. Departures: May 1–mid-Sept., daily 10–5; June 12–Aug. 2, daily 10–9.*

The hub of Gothenburg is **Kungsportsavenyn,** better known as "The Avenue." It is a broad, tree-lined boulevard flanked with elegant shops, restaurants, and sidewalk cafés. During the summer it has a distinctively Parisian air. The avenue ends at **Götaplatsen Square,** home of the municipal theater, concert hall, and library (where there's an excellent selection of English-language newspapers). Just off the avenue is **Trädgårdsföreningen,** a newly constructed Butterfly House featuring 40 different species and an attractive park with a magnificent Palm House that was built in 1878 and recently restored. *Admission to park: SEK 5. Open May–Sept. Admission to Palm House: SEK 10. Open May–Aug., daily 7 AM–9 PM; Sept.–Apr., daily 7–6. Admission to Butterfly House: SEK 20. Open Apr.–Sept., Tues.–Sat. 10–4, Sun. 11–4.*

If you're interested in shopping, the best place to go is **Nordstan,** a covered complex of shops near the central train station. Many of its businesses participate in the tax-free shopping service. In the harbor near the Nordstan shopping complex, you will find the new **Maritime Center.** The center houses a historic collection of ships, including a destroyer, a lightship, a trawler, and tugboats. *Admission: SEK 50. Open May 29–Sept. 3, daily 11–5; Feb. 29–Nov. 29, weekends 11–5.*

Kronoberg County's main town and the best center for exploring Sweden's Glass Country is Växjö. It is also an important sightseeing destination for some 10,000 American visitors each year, for it was from this area that their Swedish ancestors set sail during the 19th century. The **Emigrants' House,** located in the town center, tells the story of the migration, during which close to 1 million Swedes—one-quarter of the entire population—departed for the promised land. The museum exhibits provide a vivid sense of the rigorous journey, and an archive room and research center allow American visitors to trace their ancestry. On the second Sunday in August, Växjö celebrates "Minnesota Day." Swedes and Swedish-Americans come together to commemorate their common heritage with American-style square dancing and other festivities.

Many of Sweden's most famous glassworks are within easy reach of Växjö, and it is usually possible to take an organized sightseeing tour of the facilities. Inquire at the tourist office for information. The manufacture of Swedish glass dates to 1556, when Venetian glassblowers were first invited to the Swedish court. But it was another 200 years before glass manufacturing became a real Swedish industry. This area was chosen for its dense forest, which offered limitless wood supplies for heating the furnaces. All the major Swedish glass companies, including **Orrefors** and **Kosta Boda,** still have their works in this area, and all of them are open to the public. They also have shops where you can pick up near-perfect seconds at bargain prices. *Open weekdays 9–6, Sat. 9–3, Sun. noon–4 (no glass manufacturing on Sat. and Sun. in winter).*

To return to Stockholm from Växjö, catch the train to Alvesta (the service runs about five times a day) and change there for Stockholm. The journey takes about five and a half hours. For information call 0470/47075. Linjeflyg operates several flights per day to Stockholm from Växjö airport, located about 8 kilometers (5 miles) from the town center. The trip takes about 40 minutes. For information call 0470/58200.

Dining and Lodging

For details and price-category definitions, *see* Dining and Lodging in Staying in Sweden.

Gothenburg
Dining

Bräutigams. Near the tourist office, Bräutigams is an elegant café, ideal for a snack or light meal in a turn-of-the-century atmosphere. The restaurant specializes in homemade cakes and coffee, but light lunches—open-faced sandwiches and salads—are also available. *Östra Hamngatan 50B, tel. 031/136046. Reservations not necessary. AE, DC, MC, V. Closed Christmas Eve. Moderate.*

Weise. A centrally located restaurant with a German beer-cellar atmosphere, Weise was once a haunt of local painters and intellectuals and still retains something of that ambience. The tables and chairs date from 1892. It specializes in traditional Swedish home cooking, serving such dishes as pork and brown beans. *Drottninggatan 23, tel. 031/131402. Reservations advised. AE, DC, MC, V. Moderate.*

Lodging

Liseberg Heden. Not far from the famous Liseberg amusement park, Liseberg Heden is a popular, modern family hotel. It offers a sauna and gourmet restaurant. *Sten Sturegatan, tel. 031/200280. 160 rooms with bath. Facilities: restaurant, sauna. AE, DC, MC, V. Closed Christmas and New Year's Day. Moderate.*

Hotel Klang. This popular, family-run hotel is 10 minutes' walk from the central train station. The rooms are simple and clean. Only breakfast is served. *Stora Badhusetgatan 28, tel. 031/174050. 50 rooms with shower or bath. AE, DC, MC, V. Closed Christmas and New Year's Day. Inexpensive.*

Maria Erikssons Pensionat. Occupying an old, elegant building with high ceilings in the center of the city, the small Maria Erikssons Pensionat is a traditional Gothenburg hotel. The rooms feature old wooden furniture. Breakfast is included. *Shalmergsgatan 27A, tel. 031/207030. 9 rooms, some with showers. MC, V. Budget.*

Växjö
Lodging

Esplanad. Centrally located, Esplanad is a small, family hotel offering basic amenities; it has been recently renovated. Only breakfast is served. *Norra Esplanaden 21A, tel. 0470/22580. 27 rooms, most with shower. MC, V. Closed Christmas and New Year's Day. Inexpensive.*

Solvikens Pensionat. A family-run hotel 15 miles south of Växjö, Solvikens Pensionat is situated on Lake Torsjön. A new hotel and annex offer basic accommodations. Breakfast is not included. *Ingelstad, tel. 0470/30141. 28 rooms, some with shower. MC, V. Budget.*

24 Switzerland

Switzerland's political isolation, prosperity, and ruthless efficiency have produced a standard of living that is sometimes dauntingly high. But careful planning can open up much of the country's best: rustic coziness, medieval charm, magnificent Alpine wilderness. "Rustic" in Switzerland doesn't mean Turkish toilets and sagging mattresses; the Swiss keep their coziness under strict control. An electric eye may beam open the sliding glass door into that firelit, wood-raftered *stübli* (cozy little pub), and your knotty-pine hotel room is likely to have state-of-the-art bedding and an all-tile bath. That is the paradox of the Swiss, whose aesthetic pitches high-tech efficiency against bucolic Alpine tranquillity. Fiercely devout, rigorously clean, prompt as their world-renowned watches, the Swiss measure liquors with scientific precision into glasses marked for one or two centiliters, and the local wines come in sized carafes that are reminiscent of laboratory beakers. And as for passion—well, the "double" beds have separate mattresses and sheets that tuck firmly down the middle. (Foreigners with more lusty Latin tastes may request a French—that is, a standard double—bed.) Switzerland is a country of contrasts: While cowbells tinkle on the slopes of Klewenalp, the hum of commerce in Zürich isn't far away. As befurred and bejeweled beauties shop in Geneva, across the country in Appenzell women stand beside their husbands on the Landsgemeinde-Platz to raise their hands in the local vote—a right they didn't win until 1990.

Switzerland comprises most of the attractions of its larger European neighbors—Alpine grandeur, urban sophistication, ancient villages, scintillating ski slopes, and all-around artistic excellence. It's the heart of the Reformation, the homeland of William Tell; its cities are full of historic landmarks, its coun-

There's only one airline that offers as many travel choices as Scandinavia itself.

Scandinavia is fjords, archipelagoes, rolling countryside, ancient castles, and quaint inns. It's lively capitals, gourmet restaurants, museums, first class hotels, opera and ballet. A region of wonderful contrasts and friendly, English-speaking people.

And SAS the airline with the most nonstop flights to Scandinavia, offers the most ways for you to enjoy your visit. Select from a full range of escorted tours as well as independent fly/drive and fly/cruise packages.

There's only one place like it. Scandinavia.

Call 212-949-2333, dept. 48 to request a free Scandinavian Discovery Kit to find out more about Denmark, Finland, Iceland, Norway and Sweden.

Scandinavia

DENMARK • FINLAND • ICELAND • NORWAY • SWEDEN

No matter what your travel style, the best trips start with **Fodor's**

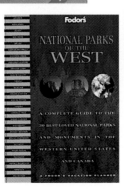

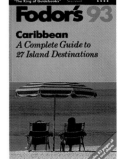

Fodor's
TRAVEL GUIDES
The name that means smart travel
Available at bookstores everywhere.
See back pages for complete title listing.

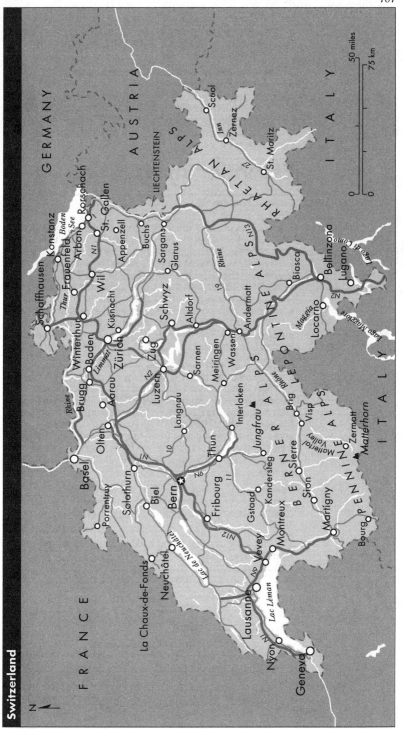

Switzerland

tryside strewn with castles. The varied cuisine reflects an ethnic mix, with three distinct cultures dominating: French in the southwest, Italian in the southeast, and German—a 70% majority—in the north and east.

All these assets have combined to create a major center of tourism, and the Swiss are happy to pave the way. A welcoming if reserved people, most of them well versed in English, they have earned their age-old reputation as fine hosts. Their hotels and inns are famous for cleanliness and efficiency, and the notorious high prices are justified, for the most part, by standards unrivaled in the world.

Essential Information

Before You Go

When to Go There's always something happening—it just depends on what you want. Winter sports begin around Christmas and usually last until mid-April, depending on the state of the snow. The countryside is a delight in spring when the wild flowers are in bloom, and the fall colors rival those in New England. In the Ticino (the Italian-speaking area) and around Lake Geneva (Lac Léman), summer stays late. There is often sparkling weather in September and October, and the popular resorts are less crowded then. After that, though, beware: They may close up altogether in November and May. Always check with the local tourist office.

Climate Summer is generally warm and sunny, though the higher you go, of course, the cooler it gets, especially at night. Winter is cold everywhere: In low-lying areas the weather is frequently damp and overcast, while in the Alps there are often brilliantly clear days, but it is guaranteed to be cold and snowy—especially above 1,400 meters (4,600 feet). Summer or winter, some areas of Switzerland are prone to an Alpine wind that blows from the south and is known as the *Föhn*. This gives rise to clear but rather oppressive weather, which the Swiss claim causes headaches.

The only exception to the general weather patterns is the Ticino. Here, protected by the Alps, the weather is positively Mediterranean; even in winter, it is significantly warmer than elsewhere.

The following are the average daily maximum and minimum temperatures for Zürich.

Jan.	36F	2C	May	67F	19C	Sept.	69F	20C
	26	- 3		47	8		51	11
Feb.	41F	5C	June	73F	23C	Oct.	57F	14C
	28	- 2		53	12		43	6
Mar.	51F	11C	July	76F	25C	Nov.	45F	7C
	34	1		56	14		35	2
Apr.	59F	15C	Aug.	75F	24C	Dec.	37F	3C
	40	4		56	14		29	- 2

Currency The unit of currency is the Swiss franc (Fr.), divided into 100 rappen (known as centimes in French-speaking areas). There are coins of 5, 10, 20, and 50 rappen and of 1, 2, and 5 francs. The bills are of 10, 20, 50, 100, 500, and 1,000 francs.

At press time (summer 1992), the Swiss franc stood at 1.45 to the dollar and 2.65 to the pound sterling.

All banks will change your money, though many impose a minimum and a slight fee. Traveler's checks get a better exchange rate, as do cash advances on major credit cards. Main airports and train stations have exchange offices (*bureaux de change*) that are open longer hours than banks and often offer equally good rates of exchange. Most hotels and some restaurants will change money but usually at a far less favorable rate. Most major credit cards are generally, though not universally, accepted at hotels, restaurants, and shops.

What It Will Cost Switzerland is generally expensive, especially for visitors spending dollars. It's extremely rare to find even the simplest hotel room for less than 100 Fr. (at press time, $72 or £40), and hot meals start at 15 Fr. ($11 or £6). Renting a holiday apartment or chalet can save on restaurant costs, but you may find yourself paying inflated prices in resort grocery stores. For instance, three raw sausage kebabs recently cost 22 Fr. in Gstaad. When possible, steer away from the flashier resorts and budget for limited stays in the biggest cities (Geneva, Zürich, Basel). And take chances off the beaten track: Many of Switzerland's most atmospheric restaurants and inns lie outside the developed tourist centers. If you really need to watch your budget, settle for rooms with bathrooms down the hall: You'll still have a sink to call your own, and can save about 30%. Calculate the cost of novelty-transit excursions carefully; those cable cars, funiculars, and cog-rail trains cost a lot to build, inspect, and maintain, and rides are priced accordingly.

Sample Prices Cup of coffee, 2.20 Fr.; bottle of beer, 2.50 Fr.; Coca-Cola, 2 Fr.; ham sandwich, 7 Fr.; a 1-mile taxi ride, 10 Fr. (except in Geneva or Zürich).

Customs on Arrival There are two levels of duty-free allowance for visitors to Switzerland. Residents of non-European countries may import 400 cigarettes or 100 cigars or 500 grams of tobacco, plus 2 liters of alcoholic beverage below 15% and 1 liter of alcoholic beverage in excess of 15%. Residents of European countries may import 200 cigarettes or 50 cigars or 250 grams of tobacco, plus 2 liters of alcoholic beverage below 15% and 1 liter of alcoholic beverage in excess of 15%. These allowances apply only to those aged 17 and above.

There are no restrictions on the import or export of any currency.

Language French is spoken in the southwest, around Lake Geneva, and in the cantons of Fribourg, Neuchâtel, Jura, Vaud, and the western portion of Valais; Italian is spoken in the Ticino, and lilting dialects of German are spoken everywhere else—in more than 70% of the country, in fact. The Romance language called Romansch has regained a firm foothold throughout the Upper and Lower Engadine regions of the canton Graubünden, where it takes the form of five different dialects. English, however, is spoken widely. Many public signs are in English, as well as in the regional language, and all hotels, restaurants, tourist offices, train stations, banks, and shops will have someone who can speak English comfortably.

Getting Around

By Plane Swissair connects the cities of Zürich, Basel, and Geneva. The airline (Box 845, New York, NY 10102, tel. 800/688–7947) offers flexible packages from April through October for the independent traveler who flies at least one way between North America and Europe on Swissair or Delta. "The Swiss Travel Invention" allows visitors to tailor-fit their Swiss holiday to include hotels, car rentals, rail vacations, and guided tours at great savings. Swissair also offers personalized ski packages consisting of round-trip flights, surface travel by rail or bus, and hotels.

By Train Switzerland's trains are among Europe's finest. Generally, they are swift (except through the mountains), immaculate, and unnervingly punctual. Don't linger between international connections: The Swiss don't wait for languorous travelers. If you plan to use the trains extensively, get the official timetable *(Offizieles Kursbuch)*, which costs 14 Fr. A small, pocket-size version *(Fribo)* covers key intercity connections and costs 10.80 Fr. A useful booklet called "Switzerland by Rail," available from the Swiss National Tourist Office (SNTO), describes 20 excursions that can be made by public transportation, as well as including timetables for the best train connections to Zürich and Geneva airports.

Trains described as Inter-City or Express, the fastest, stop only at principal towns. A *Regionalzug* is a local train, and often affords the most spectacular views. Meals, snacks, and drinks are provided on most main services. Seat reservations are useful during rush hours and high season, especially on international trains.

Fares There are numerous concessions for visitors. The **Swiss Pass,** the best value, offers unlimited travel on Swiss Federal Railways, postal buses, lake steamers, and the local bus and tram service of 30 cities. It also gives reductions on many privately owned railways, cable cars, and mountain railways. It's available from the Swiss National Tourist Office and from travel agents outside Switzerland. The card is valid for eight days (cost 220 Fr.), 15 days (260 Fr.), or one month (360 Fr.). There is also a new 3-day **Flexi Pass** (180 Fr.), which offers the same unlimited travel options of a regular Swiss Pass for any 3 days within a 15-day period. Prices are for second-class travel; first-class travel costs about 40% more.

Within some popular tourist areas, **Regional Holiday Season Tickets,** issued for 15 days, give 5 days of free travel by train, postal buses, steamers, and mountain railways, with half fare for the rest of the validity of the card. Central Switzerland offers a similar pass for 7 days, with 2 days of free travel. Prices vary widely, depending upon the region and period of validity, but if you like to cover a lot of ground, they do assure you of savings over full fare. Increasingly popular with tourists is a **Swiss Half-Fare Travel Card,** which allows half-fare travel for 30 days (85 Fr.) or one year (125 Fr.).

The new **Swiss Card,** which can be purchased in the United States through RailEurope (226–230 Westchester Ave., White Plains, NY 10604, tel. 914/682–5172 or 800/345–1990) and at train stations at the Zürich and Geneva airports and in Basel, is valid for 30 days and grants full round-trip travel from your arrival point to any destination in the country, plus a half-price reduction on any further excursions during your stay (140 Fr. first class, 110 Fr. second class). For more information about train travel in Switzerland, get the free "Swiss Travel System" or "Discover Switzerland" brochures from the SNTO.

For 9 Fr. per bag, travelers holding tickets or passes on Swiss Federal Railways can forward their luggage to their final destination—and make stops en route unencumbered.

By Bus Switzerland's famous yellow postal buses link main cities with villages off the beaten track. Both postal and city buses follow posted schedules to the minute; free timetables can be picked up at any post office.

The Swiss Pass (*see above*) gives unlimited travel on the postal buses. The **Postal Coach Weekly Card** gives unlimited travel within certain regions where train travel is limited and can be bought at local post offices.

The postal buses pay special attention to hikers. You can get a free booklet, "The Best River and Lakeside Walks," from the SNTO. The booklet describes 28 walks you can enjoy by hopping on and off postal buses. Most walks take around three hours.

By Boat Drifting across a Swiss lake and stopping off here and there at picturesque villages nestling by the water makes a relaxing day's excursion, especially if you are lucky enough to catch one of the elegant old paddle steamers. Trips are scheduled on most of the lakes, with increased service in summer. Unlimited travel is free to holders of the **Swiss Pass** (*see above*). For those not traveling by train, there is also a **Swiss Boat Pass**, which allows half-fare travel on all lake steamers for the entire summer (30 Fr., May 1–Oct. 31).

By Bicycle Bikes can be rented at all train stations and returned to any station. Rates are 16 Fr. per day or 64 Fr. per week for a conventional bike. Families can rent bikes for a single fee of 42 Fr.–48 Fr. per day, depending on the region, or for 168 Fr.–192 Fr. per week; groups get reductions according to the number of bikes involved. Reservations are necessary by 6 PM the day before use by individuals and a week ahead for groups. **Touring Club Suisse** (9 rue Pierre Fatio, CH-1211 Geneva 3, tel. 022/7371212) also rents bikes from its local offices at prices ranging from 14 Fr. to 24 Fr. per day.

Staying in Switzerland

Telephones There is direct dialing to every location in Switzerland. For lo-
Local Calls cal and international codes, consult the pink pages at the front of the telephone book.

International Calls You can dial most international numbers direct from Switzerland, adding a 00 before the country's code. If you want a number that cannot be reached direct, dial 114 for a connection. Dial 191 for international numbers and information. It's cheapest to use the booths in train stations and post offices; calls made from hotels cost a great deal more. Rates are lower between 5 PM and 7 PM, after 9 PM, and on weekends. Calls to the United States cost 2 Fr. per minute, to the United Kingdom 1.40 Fr. per minute.

| Operators and Information | All telephone operators speak English, and instructions are printed in English in all telephone booths. |

Mail
Postal Rates Mail rates are divided into first class (air mail) and second class (surface). Letters to the United States up to 20 grams cost 1.60 Fr. first class, .80 Fr. second class; to the United Kingdom, .90 Fr. first class, .70 Fr. second class. Post-cards with a written message of no more than five words cost 1.10 Fr. to the United States, .80 Fr. to the United Kingdom.

Receiving Mail If you're uncertain where you'll be staying, you can have your mail, marked Poste Restante or Postlagernd, sent to any post office in Switzerland. The sender's name and address must be on the back, and you'll need proof of identity to collect it. American Express cardholders can also have their mail sent to American Express for a small fee.

Shopping
VAT Refunds A 6.2% value-added tax (VAT) on all goods is included in the price. Nonresidents who have spent at least 500 Fr. at one time at a particular store may claim a VAT refund at the time of purchase, or the shop will send the refund to your home. In order to qualify, sign a form at the time of purchase and present it to Swiss customs on departure.

Bargaining Don't try bargaining: Except at the humblest flea market, it just doesn't work. As with everything in Switzerland, prices are efficiently controlled.

Opening and Closing Times **Banks.** Banks are open weekdays 8:30–4:30 or 5.

Museums. Museum times vary considerably, though many close on Monday. Check locally.

Shops. Shops are generally open 8–noon and 1:30–6:30. Some close at 4 on Saturday, and some are closed Monday morning. In cities, many large stores do not close for lunch.

National Holidays January 1, 2; April 9 (Good Friday); April 11, 12 (Easter); May 20 (Ascension); May 30 (Pentecost Sunday); December 25, 26. May 1 (Labor Day) and August 1 (National Day) are also celebrated, though not throughout the country.

Dining Options range from luxury establishments to modest cafés, *stübli* (cozy little pubs), and restaurants specializing in local cuisine.

Because the Swiss are so good at preparing everyone else's cuisine, it is sometimes said that they have none of their own, but there definitely is a distinct and characteristic Swiss cuisine. Switzerland is the home of great cheeses—Gruyère, Emmentaler, Appenzeller, and Vacherin—which form the basis of many dishes. *Raclette* is cheese melted over a fire and served with potatoes and pickles, *Rösti* are hash brown potatoes, and *fondue* is a bubbling pot of melted cheeses flavored with garlic and kirsch, into which you dip chunks of bread. Other Swiss specialties to look for are *Geschnetzeltes Kalbfleisch* (veal bits in cream sauce), *polenta* (cornmeal mush) in the Italian region, and fine game in autumn. A wide variety of Swiss sausages make both filling and inexpensive meals, and in every region the breads are varied and superb.

Mealtimes At home, the main Swiss meal of the day is lunch, with a snack in the evening. Restaurants, however, are open at midday and during the evening; often limited menus are offered all day. Watch for *Tagesteller* or *menus* (fixed-price lunches), which enable you to experience the best restaurants without paying high à la carte rates.

Dress Jacket and tie are suggested for restaurants in the Expensive categories; casual dress is acceptable elsewhere.

Ratings Prices are per person, without wine or coffee, but including tip and taxes. Best bets are indicated by a star ★.

Category	Zürich/Geneva	Other Areas
Moderate	30 Fr.–50 Fr.	25 Fr.–40 Fr.
Inexpensive	15 Fr.–30 Fr.	15 Fr.–25 Fr.
Budget	under 15 Fr.	under 15 Fr.

Lodging Switzerland's accommodations cover a broad range, from the most luxurious hotels to the more economical rooms in private homes. Pick up the *Schweizer Hotelführer (Swiss Hotel Guide)* from the SNTO before you leave home. The guide is free and lists all the members of the Swiss Hotel Association (comprising nearly 90% of the nation's accommodations); it tells you everything you'll want to know.

Most hotel rooms today have private bath and shower; those that don't are usually considerably cheaper. Single rooms are generally about two-thirds the price of doubles, but this can vary considerably. Remember that the no-nonsense Swiss sleep in separate beds or, at best, a double with separate bedding. If you prefer more sociable arrangements, ask for the rare "matrimonial" or "French" bed. Service charges and taxes are included in the price quoted and the bill you pay. Breakfast is included unless there is a clear notice to the contrary. In resorts especially, half pension (choice of a noon or evening meal) may be included in the room price. If you choose to eat à la carte or elsewhere, the management will generally reduce your price. Give them plenty of notice, however.

All major towns and train stations have hotel-finding services, which sometimes charge a small fee. Local tourist offices will also help.

Hotels Hotels are graded from one star (the lowest) to five stars. Always confirm what you are paying before you register, and check the posted price when you get to your room. Major credit cards are generally accepted, but, again, make sure beforehand.

The Check-In E and G Hotels are small hotels, boardinghouses, and mountain lodges that offer comfortable and often charming accommodations at reasonable prices. Details are available from the SNTO, which also offers pamphlets recommending family hotels and a list of hotels and restaurants that cater specifically to Jewish travelers.

Country Inns Country inns offer clean, comfortable, and hospitable accommodations, often in areas of great scenic beauty. Many are in the inexpensive category and are a good value.

Rentals Switzerland has literally thousands of furnished chalets. Off-season, per-day prices are around 50 Fr. per person for four sharing a chalet. In peak season, prices would be at least twice that. Deluxe chalets cost much more. For more information, pick up an illustrated brochure from the **Swiss Touring Club** (9 rue Pierre Fatio, CH-1211 Geneva 3) or from **Uto-Ring AG** (Beethovenstr. 24, CH-8002 Zürich). Or contact **Interhome** in the United States (36 Carlos Dr., Fairfield, NJ 07006) or in Britain (383 Richmond Rd., Twickenham, Middlesex TW1 2EF). You may save considerably if you write directly to the village or resort you wish to rent in, specifying your projected dates and number of beds required: Prices may start at around 20 Fr. per person without an agency's commission.

Ratings   Prices are for two people in a double room with bath or shower, including taxes, service charges, and breakfast. Budget hotels do not have baths or toilets in rooms. Best bets are indicated by a star ★.

Category	Zürich/Geneva	Other Areas
Moderate	140 Fr.–250 Fr.	110 Fr.–180 Fr.
Inexpensive	110 Fr.–140 Fr.	90 Fr.–110 Fr.
Budget	under 110 Fr.	under 90 Fr.

Tipping   Although restaurants include service charges of 15% with the taxes in your hotel and restaurant bill, you will be expected to leave a small additional tip: 1 Fr. or 2 Fr. per person for a modest meal, 5 Fr. for a first-class meal, and 10 Fr. at any exclusive gastronomic establishment. When possible, tip in cash rather than on the credit-card slip. Elsewhere, give bathroom attendants 1 Fr. and hotel maids 2 Fr. Theater and opera-house ushers get 2 Fr. for showing you to your seat and selling you a program. Hotel porters and doormen should get about 1 Fr. per bag.

Zürich

Arriving and Departing

By Plane   Kloten (tel. 01/8121212) is Switzerland's most important airport and is among the most sophisticated in the world. Several airlines fly directly from major cities in the United States, Canada, and the United Kingdom.

Swissair flies nonstop from New York, Chicago, Toronto, Montreal, Atlanta, Los Angeles, and Boston. "Fly Rail Baggage" allows Swissair passengers departing Switzerland to check their bags at any of 120 rail or postal bus stations throughout the country; the luggage is automatically transferred to the airplane. At eight Swiss railway stations, passengers may complete all check-in procedures for Swissair flights, boarding-pass issuance as well as baggage forwarding.

Between the Airport and Downtown   Beneath the air terminals, there's a train station with an efficient, direct service into the Hauptbahnhof (main station) in the center of Zürich. Fast trains run every 20 minutes, and the trip takes about 10 minutes. The fare is 4.60 Fr. and the ticket office is in the airport. There are express trains to most Swiss cities at least every hour. Trains run from 6 AM to midnight.

By Train   There are straightforward connections and several express routes leading directly into Zürich's Hauptbahnhof from Basel,

Geneva (Genève), Bern (Berne), and Lugano as well as from other major European cities.

Getting Around

Although Zürich is Switzerland's largest city, it has a population of only 362,000 and is not large by European standards. That's one of its nicest features: You can explore it comfortably on foot.

By Bus and Streetcar The city's transportation network is excellent. **VBZ Züri-Line** (Zürich Public Transport) buses run from 5:30 AM to midnight, every six minutes on all routes at peak hours, and about every 12 minutes at other times. Before you board the bus or train, you must buy your ticket from the automatic vending machines (instructions appear in English) found at every stop. A ticket for all travel for 24 hours is a good buy at 5.60 Fr. Free route plans are available from VBZ offices.

Important Addresses and Numbers

Tourist Information The tourist office is located at Bahnhofplatz 15 (Main Station), tel. 01/2114000. Open Mar.–Oct., weekdays 8 AM–10 PM, weekends 8 AM–8:30 PM; Nov.–Feb., Mon.–Fri. 8–8, weekends 9–6.

Consulates U.S. (Zollikerstr. 141, tel. 01/552566). U.K. (Dufourstr. 56, tel. 01/2611520).

Emergencies Police (tel. 117). Ambulance (tel. 144). Doctor/Dentist (tel. 01/2614700; poisoning cases, tel. 01/2515151).

Exploring Zürich

Zürich is not at all what you'd expect. Stroll around on a fine spring day and you'll ask yourself if this can really be one of the great business centers of the world: The lake glistening and blue in the sun, the sidewalk cafés, the swans gliding in to land on the river, the hushed and haunted old squares of medieval guildhouses, the elegant shops. There's not a gnome (a mocking nickname for a Swiss banker) in sight, not a worried business frown to be seen. The point is that for all its economic importance, Zürich is a place where people enjoy life. Hardworking, inventive, serious when need be, the Swiss love the good things in life, and they have the money to enjoy them.

Zürich started in 15 BC as a Roman customs post on the Lindenhof overlooking the river Limmat, but its growth really began around the 10th century AD. It became a free imperial city in 1336, a center of the Reformation in 1519, and then gradually assumed commercial importance during the 19th century. Today there is peace as well as prosperity here, and since Zürich is so compact, you can take in its variety in a morning's stroll.

Numbers in the margin correspond to points of interest on the Zürich map.

Collect your map from the tourist office (Bahnhofplatz 15), then start your walk from the nearby **Bahnhofstrasse,** famous for its shops and cafés and as the center of the banking network, though you'd be unlikely to guess it. Take Rennweg on your left, and then turn left again into the Fortunagasse, a quaint medieval street leading to the **Lindenhof,** a square where there

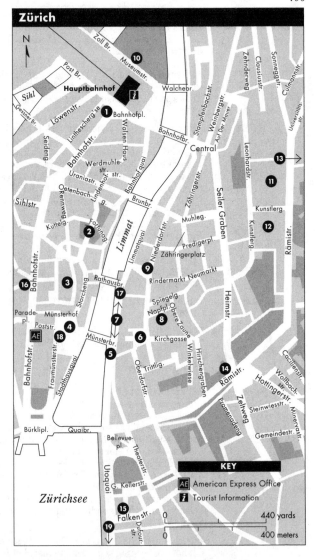

Main Attractions
Bahnhofstrasse, **1**
Fraumünster, **4**
Grossmünster, **6**
Limmatquai, **7**
Lindenhof, **2**
Niederdorf, **9**
Old Town, **8**
Peterskirche, **3**
Schweizerisches
Landesmuseum, **10**
Wasserkirche, **5**

Other Attractions
Centre Le
Corbusier, **19**
Federal Institute of
Technology, **11**
Kunsthaus, **14**
Opernhaus, **15**
Rathaus, **17**
Stadthaus, **18**
University of
Zürich, **12**
Wohnmuseum, **16**
Zoo, **13**

Zürich

KEY
[AE] American Express Office
[i] Tourist Information

0   440 yards
0   400 meters

are remains of Zürich's Roman origins. The fountain commemorates the ingenuity of the Zürich women who, when the city was besieged by the Habsburgs in 1292, donned armor and marched around the walls. The invaders thought they were reinforcements and beat a hasty retreat.

An alley on the right leads to a picturesque square dating from the Middle Ages, with the **Peterskirche,** Zürich's oldest parish church (13th century), which also happens to have the largest clockface in Europe. Walk down to the river and follow it to the 13th century **Fraumünster** (church), which has modern stained-glass windows by Chagall. There are two handsome guildhalls nearby: the **Zunfthaus zur Waag,** the hall of the linen weavers (Münsterhof 8), built in 1637, and the **Zunfthaus zur Meise**

(Münsterhof 20), built during the 18th century for the wine merchants.

Continue along Bahnhofstrasse to Bürkliplatz and cross the **Quai Bridge** to take in the impressive views of the lake and town. Now head left to the **Wasserkirche** (Water Church), dating from the 15th century and a lovely example of late-Gothic architecture. It is attached to the **Helmhaus,** originally an 18th-century cloth market.

Now turn right toward the **Grossmünster** church, which dates from the 11th century. During the 3rd century AD, St. Felix and his sister Regula were martyred by the Romans. Legend maintains that having been beheaded, they then walked up the hill carrying their heads and collapsed on the spot where the Grossmünster now stands. On the south tower you can see a statue of Charlemagne (768–814), emperor of the West. During the 16th century, the Zürich reformer Huldrych Zwingli preached sermons here that were so threatening in their promise of fire and brimstone that Martin Luther himself was frightened.

Back at the river on the **Limmatquai** are some of Zürich's most enchanting old buildings. Today most of them are restaurants. In the **Haus zum Ruden,** a 13th-century noblemen's hall, you will eat under a 300-year-old wooden ceiling. Other notable buildings here are the **Zunfthaus zur Saffran,** built in 1723 for haberdashers, and the **Zunfthaus zur Zimmerleuten,** built in 1708 for carpenters. The 17th-century Baroque **Rathaus** (Town Hall) is nearby.

Turn right into the **Old Town,** and you will enter a maze of fascinating medieval streets where time seems to have stood still. The Rindermarkt, Napfplatz, and Kirchgasse all have their charming old houses.

Head back to the river through **Niederdorf,** Zürich's nightlife district, and cross the bridge to the Hauptbahnhof. On the northern edge of the Hauptbahnhof, go to the **Schweizerisches Landesmuseum,** housed in a curious 19th-century building, for a look at Swiss history. There are fascinating pre-Romanesque and Romanesque church art, glass paintings from the 15th to the 17th century, splendid ceramic stoves, gold and silver from Celtic times, and weapons from many ages. *Museumstr. 2, tel. 01/2211010. Admission free. Open Tues.–Sun. 10–5.*

Shopping

Gift Ideas Typical Swiss products, all of the highest quality, include watches in all price categories, clocks, jewelry, music boxes, embroidered goods, wood carvings, and the famous multiblade Swiss army pocket knife. You'll also find fine household linens, delicate cotton or woolen underthings, and Zürich-made Fogal hosiery.

Shopping Districts The **Bahnhofstrasse** is one of the most bountiful shopping streets in Switzerland. Here you'll find **Jelmoli** (Seidengasse 1), Switzerland's largest department store, carrying a wide range of tasteful Swiss goods. **Heimatwerk** (Bahnhofstr. 2) specializes in handmade Swiss crafts, all of excellent quality. For high fashion, go to **Trois Pommes** (Storchengasse 6/7) and **Grieder** (Bahnhofstrasse 30), and for the finest porcelain, glass, and silverware, visit **Sequin-Dormann** (Bahnhofstr. 69a). If you have a sweet tooth, stock up on truffles at **Sprüngli** (Paradeplatz).

In the **Old Town** and off the **Limmatquai,** you'll find boutiques, antiques shops, bookstores, and galleries in picturesque byways. The **Löwenstrasse** has a diversity of upscale shops; the **Langstrasse** is another good shopping area and often has slightly lower prices. Under the central train station, **Shopville** offers a variety of middle-class stores and snack bars.

Food and Flea Markets   In many parts of town, there are lively markets where fruit, vegetables, and flowers are competitively priced. The best are at **Bürkliplatz, Helvetiaplatz,** and **Milkbuckstrasse** (open Tues. and Fri. 6 AM–11 AM) and at **Marktplatz**, on the way to the airport (open Wed. and Sat. 6 AM–11 AM).

At Bürkliplatz, at the lake end of the Bahnhofstrasse, there's a flea market that's open May through October, and a curio market is held at **Rosenhof** every Thursday and Saturday between April and Christmas.

Dining

You're likely to be served seconds in Zürich's generous restaurants, where the rest of your Rösti and Geschnetzeltes Kalbfleisch nach Zürcher Art simmer in copper pans by your table while you relish the hefty first portion. This is a Germanic city, after all, though its status as a minor world capital means that most international cuisines are represented as well. But brace yourself: The cash register rings portentously when the waiter places your order. Watch for posted *Tagesteller* specials, a good source of savings. For details and price-category definitions, *see* Dining in Staying in Switzerland.

Moderate   **Oepfelchammer.** This was once the haunt of Zürich's beloved
★   writer Gottfried Keller, and, recently restored, it still draws unpretentious literati. One room's a dark and graffiti-scribbled bar, with sagging timbers and slanting floors; the other's a welcoming little dining room, with carved oak paneling, a coffered ceiling, and pink damask linens. The traditional meats—calf's liver, veal, tripe in white wine sauce—come in generous portions; salads are fresh and seasonal. It's always packed, and service can be slow, so stake out a table and spend the evening. *Rindermarkt 12, tel. 01/2512336. Reservations advised. Dress: casual. MC, V. Closed Sun.*

Zunfthaus zur Schmiden. The sense of history and the magnificent mix of Gothic wood, leaded glass, and tile stoves justify a visit to this popular landmark, the guildhouse of blacksmiths and barbers since 1412. All the classics are served in enormous portions, and there's a considerable selection of alternatives, fish among them. The guild's own house wine is fine. *Marktgasse 20, tel. 01/2515287. Reservations advised. Dress: casual but neat. AE, DC, MC, V.*

Inexpensive   **Bierhalle Kropf.** Under the giant boar's head and century-old
★   murals that have been recently restored, businesspeople, workers, and shoppers crowd shared tables to feast on generous hot dishes and a great selection of sausages. The *leberknödli* (liver dumplings) are tasty, *apfelköchli* (fried apple slices) tender and sweet, and the bread chewy and delicious—though you pay for every chunk you eat. The bustle, clatter, and wisecracking waitresses make for a lively, sociable experi-

ence. *In Gassen 16, tel. 01/2211805. Reservations advised. Dress: casual. AE, DC, MC, V.*

★ **Zeughauskeller.** Built as an arsenal in 1487, this enormous stone and beam hall offers hearty meat platters and a variety of beers and wines amid comfortable and friendly chaos. Waitresses are harried and brisk, especially at lunchtime, when crowds are thick. They're not unaccustomed to tourists—menus are posted in English and Japanese—but locals consider this their home away from home. *Bahnhofstr. 28 (at Paradeplatz), tel. 01/2112690. Reservations advised at lunch. Dress: casual. No credit cards.*

Budget **Odeon.** A pre-Revolutionary Lenin once nursed a coffee and
★ read the house's daily papers in this historic café-restaurant, whose atmosphere is as Parisian as it gets in this Prussian town. Now the crowd is just as intense, and a tonic air of counterculture chic mixes with the no-filter cigarette smoke. You can nurse a coffee, too, or have a plate of pasta, a sandwich, or dessert from the limited menu. The restaurant is open daily to 2 AM, weekends to 4 AM. *Am Bellevue, tel. 01/2511650. No reservations. Dress: casual. AE, DC, MC, V.*

Rheinfelder Bierhaus. Mixed parties of workers, bikers, shoppers, and tourists squeeze into every wooden table at this dark, smoky spot, a solid old institution in the Niederdorf area. There's rich *rindpfeffer* (preserved beef stew) with homemade spätzli (tiny dumplings), tender liver with rösti, sausage standards, and, incongruously, once a month the chef's pride: a freshly homemade paella. *Marktgasse 19, tel. 01/2512991. No reservations. Dress: casual. No credit cards.*

Lodging

Zürich has an enormous range of hotels, from some of the most chic and prestigious in the country to modest guest houses. Prices tend to be higher than anywhere else in Europe, but you can be sure that you will get what you pay for: Quality and good service are guaranteed. For details and price-category definitions, *see* Lodging in Staying in Switzerland.

Moderate **Rössli.** Young, trendy, and completely high-tech, this hip new
★ spot in Oberdorf, near the Grossmünster, offers a refreshing antidote to Zürich's medievalism. Decor is white-on-white, with metallic-tiled baths, vivid lithographs, and splashy fabrics; hair dryers, robes, and fax connections keep services above average, especially for the price. The adjoining bar is very popular with young locals. *Rössligasse 7, CH-8001, tel. 01/2522121. 12 rooms with bath. Facilities: bar. AE, DC, MC, V.*

★ **Sonnenberg.** If you're traveling by car and want to avoid the urban rush, escape to this hillside refuge east of town. There are breathtaking views of the city, lake, and mountains, and landscaped grounds with a lovely terrace restaurant. The wood, stone, and beam decor reinforces the resort atmosphere. It's run by the friendly Wismer family. Take tram No. 3 or No. 8 to Klusplatz, then walk 10 minutes uphill. *Aurorastr. 98, CH-8030, tel. 01/2620062. 35 rooms with bath. Facilities: restaurant, terrace cáfe. AE, DC, MC, V.*

Wellenberg. Another effort at high style but not as effective as the Rössli, this new, central hotel sports a postmodern retro look, with burled wood, black lacquer, Art Deco travel posters, and Hollywood photos. Rooms are relatively roomy, if occasionally garish, and the location—on Niederdorf's Hirschen-platz—is superb. *Niederdorfstr. 10, CH-8001, tel. 01/2624300. 46 rooms with bath. AE, DC, MC, V.*

Inexpensive **Linde Oberstrasse.** Near the university in a sterile residential
★ area, this small hotel, built as a guildhouse in 1628, offers a handful of modest but agreeable rooms. The decor has been comfortably modernized, and though baths are down the hall, there is a sink, TV, and minibar in each room to compensate. The restaurant is comfortable and, though renovated to dated-modern style, maintains its traditional atmosphere and solid menu. *Universitätstr. 91, CH-8033, tel. 01/3622109. 10 rooms without bath. Facilities: restaurant. AE, DC, MC, V.*

★ **Vorderer Sternen.** On the edge of the Old Town and near the lake, this plain but adequate establishment takes in the bustle (and noise) of the city. It's steps from the opera house, theaters, art galleries, cinemas, and a shopping area; it's also close to the Bellevueplatz tram junction. There's a dependable and popular restaurant downstairs with moderate standards; none of the rooms has a bathroom. *Theaterstr. 22, CH-8001 tel. 01/ 2514949. 15 rooms without bath. AE, DC, MC, V.*

Budget **Italia.** This cozy Old World family hotel, which is located far
★ west of the river in a barren but perfectly safe neighborhood, spills over with doilies, overstuffed chairs, and mismatched antiques. Rooms have sinks only, but there's a big, homey bathroom on each floor and prices are rock-bottom. The Papagni family runs the restaurant downstairs, a picture of leather and wood, and in summer serves crowds under the chestnut pollards in the garden outside. To get there, take Bus 31 from the train station to Kanonengasse. *Zeughausstrasse 61, tel. 01/ 2410555. 36 rooms, none with bath. Facilities: restuarant, garden. No credit cards.*

St. Georges. In this simple former pension, the lobby and breakfast room are fresh and bright, but rooms and corridors are considerably more spare, with toothpaste-green walls, red linoleum, and pine furniture dating from the 1960s. Rooms with shower cost 40% more than those without. Take Tram 3 or 14 from the station to Stauffacher; it's another five minutes on foot. *Weberstrasse 11, tel. 01/2411144. 44 rooms, half without private bath. Facilities: breakfast room. AE, DC, MC, V.*

The Arts

Pick up *Zürich News*, published each week by the tourist office, to check what's on. Ticket reservations can be made through the **Billetzentrale** (Werdmühleplatz, tel. 01/2212283; open weekdays 10–6:30, Sat. 10–2). **Musik Hug** (Limmatquai 26, tel. 01/2516850) and **Jecklin** (Rämistr. 30, tel. 01/2515900) are good ticket sources as well.

The **Zürich Tonhalle Orchestra** (Claridenstr. 7, tel. 01/2011580) ranks among Europe's best. The **Opernhaus** (Falkenstr., tel. 01/2620909) is renowned for its adventurous opera, operetta, and ballet productions. The **Schauspielhaus** (Rämistr. 34, tel. 01/2511111) is one of the finest German-speaking theaters in the world. Zürich has 40 movie theaters, with English-language films appearing regularly.

Nightlife

Zürich has a lively nightlife scene, largely centered in the Niederdorf, parallel to the Limmat, across from the Hauptbahnhof. Many spots are short-lived, so check in advance. Informal dress is acceptable in most places, but again, check to make sure. The hotel porter is a good source of information.

Bars and Lounges The narrow bar at the **Kronenhalle** (Rämistr. 4, tel. 01/2511597) draws mobs of well-heeled locals and internationals for its prize-winning cocktails. The **Jules Verne Panorama Bar** (Uraniahaus, tel. 01/2111155) offers cocktails with a wraparound view of downtown Zürich. **Champagnertreff** in the Hotel Central (Central 1, tel. 01/2515555) is a popular Deco-look piano bar with several champagnes available by the glass. **Odeon** (Am Bellevue, tel. 01/2511650) serves a young, arty set until 4 AM. Some beer halls, including **Bierhalle Kropf** (In Gassen 16, tel. 01/2211805) and **Zeughauskeller** (Bahnhofstr. 28, tel. 01/2112690), serve draft beers in an old-Zürich atmosphere.

Cabaret/Nightclubs There's a variety show (dancers, magicians) at **Polygon** (Marktgasse 17, tel. 01/2521110). There are strip shows all over town, as well as the traditional nightclub atmosphere at **Le Privé** (Stauffacherstr. 106, tel. 01/2416487), **Moulin Rouge** (Mühlegasse 14, tel. 01/690730), and the slightly more sophisticated **Terrace** (Limmatquai 3, tel. 01/2511074).

Discos **Mascotte** (Theaterstr. 10, tel. 01/2524481) is, at the moment, popular with all ages on weeknights, but caters to young crowds on weekends. **Nautic Club** (Wythenquai 61, tel. 01/2026676) opens onto the lakefront in summer. **Le Petit Prince** (Bleicherweg 21, tel. 01/2011739) attracts an upscale crowd. **Birdwatcher's Club** (Schützengasse 16, tel. 01/2115058) requires jackets and a membership card. Even more exclusive is **Diagonal,** at the Hotel Baur au Lac (Talstr. 1, tel. 01/2012410), where you must be a hotel guest—or the guest of one.

Jazz **Casa Bar** (Münstergasse 30, tel. 01/472002) is the exclusive domain of jazz, with music until 2 AM.

Folklore If you're passing through Switzerland quickly and want the regional experience in a nutshell—even if it's inappropriate to this cosmopolitan and distinctly non-Alpine city—head for the **Kindli Swiss Chalet** (Oberer Rennweg, tel. 01/2114182) for evenings of yodeling, Alphorn playing, dancing, and fondue.

Excursion from Zürich: Liechtenstein

For an international day trip out of Zürich, dip a toe into tiny Liechtenstein: There isn't room for much more. Just 80 kilometers (50 miles) southeast on the Austrian border, this miniature principality covers a scant 158 square kilometers (61 square miles). An independent nation since 1719, Liechtenstein has a customs union with Switzerland, which means they share trains, currency, and diplomats—but not stamps, which is why collectors prize the local releases. It's easiest to get there by car, since Liechtenstein is so small that Swiss trains pass through without stopping. If you're using a train pass, ride to Sargans or Buchs and take a postbus across the border to Liechtenstein's capital, Vaduz. Note: Phone numbers in Liechtenstein will change in March 1993, but new versions were not available at press time.

Tourist Information The principal tourist office in Liechtenstein is at Städtle 37, Box 139, FL 9490, Vaduz, tel. 075/21443. It's open weekdays 8–noon and 1:30–5.

Exploring Liechtenstein Green and mountainous, its Rhine shores lined with vineyards, greater Liechtenstein is best seen by car. But if you're on foot, you won't be stuck: The postbuses are prompt and take you everywhere at a scenic snail's pace.

In fairy-tale **Vaduz,** Prince Johannes Adam Pius still lives in **Vaduz Castle,** a massive 16th-century fortress perched high on the cliff over the city. Only honored guests of the prince tour the interior, but its exterior and the views from the grounds are worth the climb. In the modern center of town, head for the tourist information office to have your passport stamped with the Liechtenstein crown. Upstairs, the **Prince's Art Gallery and the State Art Collection** display Flemish masters. *Städtle 37, tel. 075/22341. Admission: 3 Fr. adults, 1.5 Fr. children. Open Apr.–Oct., daily 10:30–noon and 1:30–5:30; Nov.–Mar., daily 10–noon and 2–5:30.*

On the same floor, the **Postage Stamp Museum** attracts philatelists from all over the world to see the 300 frames of beautifully designed—and relatively rare—stamps. Place subscriptions here for future first-day covers. *Städtle 37, tel. 075/66259. Admission free. Open daily 10–noon and 2–6.*

Next, move on to the **Liechtenstein National Museum,** which houses historical artifacts, church carvings, ancient coins, and arms from the prince's collection. *Städtle 43, tel. 075/22310. Admission: 2 Fr. Open May–Oct., daily 10–noon and 1:30–5:30; Nov.–Apr., Tues.–Sun. 2–5:30.*

In **Schaan,** just north of Vaduz, visit the Roman excavations and the parish church built on the foundations of a Roman fort. Or drive up to the chalets of picturesque **Triesenberg** for spectacular views of the Rhine Valley. Higher still, **Malbun** is a sun-drenched ski bowl with comfortable slopes and a low-key family ambience.

Dining For details and price-category definitions, *see* Dining in Staying in Switzerland.

★ **Wirthschaft zum Löwen.** Though there's plenty of French, Swiss, and Austrian influence, Liechtenstein has a cuisine of its own, and this is the place to try it. In a wood-shingled farmhouse on the Austrian border, the friendly Biedermann family serves tender homemade *Schwartenmagen* (the pressed pork-mold unfortunately known as headcheese in English), pungent *Sauerkäse* (sour cheese), and *Käseknöpfli* (cheese dumplings), plus lovely meats and the local crusty, chewy bread. Try the area's wines and the automatic snuff machine. *Schellenberg, tel. 075/31162. Reservations advised. V. Inexpensive.*

Lodging For details and price-category definitions, *see* Lodging in Staying in Switzerland.

Engel. Directly on the main tourist street, its café bulging with bus-tour crowds, this simple hotel/restaurant manages to maintain a local, comfortable ambience. The Huber family oversees the easygoing pub downstairs; the restaurant upstairs serves Chinese food. The rooms were renovated in winter 1991. *Städtle 13, tel. 075/20313. 17 rooms with bath.*

Facilities: restaurant, café, terrace. AE, DC, MC, V. Moderate.

Alpenhotel. Well above the mists of the Rhine in sunny Malbun, this 82-year-old chalet has been remodeled and a modern wing added. The old rooms are small and cozy; the higher-priced new rooms are modern and spare. The Vögeli family's welcoming smiles and good food have made it a Liechtenstein institution. *Tel. 075/21181 or 075/21624. 25 rooms with bath. Facilities: restaurant, café, indoor pool. AE, DC. Inexpensive.*

Geneva

Arriving and Departing

By Plane Cointrin (tel. 022/7993111), Geneva's airport, is served by several airlines that fly directly from New York, Toronto, and London. Swissair also has flights from Chicago and Los Angeles.

Swissair ticketholders departing from Cointrin can check their luggage through to their final destination from 120 rail and postal bus stations, and, at eight train stations also get their boarding passes.

Between the Airport and Downtown Cointrin has a direct rail link with Cornavin (tel. 022/7316450), the city's main train station, which is located in the center of town. Trains run about every 10 minutes from 5:30 AM to midnight. The trip takes about six minutes, and the fare is 4.50 Fr. for second class.

There is regular city bus service from the airport to the center of Geneva. The bus takes about 20 minutes, and the fare is 2 Fr. Some hotels have their own bus service.

By Train All services—domestic and international—use Cornavin Station in the center of the city. For information, dial 022/7316450.

By Bus Buses generally arrive at and depart from the bus station at place Dorcière, behind the English church in the city center.

Getting Around

By Bus and Streetcar There are scheduled services by local buses and trains every few minutes on all routes. Before you board, you must buy your ticket (2 Fr.) from the machines at the stops (they have English instructions). Save money and buy a ticket covering unlimited travel all day for 8.50 Fr. If you have a **Swiss Pass,** you can travel free (*see* Getting Around Switzerland by Train, *above*).

Tourist Information

The **Office du Tourisme de Genève** (Cornavin Station, Case Postale 440, CH-1211, tel. 022/7385200; open July–Sept., daily 8 AM–10 PM; Oct.–June, Mon.–Sat. 9–6, Sun. 4–8). **Thomas Cook** (64 rue de Lausanne, tel. 022/7324555).

Exploring Geneva

Draped at the foot of the Juras and the Alps on the westernmost tip of Lake Geneva (or Lac Léman, as the natives know it), Geneva is the most cosmopolitan and graceful of Swiss cities and the stronghold of the French-speaking territory. Just a stone's throw from the French border and 160 kilometers (100 miles) or so from Lyon, its grand mansarded mansions stand guard beside the river Rhône, where yachts bob, gulls dive, and Rolls-Royces purr beside manicured promenades. The combination of Swiss efficiency and French savoir faire gives the city a chic polish, and the infusion of international blood from the United Nations adds a heterogeneity that is rare in cities with a population of only 160,000.

Headquarters of the World Health Organization and the International Red Cross, Geneva has always been a city of humanity and enlightenment, offering refuge to writers Voltaire, Hugo, Dumas, Balzac, and Stendhal, as well as to religious reformers Calvin and Knox. Byron, Shelley, Wagner, and Liszt all fled from scandals to Geneva's sheltering arms.

A Roman seat for 500 years (from 120 BC), then home to early Burgundians, Geneva flourished under bishop-princes into the 11th century, fending off the greedy dukes of Savoy in conflicts that lasted into the 17th century. Under the guiding fervor of Calvin, Geneva rejected Catholicism and became a stronghold of Protestant reforms. In 1798 it fell to the French, but joined the Swiss Confederation as a canton in 1815, shortly after Napoleon's defeat. The French accent remains nonetheless.

Numbers in the margin correspond to points of interest on the Geneva map.

Start your walk from Gare de Cornavin (Cornavin Station) and
❶ head down the rue du Mont-Blanc to the **Pont du Mont-Blanc,** which spans the westernmost point of Lac Léman as it squeezes back into the Rhône. From the middle of the bridge (if it's clear) you can see the snowy peak of Mont Blanc itself, and from March to October you'll have a fine view of the **Jet d'Eau,** Europe's highest fountain, gushing 145 meters (475 feet) into the air.

Back at the foot of the bridge, turn right onto quai du Mont-
❷ Blanc to reach the **Monument Brunswick,** the high-Victorian tomb of a duke of Brunswick who left his fortune to Geneva in 1873. Just north are the city's grandest hotels, overlooking a manicured garden walk and the embarkation points for excursion boats. If you continue north a considerable distance through elegant parks and turn inland on the avenue de la Paix,
❸ you'll reach the enormous **International Complex,** where the Palais des Nations houses the European seat of the United Nations. (You can also reach it by taking bus No. 8 or F from the train station. For guided tour information, *see* Special-Interest Tours, *above.*)

Or turn left from the Pont du Mont-Blanc and walk down the
❹ elegant quai des Bergues. In the center of the Rhône is **Ile J.J. Rousseau** (Rousseau Island), with a statue of the Swiss-born
❺ philosopher. Turn left onto the **Pont de l'Ile,** where the tall Tour de l'Ile, once a medieval prison, houses the tourist office. Turn left again and cross the place Bel-Air, the center of the business and banking district, and follow the rue de la Corraterie to the
❻ **place Neuve.** Here you'll see the **Grand Théâtre,** which hosts opera, ballet, and sometimes the Orchestre de la Suisse Romande (it also performs at nearby Victoria Hall), and the **Conservatoire de Musique.** Also at this address is the **Musée Rath,** with top-notch temporary exhibitions. *Tel. 022/3105270. Admission*

*varies with exhibition. Open Tues.–Sun. 10–noon and 2–6;
also Wed. evening 8–10.*

Above the ancient ramparts on your left are some of the wealthiest old homes in Geneva. Enter the gated park before you, the promenade des Bastions, site of the university, and keep left **(7)** until you see the famous **Monument de la Réformation,** which pays homage to such Protestant pioneers as Bèze, Calvin, Farel, and Knox. Passing the uphill ramp and continuing to the farther rear gate, take the park exit just beyond the monument and turn left on the rue St-Leger, passing through the ivy-covered arch and winding into the **Vieille Ville,** or Old Town.

When you reach the ancient place du Bourg-de-Four, once a Roman forum, you can turn right on rue des Chaudronniers and **(8)** head for the **Musée d'Art et Histoire** (Museum of Art and History), which has a fine collection of paintings, sculpture, and archaeological relics. *2 rue Charles-Galland, tel. 022/3114340. Admission free. Open Tues.–Sun. 10–5.*

(9) Just beyond are the spiraling cupolas of the **Eglise Russe** (Rus-**(10)** sian Church) and the **Collection Baur** of Oriental arts. *8 rue Munier-Romilly, tel. 022/3461729. Admission: 5 Fr. Open Tues.–Sun. 2–6.*

Alternatively, from the place du Bourg-de-Four, head left up **(11)** any number of narrow streets and stairs toward the **Cathédrale St-Pierre,** done in a schizophrenic mix of Classical and Gothic styles. Under its nave (and entered from outside) is one of the biggest archaeological digs in Europe, a massive excavation of the cathedral's early Christian predecessors, now restored as a stunning maze of backlit walkways over mosaics, baptisteries, and ancient foundations. *Tel. 022/7385650. Admission: 5 Fr. Open Tues.–Sun. 10–1 and 2–6.*

(12) Calvin worshiped in the cathedral; he made the **Temple de l'Auditoire,** a small Gothic church just south of the cathedral toward place du Bourg-de-Four, into his lecture hall, where he taught missionaries his doctrines of reform. *Place de la Taconnerie, tel. 022/738–5650. Open Oct.–May, weekdays 9–noon and 2–5, Sat. 9:30–12:30 and 2–5, Sun. 2–5; June–Sept., weekdays 9–noon and 2–6, Sat. 9:30–12:30 and 2–6, Sun. 2–6. English-speaking hostess available Sun. and Mon.*

Behind the Temple de l'Auditoire, on the rue de l'Hôtel de **(13)** Ville, is the 16th-century **Hôtel de Ville,** where in 1864, in the Alabama Hall, 16 countries signed the Geneva Convention and laid the foundations for the International Red Cross. *Individual visits by request. Guided group tours by advance arrangement, tel. 022/272209.*

The winding, cobbled streets leading from the cathedral down to the modern city are lined with antiques shops, galleries, and unique but often expensive boutiques. The medieval Grand' Rue is the oldest in Geneva, the rue de l'Hôtel de Ville features lovely 17th-century homes, and the rue Jean Calvin has noble mansions of the 18th century (No. 11 is on the site of Calvin's **(14)** house). No. 6 on the rue du Puits-St-Pierre is the **Maison Tavel,** the oldest building in town and home of an intimate re-creation of daily life and urban history. *Tel. 022/3102900. Admission free. Open Tues.–Sun. 10–5.*

Down the hill, plunge back into the new city and one of the most luxurious shopping districts in Europe, which stretches tempt-

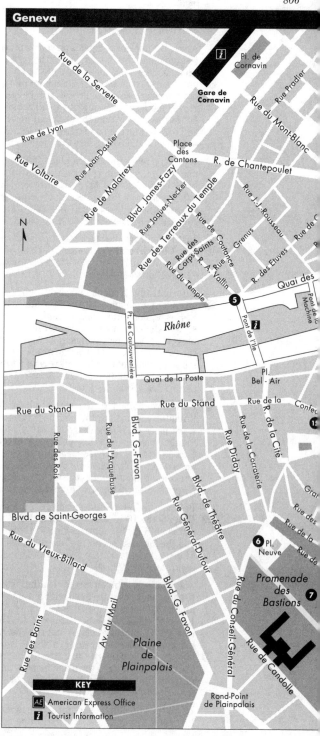

Geneva

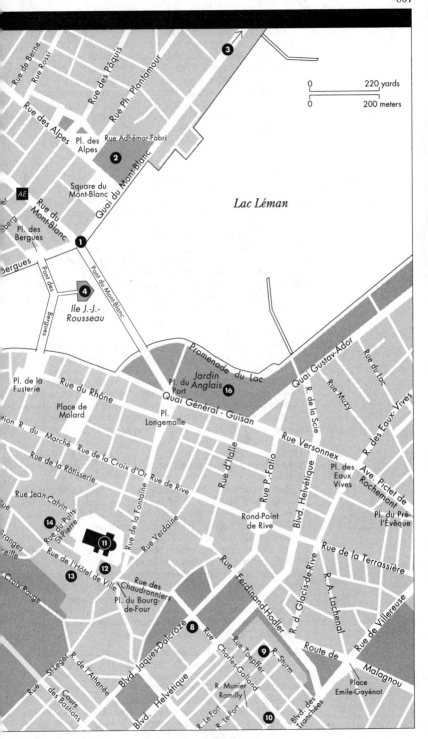

0 | 220 yards
0 | 200 meters

Rue de Berne
Rue Rossi
Rue des Pâquis
Rue Ph. Plantamour
Rue des Alpes
Pl. des Alpes
Rue Adhémar-Fabri
2
3
Square du Mont-Blanc
AE
Rue du Mont-Blanc
Quai du Mont-Blanc
Pl. des Bergues
Bergues
1
Pont des Bergues
Pont du Mont-Blanc
4
Ile J.-J.-Rousseau

Lac Léman

Quai Gustav-Ador
Rue du Lac

Promenade du Lac
Jardin Anglais
16
Pl. de la Fusterie
Rue du Rhône
Pl. du Port
Quai Général - Guisan
Rue Muzy
Place de Molard
Pl. Longemalle
R. de la Scie
R. des Eaux-Vives
...tion R. du Marché
Rue de la Croix d'Or Rue de Rive
Rue Versonnex
Rue de la Rôtisserie
Rue d'Italie
Rue P.-Fatio
Blvd. Helvétique
Pl. des Eaux Vives
Ave. Pictet de Rochemont
Rue Jean-Calvin
Rue de la Fontaine
Pl. du Pré-l'Évêque
...e ...ranges ...eille
14
Rue du Puits St-Pierre
11
Rue Verdaine
Rond-Point de Rive
...-Croix-Rouge
Rue de l'Hôtel de Ville
12
13
Rue des Chaudronniers
Rue de la Terrassière
R. A. Lachenal
Pl. du Bourg-de-Four
Rue Ferdinand-Hodler
R. d. Glacis-de-Rive
Rue de Villereuse
St-Léger R. de l'Athénée
Blvd. Jaques-Dalcroze
Rue Jaques-Dalcroze
8
Rue Toepfer
R. Sturm
9
Route de
Rue Charles-Galland
Malagnou
Cours des Bastions
Blvd. Helvétique
R. Munier Romilly
Place Emile-Gayénot
R. Le-Fort
R. Le-Fort
Blvd. des Tranchées
10

ingly between the quai Général-Guisan, rue du Rhône, rue de la Croix d'Or, and rue du Marché. It's tough enough to resist top name *prêt-à-porter* (ready-to-wear clothing), dazzling jewelry and watches, luscious chocolates, and luxurious furs and leathers, but the glittering boutiques of the new three-story ⓯ **Confédération-Centre**—where all the above are concentrated with a vengeance—could melt the strongest resolve. Escape across the quai, head back toward the lake, and come to your ⓰ senses in the **Jardin Anglais,** where the famous floral clock will tell you that it's time to stop.

Dining

Moderate **Boeuf Rouge.** Despite its decor—a consciously contrived send-★ up of a Lyonnais bistro, jam-packed with kitschy ceramics and Art Nouveau posters—this cozy and popular spot delivers the real thing: rich, unadulterated Lyon cuisine, from the bacon, egg, and greens *salade Lyonnaise* to the homemade *boudin blanc,* a delicate, pistachio-studded white sausage in morel cream sauce. There's sausage with lentils, too, and duck pâté served with a crock of *cornichons,* and authentic *tarte tatin.* Service—by the proprietors and the chef himself—is flamboyant (they present all dishes on a flower-crowded tray before serving tableside), but the ambience is relaxed. Dine late to avoid crowds of sauce-on-the-side Americans. *17 rue Alfred-Vincent, tel. 022/7327537. Reservations advised. Dress: casual. V. Closed weekends.*

★ **La Favola.** Run by a young Ticinese couple from Locarno, this quirky little restaurant may be the most picturesque in town. The tiny dining room, at the top of a vertiginous spiral staircase, strikes a delicate balance between rustic and fussy, with its lace window panels, embroidered cloths, polished parquet, and rough-beamed ceiling sponge-painted in Roman shades of ochre and rust. The food finds the same delicate balance between country simple and city chic: carpaccio with olive paste or white truffles, ravioli of duck à l'orange. Lunch menus represent excellent value. *15 rue Jean Calvin, tel. 022/217437. Reservations advised. Dress: casual. No credit cards. Closed weekends.*

Le Pied-de-Cochon. While visiting antiques shops and art galleries in the Vielle Ville, stop for lunch or supper in this old bistro, which retains its original beams and zinc-top bar. Crowded, noisy, smoky, lively, it faces the Palais de Justice and shelters famous lawyers who plead celebrated causes; there are artists and workers as well. The good, simple fare includes *pieds de cochon* (pigs' feet), of course, either grilled, with mushrooms, with lentils, or *dessossés* (boned), as well as simple Lyonnais dishes, including *petit salé* (pork belly), ham, grilled *andouillettes* (little pork sausages), tripe, and salads. The ambience is *sympa,* as the locals say—congenial. *4 place du Bourg-de-Four, tel. 022/204797. Reservations advised. Dress: casual. AE, DC, MC, V. Closed weekends.*

Inexpensive **Les Armures.** In the picturesque and historic Les Armures ho-★ tel at the summit of the Old Town and two steps from the Cathédrale St-Pierre, this atmospheric restaurant offers several dining halls, all decorated with authentic arms from the Middle Ages. The broad menu of Swiss specialties ranges from fondue to *choucroute* to *rösti,* but some of the dishes are pure Genevois. There also are inexpensive pizzas and a good selection of salads. Everyone comes here, from workers to politicians—Jimmy Carter adored the place on his last visit. *1 rue du Puits-St-Pierre, tel. 022/3103442. Reservations advised. Dress: casual. AE, DC, MC, V.*

L'Echalotte. Big and brightly lit, with warm polished wood banquettes and paper mats, this is a casual, comfortable meeting place with a generous, impulsive menu; fixed-price meals may offer a choice of no less than six first courses, three seconds. Cooking is eclectic and homey (turkey with chestnuts, zucchini flan, lemon bavarian), and everything is highly seasoned and served with casual flair. *17 rue des Rois, tel. 022/ 205999. No reservations. Dress: casual. No credit cards. Closed weekends.*

★ **Taverne de la Madeleine.** Tucked into the commercial maze between the Rue de la Croix d'Or and the Old Town, by l'Eglise de la Madeleine, this casual, alcohol-free café claims to be the oldest eatery in Geneva. It's run by the city's temperance league, and thus loses the business clientele that insist on a pitcher of Fendant with their meals: All the more room for you to relax over homemade *choucroute*, perch, or fresh-baked fruit tarts in the charming Victorian upstairs dining room. There are big, fresh salads, vegetable plates, and a variety of loose-leaf teas. Summer brings crowds to the terrace, overlooking the *place*, and diners are served until up to 10 PM; the rest of the year, the kitchen closes at 7. *20 rue Toutes-âmes, tel. 022/7284032. Reservations advised. Dress: casual. No credit cards.*

Budget **Manora/Placette.** There's nothing of Old Geneva in this Swiss Woolworth's, but you *will* find much of New Geneva, crowding elbow to elbow around the islands in the store's cafeteria to fill trays with fresh-cooked chicken curry, grilled chops, cheese tarts, fruits, salads, and pastries. Portions are generous, ingredients and preparation straightforward (some dishes are browned before your eyes in industrial-sized woks), and prices are rock-bottom. It's upstairs in the department store, but attractive and welcoming nonetheless. *6 rue Cornavin, tel. 022/ 7313146. No reservations. Dress: casual. No credit cards.*

★ **Taverne de la Madeleine.** Tucked into the commercial maze between the rue de la Croix-d'Or and the old town, near l'Eglise de la Madeleine, this casual, alcohol-free café run by the city's temperance league claims to be the oldest eatery in Geneva. The business folk who insist on a pitcher of Fendant with their meals go elsewhere—which leaves all the more room for you to relax over homemade choucroute, perch, or fresh-baked fruit tarts in the charming Victorian upstairs dining room. There are big, fresh salads and vegetarian plates, as well as a variety of freshly brewed loose-leaf teas. In summer, the terrace—overlooking the *place*—is in demand, and dinners are served until up to 10 o'clock; the rest of the year, the kitchen closes at 7. *20 rue Toutes-âmes, tel. 022/7284032. Reservations advised. Dress: casual. No credit cards.*

Lodging

For details and price-category definitions, *see* Lodging in Staying in Switzerland.

Moderate **d'Allèves.** On a quiet square between the station and the Right Bank, this simple hotel has been lovingly crowded with the art and antiques collection of the owner, and done in a kind of dark elegance no longer in vogue (velour, red carpet, chenille). *Rue*

Kléberg 13, CH-1211, tel. 022/7321530. 80 beds. Facilities: restaurant, café. AE, DC, MC, V.

Strasbourg-Univers. A stylish oasis in the slightly sleazy train-station neighborhood, this just-renovated spot offers sleek decor, convenience, and four-star quality at a three-star price. The new look is marble and faux exotic wood; a few older, less flashy rooms, redone eight years ago, still don't show the wear. *10 rue Pradier, tel. 022/7322562. 58 rooms with bath or shower. AE, DC, MC, V.*

★ **Touring-Balance.** The lower floors are tired but gracious, with French doors and a chic new paint job; ask to stay in the slick, solid high-tech rooms on the higher floors. There are gallery-quality lithos in every room. *13 pl. Longemalle, tel. 022/3104045. 64 rooms with bath. Facilities: restaurant, café. AE, DC, MC, V.*

Inexpensive **De la Cloche.** This once luxurious walk-up flat has tidy, tasteful
★ new decor and a quiet courtyard setting. Good-size rooms share a bath down the hall. The price may be the lowest in town. *6 rue de la Cloche, tel. 022/7329481. 8 rooms without shower. Facilities: breakfast served in rooms. No credit cards.*

Des Tourelles. Once worthy of a czar, now host to the backpacking crowd, this fading Victorian offers enormous bay-windowed corner rooms, many with marble fireplaces, French doors, and views over the Rhône. The furnishings are sparse and strictly functional, but the staff is young and friendly. Bring earplugs: The location is extremely noisy, over roaring bridge traffic. *2 blvd. James-Fazy, tel. 022/7324423. 25 rooms, some with shower. AE, DC, MC, V.*

International et Terminus. Although it's in the busy station area, this modest lodging has warm public areas scattered with antiques and fresh-looking rooms with clean, neutral decor. The restaurant is moderate and there's a terrace café. Rooms without bath cost considerably less. *Rue des Alpes 20, CH-1201, tel. 022/7328095. 83 beds. Facilities: restaurant, terrace café. AE, DC, MC, V.*

Lido. Despite the red linoleum and black-and-white tile baths that show this hotel's age, rooms are freshly done with light carpet and wood-veneer furniture. Though windows are double-glazed, rooms over the square are quieter; those in the 33-43 series are largest. *8 rue Chantpoulet, CH-1201, tel. 022/7315530. 60 beds. Facilities: breakfast room. AE, DC, MC, V.*

★ **Montana.** Following a slick renovation inside and out, rooms in this station-area property are snazzily decorated in taupe and salmon and have double-glazed windows and bright tile baths. Only breakfast is served. *23 rue des Alpes, CH-1201, tel. 022/7320840. 70 beds. Facilities: breakfast room. AE, DC, MC, V.*

Budget **Central.** The location at the top of an anonymous, urban build-
★ ing on a back shopping street is unpromising. But this bargain hotel merits the ride to the top floor: Rooms are freshly decorated with nice carpet and gleaming tile baths. Only breakfast is served. *2 rue de la Rôtisserie, CH-1204, tel. 022/214594. 40 beds. Facilities: breakfast room. No credit cards.*

★ **St. Gervais.** This budget inn on a historic block in the Right Bank town center has attic-like rooms that are neat, tidy, quaint, and well-maintained, with fresh linens on the beds and framed prints on the walls. Families should ask for the large, old room with ancient beams. A tiny pub on the ground floor serves snacks. *20 rue Corps-Saints, CH-1201, tel. 022/7324572. 52 beds, two with bath. Facilities: café. AE, MC, V.*

Lugano

Arriving and Departing

By Plane There are short connecting flights by **Crossair**—the Swiss domestic network—to Lugano Airport (tel. 091/505001) from
Zürich, Geneva, Basel, and Bern, as well as from Paris, Nice,
Rome, Florence, and Venice. The nearest intercontinental airport is at Milan, Italy, about 56 kilometers (35 miles) away.

Between the There is no longer a regular bus service between the local air-
Airport and port and central Lugano, 7 kilometers (4 miles) away; taxis,
Downtown costing about 25 Fr. to the center, are the only option.

By Train There's a train from Zürich seven minutes past every hour, and
the trip takes about three hours. If you're coming from Geneva,
you can catch the Milan express at various times, changing at
Domodossola and Bellinzona. Daytimes, there's a train 30 minutes past every hour from Milan's Centrale Station; the trip
takes about 1½ hours. Always keep passports handy and confirm times with the SNTO. For train information in Lugano,
tel. 091/226502 or 091/237501.

Getting Around

By Bus Well-integrated services run regularly on all local routes. You
must buy your ticket from the machine at the stop before you
board. Remember that with a **Swiss Pass** you'll be able to travel
free.

By Train With or without a Swiss Pass, get a **Regional Holiday Season
Ticket** for Lugano from the tourist office. One of these gives unlimited free travel for seven consecutive days on most rail and
steamer routes and a 50% or 25% discount on longer trips. It
costs 78 Fr. for adults (68 Fr. for holders of a Swiss Pass) and 39
Fr. for children 6 through 16. The newest version offers any
three out of seven days free on most routes, with 50% or 25%
reductions on the remaining four days. Its price is 60 Fr. for
adults, 50 Fr. for Swiss Pass holders, and 30 Fr. for children.

Tourist Information

Ente Turistico Lugano (riva Albertolli 5, CH-6901, tel. 091/
214664; open weekdays 8–noon and 2–6, and Easter–Oct., Sat.
9–noon and 2–5).

Exploring Lugano

Its sparkling bay, with dark, conical mountains rising from the
beautiful Lago di Lugano, has earned Lugano the nickname
"Rio of the Old World." The largest city in the Ticino—the Italian-speaking corner of Switzerland—Lugano has not escaped
some of the inevitable overdevelopment of a successful resort
town. There's thick traffic, right up to the waterfront, much of
it manic Italian-style, and it has more than its share of concrete
waterfront high-rise hotels, with balconies skewed to claim
rooms with a view no matter what the aesthetic cost.

But the view from the waterfront is unforgettable, the boulevards are fashionable, and the old quarter is still reminiscent of
sleepy old towns in Italy. And the sacred *passeggiata*—the af-

ternoon stroll to see and be seen that winds down every Italian day—asserts the city's true personality as a graceful, sophisticated Old World resort—not Swiss, not Italian . . . just Lugano.

Numbers in the margin correspond to points of interest on the Lugano map.

Start your walk under the broad porticoes of the tourist office and cross over to the tree-lined promenade, where you can stroll along the waterfront and take in stunning mountain views. Palm trees, pollards, and funeral cypresses—the standard greenery of Italian lake resorts—are everywhere. Head

❶ left along the waterfront and into the **Parco Civico** (City Park), full of cacti, exotic shrubs, and more than 1,000 varieties of roses. There's an aviary, a tiny "deer zoo," and a fine view of the bay from its peninsula. The **Villa Ciani,** temporarily closed for renovations, contains paintings and sculpture from Tintoretto to Giacometti.

❷ There's also the canton's **Museum of Natural History,** which contains exhibits on animals, plants, and mushrooms. *Viale Cattaneo 4, tel. 091/237827. Admission free. Open Tues.–Sat. 9–noon and 2–5.*

❸ If you continue left along the waterfront, you'll find the **Lido,** with a stretch of sandy beach, several swimming pools, and a restaurant. *Admission: 5 Fr. adults, 2 Fr. children 2–14.*

Or follow the promenade right until you reach the **Imbarcadero Centrale,** where steamers launch into the bay, and turn inland

❹ to the **Piazza della Riforma,** the scene of Lugano's vigorous Italian life, where the modish locals socialize in outdoor cafés. From here, enter the **Old Town** and follow the steep, narrow streets lined with chic Italian clothing shops and small markets offering pungent local cheeses and porcini mushrooms. Swiss culture asserts itself only at lunch stands, where *panini* (small sandwiches) are made not only of prosciutto, tuna, or mozzarella but of sauerkraut and sausage as well.

❺ On the street of the same name, you'll find the **Cathedral San Lorenzo,** with its graceful Renaissance facade and noteworthy frescoes inside. Then shop your way down the Via Nassa until

❻ you reach the **Church of Santa Maria degli Angioli** in Piazza Luini, started in 1455. Within, you'll find a splendid fresco of the *Passion and Crucifixion* by Bernardino Luini (1475–1532).

❼ Across the street, the waterfront **Giardino Belvedere** (Belvedere Gardens) frame 12 modern sculptures with palms, camelias, oleanders, and magnolias. At the far end, to your right, there's **public bathing** on the Riva Caccia. *Admission (bathing): 3 Fr., 2 Fr. children.*

If you want to see more of Lugano's luxurious parklands, take the funicular from the Old Town to the train station: Behind the

❽ station, deer greet you as you enter the floral **Parco Tassino.** Or take bus No. 2 east to the San Domenico stop in Castagnola to

❾ reach the **Parco degli Ulivi** (Olive Park), where you can climb the olive-lined slopes of Monte Brè for views of the surrounding mountains.

❿ If you're lucky, the dust will have settled at the **Villa Favorita,** owned by art baron and *real* Baron Heinrich von Thyssen, and you'll find the villa not only completely renovated but also with

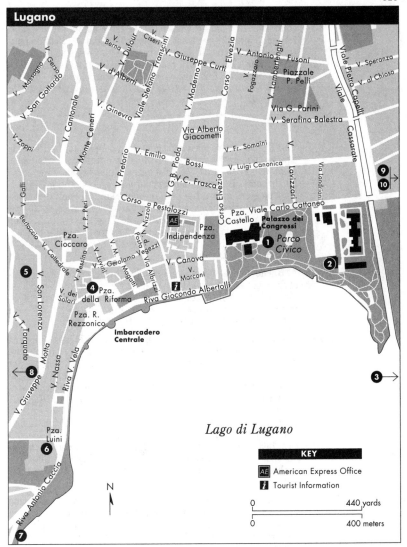

Lugano

Cathedral San
Lorenzo, **5**
Church of Santa Maria
degli Angioli, **6**
Giardino Belvedere, **7**
Lido, **3**
Museum of Natural
History, **2**

Parco Civico, **1**
Parco Tassino, **8**
Parco degli Ulivi, **9**
Piazza della Riforma, **4**
Villa Favorita, **10**

a portion of its magnificent art collection back on the walls. In a controversial bidding war, much of the collection was transferred to Madrid—at least temporarily—and which of its masterworks will stay in Lugano remains to be seen. The latest projection: The villa will reopen at Easter 1993 with some of the collection's fine drawings and watercolors on display. *Strada Castagnola, tel. 091/521741. Admission and hours to be announced.*

Dining

The Ticinese were once poor mountain people, so their cuisine shares the earthy delights of the Piemontese: *polenta* (cornmeal mush), *gnocchi* (potato-based dumplings), game, and mushrooms. But as in all prosperous resorts, the mink-and-Vuarnets set draws the best in upmarket international cooking. Fixed-price lunches are almost always cheaper, so dine as the Luganese do—before your siesta. That way you can sleep off the fruity local merlot wine before the requisite passeggiata. For details and price-category definitions, *see* Dining in Staying in Switzerland.

Moderate **Al Barilotto.** Despite its generic pizzeria decor and American-★ style salad bar, this restaurant draws local crowds for grilled meats, homemade pasta, and wood-oven pizza. Take bus No. 10 from the center. *Hôtel de la Paix, Via Cattori 18, tel. 091/542331. Reservations advised. AE, DC, MC, V.*

Inexpensive **Sayonara.** There's nothing Japanese about it: This is a modern urban pizzeria whose several rooms are crowded at lunchtime with a mix of tourists and shoppers. The old copper polenta pot stirs automatically year-round, with polenta offered in several combinations, one of them with mountain hare. *Via F. Soave 10, tel. 091/220170. Reservations not necessary. AE, DC, MC, V.*

★ **La Tinera.** This tiny taverna crowds loyal locals, tourists, and families onto wooden benches for authentic regional specialties, hearty meats, and pastas. Regional wine is served in traditional ceramic bowls. It's tucked down an alley off Via Pessina in the Old Town. *Via dei Gorini 2, tel. 091/235219. Reservations advised. AE, DC, MC, V.*

Budget **Federale.** You may choose to spend the whole afternoon at this popular outdoor café-bar, which offers light meals and cheap daily specials as well as drinks to the diverse and often glamorous crowds who all face forward, as if an audience for the real-life theater passing by. Homemade pastas include gnocchi alla romana (flour dumplings, not the traditional potato version). *Piazza Riforma 9, tel. 091/239175. Reservations not necessary. Dress: casual. No credit cards.*

Lodging

Since this is a summer resort, many hotels close for the winter, so call ahead. For details and price-category definitions, *see* Lodging in Staying in Switzerland.

Moderate **Alba.** This solid little hotel, with landscaped grounds and an in-★ terior that is lavish in the extreme, is ideal for lovers with a sense of camp or honeymooners looking for romantic privacy. Mirrors, gilt, plush, and crystal fill the public areas, and the beds are all ruffles and swags. The garden is studded with palms, a lovely place for a drink. *Via delle Scuole 11, tel. 091/ 543731. 25 rooms with bath. Facilities: restaurant, bar, garden. AE, DC, MC, V.*

International au Lac. This is a big, old-fashioned, friendly city hotel, half a block from the lake, with many lake-view rooms. It's next to Santa Maria degli Angioli, on the edge of the shopping district and the Old Town. *Via Nassa 68, tel. 091/227541. 86 rooms with bath. Facilities: restaurant, garden. AE, DC, MC, V.*

★ **Park-Hotel Nizza.** This former villa, modernized in 1974, affords panoramic views from its spot on the lower slopes of San Salvatore, well above the lake, and thus is an uphill hike from town. The mostly small rooms are decorated with antique reproductions; you don't pay extra for rooms with lake views. An ultramodern bar overlooks the lake, and a good restaurant serves vegetables and even wine made from grapes from the hotel's own garden. There's a shuttle service to Paradiso. *Via Guidino 14, tel. 091/541771. 30 rooms with bath. Facilities: 2 restaurants, bar, outdoor pool, fitness center, solarium, garden. AE, DC, MC, V.*

Inexpensive **Flora.** Though it's one of the cheapest hotels in town, this 70-★ year-old lodging has been reasonably well maintained. The room decor is minimal, a holdover of the '60s (red-orange prints, wood-grain Formica), and the once-elegant dining hall has seen better days. But some rooms have balconies, and there's a sheltered garden terrace that's lovely on balmy nights. *Via Geretta 16, tel. 091/541671. 33 rooms with bath. Facilities: restaurant, bar, terrace. AE, DC, MC, V.*

San Carlo. The San Carlo offers one of the better deals in a high-priced town: It's small, clean, freshly furnished, and right on the main shopping street, a block from the waterfront. There are no frills, but the friendly atmosphere compensates. *Via Nassa 28, tel. 091/227107. 22 rooms with bath. Facilities: breakfast only. AE, DC, MC, V.*

Budget **Rex.** Although its comforts are minimal and its location strictly urban, this no-nonsense shelter is convenient—near museums, parks, beaches, and bus lines. Only breakfast is served. *11 Viale Cattaneo, CH-6900, tel. 091/227608. 30 beds. Facilities: breakfast room. AE, DC, MC, V.*

Bern

Arriving and Departing

By Plane **Belp** is a small airport, 9 kilometers (6 miles) south of the city, with flights from London, Paris, Nice, Venice, and Lugano. A bus from the airport to the train station costs 12 Fr., a taxi about 35 Fr.

By Train Bern is a major link between Geneva, Zürich, and Basel, with fast connections running usually every hour from the enormous central station. The high-speed French TGV gets to Paris in 4½ hours.

Getting Around

By Bus and Bern is a small, concentrated city, and it's easy to get around on **Streetcar** foot. There are 6½ kilometers (4 miles) of covered shopping arcades in the center. Bus and tram service is excellent, however, if you don't feel like walking. Fares range from 1.10 Fr. to 1.70 Fr. Buy individual tickets from the dispenser at the tram or bus stop; the posted map will tell you the cost. Tourist cards for unlimited rides are available at 4 Fr. for one day, 6 Fr. for two, and 9 Fr. for three. Buy them at the bahnhof tourist office or from the public-transportation ticket office in the subway leading down to the main station (take the escalator in front of Loeb's department store and turn right through the Christoffel Tower). A **Swiss Pass** allows you to travel free.

Important Addresses and Numbers

Tourist Information The tourist office is located at Bahnhofplatz (main station, tel. 031/227676); it's open May–Oct., Mon.–Sat. 8 AM–8:30 PM and Sun. 9–8:30; Nov.–Apr., Mon.–Sat. 8–6:30 and Sun. 10–5.

Embassies U.S. (Jubiläumsstr. 93, tel. 031/437011). **Canadian** (88 Kirchenfeldstr., tel. 031/446381). **U.K.** (Thunstr. 50, tel. 031/445021).

Emergencies Police (tel. 117). **Ambulance** (tel. 144). **Doctor/Dentist** (tel. 229211).

Exploring Bern

No cosmopolitan nonsense here: The local specialties are fatback and sauerkraut, the annual fair features the humble onion, and the president takes the tram to work. Walking down broad, medieval streets past squares teeming with farmers' markets and cafés full of shirt-sleeved politicos, you might forget that Bern is the federal capital—indeed, the geographic and political hub—of a sophisticated, modern, and prosperous nation.

It earned its pivotal position through a history of power and influence that dates back to the 12th century, when Berchtold V of the Holy Roman Empire established a fortress on this gooseneck in the river Aare. By the 15th century the Bernese had overcome the Burgundians to expand their territories west to Geneva. Napoleon held them briefly—from 1798 until his defeat in 1815—but by 1848 Bern was back in charge, as the capital of the Swiss Confederation.

Today it's not the massive Bundeshaus (capitol building) that dominates the city, but the perfectly preserved arcades, the fountains, and the thick, sturdy towers of the Middle Ages. They're the reason UNESCO granted Bern World Landmark status, ranking it with the Pyramids and the Taj Mahal.

Numbers in the margin correspond to points of interest on the Bern map.

❶ Start on the busy **Bahnhofplatz** in front of the grand old Schweizerhof hotel, facing the station. To your left is the
❷ **Heiliggeistkirche** (Church of the Holy Spirit), finished in 1729 and contrasting sharply with both the modern and the medieval in Bern.

Head right up Bollwerk and turn right into Kleeplatz and
❸ Hodlerstrasse, where you'll come to the **Kunstmuseum Bern** (Bern Art Museum) on your left. Originally dedicated to Swiss art, it houses an exceptional group of works by Ferdinand

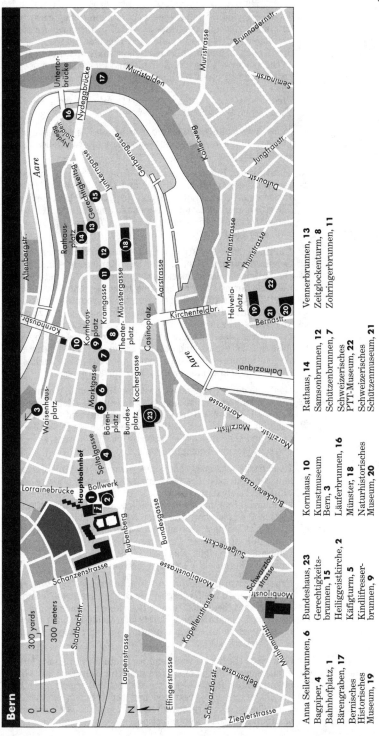

Bern

0 ___ 300 yards
0 ___ 300 meters

Anna Seilerbrunnen, **6**
Bagpiper, **4**
Bahnhofplatz, **1**
Bärengraben, **17**
Bernisches Historisches Museum, **19**

Bundeshaus, **23**
Gerechtigkeitsbrunnen, **15**
Heiliggeistkirche, **2**
Käfigturm, **5**
Kindlifresserbrunnen, **9**

Kornhaus, **10**
Kunstmuseum Bern, **3**
Läuferbrunnen, **16**
Münster, **18**
Naturhistorisches Museum, **20**

Rathaus, **14**
Samsonbrunnen, **12**
Schützenbrunnen, **7**
Schweizerisches PTT-Museum, **22**
Schweizerisches Schützenmuseum, **21**

Vennerbrunnen, **13**
Zeitglockenturm, **8**
Zähringerbrunnen, **11**

Hodler, including some enormous, striking allegories; there are landscapes and portraits as well. But the concentration is no longer entirely Swiss, and early Bern masters mingle with Fra Angelico, and Böcklin and Anker share space with artists of the caliber of Cézanne, Rouault, and Picasso. The museum's pride—and its justified claim to fame—is its collection of more than 2,000 works by Paul Klee, who spent years in Bern. *Hodlerstrasse 8–12, tel. 031/220944. Admission: 4 Fr. Open Tues. 10–9; Wed.–Sun. 10–5.*

Walk down Spitalgasse outside the arcades to see some of the city's stunning architecture; inside the sheltered walkways are modern shops and cafés.

④ Head for the **Bagpiper,** the first of the city's many signature
⑤ fountains erected between 1539 and 1546, and the **Käfigturm** (prison gate), which dates from the 13th and 14th centuries. There's a small museum of economic and cultural life inside. *Tel. 031/222306. Admission free. Open Tues.–Sun. 10–1 and 2–6, also Thurs. 6–9.*

⑥ Continue down Marktgasse past the **Anna Seilerbrunnen** and
⑦ **Schützenbrunnen** (Anna Seiler and Marksman Fountains) to
⑧ the **Zeitglockenturm** (clock tower), built as a city gate in 1191 but transformed by the addition of an astronomical clock in
⑨ 1530. To your right is the Theaterplatz, to your left the **Kindlif-resserbrunnen** (Ogre Fountain) and the Kornhausplatz, where
⑩ you will see the imposing 18th-century **Kornhaus** (granary), its magnificent vaulted cellar a popular beer hall today. Now walk past the clock tower and observe the clock from the east side. At four minutes before every hour, you can see the famous mechanical puppet bears perform their ancient dance.

Continue down Kramgasse, past fine 18th-century houses and
⑪ ⑫ the **Zähringerbrunnen** and **Simsonbrunnen** (Zähringer and Samson Fountains). Turn left at the next small intersection and
⑬ head for Rathausplatz, with its **Vennerbrunnen** (Ensign Foun-
⑭ tain), and the late-Gothic **Rathaus** (city hall), where the city and cantonal government meet.

Head back to the main route, here named Gerechtigkeitsgasse,
⑮ and continue past the **Gerechtigkeitsbrunnen** (Justice Fountain) and lovely patrician houses. Artisan shops, galleries, and antiquaries line this leg of the endless arcades. Turn left at the bottom and head down the steep Nydegg Stalden through one
⑯ of the city's oldest sections, past **Läuferbrunnen** (Messenger Fountain), to the river Aare. Here the **Nydeggkirche** (Nydegg Church), on the right, was built from 1341 to 1571 on the foundations of Berchtold V's ruined fortress.

Cross the river by the Untertorbrücke Bridge, then turn right and climb up to the **Nydeggbrücke** Bridge. Here you'll find the
⑰ **Bärengraben** (bear pits), where Bern keeps its famous live mascots. According to legend, Berchtold named the town after the first animal he killed while hunting—a bear, since the woods were thick with them.

Now cross the bridge and head back into town, turning left up
⑱ Junkerngasse to the magnificent Gothic **Münster** (cathedral), begun in 1421. It features a fine portal (1490) depicting the *Last Judgment*, recently restored and repainted in extravagant hues. There also are stunning stained-glass windows, both originals and period reproductions.

Arty boutiques line the Münstergasse, leading to the **Casino,** which houses a concert hall and restaurants, but no casino. If you head even farther south (across the river yet again), you'll find Helvetiaplatz, a historic square surrounded by museums.

⑲ The **Bernisches Historisches Museum** (Bern Historical Museum) has a prehistoric collection, 15th-century Flemish tapestries, and Bernese sculptures. Its fine Islamic holdings are imaginatively displayed. *Helvetiaplatz 5, tel. 031/431811. Admission: 3 Fr. Open Tues.–Sun. 10–5.*

⑳ The **Naturhistorisches Museum,** one of Europe's major natural history museums, has enormous wildlife dioramas and a splendid collection of Alpine minerals. *Bernastr. 15, tel. 031/431839. Admission: 3 Fr. Open Mon. 2–5, Tues.–Sat. 9–5, and Sun. 10–5.*

㉑ The **Schweizerisches Schützenmuseum** (Swiss Shooting Museum) traces the development of firearms from 1817 and celebrates Swiss marksmanship beyond the apple-splitting accuracy of William Tell. *Bernastr. 5, tel. 031/430127. Admission free. Open Tues.–Sat. 2–4, Sun. 10–noon and 2–4.*

㉒ The **Schweizerisches PTT–Museum** (Swiss Postal and Telecommunications Museum), now housed in its striking new building behind the Bernisches Historisches Museum, offers detailed documents, art, and artifacts of early technology to trace the history of the mail system in Switzerland, from Roman messengers to telegraph and radio. *Helvetiastr. 16, tel. 031/627777. Admission: 2 Fr. adults. Open Tues.–Sun. 10–5.*

Alternatively, head back from the casino on Kochergasse past
㉓ the enormous domed **Bundeshaus** (Capitol). By night, be sure to stick to Kochergasse instead of the riverview promenade behind the capitol building; some visitors have been annoyed by obvious drug traffic.

Dining

While Bern teeters between two cultures politically, Teutonic conquers Gallic when it comes to cuisine. Dining in Bern is usually a down-to-earth affair, with Italian home cooking running a close second to the local standard fare of meat and potatoes. Specialties include the famous *Bernerplatte* (sauerkraut with boiled beef, fatty pork, sausages, ham, and tongue), *Buurehamme* (hot smoked ham), and *Ratsherrentopf* (rösti with roast veal, beef, liver, and sausage). Coffee and *Kuchen* (pastry) are standard four-o'clock fare.

For details and price-category definitions, *see* Dining in Staying in Switzerland.

Moderate **Della Casa.** You can stay downstairs in the steamy, rowdy
★ stübli, where necktied businessmen roll up their sleeves and play cards, or head up to the linen-and-silver restaurant, where they leave their jackets on. It's an unofficial Parliament headquarters, and serves generous portions of local and Italian specialties—including a good Bernerplatte. *Schauplatzgasse 16, tel. 031/222142. Reservations advised. Jacket advised. DC, MC, V. No credit cards downstairs.*

★ **Lorenzini.** In a town where the cozy and the stuffy hold sway, this hip, bright spot stands apart. Delicious homemade pasta and changing menus featuring the specialties of different Italian regions are served with authentic, contemporary flair.

Marktgass-Passage 3, tel. 031/227850. Reservations advised.
Dress: casual but neat. DC, MC, V.

Zunft zu Webern. Founded as a weavers' guildhouse and built in
1704, this classic building has been renovated on the ground
floor in a slick but traditional style, with gleaming new wood
and bright lighting. Its culinary style is simple but sophisticated, and it serves generous portions of reinterpreted standards such as lamb stew with saffron. *Gerechtigkeitsgasse 68,*
tel. 031/224258. Reservations not necessary. Dress: casual.
MC, V.

Inexpensive **Brasserie zum Bärengraben.** Directly across from the bear pits,
★ this popular, easygoing little local institution, with the thin-
nest veneer of a French accent, serves inexpensive lunches to
shoppers, tourists, businesspeople, and retirees, who settle in
with a newspaper and a *dezi* (deciliter) of wine. The menu offers
many old-style favorites—*Kalbskopf am Vinaigrette* (chopped
veal in vinaigrette), pig's feet, stuffed cabbage—and wonderful pastries. *Muristalden 1, tel. 031/414218. Reservations ad-*
vised. Dress: casual. No credit cards.

Harmonie. Run by the same family since 1900, this leaded-glass
and old-wood café-restaurant serves inexpensive basics: fondue, sausage-and-rösti, *Käseschnitte* (cheese toast), and
bauern omelets (farm-style, with bacon, potatoes, onions, and
herbs). It's lively, very friendly, and welcoming to foreigners if
a little dingy. *Hotelgasse 3, tel. 031/223840. Reservations not*
necessary. Dress: casual. No credit cards.

Budget **Klötzlikeller.** A cozy muraled wine cellar, this is much more in-
★ timate than the famous Kornhauskeller and just as lovely.
There's a good, limited menu of hearty meat dishes. *Gerecht-*
igkeitsgasse 62, tel. 031/227456. Reservations not necessary.
Dress: casual. AE, MC, V.

Kornhauskeller. This spectacular vaulted old wine cellar, under the Kornhaus granary, is now a popular beer hall with live
music on weekends. Decent hot food is served as an after-
thought. *Kornhausplatz 18, tel. 031/221133. Reservations not*
necessary. Dress: casual. AE, DC, MC, V.

Lodging

For details and price-category definitions, *see* Lodging in Staying in Switzerland.

Moderate **Goldener Adler.** The exterior of this 1764 building is a magnifi-
★ cent patrician town house, but its interior is modern and modest, with linoleum-floor baths and severe Formica furniture.
The ambience is comfortable and familial nonetheless: The
same family has run the place for more than 100 years.
Gerechtigkeitsgasse 7, tel. 031/221725. 40 rooms with bath. Fa-
cilities: restaurant, terrace café. AE, DC, MC, V.

★ **Krebs.** A classic, small, Swiss hotel, Krebs is impeccable and
solid, managed with an eye on every detail. The spare decor is
warmed with wood and made comfortable by the personal,
friendly service of the Buri family. A handful of inexpensive
rooms without bath offer excellent value. *Genfergasse 8, tel.*
031/224942. 44 rooms, 41 with shower. Facilities: restaurant.
AE, DC, MC, V.

Inexpensive **Glock.** Though it's very plain and occasionally shabby, there's a
young, friendly management here and two lively restaurants,
one a "Swiss Chalet," with dancing and folklore shows, the

other Italian. The rooms have a fresh paint job, tile baths, and homey, unmatched towels. A few rooms without baths cost even less. *Rathausgasse 75, tel. 031/223771. 20 rooms, some with bath. Facilities: 2 restaurants, entertainment. AE, DC, MC, V.*

Goldener Schlüssel. This is a bright, tidy spot with its abundance of wood, crisp linens, and tiled baths. It's in the heart of the Old Town, so the rooms are quieter in the back. The two good restaurants serve Swiss and international specialties. Rooms without baths are a bargain. *Rathausgasse 72, tel. 031/ 220216. 29 rooms, some with shower. Facilities: 2 restaurants. DC, MC, V.*

★ **Hospiz zur Heimat.** The elegant 18th-century exterior promises better than the dormitory gloom inside, but the baths are new, the rooms are immaculate, and the Old Town location is excellent. *Gerechtigkeitsgasse 50, tel. 031/220436. 40 rooms, some with bath. Facilities: restaurant (no alcohol). AE, DC, MC, V.*

Jardin. This solid, roomy middle-class hotel, in a commercial neighborhood far above the Old Town, has fresh decor and baths in every room. It's easily reached by tram No. 9 to Breitenrainplatz. *Militärstrasse 38, tel. 031/400117. 17 rooms with bath. Facilities: AE, DC, MC, V.*

Budget **Marthahaus.** Take bus No. 20 over the Kornhaus Bridge to this spare, old-style pension in a residential neighborhood north of the Old Town. Rates are low and the service is friendly. *Wyttenbachstrasse 22a, tel. 031/424135. 40 rooms without bath. Breakfast only. No credit cards.*

Zermatt

Lying at an altitude of 1,616 meters (5,300 feet), Zermatt offers the ultimate Swiss-Alpine experience: spectacular mountains, a roaring stream, state-of-the-art transport facilities, and a broad range of high-quality accommodations, some of them radiating rustic atmosphere, plus 230 kilometers (143 miles) of downhill runs and 7 kilometers (4 miles) of cross-country trails. But its greatest claim to fame remains the **Matterhorn** (4,477 meters/14,690 feet), which attracts swarms of package-tour sightseers pushing shoulder to shoulder to get yet another shot of this wonder of the Western world.

Arriving and Departing

Car-free Zermatt is isolated at the end of the Mattertal, a rugged valley at the eastern end of the Alpine canton of Valais. A good mountain highway and the Brig–Visp–Zermatt Railway cut south through the valley from Visp, the crossroads of the main Valais east–west routes. The airports of Zürich and Geneva are roughly equidistant from Brig, but by approaching from Geneva you can avoid the time-consuming business of crossing the mountain passes.

By Train The Brig–Visp–Zermatt Railway, a private narrow-gauge rail system, runs from Brig to Visp, connecting on to Zermatt. All major rail routes connect through Brig, whether you approach from Geneva or Lausanne in the west, from the Lötschberg line that tunnels through from Kandersteg and the Bernese Oberland, or from the Simplon Pass that connects from Italy.

Getting Around

Because Zermatt permits no private cars, your only means of transit are electric taxis that shuttle arriving guests to their hotels and back. The village is relatively small and easily covered on foot. Yet, surprisingly enough, Zermatt remains a resort with its feet on the ground, protecting its regional quirks along with its wildlife and its tumbledown *mazots* (little grain-storage sheds raised on mushroomlike stone bases to keep the mice away), which crowd between glass-and-concrete chalets like old tenements between skyscrapers. Streets twist past weathered wood walls, flower boxes, and haphazard stone roofs until they break into open country that inevitably slopes uphill. Despite the crowds, you are never far from the sound of the river and the peace of a mountain path.

By Cable Car or Mountain Rail Skiing and hiking are Zermatt's raison d'être, but you may want to get a head start into the heights by riding part of the sophisticated network of cable cars, lifts, cogwheel rails, and even an underground tram that carry you above the village center into the wilderness. Excursions to the Klein Matterhorn and Gornergrat are particularly spectacular.

Important Addresses and Numbers

Tourist Information The main tourist office, the **Verkehrsbüro Zermatt,** is across from the train station (Bahnhofplatz, CH-3920 Zermatt, tel. 028/661181).

Emergencies **Police** (tel. 028/672197). **Ambulance** (tel. 028/673487).

Exploring Zermatt

Zermatt lies in a hollow of meadows and trees ringed by mountains—among them the broad **Monte Rosa** (4,554 meters/14,940 feet) and its tallest peak, the **Dufourspitze** (at 4,634 meters/15,200 feet, the highest point in Switzerland)—of which visitors hear relatively little, so all-consuming is the cult of the Matterhorn. But the Matterhorn deserves the idolatry: Though it has become an almost self-parodying icon, like the Eiffel Tower or the Statue of Liberty, this distinctive snaggle-toothed pyramid, isolated on all sides from surrounding peaks, is larger than life and frankly awe-inspiring as it rears up over the village.

In 1891, the cog railway between Visp and Zermatt took its first summer run and began disgorging tourists with profitable regularity—though it didn't plow through in wintertime until 1927. But what really drew the first tourists and made Zermatt a household word was Edward Whymper's spectacular—and catastrophic—conquering of the Matterhorn in 1865. Whymper and his band of six made the successful trek to the mountain's summit before tragedy struck. During the treacherous descent, four of them slid against one another and fell to their death. The body of one was never recovered, but the others lie in the grim little cemetery behind the Zermatt church in the village center, surrounded by scores of other failed mountaineers, including a recent American aspirant whose tomb bears the simple epitaph: "I chose to climb."

But if you want to gain the broader perspective of high altitudes without risking life or limb, take the trip up the

Gornergrat—a tram is used for excursions as well as ski transport. Part of the rail system completed in 1898 and the highest
open-air rail system in Europe (the tracks to the Jungfraujoch,
though higher, bore through the face of the Eiger), it connects
out of the main Zermatt train station and climbs slowly up the
valley to the **Riffelberg,** which at 2,582 meters (8,469 feet) offers wide-open views of the Matterhorn. From **Rotenboden,** at
2,819 meters (9,246 feet), a short downhill walk leads to the
Riffelsee, which obligingly provides photographers with a
postcard-perfect reflection of the famous peak. At the end of
the 9-kilometer (5½-mile) line, the train stops at the summit
station of **Gornergrat** (3,130 meters/10,266 feet), and passengers pour onto the observation terraces to take in the majestic
views of the Matterhorn, Monte Rosa, Gorner glacier, and
scores of other peaks and glaciers. There's a departure every 24
minutes between 8 AM and 7 PM. The round-trip fare is 50 Fr.
Bring warm clothes, sunglasses, and sturdy shoes.

Dining

Located at the German end of the mostly French canton of
Valais, Zermatt offers a variety of French and German cooking,
from veal and rösti to raclette and fondue. Specialties often feature pungent mountain cheese: *Käseschnitte,* for instance, are
substantial little casseroles of bread, cheese, and often ham,
baked until the whey saturates the crusty bread and the cheese
browns to gold. Air-dried beef is another Valais treat: The meat
is pressed into a dense brick and dried in mountain breezes. It
is served in thin, translucent slices, with gherkins and crisp
pickled onions. Naturally, the international influence and
wealth that pour into Zermatt every year bring cosmopolitan
cooking as well, especially to the first-class hotel restaurants.
For price-category definitions, *see* Dining in Staying in Switzerland.

Moderate **Enzo's Hitte.** Whether for long lunches between sessions on the
★ slopes or for the traditional wind-down après-ski, this mountain restaurant in tiny Findeln, between the Sunnegga and
Blauherd ski areas, is de rigueur, especially with the hip young
English and Americans. The Matterhorn views are astonishing, the decor stylish, the staff chic—and the food surprisingly
fine. Traditional hot dishes and nontraditional pastas share
billing with good homemade desserts. The nice wine list makes
for a lazy descent back to town. It is also accessible on foot during the summer. *Findeln, tel. 028/672588. Dress: casual. No
credit cards. Closed May–mid-June, Oct.–Nov.*

★ **Zum See.** Beyond Findeln in a tiny village (little more than a
cluster of mazots) by the same name, Zum See has become
something of an institution, serving light meals of a quality and
level of invention that would merit acclaim even if the restaurant weren't in the middle of nowhere at 1,766 meters (5,792
feet). During the summer its shaded picnic tables draw hikers
who reward themselves at the finish of a day's climb; during the
winter its low, cozy log dining room gives skiers a glow with an
impressive assortment of brandies. Regional specialties are
prepared with masterly care, from wild mushrooms in pastry
shells to rabbit, rösti, and *foie de veau* (veal liver). The homemade tortellini with garlic, basil, and cream are worth the trek,
as are the variety of homemade ice creams. *Tel. 028/672045.*

Reservations suggested in the evening. Dress: casual. No credit cards. Closed May–June, Oct.–mid-Nov.

Inexpensive **Elsie Bar.** Directly across from the church, this popular après-ski haunt looks like a log cabin inside and draws an international crowd into its barroom for cocktails, American-style. Light meals include cheese specialties and snails. *Tel. 028/672431. Dress: casual. AE, DC, MC, V.*

Lodging

At high season—Christmas and New Year's, Easter, and late summer—Zermatt's high prices rival those of Zürich and Geneva. But read the fine print carefully when you plan your visit: Most hotels include half-pension in their price, offering breakfast and your choice of a noon or evening meal. Hotels that call themselves "garni" do not offer pension dining plans. For price-category definitions, *see* Lodging in Staying in Switzerland.

Price categories below are based on a rough average of high-, middle-, and low-season rates, subtracting the estimated value of half-pension, which normally is included in the price.

Moderate **Julen.** Its 1937 chalet-style construction, knotty-pine decor,
★ and impeccable 1981 renovation qualify this lodge for membership in the Romantik chain, which signals authentic regional comforts. The main restaurant offers French cooking, and the welcoming stübli serves lamb specialties from locally raised flocks. *CH-3920, tel. 028/672481. 37 rooms with bath. Facilities: restaurant, café, terrace, sauna, solarium. AE, DC, MC, V.*

Romantica. Among the scores of anonymous modern hotels around Zermatt, this modest structure offers an exceptional location directly above the town center. Its tidy gardens and flower boxes, game trophies, and old-style stove soften the cookie-cutter look, and its plain rooms benefit from big windows and balconies. Views take in the mountains (though not the Matterhorn) over a graceful clutter of stone roofs. *CH-3920, tel. 028/671505. 14 rooms with bath. Facilities: bar. AE, MC, V.*

Inexpensive **Alphubel.** Although it is surrounded by other hotels and is steps from the main street, this modest, comfortable pension feels off the beaten track—and offers large sunny balconies in its south-side rooms. The interior reflects the 1954 construction—a little institutional—but there's a sauna in the basement guests can use for a slight surcharge. *CH-3920, tel. 028/673003. 32 rooms, 16 with bath. Facilities: restaurant, sauna. AE, MC, V.*

★ **Touring.** Its reassuringly traditional architecture and snug, sunny all-pine rooms, combined with an elevated location outside town and excellent Matterhorn views, make this an appealing choice for travelers who want to opt out of the chic downtown scene. Built in 1958 and tastefully updated in 1989, Touring is family-run, and rooms with Matterhorn views cost only 2 Fr. extra. *CH-3920, tel. 028/671177. 24 rooms, 10 with bath. Facilities: restaurant, stübli. MC, V.*

Budget **Mischabel.** This proud old budget pension—run by the same
★ family for 40 years—provides comfort, atmosphere, and a central location few places can match at twice the price, with balconies on the south side framing a perfect Matterhorn view (the higher, the better). Creaky, homey, and covered with knotty

pine aged to the color of toffee, its rooms have sinks only, though you'll find linoleum-floor showers on every floor. There's a generous daily menu, a lovingly manicured lawn, tidy flower boxes, and lettuce grown by the elderly owner herself. *CH-3920, tel. 028/671131. 28 rooms with bath. Facilities: restaurant. No credit cards.*

WHEREVER YOU TRAVEL, *H*ELP IS NEVER FAR AWAY.

From planning your trip to

providing travel assistance along

the way, American Express®

Travel Service Offices* are

always there to help.

**American Express Travel Service Offices are
found in central locations throughout
Europe.**

Index

Personal Itinerary

Departure *Date*

Time

Transportation

Arrival *Date*   *Time*

Departure *Date*   *Time*

Transportation

Accommodations

Arrival *Date*   *Time*

Departure *Date*   *Time*

Transportation

Accommodations

Arrival *Date*   *Time*

Departure *Date*   *Time*

Transportation

Accommodations

Fodor's Travel Guides

U.S. Guides

Alaska

Arizona

Boston

California

Cape Cod, Martha's
Vineyard, Nantucket

The Carolinas & the
Georgia Coast

Chicago

Disney World & the
Orlando Area

Florida

Hawaii

Las Vegas, Reno,
Tahoe

Los Angeles

Maine, Vermont,
New Hampshire

Maui

Miami & the Keys

New England

New Orleans

New York City

Pacific North Coast

Philadelphia & the
Pennsylvania Dutch
Country

San Diego

San Francisco

Santa Fe, Taos,
Albuquerque

Seattle & Vancouver

The South

The U.S. & British
Virgin Islands

The Upper Great
Lakes Region

USA

Vacations in New York
State

Vacations on the
Jersey Shore

Virginia & Maryland

Waikiki

Washington, D.C.

Foreign Guides

Acapulco, Ixtapa,
Zihuatanejo

Australia & New
Zealand

Austria

The Bahamas

Baja & Mexico's
Pacific Coast Resorts

Barbados

Berlin

Bermuda

Brazil

Budapest

Budget Europe

Canada

Cancun, Cozumel,
Yucatan Penisula

Caribbean

Central America

China

Costa Rica, Belize,
Guatemala

Czechoslovakia

Eastern Europe

Egypt

Euro Disney

Europe

Europe's Great Cities

France

Germany

Great Britain

Greece

The Himalayan
Countries

Hong Kong

India

Ireland

Israel

Italy

Italy's Great Cities

Japan

Kenya & Tanzania

Korea

London

Madrid & Barcelona

Mexico

Montreal &
Quebec City

Morocco

The Netherlands
Belgium &
Luxembourg

New Zealand

Norway

Nova Scotia, Prince
Edward Island &
New Brunswick

Paris

Portugal

Rome

Russia & the Baltic
Countries

Scandinavia

Scotland

Singapore

South America

Southeast Asia

South Pacific

Spain

Sweden

Switzerland

Thailand

Tokyo

Toronto

Turkey

Vienna & the Danube
Valley

Yugoslavia

Special Series

Fodor's Affordables

Affordable Europe

Affordable France

Affordable Germany

Affordable Great
Britain

Affordable Italy

**Fodor's Bed &
Breakfast and
Country Inns Guides**

California

Mid-Atlantic Region

New England

The Pacific Northwest

The South

The West Coast

The Upper Great
Lakes Region

Canada's Great
Country Inns

Cottages, B&Bs and
Country Inns of
England and Wales

The Berkeley Guides

On the Loose in
California

On the Loose in
Eastern Europe

On the Loose in
Mexico

On the Loose in the
Pacific Northwest &
Alaska

**Fodor's Exploring
Guides**

Exploring California

Exploring Florida

Exploring France

Exploring Germany

Exploring Paris

Exploring Rome

Exploring Spain

Exploring Thailand

Fodor's Flashmaps

New York

Washington, D.C.

Fodor's Pocket Guides

Pocket Bahamas

Pocket Jamaica

Pocket London

Pocket New York
City

Pocket Paris

Pocket Puerto Rico

Pocket San Francisco

Pocket Washington,
D.C.

Fodor's Sports

Cycling

Hiking

Running

Sailing

The Insider's Guide
to the Best Canadian
Skiing

**Fodor's Three-In-Ones
(guidebook, language
cassette, and phrase
book)**

France

Germany

Italy

Mexico

Spain

**Fodor's
Special-Interest
Guides**

Cruises and Ports
of Call

Disney World & the
Orlando Area

Euro Disney

Healthy Escapes

London Companion

Skiing in the USA
& Canada

Sunday in New York

**Fodor's Touring
Guides**

Touring Europe

Touring USA:
Eastern Edition

Touring USA:
Western Edition

**Fodor's Vacation
Planners**

Great American
Vacations

National Parks of the
West

**The Wall Street
Journal Guides to
Business Travel**

Europe

International Cities

Pacific Rim

USA & Canada

CNN TRAVEL GUIDE

PASSPORT TO THE WORLD

Join host Valerie Voss for an entertaining and informative program that takes you to the four corners of the earth. With expert advice from Michael Spring, Fodor's Editorial Director, *CNN Travel Guide* is the perfect companion for anyone planning a trip or just interested in travel.

Drawing on CNN's vast network of international correspondents, you'll discover an exciting variety of new destinations from the most exotic locales to some well-kept secrets just a short trip away. You'll also find helpful tips on everything from hotels and restaurants to packing and planning. So tune in to *CNN Travel Guide*. And make it your first stop on any trip.